THE OXFORD HANDBOOK OF
PRACTICAL
ETHICS

THE OXFORD HANDBOOK OF

PRACTICAL ETHICS

Edited by

HUGH LaFOLLETTE

OXFORD
UNIVERSITY PRESS

*This book has been printed digitally and produced in a standard specification
in order to ensure its continuing availability*

OXFORD
UNIVERSITY PRESS

Great Clarendon Street, Oxford OX2 6DP

Oxford University Press is a department of the University of Oxford.
It furthers the University's objective of excellence in research, scholarship,
and education by publishing worldwide in

Oxford New York

Auckland   Cape Town Dar es Salaam   Hong Kong   Karachi
Kuala Lumpur Madrid Melbourne Mexico City   Nairobi
New Delhi Shanghai Taipei Toronto
With offices in
Argentina Austria Brazil Chile Czech Republic France Greece
Guatemala Hungary Italy Japan South Korea Poland Portugal
Singapore Switzerland Thailand Turkey Ukraine Vietnam

Oxford is a registered trade mark of Oxford University Press
in the UK and in certain other countries

Published in the United States
by Oxford University Press Inc., New York

ISBN 978-0-19-928423-8

ACKNOWLEDGEMENTS

I thank Peter Momtchiloff for his consistent encouragement, support, and assistance throughout this project, for his aid in overcoming several significant obstacles, and for his astute editorial and philosophical insight. I also thank Rebecca Bryant for her efficient assistance and helpful advice in the production of this volume, and Hilary Walford for her careful copy-editing of the text.

Finally, I thank Eva LaFollette for her patience, ideas, feedback, and keen editorial eye.

CONTENTS

Notes on the Contributors   xi

Introduction   1

PART I OUR PERSONAL LIVES

1. Sexuality   15
   NANCY TUANA AND LAURIE SHRAGE

2. Love   42
   NEERA K. BADHWAR

3. Family   70
   BRENDA ALMOND

PART II MORAL STATUS

4. Children   91
   DAVID ARCHARD

5. Abortion   112
   JOHN HARRIS AND SØREN HOLM

6. Reproductive Technology   136
   ROBERT WACHBROIT AND DAVID WASSERMAN

7. Animals   161
   R. G. FREY

8. Environmental Ethics   188
   KRISTIN SHRADER-FRECHETTE

PART III EQUALITY

9. Gender and Sexual Discrimination   219
   ROSEMARIE TONG

10. Race and Racial Discrimination   245
    NAOMI ZACK

11. Affirmative Action   272
    WALTER FEINBERG

12. People with Disabilities   300
    ANITA SILVERS

PART IV THE JUST SOCIETY

13. Punishment   331
    R. A. DUFF

14. Freedom of Speech and Religion   358
    ANDREW ALTMAN

15. Legal Paternalism   387
    DOUGLAS N. HUSAK

16. Multiculturalism   413
    JOHN ARTHUR

17. Economic Justice   433
    JONATHAN WOLFF

18. Intergenerational Justice   459
    AXEL GOSSERIES

19. Privacy   485
    ANITA L. ALLEN

20. Corporate Responsibility   514
    PATRICIA H. WERHANE AND R. EDWARD FREEMAN

21. Whistleblowing   539
    MICHAEL DAVIS

PART V JUSTICE AND
INTERNATIONAL RELATIONS

22. Immigration   567
    CHANDRAN KUKATHAS

23. National Autonomy   591
    WAYNE NORMAN

24. International Economic Justice   620
    DEBRA SATZ

25. World Hunger   643
    NIGEL DOWER

PART VI LIFE AND DEATH

26. Euthanasia and Physician-Assisted Suicide   673
    MARGARET P. BATTIN

27. Capital Punishment   705
    HUGO ADAM BEDAU

28. War   734
    HENRY SHUE

Index   763

NOTES ON THE CONTRIBUTORS

Anita L. Allen is Professor of Law and Philosophy at the University of Pennsylvania. She is a graduate of New College (BA), the University of Michigan (Ph.D.), and Harvard Law school (JD). Professor Allen is co-author with Richard Turkington of a comprehensive textbook, *Privacy Law* (2nd edn., 2002). She has also published 'Uneasy Access: Privacy for Women in a Free Society' (1988) and several dozen articles on ethical, legal, and social dimensions of personal privacy and private choice.

Brenda Almond is Vice-President of the Society for Applied Philosophy and President of the Philosophical Society of England. She received an Honorary Doctorate for Philosophy from Utrecht University and is an elected Corresponding Member of the Austrian Academy of Sciences. Her books include *Exploring Ethics: A Traveler's Tale* (1998), *Moral Concerns* (1987), and *The Philosophical Quest* (1990/1992). She has served on the Human Fertilisation and Embryology Authority and engaged in research on the family as Director of the Social Values Research Centre at the University of Hull.

Andrew Altman is Professor of Philosophy at Georgia State University. He received his Ph.D. from Columbia University in 1977 and was a Fellow in Law and Philosophy at Harvard Law School in 1984–5. Professor Altman is author of *Critical Legal Studies: A Liberal Critique* (1990) and *Arguing about Law: An Introduction to Legal Philosophy* (2001). His articles on sexual harassment, hate speech, and hate-crimes legislation have appeared in *Philosophy and Public Affairs, Ethics*, and *Law and Philosophy*.

David Archard is Reader in Moral Philosophy and Director of the Centre for Ethics, Philosophy, and Public Affairs at the University of St Andrews. He previously taught in Northern Ireland for many years. He is the author of *Children, Rights and Childhood* (1993), *Sexual Consent* (1998), and the forthcoming *Children, Family and the State*, as well as numerous articles and essays in social, legal, political, and applied moral philosophy.

John Arthur is Professor of Philosophy and Director of the Program in Philosophy, Politics, and Law at Binghamton University. He received his Ph.D. in Philosophy from Vanderbilt University, and spent two years as a Liberal Arts Fellow at Harvard Law School. In addition to numerous articles, he is the author of two books, *The Unfinished Constitution* (1989) and *Words that Bind* (1996), and editor or co-editor of six others.

His interests are in legal philosophy (especially constitutional law and interpretation), political theory, and ethics. He is visiting fellow of Balliol College in 2002/3.

Neera K. Badhwar (Ph.D., Toronto) is Associate Professor of Philosophy at the University of Oklahoma. Her articles on friendship, liberalism, and communitarianism, self-interest and altrusim, virtue et al. have appeared in *Ethics, Nous, APQ*, and other journals. She also edited *Friendship: A Philosophical Reader* (1993), and is currently in pursuit of happiness and virtue. She has held fellowships at Dalhousie University, 1986–7, Social Philosophy and Policy Center, BGSU, Spring 1994, and the University Center for Human Values, Princeton University, 1996–7. In Fall 1999 she was NEH Distinguished Visiting Professor at SUNY Potsdam, and in January–December 2002 a Visiting Scholar at Liberty Fund.

Margaret P. Battin is Distinguished Professor of Philosophy and Adjunct Professor of Internal Medicine, Division of Medical Ethics, at the University of Utah. She has authored, edited, or co-edited twelve books, including *The Least Worst Death* (1994), *Ethical Issues in Suicide* (1982/1990), trade-titled *The Death Debate* (1986), as well as several co-edited collections, including *Drug Use in Assisted Suicide and Euthanasia* (1986), and *Physician-Assisted Suicide: Expanding the Debate* (1998). She has also published *Praying for a Cure* (1999), a jointly authored volume on the ethics of religious refusal of medical treatment. She is currently working on a historical sourcebook on ethical issues in suicide.

Hugo Adam Bedau (Ph.D., Harvard), has taught at Tufts University since 1966. He is the co-author of *Current Issues and Enduring Questions* (4th edn., 1996), of *Critical Thinking, Reading, and Writing* (2nd edn., 1996), and *In Spite of Innocence* (1992); and the author of *Death is Different* (1987), *The Death Penalty in America* (4th edn., 1997), and is a contributor to many other volumes. His Romanell–Phi Beta Kappa lectures delivered at Tufts in the spring of 1995 (1997), were published by Oxford University Press under the title *Making Moral Choices* (1997).

Michael Davis is Senior Fellow at the Center for the Study of Ethics in the Professions and Professor of Philosophy, Illinois Institute of Technology. Before coming to IIT in 1986, he taught at Case-Western Reserve, Illinois State, and the University of Illinois at Chicago. Davis has published more than 120 articles (and chapters), authored five books, and co-edited three others. Among his recent publications are: *Justice in the Shadow of Death* (1996), *Thinking Like an Engineer* (1998), *Ethics and the University* (1999), *Conflict of Interest in the Professions* (2001), and *Profession, Code, and Ethics* (2002).

Nigel Dower is Senior Lecturer in Philosophy in the University of Aberdeen, Scotland. His research and teaching interests have focused over the last twenty years on the ethics of international relations, development, and the environment and related issues. His publications include *World Poverty: Challenge and Response* (1983), *World Ethics: The New Agenda* (1998), and *An Introduction to Global*

Citizenship (forthcoming). He edited *Ethics and Environmental Responsibility* (1989), and co-edited *Global Citizenship: A Critical Reader* (2002), and he edits the Edinburgh Studies in World Ethics. He is currently President of the International Development Ethics Association.

R. A. Duff was educated at Oxford and (after a visiting year at the University of Washington) has taught philosophy at the University of Stirling since 1970. He held a British Academy Research Readership, 1989–91, and holds a Leverhulme Major Research Fellowship, 2002–5. His publications include *Trials and Punishments* (1986), *Intention, Agency, and Criminal Liability* (1990), *Criminal Attempts* (1996), and *Punishment, Communication, and Community* (2000).

Walter Feinberg is Professor of Philosophy of Education at the University of Illinois in Urbana. His books include *Education and Democratic Theory* (with A. B. Fields 2001), *Common Schools/Uncommon Identities* (1998), *On Higher Ground: Education and the Case for Affirmative Action* (1998), *Japan and the Quest for a New American Identity* (1993), and *Understanding Education* (1982). Feinberg has been President of the American Educational Studies Association and the Philosophy of Education Society.

R. Edward Freeman is Elis and Signe Olsson Professor of Business Administration and Director of the Olsson Center for Ethics, at the Darden School, University of Virginia. He works in the area of business ethics and business strategy. Freeman's books include *Strategic Management: A Stakeholder Approach* (1983), *Corporate Strategy and the Search for Ethics* (1988), and *Environmentalism and the New Logic of Business: How Firms Can be Profitable and Leave Our Children a Living Planet* (2000). He is the editor of the Ruffin Series of Business Ethics published by Oxford University Press. Mr Freeman has received outstanding teacher awards at the Wharton School, the Carlson School University of Minnesota, and Darden. He has been a consultant and speaker for companies across the world.

R. G. Frey (D.Phil., Oxford) is the author of numerous books and articles in normative and applied ethics and in the history of ethics. He is Professor of Philosophy at Bowling Green State University and a Senior Research Fellow in the Social Philosophy and Policy Center there.

Axel Gosseries is a post-doctoral research fellow with the Belgian National Fund for Scientific Research. He is based at the Université Catholique de Louvain. He holds degrees in law (Louvain and London) and a Ph.D. in philosophy (Louvain 2000), with a dissertation on intergenerational justice. His areas of specialization are moral and political philosophy and he is currently working on the ethical aspects of tradable quotas schemes.

John Harris is Sir David Alliance Professor of Bioethics at the University of Manchester. He is a member of the United Kingdom Human Genetics Commission and the Ethics Committee of the British Medical Association. He was recently elected a Fellow of the United Kingdom Academy of Medical Sciences, the first philosopher to have been so honoured. He is editor of numerous anthologies, and the author of many books and essays. His most recent books are *Clones, Genes, and Immortality* (1998) and *Bioethics* (2001).

Søren Holm is Professor of Clinical Bioethics at the University of Manchester, and Professor of Medical Ethics at the University of Oslo, Norway. He has written extensively on issues in reproductive ethics and on the moral status of the fetus.

Douglas N. Husak is Professor of Philosophy and Law at Rutgers University, where he teaches courses in philosophy of law, ethics, applied ethics, and criminal law. He is the author of approximately seventy articles and three books: *Philosophy of Criminal Law* (1987), *Drugs and Rights* (1992), and *Legalize This! The Case for Descriminalizing Drugs* (2002). His current interest is the theory of criminalization, especially its application to questionable uses of the criminal sanction such as the punishment of drug offenders.

Chandran Kukathas teaches in the School of Politics, University College, University of New South Wales, at the Australian Defence Force Academy. He is co-editor of the *Journal of Political Philosophy*, the author of *Hayek and Modern Liberalism* (1998), and *Rawls: A Theory of Justice and its Critics* (1990) (with Philip Pettit), as well as several papers on liberal political theory and multiculturalism, and edited *Rawls: Critical Assessments* (2002). His latest book, The *Liberal Archipelago*, is to be published by Oxford University Press.

Wayne Norman holds a Chair in the Centre for Applied Ethics, University of British Columbia. He taught previously at the University of Ottawa and the University of Western Ontario, and has held visiting positions at Stanford University, the Universitat Pompeu Fabra, Université de Paris, the Université Catholique de Louvain, and at the London School of Economics, where he did his Ph.D. in Philosophy. He has written extensively on multiculturalism, nationalism, federalism, and secession, and co-edited (with Will Kymlicka) *Citizenship in Diverse Societies* (2000) and (with Ronald Beiner) *Canadian Political Philosophy* (2001). His next book is tentatively entitled *Thinking through Nationalism*.

Debra Satz is Associate Professor of Philosophy and, by courtesy, Political Science at Stanford University. She also directs Stanford's program in Ethics in Society. Her interests are in political and moral theory, feminist philosophy, philosophy of economics, and Marxism. She has published articles on the moral limits of the market, rational choice theory, and global justice.

Kristin Shrader-Frechette, O'Neill Professor of Philosophy and Concurrent Professor of Biological Sciences at the University of Notre Dame, specializes in normative ethics and philosophy of science. Current President of the International

Society for Environmental Ethics, she is Past President of the Risk Assessment and Policy Association and of the Society for Philosophy and Technology. She has authored fourteen books and approximately 300 articles. Her latest book is *Environmental Justice: Creating Equality, Reclaiming Democracy* (2002). Her articles have appeared in journals such as *Philosophy of Science, Synthese, Biology and Philosophy, Journal of Philosophy*, and *Ethics*, as well as numerous scientific journals, including *Science*. Web site: www.nd.edu/~kshrader.

Laurie Shrage is Professor of Philosophy at California State Polytechnic University, Pomona. She is the author of *Abortion and Social Responsibility: Depolarizing the Debate* (forthcoming) and *Moral Dilemmas of Feminism: Prostitution, Adultery, and Abortion* (1994). She has published articles in a number of philosophy and women's studies journals. She is currently co-editor of *Hypatia: A Journal of Feminist Philosophy*.

Henry Shue is Senior Research Fellow, Department of Politics and International Relations, Oxford University, and Fellow, Merton College. He was a founding member, and later Director, of the Institute for Philosophy and Public Policy at the University of Maryland (1976–87) and was then the first Director of the Program on Ethics and Public Life at Cornell University (1987–2002). Best known for *Basic Rights* (2nd edn., 1996), he first wrote about the morality of violence in 'Torture', *Philosophy and Public Affairs* (1978). His other main current interest is international justice and climate change.

Anita Silvers, Professor of Philosophy at San Francisco State University, has written extensively about ethics and bioethics, and disability theory. Among her books on these subjects are *Disability, Difference, Discrimination: Perspectives on Justice in Bioethics and Public Policy* (with David Wasserman and Mary Mahowald) (1998), *Americans with Disabilities: Implications of the Law for Individuals and Institutions* (with Leslie Francis) (2000), and *Medicine and Social Justice* (with Margaret Battin and Rosamond Rhodes) (2002). She is currently writing (with Michael Ashley Stein) a series of law review articles on protection from disability discrimination and genetic discrimination, of which two have already been published, and a book of essays titled *Odd Ones Out: Normality and Singularity in Law, Medicine, and Art.*

Rosemarie Tong is Distinguished Professor of Health Care Ethics in the Department of Philosophy at the University of North Carolina at Charlotte. She is the author of *Women, Sex, and the Law* (1984), *Feminine and Feminist Ethics* (1993), *Feminist Approaches to Bioethics: Theoretical Reflections and Practical Applications* (1997), *Feminist Thought: A More Comprehensive Introduction* (1998), and *Globalizing Feminist Bioethics: Crosscultural Perspectives* (with Aida Santos and Gwen Anderson 2000). She is also a Board Member of a grassroots citizens group in North Carolina dedicated to increasing the public's knowledge about health care. She is currently writing a book on Health Care Ethics for Allied Health Professionals.

Nancy Tuana is the Dupont/Class of 1949 Professor of Philosophy and Women's Studies at The Pennsylvania State University and Director of the Rock Ethics Institute. Her books include *Engendering Rationalities* (2001), *Feminism and Science* (1998), *The Less Noble Sex: Scientific, Religious, and Philosophical Conceptions of Woman's Nature* (1993), *Revealing Male Bodies* (2002), and *Women and the History of Philosophy* (1992). She is currently co-editor of *Hypatia: A Journal of Feminist Philosophy* and series editor of the Penn State Press series *Re-Reading the Canon*.

Robert Wachbroit is a Research Scholar at the Institute for Philosophy and Public Policy at the University of Maryland's School of Public Affairs. He is also an Adjunct Associate Professor of OB/GYN in the University's School of Medicine. Wachbroit has written numerous articles in the areas of science and technology policy, philosophy of science, and medical ethics, including articles on the principles of disease classification, the challenges of genetic testing and diagnosis, the problems inherent in risk characterization and risk communication, the changing relationships between experts and the public, and the impact of the Internet on civil society.

David Wasserman (BA (Philosophy), Yale University; MA (Psychology), University of North Carolina; JD, University of Michigan) is a research scholar at the Institute for Philosophy and Public Policy at the University of Maryland's School of Public Affairs. His current work focuses on ethical and policy issues in genetic research and technology, assisted reproduction, health care, and disability. He has also written extensively about issues in procedural and distributive justice. In addition to numerous articles and book chapters, he is co-author of *Disability, Difference, Discrimination* (with Anita Silvers and Mary Mahowald, 1998) and co-editor of *Genetics and Criminal Behavior* (with Robert Wachbroit, 2001).

Patricia H. Werhane is the Ruffin Professor of Business Ethics and Co-Director of the Olsson Center for Applied Ethics in the Darden School at the University of Virginia. She formerly taught at Loyola University Chicago, and held visiting appointments at Dartmouth, Cambridge, and the University of Canterbury (New Zealand). Professor Werhane has published numerous articles and is the author or editor of thirteen books including *Ethical Issues in Business* (with T. Donaldson, 6th edn.) (2002), *Persons, Rights and Corporations* (1985), *Adam Smith and his Legacy for Modern Capitalism* (1991), and *The Business of Consumption* (with Laura Westra) (1998), and *Moral Imagination and Managerial Decision-Making* (1990). Her latest book is *Organization Ethics in Health Care*, edited with E. Spencer, A. Mills, and M. Rorty (2000).

Jonathan Wolff is Professor of Philosophy at University College London (UCL). He is the author of *Robert Nozick: Property, Justice and the Minimal State* (1991), *An Introduction to Political Philosophy* (1996), and *Why Read Marx Today?* (2002); and co-editor (with Michael Rosen) of *Political Thought* (1999) and (with Martin Stone) of *The Proper Ambition of Science* (2000). He is joint editor (with Tim Crane) of the

Routledge Philosophical GuideBook series. He is currently working on questions concerning the rectification of injustice.

Naomi Zack (Ph.D, Columbia University, New York) is Professor of Philosophy at the University of Oregon, Eugene. Her most recent book is *Philosophy of Science and Race* (2002) and she is also the author of *Race and Mixed Race* (1993), *Bachelors of Science: Seventeenth Century Identity* (1996), *Then and Now* (1996), and a textbook, *Thinking About Race* (1998). She is the editor of *Women of Color and Philosophy* (1998), *American Mixed Race: The Culture of Microdiversity* (1995), and other anthologies, and has written articles on race, racism, mixed race, gender, and seventeenth-century philosophy. Zack's current project is an existentialist theory of mind.

INTRODUCTION

HUGH LaFOLLETTE

1. THE EMERGENCE OF PRACTICAL ETHICS

PRACTICAL ethics has only recently come into its own as a sub-discipline within philosophy. When I began graduate school in the early 1970s, practical ethics was still in its infancy: the first journal in the field had just been launched; the first anthology, just published. The idea that practical ethics was then a serious sub-discipline, worthy of full membership in the philosophical community, would have been ludicrous. After all, even normative ethics, which had a rich intellectual history going back to the ancients, had itself only recently re-emerged as a recognized part of professional philosophy.

In the 1940s and 1950s ethicists were centrally concerned with the nature of moral language: they sought to identify the meaning of central moral terms like 'good' and 'right', and to explore the truth conditions, if any, for moral utterances. Old-fashioned normative ethics was largely delegated to historians of philosophy. As P. H. Nowell-Smith (1957: 24) expressed the then-common view:

The moral philosopher's task is now conceived, not to be one of conducting a theoretical inquiry into practical wisdom, but to be one of investigating questions, judgements, doubts, and beliefs that are themselves theoretical. The moral philosopher not only makes theoretical statements about his subject-matter; his subject-matter consists of theoretical statements.

It was not surprising, then, that at that time practical ethics could not be a serious academic possibility. However, by the late 1960s and 1970s, pressures within and outside the academy—most especially the appearance of a bevy of social movements—allowed normative ethics to reclaim a place at the philosophical table. But it was initially a secondary place. Still late into the twentieth century some philosophers thought meta-ethics was the apex of philosophical enquiry. For them normative ethics—and therefore indirectly practical ethics—was dependent upon a well-worked-out meta-ethics. As Michael Smith (1995: 2) put it:

> Despite their interest in normative ethics, however, philosophers have not tended to think that these sorts of questions are of the first importance in moral philosophy.... rather they have thought we should do normative ethics only after we have given satisfactory answers to certain questions in meta-ethics.... Philosophers have surely been right to give meta-ethical questions a certain priority over questions of normative ethics.

By that time, however, practical ethics had already begun to emerge as a serious sub-discipline. The aforementioned re-emergence of normative ethics, coupled with significant social upheavals, opened a space within which practical ethics could appear. In the 1960s, popular culture and college campuses were the scene of heated debates about racial and sexual discrimination, the war in Vietnam, abortion, and the degradation of nature. In this environment, courses dedicated to the careful discussion of these issues could bolster falling enrolments. Even those suspicious of practical ethics's philosophical pedigree recognized its drawing power in the classroom.

Nonetheless, it would be a mistake to infer that its heightened status simply reflects a prudential decision to boost departmental enrolments. There has also been a significant shift in professional attitudes. In general, philosophers conceive of their role more broadly than did philosophers of the 1940s. The increasing interest in practical ethics since the early 1970s is just one instance of this change. Philosophers known primarily for their work in normative and meta-ethics are now making forays into practical ethics. They are peering over—and even tearing down—the once high walls between meta-, normative, and practical ethics. Some are *doing* practical ethics and many others are proclaiming its relation to normative and meta-ethics. For instance, Stephen Darwall (1998: 12) rejects any clear separation between meta-ethics and normative ethics, while Shelly Kagan not only eschews the distinction between meta-ethics and normative ethics (1998: 7), but also renounces any firm distinction between normative and practical ethics (1998: 5). One indication of its heightened status is that the most recent—and admittedly controversial—Leiter Report identifies the top two philosophy departments in the English-speaking world as either good or excellent in applied philosophy (Leiter 2001). Practical ethics is here to stay. The changed status of the field has doubtless driven some shifts in the nature of the field, shifts I now discuss.

2. THE NATURE OF PRACTICAL ETHICS

Practical ethics at its best exhibits the virtues of any good philosophy: it eschews unqualified grand claims; it is careful, clear, thoughtful, and theoretically informed. Specifically, it is the explicit discussion of practical ethical issues, by philosophers, in their capacity as philosophers. That definition, of course, covers considerable conceptual turf. That is as it should be. We should not exclude important work from the realm of practical ethics on narrow ideological grounds, especially since, as a new sub-discipline, it is still defining itself. And, like all new sub-disciplines, it defines itself more by how it is practised than by bare self-description.

Of course there is a clear family resemblance between what practical ethicists are doing at the beginning of the twenty-first century and what they were doing in the 1970s. However, there are also significant alterations in the way it is practised, at least changes in emphases. These are both the product of, and partly responsible for, its enhanced status within philosophy more generally.

The four most important changes, to my mind, have been (*a*) the emergence of sub-fields, (*b*) a diminishing role for bare intuitions, (*c*) a heightened concern for and reliance on empirical data, and (*d*) a more robust relation between ethical theorizing and practical ethical discussion. These changes have been gradual, and, in some cases, their nature is apparent only in retrospect. I predict each of these tendencies will continue into the foreseeable future. Understanding them will help better understand what practical ethics is and what practical ethicists do.

2.1 The Emergence of Sub-Fields

People who now work in practical ethics are increasingly inclined to identify themselves as working in one of its sub-fields. Indeed, there are probably few of us who think of ourselves more as generalists in practical ethics than as a specialist in one of those sub-fields. Medical ethics and business ethics are the best established, with environmental ethics arguably the fastest growing; the prominence of this triumvirate is signalled by the facts that (*a*) each now has four or more specialized journals, (*b*) an increasing number of academic and non-academic jobs now require one of these sub-specialities, and (*c*) there are specialized programmes and even degrees in each. Still other practical ethicists now describe themselves as working in legal ethics, journalistic ethics, engineering ethics, research ethics, or professional ethics more broadly. Within these newer areas, there are also a growing number of journals, programmes, and advertised jobs. The emergence of these areas of sub-specialization indicates practical ethics's professional maturation. But specialization has its costs.

First, much of the work in early years of a sub-field is spent trying to define the field: to differentiate itself from other disciplines, to identify core issues, to categorize the basic options, to trace important argumentative lines, and to expose wholly untenable positions. Work at this stage can be very exciting, but is often deeply flawed. Since the central issues have not yet been clearly delineated, philosophers may be prone to two opposite mistakes. Some may blindly embrace and defend the status quo, while others may cavalierly reject it without fully understanding or appreciating its insights or rationale (Gaita 1991: 315–16). Arguably early work in biomedical ethics (formerly called simply 'medical ethics') exhibited both tendencies. Some practitioners, suffering from science envy, blindly defended current medical practice, while others, who failed to understand the operation of modern medicine, advocated changes that, in the light of the medical institution's operation, were simply untenable. Then, once a field moves into professional adolescence, practitioners may become unduly adversarial; they may also get bogged down into argumentative ruts dug by their predecessors (see, for example, Battin's discussion (Chapter 26, this volume) of the current status of the debate over physician-assisted suicide).

Secondly, the appearance of sub-fields can encourage inappropriate and misleading specialization where the problems within each are thought to be—or treated as if they were—*sui generis*. Practitioners may say or imply that they can satisfactorily resolve *this* issue while effectively ignoring others. This tendency is in tension with the third change, which I discuss later.

2.2 The Role of Intuitions

Since the 1930s philosophers have debated the role of intuitions in ethics. Some have derided them, while others see them as essential epistemological tools. Among the latter group, some see intuitions as the central element of a formal moral theory, while others see them as having a vital, but more limited, role in moral reasoning. Those who see them as the central elements of moral theory are intuitionists. Intuitionism gained its full expression in the work of Ross (1930/1988). According to Ross and his followers 'there are a number of distinct moral principles or duties.... some of these duties are fundamental or underivative. These principles are not themselves grounded in, or derived from, some more general theory' (McNaughton 2000: 269). Although Intuitionism, as a formal theory, has been out of favour, it is making a bit of a philosophical comeback (Stratton-Lake 2002). Were it again to become a lively theoretical option, there is nothing in principle that would prevent its adherents from engaging in practical ethics. Nonetheless, few do, perhaps because many also embrace particularism (Hooker and Little 2000), and those committed to stronger forms of particularism will, because of their views of moral reasoning, be unable to say anything general about particular issues (Hooker 2000: 16–21).

Although most philosophers are wary of full-blown intuitionism, most also believe intuitions of some form are crucial elements of sound moral reasoning, important tools for constructing or testing a moral theory. As Kamm (1995: 84) put its:

A second idea that people may have in mind when they discuss the relations between theory and practice is the view that the correctness of a theory can be tested, and a theory be changed, by seeing its implications for hypothetical cases and also for real cases. I believe theories should be tested, at least in part, in this way.

Kamm suggests that we begin with a (proto-)theory, and then explore the implications of that theory. If the implications clash with our intuitions (our pre-theoretical moral beliefs, whether specific, general, or abstract), then the theory must be rejected or modified. Theory, in this view, is thus a way of unifying our intuitions about which we are confident, so that we will be empowered to act rationally when we face issues or circumstances about which we are not so confident.

The idea that we must use intuitions in framing our moral theories is clearly in the air. The best-known way of describing their role, made popular by Rawls, gives intuitions a somewhat more circumscribed role. Bare intuitions, Rawls claims, are illegitimate starting points for moral deliberation since they may be unduly influenced by 'extraneous factors'—personal quirks, societal indoctrination, and bias. Intuitions, duly pruned of these factors, are 'considered judgements'; these are starting points for sound moral deliberation. However, they are not simply tests for theories; they, too, are subject to theorizing. Here's how. We begin with considered judgements as a first test for our theories: sometimes an intuition is very strong and our theoretical commitments weak. If so, barring any further information, we (temporarily) abandon the theoretical 'commitment'. In other cases, however, even our considered judgements are weak or fuzzy and our theoretical commitments are strong. If so, barring any further information, we abandon or at least modify them. We work back and forth between our 'considered judgements' and further theorizing, until we finally reach 'reflective equilibrium' (Rawls 1971: 48–51).

There are three important lessons about this Rawlsian method for the way that practical ethics is practised: (1) we begin ethical enquiry by reflecting upon our 'inherited' moral beliefs—what we were taught by our parents or cultures—there is nowhere else to begin; (2) those beliefs, as embodied in our intuitions, are not inerrant; and (3) the best theory is the one that makes the best overall sense of all our beliefs—moral and otherwise. However appealing this methodology is, it does not easily yield specific answers to practical ethical issues. Not even in Rawls's view. But it does help motivate the need for more extensive empirical knowledge and more careful theorizing. After all, this model presupposes that knowledge is importantly holistic: that no knowledge stands entirely on its own; it is shaped and sometimes rejected because of other knowledge we have. Seen in this way, Rawlsian reflective equilibrium is a practical adaptation of Quine's idea of a 'web of belief' (Quine and Ullian 1978) and Peircian 'ideal inquiry'. It is a recognition—if I may paraphrase Wilfred Sellers—that 'The aim of (moral) philosophy, abstractly for-mulated, is to understand how... (moral phenomena) in the broadest sense of the term, hang together in the broadest possible sense of that term' (Sellars 1963: 1).

Intuitions, then, are not themselves solutions to practical ethical issues, not even for intuitionists. No one doing practical ethics thinks, talks, or acts as if she can adequately resolve a practical ethical controversy *simply* by appealing to her intu-itions. If nothing else, she must argue from those intuitions before she can reach conclusions about practical ethical issues. People do not simply intuit the proper answer to abortion, physician-assisted suicide, capital punishment, or affirmative action. Or, if they think they do, their intuitions are unreliable.

It is not only that intuitions do not do all the work in practical ethics. I sense that intuitions, in any robust sense—where they are thought to be more than summaries of previous ethical experience, and thus, starting points for ethical deliberation—play a diminishing role. When perusing the essays in this volume, you will notice, I think, just how limited a role intuitions play in the current description of, or ten-tative solutions to, these issues. Those currently working in the field are less likely to resort to intuitions; they are especially less likely to employ highly fictionalized examples as 'intuition pumps' (Dennett 1984) to defend certain positions on prac-tical ethical issues. To the limited extent that some use such examples, they stand-ardly use them to explain a position rather than offering them as the principal premises defending that position. In fact, the best work in practical ethics is now more inclined to exhibit considerable familiarity with relevant empirical details.

2.3 The Role of Empirical Data

Just as many philosophers of science once thought—or wrote as if they thought—that they could ply their trade in relative ignorance of the actual practice of science, many practical ethicists once thought—or wrote as if they thought—that they could solve practical ethical issues without any detailed awareness of the practical details of the problem they were discussing. Both sub-disciplines have realized the error of their ways. Philosophers of science now standardly understand scientific practice and are usually well acquainted with recent scientific developments. They read not only other philosophers but also practising scientists. And their awareness of the practice of sci-ence shapes their philosophical work. Practical ethicists are likewise more prone to know relevant empirical details (legal, political, sociological, and economic) about ethical issues they discuss. And those details shape their philosophical discussion. Perhaps not as much as they should; but more than they once did (Glover 1999: 6).

These empirical details serve two related purposes. First, since practical ethics aims to say something informative about the moral appropriateness of individual behaviours and institutional structures or actions, then, on virtually any moral theory, we need adequate empirical data to know when and how the moral theory is relevant to that behaviour or institution. If we do not understand the circumstances under which many people die or in which most people make decisions about the end of life, then we will fail to fully understand and appreciate both the appeal of, and disquiet about, physician-assisted suicide. Unless we understand the circumstances in which people are impoverished and starve, we will not know how to evaluate either individual actions or political and economic institutions that might cause or prevent such impoverishment. And, unless we understand the nature and long-term effects of systematic discrimination, we cannot seriously entertain arguments for affirmative action. In short, without these (and many other) empirical details, abstractly asking whether physician-assisted suicide is justified, whether we have an obligation to help the starving, or whether affirmative action is justified will tell us little. It will probably lead us on misleading argumentative tracks.

Secondly, awareness of detailed empirical data will guide moral theorizing in at least two different ways. First, it gives content to our moral principles and moral considerations. Without knowledge of empirical details, our principles and considerations remain unacceptably amorphous. We may say, for example, that we should maximize the greatest happiness of the greatest number or that we should respect people's rights. However, those claims are little more than vague objects of our homage unless we have some knowledge of human psychology, the nature of human happiness and autonomy, and an awareness of the ways that our, others', and institutions' actions shape people's abilities to be happy or to live autonomously. Often, though, we do not notice the importance of this empirical knowledge because we normally converse about these issues with others of similar background, education, inclination, and information. Imagine, though, trying to discuss these moral principles with the average 6 year old; children of that age simply cannot understand these principles in any robust way.

Second, a serious acquaintance with the empirical details is one of, and arguably the best, means of ensuring that we do not blindly adopt the moral status quo. If we do not understand the way people act and the way our world works, we will lack a plausible standpoint from which rationally to evaluate current practices, and will therefore be more inclined to embrace that status quo. If our extant 'moral principles' condone slavery, or forbid women or ethnic minorities from voting—as they once did—then one (and perhaps the only) way of undermining those 'principles' is to become vividly aware of the practice of slavery and systematic discrimination, and to understand the nature, abilities, intelligence, and feelings of slaves, minorities, and women. Such knowledge and experience impel us to rethink our theoretical commitments, and surely one of the central aims of ethical theorizing is to help us battle bias, ignorance, short-sightedness, and selfishness (Nussbaum 2000). Anyone who teaches introductory ethics students knows just how often the students' moral views are skewed because of their relative ignorance of human psychology, and complete unfamiliarity with economic, social, and political institutions.

2.4 Theory and Practice

When people talk about the relation of theory to practice, they sometimes speak, or suggest, that we merely apply a theory, perhaps the way an engineer might apply a mathematical formula in designing a bridge. The old (and still widely used) name 'Applied Ethics' feeds this supposition. It implies that we have a theory, and that from that theory, in conjunction with the description of the current situation, we can straightforwardly derive the appropriate action. Thus, the relation between ethical theory and practical ethical deliberation is roughly the relationship between Newton's second law and the force of an accelerating car. By using the law and the statement of initial conditions, we can calculate the force of the moving vehicle. What is crucial in both the moral and the scientific cases is that we must first have the correct theory. The theory dictates the answer to the practical issue.

That is not, I think, the proper account of the relation between practical ethics and ethical theory. However, the proper alternative is not to jettison theory, as some philosophers claim or suggest (e.g. Williams 1985; Baier 1989), and as some early practitioners of practical ethics seemed to do. Both approaches err in assuming that theory and practice are fundamentally separate enquiries. However, practice without theory lacks direction; it becomes little more than a loose amalgam of reactions to specific cases, while theory without practice runs the danger of 'building castles in the air that nowhere touch the ground.' It becomes an intellectual game only vaguely connected to the very phenomena it is supposed to understand and explain. What we must do is acknowledge that theory and practice are deeply related. Sound practical ethics must be theoretically sophisticated, and a workable moral theory must understand how that theory might be embodied in practice. The best work in practical ethics is increasingly theoretically sophisticated, and, when done well, helps illuminate that theory.

When we think carefully about practical issues, we are impelled to theorize—although that does not mean that we merely 'apply' a theory. Such reflection reveals the connections between particular cases, isolates the contrasts between competing theoretical perspectives, and becomes aware of tensions between what we were taught and what experience and reflection reveal. These require us to step back from our preconceptions to examine an issue more abstractly. We begin to see that we cannot think clearly about racial and sexual discrimination unless we think about the moral status of groups; that thinking about love, friendship, and families requires us to think about the nature and role of impartiality in ethics; that we cannot evaluate competing theories of punishment unless we think more broadly about the nature of responsibility; that we cannot evaluate corporate responsibility or the practice of whistleblowing unless we also think about the moral status of corporations; that, in resolving the issue of world hunger, we must discuss the demandingness of morality; and that we cannot think about any of these issues unless we explore competing major theories and determine the moral relevance, if any, of the act/omission distinction, the principle of double effect, and so on. Then when we are theorizing, we are further led to think about still other practical ethical issues—to see how theoretical considerations are raised and realized within them. That constrains how we should think about each of these issues. For instance, if we employ the act/omission distinction to explain why we are not obliged to help the starving, how can we then reject that distinction when advancing the 'Best Bet' argument about capital punishment? Or, if we employ consequentialist considerations when defending our view on abortions, how can we then reject those same considerations when arguing against affirmative action? In short, we find we must think more holistically about ethical theory, meta-ethics, and practical ethics—to conceive of ethical thought, broadly understood, as a web of belief.

Finally, sustained and careful discussion of practical ethical quandaries can heighten our moral understanding and moral imagination, and therefore increase the chance that we will act appropriately. One benefit of higher cognitive thought is, as Popper was fond of saying, that hypotheses can die in our stead. We can learn from imagination: we need not have an experience to know what might have happened if we had. If we think carefully about and reflect upon our own experience—and the chronicle of others' experience—we can go some distance towards identifying the best ways to behave. Practical ethics, as the systematic discussion of practical moral issues, thus becomes a fountain of hypothetical experience that enriches our moral imaginations and makes us vividly aware of the subtleties of both theory and practice.

When seen in this way, practical ethics is—or could become—the ideal bridge between practice and ethical theorizing. If we approach ethics more holistically, we increase the likelihood that discussion of practical cases does not become unprincipled, and that theory does not become empty.

Each of these four changes helps drive the development of debates within practical ethics. Some options that once seemed defensible have been abandoned, and replaced by more careful, and more theoretically and empirical sensitive analyses. My aim is that the essays in this volume will serve as a suitable guide to professionals who want to know about these developments, and that the contributors to this volume will further advance those debates.

3. The Structure of the Volume

The Oxford Handbooks are designed for professionals and graduate students—not (primarily) for undergraduates or the general public. Each handbook will include chapters profiling and evaluating the current work in some segment of a professional field. Taken as a whole, each will give professionals a firm understanding of the current status of work within that field. The *Oxford Handbook of Practical Ethics* is one of the first philosophy books in that series. It includes twenty-eight lengthy chapters on key issues in practical ethics. In each case I have invited authors who can not only map the conceptual territory, but are themselves active explorers on that landscape. The plan is to provide a handbook that allows professionals and graduate students who want to familiarize themselves with a practical ethical issue to have one chapter that provides that relevant background, and that gives them a sense of the main moves and main participants in that debate, while also advancing that debate.

To provide some structure to the volume, I have arranged chapters into six broad categories running the gamut from the intensely personal through the social to the international: Our Personal Lives, Moral Status, Equality, The Just Society, Justice and International Relations, and Life and Death. This reveals the range of issues that properly come under the rubric of 'practical ethics'. However, we should not take these categories too seriously; after all, they do not carve the moral universe at its joints. There are alternative schemes I could have used, schemes that would also have made sense.

Certainly I do not want to beg too many practical or theoretical questions by this categorization. For instance, by placing abortion in the category called 'Moral Status', I am not, for instance, merely assuming the 'right-to-life' position. I might have placed it in the 'Equality' part, but then it might have seemed that I was begging the question in favour of the 'right-to-choose' position. In the end, I decided to categorize abortion as I did largely because of historical considerations—that this is the way, rightly or wrongly, that the problem was first characterized. That does not mean that characterization is correct. It does mean, however, that we can best understand the debate by first understanding its history, even if we eventually conclude that the history was misguided. Minimally, we should understand that any adequate 'solution' to the issue must address both types of considerations, even if it is only to argue that some of them are morally irrelevant.

Likewise, by putting war under 'Life and Death' I do not mean to deny that it is also or even primarily a question of 'Justice and International Relations', or even of 'Equality'. I put it there because one crucial set of issues we must address to resolve this issue comprises issues it shares with euthanasia and capital punishment. But it certainly does not exhaust the issues one must resolve to think morally about war.

I do not find this overlap either confusing or undesirable. Rather, I see this as one important indication of the extent to which (and the ways in which) practical ethics has advanced. Philosophers concerned about any of these issues are becoming increasingly aware of the complexities of the issues, and increasingly attentive to the interconnections between seemingly disparate moral issues. No issue is an island unto itself. Each engages both empirical data and theoretical considerations that are common to other practical moral issues. These connections will be apparent as you read many of these chapters. This now gives us another way to see one earlier expressed worry about undue specialization: it leads practitioners to assume they can resolve one practical ethical issue without confronting underlying theoretical issues and without thinking about other practical issues. Practical ethics, well done, combats this danger of specialization by keeping us well aware of the interconnection between different issues and between theory and practice.

References

Baier, A. (1989). 'Doing without Moral Theory?', in S. Clarke and E. Simpson (eds.), *Anti-Theory in Ethics and Moral Conservatism*. Albany, NY: SUNY Press, 29–48.

Darwall, S. (1998). *Philosophical Ethics*. Boulder, CO: Westview Press.

Dennett, D. C. (1984). *Elbow Room: The Varieties of Free Will Worth Wanting*. Oxford: Oxford University Press.

Gaita, R. (1991). *Good and Evil: An Absolute Conception*. New York: St Martin's Press.

Glover, J. (1999). *Humanity: A Moral History of the Twentieth Century*. New Haven: Yale University Press.

Hooker, B. (2000). 'Moral Particularism: Wrong and Bad', in B. Hooker and M. O. Little (eds.), *Moral Particularism*. Oxford: Oxford University Press, 1–22.

——and Little, M. O. (2000) (eds.). *Moral Particularism*. Oxford: Oxford University Press.

Kagan, S. (1998). *Normative Ethics*. Boulder, CO: Westview Press.

Kamm, F. M. (1995). 'High Theory, Low Theory, and the Demands of Morality', in I. Shapiro and J. W. DeCew (eds.), *Theory and Practice*. New York: New York University Press, 72–90.

Leiter, B. (2001). 'The Philosophical Gourmet Report', http://www.blackwellpublishers.co.uk/ gourmet/ranking.htm.

McNaughton, D. (2000). 'Intuitionism', in H. LaFollette (ed.), *The Blackwell Guide to Ethical Theory*. Oxford: Blackwell, 268–87.

Nowell-Smith, P. H. (1957). *Ethics*. New York: Philosophical Library.

Nussbaum, M. (2000). 'Why Practice Needs Ethical Theory: Particularism, Principle, and Bad Behavior', in S. J. Burton (ed.), *The Path of the Law and its Influence: The Legacy of Oliver Wendell Holmes, Jr.* Cambridge: Cambridge University Press, 50–86.

Quine, W. V., and Ullian, J. S. (1978). *The Web of Belief*. 2nd edn. New York: Random House.

Rawls, J. (1971). *A Theory of Justice*. Cambridge, MA: Harvard University Press.

Ross, W. D. (1930/1988). *The Right and the Good*. Indianapolis: Hackett Publishing Company.

Sellars, W. (1963). 'Philosophy and the Scientific Image of Man'. In Sellars, *Science, Perception, and Reality*. New York: Humanities Press, 366.

Smith, M. (1995). *The Moral Problem*. Oxford: Blackwell.

Stratton-Lake, P. (2002) (ed.), *Ethical Intuitionism: Re-Evaluations*. Oxford: Oxford University Press.

Williams, B. A. O. (1985). *Ethics and the Limits of Philosophy*. Cambridge, MA: Harvard University Press.

PART I

OUR PERSONAL LIVES

CHAPTER 1

SEXUALITY

NANCY TUANA

LAURIE SHRAGE

1. INTRODUCTION

NOT long ago, impeachment proceedings were underway in the USA because of Bill
Clinton's extramarital affair. Those opposing him claimed his behaviour violated
deeply held norms of trust, decency, honesty, responsibility, and integrity. By contrast, many supporting the president argued that his conduct, while perhaps indiscreet and politically unwise, should not be morally judged by non-intimate others.
Some supporters found questionable the voyeuristic attention the public devoted
to the president's intimate life. For many opponents, however, ways of being intimate say something important about our moral character, as individuals and a society. The president's conduct, plus his attempt to keep it from public view, led many
to question his fitness for high public office. Though the president survived his sen-
ate trial, his affair attracted persistent public criticism in ways that articulate and
rearticulate sexual values in the USA.

In this chapter, we will trace public debates about sexual practices that have
found their way into recent philosophical and other academic publications. We will
examine the ideals and standards some ethicists have proposed for guiding our
sexual lives, even those lived away from the public spotlight. Many debates about
sex concern sexual practices that transgress long-standing sexual mores, practices
such as extramarital sex, same-sex sex, and paid sex. Debates about transgressive

sexual acts often focus on whether the traditional social barriers against them are rationally defensible. Other debates about sex concern sexual practices that involve harm, coercion, or social subordination, such as rape, pornography, harassment, and 'unsafe' sex. Debates about harmful sexual acts focus on just how harmful they are and how to prevent these practices or their ill effects. Some sexual practices are viewed as both transgressive and harmful, some as neither, and some as one or the other but not both. Indeed, one strategy for demonstrating the rationality of a particular social rule is to show that transgressions of it are harmful, and one strategy for demonstrating that a sexual act is not genuinely harmful is to demonstrate that its harmful effects result primarily from cultural intolerance—that is, its transgressive status. For example, Clinton opponents pointed to the pain that his transgressive act caused others, while Clinton supporters alleged that the suffering inflicted was caused primarily by the public's puritanical reaction.

As the Clinton controversy shows, debates about sex often reflect two goals that are sometimes in conflict with one another: the desire to curtail the social policing of our intimate pleasures and the need to understand the damage some sexual practices can cause. To explore both of these goals, we will divide this overview into three parts. In Section 2, we examine philosophical arguments that challenge traditional social rules and intolerance regarding transgressive sexual acts. In Section 3, we examine debates about the harmfulness of particular practices. In Section 4, we explore some new areas of discussion about sexual ethics.

2. Moral Sex

In the *Summa theologica*, St Thomas Aquinas proclaimed that sex was designed by God solely for procreation. Aquinas's position was grounded in the deep-seated belief that sexual desire was fundamentally evil. Earlier, Augustine had argued that humans in the pre-fall state would have experienced no desire when performing the act of sex. Lust and sexual pleasure were, for both Augustine and Aquinas, a result of sin. Intercourse, then, came to be seen as a necessary evil—required for the propagation of the human race, but always tainted by sin and thus in need of strict social regulation. Following Aquinas, natural law theorists concluded that sex performed for any reason other than procreation violated God's will and was, therefore, unnatural and immoral. Moreover, procreation was deemed permissible only for married couples, whom natural law proponents regarded as the proper social unit for rearing children. Aquinas's arguments placed sex firmly and unquestioningly within the moral realm in Western theorizing and social customs.

Centuries later, Immanuel Kant embraced Aquinas's link between moral sex and marriage. Kant connects moral sex and marriage by appealing to the immoral nature of sexual relationships. According to Kant (1924/1963: 163):

Sexual love makes of the loved person an Object of appetite; as soon as that appetite has been stilled, the person is cast aside as one casts away a lemon which has been sucked dry... Taken by itself ... [sexual love] is a degradation of human nature; for as soon as a person becomes an Object of appetite for another, all motives of moral relationship cease to function, because as an Object of appetite for another a person becomes a thing and can be treated and used as such by every one.

By acting in accordance with our sexual desires, Kant argues that we inevitably treat others immorally. We make 'humanity an instrument for the satisfaction of ... lusts ... and dishonour it by placing it on a level with animal nature' (1963: 164). Yet, the civil institution of marriage, for Kant, provides a context in which human beings can satisfy their sexual appetites for each other without reducing their partners to mere things. According to Kant (1963: 167):

if I yield myself completely to another and obtain the person of the other in return, I win myself back; I have given myself up as the property of another, but in turn I take that other as my property, and so win myself back again in winning the person whose property I have become. In this way the two persons become a unity of will. Whatever good or ill, joy or sorrow befall either of them, the other will share in it. Thus sexuality leads to a union of human beings, and in that union its exercise is possible. This condition of the use of sexuality, which is only fulfilled in marriage, is a moral condition.

Marriage prevents us from using others merely as instruments for fulfilling our sexual appetites, for marital partners satisfy their sexual desires as part of a lasting relationship in which each treats and regards the other as a human being.

Although sexual practices in contemporary Western societies do not limit sex to marriage or to procreation within marriage (Janus and Janus 1993), the idea that sex is redeemable only by marriage and procreation has had a profound impact on what we teach, preach, and legally permit regarding sexuality. For example, extramarital sex (including adultery, premarital sex, same-sex sex, and prostitution) exposes individuals to negative legal sanctions. Adultery can be grounds for losing a contested divorce or the custody of children, non-marital procreation produces 'illegitimate' children whose claims on support and inheritance are weak, and taking or giving money for sex (outside marriage) is a criminal offence in many places. 'Sodomy', understood as 'unnatural sex' or sexual acts other than heterosexual genital intercourse (i.e. sex that cannot be procreative), is also criminal in many US states. Moreover, laws against sodomy tend to be enforced primarily against unmarried—especially gay and lesbian—couples, reflecting less tolerance for 'unnatural sex' when it is performed outside marriage or by those considered to have unnatural sexual tastes. In *Adams* v. *Howerton*, the US Supreme Court argued against same-sex marriage on the ground that 'the state has a compelling interest in encouraging and fostering procreation of the race and providing status and stability to the environment in which children are raised' (*Adams* v. *Howerton*, 1975). Laws banning same-sex marriage reinscribe the association between marriage, sex, and procreation. And, though same-sex couples sometimes procreate, they generally do so by means divorced from sex. Yet, for natural law theorists and some contemporary Christians, procreation without sex, like sex without procreation, is also unnatural. A generation ago, contraception and abortion were illegal, and the continuing controversy over abortion can be seen as a form of resistance to the separation of sex, procreation, and marriage.

In 1929 Bertrand Russell challenged Christian orthodoxy on sex and marriage. Though he held marriage to be 'the best and most important relation that can exist between two human beings' (1929/1970: 143), Russell was notorious for promoting premarital sex. He states, 'I should not hold it desirable that either a man or a woman should enter upon the serious business of a marriage intended to lead to children without having had previous sexual experience' (1929/1970: 166). Russell advocated premarital sex to give people a chance to experiment sexually before making the commitment of marriage. For Russell, a more liberal sexual ethic would lead to more stable and happier marriages. Russell (1929/1970: 167) acknowledges that:

This view depends, at least in part, upon that separation between procreation and mere sex which has been brought about by contraceptives. Contraceptives have altered the whole aspect of sex and marriage, and have made distinctions necessary which could formerly have been ignored. People may come together for sex alone, as occurs in prostitution, or for companionship involving a sexual element. . . or finally, for the purpose of rearing a family. These are all different, and no morality can be adequate to modern circumstances which confounds them in one indiscriminate total.

Russell argued that there was no need to restrict sex to procreation or marriage. For Russell, 'sex is connected with some of the greatest goods in human life. The three that seem paramount are lyric love, happiness in marriage, and art' (1929/1970: 292). Russell thought that social tolerance for sex outside marriage, but based on love or mutual desire, would help to minimize 'unhealthy' practices such as prostitution (1929/1970: 155).

Much philosophical scholarship on sexuality in the early 1970s and 1980s was directed at questioning the belief that sexual acts were moral only within legal marriage or marriage-like relationships (that is between committed, sexually monogamous, potentially procreative, mutually loving couples). Russell Vannoy's *Sex without Love: A Philosophical Exploration* seeks to dissolve the moral connection not only between sex and marriage, but also between sex and affection. Vannoy examines a series of arguments that support the moral acceptability and experiential preferability of sex without love. He insists that a fair analysis requires that the reader 'not see sex as so sinful that it can be redeemed only by love' (Vannoy 1980: 13). Vannoy then critiques the claim that sex with love provides a richer experience than sex without love. For Vannoy, this claim rests on a fallacious dualism between sex with love and 'crude, manipulative, exploitative sex' (1980: 28). He offers numerous arguments to support his position that sex without love can be equally or even more fulfilling an experience as sex with love, and offers a liberal sexual philosophy in which he denies that there is anything inherently sinful or disgusting about sex.

The poem 'Sex without Love', by Sharon Olds, captures the values of those promoting this practice of sex primarily for pleasure:

> How do they do it, the ones who make love
> without love? Beautiful as dancers,
> gliding over each other like ice-skaters
> over the ice fingers hooked
> inside each other's bodies...
> These are the true religious,
> the purists, the pros, the ones who will not
> accept a false Messiah, love the
> priest instead of the God. They do not
> mistake the lover for their own pleasure,
> they are like great runners; they know they are alone
> with the road surface, the cold, the wind,
> the fit of their shoes, their over-all cardio-
> vascular health—just factors, like the partner
> in the bed...
>
> (Olds 1989)

In the images of sex presented here, an emotional, social, or legal relationship between the partners is not necessary for each to experience the psychic and physical pleasures of sex. The poem acknowledges the selfish, solitary, objectifying nature of sex that Kant feared, but, rather than see these aspects of sex in morally negative terms, it presents them in aesthetically positive ones.

Critiques, like Russell's and Vannoy's, of the moral links between sex and marriage or love supported other defences of extramarital sex, with and without love. In his influential essay, 'Is Adultery Immoral?', Richard Wasserstrom (1975) argues that there is nothing inherently immoral about adulterous sex. While acknowledging that some acts of adultery involve lying or breaking a promise and thus are immoral, Wasserstrom argues that deceit and betrayal are not necessary features of extramarital sex. To demonstrate this, Wasserstrom introduces the model of the 'open marriage'. He defines an open marriage as one in which neither spouse views extramarital sexual relations as a violation of their relationship and in which neither spouse desires or promises sexual fidelity. Wasserstrom argues that, within such a marriage, an extramarital affair would not involve dishonesty and betrayal as long as there is 'openness' with the non-marital lover as well. Another philosopher, Richard Taylor, wrote an entire book, *Having Love Affairs*, based on the claim that adultery is not inherently immoral. His main goal was not to support this claim, but rather to clarify the contexts in which 'love affairs' were ethical and provide guidelines for having more fulfilling affairs.

Other theorists interrogated monogamy rather than adultery. In 'Monogamy: A Critique', John McMurtry insists that the tenets of monogamy that restrict marriage to two and only two individuals and require sexual fidelity constitute 'a massive social-control mechanism' that inhibits ' "profound affection" between the partners or a "loving context" for child-upbringing' (1972: 588, 592). More recently, Linda LeMoncheck questions the value of monogamy, especially for women. She argues that the alternative of 'promiscuity. . . provides one way for individual women to begin reclaiming and reevaluating their own sexual pleasure' (LeMoncheck 1997: 66). LeMoncheck suggests that having sexual relationships with a variety of partners can allow some women to learn more about their sexual enjoyments, to assert their own sexual agendas, and to challenge gendered sexual expectations and norms. She states, 'promiscuous sex can also bring sexual satisfaction, sexual growth, and sexual empowerment to women who would otherwise feel physically and emotionally trapped by the constraints of monogamy' (1997: 65). LeMoncheck contests the denigration of promiscuity not only by conservative moralists, but also by those feminists who see promiscuity as behaviour that serves male interests or conforms to male sexual norms. Non-monogamous sex need not be exploitative of women or men, and it can be intimate, caring, and respectful, according to LeMoncheck.

Such unconventional views have not escaped critique. Richard Wreen (1986), for example, rejects Wasserstrom's claim that adultery is not inherently immoral, arguing that a necessary condition for something to be a marriage relationship is that it involve sexual fidelity. On this view, 'open marriages' are a kind of legal fiction. Wreen's view of marriage, though, is rather ethnocentric, as it would not only count the 'open marriages' of a small subculture as not real, but probably the polygamous marriages of other societies as well. Michael Bayles (1984) attacks what he labels 'the vulgar hedonism' of sexual liberation. Focusing his critique on McMurtry's rejection of monogamy (1972), Bayles argues that McMurtry presupposes a Kantian conception of the marriage contract—namely, Kant's view that marriage 'is the Union of two Persons of different sex for life-long reciprocal possession of their sexual faculties' (see also Herman 1993: 60–1), which leads McMurtry to reject marriage 'as chiefly concerned with private ownership of the means to sexual gratification' (Bayles 1984: 132). Bayles rejects the Kantian view of marriage, and McMurtry's interpretation of it, and instead argues that marriage serves the purpose of 'providing legal recognition of some of the most valuable interpersonal relationships' (1984: 137). For Bayles, 'valuable interpersonal relationships require intimacy and usually physical privacy from others, and at the very least nonintrusion upon the relationship' (1984: 135). Bayles claims that sexual intercourse is traditionally one of the most important ways to express concern for one's intimate partner, and thus serves a symbolic purpose, which will be compromised in adulterous or polygamous arrangements. He states, 'If sexual intercourse ceases to have this function in society, some other act will undoubtedly replace it in this function. Moreover, sexual intercourse will have lost much of its value' (1984: 135). This statement can be read as a tautology—if sex ceases to have a certain symbolic value in interpersonal relationships owing to the acceptance of adultery, it will lose its symbolic value— or it can be read as—if sex ceases to have a certain symbolic value in interpersonal relationships it will lose other forms of value, perhaps instrumental value, intrinsic value, and so on. Presumably Bayles means the latter, but he does not explain or support this more substantive claim.

2.1 Same-Sex Sexual Acts

Same-sex sexual acts were condemned as sinful by both the Jewish and the Christian traditions, and thus there is a long history of treating them as violations of the moral order. Recently, a number of theorists have turned to Ancient Greece to show that there are cultures that view same-sex relations in a positive light. For example, in Plato's *Symposium*, the characters discuss the superiority of sexual relations between males over those between males and females. This work depicts the latter as acts that aim primarily to satisfy feelings of lust or are for purposes of reproduction. It is only male 'lover–beloved' relations that are depicted as having the potential to be grounded in 'higher' principles of wisdom and good character. According to Morris Kaplan (1997: 82), 'Plato's *Symposium* is a queer text and demands a queer reading . . . Plato's *Symposium* is charged with homoerotic energy . . . At the same time, Plato's queerness cannot coincide with the contemporary variety . . . defined by our deviations from a matrix of compulsory heterosexuality . . .'. Kaplan points out that this text helps us understand both the cultural and the historical limits of our own homophobia and the unique social context of contemporary same-sex practices. The unique context of contemporary same-sex practices, in which heterosexuality is compulsory and same-sex sexual relations are queer, has been shaped by centuries of Christian teachings that limit natural and thus moral sex to procreative sex. These views were taken up by modern philosophers such as Kant (1963: 170):

A second *crimen carnis contra naturam* is intercourse between *sexus homogenii*, in which the object of sexual impulse is a human being but there is homogeneity instead of heterogeneity of sex, as when a woman satisfies her desire on a woman, or a man on a man. This practice too is contrary to the ends of humanity; for the end of humanity in respect of sexuality is to preserve the species without debasing the person; but in this instance the species is not being preserved . . . the self is degraded below the level of the animals, and humanity is dishonored.

Kant viewed masturbation with equal moral disdain as being another instance of unnatural sex in which 'the species is not being preserved'. While some in the USA currently view homosexuality with a contempt similar to Kant's, few would rank masturbation as degrading one below the level of animals. Both the example of masturbation and same-sex sexual relations show how attitudes and understandings of sexual practices can change radically over time and across cultures.

There are two ways to object to views, like those of Kant, that same-sex sex is unnatural and hence immoral. One can deny that same-sex sex is unnatural by rejecting the tenet that the purpose of sex is reproduction. The second approach is to retain the belief that natural sex acts are reproductive, but to deny that unnatural acts are immoral. In 'Sexual Perversion', Thomas Nagel embraced the first position. Nagel contends 'that the connection between sex and reproduction has no bearing on sexual perversion'—that is, on whether sex is unnatural or immoral (1969: 5–6). Instead, for Nagel sex is unnatural or perverse when it lacks a kind of intersubjective complexity constitutive of normal sexual interactions. Normal sexual interactions involve, according to Nagel, an escalating responsiveness to another's desire for physical intimacy. Beastiality, necrophilia, paedophilia, masturbation, and object fetishes are paradigmatic of sex acts that lack the intersubjective dynamic Nagel viewed as essential to a complete sexual relationship, and thus were seen by him as perverse. Homosexual relationships, however, are no less likely than heterosexual relationships to manifest the psychological and relational 'completeness' that Nagel requires for non-perverse sex. Hence Nagel's model of normal sex denies that same-sex relationships are inherently unnatural or immoral.

Sarah Ruddick adopts the second approach in her analysis of same-sex relationships. Ruddick retains the more traditional view that non-reproductive sex is unnatural and perverse, but denies that perverse sex is morally bad. Ruddick reiterates the traditional Western view that, ' "Natural" sexual desire has as its "object" living persons of the opposite sex, and in particular their postpubertal genitals. The "aim" of natural sexual desire—that is, the act that "naturally" completes it—is genital intercourse' (1984: 287). In this view, same-sex sex (understood normally to include oral or anal intercourse, and intercourse with other body parts or dildos, but not 'genital–genital' intercourse) is unnatural and perverse. Ruddick, however, denies that same-sex sex is immoral: 'Though perverted sex may be "unnatural" both from an evolutionary and developmental perspective, there is no connection, inverse or correlative, between what is natural and what is good' (1984: 291). Though good sex can be unnatural or perverse, Ruddick, like Nagel, argues that good sex should be complete; that is, it requires a mutuality of desire and response. She provides three reasons for the goodness or superiority of complete sex acts: they 'tend to resolve tensions fundamental to moral life; they are conducive to emotions that, if they become stable and dominant, are in turn conducive to the virtue of loving; and they involve a preeminently moral virtue—respect for persons' (1984: 294). For Ruddick, as for Kant, one should not treat one's sex partner as a mere means, though Ruddick does not appear to hold that marital commitment is necessary to preserve respect for persons (1984: 295–6).

2.2 The Question of a Sexual Morality

Although Nagel and Ruddick both support the equal moral integrity of same-sex relationships, both base their position on a conception of 'good sex' defined via notions of mutuality and completeness, rendering such sex morally superior. While both would deny the traditional view that sex is inherently evil, they retain a moral stance concerning the value of good sex.

In *Sex and Ethics*, Igor Primoratz (1999) argues that many ideals of good sex are prudential not moral ideals. He points out that many arguments against prostitution, same-sex sex, and other unconventional practices aim to show that these practices lack some important feature of good sexual relations. But all this amounts to, Primoratz maintains, is advice on what kinds of sex are likely to advance our interests, not a moral condemnation of the practices deemed inferior (Primoratz 1999: 169). For example, Primoratz analyses Roger Scruton's critique of same-sex sex, which alleges that 'homosexual experience lacks the sort of mystery, risk and adventure that enriches heterosexual sex'. Primoratz (1999: 169) argues that

One of the flaws of this argument is that, if the factual claim is true, the argument can only show that if one has the choice, other things being equal, one should choose heterosexual rather than homosexual sex, or heterosexual rather than homosexual orientation, since it will provide a deeper, richer sexual experience. But to say this is to offer prudential advice, rather than to lay down a moral rule.

Primoratz endorses Alan Goldman's 'plain sex' approach to sexuality. Goldman (1980) alleges the purpose of sex is the production of a distinctive form of physical pleasure, rather than procreation or the expression of love. This account of sex has been elaborated by Alan Soble (1996), who associates the primary value of sex with the opportunity for bodily pleasure. Given that pleasure is inherently valuable, sexual pleasure need not be redeemed by assigning it a more noble purpose. Primoratz goes farther than Goldman and Soble and rejects all attempts to assign a purpose to sex, whether that aim be high or low. He states,

We have no reason to believe that there is only one morally acceptable aim or purpose of human sexual experience and behavior, whether prescribed by nature or enjoined by society...Sex has no special moral significance; it is morally neutral. No act is either morally good or bad, right or wrong, merely in virtue of being a sexual act. ...Accordingly, there is neither need nor room for a set of moral considerations that apply only to sex and constitute sexual morality in the strict sense of the terms. What does apply to choices, acts, and practices in the field of sex are the same moral rules and principles that apply in non-sexual matters.   (Primoratz 1999: 173)

Primoratz holds that, whatever our moral duties are—not to harm, deceive, exploit, betray others, and so on—these duties apply in the sexual realm in the same way that they apply in other areas of life. Sexual acts are condemnable only if they violate a general moral precept, rather than in virtue of some special sexual moral code.

2.3 Compulsory Heterosexuality

Rather than looking to internal features of sex to define its morality, many theorists focused on the external features, the social institutions and practices, that define and limit sex. In the USA, radical feminist philosophers turned to institutions and practices that normalize sex in US culture. In *Lesbian Ethics*, for example, Sarah Hoagland argued that 'dominance and subordination lie at the heart of social inter-actions in the form of the institution of heterosexuality, and so long as that axis remains intact, oppression will be a reality—all forms of oppression, not just male domination of women' (1988: 21). In her influential essay 'Compulsory Heterosexuality and Lesbian Existence', Adrienne Rich (1980) maintained that het-erosexuality is a political institution designed to enable males, or at least powerful males, sexual, emotional, and economic access to women. Hoagland elaborates upon Rich's position by arguing that heterosexualism is based on a complex system of male protection and predation of women, which both oppresses women and robs them of their agency. Hoagland points to the pervasiveness of sexual violence and the threat of sexual violence against women—rape, incest, sexual harassment, sexual slavery, wife-beating—as linked to the logic of predation, namely that men, or at least some men, find sexual violence against women desirable. Rich, for exam-ple, discussed the ways sexual violence against women was eroticized not only in pornography but even, for example, in mainstream movies. Hoagland points out that 'the logic of protection is essentially the same as the logic of predation . . . to protect women, men do things to women and against women; acting "for a woman's own good", they violate her integrity and undermine her agency' (1988: 31).

In critiquing compulsory heterosexuality, Hoagland and other radical feminists were not arguing for lesbian or gay 'liberation'. They rather argued for resistance to dominant values, categories, and institutions. In this way, radical feminist critiques of heterosexism were similar to the politics of Michel Foucault and his followers, who argued for resistance over liberation. David Halperin (1995: 61), for example, argued that

The most radical reversal of homophobic discourses consists not in asserting, with the Gay Liberation Front of 1968, that 'gay is good' (on the analogy with 'black is beautiful') but in assuming and empowering a marginal positionality—not in rehabilitating an already demarcated, if devalued, identity but in taking advantage of the purely oppositional loca-tion homosexuality has been made to occupy.

This position of resistance to established categories and practices became the foun-dation of queer theory and politics, a politics of opposition and resistance rather than identity, designed to expose the problematic and often immoral features of the social normalization of sexual practices. Foucault's *History of Sexuality* (1976/ 1990) provided a historical genealogy of the homosexual that would become the founda-tion of the resistance strategies of queer theory. Foucault argued that the emerging medical science of sexology in the nineteenth century transformed our under-standing of a number of sexual practices, including same-sex sexual acts. What had previously been seen as a forbidden act, came to be defined as a 'species'.

The nineteenth-century homosexual became a personage, a past, a case history, and a child-hood, in addition to being a type of life, a life form, and a morphology, with an indiscreet anatomy and possibly a mysterious physiology. Nothing that went into his total composition was unaffected by his sexuality. It was everywhere present in him: at the root of all his actions because it was their insidious and indefinitely active principle. (Foucault 1976/1990: 43)

Foucault argued that the modern view of sexuality that not only marks a distinction between a homosexual and a heterosexual, but views sexuality as a constitutive principle of the self, is a modern invention that emerged out of a particular time and culture, and was the result of various axes of power, including both the medical and the judicial institutions.

The view that sexuality itself has a history transformed theorizing about sex. Rather than questioning whether homosexuality was or was not natural or inherently moral, theorists began to examine the morality of the various institutions and social practices that gave rise not only to homosexuality but also to heterosexuality. David Halperin, for example, argued that there were three steps in this invention of heterosexuality and homosexuality. First, sexuality is defined as 'a separate, sexual domain within the larger field of man's psychophysical nature. Second, sexuality effects the conceptual demarcation and isolation of that domain from other areas of personal and social life... finally, sexuality generates sexual identity: it endows each of us with an individual sexual nature' (Halperin 1990: 25). Halperin concludes that sexuality is not a universal feature of humans, but is a specific cultural production that may not exist in some cultures and may exist but not be configured along the lines of the Western distinction between heterosexuality and homosexuality in other cultures. Sexual identity is thus not seen as simply a biological drive or instinct nor as only a force of culture, but as a complex interweaving of the two.

Fuelled by Foucault's genealogy, theorists began to investigate forms of sexuality and sexual identity in other cultures and in other time periods. While many, like Foucault and Halperin, returned to the Ancient Greeks, others focused on the diversity of identities within contemporary US culture. Thomás Almaguer, for example, argued that forms of homosexual desire, practice, and identity among contemporary Chicano men are formed by two different sexual economies—the Mexican/Latin-American sexual system and the European-American sexual system. Each system has different categories, sexual meanings, and practices that circumscribe sexual behaviour. And each defines homosexual behaviour differently. While the sexual system in the USA divides sexual identity into

discrete sexual categories and personages defined in terms of sexual preference or object choice: same sex (homosexual), opposite sex (heterosexual), or both (bisexual). . . . the Mexican/Latin-American sexual system is based on a configuration of gender/sex/power that is articulated along the active/passive axis and organized through the scripted sexual role one plays. (Almaguer 1991: 77)

Almaguer explains that male same-sex sexual practices in the Mexican/Latin-American system is configured around anal sex, where each partner adopts either an active or a passive role in the sexual act, one who is penetrated and one who penetrates. Although the anal-passive individual, the *cochón* or *pasivo*, is stigmatized for adopting a subservient, feminine role, his partner, the *áctivo* or *machista*, is not stigmatized and is viewed as a normal male. 'A Mexican man's masculine gender and heterosexual identity are not threatened by a homosexual act as long as he plays the inserter's role' (Almaguer 1991: 81). Almaguer notes how problematic an Anglo gay identity is for a Chicano man who must navigate two different sexual economies.

Queer theory not only encouraged the examination of other cultural configurations of sexuality; it urged a politics of 'queering' sexuality, of questioning the current norms and categories that shape sexuality and sexual identity in order to uncover and critique the politics that underlie them. The goal in doing so is not to uncover a true sexuality underlying culture or any inherent sexual morality, but to explore and highlight 'the legitimacy of a plurality of forms of erotic life' (Kaplan 1997: 9). Queer theory replaces the natural/unnatural, normal/pathological distinctions underlying much moralizing about sex, with a notion of sexual variation that is culturally rather than biologically based (see also LeMoncheck 1997: 108). As Mariana Valverde comments, this is an improvement 'because the pathology approach has reactionary political implications, while the "variation thesis" legitimates liberal approaches to sexual regulation' (1995: 184). This liberal (in the sense of tolerant) approach opposes the oppression of minority erotic communities, whose sexual orientations, practices, identities, and ideas about the meaning of sex differ from those that have become familiar or normalized. While feminists generally support this more tolerant approach to sexuality, especially same-sex sexuality, feminists are wary that this approach does not allow us to talk about oppressive sexual practices, but only about oppressive social institutions. Robin West summarizes this concern in her discussion of Foucault's account of

a nineteenth-century half-wit who fondles a young girl and is consequently arrested . . . Far from having his sexuality 'repressed' or 'driven underground', Foucault argues that the half-wit is forced to speak and speak and speak—literally for the rest of his life and metaphorically for centuries—of his own sexuality. He speaks of his sexual pleasures first to the constabulary, then to the judiciary, then to the priesthood, then to the medical community, and finally to the psychoanalytic and psychiatric establishment . . . In the twentieth century . . . this half-wit is still speaking: we speak of the 'unspeakable' subject—sex—more than absolutely anything. This is the irony which consumed Foucault, and which he explores so forcefully in his history . . . But there is a greater irony revealed by Foucault's story: with all the attention given to 'discourses', neither the French officials, nor Foucault himself, nor the vast majority of social and legal critics he has influenced, have yet heard scarcely a word from the child who was molested in that eerie scene or from the millions of children who have been molested since . . . While we discourse endlessly on the *pleasure* of sex so central to masculine sexuality . . . we still speak almost not at all of the violence of sex so central to childhood and femininity . . . This inattentiveness to silence is not only a massive injustice, but it also distorts understanding.   (West 1997: 270–2)

In the following sections of this chapter, we will explore various feminist discourses that seek to end the silence of those 'from whom sex has been taken' (West 1997: 272) and the ways their oppression is tightly woven into the fabric of normalized sexual practices.

3. SEXUAL ASSAULT

The link between the oppression of women and normalized sexual practices first became clear in feminist analyses of rape. While few in our culture would deny the immorality of rape, many feminists were concerned to demonstrate that rape was more than a rare and isolated attack of one man against one woman. Susan Rae Peterson in 'Coercion and Rape: The State as a Male Protection Racket' (1977) argues that the frequency of rape together with the pervasive threat of sexual violence is a form of social coercion that restricts women's freedom of bodily movement. Peterson calls attention to the sexual double standard that treats women who would 'walk anywhere they want at any hour they want, drink in bars alone, or travel without a companion' as bad women who 'deserve punishment and disrepute; if they get raped, they only "get what is coming to them"' (1977: 362, 361). In this way rape and the threat of rape functions to ensure men's control over women's sexuality, for 'if women had the same kind of freedom of bodily movement as men, it would be difficult for the current social mechanisms (like marriage, divorce, and parental custody of children) to control reproduction' (1977: 362).

While some feminists argued that rape was wrong because it denied women their full rights of personhood and treated them as objects, others, like Pamela Foa, argued that 'the special wrongness of rape is due to, and is only an exaggeration of, the wrongness of our sexual interactions in general' (1977: 347). Boys, for example, are raised to be sexually aggressive and girls to be the 'gate-keepers' of sexuality who control male sexual advances. According to Foa, 'Boys are instructed *not* to be attentive to the claims of girls with respect to their desires and needs. And girls are instructed *not* to consult their feelings as a means of or at least a check on what behavior they should engage in' (1977: 355). This situation results in many sexual encounters that are closer to rape than to fully consensual sexual intercourse.

The critique of normalized sexual behaviour enabled feminists to argue that we had to expand our understanding of rape beyond the model of random and rare attacks by strangers or social deviants and instead to see the ways typical and socially sanctioned sexual practices themselves often perpetuate a rape culture. Feminists introduced terms like marital rape, date rape, and acquaintance rape to identify types of sanctioned sexual practices that are morally unacceptable.

In 'Date Rape: A Feminist Analysis' Lois Pineau argues that both the old and new laws on sexual assault are inadequate because they do not include as a crime those rapes that involve 'nonaggravated sexual assault, nonconsensual sex that does not involve physical injury or the explicit threat of physical injury' (1989: 217). When physical injury or the threat of physical injury is absent, the sexually predatory behaviours associated with date or acquaintance rape usually fall within the bounds of normal sexual seduction. This makes it almost impossible to get the criminal justice system to prosecute such rapists. The lack of seriousness with which 'date rape' is often approached is reflected in the widespread belief that some women are 'asking for sex', especially if they allow themselves to drink alcohol or dress provocatively around men. The sexual assaults on women by male mobs in Central Park, New York, in June 2000, illustrate this mentality, as well as the many commentators who suggested that the provocative dress of the women could have led to the attacks. This myth that women who dress sexily or drink are 'asking for sex' is tied to the belief that males, after a certain point of arousal, are unable to control their sexual urges. While a man loses self-control, a woman is expected to be the 'gatekeeper', a function she may not be able to execute effectively if she loses self-control or gets her man too aroused. If she says 'no' to sex, a properly socialized man will interpret her non-submissiveness as the expression of her official 'gate-keeping' role, not as the sign of her true desires. Some men then assume that their job is to get beyond a woman's 'natural' reluctance and overcome her sexual control.

Pineau argues that this complex of myths about female and male sexuality widely accepted in US culture 'sets up sexual encounters as contractual events in which sexual aggression is presumed to be consented to unless there is some vigorous act of refusal' (1989: 233). She argues that this aggressive, high-pressure model of sex is in tension with the goal of mutual sexual enjoyment. Pineau insists that 'if a man wants to be sure he is not forcing himself on a woman, he has an obligation either to ensure that the encounter really is mutually enjoyable, or to know the reasons why she would want to continue the encounter in spite of her lack of enjoyment' (1989: 234). To foster such behaviours, Pineau contends that we need to replace the aggressive seduction model of sex, which sees sexual play as involving the desire of one partner overcoming the resistance of the other, with a conversational model, which treats sexual interaction as the mutual interpretation of and response to desire. Pineau argues that, if we saw dating 'more like a friendship than a business contract, then clearly respect for the dialectics of desire is incompatible with the sort of sexual pressure that is inclined to end in date rape' (1989: 238).

The feminist analysis of rape as a socially ingrained practice has not been accepted without protest. Perhaps the most widely publicized critique is that of Katie Roiphe, who argues for greater responsibility on the part of women.

The idea is that women get too drunk to know what they are doing, while men stay sober and lucid. If we assume women are not all helpless and naïve, then shouldn't they be held responsible for their choices to drink or take drugs? If a woman's judgement is impaired, as they say, and she has sex, it isn't necessarily always the man's fault; it isn't necessarily always rape. (Roiphe 1993: 53–4)

Roiphe is concerned with the image of women presented by much feminist critique of normalized dating behaviour.

We do not have the mind of an eleven-year-old in the body of a twenty-year-old. All competent female college students are compromised by the association of gullibility, low self-esteem, and the inability to assert ourselves with our position in relation to men . . . whether or not we feel pressured, regardless of our level of self-esteem, the responsibility for our actions is still our own.   (1993: 68)

While not sympathetic with what she calls Roiphe's unwillingness to acknowledge the experiences of those women who have felt violated by aggressive sex, Mary Gaitskill nonetheless agrees with Roiphe's call that women accept responsibility for their actions. Gaitskill argues for the importance of both women and men learning to be respectful of themselves and of others as the key to taking responsibility for our actions. She advocates women being attuned to their feelings, even their ambivalences, making a decision, and voicing it clearly. She gives an autobiographical example of a man she was dating who became more sexually aggressive when she began to say 'no'. She said very clearly, 'If this comes to a fight, you would win, but it would be very ugly for both of us. Is that really what you want?' (Gaitskill 1994: 44). But she also thinks men share an equal burden of responsibility.

I am not idealistic enough to hope that we will ever live in a world without rape or other forms of sexual cruelty; I think men and women will always have to struggle to behave responsibly. But I think we could make the struggle less difficult by changing the way we teach responsibility and social conduct. To teach a boy that rape is 'bad' is not as effective as making him see that rape is a violation of his own masculine dignity as well as a violation of the raped woman.   (Gaitskill 1994: 42)

3.1 Pornography

In *Feminism Unmodified*, Catharine MacKinnon (1987: 134) expanded the feminist attack on normalized sexual practices by denouncing the sale of women's sexuality for male entertainment. MacKinnon accused mainstream publications, such as *Playboy*, of participating in a practice that eroticizes the social subordination and sexual molestation of women. According to MacKinnon (1987: 148),

Pornography, in the feminist view, is a form of forced sex, a practice of sexual politics, and institution of gender inequality. In this perspective, pornography is not harmless fantasy or a corrupt and confused misrepresentation of an otherwise natural and healthy sexuality. Along with the rape and prostitution in which it participates, pornography institutionalizes the sexuality of male supremacy, which fuses the erotization of dominance and submission with the social construction of male and female. Gender is sexual. Pornography constitutes the meaning of that sexuality. Men treat women as who they see women as being. Pornography constructs who that is.

Some pornographic materials depict women as aroused and sexually fulfilled by aggressive and violent sexual treatment by men. MacKinnon and other feminists allege that such materials mis-educate men about women, because pornography teaches men to sexually assault women and then to expect women to be aroused by such behaviour. By shaping male attitudes to sex and women, pornography encourages behaviours that threaten women's and girls' personal safety and well-being. Moreover, 'pornography turns a woman into a thing to be acquired and used' (1989: 199). It dehumanizes women, and thus socially stereotypes women as inferior because of their gender.

MacKinnon's critique of pornography is not based on the notion of 'obscenity', or the violation of community standards of decency. For MacKinnon, 'The harm of pornography, broadly speaking, is the harm of the civil inequality of the sexes made invisible as harm because it has become accepted as the sex difference' (1987: 178). Because pornography negatively influences attitudes and behaviours towards women, it violates women's basic civil rights to equality and freedom. Yet the harm done to women's civil standing by pornography remains invisible, according to MacKinnon, because pornographic sexuality shapes our understanding of gender difference and thus how women are socially defined. Like Kant, MacKinnon sees sexuality as a force that objectifies persons and thus leads to the immoral treatment of others. Unlike Kant, MacKinnon regards the culturally constructed norms of heterosexual male sexuality, expressed graphically in pornography, rather than the sexual appetite *per se*, as the culprit (cf. Herman 1993: 56).

Feminists were not the first to take offence at pornography or to treat it as a serious problem. Many conservative moral theorists have attacked pornography because of its potential to foster harmful attitudes towards sex, attitudes that can indirectly affect people who do not use pornography. MacKinnon merely gives a new slant to an old objection. According to Fred Berger, 'The traditional form of the claim can be labeled "incitement to rape" theory. It holds that pornography arouses sexual desire, which seeks an outlet, often in antisocial forms such as rape' (1983: 85). In MacKinnon's view, pornography incites rape, not by arousing some natural sexual desire that then needs an outlet, but by arousing a desire to dominate and degrade women sexually. In defence of pornography, Berger argues that 'Pornographic materials, *by their nature* . . . are an unlikely source or means of altering and influencing our basic attitudes toward one another' (1983: 87). Berger explains that pornography does not encourage dehumanizing sex or harmful sexual attitudes because

It usually depicts people as enjoying physical activity, that is, as mutually experiencing *pleasure*. Typical pornography displays sex as something people take fun in and enjoy. There is usually little doubt the persons involved are *liking* it . . . Even sadistic pornography, it should be noted, depicts people as having enjoyment; and, it is usually sado-*masochistic* pleasures which are portrayed, with a resultant equalizing of the distribution of the pleasure (if not pain). In this respect, most pornography does not portray humans as *mere* instruments of whatever ends we have.   (1983: 97)

Berger admits that much pornography is tied to fantasies 'that treat women in conventional male chauvinist ways' (1983: 97). For MacKinnon, because the fantasies pornography projects involve women enjoying being ravished and raped, or taking pleasure in being dominated, the depiction of mutual pleasure in pornography dehumanizes women, portraying them as the mere instruments of men's sexual desires.

In 1970, a Presidential Commission on Obscenity and Pornography also challenged MacKinnon's feminist Kantian attack. Their report states 'It has been argued that erotic materials describe the female as a mere sexual object to be exploited and manipulated sexually. . . Recent experiments suggest that such fears are probably unwarranted' (Garry 1983: 63). In 'Pornography and Respect for Women' Ann Garry examines the empirical studies on which the Commission based its conclusions. Though Garry points out a number of flaws in these studies, she agrees that 'our fears about being molested on street corners by users of pornography' are not warranted or backed up by empirical data (1983: 64, 70). Garry then considers whether pornography might be objectionable because of its content rather than its presumed effects. The content of pornography would be immoral if it 'recommends behavior that violates the moral principle to respect persons' (1983: 70). Movies that depict women as desiring rape imply that their resistance is not to be believed and, in this way, recommend behaviours that disrespect women's autonomous agency whether or not anyone is influenced by the films. Moreover, by depicting women as engaging in activities that 'respectable' women do not, according to patriarchal sexual moralities, pornography promotes a loss of respect for women as women, which further promotes a loss of respect for women as autonomous individuals. Garry points out that the harm of pornography to women is partly the result of the social asymmetry between men and women: if sex is viewed as degrading to women, then depicting women having sex will degrade them. In a culture that treats sex as dirty, then depicting someone as a sex object is degrading. According to Garry, because our society fails to treat women—even 'respectable' women—as fully-fledged persons in many contexts, and because sexual activity can more easily stigmatize women socially, material that sexually objectifies women is more damaging to women than similar material sexually objectifying men would be to men. Garry's argument supports changing the content of pornography, as well as the social context in which it is received, not censoring it. She ends her article by imagining what non-sexist pornography would look like:

non-sexist pornography would treat men and women as equal sex partners. The man would not control the circumstances in which the partners had sex or the choice of positions or acts; the woman's preference would be counted equally. There would be no suggestion of a power play or conquest on the man's part, no suggestion that 'she likes it when I hurt her'. Sexual intercourse would not be portrayed as primarily for the purpose of male ejaculation—his orgasm is not 'the best part' of the movie.   (Garry 1983: 77)

In 'Objectification', Martha Nussbaum also examines how the sexual objectification of women in pornography is damaging to women. Nussbaum argues that

'Under some specifications, objectification ... is always morally problematic. Under other specifications, objectification has features that may be either good or bad, depending on the overall context' (1999: 214). Nussbaum distinguishes seven different components of objectification, not all of which are present in each case: instrumentality, denial of autonomy, inertness, fungibility, violability, ownership, and denial of subjectivity (1999: 218). Nussbaum then restates the problem of objectification in terms reminiscent of Kant:

a certain sort of instrumental use of persons, negating the autonomy that is proper to them as persons, also leaves the human being so denuded of humanity, in the eyes of the objectifier, that he or she seems ripe for other abuses as well—for the refusal of imagination involved in the denial of subjectivity, for the denial of individuality involved in fungibility, and even for bodily and spiritual violation and abuse, if that should appear to be what best suits the will and purposes of the objectifier.   (Nussbaum 1999: 223)

Citing passages drawn from erotic works in which one person sexually objectifies another, Nussbaum argues, contra Kant, that sexual desire is not necessarily objectifying in a morally problematic way. A person can sexually desire another's body, in a way that momentarily treats another as merely a body, without treating another as a mere instrument for the first person's ends, and without denying another's autonomy, subjectivity, or rendering him or her vulnerable for moral abuse. In the context of an equal relationship (not necessarily marriage) in which there is mutual desire and mutual respect for each other as persons, intermittent uses of another's body, primarily as a body, are not harmful.

3.2 Prostitution

Another culturally entrenched practice that has been the target of much feminist criticism is prostitution. Elizabeth Anderson argues that prostitution allows the norms of the market to corrupt and degrade activities that properly belong to different spheres of social life, such as the family and personal friendships. Anderson (1993: 154) states:

prostitution is the classic example of how commodification debases a gift value and its giver. The specifically human good of sexual acts exchanged as gifts is founded upon a mutual recognition of the partners as sexually attracted to each other and as affirming an intimate relationship in their mutual offering of themselves to each other. This is a shared good. The couple rejoices in their *union*, which can be realized only when each partner reciprocates the other's gift *in kind*, offering her own sexuality in the same spirit in which she received the other's—as a genuine offering of the self. The commodification of sexual 'services' destroys the kind of reciprocity required to realize human sexuality as a shared good. Each party values the other only instrumentally, not intrinsically. But the nature of the good exchanged implies a particular degradation of the prostitute. The customer's cash payment is impersonal and fully alienable. In paying the prostitute he yields no power over his person to her. The prostitute sells her own sexuality, which is necessarily embodied in her person. In appropriating her sexuality for his own use, the customer expresses a (de)valuation of women as rightfully male sexual property, as objects to be used for men's own sexual purposes, which need not respond to the woman's own personal needs.

Anderson contends that, in commercial sexual transactions, the customer treats the provider immorally, for he appropriates her sexuality for his purposes, like an object or piece of property. For Anderson, sex that is reciprocally exchanged, based on mutual attraction, does not treat others instrumentally and is also a more valuable kind of human experience.

Anderson holds that exchanges of sexuality as a commodity using primarily women sexual providers can affect how sexuality and women are valued in spheres of life beyond the market. She states, 'If women's sexuality is legally valued as a commodity anywhere in society, it would be even more difficult than it already is to establish insulated social spheres where it can be exclusively and fully valued as a genuinely shared and personal good, where women themselves can be sexually valued in ways fully consonant with their own dignity' (Anderson 1993: 155). Margaret Radin describes the corrupting effect of commercial sex in terms of the 'discourse contagion of market rhetoric' (1996: 132–3). She asks,

What if sex were fully and openly commodified? Suppose newspapers, radio, TV, and billboards advertised sexual services as imaginatively and vividly as they advertise computer services, health clubs, or soft drinks. Suppose the sexual partner of your choice could be ordered through a catalog . . . If sex were openly commodified in this way, its comodification would be reflected in everyone's discourse about sex, and in particular about women's sexuality. New terms would emerge for particular gradations of sexual market values . . . With this change in discourse, when it became pervasive enough, would come a change in everyone's experience, because experience is discourse dependent.   (Radin 1996: 133)

Both Radin's and Anderson's arguments suggest that it is not possible to allow market exchanges of sexuality without destroying or deforming some important aspects of non-commercial sexuality.

These arguments against prostitution rest on the assumption that sexuality is a good more like children and less like food or entertainment, a good that is best distributed by non-market principles, such as in accordance with love, affection, ability to nurture, and so on. These arguments also rest on the assumption that sexuality is non-alienable, like one's children or bodily organs, because sexuality is a part of oneself or intimately connected with one's person, integrity, and dignity. However, many advocates for the decriminalization of prostitution emphasize that what the prostitute alienates in her transaction with a customer is not her sexuality, but her labour, labour that may involve using parts of her body that our culture sees as sexual or 'private' (Kempadoo 1998: 4–5). Labour is a renewable and replaceable resource, unlike a bodily organ or a child. Anderson's and Radin's arguments also rest on the assumption that any market encroachments on sexuality will always negatively affect the value and significance of sexuality in our lives. Given that current markets in sexuality are typically organized by sexist and racist values and assumptions, this concern is quite legitimate (Shrage 1992, 1994). Yet there is currently an international movement of 'sex workers', mostly organized by feminist, pro-labour, prostitutes, that aims to transform the sex industry, especially its legal and social status and working conditions in the industry (Kempadoo 1998). Many leaders of this movement and its regionally diverse organizations are attempting to challenge sexism and racism in the industry (Aarens et al. 1997; Leigh 1997). Commodified sexual transactions organized by non-sexist, non-racist, non-heterosexist, non-ageist, non-ableist, and so on commercial enterprises might not always have a negative influence on non-commodified exchanges that take place between lovers, friends, and marital partners. The latter exchanges are themselves not typically free of sexist, racist, heterosexist, ageist, and ableist values, as many feminist and anti-racist theorists have demonstrated. For example, in many contemporary societies, persons who have a bodily disability are desexualized and face intense social discrimination in their pursuit of sexual partners. Yet, currently, a significant number of sex workers cater to customers who are disabled (Shrage n.d.). Commercial sexual transactions that sexualized, in respectful ways, for example, people who use wheelchairs could have a salutary effect on private sexual transactions.

4. OTHER DIRECTIONS

Since the mid-1980s, feminist critiques of pornography and prostitution have been robustly challenged by other feminists and by self-proclaimed 'pro-sex' advocates who are concerned to address the persecution of minority sexualities and erotic communities. 'Pro-sex' advocates tend to treat sex as a morally neutral activity that has been too long burdened by doctrines that regard sex as inherently shameful, harmful, and redeemable only by important social ends such as procreation or marital stability. More recently, advocates for sexual minorities are challenging attitudes to non-conventional sexual practices that appear, like pornography, to endorse subordination and rape. In 'Rethinking Sadomasochism: Feminism, Interpretation, and Simulation' Patrick Hopkins argues that feminist critics of SM have fundamentally misunderstood the practices that SM participants engage in. A number of feminist critics have alleged that SM activities eroticize sexual violence and thereby reproduce heterosexist behaviours and relationships that oppress women. Hopkins argues that SM participants do not eroticize sexual violence but only 'simulations' of violence or domination. He states:

SM participants do not rape, they do rape scenes. SMists do not enslave, they do slave scenes. SMists do not kidnap, they do capture and bondage scenes . . . SM is constructed as a performance, as a staging, a production, a simulation in which participants are writers, producers, directors, actors, and audience . . . Participants know they are doing a scene. They have sought out other performers.   (Hopkins 1994: 123)

Hopkins explains that SM actors negotiate and agree in advance about how a 'rape' will take place, and often establish 'safe words' to use in a scene so that they can 'slow down or stop the action if it gets too intense' (1994: 124). According to Hopkins, 'SM scenes gut the behaviors they simulate of their violent, patriarchal, defining features. What makes events like rape, kidnapping, slavery, and bondage evil in the first place is the fact that they cause harm, limit freedom, terrify, scar, destroy, and coerce. But in SM there is attraction, negotiation, the power to halt the activity, the power to switch roles and attention to safety' (1994: 124). SM thus does not involve force, subordination, or terror, although Hopkins admits that it may involve some physical pain (1994: 128).

Hopkins compares participating in an SM scene with riding on a roller-coaster. 'There is intense emotion—fear, tension, anticipation, thrill. There is physiological arousal—adrenaline rush, headiness, gut twisting, a body high. All this because one has placed herself in the position of simulating plummeting to her death, of simulating flying off into space, of simulating the possibility of smashing into trees or metal railings' (1994: 125). He argues that, just as we do not infer that the roller-coaster rider really desires to fall, die, or smash into something, we should not infer that an SM participant really desires to be raped, kidnapped, or enslaved. Hopkins claims 'the SM practitioner may find actual violence and humiliation repugnant and horrible, but finds the simulation of that event thrilling and exciting' (1994: 126), just as the roller-coaster rider is likely to be horrified at the thought of really falling, crashing, and dying. Because SM involves simulations of violent acts and not violence, it is not difficult to understand how participants can consent to SM practices. Moreover, because the participants in SM generally have an equal say in their productions, and because they need to articulate their sexual desires clearly and honestly, and establish bonds of trust, Hopkins concludes that SM practices may have a beneficial influence on 'vanilla' sex rather than a negative one.

4.1 Uncharted Zones

Although there are many analyses of various aspects of sexuality, certain topics have received less attention in the literature. The reasons for this relative omission are disparate and we will only identify some issues in need of additional philosophical attention.

While analyses of rape, identification of social myths surrounding rape, and refigurations of the meanings of rape have been prevalent in the literature, so far there has been too little philosophical attention directed to the topic of incest and child sexual abuse. Linda Martín Alcoff has taken issue with those like Foucault and

Gayle Rubin who advocate so-called 'cross-generational' sex. Alcoff interrogates the relations between power and discourse relative to communication between adults and children and concludes that

When we incorporate the discourse of children with our own, and translate their desires within an economy of adult sexuality characterized by genital, orgasmic sex, we are exerting our force once again to eradicate any possible difference that may be there. The only way to avoid this is to leave children alone sexually... (1996: 126)

Sue Campbell has also begun a much-needed analysis of contemporary cultural discourses about incest, particularly the politics of debates about recovered versus false memories of childhood incest. Campbell illustrates how the discourses of the supporters of the False Memory Syndrome Foundation target the competence and epistemic authority of those who experience memories of abuse. She argues that a consequence of this is to exclude a woman who has been a victim of incest 'from participating as an epistemological agent in an understanding of her past and in contributing to social knowledge of childhood sexual abuse' (Campbell 2001: 157).

There has been some, though not a lot, of discussion about the ethical issues raised by scientific research on sexuality. In *Gay Science*, Timothy Murphy (1997) analyses the moral issues raised by research on the causes and nature of different sexual orientations. Research on the causes of homosexuality, in particular, has been criticized because such investigations appear to assume that same-sex eroticism is unnatural or abnormal, and some argue that these investigations ultimately aim to find 'cures' for homosexuality, or to find ways to prevent the development of homosexuality or the existence of gay people. In this way, the intended applications of research on sexual orientation could harm lesbians and gay men. Murphy points out that some research on sexual orientation has had liberating effects. Evelyn Hooker's work, he states, has provided 'invaluable evidence regarding the psychological normalcy of gay men... The research went a great way toward dispelling the prevailing but erroneous notions that gay men and straight men differed in fundamental psychological ways' (Murphy 1997: 57). According to Murphy (1997: 57), other research has challenged the idea that gays are unfit to raise children, that gay men and lesbians are somehow more predatory than heterosexuals, and that same-sex eroticism is disruptive. Murphy (1997: 58) acknowledges that much research on sexual orientation has operated with suspicious motives, but argues that sexual orientation research might be conducted that would serve the interests of gays and lesbians, such as research on the causes of homophobia.

Moral philosophers have not given much attention to the moral issues raised by efforts to educate children about sex. In 'How should we Teach Sex?' David Archard (1998) explores the question of what sorts of programmes of sex education should be offered in state schools, given substantial differences among citizens on matters of sexual morality. He considers two strategies for teaching about sex: one 'strategy consists in the adoption and communication to young persons of an agreed, basic code of sexual morality, a set of uncontroversial prescriptions and proscriptions' (1998: 441). A second strategy 'advocates combining a strictly neutral description of possible sexual activities with a listing of the alternative moral outlooks on each' (1998: 444). Archard questions the first strategy because, even if a set of uncontroversial moral prescriptions can be formulated, students will need to be given reasons for particular prescriptions, and there are profound differences of opinion about what makes a particular act right or wrong. Thus the problem of how to deal with disagreement will reassert itself at another level. Archard questions the second strategy, because of the lack of good criteria for determining what sexual behaviours and moral perspectives on them should be included. Archard concludes by suggesting that the ideal of autonomy should guide how children are taught about sex in a liberal society. He states:

If we believe ourselves to live within a society which privileges liberty so long as its exercise by an individual is consistent with a like exercise of liberty by all then there should be no sphere of our lives which is exempt from the scope of that liberty principle. We should be as free in our sexual lives as it is alleged we should be in every other part of our life. And we should teach sex in a way that is consistent with that ideal.   (Archard 1998: 448)

Though Archard does not say much about how this principle would guide those who make policy on sex education in the state schools, he indicates briefly that his approach involves providing students with information that would allow them to make informed choices (see also Morgan 1996).

Another relatively new area of debate is comparative sexual ethics. In 'Zhu Xi and Confucian Sexual Ethics' Ping-Cheung Lo states 'that the sexual ethics of Zhu Xi (1130–1200), the most influential Neo-Confucian philosopher, had a strong ascetic tendency. Hence it is no surprise that under the sway of Zhu Xi's philosophy in Ming and Qing Dynasties, most Chinese intellectuals adopted a rather negative and mortifying attitude toward sexual desire' (1993: 465). Lo compares Zhu Xi's philosophy to that of natural law theorists. For both, it is permissible to satisfy appetites in ways that serve natural purposes such as survival. Thus one can have sex for procreation but not for pleasure. Lo concludes that Zhu Xi has a non-absolute or 'conditional ascetic attitude toward sex' (1993: 473). He claims not only that such a view is untenable for contemporary people, but that 'The unprecedented proliferation of pornographic novels and pictures in the Ming Dynasty can be interpreted as mass culture's revolt against the sexual asceticism advocated by Ming high culture' (1993: 473). Some might see the proliferation of pornography in the contemporary world, especially via the Internet, as a mass cultural revolt against the elements of Christian asceticism that remain ingrained in our laws and social institutions.

There has been some discussion among ethicists regarding the ethical issues raised by sexually transmitted diseases (STDs). Are we morally obligated to inform our partners about our sexual histories and medical conditions? Given that there is no cure for AIDS, should people who have it or who are HIV positive have sex with those who are HIV negative? Are people who have multiple partners morally required to get regular tests for STDs? Can sex be made safe enough, with condoms and by avoiding certain practices, so that a person need not be tested or disclose to others personal information such as test results or sexual contacts? Should condom use be legally required for commercial sex providers and their customers, and perhaps for all those who have multiple sex partners? How should our criminal justice system treat those who have knowingly engaged in unsafe sex practices with harmful results? Do STD epidemics often serve as excuses to persecute those with unconventional sexual practices? There needs to be more discussion of these questions.

Ethical issues raised by pregnancy have received a great deal of attention by ethicists debating the morality of abortion. Yet there could be some useful discussion about how we determine ethical responsibility for pregnancy, independently of considerations regarding whether or not it is permissible to terminate a pregnancy. For example, who, if anyone, is morally responsible when a woman becomes pregnant? Does one's use of contraceptives affect one's degree of responsibility for a pregnancy? If a person deceives another about one's potency or fertility, or about one's use of contraception, does this affect who is morally responsible for a pregnancy that results or what kinds of claims we can make on others? Perhaps some answers to these questions can help us address questions about the morality of abortion, which will be taken up later in this book.

Another area that needs more discussion is the ethics of 'outing' people for their sexual identities or behaviours. Given that information about a person's sexual behaviour can negatively affect how she is perceived and treated by others, how should we handle information that we may happen uniquely to possess about another's sexual habits, interests, or partners? In *Gay Ideas*, Richard Mohr (1992) discusses the moral issues involved in outing a lesbian or gay man. Though he acknowledges that there are many bad reasons for outing, he asserts that outing does not violate general moral principles of privacy and trust. Since living in the closet is a debased moral existence, outing does not destroy the dignity of the person outed. Mohr (1992: 37) states:

In not leading a life of lies, in simply 'living in the truth', one will make known the sexual orientation of others because one does not think, and rightly does not think, that there is anything wrong with being gay and because one will not play along with conventions that degrade gay existence, even if they are the conventions of gays themselves as a community of self-hating and self-oppressing persons. . . The core question in the outing debate is, 'Whose values shall count?' . . . Like civil disobedience, outing violates a community's conventions so that the community may come to live more morally.

By treating potentially damaging information about a person's sexuality as a secret—information that would not be damaging in a more enlightened world—we validate bigotry and lose opportunities for moral progress, according to Mohr. Do Mohr's views on outing apply to exposing other stigmatized sexual conduct, such as a person's work as a prostitute, or someone's extramarital relationship?

Going back to the example with which we began, how shall we morally evaluate Linda Tripp's 'outing' of Clinton's relationship with her friend? Interestingly, Mohr does not justify outing by its political goals, as do some gay and lesbian activists. Instead, for Mohr, 'outing is a simple consequence of living morally' (1992: 43).

We have focused on challenges both to conventional sexual moralities and to exploitative sexual practices. Debates about the rationality of particular sexual mores and the real harm of various practices will of course continue, though new laws and practices may come under attack. And new sexual scandals will certainly occur and provide us with occasions to rethink our sexual ethics.

REFERENCES

Aarens, Blake, Hima, B., Gold, Gina, Irie, Jade, Lawson, Madeleine, and Lockett, Gloria (1997). 'Showing Up Fully: Women of Color Discuss Sex Work', in J. Nagle (ed.), *Whores and Other Feminists*. New York: Routledge, 195–209.

Alcoff, Linda Martín (1996). 'Dangerous Pleasures: Foucault and the Politics of Pedophilia', in S. Hekman (ed.), *Feminist Interpretations of Foucault*. University Park, PA: Penn State University Press, 99–135.

Almaguer, T. (1991). 'Chicano Men: A Cartography of Homosexual Identity and Behavior'. *Differences: A Journal of Feminist Cultural Studies*, 3/2: 75–100.

Anderson, Elizabeth (1993). *Value in Ethics and Economics*. Cambridge, MA: Harvard University Press.

Aquinas, Thomas (1991). *Summa theologica*, trans. Fathers of the English Dominican Province. Allen, TX: Thomas More Press.

Archard, David (1998). 'How should we Teach Sex?'. *Journal of Philosophy of Education*, 32/3: 437–49.

Bayles, M. D. (1984). 'Marriage, Love, and Procreation', in R. Baker and F. Elliston (eds.), *Philosophy and Sex*. Rev. edn. Buffalo, NY: Prometheus, 130–45.

Berger, Fred (1983). 'Pornography, Sex, and Censorship', in David Copp and Susan Wendell (eds.), *Pornography and Censorship*. Buffalo, NY: Prometheus, 83–104.

Bogart, J. H. (1991). 'On the Nature of Rape'. *Public Affairs Quarterly*, 5: 117–36.

Campbell, Sue (2001). 'Memory, Suggestibility, and Social Skepticism', in N. Tuana and S. Morgen (eds.), *Engendering Rationalities*. Albany, NY: SUNY Press, 151–74.

Foa, P. (1977). 'What's Wrong with Rape', in M. Vetterling-Braggin, F. A. Elliston, and J. English (eds.), *Feminism and Philosophy*. Totowa, NJ: Littlefield, Adams & Co., 347–59.

Foucault, Michel (1976/1990). *The History of Sexuality: An Introduction*, trans. Robert Hurley. New York: Vintage Books.

Freud, S. (1908/1964). ' "Civilized" Sexual Morality and Modern Nervous Illness', in Freud, *Standard Edition of the Complete Psychological Works*, ix. London: Hogarth Press, 177–204.

Gaitskill, M. (1994). 'On Not Being a Victim'. *Harper's*, 288/1726 (Mar.), 35–44.

Garry, Ann (1983). 'Pornography and Respect for Women', in David Copp and Susan Wendell (eds.), *Pornography and Censorship*. Buffalo, NY: Prometheus, 61–81.

Goldman, A. (1980). 'Plain Sex'. In Alan Soble (ed.), *The Philosophy of Sex*. Totowa, NJ: Rowman & Allanheld, 119–38.

Halperin, David (1990). *One Hundred Years of Homosexuality and Other Essays on Greek Love*. New York: Routledge.

—— (1995). *Saint Foucault: Towards a Gay Hagiography*. Oxford: Oxford University Press.

Herman, Barbara (1993). 'Could it be Worth Thinking about Kant on Sex and Marriage?' in Louise Antony and Charlotte Witt (eds.), *A Mind of One's Own: Feminist Essays on Reason and Objectivity*. Boulder, CO: Westview Press, 49–67.

Hoagland, Sarah Lucia (1988). *Lesbian Ethics: Toward New Value*. Palo Alto, CA: Institute of Lesbian Studies.

Hopkins, Patrick (1994). 'Rethinking Sadomasochism: Feminism, Interpretation, and Simulation'. *Hypatia: A Journal of Feminist Philosophy*, 9/1: 116–41.

Hume, David (1739/1978). 'Of Chastity and Modesty', *A Treatise of Human Nature*. 2.330. Oxford: Oxford University Press.

Janus, Samuel, and Janus, Cynthia (1993). *The Janus Report on Sexual Behavior*. New York: John Wiley.

Kant, Immanuel (1924/1963). *Lectures on Ethics*, trans. L. Infield. New York: Harper & Row.

Kaplan, Morris (1997). *Sexual Justice: Democratic Citizenship and the Politics of Desire*. New York: Routledge.

Kazan, P. (1998). 'Sexual Assault and the Problem of Consent', in S. G. French, W. Teays, and L. M. Purdy (eds.), *Violence against Women: Philosophical Perspectives*. Ithaca, NY: Cornell University Press, 27–42.

Kempadoo, Kamala (1998). 'Introduction: Globalizing Sex Workers' Rights', in K. Kempadoo (ed.), *Global Sex Workers: Rights, Resistance, and Redefinition*. New York: Routledge, 1–28.

Ketchum, S. A. (1977). 'Liberalism and Marriage Law', in M. Vetterling-Braggin, F. A. Elliston, and J. English (eds.), *Feminism and Philosophy*. Totowa, NJ: Littlefield, Adams & Co., 264–76.

LeMoncheck, Linda (1997). *Loose Women, Lecherous Men: A Feminist Philosophy of Sex*. New York: Oxford University Press.

Leigh, Carol (1997). 'Inventing Sex Work', in J. Nagle (ed.), *Whores and Other Feminists*. New York: Routledge, 225–31.

Lo, Ping-Cheung (1993). 'Zhu Xi and Confucian Sexual Ethics'. *Journal of Chinese Philosophy*, 20/4: 465–77.

MacKinnon, Catharine (1987). *Feminism Unmodified: Discourses on Life and Law*. Cambridge, MA: Harvard University Press.

—— (1989). *Toward a Feminist Theory of the State*. Cambridge, MA: Harvard University Press.

McMurtry, J. (1972). 'Monogamy: A Critique'. *Monist*, 56: 587–99.

Mohr, Richard (1992). *Gay Ideas: Outing and other Controversies*. Boston: Beacon Press.

Morgan, Kathryn Pauly (1996). 'The Moral Politics of Sex Education', in A. Diller, B. Houston, K. P. Morgan, and M. Ayim (eds.), *The Gender Question in Education: Theory, Pedagogy, and Politics*. Boulder, CO: Westview Press, 170–8.

Murphy, Timothy (1997). *Gay Science: The Ethics of Sexual Orientation Research*. New York: Columbia University Press.

Nagel, T. (1969). 'Sexual Perversion'. *Journal of Philosophy*, 66: 1, 5–17.

Nussbaum, Martha (1999). 'Objectification'. In Nussbaum, *Sex and Social Justice*. New York: Oxford University Press.

Olds, Sharon (1989). 'Sex without Love', in Carole Vance (ed.), *Pleasure and Danger: Exploring Female Sexuality*. London: Pandora, 425.

Peterson, S. R. (1977). 'Coercion and Rape: The State as a Male Protection Racket', in M. Vetterling-Braggin, F. A. Elliston, and J. English (eds.), *Feminism and Philosophy*. Totowa, NJ: Littlefield, Adams & Co., 360–71.

Pineau, L. (1989). 'Date Rape: A Feminist Analysis'. *Law and Philosophy*, 8: 217–43.

Primoratz, Igor (1999). *Ethics and Sex*. London: Routledge.

Radin, Margaret (1996). *Contested Commodities*. Cambridge, MA: Harvard University Press.

Rapaport, E. (1976). 'On the Future of Love: Rousseau and the Radical Feminists', in C. C. Gould and M. W. Wartofsky (eds.), *Women and Philosophy: Toward a Theory of Liberation*. New York: Putnam's, 185–205.

Rich, Adrienne (1980). 'Compulsory Heterosexuality and Lesbian Existence'. *Signs: A Journal of Women in Culture and Society*, 5/4: 631–60.

Roiphe, K. (1993). *The Morning After: Sex, Fear, and Feminism*. Boston: Little, Brown, & Co.

Ruddick, S. (1984). 'Better Sex', in R. Baker and F. Elliston (eds.), *Philosophy and Sex*. Buffalo, NY: Prometheus, 280–99.

Russell, Bertrand (1929/1970). *Marriage and Morals*. New York: Liveright.

Shrage, Laurie (1992). 'Is Sexual Desire Raced? The Social Meaning of Interracial Prostitution'. *Journal of Social Philosophy*, 23: 42–51.

—— (1994). *Moral Dilemmas of Feminism: Prostitution, Adultery, and Abortion*. New York: Routledge.

Shrage, Laurie (n.d.) 'Are Sex Workers' Rights Human Rights?'. Unpublished typescript.

Soble, Alan (1996). *Sexual Investigations*. New York: New York University Press.

Taylor, R. (1982). *Having Love Affairs*. Buffalo, NY: Prometheus.

Valverde, Mariana (1995). 'Beyond Gender Dangers and Private Pleasures: Theory and Ethics in the Sex Debates', in Susan Dwyer (ed.), *The Problem of Pornography*. Belmont, CA: Wadworth, 177–91.

Vannoy, R. (1980). *Sex without Love: A Philosophical Exploration*. Buffalo, NY: Prometheus.

Wasserstrom, R. (1975). 'Is Adultery Immoral?' in R. Wasserstrom (ed.), *Today's Moral Problems*. New York: Macmillan, 240–8.

West, Robin (1997). *Caring for Justice*. New York: New York University Press.

Wreen, M. J. (1986). 'What's Really Wrong with Adultery'. *International Journal of Applied Philosophy*, 3/2: 45–9.

Case Cited

Adams v. Howerton, 486 F. Supp. 1119 (CD Cal. 1980), aff'd, 673 F.2d 1036 (9th Cir.), cert. denied, 458 US 1111 (1982).

CHAPTER 2

LOVE

NEERA K. BADHWAR

Love is not merely a contributor—one among others—to
meaningful life. In its own way it may underlie all other forms of
meaning. . . . by its very nature love is the principal means by which
creatures like us seek affective relations to persons, things, or ideals
that have value and importance for us.

(Singer 1994: 2)

1. THE LOOK OF LOVE

FROM Michelangelo's *Madonna con bambino* to Jamini Roy's *Mother and Child*,
from Lucien Levy-Dhurmer's *Salome* to Picasso's and Chagall's *The Lovers* and
many of the erotic sculptures of Khajuraho, we see the same look of love on the
faces of the lovers. Stated thus, the claim seems surprising, for it is commonplace to
think of the emotions of erotic and maternal love as discontinuous. Yet the fact that
we perceive as love the emotion depicted on all these faces suggests an implicit
awareness of a primordial emotion of love that is common to both types of love.
And on reflection this is just as it should be, since for most of us the first look of

I thank Hugh LaFollette for his editorial patience as I revised and re-revised this paper, David Braybrook,
Adam Morton, Louke van Wensveen, and Linda Zagzebski for their many helpful comments on earlier
drafts, Richard Terdiman for reading the paper with a literary eye, and Jan Narveson and C.D.C. Reeve
for making me see how much more needs to be said about the role of sex in romantic love (all love?)
than I could say here. I also thank the Departments of Philosophy at the University of Reading, Bowling
Green State University, and the University of Texas at Austin for the helpful discussion of several key
points following presentations of earlier versions.

love, forming an indelible image of love, is the look of delight and tenderness on the mother's face. If this look is the primordial experience of being loved and the first lesson in learning to love, then one would expect delight or tenderness to be present as a strand in different sorts of loving relationships. It may have been his recognition of this commonality in all love that led Aristotle to describe as *philia*—variously translated as love or friendship (Vlastos 1981: 3)—the love that exists between parent and child, wife and husband, siblings, as well as 'just friends' (*Nicomachean Ethics* (*NE*), bk. VIII). And, indeed, cross-cultural studies of the facial expressions of men and women in situations where they might be expected to feel *philia* for each other bear this out. 'When men and women are experiencing companionate love their faces . . . take on the expression mothers often display when they are happily, tenderly gazing at their young infants. They gaze downward. . . . Their faces soften, and a slight, tender smile plays about their lips (Hatfield and Rapson 1993: 109). No wonder, then, that God's love (agape) for his creation, and most of all human beings, is often depicted as a joyous contemplation of this creation, and the human love of God as a delighted apprehension of God. Indeed, Augustine calls the love of God *frui-love* (enjoyment love) as contrasted with *uti-love* (utility love). Similarly, Irving Singer (1994: 2) sees delighting in a person as a central feature of personal love, and C. S. Lewis makes pleasure in a thing essential to all loves and likes, whether it is the need-pleasure of need-love, such as the child's love for the parent, or the appreciative pleasure of appreciative love, which sees the loved object as lovable because of its inherent goodness (Lewis 1960/1988: 25–30). Beloved pets and inanimate or abstract objects of love—a story, a song, a joke, an ideal, a smart new computer program, a mathematical proof—can evoke the same feeling of pleasure or delight. It would seem, then, that some form of pleasure in (the thought of) the loved object's existence, whether the pleasure take the intense form of joy or delight or the quieter form of gladness, and pain in (the thought of) its non-existence, is central to the most general and basic expression of the emotion of love. In love of persons or animals, this basic emotion of love also includes pleasure in the well-being, and pain in the ill-being, of the loved object.

There is more to be discerned from the look of love in the art works mentioned. The look is a perceptive look, a look that seems really to *see* the loved object, not a falsifying look of projection and fantasy, or a self-centred look of appropriation. And, in seeing the loved object as it is, the look of love seems to affirm the object's value in its own right.

Reflection on the look of love, then, serves as a good entry point into various philosophical issues surrounding love of persons: how to define love, the question whether love is a response to the loved object's value or a bestowal of value, the epistemic significance of love, the metaphysics of love, and the importance of romantic love. For reasons of space, I confine myself to these issues in the sections that follow, even though it means neglecting some worthy contributions in the abundant contemporary philosophical literature on love. And, unless otherwise stated, the love I address is love of particular individuals, rather than love of God or of human beings qua human beings (agape).

2. DEFINING LOVE

When we think of the value of love in our lives, it is loving *relationships* that we have in mind rather than the dispositional or occurrent *emotions* of love. However, what makes a relationship one of love is the presence in it of the disposition of love, a disposition that leads to recurring emotions of love for the loved individual. Like other adult emotions, the emotion of love is not simply a feeling, but a complex, structured pattern of attention, perception, evaluation, and feeling (de Sousa 1987), which may or may not be (fully) conscious (Greenspan 1988: ch. 2). What, then, is the emotion of love?

I proposed above that pleasure in (the thought of) the existence and well-being of the loved individual, whether the pleasure take the intense form of joy or delight or the quieter form of gladness, and pain in (the thought of) his non-existence or ill-being, is central to the emotion of love. Of course, these claims are unqualifiedly true only in the paradigmatic cases of love; for instance, the pain-ridden existence of the loved individual may well lead one, as it leads him, to take no pleasure in his existence. Hence, depending on the facts of the case, the presence of such pleasure or pain as a primary strand in one's attitudes or dispositions towards an individual is necessary (though not sufficient) for a loving relationship. Conversely, pleasure in (the thought of) his ill-being or non-existence, and pain in (the thought of) his existence or well-being, are central to the emotion of hate. It is true, of course, that even in a loving relationship people can sometimes feel hatred for each other, but to the extent that they do, their emotions are contrary to their overall dispositions of love. I also remarked in Section 1 that the look of love seems to be a look that really *sees* the loved individual and affirms her as valuable in her own right. It seems to say that the loved individual's life is a blessing on one's existence—indeed, on all existence. As Ortega y Gasset (1957: 19) puts it, love is an ongoing affirmation of the loved object as worthy of existence, whereas hate is irritation at the mere existence of the hated object. More precisely, this sort of affirmation is of the essence of loving someone for her own sake—that is, non-instrumentally or as an end in herself. In such 'end love' one responds to the other primarily as a subject—a (potential) or actual centre of valuation and agency whose interests and perspectives on the world have weight in one's scheme of values. The heightened awareness of the loved individual as valuable in her own right and the delighted affirmation of this value in dispositional love imply an empathy, imagination, and understanding of the other that are part of the virtues of end love. By contrast, in instrumental or means love one sees the other primarily in relation to one's own purposes rather than as valuable in her own right. Accordingly, in such love one's empathy for, and understanding of, the other is partial, restricted to those features that are relevant to one's purposes. Hence, the virtues of instrumental love are also limited.

The idea that love is, at least in part, a response to value is now fairly widely accepted. But, with the notable exceptions of Lewis and Singer, the idea that love centrally involves pleasure in the valued individual's existence and well-being is conspicuous by its absence from modern and contemporary discussions of the topic. This stands in such sharp contrast to ancient discussions that it calls for an investigation.

2.1 Love as Concern for the Loved Person's Well-being

In his 'Autonomy, Necessity, and Love' (1994/1999a) and 'On Caring' (1999b) Harry Frankfurt proposes that love of a person for his own sake—rather than as means to our own—is a matter of being captivated by him and by one's disinterested devotion to his well-being. To be captivated is to have one's will 'rigorously constrained' by the beloved and by one's devotion to him, to regard the imperatives of love as having authority (Frankfurt 1994/1999a: 135). Contrary to Kant, it is not only the commands of reason that are categorical, but also 'the commands of selfless love' (Frankfurt 1994/1999a: 135–6). Understood thus, love is 'an element of ... [the] established volitional nature' of a person, 'and hence of his identity as a person' (Frankfurt 1994/1999a: 137). Since a person determines his identity through voluntary acts of endorsement of his motivations, passions, and other psychic elements, a person whose will is constrained by his love is, nevertheless, free rather than enslaved (Frankfurt 1994/1999a: 137). This is the difference between being captivated by love and being enslaved by passion. Frankfurt states that, whereas love 'ordinarily' involves 'strong feelings and beliefs that express, reveal, and support it', the 'heart of love ... is neither affective nor cognitive ... but volitional' (1994/1999a: 129).

But is such categorical, volitional devotion to a person's well-being sufficient to distinguish love from obligation or admiration? I think not. My devotion to my child's interests—the central case of love in Frankfurt's analysis—may well be part of my identity, but it may be motivated by a sense of duty rather than love, a duty that is experienced as an unpleasant burden, no matter how kindly I perform it (doing it kindly being part of the burden of duty). I may even love the self-sacrifice that my mothering involves without loving my child. Again, I may be devoted to someone's welfare out of admiration for his moral character or talents rather than out of love. And not only is admiration in itself different from love (mothers do not usually admire the infants they love), it is consistent with a fundamental, pervasive resentment, even antipathy, towards an individual. No doubt, love can coexist with some feelings of resentment towards an individual, or antipathy towards some of his qualities. But it cannot coexist with a fundamental resentment or antipathy towards him, no matter how devoted one may be to his well-being. One's overall emotional orientation towards a person—the complex of perceptions, thoughts, and feelings mentioned above—is all-important in determining whether or not one loves him.

This analysis bears out Stocker's well-known argument (1981) against purely teleological theories of friendship (and, more generally, of ethics)—that is, theories that seek to understand friendship entirely in terms of desires and goals. Using an example of an act of friendship—visiting a friend in hospital—Stocker shows that, although the act involves acting for the sake of the friend's well-being, it cannot be reduced to it. Indeed, it cannot be reduced to acting for the sake of anything, not even for the sake of acting out of friendship. As he points out, for an act to be an act of friendship, it must come out of a certain 'character structure', and this involves 'forms of directed attention and sensitivity' that cannot be captured by an analysis in terms of desires and goals alone. This point can be applied to all forms of love.

Yet teleological analyses of love, in particular analyses in terms of desire or concern for the loved individual's well-being, are prominent in the philosophical and popular literature. Thus we read that 'if x loves y, then x wants to benefit and be with y, etc., and he has these wants . . . because he believes y has some determinate characteristics x in virtue of which he thinks it worthwhile to benefit and be with y' (Taylor 1976: 157). Or, again, that love is 'a particularized altruism' as contrasted with 'general benevolence towards humanity' (Martin 1996: 39) or that 'love is the will to extend one's self for the purpose of nurturing one's own or another's spiritual growth' (Peck 1978: 81).

One reason for the prevalence of such analyses may lie in a failure to distinguish between love as an *emotional disposition* and love as a *relationship*. Undeniably, concern for the loved individual's well-being is essential to a loving *relationship*—that is, to the totality of attitudes, actions, and interactions that join people together in love over time. But it does not follow that it is an essential part of the *emotion* of love. Rather, given the contingencies of life, it is a common *consequence* of love. Hence, a loving relationship cannot be analysed entirely in terms of concern or desire for the loved individual's well-being.

That such a desire is not of the essence of love is readily seen when we consider that we can continue to love someone long after death has taken him beyond harm or benefit. What remains in such a case is pleasure in the thought that the loved individual existed and (as the case may be) flourished. There is another reason why love, as such, does not entail the desire for the loved individual's well-being, a reason that has to do with the nature of desire. The object of desire is something we lack, or have but could lose. But, as Aristotle famously pointed out, life is not an endless series of lacks and strivings to satisfy lacks (NE, bk. I). Life offers resting points of fulfilment, moments of pure happiness when we experience our lives as complete and lacking in nothing, and all desire and concern are stilled. If love implied desire or concern, then love, too, would be stilled at such moments. But this is clearly absurd. Indeed, in our own case, it is precisely at such moments that we feel most strongly that love of existence that may be present at other times as only a positive undertone in our lives. Likewise, love of another can also be simply a joyous contemplation of her existence, a delighted awareness of her life as complete and lacking in nothing. Love of persons, then, can be—as love of God must be— devoid of any concern for their well-being. Love for a person typically gives *rise* to such concern, as it does other desires, such as the desire for reciprocity, but it does not *entail* it. Love is essentially an emotional attitude or orientation towards an individual, not a desire or set of desires.

2.2 Love and Value

David Velleman also sees love as 'essentially an attitude toward the beloved himself but not toward any result at all', arguing that any conative—aim-oriented—definition is fundamentally mistaken (Velleman 1999: 354). Love, he says, is 'a state of attentive suspension, similar to wonder or amazement or awe', an appreciative apprehension of a self-existent end (1999: 360). Concern for the loved individual's well-being, desire for his company, and feelings of attraction, sympathy, empathy, or fascination, do usually accompany love, but they are 'independent responses that love merely unleashes'. Hence, one can love cranky grandfathers and meddlesome aunts without enjoying their company or having any concern for their well-being except when occasion demands (1999: 353). The essence of love is 'an arresting awareness of…the value inhering in its object…[that] disarms our emotional defenses … [and] makes us vulnerable to the other' (1999: 360–1). Just as reverence, according to Kant, is the awareness of a person's value that arrests our self-love and prevents us from using him as a mere means to our ends, so love, on Velleman's analysis, is an awareness that 'arrests our tendencies toward emotional self-protection from another person' and prevents us from closing ourselves off 'from being affected by him' (1999: 361).

The idea that love is 'an arresting awareness' of a person's inherent value that 'disarms our emotional defenses' and 'makes us vulnerable to the other' strikingly and illuminatingly captures something fundamental to love. Although the claim that love is a *response* to a person's *inherent value*, rather than a *bestowal* of value, requires qualification (see below), undoubtedly one largely *experiences* love as such a response. And the claim that love makes us vulnerable to the other is obviously true: a 'love' that left us unaffected by the loved individual's actions, emotions, and thoughts, by her joys and sorrows, would not be love. Such vulnerability characterizes not only adult love but also children's love for their caretakers and companions, within the limits of their cognitive and emotional capacities. However, does

Velleman's definition suffice to distinguish love from awe or fear? An arresting awareness of value that strikes down our emotional defences and makes us responsive to another's subjectivity can be an awesome or fearful rather than loving awareness. Indeed, this is often the case when one partner is severely lacking in self-esteem. The self-sacrificing, deferential wife, quick to perceive and respond to the needs, feelings, and thoughts of the husband she values, might all the same regard him with a pervasive resentment and fear mixed with her admiration and respect. Whatever love might be, it is surely not this.

Could we save Velleman's account by adding that the vulnerability of love includes not only an openness *to* the loved individual, but also an openness *of* ourselves—our needs and thoughts—to the loved individual? Such openness certainly serves to distinguish love from awe and fear, both of which tend to close us up. But it is hard to imagine this kind of two-way openness to an individual one values without pleasure in his existence and well-being. And, even if one could, this characterization would still not give us the essence of love, because it would leave out all loves—such as that of parents for their young children, or teachers for students—from which such openness is absent.

So far as I can see, then, Velleman can distinguish love from awe, fear, or admiration only by making pleasure in the loved person's well-being or existence, or pain in her ill-being or non-existence, part of the essence of love. In other words, it seems that an 'arresting awareness' of the inherent value of another person that 'disarms our emotional defenses' can be constitutive of love only with the addition that the awareness is pleasurable. An examination of some other attempts to define love without reference to pleasure should serve to strengthen this point.

2.3 Love and Love-Comprising Relations

John Brentlinger (1970/1989: 137–8) casts his net wider, seeking to characterize all love, and not only love of persons, as a positive emotional response to the intrinsic value of the object. The loved object may be general, such as mankind, animals, and kinds of activities, or it may be individual, such as a person, animal, or thing. What distinguishes love of individual objects from that of general objects is that in the former the positive emotion is some form of attachment. However, like Velleman's definition of love, Brentlinger's definition is also too broad, since reverence or admiration for an individual also satisfies his definition of love as a positive emotional attachment to an individual seen as inherently valuable. If, on the other hand, we adopt Brentlinger's suggestion that the emotional attachment in love is affection (1970/1989: 137), then his definition becomes circular, since 'affection' is simply a form of love.

A similar problem may be found in W. H. Newton-Smith's analysis of personal love in terms of certain relations—love-comprising relations or LCRs—including knowledge of the loved individual, concern for his welfare, affection, commitment, respect, liking, and attraction (1973/1989: 199–217). The most important of these LCRs, Newton-Smith states, the only ones entailed by the concept of love, are knowledge and 'possibly' affection. The others are only *generally* necessary; hence, they may be absent, or present only to a minimal extent, without defeating the claim that the relationship is one of love (1973/1989: 204).

Can love be defined satisfactorily in terms of knowledge of, and affection for, the loved individual? I believe not. In making knowledge necessary to love, Newton-Smith obviously intends to define genuine love, as opposed to infatuation or blind love. But knowledge is also necessary to genuine hate. So what must do all the work of distinguishing genuine love from genuine hate in Newton-Smith's definition is affection. But, as we have seen, we cannot define love in terms of affection without circularity. Nor can we define love as knowledge plus the other LCRs—commitment, respect, liking, attraction, and concern for welfare—unless we construe 'liking' and 'attraction' as affection, which brings us back to the problem of circularity.

Once again, then, it seems that an adequate definition of love requires reference to pleasure. And, since love is a form of valuation, to love someone for her own sake implies valuing her for her own sake, for who she is. An obvious interpretation of this idea is that love affirms the inherent value of the individual. We certainly largely *experience* love as responding to and affirming the inherent value of the individual. But, as the next section shows, this is neither the only possible interpretation of loving someone for her own sake, nor all of the experience of love.

3. Love in Relation to the Object of Love

3.1 Love as an Affirmation of Value

The claim that love is a response to value has been rejected by a long line of Christian thinkers. Starting with Luther, these thinkers have argued that a love that responds to the beloved's value (whatever the ground or nature of this value) is acquisitive or egoistic and, hence, devoid of moral worth. A love that is conditional on the beloved's value is tainted with the expectation of, and desire for, gain.

Contrary to Augustine's view, then, it follows that even agape, God's love for us and our love of neighbour, cannot be directed at the inherent goodness of human beings. How, then, should we understand agape—or any love—if it is to have moral worth? Following Luther, Anders Nygren summarizes its main features thus. Agape is 'spontaneous' and 'unmotivated', given not as a response to the value of the loved object, but rather, out of its own creative force (1953: 75–80). Agape is a love that bestows value on the object by loving. Agape stands 'in contrast to all activity with a eudaemonistic motive' and 'in contrast to all legalism' (1953: 726–7). Agape gives with no thought of gain. Christian love is 'a lost love', 'the direct opposite of rational calculation' (1953: 732). In Kierkegaard's words, 'love to one's neighbor makes a man blind in the deepest and noblest and holiest sense, so that he blindly loves every man' (1847/1962: 80).

The interest of this ideal of love is more than historical. The idea that the 'highest' love is unconditional and selfless is widespread both in philosophy and in everyday thought. Whereas Nygren directs his criticism of *eros* to Plato's theory of love in the *Lysis* and the *Symposium*, Gregory Vlastos (1981) and George Nakhnikian (1978) explicitly extend it to Aristotle's friendship as well. To understand the criticism, a brief summary of Aristotle's theory would be helpful.

According to Aristotle, adult friendships involve a mutually recognized goodwill based on each other's virtue, pleasantness, or usefulness (*NE* III. 3). Perfect or complete friendship is one that is based on the virtue of both parties (*NK* III. 3–4). It is in such friendships, and only in such friendships, that friends take pleasure in each other for what they truly are—that is, their virtuous characters. And it is only in such friendships that friends wish each other 'to be and to live' (*NE* IX. 4) and flourish—for their friends' sake, not their own. They are also useful to each other in various ways, both through their incidental qualities—wealth, talent, position— and through their good character. As Aristotle puts it, 'good people are both unconditionally good and advantageous for each other. They are pleasant in the same ways too, since good people are pleasant both unconditionally and for each other' ($1156^{b}12$–15). By contrast, in utility and pleasure friendships, friends care for each other only or primarily for their incidental qualities, the qualities that make them useful or pleasurable. And so they love their friends for their own sakes, not their friends', and they care about each other's good or bad character only in so far as it profits or pleases them, and not for itself.

Thus, Aristotle's utility and pleasure friendships are forms of what I earlier called instrumental love, and his perfect friendship is a form of non-instrumental or end love. In all forms of end love—friendship, agape, eros, or filial love—one loves the other for his own sake. What distinguishes these loves from each other is the specific intentional object of love—that is, the description under which the other is loved. Thus, in an intimate relationship of friends and lovers, the object of love is the individual as defined by her central character and personality traits, traits that make her, in a significant sense, 'another self'. In Aristotle's view, the object of love in perfect friendship is the virtuous individual who is 'another self', a 'mirror of the soul' (*NE* $1169^{b}28$–$1170^{a}4$, $1170^{b}1$–14; *Magna Moralia* $1213^{a}10$–26; Cooper 1980: 317–34).

Vlastos and Nakhnikian argue that love of another because of his virtues falls short of true love of another for his own sake, because, as Aristotle says, 'in loving their friend they love what is good for themselves' (*NE* $1158^{a}33$–35). Such love, according to Nakhnikian, is no less 'transactional' or instrumental than love of another 'because of his usefulness', for both are 'supposed to rebound [*sic*] to the satisfaction or benefit of the one who loves' (1978: 287). In loving people for their goodness or lovability, what we seek, ultimately, is our own happiness. We love a person non-instrumentally, for his own sake, according to Nakhnikian and Vlastos, only when we love him for whatever he is—that is, unconditionally. Further, only such a love, according to Vlastos, takes as its object the 'whole' person, the individual 'in the uniqueness and integrity of his or her individuality' (1981: 31). In such 'undemanding love', as Nakhnikian calls it, there can be 'no thought of expected returns and no requirement that the person loved be a good [or lovable] human being' (1978: 294). Both Vlastos and Nakhnikian give as an example of such love Aristotle's own example of the mother who loves and wishes well to the child she will never see again, the sort of love that they regard as regrettably absent from his conception of adult friendships.

It would be easy to point out that, even for the mother, this is not the ideal situation—the ideal is to love and be loved. It would also be easy to show, citing Aristotle's example of giving up one's life so that one's friend may live and flourish, that the sort of love the mother shows is not only compatible with Aristotle's perfect friendship, but also necessary to it. Last but not least, although the object of parental love is 'my child', with all the bonds of nurture and responsibilities that implies, rather than 'a virtuous other self', one could question the easy assumption that a parental love that remains *entirely* unaffected by the child's virtue or vice is the best kind of love—if it is love at all. (Here it is instructive to consider that loving parents who have lost their children tend to remember them as *good*—good children, or good human beings.) But I will leave these issues aside to focus on the claim that loving someone for his goodness makes the love instrumental because such love is sought as a good to oneself, a source of satisfaction or happiness.

This disapproving view seems both unappealing and implausible. But it cannot be met by the common argument that getting happiness from loving someone for his goodness does not make the love instrumental because the happiness *results* from the love, it does not *motivate* it. This counter-argument fails on three counts. For one, even if it is true that happiness is entirely the *result* of love, surely the *belief* that it has this result is central to the motivation for seeking love in the first place, despite the well-advertised burdens and hazards of love. And it is central to the motivation for maintaining love. After all, we are not astounded to find ourselves feeling happy when we find someone to love, or when we see our loved ones flourishing—we knew this all along (even though the joy we feel when we actually find love is, in Dante's words, 'a new and gentle miracle').[1] Secondly, the argument that love is not instrumental *because* happiness is a result, not a motivation, of love implicitly concedes the unwarranted premise that, if happiness were any part of the motivation for seeking or keeping love, love would be instrumental. Thirdly, the argument wrongly concedes the even more crucial premise that happiness is entirely the *result* of loving another. If I am right that loving someone implies

---

[1] 'si e novo miracolo e gentile' (Dante, *Vita nuova*, sect. 21).

taking pleasure in her existence and well-being, and pleasure is an element of happiness, then loving is not only a *source* of happiness but itself one of the emotions and activities *constitutive* of happiness. Hence, even if agape is unconditional, to count as love at all it must be inherently pleasurable and happiness making. And, indeed, this is close to Nakhnikian's own view. The 'mental states and dispositions' of those who love undemandingly, he says, are 'suffused with intrinsically good feelings', and 'the degree to which a human being is undemandingly loving is the degree to which he is joyful and unhysterically energetic' (Nakhnikian 1978: 314). Presumably, Nakhnikian would not say that those who are motivated by their awareness of the intrinsic benefits of unconditional love to seek to remain or become (more) unconditionally loving thereby turn their love into instrumental love. But if they can be absolved of the charge of instrumentality, then so can the Aristotelian friend.

How, then, can Nakhnikian consistently disparage Aristotle's virtue friendship on the grounds of its alleged instrumentality? He might say that what makes Aristotle's virtue friendship—as, indeed, all non-agapaic loves—instrumental is that they are conditional on the loved individual's value. Since agape is independent of the loved individual's value, the happiness derived from agapaic love is also independent of the individual's value. In other words, this crucial benefit of love is self-generated, and so the loved person cannot be seen as an instrument to the benefit.

But is there any such thing as unconditional love? Can even God love unconditionally? We can agree with Yeats (1933) that God loves us for ourselves alone and not our yellow hair—if loving people for themselves alone means loving them for who they truly are, and who they truly are makes them worth loving. Indeed, contrary to Yeats, even we *humans* can love others for themselves alone and not their yellow hair. But it seems impossible for even God to love us completely unconditionally, independently of any worth in us. For if God's love is not *motivated* by our goodness or lovability, it becomes mysterious why it is selectively *directed* at us (Kosman 1976/1989; Badhwar 1987/1989).[2] If, as Luther puts it, agape is 'an overflowing love . . . which says: I love thee, not because thou art *good*, for I draw my love not from thy goodness [*Frommigkeit*] as from an alien spring; but from mine own well-spring', then why should God single out us humans for his love? Why should he not love all his creation equally? But let us say that he does love everything equally. Does this solve the problem? Not quite. For surely *we* are not supposed to love all things equally, from rocks to roaches to Rolling Stones. So the mystery remains how our preferential love for human beings over rocks and roaches can be completely unconditional. To dispel the mystery, the defenders of unconditional love must at least concede that agape—understood now as love of humans

---

[2] Many of the ideas in this and the following paragraph are taken, with changes, from Badhwar (1987/1989).

qua humans—takes as its object the good or God—the humanity—in each individual. On this older, Augustinian interpretation, agape is no longer completely unconditional, and we can explain why God loves us selectively (if he does): he loves us selectively because humanity as such is worth loving.

We may conclude, then, that agape can be unconditional only in the sense of being unmotivated by the worth that distinguishes one human being from another, but not in the sense of being unmotivated by his *human* nature and worth, of the worth that distinguishes him from non-humans. So, once again, either agape is also instrumental, or conditional love can be non-instrumental, and the identification of the conditional with the instrumental is mistaken. Both instrumental love and non-instrumental love are conditional on features that make the other worth loving to the lover, whatever these features might be, and both are a good to those who love. As discussed in Section 1 above, what makes love of someone end love is that the individual is valued for her own sake—that is, as a subject, a centre of valuation and agency. And in friendship the intentional object is the individual as defined by her character and personality traits.

So far I have argued that love is necessarily a good to the lover because it is an inherently pleasurable affirmation of value. But this is only one aspect of the benefit of love. Love is also a good to the lover because to love someone is necessarily to experience the loved object as good for oneself; something experienced as bad for oneself (or neither good nor bad) is an object of aversion (or indifference). Finally, love is a good to oneself because it involves self-expression and self-creation. As Aristotle puts it, 'loving is like production' because in loving we actualize ourselves and, thus, live our lives more vividly and enjoyably than as mere receivers of love (*NE* 1168^{a}5–20). All creation or production of value—material, intellectual, artistic, spiritual, or biological—in activities we love expresses and shapes our identities. Indeed, love seems to be a necessary condition of a strong identity and appropriate self-love (Brown 1987: 22; Lear 1990; Frankfurt 1994/1999a: 24–5). Nothing calls for the investment of self in valued objects and activities as love does, an investment that shapes the contours of our identities and creates a self worth loving. In short, love is the fuel that feeds our lives, and the primary source of identity and meaning and, thus, of happiness. A particular love may not be a net good, of course, since it may bring grief—even devastating grief and loss of identity—in its wake. But, as the primary affective bond 'to persons, things, or ideals that have value and importance for us' (Singer 1994: 2), love is an indispensable part of a meaningful life. And, if this is the fundamental reason that we are motivated to seek and maintain love, as both common sense and philosophy suggest, then, once again, our desire for love is fundamentally self-interested. In short, contrary to the advocates of unconditional love, love is selfless neither in its motivation nor in its psychological structure. We desire love for our own good, and in loving another for her own sake, we also love her as a good to ourselves. Yet what is called into question by this analysis may be not the moral status of love, but the moral status of the ideal of selflessness, and the cogency of the conception of the moral self that lurks behind this ideal.[3]

3.2 Love as Bestowal of Value

The idea that love is a response to the value inherent in the individual has been rejected not only by the Lutheran interpreters of agape, but also by romantic writers like Stendhal and Proust. According to these writers, love *creates* or *bestows* value on the loved object. But how exactly does loving someone make her valuable? One might understand how in the case of God, if we see him and his acts and attitudes as the bearers of all value (although it is then hard to see why the act of creating human beings did not invest them with value). On this picture, God's love for humans makes them worth loving the way a gifted musician's love of performing makes an otherwise nondescript composition worth performing. In a sense, then, in loving us, what God loves is the effects of his own love. Likewise, if we are mere conduits for God's love, so that our love for other human beings is, at bottom, the love of God flowing through us, as Luther and Nygren hold, then in loving others what we love are the effects of God's love. Unfortunately, this does not help in a secular understanding of human love. A human being who thought of his love as investing inherently value-less human beings with value through his love would be a megalomaniac—not exactly the ideal lover.

How, then, does Stendhal understand the idea of the lover bestowing value on his beloved? As crystallization, the process of attributing greater and greater perfections to the beloved on the basis of his own desires—while believing that he is actually discovering these perfections in the beloved. The lover's passion endows the beloved with perfections the way the salt mines of Salzburg encrust the barren bough with shining crystals. On Stendhal's view, then, love is a form of projection rather than perception, and the object of love is a fantasy, a creature of one's own imagination, rather than the actual individual.

Such blindness is no doubt true of some people's loves, especially in the first stages of love—in the process of 'falling in love' that Ortega y Gasset (1957: 48–54) describes as an impoverishment of consciousness. But in identifying all love with blind, unrealistic love, Stendhal implies either that we are incapable of loving people for their inherent worth, the worth they possess independently of our projections—or else, that no one has any such worth. But why we should believe either proposition he does not say. Nor does there seem to be any good reason to believe it.

Is there anything to be said for bestowal if Stendhal's view is false—if, in fact, genuine love is not blind? I think there is. Reflection reveals a rich array of creative

---

[3] These issues are too vast to go into here, but I have addressed them elsewhere (Badhwar 1993: 90–117).

possibilities in an intimate relationship of friends or lovers, possibilities that are not only *compatible* with clear-sightedness but that *require* it. In such a relationship, love creates value in the loved individual by helping to actualize a potential that may be hidden even from her. Such a creation rests on a discovery of the potential for that value—a gift that rests on an acknowledgement. This idea is powerfully expressed in the *Symposium*, where love is seen as 'the power by which, recognizing the beauty in another, we bring forth that beauty by eliciting it' (Kosman 1976/1989: 159). To love is not only to *respond* to value but also, thereafter, to *seek* value and to expect to find it. This optimistic, value-seeking spirit makes love imaginative and discerning, thereby enabling the lover to perceive potentials that even the beloved cannot see. This is the 'formative attentive regard' that Leila Tov-Ruach sees as central to love, the 'intensely focused attention' on the individual's (potentially) constitutive traits that helps to form and maintain those traits (Tov-Ruach 1980: 468). The value-seeking spirit also makes love generous and trusting, enabling the lover to 'take a bet' on the actualization of her beloved's potential and act in the expectation of its actualization. If the beloved also acts in the spirit of love—love of his beloved and love of his own self—he will respond by fulfilling this expectation. The value that emerges, then, is a joint creation of the lover and the beloved.

This is one of the ways in which deep, ongoing love can help create not only one's own identity, but also the identity of the other. As Robert Solomon puts it, 'A theory of love is . . . primarily a theory of the . . . *shared self*, a self mutually defined and possessed by two people' (1988: 24). But love could not play this creative role if it were not perceptive and honest in its evaluation of the beloved's potential; a bestowal based on wishful thinking creates a fantasy, not a shared self.

There is a second sense in which love can bestow value—namely, by endowing the beloved's desires and ideals with value not because they are objectively lovable, but just because they are hers. This is what Singer (1989, 1994) means by bestowal when he states that human love is both a response to value (or, as he puts it, an 'appraisal') and a bestowal of value. This kind of bestowal encapsulates the grain of truth in Stendhal's view of love as projection. However, the projection is realistic and benign so long as the lover realizes that it is grounded in his love, and his love is grounded in features that give him good reason to love his beloved. This is one of the ways in which love can be non-rational without being irrational or inexplicable. It would become an irrational projection only if the lover thought that, for example, his beloved's absent-mindedness and untidiness were lovable independently of his love for her so that those who failed to find them lovable were simply obtuse.

What I have said about the first kind of bestowal—the bestowal that consists in bringing out the best in the other—is also true, *mutatis mutandis*, of agapaic love of humans qua humans, and love of associates, students, or teachers. And both kinds of bestowal are also to be found in familial love, especially parental love. Loving parents are creative the way good artists are creative with their material: they endeavour to form the child in the light of their values, but within the limits set by the child's temperament and, later, by her own interests and values. Indeed, in the case of parental love the question often asked is not how it can *bestow* value, but how it can be a *response* to inherent value. Frankfurt (1994/1999a) thinks it obvious that our children are valuable to us only because we love them, that our love is not a response to their inherent value. This would be true if 'inherent value' was identical with moral value—that is, the value of good character. However, the value or lovability of an individual is not limited to her moral value, or even her *capacity* for moral value. The inherent value parents respond to when they 'fall in love' with their newborns is the wonder of an independent life unfolding according to the laws of its own nature—a value we respond to in other forms of life as well. But their love (like the love of friends or lovers) is also a response to a *relational* value, the value of this wonderful life being *theirs* to nurture and guide. And for biological parents there is the additional relational value of being the 'first cause' of this marvellous life—the value of being a creator.

To summarize the discussion so far: love as an emotion is both a delighted, affirming, response to an individual's inherent and relational value, and a realistic and benign projection of value, whereby formerly aversive or indifferent features become lovable simply because they belong to the beloved. In an ongoing loving relationship there is also another kind of bestowal: bestowal through an actualization of the other's potential. Ongoing love, we may say, is a response to both actual and potential value. Finally, loving someone as an end is not the same as loving him unconditionally. The end/instrumental distinction is a different distinction from the conditional/unconditional distinction. The conditions or reasons for instrumental or non-instrumental love vary, but all love, including agape, is conditional. There is no such thing as 'love full-stop'—a love without reasons (Hamlyn 1978/1989).

This is not to deny the powerful role of non-rational factors in erotic love, or even in friendship. In so far as our early loves play an important role in our lives, some of the incidental qualities of those early love objects—a familiar gesture, a tone of voice, a fragrance, a smile—can serve, initially, to attract us to an individual, and then, if the attraction turns to love, to continue to act as powerful attractors and add to the phenomenological richness of love. The same observations apply to the role of chemical factors, especially (but not only) in romantic love (Crenshaw 1996). But when these incidental qualities attract us to someone we can neither love, nor even like, for her central qualities, the qualities that define her self, and we fail to understand (or care about) the nature of our attraction, we may be led to the kind of projection that makes for blind love, and turns love's bonds to bondage. Blind love, a love based on illusion, whether self-induced or innocent, is like a conversation with a make-believe interlocutor—love for a make-believe beloved—for the description under which we love the other fails to capture the real person. Genuine love of another is love of a real other—a love that succeeds in hitting its target by seeing the beloved veridically. In what follows, then, I will talk only about such love.

4. The Epistemic Significance of Love

4.1 Love as Offering Reliable Testimony

The look of love does more than see the loved individual veridically: it also shows the loved individual what it sees. The psychoanalyst D. W. Winnicott (1971/1991: 111–18) talks about the loving mother reflecting the baby's facial expressions and mental states on her own face, thereby giving the baby a concrete image of its own psychological states. The mother's look of love, then, is the first avenue to self-awareness and self-understanding. But all love is such an avenue, and especially the love of friends—both those who are 'just friends', and those who are also lovers. For friends serve, in Aristotle's metaphor, as mirrors of each other's souls. No doubt strangers, even enemies, can also see veridically and offer self-understanding—to know is not to love even if to love is to know. But strangers and enemies may distort as often as they reflect. Friends, on the other hand, must bear reliable testimony about each other (Friedman 1993: 197–200).

To say that friends 'must' bear reliable testimony is to make both a conceptual and a moral point. In Adrienne Rich's words, 'an honorable human relationship—that is, one in which two people have the right to use the word "love"—is a process . . . of refining the truths they can tell each other' (1979: 185–94). To the extent that a relationship is dishonest, it is lacking both in love and in honour, for it is lacking in trustworthiness. 'We take so much of the universe on trust'—and especially the trust of those we love. We allow our 'universe to change in minute, significant ways' on the basis of what we are told by those we love. When we find the ground cut out from under our trust, we are forced to 're-examine the universe, to question the whole instinct and concept of trust'. This is especially so when the other's dishonesty is about her very self, about who she is—or when it is about who she thinks we are and why she loves us. Such dishonesty strikes at the very heart of the relationship—the shared and mutually discovered and created self. Aristotle declares that those who pretend to be friends for our character, but in fact are friends for other reasons, are worse than 'debasers of currency, to the extent that . . . [their] evildoing debases something more precious' (NE 1165^{b}10 ff.). Genuine friends, then, offer reliable testimony—about each other, about themselves, and about the world. Enemies need not, and often do not.

The epistemic role of friendship in our lives is often recognized as one of its chief values (LaFollette 1996: 133–5); for seeing ourselves and the world veridically—being in touch with our values, desires, and traits, and the world around us—is necessary for living authentically and acting rightly.[4]

But why is friendship—whether between lovers or between 'just friends'— thought to play a privileged role in self-understanding? Surely parental or agapeic love can also give us insight into ourselves. Thus, an agapeic act from a stranger may show a person her fundamental strength as a human being in a way that changes her perspective on her abilities, and parental love may reveal her history to her in a way that illuminates her present. However, friendship has features that make it a privileged source of self-understanding and even, perhaps, necessary for *adequate* self-understanding.

One feature is simply that friendships are based on deeply shared values that make the friend 'another self'. It is by virtue of this fact that the friend serves as a 'mirror of the soul' and makes the other 'psychologically visible' to himself—that is, aware of himself 'as an objective existent' (Branden 1980: 72–7). We do, of course, gain a sense of ourselves 'out there' in the world when we express our values and ideas in word and deed. But, as Branden explains, it is only when we see ourselves mirrored in another consciousness that we achieve something akin to a perceptual self-awareness, to seeing our faces reflected in a mirror. In the words of a biblical writer, as 'Iron sharpeneth iron; so a man sharpeneth the countenance of his friend' (Prov. 27: 17). When we meet someone who responds to the world as we do, and responds to us in consonance with our self-concept, we perceive ourselves reflected in that person, and achieve a more vivid sense of our selves (Branden 1980: 97–105). We can also better understand our own traits and actions by observing them in a friend, where we are free of the biases and self-doubts that can mask them from ourselves (Sherman 1989: 142–3). To be a mirror of a friend's soul, one need not share *all* the friend's traits or values—in the context of a fundamental harmony of deep values, complementary traits and values can be just as revealing. The obstacle to mutual understanding and self-understanding is not *differences* as such, but differences that create *dissonance*, so that what one finds repugnant the other finds admirable.

That such value dissonance is not a barrier to agape or parental love simply shows the crucial difference between friendship and these other loves. Agape and parental love are independent of the loved individual's fundamental characteristics as the particular person she is; neither love is focused on the joys, griefs, needs, and achievements of the individual as defined by her central character and personality traits. Agape as such is based on, and responds to, the other's humanity, not on individuating traits. Witness the priest's act of loving kindness to Jean Valjean in *Les Misérables*. Again, parents' love for their children is for individuals they have nurtured and played a primary role in forming, individuals for whose well-being and

---

[4] My discussion in this section revisits some themes discussed in Badhwar (1993: 1–36).

actions they consequently bear—or feel they bear—a special responsibility, regardless of their values. In so far as this perspective informs their love for their adult children, their love is parental love. And in so far as our love for our parents is love for those who have nurtured us, our love for them is the love of children.

Literature is more akin to friendship in many ways than agape or parental love. Books provide us with whole worlds of people, events, and thoughts to explore and, sometimes, to identify with. 'We read to know that we are not alone', says Lewis in the biographical movie *Shadowlands*, repeating a line told him by a student, adding, 'We love [another] to know we are not alone.' Through identification with a friend, we learn to look at things from another point of view, to understand and feel in new ways and, thus, to realize the vast potentiality for different forms of experience (Telfer 1970–1: 240–1). Literature, too, enables us 'to see with other eyes, to imagine with other imaginations, to feel with other hearts...[to] become these other selves' (Lewis 1961: 137, 139). Wayne Booth (1988) explicitly likens the reader's relationship to fiction to a friendship, even classifying this relationship along the lines of Aristotle's pleasure, utility, and character friendships. Like human friends, the books we read and reflect upon, both fiction and non-fiction, can also encourage us to lead the examined life. Francine Hughes's story of liberation from a sadistic husband is a particularly dramatic example of this (McNulty 1980).

But friendship has a feature that neither books nor other loves—nor, again, psychoanalysis—have: the intimate, mutual self-disclosure that Laurence Thomas calls 'privileged self-disclosure' (1989: 104–8). Books disclose themselves to us, but cannot hear us—therapists hear us but do not disclose themselves to us. Unlike analysts or books, friends neither analyse us nor serve as objects for our contemplation or analysis. They are other selves who interact with us, responding to us and requiring that we respond to them in appropriate ways. This is why, as Martha Nussbaum puts it in her discussion of Plato's theory of love, 'only personal love draws a person into the exchange of choices and thoughts that will suffice to reveal, over time, the nature of ... values' like justice or wisdom, in oneself and in the world (Nussbaum 1990: 328). And the personal love best suited to such an exchange is that of equals—that is, the love of friends and lovers. The inequality of parent–child love, stemming from the difference in perspectives and responsibilities, prevents such privileged self-disclosure. Friendship and romantic love, by contrast, are based on shared perspectives and responsibilities, relating independent and interdependent adults, equally giving and receiving. And so it makes possible the sharing of lives and privileged self-disclosure that enable deep mutual understanding, self-understanding, and understanding of the world.

Being seen as we are is also a source of deep pleasure (*NE* IX. 9). Paradoxically, however, we can satisfy the need for psychological visibility and take pleasure in being seen only if we are already largely visible to ourselves—and like what we see. Those who do not like themselves can take pleasure neither in *being seen*, nor in *seeing themselves*, as they are. Nor does it help if they self-deceptively construct a more likable self and succeed in passing it off for the genuine article, for then they cut themselves off from true friendship. For reasons we have already seen, to the extent that others are deceived about us, we fail to be the actual objects of their love. The same is true of self-love: to the extent that we are self-deceived, our self-love fails to hit its target.

4.2 Love as a Flattering Mirror

However, the claim that true friends and lovers see each other veridically and bear reliable testimony is open to challenge even if we reject the love-as-projection thesis of writers like Stendhal. On some views, the daily wear and tear of life make sustaining a relationship of friendship or romantic love a matter of selective focus, a judicious mixture of rememberings and forgettings, of perceptiveness and blindness. Thus, William Hazlitt describes true friendship as 'a flattering mirror' in which we see 'our virtues magnified and our errors softened' (1991: 153). Hence, even if it is false that 'love is blind', it may still be true that love often 'closes its eyes'.[5] If this is the nature of love, it follows that those who see us with steadily open eyes cannot love us. (By the same logic it follows that we can love ourselves only if we often close our eyes to ourselves.) On this view, then, the fabric of a close friendship or romantic relationship is shot through with self-deception and mutual deception.

What can be said for this view? It is true that there are such relationships: 'mutual admiration societies' in which the parties are blissfully oblivious to each other's faults and to the views and needs of 'outsiders' (Lewis 1960/1988: 112–16). It is also true that friends and lovers who hold up 'flattering mirrors' to each other are more truly loving than those who, in a spirit of jealous competitiveness, hold up *unflattering* mirrors to each other. But these are not the only alternatives. There *are* relationships that avoid both pitfalls, combining perceptiveness and honesty with a strength of spirit that rejoices in the admirable more than it laments the unadmirable. A love that needs neither self-deception nor deception to survive is surely stronger than a love that does. And it is only such relationships that have the honesty and mutual trust necessary for true intimacy (LaFollette 1996: 129–31; Martin 1996: 120–7). Further, the view that a truly loving relationship requires exaggeration of each other's virtues and blindness to each other's faults seems incoherent. It suggests both that we can love someone only if we think of him as perfectly virtuous— and that we require him to have the vices of deception and self-deception. There is, to be sure, a desperate way out of this incoherence—namely, to adopt the view that such deception is not a vice but a virtue in a close relationship. But the implausibility of this view is a measure of the implausibility of the view that love is a flattering mirror. An internally consistent and plausible view of love implies that it is

---

[5] 'L'amour est aveugle; l'amitié ferme les yeux' (anon.).

in the nature of love to *discourage* mutual deception and self-deception, and that, to the extent that it does not, it is deficient as love. In short, genuine love both presupposes self-understanding and understanding of the other, and leads to greater understanding of oneself and of the other.

But what is this self that is made visible, understood, and recreated in love? What is the ultimate object of love?

5. Love and Metaphysics

5.1 Persons, Properties, and Bare Particulars

I said earlier that the basis and object of end love in friendship and eros is the individual as constituted by her central features, the properties that make her the distinct person she is.[6] But this seems to imply that, if someone with essentially the same central properties came along, the newcomer could replace the old love. Like two equally valuable pieces of gold, two equally lovable loves should be interchangeable. But this conclusion contradicts the widespread intuition that love of someone as an end is non-fungible and irreplaceable.

Robert Nozick's strategy for preserving irreplaceability is simply to deny that love of individuals is love of their characteristics: 'An adult may come to love another because of the other's characteristics; but it is the other person, and not the characteristics, that is loved. . . . One loves the particular person one actually encountered. . . . love is historical, attaching to persons . . . and not to characteristics' (1974: 168).

There is much to be said for Nozick's point that love is historical and cannot just be transferred 'to someone else with the same characteristics, even to one who "scores" higher for these characteristics'. But how well taken is his distinction between persons and their properties? Are persons bare particulars, Metaphysically Changeless and Simple Essences? Again, how does his conception of love as historical account for the demise of love? Nozick's dichotomy between the role of properties in love's origin and of history in love's continuation leaves no room for the fact that a shared history itself gives rise to new properties, properties that partly explain both the continuation and the demise of love. Last but not least, his explanation of the continuation of love runs afoul of the fact that a friendship or romantic relationship that attaches itself to a person *just because* that was the person initially encountered, regardless of who he has become, is simply irrational. Indeed, it cannot be understood as love at all rather than addiction (Peele 1977).

---

[6] Some of what follows is a revised version of my discussion in Badhwar (1987/1989).

5.2 Persons as Rational Natures

Velleman also seeks to preserve irreplaceability by developing a Kantian account of love of persons: he denies that loving persons as ends requires seeing them as unique. According to Velleman, love of a person is love of his rational nature, and this is, at bottom, 'a capacity of appreciation or valuation—a capacity to care about things in that reflective way which is distinctive of self-conscious creatures like us' (1999: 365). A person's rational nature is 'his core of reflective concern' and the ground of his special value: dignity (1999: 366–7). Love and respect are different responses to the same value.

Velleman's analysis of loving a person as an end in terms of loving his rational nature, and of his rational nature in terms of his 'core of reflective concern' and dignity, captures in striking language the fact that love is, in whole or in part, an attitude towards the irreplaceable value of a person, and that this value has to do with his inner self, his integrity as a subject. However, a person's dignity is something that is shared by all rational persons; it is not something that distinguishes one from another. How, then, can love of one individual fail to be replaceable by love of another? Following Kant, Velleman answers that both love and respect are modes of 'appreciation, in which we respond to . . . [a person's] value with an unwillingness to replace her or to size her up against potential replacements' (1999: 368). This, he says, is the only proper response to the special value of persons: their dignity.

I agree with Velleman that seeing a person as an irreplaceable centre of reflective concern is the only proper response to his value, and that this response does not require uniqueness of value; numerical uniqueness suffices. To respond to a person's dignity is to see her as a numerically distinct centre of reflective valuation, with (I would add) a distinct capacity for creating value and a distinct perspective on the world. It is this response that lies at the heart of both *respect* and *agape*, in which we value all persons as ends in themselves on account of a certain capacity. But how does Velleman's analysis account for the selectivity of other forms of love? On the view I have defended so far, what distinguishes friendship and eros from agape is that, in these loves, the object of love is not simply the individual as a centre of reflective concern, but, rather, the embodied individual with certain character and personality traits that, in part, express her reflective concern. For Velleman, these individuating properties are only the 'empirical persona' through which we see the inner person (1999: 371), and love is selective only because 'the human body and human behavior are imperfect expressions of personhood, and we are imperfect interpreters' (1999: 372). My finding you lovable depends upon how well your empirical persona expresses your inner value to me; your empirical persona has no essential connection to your value as a person and, hence, cannot be any part of the ultimate object of my love.

On this Kantian analysis, both character and personality, the set of dispositions to think, feel, and act that individuate us, are swept into the category of the empirical persona and contrasted with the purely rational self. But the adequacy of this metaphysics of the person and of Velleman's explanation of the selectivity of love are called into question when we consider their implications. His explanation implies that, *ceteris paribus*, the better we are at interpreting personhood, the less discriminating we must be as friends and lovers. Hence, for example, those who are put off by scoundrels are those who are simply unable to see and value the rational self within. Barring the constraints of time and energy, the most insightful of us must be the most inclusive lovers. Just as Plato's lover in the *Symposium* progresses from love of one beautiful body to love of all beautiful bodies, so Velleman's lover, given enough time and energy, must progress from love of one person's value to love of all persons' value.

There is yet another problem with Velleman's conception of the self, a problem that brings us back to the issue of irreplaceability. As already noted, Velleman's account is invaluable in showing that irreplaceability in end love does not imply uniqueness of value. It helps us to see that it is only in instrumental love that having the same value implies replaceability: one gold coin is as good as another. But his rational/empirical dichotomy implies that all the rich phenomenological differences between, say, two friendships are connected to the friends' non-essential features, and have no connection to that which he regards as the sole ground of their value: their rational natures. In other words, Velleman's account implies that the experience of the non-fungibility of love is not connected to what he regards as the deep facts about persons or our love for persons. But this sits ill with the experience of love in friendship and other non-agapaic loves. For while it is true that we love our friends as numerically irreplaceable persons with the same rational natures, it also seems true that we love them not just as rational natures (in Velleman's Kantian sense) but also as individuals with distinct character and personality traits. It is this that explains why we typically see individuals as qualitatively irreplaceable and experience our (non-agapaic) love for them as phenomenologically non-fungible. For example, my love for Alpha seems to be not completely commensurate with my love for Zeta because they are essentially different *persons*. The patterns of attention, perception, evaluation, and feeling that constitute my love for Alpha and Zeta seem to have qualitatively distinct and irreplaceable value because their *selves* have qualitatively (and not just numerically) distinct, irreplaceable value.[7] If I lose Alpha, I will mourn his loss as a distinct loss that cannot be completely made up by my love for Zeta; if I gain a new love, I will celebrate it as a distinct gain, and not simply as a replacement for Alpha.

---

[7] Needless to say, not everything I value in Alpha and Zeta need have objective value. Hence, not everything I find lovable need be objectively lovable or even admirable, and some may be objectively unlovable or unadmirable.

5.3 The Irreplaceable You

But is such qualitative uniqueness possible? The fundamental character and personality traits that define a self make up a finite list; how can two honest, optimistic, fair-minded, bright, generous friends be different in any essential respect? One might like tennis, the other swimming, one might like Chinese cabbage, the other Brussels sprouts, one might be neurotic about flying, the other about elevators. But this does not make them unique as persons.

My suggestion is that the route to qualitative uniqueness as persons lies through a 'thicker' conception of the person, the conception we use in making everyday distinctions when, for example, we say of two siblings that they are both wonderful 'in their own ways', or that Jo March, Elizabeth Bennett, and Jane Eyre are all spunky characters, but no one could mistake one for another. On this conception of the self or person, the fundamental properties that define a person include both the abstractly described central properties, and the concrete style of their expression. Of course, the distinction between abstractly described properties and style, like the distinction between matter and form, is only a relative one: the style in which one expresses certain properties can itself be described as a set of properties, and the properties expressed can be described as a style of facing life. The important point is that abstractly described properties do not give the essence of a person as the object of (non-agapaic) love.

This way of individuating persons seems right when we consider that an individual's properties are the result of his encounters with the world, coloured by and expressed in his particular, historical, existence. Thus, for example, Cyrano de Bergerac would not be the person he is without his poetic wit and physical daring. His wit and daring are an expression of his independence of mind, his courage and loyalty, his passion for the 'white plume of freedom'. What makes these properties uniquely his is the style of their expression; what makes his poetic wit and physical daring uniquely his is the properties they express. Only those who understand this about Cyrano love him for what he essentially is.

This thick description of the object of love makes love of persons as ends irreplaceable for all practical purposes. However, it does not block the logical possibility of replaceability in someone's affections, because it does not block the logical possibility of spiritual twins. As studies of identical twins suggest, two people with essentially the same genetic endowment, living in essentially the same circumstances, will probably make essentially the same choices and become essentially the same persons. So we cannot deny the possibility, as Nozick does in a later work, that the totality of a person's fundamental properties can be duplicated (Nozick 1989: 81). Even the fact that over time two people in a love relationship can change each other in essential ways does not show that duplicability is logically impossible. Had I encountered Beta instead of his spiritual twin, Alpha, Beta would have acquired the same properties as Alpha. And so my love of Alpha *would have been replaceable* by my love of Beta. The fact that it is not is due to purely contingent—though deeply grounded—reasons.

However, such deeply grounded contingent phenomenological irreplaceability seems to give us all we want: when people wonder if they are replaceable in their loved ones' lives, they are not asking the philosopher's question whether it is *logically* possible that they are replaceable. Hence it is hasty to conclude that the intuition that 'the beloved is irreplaceable is just a bit of popular ideology, an illusion' (Soble 1997a: 357).

6. ROMANTIC LOVE

6.1 Friends and Lovers

We have seen how love, and especially friendship and romantic love, both creates the self and illuminates it. Is there a significant difference between friendship and romantic love in these or other respects? Certainly this is the common-sense view of the matter, one that philosophers tend to share. On this view, it is most of all in romantic love that two autonomous individuals with well-defined selves both discover their separate selves, and redefine themselves in terms of each other. As many writers have noted, love 'involves a transition ... from I and he to I and thou' (Scruton 1986: 231), a 'desire to form and constitute a new entity in the world, what might be called a *we*' (Nozick 1989: 70). At the same time, 'love is ultimately a matter of personal identity, and falling in love, including love at first sight, is a kind of ... reaching or (in Plato's terms) "grasping" for one's future and better self' (Solomon 1988: 146). Lewis notes that, unlike friends, lovers are intensely absorbed in each other and in their love: 'Lovers are normally face to face, absorbed in each other; Friends, side by side, absorbed in some common interest' (1960/1988: 91).

Have Lewis and the others captured an essential difference between friendship and eros? Or have they merely expressed the *male* view of friendship? Male friends, says Louise Bernikow, 'are shoulder to shoulder. Female friends are more often eye to eye' (1981: 119). Bernikow has a point, although some male friendships are also 'eye to eye': witness Montaigne's love for his friend, Étienne de La Boétie (Montaigne 1580/1991: 187–99). But Lewis and the other writers cited here also have a point: there *are* important differences between friendship and eros. The absorption of lovers in each other contains a passion and yearning for union missing from friendship as such, a yearning to merge with one another that is hypostasized in Aristophanes' myth of love as the desire to unite with one's 'other half' (Plato,

Symposium: 189a–193d). Again, in contrast to friendship, imagination and fantasy play a large role in eros, creating for the lovers 'a world of their own' (Solomon 1988: 162). Except in childhood and youth, the desire for identification with a friend falls short of the desire for union, and the world that adult friends create together is more the work of shared values than fantasy.

6.2 The Desire for Union

But what is it about eros that explains the desire for union, the importance of fantasy, and the intensity of feeling and experience? The obvious answer is 'sex': eros is sexual or genital love. Eros is 'sexual in origin and motivation', says Solomon, 'it depends upon sex, thrives upon sex, utilizes sex as its medium, its language and often its primary content' (1988: 43). But sex is 'a spiritual impulse as well as a physical one' (Solomon 1988: 43–4), and the visibility and the pleasures it affords are unique in their 'integration of . . . perceptions, emotions, values, and thought' (Branden 1980: 85, 87). Erotic love involves and celebrates the self more completely and thoroughly than other loves, because it involves and celebrates the individual as a bodily, spiritual, and aesthetic being. The desire for 'carnal knowledge', for knowledge of the beloved through sexual union, is a desire for his intimate presence, for a total experience of him and of oneself (Pieper 1904: 70). For all these reasons, erotic love is 'the most vivid reminder that we exist as centers of value *here and now*, in the condition of mortality' (Scruton 1986: 251).

All these writers eloquently express the fundamental importance of sexual desire and satisfaction to erotic love, and of erotic love so understood to our sense of who we are, as human beings and as individuals. More precisely, they eloquently express the fundamental importance of sexual (genital) satisfaction in erotic love to *most* of us. There is no reason to rule out the possibility that those who lack sexual desire are still capable of the desire that is central to erotic love, the desire for psychological and physical union with another. Nor should we reject the possibility that they can achieve a full experience and expression of themselves as embodied beings through non-sexual (non-genital) bodily involvement. Both experience, and the diversity of human biology and psychology, support these propositions. We can imagine forms of ritualized physical touching between lovers that express and satisfy the same intense desire for physical and psychological union and provide the same 'reciprocated physical delight' (Delaney 1996: 347) through the same 'integration of . . . perceptions, emotions, values, and thought' (Branden 1980: 137) that sexual union provides. Hence, unless and until this possibility is ruled out by psychological evidence, it seems hasty to make the desire for sexual union essential to erotic love, much less 'fundamental to a full understanding of what it is for persons to be "ends in themselves"' (Scruton 1986: 251).

On the other hand, the thought that sexual union is not essential to the full experience of erotic union does not imply that the experience can be understood entirely in psychological terms, as some writers seem to believe (e.g. Soble 1997b: 385–401). For this view, as Soble himself notes (1997b: 401), leaves the yearnings for union in erotic love indistinguishable from the yearnings for union in the love of God. If there is a difference between the yearning for union in the two loves, it must lie in the desire for physical union in erotic love, through genital sex or some other form of physical interaction.

It might be thought that my equation of sexual union with genital union is naive. On this view, any kind of physical interaction between two people that enables them to experience a sense of physical union counts as sexual. Perhaps it is this wider sense of sexuality that explains Solomon's statement that erotic love is sexual even if the sexual component is 'inhibited, chaste or sublimated' (1988: 43). I have no stake in rejecting this wider understanding of sexuality, much less in inviting the charge of naivety; the point I want to stress is simply that the desire for physical and spiritual union with the beloved is of the essence of erotic love, and that this desire may be satisfiable in ways often (if naively) called non-sexual.

7. Loving under the Influence (of Philosophy)

The love we want and give in our lives is inevitably coloured by our understanding of love, just as our understanding of love is inevitably coloured by our experience of love—or its simulacra. A philosophical examination of love, then, can amend both our understanding and our experience of love. Thus, if genuine love requires veridical perception of the other, and this requires empathy, imagination, and honesty with oneself, then one cannot love another without cultivating these qualities; in their absence, 'love' is mere sentiment. Nor can we get any satisfaction from being loved blindly, from a love that fails to hit its target. For lack of space, I have not discussed the virtues of friendship and romantic relationships. But if it is true, as is often argued, that the virtues of benevolence (sympathy, compassion, kindness, and generosity) (Blum 1980), as well as the virtues of justice (Badhwar 1985; Friedman 1993; LaFollette 1996; Martin 1996), are partly constitutive of such relationships, then we know that friendship and romantic love are moral achievements and cannot be had just for the asking. Hence, we should neither ask for unconditional love nor blame ourselves for being unable to grant it.

REFERENCES

Aristotle. *Nicomachean Ethics* (*NE*) and *Magna Moralia*. Many editions.

Badhwar, Neera K. (1985). 'Friendship, Justice, and Supererogation'. *American Philosophical Quarterly*, 22: 123–31.

Badhwar, Neera K. (1987/1989). 'Friends as Ends in Themselves', in A. Soble (ed.), *Eros, Agape and Philia*. New York: Paragon House, 165–86.

——(1993). 'Introduction: The Nature and Significance of Friendship', in Badhwar (ed.), *Friendship: A Philosophical Reader*. Ithaca, NY: Cornell University Press, 1–36.

——(1993). 'Altruism vs Self-Interest: Sometimes a False Dichotomy'. *Social Philosophy and Policy*, 5: 10; also in E. F. Paul (ed.), *Altruism*. Cambridge: Cambridge University Press, 90–117.

Bernikow, Louise (1981). *Among Women*. New York: HarperCollins.

Blum, Lawrence (1980). *Friendship, Altruism, and Morality*. London: Routledge & Kegan Paul.

Booth, Wayne (1988). *The Company We Keep: An Ethics of Fiction*. Berkeley and Los Angeles: University of California Press. Cited in M. Nussbaum, 'Reading for Life', in Nussbaum, *Love's Knowledge*. Oxford: Oxford University Press, 231, 234.

Branden, Nathaniel (1980). *The Psychology of Romantic Love*. New York: Bantam.

Brentlinger, John (1970/1989). 'The Nature of Love', in A. Soble (ed.), *Eros, Agape and Philia*. New York: Paragon House, 136–48.

Brown, Robert (1987). *Analyzing Love*. Cambridge: Cambridge University Press.

Cooper, John (1980). 'Aristotle on Friendship', in A. O. Rorty (ed.), *Essays on Aristotle's Ethics*. Berkeley and Los Angeles: University of California Press, 301–40.

Crenshaw, Theresa L. (1996). *The Alchemy of Love and Lust*. New York: Simon & Schuster.

de Sousa, Ronald (1987). *The Rationality of Emotion*. Cambridge, MA: MIT Press.

Delaney, Neil (1996). 'Romantic Love and Loving Commitment: Articulating a Modern Ideal'. *American Philosophical Quarterly*, 33: 339–56.

Frankfurt, Harry (1994/1999a). 'Autonomy, Necessity, and Love', in Frankfurt, *Necessity, Volition, and Love*. Cambridge: Cambridge University Press, 129–141.

——(1999b). 'On Caring', in Frankfurt, *Necessity, Volition, and Love*. Cambridge: Cambridge University Press, 155–80.

Friedman, Marilyn (1993). *What Are Friends For?* Ithaca, NY: Cornell University Press.

Greenspan, Patricia (1988). *Emotions and Reasons*. New York: Routledge.

Hamlyn, D. W. (1978). 'The Phenomenon of Love and Hate' *Philosophy*, 53: 5–20.

Hatfield, Elaine, and Rapson, Richard (1993). *Love, Sex, and Intimacy*. New York: HarperCollins.

Hazlitt, William (1991). 'On the Spirit of Obligations', in D.J. Enright and D. Rawlinson (eds.), *The Oxford Book of Friendship*. Oxford: Oxford University Press, 153.

Kierkegaard, Soren (1847/1962). *Works of Love*, trans. H. Hong and E. Hong. New York: Harper & Row.

Kosman, L. A. (1976/1989). 'Platonic Love', in A. Soble (ed.), *Eros, Agape and Philia*. New York: Paragon House, 149–64.

LaFollette, Hugh (1996). *Personal Relationships: Love, Identity, and Morality*. Oxford: Blackwell.

Lear, Jonathan (1990). *Love and its Place in Nature*. New York: HarperCollins.

Lewis, C. S. (1960/1988). *The Four Loves*. San Diego: Harcourt Brace Jovanovich.

—— (1961). *An Experiment in Criticism*. Cambridge: Cambridge University Press. Cited in Telfer (1970–1).

McNulty, Faith (1980). *The Burning Bed*. New York: Avon Books.

Martin, Mike W. (1996). *Love's Virtues*. Lawrence, KS: University Press of Kansas.

Montaigne (1580/1991). 'Of Friendship', in M. Pakaluk (ed.), *Other Selves: Philosophers on Friendship*. Indianapolis: Hackett Publishing Co., 187–99.

Nakhnikian, George (1978). 'Love in Human Reason', *Midwest Studies in Philosophy*, 3: 286–317.

Newton-Smith, W. H. (1973/1989). 'A Conceptual Investigation of Love', in A. Soble (ed.), *Eros, Agape and Philia*. New York: Paragon House, 199–217.

Nozick, Robert (1974). *Anarchy, State, and Utopia*. New York: Basic Books.

—— (1989). *The Examined Life*. New York: Simon & Schuster.

Nussbaum, Martha (1990). 'Love and the Individual', in Nussbaum, *Love's Knowledge*. Oxford: Oxford University Press, 314–34.

Nygren, Anders (1953). *Agape and Eros*, trans. P. Watson. Philadelphia: Westminster Press.

Ortega y Gasset, José (1957). *On Love*. New York: Meridian Books.

Peck, M. Scott (1978). *The Road Less Traveled*. New York: Simon & Schuster.

Peele, Stanton, with Brodsky, Archie (1977). *Love and Addiction*. London: Abacus.

Pieper, Josef (1904). *Happiness and Contemplation*. South Bend, IN: Indiana, 1998.

Rich, Adrienne (1979). 'Women and Honor: Some Notes on Lying', in Rich, *On Lies, Secrets, and Silence, Selected Prose 1966–78*. New York: W. W. Norton.

Scruton, Roger (1986). *Sexual Desire: A Moral Philosophy of the Erotic*. New York: Free Press.

Sherman, Nancy (1989). *The Fabric of Character*. Oxford: Oxford University Press.

Singer, Irving (1966). *The Nature of Love: Plato to Luther*. New York: Random House.

—— (1987). *The Nature of Love: The Modern World*. Chicago: University of Chicago Press.

—— (1994). *The Pursuit of Love*. Baltimore: Johns Hopkins Press.

Soble, Alan (1997a). 'Irreplaceability', in Alan Soble (ed.), *Sex, Love, and Friendship: Studies of the Society for the Philosophy of Sex and Love 1977–1992*. Atlanta: Rodopi, 355–7.

—— (1997b). 'The Unity of Romantic Love', in Alan Soble (ed.), *Sex, Love, and Friendship: Studies of the Society for the Philosophy of Sex and Love 1977–1992*. Atlanta: Rodopi, 385–401.

Solomon, Robert (1988). *About Love: Reinventing Romance for our Times*. New York: Simon & Schuster.

Stocker, Michael (1981). 'Values and Purposes: The Limits of Teleology and the Ends of Friendship'. *Journal of Philosophy*, 78: 747–65.

Taylor, Gabrielle (1976). 'Love'. *Proceedings of the Aristotelian Society*, 76: 147–64.

Telfer, Elizabeth (1970–1). 'Friendship'. *Proceedings of the Aristotelian Society*, 223–41.

Thomas, Laurence (1989). *Living Morally*. Philadelphia: Temple University Press.

Tov-Ruach, Leila (1980). 'Jealousy, Attention and Loss', in A. O. Rorty (ed.), *Explaining Emotions*. Berkeley and Los Angeles: University of California Press, 465–88.

Velleman, David (1999). 'Love as a Moral Emotion', *Ethics*, 109: 338–74.

Vlastos, Gregory (1981). 'The Individual as Object of Love in Plato', in Vlastos, *Platonic Studies*, 2nd edn., Princeton: Princeton University Press, 3–34.

Winnicott, D. W. (1971/1991). 'Mirror-Role of Mother and Family in Child Development', in Winnicott, *Playing and Reality*. New York: Routledge. Cited in Velleman (1999), 344 n. 18.

Yeats, William Butler (1936). 'For Anne Gregory', in Michael Roberts (ed.), *Faber Book of Modern Verse*, London: Faber & Faber, 1936.

CHAPTER 3

FAMILY

BRENDA ALMOND

1. The Family as a Social Institution

THE traditional family is widely held to be in crisis in Western societies, but there has been little direct philosophical discussion of the matter. Parents' and children's rights and responsibilities have indeed been debated, especially in relation to issues in education and medicine, but philosophical interest has tended to focus on aspects of adult personal life and relationships, including analysis of the concept of marriage, discussion of the ethics of adultery, and debate about alternative lifestyles, the role of gender, and the nature of sexuality, the latter often influenced by trends in postmodernist philosophy. The family as an institution, however, has provided a focus for other disciplines, including social anthropology, sociology, and demography, and philosophical comment, too, needs to be grounded in some knowledge and understanding of past and present cultural practices—our own and those of other people. Also relevant is awareness of the role played by law in specifying rights, duties, and obligations and of the way in which economic factors, too, help to shape family structure. Both of these depend to a considerable extent on political decisions, especially in relation to the way in which provision is to be made for the non-earning members of society: the young, the old, the ill or disabled. But before turning to the fast-moving contemporary scene, it would be useful to set out briefly the historical context in which today's changes in the concept and practice of family life are set.

The family is a ubiquitous social institution, not only in human life, but also in that of other mammals and species. In strictly biological terms, 'family' is a concept that centres on the physical coming-together of male and female and on the cluster of offspring that results from that connection. In many species, a pair, once established, continues its relationship while fostering the young to independence. These are such trite and obvious facts that the necessity to set them out arises only because they are currently considered by many people irrelevant to the lives of humans, and also because there is a socio-legal conception of family that may, in some situations, be in conflict with the biological one. In the human case, too, while most societies have sought to regulate arrangements and to impose a framework of law within which people's choices may be made, history and culture have provided many variations in basic arrangements. In ancient times, for example, the Egyptian family was matriarchal, not determined by surnames or patronymics; the Chinese family, in contrast, was patriarchal and based on deference, of young to old, of female to male; while in the family of the ancient Romans, the *patria potestas* of the father was unchallengeable, giving him the right of life and death over his children, even in adulthood. Some anthropologists have debated the hypothesis that very early primitive societies were communistic in the sense of holding women in common, although others have rejected the idea as unsupported by evidence. Certainly, however, in some cultures, partnering has not been one–one but one–many, so that polygamy (having more than one wife), or, in a very few cases, polyandry (having more than one husband), have been institutionalized. In some societies, too, children have been cared for by the wider family group, or by a woman and her relatives without the male progenitor, or (as in the case of Sparta) male children have been raised in all-male groups. But these are the exceptions rather than the rule, and the cultural foundation of most civilizations has been the existence of groupings centred on a couple and their offspring. Households have often consisted of these, together with an extended family: grandparents, aunts, uncles, and, in the past, depending on wealth, servants and retainers. Hence 'family' has often come to refer to all who share a common roof.

2. The Contemporary State
of the Family

In turning to the contemporary state of the family, the picture is best sketched in terms of some of the statistical shifts from the traditional pattern of the family that took place in the last few decades of the twentieth century. In the Western world, the term 'traditional family' has until recently meant a grouping of two parents, married to each other and living with their dependent children—the so-called 'nuclear family'. Less essentially, but commonly, the economic basis for the traditional unit has consisted of one main earner, the husband, and a wife who is not in full-time employment outside the home and who can take responsibility for domestic matters and childcare. Increasingly, however, a pattern of unmarried cohabiting has become both common and widely accepted, as well as a situation in which both partners are in the workforce outside the home. But first it must be said that the traditional pattern is more persistent than is often recognized. Figures from Britain provide an illustration of trends in most of the industrialized world. There, it is still the case that four out of five dependent children are in two-parent families, and that nine out of ten of those parents are married. Nevertheless, looking at the picture from the other side, it is also true that, in Britain at the end of the twentieth century, 38 per cent of babies were born outside marriage compared to only 7.2 per cent in 1974 and that the annual marriage rate was at its lowest since records began 160 years earlier. Amongst Britain's 1.6 million lone parents at the turn of the millennium, the fastest growing group consisted of single never-married mothers. As far as those who are currently married are concerned, statistics are no more encouraging for those who favour the traditional pattern: two marriages in five are predicted to end in divorce and 28 per cent of children may be expected to experience the divorce of their parents (Family Policy Studies Centre 2000). Prospects for children who find themselves part of a new step-parent family following the divorce of their parents are not easy either. In Britain, Downing Street's Social Exclusion Unit, set up to look into the problem of homelessness and rough sleeping, published some surprising figures that showed that one child in five in step-families runs away from home—these runaways are in general aged between 13 and 15 (*The Times*, 23 March 2001).

These are not matters of purely private and personal interest, nor is it only a matter of morals, public or private. The feelings and attitudes of individuals are, of course, involved, but these personal choices have wider social consequences— ripple effects that can distort the structural basis of community life. Politicians must either accept the need to cope directly with the results of family breakdown, which in most Western countries include an increase in crime, drug use, prostitution, and homelessness, or else seek to mitigate these effects by welfare provision of one sort or another. In Britain, where the choice has been to make provision for unsupported mothers and children, the cost of family breakdown to the public purse is estimated at £5 billion per year. But there are also demographic consequences that again have economic implications. In the USA, for example, children under 18 make up a quarter of the population, but in most of the countries of the European Union, the birth rate has fallen well below the replacement rate of 2.1 per couple that is needed to maintain the current population level, and this means that, in Europe, more and more elderly must be supported by fewer and fewer young people.

One reaction to these figures is to dismiss the importance of marriage as a formal institution at the nub of family formation and to favour 'stable relationships'. But while, superficially, marriage may be seen as no more than a piece of paper, research from most sources is agreed in finding that formal marriage is more stable than cohabiting, and that unmarried couples are three or four times more likely than married ones to split up. In Europe, for example, figures indicate that less than 4 per cent of cohabiting unions last ten years or more, as compared with 71 per cent of legally constituted marriages, while, in the USA, the median duration of cohabiting has been estimated at around fifteen months. Nor is the potential to split up diminished by the presence of children. Indeed cohabitees with children are between four and five times more likely than married couples to split up. Of course, some cohabiting relationships are resolved by marriage rather than separation, but, in general, cohabiting represents a positive preference for lack of commitment, rather than, as is often supposed, a serious preliminary to it (Morgan 2000).

So much for facts and figures. It might be tempting to account for the trends they reveal in terms of shifts in the preferences of individuals. But other more general and public factors have pushed forward the changes in the way of life of the industrialized countries. Of these, the rise of the feminist movement, the drive for gay parity and recognition, the liberalization of divorce laws, the tax and benefits policies of the governments of the liberal democracies, and the impact on family formation and structure of reproductive medicine, from pill to IVF, have all played a part. While this is not the place to say a great deal about any of these topics, some of which are covered in detail elsewhere in this volume, any serious philosophical and ethical reflection on the family must take some account of them.

3. FEMINISM AND THE FAMILY

There are diverse and distinctive strands in the theoretical grounding of feminism, in the Western world. One widely accepted taxonomy identifies four ideological positions: a conservative feminism, which is directed at protecting the interests of women who adopt a traditional home-based role; liberal feminism, which is aimed at opening up opportunities for equality in the world outside the home by removing any political or legal obstacles to employment and promotion; socialist feminism, which aims to do this through the transfer of domestic and family responsibilities to the state; and separatist feminism, often lesbian separatism, which seeks to develop a wholly independent mode of female existence (Jaggar 1978, 1994). In practice, the first and to some extent the second position are viewed by some activist groups as anti-feminist, while sympathizers with the third and fourth positions have more recently turned to a form of postmodern feminism, some with psychoanalytic roots owing much to the writings of the French structuralist Jacques Lacan, some more strictly based in philosophy and epistemology, where the ideas of philosophers such as Jacques Derrida and Michel Foucault in France and Richard

Rorty in the USA have been influential. The American feminist philosopher Nancy Chadorow writes from a viewpoint that is sympathetic to the psychoanalytic tradition, while the radical French feminist Luce Irigaray combines a psychoanalytic approach that is critical of Lacan with a deconstructionist perspective (Irigaray 1977; Chadorow 1978; selections from both reprinted in Nicholson 1997). While not always directly addressing the question of the family, there is a strong patriarchal hypothesis embedded within many such new feminist approaches in both ethics and epistemology. Taking their inspiration from anti-Enlightenment or revisionist sources, many feminist philosophers have argued that both reason and the notion of universal morality are gender based. They see these concepts as created by men and imposed by them through oppressive power structures. Linda Nicholson sums up these developments: 'They [feminists] have criticized modern foundationalist epistemologies and moral and political theories, exposing the contingent, partial and historically situated character of what has passed in the mainstream for necessary, universal and ahistorical truths' (Fraser and Nicholson 1990: 26).

However, the move from universality to particularity, while it was at first fruitful, began to reveal a widening gap between philosophical critique and feminist political goals, and to pose some unexpected practical problems for a universal women's movement. If the concept of 'man' as a universal term is dissolved or deconstructed, the concept of 'woman', too, breaks down into a range of competing categories: black, white; old, young; rich, poor; fit, disabled; working class, middle class; Muslim, Jew, Christian, and so on. This means that the postmodernist approach, with its rejection of the defining features of Enlightenment—rationalism, essentialism, and universality—fits ill with the goals of a broad international women's movement. At a minimum, such a project must include an attempt to provide a universal analysis of women's needs that cuts across differences in culture, class, and ethnicity. In other words, the dismissal of essentialism seems to dissolve away the notion of 'woman' on which a global women's movement depends (Flax 1990; Young 1990).

Some have tried to avoid these consequences politically by adopting a strategy of alliances and coalitions, with the development of what has been called an 'oppositional consciousness'. But in practice the programme for Western feminists has been based politically on a common goal: the drive for justice in terms of equality. Susan Moller Okin speaks of 'the oppressive myth of an idealized natural "family"', describing it as 'often a school of day-to-day injustice' (Okin 1989: 186). The remedy she and other Western feminists have sought is to free women from economic dependence on individual men, and two strategies have been promoted as a means to this end: (1) ensuring legally enforceable anti-discrimination policies in the workplace and (2) minimizing the impact on individuals of dependency resulting from childcare. So equality has been interpreted as having freedom to work outside the home on equal terms with men; having ready access to abortion and contraception as a means of family limitation; and having access to state-provided childcare facilities from the child's earliest months—this care extended to cover parents' long working days. Paradoxically, perhaps, this was a framework for living that already existed in the communist countries, where, in contrast to the campaign in the West, women concerned about the conditions of their lives were more likely to aspire to freedom from the economic need for both parents to work, and in particular to consideration for their dual role as working mothers. For women in those East European countries, it may have seemed less obvious that transferring responsibility to the state does, in fact, make women independent, rather than merely making their dependency more diffuse. In the Western democracies, however, recourse to the taxpayer has tended to obscure some of these issues, producing the social trends already described, which in practice often conflict with female welfare, concern for which might well be taken as another way of defining feminism.

Even in the 1980s, however, some revisionist feminists had begun reappraising the feminist programmes of the 1960s and 1970s in relation to the family, and Betty Friedan, one of those who had inspired the original feminist impetus with her book *The Feminine Mystique*, was prepared to define the family, not as a reactionary relic, but as 'that last area where one has any hope of individual control over one's destiny, of meeting one's basic human needs, of nourishing that core of personhood threatened by vast impersonal institutions and uncontrollable corporate and government bureaucracies' (Friedan 1982: 229). Later Germaine Greer, too, saw reason to revise the views she had famously advanced in *The Female Eunuch* (Greer 1970, 1999).

4. THE GAY PARITY ISSUE

Running in parallel with pressure from women's groups has been a new openness and assertiveness for male and female homosexual rights. The concept of the 'gay community' arose in the USA in the early 1980s but gay pressure groups have campaigned for gay parity in law in many countries. This has led, in France, to the 'Pacte Civile', which gives some of the rights and privileges of heterosexual marriage to same-sex relationships, in some parts of the USA, for example, the state of New Hampshire, to recognition of a formal marriage ceremony for same-sex couples, and to legislation in the Netherlands that validates alternative quasi-family structures. In the United Kingdom, opinion on these matters has crystallized around the issue of sex education in schools, one view being that heterosexual marriage should be promoted as the basis of the family, the other being that homosexual and other arrangements should be given equal standing with marriage as lifestyle alternatives, or as alternative ways of restructuring families. Within philosophical feminism, these policy objectives have as an underpinning a theory in which gender is seen as socially constructed. In the much-quoted words of Simone de Beauvoir, 'One is not born, but rather becomes a woman' (1974: 301). This view, of course, would have implications for men as well, for the basic claim is that there is no essential biological basis to being a man or a woman in any way that determines lifestyles, rights, or responsibilities.

5. LEGAL AND GOVERNMENTAL INTERVENTIONS

Public policy initiatives, too, have had a visible and direct impact on personal attitudes and behaviour. Changes in divorce law, particularly no-fault divorce, have in effect made the guaranteed permanency of marriage a thing of the past, even for those who might wish to offer such permanency. Taxation policy has moved further and further away from favouring the wage-earner with dependent spouse and children to treating taxpayers as individuals, whatever their circumstances. At the same time, in the welfare and benefits area, the economic sanctions that previously operated as a deterrent to or restraint upon family foundation (whether of first or second and subsequent families) have been adjusted to protect the position of the parent who is single from whatever cause. An unintended and unanticipated result of this has been the evolution of a system of matriarchy—a pattern of life developing, not only amongst affluent intellectuals but also, with more socially damaging consequences, in areas where poverty, unemployment, and welfare dependency are the norm (Dennis and Erdos 1993). A not uncommon feature of this new pattern or lifestyle is for the children living with their mother to be the offspring of different fathers who have moved on and lost touch with them (Morgan 2000).

6. IMPACT OF NEW REPRODUCTIVE MEDICINE

Advances in reproductive medicine, in particular contraception and the availability of abortion, offer unprecedented control to individuals over their reproductive options, and have now made possible the separation of reproduction from sex and personal sexual relations. IVF and other means of transferring gametes (eggs and sperm) have also made it possible for children to be born to people to whom they are not genetically related, and these children are consequently cut off in an unprecedented way from the wider network of genetic relations—siblings, half-siblings, grandparents, aunts, cousins—who previously contributed to an individual's concept of identity, and who made up the wider notion of family (Strathern 1992). These new techniques also make it possible for same-sex couples to create families via gamete purchase or donation or by paid surrogacy arrangements. The issues raised by new reproductive technologies are too extensive to be discussed in detail in this chapter, and some are discussed elsewhere in this volume. As far as family implications are concerned, however, they raise some important questions. To begin with, where the legal relationship between parent and offspring is explicitly set aside and transferred to adoptive or commissioning parents, the biological (or genetic) relationship ceases to support the customary commitments and responsibilities. The consequences for people's lives have not been completely thought through, however, and children's interests may be lost in the limbo of the new legality. An extreme example is provided by the case of Jaycee Buzzanca (*In re Marriage of Buzzanca*, 1998), a child born in the USA, who, through an extraordinary combination of circumstances, found herself in the legal void of the *filius nulli* when the couple who commissioned her existence separated and she was deemed to be the responsibility of neither the individuals who donated their gametes, nor the surrogate who bore her, nor the couple who no longer wanted her, and had no genetic or biological connection with her (Capron 1998).

But even where arrangements work out more satisfactorily, there are difficult questions of a different kind to consider. For example, do people born in this way (from donated gametes) have a right to know their genetic origins (Almond 1995)? Some jurisdictions—for example, New Zealand and Sweden—regard this as a basic human right, while, for others, donation is still covered by the rules of medical confidentiality. Other ethical questions are raised by the commercial advertising and sale of gametes, given that the sale of children or babies is generally regarded as wholly ethically unacceptable—a vestige of the universally condemned practice of the slave trade in human beings (Warnock 1985, 1987; Overall 1993). Underlying these debates, however, is the fundamental conceptual and philosophical question of which has priority: the biological or genetic basis of the family or the family as a social and legal construct—a question to which we will return when considering public policy on the family.

7. Philosophical and Religious Views: The Historical Background

If the family, and family relationships, provide a contentious forum today for ethical, political, religious, and philosophical debate, it is interesting to turn back the page and to find that the history of philosophical discussion has itself provided almost as much diversity and disagreement.

Plato (427–348 BC) was unusual for his day and age, the Athens of the fifth century BC, in recognizing the potential equality of women in capacities and abilities, and also in holding that the fulfilment of that potential would be difficult unless the family structure was radically changed. So he recommended communal crèches, and the abolition of continuing male–female relationships either in their own right or for the purpose of raising offspring. Indeed, it was a unique aspect of his ideal arrangements as outlined in the *Republic* that neither men nor women would be able to identify their own offspring; women who had gained equality with men as rulers and had recently given birth would attend the public crèche to feed without distinction or discrimination any child handed to them by a nurse.

Plato remains the most radical of any thinker on the family implications of sex equality, but, historically, Aristotelian teleology combined with natural law theory has been more influential in shaping Western attitudes to the family, particularly through the teachings of the Catholic Church as inspired by the writings of St Augustine (354–430) and St Thomas Aquinas (1224–74) (for a modern interpretation, see Finnis 1991). The Christian concept of marriage, however, looks back as well to the Hebraic tradition according to which marriage creates 'two in one flesh' (Gen. 2: 24) and, again, assumes as its object the creation of offspring. The Christian view, then, is that marriage is a sacred, monogamous, and permanent arrangement, the purpose of which is the raising of children. It is a view at the root, too, of most other mainstream religions.

Liberal political theory in the seventeenth century produced a more individualistic view of matters, based on the idea of a social contract. As far as family matters were concerned, it emphasized the contractual aspects of the institution of marriage. The English political philosopher John Locke (1632–1704) took a narrow and relatively limited view of this, seeing the roles of husband and wife as social roles that could in theory be abandoned when the purpose for which the marriage was entered into—having and raising children—had been completed. In *Of Civil Government* he wrote: 'conjugal society is made by voluntary compact between man and woman' and 'consists chiefly in such a communion and right in one another's bodies as is necessary to its chief end, procreation' (1680/1960: paras. 52–69). The German philosopher Immanuel Kant (1724–1804), while also emphasizing contract, saw the judicial status of the partners as establishing lifelong rights, analogous to property rights, with respect to one another—especially to one another's sexual attributes. Kant's views on ethics and marriage can be found in his *Metaphysics of Morals* (1797/1887: Sect. 25).

In contrast, the German idealist philosopher G. W. F. Hegel (1770–1831) found the emphasis on contract offensive, particularly as put forward by Kant. He held that the contract involved in marriage goes beyond the prosaic nature of ordinary legal contracts; it creates a spiritual unity between two people who come to constitute an organic system, and it creates in their two selves, and in their children, a common world. He wrote: 'though marriage begins in contract, it is precisely a contract to transcend the standpoint of contract, the standpoint from which persons are regarded in their individuality as self-subsistent units' (Hegel 1882/1952: 112). This 'organic' view of marriage was shared by other idealist metaphysicians, including the English philosopher F. H. Bradley (1856–1924).

For a radically opposed conception of marriage and family, one may turn to the early English feminist Mary Wollstonecraft (1759–97), author of *A Vindication of the Rights of Woman* (1792/1985). Both she, and also the anarchist political philosopher William Godwin (1756–1836), rejected in their writings the idea that one should have a companion for life. As things turned out, however, the two did in fact marry and have a child. It was a short-lived marriage since Mary Wollstonecraft died from complications following her daughter's birth, having maintained the principle of separate residence from her husband up to that point. By an ironic twist of fate, however, family connections have particular significance here, for the poet Percy Bysshe Shelley (1792–1822), who married their daughter Mary, took Godwin's anarchist rejection of marriage seriously, but combined it with the romantic approach that links sexual union to feeling and attraction. His brief essay against legal marriage encapsulates the romantic conception that dominated nineteenth- and twentieth-century literature and popular sentiment (Shelley 1815/1980).

A succession of liberal thinkers continued the debate, including John Stuart Mill (1806–73) author of the classic defence of individual liberty and advocate of women's liberation (1859/1975 and 1861/1975). Harriet Taylor, Mill's companion and later his wife, took a yet more radical position than Mill, since, while he assumed that a married woman would not work, she argued that economic independence, through paid work outside the home, was essential if women were ever to stand equal to men. It is worth noting that, at about the same time that Mill and Harriet Taylor were writing on this subject in England, a movement for female advance and emancipation was gaining impetus in the USA, the basis of which was political and activist rather than reflective and philosophical.

Philosophical views wholly unsympathetic to the family were also current during this period. Karl Marx's (1818–83) friend and co-worker Friedrich Engels (1820–95) saw the family as a device for perpetuating and making possible capitalist patriarchy—a system that benefited men by enabling them to hand down their property to offspring who could be identified as their own, but that was ultimately exploitative of women. In his influential work *The Origins of the Family, Private Property and the State*, Engels (1884/1985) described wives and children as a proletariat within the domestic economy of the family, with husbands and fathers playing the role of the bourgeoisie.

More recently, the French existentialist writer and philosopher Jean-Paul Sartre (1905–80) and his lifelong associate the writer Simone de Beauvoir (1908–86) developed, both in theory and in personal practice, a choice-based approach to relationships that was characterized by a rejection of commitment or possessiveness, and so distinguishable as a philosophical strand of thinking about relationships quite distinct from either the contractual promise-based model or the romantic conception. It has little to say about children or the family structure as such, although its implications for such structures are clearly iconoclastic.

8. Contemporary Perspectives and the Shaping of Public Policy

If the philosophical views of earlier times are quite surprisingly diverse, the contemporary scene offers a no less varied range of opinion. This includes neo-Marxist views, the feminist anti-patriarchical views discussed earlier, liberal (or libertarian) positions, and conservative (or traditionalist) positions. At one end of the spectrum are political and religious views disposed to shore up traditional family structures. At the other, the kind of radical feminism already mentioned that denies that there are significant or fundamental differences between the sexes and so seeks to extend the child-rearing role to society as a whole, with men holding as much responsibility for it as women. The goal is to free women from what is often called the 'tyranny of reproduction'. For Shulamith Firestone, whose book *The Dialectic of Sex* was politically as well as philosophically influential, the heart of woman's oppression is her child-bearing and child-rearing role (1970/1979: 193). She acknowledges her debt, in terms of political theory, to the work of Engels; in terms of psychological theory, to that of the psychotherapist and iconoclast of family relationships, R. D. Laing (1969). Firestone endorses Laing's account of the family's oppressive and arbitrary dynamics and his attempt to expose the 'myth of the happy family'. Indeed, she goes further in describing the tie between women and their children as 'no more than shared repression' (Firestone 1970/1979: 73). But, while the rejection of traditional family roles was seen as revolutionary in the 1970s, when Firestone was writing, many of its key ideas, especially the welcoming of alternative structures, have subsequently become matters of policy for mainstream political parties. This is no doubt because policies such as flexible working hours, parental leave, and measures to guarantee equality of treament in the workplace may be used to *support* the traditional family unit as well as to facilitate alternatives to it.

These policies are central, too, to the contemporary promotion of modernization as a political programme, especially as put forward by Anthony Giddens, in his influential book, *The Third Way* (1998), seen by many as a blueprint for UK Government policy under New Labour. In a short section promoting what he calls a 'modernist' view of the family—a picture that clearly owes much to the feminist writers discussed above—he draws a contrast with the 'traditional' mode, which he sees as a depressing and unfortunate legacy of the past. He asks 'Is there a politics of the family beyond neoliberalism and old-style social democracy?' and replies 'we should be clear . . . how implausible the idea of returning to the traditional family is . . .' (Giddens 1998: 93–4). In its place, he proposes a democratized family, that he defines as one that involves 'decision-making through communication and freedom from violence' and parental authority that is 'negotiated' rather than arbitrary. This he describes as a new politics of the family quite distinct from that of either old-fashioned liberalism or social democracy. However, it is worth noticing that this claim of 'implausibility' is both ambiguous and misleading. It sounds like a claim about what is the case now and what may be possible in the future, but in fact the only reasons advanced are retrospective claims about how bad the traditional family *was*. These factual claims would need to be much more precise and evidence based to provide a justifiable ground for radical change. The idealized picture may be wrong, but the bleak portrayal is equally flawed. The only 'plausible' claim about the past, and therefore about what is inevitable in the future, must be that experiences of the traditional family were mixed, good for some people and in some respects, bad for others and in other respects. But if this is the case, then inferences to future policy should be equally cautious.

However, in place of caution, Giddens confidently advocates a major shift in public policy as far as childcare is concerned: the idea of co-parenting. He writes: 'Marriage and parenthood have always been thought of as tied together, but in the detraditonalized family . . . the two are becoming disentangled. . . . Contractual commitment to a child could thus be separated from marriage, and made by each parent as a binding matter of law, with unmarried and married fathers having the same rights and obligations' (1998: 95). There is, however, some confusion of ends implicit in this proposal: the reference is apparently to biological fathers, who would become all-important in law on the basis advocated here, but elsewhere, and in particular where same-sex couples are concerned, *social* parenting is regarded as more important than biological kinship. As was pointed out earlier, this is an unresolved difficulty that becomes apparent in relation to such issues as adoption and fertility treatment involving donors. What is more—and this is a point of wider application— if the proposals to cancel the legal differences between marriage and cohabitation are intended to impose the stability of marriage on everyone, it is worth noticing that what they *actually* do instead is to impose the insecure conditions of cohabitation on everyone.

However, the rejection of the traditional view is supported by others, albeit from a rather different point of view. One of these is the feminist writer Iris Young, who focuses on the issue of single-mother families in contrast to families that include both mother and father (Young 1999). This raises the very broad question, basic to the issue of 'reconstituted' families, and in particular for same-sex relationships: do children *need* both a father and a mother? Of course, many children have, through fate or circumstance, been raised by just one parent, but the fact that this can be successful is not sufficient in itself to justify a shift in public policy. This is more usefully guided by factual information about the *relative* success in life of children from different family backgrounds, taking into account measures like school performance, or emotional stability, or the potential to be involved in crime, to run away from home, or to suffer abuse. Even so, the facts alone are not the whole story. From an ethical point of view, there will be those who would give a higher priority to the freedom of adults to pursue without pressure or interference their chosen lifestyles. On the other side, however, and still remaining within the ethical domain, will be others who would claim on behalf of the child both a need for, and a right not to be deprived of, its two biological parents. English law, for example, included such recognition in the 1990 Human Fertilization and Embryology Act when it laid down that providers of fertility treatment must take account of 'the need of a child for a father.'

It is not difficult, however, to find in contemporary writings the view that ethics has no part to play in these matters. Rejecting an argument put forward by the British philosopher Onora O'Neill (1985) that the intimacy of sexual relations generates special obligations in treating others as persons, Igor Primoratz argues that there is no such thing as sexual morality, in the sense that there is no one morally acceptable aim or purpose of human sexual activity. Primoratz writes: 'Sex has no special moral significance; it is morally neutral.' Like other neutral actions, he acknowledges, it may have morally significant implications if, for instance, it involves hurt or betrayal (1999: 173). It is noticeable, however, that the index to his book, the theme of which is ethics and sex, does not list 'family' or 'parenthood' and that, in arguing in favour of marriage for same-sex couples, whose right to raise children he defends, he is at pains to repudiate any necessary link between marriage and procreation.

Against these views, which have a realistic claim to be considered the *Zeitgeist*, or Spirit of the Age, may be ranged those of writers who emphasize instead the *strength* of family or relational bonds. The conservative philosopher Roger Scruton writes: 'The family bond is dispensable only in the way that pleasure, industry, love, grief, passion and allegiance are dispensable—that is, only in the case of the minority which can persuade itself (for whatever reason) to renounce these things' (1986 : 31). The present writer, too, once described the family as 'a convivial multi-person entity, bonded by nature's most effective bonding agent, the sexual relationship, which also simultaneously invisibly binds to its two central agents the presexual beings who are its natural consequences' (Almond 1988: 6).

In the same spirit, the Australian philosopher Brian Trainor, echoing Hegel's organic concept, writes that married couples establish a 'shared universe'. 'The good of this shared world is their common concern. . . . a single world is formed by a husband and wife as its common members' (Trainor 1992: 137). Unlike Giddens, who offers a conception of sexuality as a 'project of self' that favours the 'advancement of self-autonomy in the context of pure relationships', Trainor says that 'to assume a role is to express one's self; the role is a medium through which an aspect of the self is realised'. Criticizing recent trends in public policy, Trainor adds a further, more technical argument in relation to no-fault divorce. This, he says, is based on the principle: since the two parties *are* apart, they *should* be free to exit without penalty, and it therefore breaches the philosophically important principle that an 'ought' cannot be derived from an 'is'.

9. CONCLUSIONS

While the concept of the family is currently a matter of disagreement and contention, it is worth noticing that most contenders take for granted its implicit connection with *children*. The conflict of views that has emerged here, however, has been largely defined in terms of adult needs. The views or interests of children have hardly featured in the philosophical discussions reviewed above, while in public debate their interest is commonly identified with that of their parents or carers. And yet, for most children, the preservation of home, neighbourhood and school through their growing years most often ranks highest in terms of what 'family' can provide, and what might be lost in family breakdown. Except in the very worst cases, they would, no doubt—if they were allowed to—vote for the 'traditional' family. If so, this might have implications for children's rights. Discussion of children's rights has, however, often proceeded on the basis of different empirical assumptions, and so reached conclusions less favourable to family continuity or permanence, including suggestions that children should be able to choose their custodial parent or 'divorce' a current one (Blustein 1979: 118; LaFollette 1999).

Talk of children's rights, however, inevitably suggests the topic of children's responsibilities, even those that may be set in the longterm future. Should children be obliged to care for their elderly parents (English 1979)? Giddens mentions a 1983 US Medicaid attempt to compel children to support needy ageing parents, calling this 'a notion whose time has come' (1998: 97). This has not been overtly taken up as a political issue although the UK Government recently imposed a *de facto* charge on children in forcing in some cases the sale of homes to pay for health care in old age that would otherwise have constituted part of a person's estate—a policy it later reconsidered. In general, though, the breakdown of families is likely to make it harder for the state to assign responsibility *directly* to children for parents in circumstances where inheritance is not involved. Who would the state, for example, pursue for parental support: a person's *social* children or his or her *biological* offspring? Would it take account of the length of time the parent–child relationship had lasted and seek out a series of multiple parents for proportionate support, picking its way through a trail of divorces, cohabitations, remarriages, and separations? Would it ignore factors like cruelty, neglect, or abuse by parents and still expect support from children who had suffered any of these?

Whatever the answer to these questions, it is certainly clear that the era of shallow relationships puts more and more of the onus of care for those suffering from poverty, or disabilities, especially age-related ones, onto the state. And, as more and more aspects of family care and provision at both ends of life become matters of public provision, the tendency grows to locate responsibility with the state. But what is it that the family *really* requires of the state? One writer who would limit the state's intervention to a minimum, seeing it as a Trojan horse of totalitarianism, is Ferdinand Mount, who writes: 'The family's demands are clear and consistent: subsistence, privacy, liberty' (1982: 176). From a more politically sensitive point of view, then, it is important to notice that the family has from time to time in the past proved the last bastion against dictatorships, and these have often deliberately sought to weaken family ties, recognizing the strength of loyalties they engender— loyaties and commitments that may be pitted against the state's own demands. Classic instances of this were provided in the twentieth century as family loyalties were put under strain in Nazi-controlled European countries, in Russia under Soviet Communism, in China for the period of the ascendancy of youthful and intolerant Red Guards, and in Cambodia under Pol Pot. Literature, too, inspired by reflection on these experiences, sometimes features the conflict between intimate bonds between persons and the impersonal claims of totalitarian rulers (for example, George Orwell's *1984*). However, even in democratic states, such tensions can surface in more muted form in educational or health-care situations where professionals and parents may be in conflict over the treatment of minors. This conflict is particularly visible in the debate about private education, denounced by some as elitism, and defended by others as the only defence against the evils of a state monopoly of education, which John Stuart Mill once described in *On Liberty* as a device for moulding people to be exactly like each other.

A number of other issues have been touched upon here only tangentially, but they remain open for further reflection and discussion. For example, is it right to give preference to your own family or family members or is this to bestow unfair privilege on them? Does this conflict with the Kantian principle of impartiality, fairness, and equality of rights? Some would defend such partiality by saying that it is morally acceptable for people to give special weight to projects essential to their self-identity. Others claim that sympathy, intimacy, and trust are concepts central to the family and legitimize its special duties, rights, and responsibilities. This 'personalist' response is defended by Hugh LaFollette, who says that partiality is part and parcel of close personal relations (1996: 199; see also Skolnick 1978; Schoeman 1980).

So this is the point the debate has reached, and it is being waged, on the whole, not in philosophy seminar rooms, but in the courts and parliaments of democratic countries. The shape of the debate is well described by Paul Gilbert, who presents it in terms of two pictures of the family. He writes:

One is a *nostalgic* picture, of relationships having once been more as they ought to be, when familial roles were accepted unquestioningly and close family bonds were forged by unreflective feeling. . . . The other is a Utopian picture, of relationships as they have never been but ought to be, in which familial roles are redefined and our attachments and sympathies to others are determined by a rational assessment of our respective needs. (Gilbert 1991: 143)

He goes on to say that the difference between the two is that the first is the view of relationships as *given*, the second that of relationships as in some sense constructed. Whichever view one takes, whichever picture has the more appeal, it is impossible to overlook another aspect of 'family'—that is the sense in which 'family' provides the archetypal image of personal continuity, and the best way for most ordinary human beings of making sense of the brevity of individual human existence. And so it is overwhelmingly only the biological understanding of the family—the family not as constructed by either custom or legislation but as given—that provides for most human beings a connecting link between their ancestors and their descendants, between personal history and personal future. As G. K. Chesterton puts this picture of the family both imaginatively and memorably: 'this frail cord, flung from the forgotten hills of yesterday to the invisible mountains of tomorrow' (1990: 224).

References

Almond, B. (1988). 'Human Bonds'. *Journal of Applied Philosophy*, 5: 3–16.
—— (1995). 'Family Relationships and Reproductive Technology', in C. E. Ulanowsly (ed.), *The Family in the Age of Biotechnology*. Aldershot: Avebury, 13–26.
Aquinas, St Thomas. *Summa theologica*, pt. II, sect. 2.
—— *Summa contra gentiles*, pt. III.
Augustine, St *The Good of Marriage*.
Blustein, J. (1979). 'Child Rearing and Family Interests', in O. O'Neill and W. Ruddick (eds.), *Having Children: Philosophical and Legal Reflections on Parenthood*. Oxford: Oxford University Press, 115–22.
Capron, Alexander M. (1998). 'Too Many Parents'. *Hastings Center Report*, 28: 22–4.
Chadorow, N. (1978). *The Reproduction of Mothering: Psychoanalysis and the Sociology of Gender*. Berkeley and Los Angeles: University of California Press.
Chesterton, G. K. (1990). *Brave New Family: G.K. Chesterton on Men and Women, Children, Sex, Divorce, Marriage, and the Family*, ed. A. de Silva. San Francisco: Ignatius Press.
Commission on Social Justice (1994). *Social Justice: Strategies for National Renewal*. London: Vintage.
de Beauvoir, S. (1974). *The Second Sex*. New York: Vintage Books.
Dennis, N., and Erdos, George (1992). *Families without Fatherhood*. London: IEA.
Engels, F. (1884/1985). *The Origins of the Family, Private Property and the State*, trans. A. West. Harmondsworth: Penguin.
English, J. (1979). 'What Do Grown Children Owe Their Parents?', in O. O'Neill and W. Ruddick (eds.), *Having Children: Philosophical and Legal Reflections on Parenthood*. Oxford: Oxford University Press, 351–6.
Family Policy Studies Centre (2000). *Family Policy Studies Centre Report*. London: Family Policy Studies Centre.

Finnis, John (1991). *Moral Absolutes: Tradition, Revision, and Truth*. Washington Catholic University of America Press.

Firestone, S. (1970/1979). *The Dialectic of Sex*. London: Women's Press.

Flax, Jane (1990). 'Postmodernism and Gender Relations in Feminist Theory', in L. Nicholson (ed.), *Feminism/Postmodernism*. London: Routledge, 39–62.

Fraser, Nancy, and Nicholson, Linda J. (1990). 'Social Criticism without Philosophy', in L. Nicholson (ed.), *Feminism/Postmodernism*. London: Routledge, 19–38.

Friedan, B. (1982). *The Second Stage*. New York: Summit Books.

Giddens, A. (1998). *The Third Way: The Renewal of Social Democracy*. Cambridge: Polity.

Gilbert, P. (1991). *Human Relationships: A Philosophical Introduction*. Oxford: Blackwell.

Greer, Germaine (1970). *The Female Eunuch*. London: McGibbon & Kee.

——(1999). *The Whole Woman*. New York: Anchor Books.

Hegel, G. W. F. (1882/1952). *The Philosophy of Right*, trans. T. M. Knox. Oxford: Oxford University Press.

Irigaray, L. (1977). *Ce sexe que n'en est pas un*. Paris: Éditions Minuit.

Jaggar, A. (1978). 'Political Philosophies of Women's Liberation', in M. Vetterling-Braggin, F. A. Elliston, A. Frederick, and J. English (eds.), *Feminism and Philosophy*. Totowa, NJ: Littlefield Adams, 5–21.

——(1994). *Living with Contradictions*. Boulder, CO: Westview Press.

Kant, I. (1877). *The Philosophy of Law: An Exposition of the Fundamental Principles of Jurisprudence and the Science of Right*. Edinburgh: T. & T. Clark.

LaFollette, H. (1996). *Personal Relationships: Love, Identity, and Morality*. Oxford: Blackwell.

——(1999). 'Circumscribed Autonomy: Children, Care and Custody' in U. Narayan and J. Bartkowiak (eds.), *Having and Raising Children*. State College, PA: Pennsylvania State University Press, 137–52.

Laing, R. D. (1969). *The Politics of the Family*. Harmondsworth: Pelican Books.

Locke, J. (1680/1960). *Of Civil Government, Second Treatise* ed. P. Laslett (Cambridge: Cambridge University Press).

McLanahan, Sara, and Sandetur, Gary (1994). *Growing up with a Single Parent*. Cambridge, MA: Harvard University Press.

Mill, J. S. (1859/1975). *On Liberty*. Oxford: Oxford University Press.

——(1861/1975). *The Subjection of Women*. Oxford: Oxford University Press.

Morgan, Patricia (2000). *Marriage-Lite: The Rise of Cohabitation and its Consequences*. London: Institute for Economic Affairs.

Mount, F. (1982). *The Subversive Family: An Alternative History of Love and Marriage*. London: Jonathan Cape.

Nicholson, L. (1990) (ed.), *Feminism/Postmodernism*. London: Routledge.

——(1997) (ed.), *The Second Wave: A Reader in Feminist Theory*. London: Routledge.

Okin, S. (1989). *Justice, Gender and the Family*. New York: Basic Books.

O'Neill, O. (1985). 'Between Consenting Adults'. *Philosophy and Public Affairs*, 14: 252–77.

Overall, Christine (1993). *Human Reproduction: Principles, Practices, Policies*. Oxford: Oxford University Press.

Primoratz, I. (1999). *Ethics and Sex*. London: Routledge.

Purdy, L. (1999). 'Boundaries of Authority: Should Children be Able to Divorce their Parents?' in U. Narayan and J. Bartkowiak (eds.), Having and Raising Children. State College, PA: Pennsylvania State University Press, 153–62.

Schoeman, F. (1980). 'Rights of Children, Rights of Parents, and the Moral Basis of the Family'. *Ethics*, 91: 6–19.

Scruton, R. (1986). *Sexual Desire*. London: Weidenfeld & Nicolson.

Shelley, P. (1815/1980). 'Against Legal Marriage', in R. Holmes (ed.), *Shelley on Love*. London: Anvil Press Poetry, 45–8.

Skolnick, A. (1978). *The Intimate Environment: Exploring Marriage and the Family*. Boston: Little, Brown.

Strathern, M. (1992). *Reproducing the Future: Anthropology, Kinship and the New Reproductive Technologies*: Manchester, Manchester University Press.

Trainor, B. (1992). 'The State, Marriage and Divorce'. *Journal of Applied Philosophy*, 9: 135–48.

Warnock, M. A. (1985). *Question of Life: The Warnock Report on Human Fertilisation and Embryology*. Oxford: Blackwell.

——(1987). 'Do Human Cells Have Rights?' *Bioethics*, 1: 1–14.

Westermark, Edward (1901). *The History of Human Marriage*. London: Macmillan.

Wollstonecraft, M. (1792/1985). *Vindication of the Rights of Woman*. Harmondsworth: Penguin.

Young, I. (1990). 'The Ideal of Community and the Politics of Difference', in L. Nicholson (ed.), *Feminism/Postmodernism*. London: Routledge, 300–23.

——(1999). 'Mothers, Citizenship and Independence', in U. Narayan and J. Bartkowiak (eds.), *Having and Raising Children*. State College, PA: Pennsylvania University Press, 15–38.

Case Cited

In re Marriage of Buzzanca, 61 Cal. App. 4th 1410, 1418 (1998).

PART II

MORAL STATUS

CHAPTER 4

CHILDREN

DAVID ARCHARD

1. INTRODUCTION

WE all once were children. Many of us have had or presently have children. Yet, whilst as adults we may be clear about what we think is owed us or about what we can legitimately claim of other adults, we are probably far less clear about what we think children are owed or can claim for themselves. No one would dispute that children should not be treated cruelly, but disagreement persists about the proper limits of parental punishment—whether, for instance, a child may be chastised by a slap. Few would dispute that children should have some say in what happens to them, but the idea that children should have the very same rights of choice as adults is defended as self-evident by some whilst dismissed as evidently mistaken by others.

The crucial questions surrounding the moral status of children are these. What is owed to children and what can they claim for themselves as of right? Do adults have rights over children? In particular, may we compel children to be educated? If so, how do we balance the claims of parents and of the state with regard to this compulsory education? If duties are owed to children, who owes them and why do the duties fall on some adults and not others? In particular, can we speak of justice for children and, if so, should we speak of justice within or between families?

These questions cannot be answered if we are not clear about who and what children are. Our understanding of the moral status of the child is thus crucially influenced by our understanding of the nature and character of childhood. This is not simply a matter of setting boundaries of age, though this is important. We can agree that a child shall be anybody under a certain age. But it is a further question as to why setting such an age defines the limits of a significant category.

2. WHO ARE CHILDREN?

Relevant here is the very influential work of the social historian Philippe Ariès. Famously he argued that the concept of childhood is an exclusively modern one lacked by pre-modern societies, which had no awareness of 'that particular nature which distinguishes the child from the adult' (Ariès 1960/1962). Ariès's evidence has been challenged and it does seem much more plausible to maintain that all human societies have marked a difference between children and adults, even if, as Ariès notes, there is a distinctive way in which that difference is marked in modern societies. We could here invoke a much used philosophical distinction between a concept and a conception (Rawls 1971: 5). A concept of something is that shared understanding of what that thing is whereas conceptions differ in their specification of the particular nature of the thing in question. Following this distinction we could suggest that all societies have a concept of childhood but different societies may have different conceptions of childhood. The concept of childhood is of that which predates and is distinct from adulthood. Conceptions of childhood share this understanding but differ in specifying where and how childhood differs from adulthood.

How exactly might conceptions of childhood differ? One fundamental line of division lies between thinking of childhood as a *state* and thinking of it as a *stage*. This is the distinction between viewing children as 'being' and as 'becoming'. On the former conception childhood is a free-standing, independently defined condition; it is not adulthood but its character is not exhausted by this privative fact. On the latter conception childhood occupies a place, or level, within a broader narrative and derives its significance from that narrative—more especially from what succeeds or supplants childhood in the longer story; childhood is not *yet* adulthood and derives much, if not all, of its character from this fact.

The former conception of childhood can be found expressed in the views of Jean-Jacques Rousseau. Criticizing those who 'are always seeking the man in the child without thinking what he is before being a man' (Rousseau 1762/1979: 34), Rousseau sought to understand the 'child in the child' and thus properly to value what is specific to childhood other than as the contrary of adulthood. This approach has been an important source for progressive educational thinking and has also inspired a 'philosophy of childhood' that views children, not as immature pre-philosophical creatures, but as able to contribute a distinctive philosophical perspective upon moral, metaphysical, and aesthetic issues (Matthews 1994).

The 'state of being' conception risks oversimplifying the issues, especially when it comes to a valuation of childhood. From the perspective of the adult, childhood may seem a magical place of uncorrupted innocence, wonder, and trust. Yet childhood is also a time of dependence and vulnerability. Of course an emphasis merely upon what childhood lacks by comparison with adulthood risks neglecting what Rousseau and his modern followers believe to be the child's 'own ways of feeling, thinking and seeing'. Yet it would be wrong to believe that adulthood and child-hood cannot be compared, and wrong to forget that a proper appreciation of child-hood can be made only from the perspective of an adult. In the celebrated words of Paul, 'When I was a child, I spoke as a child, I understood as a child, I thought as a child: but when I became a man, I put away these childish things' (I Cor. 13: 11). 'Childish things' do have their value—not least for the child—and if, as adults and in order to be adults, we must put them away, we should not forget their value. But he who speaks and understands only as a child is not in a position fully to evaluate these things, and it is the adult who can see them as 'childish'.

The other conception of childhood—as a stage on the way to adulthood—is the more widely held and has been deeply influential. On Aristotle's view, 'The common defining feature is that the child is "unfinished" relative to a human *telos*. In the biology, the child is viewed as unfinished in his or her growth as a human animal; in the ethics, unfinished in the training in virtue; in the politics unfinished in the education for adult life as a responsible citizen' (Matthews 1998: 21). That teleological characterization of childhood as a preparation for adulthood finds confirmation in the studies of developmental psychology, which Piaget, its most notable defender, defines as 'the study of the development of mental functions, in as much as this development can provide an explanation, or at least a complete description, of their mechanisms in the finished state' (1970/1972: 26).

If an adult human's moral status derives from the fact of her being rational, autonomous, and responsible, it follows that a child, which is an unfinished adult, is essentially that which is not yet fully rational, autonomous, or responsible. The 'not yet' is crucial. A child is unlike, say, an animal in lacking capacities and characteristics that it can never acquire. The child is, by contrast, incomplete but open to completion. Indeed, the work of finishing will normally be accomplished by the progress of time. But, although the 'yet' qualifies the 'not' in this crucial manner, it also indicates that what comes later is the fulfilment of a prior lack.

A stages account is influential in further and varied ways. It may be possible to discern stages *within* childhood. Infancy and adolescence are the two notable limiting subdivisions of childhood, and indeed some would restrict childhood proper to that which lies between these two further stages. If there are stages within the stage of childhood, it becomes that much harder to view childhood as one homogeneous condition. Moreover, inasmuch as each stage is a progress towards adulthood and the later stages manifest to a greater degree those abilities and skills that constitute adulthood, it is harder to view all of childhood as definitively not-adulthood. It is difficult to deny to the adolescent that status that can be readily denied the infant. Yet, on the conventional view, although an adolescent is much less clearly not-an-adult than an infant, she is still, along with the infant, ascribed the status of a child.

There are different views as to how the stages of childhood progress. One may see the process of maturation as no more than the endogenous unfolding of an innate potentiality: 'The childhood shows the man, As morning shows the day' (Milton 1671: bk. ii, l. 220). Or one may see the adult as formed exogenously by the influences of others, as a lump of clay is moulded or as a blank slate is inscribed upon. The adult shown in the child may be angelic or beastly, just as the formation of a moral adult may be with or against the grain of the child's nature. Thus one may hold with Rousseau that, 'Everything is good as it leaves the hands of the Author of things; everything degenerates in the hands of man' (1762/1979: 37). Or, as the Puritans did, one may judge it a 'fundamental error to consider children as innocent beings, whose little weaknesses may perhaps want some correction, rather than as beings who bring into the world a corrupt nature and evil disposition, which it should be the great end of education to rectify' (Hannah More, quoted in Cleverley and Philips 1976: 30).

These different views have evident relevance to the moral status of children. If one thinks that children endogeneously mature into adults of their own accord, then the exercise of adult rights and responsibilities can await the inevitable outcome of that maturation. If, on the other hand, one believes that children are a product of their environment, then one may judge that the exercise of certain responsibilities can only help children to grow into their adult status. Again, the moral pessimist will be cautious about allowing children freedom to express their nature, whereas the optimist will think that, left to their own devices, children are only disposed to do good. A realistic theory of the child's nature will surely be situated at neither extreme. Children are the products both of their environment and of their genetic inheritance; they are, as a group, neither innately good not irredeemably bad. A plausible account of their moral status should reflect such realism.

3. WHAT IS OWED TO CHILDREN?

Children may be regarded both as patients—that is, as the objects of the actions of others—and as agents—that is, as the source of actions. Children might make claims upon others in both regards. Inasmuch as children are human beings, there are things that it is wrong to do to them that it would be wrong to do to any human. Yet there may also be wrongs that can be done to children and that derive much of their wrongness from the fact that they are done to children and not to adults.

Consider, as an illustration, the wrong of using another sexually against her will. In the case of a child's being so used most would judge that there is a special wrong. This might variously be expressed as a theft of the child's innocence, as an exploitation of her vulnerability, and as an abuse of the trust that any child puts in an adult. As an innocent the child should not be exposed to forms of treatment that cause her to lose that childlike understanding of the world that gives value to being a child. Moreover, such a theft of innocence is even more wrong because a child is less able than an adult, who is independent, strong, and confident, to resist such an abuse. Nor, disposed to trust the adults she knows, will a child see such abuse by them as to be resisted. Our understanding of what childhood is presses us to acknowledge that something is owed to the child as a child and that, in consequence, a special wrong is done when that childish nature is trespassed upon.

Sexually using another against her will is wrong because it represents a refusal to respect the other's choices. Yet, whilst an adult can make sexual choices, a child is normally thought incapable of doing so. Children are below the age of sexual consent, so that their 'consent'—that is, their willingness to have sex—is not recognized. The crime of having sex with a minor is a crime not because the minor is deemed to be unwilling but because a child's willingness is without legitimating force. Now it may be appropriate to protect children against the consequences of choices they are thought incapable of making properly. But paternalism is thought wrong for its failure to respect the other's choices. Adults are wronged if *their* choices are not respected and children would be wronged if they did not deserve to be treated paternalistically.

Indeed, those who may be termed 'child liberationists' claim just that. For them children, as a group, are wronged by being maintained in an artificial state of dependence upon adults and, crucially, by being denied the same moral status as adult agents. Child liberationists would extend to children the exercise and enjoyment of all those rights that adults currently possess. The case for equal rights for children has been made most prominently by Richard Farson (1974), John Holt (1975), and Howard Cohen (1980). As Cohen says (1980: p. ix), to determine whether it is unjust to deny children rights, we must attend to their capacities. Liberationists deny what their opponents claim—that is, that children essentially lack those capacities that are a precondition for the possession and exercise of rights. The opponents do not deny that children may be entitled to some rights, most centrally the right to be protected from abuse and injury by adults. But such rights of protection are, liberationists claim, insufficient and demeaning of a child's status. Children should not be regarded as incapable of claiming as of right what may not be done to them and what they might do for themselves.

It is important to note that our understanding of what a right is determines our understanding of who or what may have them. In particular, there are two major accounts of what it is to have a right. There is an 'interest' (or 'benefit') account, which regards a right as the protection of some fundamental interest of the right-holder, so important indeed as to require, as possession of a right does, that others not impinge upon that interest. There is also a 'choice' (or 'will') theory, which sees a right as constituted by an individual's exercise of choice in some important regard, sufficiently important that others are required not to hinder that exercise (Jones 1994: ch. 20). On each account there is a different understanding of what may have a right—that which possesses interests sufficiently important to be protected by a right or that which is capable of exercising a freedom in respect of something sufficiently important. Of course, on a full picture of rights and their holders there may not be any great distance between the implications of each account. It may, for instance, be held to be in a person's interests that he should be allowed to choose, and also that a reliable guide to what is in a person's interests is what he does or would choose.

For all of that, children do seem to offer an obvious test case for both accounts (MacCormick 1976). Children will be seen by some as incapable, by contrast with adults, of making choices but as nevertheless having interests meriting protection. That, on an interest but not a choice account, qualifies them as rights-holders. On the other hand, child liberationists make the case for extending to children the liberty rights that adults have and they will deny that children do lack the capacities that, on a 'choice' account, rights-holders must demonstrate. The liberationist case is the most radical defence of children's rights, since it ascribes rights to children not despite their differences from adults but precisely by denying that there are any such relevant differences.

The liberationist case is made in two kinds of way. The most central is by pointing to the arbitrariness of a line dividing those judged to possess the relevant capacities and those judged not to do so, particularly when such a line must be that of some age: '*Any* line which uses age to distinguish people with rights from people without can be shown to be arbitrary' (Cohen 1980: 48). Of course, the mere fact of being a certain age *is* arbitrary in this respect. The point is that there is a putative correlation between being of a certain age and being possessed (or not) of the relevant qualifying capacities.

Even if this correlation is granted, the charge of arbitrariness will still be made by appeal to two interconnected thoughts. The first is that, the closer any person approaches to the qualifying age, the more unlikely it is that she should lack those capacities someone just at or over the age is deemed to have. The second is that any correlation between age and the possession of a capacity can at most be only a regular or a statistical one. There will always be those under the age who possess it and those above the age who lack it. According to both thoughts, an injustice is done to those denied rights just because of their age. It would surely be fairer directly to test for the relevant capacity. But that test should in fairness then be extended to all, including adults, and its conduct would surely be impossibly impractical. Better, then, the argument concludes to have neither test nor arbitrary line and extend to all the rights currently denied to those below the line.

Several responses can be made to this argument from the arbitrariness of age. One is that such arbitrariness is true of *all* dividing lines that have a prescriptive force and that rely on a correlation between the line and some further characteristic or fact. Levels of alcohol in the blood and speeds, for instance, are correlated with dangerous driving in the specification of motoring offences. There is nothing in the argument to show that the use of a correlation between age and a capacity (or its lack) is especially unjust. Secondly, the correlation is a statistical one and evidence that it did fail to obtain would be a reason for changing the age. If enough people below a certain age but above another can be shown to possess the relevant capacity, then that is a good reason to prefer the lower age as the appropriate dividing line.

The child liberationist case does not rest on the argument from arbitrariness alone. It also directly denies the charge that children lack the qualifying capacities. This claim will be the more implausible the younger the children are. It would be absurd to say of infants, as opposed to adolescents, that they do not differ in their capacities from adults. Or the claim will be the more plausible, the more minimally specified are the relevant capacities. Infants may thus be said to be instrumentally rational in the weak sense of striving to get what they want. Yet the onus is then on the liberationist to show how such a bare capacity can be the ground for the exercise of rights.

Child liberationists, on the other hand, may concede that presently children do not possess the capacities needed to exercise rights and yet make one of two moves. The first is made by Howard Cohen. He suggests that children should be permitted 'to *borrow* the capacities of others to secure whatever it is we are entitled to' (Cohen 1980: 56). Child agents would advise their clients with a view to ensuring that the child's right is properly exercised. The difficulty with such a move is that either such advice will amount to a paternalism that is hard to distinguish from the direct supplanting of the child's choices by her guardian in the name of her best interests. Or the agent will merely act instrumentally to secure what the child chooses for herself, choices that, it is conceded, are made by someone who lacks the adult capacities to choose wisely.

The second move is to claim that children lack the relevant capacities only in consequence of a lack of opportunity to exercise the corresponding rights. Children, it is argued, are maintained in an artificial condition of dependence upon adults. If they were allowed to exercise the rights in question, then they would develop those capacities whose present lack disenfranchises them. It is true that children may be maintained by adults in a state of dependence for too long and also true that adults can determine the character of that dependence. This much is important to acknowledge. However, it does not follow that children of any age would be able, if allowed to exercise their putative rights, to acquire the capacities of adult independence. Liberationists should respect the empirical facts of child development; it is implausible to assert that anything is possible given the opportunity to try it.

Two prominent opponents of equal rights for children are Onora O'Neill (1988) and Laura Purdy (1992). O'Neill registers a general scepticism about rights-based moralities for being silent about fundamental imperfect obligations. Obligations are fundamental in the sense of not deriving from any prior moral principle, commitment, or social relationship. They are imperfect if no specific action is owed to a specific person or persons. Such obligations lack corresponding rights. As adults, charges O'Neill, we do owe fundamental imperfect obligations of consideration

for those children for whom we do not, as parents for instance, have a clearly specified duty of care. Talk of children's rights narrows and obscures our ethical vision
by not allowing us to see these obligations whose discharge is crucial to how a child
is educated, protected, and cared for by its society.

Of course, we might as adults have perfect obligations whose counterpart are fundamental children's rights. Yet O'Neill doubts that it is appropriate to talk of such
rights. This talk is informed by a false analogy whereby children are compared to an
oppressed group maintained in its state of oppression by a more powerful ruling
group. The difference between the dependence of children and that of an oppressed
social group is 'that childhood is a stage of life, from which children normally emerge
and are helped and urged to emerge by those who have most power over them'
(O'Neill 1988: 462). For O'Neill the key to properly caring about children lies in
invoking our obligations to them not in employing the misleading rhetoric of rights.

For Laura Purdy also the case for equal rights for children misunderstands what
children are and what is in their best interests. She does not believe that it is unjust
to deny children equal rights, and argues that the consequences of giving them such
rights would be catastrophic. As adults our lives go well to the extent that we command certain skills and abilities, and can exercise self-control. These character traits
do not simply emerge over time; they require active development and training.
Children need to be protected and child liberationists fail to see the harms of
according children an unsupported freedom to do as they choose—within the family, at school, and at work. 'Granting immature children equal rights in the absence
of an appropriately supportive environment would be analogous to releasing mental patients from state hospitals without alternative provision for them' (Purdy 1992:
217). Such opposition to children's rights echoes John Locke's view that granting
fundamental liberties to a child before he possesses the capacities to be the guardian
of his own life is cruel, for it is 'to thrust him out amongst Brutes, and abandon him
to a state as wretched, and, as much beneath that of a Man, as theirs' (Locke
1690/1963: II. vi. §63).

We should be clear what the denial of equal rights to children means. It need not
amount to a denial to children of all rights. Indeed, child protectionists urge that
children be given rights of protection against mistreatment. Furthermore, even if it
is thought improper to accord children liberty rights that protect the exercise of
their freedom, it does not follow that children are denied any power to command
the actions of others in respect of their own interests. Many influential legal charters of children's rights accord to them a fundamental right, proportionate to their
maturity and ability to form views, to express their views on matters affecting them.
This, notably, constitutes Article 12.1 of the United Nations Convention on the
Rights of the Child.

Two further points should be made. First, inconsistency in the moral status
accorded children by the state is to be condemned. It is improper for a government
to allow those of a certain age to do military service but, at the same time, forbid

them sexual choice. It is unacceptable that children should be denied certain liberties but nevertheless be held criminally responsible for their actions. Secondly, rights do have a value and significance that go beyond the guarantee of that which is protected by their successful exercise. This, after all, could be ensured by the spontaneous beneficence of others. What lies beyond the guarantee of good treatment is the ascribed status of being the kind of thing that can claim or demand certain goods and not merely confidently expect them (Feinberg 1970). It should always be borne in mind that children, in lacking equal rights, lack just that status that adults as rights-holders continue to enjoy.

Rights of agency also have crucial relevance in one much discussed area, medical decision-making, and, in particular, the giving of consent by young persons to medical treatment. The principle of informed consent prescribes that no adult should be subject to any medical treatment to which she does not give her informed, voluntary consent. Are children exempt from that principle? Once again the question of competence is crucial. In practice, and also in the law of many states, children below a certain age are assumed not to be competent to give informed consent. The competence in question may be said to comprise a capacity to understand relevant information, to reason about this information, and to relate it to a conception of one's own best interests.

Without settling matters the following can be said. First, any such capacity is incrementally acquired and any policy should be sensitive to the differences between ages, not presuming that the capacity is developed all at once and completely. Secondly, the required capacity to understand is best measured against what it is that needs to be understood—the more complex the issue, the larger the capacity of understanding that is needed to grasp it. The competence needed to understand the import of some proposed medical treatment is both greater and lesser than that needed to understand the significance of other non-medical matters. Thirdly, a child lacking the competence in question should still have matters explained to her. Even if her consent is thought not to be needed, it does not follow, fourthly, that her views are without weight, nor, fifthly, that her parents' wishes are exclusively determinative of the matter. The state, as *parens patriae*, as we shall see, has a duty and a right to ensure that a child's best interests are protected and promoted.

4. Who has Rights over and Duties towards Children?

If children do not have the rights that adults have, it is still the case that adults have duties towards them. Child protectionists believe that adults must discharge basic obligations of care for children. Some of these obligations are in respect of specified children; these are the obligations of parents or designated guardians. Some of the obligations are, following O'Neill, to be thought of as imperfect—that is, owed by us all towards children in general. Some obligations are owed by the state to the children in its jurisdiction. Three sets of questions arise. The first concerns the nature and scope of the care that is owed to children. The second concerns the source and nature of any rights that might be possessed by those adults who care for children. The third concerns the proper distribution of rights and duties between individual adults, parents especially, and the state.

The duty of taking care of one's child as a parent or guardian is, at a bare minimum, that of providing the child with the means of its subsistence and development into adulthood. What, beyond this, might it require? It could be specified in terms of promoting to the greatest degree possible the child's interests. These interests can, depending on how one understands childhood, be those of the child as a child or those of the adult the child will grow into. The duty to care could be specified in terms of what the child, if it were an adult, would wish to do and have done for it. Or it could be specified as the maximization of the capacities of the future adult to exercise free and autonomous choices for herself. This last account is what Joel Feinberg describes under the child's 'right to an open future' (1980). Such a right has plausibility and is most congenial to those of a liberal outlook who view autonomy as central to their ideal of the good life. However, it will not be congenial to those who think it important that a child acquire certain values or inherit and continue a certain identity. Such people do not value the autonomous or chosen life. What matters to them is tradition, cultural inheritance, or a persisting group identity. They see their children first and foremost as the future members of their group, who must, in consequence, inherit its identity. Here we confront a fundamental difference between liberal and non-liberal understandings of the good life, which communicates itself to views on how best to bring up children. What matters then is what rights parents have, as parents, over their own children.

The duty of a parent or guardian to care for her child gives the adult a certain power or authority. This consists most obviously in a right to make those choices for the child under her care that the child is not yet competent to make for himself. The exercise of such a right also assures the parent of a freedom from the interference of others, most centrally the state, in the discharge of her duty to the child. Such a right is obviously constrained by the requirement that the duty of care, however that care is specified, is properly discharged. Jeffrey Blustein's view (1982), the 'priority' thesis, is that this duty to care is primary, and that the parental authority, the right to rear, derives its warrant, and its scope, from that prior duty. Such a view stands opposed to that which holds that any duty towards the child is subordinate to a prior parental power. Thomas Hobbes, for instance, believed that such parental power is total. Children are in 'absolute subjection' to parents who may 'alienate them . . . may pawn them for hostages, kill them for rebellion, or sacrifice them for peace' (Hobbes 1650/1994: 23.8). Hobbes's view here echoed the Roman law of *patria potestas*, which accorded to a father the absolute power of life and death over his son, this power ending not with adulthood but only with the father's death or manumission.

John Locke, who held that all civil or political authority derives from the freely given consent of those subject to it, nevertheless thought that the authority of the parent over his child is natural. He did not, like Hobbes, believe that this authority is absolute. Locke is the source of a powerful and influential idea as to why parents might be thought to have rights over their children that do not derive from a prior duty to care. Locke is the author of the celebrated labour theory of legitimate property acquisition, whereby an individual comes to own that which 'he hath mixed his Labour with, and joined to it something that is his own' (Locke 1690/1963: II. v. §27). A natural thought is that those who produce children (and labour to bring them into existence) thereby acquire rights of ownership over what, after all, is their own. Locke himself denied this, but his arguments in this regard are not convincing (Nozick 1974: 287–9). The idea of parental proprietorship continues to cast a long shadow over contemporary thinking about parental rights.

Even those who deny that parents literally own their children may believe parents have special rights over their offspring, rights that do not derive from a prior duty to care, that do have something to do with the natural fact of the procreative relationship, and that, in some sense, may be viewed as an extension of the parent's right to lead her life as she chooses. These are rights to bring the child up in the beliefs, values, and way of life that are the parent's own. Both Charles Fried (1978) and Robert Nozick (1989) provide eloquent statements of this 'extension' view that a child is an extended part of his parent. Fried writes that 'the right to form one's child's values, one's child's life plan and the right to lavish attention on the child are extensions of the basic right not to be interfered with in doing these things for oneself' (1978: 152). Nozick writes, 'Having children and raising them gives one's life substance.... The children themselves form part of one's substance. Without remaining subordinate or serving your purposes, they yet are organs of you.... Children form part of a wider identity you have' (1989: 28).

What remains unclear in this account is the warrant for moving from the claim that someone gives your life substance to the claim that they are thereby 'part of your substance', from the claim that they are part of your 'wider identity' to the claim that they are an extended part of you, such that rights you have over your own self extend to rights over this other person. After all, I am the partner of someone, and a work colleague of several. In different ways, and to different degrees, these others give my life substance and help to form my wider identity. Yet it is deeply implausible to claim that I have rights over my partner and my colleagues that are extensions of the rights I have over my own person.

How should any rights that a parent has over her child be balanced against the duty of the state to care for those children within its jurisdiction? The state has such a duty not only because it has a general duty to care for all those within its control, especially the weakest and most vulnerable, but also because children represent the literal future, and continued reproduction, of the polity. The state is *parens patriae* ('parent of the nation') responsible in the last analysis for the welfare of its young and future citizens. This role can be defined in broader or lesser terms. Amy Gutman neatly distinguishes between two contrasting ideals, that of the 'family state' in which the state takes exclusive responsibility for the rearing of children and that of the 'state of families' in which the state cedes such responsibility to individual parents (1987: ch. 1). Plato, infamously, defended the former ideal in *The Republic*, whose guardian class take collective control of both the selective breeding and the controlled education of their children. Of course, since Plato there have been various experiments in the collective rearing of children that cannot be as easily dismissed as his dystopian vision. The kibbutzim are an obvious and comparatively recent example. However, such experiments have been voluntary and they have functioned on a small scale below that of the state.

The ideal of the 'state of families', which John Locke espoused, has been the more influential, constituting what some regard as a liberal understanding of the proper relationship between the state and the family. Parents, on this view, are accorded not only a right (of autonomy) to rear their children as they think best but also a right (of privacy) to do so without interference and observation by the state (Goldstein *et al.* 1979; for a critique of the view, see Freeman 1983). That understanding has been eroded by at least three significant developments in the post-war period. The first has been the rise of the unconventional family and the corresponding decline of the traditional family unit. There has been a steady increase since the 1950s in divorce, co-habitation as an alternative to marriage, and single parenthood (whether chosen or occurring through the death or departure of one partner), together with the appearance of same-sex parenting, to the point where the number of children being raised by their married biological parents are far from being in the clear majority. The second development has been that of the new reproductive technology, which, in principle, permits adults to make considered choices about whether and whose child to bear (for a collection of essays bearing on these two developments, see Narayan and Bartowiak 1999). The impact of both developments has been such that, first, the link between biological parenthood and heterosexual marital union, perhaps once thought indissoluble, has been weakened, and, secondly, it is correspondingly less obvious that the state has no legitimate interest in the ways in which children are borne and reared.

The third development compounds these facts. This is a greater awareness of, sensitivity to, and disposition to discover the abuse of children by adults, especially those entrusted with their care. The successive stages in the discovery of child abuse—the first organized movements to protect children in the 1880s, the formulation of the 'battered child syndrome' in the 1960s, and the more recent concern with sexual abuse—have led some to think that the category of child abuse is a protean and expanding one, no longer expressing a very particular, and particularly awful, kind of behaviour towards children (Archard 1999). Nevertheless the facts of child abuse are indisputable and they reinforce two interrelated thoughts. One is that it may be unwise simply to trust to the natural love of a parent for its own child. It is true that most parents offer unconditional love to their children. But not all do, and many children are the victims of abusive parents. Parental love is natural but not universal. The second thought is that the state must be able adequately to monitor the development of every child if it is to fulfil its role as *parens patriae*. This means that the right of the family to privacy from unconsented intrusion into its affairs should not be taken as overriding.

5. JUSTICE FOR CHILDREN?

The talk thus far of what is owed to children has been only in terms of duties to care and to protect, duties that are distributed between parents and the state. But can children claim more than this? In particular, can children make claims of justice, and, if so, should these be claims of justice within or between the families to which they belong?

Since the publication of John Rawls's *A Theory of Justice* (1971) it has been accepted that any account of the good society should demonstrate which principles of justice apply to the basic institutions of that society, and why. Rawls did not in his *A Theory of Justice* (1971) or the later *Political Liberalism* (1993) make it clear whether he believed the family is a part of the basic structure to which his principles of justice apply. He has subsequently been explicit. The family is a part of the basic structure. Although political principles do not apply directly to its internal life, they do impose limits or constraints on the institutions of the family by guaranteeing the rights and liberties of its members, including those of children as future citizens (Rawls 1999: 156–64).

Notwithstanding Rawls's own view, there are three kinds of reason why one might think that the principles of justice should apply to the institution of the family. The first, following Rawls, is that any 'well-ordered' society must not only be just but one whose citizens are disposed to accept the principles of justice that regulate their institutions—that is, have the appropriate 'sense of justice'. In so far as the family will continue to be the prime site of the moral education of a society's future citizens, and in so far as we believe that citizens can only learn justice in just families, then families must be just. The claim that individuals can learn justice only within just families may be termed the 'school-of-justice' claim, and it received an exemplary statement and defence from John Stuart Mill (1869/1984: 294–5). Mill, in particular, thought that the family members should not just profess but practise, in their family life, the ideals that are also those of the constitution of the broader society. The claim that families must play a role in the moral education of future citizens should be made without prejudice to the form that families might take. That is to say, the family that is the prime site of moral education of children need not be the traditional, nuclear family.

A second reason for thinking that the principles of justice ought to apply to the family is, again following Rawls, that such principles should apply to those major institutions that have a 'profound and present from the start' effect on the life prospects and expectations of social advantage of a citizen (Rawls 1971: 7–8). The family is such a major institution inasmuch as it is the means whereby differential possession of both natural and social goods is transmitted across generations. Parents can and do pass on to their own children these goods—whether natural assets such as intelligence, skills, and talents or social goods such as status, wealth, and power—and thus crucially determine the initial starting place of these children as adults within their society.

The third reason for thinking that principles of justice ought to apply to the family is closely related to the first and derives from the thought that there is something wrong with the public sphere being regulated by principles that not only do not apply, but are violated in the private sphere. This thought goes back at least to Hegel, who sought to show how diversity and conflict of purposes in civil society were nevertheless consistent with the state's displaying unity. Critics of Hegel, most obviously Marx, believed that any divisions within civil society could be reproduced only within the state. It does, on the face of it, seem implausible, not to say undesirable for the overall good of any polity, that individuals should as citizens be motivated by ideals, say of justice, which as private members of civil society—in their employment or in the family—they gainsay.

If these three reasons have force and if principles of justice ought to apply to the family, they would do so in two quite distinct ways. On the first, justice should apply within each and every family; on the second, justice should apply between families. On the first understanding of the scope of justice, children should not be unfairly disadvantaged in relation to other family members. On the second, children should not be unfairly disadvantaged in relation to children in other families. What exactly children can claim as fair and equal treatment within the family depends very much on one's understanding of their proper status. Both a liberationist and a protectionist can agree that all children are equally owed respect but, as we have seen, disagree as to whether that means children should be given the same liberties as adults. What is owed to a child within a family may only be obligations of care and protection, however specified and even if stipulated as requiring that the child's best interests be promoted.

But perhaps thinking about the family as something that can be regulated by principles of justice may misconstrue the nature both of justice and of the family. Principles of justice are thought, following David Hume and John Rawls's influential restatement of Hume, to apply, and to need to be applied, where the circumstances of justice obtain. These are the circumstances of moderate scarcity and moderate self-interest. Critics of Rawls's claim that 'justice is the first virtue of society' have charged that there are forms of social organization in which the circumstances of justice, and thus the need for principles of justice, do not apply. Michael Sandel is one such a critic and he appeals to the examples of friendship and family to make his point (1982: 31–5). Whether or not Sandel is right to invoke the family as an appropriate model of large-scale social organization is irrelevant given the evident fact that the family is not a society in circumstances of justice. It is not a site for the distribution of goods, or at least it is not principally that. Moreover, it is characterized, at least in so far as it conforms to that ideal, which it displays in the majority of cases, by relationships and affective dispositions that are not self-interested. The family is the site of a particular, intense, and, on occasions, self-sacrificial love and mutual concern by its members for one another. Principles of justice need not apply to the familial sphere of human interrelationships, and they should not because their application might well bring about the destruction of those relationships.

The above comments gesture towards a now familiar and extensively treated contrast between justice and care. For many the contrast is overstated and there is no good reason to think that some set of relationships cannot both display attitudes of care and at the same time be constrained by principles of right and justice. A marriage, after all, can be both loving and ordered in accordance with precepts of fairness. Having said that, however, it is not clear which particular principles of justice might be thought appropriate to regulate the order and daily affairs of a particular family. Should the situation of children, as arguably the least favoured individuals within any family, be the subject of a familial difference principle such that it is always at least as good as it could be? Robert Nozick (1974: 167) has remarked on the evident inappropriateness of a difference principle for governing a family of loving individuals—if this meant, for instance, that parents should maximize the position of their least well-off and least talented child by holding back resources from the other children.

With regard to the question of justice between families, there does not seem to be the same problem of inapplicability. Families do not, of their nature, care for and love other families. What then should be the scope and character of interfamilial justice? Here there is a problem for the liberal that has been well exposed by James Fishkin (1983). Fishkin demonstrates that there is 'trilemma' for the liberal constituted by the impossibility of satisfying all of three plausibly liberal principles. These are the principle of merit, that positions within society should be allocated only on the basis of appropriate qualifications, the principle of equal life chances, that children with the same potential should have the same life prospects for social advantage, and the principle of family autonomy, that the state should not interfere with family relations except to secure the minimum preconditions for the child's eventual adult participation in society. The essential incompatibility lies between equal opportunity and family autonomy, and derives from the claim, already made, that the family is a means whereby the differential possession of natural and social goods is passed on to children.

It is hard to see how the trilemma can be resolved, since none of the principles suggests itself as one obviously to be abandoned. With regard to the question of equal opportunity, it is undeniable that membership of one family rather than another does make a significant difference to an adult's life prospects, and that such membership is a matter of that 'brute luck' affecting individuals that is now conventionally accepted as properly compensated by a principle of equality. A public education system can obviously make some difference to the prospects of an adult but, arguably, it cannot outweigh the initial distribution of familial advantages, and within any educational system that grants parents freedom of choice of school that initial distribution of advantage is likely to be reinforced.

With regard to the question of family autonomy, at least two things can be said. The first, negatively, is that the alternatives to allowing individuals to form families—such as a Platonic 'family state'—are not feasible, or at the least could be put in place and sustained only by an unacceptable degree of official coercion and interference in the lives of individuals. Conceivable are arrangements whereby children would be allocated to their primary carers. For instance, to equalize life opportunities, initially disadvantaged children would be placed in a compensatingly better-placed familial context and vice versa for initially advantaged children. Such an arrangement might equalize subsequent opportunities, but it would do so at significant costs—both to the children and to their biological parents—which did not justify the gains in equality of life chances.

The second thing, positively, to say about family autonomy is that many will regard the right to found a family—to enter into consensual relations with another adult, to bear and to rear children—as a fundamental right. Indeed, such a right is recognized in many legal charters. It is surely plausible to think that adults do have a strong interest both in having children and in raising them as they see fit. As Eamonn Callan notes, 'raising a child engages our deepest values and yearnings', and, whilst parents must discharge certain duties towards their child, no moral theory of the family should interpret 'the parent's role in ways that make individual parents no more than instruments of their children's good' (1997: 144–5). Such sentiments do not amount to an endorsement of the 'extension' view that children are no more than a part of the parent's substance, nor of the 'proprietarian' view that children are owned by their parents. They do give expression to the thought that it matters to people that they can have and raise children, and that, in consequence, the interests of parents as parents should not simply be discounted beside those of their children.

Of course, a dilemma results only if, in a conflict between two principles, neither can easily be abandoned or if there is no higher-order principle dictating which of the two principles should yield to the other. In the present case it would seem that there is a straightforward and familiar conflict between a principle of equality and one of liberty. If there is more to be said, it may lie in challenging the principle of family autonomy. The principle is, after all, already constrained by the requirement that the state secure the minimum preconditions for the child's eventual adult participation in society. Furthermore, it is important to be clear what exactly are the grounds for the principle. It may derive its support not from some ulterior right of the individual parent—to rear her own, for instance—but from the value to society of having particular families take responsibility for the upbringing of children. To the extent that this is true, an argument for the principle of family autonomy may be founded upon, and constrained by, considerations of the public good, and not the freedom of individual parents. The words of J. S. Mill are especially apposite:

It is in the case of children that misapplied notions of liberty are a real obstacle to the fulfilment by the state of its duties. One would almost think that a man's children were supposed to be literally, and not metaphorically, a part of himself, so jealous is opinion of the smallest interference of law with his absolute and exclusive control over them. (Mill 1859/1974: 175)

6. Educating Children

Should we compel children to be educated and how should we balance the state's interest in having its future citizens educated against that of the parents' interest in seeing their children acquire a certain identity, or a particular set of beliefs and values? The liberationists will deny that a child may be compulsorily educated; a child should have the right to decide whether or not she goes to school. Their liberal critics will insist that a right to compulsory education is a fundamental welfare right. Their argument will turn on the acquisition of the capacity of self-determination or autonomy. Children lack this capacity. That is why they do not have a right to choose whether or not to be educated. However, they will acquire the capacity, and the associated rights of choice, only if they are educated. Present compulsion is thus a necessary precondition of subsequent freedom. Compulsory universal education is an entirely legitimate paternalist measure of a liberal state enforceable against the child's parents (Gutman 1980; Hobson 1983).

However, it is entirely consistent with the compulsion of children to be educated that children should have a measure of choice, or at least control, with regard to the actual process of education. Radical child-centred educational theory and practice lay great stress on children having the power to determine the pace, direction, and even the broad content of their learning. A famous British experiment in such radical education is Summerhill (Neill 1968). Liberals will certainly be careful to distinguish between the need for state enforcement of education and the question of state direction of the content of any education (Mill 1859/1974: 175–9). This is because a parent may have as much of a legitimate claim as the state to determine what a child learns.

What then are the relevant interests? As we have seen, parents can claim an interest in rearing their own children where this involves the transmission to them of those beliefs and values to which the parents subscribe. Indeed, what has been termed the 'extension' claim is the view that forming a child's identity, transmitting to the child certain values and beliefs, is an extension of the fundamental right of the adult parent to live her life as she chooses. Parents would thus want any public education at least to be consistent with their own way of life. On the other hand, the state has an interest in ensuring that it is reproduced in good order over time. That means that a state must ensure that its present children can play their future part as citizens. A liberal state will thus demand 'an education adequate to serve the life of a free and equal citizen in any modern democracy' (Gutman 1992: 14). Finally, the child has a set of interests that may or may not found rights and that, arguably, include the following: an interest in acquiring a certain identity, an interest in becoming an adult possessed of certain capacities, and an interest in being reared in a loving and caring environment.

It is entirely understandable that there should be conflicts between these various interests. The most notable have been those between the putative interests of parents and the state. For instance, the celebrated American Supreme Court case *Wisconsin* v. *Yoder* (1972) was about whether a community's children might be compelled to remain in school beyond a certain age. It considered the proper balance between the state's legitimate interest in the preparing of citizens able 'to participate effectively and intelligently' in the political system, to be 'self-reliant and self-sufficient participants in society' (*Wisconsin* v. *Yoder* 1971) and the interests of a set of parents in ensuring that their children remained within a distinctive community defined by a set of values and beliefs that might be eroded by extended exposure to a certain kind of education. Yet another American case, *Mozert* v. *Hawkins* (1987), dealt with a direct conflict between the content of a compulsory curriculum and those values the parents wished to see transmitted to their children. In particular, a group of conservative Christian parents took their local school board to court, wanting to have their children exempted from a reading programme that they claimed instilled beliefs that were in conflict with their own fundamentalist faith.

There are three sets of issues that arise from these kinds of conflict. The first concerns the content of any public education. Does it need only to be a thin or minimal one concerned to ensure that children acquire the most basic of capacities, or must it be a thicker one inculcating a very particular collection of beliefs, values, and skills? Relatedly there is the question of whether an education for citizenship is principally an education in autonomy, a general capacity to understand and appraise one's own life so as to be able to participate in the collective shaping of one's society (Gutman 1989). Or does any education for citizenship need to be a more particularistic grounding of future citizens in the identity of their own society, its history, constitutive values, and defining outlook. Such an education may valorize that particular identity in a way that seems prima facie inconsistent with the requirement of education that it encourage critical reflection upon and thus detachment from all partial commitments (Galston 1991: 243–4; Callan 1997: ch. 5).

The second set of issues concerns the proper balance between the interests of the state and parents—that is, what principles should determine whose interests take priority. In the last analysis who may determine what kind of adult the child becomes?

The third set of questions are about the respective influences upon the child of parents and public education, particularly when they are not, as it were, pulling in the same direction. It might seem that a public education can correct the failings or omissions of a parental upbringing. But some worry that it is mistaken to trust to nonfamilial institutions to fill the large hole in the education and socialization of the family left in this manner by a familial failing (Okin 1994: 35). On the other hand, the metaphor of a hole to be filled may get it wrong. It is rather that an attempt to build on two different sites or foundations—the family and the school—will result in a fundamentally fractured construction. Either way it would surely be a mistake to think that education alone can secure the ends of justice both within and between families. If children ought to be within the scope of any principles of justice that regulate their society, then the efforts of education must complement and not have to outweigh the effects of broader social and economic institutions and practices.

All three kinds of issues are fundamental to a full understanding of educating citizenship. Yet there is a danger of concentrating solely on the interests of the parents and the state, thereby omitting to give proper consideration to those of the child. Any interest a child might have in acquiring a particular identity is quite distinct from the interest a parent might have in seeing that his child acquire some identity. Similarly any interest a child has in acquiring a certain set of competencies is quite distinct from the interest a state has in seeing that children acquires these capacities. There is a risk of losing sight of children and their interests. Once again perhaps the extension claim and the proprietarian view cast long shadows, leading us, mistakenly, to think that somehow a child's interests are just an extension of their parents' or that a child being just the property of his parents is not the distinct source of valid moral claims upon others.

7. Concluding Remarks

Many historians of childhood assert that children in the past were the systematic victims of parental indifference, cruel treatment, and abuse, which was nevertheless seen as entirely normal (de Mause 1976; Stone 1977). That view has been disputed (Pollock 1983). Nevertheless an influential understanding of modernity is as the terminus of a long passage to moral enlightenment, and it would be easy in consequence to regard our own present treatment of children as evidence of that more general moral improvement. It is certainly true that our treatment of children probably says most about our moral practice as individuals and as societies. The foregoing has shown, however, that it is not entirely clear what the moral status of children is. More particularly it has been suggested that a proper understanding of this status requires, on the one hand, a proper understanding of childhood itself, and, on the other, a clearer appreciation of what exactly parents can lay claim to in respect of their own children.

References

Archard, D. (1999). 'Can Child Abuse be Defined?', in M. King (ed.), *Moral Agendas for Children's Welfare*. London: Routledge, 74–89.

Ariès, P. (1960/1962). *Centuries of Childhood*, trans. Robert Baldick. London: Jonathan Cape.

Blustein, J. (1982). *Parents and Children: The Ethics of the Family*. Oxford: Oxford University Press.

Callan, E. (1997). *Creating Citizens: Political Education and Liberal Democracy*. Oxford: Oxford University Press.

Cleverley, J., and Philips, D. C. (1976). *From Locke to Spock: Influential Models of the Child in Modern Western Thought*. Melbourne: Melbourne University Press.

Cohen, H. (1980). *Equal Rights for Children*. Totowa, NJ: Littlefield, Adams & Co.

de Mause, L. (1976). 'The Evolution of Childhood', in de Mause (ed.), *The History of Childhood*. London: Souvenir Press, 1–73.

Farson, R. (1974). *Birthrights*. London: Collier Macmillan.

Feinberg, J. (1970). 'The Nature and Value of Rights'. *Journal of Value Inquiry*, 4: 243–57.

——(1980). 'The Child's Right to an Open Future', in W. Aiken and H. LaFollette (eds.), *Whose Child? Children's Rights, Parental Authority and State Power*. Totowa, NJ: Rowman & Littlefield, 80–98.

Fishkin, J. (1983). *Justice, Equal Opportunity, and the Family*. New Haven: Yale University Press.

Freeman, M. D. A. (1983). 'Freedom and the Welfare State: Child-Rearing, Parental Autonomy and State Intervention'. *Journal of Social Welfare Law*, 70–91.

Fried, C. (1978). *Right and Wrong*. Cambridge, MA: Harvard University Press.

Galston, W. (1991). *Liberal Purposes: Goods, Virtues, and Diversity in the Liberal State*. Cambridge: Cambridge University Press.

Goldstein, J., Freud, A., and Solnit, A. J. (1979). *Before the Best Interest of the Child*. New York: Free Press.

Gutman, A. (1980). 'Children, Paternalism and Education: A Liberal Argument'. *Philosophy and Public Affairs*, 9: 338–58.

——(1987). *Democratic Education*. Princeton, NJ: Princeton University Press.

——(1989). 'Undemocratic Education', in N. L. Rosenblum (ed.), *Liberalism and the Moral Life*. Cambridge, MA: Harvard University Press, 71–88.

——(1992). 'Introduction', in C. Taylor, *Multiculturalism and 'The Politics of Recognition'*. Princeton, NJ: Princeton University Press, 3–24.

Hobbes, T. (1650/1994). *The Elements of Law, Natural and Politic*, ed., with an Introduction by J. C. A. Gaskin. Oxford: Oxford University Press.

Hobson, P. (1983). 'Paternalism and the Justification of Compulsory Education'. *Australasian Journal of Education*, 27: 136–50.

Holt, J. (1975). *Escape from Childhood: The Needs and Rights of Children*. Harmondsworth: Penguin.

Jones, P. (1994). *Rights*. London: Macmillan.

LeBlanc, Lawrence J. (1995). *The Convention on the Rights of the Child*. Lincoln, NE: University of Nebraska Press, app. C.

Locke, J. (1690/1963). *Two Treatises of Government*. A critical edition with an Introduction and *apparatus criticus* by Peter Laslett. Cambridge: Cambridge University Press.

MacCormick, N. (1976). 'Children's Rights: A Test-Case for Theories of Rights'. *Archiv für Rechts und Sozialphilosophie*, 62: 305–17.

Matthews, G. B. (1994). *The Philosophy of Childhood*. Cambridge, MA: Harvard University Press.

——(1998). 'Socrates's Children', in S. M. Turner and G. B. Matthews (eds.), *The Philosopher's Child: Critical Essays in the Western Tradition*. Rochester, MN: University of Rochester Press.

Mill, J. S. (1859/1974). *On Liberty*. Harmondsworth: Penguin.

——(1869/1984). 'The Subjection of Women', in *Collected Works of John Stuart Mill*, ed., J. M. Robson. Toronto: University of Toronto Press, xxi.

Milton, John (1671). *Paradise Regained*.

Narayan, U., and Bartowiak, J. (1999) (eds.), *Having and Raising Children: Unconventional Families, Hard Choices, and the Social Good*. University Park, PA: Pennsylvania State University Press.

Neill, A. S. (1968). *Summerhill*. Harmondsworth: Penguin.

Nozick, R. (1974). *Anarchy, State, and Utopia*. Oxford: Blackwell.

——(1989). *The Examined Life: Philosophical Meditations*. New York: Simon & Schuster.

Okin, S. M. (1994). 'Political Liberalism, Justice and Gender'. *Ethics*, 105: 23–43.

O'Neill, O. (1988). 'Children's Rights and Children's Lives'. *Ethics*, 98: 445–63.

Piaget, J. (1970/1972). *Psychology and Epistemology*, trans. P. Wells. Harmondsworth: Penguin.

Pollock, L. (1983). *Forgotten Children: Parent–Child Relations from 1500–1900*. Cambridge: Cambridge University Press.

Purdy, L. M. (1992). *In their Best Interest? The Case against Equal Rights for Children*. Ithaca, NY: Cornell University Press.

Rawls, J. (1971). *A Theory of Justice*. Cambridge, MA: Harvard University Press.

——(1993). *Political Liberalism*. New York: Columbia University Press.

——(1999). *The Law of Peoples with 'The Idea of Public Reason Revisted'*. Cambridge, MA: Harvard University Press.

Rousseau, Jean-Jacques (1762/1979). *Émile, or On Education*. Introduction, Translation and Notes by A. Bloom. Harmondsworth: Penguin.

Sandel, M. (1982). *Liberalism and the Limits of Justice*. Cambridge: Cambridge University Press.

Stone, L. (1977). *The Family: Sex and Marriage in England 1500–1800*. London: Weidenfeld & Nicolson.

Cases Cited

Mozert v. Hawkins County Bd of Education, 827 F. 2d 1058 (6th Cir. 1987).

Wisconsin v. Yoder, 406 US 205 (1971).

CHAPTER 5

ABORTION

JOHN HARRIS

SØREN HOLM

1. INTRODUCTION

ABORTION is one of those classic problems that has been discussed in all of the major 'fertile periods' of practical philosophy, from the flourishing of Greek thought, through the medieval period, in the Renaissance and from the start of modern applied ethics in the 1960s. According to *The Oxford English Dictionary* abortion is: 'The act of giving untimely birth to offspring, premature delivery, miscarriage; the procuring of premature delivery so as to destroy offspring. (In [medicine] abortion is limited to a delivery so premature that the offspring cannot live, i.e. in the case of the human fetus before the sixth month)' (*Oxford English Dictionary, OED Online* 2001). This definition encompasses both spontaneous abortion and abortion caused by some form of (usually medical) intervention. It is the latter type of abortion that has interested philosophers and policy-makers, and when in the following we use the term 'abortion' it is always in the sense of 'abortion caused by human intervention'.

The chapter begins with a brief historical overview of the discussion of the ethics of abortion, and then proceeds to a range of questions that have been prominent in the philosophical discussion about abortion since the 1960s. The two main areas of controversy have been (1) how to understand the moral status of the fetus, and (2) whether a right to abortion can be based in the mother's right to autonomy (or

Thanks to Jeff McMahan for helpful suggestions and comments on an early version of this chapter.

some other right the mother holds)? Other debates have concentrated on whether there is a moral difference between early and late abortions, whether abortion after prenatal diagnosis is morally different from other forms of abortion, and whether there should be a legal right to abortion even if our ethical analysis shows that abortion is ethically problematic.

The modern literature on the ethics of abortion is extensive, and it is impossible in this chapter to do justice to all the arguments that have been presented. Taking as a basis our view of what issues are most important, we therefore look at the first two areas of controversy identified above in some detail, and give a shorter overview of the other questions mentioned.

How we resolve the moral issues concerning abortion, and the arguments that are found to be the most convincing in this context, have implications for a wide range of other issues in reproductive ethics. The analysis of the moral status of the fetus does, for instance, have implications for the ethics of many of the techniques involved in *in vitro* fertilization, research on embryos, and pre-implantation genetic diagnosis. We have, however, decided to concentrate on the issue of abortion, since this raises more than sufficient issues of its own.

This chapter has been co-authored by two people with very different views about the ethics of abortion, and about the final merits of many of the arguments presented here (see e.g. Harris 1985; Holm 1996). We hope that this has resulted in a chapter that will help our readers to make up their own minds. That is, after all, the main purpose of practical ethics.

2. A Brief Historical Introduction

Abortion has been discussed as an ethical and legal question as far back as we have a written record. Even during the earliest parts of this history we can find the whole range of views concerning the ethical analysis of abortion from the most restrictive to the most permissive.

Plato, for instance, mentions abortion performed by midwives in *Theaetetus* (149d) and advocates abortion (and infanticide) for those who have passed the age of lawful procreation in the *Republic* (bk. V, 461c):

But when, I take it, the men and the women have passed the age of lawful procreation, we shall leave them free to form such relations with whomsoever they please . . . first admonishing them preferably not even to bring to light anything whatever thus conceived, but if they are unable to prevent a birth to dispose of it on the understanding that we cannot rear such an offspring.   (Plato 1994: 700)

In a given time period the philosophical discussion is often coloured by the most fashionable philosophical and religious views during that period, and by the most recent beliefs about the intricacies of reproductive biology.

Until the invention of the microscope and the discovery of the human egg, most philosophers, for instance, based their ethical analysis of abortion on the mistaken factual belief that the woman provided only unformed matter to the fetus, whereas the generative principles giving form to the fetus were exclusively present in the sperm.

When Aquinas therefore believed that the fetus received a soul only some time after conception, it was partially because he believed that a soul could be received only by a suitably formed individual, and that the generative (male) forces in the sperm needed time to form the unformed (female) matter.

In the Western world the philosophical debate about abortion has until recently been carried out within a Christian framework, where it could be taken as a given that killing an innocent human being was ethically wrong, and where the two main questions therefore became (1) when does the fetus become a human being, and (2) under what conditions can a fetus be killed when it has become a human being.

One of the arguments that has been prominent in the historical debate about the second of these questions is the argument from double effect, an argument that has also been prominent in debates about active euthanasia. This argument has been used to show that there may be cases where it is morally permissible to kill a fetus as a side effect of some other medical intervention—for instance, the removal of a cancerous womb in a pregnant woman.

According to the argument from double effect it is permissible to perform an act which has two effects one good and one bad if:

- the act is intended to produce the good effect;
- the bad effect is an unintended side effect of the act;
- there is no way of producing the good effect without producing the bad effect;
- the badness of the side effect does not outweigh the goodness of the intended effect.

There is an extensive literature on the argument from double effect and it is rejected by most modern consequentialists. What is rehearsed in most of the literature is the more general underlying question whether only the consequences of an act matter in the moral evaluation of that act, or whether other factors (in this case the intention of the act) are also morally relevant. The critics of the 'double-effect' argument point mainly to two problems with the argument. Their first claim is that it is superfluous, since, if the goodness of the intended effect outweighs the badness of the side effect, you ought to perform the action, even if you do not intend to do so. Their second claim is that, if it is not superfluous, it is pernicious, since it allows the agent to do bad things (all things considered) as long as his intentions are pure.

At the beginning of the modern era of practical ethics discussions about abortion were very prominent. Many of the most prominent figures in the early phase of medical ethics wrote extensively on abortion (see e.g. Joseph Fletcher 1966; Paul Ramsey 1970, 1978; Daniel Callahan 1972; James Gustafson 1975; Richard McCormick 1981); and it was also an issue of intense public debates in the late 1960s and early 1970s. At the public policy level many Western countries changed their legal regulation of abortion around this time, either by legislation passed by national parliaments, or by judicial decision (like the famous *Roe* v. *Wade* decision of the US Supreme Court in 1973).

3. THE STATUS OF THE FETUS

One of the main strategies for showing the moral respectability of abortion or at least its moral neutrality is to show that the killing of the fetus that is part of the abortion procedure is not morally wrong. The main class of arguments trying to show this are the so-called 'personhood arguments.' These build on ideas in John Locke, and were first used in the abortion debate by Joseph Fletcher (1966, 1972), and later developed by Mary Anne Warren (1973), Jonathan Glover (1977), Peter Singer (1979), John Harris (1980, 1985), Michael Lockwood (1985), and H. Tristram Engelhardt (1986). A useful book-length analysis of the whole question of moral status and personhood can be found in Mary Anne Warren's *Moral Status: Obligations to Persons and Other Living Things* (1997).

In the following sections we will first lay out the personhood arguments and then look at arguments trying to show that killing a fetus is actually wrong, and that the personhood analysis is misguided.

4. WHAT IS 'PERSONHOOD'?

In the middle of the seventeenth century in his *Essay Concerning Human Understanding* the philosopher John Locke attempted to give an account of the sorts of features that make an individual a person:

We must consider what person stands for; which I think is a thinking intelligent being, that has reason and reflection, and can consider itself the same thinking thing, in different times and places; which it does only by that consciousness which is inseparable from thinking and seems to me essential to it; it being impossible for anyone to perceive without perceiving that he does perceive.   (Locke 1690/1964: 188)

This account of personhood identifies a range of capacities as the preconditions for personhood. These capacities are interesting in that they are species, gender, race, and organic-life-form neutral. Thus persons might, in principle, be members of any species, or indeed machines, if they have the right sorts of capacities. The connection between personhood and moral value arises in two principle ways. One of these ways involves the fact that the capacity for self-consciousness coupled with a minimum intelligence, identified by Locke, is not only necessary for moral agency but is also the minimum condition for almost any deliberative behaviour. More significantly, however, is the fact that it is these capacities that allow individuals to value their own existence and that of others. It allows individuals to take an interest in their own futures, and to take a view about how important it is for them to experience whatever future existence may be available (Harris 1980, 1985, 1992).

In this view, the wrong done to an individual when his existence is ended prematurely is the wrong of depriving that individual of something that he values. On the other hand, to kill or to fail to sustain the life of a non-person, in that it cannot deprive that individual of anything that he, she, or it could conceivably value, does that individual no harm. It takes from such individuals nothing that they would prefer not to have taken from them. This does not, of course, exhaust the wrongs that might be done in ending or failing to sustain the life of another sentient creature. Some of these wrongs will have to do with causing pain or suffering or apprehension to a creature, others will have to do with wrongs that may be done to those persons that take a benevolent interest in the individual concerned (Marquis 1989; Harris 1992).

This account gives one answer to the ethics of abortion and this is why theories of personhood have come to figure significantly in the abortion debate. To this extent, it does what a theory of personhood should try to do. It explains many of the judgements that we intuitively make about these issues, resolves some of the dilemmas that we have about the ethics of decision making, and gives us ways to approach new and possibly unforeseen dilemmas. In uniting and explaining some of our basic intuitions in biomedical ethics, it of course also violates some of these intuitions. In telling us how to handle existing hard cases, it creates some new hard cases.

4.1 Criteria for Personhood

This account offers criteria for personhood in that any self-conscious, minimally intelligent being will be a person. The problem is that we not only want reliable criteria for personhood, but we want *detectable evidence of personhood*. Here matters are not so simple, and we need to know whether and why we should assume that the sorts of creatures that we know to be normally capable of developing self-consciousness—namely, human creatures—are persons at some time prior to the manifestation of the 'symptoms' of personhood.

Those who give prominence to theories of personhood, do so because they think that accounts of personhood help with questions about the ethics of killing and letting die. Many people who have been interested in the distinctions between different sorts of creatures that personhood highlights have followed John Locke in emphasizing a particular sort of mental life as characterizing personhood. Personhood provides a species-neutral way of grouping creatures that have lives that it would be wrong to end by killing or by letting die. These may include animals, machines, extraterrestrials, gods, angels, and devils. All, if they were capable of valuing existence, would, whatever else they were, be persons.

Personhood applied to human individuals implies that the life cycle of a given individual passes through a number of stages of different moral significance. The human individual comes into being before it acquires personhood. This individual will gradually move from being a potential or a pre-person into an actual person when she develops whatever characteristics are thought to be distinctive of personhood. And if, eventually, she permanently loses these characteristics prior to death, she will have ceased to be a person.

Personhood then is an idea used to characterize individuals who have the highest moral importance or value. The term 'respect for persons' encapsulates this 'ultimate' moral importance and attempts to give it content—to explain just what those who accept the moral importance of persons are committed to in concrete terms. Respect for persons understood as a moral principle sets out the ways in which it is appropriate to behave towards those who matter morally in this 'ultimate' sense. Non-persons may, of course, be harmed in other ways; by being caused pain, for example. Respect for persons then not only describes the outcome—treating others in morally appropriate ways—but also points to the origin of this obligation in the ultimate or supreme moral value of particular sorts of individuals. We have examined one account of personhood derived from John Locke, which attempts to connect personhood with value and which gives one account of the wrongfulness of ending the lives of persons and hence one account of the rights and wrongs of abortion. On this account of personhood, abortion is permitted so long as neither the embryo nor the fetus is an individual possessing self-consciousness and an intelligence sufficient to value its own existence.

This account of personhood has a number of disadvantages. The first is that, depending on how the criteria for personhood are interpreted, it can lead to the conclusion that infanticide is permissible, since it is difficult to show relevant differences between the capacities of the late fetus and the newborn. For those who are clear that infanticide is morally impermissible, this will tend to rule out adoption of personhood as a criterion of moral worth. Whether accounts of personhood also permit ending the lives of severely mentally retarded adults will depend on whether the degree of retardation is such as to totally rule out self-consciousness and rudimentary intelligence. There will be few such cases. However, those in a permanent vegetative state (PVS) will have lost their personhood.

Are there other accounts of when a creature is a person?

5. PERSONS EXIST WHEN HUMAN LIFE BEGINS

Many people have thought that the problem of when life becomes morally important, in the ultimate sense that personhood demands, is answered by knowing when life begins. When can human life be said to begin and is it plausible to believe that the life of a person begins simultaneously with human life? Human sperm and eggs are both alive prior to conception, and the egg undergoes a process of maturation without which conception would be impossible. Both sperm and egg are alive and are human, although this does not, of course, mean that either of them individually constitutes 'human life'. The event most popularly taken to mark the starting point of human life is conception. But conception can result in a hydatidiform mole, a cancerous multiplication of cells that will never become a person, and, even when human life does begin at conception, it is not necessarily the life of an individual; twins may form at any point up to approximately fourteen days following conception.

Cloning also has raised problems for our understanding of when life begins. If one has a pre-implantation embryo in the early stages of development when all cells are toti-potent—that is, where any of the cells could become any part of the resulting individual, or indeed the whole individual—and one splits this early cell mass (anything up to the sixty-four-cell stage) into, say, four clumps of cells, each of the four clumps would constitute a new, viable embryo that could be implanted with every hope of successful development into adulthood. Each clump is the clone or identical 'twin' of each of the others and comes into being not through conception but because of the division of the early cell mass. These four clumps of cells can be recombined into one embryo. Thus, without the destruction of a single human cell, one human can be split into four and can be recombined again into one. Did 'life' in such a case begin as an individual, become four individuals, and then turn into a singleton again? All this occurred without the creation of extra matter and without the destruction of a single cell. Those who think that ensoulment, the point at which the divinely sent immortal soul is supposed to enter and animate the body, takes place at conception have an interesting problem to account for the splitting of one soul into four, and for the destruction of three souls when the four embryos are recombined into one, and to account for the destruction of three individuals without a single human cell being removed or killed.

5.1 Speciesism and Natural Kinds

It is possible simply to stipulate that membership of the human species confers moral importance and hence personhood (Warnock 1983). This stipulation of a preference for one kind of creature over another (particularly when this preference is asserted by self-interested individuals on behalf of their own kind) requires justification. Claims in which the moral priority and superiority of 'our own kind' have been asserted on behalf of Greeks at the expense of barbarians, whites over blacks, Nazis over Jews, and men over women have been common and seem of doubtful logic and more doubtful morality. Assertion of the superiority of our own kind, whether defined by species membership, race, gender, nationality, or religion, seems not only unjustified but unjustifiable. What then would support assertion of moral priority for membership of a natural kind?

5.2 Potentiality

How then to distinguish, in some morally significant respect, human embryos from the embryos and indeed the adult members of any other species? One feature of human embryos that members of other species do not share is their potential, not simply to be born and to be human, but to become the sort of complex, intelligent, self-conscious, multifaceted creatures typical of the human species.

There seem to be two problems with potentiality interpreted as the idea that human embryos or fetuses are morally important beings in virtue of their potential. The first is logical: acorns are not oak trees, nor eggs omelettes. It does not follow from the fact that something has potential to become something different that we must treat it always as if it had achieved that potential. We are all potentially dead but it does not follow that we must be treated now as if we are already dead.

The second difficulty with the potentiality argument involves the scope of the potential for personhood. If the human zygote has the potential to become an adult human being and is supposedly morally important in virtue of that potential, then what of the potential to become a zygote? Something has the potential to become a zygote, and whatever has the potential to become the zygote has whatever potential the zygote has. It follows that the unfertilized egg and the sperm also have the potential to become fully functioning adult humans. In addition, it is theoretically possible to stimulate eggs, including human eggs, to divide and develop without fertilization (parthenogenesis). As yet it has not been possible to continue the development process artificially beyond early stages of embryogenesis, but if it ever does become possible, then the single unfertilized egg, without need of sperm or cloning, would itself have the potential of the zygote.

Cloning by nuclear transfer, which involves deleting the nucleus of an unfertilized egg, inserting the nucleus taken from any adult cell, and electrically stimulating the resulting newly created egg to develop, can, in theory, produce a new human. This was the method used to produce the first cloned animal, Dolly the sheep, in 1997. This means that any cell from a normal human body has the potential to become a new 'twin' of that individual. All that is needed is an appropriate environment and appropriate stimulation. The techniques of parthenogenesis and cloning by nuclear substitution mean that conception is no longer the necessary precursor of human beings.

Thus, if the argument from potential is understood to afford protection and moral status to whatever has the potential to grow into a normal adult human being, then potentially every human cell deserves protection.

However, defenders of the argument from potential will claim that this view of potentiality misrepresents their position. John Finnis, for example, has argued that: 'An organic capacity for developing eye-sight is not "the bare fact that something will become" sighted; it is an existing reality, a thoroughly unitary ensemble of dynamically inter-related primordia of, bases and structures for, development'. He concludes that 'there is no sense whatever in which the unfertilized ovum and that sperm constitute one organism, a dynamic unity, identity, whole' (1995: 50).

However, it is surely the case that A has the potential for Z if, when a certain number of things do and do not happen to A (or to A plus N), then A (or A plus N) will become Z. Even a 'unitary ensemble of dynamically inter-related primordia of, bases and structures, for development' must have a certain number of things happen to it and a certain number of things that do not happen to it if its potential is to be actualized. If A is a zygote, it must implant, be nourished, and have a genetic constitution compatible with survival to term and beyond. Moreover, insistence on a 'unitary ensemble', on 'one organism', seems also to apply to cloning by nuclear substitution, surely an embarrassing fact. In any adult cell there is a complete single human genome, which, if treated appropriately, might be cloned. Thus this method of cloning allows for the 'existing reality' of a complete genome that exhibits the 'dynamic unity, identity, whole[ness]' that the Finnis analysis requires and we can therefore now ascribe potentiality in the Finnis sense to the nucleus of every cell in every body.

The moral importance of drawing attention to the potentiality of something suggests that it is actualizing a particular potential that matters. Our moral concern with what it is that has the potential to become an adult human being would be inexplicable if persons or adult humans did not matter. We are interested in the potentiality argument because we are interested in the potential to become a particular, and particularly valuable, sort of thing. If the zygote is important because it has the potential for personhood, and *that* is what makes it a matter of importance to protect and actualize its potential, then whatever has the potential to become a zygote must also be morally significant *for the same reason*. Those who value potentiality for personhood surely do so not because the potential is contained within 'one organism', but because it is the potential to become something the actualization of which has moral importance.

6. THE REJECTION OF ABORTION

Traditionally rejection of abortion has been based on the idea that killing innocent human beings is ethically wrong, and that the fetus obviously falls within the class of innocent human beings. As we have argued above, personhood arguments attempt to show this traditional argument to be false by showing that the wrongness of killing is based in the possession of features that the fetus does not have.

We will now look at the positive arguments that support the traditional view that there is something seriously wrong involved in killing the fetus.

7. RELIGIOUSLY BASED ARGUMENTS

There is a plethora of religiously based arguments that have been deployed in the abortion debate on both sides of the argument. Here we will outline only one of them, the position held by the Catholic Church at present. The reason for choosing this argument is that it has been prominent in the debates about abortion and that it is very often misunderstood and misquoted.

According to Catholic moral theology, certain basic moral truths are available to all human beings through rational deliberation, and to some through divine revelation within the Church. Among these is the idea that killing innocent human beings is wrong. Within the Church the combination of these two sources of moral truth enables moral theologians to see that the killing of innocent human beings is a special case of the killing of any innocent beings in possession of a rational soul (including any non-human beings with this characteristic).

Within the Catholic tradition the question about the wrongness of abortion therefore centres on the question of at what time the embryo or fetus becomes ensouled. The Catholic position is often described to be one of 'immediate ensoulment'—that is, that the soul is present from the time of fertilization, but this is actually not the case.

Another common misconception is that the views of the Pope on this matter have to be followed by all Catholics because the Pope's view is infallible in moral matters. According to Catholic theology, the Pope is infallible only when he declares new dogmas *ex cathedra*. Normal pronouncements of the Pope, even on matters of faith and morals, are not infallible, although they are, of course, seen as important. No Pope has ever spoken *ex cathedra* on the matter of the moral status of the fetus, and it is unlikely that it will ever happen, since the status of the fetus is not something that is likely to give rise to an important dogmatic dispute.

While immediate ensoulment has been defended by some Catholic theologians, the position held by the Church is actually more complicated. Within a rich theological tradition like the Catholic one, a problem very quickly occurs with regard to what one should do in cases of uncertainty, either factual uncertainty or moral uncertainty where *bona fide* moral authorities disagree on what the right analysis or course of action is. In the case of the ensoulment of the fetus, we have both factual and moral uncertainty. Some authorities defend immediate ensoulment, whereas others defend delayed ensoulment, with different views among the latter on when ensoulment actually occurs. In this situation the Church has adopted the position that, because killing is such a grave moral wrong, one should act cautiously and presume that there may be ensoulment from conception. Abortion and the destruction of embryos should therefore be treated as the killing of an ensouled being.

8. A LIFE LIKE OURS

Personhood arguments claim that the wrongness of killing should be dissociated from species membership and membership of any other natural class, and should instead be located in the thwarting of an interest that the individual who is killed possesses. It is, however, possible to develop arguments with a similar structure that leads to the conclusion that killing the fetus is morally wrong.

One such argument has been proposed by Marquis (1989). He suggests that what is wrong with killing adult human beings is that we deprive them of their future, and that this can be further explicated as depriving them of 'a life like ours'. The harm done to someone who is killed is not just that we go against their desire to keep on living (which may conceivably have many different levels of strength and importance, thereby making the magnitude of the wrongness of killing different in each case), but that we deprive them of their whole future, a future that is so multifaceted that it only makes sense to describe it in broad terms like 'a life like ours'. We do, for instance, deprive them not only of the future fulfilment of their present desires, but also of the future formation of new desires and preferences.

This analysis of the wrongness of killing has the great advantage that it can explain why it would be wrong to kill someone who temporarily has no preferences for going on living. It also avoids being speciesist, because it would make it wrong to kill any being or machine having a future sufficiently like the one we have.

On this analysis, the fetus that is killed is deprived of a life like ours in exactly the same way as any other human being who is killed. There may be other wrong-making factors involved in killing adults (for instance, relating to their preferences not to be killed), but the basic wrong-making factor is involved in killing both fetuses and adults. Killing a fetus is, therefore, seriously wrong and the same is *eo ipse* true for abortion. What is wrong in killing the fetus is not that we kill a being with potentiality for attaining the feature that would make it wrong to kill it, but that we kill a being that already has this feature (that is, a future like ours). The future of the fetus is no more logically uncertain or contingent than the future of any other biological individual.

This analysis faces two difficulties. One involves the apparent arbitrariness of the stipulation of a future 'like mine'. We can imagine the future of persons from other planets—brainy fish, for example—being very unlike 'mine' but morally important in ways we could recognize. One way out is to attach importance to the content of the future that then becomes the person-making feature or to make personhood turn not on the character of the future but on the present capacity to want to experience it. A second difficulty may be to stop this argument collapsing into a form of the potentiality argument in that a given unfertilized egg and a sperm (or even the nucleus of one of my own cells) may also be said to have 'a future like mine', a future that would include fertilization or cell nuclear substitution (cloning) as one of its events (see the discussion of this above).

9. BECOMING A PERSON

A certain puzzle seems to be inherent in the idea that I at some point in my biological life become a person, and then at some later point before my death may again become a non-person. The puzzle is the following. There seems to be no doubt that I am presently both a biological being and a person, and it would be difficult to argue that only one of these is essential to who I am. In a computer it may be possible to separate hardware and software, but in human beings and all other biological beings the two aspects of me seem to be inextricably and necessarily linked. However, if any personhood view is correct, then we can trace my biological identity as an individual further back in time than we can trace my personal identity. But if 'person' is part of what I essentially am, this is a peculiar result, because it would mean that the two sortals—both describing what I essentially am: that is, 'Peter Jones (biological individual)' and 'Peter Jones (person)'—would have a different analysis. The first would be a substance sortal, whereas the second would be a phase sortal (like 'child' or 'adult'). This problem can be resolved in three ways: (1) by denying that I am essentially a biological being, (2) by denying that I am essentially a person, or (3) by admitting that both sortals must be of the same type. Of these options only the third is attractive, and, since there is no doubt that 'Peter Jones (biological individual)' is a substance sortal, this entails that 'Peter Jones (person)' must also be a substance sortal—that is, that, if I am now essentially a person, then I must have been a person for as long as I have been a biological individual.

Against this it can be argued that I cannot have a biological identity and a personal identity. If I am essentially a person, I cannot also be essentially a living organism; if I am essentially a living organism, I cannot also be a person, unless 'person' is a phase sortal.

There are a number of other arguments aimed at showing that the idea that we become persons at some point in our biological life creates inconsistencies. Many of these are discussed by Lee (1996).

10. PARENTAL RIGHTS

Entitlement to abortion is often thought to be a derivative of rights possessed by adults, usually the mother. There are a number of candidate rights here, which would include 'a woman's right to choose', the right to control one's own body and what happens in and to it, the right to control reproduction (Dworkin 1993; Robertson 1994), the right to self-defence, and the right to autonomous control of one's life.

A first thing to notice is that all of these rights are limited by the requirement that they be generalizable, that they are compatible with a similar right or rights for all others. If the embryo or fetus is one of those others, then all of these other rights have to compete with similar rights claimed by or on behalf of the fetus. Thus the question of parental rights can arise only in a form that would readily permit abortion once the prior question of the moral status of the fetus has been settled. If the fetus has the same moral status as the mother, then their rights are in competition, and where they are incompatible one with another, some fair method of choosing between them must be found. Just as, for example, a woman's right to control her own body might involve ejecting the fetus, so the like right possessed by the fetus might involve retaining possession of the mother's body until birth.

A possible exception here might be the right to self-defence, famously invoked by Judith Jarvis Thomson (1971). Thomson suggested that the mother was entitled to view her fetus as a wrongful trespasser, which, in virtue either of her right of self-ownership or her right of self-defence, could legitimately and consistently with justice be ejected from her body. She asks us to imagine that you wake up in the morning and find yourself back to back in bed with an unconscious famous violinist. He has been found to have a fatal kidney ailment, and the Society of Music Lovers has canvassed all the available medical records and found that you alone have the right blood type. Now to save his life you have to remain plugged in. If you unplug him he will die. Thomson suggests that you may unplug him.

However, the plausibility of Thomson's suggestions depends upon acceptance of a highly individualistic interpretation of such rights. For most people, even a right to self-defence requires proportionality of force. The fetus is, after all, an innocent threat, and there is only a relatively small chance that it constitutes a life-endangering threat. It is far from clear that a right to defend oneself from temporary trespassers extends to killing them.

This raises a further interesting question about the scope of the right to an abortion if such a right exists. Is it a right to kill the fetus or simply a right to eject it from one's body? In the case of most pregnancies this amounts to the same thing, for until around 23–24 weeks the fetus will not be viable outside the womb. But this non-viability is contingent on technology and we may see further reductions in the age of viability. Where fetuses might survive alive outside the body, does the right to abortion extend to a right to pursue the fetus into the world and ensure that it does not survive? Most of the rights-based arguments we have considered, like the right to control one's own body, would seem to embrace only a right to eject the fetus and not a right to kill it (see below).

One newly fledged right might yield a different conclusion. That is the right that is sometimes claimed to control the destiny of one's genes. Such a right if it can be sustained might embrace abortion, but such a right is highly problematic and is unlikely to have the requisite force. For example, it is sometimes invoked in defence of reproductive autonomy (Dworkin 1993; Robertson 1994), but if it includes the right to have children it must also constrain the right of those children to reproduce, for my daughter, in exercising the right to pass on her genes, will also pass on mine. A right that is extinguished by my daughter's right to reproduce is unlikely to justify my choice to extinguish my daughter's life.

10.1 Father's Rights

Although fathers have often claimed the right to control the reproductive destiny of their sexual partners, it seems unlikely that any such claim either to insist on or to prevent an abortion has any ultimate force. The claim by a father to prevent an abortion could be sustained only by demonstrating that an abortion was unacceptably immoral. Such a claim, if it could be sustained, would not be peculiar to fathers but could be made by any third party. If, on the other hand, it is a claim by a father to procure an abortion against the will of the mother, this would involve an assault on the mother's bodily integrity at least equivalent to rape and is unlikely to be sustainable in law or ethics. This is not, of course, to say that fathers do not have an *interest* in the fetus to which they have contributed twenty-three sets of chromosomes. The question is what is the ultimate force of this interest? We will leave aside the question of the possibility of non-paternity—that is, the possibility that the man who thinks he is the genetic father of a fetus *en ventre sa mère* is not in fact its genetic father—and look at the clearest case of a father's claims. Suppose a pregnancy has arisen from a clear agreement between a man and a woman to have a child together and that subsequently the women decides to renege on the agreement and to have an abortion. Certainly the father has an interest and even a quasi-contractual claim against the mother. However, to enforce the claim in the sense of compelling the mother to forgo her termination and give birth is surely out of the question. There are a number of reasons for this. Giving birth is almost always more risky to the mother's health than termination of pregnancy. It is doubtful whether any moral claim by a man that involved subjecting a woman to involuntary risks to her health could succeed. Moreover, for the claim to succeed against the mother's will we would have to accept the denial of very basic rights to physical integrity for the mother. This is not to say that fathers may not be entitled to some form of compensation when such agreements are broken, but this is a long way from suggesting that they have enforceable moral rights.

11. SPECIAL ETHICAL PROBLEMS IN LATE ABORTION?

In the debate about abortion it is often claimed that late abortions are more ethically problematic than early abortions, and in this section we want to consider the arguments supporting such a view.

The arguments fall into three major categories focusing on:

- increased risk to the pregnant woman;
- developing features of the fetus;
- developing relation between the fetus and others.

The first category of arguments is uncontroversial, but with limited scope. It simply states that, because the medical risks to the pregnant woman of an abortion increases with the length of gestation, early abortions are preferable to late abortions from both a technical and an ethical point of view. If the woman accepts the increased risk, it is unlikely that this line of argument could override that consent and make late abortion ethically prohibited.

Arguments based on features that the fetus develops during the pregnancy are usually based on either (1) sentience, or (2) viability. We will look at these in turn.

11.1 Sentience

It is generally accepted that the human fetus becomes sentient some time during pregnancy and that one of the abilities that develop is the ability to feel pain. There is disagreement about exactly when sentience and the ability to feel pain develops, but this does not affect the basic structure of the arguments based on sentience, but only exactly when they become valid.

The simplest argument based on sentience is the argument that inflicting pain on any kind of being is a morally bad thing to do, and that methods of abortion that create fetal pain are therefore morally problematic. This would rule out pain-producing methods of abortion after the development of fetal sentience, at least if it is the case that alternative methods are available that do not entail increased risk to the mother. If the only painless methods of abortion do entail increased risks for the mother, we would then have to balance these against the fetal pain produced by the standard methods of abortion.

A more complex sentience-based argument relies on the idea that personal identity is based on psychological continuity between successive stages of the same person. If this is accepted, it can then be argued that, although I am not personally identical to the early embryo, I am personally identical to the late-stage fetus, because its mental experiences have contributed to forming my present psychology, and that there is no discernible break between those early experiences (even though I may not be able to remember them) and my present mental life. If I am personally identical with the late-stage fetus, it must then follow that I was already a person at that time, and that I already possessed the rights that persons possess.

A third sentience-based argument draws an analogy between brain death and brain life and argues that the beginning of human personal life begins with the beginning of significant brain function. If I have died when my brain has died, it seems to make sense to say that I have started to live when my brain has started to live as a brain. This argument has been put forward by Kluge (1978) and by Lockwood (1985). The problem with the argument is that 'brain death', although almost universally accepted as a criterion of death, seems less acceptable as a criterion of loss of moral status, since many believe moral status to be lost without brain death. Moreover, brain death and for that matter brain birth seem important because the brain is required to support some capacities that are deemed morally relevant. If we identify these capacities, we might have reason to suppose that they develop at some point after the development of the brain and may be lost some time before the brain dies, just as legs are required by humans for running but humans have legs before they can run, and may cease to be able to run while still retaining these limbs.

11.2 Viability

A human fetus becomes viable outside the womb of the pregnant woman a considerable time before birth, as evidenced by our success in keeping pre-term babies alive in neonatal intensive care units from about 23–24 weeks into gestation. It has been argued that abortion becomes morally impermissible after viability.

The basic structure of the viability argument is the following, although each proponent of this argument has his own favoured variations.

1. The argument for abortion is an argument leading to the conclusion that a woman has a right to have her pregnancy terminated.
2. After viability the pregnancy can be terminated without killing the fetus either directly or indirectly by expelling it from the uterus in a non-viable state.
3. The woman has no independent rights to have the fetus killed.
4. Therefore: after viability there is no right to have the pregnancy terminated in a way that results in the killing of the fetus.

This argument has force only if premises 1 and 3 are accepted, and these are resisted by some proponents of abortion who base their arguments for abortion on the personhood analysis discussed above.

One difficulty with the viability argument is that the fetal age where viability is attained depends on the technological development in neonatal intensive care. This means that the ethical status of a given abortion may change according to context. It might be ethically acceptable in a context where there is no access to neonatal care, and ethically unacceptable if there is such access.

11.3 Late Abortion and Social Bonding

The third category of arguments concerning late abortions relies on the idea that our moral obligations towards other individuals depend not only on their attributes but also on our relationship to them. This type of argument is related to an analysis of personhood and personal continuity that claims that personhood is, at least partially, constructed through the narratives we tell about persons (including their own self-narrative). Many of the things that I as a person believe about myself and that shape my life I only know through what I have been told by others, and from the reactions I experience in others to my actions and my telling of my own narrative. Personhood, personal identity, and moral status are, therefore, based not on some property or capacity of my body or my mental life, but on the personal narrative that I co-construct with others.

The core premise of the argument linking this narrative understanding of personhood to the ethics of abortion is that during pregnancy the fetus gradually becomes part of our social networks and obtains the beginnings of a specific personal narrative, and that this creates obligations on our part (and later may create obligations on the part of the present fetus towards the gestational mother).

12. ABORTION JUSTIFIED IN TERMS OF FEATURES OF THE FETUS

There is a persistent strand of thinking about abortion that locates the justification in terms of features of the fetus—particularly fetal abnormality or the presence of adverse genetic conditions. Much legislation on abortion specifically provides for abortion where there is evidence of fetal abnormality (e.g. United Kingdom Human Fertilization and Embryology Act 1990). While it is true that such considerations often constitute the reasons people have for opting for a termination of pregnancy, it is difficult to see how they could operate as justifications for abortion unless they are such as to change the moral status of the fetus.

12.1 Pre-natal Genetic Diagnosis

The question 'what reproductive choices would be legitimate and which, if any, reproductive choices would be wrongful?' is perhaps more helpful than the question 'what degree of fetal abnormality would justify abortion'. To see why this is so we should consider pre-implantation genetic diagnosis (PIGD). Suppose a woman has six pre-implantation embryos *in vitro* awaiting implantation. PIGD has revealed that three have various genetic disorders and three seem healthy. Which should she implant? Does she have any moral reasons to avoid implanting those with genetic disorders? Notice two features of this case. Few would judge women to be under any moral or any legal obligation to implant any embryos. The decision to implant some or none is entirely within her unfettered discretion. She does not have to offer legal, moral, or any other justifications to anyone if she decides to implant none of the embryos. Under English Law, for example, she may implant only up to three without a special medical reason for implanting more. Which three should she implant? Can she say: 'It is a matter of moral indifference whether or not my resulting child has a genetic disorder and therefore *I* have no reason to select the healthy embryos.' This seems implausible. Since none of the embryos has a right or an entitlement to be chosen rather than the others, since none is a person, nor yet a moral agent, and none has begun the sort of biographical life that would give it interests, her choice is relatively free. She has a reason to do what she can to ensure that the individual she chooses is as good an individual as she can make it. She has a reason therefore to choose the embryo that is not already harmed in any particular way and that will have the best possible chance of a long and healthy life and the best possible chance of contributing positively to the world it will inhabit.

If, on the other hand, she chooses to implant an individual destined to suffer an illness, she will have created that illness and any harm that it will do. This woman has the same reason to select against an embryo with a genetic disease as her sister who is told that, if she conceives immediately, she will have a child with a genetic defect, but that if she postpones pregnancy and takes a course of treatment she will have a healthy child (Parfit 1984: 366 ff.).

12.2 Unfair Discrimination against the Disabled

It is sometimes claimed that to choose not to have a child because of some adverse feature that will affect it is not only unfair discrimination against that particular feature but may also be self-defeating in terms of other values that we hold. Here the famous 'aborting Beethoven' fallacy (Harris 1992: 179) is often invoked. We are asked whether it would be reasonable to abort a child because it was congenitally deaf and if we agree we are triumphantly told that we have just aborted Beethoven. However, it is as senseless to think that aborting any particular deaf child would involve the non-existence of Beethoven as it would be to celebrate the fact that, by practising contraception, we have just prevented the birth of a Hitler.

If abortions occur, we know that as a result both healthy fetuses and some with genetic diseases will never become persons. That does not mean that we deprive society of people like Einstein or Gandhi, nor does it mean that we pre-empt the existence of a Hitler or a Bin Laden, nor does it mean that we discriminate against such people nor against people like them.

12.3 Choosing who shall Exist

Choosing between existing people for whatever reason always involves the possibility of unfair discrimination because there will, inevitably, be people who are disadvantaged by the choice. Choosing which sorts of people to bring into existence or choosing which embryos or fetuses to allow to become persons can never have this effect because there is no one who suffers adversely from the choice.

Readers should consider the question of whether their own parents were under any obligation to attempt to conceive in any particular month. If they had conceived in any month other than the one in which the reader was conceived, he or she would never have existed.

Suppose your parents had been told that by postponing pregnancy and changing their diet they would probably have a much healthier and longer-lived child. Had they done so you would never have existed but would you have had any ground for complaint? Would that have constituted discrimination against people with your genetic condition. It is surely a fallacy to think that choosing between pre-implantation embryos or choosing to terminate pregnancies of embryos because other embryos would have a better chance in life constitutes unfair discrimination.

13. ENHANCEMENTS

Consider again not the issue of disabilities or impairments but rather the issue of enhancements. Suppose some embryos had a genetic condition that conferred complete immunity to many major diseases—HIV/AIDS, cancer, and heart disease, for example, coupled with increased longevity. Any parent would surely have moral reasons to prefer to implant such embryos given the opportunity of choice. But such a decision would not imply that normal embryos had lives that were not worth living or were of poor or problematic quality. If I would prefer to confer these advantages on any future children that I may have, I am not implying that people like me, constituted as they are, have lives that are not worth living or that are of poor quality.

Most disabilities fall far short of the high standard of awfulness required to judge a life to be not worth living. This is why we must distinguish between having moral reasons for avoiding producing new disabled individuals and the question of enforcement, regulation, or prevention of the birth of such individuals.

13.1 The Moral Reasons We Have to Avoid Harm

There is continuum between harms and benefits such that the reasons we have to avoid harming others or creating others who will be unnecessarily harmed are continuous with the reasons we have for conferring benefits on others if we can. In short, to decide to withhold a benefit is in a sense to harm the individual we decline to benefit. We have reasons for declining to create or confer even trivial harms, and we have reasons to confer and not withhold even small benefits. But to say that it would, other things being equal, be better not to create an individual who will suffer an unnecessary harm is not to say that it would be better for that individual had he or she never been born, nor is it to say that the world would have been a better place had he or she never been born, nor is it to say that individuals with disabilities are somehow less valuable or lesser persons than others.

13.2 Gender Selection

Infanticide has been practised as a method of gender selection for millennia. Abortion has been added to the methods of gender selection, since it has been possible to determine gender *in utero* since the 1960s. For some the ethics of gender selection are a function of the methods chosen, for others gender selection is always wrong. The ethics of gender selection are beyond our purview here (Harris 1998). What can be said is that, while abortion seems a costly and inefficient method of achieving this end, it will be ethical if abortion is permissible for a number of the reasons considered above, if, for example, the moral status of the embryo or fetus is such as to permit it, or if abortion is legitimate because it is a dimension of the rights or autonomy of the mother.

14. ABORTION, SOCIAL CONSEQUENCES, AND LEGALIZATION

A very frequent argument in the abortion debate claims that, although all (or most) abortions are ethically wrong, all things considered they should nevertheless not be legally prohibited.

The relation between the ethical wrongness of an act and its legal prohibition is not straightforward. It is a problem that has vexed political philosophers for many years, and an in-depth analysis is outside the scope of this chapter. It is, however, important to note that ethical wrongness is not in and of itself a sufficient reason for legal prohibition in all circumstances. It can, for instance, be ethically wrong in many situations to tell people the truth about themselves, but this does not seem to be sufficient to try to draft legislation prohibiting this specific class of truth-telling actions.

In general the arguments for not legally prohibiting an ethically bad type of action fall into three categories: (1) it is impossible to draft legal rules that accurately delineate the problematic acts from acts that are not problematic, (2) it is impossible to police the resultant legislation, either because it is very difficult or because the intrusions in private life necessary for policing the legal rules far outweigh the good to be gained, or (3) the prohibition will have such serious side effects that allowing the problematic act is on balance preferable.

The arguments trying to disassociate the ethical wrongness of abortion (assumed for the sake of argument to be firmly established) and its legal prohibition generally point to the bad effects of not allowing abortions as the justification for not prohibiting it.

The alleged bad effects if abortion is not permitted are (1) a large number of back-street abortions with consequent threat to the life or welfare of the mother and (2) a negative effect on the status of women and their opportunities to participate fully in society.

14.1 Back-Street Abortions

Historically there seems to be no doubt that abortions do take place in large numbers in societies where abortion is prohibited, and that this causes great suffering to women because these abortions are carried out in unsuitable conditions by unqualified persons. Some women are killed by botched abortions and many more are permanently damaged in various ways.

It is, on the other hand, evident that, when abortion is legalized (especially if it is legalized as 'abortion on demand'), the number of abortions increases substantially. This creates a problem for the first type of argument based on the bad effects of prohibiting abortion. If a large increase in the number of abortions is acceptable to avoid the suffering to women caused by the prohibition of abortions, then abortion cannot be very wrong. But the argument is usually put forward by people who argue that abortion is seriously wrong, and they thereby seem to involve themselves in inconsistency.

14.2 The Status of Women in Society

A different argument for the dissociation between the ethical and the legal status of abortion is based on the more general effects of preventing women from controlling their reproduction. If the participation of women as equals in all aspects of society is an important good, then any law or social custom that makes such participation more difficult is prima facie problematic. The question then becomes one of balancing the bad of abortion against the good of equal participation. In this balancing it seems to be the case that, if abortion is a serious moral wrong, then the absence of a legal right to abortion would have to have a marked influence on women's opportunities to participate in society. It would furthermore have to have this effect, even if other means of reproductive control like contraception are freely available.

14.3 The Role of the Medical Profession

Any legal regulation of abortion must explicitly or implicitly deal with the role of the medical profession, since it is usually members of this profession who perform legal abortions. Should there be a conscience clause allowing persons with ethical objections to performing abortions to opt out, and how wide should the scope of this conscience clause be?

This is, again, a difficult question, involving both ethics and political philosophy, which we are unable to analyse in full within the scope of this chapter.

One point is nevertheless worth noting. Most (or perhaps all?) conscience clauses allow doctors and other health-care professionals to opt out of any direct involvement in abortions, but do at the same time require them to refer the patient to a colleague who is willing to perform the abortion. This requirement is clearly inconsistent. If the reason for allowing persons to opt out is that it is wrong to force someone to perform acts they believe to be seriously ethically wrong, it might seem inconsistent to force them to be causal agents in a chain of events leading to the performance of the act in question. However, this inconsistency can be resolved by only requiring doctors with moral objections to abortions to tell the patients of their entitlement to go elsewhere for advice, but not requiring them to give any specific advice concerning where to go.

A more radical solution to the problem of conscience clauses is to remove the whole area of abortion provision from the medical field. Early abortions are not technically difficult to perform, and the requirements for performing them safely and effectively have more to do with manual skill and training than with medical knowledge. We can, therefore, easily imagine 'abortion by philosopher' as an option—that is, a system where philosophers convinced by the personhood analysis or by Judith Jarvis Thomson's arguments outlined above are given the necessary training in abortion techniques and allowed to perform abortions according to their philosophical convictions.

15. The State of the Debate

Although the ethics of abortion remains one of the problems that most divides societies, the arguments for and against are well rehearsed and understood and there seems little room for new and convincing arguments on either side. Although opponents of abortion often see killing embryos as a form of murder and proponents view anti-abortionists as committed not only to enslaving women but as opponents of basic public-health measures that save many lives, both pro- and anti-abortionists are usually otherwise good citizens and highly moral beings. In such circumstances, where basically decent, moral people disagree and where there are no compelling or clearly decisive arguments on either side, the requirements of tolerance should surely prevail. This means that neither side should seek to impose its position on the other. No one who has conscientious objections to abortion should be forced either to have an abortion or to assist or support the abortion process. Equally no one who sees abortion as unproblematic should be denied access to abortion nor should he seek to impose his views on others.

References

Callahan, D. (1972). *Abortion: Law, Choice and Morality*. New York: Macmillan.

Dworkin, R. (1993). *Life's Dominion*. London: HarperCollins.

Engelhardt, H. T. (1986). *The Foundations of Bioethics*. New York: Oxford University Press.

Finnis, J. (1995*a*). 'A Philosophical Case against Euthanasia', in J. Keown (ed.), *Euthanasia Examined: Ethical Clinical and Legal Perspectives*. Cambridge: Cambridge University Press, 23–36.

——(1995*b*). 'The Fragile Case for Euthanasia: A Reply to John Harris', in J. Keown (ed.), Euthanasia Examined: Ethical Clinical and Legal Perspectives. Cambridge: Cambridge University Press, 46–56.

Fletcher, J. (1966). *Situation Ethics*. London: SCM Press Ltd.

——(1972). 'Indicators of Humanhood: A Tentative Profile of Man'. *Hastings Center Report*, 215: 1–4.

Glover, J. (1977). *Causing Death and Saving Lives*. Harmondsworth: Penguin.

Gustafson, J. M. (1975). *The Contributions of Theology to Medical Ethics*. Wisconsin: Marquette University Press.

Harris, J. (1980). *Violence and Responsibility*. London: Routledge & Kegan Paul.

——(1985). *The Value of Life*. London: Routledge & Kegan Paul.

——(1992) *Wonderwoman and Superman*. Oxford: Oxford University Press.

——(1998). 'Rights and Reproductive Choice', in J. Harris and S. Holm (eds.), *The Future of Human Reproduction*. Oxford: Oxford University Press.

Holm, S. (1996). 'The Moral Status of the Pre-Personal Human Being—the Argument from Potential Reconsidered', in D. Evans (ed.), *Conceiving the Embryo*. Dordrecht: Kluwer, 193–220.

Kluge, E.-H. W. (1978). 'Infanticide as the Murder of Persons', in M. Kohl (ed.), *Infanticide and the Value of Life*. Buffalo, NY: Prometheus.

Lee, P. (1996). *Abortion and Unborn Human Life*. Washington: Catholic University of America Press.

Locke, J. (1690/1964). *Essay Concerning Human Understanding*, ed. A. S. Pringle-Pattison. Oxford: Clarendon Press.

Lockwood, M. (1985). 'When does Life Begin', in M. Lockwood (ed.), Moral Dilemmas in Modern Medicine. New York: Oxford University Press, 9–31.

——(1988). 'Warnock versus Powell (and Harradine); When does Potentiality Count?' *Bioethics*, 2: 187–213.

McCormick, R. A. (1981). *How Brave a New World?* London: SCM Press.

Marquis, D. (1989). 'Why Abortion is Immoral'. *Journal of Philosophy*, 86: 183–202.

Parfit, D. (1984). *Reasons and Persons*. Oxford: Oxford University Press.

Plato (1994). *Plato: The Collected Dialogues Including the Letters*, ed. E. Hamilton and H. Cairns. 15th Printing. Princeton: Princeton University Press.

Ramsey, P. (1970). *Fabricated Man*. New Haven: Yale University Press.

——(1978). *Ethics at the Edges of Life*. New Haven: Yale University Press.

Robertson, J. A. (1994). *Children of Choice*. Princeton: Princeton University Press.

Singer, P. (1979). *Practical Ethics*. Cambridge: Cambridge University Press.

Thomson, J. J. (1971). 'A Defence of Abortion'. *Philosophy and Public Affairs*, 1/1 (Fall), 47–66.

Tooley, M. (1985). *Abortion and Infanticide*. Oxford: Oxford University Press.

——(1998). 'Personhood', in H. Kuhse and P. Singer (eds.), *A Companion to Bioethics*. Oxford: Blackwell, 117–27.

Warnock, Mary (1983). 'In Vitro Fertilization: The Ethical Issues'. *Philosophical Quarterly*, 33: 241.

Warren, M. A. (1973). 'On the Moral and Legal Status of Abortion'. *Monist*, 57/1: 43–61.

——(1997). *Moral Status: Obligations to Persons and Other Living Things*. Oxford: Oxford University Press.

Case Cited

Roe v. *Wade*, 410 US 113 (1973).

CHAPTER 6

REPRODUCTIVE TECHNOLOGY

ROBERT WACHBROIT

DAVID WASSERMAN

1. INTRODUCTION

THE last three decades of the twentieth century witnessed remarkable advances in reproductive technologies. One of the most striking of these developments was the successful *in vitro* fertilization (IVF) that took place in England in the late 1970s. IVF is a procedure where an egg is removed from the woman's ovaries and placed in a Petri dish with semen. The resulting fertilized egg is then inserted into the woman's uterus, where, it is hoped, the egg will be implanted and lead to a successful pregnancy. While the overall success rate for this procedure remained less than 25 per cent at the end of the century (Centers for Disease Control and Prevention, Division of Reproductive Health, 2001), these techniques for manipulating eggs and sperm—that is, gametes—outside the body led to other reproductive possibilities: not only the option of reinserting the egg into the uterus of the woman who produced the egg, but also the option of inserting it into the uterus of a different woman. This use of 'surrogate mothers' received much attention during the 1980s. Alternatively, the egg to be implanted in the prospective mother could be taken from a different women, or could be fertilized by a man other than the prospective father.

IVF has since been supplemented by a number of other techniques for increasing the probability of successful conception and gestation. But it can be seen as the culmination of decades of efforts to isolate the distinct functions involved in human reproduction, in order to 'fix' or supersede those functions that were not working. The primary goal of these technologies was to assist married couples who could not have children *on* their own to have children *of* their own. But the social impact of these technologies went well beyond their original purpose. In separating the biological contributions to making a child, they raised questions about the claims of contributing 'third parties' to that child, and, more broadly, about the meaning and significance of biological connections. Moreover, by allowing early embryos to survive outside a woman's body, they drove a wedge between the issues of women's autonomy that had dominated the abortion debate and the issues about the moral status of the embryo that had always lurked in the background, throwing the latter issues into sharp relief.

Finally, these advances in reproductive technology have begun to converge with a series of developments in genetic technology, which make it feasible to predict, and perhaps eventually to alter, some of the disease propensities and other characteristics of the fetus. By isolating early embryos from the wombs in which they might gestate, and by allowing indefinite delay in the gestational process, IVF provided the new technologies for genetic diagnosis and manipulation with a far more extensive foothold than they would otherwise have had. These emerging genetic technologies have further complicated issues about the role of biological contributions in creating social and legal responsibilities.

The advent of reproductive technologies in the last third of the twentieth century thus raised or sharpened a wide range of ethical and philosophical issues, from parental rights and autonomy to children's rights, from the nature of the family to the basis of personal identity, from the impact of disease and disability on individuals and society to the promise and threat of genetic enhancement. In this chapter, we will focus exclusively on these ethical and philosophical issues. Because of space limitations, we will have little to say directly about the important, unresolved legal, social, and policy issues raised by these new technologies, from their role in reducing the disparities between the legal treatment of adoption and 'unassisted' reproduction, to their role in liberating or oppressing women. Many writers, including the present ones, have addressed these issues at length (e.g. Corea 1985; Andrews 1989; Katz-Rothman 1989; Wasserman and Wachbroit 1992; Charo 1994; Blank 1995; Callahan 1995; Harris and Holm 1998; New York State Task Force on Life and the Law 1998; Donchin and Purdy 1999), and their writings should be consulted as a complement to the more theoretical analysis we undertake here.

In order to impose some organization on the ethical and philosophical issues associated with reproductive technology, we can divide them into four groups.

One group consists of those issues that arise with any new medical technology—that is, issues about the risks created by the technology. In the case of reproductive technologies, identifying who is at risk will depend upon the specific technology: often it will be the mother, especially if she has to undergo a surgical procedure or a high-dose regimen of hormone treatment, but sometimes it will be the child, especially if the technology can cause mutations. What is an acceptable level of risk and who should make this decision? This question can be particularly difficult, because the desire of some people to have a biologically related child is so powerful, and thus the benefit of the technology so great, that those benefits appear to justify an undertaking with a very high level of risk.

A second group of issues is presented by reproductive technologies that require third parties to be directly involved in the biological creation or development of the child. Surrogacy is a good illustration of this type of technology. Although a couple might be able to create a fertilized egg without technological assistance, the woman may not be able to bring that egg to term in her womb. Rather than giving up on the pregnancy, the couple could utilize technology to transfer the fertilized egg to the womb of another woman who is able to bring it to term. If the second woman succeeds in bringing the egg to term, we might ask whether the mother of the child is the one who produced the egg or the one who carried and gave birth to the child. Does surrogacy, especially if it is contractual or commercial, treat babies as commodities and so undermine some of the values informing the parent–child relationship (Murray 1996)? In sum, this second group of issues centres around the meaning of, and the risks to, family integrity, the importance of different biological contributions to parental rights and responsibilities, and the threat of commodification brought about by involving third parties in the making of babies.

A third group consists of issues that arise when reproductive technologies generate 'surplus' reproductive material—for example, sperm, eggs, embryos. For example, because of the low success rate of IVF, the typical procedure is to make the woman superovulate so as to produce a large number of eggs. These are then fertilized via IVF and inserted in the womb, only some at a time, until a successful implantation occurs. What should be done with the remaining fertilized eggs, assuming the couple does not want any more children? How we answer this question will depend in part on what we believe is the moral status of such material. If it is the moral equivalent of blood and hair, then disposing of it would seem to raise no special issues. But if the material—for example, a surplus embryo—has the moral status of a person, then destroying it will be subject to many of the same objections as abortion. If destroying an embryo that is residing in a womb is morally objectionable, then it is unclear how destroying an embryo that is residing in a laboratory container is less so, unless the embryo's moral status depends not only on its genetic constitution but on its involvement in the gestational process (e.g. Sen. Orrin Hatch, quoted in Brody 2001; Barbara Katz-Rothman, quoted in Angier 2001: D6). Comparable concerns arise even if disposal does not mean (immediate) destruction. Can such material be sold or experimented upon? Moreover, who should decide upon this matter? When the embryo resides in the womb, the woman's preferences or desires are given much greater weight than the man's. But if the embryo is no longer physically attached to the woman, is her authority to decide on the disposition of the embryo any greater than that of the man's? Is it any greater than her authority over other discarded biological material, such as hair or skin?

Finally, a fourth group of issues arise from technologies that enable a couple to have, or avoid having, a particular kind of child. Couples can learn much about some of the medical problems their offspring might have even before their child is born; and, in some cases, even before conception. These developments have had a profound effect in framing reproductive decisions: couples can decide not only whether to have children but whether to terminate a particular pregnancy. These developments may also lead to techniques for genetic intervention and modification. We may soon have the ability not only to learn about our offspring before they are born but also to make changes in their genes, eliminating the need to terminate a pregnancy because of a problem with the fetus. Although not yet feasible, these techniques hold out the prospect of altering or designing the child—from removing the threat of certain diseases to selecting the colour of its eyes and hair.

Of these groups of issues, the fourth is perhaps the most challenging and complex. Genetic technologies seem to promise an ever-increasing control over the creation of children, altering the nature of reproduction in a fundamental way. The use of genetic diagnosis, therapy, and screening on embryos and gametes may transform, or complete the transformation, of reproduction into manufacture, threatening to eliminate or radically to alter the role of biological parent. In modifying the parental role in the creation of children, these developments also have implications for the second set of issues outlined above, concerning the roles and claims of 'third parties'. Genetic engineering enlarges the roster of biological contributors to the creation of a child—not only those who donate gametes and lend wombs, but those who supply the germ-lines from which the replacement genes are developed. Genetic engineering may also affect the appraisal of the embryo's moral status and identity, adding complexity to the third set of issues outlined above. Instead of a well-defined moment (or brief process) in which a unique entity is formed from the partial combination of two parental genomes, genetic engineering raises the spectre of the ongoing modification of biological material from various sources, making it difficult to say when a new organism comes into being, let alone what moral status it has when it does. For related reasons, genetic engineering will also complicate the first set of issues outlined above. The assessment of risk in reproductive technologies is always difficult when the risk is imposed by action necessary for the very existence of the entity placed at risk. That assessment will become even more complex if we are uncertain when or whether the deliberate modification of the genome creates a new entity or merely modifies an old one.

For these reasons, we will focus our discussion on the fourth group of issues, which arise directly from the convergence of reproductive and genetic technologies (for other discussions of ethical, legal, and policy issues raised by this convergence, see Hildt and Graumann 1999). But we will also explore some important, and related, implications that convergence has for the other three groups of issues: the moral assessment of risks, the involvement of third parties, and the status and disposition of various reproductive materials. In examining these issues, we will distinguish concerns about the products, processes, and reasons involved in the use of new reproductive and genetic technologies, an approach we describe below. First, however, we need to take up an important preliminary matter.

2. The Limitations of Genetics

Before we can examine the issues arising from the convergence of reproductive and genetic technologies, we need to be clear about what genes can and cannot do. The fundamental doctrine of genetics is that, in general, nearly every physical trait (hair colour, body shape, disease susceptibility) and many mental traits (memory capacity, cognitive functioning) of a person are the product of genetic and environmental factors (e.g. Plomin et al. 1997) The major research programme in genetics is identifying which genes (and environmental factors) are linked to which traits. But we are a long way from making this identification in many cases, and we are even further from understanding how these factors yield the traits they do (Schaffner 2001). Consequently, our ability to predict a person's traits on the basis of knowledge about her genetic structure or genome is very modest. In a few cases—single-gene disorders of high penetrance, such as Huntington's disease—we can indeed predict whether an individual will acquire the disease, although we cannot predict when. But in the vast majority of cases, we can at best make only claims of probability, not only because of our ignorance regarding the complex interaction of genes on each other but also because of our ignorance about the effect of various environmental factors.

This view regarding the limitation of genetics is sometimes referred to as the rejection of genetic determinism, a rejection that a person's genes alone determine that person's traits and conditions (Wachbroit 2001). The case of identical twins who have the same genes can offer a vivid illustration: as people who know identical twins can attest, they often have very different personalities and skills; they also have clear differences in certain physical traits, such as fingerprints. These differences are presumably due at least in part to differences in environment or in the stochastic processes of development (e.g. Schaffner 2001).

While we can expect our knowledge and understanding of genetics to improve, we do not yet know which traits or conditions we might be able eventually to predict or manipulate using genetic technologies. Quite probably we will be able to make probabilistic predictions regarding some cancers, but even probabilistic predictions may not be possible for many personality traits.

In sum, apart from rare diseases that can be associated with single-gene abnormalities, the human traits and conditions that most people are interested in—from common diseases to personality traits—cannot be predicted or manipulated simply through the use of genetic technologies. But this does not mean that genetic technology cannot exercise a profound influence on the characteristics of new human beings; it merely means that, for most characteristics worth influencing, it cannot do so by itself, and that we are uncertain how much it can do in conjunction with environmental interventions from other fields—for example, embryology or pedagogy. The hopes and fears raised by human genetic engineering are certainly exaggerated, but that does not mean that they are insignificant.

3. GENETIC TECHNOLOGIES AS REPRODUCTIVE TECHNOLOGIES

There are three different types of technology, much discussed in the literature, with which one might try to have the kind of child one wants—or, more accurately, the child with the kind of genes one wants: genetic engineering, selection technology, and cloning. (An overview of human genetic technologies in the late 1990s can be found in Howard Hughes Medical Institute 1999.)

The most direct approach would be genetic engineering or gene manipulation. For example, a couple could have a genetic test done on their fetus to determine if it had the genes associated with some undesirable condition. If the test were negative, the couple would allow the pregnancy to go to term. But, if the test were positive, the offending genes would be appropriately modified or replaced and then the pregnancy allowed to go to term. (A variation on this approach would be to perform the modification before conception: test the gametes, genetically modify them if necessary, and then allow conception to take place.)

This procedure, while easy to state abstractly, would be enormously difficult to carry out. Not only must the replacement gene be placed on the right chromosome, it must be placed on the right spot on the chromosome. Off by only a few molecules and the result could well be lethal. Furthermore, the gene must be 'turned on' in certain cells and turned off in the others, even though nearly every cell of a person has the same genes. Although the genes affecting hair colour and texture are present in lung cells, they had better be turned off. Such prenatal 'molecular surgery' is largely beyond turn-of-the-century technology, though research in gene replacement technologies is quite active. But even though gene modification is not a current option in reproductive planning, its significance and implications need to be discussed. There is no reason to doubt that gene replacement or modification will become technologically feasible, at least for some genes, at which point its power and promise for affecting the conditions associated with those genes will be overwhelming. Parents will have the option to rid their child of certain diseases or disease suscepti-bilities as well as to ensure the presence of certain other, non-disease traits. Successful prenatal gene replacement will probably affect not only the child but also that child's progeny, since such early modification can easily be transmitted and reproduced in the child's gametes. Of course, as we emphasized in the previous section, we cannot, in 2002, say which conditions this technology could be applied to. Nevertheless, gene modification and replacement as a reproductive technology raise some of the most difficult questions about what limits there should be on the choices parents can make about what kind of children they have (see Robertson 1994).

While gene modification technology lies in the future, there are other procedures that may be used to achieve similar results in a far cruder way. One such procedure is selection. The couple has the appropriate genetic test performed on the fetus. If the test reveals the desired result, the pregnancy is brought to term; if not, the pregnancy is terminated and the couple tries again. The hope, of course, is that, the next time the couple conceives, the results will have the correct genes. For example, suppose a couple learns that one of them has a family history of Duchenne Muscular Dystrophy (DMD)—a disease that usually begins at 3–5 years of age, involving muscle weakness, inability to walk, and death by the second or third decade. Suppose they do not want to give birth to a child with that disease. They can proceed to have the fetus tested, and, if the test is positive, terminate the pregnancy. If one of the prospective parents has the gene associated with that disease, then there is a 50 per cent probability that a male child will have the disease and no chance that a female child will. Thus, the cou-ple has at least a 75 per cent chance of conceiving a child without DMD next time.

A variation on this procedure uses it in conjunction with IVF. Since in IVF the woman is superovulated, so that she can produce a large number of eggs for the technicians to work with, the selection procedure can be done all at once on the set of fertilized eggs. After discarding those that test positively, the others can be inserted in the womb, one by one, until a successful implantation occurs. Eventually, it may be possible to do such screening on the couple's gametes, so that none of the embryos produced will have the offending genes.

A procedure different from either selection or gene modification is nuclear trans-plantation—commonly called 'cloning'. Cloning can be seen as lying between genetic engineering and selection in the degree of control over reproduction it con-fers. But, unlike selection, cloning is not yet technologically feasible in humans, although it has been successfully performed in some mammals and it may prove eventually to be less technically challenging than gene replacement or modification. The procedure consists of removing the nucleus of an egg cell and replacing it with the nucleus from an adult cell. The resulting cell, if successfully implanted in a womb and brought to term, will be a child with the same genetic make-up as the adult who provided the cell nucleus. The child is in effect a delayed identical twin of the adult. This is not selection for a particular trait or condition or replacing a few genes; cloning is the replication of the entire genetic package.

Although less powerful than gene replacement, human cloning has captured many people's imagination ever since the announcement of the successful cloning of a sheep. Part of the reason for this may be that some people believed that actual human cloning was imminent. Part of the reason may also be that the mere prospect of human cloning vividly conveys some of what genetic technology could do. Thus, although many of the issues concerning human cloning could be subsumed under the topic of gene replacement technology, many commentators give it a separate discussion (e.g. Winters 1998; MacKinnon 2000).

4. ASSESSING TECHNOLOGIES

It is helpful to assess the concerns raised by new reproductive and genetic technologies under three general rubrics: product, process, and reasons. For example, with regard to genetic engineering and cloning, we can wonder about the *product* of the technology: is there something wrong with genetically modified or cloned humans, or with the existence of significant numbers of such humans? We can wonder about the *process* of the technology: even if there is nothing problematic about the fruits of this technology, is there something unacceptable about the process itself? Is it wrong to use technology to get a particular kind of child? Finally, we can wonder about the *reasons* or *motives* that someone would have for employing the new reproductive technologies: is there something suspect or objectionable in the reasons that some might have for using technology in order to have a particular kind of child?

Of course, these concerns are not entirely independent of each other. Someone might judge a process on the basis of its product, or on the basis of the motives that support or are supported by it. Or we might assess reasons in the light of the processes a person is willing to employ in their service. Nevertheless, for our purposes, it is useful to keep the exposition of these three concerns separate since it helps to clarify what is at stake in various arguments about new reproductive and genetic technologies.

All three of these questions were raised by IVF. The product of IVF—the successfully gestated child—turned out to be indistinguishable from children produced by standard *in-vivo* fertilization. Nothing but her (pre)-history distinguished Mary Louise Brown, the first 'test tube baby', from the average members of her birth cohort. Indeed, the very phrase 'test-tube baby' is anachronistic, a relic of a time when the product of IVF was seen as a laboratory artefact, even a freak. Concerns about process and reasons, however, have not been so easily laid to rest. In the two decades following the introduction of IVF, the success rate for a round of IVF has inched up from a dismally low 15 per cent to less than 25 per cent (for recent statistics, see Centers for Disease Control and Prevention, Division of Reproductive Health, 2001). Most attempts still fail, and the successes have left in their wake thousands of 'excess' embryos, whose disposition poses a vexing social and moral problem. But it is noteworthy that even staunch defenders of the moral status of early embryos, such as George W. Bush, have not seen the risk of their routine destruction as a basis for opposing IVF. Finally, the willingness of couples to undergo the largely uninsured expense and likely initial failure of IVF suggests that they are placing, and being encouraged to place, an excessive premium on having a genetic and gestational link to their children. But, although controversies remain about IVF, they concern its promotion, funding, and regulation, not its basic legitimacy.

This is hardly the case for the new genetic technologies: prenatal and pre-implantation genetic diagnosis, genetic engineering, and cloning. The application of the product/process/reasons framework for assessing these technologies will be helpful in distinguishing the empirical and moral issues in the debate, and in identifying the most intractable sources of conflict.

We will begin by systematically assessing human genetic engineering and cloning under these three rubrics. Although there are important practical differences between these technologies, they raise many of the same issues (Wachbroit 1998). As we noted earlier, cloning is in effect crude genetic manipulation. Consequently, we can discuss the two technologies together, noting when their differences affect their ethical appraisal. Once we have an overview of the ethical issues in these two areas, we will look at selection technologies, which, we will see, raise distinct but overlapping issues.

We will focus on the fourth group of issues discussed at the beginning of this chapter—concerning control, selectivity, and discrimination in the creation of new human lives. But we will also discuss issues from the other three groups, concerning the risks of the new technologies, their role in creating or attenuating family bonds and parental rights and responsibilities, and the complications they raise in assessing the moral status of the early embryo.

5. Genetic Manipulation and Human Cloning

5.1 Product

When the concern with a reproductive technology is with the result or product— that is, the child—the question 'What is wrong with there being such individuals?' is typically understood to be a question about harms or rights. Is the cloned or genetically modified child necessarily suffering a harm or, by existing, does the child necessarily suffer some rights violation?

Let us begin with the concern over physical harm. In the case of human cloning, the National Bioethics Advisory Commission (1997) made this the primary reason for its recommendation for a temporary moratorium on any efforts at human cloning. Thus far cloning in mammals has had an extremely low success rate—it took nearly 300 attempts to clone the sheep in Edinburgh. This suggests that human cloning is simply too risky at this time, since we do not know enough about this technology. The theme of ignorance and risk also looms large over any attempt genetically to modify a child. Since we are still in the dark about a great deal in genetics, we have to acknowledge that it is risky to employ any such procedure now. Have we identified the right set of genes? Have we placed them in exactly the right spot on exactly the right chromosome? Have we ensured that only the right cells will express this gene?

The concerns about physical risk go beyond worries over whether the intervention itself fails or harms the child. We cannot say what the long-term consequences of altering genes will be. Many genes have multiple effects, some bad and some good. Because of our ignorance, we cannot be confident that there will not be unintended bad consequences; that by replacing a gene associated with a particular disease we will not have placed the child at risk for a worse disease.

The practical conclusion to be drawn from concerns about risk of physical harm is that we should proceed cautiously in developing this technology. Nearly every medical technology was risky in the beginning. It is plainly common sense to be cautious in the beginning and not permit the technology to be used until it has a proven record of safety and efficacy. But underlying this response is the deeper issue—what constitutes sufficient caution? Raising a concern about risk is often a call to balance possible harms against possible benefits. What principles should govern a justifiable balancing and who should determine the balance?

Conventional principles of risk assessment may be difficult to apply to genetic engineering. Even if the technical challenges to that technology can be overcome, the assessment of its benefit and harm will be complicated by the effect that pre-conception or prenatal genetic modifications may have on fetal or personal identity: in preventing disease or disability, such modifications may alter the identity of the fetus or child for whose benefit they are undertaken.

Several commentators (e.g. Zohar 1991) have raised concerns about this 'non-identity problem' or 'paradox of genetic harms'. The paradox starts with the idea that some genetic replacements can result in a different human being. While replacing some genes in a human being merely results in a change in some of the traits or properties of that human being, it may be that replacing certain genes—so-called essential genes—or replacing a sufficiently large number of important genes means replacing one human being by another. There is no consensus over when change becomes replacement—which or how many genes are essential to an individual's identity. Most people would agree that, if we replaced all of the genes, we have replaced the individual. And if we replaced only the genes affecting hair colour, we have changed, not replaced, the individual. But suppose we replace the genes located on the 23rd chromosome, which determine the child's sex. Have we changed the boy into a girl or have we replaced the boy with a girl?

The paradox does not depend on the location of the line between modifying and replacing the embryo, merely on its existence. We recognize such a line if we regard some genes as essential. Suppose some essential gene of a child is associated with a disease. We might think that this gene was harmful because, presumably, the disease is harmful. But changing the essential gene could not possibly make the child better—instead it would destroy the child and replace it with a different one. Hence, because this genetic condition cannot possibly be improved, it cannot possibly be harmful (in one familiar sense of 'harmful'), even though it is associated with a disease condition. In other words, an individual is harmed by a gene or genetic condition only if that individual would be better off if that gene or genetic condition were different. Because an individual's identity is tied to his essential genes, such genes or genetic conditions could never be harmful, appearances to the contrary notwithstanding.

The paradox arises, though less dramatically, even if we reject the idea of some genes being essential. All that is needed for the paradox is that replacing a sufficient number of genes in a person results in a different person and not simply in the same person with different properties. Any apparent harm that can be treated only by replacing this number of genes cannot be harmful to that individual, for the reasons given above.

There seems to be little disagreement that one ought to treat the disease even if that requires affecting essential genes. The problem is in explaining why this course of action is morally justified if the replacement of a fetus is not a morally negligible loss. Some commentators have suggested that we should not think in terms of the harm done to the child—which would then generate the paradox—but rather in terms of the harm done to the other people involved. (This seems to be Zohar's position.) Others (like Brock 1995) have suggested that in order to avoid the paradox we should think about the situation in terms of 'non-person-affecting principles'. The discussion of these matters has led to subtle and complex disputes in moral theory generally, about the integration of 'person-affecting' moralities, concerned with conduct that makes people better or worse off, with more 'impersonal' moralities, concerned as well with conduct that causes there to be better- or worse-off people (McMahan 1998). This theoretical debate may be complicated by the manifest difficulty of determining when a series of genetic modifications is identity affecting (Wasserman forthcoming).

In addition to physical harms, some commentators have worried that children resulting from the new reproductive technologies will suffer distinctive psychological harms. One harm that has sometimes been mentioned is the burden of parental expectations. In particular, if the parents have gone to such effort as to use technology to affect the kind of child they have, the child may come to be burdened by the parents' expectations. This burden may seem more likely in the case of cloning than in the case of gene manipulation to engineer a single trait. Since the clone is in effect the delayed identical twin of the adult cloned, the parents may well have a more vivid expectation of what the child will grow into—they can see in the adult what the child will probably look like and, so they may believe, how the child may come to act. For example, such a child might be constantly compared to the adult from whom he was cloned, and thereby burdened with oppressive expectations.

The objection here need not be confined to a worry about the psychological burden of parental expectations. The parents might actually limit the child's opportunities for growth and development: a child cloned from a basketball player or a child who was genetically manipulated to have certain athletic abilities, for instance, might be denied any educational opportunities that were not in line with a career in athletics. Moreover, regardless of the parents' conduct or attitudes, a child might be burdened by the *thought* that he is a copy and not an 'original' or that some of his traits were the result of parental choice. The child's sense of self-worth or individuality or dignity would thus be difficult to sustain.

This objection has sometimes been phrased not so much as a concern about the child suffering from psychological harms as a right of the child's being violated—the child's right to 'an open future'. This right is invoked to argue that an action taken on a child, even though it may have little impact at the moment, could wrongfully deny the child significant opportunities later in life. For example, the wrong of sterilizing a child lies not in the present harm incurred but in the important future possibilities that are thereby eliminated. As Davis (1997) argues, limiting a child's opportunities can in certain cases constitute a violation of the child's right to an open future.

How should we assess these concerns? First of all, we should note that children are often born in the midst of all sorts of hopes and expectations; the idea that there is a special burden associated with being the product of a reproductive technology is necessarily speculative. Moreover, given the falsity of genetic determinism, any conclusions a child might draw about how he will develop would be tentative at best. His knowledge of his future would differ only in degree from what many children already know once they begin to learn parts of their family's (medical) history. Some of us know that we will almost certainly be bald, or that we will be susceptible to certain diseases. To be sure, the cloned or genetically modified individual might know more about what he or she could become. But, because our knowledge of the effect of the environment on development is so incomplete, the genetically modified or cloned individual would certainly be in for some surprises.

The existence of a right to an open future has a strong intuitive appeal. We are troubled by parents who radically constrict their children's possibilities for growth and development. Obviously, we would condemn a cloning parent for crushing a child with oppressive expectations, just as we might condemn fundamentalist parents for utterly isolating their children from the modern world, or the parents of twins for inflicting matching wardrobes and rhyming names. But how far do these concerns take us regarding the new reproductive technologies? Is the claim that bad parenting is the unavoidable consequence of these technologies? Are the alleged harms or violations of rights sufficient to conclude that the child should not have been born?

It would seem that, even if we were convinced that cloned or genetically modified individuals were likely to suffer particular burdens, that would not be enough to show that it is wrong to create such individuals. The child of a poor family can be expected to suffer specific hardships and burdens, but we do not thereby conclude that such children should not be born. Despite the hardships, poor children can experience parental love and many of the joys of being alive: the deprivations of poverty, however painful, are not decisive. No one's life is entirely free of difficulties or burdens. In order for these considerations to have decisive weight, we have to be able to say that life does not offer compensating benefits.

A different set of objections raised about genetically modifying or cloning children focuses on the 'product' in a broader sense; not on any particular case but rather on the biological or social impact of widespread use of these technologies. For instance, one might allege that widespread use of these technologies will threaten human genetic diversity. If a significant number of parents choose to have children with a particular genetic composition—either in part through gene manipulation or entirely through cloning—then the prevalence of certain genes in the population will decrease. The worry here is that reduced diversity in the human genome renders the human species less resilient to environmental changes. Vulnerability to many diseases varies with genetic structure. For example, people with the genes associated with sickle-cell anemia have a greater resistance to malaria. Part of the explanation of why the US corn crop in 1970 was devastated is that so much of it was vulnerable to a particular fungus because the corn crop, owing to agricultural biotechnology, was genetically similar. The worry here is that, because of reduced diversity, the human species could be wiped out by a disease that would otherwise have killed only a fraction of the species. (For a discussion of the medical value of human genetic diversity, see National Research Council 1997.)

The earlier objection concerned individual risk of physical harm from a single use of the technology; this objection concerns species-wide risk of harm from widespread use. Unless this objection is framed in terms of a specific threat or vulnerability, rather than the mere possibility of a threat, the appropriate response may well be the same. Unless we hold that any change in the frequency of any gene in the population is disastrous, we should proceed slowly and cautiously as we learn more about how genes work.

Nevertheless, physical harm is not the only concern about widespread use of reproductive technologies. Suppose, for example, their use was confined to certain social groups or economic classes. Only the elites could choose the kind of child they would have; the poor and underclass would have to make do with the results of the 'natural lottery'. The rich would not only be economically different from the poor; they would also become biologically different.

We should note that the role of economic inequality in exacerbating disparities in health and fitness was recognized long before the advent of cloning and other reproductive technologies. Since the rich have greater access to health care and nutrition, they are generally healthier than the poor. This suggests that the problem is part of a broader one regarding the distribution of health-care services (see e.g. Buchanan et al., 2000).

5.2 Process

Even if there are no concerns about the child resulting from the new reproductive technologies, objections could be raised about the process itself. Many objections to gene-modifying technologies begin with the thought that they are unnatural or artificial. Of course, being unnatural or artificial is not by itself an indictment, otherwise much of modern medicine would have to be condemned. Being unnatural is an indictment only in certain religious contexts. Consequently, if that were the extent of the objection, it plainly would have limited appeal and it would not be open to secular assessment.

But some, like Kass (1985), have tried to cast the concern about unnaturalness of genetic technologies in secular terms. Employing these technologies demystifies or deromanticizes the procreative act. The result is a dehumanizing effect on everyone involved. Babies are not born, they are manufactured.

Such concerns are difficult to assess, once they are distinguished from predictions about physical or psychological harm to children conceived through the new reproductive technologies (product) or objections to the moral posture of parents who employ those technologies (reasons). The idea is not simply that there is something inherently valuable in the 'natural' way of making babies. The claim is that the recourse to artificial means so corrupts or debases our values that it would be better if the children resulting from the use of this technology had never been brought into existence. This is a very strong claim. Admittedly, IVF and its kindred technologies lack the beauty and mystery found in the creation of a child through the physical expression of a couple's love and commitment. But much 'natural' procreation cannot be seen as expressing love and commitment, while much assisted reproduction can be an expression of love and commitment all the greater for its difficulty, risk, and expense. And, even if the process of IVF is cumbersome and impersonal, these infelicities seem quite trivial in the face of the many people who would not have been born but for these technologies and their parents, who in many cases are very glad that these people were born.

The issue of 'unnatural' means also arises in the context of reproductive technologies used for enhancement purposes. If there is nothing wrong in cultivating a special ability or talent in one's child through training and practice, is it morally objectionable to 'cultivate' it through biological manipulation or genetic enhancement? Some writers view the use of reproductive technologies to have a 'better' child to be little different than using post-natal, environmental methods such as education, athletics, and nutrition in order to have a better child. We would not generally regard a couple who try to enhance their child's memory through special training as bad parents. Why should we think any worse of the parents if they employed reproductive technologies? Some argue that the chosen means of enhancement differ in critical respects—that conventional enhancement requires struggle, discipline, and commitment, while genetic enhancement does not. (Such an argument is made about biological and pharmacological enhancement generally by Cole-Turner 1998.) This distinction, however, may rest on a mistaken conception of the way genes operate, a false determinism that sees the genome as doing all the work. Someone with 'superior' genes for athletics or music still has to do a lot of practising.

But this concern about process does not exhaust the issue of means. Even if genetic modifications cannot be phenotypically expressed without some effort on the part of parent and child, they will be introduced without the natural resistance offered by an existing child, with its own, often conflicting, desires and values. Lacking that resistance, genetic enhancement may turn out to be a fundamentally more impersonal enterprise than even the most driven and obsessive parental efforts to cultivate excellence in their existing children. Even when it is not identity altering, genetic enhancement may have more to do with making excellent children than with making children excel.

Fears about the integrity of the reproductive process can sometimes be linked to fears about the integrity of the family. This is particularly evident in the objections to cloning that accuse it of undermining the structure of the family by obscuring identities and lineages. On the one hand, the relationship between the adult and the cloned individual could be described as that between a parent and offspring. Indeed, some commentators have called cloning 'asexual reproduction', which clearly suggests that cloning is a way of generating *descendants*. The cloned individual, in this view, has only one biological parent. On the other hand, from the point of view of genetics, the cloned individual is a *sibling*, so that cloning is more accurately described as 'delayed twinning' rather than as asexual reproduction. The cloned individual, in this view, has two biological parents, not one—they are the same parents as those of the person from whom that individual was cloned.

Against the claim that cloning threatens family integrity, it has been argued that it in fact helps to preserve it. The argument rests on the same assumptions as the claim that IVF with donor gametes subverts family integrity: in the case of donor IVF, a couple with one member who is infertile or has a dominant disease gene must bring in a third party to provide gametes. Cloning eliminates this recourse to third parties, and thereby eliminates any genetically based claim to the child from those outside the extended family (Orentlicher 1999). At the same time, however, it may ground claims to the child from relatives beyond the nuclear family, especially grandparents. Moreover, if a genetic contribution were so important, one might fear that cloning, as well as IVF, could give rise to a disturbing asymmetry of care, attachment, and responsibility between the contributing and non-contributing parents. Angry references to 'your child' might take on a more literal meaning than they have for ordinary biological parents. The concern is that the non-contributing parent would be relegated to the status of a step-parent, who likewise has no genetic link to the child. But this does not appear to have happened in the case of donor IVF, suggesting that rearing plays a far more important role than breeding in parental bonding, responsibility, and authority.

In any case, it seems clear that cloning will result in some ambiguities about lineage and relationship. Is the cloned individual an offspring or a sibling? Does the cloned individual have one biological parent or two? The moral significance of these ambiguities lies in the fact that in many societies, including our own, lineage identifies responsibilities. Typically the parent, not the sibling, is responsible for the child. But if no one is unambiguously the parent, so the worry might go, who is responsible for the cloned child? In so far as social identity is based on biological ties, will not this identity be blurred or confounded?

One might reply that the answer to the question of who is responsible for the child is a social one: even though, in our society, certain biological ties indicate certain responsibilities, that indication is only presumptive (Wasserman and Wachbroit 1992; Charo 1994). Duties of care and rearing arise within a family, understood as a social institution. As the practice of adoption makes clear, the faithful execution of these duties does not depend upon the existence of biological ties. A fortiori, it does not depend upon the existence of unambiguous biological ties. Still, the general point is important: throughout the development of reproductive technologies we must be clear in our understanding of who is responsible for the child.

The 'process' of genetic engineering, though it can now only be imagined, would not complicate lineage in the same way as cloning, if the parents merely modified their own genetic material. But the greater the extent of the modification, the more it would attenuate the biological connection. Children whose striking physical or psychological differences from their parents arose not from the vagaries of genetic recombination but from the deliberate selection of non-parental alleles would not only look adopted, they would be somewhat akin to adopted children in their lack of genetic commonality with their parents. And if parents actually chose their children's genomes from a 'genetic supermarket'—a possibility that still seems quite fanciful—their bonds with their children would have less to do with biology and more with composition or authorship.

The spectre of a genetic supermarket also raises questions about the role of third parties, questions that obviously do not arise in the case of cloning. One does not need to be a genetic determinist to expect that certain distinctive phenotypic features will be attributable to certain genetic alleles, derived from identifiable individuals. It is not hard to imagine that certain features, reliably expressed by certain alleles, will become extremely popular. If 'Betty Davis' eyes were derived from Betty Davis's genes, those endowed with 'her' eyes might look on the movie star as more of an ancestor than a role model; she, in turn, could see them more as descendants than fans. But if such feature-specific contributions became common, it might do more to reduce the social significance of genetic links than to increase the bonds between those who bore them.

Both the failures and the successes of genetic engineering may attenuate the genetic mystique that gives it so much of its impetus (Nelkin and Lindee 1995). The difficulty of engineering such characteristics as intelligence and empathy may highlight the limited role that genes play in the development of many of our most valued characteristics. And the prospect of an indefinite number of contributors to the modified genome of a child may complicate the notion of a 'genetic parent'. In the past decade, the conflicting claims of different biological contributors were sometimes resolved by giving priority to the genetic over the gestational mother, most famously in the California case of *Johnson* v. *Calvert* (1993). This preference, denounced by some commentators as 'genetic essentialism' (Dreyfuss and Nelkin 1992), may be far harder to sustain in the face of multiple genetic contributions.

5.3 Reasons

The reasons or motives for why a couple would employ technology to have a particular kind of child is an important element in the moral assessment of reproductive technologies. It widens the discussion beyond considerations of who or what is benefited, harmed, or wronged to an examination of the impact that such technologies might have on how we see ourselves, our children, and reproduction.

Nevertheless, before examining these reasons, we need to consider a general argument restricting such an examination. Couples in the USA have a great deal of freedom and autonomy regarding reproduction. They are free to decide whether to have children, when to have children, and how many children to have. Couples have children for all sorts of reasons, including no reason at all. If the child suffers no harm or violation of his rights and if there is no objection to the process itself, why should the couple's reasons for having a (particular kind of) child matter? Is not an assessment of reasons an objectionable paternalism, a failure to respect a couple's autonomy regarding reproduction?

The concern with reproductive autonomy has a history. The beginning of the twentieth century was marked by an enthusiasm over 'eugenics', a word coined by Francis Galton, a cousin of Charles Darwin. By applying the wisdom of animal breeders to people, we could improve the human stock, or so it was argued. The programme had two components: a negative one, under which people with undesirable traits would not reproduce, and a positive one, under which people with desirable traits would breed only with each other. Countries such as the USA and Germany caught the enthusiasm for the eugenics programme, and so carried out some of the most chilling coercive measures of the century—including the

US sterilization programmes and the Nazi 'euthanasia' campaigns. The widespread revulsion over these programmes after the Second World War led to a general repudiation of anything that smacked of eugenics. (The leading accounts of the history and legacy of the eugenics movement are Kevles 1985; Paul 1995, 1998.)

Consequently, one of the legacies of the dismal history of eugenics is the general support available to couples to ensure that they are free and autonomous regarding their reproductive decisions. Although doubts have been expressed about the extent to which economic, social, and cultural pressures undermine autonomy, and about the extent to which eugenic objectives have been internalized by the individual consumers of reproductive services (Duster 1990), the rejection of state and institutional coercion is a virtual tenet of reproductive law and practice in modern Western societies. Indeed, the dominant position in counselling couples is 'non-directive counselling'—wherein the professional avoids disclosing his or her own opinions about what to do when counselling a couple over a reproductive issue.

Nevertheless, the degree that the (reproductive) autonomy of couples should be respected is limited; it is not as great as the degree of autonomy that an individual can demand regarding decisions over his or her own medical treatment. The reason for this limitation is plain—the presence of a third party's interests and rights. Once the interests or rights of the child can be taken into account, the couple's reproductive autonomy is restricted. At what point that occurs is, of course, controversial, and reflects some of the controversy over abortion and over what constitutes 'fetal abuse'. For example, at what point if any should the state intervene to prevent the pregnant woman from engaging in behaviour (for example, smoking) that might harm the fetus?

But even in those areas where one believes that reproductive autonomy should be respected, that respect does not mean that the couple's decision is above criticism. Respecting their autonomy means not interfering with their decisions, especially by law, but that is perfectly compatible with morally assessing the reasons, if any, for the couple's decision (Clarke 1991; Wachbroit and Wasserman 1995).

As we noted in the beginning of this section, it is important to recognize that the reason or intention motivating the use of the technology raises issues that are not captured by simply examining the product or process of the technology. A good illustration of the case for assessing the couple's intent is that of sex selection. Most writers have condemned the use of reproductive technologies simply to ensure that a couple has a child of a desired sex. The objection is not based on any misgivings about the child resulting from a single sex selection, the possible sex imbalance resulting from aggregate selection, or even, necessarily, about the process itself, especially if it does not involve the destruction of embryos. The objection turns more on the reasons for sex selection. If, for example, the couple acts on a belief that a male child is more valuable than a female, that a boy gives the couple greater prestige or other benefits, then their reason is objectionable. It treats being female as if it were a disease, and feeds into a culture of prejudice and discrimination against women.

Despite this concern, in some instances choosing a child because of its sex may be justifiable as selection against disease, since sex can be a marker for some diseases. As we noted earlier, a couple with a family history of DMD may use sex-selection techniques to ensure they have a female child, because a male child would have a 50 per cent chance of having the disease whereas a female would not be at risk. In such cases, sex selection may seem less objectionable because the reason for it is less objectionable (but see our discussion in the next section on selection against disability). Hence, even though public policy should not rest on the assessment of the reasons for particular reproductive decisions, such assessments can nonetheless be a significant element in the moral assessment of reproductive technologies.

There are many reasons why a couple would use reproductive technologies to have a child, or avoid having a child of a particular kind, but the consideration that underlies most of these reasons is the desire for a child that is biologically related. If all that a couple wanted was a child who, for example, was not at risk for a disease that ran in the couple's family, adoption would seem to be a more straightforward solution than cloning, genetic modifications, and so on. That adoption is not seen as an option, or only as the very last option, testifies to the importance many people place on being biologically connected to the child they raise. It is, therefore, worth keeping in mind this desire for biological connection when considering the various objections to the reasons for employing reproductive technology. Is the importance some people attached to having a biologically related child a fact to be accepted and respected? Should such desires be subject to moral assessment?

Let us now look more closely at some of the reasons for having a particular kind of child. One important class of reasons that couples might have for wanting to have or avoid a particular kind of child is to prevent the burden of a certain disease or disability. As we noted already, couples often know—either from prenatal testing or from family history—whether they are at risk of having a child with a disease or disability. And the range of diseases and disabilities that can be predicted will increase with developments in genetic and reproductive technology. The new technologies can help the couple respond to this knowledge. If the disease or disability is associated with some problematic genes, then the couple, at least theoretically, could have those genes appropriately modified and the disease or disability removed, or they could decide not to have that child by having a clone of someone without the disease or disability instead.

There is little controversy about such efforts at avoidance when the conditions are recognized by all as terrible and severe—when, to use a standard phrase, they would result in a life not worth living. The matter becomes much more complicated when we consider other conditions—that is, less severe disabilities.

Consider, for example, the case of a couple who uses cloning to avoid giving birth to a child with paraplegia or with mild cognitive dysfunction. Some have argued that such a child could well have a life not merely worth living, but full of as many pleasures, achievements, and satisfactions as a person without that disability would enjoy (e.g. Asch 1986, 2000). The preference to eliminate the disability reflects, they

argue, negative stereotypes about life with that disability, and the use of reproductive technology to satisfy that preference has expressive significance. It feeds a culture of stigmatization and discrimination that many people with disability suffer
under by expressing the belief that it would be better if such people were not born.

Even if we were concerned with gene modification rather than cloning—so that
the aim was to eliminate the disability rather than ensure that a certain type of individual was not born—similar concerns might be raised. In many cases, what makes
a disability a burden can be traced to the way the environment has been constructed,
rendering places and activities less accessible than they should be for people with
various disabilities. Gene-modification technologies, by reducing the number of
people with a particular disability, may reduce the urgency of constructing our environments so as to be more accommodating. The result is that the remaining people
who do have the disability suffer. And the investment in those preventative and corrective technologies, rather than in social and environmental reconstruction, may
give expression to a very negative view of life with that disability.

How we respond to these issues will greatly depend upon how we see the alleged
burdens of disability. While the distribution of normal and abnormal genes associated with disability may be a matter of the 'natural lottery', the distribution of the
associated burdens need not be. To what extent should this distribution be regarded
as a matter of justice? The expressive significance of prenatal genetic therapy, as of
prenatal genetic selection, is a matter of sharp debate, as we discuss below. (For further discussion on these issues, see Chapter 12, this volume.)

Let us turn to an arguably different kind of reason for wanting a particular child,
one that goes beyond the avoidance of certain diseases or disabilities to the
enhancement of the various talents and capacities. Parents typically want what is
best for their children and some reproductive technologies—particularly, gene-
modification technologies—suggest new possibilities of providing the best for one's
child. To some extent, the effort to avoid disability through selection or therapy can
be seen as arising from the same perfectionist attitudes—the quest for a perfect, or
at least a superior child requires the exclusion of significant imperfections. But
many parents who attempt to avoid having children with disabilities are motivated
less by ambition than by fear or dread, however exaggerated. And, even if the desire
to avoid disabilities is sometimes subsumed under the desire to achieve superior
abilities, it is useful to look at the latter as a distinct motivation.

Some concerns about the motives for genetic enhancement remain even if we
assume parity between different processes of enhancement and discount fears
about the results (for example, risks, open future) and process. Given the current
stigmatized cultural status of reproductive technologies, their use would indicate a
stronger desire to have a better child than the use of more widely acceptable environmental, post-natal methods. One might well wonder whether it could be an
excessive desire. While it is certainly good that couples want the best for their child,
we rightly become suspicious if this desire becomes too powerful.

We are concerned that parents so motivated would love and care for their child only because the child exhibited the traits the parent wanted, that their love was contingent on their child being made to order. It is difficult to assess the significance of this concern, given the transformative effects of child rearing. That is to say, the motives people have for bringing a child into the world do not determine the manner in which they raise him or the attitudes they have towards him. Couples who have children without using any of the new reproductive technologies can be deeply narcissistic, and yet the experience of parenthood sometimes makes them caring, respectful, and even self-sacrificing. In the process of raising a child, of seeing her grow and develop, they learn that she is not merely an extension of themselves. Then again, it is also true that some parents never make this discovery, and that others, having done so, never cease to resent it. Some parents relentlessly drive their children to excel, sacrificing their childhood to the pursuit of their achievement. The pace and extent of moral development among parents, as well as among children, are infinitely variable. Perhaps all we can say is that those who employ technology will not, by virtue of this fact, be immune to the transformative effects of child rearing—even if it is the case (and it will not always be) that they begin with more problematic motives than those of parents who engage in the 'natural lottery'.

One final concern is that the investment in, and promotion of, cloning and genetic engineering may be seen as giving social support to some of the most problematic reasons for having children—as trophies or replicas. No matter that these technologies could not possibly achieve the desired ends; the harm would be in encouraging their pursuit. There are, however, a variety of practical measures that could blunt or mitigate such an effect: the technologies could be restricted in various ways to withhold any endorsement of or support for objectionable parental motives. Cloning, for example, could be limited to cases of infertility (including the 'infertility' of same-sex couples) and hereditary disease, so that it was not available to those merely drawn to the illusory prospect of self-replication or immortality.

6. SELECTION

Many of the issues we have discussed regarding genetic manipulation and cloning can also arise in the case of selection, but not all of them. For example, if the selection proceeds by terminating pregnancies containing undesired fetuses until one results with the desired kind, then special concerns about the risk of physical harm to the resulting child do not arise. The child would seem to be no more at risk than one who was not born via a selection procedure. This is not to deny, however, that issues such as excessive parental expectations or concerns about an open future might still arise.

In some cases, selection raises distinctive issues, particularly concerning processes and reasons. In so far as the process of embryo selection results in the unselected embryos being destroyed, it involves abortion. The destruction of 'surplus' or unwanted embryos in selective implantation raises the same or similar concerns if one regards an unimplanted embryo as having the same moral status as an implanted one, or as having lower but still significant status. But other concerns raised by selective abortion and implantation are distinct from those raised in the general debate about abortion; they have more in common with the concerns raised about engineering and cloning to avoid disability, and about the more imminent prospect of gamete selection for that purpose. In the standard abortion debate, it is assumed that the pregnancy is unwanted. In the selective abortion debate, it is assumed that the pregnancy is wanted, but not with *that* kind of fetus. Criticism of selective abortion focuses on the expressive significance of efforts to avoid creating children with the disability; and about the appropriateness of such selectivity at the outset of a relationship that is supposed to be characterized in its later stages by unconditional love and acceptance.

These distinct concerns have resulted in some interesting combinations of positions. Someone might be 'pro-choice' in the standard abortion debate but 'anti-abortion' in the selective abortion debate, because a selective abortion may well have very different expressive significance from a standard one (Asch 1986). Those who embrace this combination of views vary in their prescriptions. Few would actually restrict abortions based on parental reasons, but some would restrict the prenatal tests that could be offered to prospective parents, while others would merely require more balanced counselling and more extensive opportunities for education and reflection (see Parens and Asch 2000).

While the concerns about expressive significance and equivocal commitment are distinct from those about the moral status of the fetus, they are not entirely independent. Those who regard the fetus as having some moral status, even considerably less moral status than a child or adult, may see a more negative view of disability expressed by selective abortion or embryo selection than by gamete selection or genetic therapy—the aversion to having a child with a disability may seem that much greater if one is willing to prevent that outcome by destroying an embryo rather than merely discarding a gamete. On the other hand, it may not be the moral status of the embryo that lies behind that perceived difference so much as the extent to which one has already undertaken the project of creating a child—that project is further along after *in vivo* or *in vitro* fertilization than it is before conception, and its interruption at a later stage suggests a greater aversion to the prospect of having a child with a disability (see Asch 2000).

The advent of routine gamete screening and pre-implantation diagnosis might blur the line between selecting against and selecting for traits. Although they would not alter or enhance a single gene, pre-conception and pre-implantation diagnosis might fall closer to genetic engineering than to cloning or prenatal selection in their selectivity. Confronted with a wide array of gametes or embryos, prospective parents might well choose the ones with desired characteristics after eliminating those with undesirable characteristics. Indeed, the decision process might be more readily seen as having one stage rather then two—the selection of the 'best' gametes or embryos. For some critics, this increased selectivity would be a disturbing development, encouraging a noxious perfectionism on the part of prospective parents, and a further commodification of the (future) child. For others, however, increased selectivity would have a silver lining—it would shift the focus away from a stigmatizing preoccupation with the avoidance of disability (see Asch 2000). It is even possible to imagine parents selecting, for example, an embryo that had a genetic predisposition to musical or mathematic ability, but also to asthma or depression.

7. Anticipating Future Developments

Reproductive technology is a rapidly developing field, and in many ways this development influences what issues get attention. For example, if this chapter had been written in 1996, it is unlikely that it would have had much discussion of cloning. Up to that time, many biologists had assured people, wrongly as it turned out, that the cloning of mammals was not feasible and so the discussion regarding its ethics was pointless. Five years later, because of developments in the technology, there are books, articles, and a President's Commission Report on cloning. The lesson to be drawn from this is that we cannot identify which issues will become prominent in five or ten years. Our assumption has been, however, that, regardless of what emerges, the general analysis of issues in terms of product, process, and reason will still be useful.

This framework becomes especially important in analysing the controversies that will arise with respect to attempts to modify or replace genes associated with specific traits and conditions. We do not know of most traits or conditions whether they can be controlled by genetic intervention, and so we do not know where specifically the controversies may cluster. Will we be able to affect memory capacity, impulsivity, obesity, or longevity? We cannot assume that the same issues will arise in each case. For now we must rely on general approaches such as the ones we have suggested.

References

Andrews, Lori (1989). *Between Strangers*. New York: Harper & Row.

Angier, Natalie (2001). 'Defining the Undefinable: Being Alive'. *New York Times*, 18 Dec., D1, D6.

Asch, Adrienne (1986). 'Can Aborting "Imperfect" Children be Immoral?' *Christianity and Crisis*, 14 July.

——(2000). 'Why I Haven't Changed my Mind about Prenatal Diagnosis: Reflections and Refinements', in Erik Parens and Adrienne Asch (eds.), *Prenatal Testing and Disability Rights*. Washington: Georgetown University Press, 234–58.

Blank, Robert (1995). *Human Reproduction, Emerging Technologies, and Conflicting Rights*. Washington: CQ Press.

Brock, Dan (1995). 'The Non-Identity Problem and Genetic Harms: The Case of Wrongful Handicaps'. *Bioethics*, 9: 269–75.

Brody, Jane (2001). 'Weighing the Rights of the Embryo against Those of the Sick'. *New York Times*, 18 Dec., D8.

Buchanan, Allen, Brock, Dan, Daniels, Norman, and Wickler, Daniel (2000). *From Chance to Choice*. Cambridge: Cambridge University Press.

Callahan, Joan (1995). *Reproduction, Ethics, and the Law*. Bloomington, IN: Indiana University Press.

Centers for Disease Control and Prevention, Division of Reproductive Health (2001). '1999 Assisted Reproductive Technology Success Rates'. *National Summary and Fertility Clinic Reports*; www.cdc.gov/nccdphp/drh/art.htm.

Charo, Alta R. (1994). 'And Baby Makes Three—or Four or Five or Six: Defining the Family after the Genetic Revolution'. In Mark Frankel and Albert Teich. (eds.), *The Genetic Frontier: Ethics, Law, and Policy*. Washington: American Academy for the Advancement of Science, 25–44.

Clarke, Angus (1991). 'Is Non-Directive Genetic Counselling Possible?' *Lancet*, 19 Oct., 998–1001.

Cole-Turner, Ronald (1998). 'Do Means Matter?', in Erik Parens (ed.), *Enhancing Human Traits: Ethical and Social Implications*. Washington: Georgetown University Press, 251–61.

Corea, Gena (1985). *The Mother Machine: Reproductive Technologies from Artificial Insemination to Artificial Wombs*. New York: Harper & Row.

Davis, Dena (1997). 'Genetic Dilemmas and the Child's Right to an Open Future'. *Rutgers Law Journal*, 28: 549–92.

Donchin, Anne, and Purdy, Laura (1999). *Embodying Bioethics: Recent Feminist Advances*. Lanham, MD: Rowman & Littlefield.

Dreyfuss, Rochelle, and Nelkin, Dorothy (1992). 'The Jurisprudence of Genetics'. *Vanderbilt Law Review*, 45: 313–48.

Duster, T. (1990). *Backdoor to Eugenics*. New York: Routledge.

Harris, John, and Holm, Søren (1998) (eds.), *The Future of Human Reproduction: Ethics, Choice, and Regulation*. Oxford: Oxford University Press.

Hildt, Elisabeth, and Graumann, Sigrid (1999) (eds.), *Genetics in Human Reproduction*. Brookfield, VT: Ashgate.

Howard Hughes Medical Institute (1999). *Exploring the Biomedical Revolution*. Baltimore: Johns Hopkins University Press.

Katz-Rothman, Barbara (1989). *Recreating Motherhood: Ideology and Technology in a Patriarchal Society*. New York: W. W. Norton.

Kass, Leon (1985). *Towards a More Natural Science*. New York: Free Press.

Kevles, D. J. (1985). *In the Name of Eugenics: Genetics and the Uses of Human Heredity*. New York: Knopf.

MacKinnon, Barbara (2000) (ed.), *Human Cloning: Science, Ethics, and Public Policy*. Champaign, IL: University of Illinois Press.

McMahan, Jeff (1998). 'Wrongful Life: Paradoxes in the Morality of Causing People to Exist', in Jules Coleman and Christopher Morris (eds.), *Rational Commitment and Social Justice*. Cambridge: Cambridge University Press.

Murray, Thomas (1996). *The Worth of a Child*. Berkeley and Los Angeles: University of California Press.

National Bioethics Advisory Commission (1997). *Cloning Human Beings*. Rockville, MD.

National Research Council (1997). *Evaluating Human Genetic Diversity*. Washington: National Academy Press.

New York State Task Force on Life and the Law (1998). *Assisted Reproductive Technologies*. Analysis and Recommendations for Public Policy. New York.

Nelkin, Dorothy, and Lindee, M. S. (1995). *The DNA Mystique: The Gene as a Cultural Icon*. New York: Freeman.

Orentlicher, David (1999). 'Cloning and the Preservation of Family Integrity'. *Louisiana Law Review*, 59: 1019–40.

Parens, Erik, and Asch, Adrienne (2000). 'The Disability Rights Critique of Prenatal Testing: Reflections and Recommendations' in Erik Parens and Adrienne Asch (eds.), *Prenatal Testing and Disability Rights*. Washington: Georgetown University Press, 3–43.

Paul, Diane (1995). *Controlling Human Heredity: 1865 to the Present*. Atlantic Highlands, NJ: Humanities Press.

——(1998). *The Politics of Heredity*. Albany, NY: State University of New York Press.

Plomin, R, deFries, J. C., Mclearn, G., and Rutter, M. (1997). *Behavioral Genetics*. 3rd edn. New York: Freeman.

Robertson, John (1994). *Children of Choice*. Princeton: Princeton University Press.

Schaffner, Kenneth (2001). 'Genetic Explanations of Behavior of Worms, Flies, and Men', in David Wasserman and Robert Wachbroit (eds.), *Genetics and Criminal Behavior*. New York: Cambridge University Press, 79–116.

Wachbroit, Robert (1998). 'Genetic Encores: The Ethics of Human Cloning', repr. in M. Winston and R. Edelbach (eds.), *Society, Ethics, & Technology*. Belmont, CA: Wadsworth, 1999, 210–15.

——(2001). 'Understanding the Genetics of Violence Controversy' in David Wasserman and Robert Wachbroit (eds.), *Genetics and Criminal Behavior*. New York: Cambridge University Press, 26–46.

——and Wasserman, David (1995). 'Patient Autonomy and Value Neutrality in Nondirective Genetic Counseling', *Stanford Journal of Law and Social Policy*, 612: 103–11.

Wasserman, David (forthcoming). 'Personal Identity and the Moral Appraisal of Prenatal Genetic Therapy', in Lisa Parker and Rachel Ankeny (eds.), *Mutating Concepts, Evolving Disciplines: Genetics, Medicine, and Society*. Dodrecht: Kluwer.

——and Wachbroit, Robert (1992). 'The Ethics, Law, and Technology of IVF, Surrogate Parentage, and Gamete Donation'. *Clinics in Laboratory Medicine: Technology Applied to Problems of Human Reproduction*, 1213 (Sept.), 429–48.

————(2001). 'Introduction: Methods, Meanings, and Morals', in David Wasserman and Robert Wachbroit (eds.), *Genetics and Criminal Behavior*. New York: Cambridge University Press, 1–21.

Winters, Paul (1998) (ed.), *Cloning*. San Diego: Greenhaven Press.

Zohar, Noam (1991). 'Prospects for "Genetic Therapy": Can a Person Benefit from Being Altered?' *Bioethics*, 5: 275–88.

Case Cited

Johnson v. *Calvert*, 851 P2d 776 (Cal. 1993).

CHAPTER 7

ANIMALS

R. G. FREY

1. INTRODUCTION

Issues of animal welfare, grouped loosely together under the heading of 'animal rights', constitute one of the major areas of growth in applied ethics today. All kinds of books and articles on our treatment of animals have appeared since 1975, and while it would be an exaggeration to say that all this work was set off by the appearance in that year of Peter Singer's *Animal Liberation* (1975), that book sparked interest in animal issues to such an extent that other writers could feed off that interest (e.g. Frey 1980). Since then a veritable industry in works on 'animal rights' has developed, both within and outside the academic world; learned journals as well as newspapers and popular magazines carry features on animal welfare issues as a matter of course.

So many different strands of thought have been put forward in this explosion of writing that it is not possible in the space allotted here to do justice to them all. I certainly can give the flavour of several important ones, however, in the course of trying to set out the current state of play in the area and of indicating which lines of development I think most promising.

2. MEDICAL RESEARCH

It is necessary to choose among the many uses we make of animals upon which to focus. If, for example, one chose to focus upon our use of animals as pets, then there is a psychological literature about interactions between humans and animals that would become relevant, whereas if the focus were upon our use of animals as exhibits in zoos, then the literatures on preservation of species in the wild, on breeding practices in the wild and in captivity, and on the effects of poaching become relevant. And all kinds of interesting works and in different areas of thought, including religion, would become relevant to a focus upon our practice of eating meat. Space prevents me from going into all these materials, even if I were competent to do so.

What I will do instead is to focus upon what I take to be that use of animals that I think raises many of the important philosophical/ethical questions revolving around our treatment of animals and that I think poses the greatest challenge for those who would on ethical grounds do away with our reliance upon animals— namely, their use in medical experimentation generally, including their use in surgical instruction and modelling. While this use certainly uses up animal lives, sometimes in a painful way, it is also the use that seems most resistant to the thought that we could dispense with a reliance upon animals altogether and still lead healthy, productive lives.

Eating meat, I think, is not very resistant to this thought, since there seems little doubt that we could lead healthy, productive lives as vegetarians or vegans. This is not to say that we could obtain so easily the protein and other nutrients that meat provides, and it is certainly not to say that the main arguments for vegetarianism on ethical grounds are compelling (Frey 1984); but it is not typically the search for healthy, productive lives that leads us to eat meat. Nor can it be said of each and every instance of medical/scientific research that life enhancement/life entension is the aim; but the general idea that underlies such research appeals to these notions in a way that eating meat does not.

No one who has witnessed the extraordinary developments of new medicines, techniques, and feats of genetic engineering and cloning in recent years can doubt that the attempt to enhance and extend our lives is coming at the direct expense of animals—certainly not of animals in the wild for the most part, but of animals bred for the very purpose of helping to enhance and extend our lives. I take it that no one can fail to realize that this use of animal lives, whether painful or not, raises important moral questions that need to be addressed by those who would support this use, just as it raises important moral questions for those who would eliminate such use. This latter group does not escape the necessity of argument by some default moral assumption that any and all uses of animals by humans is objectionable, without it being stated what it is that forms the basis of that objection. Still, I assume the burden of argument here lies with those who would continue this use and claim that what they were doing was morally permissible, and this is how I shall proceed.

There appear to be three main sets of issues that arise upon such a focus as this: the moral standing or moral considerability of animals, the value of animal life, and the argument from marginal cases (or unfortunate humans). But these issues all arise, and in various ways, in the confines of a larger argument concerned with human benefit that proponents of animal use accept to justify animal experimentation in medicine (Frey 1993) and that opponents of animal use reject to scuttle that attempted justification (Ryder 1976). In fact, these main sets of issues are all interconnected, as we shall see, and the ultimate issue in dispute in this general area will turn out to be the comparative value of human and animal life.

Certainly, the different uses we make of animals, whether as subjects for cosmetic and product testing, as the source of food, leather, and fur, and as vehicles of medical and scientific research may raise particular moral questions that the other uses do not. Each use involves, however, at some level or other, the fundamental question of the moral status of animals, and this question is itself part of a larger question, I contend, about the comparative value of animal and humans lives and about the benefits we can justifiably derive from using animals as we do. My aim, then, is not to survey all the potential uses we make of animals but rather to focus upon the deep philosophical/ethical issues that reside here. That end is best achieved, I think, by focusing upon the use of animals in biomedical research. For of all the issues, this one is arguably both the most important and the most intellectually interesting (Langley 1989; Smith and Boyd 1991). It requires thinking clearly about the appropriateness of inflicting pain on animals and taking their lives. It has the added advantage of considering a use of animals in which, while animals are indisputably harmed, there is an especially compelling case that such uses benefit humans. Because it is the central moral case, a more careful examination of it will illuminate the other uses of animals. For if there are serious doubts about whether animal experimentation is justified, then that would suggest that these other uses of animals are even more suspect. On the other hand, if the practice of animal experimentation in medicine is morally justified, then at least we can know that a strong abolitionist view about our use of animals is indefensible.

Moreover, the philosophical literature on the other uses of animals is thin, while the literature on experimentation is rich. Thus, there are only a couple of essays on, for example, animals as pets. And while there is a burgeoning literature on our use of animals as food, these writings do not add any new insights into the moral status of animals or into the trade-offs between animal lives and the enhancement and extension of human lives but simply add more empirical details about what happens to animals on their way through the food chain. By contrast, the issue of animal experimentation gives us the opportunity to confront not only the issue of moral status (Cohen 1986) but also those trade-offs between human and animal lives that lie at the centre of attempts to justify our using animals to certain of our ends. So I will focus upon this issue.

Medical and scientific experimentation, including genetic engineering, clearly involves using up animal lives, and this we need to justify, whatever the role of pain in what is being done. This leads us inevitably into discussion not only of the moral standing of animals but also of the value of their lives, since I assume that, if a life had no value, there would be nothing wrong in using it to the worthy ends of the enhancement and extension of human life. It leads as well into a discussion of the difference between human and animal lives in this regard, since I also assume that most of us who think we are permitted to use up animal lives in the course of conducting medical research do not think we are equally permitted to use up human lives in this research, in the same way, to the same degree. Why not? What is the difference between the cases? Most especially, what is the difference between the cases when the human lives being discussed are those whose quality of life has fallen so low as to be such that no one would ever choose such a life for oneself or one's family and friends and that we waver over whether we should permit those living such lives to ask for assistance from others in terminating them? Questions of these sorts are unavoidable, once we get into the animal case. In a curious way, then, a concern with the use of animals in medical experimentation leads back to a discussion of humans and the value of the lives they live in the midst of illness, disease, and physical and mental degeneration. This is why the argument from marginal cases (or unfortunate humans), to my mind, looms so large in the animal welfare debates.

Two important questions will be set aside here, for reasons of space. First, there is the question of whether, if the justification we offer for experimenting upon animals in the first place runs through the benefits this experimentation confers upon humans, this or that is indeed a benefit or is a large enough benefit to offset what we propose to do to the animal. I do not deny that such a question has point or that, at times, what we propose to do is not a benefit or a sufficiently large one; Barbara Orlans (1993) has made this point particularly effectively over certain pieces of research and over certain uses of animals, including dissection, in education and teaching. I assume here that there are pieces of medical research, however, where this is not true, where the potential benefits, say, of genetic engineering and xeno-transplantation would be agreed to be substantial, in terms of life enhancement and life extension (as in some examples that follow).

Secondly, there is the whole issue of whether animal models are suitable models in the first place for this or that human ailment or whether extrapolations from such models in the human case are always sufficiently reliable to relieve all doubts, of the sorts raised by LaFollette and Shanks (1997), about suitability of model. I accept that there are cases where such doubts are both genuine and persuasive; I assume here, however, that there are pieces of medical research where animal models are perfectly suitable to the research being carried out, in that they sufficiently approximate the human case to make extrapolations from them reasonably reliable to the human condition. Thus, in genetic engineering, we create new creatures by inserting a new gene, from another animal and/or species, into an animal's DNA, and the goal often is to enable us to study the progress and pathology of illnesses in living creatures with a reasonably close genetic and physiological structure to our own. In inserting a human gene into a mouse's DNA, we seek to develop a creature that will now be able to contract an illness or be subject to a condition to which it would otherwise not be subject, as, say, in the mouse engineered to be subject to amyotrophic lateral sclerosis. Elimination of this disease and of other dreadful diseases, such as Huntington's and Tay-Sachs, that genetic engineering might help us to understand and gene therapy to treat would enormously enhance both life expectancy and our condition or quality of life. As genetic engineering gathers pace in the research community, I suspect animal use in the search for such obvious benefits to humans, far from diminishing, is going to increase substantially. So how 'close' the animal is to us, while a matter of degree, appears to be 'sufficiently close' to enable genetic engineering to hold out prospects for the elimination of certain diseases that only a few years ago were thought of as inescapable scourges of the human condition.

Another development that is likely to spur our use of animals in medicine is their use as a repository of organs for human transplant. Xenograft, or cross-species transplantation, is set to play an increasingly important part in our medical uses of animals. (While a number of people object to harvesting animal organs for aphrodisiacs and to the use of animals in tribal, cultural, or religious ceremonies, their objections disappear when it is matter of our health.) We could breed baboons for, say, hearts for transplant into human infants, as in the Baby Fae experiment (Frey 1988; Pence 1995); we could genetically engineer pigs so that human organs are bred into the pig. In both cases, we would not be using creatures in the wild or otherwise existent creatures, but creatures who would not exist, except for their being bred for organ transplants.

The mention of a baboon raises the whole issue of primates, and today many in the animal welfare community are seeking a complete ban on their use in medical research. Indeed, the Great Ape Project, fostered by Singer, Jane Goodall, Paola Cavalieri (Cavalieri and Singer 1994), and others, is an attempt to extend the protection of 'personhood' to the great apes and so the greater protections that personhood would encompass, and discussions increasingly are heard that advocate the extension of certain legal rights to the great apes (and other animals) as well (Wise 2001). Yet, in the USA a good deal of genetic engineering already takes place in primates, and I suspect the amount is bound to increase. The very similarities of primates to ourselves genetically, physiologically, pathologically, metabolically, neurologically, and so on make them the model of choice for research into numerous human conditions. With stem cells from rhesus monkeys and marmosets isolated in 1994, we took a step towards the possibility, through inserting into the monkey the gene correlated with a certain disorder, of genetically engineering monkeys that had amyotrophic lateral sclerosis, cystic fibrosis, and so on. It is precisely because of their similarities to ourselves in the ways indicated that the ability to produce primates that have human illnesses stirs the medical community. Thus, while genetic engineering in medicine may at times focus upon non-primates, I think animal rights advocates are quite correct to think that the whole thrust of the enterprise, if we are to find models similar to ourselves in the relevant respects, in order to study and understand the progression and pathology of illnesses, is to take this research into primates.

Yet it is precisely because of their similarities to ourselves that people have come to object to the use of primates in medical research at all. Certainly, this is the trend in the United Kingdom. A tension obviously arises: similarity to ourselves is both the reason to use (in the USA) and not to use (in the UK) primates in medical research. I suspect that this tension is going to increase, as animal studies reveal further both the depth and the extent of primates's similarities to ourselves and as the European Union begins to implement further protections against the use of primates in medical research. An interesting sidelight to this tension will be the extent to which, say, countries in the European Union that curtail the use of primates continue to buy the results of medical research involving primates from the USA, the extent to which companies with labs in the USA do the research in primates there and then make the results of those studies available to their labs elsewhere, and so on.

3. THREE POSITIONS ON EXPERIMENTATION

We can distinguish (at least) three positions on animal experimentation, though there are permutations on each.

3.1 Abolitionism

There are two different types of view to be distinguished here. First, there is immediate abolitionism, to the effect that any and all animal experimentation should cease at once, no matter what the experiment or how promising it may be so far as human benefit is concerned or how far it has progressed. If something is wrong, it should be stopped. Tom Regan (1983) takes this position. Secondly, there is progressive abolitionism, of the sort advocated by FRAME (see Balls et al. 1983), in which animal experiments are eliminated as replacements become available by which to do the research in question. Sometimes, Regan (1997) has been ambivalent between these positions, but I see no reason why he should be. If he thinks it is wrong to experiment upon animals, then what permits us to continue to experiment upon them until we find replacements? In fact, an abolitionist who holds the progressive form can be accused by immediate abolitionists of having truck with evil. After all, it might be urged, who would accept the progressive closure of a concentration camp? Yet, in most public discussion, it is the progressive variety of abolitionism that is presented: as we develop alternative methods of obtaining the results or benefits of medical research, we can progressively shift away from the use of animals. But that is something that even defenders of experimentation can—and should—hold. As alternative methods become available, it becomes immoral to continue to use animals to obtain results that could be obtained by non-animal means.

The progressive form is preferred, of course, because the immediate form of abolitionism is too extreme: the removal of illnesses, the dramatic enhancement of human quality of life, and the extension of human life are clear benefits for most of us and so held to be worth having, even at the cost of animal lives. (I am not here concerned with extension of human life beyond what the person in question wants to live, cases that today propel the discussion of euthanasia and physician-assisted suicide.)

3.2 Anything Goes

If immediate abolitionism is too extreme for most people, so, too, is the 'anything-goes' position. Here, the claim would be that we can do anything we please to research animals. If this position were ever in vogue, it clearly is no longer. Thus, very few people today would claim that animals do not feel pain, and those who might be so tempted, as Peter Carruthers (1992) is thought to be, usually go on at once to qualify the sense in which they might be understood to intend such a claim. Certainly medical people give every evidence of believing exactly the opposite. Hospital and research facilities have ethics review committees that oversee the institutional use and care of animals, and they have in place guidelines governing the infliction of pain and suffering upon animals. Medical periodicals have peer review policies that ask about what was done to animals in the course of research and about what in the experiment justifies the infliction of pain and suffering. Guidelines demand that animal suffering be controlled, limited, mitigated where feasible, and justified in the course of research, and where these guidelines are ignored or violated, government and institutional oversight committees can deny further funding for the research and so effectively terminate it. Of course, none of this denies that animals can be used and, at times, painfully, but the 'anything-goes' position, in which the infliction of pain is viewed as uncontrolled and in which the value of animal life is held to be negligible or non-existent, can again seem too extreme.

Today, of course, the three-R approach, associated with the names of W. M. S. Russell and R. L. Burch (Russell and Burch 1959), is very much to the fore in animal welfare circles. The idea is to try to achieve *reduction* in the number of animals used and the pain and suffering inflicted, *refinement* in the experiment in order to eliminate, for example, repetitive uses of animals, continual duplication of results, and, ultimately, the number of animals used, and *replacement* of animals with non-animal models (such as tissue cultures, computer adaptations, and so on). The three-R approach is widely endorsed today as the embodiment of a humane research ethic, so far as animals are concerned. But it must be understood clearly that, far from being an abolitionist position, it is in fact a pro-research position. It aims at forming a 'humane' research ethic, one that animal welfarists can endorse but that working scientists can also attempt to achieve in their working lives.

3.3 Middle Position

To many people, of course, there has to be middle ground between the abolitionist and anything-goes positions. This middle ground needs to be described and defended, a task to which I now turn. It is characterized by several claims: animals possess moral standing and so are part of the moral community; therefore, their pains are to be taken seriously and their lives accorded value; progressive abolition occurs as replacement of animal models occurs; and trade-offs between benefit and loss with regard to humans and animals are accepted. This middle ground, adequately defended, constitutes, I think, a moral justification of animal experimentation.

4. HUMAN BENEFIT

Human benefit drives animal research (though benefit to animals is, of course, also a consideration), and virtually all attempts to justify animal research inevitably go through this appeal to benefit. This appeal, however, requires supplementation, and for an obvious reason: the benefits that animal research confer on us could be obtained from doing the research in humans. Indeed, using humans could confer those benefits as well, if not better, than doing the research in animals, since extrapolations from animals to humans are bound in some sense to be more problematic than extrapolations from humans to humans. Yet, everyone would agree, I presume, that it is wrong to do to humans what we presently do to research animals. Therefore, the claim of benefit needs to be supplemented with an argument that shows why, given some particular benefit, it would be wrong to do the research that obtains that benefit in humans but not in animals.

5. REJECTION OF THE TRADITIONAL JUSTIFICATION

This line of argument is sufficiently powerful, I think, that those in the pro-research camp are liable to be tempted to an extreme position here—namely, to suggest that humans are morally considerable or possess moral standing and that animals do not. Accordingly, what is done to animals will not matter morally, or, if it matters, it does so only derivatively, in terms, as Kant implied, of what it may lead us to do to humans. If, then, animals do not matter morally, then there is nothing wrong with using them to our research ends by, for example, giving them certain illnesses and then studying the progress and pathology of those illnesses in their lives. This extreme position does indeed differentiate humans from animals: humans are morally considerable in their own right and not derivatively; therefore, what is done to them counts morally in a way that what is done to animals does not.

What we might think of as the traditional justification of animal experimentation incorporates this extreme position. That justification rests upon three claims: first, animals are not members of the moral community and lack all moral standing; secondly, their lives have no or only very little value; and, thirdly, since humans are members of the moral community, we cannot use them in the way we presently use animals.

Behind these claims lay the Judaic/Christian ethic that posited a sharp break between humans and animals. The first two claims would indeed mark out a sharp moral difference. If animals are not members of the moral community, then what we do to them, including using them in painful ways, is not of moral concern (except in so far as it might lead us to use humans in painful ways), and if their lives had no or only very little value, then the destruction of those lives, lives that in any event lay outside the moral community, is also of little concern. The third claim simply applied the first two: no human who is a member of the moral community and whose life is of (considerable) value can be treated as we presently treat research animals.

This traditional justification must, I think, be given up. In very general terms, as we learn more about animals, it becomes more difficult to maintain a sharp break between animals and ourselves. From one side, as we learn more about animals and the feats they can perform, especially primates, it becomes difficult in the light of those feats to maintain a sharp break; from the other, as we learn more about the conditions in which humans can find themselves through illness, disease, and degeneration, conditions in which some humans can do little of what primates customarily do, it becomes equally difficult to maintain a sharp break. Besides, there is the sheer convenience of it all, of how our religious ethic advantages ourselves at the expense of the animate (and, indeed, inanimate) environment.

The main problem with the traditional justification of animal experimentation, of course, is that we cannot take for granted any longer the religious underpinning of the first two claims. In a pluralistic society, unanimity in religious opinion is no longer the case; not only do different religions, especially Eastern ones, take different views about animals, but the number of non-religious people also appears to have risen as well. In fact, those who offer a religious ethic sometimes do so in terms, for example, of distinctly human goods and conceptions of human flourishing, notions that are more amenable to non-religious people. In short, I do not think we can simply take for granted that the traditional justification of animal experimentation will any longer carry the day, and I think that any new attempt at justification, including one that involves appeal to human benefit, will almost certainly start by denying the first two claims of the traditional justification. That is, I think any justification must accept that animals have moral standing and so are members of the moral community and that their lives have value. In this regard, I think Singer, Regan, Clark (1982), and others are right to criticize past efforts to read animals out of the moral community.

They were read out of the moral community because their pain and suffering and their lives were postulated as being of no moral signficance. But pain and suffering are moral-bearing characteristics for us, and throughout the USA and Europe there are guidelines that mandate that animal suffering be controlled, limited, mitigated, and justified in the research protocol and/or experiment. Moreover, the great care researchers extend to their experimental animals and their concern that such animals be euthanized before recovering from anaesthetic indicate that they take animal suffering seriously.

Besides, there is something odd about maintaining that pain and suffering are morally significant when felt by a human but not when felt by an animal. If a child burns a hamster alive, it seems quite incredible to maintain that what is wrong with this act has nothing essentially to do with the pain and suffering the hamster feels. To maintain that the act was wrong because it might encourage the child to burn other children or encourage anti-social behaviour, because the act failed to exhibit this or that virtue or violated some duty to be kind to animals—to hold these views seems almost perverse, if they are taken to imply that the hamster's pain and suffering are not central data bearing upon the morality of what was done to it. For us, pain and suffering are moral-bearing characteristics, so that, whether one burns the child or the child burns the hamster, the morality of what is done is determined at least in part by the pain and suffering the creature in question undergoes. Singer's utilitarianism picks this feature up quite nicely, and it seems to me exactly right. Of course, there may be other moral-bearing characteristics that apply in the case, but that fact in no way enables us to ignore, morally, the hamster's pains.

If the hamster's pain and suffering count morally, however, then it seems implausible to suggest that its life does not. The very reason that suffering so concerns us, in the case of any creature who can undergo it, is how it can blight and ruin a life (Rollin 1989). If the lives of experimental animals had no value, then why do researchers go to such lengths to justify the sacrifice of those lives? Why would we even bother to point to the benefits that such sacrifice can bring, if the lives sacrificed had no value whatever? If, however, those lives do have some value, then we certainly need to justify their destruction and the deliberate lowering through experimentation of their quality of life.

Though it perhaps sounds slightly offensive, I do not think the first two claims of the traditional justification of animal experimentation are even plausible beginnings of a defence of animal experimentation. As we shall see, I think what confers moral standing upon animal lives and gives them value is precisely what does these things in our lives—namely, their experiential content.

6. THE CENTRAL PROBLEM: HUMANS, NOT ANIMALS

There is an obvious way of making plain, so far as moral standing is concerned, the difficulty of separating the human and animal case. For example, it is widely agreed today that there are features of human lives, such as intelligence, sentiency, and self-direction, that bar using such beings in research without their consent (or, indeed, in certain cases, even with their consent), and a number of writers on 'animal rights' have tried, not surprisingly, to find such features in animal lives, including some of the main types of research animals. In the face of this attempt, one might, I suppose, simply insist that animals do not share in the relevant characteristics picked out 'to the same degree' or 'enough' to warrant a similar bar to research in their cases. But the central problem with this kind of move has little to do with the success of those writers on 'animal rights'; it has rather to do with the fact that not all human beings share in the characteristics picked out to the same degree. What do we do about these humans? If animals do not gain protection from research because they lack the relevant degree of the relevant characteristics, then what about those humans who lack that degree of those characteristics?

One suggestion here, of course, is that, side effects apart, we may use the humans in question as we use animals in research. But most people would be outraged by this suggestion. Yet, these same people are not outraged by the thought of using animals in medical research. So what can be the difference? What can make it wrong to use humans but right to use animals? An answer to this question simply must be forthcoming. The appeal to human benefit cannot stand alone as a justification of animal experimentation, since it would also justify human experimentation. It must be supplemented, therefore, with some account of why it would be wrong to use humans, any humans whatever, in order to obtain the benefits in question but not wrong to use animals.

What is driving the argument here is what I take to be a justified assumption—namely, that, for any characteristic selected as that around which to formulate a claim of protection, humans will be found who lack the characteristic altogether, or lack it to a degree sufficient to protect them from being used in medical experiments, or lack it to a degree that in fact means that some animals have it to a greater degree. Thus, any number of primates give evidence of being more intelligent than many severely mentally enfeebled humans, of being sentient to a degree beyond anything we associate with anencephalic infants, and of being better able to direct their lives than humans fully in the grip of senile dementia. Indeed, depending upon the characteristic selected, all kinds of animals, and of different species, will exceed the human case.

Certainly, the characteristic of having had two human parents may favour humans, but it does not appear to be the kind of characteristic required. For the nature of one's parentage says nothing about one's present quality of life, intelligence, capacity for pain and distress, the ability to direct one's life, and so on, and these sorts of characteristics appear much more like the kinds of things that would justify not treating a human life as we presently treat animal lives. For these sorts of characteristics say something about the life being lived, not what produced that life, something, that is, about the quality of the life being lived and so the welfare of the creature whose life it is. Thus, while anencephalic infants have had human parents, the nature and quality of their lives, by all the usual standards, appear to be far worse than the lives of many animals. Much the same appears to be true in the cases of all those who suffer from radically debilitating, degenerative illnesses, such as Huntington's disease, amyotrophic lateral sclerosis, and so on.

The central problem, then, in this discussion of animals turns out to be certain humans. Whatever characteristic we select around which to formulate some claim of protection from research, we seem inevitably to come across humans who lack that characteristic and animals who to a greater or lesser degree have it. Do we use these humans as we presently use animals in research? Or do we use neither humans nor animals, since the latter possess the characteristic selected around which to formulate the claim of protection? The first option will be repugnant to most; the second will virtually bar animal research. The problem, then, is that, if we cannot separate fully, in a morally significant way, the human and animal cases (Rachels 1990), then we must either endorse some version of animal research on humans or cease, whether in an immediate or progressive fashion, research on all those animals who share in the characteristic selected. In this sense, the sense in which the argument from marginal cases (or unfortunate humans) looms large, the case for antivivisectionism, as I have always maintained, is stronger than most people allow.

It is obvious why the usual tactic at this juncture—namely, to select some strongly cognitive characteristic in order to bar all animals from the protected class—fails completely (Beauchamp 1992, 1997). The number of humans who fall outside the protected class will significantly increase, as the complexity of the cognitive task required for protection from research mounts; whereas to go in the other direction and to select a very much less complex task to acquire the relevant protection runs the obvious risk of including a good many animals in the protected group, even as some humans are excluded from it. Thus, the difficulty here is not that protection would be extended to some animals by this argument; it is that protection would not be extended to all humans. And those outside the protected class would then fall subject, side effects apart, to the benefit argument for experimentation.

In short, the search for some characteristic or set of characteristics, including cognitive ones, by which to separate us from animals runs headlong into the problem of marginal humans (or, in my less harsh expression, unfortunate humans). Do we use humans who fall outside the protected class, side effects apart, to achieve the benefits that animal research confers? Or do we protect these humans on some other ground, a ground that includes all humans, whatever their quality and condition of life, but no animals, whatever their quality and condition of life, a ground, moreover, that is reasonable for us to suppose can anchor a moral difference in how these different creatures are to be treated? But then what on earth is this other ground?

What in part bedevils the case of animals, then, is the case of humans. I shall return to this argument about marginal or unfortunate humans below, but first it is necessary to go back to the issue of moral standing, of who or what is morally considerable or a member of the moral community, in order now to indicate why I think animals have moral standing and lives of value and in what the value of their lives consists.

7. MORAL STANDING

In recent years, the search for a characteristic (or set) that transforms a creature from one that does not count morally into one that does so count has been protracted and heated. In some respects, this search has resembled that earlier in the abortion controversy, as claims about whether the fetus is a person, can feel pain, has rights, and so on all became ways of trying to give the fetus moral standing. In the case of animals, however, where many did not feel inclined to grant the fetus independent moral standing, no such reluctance was felt here. Numerous options have surfaced. Singer (1986) and a good many others have followed Bentham and urged sentiency or the ability to feel pain as the characteristic in question; Regan (2001) has talked about things that have inherent worth and a biography, with moral rights then used to protect such worth; Mary Anne Warren (1997) has urged a multiplicity of criteria, in addition to sentiency, as the required feature. A host of people, including Sapontzis (1987), De Grazia (1996), and to some extent Rollin (1981), have urged the possession of interests as the crucial feature required for moral standing, with or without rights then deployed as the device by which interests are protected. Clark (1997), Linzey (1987), and others have urged a more theocratic view be taken of our relationship with both animate and inanimate nature and that moral standing be seen in the light of this relationship to God. Carruthers (1992) has put forward contractualist concerns and the ability to enter into voluntary agreements as a condition of standing, with the result that animals turn out to have moral standing only derivatively. Others treat this implication as a kind of *reductio* of the contractualist position. Scruton (1996) has talked of moral community in a more traditional sense, in which the interplay of reciprocity among persons, duty, responsibility, and virtuous action is characteristic, with some allowance then made for children and certain adults. John Harris (1988) takes being a person to be the central datum, where that notion is not identical with that of being human, and others have followed his lead. And Rosalind Hursthouse (2000) has even given, though in more indistinct form, some account of how a virtue theorist might try to address the issue of moral standing (given that the virtuous agent is the prime datum in the theory and animals are not virtuous agents) and the virtuous agent's treatment of animals. In short, all kinds of suggestions have been put forward over moral standing. I have not space to go into all these. It seems to me, however, that there is a central notion that many of these different accounts strive to capture in some form or other, one that enables us as well to keep the focus upon the interplay between our treatment of research animals and the claim that the benefits that research confers can be obtained through the use of (certain) humans.

Moral standing, I think, has nothing to do with agency on the part of the subject, nothing to do with the capacity to display virtues in the course of one's behaviour or with the capacity to make contracts, nothing to do with the possession of moral rights. Humans fully in the grip of Alzheimer's disease may cease to be agents, making choices and directing their own lives, but we do not think thereby that they cease being members of the moral community. In certain cases, the severely subnormal may never have risen to the station of agent in the first place, but they do not thereby cease being morally considerable and so part of the moral community.

In my view, moral standing or moral considerability turns upon whether a creature is an experiential subject, with an unfolding series of experiences that, depending upon their quality, can make that creature's life go well or badly. Such a creature has a welfare that can be positively or negatively affected, depending upon what is done to it. With a welfare that can be enhanced or diminished, a creature has a quality of life. People in the grip of senile dementia or who are severely subnormal nevertheless are beings with a quality of life that can be positively or negatively affected by what we do to them. At the same time, however, most people today would concede that hamsters, rabbits, and rodents, let alone chimps and other primates, are such creatures. They are experiential subjects with a welfare and quality of life that our actions can affect, and this is true whether they have rights, whether they are thought of as agents, and whatever their capacities for displaying virtues in their behaviour or making contracts. Of course, there are likely to be cases where we are doubtful about whether a creature is an experiential one (say, earthworms), but I cannot see that the usual experimental animals, such as rodents, rabbits, pigs, and primates, are doubtful cases at all. Accordingly, in this view, creatures who are experiential subjects have moral standing and are members of the moral community in exactly the same way that we are.

As I noted earlier, pain is a moral-bearing characteristic for us, and I cannot see what difference it makes as to which species feels pain. Pain is pain: to experiential creatures, it represents an evil in life, if not intrinsically, then certainly instrumentally, with respect to their quality of life. But, if the pains of animals count morally, then it is rather odd to conclude that their lives do not. As I indicated above, part of what matters about pain so much is how it can ruin a life and seriously reduce its quality, and this possibility of reduced quality exists in the cases of all those who can experience pain. After all, it would be absurd, whether in ourselves or in animals, to take excruciating agony to be an indication, other things being equal, of a high or desirable quality of life. Animals, then, are living creatures with experiential lives, creatures with a welfare and quality of life, and they are, therefore, creatures whose lives can be blighted and radically diminished in quality. For these reasons, I think that animal lives have value.

Given that animals and humans are experiential creatures, I see no reason to offer an account of the value of their respective lives that is different (Frey 1988), and quality-of-life views will typically treat them the same. What matters is the quality of life lived. Such a view makes the value of a life turn upon its content or experiences, whether that life be human or animal, and this in turn raises the interesting issue of the nature of, and the nature of our access to, the subjective lives and inner experiences of animals. Today, most informed people accept that animals—certainly, primates—have such experiences. It is these unfolding experiences that constitute their inner lives and make them, so to speak, psychological beings, in the way that we are psychological beings, and the difficulty of determining the exact nature of these experiences in their cases does not, in and of itself, undermine this fact.

In sum, animals and humans are living creatures with experiential lives and so things with a welfare and a quality of life. For these reasons, I take animal lives to have value, where the value of a life is a function of its quality. It is not just true of human lives that they can go well or badly: this is true of the lives of all experiential creatures. So, I think quality of life determines the value not only of human but also of animal lives, and I think that quality of life is a function of the scope and capacities of a creature for different kinds of experiences.

If the value of a life is a function of its quality, the quality of its richness, and the richness of its scope and capacities for enrichment, then the lives of normal adult humans are almost certainly going to turn out to be of a higher value than the lives of most animals. The capacities of enrichment of life in the normal adult case exceed anything we find in the animal case, or so the evidence suggests; thus, though we live lives with basic human needs, many, if not most, of which we share with animals, we also live lives at a level at which our mental, cultural, academic, and artistic talents, to name only a few things, deeply affect the texture of our lives. I do not have space here for more detail, but the general idea may be captured by a thought about death. When we say of a man after death that he lived a rich, full life or that he lived life to the full, we refer to things far beyond what evidence suggests that rodents, our main research animal, can enjoy. We cannot on a quality-of-life view, however, be dogmatic in the matter: if evidence turns up to suggest otherwise of rodent lives, then we shall have to change our view of their richness, quality, and value.

8. Questioning Tradition and Avoiding Speciesism

I cannot here go into all the qualifications that must attend any discussion of quality of life, including the obvious fact that, if this is often difficult to determine in the human case, how much more difficult it is likely to be in the animal case. Still, we use the notion constantly with regard to humans and in all kinds of contexts, from discussions about treatment and the allocation of medical goods to the evaluation of social policies as they affect the well-being of those they are intended to help. Granted that the concept is not an easy one to unravel, it is not, however, completely beyond us to do so. Yet, I do not need to go into these various qualifications here in order to show, if the notion of quality of life can be defended, how it can supply what is needed with the appeal to benefit in order to justify animal experimentation.

Why can we not do to humans what we presently do to experimental animals? The answer the traditional justification gave was that humans are members of the moral community and have lives of some value. On the view just sketched, however, animals are members of the moral community, because they, too, are experiential creatures, and they have lives of some value, because they, too, have a quality of life and welfare that our actions can augment or diminish. The fact is that these things are true of both humans and animals, and it is only speciesism that makes us think otherwise. By 'speciesism', I mean discrimination on the basis of species alone.

So, whether we use animals to achieve the benefits of experimentation or we use humans, we shall be using creatures who are members of the moral community and who have lives of value. How, then, do we choose between them, in a non-speciesist way?

Any number of things may be said at this point, but virtually all of them strike me as attempts to hang on to past practices, when we have discarded the rationale and ethic that underlay those practices. For example, can we not just prefer humans to animals, say, because of the tradition (moral, social, cultural, religious) out of which we come? But how can this sort of thing make something, such as regarding black people as inferior to white, right? No one really believes today that citing tradition justifies the continuance of racism. So why should we think that it justifies a perpetual preference of animals over humans, in the case of experimentation?

How, then, are we to choose which creatures to use in order to achieve the benefits of the enhancement and extension of human life? The thought that underlies the quality-of-life position is that we use quality of life to decide. Other things being equal, in a hospital, if we can save one of two lives, we save the life of higher quality (actual and/or prospective); in taking life, other things being equal, we sacrifice the life of lower quality. Accordingly, we achieve the benefits of experimentation by using creatures of lower rather than higher quality of life. Plainly, then, a good deal of work needs to be done on the notion of quality of life, on how to determine it in humans and animals, and on gaining access to the inner lives of animals. This way of proceeding is non-speciesist, since we are preferring (most) human lives to (most) animal lives not in virtue of species but in virtue of quality of life.

I accept, then, that animals, and certainly the 'higher' animals, have subjective experiences, that those experiences determine their quality of life, and that the quality of lives determines the value of those lives. This is exactly what I accept in the human case. We use behaviour and behavioural studies to gain access to the interior lives of animals, and we move slowly forward as these empirical studies of animal behaviour yield more information about them. If I can never know exactly what it is like to be a hamster, I can nevertheless come to know more and more in this regard, as we learn more about them and their responses to their environment.

Most of us do not think, however, that animal life is as valuable as human life, and a quality-of-life view of the value of a life can explain why. The richness of normal adult human life greatly exceeds that of animal life, in that the capacities for enrichment, in all their variety, extent, and depth, exceed anything that we associate with mice or even chimps. That an animal has a more acute sense of hearing than we do does not make up for this difference in variety, extent, and depth of capacities; for that to happen we should have to think that the animal's more acute hearing confers on its life a quality that approximates the quality that all of our capacities for enrichment along multidimensions that appear unavailable to the animal, on present scientific evidence, confer on our lives. Once again, however, we cannot be dogmatic on this score and must be prepared to revise our view of animal lives as more and better information on them becomes available to us.

Most importantly, the claim that the animal's capacities provide it with a perfectly full life for a creature of its kind is not to the point, for what quality-of-life concerns are being used to do here is to make comparative judgements about the value of different lives. The concession that animals lead full lives for creatures of their kind does not, in and of itself, answer the question about the comparative value of the animal's life versus the value of a normal adult human's life. Moreover, while one can object to making such comparative judgements, at least with any very great degree of refinement, we certainly make such judgements daily, whether in our hospitals, as we evaluate the comparative conditions of two patients, or in our veterinary schools, as we evaluate the comparative conditions of two animals. But the degree of refinement I am talking about does not need to be very great, in order for me to suggest that it is the comparative value of lives, not species, that supplements the argument from benefit.

Thus, in addition to the fact that pain is a moral-bearing characteristic for us, animals are members of the moral community because they are experiential creatures with a quality of life and welfare that can be affected by what we do to them. But they do not have the same moral standing as normal adult humans, since the value of these human lives far exceeds that of animals. The truth is that not all creatures who have moral standing have the same moral standing, and this truth, as we shall see, has as dramatic implications for human lives as it does for the comparative-value question for animal lives. Even so, animals are members of the moral community and have lives of some value; they are morally considerable. The 'anything-goes' position on animal research, then, a position that might seem desirable from the point of view of research scientists, will not do: it simply fails to take account of the moral considerability of animals and the fact that their lives have value.

9. COMPARING LIVES

If one can kill a mouse or a man and obtain the relevant benefits, then, other things being equal, it is worse to kill the man. What makes it worse is not species membership, but the fact that human life is more valuable than animal life. While the mouse's life has value, it does not have the same value as the man's life, and it is worse to destroy lives of greater rather than lesser value. This comparative view of the value of a life will be speciesist, however, unless something other than species membership confers greater value on the man's life. Richness, capacity for enrichment, and quality of life are such things.

What matters, then, is how pronounced the capacities of an experiential creature are for a rich life, and science and observation teach us different things about mice and men. Neither the behavioural sciences nor observation give us reason to believe that the mouse, given the variety and extent of its capacities and the life appropriate to its species, approaches our own in richness, quality, and value, given the variety, extent, and depth of our capacities. So far as we know, the capacities for enrichment of the mouse are just too limited in number, scope, and variety to lead us to think differently, though we must retain an open mind on the matter and pay attention to opposing evidence. Where this evidence comes in the form of detailed observation of primates, we might have to be prepared, I think, to envisage something radically different from the case of the mouse, based on the accruing evidence of primate studies both in the wild and in captivity.

Certainly, much here is difficult because it is difficult to gain access to the inner lives of animals. It is quite wrong to suggest, however, that we can know nothing of the richness of animal lives, so that I am barred from using the notion. Animal behaviourists sympathetic to the 'animal rights' cause, such as Donald Griffin (1981, 1992), Rosemary Rodd (1990), Marian Dawkins (1993), and Marc Bekoff (1998), all think that we can know something of the richness and quality of life of the 'higher' animals. Certainly, all laymen think this, when they point out that pain and suffering, boredom, inability to scratch or peck, and so on, affect a creature's quality of life, something to which veterinarians, such as David Morton (1995), also attest. The fact that we cannot know everything about an animal's inner life does not mean that we cannot know a good deal. Yet, what we know leads us to think that the capacities associated with normal adult human life exceed anything we associate with the lives of mice, pigs, or baboons. This difference in capacities for enrichment affects the content of a life and so its quality and value. This, then, is why it is morally worse to kill the man rather than the mouse: it amounts to the destruction of something of greater value.

10. Intra- and Inter-Species Comparisons

Difficulties arise, of course, with quality-of-life judgements even within our own species, as when we try, for example, to compare the quality of lives of two patients in a hospital. Such comparisons are not, however, entirely beyond us, and medical people make such judgements daily, often as a basis for treatment and decisions about allocation of scarce goods. Nor do I deny that different factors can be taken into account, especially as between subjective impressions as to how well one's life is going versus objective criteria about that life. One area where interesting work is being done on this kind of problem is in the quality-adjusted-life-year (QALY) literature, where the scales of measurement of quality of life, in order to assign a QALY ranking and so to be able to compare and contrast different lives, weave together subjective and objective criteria of richness of content (Mooney 1986). The point is that such weaving together is not entirely beyond us.

If intra-species comparisons are difficult, inter-species comparisons are likely to be more so, though, again, not impossible. Once we depart very far from the 'higher' animals, we lose behavioural correlates that give us access to the interior lives of animals. Behavioural science and observation, both in captivity and the wild, have added enormously to our knowledge of the subjective lives of animals, and there is no doubt that this work has suggested that the interior lives of at least some animals are far richer than the traditional justification of animal experimentation ever envisaged. Yet, even so, ethologists and others are very hesitant to posit anything like similarity of richness of content with normal adult human life.

On two important points, we must be careful not to mistake what is at issue. First, to claim that I cannot be certain that the hamster's life is not as rich as the normal adult human's is not to meet the thrust of the capacities argument. If one wants to maintain that the two lives are equally valuable, then one must cite something that, however limited the capacities of the hamster in number and variety, confers on its life a richness comparable to what the differing capacities of the normal adult human confer on his life. The fact that the hamster has a keener sense of smell, the dog a keener sense of hearing, the eagle a keener sense of sight does not readily make us think otherwise. And to assume that the keener sense of smell confers on the hamster's life a vast dimension of joy that exceeds the various dimensions of richness conferred on human life by all its differing and extended capacities is again not something that science or observation will lead us readily to think. Secondly, we must be careful not to take the claim that both the hamster and we ourselves have but one life to live and that its value should be judged by the capacities appropriate to it as if it answered the comparative point. It does not. Based on what we know, we have no reason to believe that the hamster possesses anything like the extent, variety, and depth of ways of enrichment typical of normal adult humans, and we need some reason to believe that its keener sense of smell can confer on its life a richness similar to our own. There is nothing incommensurable here, nothing that as a matter of principle denies me access to the richness and quality of the hamster's life, even if it is difficult to gain that access. This fact supports the view that the difficulties in comprehending the richness and quality of life of (at least the 'higher') animals is one of degree and not of kind.

Nor must we overlook several features of normal adult human life that enable us to add enormously to the value of our lives. First, no account of all the activities we share with animals, such as eating, sleeping, and reproducing, comes anywhere near exhausting the richness of a life in which art, music, literature, family, friendship, love, intellectual endeavours, and so on inform it. Indeed, the fact that we can mould our lives in particular ways, to live out certain conceptions of the good life, such as a painter, is an important fact about us. Even if ultimately all this is cashed out in terms of experiences, it shows that we can shape our lives in ways of our own choosing, that we are not condemned to a life appropriate to our own species, even if it is true that there are limits on the sorts of life we can make for ourselves. Secondly, this feature of our lives lies beyond any mere concern with our capacities. In fact, we can integrate our lives into wholes whose value is enhanced as a result. This integrative task is partly an intellectual one, governed by some conception of the good life, and by a psychological awareness of how we are as people, in terms both of our similarities to other people and creatures and of our differences from them. This integration of our lives is part of what makes them worth living, a part that we do not share with other animals, as far as we know. Yet, no account of the richness of our lives could ignore it, since we should fail to understand how people have moulded their lives into lives they take appropriate to being teachers, athletes, and artists. Thirdly, we cannot ignore the role of agency in our lives. Not every being who is an experiential one and a member of the moral community is also an agent; some are, and always remain, patients. Among agents, however, there is a further sense of moral community that informs their lives. In this further sense of community, members have duties to each other, reciprocity of action occurs, standards for the assessment of conduct occur, and reasons for action are proffered and received. The absence of agency in this sense means that the creature in question is not regarded as a moral being in the full sense of being held accountable for its actions. To be accountable for what one does, in a community of others who are accountable for what they do, is not the same thing as having moral standing, nor is agency construed as acting and weighing reasons for action in the light of stand-ards required in order to be morally considerable.

Nevertheless, agency in this sense matters to the value of a life. The moral rela-tions in which normal adult humans stand to each other are part of whom they take themselves to be. They are husbands and wives, sons and daughters, family and friends. These are important roles we play in life, and they are composed in part by a view of the moral burdens and duties they impose on us, as well as the opportu-nities for action they allow us. In these relations, we come to count on others, to see ourselves as interlocked with the fate of at least some others, to be moved by what happens to these others, and to be motivated to affect the fate of these others to the extent that we can. While there is nothing fixed about all this, being a functioning member of a community in this sense can be one of the great goods of life, enrich-ing the very texture of the life one lives.

Our participation in a community of such agents enriches our lives. At a mini-mal level, it achieves this by allowing us to cooperate to achieve our cooperative ends. But the very way we live our lives—for example, as husbands and fathers—in order to fulfil what we see as our obligations within these moral relations in which we take ourselves to stand to others forms part of the texture and richness of our lives and so part of what we look at in order to determine whether our lives are going well or badly. In fact, these relations partly inform many of our prized ends in life, and we often find it difficult to explain why we did something at such obvi-ous cost to ourselves except through citing how we see ourselves linked to certain others.

The above barely scratches the surface of the sorts of things that come to consti-tute the richness of our lives. Yet, they show clearly that, when we speak of some-one as having led a 'rich, full' life, we refer to something that we understand to be beyond the animal case. The relations in which we stand to each other aid us in pur-suit of our ends and projects, many of which require the help of others to achieve, and the pursuit of these ends and projects, sometimes referred to collectively as one's 'conception of the good life', adds enormously to how well we take our lives to be going. Since our welfare is bound up with these kinds of pursuits, to ignore this fact is to give an impoverished account of a characteristically human life. Since all these ends and projects can vary between persons, there is no life 'appropriate' to our species, no single way of living to which every human being is condemned to conform. Agency enables us to make different lives for ourselves and so reflects, in this sense, how we want to live. Accomplishment of ends so moulded and shaped by ourselves is one of the important factors that can enrich individual human lives.

Agency, then, enables normal adult humans to enhance the quality and value of their lives in ways that no account of the activities we share with animals captures, and in seeking to give some account of the comparative value of human and animal life this kind of difference—to mention only one thing—is obviously important. It is just such a difference as this that evolutionary accounts of morality today can all too easily overlook, in their urge to show the common holdings of humans and animals.

Of course, on the comparative value of lives, we must be careful not to use in some unreflective manner criteria for assessing the richness of human lives as if they applied automatically to the animal case. This would be to make oneself into a speciesist in a second-order sense. We must use all we know about animals, especially primates, to try to gauge the quality of their lives in terms appropriate to their species. We must then try to assess the differences we allude to when we say, first of a rodent, then of a human, that each has led a rich, full life. What I am suggesting here is not merely that such assessments are within our capabilities, as we learn more about the subjective lives of animals, but also that they need to be informed by what we know in our own case about dimensions of our lives that neither science nor observation leads us to believe are characteristic of animal lives. For these differences will bear upon the issue of the comparative value of human and animal life.

We have, then, a non-speciesist reason for thinking that normal adult human life is more valuable than animal life. Its richness and quality exceed that of animal life. I said earlier that killing—between two lives, we take the life of lower quality and value—and saving—between two lives, we save the life of higher quality and value—are two sides of the same coin. Quality-of-life judgements dictate this. Accordingly, we have a non-speciesist reason for using the animal in preference to the human in medical experimentation, if we have to use some creature or other.

11. THE ARGUMENT FROM MARGINAL CASES

Yet, it should be apparent, as I remarked earlier, that there is a problem involving humans. Take the issue of moral standing: if those in the final stages of senile dementia or the very severely mentally enfeebled remain experiential creatures, it is unclear that those in permanently vegetative states or anencephalic infants do. Where the value of life is concerned, matters are even worse. It seems reasonably clear that many human lives, devastated by illness and disease, have diminished radically in richness and quality, quite apart from PVS patients and anencephalic infants, and it seems reasonably clear that numerous people undone by their medical conditions cannot adduce standards for the evaluation of conduct or conform their behaviour to such standards or receive and weigh reasons for action. (Indeed, even perfectly normal children and many of the very severely mentally enfeebled cannot do these things.) Today, of course, when the issue of physician-assisted sui-cide is much debated, virtually everyone is familiar with cases in which people liv-ing out certain lives seek relief from them, as they worsen, and where the quality and value of their lives are in inexorable decline. Such lives, even as they remain morally considerable, have plummeted in quality and value, and the fact is that they can plummet to such an extent that the quality and value of a perfectly healthy ani-mal's life can exceed these things in their lives.

In truth, not all human lives have the same richness or scope for enrichment; they do not, therefore, have the same value. What the prominence of medical cases has taught us today is that the quality of human life can plummet to such a degree that neither we nor the people forced to live those lives wish to see them condemned to do so. Tragic cases abound, from infants with AIDS to adults dying from amy-otrophic lateral sclerosis, cardiomyopathy, or pancreatic cancer. It seems absurd to pretend that lives of these sorts, lives that no one, not even the people living them, would wish to live, are as valuable as normal adult human life. Whereas, with ordin-ary children, we might appeal to some potentiality argument, in order to address the issue of the value of their lives, no such appeal is possible in the cases of some children or with adults stricken with severe, devastating illnesses. The truth seems to be that human lives vary in richness, quality, and value, and, when their value plummets drastically in severe cases, while these lives remain members of the moral community, their value can reach a point such that the value of quite ordinary ani-mal lives appears to exceed that of the human. If, therefore, research involving the use of lives is required, a terrible problem confronts us.

Dombrowski (1997) and others (Pluhar 1995) think well of the argument from marginal cases, but I reject it. If the argument is supposed to show the moral con-siderability of animals because we cede moral considerability to humans of low quality of life, then the argument is beside the point, since we include neither humans nor animals in the moral community for that reason. We include them because they are experiential creatures, with a welfare and a quality of life that can be increased or diminished by what we do to them. If, however, the argument is sup-posed to show that animals have lives of equal value to those of normal adult humans, then it fails outright, since not even all humans have lives of equal value.

On the latter side of the argument, massively diminished human life, where the scope and capacity for enrichment are radically diminished, is not of equal value with normal adult human life; there is no question, therefore, of ceding animal life similar value. Indeed, with a focus upon the medical cases, there is something dis-tinctly odd about the attempt to hold all human lives equally valuable, including those lives that no one would choose to live and about which we argue today whether we are justified in helping people condemned to live them to end their lives. It used to be said that deciding between humans on the ground of social worth, or their usefulness to society, was both distasteful and immoral; who, after all, are we to say of someone else's life that it is less valuable than another life? But talk of quality of life is rife in medical cases; and, though no one would want to be in the position of having to tell the patient in the grip of pancreatic cancer that an unpleasant end was in the immediate future, there are people who do this. And such an end is ahead. One can be sensitive in all this; but one can also be realistic. To treat all human lives as equally valuable fails the realism test.

It fails that test, that is, UNLESS one can come up with something that converts all human lives, *whatever their quality*, into lives of equal value. I do not have space here to explore this possibility, but certain metaphysical claims attempt to do just this. For example, it might be claimed that all human lives, whatever their richness and quality, are equal in the eyes of God. Or it might be claimed that all human lives, whatever their richness and quality, have equal inherent worth, where the notion of inherent worth amounts to a secular analogue to God. Here, inherent worth is separated from quality of life, thereby enabling two lives to have radically different qualities but equal worth (Regan 2001). Then the value of a life is tied to its worth, not its quality, thereby enabling one to tell a patient in the terminal stages of AIDS, suffering from Karposi's sarcoma, that his life is as valuable as the life of a normal adult human and, perhaps even, that he is wrong to seek relief from a valuable life. With space, I should want to argue that these and other metaphysical attempts to give renewed force to the argument from marginal cases fail. They increasingly appear to many of us, well and unwell alike, as bits of wishful thinking, in the face of medical conditions that bite drastically and irreversibly into what we take to comprise a rich, full life.

The argument from benefit, then, does not tell us which life to use; it needs to be supplemented with an argument that enables us to choose between lives, which I have attempted to provide. It turns out that lives of higher quality have greater value than lives of lower quality and that taking a life of higher quality in preference to a life of lower quality is worse. Assuming we have to use some lives in research in the first place, this tells us which lives to use. We should use lives of lower rather than higher quality. Typically, this will mean that we use animal lives. We simply cannot guarantee that this will always be so, however, unless we can find something that always ensures, whatever the richness and quality of human life, that it exceeds in value the lives of any and all animals. Unfortunately, I know of no such thing.

I do not advocate that we conduct experiments upon humans. Mine is not a recipe for action, but an attempt to understand what underlies one major effort at or argument for justifying the use of animals in medical experimentation. After all, the adverse side effects of experiments on certain humans—admittedly, the weakest amongst us—would be immense, and public outrage would be vociferous. Yet, if the benefits of animal research are all that researchers would have us believe, how do we avoid envisaging this terrible outcome? The claim would be not that we replace animals with humans, but that we follow the logic of the argument and use creatures with lower qualities of life. If one cannot bring oneself to do this, then I think one is forced to re-examine the case for animal experimentation, at least if that case is held, either directly or indirectly, to run through the appeal to benefit. As I indicated at the outset, the case against using animals in medical research can exert a stronger pull than is usually realized. One needs, then, in urgent fashion, that which transforms any and all human lives to a richness, quality, and value beyond the life of any animal, however tragic the condition of those human lives.

Of course, it may be said that this outcome here over animal experimentation just shows the folly of using quality-of-life concerns to determine the value of a life. If the use of quality-of-life concerns in the argument could expose some humans to experimentation, then we should jettison those concerns. Yet, every hospital and medical establishment uses quality-of-life considerations in making all kinds of judgements, including ones of life and death, with regard to humans. Indeed, such concerns are ubiquitous in the health-care system. So how can we simply jettison the very concerns that are part of the foundations of health-care decisions generally? And jettison them for what? For metaphysical claims that not all of us share? Or do we revert in the end merely to a brute preference for our own kind? But who gets to determine what counts as 'our own kind' and when we get to use it? Could the protected class turn upon a person's brute preference for white males?

Finally, I think one can now see in retrospect something about ceding animals moral status and granting that they have lives of value that, realizing what the implications of these on the quality-of-life position outlined will be, a research scientist may now want to go back and simply deny these things, go back to the Judaic/Christian ethic and assert the first two claims that we identified as comprising it. Put differently, it can appear that the only way to hold fast to one's ability to justify animal research, given that one does not want to go down my path, is simply to insist that animals lack moral standing, to deny that pain is a moral-bearing characteristic in their cases, and to deny that their lives have any value. But how does one now do this? That is, I think one of the powerful factors in favour of a quality-of-life view of the value of a life is that it faithfully replicates modern views about the value of human life and the way in which illnesses and disease can affect that value, and once the value of a human life begins to plummet the argument above starts to exert its pull, in the absence of some rather stout defence of metaphysical claims of a kind that are today contentious. Then one is left simply having to explain something: what is it that makes setting a child alight wrong but not setting a hamster alight? The screeching, the writhing, the uncontrolled movements: what is the difference?

REFERENCES

Balls, M. et al. (1983) (ed.), *Animals and Alternatives in Toxicity Testing*. London: Academic Press.

Beauchamp, T. L. (1992). 'The Moral Standing of Animals in Medical Research'. *Journal of Law, Medicine, and Ethics*, 20: 7–16.

Beauchamp, T. L. (1997). 'Opposing Views on Animal Experimentation: Do Animals Have Rights?' *Ethics and Behavior*, 7: 113–21.

Bekoff, M. (1998). 'Cognitive Ethology: The Comparative Study of Animal Minds', in W. Bechtel and G. Graham (eds.), *Blackwell Companion to Cognitive Science*. Oxford: Blackwell, 371–9.

Carruthers, P. (1992). *The Animals Issue*. Cambridge: Cambridge University Press.

Cavalieri, P., and Singer, P. (1994) (eds.), *The Great Ape Project*. New York: St Martin's Press.

Clark, S. R. L. (1982). *The Nature of the Beast*. Oxford: Oxford University Press.

——(1997). *Animals and their Moral Standing*. London: Routledge.

Cohen, C. (1986). 'The Case for the Use of Animals in Biomedical Research'. *New England Journal of Medicine*, 315: 865–70.

Dawkins, M. S. (1993). *Through our Eyes Only: The Search for Animal Consciousness*. New York: W. H. Freeman.

DeGrazia, D. (1996). *Taking Animals Seriously*. Cambridge: Cambridge University Press.

Dombrowski, D. (1997). *Babies and Beasts: The Argument from Marginal Cases*. Urbana, IL: University of Illinois Press.

Frey, R. G. (1980). *Interests and Rights*. Oxford: Oxford University Press.

——(1984). *Rights, Killing, and Suffering*. Oxford: Blackwell.

——(1987). 'Animal Parts, Human Wholes: On the Use of Animals as a Source of Organs for Human Transplant', in J. M. Humber and R. F. Almeder (eds.), *Biomedical Ethics Reviews*. Clifton, NJ: Humana Press, 89–101.

——(1988). 'Moral Standing, the Value of Lives, and Speciesism'. *Between the Species*, 4: 191–201.

——(1993). 'The Ethics of the Search for Benefits: Animal Experimentation in Medicine'. in R. Gillon (ed.), *Principles of Health Care Ethics*. New York: John Wiley, 1173–83.

Griffin, D. 1981. *The Question of Animal Awareness*. New York: Rockefeller University Press.

——(1992). *Animal Minds*. Chicago: University of Chicago Press.

Harris, J. (1988). *The Value of Life*. London: Methuen.

Hursthouse, R. (2000). *Ethics, Humans, and Other Animals*. London: Routledge.

LaFollette, H., and Shanks, N. (1997). *Brute Science: Dilemmas of Animal Experimentation*. New York: Routledge.

Langley, G. (1989) (ed.), *Animal Experimentation: The Consensus Changes*. London: Chapman & Hall.

Linzey, A. (1987). *Christianity and the Rights of Animals*. London: Herder & Herder.

Malouin, R. (1994). 'Surgeons' Quest for Life: The History and Future of Xenotrans-Plantation'. *Perspectives in Biology and Medicine*, 37: 416–28.

Mooney, G. (1986). *Economics, Medicine, and Health Care*. Atlantic Heights, NJ: Humanities Press International.

Morton, D. (1995). 'Recognition and Assessment of Adverse Effects in Animals', in N. E. Johnston (ed.), *Proceedings of Animals in Science Conference Perspectives on their Use, Care, and Welfare*. Melbourne: Monash University, 131–48.

Orlans, F. B. (1993). *In the Name of Science: Issues in Responsible Animal Experimentation*. New York: Oxford University Press.

Pence, G. (1995). *Classic Cases in Medical Ethics*. New York: McGraw-Hill.

Pluhar, E. B. (1995). *Beyond Prejudice: The Moral Significance of Human and Nonhuman Animals*. Durham, NC: Duke University Press.

Rachels, J. (1990). *Created from Animals: The Moral Implications of Darwinism*. Oxford: Oxford University Press.

Regan, T. (1983). *The Case for Animal Rights*. Berkeley and Los Angeles: University of California Press.

—— (1997). 'Animals and Morality'. *Ethics and Behavior*, 7: 95–110.

—— (2001). *Defending Animal Rights*. Urbana, IL: University of Illinois Press.

Rodd, R. (1990). *Biology, Ethics, and Animals*. Oxford: Oxford University Press.

Rollin, B. (1981). *Animal Rights and Human Morality*. Buffalo, NY: Prometheus.

—— (1989). *The Unheeded Cry: Animal Consciousness, Animal Pain, and Science*. Oxford: Oxford University Press.

Russell, W. M. S., and Burch, R. L. (1959). *The Principles of Humane Experimental Technique*. London: Methuen.

Ryder, R. (1976). 'Experiments on Animals', in T. Regan and P. Singer (eds.), *Animal Rights and Human Obligations*. Englewood Cliffs, NJ: Prentice Hall, 72–84.

Sapontzis, S. F. (1987). *Morals, Reason, and Animals*. Philadephia: Temple University Press.

Scruton, R. (1996). *Animal Rights and Wrongs*. London: Demos.

Singer, P. (1975). *Animal Liberation*. New York: New York Review, distributed by Random House.

—— (1986). *In Defense of Animals*. New York: Perennial Library.

Smith, J. A., and Boyd, K. M. (1991) (eds.), *Lives in the Balance: The Ethics of Using Animals in Biomedical Research*. Oxford: Oxford University Press.

Warren, M. A. (1997). *Moral Status: Obligations to Persons and Other Living Things*. Oxford: Oxford University Press.

Wise, S. M. (2001). *Rattling the Cage: Toward Legal Rights for Animals*. New York: Perseus Books.

CHAPTER 8

ENVIRONMENTAL ETHICS

KRISTIN SHRADER-FRECHETTE

1. DEVELOPMENT OF A NEW FIELD OF PHILOSOPHY

ENVIRONMENTAL ethics, as a field of philosophical study, began in the 1970s and 1980s, in part as a result of the environmental movement and largely in Anglo-American work. Its roots trace to the monumental technological discoveries of the twentieth century, such as nuclear power and chemical pesticides; their overuse or misuse; and recognition of the environmental degradation these technologies have caused.

1.1 Technological Threats and New Ethical Issues

Two paradigm examples of how misuse of technology has caused massive environmental damage and consequently raised new ethical questions are DDT and nuclear power. Paul Muller discovered the pesticide DDT, for which he received patents in 1942. Billions of pounds of the chemical were spread around the globe to protect people from malaria and typhus and their food supplies from the ravages of insects. By the 1960s, DDT and its by-products were discovered in the polar ice caps and in human breast milk. The World Health Organization estimates that pesticides kill approximately 40,000 people per year in developing nations alone.

In 1942, Enrico Fermi produced the world's first nuclear chain reaction, and then helped the USA to build the nuclear weapons, dropped on Hiroshima and Nagasaki, that ended the Second World War. Physicians estimate that one million premature cancers have been caused globally by above-ground nuclear-weapons testing and that the 1986 Chernobyl nuclear power accident will cause half a million premature fatal cancers, worldwide. Moreover, there is no established method for dealing with the billions of tons of high-level radioactive waste from the technology, waste that will remain lethal in perpetuity.

Ethical issues related to technologies such as DDT and commercial nuclear fission—issues such as whether there are duties to future generations, rights to a liveable environment, animal rights, and duties to prevent environmental injustice (inequitable distribution of environmental pollution and resources)—came to light in the 1960s not only because of technological failures but also because, in 1950, the human cancer rate began increasing by roughly 1 per cent per year. People and animals also began dying of air and water pollution. E. O. Wilson of Harvard claimed that human-induced species losses have numbered 1,000 per day since the Industrial Revolution. In 1962 Rachel Carson wrote her classic *Silent Spring*, an indictment of chemical pesticide technologies and the environmental and public-health harm they caused, and many people credit her volume with awakening environmental consciousness.

Recognizing the rising cancer deaths, the species losses, and the damaging technological impacts, scholars began asking about the causes of the environmental crisis. Their analyses began one of the major themes of environmental ethics: the degree to which human-centred or anthropocentric ethics have caused environmental problems. Historian Lynn White (1967) argued that Judaeo-Christian ethics, with its emphasis on anthropocentrism, its biblical injunction to subdue the earth, and its destruction of pagan animism, was responsible for environmental destruction. Philosopher Alan Donagan (1977) agreed in part with White, arguing that Judaeo-Christianity gave humans dominion over nature. Other philosophers, like John Passmore (1974), argued that White ignored the environmental stewardship practised by Francis of Assisi and many monasteries. He said greed and short-sightedness caused the environmental crisis, causes not unique to Judaeo-Christian ethics.

In 1979 Eugene Hargrove, then of the University of Georgia, began the first journal in the new field, *Environmental Ethics*, and Kristin Shrader-Frechette completed the first text book, *Environmental Ethics*. It took two years for it to be published, in 1981, because publishers initially said there was no such field.

1.2 Main Approaches to Environmental Ethics

From the point of view of the relative importance of human interests, the new field of environmental ethics can be divided roughly into anthropocentric, non-anthropocentric, and mixed approaches. Those in the first camp believe that environmental ethics is or ought to be human centred. That is, they argue either that environmental values are merely human preferences or that one ought to put most human considerations ahead of those of nature and the environment. Those in the second camp believe either that environmental values are not merely the product of human preferences or that traditional ethics has erred in placing human interests first. Ethics, they say, must undergo a massive transformation in order to address contemporary environmental problems. Those in the third, or mixed, camp argue that, while ethics ought to be amended to address environmental problems, nevertheless some human concerns ought to take preference over environmental interests, and some ought not.

Among those in the first, or anthropocentric, camp, John Passmore (1974) argues that Western anthropocentric ethics is adequate to solve environmental problems, provided people recognize that what harms the environment also harms humans. Passmore reasons that, to protect human welfare, everyone ought to protect the environment. Bryan Norton (1984) defends a weaker anthropocentrism, an attitude of *noblesse oblige* towards the environment. Although he recognizes that all environment-related choices must be made by humans and consistent with human preferences, he has a mixed theory in so far as he does not believe that environmental ethics ought to count only human interests. He maintains that, if humans take an attitude of beneficence towards the environment, this would both protect the planet and enhance human character.

Eugene Hargrove (1989) and Mark Sagoff (1988) also defend a weak anthropocentric account of environmental ethics. Arguing that there are no clear non-anthropocentric scientific norms that govern the environment, they claim the value found in nature is human centred because it is based on human aesthetic judgements.

Non-anthropocentric environmental ethicists include extensionists, zoocentrists, biocentrists, and ecocentrists. Extensionist Peter Singer (1990) pioneered the first approach, extending traditional utilitarian ethics to include all sentient beings, on the grounds that all beings capable of suffering ought to have moral standing. Zoocentrists such as Tom Regan (1988) argued that sentience is a sufficient but not a necessary condition for moral standing or rights, and they argued for development of necessary conditions. Biocentrists such as Kenneth Goodpaster (1978) maintain that the capacity to live is the criterion of moral considerability, presumably possessed by all beings capable of moral striving towards a goal. According to Paul Taylor (1986), the best-known exponent of the biocentric position, even plants have interests because they are teleological centres of life that strive to grow and reproduce. One of the obvious questions raised by Taylor's position, however, is whether use of language like 'striving' is more anthropomorphic and metaphorical than metaphysical or scientific.

For ecocentrists such as Baird Callicott (1987) and Holmes Rolston (1988), the extensionists, zoocentrists, and biocentrists provide an inadequate account of what is morally considerable in environmental ethics, largely because they do not treat the environment as an organic whole. Callicott argues that nature is indifferent to individual life and hence that environmental ethics, according to which individual life is the highest good and death is the greatest evil, is fundamentally flawed. Focusing on the 'land ethics' of Aldo Leopold (1970), Callicott (1987) argues that Humean moral sentiment is the basis of ethics and that environmental ethics requires extending the boundaries of moral community to include soil, waters, plants, and animals, or, collectively, the land.

Rejecting both the anthropocentrism of Passmore and the varieties of biocentrism and ecocentrism just discussed, proponents of mixed theories, like Christopher Belshaw (2001) and Kristin Shrader-Frechette (1995), adopt a more conciliatory or moderate position. Belshaw (2001: 121–46) argues against radically egalitarian or biocentric positions, like Taylor's, on the grounds that, just because one ought to extend the sphere of moral concern to other living things, nevertheless people ought to count for more, in part on grounds of sentience. Shrader-Frechette (1995) also defends a mixed ethical theory that recognizes both anthropocentric and biocentric values, provided that strong human rights, such as rights to life, are given first priority. According to her scheme, strong human rights have priority over environmental welfare, and serving environmental welfare has priority over weak human rights, such as rights to property (Shrader-Frechette and McCoy 1993: 173–6). In general, analytic philosophers, like Bryan Norton (1984), tend to hold more anthropocentric or mixed theories in their approaches to environmental ethics, perhaps because they take more account of the many philosophical problems associated with various criteria for moral considerability. However, non-philosophers, such as biologists, and philosophers outside the mainstream analytic tradition, like Baird Callicott (1987), tend to be more biocentric in their approaches.

Although work in environmental ethics includes questions about meta-ethics, normative ethics, and practical ethics, as the preceding overview suggests, the field has been dominated by the metaphysical or meta-ethical question of how to define the beings that ought to have 'moral standing' in environmental ethics. Although there are a variety of alternative approaches to environmental ethics that do not deal explicitly with such metaphysical or meta-ethical approaches, two of them perhaps deserve mention, in part because they are so well known. One alternative approach is ecofeminism, pioneered by philosophers such as Val Plumwood (1988) and Karen Warren (1996) and by historian Carolyn Merchant (1995). Although there are varieties of ecofeminism, its central precept is that the oppression of both women and nature is caused in part by glorification of domination and by a faulty account of rationality, one that overemphasizes purely intellectual modes of knowing. To remedy such oppression, ecofeminists argue for ways to reconceptualize accounts of rationality and to reform behaviours of dominance and control.

Another alternative approach to environmental ethics is the deep ecology of Norwegian philosopher Arne Naess (1989) and of George Sessions. Rather than espousing precise principles, deep ecologists support the 'deep' themes of being at one with nature; rejecting materialism, capitalism, and imperialism; showing respect for nature; and engaging in environmental activism. Whereas many people agree with such emphases, rather than the 'shallow' behaviour associated with egoism or materialism, other philosophers (e.g. Belshaw 2001: 179–203) have complained that deep ecology is more like ideology or religion than philosophy. They also have argued that it is grounded on opposition among people, rather than cooperation, and that it is vague and therefore difficult to apply, especially in troublesome cases.

1.3 Recent Developments in the Field of Environmental Ethics

As the field has developed over the last thirty years, four main changes have occurred in environmental ethics. First, later thinkers have gradually tended to avoid some meta-ethical errors that typified early work on environmental ethics, such as that of historian Roderick Nash. Failing to take account of various criteria for use of the term 'right', and not recognizing the theoretical difficulties arising when everyone and everything is said to be a rights-holder, Nash (1989) argued that even rocks have rights. Several philosophers have pointed out logical and meta-ethical problems with Nash's position.

A second change in environmental ethics is that more recent authors have resorted less to hand-waving environmental advocacy and instead are providing more philosophically defensible arguments. Often the early, philosophically naive 'preaching' consisted of enjoining people to accept a number of uncontroversial first-order ethical directives such as 'preserve biodiversity' or 'think small' or 'practise biotic equality among all living things'. Baird Callicott (1987), for example, made early appeals to equality within the biotic community. After criticism, he modified his position so that he discussed second- and higher-order ethical claims for adjudicating controversies among different beings within the biotic community. His move is important because the more controversial and interesting questions in ethics typically arise at the level of second- and higher-order analyses. These analyses attempt to illuminate decisions one faces when goals like preserving biodiversity or recognizing biotic equality, for example, conflict with other ends, such as economic development.

Callicott's theoretical modification of his ecocentric position also made him more able to handle the main objection of zoocentrist Tom Regan (1988). This objection is that, in asserting the equality of all human and non-human members of the biotic community, Callicott and other biocentrists have left themselves open to the charge of 'environmental fascism' (1987). According to Regan (1988), 'environmental fascism' refers to the dangerous consequences that arise if one attempts to maximize biotic welfare. If one maximizes biotic welfare, independent of human interests, then under some circumstances one could fail to recognize human rights and allow humans to die, whenever human welfare seemed at odds with biotic welfare.

Beginning in the early 1990s many environmental ethicists began to realize that they needed to provide second- and higher-order ethical criteria to help adjudicate environmental controversies. As a result, environmental ethics has become considerably less ideological and question begging than it was in the early days. Not all environmental philosophers fell into this ideological or question-begging approach, but enough did, so that the field has often been perceived as analytically weak.

Thirdly, environmental ethics became more scientifically sophisticated, as ethicists realized the sorts of objections to which their early theories were open. Holmes Rolston (1988), for example, made early appeals to 'the balance of nature' to defend his environmental ethics. He suggested that humans were disrupting an existing balance and that environmental ethicists simply had to urge people to conform to this balance. Rolston later modified his position when he realized that contemporary ecologists have rejected the notion of a balance of nature in favour of a stochastic concept of biological organization.

Fourthly, some environmental ethicists, such as Bryan Norton (1991) and Andrew Light (Light and Katz 1996), are adopting more pragmatic approaches. Arguing from a nominalist perspective and against any metaphysical or scientific foundations for environmental ethics, Norton maintains that environmental ethicists should pursue whatever theories 'work'. He says that no one ethical theory is inherently better than another, and that philosophers instead should attempt to choose environmentally protective theories on the basis of political and case-specific considerations.

2. CENTRAL CONTROVERSIES AND ARGUMENTS IN ENVIRONMENTAL ETHICS

Most environmental ethicists tend to agree, at least generally, on broad practical issues, such as opposition to chemical biocides or commercial nuclear power and support of solar energy and environmental justice. ('Environmental justice' refers to the goal of attaining equal protection for all humans against environmental pollution and degradation. Because most environmentally noxious facilities are sited among indigenous people and among the poor, environmental injustice often occurs in these communities; see Wenz 1989.) On theoretical issues there is much greater disagreement among ethicists. Often these disagreements occur in one of three areas: meta-ethics, normative ethics, and epistemic foundations of ethical problems.

Meta-ethical controversies in environmental ethics tend to focus on moral criteria for assigning worth or value to various inhabitants of the planet, whereas normative debates in the field often address the precise nature of duties to these inhabitants. The epistemological controversies in environmental ethics usually centre on the logical and scientific warrants for different claims in environmental ethics.

2.1 Meta-Ethical Controversies

A main meta-ethical question in the field concerns how to define the worth or value of natural objects. Do they have intrinsic value, inherent value or worth, or instrumental value? How is that value or worth best defined? Robert Elliot (1992) argues that wild nature has intrinsic value, for example, but Paul Taylor (1986) argues that, because possessing value presupposes a valuing subject, instead all living beings have inherent worth (rather than intrinsic value). That is, he says their worth, as ends in themselves, is neither dependent on any consciousness to recognize it, nor merely instrumental to some human end. Baird Callicott (1987), however, believes that beings have value only because of a valuing subject. On the one hand, Taylor defines the locus of worth in environmental ethics as he does because of his Kantian account of value, including his commitment to the metaphysical reality of worth. On the other hand, Callicott defines the locus of worth in environmental ethics as he does because of his Humean account of value as sentiment depending on the conscious subject.

Another meta-ethical controversy in environmental ethics concerns how to define or specify the intuitions allegedly providing grounds for accepting or rejecting particular accounts of environmental ethics. This controversy has been most heated between Norwegian philosopher Arne Naess (1989) and US philosopher Richard Watson (1983). On the one hand, Naess claims that environmental ethics is founded on basic intuitions about ourselves and nature that comprise 'ecological consciousness'. His resultant 'deep ecology' consists of asking more searching questions about the relationship between humans and nature, questions that focus on the spiritual or 'earth wisdom' intuitions that all earth is one. For Naess and his followers, such intuitions are beyond the realm of mere factual understanding. They say two such intuitions ground deep ecology and environmental ethics. One intuition is that self-realization depends on one's ability to identify with the larger organic whole of all beings, not just humans. The other intuition is that all things in the biosphere have an equal right to live and blossom. These might be called the intuitions of self-realization and biocentric equality.

According to Naess (1989), neither of these intuitions can be validated according to traditional scientific or philosophical reasoning but only according to the deep-ecology method of searching questioning, according to which the spiritual wisdom of these intuitions will reveal itself. To explicate their intuition-based account of environmental ethics, many deep ecologists appeal to the work of Spinoza and to his belief that real happiness consists of higher knowledge of oneness with God or nature. According to Naess, knowledge of this organic wholeness is knowledge, in part, of ecological harmony or equilibrium.

Contrary to Naess, many environmental ethicists reject both intuition in general and deep ecology in particular as providing the foundation for their meta-ethical and normative claims. In his classic criticism of deep ecology, Richard Watson (1983) rejects the notion that deep-ecology intuitions can ground environmental ethics. For one thing, Watson argues that the self-realization intuition of Naess, especially as grounded in Spinoza, seems to lead to a contemplative, non-activist, passive environmental ethics, yet Naess is a celebrated environmental activist. Thus Watson charges not only that deep ecologists are inconsistent in appealing both to passivity and to activism but that, more generally, the intuitions on which their views are based are not clear. Not only are the intuitions incoherent, says Watson, but they are not realistic. In appealing to biotic equality in the second intuition, Watson argues that Naess underestimates human potential for evil. He warns that, if humans are treated equally with other members of the planet, great harm will occur because of human propensity to propagate and thrive at the expense of many other inhabitants of the planet.

Paul Taylor (1986) also offers at least two arguments against the intuitionistic approaches of the deep ecologists. For one thing, he claims that many intuitions—such as that it is not wrong to dig weeds out of gardens or clams out of the shore—are flawed because they are psychologically dependent on basic attitudes towards nature that people acquired during childhood. Taylor claims they merely reflect the particular social group within which people were raised. Moreover, he argues that such intuitions often conflict with those of others who instead maintain that their views are also 'self-evident'. For Taylor, only good reasons, not appeal to intuitions, can ground environmental ethics. Like Naess, Taylor believes that humans' attitudes towards nature need to be transformed but, unlike Naess, he believes that intuitions cannot be the primary guide.

2.2 Normative Controversies

In addition to questions of meta-ethics, many environmental ethicists disagree about particular normative questions, such as whether animals or members of future generations have moral rights, whether humans have duties to natural objects, how one ought to balance economic and environmental welfare, and how natural resources ought to be distributed across space and time.

Martin Golding (1972) has perhaps the most thoughtful negative response to the question whether contemporary people have obligations to future people. He argues that, in order for present people to have obligations to future ones, they must be members of the same moral community or else have a shared conception of the human good. But present and future people cannot be members of the same moral community, says Golding, because such membership presupposes reciprocity, and future people cannot reciprocate present people for their sacrifices. Moreover, because the precise nature of the good that present and future persons might share is unclear, Golding argues that responsibilities to future persons are minimal.

Feinberg (1980) disagrees. He claims contemporary individuals do have a relatively clear sense of the good that they will share with future people. He says they know that members of future generations will need clean air, clean water, various natural resources, and so on. Hence Feinberg reasons, contrary to Golding, that members of the current generation have some fairly extensive obligations to future people, in large part because they can and will share a common conception of the good, one that is precise enough to enjoin or prohibit certain actions in the present. Similarly, Gregory Kavka (1978) takes issue with Golding's arguments and claims that duties to ancestors provide a basis for duties to members of future generations.

The two leading environmental ethicists writing about the moral status of animals are Peter Singer (1990) and Tom Regan (1988). Defending a utilitarian point of view, Singer follows Bentham and argues that, because all sentient beings have the ability to suffer, they have interests. He claims that, because there is no sort of factual equality among humans and other beings, one's opposition to racism or sexism cannot be based on some scientific criterion like rationality. Nevertheless, he says, because all sentient beings can suffer, it makes sense to base ethics on ameliorating this suffering. He argues that there is no moral justification for failing to take this suffering into account, apart from whether the suffering threatens the interests of animals or humans. Singer (1990) also argues that, in order to maximize the satisfaction of interests and to minimize suffering, one might be equally justified in experimenting not only on animals but also on retarded children.

Disagreeing with Singer on the issues of experimentation, Tom Regan (1988) argues that both animals and humans are ends in themselves, not merely resources to be used, and therefore that utility cannot override either animal or human rights. As a deontologist, Regan defends animal rights by arguing that both humans and non-human animals possess the same essential psychological properties, such as desires, memories, intelligence, and so on, even though non-human animals do not possess a human-like language. These properties, says Regan, give all animals (that have desires, memories, and so on) and humans equal inherent value and therefore equal rights.

The differences between Singer and Regan appear to emerge primarily from their different theoretical stances (utilitarian versus deontological). However, one could also question the factual assumptions on which the views of Singer or Regan are based. Ray Frey (1983) challenges Singer's empirical views, while Mary Anne Warren challenges those of Regan. Frey supports Singer's utilitarian methods but argues that his calculation of the relevant interests of animals and humans is not correct. He maintains that, because of the greater complexity of the human psyche and because of humans' more complex social organization, humans and animals do not suffer equally. And if not, says Frey, then it makes no sense to argue that experimenting on retarded humans is no worse than experimenting on animals.

Reasoning from a deontological point of view, Mary Anne Warren (1987) agrees with Frey that there are important differences between humans and non-human animals. Because of these important differences, such as the ability to reason, Warren argues that there are important variations in human duties to animals and to humans. Therefore she reasons that Regan, who argues for equal rights among humans and non-human animals who have memories, desires, and so on, is wrong. Moreover, says Warren, even if one admits that animals have inherent value, as Regan does, it is not clear that one ought to argue that these animals also have rights, particularly because the notion of inherent value is not clear.

On the issue of whether humans have duties to natural objects, the main controversy is among Christopher Stone (1974), Roderick Nash (1989), and other ethicists such as Christopher Belshaw (2001). Stone argues that natural objects like rivers ought to have legal rights, in part because society already grants rights to inanimate objects such as corporations and municipalities. He maintains that implementing a system of legal rights for natural objects such as mountains could be accomplished through a system of legal guardians, analogous to the guardians that the legal system provides for mentally incompetent people. Moving significantly beyond Stone, environmental historian Rod Nash (1989) argues that natural objects like rivers ought to have moral as well as legal rights. He claims that, just as society has been slow to recognize the rights of women and children, so also society has been slow to recognize the rights of natural objects. Hence he argues for an extension of the historical expansion of (moral) rights-holders.

Whereas many philosophers believe Nash's expansion of legal rights is reasonable, they argue that it requires justification on moral, and not merely prudential, grounds. They also note that Nash has provided no epistemic criterion for admission to the class of rights-holders. For Belshaw (2001), this criterion is being sentient. Without some such criterion, there is no conceptually defensible way for Nash to argue for extension of moral rights to natural objects. Other philosophers have noted that Nash fails to take account of the fact that, if he extends moral rights to all natural objects, he needs second- and third-order ethical criteria for adjudicating controversies among rights-holders; otherwise, the extension of rights would become arbitrary and incapable of operationalization. Moreover, if virtually everything is said to have rights, as in Nash's scheme, then environmental fascism might occur, because a rock, a tree, and a human all could be said to have equally legitimate rights claims. Extending the class of rights-holders to include virtually everything would also probably result in a devaluation of the concept of rights. Hence they argue that Nash overlooks the historically and politically specific concept of rights and has no philosophical principles necessary for implementing his expansion of moral rights.

Questioning Property Rights in Natural Resources

To determine whether natural objects can be said to have legal or moral rights, one approach is to investigate whether humans may be said to have property rights to natural resources like land. Following Aldo Leopold, many environmental ethicists accept the claim that one cannot own land (meaning soil, waters, trees, and the entire earth). Leopold argues that, just as members of current generations express dismay and surprise that our ancestors hanged slaves for misbehaviour and treated them as mere property, so also he says that subsequent generations will express surprise and dismay that this generation continues to treat land as merely property, as a commodity.

On the question of whether humans can claim full property rights to land and other natural resources, there are three main positions among environmental ethicists. The major proponents of these positions, respectively, are the late Harvard philosopher Robert Nozick; Texas Tech philosopher Eugene Hargrove; and Notre Dame philosopher Kristin Shrader-Frechette.

The Nozick (1974) position is that one ought not to argue for some end state or distributive principles for assigning property rights in land. For Nozick, the moral acceptability of human actions, such as claims to property rights in land, is based not on distributive principles but on whether these actions and claims are the product of lying, cheating, stealing, or some other unjust procedure. If no unjust procedure is involved, then Nozick (1974: 262) argues that the act or claim is morally defensible. He does not believe that appeals to distributive justice or to end-state principles, such as environmental protection, are ever ethically defensible grounds to restrict property rights, because he says appeals to end-state principles are arbitrary, not accepted by everyone, and amount to unjust restrictions on human liberty and dignity (Nozick 1974: 3–30, 238). Hence, for Nozick, the only ethically non-question-begging basis for moral appeals is that of procedural justice. And if people acquire their property rights to land without lying, cheating, or stealing— thus without violating procedural justice—then Nozick believes their property rights are legitimate.

In response to Nozick's defence of full property rights, it can be argued that he errs in believing that appeals to environmental welfare rely only on end-state principles. Shrader-Frechette (2002), for example, argues that such appeals do not rely only on end-state principles because they do not specify any particular distribution of land or goods but focus merely on just procedures and on removing disadvantages affecting particular people, as Nozick (1974: 343) requires. Moreover, she argues that no end-state principles need be involved in limiting property rights, in part because such limitations typically focus on a particular way that appropriative actions affect other people or the environment; they do not focus on the end state or the structure of the situation that results. Admittedly, if one does not have some specific end-state principles to guide limitations on property rights in land, then there may be no clear criterion for when social processes are truly voluntary and procedurally just. Nevertheless the absence of end-state principles need not be a flaw in deciding how to apportion property rights in land and natural resources. In fact, a similar problem faces someone who argues, for example, for reparation for African-Americans who have been victimized by illegal discrimination. Just as there is no clear criterion for when social processes are truly non-racist, likewise there is no clear criterion for when social processes are voluntary or procedurally just. In both the racism case and the property-rights case, it is possible to make reasonable judgements, based on the analysis of the situation, that particular social transactions are either racist or violations of procedural justice.

Reacting to the previous argument, that limitations on property rights in land need not be based on end-state, and therefore questionable, principles, Nozick (1974: 238) responds that no one has a right to something, such as environmental welfare, whose realization requires certain uses or property and certain activities over which other people have rights and entitlements. Nozick's response, however, seems to beg the relevant question. This question is whether people continue to have rights over things, such as natural resources, when their exercise of these alleged rights limits the autonomy, equal opportunity, or welfare of someone else. Nozick's account seems doubtful in that it presupposes that one need not analyse or adjudicate rights claims and that there are no competing rights claims.

Also arguing against the Nozickean account, Eugene Hargrove maintains that appeals to near-absolute property rights in land are flawed because such appeals often rely on assumptions and positions of John Locke that are false. Hargrove (1989: 64–73) claims that Locke's views on property, as expressed in *The Second Treatise on Civil Government*, were really the partisan product of English history and were written for political purposes. Prior to the time of Locke, Hargrove notes, property rights had been tied to inheritance and to the divine right of kings. By virtue of this right, someone allegedly owned property in land because some ancestor had received the land from the king. As a descendant of Adam and as God's designated agent, the king was said, because of the divine right of kings, to be executor of all land. Because the English Parliament had rescinded the divine right of kings, says Hargrove (1989: 65), Locke had to devise a new theory of property to take the place of the older one. This new theory is based on labour: Locke says that, whenever someone uses his labour to move something out of the state of nature, as by tilling land, he thereby acquires property rights over it. This labour theory of property rights, says Hargrove, thus served the interests of Locke and his friends because it made the rights completely independent of all outside interests, such as that of the king and nobles, other people, and governments. Seeking to throw off the yoke of British rule, Americans like Thomas Jefferson were quick to appropriate Locke's views on private property.

Hargrove (1989: 64–73) rejects the Lockean theory, which has been used to justify virtually unlimited property rights in land and natural resources, not only because it allegedly arose in a partisan context, for expedient purposes, but also because he claims that Locke ignores the social context of property rights, and he makes them a matter of mere individual labour. Hargrove also faults Lockean property rights, and resultant claims to natural resources, on the grounds that he makes property rights prior to, and more important than, society. In fact, notes Hargrove, Locke says that the purpose of the state is to make it possible for individuals to enjoy their own property. Hargrove says that Locke errs in arguing that the landowner has 'absolute dominion without any obligation to a superior', a position that Hargrove claims is obviously false. Hargrove likewise faults Locke for the claims that there is enough land for everyone; that land on which no one has laboured is virtual waste; that one ought to seek maximum agricultural productivity; and that land was given by God to humans for their support and comfort.

Evaluating Locke's labour theory of value, Shrader-Frechette (2002) disagrees both with Nozick's view that property rights in land and natural resources ought to be virtually absolute and with Hargrove's claim that Locke defends unlimited appropriation. Although Locke is wrong about certain factual claims, such as that there is enough land for everyone and that land on which no one has laboured is virtual waste, she says there are no serious ethical shortcomings of his view. For example, although Hargrove (1989: 70) criticizes Locke for saying that God gave property to humans for their support and comfort, Hargrove ignores the fact that Locke did not say God gave humans property *only* for their support and comfort. Yet Hargrove's criticisms seem to presuppose this exclusivist interpretation not found in Locke. Moreover, for Hargrove to assume that Locke's position is a result merely of expediency is to fall victim to the genetic fallacy, to confuse the origin of a position with its justification.

Hargrove misinterprets Locke most seriously, according to Shrader-Frechette, when he argues that Locke has no social account of property rights and gives humans absolute dominion over property. Both these claims of Hargrove (1989: 70–3) are questionable. For one thing, she notes that Locke never gave humans absolute dominion over resources because he explicitly says labour creates the value in things, and he admits that human labour did not create all the value in natural resources. Thus, if only human labour can create property rights, and if human labour did not create natural resources, then there can be no full or absolute property rights to natural resources, even on Lockean grounds. Instead there can be property rights only to the value added to the resources by labour. Locke also explicitly says, in his first 'proviso', that one can appropriate property out of the commons only if there is 'as much and as good' left for others (Shrader-Frechette 2002). Hence, he appears to have something like an 'equal-opportunity' criterion for appropriation of natural resources through property rights.

Environmental Justice

Still another normative issue that has gained prominence in contemporary environmental ethics is the degree to which there is a problem of environmental injustice and the extent to which humans have duties to remedy it. 'Environmental injustice' refers to any situation in which poor or minorities bear disproportionate burdens of pollution or resource depletion. In the early days of environmental-ethics research, authors used to focus on images of backpackers and birdwatchers, Boy Scouts and nature lovers. These images were of white upper- or middle-class people concerned with conserving a pristine wilderness or an important sanctuary. Environmental ethics, in this early sense, often meant using philosophy to protect forests, rivers, and trees. Rather than being directed at the human and public-health toll of environmental abuse, environmental ethicists in the early days frequently addressed more meta-ethical notions, such as whether non-human beings have intrinsic or inherent worth, and more biocentric questions, such as whether ethics ought to be zoocentric or ecocentric. At least since 1990, however, environmental ethicists have begun to focus more on environmental injustice—for example, on farmworker communities victimized by pesticides, on indigenous people devastated by radioactive waste, on Brazilian tribes harmed by rainforest destruction, on African nations ruined by oil-drilling damage, or on Latino settlements plagued with hazardous-waste incinerators. All of these cases of disproportionate environmental pollution have arisen because the poor have been forced to trade jobs for environmental pollution, support for the local tax base in exchange for environmental toxins, a bloody loaf of bread rather than no loaf at all. As sociologist Bob Bullard (1990) notes, this situation has changed, and poor people are fighting for environmental justice. They are no longer willing to bear the lion's share of environmental degradation.

Problems of environmental justice came to the fore in the USA in the 1980s when Bullard (1990) showed that Houston had placed all of its city-owned landfills, and 75 per cent of its waste incinerators, in African-American communities, even though African-Americans made up only about a quarter of the Houston population. Other researchers showed that the environmentally dirtiest zip codes in California are those whose population is 60 per cent African-American and 40 per cent Latino. In these zip codes, total air pollution is five times greater than in other zip-code areas (see Wenz 1988).

Typically the worst environmental degradation exists in the places where people are the least able to stop it. One famous instance of environmental injustice occurred in 1984 when the Union Carbide plant in Bhopal, India, had a chemical spill that leaked a toxic gas, MIC. The gas killed roughly 4,000 people and permanently disabled another 50,000. Other environmental injustices occur when polluters covertly ship hazardous wastes from developed nations to Africa and to the Caribbean. In fact, in some instances, the World Bank has been encouraging migration of dirty industries abroad, on the grounds that citizens in such countries already have a lower life expectancy and that impairing the health of those with the lowest wages makes the most economic sense.

Responding to such environmental injustices, environmental ethicists such as Peter Wenz (1988) have argued that allowing the poor and the powerless to bear dispro-portionate environmental burdens violates traditional ethical norms of equal treat-ment, just compensation, and informed consent. Often these authors point to the ways in which background conditions allow disproportionate environmental burdens to fall on those who least deserve them and who can least afford to avoid them.

In response to ethicists' charges of environmental injustice, libertarians such as Christopher Boerner and Thomas Lambert (1997) typically make two replies. First, they claim that evidence for particular cases of environmental injustice is not com-pelling (Boerner and Lambert 1997: 74–5). Secondly, they argue that, even if some environmental injustices exist, the benefits of avoiding environmental injustice do not outweigh the costs (Boerner and Lambert 1997: 79). They also say that much evidence for environmental injustice is anecdotal and that the mere presence of a noxious facility in a particular neighbourhood does not prove that actual environ-mental exposures are more dangerous (Boerner and Lambert 1997: 73–5). Those who are sceptical about claims of environmental injustice also say the poor would suffer more if the injustice or the polluting facility were removed. They claim that higher employment and lower housing costs result from having environmentally noxious facilities nearby (Boerner and Lambert 1997: 79).

In response to the previous arguments, environmental ethicists like Wenz (1989) and Shrader-Frechette (2002) point out that, regardless of whether people want cheap housing, it is clear that no one makes a free choice to live in a dangerous or heavily polluted neighbourhood. Apart from the ultimate scheme of costs and bene-fits, they argue that the real issue is not aggregate costs and benefits but the equity of their distribution. As a result, they accuse critics of environmental-justice efforts of ignoring both questions of distributive justice and the fact that people have rights to equal protection and rights to control the risks that others impose on them.

In addition to environmental-justice controversies over whether genuine dis-crimination is occurring in a given situation, environmental ethicists also have opposed positions on the role that those in developed nations ought to play in rem-edying social and environmental ills in developing nations. Holmes Rolston, for example, argues that saving particular species is sometimes a higher value than pro-tecting human life in poor areas; he says that African poachers in poverty-stricken nations should be shot on sight. Andrew Brennan (1988), however, disagrees sharply with Rolston and argues that he ignores the institutional and colonial structures that have caused many environmental problems in developing nations. He also argues that Rolston's views, like those of the deep ecologists, rely on elitist and Puritanical assumptions. In criticizing Rolston, Brennan appeals to some of the same themes that appear in other contemporary work in ethics, notably that of

Peter Singer (1993) and Peter Unger (1996). Both Singer and Unger argue that contemporary people have duties to help save the poor from death, especially in developing nations. On the one hand, the appeals of philosophers like Brennan, Singer,
and Unger point to a vision of environmental justice that includes concern for the
poor and for the unhealthy environments in which they live and die. On the other
hand, the views of philosopher Rolston, like those of biologist Garrett Hardin, point
to a quite different, more biocentric vision of environmental justice, one that
Brennan says follows from the sporting-elitist tradition of environmentalism,
rather than the social-justice tradition of environmentalism.

2.3 Epistemological Controversies

Besides the meta-ethical controversies over issues such as whether non-human
beings have intrinsic or inherent worth, and normative debates over issues such
as whether society adequately compensates victims of environmental injustice,
another central area of conflict in environmental ethics focuses on epistemology.
These controversies arise because of differing ethical positions on how to assess
environmental problems. Often environmental ethicists will support or criticize
particular scientific techniques, such as benefit–cost analysis, quantitative risk
assessment, or island biogeography (in ecology). For example, in the ethical battle
over benefit–cost analysis, philosophers Mark Sagoff (1988), Alasdair MacIntyre
(1983), Douglas MacLean (1986), and Hubert Dreyfus (1982) are critical of the technique and argue that there are normative grounds for abandoning it, whereas
Robert Goodland (Goodland and Ledec 1999) and Kristin Shrader-Frechette (1991)
have defended it.

Environmental Ethicists' Disagreements over Economic Methods

University of Maryland philosopher Mark Sagoff, especially in his volume *The
Economy of the Earth* (1988), has been sharply critical of neoclassical economic
methods, chiefly on the grounds that most values, especially environmental values,
are not amenable to economic or quantitative measurement. With Douglas
MacLean (1986) and Hubert Dreyfus (1982), he argues that such values can be presented adequately only within a more deontological, political, and phenomenologically correct framework, rather than an economic one. Alasdair MacIntyre (1983)
criticizes benefit–cost analysis on the grounds that it embodies utilitarian presuppositions and hence is fatally flawed.

   In response to these criticisms of benefit–cost analysis, as used in environmental
decision making, Goodland and Ledec (1999) and Shrader-Frechette (1991: 169–96)
point out that it is ethically better to attempt to represent environmental values
through this quantitative technique than to fail to quantify them. In the latter case,

they say environmental values would probably be accorded zero worth in the societal calculations underlying decision making. Following Aristotle, they also argue that, without some common denominator (like money or preferences) to evaluate all environmental costs and benefits relative to each other, no rational ethical decision is possible. They admit that benefit–cost analysis has many problems, but they see no more desirable mechanism for achieving its goals.

With respect to the criticism that using benefit–cost analysis to measure environmental values is flawed because it is a utilitarian scheme, Shrader-Frechette (1991: 182) disagrees. She points out, following Patrick Suppes, that benefit–cost analysis is merely a formal calculus for measuring any types of benefits or costs. One could include ethical values like equity within this calculus, just as one could also include deontological or aesthetic values. One could place an infinite value on any negative consequences, such as violations of rights to life, and thereby one could make benefit–cost analysis amenable to almost any sort of value system. Moreover, she says, the calculus does not create or measure particular values, but it merely represents them, once people already subscribe to them.

Environmental Ethicists' Disagreements over Ecological Methods

In addition to their disagreements over whether economic methods can reliably represent environmental values and assist in environmental policy making, environmental ethicists are also sharply divided over the extent to which ecological science can provide a foundation for environmental ethics. Robert Henry Peters (1991) and Mark Sagoff (1988), for example, believe that ecological science provides very little help to environmental ethics, while Henry Regier (1993) and Laura Westra (1994) claim that it offers significant assistance.

Peters (1991: 11) claims that ecology is a 'weak science' that needs to be strengthened by assessing it in terms of its predictive power. He says that, because ecology has very little predictive power, it can contribute little, as a science, to environmental ethics (Peters 1991: 290).

According to most ecologists and environmental ethicists, Peters's position is correct in at least two respects. First, it is true that prediction is often needed for applying ecology to environmental problem solving. Secondly, if scientists did not seek prediction, at least in some cases, they would probably foreclose the possibility of ever having any predictive scientific theories. Nevertheless, Peters's argument is misguided in several ways. (1) He is wrong to use prediction as a criterion for, rather than a goal of, ecological theorizing, because not all sciences are equally predictive. Many geological phenomena—such as whether a given rock formation will be intact in 10,000 years—are not susceptible to precise, long-term prediction. In overemphasizing the importance of prediction in ecology, Peters seems to have erred in underemphasizing the role of explanation. (2) No sciences can be perfectly deductive in method because they depend on methodological value judgements, such as whether certain data are sufficient or whether a given model fits the data. Because such value judgements render strict deduction impossible, using prediction in falsification and confirmation of hypothesis is always somewhat questionable. A major source of value judgements in ecology is the fact that the island-biogeographical theory, underlying a major ecology paradigm, has rarely been tested and is dependent on ornithological data, on correlations rather than causal explanations, on assumptions about homogeneous habitats, and on unsubstantiated turnover rates and extinction rates. As a result, ecologists who use island biogeography must make a number of value judgements about the representativeness and importance of their particular data. And, if so, then, although Peters's demanding prediction of ecology may represent an important ideal, it demands too much of ecology, and it overestimates its non-reliance on value judgements (Shrader-Frechette 1995).

At the other extreme of positions, on the power of ecology to provide a foundation for environmental ethics, are Henry Regier (1992) and Laura Westra (1994). They claim that ecological science can adequately ground environmental ethics and provide a standard for desirable versus undesirable environment-related actions.

Explicating the account of 'integrity' that is central to his and Westra's account, Regier (1993) admits that ecological integrity has been defined in a variety of ways: to refer to open-system thermodynamics, to networks, to Bertalanffian general systems, to trophic systems, to hierarchical organizations, to harmonic communities, and so on. Obviously, however, a clear, operational scientific theory cannot be explicable in a multiplicity of ways, some of which are mutually incompatible, if one expects a theory to be useful in doing environmental ethics and in resolving environmental controversies. Often the best account of ecological integrity that scientists can provide is necessary conditions for its presence, such as healthy indicator species. For example, the 1987 Protocol to the 1978 Great Lakes Water Quality Agreement formally specified lake trout as an indicator of a desired state of oligotrophy. Nevertheless, tracking the presence or absence of an indicator species, alone, is not sufficient to characterize everything that might be meant by ecosystem 'integrity' (Shrader-Frechette 1995).

The integrity theory proposed by environmental ethicists Regier and Westra is also questionable because many ecologists measure integrity by means of the Index of Biotic Integrity (IBI). Yet this IBI relates directly to nothing that is either observable by the non-expert, or included within a theoretical or empirical synthesis. As a conceptual mixture put together according to judgement or knowledgeable observers, it is not understandable in a theoretical sense. It is conceptually opaque in that it provides only a number on a scale, a number chosen by the ecologist and then interpreted as bad or good according to practical considerations. In short, the IBI is problematic because even integrity proponents admit that only very general, qualitative judgements of experts provide the basis for understanding the theory. But, if so, then it is not clear how it can provide a foundation for environmental ethics.

Problems with the Balance of Nature. One reason for the epistemological problems in the theories of Peters, Regier, and others is that they rely on ecological concepts that are vague or incoherent, such as 'balance of nature'. If environmental ethics is supposed to preserve some such balance, but if ecologists have no clear definition of the term, then ethicists face difficult epistemological problems in attempting to ground their theories.

Perhaps the greatest problem with appealing to balance or stability is that there is no precise, confirmed sense in which one can claim that natural ecosystems proceed toward homeostasis, stability, or some balance. Admittedly the concept of a balanced or stable ecosystem has great heuristic power, and there appears to be some general sense in which nature is balanced or stable. Nevertheless, in the specific case of the ecosystemic view of the balance of nature, there is no consensus among ecologists. Nor is there support for the diversity-stability view held by MacArthur and Hutchinson. The reasons for the disfavour attributed to the view of MacArthur et al. are both empirical and mathematical. Salt marshes and the rocky intertidal provide only two of many classical counterexamples to the diversity-stability view. Salt marshes are simple in species composition, but they are stable, and they are not diverse ecosystems. On the other hand, the rocky intertidal is one of the most species-rich and diverse natural systems, yet it is highly unstable, since it may be perturbed by a single change in its species composition. Empirically based counterexamples of this sort have multiplied over the last twenty years, and May, Levins, Connell, and others have seriously challenged the diversity-stability hypothesis on both mathematical and field-based grounds (McIntosh 1985: 187–8). Diversity, for example, can be defined to suit almost any conclusion. Yet numerous environmental ethicists continue to cite the diversity-stability hypothesis, the most famous version of the balance of nature, as grounds for supporting many tenets of environmental ethics and law, including the Endangered Species Act. Most ecologists say it cannot be defined, at least at present.

'Defining some balance of nature' is difficult because it is impossible to say, in all cases, what it would be to hinder the balance of nature. Ecosystems regularly change, and they regularly eliminate species. How would one use an ethics based on some balance of nature to argue that humans ought not to modify ecosystems or even wipe out species, for example, when nature does this herself, through natural disasters such as volcanic eruptions and climate changes like those that destroyed the dinosaurs? Nature does not appear merely to extirpate species or cause them to move elsewhere because their niches are gone. But, if not, then one cannot obviously use science, alone, to claim that it is always wrong, on ecological grounds, for humans to do what nature does, wipe out species. However, given a number of ecocentric or biocentric ethics based on notions such as teleology, inherent worth, or intrinsic value—none of which is based solely on science—it is possible to argue against species extinctions. Likewise there are anthropocentric grounds for arguing against species extinctions (see Norton 1986, 1987).

But if one's main basis for condemning actions resulting in species extinction is anthropocentric, because there are no adequate and universal theories of ecological balance, then it is not clear how ecological theory can support purely ecocentric or biocentric environmental ethics. Moreover, the criterion for justifiable species extinction, for those who appeal to the notion of balance, cannot be that what happens naturally is good, while what happens through human intervention is bad. Using this criterion would saddle scientific and ethical meanings with purely stipulative and *ad hoc* definitions of the foundational ecological concepts. Nor can the difference be merely that humans do quickly (for example, cause lake eutrophication) what nature does slowly. One must have some arguments to show that accelerating ecosystemic changes is bad, even if the changes themselves, such as wiping out species, are natural. With medical science, it is relatively easy to specify the well-being of the individual patient or organism. Environmental ethics, however, almost never focuses on the health of one individual or species. Maintaining the alleged balance of the entire system is usually the goal, and it is a far more difficult enterprise than specifying the health of an individual, in part because ecologists are not sure about the 'whole' whose welfare is to be sought (Shrader-Frechette 1995).

Problems with Ecological Wholes. Specifying the 'whole' whose welfare is to be maximized in environmental ethics is difficult (see Botzler and Armstrong 1998; Belshaw 2001). There are communities, species, ecosystems, biomes, and so on, all at different levels of scale, and it is not clear which scale, if any, is more appropriate. Most ecologists have either remained agnostic or rejected the GAIA hypothesis, for example, the basis of many accounts of holism. They regard it as possibly correct, but at present only unproved speculation. Of course, they admit the ecological facts of interconnectedness and coevolution on a small scale. Moreover, an ecosystem, as the same collection of individuals, species, and relationships, certainly does not persist through time. Hence any notion of the dynamic stability of an ecosystemic whole is somewhat imprecise and unclear. Also the selection of the ecosystem as the unit that is or ought to be maximized is peculiar. Why not choose, as the unit, the community, or the association, or the trophic level? Early ecologists, like Clements, said the community is an organism, and, if so, then why do some ecologists say the ecosystem also is an organism? Which is it, and what are the criteria for a holistic organism? Or, if one is a holist, why not choose the collection of ecosystems, the biosphere, as that which is maximized in nature and which we are morally enjoined to optimize? Once one abandons an individualistic ethics, from a scientific point of view, how does one choose among alternative non-individual units to be maximized (see Shrader-Frechette 1995; Botzler and Armstrong 1998: 346–407).

Moreover, a given ecological conclusion regarding balance typically holds for some, but not other, wholes, such as for populations but not for communities. For example, there may be some sort of stability or balance for a given species within a certain spatial scale, but not for other species or not within another such scale. Ecologists cannot optimize the welfare of all species for all wholes, because each whole has a different spatial and temporal scale. Because they cannot, there is no general level at which environmental ethics takes place, and no general scale within which a stable whole is exhibited.

Another problem with holistic notions in environmental ethics is that it is scientifically wrong to suggest that ecosystems, rather than populations, adapt. Although species may evolve in a way that benefits a given ecosystem, there is no selection at the level of the ecosystem. Adaptation is restricted to heritable characteristics; no alleged knowledge of the past operates in natural selection, and the individual that is better adapted to the present environment is the one that leaves more offspring and hence transmits its traits. Thus anyone like Lovelock (1979) or Rolston (1988) is scientifically wrong to suggest either that natural selection operates to produce organs of a given kind because their presence gives rise to certain effects, or that ecosystemic processes operate in certain ways because they maximize ecosystemic excellence. Moreover, although it is possible to claim that adaptation maximizes individual survival, in the sense already discussed, it is not clear what a community or an ecosystem maximizes. Traits advantageous to the individual are not always advantageous to the species or the ecosystem, as in the individual's 'taking all the good'. And what are advantageous to the species or to the ecosystem are not always advantageous to the individual, as in the case of 'dying young to hasten the cycling of nutrients'. Such observations suggest that holism and organicism, despite their apparent heuristic power, are arbitrary and imprecise notions that may block progress in environmental ethics (Shrader-Frechette and McCoy 1993: 11–31).

A Middle Ecological Path for Environmental Ethicists. Given the disagreements among ecologists and the epistemological problems inherent in notions such as 'balance of nature' and 'ecosystem', it appears that Sagoff (1988) and Peters (1991) err in demanding too much of current ecology—namely, predictive power. It also is clear that Westra (1994) and Regier (1993) also err in demanding too little of current ecology—namely, stipulative definitions of terms such as ecosystem 'integrity'. Because so much of scientific ecology is uncertain, anyone who practises or studies environmental ethics needs, at a minimum, a procedure for making ethically responsible decisions under conditions of scientific uncertainty, and a procedure for using ecology, in a practical sense, to direct environmental ethics.

One procedure for dealing with ecological uncertainty is to minimize type II statistical errors (false negatives) rather than type I errors (false positives), when both cannot be avoided. Contrary to current scientific norms, this new rule of thumb places the burden of proof not on anyone who posits a damaging environmental effect, but instead on anyone who argues that there will be no damaging effect from a particular environment-related action. Because ecologically related decisions affect welfare, and because ethics requires, at a minimum, that one do no harm, it is arguable that in matters of environmental controversy or uncertainty about an action—provided it has potentially catastrophic consequences and provided it is only one of several ways to obtain particular benefits—one ought to minimize false negatives under conditions of uncertainty when both false negatives and false positives cannot be avoided (Cranor 1993; Shrader-Frechette and McCoy 1993: 149–69).

Another means of dealing with scientific uncertainty in environmental ethics would be to follow the recommendation of a recent US National Academy of Sciences committee and use case-specific, empirical, ecological knowledge, rather than an uncertain, general, ecological theory or model. According to a recent US National Academy of Sciences' committee, ecology's greatest predictive successes occur in cases that involve only one or two species, perhaps because ecological generalizations are most fully developed for relatively simple systems (Orians et al. 1986). That is why, for example, ecological management of game and fish populations through regulations of hunting and fishing can often be successful. Applying this insight to environmental ethics, ecology might be most helpful to ethics when it does not try to predict complex interactions among many different species but instead attempts to predict only what will happen for one or two taxa in a particular case. Predictions for one or two taxa are often successful because, despite the problems with general ecological theory, there are numerous lower-level theories in ecology that provide reliable predictions. Application of lower-level theory about the evolution of cooperative breeding, for example, has provided many successes in managing red-cockaded woodpeckers. In this case, successful management and predictions appear to have come from natural-history information such as data about the presence of cavities in trees that serve as habitats (Orians et al. 1986).

In one National Academy study, for example, the goal was to find a control agent for the vampire bat, the 'pest' species of concern that was killing cattle. Using natural-history information about the bat, ecologists were able to provide a firm scientific foundation for ethical discussion about whether control of the bat was rationally defensible and desirable. If the bat case study is representative, then it suggests that philosophers interested in the epistemological and scientific grounding for their environmental ethics would do well to focus on practical applications and on unavoidably human judgements about environmental welfare, rather than on complex general ecological theory that is uncertain (Orians et al. 1986).

3. RELATED ETHICAL ISSUES

In addition to the controversies over meta-ethics, normative ethics, and the scientific or epistemological foundations for environmental ethics, there are a number of issues that arise in related areas but that have great relevance for environmental ethics. As the previous discussion of epistemological problems underlying environmental ethics made clear, one of the most important areas related to environmental ethics is that of philosophy of science. By uncovering the epistemic and ethical presuppositions of various scientific methods, like benefit–cost analysis, especially those used in environmental policymaking and management, philosophers of science can make a direct contribution to the clarification and resolution of epistemological controversies that underlie environmental ethics. For example, philosophers of geology can assess the reliability of hydrogeological models of groundwater transport, so that they can evaluate, in turn, the likely success of proposed models of deep geological storage of radioactive waste. To the degree that the science in this area is problematic, to that same extent will the ethical judgements of repository safety be uncertain, and therefore something that environmental ethicists ought to evaluate. Likewise, to the degree that the databases for evaluating epidemiological effects of toxic chemicals are uncertain, to that extent will the safety assessments of environmental policymakers be uncertain and therefore open to ethical questioning.

In general, because ethical analysis of environmental problems always relies on scientific knowledge about those same problems, environmental ethics will always be dependent, to some degree, on philosophy of science for its assessment of the uncertainties and methods in the relevant environmental science. For instance, if philosophers of science debate the rationality of using a discount rate to compute future costs of some environment-related action, then environmental ethicists' controversies over duties to future generations are likely to rely both on the ethical legitimacy of using such a discount rate and on the more foundational controversy in philosophy of science.

Similarly, to the degree that environmental-ethics debates concern questions of social choice, such as whether to ban particular pesticides or whether to use onsite solar, rather than nuclear, power, these debates will rely, in part, on related discussions among decision theorists, since decision theory is widely used to help resolve and clarify societal problems. One of the most famous such controversies, still not resolved to date, is that between John Harsanyi (1975) and John Rawls (1971: 75–83, 321–4, 586) over the appropriate decision rule that one ought to use in a situation of probabilistic uncertainty, like that characterizing many environmental problems.

On the one hand, Harsanyi (1975) argues for using the rule of maximizing average expected utility, rather than maximin rule, on the grounds that not doing so would be to ignore probabilities, an irrational move (Harsanyi 1975: 595). He also argues that failure to follow this Bayesian strategy of maximizing average expected utility would lead to impractical and irrational consequences, such as avoiding extremely small risks, even when their associated benefits are extremely large, and that following this strategy would enable one to assign equal apriori probability to everyone's interests (Harsanyi 1975: 598).

On the other hand, Rawls (1971: 586) argues for using the rule of maximin, rather than that of maximizing average expected utility, in situations of uncertainty characterized by probabilistic uncertainty, potentially catastrophic consequences, and no overarching benefits to be gained from the action that could not be obtained in other ways. Rawls (1971: 12–17, 58–82, 94) justifies his position on the grounds that the latter rule would violate fairness, that it would not give the interests of the least advantaged people the highest priority; and that it would employ a utility function in an area, ethics, where it does not belong. Rawls's view is also defensible in the light of the fact that the Harsanyi or Bayesian position would sanction subjective probabilities; that it would rely on controversial interpersonal comparisons of utility; that it would make supererogatory actions a matter of duty, as do utilitarian theories; and that it would depend on uncertain predictions about the consequences of alternative actions.

In addition to philosophy of science and decision theory, many controversies related to environmental ethics also arise in philosophy of law. One case in point is ethicist Carl Cranor's volume, *Regulating Toxic Substances* (1993), in which he argues for weakening the evidentiary burden that plaintiffs face in toxic tort suits that they bring against polluters. Elizabeth Whelan (1993) argues against proposals like Cranor's on the grounds that society overestimates environmental burdens and that such a weakening is not needed in order to ensure the greatest good.

Other environmental-ethics-related controversies arise in philosophy of technology. One example of work in philosophy of technology that has dominated environment-related issues is Langdon Winner's *Autonomous Technology* (1977), in which he argues that technology has moved beyond human control and that people have duties to attempt ethical control of technology through more participatory decision making. Joseph Pitt (2000) challenges the Winner argument and maintains that technology assessment shows that technology is still largely within human ethical control and that experts, not members of the public, are better able to make such ethical decisions regarding environmental effects of particular technologies.

Still another area of philosophy in which its controversies are of great relevance for environmental ethics is environmental risk assessment. One of the more famous ethical debates in risk assessment is that between Roger Ames (Ames et al. 1995) and Samuel Epstein (1998). Ames argues that the current increase in cancers has not been caused by environmental pollutants but mainly by lifestyle choices and by natural hazards and that, as a consequence, government ought not to regulate polluters so strictly. Epstein claims that reliable epidemiological evidence, while not complete, shows that cancer deaths increase, all things being equal, in areas of highest pollution and, therefore, government ought to regulate polluters much more strictly.

4. THE FUTURE OF THE FIELD

Given the controversies discussed earlier in this article, future work in environmental ethics is likely to develop in six distinct ways. *First*, given the importance of philosophy of science in examining environmental science, as illustrated in the two previous sections, work in environmental ethics is likely to become far more attuned to, and dependent upon, scientific findings to shore up its conclusions about environment-related harms and benefits, rights and wrongs. This development is already beginning to take place as a number of philosophers of science are turning their talents to environmental ethics, given the strong relevance of philosophy of science for the field. These philosophers include Gregory Cooper, Deborah Mayo, and Isaac Levi.

Secondly, given the strong pragmatic turn in contemporary philosophy, environmental ethics is likely to continue in the pragmatic direction already begun by Georgia Tech philosopher Bryan Norton (1991; see also Light and Katz 1996). This turn means not only that future environmental ethicists are likely to try to avoid begging any metaphysical questions in their work, but also that they are probably going to attempt to provide rationales for their positions that rely less on foundationalist claims in ethics and metaphysics and more on the practical consequences of their positions.

Thirdly, given the fact that, to date, environmental ethicists have had very little effect on practical environmental policy decisions, future work is likely to focus on the practical policy applications of environmental ethics, just as Avner de Shalit (2000) recommended in his recent book. The trend towards applied and practical philosophy is likely to continue, with philosophers generally and environmental ethicists specifically looking for ways to make their ethical conclusions more relevant to real-world issues.

Fourthly, because so many decisions in areas of technology and environment are plagued with scientific and probabilistic uncertainties, environmental ethicists are likely to develop more analyses of appropriate ethical behaviour under conditions of uncertainty. More specifically, they are likely to sharpen and to elaborate on the excellent debate on this topic already begun by John Rawls (1971) and John Harsanyi (1975) and to search for other default rules. The recent prominence of the precautionary principle—the tenet that, in situations of uncertainty, one should take precautions to avoid harm rather than to assume harm has not been proved—also illustrates some of the tendencies of environmental ethicists to begin looking for default rules for behaviour under uncertainty.

Fifthly, given the continuing development of interest in questions of environmental justice, environmental ethics is likely in the future to continue to expand and articulate norms for appropriate ethical behaviour across national boundaries. The passage of the agreements implementing the 1995 World Trade Organization (WTO) and the earlier North American Free Trade Agreement (NAFTA) are also likely to contribute to this globalization of environmental ethics, as well as to its merger with development ethics, as signalled by Peter Unger's recent volume, *Living High and Letting Die* (1996).

Sixthly, given the recent prominence of virtue ethics, environmental ethics is likely in the future to begin to incorporate some of these insights into schemes of environmental virtue. In the past most of the work of environmental ethicists has been deontological, as illustrated by Tom Regan, or utilitarian, as illustrated by Peter Singer. The scope of environmental ethics is likely to expand to incorporate insights from the recent rediscovery of both Aristotelian and virtue-theoretic accounts.

REFERENCES

Ames, B. N., Gold, L. S., and Willett, W. C. (1995). 'The Causes and Prevention of Cancer'. *Proceedings of the National Academy of Science, USA*, 92: 5258–65.

Attfield, Robin (1983). *The Ethics of Environmental Concern*. New York: Columbia University Press.

Belshaw, Christopher (2001). *Environmental Philosophy*. Chesham: Acumen.

Boerner, Christopher, and Lambert, Thomas (1997). 'Environmental Injustice', in Theodore Goldfarb (ed.), *Taking Sides: Clashing Views on Controversial Environmental Issues*. Guilford, CT: Dushkin/McGraw, 72–84.

Botzler, Richard, and Armstrong, Susan (1998) (eds.), *Environmental Ethics*. New York: McGraw-Hill.

Brennan, A. (1988). *Thinking about Nature*. Arthens, GA: University of Georgia Press.

Bullard, Robert (1990). *Dumping in Dixie*. Boulder, Co: Westview.

Callicott, Baird (1987) (ed.), *A Companion to the A Sand County Almanac*. Madison: University of Wisconsin Press.

——(1989). *In Defense of the Land Ethic*. Albany, NY: SUNY Press.

Carson, Rachel (1962). *Silent Spring*. Boston: Houghton Mifflin.

Cranor, Carl (1993). *Regulating Toxic Substances*. New York: Oxford University Press.

de Shalit, Avner (2000). *The Environment in Theory and in Practice*. New York: Oxford University Press.

Donagan Alan (1977). *The Theory of Morality*. Chicago: University of Chicago Press.

Dreyfus, H. E. (1982). 'Formal Models versus Human Situational Understanding', *Technology and People*, 1: 135–65.

Elliot, Robert (1992). 'Intrinsic Value, Environmental Obligation, and Naturalness'. *Monist*, 75: 132–51.

Epstein, S. S. (1998). *The Politics of Cancer*. Fremont Center, NY: East Ridge Press.

Feinberg, J. (1974). 'The Rights of Animals and Unborn Generations', in W. Blackstone (ed.), *Philosphy and Environmental Crisis*. Athens, GA: University of Georgia Press, 43–68.

Frey, R. G. (1983). *Rights, Killing, and Suffering*. Oxford: Blackwell.

Golding, Martin (1972). 'Obligations to Future Generations'. *Monist*, 56: 85–99.

Goodin, Robert (1992). *Green Political Theory*. Cambridge: Polity.

Goodland, R., and Ledec, G. (1999). 'Neoclassical Economics and Principles of Sustainable Development', in Louis Pojman (ed.), *Environmental Ethics*. Boston: Jones & Bartlett, 450–7.

Goodpaster, Kenneth (1978). 'On Being Morally Considerable'. *Journal of Philosophy*, 75: 308–25.

Hargrove, Eugene (1989). *Foundations of Environmental Ethics*. Englewood Cliffs, NJ: Prentice Hall.

Harsanyi, J. (1975). 'Can the Maximin Principle Serve as a Basis for Morality?' *American Political Science Review*, 69: 594–605.

Kavka, Gregory (1978). 'The Futurity Problem', in R. I. Sikora and Brian Barry (eds.), *Obligations to Future Generations*. Philadelphia: Temple University Press, 186–203.

Kingsland, Sharon (1995). *Modelling Nature*. Chicago: University of Chicago Press.

Leopold, Aldo (1970). *A Sand County Almanac*. New York: Ballantine Books.

Light, Andrew, and Katz, Eric (1996) (eds.), *Environmental Pragmatism*. London: Routledge.

Lovelock, J. E. (1979). *Gaia*. New York: Oxford University Press.

McIntosh, R. P. (1985). *The Background of Ecology*. Cambridge: Cambridge University Press.

MacIntyre, A. (1983). 'Utilitarianism and Benefit-Cost Analysis'. in D. Scherer and T. Attig (eds.), *Ethics and the Environment*. Englewood Cliffs, NJ: Prentice Hall, 139–51.

MacLean, D. (1986). 'Social Values and the Distribution of Risk'. in D. MacLean (ed.), *Values at Risk*. Totowa, NJ: Rowman & Allenheld, 75–93.

Merchant, Carolyn (1995). *Earthcare*. New York: Routledge.

Naess, A. (1989). *Ecology, Community, and Lifestyle*, ed. David Rothenberg. Cambridge: Cambridge University Press.

Nash, Roderick (1989). *The Rights of Nature*. Madison: University of Wisconsin Press.

Norton, B. G. (1984). 'Environmental Ethics and Weak Anthropocentrism'. *Environmental Ethics*, 6: 131–48.

——(1986). *The Preservation of Species*. Princeton: Princeton University Press.

——(1987) (ed.), *The Spice of Life: Why Preserve Natural Variety?* Princeton: Princeton University Press.

——(1991). *Toward Unity among Environmentalists*. New York: Oxford University Press.

Nozick, R. (1974). *Anarchy, State and Utopia*. New York: Basic Books.

Orians, G. H. et al. (1986). *Ecological Knowledge and Environmental Problem Solving*. Washington: National Academy Press.

Passmore, John (1974). *Man's Responsibility for Nature*. New York: Scribner's.

Payne, Henry (1977). 'Environmental Injustice'. *Reason*, 29: 53–6.

Peters, Robert Henry (1991). *A Critique for Ecology*. Cambridge: Cambridge University Press.

Pitt, Joseph (2000). *Thinking about Technology*. New York: Seven Bridges Press.

Plumwood, Val (1988). 'Women, Humanity, and Nature'. *Radical Philosophy*, 48: 16–24.

Pojman, Louis P. (1999) (ed.), *Environmental Ethics: Readings in Theory and Application*. Boston: Jones & Bartlett.

Rawls, J. (1971). *A Theory of Justice*. Cambridge, MA: Harvard University Press.

Regan, Thomas (1988). *The Case for Animal Rights*. London: Routledge.

Regier, H. A. (1992). 'Indicators of Ecosystem Integrity', in D. H. McKenzie, D. E. Hyatt, and V. J. McDonald (eds.), *Ecological Indicators*. Fort Lauderdale, FL: Elsevier, 183–200.

——(1993). 'The Notion of Natural and Cultural Integrity'. in S. Woodley, J. Francis, and J. Kay (eds.), *Ecological Integrity and the Management of Ecosystems*. Delray Beach, FL: St Lucie Press, 3–18.

Rolston, Holmes (1988). *Environmental Ethics*. Philadelphia: Temple University Press.

——(1986). *Philosophy Gone Wild*. Buffalo, NY: Prometheus.

Sagoff, Mark (1988). *The Economy of the Earth*. Cambridge: Cambridge University Press.

Shrader-Frechette, K (1991). *Risk and Rationality*. Berkely and Los Angles: University of California Press.

——(1995). 'Practical Ecology and Foundations for Environmental Ethics', *Journal of Philosophy*, 92: 621–35.

——(2002). *Environmental Justice: Creating Equality, Reclaiming Democracy*. New York: Oxford University Press.

——and McCoy, E. D. (1993). *Method in Ecology: Strategies for Conservation*. Cambridge: Cambridge University Press.

Singer, Peter (1990). *Animal Liberation*. New York: New York Review of Books.

——(1993). *Practical Ethics*. 2nd edn. Cambridge: Cambridge University Press.

Stone, Christopher (1974). *Should Trees Have Standing?* Los Altos, CA: William Kaufmann.

Taylor, P. W. (1986). *Respect for Nature*. Princeton: Princeton University Press.

Unger, Peter (1996). *Living High and Letting Die*. New York: Oxford University Press.

Warren, Karen (1996) (ed.), *Nature, Self, and Gender*. Bloomington, IN: Indiana University Press.

Warren, Mary Anne (1987). 'Difficulties with the Strong Animal Rights Position'. *Between the Species*, 2: 433–41.

Watson, Richard (1983). 'A Critique of Anti-Anthropocentric Biocentrism'. *Environmental Ethics*, 5: 245–56.

Wenz, Peter (1989). *Environmental Justice*. Albany, NY: SUNY Press.

Westra, Laura (1994). *An Environmental Proposal for Ethics: the Principle of Integrity*. Lanham, MD: Rowman & Littlefield.

Whelan, Elizabeth (1993). *Toxic Terror*. Buffalo, NY: Prometheus.

White, Lynn (1967). 'The Historical Roots of our Ecological Crisis'. *Science*, 155: 1203–7.

Winner, Langdon (1977). *Autonomous Technology*. Cambridge, MA: MIT Press.

PART III

EQUALITY

CHAPTER 9

GENDER AND SEXUAL DISCRIMINATION

ROSEMARIE TONG

1. INTRODUCTION

Sex discrimination is the disadvantaging of a member or members of one sex over a member or members of the other because of their sex. Although either men or women may be the victims of sex discrimination, throughout history and in most societies, women have been the victims (Benokraitis and Feagin 1986: 30–2). Discrimination against women is usually predicated on the claim that men and women are biologically different, and that these differences justify the lesser status of women. Throughout the eighteenth, nineteenth, and twentieth centuries, however, feminists increasingly challenged not only the view that women's biological status is somehow worse or weaker than men's, but also the view that feminine and masculine gender identities and behaviours are the inevitable consequence of female and male biology, respectively. In particular, they claimed that femininity and masculinity are primarily socially constructed rather than biologically determined phenomena. Therefore, they urged their contemporaries to reserve the term 'sex' for those chromosomal, hormonal, and anatomical features that make humans biological males or females, and the term 'gender' for those ways of thinking, looking, and acting that society deems appropriate for men and women respectively (Nicholson 1998: 289–90).

Regarding the sex/gender distinction as a significant advance over the view that one's gender is determined by one's sex, feminists encouraged women and men to become well-integrated androgynous persons; to mix and match within themselves a variety of feminine and masculine personality traits and behaviours, thereby demonstrating that anatomy does not constitute destiny. Beginning in the 1980s, however, feminists began to question, as they had in the nineteenth century, whether androgyny is necessarily a worthwhile goal for women to achieve. Specifically, feminists began to debate in earnest what it means to say that women should be treated as men's equals.

2. FEMINIST THOUGHT: THE SAMENESS–DIFFERENCE– DOMINANCE–DIVERSITY DEBATE

In their attempts to articulate the terms of women's and men's equality, feminists have moved through three major stages of thought. Within each period, they have offered different explanations for and understandings of sex discrimination, and, correspondingly, different prescriptions for coping with its unfortunate consequences. Dominant in the first stage of feminist thought, though by no means unchallenged, is the view that women have to become the *same* as men in order to become men's equals.

During the second stage of feminist thought, the initial recommendation flows in an opposing direction. According to this view, often called the *difference* view, women do not have to become like men in order to become men's equals. Gender equality will be achieved when society esteems 'womanly' ways as highly as it esteems 'manly' ways. Later, but still during the second stage of feminist thought, a so-called *dominance* view of equality emerges. This view maintains that equality for women consists neither in women becoming the same as men nor in women maintaining their differences from men; but rather in women liberating themselves from men. In order to achieve equality with men, women need to identify and explode those attitudes, ideologies, systems, and structures that keep women less powerful than men.

Finally, yet another recommendation for gender equality surfaces in the third stage of feminist thought, the stage that best characterizes feminist thought today. According to this perspective, sometimes called the *diversity* view, the equality problem for women is a matter of eliminating disparities not only between men and women but also between rich women and poor women, white women and minority women, young and old women, heterosexual and lesbian women, and so on.

2.1 First-Stage Feminist Thought about Sexual Equality

In the eighteenth and nineteenth centuries, first-stage feminists split on the so-called sameness–difference question, with the advocates of the sameness perspective ultimately gaining the upper hand. In her 1792 monograph, *A Vindication of the Rights of Women*, the philosopher Mary Wollstonecraft noted that whereas men are taught 'morals, which require an educated understanding', women are taught 'manners', specifically a cluster of traits such as 'cunning', 'vanity', and 'immaturity' that offend against real morals (Wollstonecraft 1792/1988: 106). Denied the chance to become moral persons who have concerns, causes, and commitments over and beyond their own personal convenience and comforts, women become hypersensitive, extremely narcissistic, and excessively self-indulgent individuals. So disgusted was Wollstonecraft by her female contemporaries' 'femininity' that she reasoned women would never become truly moral unless they learned to be, think, and act like men (Wollstonecraft 1792/1988: 259).

Like his eighteenth-century predecessor, nineteenth-century philosopher John Stuart Mill argued that women need to become like men in order to become fully human persons. Mill noted that society's high praise of women's virtue does not necessarily serve women's best interests. To praise women on account of their gentleness, compassion, humility, unselfishness, and kindness is, he said, merely to compliment patriarchal society for convincing women 'that it is their nature to live for others', but particularly for men (Mill 1869/1911: 168). Thus, Mill urged women to become autonomous, self-directing persons with lives of their own; and he demanded that society give women all the rights and privileges it gives men.

In contrast to Mill, other nineteenth-century feminists such as Catherine Beecher denied that women had to become like men in order to be viewed as men's equals. Beecher reasoned that, because women are insulated in the domestic sphere, they do not hear the siren calls of wealth, power, and prestige that pervade the marketplace and political forum in which men preside. Consequently, women remain 'purer' than men and, therefore, more capable of civilizing, indeed 'Christianizing' the human species. Women's differences from men had best be maintained, insisted Beecher, lest the human species sink back into its animal origins (Beecher and Stowe 1869/1971: 234).

Like Beecher, the nineteenth-century feminist Elizabeth Cady Stanton viewed women as men's moral superiors. Nevertheless, Stanton expressed the view that, in a patriarchal society, women's self-sacrificial behaviours tend to perpetuate their second-class status. Thus, she urged women to adopt the motto, 'self-development is a higher duty than self-sacrifice' (Buhle and Buhle 1978: 252–3).

Stanton's motto previewed the eventual consensus of most first-stage feminists that, on balance, women must become like men before women can dare to be different from men. Thus, when Stanton joined forces with Lucretia Mott to convene a women's rights convention at Seneca Falls, NY, the aim of the convention was to secure for women the *same* rights and responsibilities typically enjoyed by men. Although the 1848 convention did not secure for women even so basic a political right as the right to vote, it generated enough passion and thought among women to sustain the woman's suffrage movement for several decades. When women at last won the right to vote in 1920, the first stage of feminist activism ended in the USA. Not until the second half of the twentieth century, during a period of great social ferment, did women realize just how little women's suffrage had changed women's status as the 'second sex'.

2.2 Second-Stage Feminist Thought about Sexual Equality

With the emergence of second-wave feminism came new developments in the sameness–difference debate, and the gradual emergence of what is most often termed a 'dominance' approach to gender equality. During the 1960s a wide variety of women joined what came to be known as the Women's Liberation Movement in the USA. Among the leaders of this Movement was Betty Friedan, the first president of the National Organization for Women (NOW). In 1967 NOW forwarded a Bill of Rights for women, demanding that American women be granted all the rights enjoyed by American men. But because this Bill focused primarily on work-related and education-related issues, and because it was predicated on the assumption that the system of social, political, and economic relations is basically good and simply in need of reform, it caused a split between *reformist* liberal feminists, on the one hand, and *revolutionary* radical feminists, on the other.

According to liberal feminists, female subordination is rooted in a set of social and legal constraints that block women's entrance to, and success in, the public world. Because society has the false belief that women are by nature less physically and intellectually capable than men, it fails to provide women with the educational and occupational opportunities it provides to men. As a result of this policy of exclusion, the true potential of many women goes unfulfilled. Since this is unfair to women, women should be given the same opportunities as men.

Radical feminists countered that the liberal-feminist position on gender equality was misguided; that it would result in equality only for some women—and a flawed form of 'equality' at that. In other words, as radical feminists saw it, the liberal-feminist position on gender equality would purchase for a small group of 'winner' women the right to be like men; that is, to subordinate others to them. Claiming that the American system, like all patriarchal systems, is built upon a variety of unjust, hierarchical power relationships, and in particular the domination of women by men, radical feminists insisted that so corrupt is this system that it cannot be reformed. It must simply be destroyed.

Although all radical feminists espoused the position that the battle for true gender equality must be fought in the personal realm of sex and reproduction as well as in the academy, political forum, and marketplace, it soon became clear that radical feminists were not a monolithic group. Indeed, before the second stage of feminist thought had peaked and begun to ebb, radical feminists had divided into three distinct subgroups: so-called radical-libertarian, radical-cultural, and radical-dominance feminists.

Radical-libertarian feminists advocated androgyny, stressed the pleasures of all kinds of sex (heterosexual, lesbian, and autoerotic), and viewed developments in reproductive and genetic technology as unmitigated blessings for women. Specifically, radical-libertarian feminists claimed that, if society permitted men and women to engage in polymorphous, perverse sex, it would no longer be necessary for men to display only masculine identities and behaviours and for women to display only feminine ones. Freed from their gender roles, women would no longer have to be passive, receptive, and vulnerable, sending out signals to men to dominate, possess, and penetrate them in order to keep the wheels of human procreation spinning. Instead, men and women would be able to become either equally masculine and feminine (monoandrogynous) or as differently masculine and/or feminine as they wished (polyandrogynous) (Firestone 1970).

Radical-cultural feminists dismissed radical-libertarian views as the wrong ones for women to embrace. First, they rejected the ideal of androgyny. They urged women to eschew the identities, behaviours, and attitudes traditionally associated with masculinity, including 'assertiveness, aggressiveness, hardiness, rationality or the ability to think logically, abstractly and analytically, ability to control emotion' (Vetterling-Braggin 1982: 6). In the place of the ideal of androgyny, radical-cultural feminists offered women the concept of *essential* femaleness. They invited women to celebrate the identities, behaviours, and attitudes traditionally linked with femininity, including 'gentleness, modesty, humility, supportiveness, empathy, compassionateness, tenderness, nurturance, intuitiveness, sensitivity, unselfishness' (Vetterling-Braggin 1982: 6). Next, radical-cultural feminists emphasized the dangers of sex, particularly heterosexual sex, which they viewed as the paradigm for all forms of male domination and female subordination and all types of male sadism and female masochism. Finally, they advised women not to use reproduction-controlling and reproduction-assisting technologies, but to rely instead on their 'natural' abilities to give or deny life. Women, they said, must guard their reproductive powers jealously, for without them men will have even less respect and use for women than they have now (Corea 1985).

Although *radical-dominance feminists* agreed with radical-cultural feminists that, in and of themselves, the traditional feminine virtues were indeed excellent, they nonetheless cautioned that, as practised, these virtues were not necessarily women's 'best friends'. Much like Stanton in the nineteenth century, twentieth-century radical-dominance feminists claimed that women's capacities for relating to other people and to meeting their needs could all too easily set women up for exploitation and misery. In Robin West's words, 'Invasion and intrusion, rather than intimacy, nurturance, and care, is the "unofficial" story of women's subjective experience of connections' (West 1988: 29). In particular, the uninvited penis and the unwanted fetus are women's relational woe. Thus, according to radical-dominance feminists, gender equality consists in women disconnecting as much as possible from men, and in looking to themselves rather than to men for their self-definition, self-esteem, and self-respect.

2.3 Third-Stage Feminist Thought about Sexual Equality

In proposing that women share an essential nature—that of connectedness—radical-cultural and radical-dominance feminists implied that all women are the same. But, in the opinion of third-stage feminists, most of whom were born after the Women's Liberation Movement of the 1970s had peaked, women are not *simply* women. A woman's 'femaleness' is substantially modified and differentiated by factors such as race, ethnicity, class, age, and religion. Thus, in the estimation of third-stage feminists, to achieve gender equality without simultaneously achieving race and class equality is to achieve very little for those women whose class or ethnicity is the primary source of their oppression.

Still in the process of development, third-stage feminists willingly acknowledge the ways in which privileged women have sometimes oppressed less privileged women and men. Among the most vocal third-wave feminists are so-called postmodern feminists. They agree with radical-dominance feminists that the traditional measure, Man, should indeed be rejected as women's point of departure for self-understanding. So too should the radical-cultural and radical-dominance feminist ideal, Woman, be rejected. The idea of an essential female is of no help to women who need to understand their differences from each other as well as from men. Thus, postmodern feminists maintain that, just as we have no access to the Triangle as it exists in itself, but only to the enormous variety of triangles we construct, postmodern feminists maintain we have no access to Woman as she is in Herself, but only to the enormous variety of women who take shape before our eyes. Yet, despite women's differences, in the same way that we can recognize a triangle when we see one—be it scalene, isosceles, or equilateral—we can recognize a woman when we see one (Grosz 1994: 91).

Postmodern feminists' decision to emphasize women's diversity has generated a crisis in confidence among many feminists. If women's interests are radically divergent, they wonder whether feminist political action on behalf of women's collective best interests is still possible. According to Teresa de Lauretis, one way to address this important concern is to view gender neither as the automatic consequence of biology nor as the arbitrary construction of society, but as a *perspective* or conceptual grid through which values and meanings can be interpreted or (re)constructed (Lauretis 1994: 10). If third-wave feminists wish to remain *feminists*, they must, says

Lauretis, in some way privilege the category of gender over other worthy contenders (for example, race and class), for, without the category of gender, feminism is absorbed into humanism.

3. Applications of Feminist Thought to Contemporary Public Policy Issues

Both the debates over whether women should be treated the same or differently than men, and whether women's differences from one another should be emphasized or de-emphasized, significantly shape a variety of women-sensitive public policy issues. Although gender inequality is pervasive in the arts, the Church, professional sports, and the military, it is in the areas of education, work, sexuality, reproduction, and the family that public policy has had the greatest effect on women's private and personal lives. Thus, it is these areas of life that require particularly intense scrutiny.

3.1 Education

One way to understand how sameness, difference, dominance, and diversity models surface in discussions of women's education is to focus on Jane Roland Martin's historical study entitled *Reclaiming a Conversation: The Ideal of the Educated Woman* (1985). Martin puts thinkers such as Plato, Jean-Jacques Rousseau, Mary Wollstonecraft, Catherine Beecher, and Charlotte Perkins Gilman in conversation, asking them to comment on whether women should be given the same education as men or one more suited to women. Whereas Plato and Wollstonecraft insisted that society's well-being depends on men and women receiving the same education, Rousseau and Beecher claimed that, unless men and women are educated differently, society will fragment. As the latter two thinkers saw it, the stability of basic social institutions such as marriage and the family requires men and women to think that each gender has something the other one lacks. Simply put, couples will stay together only if they feel they need each other to constitute a whole.

Seeking to raise some new points about men's and women's education as well as their respective roles and identities, Charlotte Perkins Gilman portrayed an all-female society in her early twentieth-century feminist utopian novel, *Herland* (1979). All the women in Gilman's fictional world do both traditionally male and traditionally female work, and all of them are ideally feminine and masculine. When three male explorers stumble into Herland, however, two questions arise: (1) whether men can function in it without becoming like women; and (2) whether the possibility of heterosexual relationships will destabilize it. Since each of the three explorers finds a woman in Herland, and since only one of the couples decides to remain there, the implication is that single-sex societies are less than completely satisfying for most people, and that co-education rather than single-sex education is more likely to lead to the creation and maintenance of a sustainable society.

Plato, Rousseau, Wollstonecraft, Beecher, and Gilman all addressed a question about education that remains significant for today's sameness, difference, dominance, and diversity feminists. Namely: is an equal education for women one that provides women with the same or a different education from the one men receive? Sameness feminists have observed that, in the main, boys and girls are cued about appropriate masculine and feminine roles and responsibilities. Boys are supposed to be good in science and mathematics; to excel in all types of engineering and computing; and to be physically strong. In contrast, girls are supposed to be good in the arts, literature, and writing; to excel in communication skills; and to be physically weak. In addition, boys are pushed to work in high-pressure, competitive environments, whereas girls are encouraged to seek positions in low-stress, cooperative environments.

But, as sameness feminists see it, irrespective of what is said to be true about men and women in general, there are many men and women in particular who are exceptions to the rules governing appropriate masculine and feminine behaviour. Such individuals deserve the opportunity to excel in, for example, occupations and professions traditionally reserved for one sex only. Thus, sameness feminists have recommended that school officials encourage women to major in maths, science, and engineering and men to major in the humanities and the social sciences. Moreover, they have insisted that male-dominated professional schools such as law, medicine, and business be open to women; and, in those instances that women's entrance to them is blocked or resisted, that affirmative action legislation should be put in place.

Although difference, dominance, and diversity feminists have agreed with sameness feminists that women should be permitted to pursue whatever line of work they wish, they have not also agreed that women's development is better fostered in single-sex rather than co-ed contexts. According to difference feminists, co-ed classrooms are one of the primary places where men's gender dominance over women is created and maintained. For example, a significant percentage of teachers (female as well as male) tend to praise boys more than girls for equal-quality work; encourage boys to try harder; and give boys more interactive attention (Hall and Sandler 1982: 294). Thus, girls and women need same-sex classrooms, not because female students are less academically capable than male students, but because such classrooms constitute an environment friendly to women's concerns, issues, interests, needs, and values.

For all of their apparent benefits, same-sex classes have nonetheless come under attack. Sameness feminists have asserted that it is misguided to insist women learn best when men are absent. As they see it, such a claim bolsters the view that the two sexes cannot come together to work on intellectual things without letting sexual thoughts distract them. In addition, dominance feminists have reasoned that the sensible way to increase women's power base in society is not to shelter women from men but to eliminate the androcentric biases that presently permeate the co-ed environment. Women's Studies programmes, mentoring programmes for women interested in science, maths, and technology, and challenging, well-funded athletic programmes for women can all help co-ed classrooms become good places for women as well as men to learn (Culley 1985: 213). Finally, diversity feminists have noted that the more the academy erases the boundaries that separate racially and socio-economically privileged groups from racially and socio-economically disadvantaged groups, the more opportunities all sorts of women will have to become who they want to be.

3.2 Work

Sex discrimination in the workplace has a very long history. As early as the 1848 Seneca Falls Convention, feminists declared as one of their sentiments that 'He [man] has monopolized nearly all the profitable employments and from those she is permitted to follow, she receives but a scanty remuneration' (Lindgren and Taub 1988: 109). Although women have always worked within the home and alongside men on farms or in small family-operated entrepreneurial establishments, American women did not enter the *paid* labour force *en masse* until the 1950s and the 1960s.

Among the factors that account for women's massive entry into the workplace were books such as Betty Friedan's *The Feminine Mystique* (1974) and Simone de Beauvoir's *The Second Sex* (1974). These and other publications motivated middle-class, white, heterosexual women to seek employment, independence, and meaning outside the home environment. Certainly, according to diversity feminists, significant numbers of poor, working-class, and minority women were already labouring in factories or the service industry; but it was not until relatively privileged women entered the workplace that paid work for women was deemed to be a source of personal fulfilment as well as economic survival. Unlike lower-class women, who had to work in order to support themselves or their families, middle-class and upper-class women insisted they wanted to work because they had aspirations that transcended *kinder, kòche, and kirche* (children, the kitchen, and the Church). Moreover, as the desire for material goods increased, men as well as women began to view women's work outside home as something of a necessity, a means to purchase the family unit a suburban home, a second car, or a luxury holiday, for example.

The Wage Gap

As the number of women in the paid workforce swelled, sex discrimination in employment became more visible. The first inequality that captured women's attention was the male–female wage gap. In 1955 full-time female workers earned

64.5 per cent as much as full-time male workers; 59.7 per cent in 1975; 65 per cent in 1986; and in 1996, 76 per cent. Since women are more likely to work part time than men, these percentages would probably go down were all female workers (full and part time) contrasted with all male workers (full and part time). Further exacerbating the gender wage gap is the fact that women often get less ample benefit packages than men (Richmond-Abbott 2000: 162).

The standard explanations for the wage gap are twofold. First, women's lower wages are due to 'human capital' differentials. Because men have accumulated more than women in the way of education, on-the-job training, and work experience, they can produce more for their employers than women can. Therefore, it is only fair that employers pay their male employees more than their female employees. Secondly, women earn less than men because women with families cannot usually work extra hours, choose jobs involving travel, or accept demanding promotions without leaving many of their domestic and child-rearing duties undone.

Although these two explanations for the wage gap persuasively account for two-thirds of it, they leave the last one-third of it unexplained (Lindgren and Taub 1988: 193). The remaining fraction of the wage gap is increasingly explained as the direct result of sex discrimination. Numerous studies report that employers' attitudes towards female employees are unduly influenced by the stereotypes that women are less serious about their work than men are; that women's wages are second incomes and not really needed; and that women cannot handle job-related stresses and strains (Richmond-Abbott 2000: 168–9).

Occupational Sex Segregation

The second disparity that women noted in the workplace was the degree of occupational sex segregation there. For decades women have tended to work as librarians, nurses, primary schoolteachers, sales clerks, secretaries, bank tellers, and waitresses—lines of work that are either low paid and/or low status. In contrast, men have tended to work in executive, administrative, and managerial positions— lines of work that are high paid and/or high status. Thus, it is not surprising that, in the USA in the 1990s, 91.6 per cent of the clergy, 75.6 per cent of lawyers and judges, and 79 per cent of physicians were men, while more than 94.3 per cent of nurses, 81.3 per cent of librarians, and 98.6 per cent of pre-kindergarten and kindergarten teachers were women. Moreover, most of the women in the male-dominated professions tended to cluster at the bottom of the wage hierarchy. For example, female physicians typically serve as relatively low-paid primary-care doctors, while male physicians gravitate towards one of the high-paying specialities (Kaufman 2000: 190–2).

One of the standard explanations for occupational sex segregation is that women choose to segregate themselves in jobs that are structured for and/or compatible with the kinds of lives they typically lead. For example, career continuity is not particularly essential in the blue-collar and pink-collar occupations, such as factory worker and file clerk, respectively. Hence, such jobs fit women's decisions to take time off from work for child bearing and child rearing. Moreover, service-oriented jobs (most of which are low paying or low status) are said to suit women's caring, nurturant, and emotional 'nature' better than high-status, high-prestige jobs, which supposedly suit men's competitive, independent, and rational 'nature' (Kaufman 2000: 166).

A third explanation for occupational sex segregation is that women are discriminated against. When women are not excluded altogether from certain male-dominated jobs, they tend to be left out of the power networks controlling promotions, partnerships, tenure, research grants, and co-editorships. The women who manage to break through such barriers will do so only because they have paid some extremely high dues. Women who work in traditionally male-dominated lines of work often give up personal relationships, delay having children, and/or add on major domestic responsibilities to their already demanding workday.

Thus, it is no wonder that many women choose not to enter or to leave male-dominated jobs.

Feminization of Poverty

The third gender-based disparity that women observed inside (as well as outside) the workplace was the so-called feminization of poverty. This phrase captures how social factors coalesce to create economic conditions unfavourable to women. As a result of women's general economic dependency on men, many never-married, divorced, and widowed women and their children find themselves increasingly dependent on state subsidies (Sidel 1986: 15). In diversity feminists' estimation, minority women and poor women of any race in blue-collar jobs are particularly hard hit by sex discrimination in the workplace. Many of these women have to work because they are the primary or sole support of one or more child. This often leads to another serious abuse of women—one I discuss later in more detail. Too often, an employer or manager may force himself upon a female worker precisely because he knows how much she needs a job. Faced with a choice between giving in to her employer's sexual advances or being fired, a poor, single mother might reasonably choose the former course of action.

Strategies for Eliminating Gender-Based Inequities in the Workplace

Equal Pay for Equal Work. When a woman works alongside a man, performing the same job he performs equally well, and then receives lower pay, an injustice is done. Among the legal strategies that have been used to combat workplace sex discrimination in the USA are equal-pay-for-equal work remedies, including the Equal Pay Act of 1963, Title VII of the Civil Rights Act of 1964, and Executive Order No. 11246. These Acts require employers to pay employees of one sex the rate at which they pay wages to employees of the opposite sex. Although such Acts have helped to reduce sex discrimination in the workplace, they have by no means eliminated it. Employers who pay men and women unequally are provided with various 'affirmative defences' to justify their action: (1) seniority; (2) merit; (3) a system that measures earnings by quantity or quality of production; or (4) 'a differential based on any other factor other than sex' (Lindgren and Taub 1988: 193). Thus, employers may argue that the men who do job *X* receive higher wages than the women who do job *X* because the men are longtime employees, whereas the women are new hires.

Equal Pay for Work of Comparable Worth. Seeking to combat employers who manipulate job categories to make it look as though men and women are performing *different* work, when in fact they are performing essentially the *same* work, feminists have been strong supporters of comparable worth initiatives. The assumption that guides these initiatives is that many low-paying and/or low-prestige female-dominated jobs require at least as much in the way of skill, effort, responsibility, and taxing working conditions as many high-paying and/or high-status male-dominated jobs do. For example, when Washington state analysts used worth points to ascertain specific jobs' values, they discovered that pay for female-dominated jobs averaged only 80 per cent of that for male-dominated jobs, despite the fact that many low-paying female-dominated jobs scored far more worth points than many high-paying male-dominated jobs. Specifically, nurse practitioners netted 385 worth points, while boiler operators netted only 144 worth points. Yet boiler operators were paid exactly the same as nurse practitioners—namely, $832 a month. As a result of this Washington state study and studies like it, sameness feminists concluded that employers must pay women what they are worth, or expose themselves to sex discrimination suits.

Affirmative Action. Because neither equal-pay remedies nor comparable-worth initiatives have done much to break down occupational sex segregation, many sameness and diversity feminists have concluded that, in addition to such efforts, affirmative action programmes for women are probably necessary. Within the USA, affirmative action programmes are manifestly visible. Companies seeking to fill available positions place advertisements where women of all races and ethnicities and non-white males are likely to see them. Often these advertisements include a familiar clause that assures the use of non-racist and non-sexist criteria in evaluating and selecting applicants. Some critics have erroneously interpreted such clauses as indicating that a quota system exists, whereby a certain number of minorities or white women must be hired regardless of the qualifications of the entire pool of applicants. In fact, there are no laws or regulations that require employers to hire minorities or white women if more qualified white male candidates are available. All that affirmative action supports is the hiring of minorities or white women if their qualifications are equal to those qualified males.

According to long-time participants in the debate over affirmative action, the same arguments for and against it are repeatedly made. Advocates argue that affirmative action is needed to permit fairer competition, and that it is necessary to break the cycle that keeps minorities and white women locked into low-paying, low-prestige jobs. Opponents point out that affirmative action violates white men's rights and stigmatizes its female beneficiaries as having received an opportunity they do not really deserve. They also claim that strict policies of non-discrimination, which favour neither white men on the one hand nor white women and minorities of both sexes on the other, are the best way to achieve social justice.

At present, dominance feminists are increasingly dubious about the value of affirmative action, not so much for the reasons just cited, as because affirmative action tends to help mostly women who have succeeded in constructing a lifestyle and way of thinking that meets the demands of the 'male norm'. According to dominance feminists, the kind of programmes, laws, and attitudinal shifts most likely to decrease *all* women's subordination to men are those that permit women to combine family and career without sacrificing one to another. Their view is that disadvantaged as well as privileged women would benefit if companies offered maternity/paternity/parental leave, flexitime, telecommuting opportunities (work from home), job sharing, and on-site daycare for children and elders. In addition, government programmes should subsidize poor women with children so that they can work in decent paying jobs without jeopardizing their children's well-being.

3.3 Sexuality

Like work, sex is an area of major concern for women (Person 1980: 606). Supposedly, 'normal' women not only bear children and exhibit culturally selected feminine characteristics (gentleness, modesty, humility, supportiveness, empathy, sensitivity, unselfishness); they also pursue men as the object of their sexual desires. In contrast, 'abnormal' women avoid having children; exhibit culturally selected masculine characteristics (strength of will, ambition, courage, independence, assertiveness, aggression, hardiness, the ability to think abstractly and analytically, and the ability to control emotion); and pursue women as the object of their sexual desires (Vetterling-Braggin 1982: 4).

If one contrasts 'normal' women with their 'abnormal' counterparts, it becomes clear that 'normal' women adhere to the rules of the institution Adrienne Rich (1986: 631–60) termed the institution of compulsory heterosexuality. This institution mandates a unilateral arrangement according to which 'female sexuality cannot be lived or spoken or felt or even somatically sensed' apart from its definition as that which has the 'capacity to arouse desire' in men (MacKinnon 1980: 533). In other words, female sexuality has no meaning or use apart from male wants and needs—a state of affairs that seems manifestly unfair to women.

Sexual Double Standard

According to sameness feminists, a specific feature of the institution of compulsory sexuality is the so-called sexual double standard that imposes far more restrictions on women's sexual behaviour than men's. Whereas society winks at boys who 'sow their oats', it condemns as 'whores' girls who experiment sexually. Viewing such a state of affairs as unfair to women, sameness feminists have claimed that women's sexual desires should be given just as much 'free play' as men's. Although difference feminists have agreed with sameness feminists that society has unfairly restricted women's sexual activities, they have nonetheless cautioned that some forms of sex (particularly heterosexual relationships) are dangerous for most women. As they see it, male–female sexual relationships are the paradigm for all domination–subordination relationships, especially those that involve violence. Thus, difference feminists have generally espoused the position that women should focus on developing a 'female' sexuality, which would presumably be more about intimacy, emotional bonding, and love than performance, orgasm, and conquest (Ferguson 1984: 108–10).

Persuaded in the main by difference feminists' views on sexuality, dominance feminists have nonetheless stressed that, as it stands, the only sexuality women can possibly know now is the 'false' sexuality that has been constructed under conditions of male dominance and female subordination. Only in a society in which men and women have the same rights, responsibilities, and opportunities would it be possible for women to know the 'truth' about their own sexuality—whether, for instance, women are, 'by nature', more sexually attracted to women than to men, or more interested in love than sex. Diversity feminists have added the further point that race and ethnicity also shape women's sexual desires and practices.

Pornography

Another specific sex-related issue about which sameness, difference, dominance, and diversity feminists have disagreed is pornography. Sameness feminists have generally espoused the liberal view on pornography, according to which women as well as men have the right to view and read whatever pleases them, provided that their doing so does not significantly harm others. In contrast to sameness feminists, both dominance and difference feminists have adopted an anti-pornography position. As they see it, all pornography, but particularly pornography that depicts admixtures of sex and violence, can harm women in several possible ways. First, it can prompt men to abuse women sexually. Secondly, pornography can defame women by portraying them as persons who have so little regard for themselves that they willingly accept and even invite sexual abuse from men. Thirdly, and most seriously, it can lead men not only to think less of women as human beings but also to treat them as second-class citizens unworthy of the same due process and equal treatment to which men are accustomed.

Convinced that pornographers can and ought to be viewed as agents of sex discrimination, dominance feminists worked for the passage of anti-pornography ordinances in some American cities (MacKinnon 1987: 176). The initial success of their efforts notwithstanding, a coalition of sameness and diversity feminists called the Feminist Anti-Censorship Taskforce (FACT) helped convince the US Supreme Court that anti-pornography ordinances violate the First Amendment. FACT argued that phrases such as the 'sexually explicit subordination of women' have no context-free, fixed meaning. A photo that, in the eyes of a dominance feminist, depicts the sexual terrorization of a woman might in the view of a sameness feminist portray a woman in sexual ecstasy (Hunter and Law 1985: 9–18). Similarly, a pornographic photo that horrifies a woman in Saudi Arabia might titillate a woman in Norway.

Prostitution

Men are the primary purchasers not only of sexually explicit material but also of sexual services. Typically, homosexual men buy the sexual services of men and boys, whereas heterosexual men buy the sexual services of women and girls. Men often pay to see exotic dancers, to be entertained by Playboy bunnies, to be massaged by lap dancers, and to be escorted by beautiful and intelligent call girls. In addition, they pay for sexual intercourse.

In general, difference feminists have viewed all female sex workers, but particularly female prostitutes, as casualties of a society in which women with no other viable means to support themselves sell the only thing they have at their immediate disposal: their bodies.

In the estimation of difference feminists, this already bad state of affairs is worsened by the fact that many prostitutes, including poorly treated ones, believe that women's lot is truly one of sexual submission to men, and that it is women's role and responsibility to please men sexually. In short, prostitutes are not born. They are created by a society that teaches girls that, if all else fails, a woman can always use her body to gain money, attention, or even what passes for love.

Sameness feminists have disagreed, at least in part. Admitting that some sex workers and prostitutes are indeed 'sexual slaves', they have nonetheless stressed that a significant percentage of these women freely choose their line of work. The best way to help the latter group of women is, in the estimation of sameness feminists, to work for the decriminalization and destigmatization of sex work. Women who sell sex should be able to earn their living without being systematically hassled by the police, routinely imprisoned, and/or callously separated from their children. At the very least, women who sell 'sex' should not be punished more severely than the men who buy it.

With respect to prostitutes, dominance feminists have pressed the view that, in a patriarchal society, the only kind of sexual freedom women really have is the 'freedom' to choose the form of sexual bondage (such as dating, cohabitation, marriage, or prostitution) that most suits them. They have further reasoned that, because this is so, the law should not make life any more difficult for women who sell sex than it does for women who give sex away for free. Thus, feminists should lobby not only for the decriminalization of prostitution and other kinds of sex work but also for legal measures aimed at increasing the independence, health, and safety of the women who sell their sexual services. In particular, police and judicial authorities should be required to provide better protection for sex workers who lodge complaints against abusive 'pimps' and 'johns', and to punish any man who rapes, beats, or otherwise harms a sex worker (Jaggar 1986: 139).

Sexual Harassment

As varied and serious as are feminist concerns about pornography and prostitution, their concerns about sexual harassment are even greater. Before feminists began to focus on the coercive, manipulative, and exploitative dimensions of sexual harassment, society viewed this type of behaviour as a matter of offended sensibilities. In other words, up to the mid-twentieth century, a man's unwanted, repeated solicitations for sexual intercourse from a woman were addressed by a so-called tort approach. A woman could sue her harasser for damages on the grounds that he intentionally inflicted mental or emotional 'disturbance' upon her.

Such suits were not always successful, however, because the harasser had three defences. First, he could claim that the woman wanted or consented to his sexual advances. Secondly, the harasser could argue that the disturbance he inflicted upon the woman was small. Thirdly, and most significantly, he could claim he had no reason to believe that the woman whom he touched or threatened to touch would be offended or frightened. That is, he could insist he had no idea that his target was a hypersensitive individual. In such cases, the harasser would escape penalties on the grounds that a person with *ordinary* sensibilities would not have been offended by his remarks and/or actions. But because the law uses a so-called ordinary *man* test to determine whether a person is hypersensitive or not, problems can easily arise for the ordinary woman. Her reactions to men's comments about the size of her breasts are likely to differ from the ordinary man's reactions to women's comments about the size of his pectoral muscles. In this society, says Catherine MacKinnon, sex is an area where presumptions about gender sameness work against women's interests, 'since to remind a man of his sexuality is to build his sense of potency, while for a man to remind a woman of hers is often experienced as intrusive' (MacKinnon 1979: 171).

Disenchanted with the tort approach to sexual harassment, feminists have increasingly looked to anti-discrimination law for the conceptual tools women need to combat sexual harassers in both the workplace and the classroom. Whereas tort law views sexual harassment as an outrage to an individual woman's sensibilities, anti-discrimination law casts the same act either as one of *economic* coercion, in which the material survival of all women is threatened, or as one of *intellectual* coercion, in which the spiritual survival of all women is similarly jeopardized. If a woman wishes to argue that she has been sexually harassed not because she is vulnerable Sally Jones, but because she is a member of a gender that suffers from institutionalized inferiority and relative powerlessness, then the anti-discrimination approach obviously suits her purposes best (MacKinnon 1979: 173).

Despite feminists' shared view that sexual harassment impedes women's success in both the workplace and the classroom, they have disagreed about whether some purported instances of sexual harassment are truly sexual harassment. Sameness feminists have stressed that just because one person has more formal power over someone else does not mean that any sexual relationship between them is necessarily coercive; and that it is important to leave room in the academy, and certainly in the office, for genuine sexual attraction. In contrast to sameness feminists, dominance, difference, and diversity feminists have insisted that, whenever the person who makes a sexual advance has more economic, legal, or social power than the person he (or she) approaches, chances for a genuine sexual relationship are virtually nil. Thus, the safest policy is simply to conclude that teacher–student or boss–secretary 'dating' for example, is a form of sexual harassment.

In addition, feminists have debated whether women can sexually harass men, generally conceding that it is indeed possible for powerful female employers and teachers sexually to harass powerless male employees and students. Nonetheless, virtually all feminists stress that female-on-male harassment is relatively rare, not only because few women are powerful enough to engage in sexually harassing behaviour but also because few men are as bothered and distressed by sexual advances as women are. There is, in other words, no history or tradition of men losing their jobs or graduate assistantships because they rejected their female superiors' sexual advances.

Rape

Feminists have rethought the nature of rape as well as sexual harassment. Specifically, they have reinterpreted rape as a crime of violence as opposed to a crime of passion. This paradigm shift has led to major changes in rape law.

In the past, Anglo-American rape law was tainted by two misogynistic images of women: woman as sexual temptress and woman as liar. As a result, rape law was written in ways that required women to prove that they had indeed been raped. One assumption was that many of the women who cried 'rape' had 'asked for it', protesting 'No' when they meant 'Yes'. Another assumption was that some women accused men of rape to get even with them for ending a relationship. For the most part, judges and juries were not likely to believe a woman who claimed she had been raped unless she was a virgin, had been raped by a stranger, and showed signs of severe physical trauma. As a result, many rapists went free until rape law was reformed in ways that made it easier to prosecute rapists, and that encouraged rather than discouraged rape victims from complaining. Among these reforms were those that changed the three 'special rules' that had traditionally been invoked in rape cases. These rules had: (1) required the victim's testimony to be corroborated or substantiated by independent evidence; (2) allowed evidence regarding the victim's reputation and/or past sexual conduct (is she a virgin or a whore?); and (3) authorized cautionary jury instructions impugning the victim's credibility or questioning her veracity (Tong 1984: 105).

Although all feminists were relieved to see these rules reformed, sameness feminists resisted other, even more revolutionary attempts to reform rape law. In particular, they rejected a so-called criminal-circumstances approach to rape according to which, given certain circumstances, including a more powerful differential, one can simply *assume* that a rape has occurred. Conceding that sexual intercourse accomplished by means of a weapon, or sexual intercourse with an unconscious or drugged victim, constitutes circumstances indeed indicative of rape, sameness feminists nonetheless challenged the assumption that simply 'being in a position of authority' over someone is enough of a circumstance automatically to constitute rape. They insisted that competent, adult women *can* freely choose to have sexual intercourse, for example, with male employers or male professors to whom they are sexually attracted. Finally, sameness feminists pressed the view that rape should be viewed as a *standard* assault rather than a *special* kind of assault. In their estimation, 'the perceived need for a special set of laws to protect a woman's genitals is one of the barriers that prevent women from being the equals of men under the law, just as do female labor laws or combat restrictions' (Schwartz and Clear 1980: 148).

Unlike sameness feminists, difference feminists continued to insist that rape *is* a very *special* kind of assault. They objected that, by downplaying the *sexual* aspect of rape, sameness feminists implied that the rapist's choice of a woman's sexual organs as the direct object of his aggression is accidental rather than essential. Nothing could be further from the truth in difference feminists' estimation. They claimed that a rapist's choice to penetrate a woman's vagina, rather than to punch her body randomly, shows that he is interested not simply in assaulting her but in reminding her that women's bodies exist for men.

Going several steps further than difference feminists, dominance feminists argued that, no matter how many reforms are made in rape law, the incidence of rape is not likely to decrease noticeably unless society radically changes its view about male and female sexuality, about whose body (if anyone's) exists for whom. Specifically, Andrea Dworkin claimed that rape is the form heterosexual intercourse takes in an unequal society that subordinates women to men. In such a society, the rapist is not a psychopath or deviant but, literally, the boy next door or the man with whom one sleeps (Bienen 1980: 454–5).

3.4 Reproduction

Of all the factors that play a role in the unequal status of men and women in society, women's role in child bearing and child rearing is probably the largest one. The fact that only women can get pregnant, gestate, give birth to, and nurse a child, coupled with the fact that women typically shoulder the bulk of a family's child-rearing responsibilities, means that women's reproductive responsibilities are far heavier than men's. Therefore, unless extraordinary technological means are developed and taken, and/or unless parenting arrangements become more gender equal, women will continue to have far less time than men have for leisure as well as work in the public arena.

Contraception, Sterilization, and Abortion

In the main feminists have viewed birth control through contraception, sterilization, and abortion as a necessary condition for the emancipation of women. Throughout the nineteenth century and the early part of the twentieth, many feminist groups in the USA fought strenuously for so-called voluntary motherhood and women's right to control their reproductive destiny. Yet, despite all their efforts, and the fact that a large number of American women used a variety of birth-control methods, anti-birth-control legislation became increasingly restrictive. One of the more notorious examples of such legislation were the Comstock laws of the 1870s, which defined practising, advertising, or even owning, lending, or giving away literature on contraception or abortion as pornography, punishable by six months to five years imprisonment at hard labour, or a fine of between $100 and $2,000. Not until 1963 in *Griswold* v. *Connecticut* did even *married* women gain the right to purchase and use contraceptives, and it was only in 1973 that American women gained the legal right to have an abortion 'on demand' during the first trimester of their pregnancies.

Birth control has come not only slowly but also unevenly to American women. For many white, relatively privileged American women, it has been emancipation indeed, but for many minority women, it has proved to be a mixed blessing. Many African-American and Hispanic women, for example, use contraceptives, get sterilized, or have abortions not because they do not want a child or the responsibilities of motherhood, but simply to prevent the birth of a child destined to live in unfavourable social conditions—indeed, the same conditions that limit them. In addition, many of these women, as well as women from other disadvantaged minority groups, and poor women in general, have been provided with and encouraged to use birth control for eugenic purposes—as a means of preventing the proliferation of the 'lower classes'. Far from being freely chosen, this type of birth control has frequently included 'elective sterilization', but without informed consent, or even forced sterilization, paid for and sanctioned by the government.

In so far as abortion is concerned, feminists have generally stressed that it is the ultimate means that assures women that, like men, they do not have to *bear* an unwanted child. This is not to say that feminists have agreed among themselves about how to strike a proper balance between a woman's right to control her reproductive destiny, on the one hand, and the developing fetus's right to life, on the other. Whereas some feminists have insisted that women's abortion rights are absolute, others have maintained that abortion is justified only in the event of failed or inaccessible contraceptives; an unfortunate contingency such as the severely defective state of the fetus; risks to the woman's health or life; or an intensely personal reason such as pregnancy due to rape or incest. Nevertheless, even though some feminists have objected to late-term abortions or abortions for reasons of convenience, one would be hard pressed to find any feminist who has supported, for example, a husband's right to veto his wife's abortion decision. Similarly, one would have a hard time finding a feminist in favour of overturning *Roe* v. *Wade*, the 1973 Supreme Court decision that ruled that states may not enact laws to interfere with a woman's and her physician's abortion decision during the first trimester of pregnancy (Lindgren and Taub 1988: 394–6).

Yet not all feminists are enthusiastic supporters of American abortion law. Dominance feminists have noted that Hugh Hefner's Playboy Foundation has actively supported permissive abortion laws. According to Catharine MacKinnon, this fact is not surprising since 'the availability of abortion . . . removes the one remaining legitimized reason that women have had for refusing sex besides the headaches. As Andrea Dworkin put it, "Getting laid was at stake . . ."' (MacKinnon 1993: 223). In addition, difference and diversity feminists have noted that for most women abortion is a traumatic, difficult decision, and that the choice to have an abortion is not truly *free* unless the choice *not* to have an abortion is also available.

Insemination, Fertilization, Transfers, and Surrogacy

Although many women are interested in *not* procreating, an increasing number of women are just as interested in procreating. In the 1970s sameness feminists welcomed the advent of the new reproduction-assisting technologies. They stressed the ways in which donor insemination, *in vitro* fertilization, egg and embryo transfer, and surrogate mother arrangements permitted women who had trouble conceiving and/or bearing a child nonetheless to have a much wanted child. For sameness feminists the primary issues to address about collaborative reproduction involve informed consent and access issues. As they see it, both the women who need reproductive services and the women who provide them should be fully informed about the psychological and physical risks and benefits of them. Moreover, women of modest means as well as wealthy women should have access to infertility services if they need them to procreate.

Difference and dominance feminists have argued that, contrary to appearances, collaborative modes of reproduction actually decrease rather than increase women's reproductive freedom. Commercial surrogacy is held out for special scrutiny on the grounds that it cannot be distinguished either from selling babies or from selling (or renting out) women's bodies; and that it raises the spectre of rich infertile couples 'harvesting' the babies of poor contracted mothers. Also of concern is the tendency in these contractual arrangements to focus on the interests of the contracting parents and, correspondingly, to lose sight of the interests of the gestational mothers, their families, and the offspring produced in the process. For these reasons and others like them, dominance and diversity feminists have recommended the prohibition and/or the non-enforcement of at least *commercial* surrogacy arrangements.

Difference, dominance, and diversity feminists have also been concerned about the general coercive potential of the new reproductive technologies. The increasing 'medicalization' of pregnancy and birth that these technologies entail make women dependent on experts, thereby robbing women of meaningful control over their own reproductive processes. In fact, the very availability of these new technologies can serve as a social and even legal pressure for women to use them. In some instances, infertile women have felt that it was their duty as 'good' women to try every available means to have a baby, no matter how physically and psychologically taxing or how economically costly. In other cases women have been forced to use diagnostic or therapeutic procedures intended to improve the health of their fetuses.

Disturbed by these impositions on women, biologist Ruth Hubbard stresses that, for all we know, some of these new technologies might turn out to be more harmful than beneficial. For example, the long-term consequences of taking certain infertility drugs, or the current, sometimes indiscriminate use of ultrasound or *in utero* fetal surgery, might prove to have the kind of unfortunate outcomes that the indiscriminate use of DES and thalidomide had in the past. Finally, concludes Hubbard, the highest price some women might have to pay for the uncertain benefits of the new technologies might be their own emotional well-being. Encouraging women to use every available prenatal diagnostic procedure and treatment may, for example, cause many pregnant women to 'look on every fetus as potentially disabled and in need of ongoing medical surveillance' (Hubbard 1990: 144–5).

3.5 The Family

Marriage as a cultural practice accomplishes a variety of public functions from the procreation of humanity to fuelling the economy. In societies such as ours, where marriages are not arranged, girls are from the earliest ages invited to dream about their 'big day'. In order to ensure that young women will continue to walk down the aisle, girls are exposed to imagery in movies, bridal magazines, and romance novels, all of which glorify the status of the wife. Yet, throughout the decades, women (and, to a lesser degree, men) have written personal accounts and serious literature about failed marriages as well as successful ones. For all its positive features, the institution of marriage has some negative ones for both husbands and wives, but particularly for full-time wives and mothers who are economically dependent on their spouses.

Although all feminists have expressed concerns about the institution of marriage, beginning with the tradition of wives replacing their familial surname with their husbands', dominance feminists have probably levelled some of the most devastating critiques. In her *Intergalactic Wickedary of the English Language*, Mary Daly defined 'family, patriarchal' as the 'primary unit of the sadosociety, consisting of slaves organized in domestic and sexual service to a snool [bully] as their head' (Daly 1985: 197). For Daly and many other dominance feminists, heterosexual marriage is a purely cultural construction that serves only husbands well. Sanctioned as 'head of the household', the husband has had legal rights to dominate, or to be, as the authors of the 1848 Seneca Falls Declaration said, the 'master of his wife and children' (Lindgren and Taub 1988: 307). For dominance feminists, marriage is at its worst simply 'as a mechanism for the domination of women because it forces individual women into dependence on individual men while isolating women from each other' (Baker 1994: 506). Thus, they have sometimes argued that the only effective means that women have to resist this kind of gender oppression is to not get married.

Whereas dominance feminists are fundamentally opposed to the institution of marriage, difference feminists are not naysayers of the institution itself. On the contrary, they have argued that full-time marriage and motherhood are not only a choice that women can *freely* make, but often a *good* choice in comparison to some of their other options. Indeed, as difference feminists see it, it makes perfect sense for a woman to focus exclusively on her family and home rather than trying to add that full-time job to another full-time job outside the home.

Disagreeing with difference feminists that a marriage-and-motherhood-only decision may serve women's best interests, sameness feminists have instead sought to equalize the benefits and burdens of married life. Specifically, they have argued that a married couple should both work outside the home and within the home, thereby overcoming traditional gender roles and responsibilities. The hope of sameness feminists is that, if husbands and wives equalize the amount and even *kind* of work they do outside and inside the home, their children will be able to overcome the sexist attitudes and behaviours present in the larger society.

As promising as the egalitarian marriage sounds, the egalitarian divorce is not so good for women, in the estimation of many feminists, including many sameness feminists. The old divorce laws assumed that a husband's role was to support a wife and child during marriage and to continue to support them after divorce; and that a wife's role was to take care of home and children during marriage and to continue to care for them after divorce. In contrast, the new no-fault divorce laws treat wives and husbands as fully equal partners in marriage *and* divorce. Thus, at divorce both persons are responsible for self-support and child support, and both are eligible for child custody. Alimony is awarded only according to need, and property is divided equally. Moreover, in most states no ground or 'fault' is necessary to obtain a divorce. All that is required, according to the new divorce laws, is the desire of at least one partner in the marriage to end it. This is in sharp contrast to the old divorce laws, according to which a marriage could be dissolved only if at least one of the parties was judged guilty of some serious indiscretion, such as adultery, phys-ical abuse, or mental cruelty. In such cases, the law punished the guilty party and rewarded the innocent one through suitable alimony and property awards.

Initially, the new no-fault divorce laws seemed like a boon to women who wanted a relatively easy and quick way out of a bad marriage. But, according to Lenore Weitzman (1985: 232), it soon became clear that the new no-fault divorce laws were not an unalloyed blessing for all women. Even when both members of a married couple work outside the home, the woman's job is usually the second job: the part-time job, the dead-end job, the luxury job. Women still tend to choose family respons-ibilities over career opportunities when push comes to shove, a tendency that is far less prevalent among men. As a result, at the time of a divorce a woman's earning capacity may have been impaired by the marriage relationship, while a man's earn-ing capacity may have been enhanced. But the new divorce laws do not take this phe-nomenon into account. Instead, divorce courts decide property settlements, alimony awards, and child support as if the two divorcing spouses were fully the other's equals. What makes this 'new deal' a particularly difficult one for many ex-wives, who get child custody 90 per cent of the time, is that their ex-husbands rarely pay even half of the expenses associated with rearing a child to adulthood. As a result, many women and children tend to experience a sharp decline in their standard of living subsequent to a divorce while many men often experience a rise in theirs.

4. CONCLUSION

In the USA and in most developed, industrial nations, sex discrimination has noticeably diminished, but it remains markedly present in many developing nations. Thus, although American women have some way to go before they are entirely equal to American men, the wait should be relatively short compared to the wait of women in less free societies. For all women, however, justice is not simply a matter of political, economic, and educational parity, but also of sexual, reproduct-ive, and familial parity. In many ways, it is easier for women to achieve equality with men in the workplace, forum, and academy than in the home. Given that this is the case, it is important that theories of justice stop focusing on the redistribution of legal rights, economic resources, and educational opportunities, and that they incorporate other key components of gender injustice.

Although sameness, difference, dominance, and diversity feminists have each contributed to reducing overt, subtle, and covert sex discrimination, perhaps the most promising approach to eliminating residual gender disparities is what Eva Kittay has termed a 'dependency' approach to human existence. According to Kittay neither the sameness approach nor its standard critiques (difference, dominance, and diversity) recognize just how problematic the traditional conception equality is and how it usually works against women's best interests. The standard view about equality presumes that all persons are independent, symmetrically situated, and wanting the kind of life privileged white men have traditionally had. The problem with this view of equality is not only that people are more or less dependent on each other and asymmetrically situated, but also that the kind of life the most privileged members of society lead would not be possible were it not for the 'dependency work' others do for them. In other words, the success of the 'successful' is made possible by the caring, nurturing work done on their behalf, traditionally by all women, but increasingly by economically and socially disadvantaged women as more advantaged women achieve 'equality' with men (Kittay 2000).

Although Kittay does not say so explicitly, her work suggests that sex discrimination will persist unless we abandon the traditional conception of equality, the ethics of justice that bolsters it, and the ontology of the separate and independent self that masterminds it. In their places we must substitute a concept of reciprocity, supported by an ethics of care and an ontology of connectedness and independency. In particular, we need to ask ourselves why men do not want to be equal to women. The fact that most men continue to eschew service-oriented jobs, that they avoid taking parental and family leave from work, and that they view unwanted pregnancies as primarily the 'woman's' problem says that men remain dependent on women to take care of them. After all, no society worth living in can survive, let alone thrive, unless someone cooks, cleans, tends the children, assists people with illnesses and disabilities, and so on. Kittay implies that the only way to eliminate sex discrimination once and for all is to focus our concerns about justice on society's 'dependency workers' (male as well as female), and to restructure our schools, workplaces, and homes in ways that enhance the freedom and well-being of 'dependency workers'. In short, Kittay proposes a 'trickle-up' approach to justice— an approach that, in my estimation, offers our society the opportunity to achieve the goal that has eluded it for too long: a fully human life for all women and men in a truly just society.

REFERENCES

Baker, K. (1994). 'Bisexual Feminist Politics: Because Bisexuality is Not Enough', in A. M. Jaggar (ed.), *Living with Contradictions: Controversies in Feminist Social Ethics*. Boulder, CO: Westview 504–10.

Beauvoir, S. de (1974). *The Second Sex*. New York: Vintage Books.

Beecher, C. E., and Stowe, H. B. (1869/1971). *The American Woman's Home: Principles of Domestic Science*. New York: Arno Press and the *New York Times*.

Benokraitis, N. V., and Feagin, J. R. (1986). *Modern Sexism: Blatant, Subtle, and Covert Discrimination*. Englewood Cliffs, NJ: Prentice Hall.

Bienen, L. (1980). 'National Developments in Rape Reform Legislation', in J. R. Lindgren and N. Taub (eds.), *The Law of Sex Discrimination*. St Paul, MN: West Publishing Company, 453–63.

Buhle, M. J., and Buhle, P. (1978) (eds.), *The Concise History of Women's Suffrage*. Urbana, IL: University of Illinois Press.

Corea, G. (1985). *The Mother Machine: Reproductive Technologies from Artificial Insemination to Artificial Wombs*. New York: Harper & Row.

Culley, M. (1985). 'Anger and Authority in the Introductory Women's Studies Classroom', in M. Culley and C. Portuges (eds.), *Gendered Subjects: The Dynamics of Feminist Teaching*. Boston: Routledge & Kegan Paul, 209–17.

Daly, M. (1985). *Webster's First New Intergalactic Wickedary of the English Language*. New York: HarperCollins.

Ferguson, A. (1984). 'Sex Wars: The Debate between Radical and Libertarian Feminists'. *Signs: Journal of Women in Culture and Society*, 10/1: 108–10.

Firestone, S. (1970). *The Dialectic of Sex*. New York: Bantam Books.

Friedan, B. (1974). *The Feminine Mystique*. New York: Dell.

Gilman, C. P. (1979). *Herland: A Lost Feminist Utopian Novel*. New York: Partheon Books.

Grosz, E. (1994). 'Sexual Differences and the Problem of Essentialism', in N. Schor and E. Weed (eds.), *The Essential Difference*. Bloomington, IN: Indiana University Press, 82–97.

Hall, R. M., and Sandler, B. R. (1982). 'Outside the Classroom: A Chilly Campus Climate for Women?', in J. R. Lindgren and N. Taub (eds.), *The Law of Sex Discrimination*. St Paul, MN: West Publishing Company, 296–300.

Hubbard, R. (1990). *The Politics of Woman's Biology*. New Brunswick, NJ: Rutgers University Press.

Jaggar, A. M. (1986). 'Prostitution', in A. M. Jaggar (ed.), *Living with Contradictions: Controversies in Feminist Social Ethics*. Boulder, CO: Westview, 102–12.

Kaufman, D. R. (2000). 'Professional Women: How Real Are the Recent Gains?', in J. A. Kourany, J. P. Sterba, and R. Tong (eds.), *Feminist Philosophies: Problems, Theories, and Applications*. Upper Saddle River, NJ: Prentice Hall, 189–202.

Kittay, E. F. (2000). *Love's Labor: Essays on Women, Equality, and Dependency*. New York: Routledge.

Lauretis, T. de (1994). 'The Essence of the Triangle, or Taking the Risks of Essentialism Seriously', in N. Schor and E. Weed (eds.), *The Essential Difference*. Bloomington, IN: Indiana University Press, 1–39.

Lindgren, J. R., and Taub, N. (1988). *The Law of Sex Discrimination*. St Paul, MN: West Publishing Company.

MacKinnon, C. A. (1979). *Sexual Harassment of Working Women*. New Haven: Yale University Press.

——(1980). 'Feminism, Marxism, Method, and the State: An Agenda for Theory'. *Signs: Journal of Women in Culture and Society*, 5: 631–60.

——(1987). 'Francis Biddle's Sister: Pornography, Civil Rights, and Speech', in C. A. MacKinnon, *Feminism Unmodified: Disclosures on Life and Law*. Cambridge, MA: Harvard University Press, 163–97.

——(1993). 'Roe v. Wade: A Study in Male Ideology', in L. H. Schwartz (ed.), *Arguing about Abortion*. Belmont, CA: Wadsworth, 188–201.

Martin, J. R. (1985). *Reclaiming a Conversation: The Ideal of the Educated Woman*. New Haven, CT: Yale University Press.

Mill, J. S. (1869/1911). *On the Subjection of Women*. New York: Frederick A. Stokes Company.

Nicholson, L. (1998). 'Gender', in A. M. Jaggar and I. M. Young (eds.), *A Companion to Feminist Philosophy*. Oxford: Blackwell, 289–97.

Person, E. S. (1980). 'Sexuality as the Mainstay of Identity: Psychoanalytic Perspectives'. *Signs: Journal of Women in Culture and Society*, 4: 606.

Rich, A. (1986). 'Compulsory Heterosexuality and Lesbian Existence', in A. M. Jaggar (ed.), *Living with Contradictions: Controversies in Feminist Social Ethics*. Boulder, CO: Westview, 487–90.

Richmond-Abbott, M. (2000). 'Women Wage Earners', in J. A. Kourany, J. P. Sterba, and R. Tong (eds.), *Feminist Philosophies: Problems, Theories, and Applications*. Upper Saddle River, NJ: Prentice Hall, 162–79.

Schwartz, M. D., and Clear, T. R. (1980). 'Toward a New Law on Rape'. *Crime and Delinquency*, 27: 148.

Sidel, R. (1986). *Women and Children Last: The Plight of Poor Women in Affluent America*. New York: Penguin.

Tong, R. (1984). *Women, Sex, and the Law*. Totowa, NJ: Rowman & Allanheld.

Vetterling-Braggin, M. (1982). *'Femininity', 'Masculinity', and 'Androgyny': A Modern Philosophical Discussion*. Totowa, NJ: Rowman & Littlefield.

Weitzman, L. J. (1985). 'The Divorce Law Revolution and the Transformation of Legal Marriage', in J. A. Kourany, J. P. Sterba, and R. Tong (eds.), *Feminist Philosophies: Problems, Theories, and Applications*. Upper Saddle River, NJ: Prentice Hall, 230–40.

West, R. (1988). 'Jurisprudence and Gender'. *University of Chicago Law Review*, 55/1: 1–72.

Wollstonecraft, M. (1792/1988). *A Vindication of the Rights of Women*. London: Penguin.

Cases Cited

Griswold v. *Connecticut*, 381 US 479 (1965).

Hunter, N. D. and Law, S. A. (1985). Brief Amici Curiae of Feminist Anti-Censorship Task Force et al. To U.S. Court of Appeals for the Seventh Circuit, *American Booksellers Association, Inc.* et al. v. *William H. Hudnut III* et al. 18 April, 9–18.

Roe v. *Wade*, 410 US 113 (1973).

CHAPTER 10

RACE AND RACIAL DISCRIMINATION

NAOMI ZACK

1. INTRODUCTION

THERE is often a lack of knowledge about contemporary academic analyses of racism and race, in American power structures where whites occupy dominant positions. Whites in positions of power conduct their most serious discussions about racism and race among their peers. Activists who are committed to resisting white racism rarely apply the academic analyses to their own situations. And academics talk mainly to one other. When something sufficiently terrible happens, which the media is able to reprocess for the masses, renewed general interest in racism and race is sparked. But, without careful understanding of underlying social causes and their history, there is nothing to sustain such a spark. Needed is a coherent and cohesive approach to race and racism, which would be accessible to all interested parties who considered it.

This chapter is an attempt to develop an accessible approach to race and racism in the US at the beginning of the twenty-first century. Section 2, 'Racism', is about the concept of racism, and, by derivation, racists and racist behavior. Any acceptable definition of racism would seem to presuppose the existence of races and racial difference. Therefore, Section 3, 'Race', is an examination of those concepts. Section 4, 'Remedies', is a discussion of practical correctives to racism in the light of the progress made in Sections 2 and 3.

2. RACISM

It is important to begin with racism, because, when the subject of race comes up, the general response is to focus on racism. At present, most educated and benevolent people believe that racism is wrong, racists are immoral, and racist actions are unjust. It follows that racism ought to be morally condemned and that racist actions ought to be punished. There is also widespread agreement that the victims of racism are entitled to something, although proposals about what they are entitled to range from the enforcement of laws protecting civil rights, to compensation, reparation, and pro-active, anti-racist remedies. Not everyone thinks that racism can be eliminated, although most agree it would be desirable to do so. Furthermore, in discussions about the elimination of racism, there is disagreement about defining racism, and how to apply accepted definitions.

2.1 Importance of the Concept of Racism

Racism, a multiplicity of morally blameworthy attitudes and dispositions, and the specific beliefs, emotions, and actions that instantiate them, is usually assumed to be of some duration in human history. Racism is also commonly regarded as a type of injustice. Within the Western moral tradition, justice is the cardinal individual and social virtue, so injustice must be the cardinal individual and social vice. As a type of injustice, racism is a moral defect in individuals and a distortion of the social order. As a type of injustice, racism therefore must be recognized as a serious individual and social vice.

The term 'racism', as we now use it, describes injustice associated with recognized racial difference. The concept of racism is applied as a reason for blame or censure against individuals and groups. The term 'racism' is also used as a means to achieve further liberation or empowerment of those believed to have been treated unjustly on the grounds of race. Whenever it is agreed that racism is present, it is usually also agreed that something ought to be done to lessen or eliminate it. Thus, it is expected that, if people understand they are agents of racism, they will change their unjust behavior; and, if others understand they are victims of racism, they will be better able to resist injustice. In this way, the identification of an action, rule, or social practice as 'racist' is intended to cure ignorance and prevent further harm, as well as make a moral evaluation.

2.2 Critical and Historical Uses of the Concept of Racism

For millennia, members of dominant groups have oppressed, and abused, members of subordinate groups on the basis of differences that we would today identify as racial; and members of subordinate racial groups have sometimes defended themselves, and less frequently behaved unjustly, against members of dominant racial groups. But such wrongs have not always been identified as racism, because that identification requires prior background assumptions about human equality and universal rights. Those assumptions are relatively recent in Western history. Moreover, different concepts of race, in modern times, have been accompanied by different forms of racism. Still, some philosophers identify as racist, beliefs or behavior from historical periods pre-dating the modern concept of race. For instance, Berel Lang claims that a general form of racism is historically prior to modern concepts of race. Although Lang identifies racism in contexts doubly removed from contemporary applications of the term—because they are historically prior to both the present concept of race and its accompanying racism—he avoids anachronism by positing racism as a (transhistorical) metaphysical conceptual scheme, capable of appropriating historically changing empirical concepts of race, for unjust ends (Lang 1997). Along similar lines, Charles Mills argues that modern Western history has been based on a (not always explicit) *racial contract* that has positioned Europeans and Americans at the apex of an industrial and technological project that has exploited indigenous Americans, Africans, and Asians, and their descendants (Mills 1997).

Lang's notion of metaphysical racism and Mills's idea of a racial contract are interesting critical devices, but they fail to provide non-metaphorical and empirically grounded descriptive analyses of racism that could be of practical use in contemporary public and private life. An empirical analysis of racism should begin with the history of the concept. Before the 1950s in the US, social custom and public policy, generally, supported beliefs and behavior that would now be identified as racist, such as slavery, and reduced civil and social status for non-whites. During the nineteenth century, concepts of racial taxonomy differed even more from the scientific and educated views prevailing today. (I will address some of the specific intellectual connections between racism and ideas about race in Section 3.) Between the 1950s and the 1970s, what is today called racism would have been called bigotry, intolerance, discrimination, or prejudice (BIDP). BIDP may occur on the grounds of racial differences, but not merely on those grounds. For instance, people may be intolerant or prejudiced against those who differ from them in religion, nationality, gender, or any of a myriad number of human traits, preferences, and conditions that include physical able-ness, body size, age, education, income, wealth, and sexual orientation or 'preference'. Members of groups we now recognize as racial groups were victims of BIDP before the modern concept of race was constructed. Slavery was practiced in the ancient world, before there was a concept of biological race (Finley 1983). During the European slave trade prior to the eighteenth century, Europeans, as well as Africans, were enslaved, and religious and cultural differences were considered more important than physical differences as a justification for the development of the (specifically) African slave trade (Zack 1996: ch. 12). Therefore,

BIDP, the closest ancestors of racism, are more broad in (non-anachronistic) application than 'racism'. This suggests another important requirement for an empirical definition of racism: it should reflect contemporary practice in a way that is tied to present beliefs about races and racial difference.

2.3 Competing Definitions of Racism

Racism is a type of injustice, and, as such, morally wrong. Racism is a vice. Therefore, its definition can be expected to have practical effects concerning the kinds of attitudes and behavior that are morally blameworthy. Americans have different, and sometimes conflicting beliefs about the nature of racial differences, the desirability of social change, and the extent of existing social injustice based on racial difference. Since the civil-rights movement there has also been varied intensity in race-based social and political conflict. It is, therefore, not surprising that there are competing definitions of racism at this time, or that definitions are to some extent preferred according to racial identities and race-based 'agendas'.

Foremost is what could be called *classic racism*: unjustified feelings of hatred and contempt for members of races different from one's own, resulting in insult, exclusion, discrimination, and/or violence against them. Intellectually, classic racism has been connected with doctrines of white supremacy. Among educated Americans, today, classic racism is morally condemned and associated with political and ideological extremists who, as classic racists, are not publically accepted by the majority in civic or private life. Members of educated communities disagree about whether classic racism is the only important kind of racism—that is, the only kind deserving of legal action or moral blame.

The Kantian moral tradition yields a *mens rea* definition of racism that is useful for analyzing the concept of classic racism. Jorge Garcia and others have argued that racism should be defined as a kind of ill will or contempt in the hearts and minds of individuals, precisely because it is a moral wrong for which people are, and ought to be, held responsible. Garcia argues that racism may be present when others are not harmed by it, and that it may not be present when others are harmed in ways tied to their race. In this view, racism is not necessarily connected to its effects on other people (Garcia 1997).

The *mens rea* definition of racism is perhaps a direct descendant of BIDP. But, racism as *mens rea* is located in individuals, while BIDP could be characteristic of groups. The *mens rea* definition requires that someone actually be a racist in order for racism to exist, but there is indeterminacy in how aware of their own racism people need to be in order to be judged racists. This indeterminacy in the definition allows for 'unconscious' racism, as well as racist feelings and thoughts that individuals may have in some contexts but not others. Behaviorists and pragmatists might wish to eliminate the *mens rea* component of traditional racism—because it is metaphysical and suggestive of old-fashioned concepts of virtue and vice in the soul—and restrict the definition of racism to *behavior* or action by individuals that is insulting, discriminating, or harmful, in ways tied to race. But, even if all cases of racism were defined in terms of behavior or action, there would have to be criteria for distinguishing between deliberate behavior that had racist motivation and intent and behavior or action that was inadvertently racist. This distinction could be made by specifying different prior, attendant, or subsequent behaviors or actions for the motivated and inadvertent cases. But, even if these specifications could be precisely met, a perceived need for them suggests lingering importance of the *mens rea*.

Judith Lichtenberg's notion of *less-than-conscious racism* seems to steer clear of the metaphysical and epistemological problems raised by the *mens rea* definition of racism. Less-than-conscious racism includes race-based aversive behavior, stereotyping, and accommodation of the *mens rea* racism of others, by people who would not consider themselves racists, or be so considered by their peers (Lichtenberg 1998).

Other philosophers have argued that racism need not be the result of any conscious or explicit mental state in individuals, because harm to members of non-white groups in situations where whites are not harmed is sufficient proof of its presence. According to that view of racism, the most important form of racism is *institutional racism*, or social, economic, and political conditions in which established norms and practices disadvantage non-whites in comparison to whites. Race need never be mentioned or even thought about in cases of institutional racism. Moreover, its *institutional* aspects are underscored when well-developed social institutions (which are but parts of the whole of society, or 'the system'), such as schools, governmental entities, and business corporations, disproportionately include and reward whites, in comparison to non-whites, based on requirements or criteria that whites are more likely to fulfil because of a history of racial inequality that has privileged them.

Different kinds of institutional racism interact and compound racist effects. Segregation in housing and unequal educational opportunities are two kinds of institutional racism that regularly reinforce one another. Since whites, as a group, earn more money and have more financial assets than blacks, the prices of houses that they can afford are too expensive for many blacks. Because schools are funded by local taxes, schools in predominantly white neighborhoods have bigger budgets than schools in predominantly black neighborhoods. Parents who can afford high-priced houses are attracted to neighborhoods with better schools. As a result, segregation in education, as well as in housing, is reinforced by economic disparity that is connected to racial difference (Kozol 1991). This may happen without conscious, explicit, or intentional racism against those excluded. The *mens rea* form of racism may also be present and active in cases of institutional exclusion and segregation, but the point for those who advocate a definition of racism as institutional racism—the present majority of liberatory scholars and activists—is that determination of the *mens rea* component is not necessary to determine that racist injustice has occurred.

Critical race theorists have brought a legal dimension to the concept of institutional racism. Derek Bell insists that the American legal system has always had
different effects on different racial groups. Slavery was accepted in the US
Constitution, via the stipulation that a slave would count as two-thirds of a person
for the purpose of determining the number of congressional representatives in a
district (Bell 1998).

Patricia Williams argues that the omission of racial terms in laws protecting civil
liberties often has the effect of covert discrimination against blacks. The social and
economic disadvantage within which blacks live precludes their ability to start off
on an equal footing with whites, in many contexts. Then, when blacks fail or are
automatically excluded, we infer that racial bias is not a cause, since legal neutrality about race is assumed to guarantee the absence of racial bias. Thus, the presumption of racial neutrality in the law may have the same force as an agreement
not to address race-based structural inequalities, and, without specific address,
these inequalities tend to remain unchanged (Williams 1991).

Angela Davis, and others, have argued that present disproportional incarceration
rates for African-Americans are the effect of a legal system that criminalizes behavior within non-white groups that have high rates of poverty. Some of this poverty
is the result of unemployment in inner cities, caused by the exportation of low-
paying jobs to the third world, by the multinational corporations that are now
the effective agents of capitalism. The bottom of the labor force is always most
vulnerable to unemployment, and the educational disadvantages of non-whites,
as well as the social effects of a long history of racial injustice, relegate them to
the bottom of the labor force. The harm to American non-whites may not have
been intended by corporate decisions-makers, but it results from the disproportionately high numbers of non-whites among unskilled and semi-skilled workers
(A. Davis 1998).

The contending definitions of *mens rea* racism (both self-aware and less than
conscious) and institutional racism sparked debate during the last decades of the
twentieth century, which sometimes sounds as though the main problems concerning racism are semantic. Disputes in which contending parties attach different
meanings to the same words are merely semantic. But, when public policy standards
are under deliberation, differences in the meaning of 'racism' make a difference
about what will be done. Consider, for instance, a case in which the criteria for
admission to college favor white applicants, because they were more successful in
high school than non-whites. Suppose that the criteria themselves are 'color
blind'—that is, make no mention of race—and that white administrators applying
the criteria have no feelings of ill will towards non-whites. Still, year after year,
despite a racially diverse applicant pool in proportions corresponding to the general population, the student body is disproportionally white. If racism is defined as
self-aware *mens rea* racism, then the judgment that this is not a racist situation
could result in the conclusion that there is no reason to change the criteria for

admission. If racism is defined as institutional racism, or even as less-than-conscious racism, then the low number of successful non-white applicants could result in the conclusion that the criteria for admission ought to be changed. In each case, the accepted definition of racism, together with the belief that racism is morally wrong, will lead to a distinctive course of action.

Consider, also, an example that does appear to be purely semantic, because it is about words only. In late 1998, a white employee in the Washington DC mayor's office said in a business meeting that he intended to manage a budgetary matter in a 'niggardly' way. He later said he meant no racial insult by this usage, because he knew that the word 'niggardly' derived from a fourteenth-century Scandinavian word that had no etymological relation to the later racial epithet. Nonetheless, there was strong protest from the mayor's black constituents, and, when the official offered his resignation, the mayor immediately accepted it. A public debate ensued, in the press and on the Internet. Prominent whites and blacks argued about the acceptability of the word 'niggardly' even without discriminatory intent, and about whether the employee's effective dismissal was just (Henneberger 1999). The employee was eventually reinstated, but the disagreement about the word 'niggardly' raised issues that are not so simply resolved. On a self-aware *mens rea* definition of racism, the employee was not a racist and ought not to have lost his job (assuming he was telling the truth about his beliefs and intentions). But, on an effects-based, or institutional, definition of racism, the judgment becomes more complicated. The word 'niggardly' would be expected to cause distress to blacks, and people of all races, who were not aware of its etymology, but also to blacks and others who were, because they believed it would distress others. Such effects could be sufficient reason to identify the use of the word, if not the speaker, as racist.

Some might insist (as they did in the public discussion, and more than a few private ones) that distress caused by the use of a word is not in itself sufficient for censure, if the word is used correctly. That some were ignorant of the etymology, or even of the meaning itself, is their problem. There is no injustice involved if one's own correct behavior offends the ignorant or those who sympathize with them.

But, on the other hand, the adverb 'niggardly' is homonymous to 'nigger', the use of which is offensive and distressing, to everyone who counts in such deliberations. The etymological truth (which is obscure and not part of common public knowledge) has no bearing on how words sound. Most importantly, synonyms for 'niggardly' are well known. Indeed, it is unlikely that someone would know the correct usage and etymology of 'niggardly', without having first learned the words 'stingy', 'miserly', or 'parsimonious'. Why not use one of these other words in situations where even an informed use of 'niggardly' is likely to offend? What counts as racist language is in part victim identified. Given the known sensitivity of American blacks to racist language, it could be claimed that government officials have an obligation to avoid not only racist language, but what sounds like it. That obligation would imply acceptance of a definition of racism for which the *mens rea* of agents is somewhat irrelevant—but only because the *mens rea* of good will is necessary to choose language that will not be offensive. In other words, it would not be that intentions in themselves were unimportant, but that more general intentions were more important than less general ones that were supposed to be exculpatory. This would be analogous to the priority of the general rule to avoid accidents, over any specific rule that one may exercise right of way.

The problem in choosing only one of the definitions of racism results from the ways in which each definition has distinctive political consequences. Those in favor of additional administrative policies and legislation, to benefit non-whites, work backwards from their goals and choose the definition of racism that will include what they want to eliminate. The less-than-conscious and institutional definitions apply to more aspects of social life than the *mens rea* definition, and they can therefore be used to justify more social change. Those who are opposed to such change, because of beliefs about racial difference, reluctance about increasing regulations, or resistance to change itself, also work backwards, and they favor the *mens rea* definition.

And yet, the practical uses of either definition do not imply that those *theorists* who advocate the *mens rea* definition are opposed to social change, or that those *theorists* who advocate the less-than-conscious or institutional definitions are in favor of social change. A *mens rea* racism theorist might believe that change is likely to result from a strengthening of individual virtues, which requires new social or educational programs. An institutional racism (or less-than-conscious racism) theorist might think that change should be allowed to develop historically, without external interference with custom. Because the theorist usually addresses a longer period of time than the activist, it is not necessary that the theorist's goals be realized by a definition, which, if instantly applied, would have desired effects. (The theorist may even be unconcerned about outcomes, in the context of constructing his or her theory.)

2.4 Relations among Forms of Racism

All of the advocates of different definitions of racism recognize the existence of undesirable race-related behavior and situations other than the kind they want to be covered by their definition of 'racism'. Particular and immediate political aims aside, it is difficult to see why all three definitions cannot be accepted. We all know that *mens rea* racism persists in some people and that there are predominantly white institutions, in which whites have a better chance of succeeding than non-whites. We all know people whose lack of concern about, and attention to, important matters over which they are responsible causes harm to others. Negligence occurs in the discharge of all kinds of duties, and there is no reason to believe it is confined in special ways to duties that affect people on the grounds of race, or that it fails to occur in such duties. However, *mens rea*, institutional, and less-than-conscious racisms do not merely coexist in life in the US (at least); they interact. Not surprisingly, students, critics, and leaders in racial matters have been juggling their ideas of these different racisms for some time.

Even when a *mens rea* form of racism is believed to be a present cause of harm, its existence is notoriously difficult to prove in individual cases. In many institutional and corporate situations, people do not know each other well enough to make accurate evaluations about the beliefs, attitudes, or moral character of others in the same work context. Even if they could make such judgments, they could not prove them to the satisfaction of all interested parties. And, even if they could prove them, the judgments might be true of people whose positions of power and authority render them immune from the proofs, for most practical purposes.

After the US civil-rights legislation prohibiting discrimination in public institutions and business was passed in the mid-1960s, court decisions about allegations of racial discrimination became effects based. It was assumed that some racist *mens rea* was behind exclusionary and discriminatory action that had the observable effect of disproportionately low numbers of non-whites who gained access. That assumption of a *mens rea*, unprovable for practical purposes, led to the contemporary pre-analytic concept of racism, which focuses on affected victims, rather than effecting perpetrators. Administratively, the assumption of a *mens rea* led to affirmative action policies. Given the difficulty of proving the existence of *mens rea* racism, affirmative action can be viewed as a strategy to thwart it; it does not directly address or remedy *mens rea* racism. (I will discuss affirmative action in Section 4.)

The background assumption that racism has a *mens rea* component is also held by those who mainly define racism as institutional racism. If racism always lacked a mental component, and never proceeded from ill will or malign intent, then it would not be a moral problem, but a 'no-fault' type of social misfortune (which of course would not preclude remedying it). But those who use the institutional and less-than-conscious definitions of racism usually hold those who are instrumental in causing racist effects, morally responsible for them. Many non-whites believe that US society, as dominated by whites, is a racist society; and, since racism affects non-whites, personally, as individuals, they conclude that a large number of whites must be racist individuals—in their hearts and minds (Gwaltney 1980: 27–73). Responsibility in this sense of morally deserving the labels attached to one's actions does not prove that the actions were in fact intended in the required way. It does not precisely establish the *mens rea*. Yet, when an individual is harmed in a way that is connected with his or her race, because of the actions of other individuals, it is not wildly imaginative for the injured party to consider the offenders racists.

Still, we are left with the question of how to determine the point where racist effects justify the imputation of a racist *mens rea*. Consider the following case. One corporate defense of *environmental racism* that takes the form of dumping toxic waste in inner-city areas with large black and Hispanic populations has been that the cost of real estate is low in such areas. If corporate managers ought to accept responsibility for the effects of their decisions on communities, then most critics would claim they should not undertake business actions that have a dispropor- tionately harmful effect on non-white residents, and that their indifference to the plight of the poor is not a valid excuse (Westra and Wenz 1995). If managers are not distressed by disproportionate effects of their actions on non-whites—as well as on the racially undifferentiated 'poor'—critics would have grounds to question whether they take their responsibilities seriously.

A responsibility is a moral one if discharging it has an effect on human well-being. When people are unjustly harmed in ways distinctly connected with their racial membership, it makes sense at that point to impute a racist *mens rea* to those who are responsible for the harm, if they knew about it before acting, or were in a posi- tion where they should have known it was likely. In the corporate example, it is important to separate the issue of when corporate behavior has a moral dimension, from the issue of when corporate behavior becomes the responsibility of specific individuals acting for the corporation. Since a *mens rea* is something in individuals, connected with their moral responsibility, it should therefore be restricted to indi- vidual members of corporations, rather than ascribed to corporations, either in so far as they are fictitious entities, or, more importantly, in so far as they are collectiv- ities of individuals. Therefore, it is difficult to see how a corporation practicing envir- onmental racism could be guilty of anything more than institutional racism, Although its members, as individuals, might be guilty of *mens rea* racism, if their actions harm others unjustly in racially distinctive ways. This is *mens rea* guilt by imputation. Of course, it is always more tidy to have a confession or a direct avowal, but there is a legal tradition, and to a lesser extent a moral one, that allows others to 'establish' what probably went on in the mind of someone who causes harm.

In individuals, *mens rea* racism may result from temperamental and emotional disposition, and also *beliefs* about members of different racial groups. Anthony Appiah (1990) explains how such beliefs are negative judgments based on a scale of comparison with one's own racial group. The Western history of such judgments has varied with what science and common sense have presented as objective fact about racial difference. In the eighteenth and nineteenth centuries, it was falsely believed by many prominent white scientists, scholars, and educators that human- ity was hierarchically divided into biological racial groups, with the white race super- ior to all others in physical beauty, cultural, moral and intellectual talents, and achievement. On the hierarchical model, cultural differences among races were assumed to be inherited along with physical ones. Justification for the hierarchical model came from pronouncements by respected intellectual authorities. Hume, Kant, and Hegel, for instance, explicitly asserted that blacks were mentally and cul- turally inferior to whites and therefore not part of human cultural history. (Emmanuel Eze has usefully compiled the relevant philosophical excerpts in *Race and the Enlightenment* (1997).)

Twentieth-century social and biological sciences have yielded a continuous stream of information that reputable practitioners in relevant fields have accepted as disproof of all aspects of the hierarchical model of human racial taxonomy (Levi-Strauss 1965; Gould 1996). Nonetheless, many white Americans still accept all or parts of this model, as a cognitive foundation for their *mens rea* racism, and their acceptance of institutional racism. The less-than-conscious racism associated with stereotypical thinking about racial difference is often implicitly based on the hierarchical model, although its actual cognitive content may be obscured for the less-than-conscious [of her racism] racist, by ignorance, limited experience, or uncritical acceptance of racially biased custom and sensationalist media portrayals of non-whites.

Apart from false beliefs and false stereotypes, *mens rea* racism may exist as a rationalization or justification for unjust behavior against people of different races, which is motivated by a desire for gains that have nothing to do with race. (Less-than-conscious and institutional racisms cannot be used in this way because they are not proclaimed by their practitioners.) There are striking examples of *mens rea* racism as rationalization: defenders of slavery notoriously proclaimed that blacks were inferior to whites, as part of an ideology that always accompanied and sometimes masked the economic motives for slavery (Bell 1998); in the early years of the twenty-first century, competition for jobs or academic admissions may occasion bitter racist judgments about the incompetence of successful non-white candidates (who are in fact competent); innocent non-whites may be targeted as criminal suspects to allow guilty white parties to escape punishment. While a belief in false stereotypes could be called error or ignorance, a use of stereotypes to conceal other unethical purposes is a form of deception, and, in some cases, self-deception.

2.5 Unacknowledged Racism

Whites who hold or apply false beliefs about non-whites may not realize that their beliefs, and the feelings that go with them, are racist. Although this is often called 'unconscious' or 'less-than-conscious' racism, its proper name is *unacknowledged racism*, because the racist beliefs at issue are consciously held. For example, someone who thinks that most black men are dangerously violent, and as a result fears and regards with hostility any black male stranger, knows that they hold the generalization about black male violence, but fails to acknowledge that it is a negative racial stereotype, and racist on that count.

Another kind of unacknowledged racism, which has been mistakenly called 'unconscious', occurs when people unreflectively put racist beliefs and assumptions that they have not critically examined into practice, through habit, obedience to custom, or early childhood training. This could be the result of a wider moral failure of not choosing and deciding how to construct one's character. Jean-Paul Sartre famously explored a version of this kind of moral failure in the context of French anti-Semitism. The French anti-Semite enthusiastically embraces an unearned identity that he believes to be superior, because it goes back a hundred generations. He thereby proudly flaunts his larger moral failure, and probably would not be daunted if made to acknowledge his racism explicitly (Sartre 1965). A better example for present purposes would be a small business owner who always hired whites for a particular job because that is what his father did and what his customers expect. If asked, he would sincerely say that neither he nor the family business harbored any ill will against blacks, Hispanics, Asians, or American Indians.

Ought people to be held morally responsible for unacknowledged racism? Regarding other vices that harm others, we hold offenders morally responsible for their actions, even when they have failed to label them correctly, and the excuses of obedience to custom or childhood training are generally not exonerating. Parents who neglect or abuse their children are held responsible for their actions, even though they themselves may have been abused or neglected as children. A family background in which animals were routinely treated with cruelty is not a defense against present cruelty to animals. Why should not racists who fail to acknowledge their own racism be held responsible in the same way these other perpetrators are? The most racist of societies have contained individuals who choose to depart from conventions for humanitarian reasons, or to preserve consistency in their moral reasoning. The sharper the focus on racism as a condition of mind, the more does it qualify as a trait of individual character—that is, as a vice. If we grant that racism is a vice, then excuses for it based on external circumstances are weak, because good moral character is something for which those who have or lack it are held individually responsible. The point of moral responsibility is that there are things we do or do not do that properly reflect on who we are as autonomous agents. Our present view of moral virtue and vice is not that much different from Aristotle's in the *Nichomachean Ethics*: actions are virtuous or vicious to the degree that they flow from settled traits of character, or dispositions, that result from a history of similar actions, deliberately undertaken for specific reasons.

2.6 Diversity in Racism

When most Americans hear the term 'racism', they are likely to assume that the subject is white–black relations. Lewis Gordon (1995) justifies this assumption by arguing that 'antiblack racism' is the most extreme form of racism in ordinary life, because racial blackness is associated with sin and human inferiority in the Western Christian tradition. But this is not the whole story. Dominant white groups in American society have behaved in racist ways and developed racist beliefs against Asians, Native Americans, and individuals of mixed race (Zack 1993). Members of non-white groups have also been racist against members of other non-white groups. Within non-white groups, racist beliefs have been expressed and acted on by some members against others—for instance, in the practices of preference, or aversion for, light skin shades among African-Americans and Asians (Harris 1998). And, finally, some members of non-white groups hold racist beliefs about, and have committed racist acts against, white people.

It has been claimed that harmful actions and negative beliefs against whites, by non-whites, cannot be racist. Reasons for this claim may include reference to the historical fact that whites were the original aggressors against non-whites, or to present cultural structures of white dominance. Because of the broader context of white oppression, beliefs and actions by non-whites, which disadvantage or harm whites, are interpreted as justified retaliation, self-defense, or relatively ineffective harms or offenses. But, against this view, it should be remembered that racism is not simply harm against members of a distinct race, but unjust harm. If the harm to whites is intentional and based on their race, then it qualifies as racist in the *mens rea* definition. However, there are few contexts in American life where non-whites are in a position to inflict less-than-conscious or institutional racism on whites.

The concept of justice that leads to identifying racism with injustice extends from Aristotle and Plato to John Rawls (1971): justice means treating equals equally; justice means fairness. The equation of injustice with unfairness implies that it is always wrong to behave unfairly on the basis of racial difference, or to treat people differently on the basis of racial difference alone. There is no evidence from either the biological or the social sciences that racial difference in itself can represent differences that would justify unequal treatment, in any moral or political sense. Furthermore, there is even strong biological evidence against the very existence of human biological racial taxonomy. While scientific issues about race are distinct from social issues of racism, the two subjects have always been intertwined. One cannot reach a full understanding of racism without knowledge about the human biology, which racism, with great distortion, presupposes.

3. RACE

The major social problems with race concern how people of different races ought to relate to one another. There is a fundamental moral and legal presumption that all human beings have the same basic rights, such as the right to life and not to be harmed, the right to own personal property, and basic political rights. Within modern societies, ideals of justice require that people be treated the same in situations, or with regard to traits, in which they are the same or equal. Equals must be treated equally. Before and during the civil-rights movements of the 1950s and early 1960s, it was debated whether whites and non-whites were equals in the sense that would result in the same civil rights and liberties for non-whites, as for whites. Since the passage of the US civil-rights legislation in the mid-1960s, there has been a public presumption of racial equality, but disagreement about what constitutes equal treatment. Underlying both contexts of debate is an assumption that what is perceived as racial difference represents some natural difference in human typology. It is further assumed that this natural difference has a foundation in human biology that can be studied scientifically. If average Americans do not know exactly what the biological differences between or among people of different races are, they are usually confident that relevant scientists are in possession of the information. To borrow a term from Anthony Appiah (1990), the public has *semantic deference* for the discourse of science on race.

From colonial days until the present, it has been commonly assumed that the existence of a taxonomy of different human races, be they subspecies or breeds, is a scientific fact. However, over the course of the twentieth century, geneticists and anthropologists have retreated from a belief in the existence of distinct human races. It needs to be emphasized that this is not the retreat from racial hierarchy mentioned in Section 2, but a retreat from racial ontology. Human racial taxonomy could be real and races might be either equal or different, but, if the taxonomy itself is unreal, there is nothing that can be ranked. At each stage of the scientific retreat from race (both hierarchy and taxonomy itself), the public has continued to believe scientific conclusions from earlier stages of enquiry. Common sense lags behind science for many subjects and these gaps are themselves interesting sociological and psychological subjects. But, given the ongoing importance of perceived and believed racial difference in daily existence, practical ethics ought to be based on empirical assumptions that do not contradict current scientific evidence, rather than on received opinion. Social scientists may properly describe what people believe, without evaluating those beliefs, but, since ethicists seek to determine how people ought to behave, they have a special duty to evaluate received opinion. And, more generally, empirical philosophers have an obligation to accept the truth about physical reality, for which biology is the authority in the case of race (Zack 2002).

3.1 The Biological Facts about Race

What is the current scientific information about race? A comprehensive account of the relevant contemporary consensus in transmission genetics and population genetics, as well as the intellectual history of now-discarded scientific racial taxonomy, is not necessary to correct common beliefs. In the nineteenth century it was believed that individual members of human racial groups inherited their distinctive racial cultures and physical characteristics through racial 'essences' that were transmitted in the blood. Since 1900, it has been widely known in the biological sciences that human blood types do not correspond to racial types. The four major blood types are identified on the basis of transfusion compatibilities that cannot be predicted on the basis of racial membership. There is some statistical correspond-ence between blood types and continental origins of ancestral populations, but not enough correspondence to support social racial divisions (Dubinin 1965).

The inheritance of blood types, and other phenotypes socially associated with racial difference, occurs according to Mendelian laws of heredity, which were not fully understood in the nineteenth century. According to Mendelian heredity, genetic traits are subject to dispersal and recombination at conception. The genes for bone struc-ture, skin shade, and hair texture, which are associated with social racial membership, do not all get inherited together. There is greater variation within any race of these 'racial' traits than between or among any of the recognized races, as groups. Within the human species, as a whole, the genetic variation that occurs randomly—that is, between any two people—constitutes 0.2 per cent of all human genetic material. Of that 0.2 per cent, or 1/500, 85 per cent occurs locally, or between any two individuals who happen to be neighbors, 7 per cent occurs within races, and 8 per cent occurs between races. Thus, the amount of human genetic difference due to difference in race is 8 per cent of 0.2 per cent, or less than 1/6000 (Appiah 1996; Templeton 1998). Of course, that 1/6000, although small, could be important. But there is no evidence that it is. No racial essence has ever been identified. There are no general genes for race, such that, once identified, their presence could be used to predict more specific, or sec-ondary, racial characteristics. None of the physical differences associated with racial difference in society is correlated with any important difference in human talent, func-tion, or skill. This is relevant to the notoriously debated claims about correlations between racial difference and 'IQ', which I will discuss toward the close of this section.

The biological emptiness of race tends to send many contemporary social critics scrambling for a foundation on which to reconstruct social racial differences. The motivation for such reconstruction includes: preservation of white privilege; reaf-firmation of non-white liberatory efforts that are based on racial identity; preser-vation of tradition. However, none of the efforts to reconstruct a *biological* notion of race, given its empirical emptiness, succeeds (Zack 1997, 2002).

3.2 Cultural Constructions of Race

Ideas of physical racial heredity were invented at different stages of economic, polit-ical, and intellectual history, from the Age of Discovery onward. Human races were assumed to be isolated breeding populations distinguished by the continental ori-gins of their ancestors. The modern notion of race therefore contained assumptions about appearance and family ancestry. Blacks had dark skin and black children, whites had light skin and white children, and anyone could easily tell the racial differences between individuals based on cursory observation of physical appear-ance. It was overlooked that human beings vary continuously in apparent racial traits, over the surface of the globe, and that group migration and interbreeding have disrupted the generational sameness of all populations (Montagu 1965: 97–8; Smedley 1999; Zack 2002).

The social ways in which people are still sorted into races reflects the history of racial identity as determined by appearance and family descent. In American society people still sort others into races, based on their appearance and biological families. Appearance is the primary common-sense basis for racial sorting, but, at this time, almost any classroom containing more than thirty students in a college or university with a (minimally) diverse racial and ethnic population will contain at least one individual who claims a racial identity that is at odds with his or her racial appearance. Such anecdotal experience has been broadly (albeit superficially) addressed by the US Census 2000, which enabled individuals to identify racially in more than one way (Zack 2001a).

The race of an individual's family of origin works for the individual's racial identification only if all or most family members belong to the same social racial group, and appear to belong to that group. People resemble their parents if their parents resemble each other. According to the one-drop rule, which has been in effect since 1900, and which refers to 'one drop of black blood', a black person is someone with black ancestry, any number of generations back (Williamson 1980; F. J. Davis, 1991). Logically, this definition is an infinite regress, because the black ancestor would be defined as someone with black ancestry. Aside from assumptions about African ancestry, in the nineteenth century, blacks, or 'negroes' (the 'n' was not capitalized in the US until the 1930s), were, in effect, defined as slaves and the descendants of slaves. Only blacks could be enslaved at that time, and all descendants of slaves, including those of white paternity, were legally slaves (Williamson 1980). Therefore, 'slavery' became synonymous with American blackness, despite the existence of freed blacks, American blacks who had never been enslaved, and blacks from other nations who emigrated to the US.

A white person is someone with no known non-white ancestry. The key term is 'known', but, niceties of official versus unofficial family histories aside, whiteness is defined as the absence of a possible infinite regress. In other words, whiteness is defined as a negation, something that is, in principle, impossible to prove. Other racial definitions, of Native American and Asian, are problematic in different ways. Native Americans are individuals who can prove their descent from original inhabitants of the continental US. The American government has imposed 'blood quantum' requirements on those claiming Indian ancestry as a basis for entitlements according to treaty law. Not only are such requirements based on outdated and fallacious scientific speculations about race, but they have often conflicted with Native American tribal criteria for who is Indian (Jaimes 1995).

Asians are a constructed racial category that include disparate cultural groups from a variety of nations on the continent of 'Asia', and other geographical locations. In addition to the racial categories of black, white, Native American, and Asian, in recent decades an Hispanic ethnic category has been added, which is intended to include members of groups who are Spanish speaking, though many Hispanics do not speak Spanish or have no known ancestral connections to Spain (Alcoff 1995; Goldberg 1995).

Current cultural constructions of race do not rest on anything that approximates what even the average lay person considers a biological foundation. Geographical origins of ancestors cannot take the place of a physical foundation for race. Conceptual apologists for physical notions of race concede that complex migrations to and from Europe, Africa, and Asia have made it impossible to identify original populations as racial groups that correspond to the present categories of black, white, and Asian (Andreasen 1998).

Family history does not yield a foundation for physical race, because recognized or acknowledged family descent is often determined according to existing social categories of race. An interesting example is Thomas Jefferson's paternity of a child of Sally Hemings, a slave he inherited from his wife. Recent DNA testing has confirmed Jefferson's paternity of Hemings's last child, based on a deformation of a sex-linked chromosome in the male Jefferson family line, which was present both in Hemings's living black descendant and a descendant of the acknowledged white Jefferson family (Foster 1998). The Jefferson case illustrates how DNA testing does determine *biological* family relation, which is not the same thing as official and socially recognized family relation. It also illustrates how DNA testing can determine racial identity, only if racial identity has been previously determined according to non-scientific, social criteria for racial membership. Hemings's living descendant was presumed to be black because Hemings was black, and Jefferson's living descendant was presumed to be white because the Jefferson family was officially white. What the DNA testing proved was not racial membership, which was already assumed to be disparate, but biological family relation.

3.3 Race and Public Health

Contemporary genetic science has raised concerns that notions of biological race be preserved for the sake of public health, for instance, to aid in diagnosing hereditary diseases, and finding donors for tissue transplants. However, the scientific data does not support the social concerns in any simple way (Zack 2001*b*). Consider sickle cell anemia. For decades, it was believed that sickle cell anemia was present only in individuals of African and Mediterranean descent. However, in 1992, the policy-making committee of the American Medical Association recommended that all infants be tested for sickle cell anemia on the grounds that there is no independent empirical way to determine whether infants are of African or Mediterranean descent (Jarrett 1992). Similarly, all current research on bone marrow transplantation and donation is based on the premise that, although chances of matches for non-white recipients may be increased by a diverse donor registry, all transplant candidates have to be tested, individually, not for race, but for the compatibility with recipients' tissue, of the tissue they are willing to donate (Beatty et al. 1995; Mori et al. 1997).

3.4 Race and IQ

No discussion of the biological foundation for race, or lack thereof, could be complete without mention of what some believe to be race-based inherited intelligence differences. In current folklore on this subject, Asians show the highest intelligence of all groups in the subjects most valued in American society, mathematics, computer science, and basic science; whites are just below Asians; blacks are on the bottom. The difference between whites and blacks is the greatest gap. Evidence for these views consists of reading and maths levels at different grades of primary and secondary school, college entrance exams, and 'IQ' tests.

The appearance of a link between race and IQ was what catapulted *The Bell Curve*, by Richard J. Herrnstein and Charles Murray, onto the national best-seller lists in 1994. The early chapters of *The Bell Curve* present a Social Darwinist perspective that favors non-intervention in achievement disparities among social groups, on the grounds that such disparities are the result of inherited biological differences (Herrnstein and Murray 1994). However, since the biological sciences do not provide any basis on which to make physical racial distinctions, it follows that what are known as black, white, and Asian races in American society are socially constructed. If biological race as popularly understood cannot be empirically measured, because it does not exist, then it cannot be correlated with anything else. This is no more than a logical point (Zack 2001*b*).

Herrnstein and Murray did not address the difficulties in defining race as something that could be biologically determinative of something like IQ. Stephen Jay Gould has addressed the race–IQ linkage implied in *The Bell Curve* by analyzing the problems with identifying intelligence as something that is, or can be, measured by IQ tests. According to Gould, there cannot be a gene for IQ because there is no one linear measurement of intelligence. Psychologists have disagreed since the turn of the twentieth century about whether there is a general factor of intelligence ('g') that causes competence at a variety of mental tasks. It is agreed that there is a high statistical correlation among abilities to do a number of mental tasks, and IQ tests do measure that correlation. There is, as well, a high correlation between IQ scores and performance on tasks related to test tasks. However, that is something of a closed system, because the mental tasks are pre-selected. That society values some mental skills and not others does not mean that high performance at tasks requiring the valued skills is evidence for an hereditary 'something' called general intelligence (Gould 1996.)

What then can be concluded if members of the white and Asian groups consistently outperform members of the African-American group on IQ tests? It cannot be concluded that the performance is hereditary, rather than the effect of family enculturation and other environmental influences. But, even if a high performance at selected intellectual tasks were hereditary, Gould explains that this would not mean that it could not be changed. Height, for instance, is hereditary, but when nutrition is enhanced for members of a group who are short, relative to members of other groups, the average height of the shorter group increases. The facts about changes in group heights, which are well documented, suggest that, given environmental changes, IQ scores within some groups could be raised. In practice, little is done in education to boost IQ, even though IQ is commonly assumed to be no more than 60 per cent hereditary.

Gould points out that, when Alfred Binet first constructed intelligence tests in France in the early 1900s, it was his intention to measure the performance of primary school children on a variety of tasks, so that teachers could identify those children who might be in need of special assistance in educational programs (Gould 1996). However, IQ testing in the US has often resulted in 'tracking' non-white children in educational contexts in which both school facilities and family advantages are not the same for white and non-white children. In *Savage Inequalities* (1991), Jonathan Kozol describes how African-American and Hispanic children currently attend schools that are understaffed and less well equipped than those attended by white children in the same cities. In affluent neighborhoods, with racially integrated schools, non-white children are often segregated under the labels 'mental retardation' or 'developmental disability', and placed in underfunded Special Education programs (Kozol 1991). Neither such labels nor the attendant programs are constructed to develop the mental skills believed to constitute 'IQ'.

To conclude, there is no foundation in science for racial difference, either on the basis of physical traits that in American society are believed to indicate biological racial membership, or on the basis of any traits that may be presumed to determine mental and psychological capabilities. The full implications of these scientific facts probably exceed the imagination of all who base significant aspects of their lives on their own racial identities, or who influence the lives of others, based on race. But this failure of imagination does not excuse practical ethicists and other humanistic scholars from continuing to ignore or neglect the scientific facts.

4. REMEDIES

Racism and widespread ignorance concerning the scientific facts about race and racial difference overlap. There are no simple remedies, although it is clear that legal restrictions and prescriptions, education, psychological and moral persuasion, and changes in racial identities will continue to make up the mosaic of social justice concerning race.

4.1 Legal Remedies and Affirmative Action

Historically, from the Emancipation Proclamation to the US civil-rights legislation of the mid-1960s, changes in laws regarding the status of non-whites, and in acceptable treatment of them by whites, have been the cohesive basis for social change. All the legal changes have been preceded by intense public moral debate, and, in a pluralistic and variably participatory democracy, progressive laws are themselves subject to change (Grant 1983). The effectiveness of the law as an instrument of social justice or egalitarianism depends on public support, administrative implementation, executive enforcement, and judicial interpretation. While major progress against racism has followed legal change, when large segments of the public resist the spirit of liberatory laws, then racism and ignorance about race continue to determine social interactions. A democratic legal system cannot force people to think logically, accept empirical information that they do not wish to believe, or expunge irrational hatred from their hearts.

The existing legal system now generally prohibits discrimination on the basis of race, in education, employment, housing, and all public and civic aspects of American life. However, it does not exhaustively specify exactly what counts as discrimination and neither does it mandate particular strategies for eliminating discrimination. Affirmative action was developed as such a strategy and it has had varied forms: preference for non-whites who are equally qualified as whites; the expansion of applicant pools to include more non-whites, who then compete on the same terms as whites; extra places in employment or education that are specifically targeted for non-whites; specific 'quotas' of non-whites. Justifications for affirmative action have included compensation and reparation for past discrimination. Bernard Boxill argues that reparation has a moral dimension that exceeds compensation, because it requires acknowledgment of past injustice (Boxill 1998). Another justification of affirmative action is the value of role models. When non-whites occupy positions previously filled by whites only, they provide encouragement for other members of their racial groups to do the same. Claims have also been made that, were affirmative action to be eliminated, racial discrimination would reoccur in ways that could not be proved in specific instances. This brings us back to the *mens rea* definition of racism and the fact that, while affirmative action programs may frustrate its expression, they do not eliminate it.

Arguments against affirmative action have focused on the unfairness of making race a qualification for opportunities or rewards, given agreement that race is unacceptable as a disqualification. This unfairness is posited not as a violation of an abstract ideal, but as measurable harm to otherwise qualified whites who lose out to 'affirmed' non-whites (Newton 1998). Strong public objection to the alleged unfairness of affirmative action has led many to question its justice as a strategy for implementing non-discrimination. In recent years, the US courts have increasingly ruled in favor of white plaintiffs who have claimed to be the victims of 'reverse discrimination', as a result of affirmative action policies.

4.2 Remedies through Education

It is widely acknowledged that the most disadvantaged members of non-white groups will be unable to compete fairly without public policy that addresses their disadvantages. Ever since it was publically recognized that the US had a race problem, American attention has been directed to the economic and educational deficits of non-whites. Nonetheless, poverty and educational disadvantage are not problems correlated solely with racism and beliefs about race. There are poor and poorly educated whites, as well as rich and well-educated blacks. Also, there is evidence that, on every social class level, non-whites do less well and have less status than whites on the same level (Thernstrom and Thernstrom 1999). Therefore, the remedies for racism and beliefs about race are not the same as remedies for poverty and educational disadvantage. Distinct problems with racism and beliefs about race would probably remain after the poverty and educational disadvantage of non-whites had been remedied. Not that the poverty and educational disadvantages of non-whites are easy to remedy. White racism and false beliefs about race, in combination with the relative wealth and education of whites in dominant social positions, form formidable obstacles. Still, remedies for these social problems remain the primary tools for overcoming racism and false beliefs about race.

Most Americans have faith in education, generally, as a remedy for poverty. When education itself is viewed as a remedy for non-white poverty, reference is made to the inequality in educational resources for poor non-white children, as compared to middle-class white children. When educational curricula are addressed in terms of racism and race, the subject is the inclusion of multicultural materials that reflect the distinctive heritages of students from non-white racial groups. Because multicultural content in curricula affirms the identities of groups subject to white racism, it is believed to remedy racial bias within educational institutions, and thereby support the success of non-white students.

Multiculturalism has famously drawn criticism from conservatives: for political reasons, because its proponents assume the existence of white bias; for intellectual reasons, because it diverts time and resources from traditional curricula. Liberatory critics of multiculturalism have not received as much attention. Yehudi Webster, for instance, argues that multicultural content fails to empower minority students, because it does not emphasize critical thinking skills and fails to teach them effective theories with which to interpret written material or practical experience. This failure of multiculturalism increases the vulnerability of non-white students to existing and new forms of racism, and neglects the development of skills that would enable them to compete better with whites in employment as well as education (Webster 1997).

It is assumed by both proponents and critics of multiculturalism that primary and secondary school children will continue to be taught moral and legal principles of racial equality, as rules that they ought to follow. However, except for attempts to dispel stereotypical beliefs about racial inferiority or superiority, little effort is currently made to impart information about race as a false biological tax-onomy. It is therefore unknown whether wide-scale dissemination of such informa-tion, on levels appropriate to grade-based learning abilities, would be another effective remedy for white racism as well as the false beliefs about race held by members of all social racial groups.

4.3 Psychological and Moral Remedies

At present, the increase of 'diversity', or the inclusion of non-whites where they were previously excluded, is assumed to be the main practical way to disabuse people of racial stereotypes. The rationale is that, when people interact with others about whom they hold stereotypes, experience corrects their faulty generalizations. Given what is now known from biology concerning racial difference, *variety* might be a better concept for such projects than *diversity*, because diversity connotes necessary differences and divergences, whereas variety connotes mere variation, which is all that exists in terms of human biological difference.

Practical remedies aside, there is an irrational structure to racism, as well as sexism, ageism, able-ism, and all of the complexes of beliefs that privilege the presumed biological identities of those who hate or blame others who they believe to be biologically inferior to them. The persistence of these beliefs, in the face of broad evidence that biology does not determine anything of moral importance among human beings, is commonly recognized to be irrational. Less well recog-nized is the depth of the irrationality. The elements of hate and blame in these 'isms' are closely connected to negative moral judgments. The negative moral judgments accompany the assumption that the objects of hate and blame are responsible for being the race, gender, age, or whatever they are, that is deemed 'inferior'. To hold another morally responsible means that the person did something or exercised a choice in becoming worthy of hate or blame, when he or she could have chosen to do and be otherwise. But racism, sexism, able-ism, and company, are all directed toward groups of people who are believed to be defined by their biology in essen-tial ways that they did not choose *and* cannot change. Biologically defined objects of hatred are thus symbolically trapped in a despised position, for which they are punished, and from which they have no hope of escape. The punishment is there-fore cruel. It is possible that some, or many, who are cruel in holding and acting on false beliefs about biological determinism are unaware of this logic of responsibil-ity, the violation of which constitutes their cruelty. While fundamental principles of moral reasoning elude precise proof, this does not mean that everyone has the same opportunities to become intuitively aware of their truth. Perhaps the kind of intro-ductory moral theory with which philosophers bedevil undergraduates ought to be made available to all college students, and to high school and primary school students, as well. Too often, injunctions against cruelty are made on grounds of psychological compassion, or religion, and no use is made of moral argument or basic ethical principles, as intellectual matters.

Nonetheless, in at least some cases, the cruelty of racism may mean that it cannot be remedied by purely reasonable, logical, or empirical discussion, but instead requires individual corrective therapy. Clinical protocols for such therapy have not yet been developed. Therapy generally addresses the well-being of the client, rather than of those with whom he or she interacts. The kinds of racism that persist in American life on a daily basis rarely receive serious legal punishment. Even if they did, the rehabilitation of criminals has never been effective in the US. But, without punishment for the cruelty of racism, there is no reason for racists to seek corrective therapy, although public opinion and institutional policies may here and there succeed in 'sensitizing' offenders.

So far, my discussion of psychological and moral remedies for racism has focused on what whites ought to do in relation to non-whites. The other psychic dimension of racism concerns what non-whites ought to do to remedy racism. I have already discussed non-white racism against whites in Section 2. In so far as it is strictly a matter of race, separated from the correction of injustice, it would be subject to the same kind of treatment as white racism against non-whites. Members of some non-white groups also have irrational racist emotions, fed by beliefs in derogatory stereotypes, against members of other non-white groups. Here, also, psychological remedies would seem to be appropriate. In the case of racism against members of one's own group, a form of racism that is often called 'self-hatred', analyses by Franz Fanon (1967), Jean-Paul Sartre (1965), and Malcolm X (1973) suggest that the non-white racists who are cruel to themselves have internalized the ill will and stereotypical thinking of white racists.

The mirror image of psychological remedies for racism as something that people do to other people is psychological remedies for objects or victims of racism. Racism that is not identified, confronted, and resisted when possible and not highly dangerous to do so, undermines the self-esteem and self-confidence of its victims. In line with a nineteenth-century tradition of 'racial uplift' among African-Americans, much of the liberatory force of identity politics in recent decades comes from strategies of empowerment that make it possible for people psychologically to heal from racism directed toward them. The damaging effects of racism are particularly important to correct in formative years, which is partly why the US Supreme Court ruled against segregation in public schools in 1954. In so far as racism is suffered on the basis of internalized beliefs about racial identity, freedom in choosing, constructing, and rejecting falsely biological ascribed racial identities (in the sense described in Section 3, above) might be an important aspect of such recovery. Indeed, Jason Hill, in *Becoming a Cosmopolitan*, argues provocatively for the right to 'forget where one comes from' (Hill 2000: esp. ch. 4). In more traditional ways, African-Americans have trans-valued racist stereotypes into valorized and celebrated identities, a practice that Tommy Lott (1999) traces from nineteenth-century minstrelsy to twentieth-century rap.

4.4 Mixed Race as a Remedy

The visibility of a growing population of self-identified mixed-race Americans undermines traditional racial categories in the false biological sense. This represents a potential remedy for racism, because it undermines the received epistemology of race. Since the US Supreme Court struck down existing state laws against racial intermarriage in 1967, the population of children born in marriages with parents of different races has increased from approximately 500,000 to over two million. But, the facts of mixed race are more broad than this: the artificially constructed ethnic category of Hispanic Americans admits of a range of racial ancestry; an undetermined number of Native Americans are racially mixed; approximately 5 per cent of the white population is believed to have African ancestry; approximately 80 per cent of the African-American population has white ancestry. If there is no biological foundation for the three or four 'pure' racial groups that have traditionally been recognized in the US, then there is no biological foundation for categories of mixed race (Zack 1998*b*). Indeed, Ranier Spencer (1999) argues against the desirability of mixed-race identity, on the grounds that the black population has been mixed throughout American history. Nonetheless, in a society that divides people racially based on false beliefs about human biological types, those with known ancestry from more than one race would seem to be as entitled to distinctive racial identities as those presumed to be pure (Zack 1998*b*).

There are ethical tensions in claiming and recognizing mixed-race identity, between expectations of group loyalty to traditional non-white groups, and individual rights to self-identify. Since the US census for the year 2000, Americans may check as many racial categories as they believe apply to them. Given six racial choices and the choice of Hispanic or non-Hispanic ethnicity, over sixty combinations are now possible as sites for racial identity (Schemo 2000; Zack 2001*a*). If a fraction of those combinations become broadly acknowledged as legitimate racial identities, it will no longer be assumed that a person's race is a visible trait.

Practical ethical issues about race in the near future will probably revolve around the importance of self-identification and respect for the boundaries of others (Zack 1998*a*). These are issues that affect people in the most personal and private aspects of their lives. Anita Allen (2000) suggests that some of the moral controversy about interracial marriage experienced within the African-American community should be taken seriously by mainstream philosophers who find other legal but controversial issues, such as abortion, worthy of ethical debate. Barbara Hall (2000) notes that group loyalty, as a significant moral issue for African-Americans, at the very least precludes leaving the group. Those subjects and many others concerning mixed-identity are still framed in ways that make individuals of presumably pure race the main subjects of concern. If mixed-race identities achieve broad public recognition as legitimate categories of social race, that focus is likely to shift.

REFERENCES

Alcoff, L. (1995). 'Mestizo Identity', in N. Zack (ed.), *American Mixed Race: The Culture of Microdiversity*. Lanham, MD: Rowman & Littlefield, 257–78.

Allen, Anita (2000). 'Interracial Marriage: Folk Ethics in Contemporary Philosophy', in N. Zack (ed.), *Women of Color and Philosophy: A Critical Reader*. Malden, MA: Blackwell, 182–205.

Andreasen, R. (1998). 'A New Perspective on the Race Debate'. *British Journal of Philosophy of Science*, 49: 199–215.

Appiah, K. A. (1990). 'Racisms', in D. Goldberg (ed.), *Anatomy of Racism*. Minneapolis: University of Minnesota Press, 3–17.

—— (1996). 'Race, Culture, Identity: Misunderstood Connections', in A. Appiah and A. Gutman (eds.), *Color Conscious*. Princeton: Princeton University Press, 3–69.

Beatty, P. G., Mori, Motomo, and Milford, Edgar L. (1997). 'Impact of Racial Genetic Polymorphism in the Probability of Finding an HLA-Matched Donor'. *Transplantations*, 67/7: 1017–27.

Bell, D. (1998), 'The Real Status of Blacks Today', in N. Zack, L. Schrage, and C. Sartwell (eds.), *Race, Class, Gender and Sexuality: The Big Questions*. Malden, MA: Blackwell, 15–27.

Boxill, B. R. (1998). 'The Morality of Reparations', in N. Zack, L. Schrage, and C. Sartwell (eds.), *Race, Class, Gender and Sexuality: The Big Questions*. Malden, MA: Blackwell, 55–61.

Davis, A. (1998). 'Prisons, Repression and Resistance', in J. James (ed.), *The Angela Y. Davis Reader*. Malden, MA: Blackwell, 3–109.

Davis, F. James (1991). *Who is Black? One Nation's Definition*. University Park, PA: Pennsylvania State University Press.

Dubinin, N. P. (1965). 'Race and Contemporary Genetics', in L. Kuper (ed.), *Race, Science and Society*. New York: Columbia University Press, 68–94.

Eze, E. C. (1997) (ed.), *Race and the Enlightenment*. Malden, MA: Blackwell.

Fanon, F. (1967). *Black Skin, White Masks*, trans. C. L. Markmann. New York: Grove.

Finley, M. I. (1983). *Ancient Slavery and Modern Ideology*. New York: Pelican.

Foster, G., et al. (1998). 'Jefferson Fathered Slave's Last Child'. *Nature*, 396: 27–8.

Garcia, J. L. A. (1997). 'Racism as a Model for Understanding Sexism', in N. Zack (ed.), *RACE/SEX: Their Sameness, Difference and Interplay*. New York: Routledge, 45–60.

Goldberg, David T. (1995). 'Made in the USA', in N. Zack (ed.), *American Mixed Race: The Culture of Microdiversity*. Lanham, MD: Rowman & Littlefield, 237–55.

Gordon, L. (1995). *Bad Faith and Antiblack Racism*. Atlantic Highlands, NJ: Humanities Press.

Gould, S. J. (1996). 'Critique of *The Bell Curve*', in Gould, *The Mismeasure of Man*. New York: W. W. Norton, 377–89

Grant, J. (1983). *Black Protest: History, Documents and Analyses, 1619 to the Present*. New York: CBS Publications.

Gwaltney, J. L. (1980). *Drylongso*. New York: Random House.

Hall, Barbara (2000). 'The Libertarian Role Model and the Burden of Uplifting the Race', in N. Zack (ed.), *Women of Color and Philosophy: A Critical Reader*. Malden, MA: Blackwell, 168–81.

Hannaford, I. (1996). *Race: The History of an Idea in the West*. Baltimore: Johns Hopkins Press.

Harris, V. (1998). 'Prison of Color', in N. Zack, L. Schrage, and C. Sartwell (eds.), *Race, Class, Gender and Sexuality: The Big Questions*. Malden, MA: Blackwell, 66–72.

Henneberger, M. (1999). 'Race Mix-up Raises Havoc for Capital', *New York Times*, 27 Jan. 1999.

Herrnstein, Richard J., and Murray, Charles (1994). *The Bell Curve: Intelligence and Class Structure in American Life*. New York: Free Press.

Hill, Jason (2000). *Becoming a Cosmopolitan: What it Means to Be a Human Being in the New Millenium*. Lanham, MD: Rowman & Littlefield.

Jaimes, M. A. (1995). 'Some Kind of Indian', in N. Zack (ed.), *American Mixed Race: The Culture of Microdiversity*. Lanham, MD: Rowman & Littlefield, 133–54.

Jarrett, J. C. (1992). 'From the Agency for Health Care Policy and Research'. *Journal of the American Medical Association*, 70/18: 2158.

Kozol, J. (1991). *Savage Inequalities: Children in America's Schools*. New York: Crown.

Lang, Berel (1997). 'Metaphysical Racism (or: Biological Warfare by Other Means)', in N. Zack (ed.), *RACE/SEX: Their Sameness, Difference and Interplay*. New York: Routledge, 17–27.

Lévi-Strauss, Claude (1965). 'Race and History', in Leo Kuper (ed.), *Race, Science and Society*. New York: Columbia University Press, 95–135.

Lichtenberg, J. (1998). 'Racism in the Head, Racism in the World', in N. Zack, L. Schrage, and C. Sartwell (eds.), *Race, Class, Gender and Sexuality: The Big Questions*. Malden, MA: Blackwell, 43–7.

Lott, Tommy L. (1999). *The Invention of Race*. Malden, MA: Blackwell.

Malcom, X. (1973). *The Autobiography of Malcolm X*, ed. A. Haley. New York: Balantine.

Mills, Charles W. (1997). *The Racial Contract*. Ithica, NY: Cornell University Press.

Moutagu, Ashley (1965). *The Idea of Race*. Lincoln NE: University of Nebraska Press.

Mori, M., Beatty, Patrick G., Graves, Michael, Boucher, Kenneth M., and Milford, Edgar, L. (1997). 'HLA Gene and Haplotype Frequencies in the North American Population', *Transplantation*, 64/7: 1017–27.

Newton, L. (1998). 'Reverse Discrimination as Unjustified', in N. Zack, L. Schrage, and C. Sartwell (eds.), *Race, Class, Gender and Sexuality: The Big Questions*. Malden, MA: Blackwell, 50–4.

Rawls, J. (1971). *A Theory of Justice*. Cambridge, MA: Harvard University Press.

Sartre, J. -P. (1965). *Anti-Semite and Jew*. New York: Schocken.

Schemo, Diane Jean (2000). 'Biracials in the 2000 Census', *New York Times*, 12 Feb.

Smedley, Audrey (1999). *Race in North America: Origin and Evolution of a Worldview*. Boulder, CO: Westview, chs. 10, 11, 12.

Spencer, Ranier (1999). *Spurious Issues: Race and Multiracial Identity Politics in the United States*. Boulder, CO: Westview.

Templeton, A. (1998). 'Human Races: A Genetic and Evolutionary Perspective', *American Anthropologist* 100/3 (Fall), 632–51.

Thernstrom, S., and Thernstrom, A. (1999). *America in Black and White*. New York: Simon & Schuster.

Webster, J. (1997). *Against the Multicultural Agenda: A Critical Alternative*. Westport, CT: Praeger.

Westra, L., and Wenz, P. (1995) (eds.), *Faces of Environmental Racism*. Lanham, MD: Rowman & Littlefield.

Williams, Patricia J. (1991). *The Alchemy of Race and Rights*. Cambridge, MA: Harvard University Press.

Williamson, J. (1980). *New People*. New York: Free Press.

Zack, N. (1993). *Race and Mixed Race*. Philadelphia: Temple University Press.

—— (1996). *Bachelors of Science: Seventeenth Century Identity, Then and Now*. Philadelphia: Temple University Press.

—— (1997). 'Race and Philosophic Meaning', in N. Zack (ed.), *RACE/SEX*, 29–44.

—— (1998a). 'Conclusion', in Zack, *Thinking about Race*. Belmont, CA: Wadsworth.

—— (1998b). 'Mixed Black and White Race and Public Policy', in N. Zack (ed.), *Race, Class, Gender and Sexuality: The Big Questions*. Malden, MA: Blackwell, 73–84.

—— (2001a). 'American Mixed Race: Theoretical and Legal Issues'. *Harvard Black Letter Law Journal*, 17 (Spring), 33–46.

—— (2001b). 'Philosophical Aspects of the 1998 AAA [American Anthropological Association] Statement on Race'. *Anthropological Theory*, 1/4 (Dec.), December 445–65.

—— (2002). *Philosophy of Science and Race*. New York: Routledge.

CHAPTER 11

AFFIRMATIVE ACTION

WALTER FEINBERG

1. DEFINITION AND GOALS

AFFIRMATIVE action is a term used in the USA to depict a set of laws, policies, guidelines, and government-mandated and government-sanctioned administrative practices, including those of private institutions, intended to end and correct the effects of a specific form of discrimination. It seeks to end the effects of discriminatory practices that violate the inherent equality of persons who, because they share certain attributes such as sex or skin colour, have been denied opportunities on the grounds *that they are inferior or different* (Rosenfeld 1991). Affirmative action aims to reduce present discrimination against members of targeted groups such as African, Native or Hispanic Americans, women, and the handicapped, and to increase their numbers within certain occupations and professions and at universities and colleges.

Affirmative action seeks to eliminate discrimination on the basis of race or other extraneous grounds, and in this respect it is similar to laws that disallow redlining by banks or restrictive covenants by homeowner associations. But, unlike affirmative action, these non-discrimination laws do not actively seek to increase the number of people who have previously been discriminated against in a given area. They simply

My appreciation to Jason Odeshoo for his invaluable assistance with this chapter. Some parts of this chapter follow my *On Higher Ground: Education and the Case for Affirmative Action* (New York: Teachers College Press, 1998).

aim to make it illegal to exclude people based on extraneous factors, such as race, religion, ethnicity, gender, sexual orientation, and so forth. Once the laws are enacted, however, it is usually a matter of legal indifference whether members of the previously excluded groups choose to apply for a loan or move into a residential area. Jews who learn they are unwelcome in an area may choose not to relocate there even if they know that existing homeowners would be obliged to sell to them.

Affirmative action does more. In addition to eliminating legalized discrimination, it actively aims to increase the number of woman and targeted minorities in certain positions. It seeks ultimately to raise the standing of the targeted group so that the basis of their previous exclusion—race, gender, ethnicity, sexual orientation—will no longer be used in determining the distribution of the desired good.

Although some form of race and gender-based affirmative action has been practised since the 1960s in the USA, there are differing arguments for the practice. Advocates of affirmative action even differ about its ultimate goals. Some advocates seek proportionality: the distribution of benefits should approximate the group's representation within the population as a whole. Other advocates believe that this is too high a standard and that affirmative-action goals can be met by assuring that procedures for selection are fair, that artificial barriers are removed, including barriers that arise because opportunities for networking are limited, and that adequate mentoring procedures are in place. A working definition of affirmative action should allow for both possibilities. Thus we may define affirmative action as government policies that seek to end inequalities based on the status assigned to individuals by virtue of their membership in a group.

2. REQUIREMENTS

In this section I set out the different kinds of practices that are included under the rubric of affirmative action, while in the section that follows I introduce some of the contentious issues that will be addressed in the rest of the chapter. The requirements of affirmative-action policies are situation dependent and thus there are a variety of ways in which they can be met. In some cases it may be sufficient to advertise widely for a position or contract and to stipulate that applications from women and previously excluded minority members will be especially welcome. In other cases, affirmative action has allowed a company, even one that does not have a past record of active discrimination (say, for example, in cases where excluded minority members did not apply for positions), voluntarily to take active steps to recruit and advance minorities over members of the majority population. And, in still other cases, usually those where discrimination has been persistent and egregious, quotas have been mandated requiring the discriminating organization to hire a certain percentage of its workers or students from the excluded population.

One distinction that is critical in understanding different modes of affirmative action is the difference between programmes that seek to reach 'targeted goals' and those in which quotas have been mandated. Whereas quotas require that a certain percentage of workers be hired from specified groups until they represent a certain proportion of the total workforce, targeted goals require only that good-faith efforts be made to identify, select, and train potentially qualified minorities and women. The two may be related in certain instances in which there has been blatant and long-term discrimination, and where the guidelines established by targeted goals have been ignored. In such cases, quotas may replace the guidelines for targeted goals.

Quotas and guidelines are related, but there are important differences between them. Whereas both set targets on hiring members of minority groups or women, the latter is sensitive to means and procedures, and the former, to goals and results. Under a quota system an agency or a court may *mandate* that an industry hire a certain proportion of women or minority workers. However, courts may serve a more permissive role. In the past, courts have enabled companies to correct for past social discrimination, even if the company itself did not have a history of discriminatory practices. This was especially important in those industries where women and minorities simply did not apply because of a mystique that a certain industry was reserved for white males. Recently those who want courts to place a narrower restriction on such activities and allow quotas only in cases where the company has a specific history of discrimination have challenged this practice.

More common than quotas is a mandated system of guidelines in which an industry is required to examine its hiring standards and its training procedures to ensure that members of minority groups are not excluded arbitrarily from certain positions. This may entail that traditional instruments for selecting people be placed under scrutiny and evaluated in terms of their relevance to the job in question. Under a system of guidelines, a manufacturing company may, for example, set different norms for men and women on mechanical aptitude tests on the grounds that men usually have more experience with machinery than women and this experience provides them with an advantage in the test that will not necessarily translate into better performance on the shop floor. Given gendered norms, the company will probably hire more women than it otherwise would have done.

Active inclusion also has an influence on the behaviour permitted in the work place by requiring employers to maintain a non-racist, non-sexist environment. This requirement is seen as necessary in cases where such environments affect job performance and inhibit the advancement of members of the targeted groups. If, for example, a woman mechanic's efficiency and thus her prospects for advancement are reduced as a result of a sexist environment at work—say, pictures of naked women on calendars—she may have recourse on the grounds of sexual harassment. Although harassment legislation is not usually identified with affirmative action, when harassment indirectly limits the hiring or promoting of people from targeted groups, it may be subject to review under affirmative-action policies.

3. THE MORALITY OF AFFIRMATIVE ACTION

Non-discrimination measures enjoy a more stable moral consensus than do affirmative-action policies, because of the belief that affirmative action contradicts the principle of equal opportunity, the principle that non-discrimination measures are designed to enforce. Those who take this point of view believe that what they call 'reverse discrimination' is as wrong as the original acts of discrimination themselves. Some, such as the black conservative Shelby Steele (1998), argue that affirmative action is intended to assuage white guilt by patronizing blacks, and that in the process it reinforces dependency. On the other side of this motivational issue, there is some evidence to suggest that affirmative action had been advanced by President Nixon to split the democratic black/labour constituency. Yet the question of motives, while often interesting, is not the only basis on which to evaluate policy. A more basic issue has to do with the relationship between affirmative action and equal opportunity.

Supporters and critics often share one assumption—that is, that affirmative action is justified only in terms of the principle of equal opportunity. Supporters often hold that it is needed to reinstate the principle of equal opportunity by eliminating discriminatory practices, while critics argue that any group standard for advancement is inconsistent with the basic ideal of individual merit that informs the principle of equal opportunity. While affirmative action is clearly related to the principle of equality of opportunity, as we will see later in this chapter, the relationship is not a direct and straightforward one.

Nevertheless, many people, in addition to Steele, object to affirmative action on moral grounds, arguing that affirmative action is just old-fashioned discrimination in reverse. They ask, if we are not allowed to discriminate against those in the minority, why we should be expected to discriminate against those in the majority. These critics hold that, every time a less-qualified African-American or woman is hired over a more qualified white man, a morally impermissible act is committed. All people should be appointed on the basis of fair competition between individuals, and not because they belong to one group or another.

Those who accept this argument believe that affirmative action greatly advantages minorities. They claim, for example, that some minorities admitted to elite universities are granted a 400 point bonus on the SAT admissions tests (Wolfe 1998); this group favouritism, they argue, is ethically impermissible. Selective universities are not the only place where traditional standards have been adjusted to accommodate minority or women applicants. For example, the police force readjusts standards when it allows women to do certain exercise routines differently from men. These practices, though controversial, are defended on the grounds that the standards were established with certain groups in mind and that different factors may weigh as heavily in predicting the on-job performance of members of other groups.

Advocates of affirmative action also have their favourite facts. For example, a recent book by two former Ivy League College Presidents (Bowen and Bok 1998) points to the record of high achievement, both during and after college, of African-Americans admitted under affirmative action to elite universities. They point out that the maths scores of more than 75 per cent and the verbal scores of 73 per cent of blacks admitted to selective colleges and universities were higher than the national average, and that the African-American graduates of these colleges have been successful in many walks of life (Bowen and Bok 1998: 256–74). Even though the scores were lower on average than those of white students, the achievement of African-American students in these schools suggests to these authors that there is considerable room for arguments about what to count as a fair and responsible admission policy. Clearly this is not the first time that elite colleges have measured merit by a broader yardstick than academic ranking and test scores (the case of athletes and legacies are two notable exceptions).

Even though the test scores of targeted minorities were significantly lower than their white counterparts, the authors argue that the motivation, ability to overcome obstacles, and personal character made up for any deficiency in their preparation for the college admission tests (Bowen and Bok 1998: 277). Yet, as one sympathetic reviewer points out, this fact alone is not sufficient to establish a case for affirmative action. It shows the additional value that an education in an elite college may provide, but, without an additional argument that addresses the moral basis of admitting certain people over others, it does not tell us which applicants should receive this added benefit (Wolfe 1998).

Although the achievement of minority students at elite universities may not settle the issue, it highlights the central questions in this debate—what is to count as qualifications, how do we determine those qualifications, and is it justifiable to apply different standards to members of different groups.

4. Some Arguments against Affirmative Action

There are a number of different arguments against affirmative-action policy, some of which are advanced by the political right, some by the centre, and others by the political left. Many, but not all the arguments hold that affirmative action violates the basic principal of equality of opportunity and is therefore an inappropriate instrument for governing competition over scarce occupational or educational resources. One of the exceptions to this argument comes from the right of the political spectrum. It holds that affirmative action violates individual rights of property.

Another comes from the left, and it argues that affirmative action is ineffective in addressing the problems of poverty.

4.1 Affirmative Action Seen as Violating Individual Rights

Some people claim that affirmative action violates individual rights unless there is a very specific history of racial discrimination. This argument applies not only to hiring individual members of minority groups within a company, but also to affirmative-action policies that set aside a certain percentage of contacts for minority firms within an industry. Thus any policy that takes active steps to alter the representation of workers of different races in a given company is said to be unjust unless that company has a proven history of discrimination. And, similarly, any policy that insists that minority companies be favoured (say by setting aside a certain proportion of contracts for minority-owned firms) is unjust unless there has been favouritism in the past that has placed a given minority firm in an unfair and disadvantaged position. However, if a business employs fair procedures in hiring or in assigning contracts, then it has satisfied the requirements of justice. Anything more should be viewed as 'reverse discrimination' and hence unjust.

This argument is intended to counter the view of some that a lower percentage of racial representation in a field or industry is itself an indication of past discrimination and therefore must be corrected. The objection is expressed scornfully by Eastland in what he viewed as Congress's overly generous policy towards minority-owned businesses. He says: 'It did not matter to Congress that the set-aside, in remedying discrimination practiced by no one in particular, would benefit minority businesses regardless of whether or not they had actually experienced discrimination in procurement' (Eastland 1996: 121).

Some defenders of affirmative action, however, think Eastland's implicit standard—that there must be a specific victim and a specific victimizer in order for affirmative action to be justifiably triggered—is too demanding. After all, it allows members of non-discriminating groups to benefit from this discrimination and to pass those benefits on to their children and others in their group. Suppose a firm never discriminated against black workers or subcontractors because in a generally discriminatory social climate blacks knew that certain jobs and contacts were off limits for them, and hence did not apply for them. Assuming their knowledge is accurate, their behaviour is perfectly rational. Why spend time pursuing a goal that you cannot reasonably expect to attain when you could spend it in a more satisfying way. The narrow interpretation, however, would not require, expect, or even permit firms to remedy the effects of that broader discriminatory climate. The only obligation the firm has is to hire those who have been the direct victims of its own discriminatory practices. However, a climate of discrimination has indirect as well as direct effects. The knowledge that a firm will discriminate against you and your kind not only serves as a deterrent to potential applicants, but places a much greater burden on those who do apply. As mentioned above, given this knowledge, they must weigh the time they might spend training for and pursuing an elusive higher-end job against the income they could earn working in a less desirable position. Advocates of affirmative action might well object that, given this handicap—one where the choices have intergenerational costs and benefits—the very narrow policy described above is the equivalent of distributing prizes in a race according to who crosses the finishing line first, without regard to whether the runners have completed a 26-mile marathon or a 100-yard dash.

4.2 The Market Argument

Those who believe that group attributes, such as race and gender, should not be a consideration in hiring, promoting, or contracting, and who also hold to the basic principle of government non-interference and the sanctity of private property, believe that there is another way to accomplish the fairness that advocates of affirmative action seek. That is through the market and its reported bias towards efficiency.

In the market argument, a bad hiring practice is one that is inefficient in the long run within the context of a competitive market environment. Given this efficiency bias, 'discriminatory' practices should not be addressed by policy-makers. If I choose the wrong workers, the market will provide feedback quickly enough. If, as a result of my actions, I hire less than the best people, then my business will falter and those with more open hiring policies will advance. Thus, in the long run the business with discriminatory hiring practices is likely to loose out to more progressive competitors (Epstein 1995).

To those, like Epstein, who advance a market argument, affirmative action stands as an inefficient substitute for the more rational market processes of selection. When market forces are left to operate on their own without interference from externally imposed ideas of fairness, enterprises that fail to hire the most talented candidates, regardless of race, gender, or class, will fail. Accordingly, if race and gender are short-run considerations and are allowed to interrupt market selection, according to this argument, they will result in long-term distortions and inefficiencies.

According to this argument, any government intervention in the market, other than those designed to advance competition by limiting unproductive monopolies, promotes inefficiency. This includes interference in the academic marketplace of talent. The argument holds that any progress in advancing women and minorities will come through the private sentiments of individuals and the voluntary activities of business in response to market forces rather than through government intervention. Affirmative action is thus seen as self-defeating because the inefficiencies that it creates lead to a reduced standard of living for all. The argument suggests that very little is needed to empower individuals who are now the beneficiaries of elaborate affirmative-action rules. Epstein, one of the most persuasive proponents of this view, believes that the prevailing sentiment for diversity is so great that 'the strong hand of government is not needed to give women and minorities a boost' (1995: 180).

Epstein is the latest in a line of theorists (Banfield 1970) who believe that market forces alone are sufficient to correct for discrimination in the workplace, and that affirmative action serves only to distort market processes. They believe the market is sufficiently supple to allow shifts in sentiment to be disciplined by 'painful marginal calculations of how much they can have of a good thing before it becomes a bad thing' (Epstein 1995: 180). The 'good thing' includes hiring too many people who look like you.

Hence, the manager of a firm who hires only white men will supposedly find himself at a disadvantage if his competitors begin to hire more talented women and minorities, and either this disadvantage will require that he too widen his search for talent or he will begin to lose profits. Yet, should this not actually happen, Epstein has a way both to explain it and to save the good reputation of the market. There are, after all, many practices that appear to be discriminatory, but, when scrutinized adequately, prove to be otherwise.

Epstein argues, for example, that policies that seek equal pay for equal work among men and women often ignore collateral costs for different types of workers and hence distort important market considerations. If, for example, a woman can work at the same pace as a man on an assembly line but is prone to a higher rate of injury, then the true cost of labour must be weighed in terms of the cost of injuries as well as the output of goods. And if the cost of a woman worker is higher than that of a male, then, he holds, that the firm actually discriminates against men when it overlooks this cost and hires a women at the same wage. The result also militates against women, by making employers more reluctant to hire them because of the real premium that must be paid if they are to receive the same wages as men.

5. OBJECTIONS

The critical question for advocates of affirmative action is whether this faith in the market is justified. Imagine that the workforce in factories in the USA that produces widgets is white and male and that the culture in each of these enterprises is racist and sexist. Suppose, too, that there are some women who would make widgets equally as well, and would cost no more than the present workers under non-sexist conditions. However, under sexist conditions they get nervous, perhaps even irritated, possibly angry, and, as a result, their productivity falters; they produce fewer widgets, have more accidents, and contribute to the development of a discordant environment. Moreover, women's presence on the shop floor violates the men's ideas of fit and appropriateness, and the men continue to make life uncomfortable for female workers. Suppose that, when women leave because of such harassment, the men's morale and their productivity increase.

Given this situation, as the advocates of affirmative action would point out, any one firm that hires women is at a significant disadvantage. If it chose to change its sexist culture, it would have to absorb the cost of doing so and would thus have an expense that a less enlightened factory would not have. If it chose to allow the women to work without changing the culture, then it would have to put up with a slower, less efficient workforce, and again it would be at a competitive disadvantage. Of course, it may be acceptable for Epstein that the women are paid less even though the cause of their higher cost is simply the result of historical discrimination. Epstein might argue that nervousness, irritation, and anger, even if provoked, should be controlled, and that, if a worker's productivity consequently suffers, she should be replaced. However, to make this argument stick, he needs more than market economics. He needs a moral theory that addresses the issue of moral responsibility. Without such a theory, Epstein's argument is subject to important objections.

The advocate of affirmative action might object that Epstein is able to maintain this optimistic view of market forces and cultural fairness because he fails to consider the dynamics of the field created by the firms' interactions with each other. Even if the manager of every firm were personally committed to racial and gender equality, many reforms would be disadvantageous to the firm unless it could be assured that other firms would adopt similar reforms. In short, fairness is then not just a product of the decisions of individual firms taken in the aggregate. It also concerns the basic rules governing their interactions.

Because he does not consider rules of interaction, Epstein does allow that the market *as it is* may encourage companies to take advantage of discriminatory cultural practices, and to continue to be successful. For example, because of cultural assumptions that women belong at home, taking care of children, companies can hire men without providing day care for their children.

Suppose, to use Epstein's example of safety, that the reason for the greater number of accidents among women workers was that the factory was designed with the anatomy and physical requirements of men in mind—say, the height at which the controls of the machines were set. Suppose that, given this design, unless all competitors were required to make the kind of changes that would accommodate women, any single factory that did so would incur a very large capital expense that would place it at a competitive disadvantage. Under these circumstances, the only way to achieve the ideal of providing people with equal merit with reasonably similar opportunities and rewards is to mandate changes for all.

The argument should be familiar to economists from many different persuasions. The basic point is that the aggregate of individual choices, each motivated by self-interest, may lead to a very bad situation for all. The conservative theorist

Malthus (1820) was among the first to articulate this point in the context of his argument that population (the result of the aggregate of individual choices) is destined to outrun the food supply (the collective consequence of all those choices). Marx (1887/1961) and Keynes (1936) make similar points. The difference between these theories has much to do with the faith that they have in the effectiveness of government in controlling for undesirable consequences.

Advocates of affirmative action seek to eliminate situations in which one company is placed at a competitive disadvantage by doing 'the right thing' and to provide an even playing field for companies that wish to diversify their workforce. In other words, by requiring each company to take into account the effects of past discrimination on present hiring practices, it inhibits free-rider companies from taking advantage of the goodwill of their competitors.

Thus affirmative action is like anti-monopoly policies. However, in the example above, the monopoly is not that of a single company capturing the market for a certain product, but that of a single group capturing the jobs within an entire industry and thereby advantaging their children, friends, and fellow ethnics in the competition for future positions. Thus, continuing with the widget example, in response to job monopoly within the widget industry, affirmative action has government requiring that every factory make good-faith efforts to hire and retain women.

This objection to the market argument is still inconclusive. Traditional policies against monopolies are justified in terms of controlling price increases that arise when one company exercises total dominance in a given market sphere. Yet, where there are a sufficient number of competitors, there are circumstances, say when women absorb the cost of childcare, where job restrictions may be an efficiency factor serving to lower prices. Thus either to justify or to reject affirmative action on strictly economic grounds is incomplete. There is a larger issue of fairness that needs to be addressed. Ultimately, those who argue against affirmative action must rest their case on a conception of fairness.

The belief that the market is an effective alternative to affirmative action is plausible because those who advocate free markets and those who seek non-discrimination often justify their goals by appealing to the need to eliminate irrelevant distinctions—distinctions that are accidents of birth and that do not affect performance. Both those who advance the cause of stigmatized groups and those who advance the cause of free markets often cite race, sex, religious belief, and ethnicity as examples of irrelevant distinctions. There are differences though in the way in which the market advocates and the affirmative-action advocates think about irrelevant characteristics, and these differences are sufficient to disrupt the initial plausibility of a coincidence of interest between those who want efficiency and those who want fairness.

First, whereas many advocates of affirmative action hold that attending to race and sex in the short run will lead to race- and sex-free selection in the long run

(Fiscus 1992), the advocates of market selection believe that, if race and sex are short-run considerations, they will result in long-term distortions and inefficiencies (Blits and Gottfredson 1990). If one hires two people of equal ability but unequal skill levels, the person with the higher skills will require less training costs and will have a more established foundation on which to build new skill levels. Thus, market advocates hold that in both the short and the long term the market provides for fair and efficient selection. Fairness is determined by the value that the employee adds to the company or, in the case of the university, by the comparative skill level the student can be accurately expected to reach upon graduation. The trick is to eliminate present discrimination—including discrimination against white males—not to compensate for past discrimination.

Secondly, there is an important difference in the priority that affirmative-action advocates and market advocates place on non-discrimination. Advocates of markets seek first efficiency and low cost, and, in doing so, they must allow for the possibility that race or gender bias may affect production in a positive way. Given their commitment to market efficiency, they must also allow that, if such circumstances arise, discrimination is allowable (Epstein 1995).

Consider a factory in which owners, managers, and workers belong to the same ethnic group and where, as a result, certain conflicts that occur in other similar factories are absent here. Given this higher level of cultural uniformity, the company is more efficient than its competitors and seeks to maintain that efficiency by hiring from the same ethnic group. Because cultural uniformity is a factor in the efficiency of this plant and ultimately in its profits, many strong advocates of market reform should accept the hiring practices as justified.

Advocates of affirmative action must view such an advantage differently. They must hold that the hiring practices are wrong, even if they do increase the firm's efficiency, and that the fact that they provide the firm with advantages over those firms that seek fairness should make the practices impermissible. There may be slightly different reasons for taking this stance. Some may hold this position in terms only of past discrimination—culturally generated efficiency is wrong when it is a product of past discrimination. Others may hold it on present and future terms—it is wrong because it continues to bestow undeserved advantages and disadvantages and inhibits the development of talent. Whichever way one argues the case for affirmative action, market efficiency is rejected as the ultimate determinant of policy.

Neither of these objections must deny that affirmative action is compatible with market efficiency. What they must deny is only that market efficiency is the primary reason for affirmative action. For these advocates of affirmative action, efficiency needs to be constrained by a certain conception of fairness that goes beyond the value that a broader hiring policy might add to a business.

There is an additional burden that market advocates carry. Those who are sympathetic to the ideal of equality of opportunity but who believe that the market is sufficient to accomplish its goals must show that disproportionate race and gender representations have less to do with racism, sexism, or other forms of injustice than they do with the tendency of markets, when left alone, to select for the most efficient traits. However, without some independent point of validation, their claim appears circular. It says that whatever the market selects is what we will *define* as maximally efficient. Even if one holds strictly to a market view of fairness then, the question that needs to be raised is whether present practices are inhibiting the development of future productivity.

This is not a question that can be answered in a straightforward way without assuming that certain present indicators are good signs of future potential. If a great deal of talent is hidden because of educational discrimination, then the existing distribution of positions and rewards will appear fair. And this will be the case even though, under some other possible educational system, say one that compensates for differences in parental income, there would actually be a higher level of performance, more minority mobility and greater workplace efficiency. Thus the case for market efficiency and against affirmative action must rest on assumptions about talent and how it is best identified.

5.1 *The Bell Curve* and the Distribution of Talents

Herrnstein and Murray (1994) argue that existing inequalities are the result not of the suppression of hidden talents or unequal educational opportunities, but of core differences in the intellectual capacity of members of different groups. They contend that IQ tests provide an independent measure for efficient selection and they argue that such tests show that education in the USA, with the exception of affirmative-action selection, which introduces static into the process, is doing a more efficient job than ever of sorting children into programmes that are appropriate to their intellectual talents. They argue that highly selective colleges and universities are selecting, teaching, and placing into the most important and highest-paying jobs the most talented graduates and that they are doing so in greater proportion to their numbers in the general population than ever before.

Thus, according to Herrnstein and Murray, except for distortions created by affirmative-action programmes, the USA is becoming more of a meritocracy than it ever was before, and an increasing number of intelligent people are being placed in demanding colleges and in highly rewarding jobs. The cause of most of the remaining racial inequality in society, they suggest, is a stubborn and largely unchangeable difference in intelligence, a difference in which race and genetics play a sizeable role.

The argument, if correct, supports the idea that test scores and grades are more efficient selectors for college and professional school and that market selection is a more efficient and fairer way than affirmative action to allocate jobs. As one commentator puts it: 'They suggest that affirmative action has the effect of reducing the opportunity for the nation to achieve its potential because it exercises artificial constraints upon some people's cognitive ability' (Nettles 1995: 17). Equal opportunity, according to the authors, will not produce equal outcomes when people differ in their intellectual capacities. Nor will equal opportunity produce equal educational outcomes for different races if the members of the racial groups display, as an aggregate, differing and unequal intellectual capacities (Gottfredson 1992).

5.2 Problems

The research reported in *The Bell Curve* (Herrnstein and Murray 1994: 480) is not new and, in its different incarnations, has been the subject of significant challenges on both empirical and conceptual grounds (Block and Dworkin 1974*a*, *b*; Feinberg 1983; Gould 1994). One objection is that the underlying belief that intelligence can be measured on an ordinal scale is an example of misplaced precision, similar say to the idea that we can assign meaningful numbers to goodness. Dewey captured the objection of misplaced precision with the following anecdote:

Listening to these papers I was reminded of the way we used to weigh hogs on the farm. We would put a plank in between the rails of the fence, put the hog on one end of the plank and then pile up the other end of the plank with rocks until the rocks balanced the hog. Then we took the hog off; and then we guessed the weight of the rocks.   (quoted in Bredo 1995: 2).

Herrnstein and Murray believe that an intelligence test measures our capacity to learn, and they also believe that a considerable portion of this capacity is genetically grounded and thus not subject to change through education or environmental manipulation. The fundamental source of cognitive ability is just something that cannot be influenced.

One critic, Gould (1994: 139), holds that their argument rests

on the validity of four shaky premises, all asserted (but hardly discussed or defended) by Herrnstein and Murray. Intelligence, in their formulation, must be depictable as a single number, capable of ranking people in linear order, genetically based, and effectively immutable. If any of these premises are false, their entire argument collapses. For example, if all are true except immutability, then programs for early intervention in education might work to boost I. Q. permanently, just as a pair of eyeglasses may correct a defect in vision. The central argument of 'The Bell Curve' fails because most of the premises are false.

Other critics have noted the genetic essentialism that underlies the study and the assumption that 'black' and 'white' refer to genetically uniform groups. As Marks (1995: 261) notes:

the biological differences between groups are trifling compared to those within the group, and . . . the major biological divisions of humans presumed to be out there do not manifest themselves clearly. Race doesn't explain the patterns of diversity of human behavior; and ultimately even simple classifications of races emerge to be based more on cultural perceptions of who-is-more-like-whom than on biological criteria.

IQ tests are part of a general class of tests that are supposed to measure a person's aptitude for certain kinds of activity. In the case of IQ tests, the activity is anything that involves intellectual work. Tests that claim to measure more specific aptitudes are also available, and, if we turn to one of these, the medical aptitude test, we can illustrate an important concern of those who criticize such claims. With all of these tests it is important to remember that what we count as a high level of competence depends to a certain extent on what we, as a society, want. For example, when women and non-white men were largely excluded from medical school, research on diseases that affected these groups was neglected without any great outcry from within the profession. While many medical schools actively discouraged women and minority members from applying, hence creating a comfort zone for white males only, they also made a questionable assumption about the meaning of the test scores. The assumption was that, above a certain minimum, the tests were good predictors of who would make good physicians. However, since admissions officers were choosing from a group of already high-achieving students, the force of this assumption is diminished significantly. Some research suggests that the correlation between the test scores and the quality of the future physician is not especially high, although the correlation between the scores and the performance during the earlier years of medical school is better (Gottheil and Michael 1957).

If admission to medical school is not an exact science, advocates of affirmative action could argue greater initial investment in training may be required if, as a society, we value healthy woman as well as healthy men and healthy minorities as well as healthy majorities. In other word, test scores do not tell us what to do. We need to be open to circumstances where we can get more of what we want by selecting for greater gender and racial diversity even if doing so means a higher investment in initial training costs or fewer highly skilled specialists. Julian Bond, in following the minority medical students whose admission was challenged in the Bakke decision, noted that a significant number are serving under served populations (Bond 1995).

Although some advocates of market selection may believe that IQ scores serve as a good proxy for predicting future productivity, there are some factors that might lead to a reconsideration of this view even given traditional productivity targets. The basic assumptions behind IQ research are, first, that intelligence is a commodity that is distributed to individuals alone, secondly, that its expression has little to do with the way in which an enterprise is organized or the way its members interact with one another and, thirdly, that efficiency is obtained by selecting the most intelligent individuals to perform the most mentally demanding jobs. Yet these assumptions are being challenged on a number of levels.

Consider, for example, one of the factors motivating recent works on academic performance—the competition between the USA and Japan for economic superiority. Herrnstein and Murray allow us to conclude that the recent success of the Japanese is due to their somewhat higher IQ scores, a consideration to which they pay significant attention as a prelude to their reporting of the lower scores of African-Americans. A sceptic might note that their research does not explain the long recession that Japan was just beginning to experience as their book was published and that continues at the beginning of the twenty-first century, nor does it explain the sustained economic growth that was beginning to take place in the USA at the same time. If IQ scores are relatively fixed, then the reversal of the economic fortunes of the two countries during the 1990s presents a problem for those who hold that IQ scores are a good proxy for efficient market performance.

Many commentators attributed the productivity of the Japanese in the 1980s not to the individual intelligence of their workers but to the unique organization of the workplace and to the fact that many different people at all levels of production are given a voice in the process (Vogel 1979; Cummings 1980; Abegglen and Stalk 1985; Feinberg 1993). There is good evidence to support this view. As American industry has reorganized in recent years, productivity has increased without any significant increase in IQ scores. This suggests that, whatever individual or group limits there may be to intelligence, we have a long way to go before the potential of our present capacities are reached. It also suggests that an environment that seeks not to order intelligence from highest to lowest, but to make everyone think and act more intelligently and cooperatively, is the policy we should seek.

Intelligence involves the capacity to adapt to an established environment and to shape that environment in new ways so that it serves our needs and purposes (Sternberg 1985). Since a large part of this environment consists of other people, (Dewey 1916), the more understandings and information can be shared, needs and purposes coordinated, and activity mutually planned and carried out, the greater the likelihood that individual and collective goals will be met efficiently. By focusing only on individual performance, traditional IQ research simply fails to address the issue of how to organize an environment so that everyone's capacities are developed to their fullest.

Clearly individuals differ in what they can learn and in how fast they can learn it, and this is important in making decisions about selection, education, and placement. And people can learn some things more quickly and more thoroughly than they can learn others. However, the IQ research goes considerably beyond these obvious facts and reinforces the image that people can be ranked for any given position from the worst to the best. Yet this image is highly questionable. Much like marriage, there is not just one Mr or Ms Right. There are often many—some of course never to be met—and there are also many Mr and Ms Wrongs (met and unmet as well). And the right ones are not all right for the same reasons and may not be rankable according to a set standard.

Once this is faced, as it must be by any society that is not to be locked into a nineteenth-century version of science, the assumptions behind the argument presented in *The Bell Curve* become highly problematic. What those who want market efficiency should aim for is actually to maximize the number of people who are able to think and act together at high levels of proficiency and will do so in ways that provide added benefit to the society at large. Intelligence must be seen as a product of social organization. Once this goal is substituted for the Mr/Ms Right myth, then our way of thinking about the nature of intelligence and selection must change as well.

6. Affirmative Action and Poverty: The Argument from the Left

While some on the right argue that affirmative action is inefficient, some on the left are concerned that it is an inadequate instrument to end poverty. They are concerned that affirmative action does little to close the income gap or to move people out of poverty (Wilson 1987, 1996).

Wilson, a qualified supporter of affirmative action, expresses concern about the effects of programmes on the growing economic gap between lower- and higher-income black people. He argues that, while many of the race-targeted programmes have aided the more advantaged of the black population, they have done little to advance the situation of less advantaged blacks. Although this concern may underestimate the considerable and beneficial effect of affirmative action on the number of African-Americans who have entered blue-collar jobs, the larger point is that affirmative action is not a substitute for broader economic policies that would create jobs. This concern is justified for anyone who wants to relieve poverty or to reduce the income gap between the rich and the poor. Affirmative action just assures that members of targeted groups are provided opportunities to be considered for whatever number of jobs are available—however many or few. It does not have as its primary goal the elimination of poverty, and, as long as it is evaluated in those terms, it will probably come up short. Yet many who wish to address poverty and who understand the limits of affirmative action also believe that it too has an important role to play in addressing social injustices. To see what that role is we need to explore some of the central justifications for affirmative action within the context of a liberal society.

The argument from the left is a problem for affirmative-action advocates only if one holds that the primary goal of affirmative action is to eliminate poverty. However, affirmative action is not an anti-poverty programme. It seeks fairness within a given distribution. It does not address another quite important question—whether the overall pattern of distribution is fair among economic classes. Affirmative action may function within the present scheme of distribution, but it might also function under different ones—say one where the gap between social classes is much smaller than at present.

7. The Argument for Race- and Gender-Based Affirmative Action

Affirmative action and the criticism of it must be understood within the context of a liberal society—that is, it must be understood within the context of a society that seeks to reward individual talent, effort, and achievement and that basically eschews rewards based on group identity. This is one reason why both advocates and critics of affirmative action will often view it as an attempt to correct distortions in equal opportunity, and will argue the case on the basis of whether those distortions are real.

However, while there is a strong relationship between affirmative action and equal opportunity, it is not a simple or direct one. Where affirmative action is justified primarily by an appeal to equal opportunity, it requires a number of additional assumptions in order to justify the leap that seems to be entailed when it is argued that present members of group x deserve special consideration because past members of this group (many of whom are dead) have been discriminated against. It is the intergenerational break between past individual victims of discrimination and present individual beneficiaries of affirmative action that defenders of race- and gender-based affirmative action are challenged to address. How can discrimination against members of one generation long dead be compensated for by advantaging people who were not born when the initial discrimination occurred? If discrimination still exists, the argument continues, we can end it now. We cannot make amends to those who are no longer with us.

Race- and gender-based affirmative action is that form of affirmative action that gives special consideration to individuals because they belong to targeted racial and gender categories, the members of which have suffered past discrimination. Critics thus ask: if non-discrimination legislation is aimed at eliminating present discrimination directed at individuals as a result of historical prejudice, why do we need a policy that is group sensitive? How can we redress discrimination against those who are no longer living by providing additional considerations to those people living today who have the same skin colour or are the same sex? Would it not be better simply to end all present-day discrimination rather than to reach back into the past in order to justify special treatment and practise a new or reverse form of discrimination?

In addressing these questions it is important to recall the distinction made earlier between affirmative-action programmes and non-discrimination policies. Most critics of affirmative action, especially those committed to liberal individualism and merit-based equality of opportunity, have few objections to non-discrimination policies. What they ask for is a reason to go beyond such policies and to single out for special consideration people from certain groups whose members have been the victims of past discrimination. It is also important to note that affirmative action does not single out everyone who belongs to groups that have experienced past discrimination. Italians and Irish are not categories for affirmative-action consideration, even though in the past members of these groups have suffered discrimination. Thus the question that needs to be addressed is why do present members deserve special consideration because of a fate suffered by past members and why only present members of some discriminated-against groups (Scalia 1979)?

An additional question about fairness remains: affirmative action is targeted for members of certain groups regardless of their individual situations. Hence, an affluent African-American or woman has a source of appeal that in many circumstances is closed off to an equally talented but less-well-off white male. This seems unfair to many people and some would prefer an affirmative-action programme based on economic need rather than on race or gender (Kahlenberg 1996).

7.1 The Importance of History for Affirmative Action

The most publicized purpose of affirmative action is to re-establish the elements of fair competition embedded in the ideal of equality of opportunity. Yet affirmative action as it stands aims to correct only certain kinds of distortions in equal opportunity—those that result from a history involving group stigma or those that continue to have a present discriminatory impact. Because historical discrimination and its lingering effects apply only to members of some groups and not to others, the application of the principle of equality of opportunity is circumscribed by affirmative action, at least in its strictest sense, to members of these groups. This is the case even though *individuals* from outside these groups may have been the subjects of unfair treatment, bad luck, or other factors that may impact on economic well-being.

It is important to recall that those outside the targeted groups may appeal to non-discrimination laws and policies to justify individual claims to advancement and may even successfully sue to counter individual acts of discrimination that blatantly favour individual women or minority members over a more qualified white man. And they may, by accident or design, fall within a policy intended to benefit targeted groups, as, for example, when it is required that certain positions be advertised widely. Nevertheless, the focus of affirmative-action policy remains largely women, the disabled, and people of colour who continue to experience the effects of systematic discrimination and group stigmatization. The reasons for this focus are discussed below, but first it will be useful to look at one alternative to race- and gender-based affirmative action that has attracted some attention.

7.2 Affirmative Action and Economic Need

Because affirmative action is intended to correct for systematic discrimination among members of certain historically disadvantaged groups, it has not been, except in a limited sense, a needs-based policy. For example, in theory at least, the critical spotlight of affirmative action might well shine on a college that eliminates women's gymnastics even though every member of the team comes from professional and upper-middle-class homes. In contrast, it might allow a college to eliminate men's baseball even though all the members of the team come from a white lower-working-class background. However, since most men's sports are well entrenched in colleges and universities, while women's sports are not, such cases, while not unheard of, are quite rare. And, since the social class composition, as opposed to the sex, of a team is accidental, the actual elimination of the baseball team would not be a case of class discrimination.

Those who object to race- and gender-based affirmative action are concerned about the fairness of policies with these implications. Some have proposed to substitute a needs-based policy for the present race- and gender-based one (Kahlenberg 1996). However, affirmative action is not only concerned with the fact that talent is being inhibited, although it is certainly concerned with that. It is also concerned with the fact that the discrimination has been directed at people who share a certain attribute, that they have been discriminated against because of this attribute, that there has been an agent that has done the discriminating, and that the effects of this discrimination continue in the present. More than misfortune is present here. Injustice exists as well (Feinberg 1998).

7.3 Economics versus Culture

Affirmative action is often thought of as strictly an economic policy, as a way to compensate for historical injustices that have been committed against a certain racial or ethnic group. This focus has merit especially when considering the comparative position of certain African-American businesses when compared to their white counterparts. It is also this focus that led some people to believe that a needs-based policy is fairer than the present arrangement. However, not all discrimination is just economic in its origin. Some of it resides in deep cultural stigmas that have been attached to membership in certain groups. One purpose of targeting members of these groups is to remove a stigma that all members of the group have been marked with and that serves to assign individuals from these groups to positions of reduced prominence and opportunity.

Thus affirmative action differs from most other policies that are concerned to advance the ideal of equality of opportunity and that have focused attention on the impediments to advancement that arise because of economic need alone. Some of the impediments to equal opportunity are to be found at a deep cultural level, and cannot be fully addressed simply by assuring that all who apply for a position are treated fairly. Given these deep cultural factors, many will simply not apply, and, when they do, their applications will not be taken seriously.

Consider the situation of women as an example. Although raised in the same families as their brothers, and sharing largely the same economic benefits or deprivations, women have been systematically relegated to positions with less status and authority. While there are economic factors involved here, they are intertwined with cultural ones. Married women, at one point were denied rights to property—surely an economic factor—but this denial went along with the view that women were weaker or less responsible or needed to worry about children, not about running a business—all cultural attitudes. This suggests that economic disadvantage is not the only roadblock to achievement. The reduced level of opportunity for women has been grounded in cultural and educational factors as much as in material ones.

The argument for needs-based affirmative action assumes that economic deprivation is primary and that it leads to cultural and educational deprivation. This assumes a one-way causal relationship whereas the situation is probably more complex and these three elements reinforce each other. What may begin as a cultural difference results in an educational difference—which results in an economic inequality—which in turn reinforces the cultural and educational inequality. If women are expected to work in the home, then education need not be a high priority, and, without a strong education, then women have little choice but to work in the home.

7.4 Merit versus Standing

Another difference between the needs-based approach to affirmative action and the race- and gender-based approach is that, while both stress the importance of individual merit, the present practice seeks, in addition, to effect a cultural and psychological change that goes well beyond the benefits awarded to the successful individual applicants. Hence attention is focused on those who share certain 'innate' characteristics—colour or sex—and who, because of these characteristics, have been assigned reduced social standing. Because this reduced standing has negatively affected the aspirations of many and has frequently defined 'normal' institutional practice, a systematic effort is needed to effect the desired change. Targeted assignment and selection are one way to educate the larger public about what *should* count as standing and to help all members of the stigmatized groups think differently about their opportunities. A race and gender approach selects people on the basis of features that will persist even after a change in educational and economic status has occurred—namely, sex and skin colour. Among other things, the change in status serves as a reminder that such characteristics should not be taken as a sign of reduced ability or competence.

7.5 Forward- versus Backward-Looking Perspectives

Finally, those who argue for a needs-based policy of affirmative action do so from what they see as a forward-looking perspective. Their goal is to advance the idea of equal opportunity and reduce inefficiencies in the economic system by assuring that talented applicants are not overlooked because of their economic situation. Certainly, the traditional practice also advances forward-looking consequences, since any policy that finds and cultivates talent will increase the chances that society as a whole will also benefit. However, the existing policy largely, although not exclusively, focuses attention on members of certain groups on the grounds that it has a special obligation to members of these groups as a result of past acts of discrimination.

It is concerned to advance equal opportunity by aiding the search for talented individuals among those who, because of certain attributes such as race or gender, have been systematically excluded from certain positions. Thus, whereas a needs-based programme is driven primarily by a vision of the future economic benefits to the society, a race- and gender-based programme is driven to a large extent by the past treatment of certain groups and by the way such treatment impacts their present situation. In so far as the effects are forward seeking, they are so within a framework that brings specific groups into relief.

For example, to the advocates of a race- and gender-based approach it will not do simply to toss a coin to determine the educational benefits for two equally talented, equally poor students when one belongs to a group with a long history of discrimination and the other is say a child of recent immigrants. Indeed, equal talent may be an unnecessarily high standard in many cases where affirmative action is called for. This is because sometimes affirmative action may involve an obligation to a specific group of people who continue to carry the stigma first imposed on their great grandparents, whereas the selection of the most talented person among any and all applicants is best understood as a future investment for society at large and may entail selection from a different group.

Affirmative action often involves a special obligation owed to individuals as a result of their membership in certain groups. In these cases, to the extent that it is an investment, it is so within the confines of specific aggrieved groups. Affirmative action should be forward looking in the sense that, wherever a choice is available, society should seek to pay its debt in a way that will advance a relevant social interest. However, it must be emphasized that society *should* seek to pay its debts. Such a debt is due when the effects of past mistreatment have significant and lingering present effects. This means that, to the extent that debt is involved, affirmative action must involve a group-specific policy. In these cases the first aim of affirmative action should be not to maximize interests in general, but to serve the specific interests of members of the aggrieved group.

This does not mean that affirmative action is opposed to merit-based equal opportunity. Equality of opportunity is poorly served when an entire class of people is discouraged from competing for certain positions, whether such discouragement takes on a cultural, educational, or economic manifestation.

The question remains whether race- and gender-based affirmative action is justified in treating people as members of a group and in addressing group discrimination rather than responding to discrimination against individuals regardless of the group they may belong to. There are at least two reasons for a group-sensitive policy: the first involves the practical strategies needed to change the situation while the second, applicable to a subset of those who benefit from affirmative action, involves an issue of historical justice.

7.6 The Strategy of Simultaneity

What I am calling the strategy of simultaneity is a strategic move that is intended to have the effect of breaking institutional deadlock where the action of isolated decision-makers is unlikely to have the desired effect.

To see this point, consider the once-long absence of African-American quarterbacks in the professional football leagues. It is hardly plausible that black players lacked the natural talent to play that position until a few years ago. It is more likely that the prejudice of players, coaches, and owners resulted in this exclusion. What is hard to understand is why the profit motive or the desire to win did not override this prejudice long ago, at least among the poorer and least able teams.

One explanation involves what Carmichael and Hamilton (1967) call institutional racism. One feature of institutional racism is that racist consequences do not always require the biased acts of racially prejudiced people. They can happen without any overt racist intentions. To illustrate an aspect of institutional racism imagine a situation in which a well-intentioned, non-racist coach considers preparing his star eighth grader to play quarterback. However, before he does so he surveys the high school players and finds that no blacks play quarterback and concludes that there is deep racism at the high school level. As a result the coach comes to believe that preparing a talented black child for quarterback would be a disservice because the coaches at the next level would never put a black athlete in that position when there are white boys available. One consequence of this belief is that even a non-racist high school coach would have good reason not to train a black at quarterback: first, because the coaches at the lower levels have not trained any talented black players for him to develop, and, in addition, because the coach at the college level has never played a black at quarterback—because the high school coaches have not sent any along to him. And, of course, the non-racist pro coach who, for similar reasons, has never played a black quarterback adds to the incentive of the college coach to train his black athletes to play other positions. This situation has a psychological dimension as well and affects the inclinations of the athlete, who wants to be trained for a slot where he has a chance of playing. Finally, there is an added effect on fans who, seeing no black quarterbacks, have the perception reinforced that blacks are not suited for leadership positions. Thus a culture is created and maintained. Even though no one ever wished to discriminate, discriminatory practices are established and perpetuated.

Simultaneity is a strategic way to break such cycles. It is intended both to affect the way in which members of targeted minorities think about their opportunities for a good life within established institutional structures, and to change the way in which established institutional structures respond to minorities. For example, an otherwise bright girl may well decide not to pursue a career in medicine if she is unable to associate womanhood with a medical career because she is not exposed to female physicians. Similarly, even if the medical school faculties wanted to increase the number of women in medicine, they would have difficulty doing so if girls and young women, seeing few women physicians, decide to pursue different courses of study.

Simultaneity seeks to break this impasse by working on both ends at the same time. In this case it seeks ways to admit more women applicants into medical schools and into prestigious internships, while also encouraging more girls to pursue a course of study that would lead to medical school. The increase in the numbers of female medical students and physicians as a result of gender-based affirmative action is an indication that the policy can play a significant role in addressing historically generated inequalities.

Simultaneity can be a useful strategy when certain kinds of roadblocks are deeply rooted in historical and cultural practices and when, if they are to be broken, special attempts must be made to remove them. It is a way to break those instances of underrepresentation that are the result of systematic and enforced past discrimination and that have resulted in present cultural formations that continue to discriminate and reinforce reduced social standing. The policy is best understood not as reverse discrimination. Rather, it is one way to address the systematic discrimination against some groups. This disadvantage has often constrained motivation and hindered equal opportunity. The idea of affirmative action in these cases is to create the conditions where equal opportunity is possible.

7.7 Rectifying Historical Injustice

However, there is an additional argument for the practice of affirmative action for certain groups. This argument arises from the belief that there is a need to address historical injustices that have been perpetrated against certain groups. Thus the question of whether historical injustice is a relevant category for affirmative action and, if so, whether it is possible to redress such injustice when the beneficiaries are not necessarily the same individuals as those who suffered the injustice is a contentious one. How could the injustice suffered by slaves ever truly be redressed and why should we believe that providing present-day black people with affirmative-action advantages could ever really do so. Moreover, it is not at all clear why those who live in the present day and had nothing to do with slavery should be asked to pay the price of this past injustice.

This objection is made by Anthony Scalia (1979), a justice of the US Supreme Court. Scalia does not deny that there is a debt, but he is concerned whether anyone can be legitimately expected to pay for it because he suggests that the ancestors of most present-day Americans, many of them immigrants, arrived well after slavery was over and never benefited from the practice.

In responding to issues like this, some scholars make a distinction between voluntary immigrants (those who chose to move to the USA) and involuntary ones (those who were forced to go there) along with those, such as Native Americans, who, already there, were forced to adopt a system they did not choose (Kymlicka 1995). Given this distinction, the most important part about the debt is that it results from a forced, involuntary act that brings about serious and long-standing intergenerational disadvantages. Both sides of this are important. Many immigrant people suffered serious disadvantages when they came to the USA in relation to individuals from other groups who were already there. However, even though some immigrants were forced to leave their native countries, they were not forced to enter that country. They did so believing they would be better off than if they stayed in their home country. Clearly, many were discriminated against once they arrived, as Justice Scalia rightly points out, and it is still important from the point of view of fairness and equal opportunity that these discriminations, to the extent that they exist today, be removed. Nevertheless, they alone are not sufficient to warrant a targeted policy of affirmative action to address them, and this is because of a second point.

Scalia assumes that the proper point of comparison is the initial treatment between different groups. He holds that an equivalency is established by virtue of the fact that both groups suffered an initial period of discrimination. Many who would agree with Scalia that immigrants were treated very badly indeed would remind him that the slave trade was more than discrimination. It was a holocaust of the worst kind. And, while immigrants were clearly objects of discrimination, the colour of the European immigrants' skin allowed for reasonable integration within a few generations, an elevation that African-Americans could not expect (Takaki 1993).

It is not only the level of material degradation that affects the judgement about how well or poorly members of one group faired in comparison to members of another. It is also the conditions under which they arrived to begin with. To arrive as an involuntary slave in shackles, with one's family and cultural ties destroyed, with friends and relatives drowned, sometimes intentionally, at sea is an act of extreme physical and spiritual degradation that cannot be captured by the word *discrimination*, and is quite different from choosing to immigrate as a way to escape greater discrimination elsewhere.

Yet, regardless of who is owed the debt, Scalia believes that its costs are an unfair burden on the non-discriminating offspring of immigrants, and because of this he believes that affirmative action itself is unfair. It forces payment from those who were not victimizers. The assumption that Scalia makes is that those who did not benefit directly from the initial act of discrimination are not obliged to compensate for it. Yet his conception of benefits is overly narrow, myopically focusing on the individual while he also confuses guilt and obligation. Certainly he is correct to suggest that our immigrant ancestors should not be thought guilty because of a slavery that was practised before they arrived. However, this is not the same as saying that no obligation is owed.

Scalia's argument takes no account of the national capital that accrued as a result of the *forced* back-breaking labour of slaves, nor does he consider how such labour contributed to the eagerness of Europeans to emigrate to the USA. Certainly he and his father benefited from this labour—without it America would have been an even harsher place for new immigrants—and the question is whether, because of this benefit, a debt is owed.

To answer this, suppose that, instead of slavery being assigned to members of a specific racial group, it was assigned on a random basis to all new immigrants. Suppose that potential immigrants knew, before leaving home, that they would be randomly assigned to positions in the new land and that many would be wrenched from their families, chained together, and cramped into ocean ships where many would die, and where those who lived would arrive as slaves with no control over the well-being of their children. Given this random assignment, it is hard to imagine that many European immigrants who chose voluntarily to come to the USA would still have taken the chance to do so. Granted, this account might not defend only affirmative action. It provides a strong case for reparations as well (Robinson 1999; Fullinwider 2000). However, one need not necessarily preclude the other.

This above justification is obviously adapted from John Rawls (1971), who wishes us to focus on the least advantaged among us in developing our distributive policies. Yet, given the initial theft of labour and the benefits that so many of us have derived from this theft, the case could be forcefully argued from Nozicks' defence (1974) of the right to property. After all, the right to property exists only if the property was acquired justly. Surely, some of the benefits that US citizens now enjoy are derived from slavery itself and from the social, economic, and legal stigmas that burdened the slave's children and grandchildren. Hence, perhaps the best argument for compensation to African-Americans and other groups in a similar situation is not the argument of the progressive Rawls after all. It may instead be the conservative argument that holds people accountable for the way in which they acquired their wealth.

8. CONCLUSION

It is important to distinguish affirmative-action policies from anti-discrimination policies and anti-poverty policies. While anti-discrimination policies are aimed at individuals and seek to remove discriminatory impediments to individual freedom and equal opportunity, affirmative action is targeted to advance the situation of members of certain groups that have been stigmatized because they share a certain attribute. Whereas non-discrimination policies are relatively indifferent to how many people choose to take advantage of laws against discrimination, affirmative action seeks to advance people from certain groups. In doing so it has been subject to the charge that it involves reverse discrimination and hence is unfair to those who are not targeted by affirmative-action policy. There are at least two justifications that can be offered in defence of affirmative action. First, given the stigma placed on certain groups, equal opportunity requires a policy that takes special pains to advance people from these groups. The second is that some groups have been treated so poorly, discriminated against so systematically, and continuously, that there is a very significant debt owed to all who are members of such groups. While affirmative action may not be the only, or even the best way to acknowledge that debt, it is the only one available at the present moment.

References

Abegglen, J. C., and Stalk, G., Jr. (1985). *Kaisha: The Japanese Corporation*. Tokyo: Charles E. Tuttle.

Banfield, E. (1970). *The Unheavenly City: The Nature and Future of our Urban Crisis*. Boston: Little, Brown & Co.

Blits, J. H., and Gottfredson, L. (1990). 'Race Norming: Equality or Lasting Inequality'. *Society*, 27: 4–11.

Block, N. J., and Dworkin, G. (1974a). 'IQ Heritability and Inequality, Part 1'. *Philosophy and Public Affairs*, 4/1: 40–99.

—— (1974b). 'IQ Heritability and Inequality, Part 2'. *Philosophy and Public Affairs*, 3/4: 331–409.

Bond, J. (1995). 'Civil Rights: Acting Affirmatively'. Talk given before the Curry Schools of Education, University of Virginia, Charlottesville, VA.

Bowen, W. G., and Bok, D. (1998). *The Shape of the River: Long Term Consequences of Considering Race in College and University Admissions*. Princeton: Princeton University Press.

Bredo, E. (1995). 'What if the Emperor Really Has No Clothes?' Presentation at the University of Virginia.

Carmichael, S., Hamilton, C. V. (1967). *Black Power: The Politics of Liberation in America*. New York: Random House.

Cummings, W. K. (1980). *Education and Equality in Japan*. Princeton: Princeton University Press.

Dawson, Judith A. (n.d.). 'The Complexities of Selecting Medical Students: A Search for Criteria and Predictors'. School of Basic Medical Sciences, College of Medicine, University of Illinois, Urbana, IL.

Dewey, John (1916). *Democracy and Education*. New York: Macmillan.

Duster, T. (1996). 'Individual Fairness, Group Preference and the California Strategy', in R. Post and M. Rogin (eds.), *Representations 55: Special Issue Race and Representation*. Berkeley and Los Angeles: University of California Press, 41–58.

Dworkin, R. (1977). 'Why Bakke Has No Case'. *The New York Review of Books*, 10 Nov., 11–15.

Eastland, T. (1996). *Ending Affirmative Action: The Case for Colorblind Justice*. New York: Basic Books.

Epstein, R. (1995). *Simple Rules for a Complex World*. Cambridge, MA: Harvard University Press.

Feinberg, W. (1983). *Understanding Education*. New York: Cambridge University Press.

——(1993). *Japan and the Pursuit of a New American Identity: Work and Education in a Multicultural Age*. New York: Routledge.

——(1998). *On Higher Ground: Education and the Case for Affirmative Action*. New York: Teachers College Press.

Fiscus, R. (1992). *The Constitutional Logic of Affirmative Action*. Durham, NC: Duke University Press.

Fullinwider, Robert K. (2000). 'The Case for Reparations'. *Philosophy and Public Policy*, 20/2–3: 1–8.

Gottfredson, L. S. (1992) (ed.), *Dilemmas in Developing Diversity Programs*. New York: Guilford Press.

Gottheil, E., and Michael, C. M. (1957). 'Predictor Variables Employed in Research on the Selection of Medical Students'. *Journal of Medical Education*, 32: 131–47.

Gould, S. J. (1994). 'Curve Ball'. *New Yorker*, 28 Nov., 139–49.

Herrnstein, R., and Murray, C. (1994). *The Bell Curve: Intelligence and Class Structure in American Life*. New York: Free Press.

Hollinger, D. A. (1996). 'Group Preferences, Cultural Diversity, and Social Democracy: Notes toward a Theory of Affirmative Action', in R. Post and M. Rogin (eds.), *Representations 55: Special Issue Race and Representation*. Berkeley and Los Angeles: University of California Press, 31–40.

Kahlenberg, R. D. (1996). *The Remedy: Class, Race, and Affirmative Action*. New York: Basic Books.

Keynes, J. M. (1936). *The General Theory of Employment, Interest and Money*. London: MacMillan.

Kymlicka, W. (1991). *Contemporary Political Philosophy: An Introduction*. Oxford: Oxford University Press.

——(1995). *Multicultural Citizenship*. Oxford: Oxford University Press.

McDermott, R. P. (1982). 'Social Relations as Contexts for Learning in School', in E. Bredo and W. Feinberg (eds.), *Knowledge and Values in Social and Educational Research*. Philadelphia: Temple University Press, 252–70.

Malthus, T. (1820) *Principles of Political Economy*. London: John Murray.

Marks, J. (1995). *Human Biodiversity: Genes, Race, and History*. New York: Aldine de Gruyther.

Marx, K. (1887/1961). *Capital: A Critical Analysis of Capitalist Production* ed. F. Engels, vol. i, trans. S. Moore and E. Aveling. Moscow: Foreign Language Publishing House.

Nettles, M. (1995). 'How Much Can Education Do? Should We Prefer Standardized Tests of Higher Standards for Everyone?' *Planning for Higher Education*, 23: 10–18.

Nozick, R. (1974). *Anarchy, State, and Utopia*. New York: Basic Books.

Ogbu, J. (1991). 'Immigrant and Involuntary Minorities in Comparative Perspective', in M. Gibson and J. Ogbu (eds.), *Minority Status and Schooling: A Comparative Study of Immigrant and Involuntary Minorities*. New York: Garland, 3–33.

Rawls, J. (1971). *A Theory of Justice*. Cambridge, MA: Harvard University Press.

Robinson, R. (1999). *The Debt: What Americans Owe to Blacks*. New York: Dutton.

Rosenfeld, M. (1991). *Affirmative Action and Justice: A Philosophical and Constitutional Inquiry*. New Haven: Yale University Press.

Scalia, A. (1979). 'Commentary—The Disease as Cure'. *Washington University Law Quarterly*, 147–57.

Steele, S. (1998). *A Dream Deferred: The Second Betrayal of Black Freedom in America*. New York: HarperCollins.

Sternberg, R. J. (1985). *Beyond IQ: A Triarchic Theory of Human Intelligence*. Cambridge: Cambridge University Press.

Takaki, R. (1993). *A Different Mirror: A History of Multicultural America*. Boston: Little Brown & Company.

Vogel, E. F. (1979). *Japan and Number 1: Lessons for America*. New York: Harper Colophon.

Wilson, W. J. (1987). *The Truly Disadvantaged*. Chicago: University of Chicago Press.

—— (1996). *When Work Disappears: The World of the New Urban Poor*. New York: Knopf.

Wolfe, A. (1998). 'Affirmative Action: The Fact Gap, Review of William G. Bowen and Derek Bok, *The Shape of the River*'. *New York Times Book Review*, 26 Oct.

Case Cited

Brown v. Board of Education, 347 US 483 (1954).

CHAPTER 12

··

PEOPLE WITH DISABILITIES

··

ANITA SILVERS

1. THE DISABILITY PROBLEM

··

1.1 Seeking the Right to Be in the World

WRITING two years after the passage of the US 1964 Civil Rights Act,[1] Jacobus tenBroek argued that 'nothing could be more essential to personality, social existence, economic opportunity... than... the legal right to be abroad in the land'

---

[1] In understanding claims about the rights of people with disabilities, it is important to distinguish between civil rights and entitlements to benefits. The relationship(s) between these two sorts of claims is a matter of important philosophical disagreement. Among nations with an English law system, US law most clearly distinguishes civil rights from welfare system benefits. For this reason, developments in US law, culminating in the adoption of the Americans With Disabilities Act (ADA) in 1990, are emphasized here. Of course, the USA is not the only nation where disability rights are of concern. Influenced to some extent by the ADA, Australia adopted a Disability Discrimination Act (DDA) in 1992, and the UK adopted a Disability Discrimination Act (DDA) in 1995. The Canadian Charter of Human Rights brings disabled people under its broad guarantee of equality for all, but leaves it to courts to interpret the provision's scope. Disability discrimination law in Australia, Canada, and the UK relies more on arbitration and conciliation than US law does. Like Canada, Poland, the Netherlands, and Uganda have constitutional guarantees of equality for disabled people. France and Germany make special arrangements placing the disabled in the workforce. Japan and China base nonenforceable antidiscrimination provisions on the United Nations' Standard Rules for Equalization of Opportunities for People with Disabilities, which also are not legally binding. The delineation of civil rights from welfare entitlements is useful in sorting out claims about disability rights in all these systems, regardless of their differences in regard to the legal status of disabled people.

(1966: 842). TenBroek held degrees from the law schools at Harvard and Berkeley, had taught at the University of Chicago's law school, and was a tenured UC–Berkeley professor when he wrote the classic law review article entitled 'The Right to Be in the World'. Despite his status as a nationally acclaimed legal scholar, tenBroek himself had no legal right to be abroad in the land. In virtue of his being blind, his claim to the right to be in the world was unrecognized in law and in life.

Simply because he was blind, tenBroek had no legal recourse when restaurants declined to serve him, or banks refused to let him deposit his money, or he was denied carriage on a train or plane for which he had purchased a regular ticket. Regardless of his competence and accomplishments, he expected to be held the responsible party if, in traversing the university campus, he fell into any open pit thoughtlessly left unguarded by a repair crew or was injured in a collision with a recklessly speeding campus-owned vehicle. Because he was disabled, tenBroek had to absorb harms against which non-disabled peers were protected.

At the time when civil-rights protections were specified in statute for other minorities and women, the disabled had been passed over. Although tenBroek could not know it, the next two decades would witness many failed attempts to extend existing civil-rights statutes to safeguard disabled people. The reasons were both political and conceptual, with traditional civil-rights groups sometimes joining the usual opponents of government regulation to block adding disability discrimination to the list of offences against citizens' civil rights (Burgdorf 1991).

Representatives of the groups protected under earlier legislation feared that opening it to amendments protecting the disabled might diffuse the focus of anti-discrimination enforcement. Moreover, some representatives of groups traditionally disadvantaged on the basis of race or sex simply could not conceive that people with disabilities were similarly mistreated (Burgdorf 1991). They thought of the disabled as being naturally deficient rather than artificially limited by biased social practice. They thought of disabled people as definitively incompetent, even while complaining about stereotyping when this same ascription was applied to women and racial minorities. To make disability a category that activates a heightened legal shield against exclusion, it was objected, would alter the purpose of legal protection for civil rights by transforming the goal from protecting opportunity for socially exploited people to providing assistance for naturally unfit people (Burgdorf 1991).

TenBroek showed that standards of care, conduct, risk, and liability for the disabled were inferior to those non-disabled people enjoyed (tenBroek 1966: 842). Such exclusions seemed to him inconsistent with the progressive policy President Johnson declared, and the Supreme Court affirmed, in supporting the Civil Rights Act, according to which denying equal access to public facilities to any group of citizens is a wrong and a burden on commerce. 'According to the policy of integrationism, the disabled are not to be confined to their houses, asylums, and institutions—threatened, if they emerge, with not only social sanctions but legal sanctions as well, in the form of legal barriers, disadvantages, and inadequate

protections.... Such confinement would in effect be a form of house arrest'
(tenBroek 1966: 848–9).

1.2 Historical Exclusion of People with Disabilities

The system of removing people from the community because they are disabled took
hold in the USA in the middle of the nineteenth century. Before 1820, disabled people stayed with their families or found places elsewhere in their immediate communities. During the next forty years, however, residential schools meant to train
these individuals so that they could be more productive sprang up, supported by
charitable donations and government funds. Up until the US Civil War, these institutions focused on improving the skills and therefore the productivity of corpore-
ally or cognitively impaired people, and on giving them access to the Bible and
therefore to the word of God, with the goal of returning them to the community to
earn their own livings (Trent 1994; Baynton 1996; Carlson 1998).

After the Civil War, residential schools evolved into custodial facilities comparable to those that had existed for centuries in Europe. Several contributing factors
promoted the change. Waves of immigrants arrived to provide labour, making it
harder for disabled people to support themselves. As more jobs were factory based,
caring for an impaired family member interfered more and more with wage earn-
ing. So custodial institutions were enlarged to relieve private citizens of the burden
of caring for the disabled (Trent 1994; Carlson 1998). These 'homes' then vigorously
pursued the institutionalization of less impaired individuals who, once confined,
spent their lifetimes being caregivers without remuneration for more seriously dysfunctional inmates. For instance, when a new young superintendent had inmates at
the Iowa Home for Feeble-Minded Children assessed in the early 1950s, he found
more than fifty with normal IQs higher than some of the employees. They had been
institutionalized because families, physicians, or public officials found their anomalies disturbing—for example, one had been institutionalized for sixty years
because of his peculiar eyerolling (Trent 1994).

For a century, the custodial system went unchallenged. But in the mid-twentieth
century images of its inhumanities were widely circulated by the media to the public. Just after the Second World War, *Life* magazine's 'Snakepit' story revealed the
horrors of the treatment of patients in psychiatric institutions with images reminiscent of photographs of Nazi concentration camp survivors. *PM*, a progressive
New York daily, ran pictures of the horrors of Letchworth, an asylum for cognitively
impaired individuals. A quarter century later, after the Civil Rights Act, the disgusting conditions of Letchworth persisted. Within a few months of being committed to the institution, all inmates contracted hepatitis because they were forced
to live in each other's excrement. Many similar exposés, illustrated with haunting

images, appeared in printed or televised news throughout the second half of the twentieth century.

It took another quarter century, however, for the courts to affirm that this custodial system could be discriminatory as well as inhumane. In *Olmstead* v. *LC* (1999), the US Supreme Court was for the first time able to invoke an explicitly applicable federal civil-rights statute—the 1990 Americans with Disabilities Act (ADA)—in deliberating on this matter. In the Findings that preface the ADA, the Congress stipulates that 'historically, society has tended to isolate and segregate individuals with disabilities, and, despite some improvements, such forms of discrimination against individuals with disabilities continue to be a serious and pervasive social problem' (Americans with Disabilities Act 1990). Further, the ADA defines as discriminatory the failure to integrate dispensing goods and services to disabled people into their distribution to the broader public. Providing different goods or segregated services is non-discriminatory only if there is no other possible way to offer equally effective opportunity to a disabled individual.

In *Olmstead* v. *LC*, the court declared that 'unjustified institutional isolation of persons with disabilities is a form of discrimination' and that recognition of the discriminatory potential of the custodial system 'reflects two evident judgments'. First, by confining individuals capable of living in the world to institutions and isolating them, the system perpetuates unwarranted assumptions about their capability and worthiness. Secondly, confinement deprives these individuals of family relations, social contacts, work options, economic independence, educational advancement, and cultural enrichment. If people with disabilities must relinquish participation in community life to receive services, but non-disabled people need not make similar sacrifices to receive equivalent services, the court ruled, dissimilar treatment of a discriminatory nature exists (*Olmstead* v. *LC* 1999).

Only at the end of the twentieth century did the statutory climate encourage the courts to recognize that segregating the disabled is discriminatory and that people with disabilities have the same right as other people to be in the world. In the USA, even in an era of substantial commitment to furthering civil rights, it took several decades to stimulate this process. Eventually, disability advocates abandoned efforts to integrate recognition of their rights into existing civil-rights statutes. They turned instead to laws specifically addressed to the disabled. That law-making process began with the Architectural Barriers Act of 1968 to mandate access to the built public environment and reached full expression in the 1990 Americans with Disabilities Act. Even so, the bias of which tenBroek complained has yet to be dislodged from the justice system. To illustrate, a 1999 law review article revisited the tort law issues tenBroek addressed and concluded that the goal of integrating people with disabilities into society will remain a distant one because courts still do not comprehend what is entailed in the legal recognition of their right to live in the world (Milani 1999). Further, each year brings new political and legal action aimed at reducing their statutory protection.

1.3 The Conceptual Exclusion of People with Disabilities

TenBroek believed our political and legal practice should evolve to recognize the right of disabled people to full and equal places in the world. This proposal poses some enormous challenges to everyday thinking. The conceptual problems are as vexatious in the USA as in nations that do not have civil-rights traditions. Before we can fully embrace and apply the idea that disabled people are equal, we must eliminate bias from the ways we conceptualize and communicate about disability. The ways we currently think and talk about disability create barriers by making the integration of people with disabilities appear unattainable, unimaginable, or undeserved.

Our conceptualizations of disability lead us to speak or think as if being disabled were definitively bad. The source of the badness of disability commonly is thought to be its connection with physical, sensory, or cognitive impairments, those differences that mark the disabled as being other than species typical. But what do we mean when we talk about impairment? By definition, an impairment may be an absence, deletion, omission, reduction, or diminution. These states are anomalous in that they differ from what is typical, but anomalies are not necessarily harmful, disadvantageous, or otherwise bad.

However, an impairment may also be thought of as a weakness, inadequacy, or loss. In conceptualizing disability, we too easily slide down a slippery slope from attributions of anomalies to verdicts of badness. To characterize an anomaly as a weakness or loss improperly closes by definition what should be an open empirical process of particularized valuing, for whether a particular physical or cognitive difference is unfavourable should be an open question. Thus, the commonplace elision of the first meaning of 'impairment' with the second, so that the negative value of disability is assumed rather than investigated, is a source of bias.

Because listening, seeing, walking, and other such performances are commonplace in most people's daily lives, we imagine that the sheer exercise of the faculties that support them necessarily gratifies us. From this assumption, we stray to the views that sight, hearing, and mobility are good in themselves, and, consequently, their absence constitutes a net loss of intrinsically valuable experience and a reduction of the quality of life. In this regard, it is argued that not being able to hear music or look at paintings is intrinsically bad. Yet no one questions the quality of life of the many non-disabled people who could enjoy these pleasures but pass them up. It seems biased to say forgoing these pleasures is deleterious to those who cannot experience them but indifferent to those who can but do not experience them.

There are other common ways of speaking that make it difficult for most people to talk about or think of a disability as anything but bad. To illustrate, genetic counsellors call the probability that a baby will have a disability a 'risk'. This rhetorical convention places prospective parents on the defensive if they do not display reservations about having such a child. They are expected to justify continuing 'risky' pregnancies that may result in children with disabilities, but the discourse does not equally require them to defend pregnancies with no such prognosis (Silvers 1998). In other words, the discourse exerts conceptual pressure by putting the parents on the defensive if they do not exclude the option of living with (a child who has a) disability.

A series of exchanges between philosophers Bryan Magee and Martin Milligan—published under the title *On Blindness* (Magee and Milligan 1995)—further illustrates the conceptual burden borne by whoever remains neutral about disability or questions the assumption that it is intrinsically bad. Magee wanted to discover whether someone like Milligan, blind nearly from birth and with no memory of seeing, can understand what visual language means and what is conveyed by other people's reports of visual experience. Magee hypothesizes that blindness is not just a sensory impairment, but a significant epistemic deficit as well.

Sight is useful, Milligan acknowledges. Nevertheless, he demonstrates that, despite his impairment, he can understand what is involved in, and is the product of, visual judgement:

You seem to have found my claims that born-blind people can understand, at the very least, a major part of the meaning of visual terms, and that many sighted people grossly exaggerate the importance of sight, somewhat exasperating in their presumption....because the sense of which they make overwhelmingly the greatest use is sight, sighted people just cannot imagine how blind people can manage without it.   (Magee and Milligan 1995: 42–3)

Magee, though, insists that whoever considers blindness a difference rather than a handicap is 'refusing to face the reality of his situation' (Magee and Milligan 1995: 99). He advances his case not through argument but by using rhetorical conventions that privilege the sighted over the blind. For him, people with disabilities must bear the burden of proving they are not incompetent. Magee never meets Milligan's argument that blind people enjoy a more comprehensive standpoint on the subject than sighted people:

Whereas most sighted people will have known few if any blind people, and (if any) will often not have known them very well, born-blind people will usually have known a lot of other blind people, including blind people who have had sight, and also a lot of sighted people, and will have known some of both groups very well....blind people are apt to know a good deal more about sight and sighted people than the latter can know about blindness and blind people.   (Magee and Milligan 1995: 49)

Milligan explains that erroneous conceptions of blind people's competence occur because sighted people, who are in the majority, have come to rely on vision instead of practising the full range of human skills: 'because sight is in modern conditions so much more efficient than the other senses, sighted people have got into the habit of disregarding a lot of the information the other senses provide, or can provide' (Magee and Milligan 1995: 44–5). Of course, blindness does not inherently enhance hearing, nor deafness sight, any more than paraplegia inherently builds up the shoulders and arms. What deafness does do, however, is invite increased attentiveness to effective looking, as blindness does to proficient listening. Looking or listening with greater skill increases the value realized by these perceptual modes. So people with certain kinds of sensory impairments may realize more epistemic value than is typical for members of the human species, in that they are informed by sensory data non-disabled people disregard. Thus, even if an impairment occasions a specific disadvantage, we should not assume it results in a net loss of capability or of quality of life.

The problem, then, is that Magee assumes that species-typical behaviour constitutes the appropriate standard for competence. But this kind of 'normalizing' is a bias that violates Hume's prohibition against conflating 'ought' with 'is'—that is, against unreflectively equating what is desirable with what is typical. As Alexander Rosenberg points out, modern biology suggests that there is no 'base-line repertoire of abilities common to normal agents' that is adaptive for the organism (Rosenberg 1986: 5). In imposing such a groundless standard, the dialogue inflicts a grave inequity. The heaviness of the burden of proof imposed on those who, like Milligan, approach being disabled non-judgementally is patently unfair in comparison to the light burden of proof placed on those who, like Magee, normalize by assuming without proving that being deaf or blind or crippled is intrinsically bad.

This bias is not confined to philosophical dialogue. It pervades many rhetorical domains. Often, specific protections and remedies must be legislated to relieve disabled people from such bias. For example, tenBroek demonstrated that common law tort theory is biased against blind people by requiring them to adhere to an exceptionally high standard of care in respect of avoiding injury, so much so that they can be convicted of contributory negligence simply by being in a location where they are endangered by other people's thoughtlessness. To flush out this deeply embedded bias, the National Foundation of the Blind, over which tenBroek presided, lobbied for 'white cane laws'. These state statutes decree that blind (and deaf) pedestrians have the rights and privileges of other pedestrians, including the right to go abroad in the land without signalling their blindness or relying on guides. Thus these statutes abrogate the common law rule imposing an unduly high standard of precaution on disabled people.

Rectifying such bias through legislation protects against deviations from species typicality being presumptively designated as bad and thereby being assumed to underwrite unfavourable treatment. It does not preclude acknowledging that seeing well, hearing well, and moving well are valuable. Nor does such assurance ignore the fact that impairment is often experienced as a loss by those who become disabled, especially later in life. Impairment that affects a particular mode of performance may preclude exercise of some of a person's special talents or enjoyment of some of her personal pleasures. Eliminating such accustomed performance is likely to disrupt the core of how one lives one's life, just as losing any other familiar lifeplan component, a loved child or spouse, an important opportunity or possession, a respected community role, would do. These considerations reveal that badness lies in the dislocation of familiar patterns, which may—but need not—be occasioned by disability, rather than in disability itself (Fuhrer 2000: 484).

Does Disability Diminish Quality of Life?

The onset of disability can disturb the flow of individuals' lives. Such persons' distress is understandably magnified when they are subjected to biased conceptualizations that place them on the defensive, when their right to be in the world is ignored or denied, and when they must battle for recognition of their competence. They are also stressed by policies shaped by the assumption that to have a disability makes a person's life inherently less valuable.

For instance, in 1927, the US Supreme Court declared that the state has a legitimate interest in preventing the births of disabled people whose existence detracts from the welfare of the community (*Buck v. Bell*, 1927). As late as the 1930s, more than half the states in the USA had laws on the books encouraging sterilization of people with disabilities, usually those with developmental disabilities, but also those who were blind or deaf (regardless of whether their conditions were inherited or aquired). California's eugenic sterilization law may have inspired the Nazi programme of euthanizing members of these same groups (Kevles 1998: 3). In Western Europe, eugenic practices existed well past the half-century mark. The world has learned that programmes of sterilizing people designated as disabled accompanied the post-Second World War expansion of generous social service policies in Scandinavia and the Netherlands (Silvers et al. 1998).

These programmes, Kevles (1998: 3) reports, were predicated on the proposition that disabled people burdened the community by proliferating at a rate that placed great pressure on social resources and stability. In health-care practice, suggests bioethicist Leon Kass (1973: 400), a similar attitude propels the assumption that the lives of people with disabilities makes them burdensome to themselves. But it is illegitimate to assume that disability is necessarily burdensome. Despite the depleted opportunities they are offered, many disabled people equal or excede the typical social contributions of non-disabled individuals. And, though impairments may preclude some activities, such limitations need not have a deleterious impact on people's well-being.

Not every limitation is a loss—and certainly not an intolerable loss. We know, for instance, that the absence of limitations can also lead to suffering. We may well be better off if we were to be focused on a few fulfilling options than torn with indecision by many glittering ones. It is important to learn to overcome disadvantageous circumstances when faced with limited, less than desirable, options. Because one has only one life to plan, the ultimate difference between having begun with a single, several, or many equally satisfying life-plan opportunities may be negligible.

It is thus problematic to identify disability with diminished worth of life. In fact, individuals who are experienced in living with a disability very often give a much higher rating to the quality of life disabled people can achieve than the non-disabled do (Murray and Lopez 1996). The difference that a person's standpoint makes in how a health condition is experienced foregrounds an important issue about conceptual bias. 'Many of the outcome measures (used in health services research) reflect the hegemony of providers' and payers' values', and only equivocally those of disabled people (Fuhrer 2000: 487). Constructing a univocal standpoint usually means defining away the perspectives of disabled people so that these have no weight within the assessment system. 'These models do not lend themselves to providing a holistic portrayal of people's living with a disability' (Fuhrer 2000: 483).

There are further problems with the way disability is assessed in health-care service allocation. Attempting to calibrate his disability-adjusted life year (DALY) scale, Murray reports that, if invited to choose between extending the lives of a larger number of blind people or of a smaller number of seeing people, most non-disabled people choose to benefit the larger group, suggesting that they assign the same value to each life whether the individual is disabled or not. (However, the same subjects think it more important to restore sight to a blind person than to extend a non-disabled person's life by a year.)

Murray interprets these results as incoherent, and therefore as of no relevance to the appropriateness of his scale. He thinks his respondents are claiming inconsistently that disabled and non-disabled people's lives are identically valuable, and at the same time that eliminating a disability, so as to transform a person from being disabled to non-disabled, makes that person's life more valuable (Murray and Lopez 1996: 36). As is characteristic of discussions about the distribution of health care, this interpretation of respondents' replies fails to distinguish between the burden of disability and the burden of life with disability. It is not inconsistent to think that being blind is a burden, an obstacle one must constantly work around, but that being alive (while blind) is not itself a burden, regardless of the challenges associated with being blind. Analogously, being poor usually is a burden but this does not entail that it is better not to live at all than to live with poverty.

Murray reminds us that the limitation associated with an impairment may differ depending on environment. The same impairment may be more or less disabling in an advanced technological society than in a simple rural one. For example, it is well known that mild mental retardation does not disable women in environments in which a woman's role is restricted to cleaning, cooking, and bearing children. Why, then, does Murray adopt a standard that imposes an identical assessment of the quality of life of all people with the same impairment, a standard that disregards the difference having a hostile or an accepting environment can make to their lives?

Remarkably, Murray's appeal here is to justice. It would be unjust to allocate resources to rich societies to prevent a type of impairment but not to poor ones, Murray believes, even though 'in many cases [programmes] to avert impairment could exacerbate inequalities' by eliminating disabled people from reproductive roles (Murray and Lopez 1996: 33). Yet surely there is nothing unjust in acknowledging that an impairment is no burden at all where it is not experienced as one.

Murray assumes that allocating more medical care always serves justice. But it is surely less just to treat people as dysfunctional when they actually are not than to refrain from intervening where intervention harms them. Undergoing a medical intervention almost always costs the patient some pain and risk. A medical intervention is unlikely to be experienced as beneficial by individuals who were not dysfunctional prior to it and are no more functional, relative to their environment, as a result of it. To illustrate, adults with congenitally anomalous limbs, such as those occasioned by the prenatal presence of thalidomide, often believe themselves to have been injured as children by being fitted with dysfunctional artificial arms and forbidden to use the much more functional method of manipulating objects with their feet (Baughn et al. 2000). As long as the patient is competent, commensurability demands that the benefit offsetting the patient's cost be in terms of the patient's own experience of good.

But this perspective has usually been disregarded in favour of a medical point of view that gives normality priority over functionality. (Fuhrer 2000: 482). From the medicalized perspective, claims to equality are predicated on the claimants' species-typical functioning. So equal access to the world is to be achieved by functioning in a species-typical way. On this view, the claims of people who do not function at common levels and in typical ways should be, primarily for medical procedures meant to make them more normal.

2. SOLVING THE DISABILITY PROBLEM

2.1 Models of Disability

The Medical Model

In our era, a medical model of disability has pervaded political, legal, and other thought as thoroughly as it has dominated health-care policy making. This model has important implications for the assignment of rights. According to it, people are disabled when they are biologically anomalous—when they are less functionally proficient than is typical for most humans. Norman Daniels puts it this way: 'The basic idea is that...diseases (I here include deformities and disabilities that result from trauma) are deviations from the natural functional organization of a typical member of a species' (1987: 302). The job of medicine then is to maintain or restore species-typical functioning.

This medical model is applied to defeat claims that disabled people have rights to equitable access to the opportunities of the world. It is not reasonable to expect such access in the absence of species-typical functioning, Daniels (1987: 302) claims:

Life plans we are otherwise suited for and have a reasonable expectation of finding satisfying or happiness-producing are rendered unreasonable by impairments of normal functioning...if people have a higher-order interest in preserving ... opportunity...then they will have a pressing interest in maintaining normal species functioning by establishing institutions—such as health care systems—that do just that.

What could be a more natural, and modest, expectation on the part of an individual than the desire to function as her species typically does? Broad-based public support for policies that reduce whatever biological anomalies or singularities hinder adherence to the species-typical functional standard seems natural. As Tocqueville remarked, the inclination to create fair opportunity by levelling the players rather than the playing field is a strong force in egalitarian societies. There is, nevertheless, an abiding question about the propriety of making homogeneity the price of opportunity. Normalizing policies can worsen the situation, or otherwise oppress, the very individuals they purport to improve by decreeing that inequality of opportunity is the unavoidable consequence of not functioning in the normal, typical, or customary way.

Daniels (1987: 303) supposes that an objective biological principle warrants restoring impaired individuals so that they function typically for the species. However, Ron Amundson challenges Daniel's view. According to him the idea of normal function has no foundation in objective biological fact because very large amounts of heritable variation occur in natural species (Amundson 2000a: 36). In modern biology dogmas about determinate species design have given way to appreciation of rich ranges of variation. No nature-based justification underwrites making social justice conditional upon normality (or upon species typicality, which is often confused with normality). That there are average, common, or typical modes and levels of human performances does not make these the normal or natural modes and levels for humankind (Sober 1980).

The Social Model

The medical model understands the reduction of opportunity occasioned by disability in terms of the disabled individual's personal deficits, but people with disabilities often interpret their situation differently. They understand their limitations in terms of social rather than personal deficits. This social model of disability transforms the notion of 'handicapping condition' from a biological state that disadvantages unfortunate individuals to a state of society that disadvantages an oppressed minority. The social model attributes the dysfunction experienced by people with disabilities primarily to hostile social arrangements.

For instance, Richard Hull examines the condition of disabled people in the UK. Like other nations, social arrangements in the UK are such that people with disabilities incur significant extra cost to meet the conditions for social participation. Yet, disability welfare payments are insufficient to meet this cost, and institutional discrimination against disabled people is prevalent throughout the labour market (Hull 1998: 201–2). Hull observes: 'Contrary to the conventional view... functional limitation does not always secure or guarantee disadvantage.... society can be equally to blame, or more to blame, in many cases' (1998: 203).

In this social view of disability, socially constructed barriers are the primary disadvantage faced by people who do not function in species-typical ways. These obstructions range from discriminatory practices such as disability-based denial of employment through thoughtlessly inaccessible design such as the installation of steps rather than ramps. Sometimes the absence of adequate support services and health-care benefits is also construed as a barrier to the effective functioning of people with certain kinds of impairments (Silvers et al. 1998).

From this perspective, the pre-eminent strategy of the medical model—namely, altering biologically anomalous people to make them species typical or normal—unfairly disparages personal traits central to the identity of individuals with disabilities. Further, by placing a premium on medically altering them so as to bring their modes of functioning into better conformity with species-typical functioning, this medicalized approach to disability can be coercive and can expose the disabled to risky or ineffective medical interventions. Consequently, from this viewpoint, reforming social arrangements to achieve equitable opportunity and accessibility is the best route to reducing dysfunction in biologically anomalous people.

The social model thus entails that the solution to the 'disability problem' lies in fully realizing disabled people's right to be in the world. There are two competing schools of philosophical thought about this right. The first rests firmly on the social model by arguing that 'injustices may be better remedied by changing social norms and the structure of public goods than by redistributing resources' (Anderson 1999: 336). In this first view, enabling disabled people to be in the world is grounded in the collective good of achieving a democratically equitable social order based on principles that express respect for everyone. This approach emphasizes participatory rights that give disabled people claims to inclusion in social practice and to revision of such practice if needed for access.

The second straddles the medical and social models by revising the distribution of private goods to improve disabled individuals' personal capacity to cope with existing social norms. In this second view, the right of disabled people to be in the world is grounded in the individual good of achieving personal satisfaction based on principles that promote well-being for everyone. This later approach claims the disabled are due compensatory rights to repair their deficits, relieve their needs, or mitigate the consequences of their losses.

2.2 Disability Rights

Disability Rights as Participatory Rights

Philosophers like Elizabeth Anderson (1999), Anita Silvers (1995, 1997; Silvers et al. 1998), and Iris Marion Young (1990) all take justice to be about interpersonal respect and inclusive social participation. They argue that to treat disabled people equally requires reshaping the practices that exclude them. From a disability perspective, physical or cognitive limitations are not absences of talent, but instead are constraints upon the functional modes through which talents are exercised. Social arrangements that offer equivalent prospects of success to people of similar talent and ambition provide fair equality of opportunity. Fair equality of opportunity requires that people with similar talents should enjoy equitable access to the necessary social conditions for realizing their talents, regardless of whether their functional modes are normal or anomalous.

In this kind of view, equality is a social relationship that is free of exclusion, coercion, and oppression. Anderson and Silvers follow Iris Marion Young in identifying inegalitarianism with claims about the necessary dominance by some social groups of others, usually on the ground that the former have superior intrinsic worth while the latter are incompetent or otherwise intrinsically inferior (Silvers 1995: *passim*; Anderson 1999: 311–12). To secure equality, the social patterns in which people interact, and through which personal goods are actualized and interchanged, must express respect for everyone alike, whether fortunate or unfortunate, judicious or reckless, through mutual, reciprocal consultation and action (Anderson 1999: 313).

Of course, functioning as a social being requires functioning as a human being, which involves effective access to the means of sustaining one's biological existence and agency. It also requires effective access to the means of being productive, of developing talents, and of forming relationships in civil society (Anderson 1999: 318). Therefore, regardless of whether one is typically or anomalously circumstanced, everyone equally has a right to social arrangements that provide the enabling conditions for these fundamental capabilities (Anderson 1999: 331). In this way, democratic equality matches remedy to injustice. If, as tenBroek describes, the fundamental injustice done to the disabled is to exclude them from the world, the remedy lies in assigning them the direct right to the means of inclusion, not the circuitous right to be compensated for exclusion by gaining satisfaction in some alternative way (Anderson 1999: 334).

In this spirit, Anita Silvers proposes a test for the justice of specific social practices to see whether their exclusionary aspects grow out of the dominance of non-disabled people's convenience and tastes. 'Historically counterfactualizing' is a conceptual test that involves asking whether a practice would be the same if the disabled individuals it marginalizes were the majority, not a powerless minority, of people. Its purpose is to free our imaginations from the constricting routine of institutionalized behaviours so that we are not misled into assuming that the familiarity of a practice signals its biological or economic necessity (Silvers 1995, 1998, 2000; Silvers et al. 1998).

Historical counterfactualizing indicates whether, by broadening assumptions about the variety of modes in which individuals can achieve effective function, we can and should redesign a practice so that anomalous individuals can partake of the collective good it secures. For example, the practice of privileging visual over aural and tactile media for storing data disregards the functional modes in which blind and dyslexic individuals retrieve information. That this practice is exclusionary is of no moment to the majority of people. They are sighted, so for them the practice works well. If, however, blind individuals, for whom looking at texts is dysfunctional, were the majority rather than the minority, the practice would be different. The relative ease of storing and conveying information in a variety of media would make offering information in alternative formats the rule rather than the exception (Silvers 2000).

Historical counterfactualizing helps us to identify disadvantage that is the arbitrary artefact of social arrangements controlled by the standard of normality. It facilitates distinguishing arrangements that do no more than conform to the dominant group's tastes and preferences from arrangements that have more to recommend them. Tastes and preferences are transitory. The practices they elicit need not be perpetual. Exclusionary practices dominate, Silvers believes, because most often they are comfortable for the majority and disadvantage only a minority of people. Although the majority may be discomforted if restrictive practices are altered to become more inclusive, their social participation is not threatened by such change. Thus, on balance, such social reform is less burdensome for members of the majority than enduring exclusion is for members of the minority.

Some alterations of practice to repair disadvantages suffered by the disabled can be justified as necessary to counter our culture's arbitrary and oppressive affinity for normality. But historical counterfactualization also helps identify elements of our current disability policy that do not have such a warrant. To illustrate, the disabled have been disadvantaged in gaining access to the workplace. So it is sometimes thought that equity requires providing compensatory income for them. Yet there is no reason to think that, were the disabled the majority instead of the minority, they could command compensatory income. Were most people disabled, it would surely be very difficult for the able-bodied minority to care for and sustain so many people with disabilities. So, were the non-disabled in the minority, it is less rather than more likely that they could guarantee to provide subsistence for the disabled.

Counterfactualizing thus reveals nothing arbitrary nor inequitable if society does not supply such care. Indeed, counterfactualizing indicates a significant problem with the strategy of utilizing compensatory income to offset the social disadvantage disability occasions. The feasibility of doing so wanes with increases in the population of people who are excluded from the workplace because of their disabilities. This result suggests that reducing exclusion is preferable to compensating for it (Silvers 1995; Silvers et al. 1998).

Negative and Positive Disability Rights

This debate may seem to reflect the larger philosophical discussion of positive and negative rights. For philosophers who propose reshaping social practice to permit disabled people fully to participate in society, ensuring them the same liberatory rights that others enjoy is preferable to granting them special compensatory rights. Although such emancipation from social restriction is usually associated with the exercise of negative rights, it may be misleading to impose the traditional template of positive and negative rights on our consideration of disability rights.

Negative rights limit the ways in which the activities of rights-bearers may be obstructed; the state has a duty to ensure that the exercise of these rights is not restricted and consequently must ensure that rights-bearers are free of the prohibited constraints. Positive rights are entitlements to benefits the state has a duty to provide to rights-bearers (Gewirth 1992: 106–7). Ensuring the successful exercise of either kind of right has its costs: typically, allocation mechanisms, such as the social security system, must be available to support positive rights-bearers, while enforcement mechanisms, such as the judicial system, must be available to protect negative rights-bearers.

Discrimination curtails liberty by corrupting the routes of access to productivity and fulfilment. Claimants to protection against discrimination traditionally call on the resources of the state to extirpate harms that arise when the bigotry or arbitrariness of public and proprietary entities blocks this access for certain kinds of people. Their claims are to relatively 'thick' rights that command positive action to open the routes to accomplishment (Silvers 2000).

There is neither agreement nor clarity regarding the point at which a thick negative right transforms into a thin positive right. Responses to discrimination sometimes appear to proffer special preferences similar to the entitlements associated with positive rights. For instance, US disability discrimination law requires employers and programme operators to make reasonable accommodations to give disabled people meaningful access to productive, fulfilling social participation. Regulations that direct the installation of toilet stalls wide enough for wheelchairs in office buildings, or the toleration of guide dogs in restaurants and aeroplanes, may appear to entitle disabled individuals to extra cost and exertion on other people's part, rather than merely to protect their liberties. Thus, claims to such accommodations may appear to exercise positive rather than negative rights (Illingworth and Parmet 2000). From a disability perspective, however, these regulations protect disabled people's liberty to access toilets, restaurants, and planes. To make being stripped of one's mobility device (because toilet stall doorways are too narrow for wheelchairs, for example) or one's visual alerting system (because guide dogs are banned from a restaurant or plane, for example) the condition of entering a facility is as much a curtailment of one's liberty as making cutting off a person's legs or poking out his eyes the price of entry would be.

This last observation illuminates one respect in which reshaping social practice resembles implementation of a negative, rather than a positive, right. While positive rights are entitlements assigned to some among us, negative rights are shields for all citizens alike. The characteristic defence of a claim to a positive right involves differentiating those said to be deserving of it from other individuals. In contrast, the characteristic defence of a claim to a negative right involves assimilating those who lack a liberty to other individuals who already enjoy it. When disabled people pursue recognition of their right to be in the world, they seek the same freedoms of access as are afforded without question to other citizens. To alter practice so that civic and commercial facilities can be utilized by those who substitute mechanical devices or animal aides for legs and arms, or eyes or ears, is simply to give disabled people the same freedoms of social participation as other people enjoy.

Thus, when disability rights are claims for participation, they appear to fall within the negative rights tradition. For non-disabled people who need undergo no struggle in order to be in the world, being required to accommodate people with disabilities may be misperceived as privileging this minority and so may be received with resentment. To make clear that such accommodation offers disabled people only freedoms others enjoy, it is advisable (as Iris Marion Young points out) to adopt public and commercial policies aimed at fostering inclusion by accommodating the differences of all citizens, not just those certified as falling into the disability category. For instance, non-disabled and disabled workers alike should challenge employers to create more individualized, accommodating, and humane workplaces (Young 2000).

Disability Rights as Compensatory Rights

Nevertheless, philosophers who take justice to be mainly concerned with the fair allocation of resources often think that access to social opportunity is a peripheral issue when it comes to the disabled. They assert that disabled people characteristically need more than the usual resources. This to them is the main source of the problem of disability. Adherents of the view that equalizing must offer more than opportunity urge that something more than levelling the playing field must be done. Individuals must also be made capable of leaving the starting gate, even if doing so involves an unevenness in how goods and services are allocated. In general, for disabled people to flourish, extra resources are needed to remedy the results of their limitations.

Disability thus poses a philosophical challenge—namely, the question of whether the disabled can receive greater portions of goods than other people do without being unfairly privileged by the allocation scheme. Amartya Sen (1982, 1992, 1993), Bickenbach (1993, 2000), Ronald Dworkin (1994), Dan Brock (1995, 2000), Allen Buchannan (1995, 1996), David Wasserman (Silvers et al. 1998), and Richard Arneson (2000) are among the well-known contributors to the literature on this subject. Because natural differences, including impairments, affect well-being, Sen urges taking them into account in formulating just distributive arrangements. Sen believes justice requires allocating more resources to individuals who require them to enjoy basic capabilities. It is, for instance, merely just, rather than privileging, to provide more resources to people who need to purchase wheelchairs in order to mobilize than to people who can mobilize by walking. Brock thinks that some of the differences caused by impairments irremediably decrease well-being and therefore holds that resource allocation to people with these differences may be neither cost effective nor otherwise beneficial. In a more nuanced discussion, Wasserman points out that any adequate view requires constructing a metric of well-being that respects the multiplicity of ways in which people can live well. The theory that generates such a metric must convincingly explain how much inequality in the distribution of well-being can be tolerated before differences in allocations become unjust.

Arneson argues that 'what we owe to one another by way of social justice requirements goes beyond... nondiscrimination'. He believes that 'the provisions of the Americans with Disabilities Act... cannot be fully justified by appeal even to the most plausible versions of the nondiscrimination ideal' (Arneson 2000: 18). For Arneson, the pre-eminent ethical question in regard to disability is what we owe to people whose competence is so low as to compromise their well-being regardless of the excellence of their access to opportunity. Moral value is maximized by making gains in the expected well-being of individuals disadvantaged through no fault of their own. By increasing such individuals' material resources, we can sometimes reconfigure the circumstances that determine their lifetime allotment of well-being. We are obligated to strive for satisfying outcomes for all deserving people alike, regardless of their differences of merit or talent. Such social intervention promotes a fairer distribution of well-being than could be accomplished by relying on individuals' good or ill luck in making good use of their access to opportunity.

Undoubtedly, compensatory resources for goods and services conducive to well-being would benefit many people with disabilities. Nevertheless, Anderson criticizes Arneson for grounding justice for disabled people in considerations of the putative incompetence and consequent neediness of this class. Arneson creates another difficulty by particularizing allocation decisions. On the criteria he gives, deserving beneficiaries must be blameless for their deficits and must possess the capacity to capitalize on allocated resources by achieving enhanced welfare. According to Arneson, what we owe each other depends on two factors: (1) how badly off or well off each person would be in the absence of further receipt of benefits, and (2) the extent to which each person's well-being prospects would improve if further benefits were bestowed on that person. Individualized judgements are required to determine whether a particular disabled person meets these criteria and thus is qualified to exercise disability rights. Individual beneficiaries of welfare justice must show they are both most deserving and most deprived. Further, the extent of their deprivation conditions their deservingness.

However, this approach invites a counter-intuitive conclusion—namely, that of two individuals who are blind: the more talented one is more fortunate and therefore appears to deserve less justice than the less talented one. For instance, tenBroek's successful position in life would not entitle him to as much justice as a blind beggar. But having less call on justice can itself trigger neediness. Moreover, what is owed the Berkeley professor and the beggar in virtue of their being blind should be the same, as they have the same disability.

Answering Anderson, Arneson would probably respond that we should be mainly concerned about improving the welfare of incompetent or unlucky disabled individuals rather than with improving the status of the disabled as a class. In sum, Arneson criticizes Anderson and Silvers for an account on which justice invites us to treat very differently disabled people homogeneously by giving less weight to promoting deserving individuals' well-being than to avoiding actions that might stigmatize the class. On the other hand, Anderson criticizes luck egalitarians like Arneson for an account on which justice treats similarly disabled people differently, depending on the extent to which they are afflicted with personal problems.

Is it appropriate merely to level the social playing field in ways that afford fair access to disabled people as a group? Or is it unrealistic, and thereby unfair, to expect these individuals to take the field at all, let alone succeed on it? Anderson and Arneson answer these questions in different ways because they have very different ideas about what is owed to people in virtue of being disabled.

Anderson seems to construe basic disability rights as group rights. In this approach, disabled people have a collective right to a society in which the existence of their type of person is acknowledged, and where the differences that signify their group membership command respect. For example, in a society where there is respectful acknowledgement that some people do not hear, deaf people can expect information that is conveyed aurally also to be offered in a visual mode. Similarly, where practice is influenced by both the awareness that some people cannot see and the principle that their access to information is as important as anyone else's, blind people have a recognized claim to aural or tactile versions of information that is conventionally presented visually.

In addition to being grouped according to their impairments, all disabled people belong to the more comprehensive collection of individuals whose corporeal or cognitive anomalies result in some degree of non-species-typical performance. Together, they have a broad collective right to a society in which practices are generally inclusive of both species-typical and species-anomalous individuals. Within such a society, they may have derivative individual rights to enforcement or compensation as remedies for exclusion they suffer because they are disabled. Of course, even if a practice is as accessible as good will and good technology can make it, some disabled people will not engage in it successfully. But, in this view, no one is owed success in virtue of being disabled (although there may be other grounds on which disabled and non-disabled individuals alike are owed basic components of well-being).

In contrast, Arneson construes basic disability rights as individual rights. In this approach, disabled people have individual claims to a society in which each enjoys entitlements in virtue of having qualified for membership in the group of the deserving disabled. Where there is sufficient societal concern for people whose competence is compromised by disability, deaf people and blind people can, for example, expect resources to compensate for the loss of welfare occasioned by limited access to information, at least to the extent that these resources will elevate their well-being. Further, within such a society, disabled beneficiaries may have a derivative collective right to practices that make the allocation of resources effective. For example, to help make allocations of rehabilitative services to disabled individuals effective in securing the benefits of employment, disabled people may be assigned a derivative collective right to accessible public transportation to get to the workplace. However, unlike the former approach, where everyone is owed inclusion for its own sake, in this view no disabled individual is owed inclusion unless it is the most effective route to enhancement of her welfare.

2.3 Disability Rights and Disability Policy

The positions represented by Anderson and Arneson lay out disability rights very differently, not only in respect of whether they are individual or collective, but also in respect of the fundamental values to be sought and achieved by exercising them. Their difference turns in part on a disparity in their conceptions of the connection between social participation and individual flourishing. The issue is whether the successful exercise of participatory rights in itself secures intrinsic value, or whether social participation is a mere instrument, one among other possibly effective approaches, for attaining intrinsically valuable results—namely, the increased welfare that is pursued through the exercise of compensatory rights.

Philosophers who take the pre-eminent kind of disability right to be participatory suppose that individuals cannot flourish without their joining with other humans in some sorts of collective activities. Thus, for them, participation is inherently valuable, and practices should be shaped to facilitate interaction between different kinds of people. A social environment that facilitates their connectedness is important for disabled and non-disabled individuals alike. Individuals' basic needs are to be assessed in terms of cultivating the capabilities they must have to maintain their social connections. Distributing resources to satisfy these individual needs secures instrumental value only. Allocation schemes that segregate or otherwise isolate their disabled recipients are counterproductive in this view.

On the other hand, those who construe the pre-eminent kind of disability right to be compensatory suppose that participation in community activities contributes to, but is not necessary for, every human's well-being. To base disability rights on the value of social inclusion, they say, is to deny rights to very severely disabled people for whom access to participatory activities is either beside the point or not possible to achieve. Yet these are the individuals who, in virtue of the profundity of their disabilities, should be most able to have their claims on others acknowledged.

Disability rights should be meaningful for the most disabled and responsive to their individualized situations. Therefore, allocating resources to satisfy these individual needs secures intrinsic value.

Jonathan Wolff (2000) crafts a position that integrates the fair-access and fair-allocation approaches. Drawing on the work of Ronald Dworkin to propose how a society of equals should treat the disabled, Wolff identifies three acceptable responses: medical interventions remedying impairments that occasion disability, resource allocations compensating for disadvantages associated with disability, and social-practice alterations nullifying disadvantages imposed on disability. The objective is to help each disabled individual find a place in the world.

Regardless of which strategies we emphasize, Wolff reminds us, we must decide what amount of effort and resources to expend on doing so. Following Dworkin, he recommends imagining people behind a veil of ignorance, aware of the disadvantages of disability, its general prevalence, and the costs of remedial strategies, but unaware of their own disability status. We should consider how well, in what ways, and at what cost people who do not know whether they are or will be disabled would insure themselves against suffering exclusion should they become so. Tax revenues generated on this basis would be assigned to a government agency charged with pursuing the most effective combination of strategies—medical repairs, compensatory allocations and services, or reform of exclusionary social practices—both for individuals and for the general public.

Wolff's solution reflects the state of disability policy in many nations. Medical research and resources, funded by various public or private schemes, are applied to reduce the numbers of the disabled. Criteria of deservingness are applied to those who cannot be cured to determine the kind and amount of material resources and social services each should receive. Attention has turned to requiring that environments be more accommodating to people with various kinds of biological anomalies. In some nations these strategies are all pursued by a single agency charged with addressing the disability problem. In others, different branches of government execute different aspects of disability policy.

Regardless of how disability policy is administered, these components do not always coexist compatibly. There are deep conceptual tensions between viewing the disability problem as primarily caused by discrimination and therefore as susceptible to a civil rights solution, and viewing it as primarily a social safety net issue and therefore as susceptible to a needs-based benefits solution. How we credit what disabled people claim society owes them is influenced by whether the claim is framed as liberatory—that is, as a claim to opportunity all citizens should be positioned to enjoy—or as allocatory—that is, as a claim to assistance some citizens should be positioned to receive.

In the USA, disability entitlement programmes that are partially or fully needs-based pre-dated the application of the civil-rights paradigm to disability discrimination. During the quarter century that followed the Civil Rights Act of which

Jacobus tenBroek had such high hopes, few provisions to relieve people with disabilities of their exclusion from social participation were integrated into comprehensive legislation aimed at safeguarding minorities generally. (The Fair Housing Amendments Act of 1988 is a notable exception.) Instead, their protection against discrimination was fashioned mainly by enacting or amending statutes pertaining solely or principally to the disabled. Important laws of this kind included the Rehabilitation Act, the Education for All Handicapped Children Act (since 1990 the Individuals with Disabilities Education Act), and the Developmental Disabilities Assistance and Bill of Rights Act. Having waited in vain for nearly a decade to draw the disabled under the shield of the 1964 Civil Rights Act, disability leaders eventually introduced a non-discrimination provision into federal statute by amending the Rehabilitation Act. Sections 503 and 504 of the Rehabilitation Act prohibit denying individuals participation in federally funded programmes or activities in virtue of their handicaps, but enforcement mechanisms were lodged mainly in funding agencies' complaint reviews. Eventually, the idea of achieving civil-rights protection through a new federal statute specifically aimed at forbidding discrimination based on disability was adopted, and the Americans with Disabilities Act (ADA) became law in 1990.

During the two decades between the amended Rehabilitation Act and the implementation of the ADA, the statutory conceptualization of disability discrimination seemed unproblematic. In the many investigations and rare litigations pursued under the Rehabilitation Act, actions centred mainly on whether complainants had been subjected to unwarranted exclusion. Disputes most often were over whether there were unburdensome ways in which disabled complainants could be given access to the benefits federally funded programmes bestowed on non-disabled people.

Complainants were typically people who suffered from diminished prospects for employment because of some limitation of body or mind. Thus such persons already met the criteria for services under the Rehabilitation Act. The relief they sought typically was pertinent to the core purpose of that legislation, for it was commonly an action or accommodation to gain or maintain (suitability for) employment. In the context of the Rehabilitation Act, reasonably accommodating to a person's disability is generally thought of as responding to the person's special needs.

Consistent with the nature of the Rehabilitation Act as an entitlement to benefits statute, concerns that increasing the welfare of disabled complainants decreases other people's welfare are the most frequent source of contentiousness provoked by attempts to exercise the disability rights established by Sections 503 and 504. For instance, in *Southeastern Community College* v. *Davis* (1979), the Supreme Court refused to order that assessment of the plaintiff's application to a nursing programme be based solely on academic record, as other applicants' were. On the grounds that her deafness prevented her from fully practising the profession 'safely' (for instance, she could not be a surgical nurse because her colleagues' surgical masks would prevent her from reading their lips), the court decided that the public benefits of denying her this opportunity outweighed the personal benefits to Davis of being admitted.

Litigation under the ADA commonly turns on questions of classification rather than access. Most of the ADA cases heard by the Supreme Court involve this issue. (Some have concerned whether specific physical conditions meet the ADA's classificatory criterion for being protected from disability discrimination, another addressed inconsistencies in how different statutes define disability, and yet another turned on whether disability is a classification that qualifies for Fourteenth Amendment protection (Francis and Silvers 2000)). For example, in *Kirkingburg*, the court did not address the justice of denying the plaintiff employment as a driver, simply because of his monocular vision and despite his demonstrating adequate depth perception and a flawless driving record. Instead, the fact that the plaintiff had overcome the usual limitation of monocular vision and had passed the tests for depth perception meant, to the court, that he could not be classified as disabled and so had no standing under the ADA (*Albertsons, Inc.* v. *Kirkingburg* 1999). Notice that, by pursuing individualized enquiries into whether plaintiffs' impairments are sufficiently limiting so that eligibility criteria are met, the court has applied procedures characteristically applied in disputes about social welfare rights to adjudicate civil rights complaints.

In sum, US disability policy encompasses incongruous understandings of disabled people's rights. Even where civil-rights and benefit-entitlement statutes require the same compliance—for instance, the provision of a sign language interpreter for a person who cannot hear—the two kinds of laws supply quite disparate warrants for the same requirement. The ADA underwrites disabled people's equal right to the same degree of social participation enjoyed by other people. On the other hand, the Rehabilitation Act establishes disabled people's special right to the fulfilment of needs not experienced by other people. Disputes under the Rehabilitation Act focus on whether the actions required to provide disabled individuals with access are too burdensome on non-disabled people. On the whole, disputes under the ADA have, so far, assumed that such actions are required and have focused, instead, on who is included in the group for whom they must be executed.

Disability policy in other nations exhibits similar complexity. For instance, neither Australia's 1992 Disability Discrimination Act (Jones and Marks 2000), nor Section 15 of the Canadian Charter of Rights and Freedoms (enacted as the Canada Act in 1982) (Bickenbach 2000), nor the UK's 1995 Disability Discrimination Act (Silvers 1995; Corker 2000) makes clear whether captioning, ramping, and print enlarging should be thought of in general terms—as integral elements of an increasingly inclusive social climate in which the existence of deaf, vision-impaired, and mobility-limited people, and their right to equal access to the world, are acknowledged. Or whether, on the other hand, these accommodations should be understood in particular terms—as contingent responses to the petitions of singular individuals with extraordinary needs.

2.4 Are Disability Rights Redundant?

Moral theories that centre on justice typically foreground the goals of securing equality for all alike through the exercise of rights that all should recognize. There are, however, challenging reasons for thinking that assigning justice the pre-eminent moral role in ameliorating the disability problem disregards the realities of disability and especially of the dependency associated with it. Looked at in this light, grounding disability policy in other, more appropriate values should make appeals to disability rights subsidiary or even redundant.

Writing about her relation with her disabled daughter, Eva Feder Kittay considers how we can best care for people made vulnerable by significant disabilities. We should recognize that their lives have a value unrelated to productivity and profit: their contribution is the bonding that relationships of dependency create. This is an important contribution because the coherence of our sense of ourselves as persons relies on our relations with others. Supporting the bonding between seriously disabled individuals and their families helps realize the human capacity for moral connectedness (Kittay 1998, 2000).

Relating to disabled people holds further beneficial lessons. The more we stress the importance of independence, Kittay observes, the more we are inclined to feel threatened by disabled people who remind us of our own potential for dependency. We should utilize this reminder to recognize that each of us has periods in which we need to be cared for and thus are susceptible to exploitation and abuse. Then we will not be motivated by the fantasy that our lives are at all moments under our own control.

Susan Wendell also thinks feminist ethics that value care over justice, and inter-dependence over autonomy, afford disabled people a role preferable to the one they must assume under the traditional ethical standards of justice, equality, and autonomy. Within the embrace of an ethics of care, Wendell urges, disabled people would be free to acknowledge their limitations, dependencies, and other real differences. Unfortunately, cultural taboos rooted in the currently predominant value of self-determination through self-sufficiency now discourage disabled people from being honest in communicating their experiences (Wendell 1996). Far less optimistic about reforming cultural values than Kittay is, Wendell doubts that we will cease to occlude disability. She thinks fears of losing bodily control and suffering are too deeply embedded in our culture to be dislodged.

On the other hand, Alasdair MacIntyre (1999) casts the disabled as the quintessential moral insiders because rational consideration of their experience stimulates both personal and social virtue. Acknowledgement of disability plays an important role in answering the question 'Why be moral?', MacIntyre argues. The pervasiveness of human disability is a compelling reason for virtuous social conduct. Disability makes dependence an ineluctable element of human existence, and the disabled should not be relegated to the social fringe because their state is a condition we all have the potential to share.

For MacIntyre, the occlusion of disability of which Wendell complains is indicative of an irrationally driven, scarcely virtuous culture. Personal and social virtues of acknowledged dependence facilitate our flourishing as dependent animals, he thinks. Further, laws that protect the disabled will prove hollow in societies where the virtues of acknowledged dependence are not cultivated (MacIntyre 2000). In societies where this is not so, even generally benevolent people

will tend to see the cause of the disabled as something competing with other causes . . . They will not take the possibility of . . . a career as a provider of care for the disabled as having any great claim upon them and they will not understand the importance of . . . enhancing the status . . . enjoyed by those who give their lives to such caregiving. Moreover, they will not recognize what important indicators these are of the moral well-being . . . of their society. (MacIntyre, 2000: 85)

This suggests that there may be an inverse ratio between a society's virtue and the need for its disabled citizens to invoke disability rights.

Virtue theory competes with welfare theory, but complements inclusion. Inclusion theory urges reshaping communal practice to achieve more expansive goods. It can promote practices of caring for individuals at times and in aspects where their social participation is naturally unachievable rather than socially barred. In contrast, both inclusion theory and virtue theory lie uneasily with welfare theory. For inclusion theory, welfare theory's emphasis on establishing eligibility for justice is exclusionary. For virtue theory, welfare theory makes the care that should be freely and compassionately given by individuals into a public obligation discharged by an impersonal system.

3. CONCLUSION

Prior to calling attention to the urgency of recognizing disabled people's right to be in the world, Jacobus tenBroek studied and wrote about the reasons Americans of African descent should not be collectively enslaved, Americans of Japanese descent should not be collectively imprisoned, and women should not be collectively prohibited by statute from rewarding kinds of employment (Tussman and tenBroek 1949). It is no accident, then, to find him gripped by the similarities between such constraints upon the liberties of other minorities and disabled people's deprivation of social access. Nor is his supposition that all such wrongs are susceptible to similar remedies surprising. Whether his assumption in this regard is accurate remains an unresolved issue for both public policy and practical ethics.

TenBroek's proposal emerged in a climate in which a tradition of casting welfare, rather than liberatory, values as the basis of disability rights prevailed. An even older tradition, in which virtue rather than duty properly motivates interactions with disabled people, also retained influence. In such tangled circumstances, which persist, shapers of disability policy are inclined to elide competing theories of moral value and to conflate very different domains of ethical appeal.

One challenge for practical ethics, then, is to clarify the implications not only of various construals of disability rights, but also of theories on which the pursuit of certain goods, or the cultivation of certain virtues, eclipses proposals to address the social exclusion of disabled people through recognition of their rights. Equally important is the challenge of elevating both private and public efforts to address the disability problem by introducing into these exceedingly emotional and politicized debates the higher standards of lucidity, coherence, and sensitivity to nuances, associated with serious endeavours of practical ethics.

REFERENCES

Americans with Disabilities Act (ADA) (1990). Public Law 101–336 26 July, 1990 104 Stat. 327st Cong., 101st sess.

Amundson, Ron (2000a). 'Against Normal Function'. *Studies in History and Philosophy of Biological and Biomedical Sciences*, 31: 33–53.

——(2000b). 'Biological Normality and the ADA', in Leslie Francis and Anita Silvers (eds.), *Americans with Disabilities: Implications of the Law for Individuals and Institutions*. New York: Routledge, 102–110.

Anderson, Elizabeth (1999). 'What is the Point of Equality?' *Ethics*, 109: 287–337.

Arneson, Richard (2000). 'Disability, Priority and Social Justice', in Leslie Francis and Anita Silvers (eds.), *Americans with Disabilities: Implications of the Law for Individuals and Institutions*. New York: Routledge, 18–33.

Baughn, Bill, Degener, Theresia, and Wolbring, Gregor (2000). E-mails, 11 Jan. 2000, 12 Jan. 2000, 18 Jan. 2000. On file with the author.

Baynton, Douglas (1996). *Forbidden Signs: American Culture and the Campaign Against Sign Language*. Chicago: University of Chicago Press.

Becker, Lawrence (2000). 'The Good of Agency', in Leslie Francis and Anita Silvers (eds.), *Americans with Disabilities: Implications of the Law for Individuals and Institutions*. New York: Routledge, 54–63.

Bickenbach, Jerome (1993). *Physical Disability and Social Policy*. Toronto: University of Toronto Press.

——(2000). 'The ADA v. the Canadian Charter of Rights: Disability Rights and the Social Model of Disability', in Leslie Francis and Anita Silvers (eds.), *Americans with Disabilities: Implications of the Law for Individuals and Institutions*. New York: Routledge, 342–56.

Brock, Dan (1994). 'The Human Genome Project and Human Identity', in Robert Weir, Susan Lawrence, and Evan Fales (eds.), *Genes and Human Self-Knowledge: Historical and Philosophical Reflections on Modern Genetics*. Ames, IO: University of Iowa Press, 18–33.

——(1995). 'Justice and the ADA: Does Prioritizing and Rationing Health Care Discriminate against the Disabled?' *Social Philosophy and Policy*, 12: 159–85.

——(2000). 'Health Care, Resource Prioritization and Discrimination against Persons with Disabilities', in Leslie Francis and Anita Silvers (eds.), *Americans with Disabilities: Implications of the Law for Individuals and Institutions*. New York: Routledge, 223–35.

Buchanan, Allen (1995). 'Equal Opportunity and Genetic Intervention'. *Social Philosophy and Policy*, 12: 105–35.

——(1996). 'Choosing who will be Disabled: Genetic Intervention and the Morality of Inclusion'. *Social Philosophy and Policy* 13: 30–64.

Burgdorf, Robert L. (1991). 'The Americans with Disabilities Act: Analysis and Implications of a Second-Generation Civil Rights Statute'. *Harvard Civil Rights–Civil Liberties Law Review*, 418–19.

Carlson, Angela Licia (1998). 'Mindful Subjects: Classification and Cognitive Disability'. A dissertation submitted in partial fulfilment of the requirements for the doctorate in philosophy, University of Toronto.

Corker, Mairian (2000). 'The UK Disability Discrimination Act: Disabling Language, Justifying Inequitable Social Participation', in Leslie Francis and Anita Silvers (eds.), *Americans with Disabilities: Implications of the Law for Individuals and Institutions*. New York: Routledge, 357–77.

Daniels, Norman (1987). 'Justice and Health Care', Donald Van DeVeer and Tom Regan (eds.), in *Health Care Ethics: An Introduction*. Philadelphia: Temple University Press, 290–325.

Davis, Dena (1997). 'Genetic Dilemmas and the Child's Right to an Open Future'. *Hastings Center Report*, 27: 7–14.

Dworkin, Ronald (1994). 'Will Clinton's Plan Be Fair?' *New York Review of Books*. 13 Jan., 20–25.

Francis, Leslie, and Silvers, Anita (2000) (eds.), *Americans with Disabilities: Exploring Implications of the Law for Individuals and Institutions*. New York: Routledge.

Fuhrer, Marcus (2000). 'Subjectifying Quality of Life as a Medical Rehabilitation Outcome'. *Disability and Rehabilitation*, 22: 481–9.

Funk, Robert (1987). 'Disability Rights: From Caste to Class in the Context of Civil Rights', in A. Gartner and T. Joe (eds.), *Images of the Disabled, Disabling Images*. New York: Praeger, 7–30.

Gewirth, Alan (1992). 'Rights', in L. Becker and C. Becker (eds.), *The Encyclopedia of Ethics*. New York: Garland, 1103–9.

Hahn, Harlan (2000). 'Disputing the Doctrine of Benign Neglect: A Challenge to the Disparate Treatment of Americans with Disabilities', in Leslie Francis and Anita Silvers (eds.), *Americans with Disabilities: Implications of the Law for Individuals and Institutions*. New York: Routledge, 269–74.

Hull, Richard (1998). 'Defining Disability—A Philosophical Approach'. *Res Publica*, 4: 199–210.

Illingworth, Patricia, and Parmet, Wendy (2000). 'Positively Disabled: The Relationship between the Definition of Disability and Rights under the ADA', in Leslie Francis and Anita Silvers (eds.), *Americans with Disabilities: Implications of the Law for Individuals and Institutions*. New York: Routledge, 3–17.

Jones, Melinda, and Marks, Lee Ann (2000). 'A Bright New Era of Equality, Independence, and Freedom—Casting an Australian Gaze on the ADA', in Leslie Francis and Anita Silvers (eds.), *Americans with Disabilities: Implications of the Law for Individuals and Institutions*. New York: Routledge, 371–86.

Kass, Leon (1973). 'Ethical Implications of Pre-Natal Diagnosis for the Human Right to Life', in B. Hilton, D. Callahan, M. Harris, P. Condliffe, and B. Berkeley (eds.), *Ethical Issues in Human Genetics*. New York: Plenum Press, 185–99.

Kevles, Daniel (1998). 'Grounds for Breeding: The Amazing Persistence of Eugenics in Europe and North America'. *Times Literary Supplement*, 4944: 3–4.

Kittay, Eva Feder (1998). *Love's Labor: Essays on Women, Equality, and Dependency*. New York: Routledge.

——(2000). 'At Home with My Daughter: Reflections on *Olmstead* v. *L.C.*', in Leslie Francis and Anita Silvers (eds.), *Americans with Disabilities: Implications of the Law for Individuals and Institutions*. New York: Routledge, 64–80.

MacIntyre, Alasdair (1999). *Dependent Rational Animals: Why Human Beings Need the Virtues*. Chicago: Open Court.

——(2000). 'The Need for a Standard of Care', in Leslie Francis and Anita Silvers (eds.), *Americans with Disabilities: Implications of the Law for Individuals and Institutions*. New York: Routledge, 81–6.

Magee, Bryan, and Milligan, Martin (1995). *On Blindness*. Oxford: Oxford University Press.

Milani, Adam (1999). 'Living in the World: A New Look at the Disabled in the Law of Torts'. *Catholic University Law Review*, 48: 328–40.

Murray, Christopher, and Lopez, Allan (1996). *The Global Burden of Disease*. Cambridge, MA: Harvard School of Health.

Rosenberg, Alexander (1986). 'The Political Philosophy of Biological Endowments'. *Social Philosophy and Policy*, 5: 2–31.

Sen, Amartya K. (1982). *Choice, Welfare, and Measurement*. Oxford: Blackwell.

——(1992). *Inequality Reexamined*. Cambridge, MA: Harvard University Press.

——(1993). 'Capability and Well-Being', in Martha Nussbaum and Amartya K. Sen (eds.), *Quality of Life*. Oxford: Oxford University Press, 30–53.

Silvers, Anita (1995). 'Reconciling Equality to Difference: Caring (f)or Justice for People with Disabilities'. *Hypatia*, 10: 30–55.

——(1997). 'Disability Rights', in Ruth Chadwick (ed.), *The Encyclopedia of Applied Ethics*. San Diego: Academic Press, i. 781–96.

——(1998). 'On Not Iterating Women's Disabilities: A Crossover Perspective on Genetic Dilemmas', in Anne Donchin and Laura Purdy (eds.), *Embodying Bioethics: Feminist Advances*. Lanham, MD: Rowman & Littlefield, 177–202.

——(2000). 'The Unprotected: Constructing Disability in the Context of Anti-Discrimination Law', in Leslie Francis and Anita Silvers (eds.), *Americans with Disabilities: Implications of the Law for Individuals and Institutions*. New York: Routledge, 126–45.

——(2002). 'Bedside Justice: Personalizing Justice, Preserving Impartiality', in Rosamond Rhodes, Margaret Battin, and Anita Silvers (eds.), *Medicine and Social Justice: Essays on the Distribution of Health Care*. Oxford: Oxford University Press.

——Wasserman, David, and Mahowald, Mary (1998). *Disability, Difference, Discrimination: Perspectives on Justice in Bioethics and Public Policy*. Lanham, MD: Rowman & Littlefield.

Sober, Eliot (1980). 'Evolution, Population Thinking, and Essentialism'. *Philosophy of Science*, 47: 350–83.

Stiker, Henri-Jacques (1982). *Corps infirmes et sociétés*. Paris: Aubier Montage.

TenBroek, Jacobus (1966). 'The Right to Live in the World: The Disabled in the Law of Torts'. *California Law Review*, 54: 841–919.

Trent, James (1994). *Inventing the Feeble Mind: A History of Mental Retardation in the United States*. Berkeley and Los Angeles: University of California Press.

Tussman, Joseph, and tenBroek, Jacobus (1949). 'The Equal Protection of the Laws'. *California Law Review*, 37: 344–53.

Wendell, Susan (1996). *The Rejected Body: Feminist Philosophical Reflections on Disability*. New York: Routledge.

Wolff, Jonathan (2000). 'Disability in a Society of Equals'. Unpublished typescript. University College, London.

Young, Iris Marion (1990). *Justice and the Politics of Difference*. Princeton: Princeton University Press.

—— (1997). 'Asymmetrical Reciprocity: On Moral Respect, Wonder, and Enlarged Thought'. *Constellations*, 3: 340–63.

—— (2000). 'Disability and the Definition of Work', in Leslie Francis and Anita Silvers (eds.), *Americans with Disabilities: Implications of the Law for Individuals and Institutions*. New York: Routledge, 169–73.

Cases Cited

Albertson's Inc. v. *Kirkingburg*, 527 US 555 (1999).

Bragdon v. *Abbot*, 524 US 621 (1998).

Buck v. *Bell*, 274 US 200 (1927).

Cleveland v. *Policy Management Systems*, 526 US 795 (1998).

Murphy v. *United Parcel Service, Inc.*, 527 US 516 (1999).

Olmstead v. *LC*, 527 US 581 (1999).

Southeastern Community College v. *Davis*, 442 US 397 (1979).

Sutton v. *United Airlines, Inc.*, 527 US 471 (1999).

PART IV

THE JUST
SOCIETY

CHAPTER 13

....

PUNISHMENT

....

R. A. DUFF

1. INTRODUCTION

....

THE central question for this chapter is: 'What can justify a system of criminal punishment?' That question is familiar, but merits clarification.

1.1 What is to be Justified?

The chapter focuses on *criminal punishment* imposed by criminal courts for criminal offences. So narrow a focus, though typical of penal philosophy, requires justification.

First, it ignores other kinds of punishment, formal and informal, imposed by other agencies: by institutions or professions, in the family. What justifies this focus is that *criminal* punishment is distinctive in involving the state's exercise of its dominant coercive power over its citizens, and thus raises the distinctive question of what penal powers (if any) the state should have, and how they should be exercised. In what follows, 'punishment' will mean 'criminal punishment'.

Secondly, it ignores other aspects of criminal justice, and the complex processes from which punishment flows—the investigation of crime, the criminal procedure of trial and conviction. A theory of punishment must ultimately be part of an account of the whole apparatus of criminal justice (see Braithwaite and Pettit 1990). But there is room for a narrower enquiry into punishment, as a distinctive aspect of that apparatus. Punishment is the imposition of something intended to be burdensome or painful on a supposed offender for a supposed crime, by a body claiming the authority to do so (see Hart 1968: 4–6; Scheid 1980). How can such a practice be justified?

Thirdly, it focuses on responsible adult offenders, and ignores the problems presented by juvenile and by mentally disordered offenders (on which see Newburn 1997; Peay 1997).

1.2 Theory and Practice

Our question concerns the justification of a particular, pervasive human practice. We must be clear, however, about the relationship between the kind of normative theory that an answer to our question will provide, and those actual human practices.

First, normative theory is *critical*. It offers us, not a comforting rationalization of the status quo (see Murphy 1973), but a critical standard, an ideal account of what punishment *ought* to be, by which we can evaluate existing penal practices. We cannot assume that the actualities will be close to that ideal—that a plausible normative theory will justify our existing penal practices; we must recognize that a justified penal system might be very different from our own.

Secondly, however, even that way of putting the point 'begs the institution' (Mackenzie 1981: 41), by assuming that some practice of punishment must be justifiable—the task for normative theory then being to establish that justification. That tempting assumption must be resisted. Our question is not how, but *whether*, punishment can be justified, and we must face the abolitionist argument that no such practice can be justified: that we should abolish, rather than reform, the practice of punishment. (See e.g. Christie 1977, 1981; Hulsman 1986, 1991; de Haan 1990; Bianchi 1994. For discussion, see Duff 1996: 67–87.) The abolitionist challenge can in principle be met—but it must be met rather than ignored.

1.3 What Kind of Justification?

If we take ourselves to be seeking '*the* justification of punishment', we might think that we need a *unitary* justificatory theory, which will posit a coherent set of goals and values by which a penal system could be unequivocally structured. It could be plausibly argued, however, that any unitary theory will be inadequate to the complexities of punishment (see Garland 1990: 9–10; Gardner 1998: 31–3). First, why should we expect any single theory to cover all the different punishments that might be appropriate for different crimes? Secondly, it is a liberal commonplace that political life is a site of fundamentally *conflicting* values, between which we might make uncomfortable compromises, but which we cannot tidily reconcile (Nagel 1979): we should not be surprised to find such conflicts in the realm of punishment (see Hart 1968), and should mistrust any account that claims to dissolve them in a unitary 'theory of punishment'.

Nonetheless, this chapter will be structured by a search for a unitary theory of punishment. We can best progress towards an adequate normative understanding of punishment by examining competing unitary *visions* of what it ought to be, even if we must ultimately accept that a pluralistic, conflictual theory is the only plausible answer.

1.4 Punishment and Crime

Punishment presupposes crime, as that for which punishment is to be imposed. A normative account of punishment thus depends on a normative account of crime and the criminal law: what kinds of conduct should be defined as *criminal* wrongs, rather than as private matters that do not concern the law, or as *civil* wrongs for which the injured party might seek damages through the civil courts, but which are not subject to punishment? I can comment only very briefly on this issue here (see Murphy and Coleman 1984: ch. 3; *Boston University Law Review* (1996); Marshall and Duff 1998; Duff 2000: ch. 2.4).

First, the abolitionists' critique of punishment involves a critique of the concept of crime: we should, they argue, think not of 'crimes' that demand punishment, but of 'conflicts' that must be resolved by those involved in them (Christie 1977; Hulsman 1986). This argument is misguided: sometimes we should recognize, not that two people are in conflict, but that one has *wronged* the other. But it challenges us to articulate a suitable concept of crime.

Secondly, crimes are at least socially proscribed wrongdoings: breaches of authoritative social norms. But not all such wrongdoing concerns the law, and some that does concern the law counts as civil rather than criminal wrongdoing. If we ask which kinds of wrongdoing should count as *criminal*, we might say that crimes are 'public' wrongs. But what makes a wrong 'public'? One answer is that a 'public' wrong injures the community as a whole—for instance, by causing 'social volatility' (see Becker 1974), or by taking unfair advantage over all the law-abiding (see Murphy 1973); but that denigrates the wrongs done to individual victims; we should punish murderers or rapists for what they do to their victims. Another answer is that 'public' wrongs are wrongs that properly concern the whole political community, because they flout values that are essential to the community's identity: they are wrongs in which the whole community should share, counting the victim's wrong as 'ours'. We must then ask which wrongs are of this kind, and cannot expect any simple, uncontroversial answer; we should note here only that a complete normative theory of punishment depends on an answer.

1.5 Penal Theory and Political Philosophy

A further matter with which this chapter cannot deal concerns the relationship between penal and political theory. A normative theory of punishment justifies a state in maintaining a system of criminal law and punishment: it thus depends on some account of the proper functions of the state; and different kinds of political theory might generate different accounts of the proper aims of state punishment (see Philips 1986; Lacey 1988; cf. M. Davis 1989).

In particular, we might expect communitarian and liberal theorists to offer different accounts of punishment: liberals might ask what kind of penal system—if any—rational social contractors would agree to create, and would want strictly to limit the scope and aims of the penal system, to protect citizens against the state's intrusive power; communitarians would ask how punishment can serve the interests of the community, and be willing to intrude into individuals' lives for the sake of a common good in which those individuals necessarily share. Given the vagueness of the labels 'liberal' and 'communitarian', and the possibility of liberal forms of communitarianism that give a central place to versions of such liberal values as autonomy (see Duff 2000: ch. 2), we should not exaggerate the necessary differences between 'liberal' and 'communitarian' penal theories; but there will predictably be some such differences (see further Section 4. 3 below).

2. CONSEQUENTIALISM AND PUNISHMENT

For some time in the mid-twentieth century, consequentialism appeared to be the orthodoxy in penal theory; and it still seems obvious to many that an institution such as punishment can be justified only by showing that it brings about consequential goods that outweigh the harms it undoubtedly causes. There are, however, serious objections to consequentialist penal theories. (For simple examples of consequentialist accounts, see Wilson 1983; Walker 1991; Bagaric and Amarasekara 2000.)

2.1 Consequentialism

Consequentialists hold that a practice is justified if and only if its consequences are at least as good as those of any available alternative. To justify a system of punishment it must therefore be shown not only that it brings some benefits; nor just that those benefits outweigh its costs, but that no other available practice would bring as great (or greater) benefit at lower (or no higher) cost.

A thorough consequentialist theory of punishment would thus need to begin with an account of the intrinsic good(s) and evil(s) in which 'benefits' and 'costs' ultimately consist; identify and aggregate the predictable benefits and costs of different possible systems of punishment; weigh them against each other; do the same for other practices that might produce the same kinds of benefit; and so calculate which practice is likely to be the most efficient means of securing those benefits. This task would clearly require some large, complex empirical calculations, whose very possibility is doubtful; but we can for the present accept the common-sense view that the obvious benefit of a system of punishment lies in the reduction of crime, and ask whether such a system might be a cost-effective means to that good. (We need not suppose that the reduction of crime is an *intrinsic* good: only that a justified system of law will criminalize conduct that is harmful, whose prevention is therefore beneficial.)

Punishment can prevent crime by incapacitating, reforming, or deterring potential offenders. It is a contingent question whether punishment can be, in any of these ways, an efficient method of crime prevention; and some objections both to consequentialist theories of punishment, and to supposedly consequentialist penal practices (such as the 'rehabilitative' approach in California in the mid-twentieth century), are based on the claim that punishment, or this penal practice, is not an efficient method of preventing crime. A deeper objection is that consequentialist theorists too often beg the institution: they assume without adequate argument that no other crime-preventive practice that could replace punishment would be a more efficient method of preventing crime.

This objection bears most obviously on consequentialist accounts that emphasize reform or incapacitation as the means by which punishment prevents crime: for, if the aim is so to reform potential offenders that they will willingly refrain from crime, or to make it impossible for them to commit crimes by incapacitating them, why should we pursue these aims through a system of *punishment*, whose measures are imposed only on those who have already committed crimes? Why not prefer a system that imposes its measures on *anyone* who is reasonably judged likely to commit crimes if left free, whether or not he or she has already done so (see Duff 1986: 102–6, 164–9; cf. Wootton 1963)?

By contrast, deterrence as a means of crime prevention does require something like a system of punishment: the law deters potential criminals by threatening harm against those who break it, and by being seen to impose such harm on those who are not deterred—by being seen to punish them. Furthermore, whilst it is very hard to establish how effective (let alone how efficient) any deterrent system actually is (Beyleveld 1979; von Hirsch et al. 1999), it is plausible that punishment can efficiently deter some offenders (see Walker 1991: 13–20).

I will not pursue the issue of whether punishment can be a cost-effective method of crime prevention further here: my concern is, rather, with moral objections to consequentialist penal theories. So let us assume that punishment can be consequentially efficient, and ask whether this suffices to render it morally justified.

2.2 Pure Consequentialism and the Rights of the Innocent

A *purely* consequentialist penal theory holds that *only* the consequences are relevant to the justification of a system of punishment. The familiar objection to any such theory is that it would justify immoral—because unjust—kinds of punishment (the punishment of innocent scapegoats, the excessively harsh punishment of the guilty), if they would serve the system's aims. Just as it is a contingent question whether punishment is an efficient means to those aims, so it is a contingent question whether unjust punishments could sometimes efficiently serve them: but, the critic argues, an unjust punishment is unjustified whether or not it is consequentially beneficial (see e.g. Ten 1987; Primoratz 1999: chs. 2–3).

Pure consequentialists respond to this criticism in various ways. Some try to 'outsmart' it, arguing that we *should* punish the innocent if—in an extreme situation—it would be useful to do so (see Smart 1973: 69–72; Dennett 1987, s.v. 'outsmart'; Bagaric and Amarasekara 2000: 17–20). This will not impress critics, who will still insist that the deliberate punishment of an innocent is a serious injustice; and that, even if we felt impelled in a tragic situation to punish an innocent, that injustice would constitute a moral cost that consequentialists cannot recognize (see Hart 1968: 12).

Others argue that, even if their accounts could *in principle* justify such intuitively immoral kinds of punishment, *in practice* they would never do so. In our actual world it is extremely unlikely that the deliberate punishment of an innocent would be consequentially useful, and that penal officials could be trusted reliably to identify just those cases in which it would be useful: given also the harm that would ensue if it became known that innocents had been deliberately punished, we will in the long run do best if we train ourselves and our penal officials to think and act as if it was intrinsically and always wrong to punish an innocent. (For such arguments, which appeal to a 'two-level' type of consequentialism, see Rawls 1955; Sprigge 1968; Hare 1981: ch. 3 and sect. 9.7; in response, see Duff 1986: 162–4; Ten 1987: 17–32; Primoratz 1999: sects. 3.3, 6.5.) One problem for such arguments is that they depend on large empirical claims for which it is hard to find any secure foundation. Another problem is that they still make the protection of the innocent contingent on the effects of punishing them (especially on the effects if it became widely known that innocents might be deliberately punished); but, critics will reply, the wrong of punishing an innocent is an *intrinsic* injustice, whose wrongfulness does not depend on its being found out.

Other consequentialists argue that a richer account of the ends that punishment should serve, of the goods that underpin the consequentialist calculus, will ground suitable protections for the innocent. Thus Braithwaite and Pettit (1990) posit a 'republican' idea of 'dominion', the assured and equal freedom of citizens living under the law, as the good that a consequentialist system of justice should serve; they argue that this end generates a secure ground for rights, including the innocent's right not to be punished, that are problematic for other forms of consequentialism (Braithwaite and Pettit 1990: 71–6; von Hirsch and Ashworth 1992;

Duff 1996: 20–5; Pettit 1997; see also Lacey 1988, on autonomy and welfare as the goods that punishment should serve; on which see Duff 1996: 18–20). The trouble with this argument is that we cannot rule out a priori the possibility that dominion, like any other consequentialist justifying aim of punishment, might sometimes be efficiently maximized by unjust punishments. The protection of the innocent is still contingent on the effects of punishing them, or being willing to punish them. But, critics argue, their deliberate punishment is an intrinsic wrong, against which citizens should be protected by a non-contingent right not to be punished unless they are proved to be guilty.

Critics will thus insist that no purely consequentialist theory is acceptable, simply in virtue of being consequentialist: the right of the innocent not to be deliberately punished is a fundamental demand of justice whose force is independent of the consequences of flouting it. This claim will not impress committed pure consequentialists: but those who find persuasive *both* the thought that a practice such as punishment can be justified only by doing some consequential good, *and* the objection that purely consequentialist accounts fail to do justice to the rights of the innocent, still have a way out; for they can replace a pure consequentialist account by a 'side-constrained' consequentialist account.

2.3 Side-Constrained Consequentialism and the Moral Standing of the Guilty

The familiar objection to purely consequentialist penal theories is that they cannot recognize the *intrinsic* injustice of some possible methods of pursuing the end of crime prevention—that is, they wrongly think that the end always justifies the means. The side-constrained consequentialist accepts the justice of this objection, and argues that, whilst a system of punishment must find its positive justification in its efficiency as a method of crime prevention, it must also be bound by certain non-consequentialist side constraints on the means by which it pursues that end (on 'side constraints', see Braithwaite and Pettit 1990: 26–36; Scheid 1997: 448–51).

The best-known such account is Hart's (1968). The prevention of crime provides, he argues, the consequentialist 'general justifying aim' of punishment, but our pursuit of that aim is subject to non-consequentialist constraints that forbid the deliberate punishment of the innocent, and the excessively harsh punishment of the guilty (see Lacey 1988: 46–56; Morison 1988; Primoratz 1999: sect. 6.6; Scheid 1997 offers a sophisticated Hartian account). We must then ask what can justify these side constraints. One possibility is a form of 'negative retributivism', which tells us that we must not punish the innocent (because only the guilty deserve punishment), or punish the guilty more harshly than they deserve (on 'negative' versus 'positive' retributivism, see Dolinko 1991: 539–43). Hart aims to avoid such an appeal (and thus avoid the problem of making sense of retributivism; see Section 3.1 below) by grounding the prohibition on deliberately punishing the innocent in the need to protect individual freedom (Hart 1968: 23–4, 44–8; see Walker 1991: ch. 11).

Such an account certainly avoids the familiar objection to purely consequential-ist theories, since the innocent are now securely protected against deliberate injust-ice; but it faces another objection (one that also applies to purely consequentialist theories)—that it fails to do justice *to the guilty*.

This objection is sometimes expressed in Kantian terms: a side-constrained con-sequentialist system of punishment treats those who are punished 'merely as means' to the further end (crime prevention) for whose sake they are punished (see Murphy 1973: 218). Consequentialists might reply that, so long as they are punished only if they have voluntarily broken the law, they are not treated *merely* as means—whereas an innocent who is punished as a scapegoat is treated merely as a means (see Walker 1980: 80–5); but it can still be argued that consequentialist punishment does not do justice to the guilty.

The objection has most obvious force against purely reformative theories that would allow offenders to be subjected to whatever treatment was necessary to 'cure' them; and incapacitative theories that would sanction detaining or otherwise inca-pacitating offenders simply to prevent the crimes that it is predicted they would otherwise commit. As the critic argues, we owe it to each other to respect and treat each other as rational, responsible agents (this is the modern form of the Kantian demand that we treat each other as 'ends'); and we owe such respect to the guilty as well as to the innocent. Such reformative or incapacitative practices, however, treat those who are subjected to them not as rational, responsible agents, but as *objects* whose attitudes or future behaviour we aim to modify by whatever means might be efficient. For punishment to satisfy the Kantian demand, it must be something we can justify to those whom we punish as an appropriate response to their crimes; and it must leave them free to determine their own future attitudes and conduct. Purely reformative and incapacitative punishments, however, focus not on what those punished have done, but on what they might do in the future if not 'reformed' or incapacitated; and, far from leaving them to determine their own future attitudes and conduct, such punishments seek to manipulate or coerce them into conform-ity (see Lewis 1953; H. Morris 1968; von Hirsch and Ashworth 1998: chs. 1, 3).

This is not yet to argue that neither reform nor incapacitation should play *any* part in a penal system: we will attend later (Section 4.3) to an account that gives punishment a reformative aim; and it is at least problematic whether we could justifiably subject persistent 'dangerous' offenders to preventive imprisonment (see Duff 1998). It is to argue, however, that consequentialist theories that allow us to treat the guilty in whatever ways will efficiently reduce crime fail to give the guilty the respect that is their due.

Some who are impressed by the Kantian demand as a demand on our general dealings with each other, and on the state's dealings with its citizens, might think that it loses force in relation to criminals. As they argue, by breaking the law offenders forfeit their normal rights, or moral standing, as citizens: they may, therefore, be treated in ways that would normally be illegitimate, in order to prevent future crimes—and perhaps to restore them to law-abiding citizenship (see Goldman 1982; C. W. Morris 1991; on which see Duff 2000: sect. 1.3.1). This view might appeal to those who take a contractualist view of political relations—though they must specify just what rights are forfeited by what kinds of crime, and what protections criminals should still have. The critic will argue, however, that we should not be so quick to deny others the rights of responsible, autonomous agency: punishment can be justified only if it can be shown to be consistent with the respect that is owed to criminal as well as non-criminal citizens.

A version of the Kantian objection also applies to a system of deterrent punishment. Such a system treats those whom it threatens with punishment as rational agents: it offers them reason (the prudential reason provided by the prospect of punishment) to refrain from crime. But it does not address them as *moral* agents who should be moved by the moral reasons for refraining from crime on which the criminal law itself depends. It addresses them only as self-interested beings, in the language of coercive threats. To justify punishment thus as a deterrent is 'to liken it to the act of a man who lifts his stick to a dog. It is to treat a man like a dog instead of with the freedom and respect due to him as a man'. (Hegel 1821/1942: 246; see also Duff 1986: 178–86; 2000: sects. 3.1.2, 3.3.1; von Hirsch 1993: 9–14; in response see Baker 1992a). This objection concerns the moral standing not only of those who are punished, but of all who are threatened with punishment—all whose obedience is sought by such threats. A state that uses punishment as a deterrent, it argues, fails to show its citizens the respect that is due to them.

One response to this objection is to argue that we can show punishment to be consistent with the respect that is due to our fellow citizens by portraying it as analogous to self-defence. We are self-defensively justified not merely in using force to ward off an unlawful assailant, but also in threatening force to deter a potential assailant (see Alexander 1980; Quinn 1985; Farrell 1985, 1995; Montague 1995; for criticism, see Duff 2000: sect. 1.3.2.) I cannot discuss this argument in detail; but, whilst the use of force as a defensive response to an unlawful attack is consistent with a due respect for the attacker as a responsible agent, to use the *threat* of retaliatory force to deter potential attacks is open to the Hegelian objection—it treats those whom we threaten 'like dogs' rather than as responsible moral agents (although we must distinguish legitimate warnings that one would use defensive force from illegitimate threats to use retaliatory force).

I have not refuted either pure or side-constrained consequentialist theories of punishment. I have, rather, sketched the general features of these two kinds of consequentialist theory, the main objections to them, and some responses to those objections. We must now turn to retributivism.

3. Retributivism and Penal Desert

Consequentialists justify punishment as an instrumentally efficient means to some *future* benefit. Retributivists justify it as an intrinsically appropriate (because deserved) response to *past* crimes: their central slogan is that the guilty 'deserve to suffer'.

3.1 'Positive' Retributivism and the Meaning of Penal Desert

For 'negative' retributivists (see section 2.3 above) desert sets side constraints on our pursuit of the consequentialist aim of punishment: it tells us that we may *not* punish the innocent (or punish the guilty more than they deserve), but not that we *should* punish the guilty. By contrast, positive retributivism holds that we *should* punish the guilty, because they deserve it: their guilt makes it not merely *permissible* to punish them, but positively desirable or even obligatory.

For a significant part of the twentieth century, positive retributivism was taken to be defunct. Perhaps negative retributivism had a role in penal theory, as a defence against the moral excesses of pure consequentialism: but positive retributivism was merely a relic of an earlier, uncivilized age—a matter of crude retaliation that had no place in a civilized polity. A striking feature of the last decades of the twentieth century, however, was the revival of positive retributivism, which finds the positive justification of punishment primarily in its intrinsic character as a deserved response to criminal wrongdoing. (For early contributions, see H. Morris 1968; Murphy 1973; N. Morris 1974; von Hirsch 1976. For discussion, see Galligan 1981; Hudson 1987.)

The central task facing retributivists is to explain this notion of desert. It is meant to explain the justificatory relationship between crime and punishment in virtue of which punishment is an intrinsically appropriate response to crime: but what is that relationship? What is it about crime that calls for punishment, or about punishment that makes it an appropriate response to crime (see Ardal 1984; Honderich 1984: ch. 2)? The intuition that 'the guilty deserve to suffer' might be widely shared (see L. H. Davis 1972), but what does it mean—*what* do they deserve to suffer? Why should we believe it—*why* do they deserve to suffer? And why should it be the state's responsibility to make them suffer (see Murphy 1985; Husak 1992; Shafer-Landau 1996)?

Different versions of retributivism (see Cottingham 1979) offer different answers to these questions. I will comment briefly on two recent attempts, before turning to a third approach.

3.2 Removing Unfair Advantages

Suppose we see a system of law as bringing benefits (security, protected freedom) to all its citizens, by imposing on them all the burden of self-restraint involved in obeying the law. One who breaks the law then takes an unfair advantage for herself over all those who obey it: she accepts the benefits that flow from the law-abiding self-restraint of others, but refuses to accept the burden of obeying the law herself; she takes the benefits that the law brings, but refuses to bear her fair share of the burdens on which those goods depend. She now deserves, in justice, to lose that unfair advantage, and punishment deprives her of it: by imposing an extra burden on her, it restores that fair balance of benefits and burdens that her crime disturbed. (see H. Morris 1968; Murphy 1973; von Hirsch 1976; Sher 1987: ch. 5; Adler 1992: chs. 5–8; Dagger 1993).

This account has been convincingly criticized (e.g. Burgh 1982; Murphy 1985; Duff 1986: ch. 8; Falls 1987; Dolinko 1991; Anderson 1997). Apart from problems internal to it (does every crime involve the relevant kind of 'advantage'; how could we judge the seriousness of different crimes?), a central objection is that it distorts the character of crime as deserving of punishment. On this account, the rapist is punished for the unfair advantage he took over all the law-abiding who restrained themselves from crime, but the wrongfulness of his action, in virtue of which it deserves punishment, surely lies in what he did to his victim.

However, the account is interesting, as exemplifying one way in which the task facing any retributivist can be discharged. It offers an account of crime (as taking an unfair advantage over the law-abiding) and punishment (as a burden that negates that advantage) that explains how punishment is an appropriate response to crime: what the criminal deserves to suffer is the loss of her unfair advantage; she deserves this because a just distribution of benefits and burdens requires it; and the state should ensure that she suffers it because the state maintains the system of law that provides for that distribution. If we are to find a more plausible retributivist theory, we must find one that offers more plausible answers to these questions.

3.3 Punitive Emotions

An alternative approach grounds a justification of punishment in the emotions that (serious) crime typically arouses. Murphy argues that resentment and 'retributive hatred' are appropriate responses to some kinds of crime; that they involve a desire to make the wrongdoer suffer; and that punishment might then in principle be justified as a way of imposing that deserved suffering on them (Murphy and Hampton 1988: chs. 1, 3). Moore appeals to our responses not to the wrongs of others, but to our own wrongdoing—to the guilt that would lead us to judge that we ought to suffer punishment. Since virtuous emotions (of which justified guilt is one) are good heuristic guides to the truth of the moral judgements that they generate, we can conclude that those who commit such wrongs deserve to be punished (Moore 1997: ch. 4).

Such accounts also try to discharge the tasks that retributivists face. They explain what it is about crime that makes punishment an appropriate response: crime properly arouses emotions that punishment satisfies. This does not yet explain why it should be the state's responsibility to satisfy those emotions, but it at least tries to explain the supposed justificatory link between crime and punishment.

Both these accounts fail, for different reasons (on Murphy, see Murphy and Hampton 1988: ch. 2; Duff 1996: 29–31; Murphy 1999; on Moore, see Dolinko 1991: 555–9; Knowles 1993; Murphy 1999). One general point is that a range of emotions are indeed rational and appropriate responses to our own and others' wrongdoings (remorse at our own wrongdoings; resentment at wrongs done to us or those close to us; indignation at wrongs done to others). But, apart from the dangers involved in allowing such emotions to dominate us, this is not to say that we should also satisfy the desires for suffering that naturally flow from them. We need to know more about *why* they should motivate the infliction of suffering—on oneself in the case of guilt, on others in the case of resentment or indignation; about what that suffering means; and about whether the desire to inflict it is not one that we should resist, even if the emotions that generate the desire are justified (cf. Horder 1992: 194–7).

However, these accounts are suggestive. If, in trying to understand the intuition that 'the guilty deserve to suffer', we ask *what* it is they deserve to suffer, one answer will indeed refer to certain emotions. They deserve to suffer, we might say, the pangs of guilt—which are necessarily painful; or the angry condemnation of others, which expresses the emotions they appropriately feel at the wrongdoer's conduct, and which is also likely to be painful to the person condemned.

Such an answer must be explained; and we must ask how *punishment* can be an appropriate way of ensuring that wrongdoers suffer as they deserve. We can take this line of thought further by turning to a third type of retributivism that has become prominent in recent debates.

4. PUNISHMENT AND COMMUNICATION

Many theorists, both consequentialist and retributivist, have emphasized the communicative or expressive dimension of punishment. (See generally Feinberg 1970. For critical discussion, see Hart 1963: 60–9; Walker 1978; Skillen 1980; M. Davis 1991. Lacey 1988 and Braithwaite and Pettit 1990 offer consequentialist accounts of punishment as expressive.) I will focus here on the role that the idea of communication plays in recent retributivist theories.

4.1 Communicating Censure

A communicative account of punishment must tell us *what* is to be communicated, to *whom*, and *why* (see Skillen 1980). The standard answer to the 'what' question is that condemnation, or censure, is to be communicated; and to the 'to whom' question, that it is to be communicated to the offender—although, in thus communicating censure to him, we also communicate with his victim, and with the political community as a whole. As for *why* we should thus communicate, the simple answer is that the offender *deserves* censure; and this notion of desert seems readily intelligible. Wrongdoers surely deserve to be censured for their wrongdoing, by those who have the moral standing to comment on their conduct; and if crimes are 'public' wrongs (see Section 1.4 above) that concern the whole political community, that community has the standing, through the criminal law, to censure those who commit them. However, we can say more than this about why criminal wrongdoers should be publicly censured.

Someone who is committed to certain values is thereby committed to being ready to censure anyone who flouts those values. To stay silent in the face of flagrant wrongs against the values to which I claim to be committed casts doubt on my professed commitment. A polity's criminal law should embody that political community's public values; and the community's commitment to those values is expressed in part by its readiness to censure, through the criminal process of trial and punishment, those who flout them. We can also say that such censure of wrongdoers is owed to their victims, since to remain silent in the face of the wrongdoing is implicitly to condone the wrong done to the victim, rather than recognizing it as we should; and to wrongdoers themselves, since to censure them is to take them seriously as responsible moral agents, rather than ignoring them or treating them simply as harmful objects (see von Hirsch 1993: ch. 2).

We will see later that communicative punishment, which is initially justified in retributivist terms as an appropriate response to past wrongdoing, can also have forward-looking aims. First, however, we should note how a communicative account of punishment can discharge the tasks facing any retributivist account (see Section 3.1 above).

What makes punishment intrinsically appropriate as a response to crime, on communicative accounts, is that crimes are public wrongs that merit censure, and punishment communicates that censure. This explains the justificatory relationship between crime and punishment: censure is something suffered by, and normally painful to, those who are censured; the criminal deserves that kind of suffering, and punishment inflicts it. It also shows why it should be the responsibility of the state to punish criminals: as public wrongs, crimes should be authoritatively censured by the state, through the criminal process.

However, a communicative account now faces a difficult question. The authoritative censure that criminals deserve could be communicated to them in various ways.

It can be communicated through their conviction after a criminal trial: through the verdict of 'Guilty', through a judicial denunciation of their crime. It could be communicated through purely symbolic punishments, which are painful *only* in virtue of their condemnatory meaning. A pickpocket whose punishment was to have a sign saying 'I stole from my fellow citizens' stuck to his mirror would be pained by it only if he was pained by the condemnation it implied. The punishments typically imposed by our own penal systems, however, are not purely symbolic. They impose penal 'hard treatment' (see Feinberg 1970), in that they are painful or burdensome independently of their condemnatory meaning; imprisonment, fines, and other familiar punishments are burdensome even for one who is unmoved by, or unaware of, their condemnatory meaning as *punishments*. Such punishments *can* also communicate censure if they are imposed in the right context, against a background of shared understandings of their meaning. But why *should* we use this method of communication, instead of a system of formal denunciation or symbolic punishment (see Christie 1981: 98–105)?

4.2 Justifying Penal Hard Treatment

One answer to the question of why censure should be communicated through hard treatment is that only then will the communication be effective, or get through to offenders who might not listen to merely verbal censure or purely symbolic punishment (see Falls 1987; Primoratz 1989); but why is it so important to 'get through' to offenders?

One answer to that question is that we must get through to them in order to deter them. This offers a new way of mixing retributivism with consequentialism. A retributivist notion of desert now not only sets negative side constraints on our pursuit of the consequentialist aim of crime prevention (see Section 2.3 above), but provides part of the positive justification of punishment: we should punish offenders to censure them as they deserve. But that retributivist justification is not complete, since it does not justify using penal hard treatment to communicate censure. That aspect of punishment is justified in consequentialist terms, as an efficient method of deterring those who will not be dissuaded from crime by the mere prospect of censure (see Feinberg 1970; von Hirsch 1985: ch. 5).

Such an answer, however, still faces the Hegelian objection that it fails to respect the moral status of those who are threatened with punishment as responsible agents (see Section 2.3 above). The law does now initially address the citizens in appropriate moral terms. It declares certain kinds of conduct to be wrong, censurable, in the hope that citizens will refrain from such conduct for that appropriate reason. But, faced with the prospect that some will not be dissuaded from crime by such moral considerations, the law then abandons any attempt at moral discourse with them, and addresses them in the brute language of threats: it addresses them 'like dogs' (see further Duff 2000: ch. 3.3.1; but contrast Lipkin 1988; Baker 1992*a*).

Some might argue that this is the best that the state can do in the face of morally recalcitrant potential offenders who do not share or are insufficiently motivated by the values that the law embodies. The state owes its citizens protection against crime, and could provide no adequate protection by a system of law that depended only on moral appeals to the citizen (since such a system would be intolerably ineffective); and a system that combines censure and deterrence in this way does at least still address potential offenders as rational agents, by offering them what they will see as good reasons to obey the law. This argument is powerful, but might we find a justification of hard treatment punishment that completely avoids the Hegelian objection?

Von Hirsch offers a more sophisticated account of hard treatment punishment as serving a preventive purpose, which aims to avoid the Hegelian objection. We should see hard treatment not as a deterrent that *replaces* the moral voice of censure (since that provokes the Hegelian objection), but as a more modest 'prudential supplement' that adds to the law's moral appeal. Such a supplement is appropriate for morally imperfect beings like ourselves, who are not always sufficiently motivated by moral considerations; and this avoids the Hegelian objection, since the law is still engaged in essentially moral communication with its citizens (von Hirsch 1993: ch. 2; Narayan 1993; see Bottoms 1998). This is perhaps the most plausible attempt to find a place for deterrence within a communicative theory of punishment, whilst recognizing the force of the Hegelian objection, but we must ask whether, in the case of serious crimes, punishments that were mild enough to constitute mere 'supplements' to the law's primarily moral voice could be severe enough to have any real preventive efficacy (see von Hirsch 1999: 71; Duff 2000: sect. 3.3.2). I cannot discuss this further here, but turn instead to explore a different possibility.

Those who justify penal hard treatment in terms of deterrence implicitly accept that it cannot be justified in communicative terms, as being necessary to the proper communication of censure, and must therefore be justified in other terms. I will argue, however, that a communicative theory can offer a *complete* justification of punishment, including its hard treatment dimension—suitable hard treatment punishment is the appropriate medium of communication because it can serve the communicative aims of punishment more adequately than can merely verbal censure or purely symbolic punishments.

4.3 Punishment as Penance

I have talked so far as if the only purpose of communicative punishment is to communicate censure; but censure, including penal censure, has aims beyond itself.

One aim is that the person censured accept the censure as justified. We say to a wrongdoer, in effect, 'Can't you see the wrong you have done?'; internal to that censure is the intention that she will come to recognize, if she has not already done so, the wrong that she did. If she comes to recognize it (which involves not just realizing that it was somehow wrong, but understanding the kind of wrong it was, its implications for its victim and for her relationship to the victim), she must also repent it: a sincere recognition of one's own wrongdoing is a remorseful recognition. If she repents it, she must commit herself to avoiding such wrongdoing in the future, which might involve an attempt to reform herself—to remedy the moral failings that led her to do wrong. She must also look for some way to 'make up', to make reparation, to her victim (if there is one) for the wrong she did him. What this involves is not primarily *material* compensation for any material harm she caused (there might have been no such harm, or it might not be reparable, or not reparable by her), but *moral* reparation for the wrong she did; and central to moral reparation is apology—an apologetic assurance that she recognizes and repents the wrong she has done and is determined to avoid it in future. Finally, such apology should reconcile her with those she has wronged; it repairs the damage that her wrong did to her relationship with them.

Perhaps then we can understand punishment as serving these more ambitious aims: as trying to bring offenders to recognize and repent their wrongdoings, to reform themselves so as to avoid such wrongs in future, and to make apologetic reparation to those they wronged. Hard treatment punishments of appropriate kinds can serve these aims.

Consider, for instance, a 'Combination Order' under which an English court can sentence an offender to probation, plus a specified number of hours of unpaid community service. A sentence such as this can help, first, to focus the offender's attention on his crime—to confront him with what he has done, to make it hard for him to ignore it. Secondly, it can provide a structure within which he can think about how he should reform himself—and if necessary, through the probation officer, help him towards that reform. Thirdly, it can constitute an apologetic reparation to those he has wronged, an apology that is given more force by the burdensome form it is given. Finally, such reparative apology can reconcile the offender with those he has wronged—with his direct victim, and with the political community as a whole. In this view punishment constitutes a kind of secular penance—though one that imposed on or required of the offender, rather than one that it is up to him to undertake, or not, as he sees fit. (See further Duff 2000. This account has some resemblance to accounts of punishment as moral education; see H. Morris 1981; Hampton 1984; for criticism, see Deigh 1984; Shafer-Landau 1991; Duff 2000: sect. 3.4.1.)

I should emphasize three points about this account. First, it is an account of what punishment ought ideally to be, not a justification of existing penal systems (see Section 1.2 above). If punishment is to become what it ought to be, radical changes are required: in the modes of punishment that are used (see Section 5.2 below); in the way and the spirit in which punishment is imposed; and in the social, political, and legal context within which it is imposed (see Duff 2000: ch. 5).

Secondly, this account does not suggest that we should try to *coerce* offenders into repenting their crimes and reforming themselves—indeed, it forbids such coercion. Punishment is coercive in that it is imposed regardless of the offender's wishes; and it constitutes an attempt to force him to *hear* the message it communicates. How far he listens to that message, however, and how he responds to it, must be left up to him as a responsible moral agent. Punishment, as an exercise in moral communication, seeks to *persuade* him to repent, but leaves him the freedom to refuse.

Thirdly, the account is retributivist in that it justifies punishment as an intrinsically appropriate response to crime, which seeks to communicate the censure that crime deserves. It also posits a future-oriented purpose for punishment—that the offender repent her crime, and so recognize the need for reform and reparation. This does not mean, however, that it is another 'mixed' theory that combines retributivist and consequentialist concerns. What makes punishment appropriate as a way of persuading wrongdoers to repent is not that it is a contingently *efficient technique* for bringing about that outcome (as if one could ask whether there might not be more efficient, non-penal techniques), but that it is an *intrinsically appropriate* way of trying to bring a responsible wrongdoer to repentance; 'end' and 'means' are, we could say, connected internally rather than merely instrumentally. Of course it matters that punishment should be apt, at least in principle, to persuade in this way—it should not baffle us that a punished offender comes to repent. But this is not to say that punishment is appropriate only if and in so far as it is in fact likely to persuade.

This account faces, of course, a number of objections (see Bickenbach 1988; Lipkin 1988; Ten 1990; Baker 1992b; Narayan 1993; von Hirsch 1993: ch. 8; 1999; Bagaric and Amarasekara 2000): in particular that it does not really show penal hard treatment to be necessary; that penal hard treatment, even if intended as an exercise in rational communication, cannot but involve an attempt to coerce the offender's conscience; that an apologetic reparation that is imposed on an offender cannot bring reparation or reconciliation, since they require voluntary apology; that no liberal state should take the kind of intrusive interest in the consciences and the moral attitudes of its citizens that this account warrants (this leads us into the realm of political theory, since my account requires a particular communitarian background; see Section 1.5 above); and that, however far I try to disown any deterrent intentions, my justification still implicitly relies on the fact that such a system of punishment would deter at least some of those whom it did not persuade.

I cannot discuss these objections here. Instead, I want to return to the abolitionist challenge (see Section 1.2 above), to indicate how we can now respond to some salient abolitionist concerns.

4.4 Retribution and Restoration

A striking feature of recent penal theorizing has been the growth of the 'restorative-justice' movement (see Matthews 1988; Cragg 1992; Daly and Immarigeon 1998; von Hirsch and Ashworth 1998: ch. 7; Braithwaite 1999; Zedner 1994). Advocates of restorative justice argue that what is required in response to crime is some process of 'restoration' or reparation between offender and victim (and other interested parties), with a view to reconciling them; which is achieved not by a criminal process of trial and punishment, but by mediation or reconciliation programmes that bring together victim, offender, and other interested parties to discuss what was done and how to deal with it.

The account of punishment sketched in the previous subsection has much in common with these ideas, in so far as it too looks for reparation and reconciliation between offenders and those whom they wronged. However, theorists of restorative justice often portray it as an essentially non-punitive matter: they contrast 'restorative' with 'retributive' justice, and urge us to look for restoration rather than punishment (see e.g. Zehr 1990; Walgrave 1994; for a useful corrective, see Daly and Immarigeon 1998), whilst their critics argue that the criminal law should be concerned with punishment rather than restoration (see e.g. Ashworth 1993). It is indeed true that restorative justice, and victim–offender mediation programmes that seek restoration and reconciliation, are very different from the kinds of criminal punishment with which we are familiar: but I think it is a mistake to argue that they are not and should not be 'punitive' at all—just as it is a mistake to deny that punishment should serve the aims of restoration and reconciliation.

A crime involves not merely (nor always) material damage to a victim's interests, for which material compensation might be appropriate, but a wrong done by the offender to the victim. An appropriate 'restoration' or 'reconciliation' between them must then involve a proper recognition of that wrong and of its implications. If I am genuinely to repair my relationship with someone I have seriously wronged, we cannot just ignore that wrong; I must find some way of 'making up' for it, which requires an apologetic reparation. A suitable programme of 'restoration' must thus involve the offender in recognizing, repenting, and apologizing for the wrong he has done—that is, it must involve the same central elements as punishment on the account sketched above.

We can, therefore, agree with advocates of restorative justice that more use should be made of victim–offender mediation programmes. But we should insist that such programmes are *punitive*. The process itself (in which the offender has to listen to the victim explain how the crime affected her, and thus confront what he has done) is a punishment that he is required to undergo, that seeks to bring him to the painful recognition of the wrong he has done; and the reparation that, as the result of the discussion, he agrees to make to the victim is a punishment through which he can both confirm his repentance and apologize to his victim.

5. SENTENCING MATTERS

A theory of punishment must include, or generate, a theory of sentencing: how should sentencing authorities (legislatures, sentencing councils, courts) decide what sentences to attach to which crimes (see Morris and Tonry 1990; Tonry 1996; von Hirsch and Ashworth 1998; Ashworth 2000)? Here I can only note two questions that are central to sentencing theory.

5.1 How much to Punish?

One question concerns the *severity* of punishment. How severely should this or that crime be punished? How should sentencers determine the appropriate severity of punishment?

Debate on this question usually focuses on the role of the principle of proportionality—the principle that the severity of an offender's punishment should be proportionate to the seriousness of her crime (see Morris and Tonry 1990: ch. 4; von Hirsch 1993; Duff 2000: sect. 4.1). Some such principle is integral to a communicative account of punishment as censure. If punishment is to communicate the censure the offender deserves, it must (as a matter of both justice and honesty) communicate censure whose severity is proportionate to the seriousness of the crime; since the severity of the censure is determined by the severity of the punishment that communicates it, the punishment's severity must therefore be proportionate to the seriousness of the crime.

This general point, however, leaves a number of questions open about the meaning and role of a principle of proportionality in punishment, in particular the following.

First, such a principle clearly demands *relative*, or *ordinal*, proportionality (see von Hirsch 1985: ch. 4). An offender's punishment must be proportionate *relative to* those imposed on other offenders. Those who commit comparably serious crimes must receive sentences of comparable severity; those who commit more serious crimes must be punished more severely than those who commit less serious crimes. To punish one offender more severely than another is to censure him more severely, which is to portray his crime as more serious; and that portrayal must be justified. We can achieve relative proportionality in so far as we can rank crimes in terms of their (relative) seriousness, and sentences in terms of their (relative) severity, but this cannot help to fix *absolute* levels of punishment. The requirements of relative proportionality could be satisfied equally by a system whose lightest sentence was a fine of £1 and whose heaviest was a year in prison, and by one whose lightest sentence was a year in prison and whose heaviest was death. So can we also give content to an idea of *absolute* or *cardinal* proportionality, which would allow us to say that a given level of punishment is *absolutely* appropriate to a given kind of crime; or, if we cannot do this, how should we fix the absolute levels of punishment (see von Hirsch 1993: ch. 5)?

Secondly, judgements even of relative proportionality require some method of comparing the seriousness of different crimes, and the severity of different punishments. We must, therefore, ask what makes a crime more or less serious, or a punishment more or less severe; and how far we can hope to rank all crimes on a single scale of seriousness, and all sentences on a single scale of severity. If we take the demands of proportionality very seriously, and see it as the primary task of sentencers to impose proportionate sentences, we must try to work out such scales, but it is not clear that we can do so, without distorting our understanding of crimes' seriousness, and unduly limiting the range of sentences available to courts.

Thirdly, a principle of proportionality expresses a requirement of justice. But is it an *absolute* demand that can *never* be justifiably overridden; or might we sometimes be justified in imposing a sentence that is harsher, or lighter, than proportionality allows? The former possibility raises the problem of 'dangerous' offenders. Can we justifiably subject those who would predictably commit further serious crimes to longer than normal terms of preventive detention (see Floud and Young 1981; von Hirsch and Ashworth 1998: ch. 3; Duff 1998)? The latter possibility raises the question of mercy: is there any room in a just penal system for a merciful remission of deserved punishment (see Card 1972; Murphy and Hampton 1988: 157–86)?

Fourthly, should we read the principle of proportionality as a *positive*, or a *negative*, principle (see Morris and Tonry 1990: ch. 4; von Hirsch 1993: ch. 7; Frase 1997; Bottoms 1998: 55–77)? On the former reading, sentencers' primary responsibility is to impose *proportionate* sentences. Only when two or more sentences are equally proportionate may they choose between them on other grounds. On the latter reading the principle of proportionality instead forbids *disproportionate* punishments. It sets limits on the sentences that may justly be imposed, above or below which the punishment would be disproportionate; within those limits, however, sentencers can properly appeal to other kinds of consideration (of efficient crime prevention; of humanity) in determining the precise sentence.

Von Hirsch's communicative theory (see Section 4.2 above) gives proportionality a positive role, partly because it is a relatively modest communicative theory: what matters is that punishment communicate an appropriate degree of formal censure. My account, by contrast (Section 4.3 above), gives the formal demands of proportionality a negative role, because it is more ambitious in its communicative aims: if punishment is to communicate a deeper understanding of the nature and implications of the wrong done, and serve as a suitable penance for that wrong, sentencers must have the discretion to find punishments that will be substantively apt for those ambitious ends—which militates against the focus on measuring degrees of severity that a positive principle of proportionality requires. Punishments must not be *disproportionate*, but we should not strive for precise proportionality (it could be argued that our informal, personal responses to moral wrongs are informed by a negative, but not a positive, principle of proportionality).

This leads us into a further set of questions to which penal theorists have paid less attention, concerning the material *modes* of punishment.

5.2 How to Punish?

A theory of sentencing must include an account not just of how sentencers should determine levels of penal severity, but also of what modes of punishment should be available to them, and of how they should select the appropriate mode in particular cases. What could justify the use of particular modes of punishment (imprisonment, for instance), or the introduction of new modes (Community Service Orders, for instance), or the abolition of existing modes (capital punishment, for instance)? What considerations are relevant to decisions about which modes of punishment are suitable for which crimes or offenders?

Some considerations are obvious: considerations of humanity (some modes of punishment, such as torture, may be too cruel to inflict on anyone, whatever their crime; see Murphy 1979), and of practicality (others may be impossible to administer effectively). Fairly soon, however, what considerations are relevant will depend on the penal theory with which we begin. Thus, for a consequentialist, what matters is to determine which modes of punishment are most likely to be efficient methods of achieving the penal system's further ends; for communicative theorists who make positive proportionality central, what matters is to find modes of punishment that can communicate different degrees of censure, and be accurately compared in terms of their severity (so that we can ensure relative proportionality); while, for theorists who posit more ambitiously communicative, penitential goals for punishment, what matters is to find modes of punishment that could serve as suitable compulsory penances.

One central issue in this context concerns meaning—both the meaning of punishment itself (for instance, as censuring offenders), and the meanings of different modes of punishment (see Garland 1990: chs. 9–10; Waldron 1992; von Hirsch 1993: ch. 9; Kahan 1996; Duff 2000: ch. 4.2). We must ask what particular modes of punishment say about the offender, her crime, and her relations to the state and her fellow citizens—and whether what they say is appropriate. For instance, imprisonment has an *exclusionary* meaning—it excludes the offender from ordinary life and community, subjecting him to a 'total' regime of segregation and supervision (see Foucault 1975/1977). What crimes (if any; see Mathiesen 1990) can justify such a response? Or why should we be uneasy with a fine as the sentence for rape? Is it because a fine is not severe enough (but fines could be very severe)—or because it has the wrong kind of meaning in relation to that crime (see Young 1994)?

I cannot pursue these issues here, but they must be pursued by anyone who aspires to offer a complete or practicable theory of punishment.

6. Can Punishment be Justified?

To offer a theory of punishment (as I did in Section 4.3 above) is to argue that it can be justified—as against abolitionists who argue that it can in principle never be justified (see above, Sections 1.2, 1.4, 4.4). This is, however, a long way from arguing that punishment *as currently practised in our own legal systems* can be justified (see Section 1.2 above); even if we find some theory of punishment plausible as an ideal account of what punishment ought to be, we must ask what implications that theory has for existing penal practices and our attitudes to them. Suppose it turns out (as is very likely) that punishment as it actually is falls far short of punishment as it ought to be according to our favoured theory. What are we then to say or do about our existing practices?

This question is more difficult for retributivists, who believe that punishment is justified only if it is just, than for consequentialists, who believe that a penal system is justified so long as it is more beneficial, less harmful, than other available alternatives. Even if our existing practices are radically imperfect from a consequentialist perspective, and in need of radical reform (if not ultimate abolition), we should plausibly work gradually towards such reforms, maintaining those practices meanwhile: since just to abandon them would probably be disastrous, they are justified, for consequentialists, pending their gradual reform (or abolition). By contrast, if a retributivist is forced to conclude that our present penal practices perpetuate injustice rather than doing justice; that they fail to impose on the guilty the suffering that they deserve, or impose unjust kinds of suffering (because they punish those who are not properly 'guilty', or inflict the wrong kind of suffering on the guilty), she must surely conclude that those practices are unjustified, and cannot be supported (see Murphy 1973). Or could she argue that, if their abolition would be disastrous, we must maintain them (thus making ourselves complicit in the injustices they perpetrate), whilst also working for their radical reform so that they can come to do justice?

The question is whether an ideal account of punishment as it ought to be can justify, albeit provisionally and imperfectly, actual penal systems that fall far short of that ideal, so long as real efforts are made to reform them. For there is another abolitionist argument, which allows that punishment could *in principle* be justified, but argues that our existing penal practices are so irredeemably distant from the ideal that they cannot be justified: that is, that punishment cannot *in practice* be justified (see Duff 1996: 68–9).

How we respond to that argument will depend on how radically imperfect or unjust we think our present practices are, on what prospects we see for their reform, and on what alternatives we can envisage if we take this abolitionist argument seriously. I have no confident answer myself (see Duff 2000: ch. 5), but would emphasize one final point—that the question of whether any existing penal system is justifiable, or salvageable, depends not just on its internal workings, but also on the wider socio-political context in which it is set. I can illustrate this point by reference to the communicative theory sketched in Section 4.3 above; but some version of the problem arises for any plausible normative theory of punishment.

If punishment is to be justified on my account, it must constitute an attempt at an appropriate kind of moral communication with the offender. That entails some demanding requirements as to the kinds of punishment that are imposed, but it also posits demanding *preconditions* for justified punishment—conditions that must be met if moral communication is to be possible or justifiable. Several of these preconditions reflect the requirement that the person punished be a responsible agent, that she be capable of answering for her alleged wrongdoings (see Lucas 1993: ch. 1, on responsibility as 'answerability'); that she be bound by the laws that she allegedly broke (since otherwise she has nothing to answer for); and that she be answerable *to* the political community whose courts try her—that they have the moral standing to call her to answer (see Duff 2000: ch. 5.2). We must wonder how far these preconditions (especially the third) are satisfied for many of those who appear before our criminal courts, but, if they are not satisfied, the justifiability of our present penal practices is again put in serious doubt.

References

Adler, J. (1992). *The Urgings of Conscience*. Philadelphia: Temple University Press.

Alexander, L. (1980). 'The Doomsday Machine: Proportionality, Punishment and Prevention'. *Monist*, 63: 199–227.

Anderson, J. L. (1997). 'Reciprocity as a Justification for Retributivism'. *Criminal Justice Ethics*, 16: 13–25.

Ardal, P. (1984). 'Does Anyone ever Deserve to Suffer?' *Queen's Quarterly*, 91–2: 241–57.

Ashworth, A. J. (1993). 'Some Doubts about Restorative Justice'. *Criminal Law Forum*, 4: 277–99.

——(2000). *Sentencing and Criminal Justice*. 3rd edn. London: Butterworths.

Bagaric, M., and Amarasekara, K. (2000). 'The Errors of Retributivism'. *Melbourne University Law Review*, 24: 1–66.

Baker, B. M. (1992a). 'Consequentialism, Punishment and Autonomy', in W. Cragg (ed.), *Retributivism and its Critics*. Stuttgart: Franz Steiner, 149–61.

——(1992b). 'Penance as a Model for Punishment'. *Social Theory and Practice*, 18: 311–31.

Becker, L. (1974). 'Criminal Attempts and the Theory of the Law of Crimes'. *Philosophy and Public Affairs*, 3: 262–94.

Beyleveld, D. (1979). 'Identifying, Explaining and Predicting Deterrence'. *British Journal of Criminology*, 19: 205–24.

Bianchi, H. (1994). *Justice as Sanctuary: Toward a New System of Crime Control*. Bloomington, IN: Indiana University Press.

Bickenbach, J. E. (1988). Critical Notice of R. A. Duff, *Trials and Punishments*. *Canadian Journal of Philosophy*, 18: 765–86.

Boston University Law Review (1996). 'Symposium: The Intersection of Tort and Criminal Law', 76: 1–373.

Bottoms, A. E. (1998). 'Five Puzzles in von Hirsch's Theory of Punishment', in A. J. Ashworth and M. Wasik (eds.), *Fundamentals of Sentencing Theory*. Oxford: Oxford University Press, 53–100.

Braithwaite, J. (1999). 'Restorative Justice: Assessing Optimistic and Pessimistic Accounts'. *Crime and Justice: A Review of Research*, 23: 241–367.

——and Pettit, P. (1990). *Not Just Deserts*. Oxford: Oxford University Press.

Burgh, R. W. (1982). 'Do the Guilty Deserve Punishment?' *Journal of Philosophy*, 79: 193–210.

Card, C. (1972). 'Mercy'. *Philosophical Review*, 81: 182–207.

Christie, N. (1977). 'Conflicts as Property'. *British Journal of Criminology*, 17: 1–15.

——(1981). *Limits to Pain*. London: Martin Robertson.

Cottingham, J. (1979). 'Varieties of Retribution'. *Philosophical Quarterly*, 29: 238–46.

Cragg, W. (1992). *The Practice of Punishment: Towards a Theory of Restorative Justice*. London: Routledge.

Dagger, R. (1993). 'Playing Fair with Punishment'. *Ethics*, 103: 473–88.

Daly, K., and Immarigeon, R. (1998). 'The Past, Present, and Future of Restorative Justice'. *Contemporary Justice Review*, 1: 21–45.

Davis, L. H. (1972). 'They Deserve to Suffer'. *Analysis*, 32: 136–40.

Davis, M. (1989). 'The Relative Independence of Punishment Theory'. *Law and Philosophy*, 7: 321–50.

——(1991). 'Punishment as Language: Misleading Analogy for Desert Theorists'. *Law and Philosophy*, 10: 310–22.

de Haan, W. (1990). *The Politics of Redress: Crime, Punishment and Penal Abolition*. London: Unwin Hyman.

Deigh, J. (1984). 'On the Right to be Punished: Some Doubts'. *Ethics*, 94: 191–211.

Dennett, D. C. (1987) (ed.). *The Philosophical Lexicon*. 8th edn. Oxford: Blackwell.

Dolinko, D. (1991). 'Some Thoughts about Retributivism'. *Ethics*, 101: 537–59.

Duff, R. A. (1986). *Trials and Punishments*. Cambridge: Cambridge University Press.

——(1996). 'Penal Communications: Recent Work in the Philosophy of Punishment'. *Crime and Justice: A Review of Research*, 20: 1–97.

——(1998). 'Dangerousness and Citizenship', in A. J. Ashworth and M. Wasik (eds.), *Fundamentals of Sentencing Theory*. Oxford: Oxford University Press, 141–63.

——(2000). *Punishment, Communication and Community*. New York: Oxford University Press.

——and Garland, D. (1994) (eds.). *A Reader on Punishment*. Oxford: Oxford University Press.

Falls, M. M. (1987). 'Retribution, Reciprocity, and Respect for Persons'. *Law and Philosophy*, 6: 25–51.

Farrell, D. M. (1985). 'The Justification of General Deterrence'. *Philosophical Review*, 94: 367–94.

—— (1995). 'Deterrence and the Just Distribution of Harm'. *Social Philosophy and Policy*, 12: 220–40.

Feinberg, J. (1970). 'The Expressive Function of Punishment', in Feinberg, *Doing and Deserving*. Princeton: Princeton University Press, 95–118.

Floud, J. E., and Young, W. (1981). *Dangerousness and Criminal Justice*. London: Heinemann.

Foucault, M. (1975/1977). *Discipline and Punish: The Birth of the Prison*, trans. A. Sheridan. London: Allen Lane.

Frase, R. S. (1997). 'Sentencing Principles in Theory and Practice'. *Crime and Justice*, 22: 363–433.

Galligan, D. J. (1981). 'The Return to Retribution in Penal Theory', in C. F. H. Tapper (ed.), *Crime, Proof and Punishment*. London: Butterworths, 144–71.

Gardner, J. (1998). 'Crime: In Proportion and in Perspective', in A. J Ashworth and M. Wasik (eds.), *Fundamentals of Sentencing Theory*. Oxford: Oxford University Press, 31–52.

Garland, D. (1990). *Punishment and Modern Society*. Oxford: Oxford University Press.

Goldman, A. H. (1982). 'Toward a New Theory of Punishment'. *Law and Philosophy*, 1: 57–76.

Hampton, J. (1984). 'The Moral Education Theory of Punishment'. *Philosophy and Public Affairs*, 13: 208–38.

Hare, R. M. (1981). *Moral Thinking: Its Levels, Methods and Point*. Oxford: Oxford University Press.

Hart, H. L. A. (1963). *Law, Liberty and Morality*. New York: Random House.

—— (1968). *Punishment and Responsibility*. Oxford: Oxford University Press.

Hegel, G. W. F. (1821/1942). *The Philosophy of Right*, trans. T. Knox. Oxford: Oxford University Press.

Honderich, T. (1969/1984). *Punishment: The Supposed Justifications*. Rev. edn. Harmondsworth: Penguin.

Horder, J. (1992). *Provocation and Responsibility*. Oxford: Oxford University Press.

Hudson, B. (1987). *Justice through Punishment: A Critique of the 'Justice' Model of Corrections*. London: Macmillan.

Hulsman, L. (1986). 'Critical Criminology and the Concept of Crime'. *Contemporary Crises*, 10: 63–80.

—— (1991). 'The Abolitionist Case: Alternative Crime Policies'. *Israel Law Review*, 25: 681–709.

Husak, D. (1992). 'Why Punish the Deserving?' *Nous*, 26: 447–64.

Kahan, D. M. (1996). 'What Do Alternative Sanctions Mean?' *University of Chicago Law Review*, 63: 591–653.

Knowles, D. (1993). 'Unjustified Retribution'. *Israel Law Review*, 27: 50–8.

Lacey, N. (1988). *State Punishment: Political Principles and Community Values*. London: Routledge.

Lewis, C. S. (1953). 'The Humanitarian Theory of Punishment'. *Res Judicatae*, 6; repr. in W. Sellars and J. Hospers (eds.), *Readings in Ethical Theory*. 2nd edn. New York: Appleton-Century-Crofts, 1970, 646–50.

Lipkin, R. J. (1988). 'Punishment, Penance and Respect for Autonomy'. *Social Theory and Practice*, 14: 87–104.

Lucas, J. R. (1993). *Responsibility*. Oxford: Oxford University Press.

Mackenzie, M. M. (1981). *Plato on Punishment*. Berkeley and Los Angeles: University of California Press.

Marshall, S. E., and Duff, R. A. (1998). 'Criminalization and Sharing Wrongs'. *Canadian Journal of Law & Jurisprudence*, 11: 7–22.

Matthews, R. (1988) (ed.), *Informal Justice*. London: Sage.

Mathiesen, T. (1990). *Prison on Trial*. London: Sage.

Montague, P. (1995). *Punishment as Societal Defense*. Lanham: Rowman & Littlefield.

Moore, M. S. (1997). *Placing Blame: A Theory of Criminal Law*. Oxford: Oxford University Press.

Morison, J. (1988). 'Hart's Excuses: Problems with a Compromise Theory of Punishment', in P. Leith and P. Ingram (eds.), *The Jurisprudence of Orthodoxy*. London: Routledge, 117–46.

Morris, C. W. (1991). 'Punishment and Loss of Moral Standing'. *Canadian Journal of Philosophy*, 21: 53–79.

Morris, H. (1968). 'Persons and Punishment'. *Monist*, 52: 475–501.

——(1981). 'A Paternalistic Theory of Punishment'. *American Philosophical Quarterly*, 18: 263–71.

Morris, N. (1974). *The Future of Imprisonment*. Chicago: University of Chicago Press.

——and Tonry, M. (1990). *Between Prison and Probation: Intermediate Punishments in a Rational Sentencing System*. New York: Oxford University Press.

Murphy, J. G. (1973). 'Marxism and Retribution'. *Philosophy and Public Affairs*, 2: 217–43.

——(1979). 'Cruel and Unusual Punishments', in Murphy, *Retribution, Justice, and Therapy*. Dordrecht: Reidel.

——(1985). 'Retributivism, Moral Education and the Liberal State'. *Criminal Justice Ethics*, 4: 3–11.

——(1999). 'Moral Epistemology, the Retributive Emotions, and the "Clumsy Moral Philosophy" of Jesus Christ', in S. A. Bandes (ed.), *Law and Emotion*. New York: NYU Press, 149–67.

——and Coleman, J. (1984). *The Philosophy of Law*. Totowa, NJ: Rowman & Littlefield.

——and Hampton, J. (1988). *Forgiveness and Mercy*. Cambridge: Cambridge University Press.

Nagel, T. (1979). 'The Fragmentation of Value', in Nagel, *Mortal Questions*. Cambridge: Cambridge University Press, 128–41.

Narayan, U. (1993). 'Appropriate Responses and Preventive Benefits: Justifying Censure and Hard Treatment in Legal Punishment'. *Oxford Journal of Legal Studies*, 13: 166–82.

Newburn, T. (1997). 'Youth, Crime, and Justice', in M. Maguire, R. Morgan, and R. Reiner (eds.), *Oxford Handbook of Criminology*. 2nd edn. Oxford: Oxford University Press, 613–60.

Peay, J. (1997). 'Mentally Disordered Offenders', in M. Maguire, R. Morgan, and R. Reiner (eds.), *Oxford Handbook of Criminology*. 2nd edn. Oxford: Oxford University Press, 661–701.

Pettit, P. (1997). 'Republican Theory and Criminal Punishment'. *Utilitas*, 9: 59–79.

Philips, M. (1986). 'The Justification of Punishment and the Justification of Political Authority'. *Law and Philosophy*, 5: 393–416.

Primoratz, I. (1989). 'Punishment as Language'. *Philosophy*, 64: 187–205.

——(1999). *Justifying Legal Punishment*. 2nd edn. New Jersey: Humanities Press.

Quinn, W. (1985). 'The Right to Threaten and the Right to Punish'. *Philosophy and Public Affairs*, 14: 327–73.

Rawls, J. (1955). 'Two Concepts of Rules'. *Philosophical Review*, 64: 3–32.

Scheid, D. E. (1980). 'Note on Defining "Punishment" '. *Canadian Journal of Philosophy*, 10: 453–62.

——(1997). 'Constructing a Theory of Punishment, Desert, and the Distribution of Punishments'. *Canadian Journal of Law and Jurisprudence*, 10: 441–506.

Shafer-Landau, R. (1991). 'Can Punishment Morally Educate?' *Law and Philosophy*, 10: 189–219.

——(1996). 'The Failure of Retributivism'. *Philosophical Studies*, 82: 289–316.

Sher, G. (1987). *Desert*. Princeton: Princeton University Press.

Skillen, A. J. (1980). 'How to Say Things with Walls'. *Philosophy*, 55: 509–23.

Smart, J. J. C. (1973). 'An Outline of a System of Utilitarian Ethics', in J. J. C. Smart and B. Williams, *Utilitarianism: For and Against*. Cambridge: Cambridge University Press, 1–74.

Sprigge, T. L. S. (1968). 'A Utilitarian Reply to Dr McCloskey', in M. D. Bayles (ed.), *Contemporary Utilitarianism*. Garden City, NY: Doubleday, 261–99.

Ten, C. L. (1987). *Crime, Guilt and Punishment*. Oxford: Oxford University Press.

——(1990). 'Positive Retributivism'. *Social Philosophy and Policy*, 7: 194–208.

Tonry, M. (1996). *Sentencing Matters*. New York: Oxford University Press.

von Hirsch, A. (1976). *Doing Justice: The Choice of Punishments*. New York: Hill & Wang.

——(1985). *Past or Future Crimes*. Manchester: Manchester University Press.

——(1993). *Censure and Sanctions*. Oxford: Oxford University Press.

——(1999). 'Punishment, Penance and the State', in M. Matravers (ed.), *Punishment and Political Theory*. Oxford: Hart Publishing, 69–82.

——and Ashworth, A. J. (1992). 'Not Not Just Deserts: A Response to Braithwaite and Pettit'. *Oxford Journal of Legal Studies*, 12: 83–98.

————(1998) (eds.), *Principled Sentencing*. 2nd edn. Oxford: Hart Publishing.

——Bottoms, A. E., Burney, E., Wikström, P.-O. (1999). *Criminal Deterrence and Sentence Severity*. Oxford: Hart Publishing.

Waldron, J. (1992). 'Lex Talionis'. *Arizona Law Review*, 34: 25–51.

Walgrave, L. (1994). 'Beyond Rehabilitation: In Search of a Constructive Alternative in the Judicial Response to Juvenile Crime'. *European Journal on Criminal Policy and Research*, 2: 57–75.

Walker, N. (1978). 'Punishing, Denouncing or Reducing Crime', in P. R. Glazebrook (ed.), *Reshaping the Criminal Law*. London: Stevens, 391–403.

——(1980). *Punishment, Danger and Stigma*. Oxford: Blackwell.

——(1991). *Why Punish?* Oxford: Oxford University Press.

Wilson, J. Q. (1983). *Thinking about Crime*. Rev. edn. New York: Basic Books.

Wootton, B. (1963). *Crime and the Criminal Law*. London: Stevens.

Young, P. (1994). 'Putting a Price on Harm: The Fine as a Punishment', in R. A. Duff, S. E. Marshall, R. E. Dobash, and R. P. Dobash (eds.), *Penal Theory and Practice*. Manchester: Manchester University Press, 185–96.

Zedner, L. (1994). 'Reparation and Retribution: Are They Reconcilable?' *Modern Law Review*, 57: 228–50.

Zehr, H. (1990). *Changing Lenses: A New Focus for Crime and Justice*. Scottsdale, PA: Herald Press.

CHAPTER 14

FREEDOM OF SPEECH AND RELIGION

ANDREW ALTMAN

1. INTRODUCTION

FREEDOM of speech and religion are among the central values of modern constitutional democracies. Efforts to understand what these freedoms mean and why they are important, and to translate them into enduring institutional arrangements, constitute a major part of the history of such democracies. As the twenty-first century begins, the political and theoretical debates over these values are not the same as they were in the past. Although centuries of philosophical controversy and institutional experimentation have settled some issues, others have been raised, with some surprising twists. Constitutional democracies rest on the principle that all citizens are to be treated as free and equal persons under the law. The principle is the settled starting point for all reasonable debate about freedom of speech and religion, and it entails that the law must secure for each citizen an equal and extensive scheme of basic liberties, including the liberties of speech and religion.

Since the birth of liberal democratic ideals in the seventeenth century, there has been a dramatic expansion in the range of expressive activities generally regarded as instances of the exercise of free speech. Until the twentieth century, it would have been unthinkable even to strong proponents of free speech that advocating the forcible overthrow of the government was properly considered an exercise of such freedom. Today, the prevailing view is that subversive advocacy is an exercise of free speech and should be legally protected.

Similarly, freedom of religion has expanded substantially over time. Until the twentieth century, Jews were routinely denied equal political and civil rights, even in the USA. They could not hold office in North Carolina or vote in New Hampshire until after the Civil War. Today such religious discrimination is unthinkable.

2. The Status of Basic Liberties

To describe the freedoms of speech and religion as basic liberties is to accord them a special status among the various forms of human activity. Basic liberties are understood to be those whose infringement by government or official action requires an especially strong justification (Scanlon 1972; Cohen 1996).

Many philosophers construe this requirement to mean that such infringements cannot be justified simply on grounds of social utility. Restrictions on basic liberties are not simply another cost to be weighed in the overall utility calculus. This idea fits comfortably with theories that posit, at the level of fundamental principle, rights-based constraints on the pursuit of social utility. Nagel explains that violating liberty of expression and conscience 'is not a function of the balance of costs and benefits... while in some cases a right may be justifiably overridden by a sufficiently high threshold of costs, below that threshold its status as a right is insensitive to differences in the cost–benefit balance of respecting it in each particular case' (1995: 84–5).

However, utilitarians need not abandon the idea of basic liberties. They will reject any theory in which the idea of rights plays a role at the level of fundamental principle but can accept the notion that there are certain types of liberty that government must have unusually strong reasons for restricting. Utilitarians might argue, for example, that some liberties are unusually productive of social utility. Or it might be claimed that government cannot be fully trusted in its utility judgements when it comes to certain liberties, so that there should be especially strong reasons before government is permitted to restrict such liberties. Mill's arguments (1859/1978) can be construed as providing utilitarian reasons for demarcating basic liberties such as freedom of speech and conscience from those he regards as non-basic, such as freedom of trade.

3. Free Speech: Theoretical Issues

3.1 Levels of Protection

The term 'speech' has come to stand for all forms of symbolic expression. For example, burning a national flag in protest over a government policy or wearing a Nazi uniform to display support for that ideology are regarded as speech. Several current debates focus on whether certain forms of symbolic expression, such as pornography and hate speech, should receive less than full protection or even no protection at all.

Schauer (1982) usefully distinguished questions of whether a form of expression is covered by the free speech principle from questions of the degree of protection a form of speech is to receive. It is widely agreed, for example, that commercial speech is covered, but many scholars argue that it should not receive the same level of protection as the advocacy of political doctrines or as artistic expression.

Schauer's distinction can be elaborated in numerous ways. For example, Sunstein has argued for a two-tier approach in which the upper tier consists of expression that is 'both intended and received as a contribution to public deliberation about some issue' (1993: 134). Such expression is to receive the strongest protection and is subject to regulation 'only on the gravest showing of harm' (1993: 123–4). Lower-tier speech involves forms of expression that are not part of the process of public deliberation, such as advertising or pornography that involves children or violence against women, and its regulation would be subject to a less rigorous standard.

Sunstein's theory is a version of an approach developed in the mid-twentieth century by Meiklejohn, who argued that 'the principle of the freedom of speech springs from the necessities of the program of self-government' (1948: 26). Meiklejohn claimed that legal doctrine in the USA at the time was inadequately protective of speech. But critics of Sunstein's approach doubt that it is sufficiently protective of non-political forms of speech, such as works of art that are not politically intended and interpreted (Weinstein 1999: 178).

Nonetheless, Sunstein is probably right that some way of distinguishing among forms of expression and levels of protection is needed if we are to give a cogent account of why it is legitimate for government to regulate speech reasonably regarded as calling for restriction, such as child pornography and false advertising. To extend the most stringent protection to every form of expression that counted as speech would be to tip the balance too far in favour of free speech and against the efforts of government to carry out its legitimate functions.

3.2 Speech and Conduct

The distinction between speech and conduct has also been prominent in efforts to specify a reasonable balance between the expressive liberty of the individual and the authority of government. In the past, for example, it was sometimes argued that workers who walked on picket lines or civil-rights protestors who marched in the streets were engaged in conduct and not speech. In 1971, several justices on the US Supreme Court opined that wearing in public a jacket bearing the words 'Fuck the Draft' amounted mainly to conduct rather than speech (*Cohen v. California*, 1971).

Those justices' views are not tenable, but it has proved notoriously difficult to specify the distinction between speech and conduct. Some scholars have given up on the distinction entirely. Fish claims that 'there is no class of utterances separable from the world of conduct' (1994: 114). Others have argued that the distinction does not track any ordinary understanding of what 'speech' is and that it must be construed in terms of the normative theory that best explains why communicative expression should receive special protection in the first place (Greenawalt: 1995*a*). Still others have argued that a theory of communicative expression can draw the distinction without invoking normative claims about why such expression should be regarded as a basic liberty: what should count as speech is a task for linguistic theory rather than political philosophy (Tiersma 1993).

If it makes sense to regard freedom of speech as a basic liberty, then there must be some justifiable speech/non-speech distinction. Without a non-arbitrary distinction, it would be impossible adequately to defend why the liberty one calls 'free speech' should count as basic. The logical consequence would be, as Fish (1994) puts it, that 'there's no such thing as free speech'—that is, no domain of expressive activity that can be impartially demarcated and that merits heightened protection.

3.3 Free Speech Scepticism

Even granting a speech/non-speech distinction, Fish is sceptical of regarding free speech as a basic liberty. He contends that the term 'free speech' is 'just the name we give to verbal behavior that serves the substantive agendas we wish to advance. . . . Free speech . . . is not an independent value but a political prize' (1994: 102). Because the rhetoric of liberal democracy accords high status to expression that gets to wear the label of 'free speech', the label is an object of political struggle. Accordingly, Fish counsels that, if 'so-called free-speech principles have been fashioned by your enemy... contest their relevance to the issue at hand; but if you manage to refashion them in line with your purposes, urge them with a vengeance' (1994: 114).

Fish's deflationary account of free speech erases the distinction between the values ('agendas') we happen to hold and the values we *ought* to hold. Once that distinction is erased, all discussion and dialogue become a matter of strategic action: what counts is successfully outmanœuvering the opponent ('your enemy') to achieve a fixed goal, not discovering which answers can be supported by the strongest reasons. But Fish does not consistently adhere to this view. He criticizes the idea that free speech is an absolute right, arguing that it blocks dialogue about issues such as hate-speech regulation, and he suggests ways in which dialogue can proceed once the blockage is removed. Fish recommends that we consider 'each situation as it emerges' and regard any question about speech regulation as a 'local one' about the risks and gains of a particular proposal (1994: 111).

Such suggestions may be plausible, but they presuppose that his situational approach would yield those answers to speech issues that could be supported with the strongest reasons. Moreover, Fish begs the question of whether speech should be regarded as a basic liberty. A case-by-case approach rejects any special status for free speech, but the issue is whether there are good reasons for according speech that status. And a long line of thinkers have argued plausibly that a case-by-case method is inadequately protective of speech (Meiklejohn 1948; Frantz 1962; Ely 1980). Thus, Ely notes in connection with the suppression of Communism during the 1950s that majority opinion and official judgement tend to exaggerate the potential dangers posed by incidents of unpopular speech: 'The First Amendment simply cannot stand on the shifting foundation of ad hoc evaluations of specific threat' (Ely 1980: 107). Ely may be wrong, but Fish fails to engage the issue with him.

Alexander and Horton express another form of scepticism, which questions the coherence of efforts to justify the status of speech as a basic liberty. They point out that such justifications necessarily appeal to general principles that (a) apply to activities that go beyond speech and (b) do not apply to some forms of speech. For example, they claim that Mill's argument that free speech facilitates the discovery of truth is vulnerable because some speech 'contributes little toward answering . . . questions [and] some activities other than speech contribute a great deal' (Alexander and Horton 1983: 1350). More generally, the justifications for free speech do not fit the idea that speech is special and distinctive from other activities.

Alexander and Horton are right that justifications for expressive liberty will bottom out on normative principles that do not refer specifically to speech but instead involve values that are more general in scope. Yet, expression may be on some short-list of activities that such principles entail should generally be treated as basic. Thus, expression may be special, even if fundamental principles do not explicitly single it out for special treatment.

An older form of scepticism, associated with Marcuse (1969), claims that class divisions and corporate domination under capitalism make the marketplace of ideas a tool through which the powerful dominate expression and perpetuate their economic and social power. A system of expressive liberty that is 'neutral' among competing views is in fact repressive because background inequalities stifle the voices and manipulate the thinking of the oppressed. Marcuse argued that the existing political and economic structure 'rigs the rules of the game' and places at a disadvantage 'those who stand against the established system' (1969: 92). He favoured a structure that deliberately promoted the interests of the oppressed, even to the point of censoring views antagonistic to those interests. Only after the subversion of class society by a mass egalitarian movement would a truly neutral system of free expression be possible.

Elements of Marcuse's scepticism live on today in the work of critical race theorists and radical feminists, which will be examined below. His scepticism is also reflected in the current claim that corporate power poses a threat to expressive liberty that is as serious, if not more so, than the traditional threat of government. Some argue that the means of mass communication are so concentrated in the hands of a few corporate entities that free speech for the average person is virtually nonexistent. (Kairys 1998). Herman and Chomsky have argued that 'money and power are able to filter the news fit to print, marginalize dissent, and allow government and dominant private interests to get their message across to the public' (1988: 2).

Scholarly attention to the issue of corporate domination of the means of communication is likely to increase in the coming years, as globalization and the Internet alter the ways in which people communicate. Debates will focus on whether the new technologies decentralize the power of communication or further concentrate it in the hands of transnational corporations. And those who see the latter tendency at work will argue for institutional mechanisms to confine it and to build a freer marketplace of ideas.

3.4 Arguments for Free Speech as a Basic Liberty

Among the arguments for according special status to expressive freedom is that speech is less harmful than other forms of behaviour. Speech can 'hurt' but not really 'harm'. But Schauer casts doubt on the 'lesser harm hypothesis' (1993: 640). The subjective distress caused by speech can be as intense and long-lasting as that caused by many types of conduct. And the classification of speech-induced distress as mere 'hurt' involves dubious and question-begging normative judgements about the disvalue of such distress. Cohen seems right to argue, 'Denying the cost of speech is simply insulting to those who pay it' (1996: 181).

Another line of argument revolves around the claim that government is properly subjected to great suspicion whenever it seeks to restrict expression. In this view, government has strong, self-serving motives to limit expression, especially the speech of dissenters and those with unpopular views and attitudes. In particular, government will tend to exaggerate whatever harms the expression of critics or dissenters may risk causing. Treating expressive liberty as basic acts as a prophylactic to help ensure that when government restricts expression it is not simply furthering its own interests but acting for good and legitimate reasons.

This argument from distrust contains some element of truth and plays a role in current debates over pornography, hate speech, and campaign finance reform. But standing alone the argument is incomplete. Government always has a tendency to act from self-serving motives. We need some account of what makes expression, in contrast to action in general, entitled to the status of a basic liberty. Such an account would need to explain why freedom of speech is especially valuable. One way to complete the argument is to connect expressive liberty to the discovery of truth.

Prominent among the traditional arguments for the special value of free expression is the idea that the 'free marketplace of ideas' facilitates the discovery and understanding of truth, especially new truths that run against the prevailing wisdom of the day (Mill: 1859/1978).

Some contemporary thinkers argue that existing democracies do not have a truly free marketplace of ideas, because of oppression based on gender, race, and class

(Matsuda 1993). But others respond that expressive liberty has historically proved crucial for emancipatory movements and that a system of free expression is vital for exposing and eliminating the oppression that remains (Richards 1999).

This debate is sometimes cast as one between advocates of wholly different political systems, but few thinkers defend censorship. The disputes are more like debates about whether the economic market for certain goods is malfunctioning and needs specific corrections than like debates about whether to eliminate the market system and replace it with state socialism. All sides can agree with Mill's claim that a system of free expression facilitates the discovery of truth, while disagreeing over whether the current system needs a 'market correction' when it comes to racist or pornographic speech. Still, one must wonder about the consistency of a view that claims systemic oppression, on the one hand, and then argues for reformist market corrections, on the other. Some may suggest that the only consistent radical position is one that, like Marcuse's, advocates a form of censorship.

In the current literature, perhaps the most common argument for free speech emphasizes its connection to individual autonomy. The right of free expression derives conceptually from the 'moral sovereignty' of the individual (Richards 1999: 50). That sovereignty requires society to respect the conscientiously expressed views of its citizens. Dworkin (1996) takes a similar approach in arguing that freedom of speech is valuable because it is a necessary element of any society that treats its citizens as responsible moral agents who have the capacity to make up their own minds about what is good or bad, true or false.

But the autonomy arguments also threaten to undo the distinction between basic and non-basic liberties. To the extent that any activity may be an exercise of autonomy, no particular form of liberty can be accorded special status strictly on the basis of autonomy. Accordingly, the idea of autonomy must be appropriately limited or the autonomy-based arguments must be modified, if the basic/non-basic distinction is to be maintained.

Rawls argues for the special status of freedom of expression, as well as freedom of conscience and other basic liberties, by linking them to what he describes as a 'liberal' conception of the person. On his conception, persons have two fundamental moral powers that constitute them as free and equal: the capacity for a sense of justice and the capacity to formulate, pursue, and revise a conception of the good. For Rawls, special protections for the basic liberties 'are essential social conditions for the adequate development and exercise of the two powers of moral personality over a complete life' (1993: 293). It is not liberty as such but only certain forms of liberty that have the appropriate connection to the two moral powers. Accordingly, his view can be seen as a modified version of the autonomy-based approach. It is examined in greater detail in the sections below on religion.

Raz emphasizes an important autonomy-interest served by free expression for individuals with unconventional lifestyles, such as homosexuals and bisexuals. 'The public portrayal and expression of forms of life validate the styles of life portrayed and . . . censoring expression normally expresses authoritative condemnation' (Raz 1994: 10). Thus expressive liberty helps promote the public recognition and acceptance of modes of life that lie outside the mainstream.

Another argument for free expression emphasizes its connection to democracy (Ely 1980). It holds that the special status of free speech derives principally from the fact that it is indispensable for the kind of collective deliberation and decision making that is central to democratic self-government. Fiss presents an aggressive version of this approach in his interpretation of the US Constitution: 'The autonomy protected by the First Amendment and rightly enjoyed by individuals and the press is not an end in itself, as it might be in some moral code, but is a means to further the democratic values underlying the Bill of Rights' (Fiss 1996: 83). Thus, for Fiss, expressive liberty is essential for the full and robust public debate that is called for by the ideal of collective self-government by the people. In other forms of the democracy-based argument, the role of free expression in curtailing government corruption and abuse is prominent.

Sunstein develops a nuanced version of the democracy-based approach, agreeing that individual autonomy is an important intrinsic value served by free expression but arguing that the dominant justification for treating free speech as a basic liberty stems from its role in the collective deliberations of democratic self-government. He writes that 'the free speech principle should be seen through the lens of democracy' (Sunstein 1993: 252).

A pluralist approach would argue that many of the preceding arguments play some role in justifying the special status of free speech. Any one argument, in isolation, may be vulnerable to criticism, but in combination they provide strong reasons for treating speech as a basic liberty. Moreover, some of the values invoked by the arguments can be mutually reinforcing. Thus, Post has pointed out that democracy requires 'a public discourse . . . kept free for the autonomous participation of individual citizens' (1995: 7).

Still, the internal conflicts found in a pluralist approach should not be discounted. Post emphasizes the 'serious internal tension' between individual autonomy and collective self-government (1995: 7). Monistic theories can avoid such tensions, but, in doing so, they may simply be ignoring the untidy reality of moral life.

4. FREE SPEECH: APPLICATIONS

4.1 Pornography, Morality, and Harm

One of the central issues of recent years has been whether the legal regulation of adult pornography is justifiable. Some thinkers advocate regulation on the basis of the moral principles of natural law. Thus, George contends that pornography tends 'to corrupt and deprave' by harming 'people's capacity properly to channel sexual desire' (1999: 189). George's conception of natural law reflects that developed by Finnis (1997), according to which sexual acts are morally wrong if they fail to contribute to the inherent good of heterosexual, monogamous marriage. But many thinkers reject the view of sexuality that informs the natural law position, and the argument that pornography should be regulated because it promotes immorality is not central to the current debate.

Instead, the debate has revolved around the issue whether pornography subverts gender equality. The arguments have been shaped by the feminist insight that much pornography is not simply about sexual pleasure but also about the subordination of women as a vehicle for that pleasure.

Advocates of the legal regulation of pornography typically argue that it causally contributes to sexual assaults against women and makes men indifferent to the sexual aggressions other men may commit. Such harm, they contend, is more than sufficient to justify the regulation of pornographic expression. But there is deep division among scholars on whether, and to what degree, the causal claims connecting pornography to sexual aggression are warranted by the empirical evidence, and there is little prospect of any consensus on the matter. Indeed, there is a notable lack of agreement over what degree and type of evidence would be sufficient to sustain—or rebut—the claims. Opponents of regulation will typically insist on controlled studies using the quantitative techniques of mainstream social science. Accordingly, a leading critic of regulation, Dworkin, contends that 'no significant scientific study has concluded that pornography is a significant cause of crime' (1996: 230).

On the other side, advocates of regulation often charge that a much broader array of evidence should be considered than is typically examined by mainstream social science. Delgado and Stefancic claim that 'researchers fail to take account of certain types of evidence that, if counted, would tend to corroborate feminist claims'. They would include in the evidence correlations between pornography consumption and conduct considered socially 'normal', such as 'aggressive flirting' and 'conspicuous leering' (Delgado and Stefancic 1997: 34). Others would expand the evidence to include the personal accounts of sexually violent men who consume pornography and women who are their victims.

Insistence on controlled studies sets the bar unreasonably high, but sole reliance on personal accounts seems insufficient. Rapists may claim that they were provoked to act by their consumption of pornography, but they have self-interested reasons for making such claims. Moreover, the psychological causes of a person's sexual impulses are hardly transparent, even—perhaps especially—to the individual himself. And Delgado and Stefancic are simply speculating when they suggest the existence of significant correlations between pornography consumption and such behaviours as 'aggressive flirting' and between those behaviours and sexual assaults. Moreover, even if there were agreement that pornography did causally contribute to sexual aggression against women, there would be debate over the extent and normative implications of the marginal increase in sexual assaults caused by pornography.

4.2 Pornography and Equality

Aside from their complicated empirical aspects, disputes over the regulation of pornography involve competing conceptions of gender equality. MacKinnon argues that protecting pornography under the umbrella of free speech amounts to a failure to take gender equality seriously. The serious harm done to women by degrading sexual images is discounted by arguments that pornography merits the same protection as political or artistic expression.

Dworkin (1996: 237–8) argues that MacKinnon has misconstrued the idea of equality.

Because the moral environment in which we all live is in good part created by others ... the question of who shall have the power to help shape that environment, and how, is of fundamental importance. ... Only one answer is consistent with the ideals of political equality: that no one may be prevented from influencing the shared moral environment through his own private choices, tastes, opinions, and example, just because these tastes or opinions disgust those who have the power to shut him up or lock him up.

Dworkin's argument would be more convincing if we lived in a world in which there were no systemic oppression or exclusion on the basis of such factors as gender or race. But in a non-ideal world, where the combined effect of the 'private choices, tastes, opinions, and examples' of many people is to put others at a severe, systemic and unjust disadvantage, it is hardly clear that equality prohibits some measure of official regulation in how those tastes and opinions are expressed. Such regulation is defended not 'just because' the tastes or opinions are disgusting. It is defended on the claim that the tastes and opinions contribute to systemic inequality.

Dworkin counters that such an approach would justify the regulation of television commercials, movies, and the popular media generally, which contribute to women's subordinate status. In fact, he may well be right that popular media contribute much more to that status than does pornography. His views reflect Feinberg's claim (1985) that pornography is primarily a symptom, not a cause, of violence and discrimination against women: the cause is a deeply entrenched system of 'macho' cultural values. And policing the popular media in order to eliminate gender inequality would mean a gender-totalitarian state. But it does not follow that it is wrong to regulate any form of expression that contributes to women's subordination. Relatively narrow regulations that do no significant damage to the free communication of ideas and attitudes should not be ruled out of court on a priori grounds. Sunstein (1993) and Cohen (1996), for example, reasonably argue that the regulation of violent pornography should be considered permissible because it is 'low-value' expression that may cause gender-based injury.

4.3 Pornography as Subordination

Recently, some feminist advocates of the regulation of pornography have developed a new line of argument, contending that the production and consumption of pornography are forms of discriminatory conduct that subordinate and silence women and, as conduct, should not receive free speech protection. MacKinnon (1993) pioneered this line of argument, but Langton (1993) has developed it using the ideas of speech-act theory.

To regard pornographic depictions as acts of subordination may appear to conflate a depiction with the object it depicts. Moreover, some philosophers contend that the idea that pornography silences women is a strained metaphor for a contestable causal claim about the social effects of pornography on women's willingness to voice their views. But Langton seeks to vindicate the plausibility of MacKinnnon's claims about subordination and silencing. Langton concedes that depictions as such cannot subordinate, but she contends that they can be used to rank certain people as inferior and legitimize discriminatory treatment against them. Such uses amount to the 'illocutionary force' of pornography, as Langton sees it, borrowing a concept from Austin (1962). And she suggests that there is evidence that pornographic depictions are used in our society authoritatively to rank women as subordinates and rationalize the treatment accordingly. Moreover, Langton argues that it is plausible to think that pornography is used to disable women from successfully performing certain speech-acts. For example, a woman's refusal to have sex does not count as a refusal. Her utterance of 'No' is not taken to mean 'No': there is no 'uptake', and so she is effectively silenced, even if nothing is preventing her from vocalizing certain words. The woman cannot do with those words what she is intending to do—namely, to refuse sex.

Jacobson criticizes Langton by arguing that, if women were disabled from performing the illocutionary act of refusing sex, then we could not describe as 'rape' the act of a man who ignores a women's 'No' and proceeds to have sex with her. Jacobson also argues that whether a woman performs the speech-act of refusal does not depend on the idiosyncratic understanding of any particular man but rather on how a 'competent auditor'—woman or man—would understand her utterance (1995: 78). Pornography does not silence women in the way Langton suggests, Jacobson argues, because competent auditors understand that women can and do use their words to refuse sex.

Moreover, it is questionable whether consumers regard pornographic depictions as authoritative pronouncements declaring that women ought to be sexual subordinates. Sadurski argues, 'Recognition of the pornographer's special "authority" . . . does not seem to be a plausible description of the attitude held by pornography's consumers toward its producers' (1999: 132). Pornography is consumed for purposes of sexual arousal, not for receiving authoritative verdicts on the proper sexual role of women.

4.4 Hate Speech in the USA

During the 1980s, a vigorous debate began over the legitimacy of regulating speech that degrades or demeans persons on the basis of such features as race, gender, and sexual orientation. In the USA, hundreds of colleges enacted speech codes that sought to restrict such speech. Many of the codes were challenged in court as inconsistent with the free speech guarantees of the Constitution and criticized by many scholars (Shiell 1998). But the codes were supported by other scholars, including those associated with Critical Race Theory, a movement that highlights the continued existence of racial oppression and the need for more aggressive legal and political strategies in combating it. (Lawrence 1993). Campus speech codes were also defended by some liberal scholars, who argued that narrowly drawn codes directed at face-to-face racist vilification were consistent with free speech principles (Grey 1991; Sunstein 1993; Greenawalt 1995a).

Some scholars went beyond the endorsement of campus speech codes. Delgado argued for extending tort law to cover the wrong of racial insult. And Shiffrin (1999: 161) contends that certain forms of racist speech should be punishable by law.

There are many parallels between the arguments for regulating hate speech and those for regulating pornography. Both sets of arguments stress the continued existence of subordination. Both point to the importance of symbolic expression in creating and perpetuating subordination. Both contend that our culture generally discounts and dismisses the harms suffered by subordinate classes. And both make their case for regulation on the basis of a principle of equal citizenship.

Yet, courts have struck down as violating free speech rights every campus speech code that has been subject to legal challenge. The decisions came from state and lower federal courts. The US Supreme Court has not ruled directly on the constitutional validity of campus codes, but in *RAV* v. *St Paul* (1992) the court did set out legal principles that would appear to condemn virtually all the codes that schools have adopted.

RAV invalidated a city ordinance that prohibited the public display of any symbol or sign 'that arouses anger, alarm, or resentment in others on the basis of race, color, creed, religion, or gender' (*RAV* v. *St Paul* 1992: 379) The ordinance was interpreted as applying only to 'fighting words', a form of expression unprotected under US law. Such words are traditionally defined as utterances that by themselves inflict injury or tend to incite immediate violence, although courts tend to read such a definition in a very narrow way.

In *RAV* the defendant was convicted under the ordinance after burning a cross on the lawn of a black family living in a white neighbourhood. The court threw out the conviction, without rejecting traditional fighting words doctrine. It held that the ordinance impermissibly selected certain categories of fighting words. Such selection reflected a particular viewpoint—namely, that certain kinds of fighting words are worse than others. The court ruled that such an approach amounts to impermissible viewpoint bias. Writing for the court, Justice Scalia argued that, when expression is regulated on the basis of viewpoint, it raises 'the specter that the Government may effectively drive certain ideas or viewpoints from the marketplace' (*RAV* v. *St Paul* 1992: 387).

Shiffrin points out that one of the implications of the ruling in *RAV* is that it licenses a more sweeping regulation of expression than the ordinance that was struck down. The implication is that the city could enact a 'pure' fighting words ban that did not specify any particular category of such words. Such a ban would still cover the racist and sexist fighting words that the ordinance sought to prohibit and so 'would drive the very same ideas and viewpoints (along with others) from the marketplace' (Shiffrin 1999: 63).

But Shiffrin misses the central point in Scalia's analysis: the ordinance was an effort by the city to place an official stigma on certain viewpoints and attitudes. Selecting out certain classes of fighting words for prohibition was essential to the stigmatizing purpose of the law. A 'pure' fighting words ban would have undermined that purpose. And, for Scalia, the use of criminal law to stigmatize certain viewpoints violates expressive liberty.

4.5 Hate Speech in Canada

Constitutional law in the USA is unique among contemporary democracies in the degree of protection that it provides hate speech. In Canada there is a statute making it a crime to communicate in public a statement that wilfully promotes the hatred of some racial, religious, or ethnic group, and virtually every other constitutional democracy apart from the USA has similar statutes. Such laws would be invalidated as viewpoint based by courts in the USA.

In *R.* v *Keegstra* (1990) the Canadian Supreme Court accepted the claim that the nation's racial hatred statute infringed on freedom of expression, a right protected under the Canadian Charter. But it held that expressive liberty must be balanced against racial equality and that the statute represented a reasonable balancing of those two values.

Sumner defends the court's view, arguing that tolerating expression that aims at fomenting racial hatred 'would inevitably be to confer upon it a certain degree of legitimacy. This is something that no society can afford to do, if it wishes to safeguard the status of minorities as equal citizens' (1994: 172–3). But in a regime of free expression it is essential to distinguish between tolerating a message and conferring legitimacy upon it. Official toleration is a stance in which society extends neither its authoritative approval nor its disapproval of a message. The Canadian hate-speech ban might be justified, but not because the failure to ban hate speech legitimizes racism. Rather, the ban would be justified only because it plays an important role in securing equal citizenship for all.

4.6 Enforcing Speech Restrictions

Some critics of hate-speech laws point to the fact that they are rarely enforced and that, when they are, racial minorities are often the ones prosecuted (Magnet 1994: 238–9). Moreover, the anonymous and borderless nature of Internet communication will make the enforcement of rules against hate speech (and pornography) increasingly difficult. The difficulties are highlighted by a case in which a French judge ordered Yahoo's auction site to prevent web-users in France from gaining access to Nazi artefacts (Kaplan 2000). He ruled that French law prohibited displaying Nazi souvenirs for sale. But many critics doubted the feasibility of implementing the ruling.

It may be that, in the age of Internet communication, many laws against hate speech and pornography will turn out to be largely symbolic expressions of a nation's commitment to racial and gender equality. Enforcement may be uneven and difficult. Yet, the simple fact that the law has authoritatively stigmatized certain views may well have a formative influence on social attitudes. As Kahan argues, laws help to 'furnish cues about how individuals should conduct themselves to gain approval and to avoid the stigma of deviance' (1999: 487). Hate-speech laws may send a strong signal to society affirming equality and stigmatizing bigotry. The possibility of such a signal should give pause to those who see the underenforcement of hate-speech laws as sufficient grounds for rejecting them. But the same possibility also raises concerns over whether the laws are an unjustifiable departure from viewpoint neutrality. Again, free speech principles and egalitarian ones appear in some measure to conflict.

4.7 Campaign Finance Regulation

To protect against the corruption of the political process, a number of constitutional democracies have imposed legal limits on the expenditures of candidates and/or parties. Such countries include Britain, India, Israel, and Japan. In Britain, for example, expenditure limits on candidates have been in force since 1883 and operate in conjunction with a law prohibiting anyone from spending on a candidate's behalf without his specific authorization (Law Library 1991: 6, 72).

In the USA, though, the Supreme Court ruled in *Buckley* v. *Valeo* (1976) that expenditure restrictions violate free speech. When candidates and parties spend money on a campaign, they are expressing their political views. When government restricts the amount of money that can be spent on a campaign, it limits political speech, the kind that merits the fullest protection. And the court said that it was not a legitimate exercise of government power to restrict the speech of some in order to equalize the amount of speech across society. At the same time, the court ruled that contributions to campaigns may be legally restricted in order to prevent corruption and the appearance of corruption.

Most commentators argue that the court's distinction between contributions and expenditures is not viable. If spending money to run a campaign is a way of expressing political views, so is contributing money to a campaign. Money is contributed so that it will be spent. Greenawalt—an advocate of expenditure limits—expresses the consensus: 'The right to spend money to disseminate ideas is a significant aspect of freedom' (1995a: 141).

Two of the central arguments in favour of expenditure limits invoke the idea of equality. The first holds that every citizen has an equal right to participate in the political process on a fair basis. Such participation includes voting, publicly expressing one's opinions, and running for public office. The one-person/one-vote rule is generally accepted—certain exceptions aside—and scholars such as Sunstein argue that 'limits on campaign expenditures are continuous with that rule' (1994: 1392). Unlimited campaign expenditures in combination with the high cost of running a campaign mean that a candidate needs either to be independently wealthy or to rely heavily on wealthy individuals or organizations to mount a viable run for office. Such a situation violates the equal right of political participation.

The second argument contends that democracy should provide for the equal representation of the interests of all citizens. Some interests will lose in the democratic process, for example, because they are not sufficiently compelling or are outvoted by the majority. But in the democratic process all interests should matter and be weighed, in accordance with some reasonable measure of urgency or importance. The problem with unlimited expenditures is that they result in a system that skews the weighing process in favour of the interests of the wealthy. Christiano contends that campaign financing in the USA has created a society 'in which the wealthy and powerful private economic institutions . . . dominate the process of discussion'. Such a society 'simply cannot live up to the egalitarian ideals of democracy' (1996: 286–7).

A third argument for expenditure limits connects them to democracy in another way. It holds that unlimited money in politics undermines the cognitive conditions necessary for a democratic public to make well-considered political judgements. Fiss makes this argument when he refers to 'the distorting effect that unlimited political expenditures have on politics' and asserts that 'what democracy exalts is not simply public choice but rather public choice made with full information and under suitable conditions of reflection' (1996: 25, 23).

Critics of expenditure limits claim that such limits face a series of dilemmas. If the limits apply only to the expenditures of candidates, then money will flow into political parties, which will use it to influence elections. If the limits are extended to parties, then money will flow to independent organizations such as environmental, pro-choice, and anti-abortion groups, who will use it to influence elections. Even if limits on candidates and parties were acceptable, critics argue, limits on independent groups would clearly violate free speech. In short, limits that are consistent with free speech would be ineffective at stemming the influence of money on politics, and limits that might have some effectiveness would violate free speech rights.

Sullivan argues that the dilemma is only intensified because 'campaign finance reform will do nothing to cure...the disproportionate influence on elections... of the owners and management of the institutional press'. More generally, because of large economic inequalities in society, 'background wealth distortions cannot be prevented without trenching much further upon widely held First Amendment values than most reformers ... are willing to go' (1998: 1086).

Sullivan does not deny that money can harm the political process. But she argues that under a system of unlimited contributions and expenditures, combined with mandatory and immediate disclosure of donors and amounts, there would be 'reasons for modest optimism that the harm the reformers fear from unlimited political money would in fact be limited' (1997: 689).

However, once it is assumed that the cost of campaigns creates conditions in which candidates are forced to rely unduly on the wealthy, it is difficult to see how disclosure requirements by themselves are going to limit the harm. The problem is not that we do not know exactly who is giving large sums to candidates and parties. The problem is that any viable candidate for public office will need to rely on such individuals or be independently wealthy himself. Disclosure requirements would not provide what is needed: alternative candidates free of the undue influence of large wealth.

Kaminer contends that the dilemmas generated by expenditure limits argue for public subsidies to 'candidates who do not have personal fortunes or major party support'. The system would create a 'financial floor, but not a ceiling, for candidates' (Kaminer 2000: 38). Critics will respond that it should be up to each individual to decide whether and how much to support a candidate. Public subsidies force all taxpayers to support candidates, even those against whom they may want to vote. This argument has been successful in stopping Britain from adopting a system of subsidies (Law Library 2000: 73). However, the argument fails to consider that in a democracy political activity such as running for office is a public good: the activity helps to sustain a system whose benefits extend to all and cannot be limited to those who 'pay' for them through their political engagement. In such a system, the relatively minor incursion on the liberty of taxpayers is more than offset by the good of maintaining a working democracy.

But the subsidy option, regarded as an alternative to expenditure limits on candidates, supporters, and parties, does face some practical difficulties. The value of any given amount of money in a campaign is relative to the amount spent by one's opponent and her supporters. In the absence of expenditure limits, it is difficult to see how any realistic version of a subsidy programme would, by itself, significantly restrain the influence of money. Presidential elections illustrate the point: despite the fact that the law provides presidential candidates with generous subsidies, expenditures by national parties have had an enormous influence on presidential politics.

In 1843, Marx wrote that there was a fundamental conflict in capitalist societies between the political principle of equal citizenship and the economic principle that individuals have a right to the unlimited accumulation of wealth. And Marx was right that economic inequality could subvert political equality. But the conflict can be mitigated, short of instituting socialism. Expenditure limits and public subsidies are among the devices that can be used in combination to promote political equality.

5. Religious Liberty: Theoretical Issues

5.1 What is Religion?

Scholars of religion are sometimes sceptical of efforts to define 'religion'. But even some sceptics could agree that the term can be reasonably understood as essentially referring to rituals, beliefs, and ways of life oriented towards a realm of existence or experience regarded as radically different from the realm of ordinary life and as carrying ultimate normative authority (King 1987: 283). This type of radical otherness is sometimes described as the sacred, and contrasted with the secular or profane.

While religions cannot be reduced to propositional attitudes, they often incorporate what Rawls (1993) calls 'comprehensive doctrines'—that is, normative and metaphysical ideas about the meaning and value of human life. These doctrines are the grounds on which people orient their conduct, containing conceptions and principles that are taken to have normative authority over the full scope of human life. When the conceptions involve a sacred/secular contrast and vest supreme authority in the sacred, the doctrines are religious. When comprehensive doctrines vest supreme normative authority in a realm that is not conceived as sacred, they are secular.

Greenawalt objects to essentialist definitions of 'religion' on the grounds that they are too restrictive and vulnerable to a bias that favours familiar religions over unfamiliar ones. He contends that we should fix the reference of the term by beginning with the features of paradigmatic religions and then seeing 'how closely disputed beliefs and practices resemble clear instances'. He insists that 'no single feature is indispensable for religion' (Greenawalt 2000: 219).

Greenawalt (2000: 207) is right to warn that defining 'religion' carries the danger that the familiar will be favoured over the unfamiliar, and his analogical approach seeks to accommodate the many different forms that religion can assume. But the requirement of an orientation towards the sacred leaves room for an abundance of varieties of religion. Moreover, Greenawalt's analogical approach carries the very danger he seeks to avoid: if we begin with paradigm cases and then look for other instances that are close enough to those cases, the extension we ultimately attribute to 'religion' may well be skewed by the fact that our starting point consists of those religions that are familiar to us. This skewing is especially likely when there are no articulated standards specifying the respects in which disputed cases must be judged similar to the paradigmatic ones.

Such bias may well be reflected in the statement of a German official that Scientology was 'a multinational combine rather than a religion' (US State Department 2000). For that official, the extensive business operations of Scientology may have made it too different from his paradigmatic religions. In contrast, 'orientation-to-the-sacred' clearly counts Scientology as a religion, notwithstanding its business ventures.

If religion is to be understood in terms of paradigm cases plus whatever is sufficiently similar to those cases, then it would be better to enumerate the respects in terms of which similarity is to be judged. Thus, Alston takes the paradigm approach but also lists nine characteristic features of religion, such as belief in supernatural beings, the sacred/profane distinction, prayer and other rituals, and a life-organizing world view (1964: 88). To be a religion requires possessing some unspecified number of such features.

Greenawalt would probably be sympathetic to Alston's approach, as it is consistent with an important practical concern of his. Greenawalt thinks that the law should not define religion in terms of an orientation towards the sacred because it would omit groups such as Ethical Culture societies, which are organized around secular comprehensive doctrines. In his view, Ethical Culture merits equal legal protection with doctrines that invoke the sacred. But the US Constitution explicitly protects religious liberty, not freedom of conscience more broadly. So constitutional protection for Ethical Culture seems to require that it be a religion.

But, instead of stretching the idea of religion in order to gain protection for secular comprehensive doctrines, one could argue that the normative principles justifying protection for religion also justify protection for freedom of conscience more broadly. And one could contend that a constitution should be construed in terms of its underlying normative principles. Such an argument could gain protection for secular doctrines, but it would also cast doubt on the idea that there is, as a matter of fundamental political principle, something special about religion. That doubt is explored in the next section.

5.2 Arguments for Religious Liberty as Basic

Let us suppose that religion involves an inner orientation towards the sacred and its outward expression in speech, rituals, and forms of life. And let us grant that the freedoms of conscience, speech, and association are basic. Because such freedoms do not distinguish the religious from the secular, we can then ask, 'Is religious liberty no more than a particular instance of the general freedoms of conscience, speech, and association?' Or is religious liberty an independent basic liberty?

The traditional arguments for religious freedom lend credibility to the idea that it is not an independent basic liberty. One prominent argument is that we should be especially distrustful of government when it comes to regulations that infringe on religious activity. Government has a tendency to attribute without good grounds malignant secular effects to the practices of unpopular and minority religions, or to exaggerate relatively trivial effects. Protecting religious liberty as basic guards against such ungrounded and biased judgements.

Such an argument parallels the one for regarding free speech as basic but does not establish any difference in principle between religious and non-religious expression. Government tends to attribute malignant effects to any system or association that it regards as a threat to its power or its view of the social good, regardless of religious or secular character of the threat. Whether religious 'threats' are perceived as more dangerous is an empirical question to be answered with respect to a particular social-historical context. And in modern times unpopular secular doctrines have also been subject to unwarranted claims of dangerousness.

Another traditional argument for treating religious liberty as basic asserts that leaving government free to restrict religion tends to foment civil strife. Failure to protect religious liberty raises the stakes in politics, and the struggle among the different sects will intensify as they vie for state power. This argument traces back to Locke: 'it is not the diversity of opinions, (which cannot be avoided) but the refusal of toleration to those that are of different opinion . . . that has produced all the bustles and wars' (1689/1983: 55).

Nonetheless, the argument does not establish any basis for religious liberty that is independent of arguments for secular freedom of expression and association. Secular strife is also a danger when government can suppress secular views and organizations. Moreover, the question whether religion is the most important threat to civil peace is empirical, to be addressed by each society and its particular circumstances (Smith 1991; Schwarzchild 1993).

Yet another argument stresses the importance of religion in promoting the civic virtues essential to a liberal democratic order (Galston 1991). But this argument elides the fact that religions take myriad forms, only some of which promote democratic virtue. Resting arguments for religious liberty on empirical claims that cannot be generalized to all religions is an unpromising strategy for establishing that religion merits greater protection than non-religion, as a matter of fundamental principle.

In the current literature, perhaps the central argument for religious liberty links it to individual autonomy. This should not be surprising, since the main argument for free speech is also autonomy based. Richards emphasizes the common root of expressive and religious liberty in the 'inalienable right to conscience, i.e., sincere convictions about matters of fact and value' (1999: 23). But this argument clearly erases the distinction between religious and secular conduct. Sincere convictions that form the basis of action can be about the sacred or about the secular.

Nevertheless, it remains possible that religious motivations have normatively important features that they share with some, but not all, secular motivations.

Rawls's work suggests that actions motivated by a person's comprehensive doctrine—religious or secular—merit heightened protection because of the connection the actions have to the full development and exercise of the two moral powers of personhood: the capacity for a sense of justice and the ability to formulate, pursue, and revise a conception of the good (1993). Those powers are exercised, not whenever one acts on any given belief he happens to hold, but only when the belief is an element of the individual's ultimate normative orientation towards life. The term 'liberty of conscience' is appropriate in this regard, as a person's conscience is reasonably conceived as her most central normative conceptions.

Sandel criticizes the Rawlsian conception of personhood on the ground that it 'depreciates the claims of those for whom religion is not an expression of autonomy but a matter of conviction unrelated to choice'. For many religious believers, their faith is not a matter of autonomous choice but rather reflects a categorical duty that they see as 'indispensable to their identity' (Sandel 1996: 67). But Sandel misses the mark. The claims of those who understand their faith as essential to their identity are given no less weight than the claims of those who see their faith as the object of an autonomous choice. The Rawlsian conception is that, however an individual understands her faith, her right to express that faith is a basic liberty. It is up to the individual to say what is, or is not, essential to her identity. That liberal right is no less important when the individual declares, 'Here I stand. I can do no other.'

Freedom of religion is rightly considered to be a basic liberty, but there is nothing special about religion at the level of fundamental political principle. Rather, religious liberty is basic because religion instantiates more general aspects of human life and activity that merit such protection: speech, association, and conscience.

6. Religious Liberty: Applications

6.1 The Accommodation Debates

In 1972 the US Supreme Court held that Amish parents had a free-exercise right to withdraw their children from public school before the statutory minimum age of 16 (*Wisconsin* v. *Yoder*, 1972). Yet today there is much disagreement whether the exemption is illegitimate because it denies Amish females the opportunity to gain the knowledge needed to make an informed choice about remaining part of a patriarchal culture. In 1989, after considerable controversy, the French government exempted Muslim girls from the school dress code to allow them to wear their religion's traditional headscarf, the *chador*. Yet, disagreement over the wearing of the headscarf in school continues today in much of Western Europe (Seiple 2000: 10). In 1990, the US Supreme Court (*Employment Division* v. *Smith*, 1990) rejected the claim of members of the Native American church that they had a constitutional right to engage in their religion's ritual smoking of peyote. In response, Congress enacted a new law better to protect religious groups, and the Supreme Court in turn invalidated that law (*Boerne* v. *Flores*, 1997).

These cases all involve debates over 'religious accommodation'—that is, claims to an exemption, based on one's religion, from an otherwise valid, general law. Many scholars contend that, in a broad range of circumstances, religious liberty requires government to provide accommodations when some general law or policy comes into conflict with a religiously motivated activity.

Advocates of extensive religious accommodations often look for reasons to show why religion is especially important and should be accorded privileged status. One prominent line of argument contends that religions provide grounds for resisting unjust and tyrannical states by recognizing a normative authority superior to secular authority (Carter 1993: 134; McConnell 2000: 1250). However, as with other arguments we have canvassed, this one fails to distinguish religious from secular comprehensive doctrines.

A distinct line of argument for accommodation rests not on the contention that religion is special but rather on the idea that accommodation is necessary to secure equal citizenship for religious persons (McConnell 1992). Thus, Galeotti argues that equal respect requires French officials to accommodate the Muslim schoolgirls. She contends that the case involved 'the quest for public recognition' by a religious minority and that such recognition is a 'fundamental demand of equality' (Galeotti 1993: 597). This interest in public recognition is similar to the one Raz emphasized in arguing that free speech is important to those with unconventional lifestyles.

On the anti-accommodationist side, Marshall argues that religion-based exemptions give religious individuals special treatment and so violate equal citizenship. Thus, he objects to the disparity of exempting the Amish from compulsory school attendance laws on account of their beliefs but denying a similar exemption to 'a group of Thoreauians whose objection would be based on social or political grounds' (Marshall 1991: 316). And if religious liberty is taken as derivative of more general basic liberties, Marshall's Thoreauians should be treated in the same manner as the Amish: either both groups or neither should be given exemptions.

Nonetheless, there appears to be a serious dilemma with the idea that religious and secular doctrines should be treated identically when it comes to accommodation. Prohibiting all accommodation would seem to violate equal citizenship. Equality is not the same as uniformity and cannot be guaranteed by uniformity of treatment (Audi 2000: 40). Sometimes a person's deepest normative convictions make his situation relevantly different, as with the Native American peyote smokers or those whose Sabbath observance prevents them from taking a job that unemployment or welfare laws would otherwise require them to take. But, if religious and secular doctrines are treated on a par, then it seems that the result would 'make a mockery of the rule of law' (Nussbaum 1999: 111). Too many claims of accommodation might need to be granted, as both religious and secular groups press for exemptions. Thus, Nussbaum contends that, as a practical matter, we must choose between providing exemptions only to religiously motivated conduct or having no exemptions at all. And she argues for the former on the basis of the traditional vulnerability of minority religions.

But Nussbaum is not entirely convincing. Religious minorities have been historically vulnerable, even in constitutional democracies, but so have secular minorities, such as Communists. Moreover, constitutionally required religious accommodations have not been extensive, restricted mainly to matters of schooling and unemployment compensation. Extending equal protection to secular doctrines would threaten the rule of law only if much more extensive religious accommodations were recognized.

Moreover, legal rulings have counted certain secular doctrines—such as Ethical Culture and secular forms of pacifism—as equivalent to religion, as Greenawalt endorses (2000: 208–9). Although this judicial stretching of 'religion' involves a legal fiction, legal thinkers could still reasonably contend that heightened protection for religious and secular comprehensive doctrines is important for promoting the moral powers of personhood.

Today, many constitutions differ from the US Constitution in explicitly protecting freedom of conscience and not simply religious liberty. Indeed, Article 4 of the German Constitution exempts from armed war service all conscientious objectors, drawing no distinction between secular and religious objections. And it is reasonable to think that a feasible arrangement exists that treats religious and secular doctrines equally, while providing both kinds of doctrine with heightened protection and avoiding harm to the rule of law.

6.2 Religion and Politics

Related to the accommodation debates is the question whether theological claims can play a legitimate role in public political discussion and decision making. Several key thinkers argue that theological claims are, in certain respects, inappropriate for public debate and decision. These thinkers do not contend that individuals should be legally barred from making religious contributions to public debate. But they argue that persons should exercise self-restraint when it comes to such contributions so as to respect the equal standing of their fellow citizens. Thus, Audi argues that citizens should not support any coercive law unless they are motivated by 'adequate secular reasons', such as public health and safety (2000: 86–96).

Rawls (1993) contends that norms of equal citizenship require each person to bracket her belief in the truth of her own comprehensive doctrine when discussing and deciding constitutional questions and issues of basic justice. Equal citizens address such matters on grounds of public reason—that is, grounds that they can reasonably expect all their fellow citizens reasonably to endorse in principle. Rawls treats religious and secular comprehensive doctrines on a par and provides for an important exception to the bracketing requirement: comprehensive doctrines may be introduced when they help to bring about or secure free and equal citizenship for all and the arguments based on those doctrines are supplemented 'in due course' by ones that are not particular to any sectarian world view (1999: 152–5).

Greenawalt argues that 'comprehensive views... can appropriately figure in resolution of the broad range of political issues that ordinary citizens face', with the proviso that when citizens argue in the public forum for a political position they should emphasize reasons that their fellow citizens can share. Legislators may give some weight to positions of their constituents that are based on comprehensive views. But, because legislators should represent all their constituents with equal respect, they 'should probably afford more weight to a citizen position that is grounded in public reason' (Greenawalt 1995b: 160–1). Judges should exercise the greatest restraint and generally decide cases based on reasons that are 'shared in our political culture' (Greenawalt 1995b: 146).

Perry (1997) rejects restrictions on religious arguments in public discussion and argues that the idea of the sacred value of life is an admissible ground of official decision making apart from any secular rationale. However, he otherwise deems it inappropriate for officials to make decisions about human well-being on religious grounds when there is no plausible secular basis for the decision.

Wolterstorff contends that liberal views such as those of Audi, Rawls, and Greenawalt have led to an unfortunate 'silencing of religion in the public square' and fail to treat religious citizens as equals (1997: 177). Quinn adds that the public airing of religious considerations has the virtue of encouraging a public dialogue in which unexpected agreement emerges and people develop their own views more adequately as a result of 'contact and confrontation with an alien religion or metaphysics' (1997: 158). Likewise, Carter contends that public dialogue in which religious argument is welcomed could help persons to learn from others with different epistemological suppositions (1993: 232).

In assessing this complex debate, it is crucial to understand the liberal conception of equal citizenship and to ask whether the anti-liberals provide a viable alternative. When citizens call on government to deploy its coercive powers, the liberal norm of equal citizenship places on them an obligation to provide a justification resting on grounds that their fellow citizens can in principle accept. For example, reasons of public health are ones that all citizens can accept, notwithstanding the diversity of religious and secular comprehensive doctrines. Moreover, citizens generally accept the methods of empirical inquiry that are capable of providing reliable evidence about claims concerning public health. Thus, disagreement over whether a particular law is needed adequately to protect public health is one that proceeds from a broad area of common ground, and thereby conforms to the norms of liberal equality.

In contrast, reasons of personal salvation are not ones that all citizens can accept, in part because the faith of many believers holds that salvation is not among the matters that government can competently or legitimately address. And citizens of faith will disagree sharply over the appropriate methods of determining the right road to salvation. Reasons involving secular ideals of personal moral perfection— for example, the Stoic ideal of an individual indifferent to his fortune or misfortune— will also fail the test of liberal equality. Many citizens will be unable to accept them because they hold conflicting ideals of moral perfection.

Liberal equality does not obligate anyone to refrain from giving voice to their comprehensive views in political discussion. Nor does liberal equality obligate any-one to refrain from supporting a coercive law if they have sufficient sectarian reasons. But, if they do have such reasons, liberal equality obligates them to refrain from supporting the law for those reasons: they should not support the law unless they also have reasons that their fellow citizens can share.

The liberal conception of equal citizenship is an ideal. Reasons and methods of enquiry that can be shared by literally every single citizen will be impossible to find. But, for the liberal, that is a matter of a regrettable gap between the ideal and the real. If anti-liberals do not regard it as such, they need to develop a viable alternat-ive to the liberal conception of equality. And, if they do regard it as such, they need to explain why they do not turn out to be liberals after all.

7. Speech, Religion, and Equality

Discussions of freedom of speech and religion often assume the existence of a demo-cratic order devoid of explosive ethnic tensions and oppressive social hierarchies. That assumption is challenged in part by critical race theorists and radical femi-nists, who assert that Western democracies are riddled with racial and gender oppression. But, regardless of the truth of that assertion, it is undeniable that there are democracies riddled by oppressive hierarchies and violent ethnic conflicts. And it is important to examine how the principles of expressive and religious liberty should be applied under conditions that fall egregiously short of the ideal of free and equal citizenship.

In his examination of India, Jacobsohn argues that caste inequality and religious violence make it reasonable to restrict religious association and speech there in ways that would be unacceptable in other constitutional democracies. Indian electoral law prohibits candidates from promoting 'feelings of enmity or hatred between classes of citizens...on grounds of religion, race, caste, community or language' (Jacobsohn 2000: 297). The Indian Constitution protects free speech and religion, but the Supreme Court has held that a leader of an extremist Hindu party could be barred from standing for election because of campaign rhetoric directed against Muslims. The court invoked a constitutional provision providing a 'public order' exception to free speech protections.

Jacobsohn endorses the court's view but goes further to contend that it has not been vigorous enough in enforcing another provision of Indian electoral law that prohibits any candidate from appealing for votes on the basis of his race, religion, or caste. Indian constitutionalism, argues Jacobsohn, is committed to the elimination of the culture's traditional structural inequalities, and the electoral provision has a logic that can be defended on grounds of its consistency with such constitutionalism. More broadly, his point is that the principles essential to constitutional democracy—such as freedom of speech and religion—should be interpreted and applied in a manner that is sensitive to the social and historical context of each country.

Tamir (2000) takes a similar tack in discussing Israel, where the law prohibits a party for standing for election if it intentionally incites racism. She defends a ruling of the Israeli High Court barring the virulently anti-Islamic Kach Party, even though the speech in question involved readings from biblical passages. On her view, religious hate speech in the Israeli context amounts to fighting words that ought to be banned on account of the potential to ignite violence.

The realities of caste in India and Jewish/Palestinian conflict in Israel make issues of expressive and religious liberty harder cases than they typically are in democracies where the gap between the real and the ideal is not nearly as wide. Interpreting such liberties in ways that would entrench caste inequality or generate widespread religious violence would be a mistake on practical and moral grounds. Religious and expressive liberty are elements of the ideal of free and equal citizenship, and social progress towards that ideal, where the reality falls egregiously short, should not be undercut by the context-blind insistence that rights are trumps over collective goals.

Nonetheless, the incursion on basic liberties found in Israeli and Indian electoral law are substantial, because the laws deny to certain groups the right of political association based on their religious speech. This incursion is far greater than that of the hate-speech laws found in Canada and most other democracies. Thus, laws that ban extremist religious parties should face a high burden of justification, requiring clear and convincing evidence that the laws are needed to make progress in mitigating caste-like inequality or to forestall widespread violence. Neither Jacobsohn nor Tamir makes the case that such evidence is available.

8. CONCLUSION

For much of the twentieth century, thinkers developed and invoked the ideals of freedom and equality to combat social disadvantage linked to race, gender, and class. But the meaning and implications of the ideals are not transparent, and debates have emerged as to whether they require society to tolerate forms of expression that demean and degrade on the basis of race, religion, and gender. Moreover, theorists have recently taken up issues concerning the equal treatment of persons whose religious convictions have political implications.

The task of future work lies in three main areas. First, in the area of ideal theory, there is need to clarify the scope and nature of expressive and religious liberty through further examination of the ideal of free and equal citizenship. Second, in the area of non-ideal theory, there is need for sociologically informed work that examines how the political ideals of freedom and equality should guide law and policy under the real conditions of social life. Third, there is need for comparative analyses, exploring the various forms that constitutional democracy takes in different countries and how that variety illuminates questions of ideal and non-ideal theory.

REFERENCES

Alexander, Lawrence, and Horton, Paul (1983). 'The Impossibility of a Free Speech Principle'. *Northwestern University Law Review*, 78: 1319–57.

Alston, William (1964). *Philosophy of Language*. Englewood Cliffs, NJ: Prentice Hall.

Audi, Robert (2000). *Religious Commitment and Secular Reason*. New York: Cambridge University Press.

Austin, J. L. (1962). *How to Do Things with Words*. New York: Oxford University Press.

Carter, Stephen (1993). *The Culture of Disbelief*. New York: Basic Books.

Christiano, Thomas (1996). *The Rule of the Many*. Boulder, CO: Westview.

Cohen, Joshua (1996). 'Freedom of Expression', in David Heyd (ed.), *Toleration*. Princeton: University Press, 173–225.

Delgado, Richard, and Stefancic, Jean (1997). *Must We Defend Nazis?* New York: New York University Press.

Dworkin, Ronald (1996). *Freedom's Law*. Cambridge, MA: Harvard University Press.

Ely, John Hart (1980). *Democracy and Distrust*. Cambridge, MA: Harvard University Press.

Feinberg, Joel (1985). *Offense to Others*. New York: Oxford University Press.

Finnis, John (1997). 'The Good of Marriage'. *American Journal of Jurisprudence*, 42: 97–134.

Fish, Stanley (1994). *There's No Such Thing as Free Speech*. New York: Oxford University Press.

Fiss, Owen (1996). *The Irony of Free Speech*. Cambridge, MA: Harvard University Press.

Frantz, Laurent (1962). 'The First Amendment in the Balance'. *Yale Law Journal*, 71: 1424–50.

Galeotti, Elizabetta (1993). 'Citizenship and Equality'. *Political Theory*, 21: 585–605.

Galston, William (1991). *Liberal Purposes* New York: Cambridge University Press.

George, Robert (1999). *In Defense of Natural Law*. New York: Oxford University Press.

Greenawalt, Kent (1995a). *Fighting Words*. Princeton: Princeton University Press.

——(1995b). *Private Consciences and Public Reasons*. New York: Oxford University Press.

——(2000). 'Five Questions about Religion Judges are Afraid to Ask', in N. Rosenblum (ed.), *Obligations of Citizenship and Demands of Faith*. Princeton: Princeton University Press, 196–244.

Grey, Thomas (1991). 'Civil Rights versus Civil Liberties'. *Social Philosophy and Policy*, 8: 81–107.

Herman, Edward, and Chomsky, Noam (1988). *Manufacturing Consent*. New York: Pantheon.

Jacobsohn, Gary (2000). 'By the Light of Reason: Corruption, Religious Speech, and Constitutional Essentials', in N. Rosenblum (ed.), *Obligations of Citizenship and Demands of Faith*. Princeton: Princeton University Press, 294–320.

Jacobson, Daniel (1995). 'Freedom of Speech Acts? A Response to Langton'. *Philosophy and Public Affairs*, 24: 64–79.

Kahan, Dan (1999). 'The Secret Ambition of Deterrence'. *Harvard Law Review*, 113: 414–500.

Kairys, David (1998). 'Freedom of Speech', in Kairys (ed)., *Politics of Law*. 3rd edn. New York: Basic Books, 190–215.

Kaminer, Wendy (2000). 'Speech Isn't Cheap'. *American Prospect*, 11 (31 July), 38–9.

Kaplan, Carl (2000). 'French Nazi Memorabilia Case Presents Jurisdiction Dilemma'. *New York Times*, 11 Aug.

King, Winston (1987). 'Religion', in M. Eliade (ed.), *The Encyclopedia of Religion*. New York: MacMillan, 282–92.

Langton, Rae (1993). 'Speech Acts and Unspeakable Acts'. *Philosophy and Public Affairs*, 22: 293–330.

Law Library of Congress (1991). *Campaign Financing of National Elections in Foreign Countries*. Washington: Law Library of Congress.

Lawrence, Charles (1993). 'If He Hollers, Let Him Go', in Mari Matsuda et al. (eds.), *Words that Wound*. Boulder, CO: Westview, 53–88.

Locke, John (1689/1983). *A Letter Concerning Toleration*. Indianapolis: Hackett.

McConnell, Michael (1992). 'Accommodation of Religion: An Update and Response to Critics'. *George Washington University Law Review*, 60: 685–742.

——(2000). 'Religion and Constitutional Rights: Why is Religious Liberty the "First Freedom"?' *Cardozo Law Review*, 21: 1243–65.

MacKinnon, Catherine (1993). *Only Words*. Cambridge, MA: Harvard University Press.

Magnet, Joseph (1994). 'Hate Propaganda in Canada', in W. J. Waluchow (ed.), *Free Expression*. New York: Oxford University Press, 1–29.

Marcuse, Herbert (1969). 'Repressive Tolerance', in Robert Wolff et al. (eds.), *Critique of Pure Tolerance*. Boston: Beacon, 81–117.

Marshall, William (1991). 'In Defense of Smith and Free Exercise Revisionism'. *University of Chicago Law Review*, 58: 308–28.

Marx, Karl (1843/1994). 'On the Jewish Question', in Lawrence Simon (ed.), *Karl Marx: Selected Writings*. Indianapolis; Hackett, 1–26.

Matsuda, Mari (1993). 'Public Response to Racist Speech: Considering the Victim's Story', in Matsuda et al. (eds.), *Words that Wound*. Boulder, CO: Westview, 17–51.

Meiklejohn, Alexander (1948). *Free Speech and its Relation to Self-Government*. Port Washington, NY: Kennikat Press.

Mill, John Stuart (1859/1978). *On Liberty*. Indianapolis: Hackett.

Nagel, Thomas (1995). 'Personal Rights and Public Space'. *Philosophy and Public Affairs*, 24: 83–107.

Nussbaum, Martha (1999). 'A Plea for Difficulty', in Susan Okin (ed.), *Is Multiculturalism Bad for Women?* Princeton: University Press, 105–14.

Perry, Michael (1997). *Religion in Politics*. New York: Oxford University Press.

Post, Robert (1995). *Constitutional Domains*. Cambridge, MA: Harvard University Press.

Quinn, Philip (1997). 'Political Liberalisms and their Exclusions of the Religious', in Paul Weithman (ed.), *Religion and Contemporary Liberalism*. Notre Dame, IN: University of Notre Dame Press, 138–61.

Rawls, John (1993). *Political Liberalism*. Cambridge, MA: Harvard University Press.

—— (1999). 'The Idea of Public Reason Revisited', in Rawls, *Law of Peoples*. Cambridge, MA: Harvard University Press, 129–80.

Raz, Joseph (1994). 'Free Expression and Personal Identification', in W. Waluchow (ed.), *Free Expression*. New York: Oxford University Press, 31–57.

Richards, David A. J. (1999). *Free Speech and the Politics of Identity*. New York: Oxford University Press.

Sadurski, Wojciech (1999). *Freedom of Expression and its Limits*. Dordrecht: Kluwer.

Sandel, Michael (1996). *Democracy's Discontents*. Cambridge, MA: Harvard University Press.

Scanlon, T. (1972). 'A Theory of Freedom of Expression'. *Philosophy and Public Affairs*, 1: 204–26.

Schauer, Frederick (1982). *Free Speech: A Philosophical Enquiry*. New York: Cambridge University Press.

—— (1993). 'The Phenomenology of Speech and Harm'. *Ethics*, 103: 635–53.

Schwarzchild, M. (1993). 'Religion and Public Debate in a Liberal Society'. *San Diego Law Review*, 30: 903–15.

Seiple, Robert (2000). 'Testimony on the Treatment of Religious Minorities in Western Europe'. *Hearing before the Committee on International Relations, US House of Representatives*, 14 June, serial no. 106–165, 6–10.

Shiell, Timothy (1998). *Campus Hate Speech on Trial*. Lawrence, KA: University of Kansas Press.

Shiffrin, S. (1999). *Dissent, Injustice, and the Meanings of America* (Princeton: Princeton University Press).

Smith, Steven (1991). 'The Rise and Fall of Religious Freedom in Constitutional Discourse'. *University of Pennsylvania Law Review*, 140: 149–240.

Sullivan, Kathleen (1997). 'Political Money and Freedom of Speech'. *University of California at Davis Law Review*, 30: 663–90.

—— 1998. 'Political Money and Freedom of Speech: A Reply to Frank Askin'. *University of California at Davis Law Review*, 31: 1083–90.

Sumner, L. W. (1994). 'Hate Propaganda and Charter Rights', in W. Waluchow (ed.), *Free Expression*. New York: Oxford University Press, 153–74.

Sunstein, Cass (1993). *Democracy and the Problem of Free Speech*. New York: Free Press.

—— (1994). 'Political Equality and Unintended Consequences'. *Columbia Law Review*, 94: 1390–414.

Tamir, Yael (2000). 'Remember Amalek: Religious Hate Speech', in Nancy Rosenblum (ed.), *Obligations of Citizenship and Demands of Faith*. Princeton: Princeton University Press, 321–34.

Tiersma, Peter (1993). 'Nonverbal Communication and the Freedom of "Speech"'. *Wisconsin Law Review*, 1993: 1525–89.

US Department of State (2000). *1999 Country Reports on Human Rights Practices: Germany*. http://www.state.gov/www/global/human_rights/1999_hrp_report/germany.html.

Weinstein, James (1999). *Hate Speech, Pornography, and the Radical Attack on Free Speech Doctrine*. Boulder, CO: Westview.

Wolterstorff, Nicholas (1997). 'Why We Should Reject what Liberalism Tells Us about Speaking and Acting in Public for Religious Reasons', in Paul Weithman (ed.), *Religion and Contemporary Liberalism*. Notre Dame, IN: University of Notre Dame Press, 162–81.

Cases Cited

Boerne v. *Flores*, 521 US 507 (1997).
Buckley v. *Valeo*, 424 US 1 (1976).
Cohen v. *California*, 403 US 15 (1971).
Employment Division v. *Smith*, 494 US 872 (1990).
R. v. *Keegstra*, 3 SCR 647 (1990).
RAV v. *St Paul*, 505 US 377 (1992).
Wisconsin v. *Yoder*, 406 US 205 (1972).

CHAPTER 15

LEGAL PATERNALISM

DOUGLAS N. HUSAK

1. INTRODUCTION

My central interest in this chapter is to examine the special philosophical difficulties that arise in attempts to think about paternalism in legal contexts. Most moral philosophers have focused on *personal relationships* in their efforts to understand both the nature and the justification of paternalism. That is, they have endeavoured to identify the conditions under which what they define as paternalism might be justified in situations in which one person (for example, a parent, a doctor, or a friend) interacts with another person (for example, a child, a patient, or a friend). I will be largely concerned with the problems that inhere in efforts to apply to the domain of law any theories about paternalism that might be derived from these personal contexts. I will propose tentative solutions to several of these problems.

2. THE NATURE OF PATERNALISM

In this section I will describe how our understanding of what paternalism *is* becomes complicated and problematic as we move from personal relationships to

I would like to thank Professors Hugh LaFollette and Seana Shiffrin for valuable assistance with earlier drafts of this chapter.

legal contexts. In order to support my claim that the nature of paternalism itself is less clear in legal situations, I must begin with a brief discussion of how paternalism is typically defined in a personal relationship.

On most occasions in which A is justified in not allowing B to act according to his preferences, A's objective is to protect persons other than B who would be harmed or adversely affected by B's behaviour. When A treats B paternalistically, however, B is prevented from adopting some course of action on the grounds that it would be bad for B. As a rough approximation, one person A treats another person B paternalistically when A interferes with B's freedom for B's own good—to protect or promote B's health and safety, economic interests, or moral well-being. A may interfere with B's freedom by disregarding either his judgement or his preferences; for simplicity, I will suppose that A disregards B's preferences in treating him paternalistically. I will refer to any example that conforms to this description as a paradigm case of paternalism.

When philosophers attempt to be more precise about the nature of paternalism, however, the details of their definitions vary, sometimes considerably (Archer 1990). Philosophers have engaged in lively debates about whether particular examples that deviate from the foregoing paradigm do or do not qualify as genuine instances of paternalism. Accounts have been offered; counterexamples have been advanced; modifications have been proposed. I will mention two (of many) such debates briefly. Still, for reasons that will become clear, I will avoid commitment about how paternalism should ultimately be defined.

Two disagreements about the nature of paternalism may be noteworthy. First, some philosophers have argued that the paternalist need not *interfere* in the freedom of the person treated paternalistically (Gert and Culver 1976). Suppose, for example, that a doctor encounters an unconscious accident victim whose life can be saved only by a blood transfusion. This doctor happens to know that the victim has a religious objection to the treatment, but proceeds to save his life anyway. Since the patient was unconscious throughout the procedure, it is hard to conclude that the transfusion involved an interference in his liberty. Still, we are invited to conclude, the doctor treated the patient paternalistically.

Secondly, some philosophers have pointed out that paternalism need not involve the simple two-party case described in my rough characterization. In some cases, only one party is involved. Suppose that Green understands his proclivity to incur debt, so he tears up the credit cards he receives in the mail. Is his act of destroying the credit cards an instance of paternalism in which Green plays the role of both A (his present self) and B (his later self whose preferences he disregards)? In other cases, three or more parties are involved. Suppose that parent A forbids his older son C from sharing cigarettes with his younger son B on the ground that tobacco is bad for B's health. This case is unlike a typical situation in which C is coerced to prevent him from harming B, since B may be willing and eager to engage in the proscribed transaction. In this case, we again are invited to conclude, A treats B paternalistically. Paternalism in this case might be called *indirect* or *impure* (Dworkin 1972), since *A* interferes directly with the liberty of *C*, and only indirectly with that of *B*, the intended beneficiary.

Are these two kinds of non-standard cases genuine counterexamples to my rough approximation, so that modifications of my definition are required? Probably. But I am not altogether confident that a 'right answer' to such questions can be defended. That is, I am sceptical that we can decide definitively whether each non-standard case is or is not a 'real' instance of paternalism. I suspect that whether a given example is a genuine instance of paternalism is a matter of degree. That is, some cases are simply *better* or *worse* examples of paternalism than others. We should not expect decisive reasons for or against categorizing any given example as an instance of paternalism. Ultimately, a philosopher who insists on a yes-or-no answer to the question of whether a given case is or is not an instance of paternalism must simply resort to stipulation and announce that he means thus-and-so by the term. The more important issue, I submit, is whether the behaviour of *A* in the foregoing examples is justified. Generalizations about whether and under what circumstances paradigmatic cases of paternalism are justified may or may not be defensible when applied to the foregoing non-standard situations. These latter cases may present distinct justificatory issues that need not arise in paradigm cases of paternalism.

Whatever exactly paternalism is taken to be, I believe it should be understood as a person's *reason* or *motivation* for failing to regard as decisive the preference of the person treated paternalistically—a reason that aims to promote or protect the welfare or interest of the person so treated. The decision to construe paternalism as a motivation has several important implications I will briefly discuss.

First, an interference with liberty should not be construed as paternalistic in virtue of its *effects*. Consider two kinds of cases in which effect and motivation diverge. Suppose that *A* somehow succeeds in advancing *B*'s interests even though *A*'s reason for interfering in *B*'s freedom is to enrich himself. Or suppose that *A* fails to advance *B*'s interests despite *A*'s best efforts to do so. I believe that the latter, but not the former kind of case should be categorized as an instance of paternalism. This categorization follows from defining paternalism in terms of the motives that lead *A* to interfere with *B*'s freedom, rather than in terms of how *A*'s interference actually affects *B*'s welfare. Although I will contend (in Section 4) that consequences are important to decide whether legal paternalism is *justified*, I believe that consequences are unimportant to understand what paternalism *is*.

Even when construed as a reason, there is room for doubt about whether *A* can treat *B* paternalistically if *B* lacks the preference with which *A* is prepared to interfere. Consider a case in which *B* lacks the slightest inclination to perform the act that *A* would not allow. Suppose, for example, that *A* writes a will providing a large inheritance for *B*. *A* believes that expeditions to the South Pole are too risky for anyone to undertake, and makes the bequest contingent on *B*'s agreement not to attempt the perilous journey. Suppose further that *B* happens to share *A*'s opinion, and never develops any desire to leave the country. In this example, A seems to have a paternalistic reason not to treat as decisive a preference of B that is purely hypothetical—that is, A hopes to dissuade B from acting according to a preference that B need not actually have. If such cases did not qualify as genuine instances of paternalism, we could not classify A's motivation as paternalistic unless and until B formed an inclination to travel to the South Pole. Admittedly, difficulties in justifying paternalism might be somewhat less worrisome in these kinds of cases. After all, B is less likely to resent a clause in A's will that discourages him from engaging in conduct he has absolutely no desire to perform. Still, difficulties in justifying paternalism do not disappear altogether here. Many persons report strong reservations about being made to do something (for example, buckle a seat belt) that they are quick to admit they would do in any event.

For present purposes, a different implication of construing paternalism as a motivation is especially important. If paternalism is understood as a reason for failing to regard the (real or hypothetical) preference of a person as decisive, disagreements about whether a particular law (or a practice, policy, or institution) is or is not paternalistic may be misguided and futile. *Laws* do not seem to be the kinds of things that *can* be paternalistic; only *reasons* can be paternalistic. Still, allegations that a law (or a policy, practice, or institution) is paternalistic are frequently made by philosophers, and should not be dismissed as confusions or category mistakes. How should such claims be understood? Perhaps we should classify a law as paternalistic when it exists for paternalistic reasons.

Several obvious difficulties arise in this attempt to understand how a law can be paternalistic—how it can 'exist for paternalistic reasons'. Many of these difficulties are familiar to legal philosophers who defend theories of statutory or constitutional interpretation that attach significance to legislative intent. The first kinds of problems arise even when a legislator is a single individual like a monarch. A legislator is not generally required to disclose his motivation for enacting legislation. In most cases, his reason must be inferred from various sources, many of which can be ambiguous or even contradictory. In addition, a legislator may have no single reason in favour of enacting a given law; he may have several distinct purposes in mind. When a philosopher categorizes a given law as paternalistic, he is probably guessing about what he supposes to have been the most important reason of the legislator who enacted it.

The second kinds of difficulties arise in a modern democracy, in which laws are enacted by a number of legislators rather than by a single individual. These problems involve combining the separate motives of several individuals into the purpose of a group. When many individuals collaborate in legislation, whose purposes should count? Should we include only those legislators who voted in favour of the law, or should we also consider the reasons of those legislators who opposed it? Even if we agree about which legislators should count, these persons are bound to have diverse reasons for enacting the statute. One legislator may vote in favour of a Bill for paternalistic reasons, another may vote for the Bill even though he explicitly rejects this paternalistic reason, while yet a third may support the Bill for reasons having nothing to do with its merits—because he hopes to gain support from the sponsor of the Bill in the next election, for example. How can we possibly decide whether to classify such a law as paternalistic?

In addition, the *persistence* of law complicates endeavours to categorize it as paternalistic. All the legislators who passed a statute may be dead. Suppose that most of the legislators who enacted a law did so for paternalistic reasons, but this rationale is now widely discredited among legislators. Still, these legislators have non-paternalistic reasons for not repealing the law. Since the law persists for altogether different reasons from those that led to its enactment, should we continue to classify the law according to the original motivation of those who created it? In the light of these (and other) difficulties, we might well despair of any prospects of identifying 'the reason' for a law. We might go so far as to conclude that persons who speak of the reason for a law are engaged in a legal fiction.

Problems in categorizing a given law as paternalistic arise whenever particular examples are discussed. Consider, for example, a statute forbidding child labour. Presumably, many legislators favoured such a law in order to protect the welfare of children who would otherwise work. An additional reason for the statute, of course, is to protect the jobs and wages of adults who would otherwise be forced to compete with underage workers. As far as I can tell, there is simply no definitive answer to the question of whether such a statute *is* or *is not* paternalistic. A very general lesson should be learned from this example. I believe that every actual law that anyone has ever been tempted to categorize as paternalistic resembles the example of child labour in this respect.

Here, then, is the first of many difficulties that arise in attempts to apply philosophical insights about paternalism in personal relationships to contexts involving law. Admittedly, on some occasions, the motivations for interference can be complicated and unclear even in personal relationships. I assume, however, that a father who requires his 6-year-old daughter to finish her vegetables before she is allowed to eat dessert may be relatively confident about his reason for not deferring to her preference. The difficulties in classifying a given interference as paternalistic are seldom as formidable in personal relationships as in legal contexts.

This fact will become important when we turn to issues of whether and under what circumstances paternalism is justified. Most philosophers, it is fair to say, have relatively strong intuitions against the justifiability of paternalism, at least when it is imposed on sane adults. Suppose that a philosopher becomes persuaded of a theory according to which paternalism is never justified, or is justified only under a narrowly specified set of conditions. Of what value is his theory in assessing legislation in the real world? It is hard to see how his theory could be used to condemn any existing law. That is, he cannot demand that any particular law must be repealed because he is convinced that such a theory is correct. All that he is entitled to conclude is that such a law is unjustified in so far as it exists for paternalistic reasons.

Nonetheless, a theory about the conditions under which paternalism is justified will have some limited relevance in legal contexts. Such a theory might constrain the set of considerations to which legislators are allowed to appeal in their deliberations about whether to support or oppose a given piece of legislation. That is, a legislator may be persuaded that, unless given conditions are satisfied, some kinds of reasons that he might otherwise cite in support of a proposed law should not be permitted to count in its favour. Alternatively, such a theory might constrain the considerations to which citizens are allowed to appeal in making judgements about whether a given law is justified (Waldron 1989). In a democracy, I assume that citizens have special reasons to form their own opinions about whether or not given laws are warranted. A theory about the conditions under which paternalism is acceptable as a rationale should be useful for this purpose.

Despite these formidable obstacles, I remain hopeful that the label 'paternalistic' can meaningfully be applied to given laws, and that a theory of when paternalism is justified is relevant to the issue of whether such laws are justified. Perhaps the most promising proposal for interpreting the claim that a given law is paternalistic is that 'the most plausible rationale' or 'the best rationale' in favour of the law is to limit the freedom of persons for their own good. According to this proposal, a law can be paternalistic even though no one, past or present, ever thought to defend it for paternalistic reasons. 'The rationale' of a law can be something other than the reasons that actually led anyone to enact it. Of course, enormous controversy may surround the judgement that one rationale for a law is more plausible or better than another. But those who conclude that the best reason in favour of a given law is paternalistic are committed to categorizing that law as paternalistic.

Despite its promise, this proposal to understand how a law can be paternalistic is problematic. Eventually, we will struggle to decide whether and under what circumstances paternalistic laws are justified. This effort requires us to apply normative principles to particular cases of paternalism. In order to undertake this effort, we must first identify whether a law is paternalistic. The foregoing proposal to identify when a law is paternalistic will complicate the task of deciding whether any such laws are justified. According to this proposal, normative principles about whether paternalistic laws are justified will turn out to have a direct bearing on whether laws *are* paternalistic. Suppose, for example, that we conclude that no paternalistic laws can be justified. If paternalistic laws are those laws for which the best rationale is paternalistic, we are likely to decide that *no* laws are paternalistic. Our normative principles tell us that the best rationale for a law will never be paternalistic; some other rationale for a given law is almost certain to be better than a paternalistic rationale. This result should be avoided. Ideally, the criteria to identify whether a law *is* paternalistic should be independent of the criteria to decide whether such a law is justified. For these reasons, I have serious reservations about this proposal to understand how a law can be paternalistic. Nonetheless, I see no better alternative—unless we deny that laws *can* be paternalistic. Perhaps some better proposal is available, or the problem I have described can be solved. In any event, we should remain cautious and tentative whenever the label 'paternalistic' is attached to a given law (or a policy, practice, or institution).

Thus far, I have pointed out some of the difficulties in applying a definition of paternalism to particular laws. Still, I have done little to support my claim that our understanding of what paternalism *is* becomes less clear as we move from non-legal to legal contexts. My central basis for this claim is that laws are necessarily general and applicable to groups of persons whose circumstances differ widely. The fact that law is applicable to a group of persons—whereas a paradigm case of paternalism in a personal relationship is applicable only to a single individual—gives rise to many of the perplexities in understanding the nature and justification of legal paternalism. Suppose that we (somehow) decide that legislators have enacted a given law to limit the freedom of persons for their own good. Even so, we are likely to find that the law does not disregard the preferences of each and every person whose liberty is restricted. Some limitations of liberty are best construed as devices that *enable* persons to attain an objective that they want, but (for one reason or another) are not especially successful in obtaining. I am doubtful that we should understand a rationale as paternalistic when it enables a person to achieve an objective that he recognizes as desirable but is unlikely to attain in the absence of the legislation that limits his liberty (Dworkin 1972).

A good example of this phenomenon is a statute that requires persons to set aside a given percentage of their income in a retirement plan. Consider Smith, who does not want to spend all his income in the present, but is well aware of his inability to save the amount of money he realizes is optimal. Although he grumbles occasionally, he usually approves of the legislation that prevents him from succumbing to his own weakness. If the legislator who enacted this statute believed that everyone resembled Smith in these respects, I would be hesitant to categorize his motivation as paternalistic. The legislator is not disregarding Smith's preference, but helping him to attain that which he prefers or judges to be best.

Complications arise, of course, because legislators know that many of the persons to whom the law applies will *not* resemble Smith. Consider Jones, who, like Smith, is made to contribute to the retirement plan. Unlike Smith, however, Jones would prefer to spend all his income in the present. The law does not regard Jones's preference as decisive, and he is certain to perceive the law as a paternalistic interference in his freedom. How should the rationale for the law be categorized when legislators realize that the liberty of both Smith and Jones will be restricted? When the preferences of many but not all the persons whose liberty is restricted are regarded as decisive, I am not confident that we can identify a 'right answer' to the question of whether the rationale of the law is paternalistic.

I have mentioned a crucial respect in which Smith and Jones differ. Of course, the persons whose liberty is restricted by the foregoing law will vary in countless other ways as well. The foregoing statute benefits both Smith and Jones, but it actually disadvantages other individuals. Consider White, who is like Smith in that he does not prefer to spend all his income in the present, but who differs from Smith in that he is sufficiently disciplined to save the amount of money he realizes is optimal. White believes that he would be able to provide more money for his retirement if he were allowed to invest his income himself, instead of being forced to contribute to the plan mandated by the state. Suppose—as is almost certainly true—that legislators know that some of the persons who resemble White are *correct* in their belief about their ability to invest more wisely than the state. In other words, we are aware that this law will actually make such persons worse off than they would have been without the law. On these assumptions, is their rationale for the law still paternalistic? Should we continue to say that the law is paternalistic? Yet again, stipulation is needed to answer this question.

This ambivalence about the rationale of given laws—which some persons recognize as enabling them to achieve a good, and others criticize as interfering with their freedom to attain a good—can be detected throughout American legal history. Consider *Lochner* v. *New York* (1905)—perhaps the most discredited Supreme Court decision in the twentieth century. Is a statute that forbids bakery employees from working more than sixty hours a week a paternalistic interference in their freedom of contract, as Justice Peckham, who wrote the majority opinion, insisted? Or is it instead a device by which workers can gain collective protection from unwanted exploitation, as Justice Holmes, in his famous dissent, seemed prepared to believe? My inability to answer this question is only partly based on the difficulties I described in identifying 'the rationale' of a law. My inability is also due to the fact that the law is general and applicable to many different persons whose circumstances differ, so that no single answer to this question pertains to each and every baker whose freedom is restricted.

3. DIFFICULTIES IN JUSTIFYING LEGAL PATERNALISM

Since at least the time of John Stuart Mill, many moral and political philosophers in the liberal tradition have expressed strong reservations about the justifiability of paternalism, tolerating it under very narrow conditions. As I have indicated, personal relationships have typically been used to develop theories about whether and under what circumstances paternalism is justified. As I will argue in this section, however, few of the central distinctions such theories invoke are helpful in efforts to justify paternalism in legal contexts.

Perhaps the single most important distinction that has been introduced in the course of attempts to justify paternalism in personal relationships is that between hard and soft paternalism (Feinberg 1986). According to the *soft* paternalist, *A* may treat *B* paternalistically only when *B*'s conduct is *non-voluntary*. According to the *hard* paternalist, *A* sometimes may treat *B* paternalistically even though *B*'s conduct is *voluntary*. Many philosophers, of course, believe that some instances of hard paternalism can be justified (Kleinig 1984). Still, the appeal of soft paternalism is evident. The soft paternalist favours intervention in B's choice for his own good only when there is a sense in which B's choice is not really his own. If B's conduct is fully voluntary—and expresses his will—soft paternalists insist that no interference for B's own good is warranted.

Clearly, the significance of the distinction between hard and soft paternalism depends on a theory of what choices are truly ours—on an account of the voluntary. According to a sensible proposal by Joel Feinberg (1986), voluntariness should be conceptualized as a matter of degree. Feinberg develops a model of a *perfectly voluntary choice*, in which the agent is fully informed of all the relevant facts and contingencies, and makes a decision in the absence of any manipulation or coercive pressure. Perhaps no choice in the real world fully corresponds to this ideal; particular choices are relatively non-voluntary to the extent that they deviate from it. Inevitably, troublesome cases on this continuum will arise in which we are unsure whether a choice is sufficiently voluntary to render paternalistic interference unjustifiable (according to the soft paternalist). For example, philosophers have struggled to decide when consent to medical treatment is sufficiently voluntary (Buchanan 1989).

Feinberg illustrates how the distinction between hard and soft paternalism should be used to decide whether a given paternalistic interference is justified by presenting three scenarios in which Doctor Doe refuses to prescribe to patient Roe a drug that Doe knows will cause Roe physical harm (Feinberg 1986). In the first scenario, Roe responds: 'You are mistaken. [The drug] will not cause me physical harm.' According to Feinberg, Roe's decision is not fully voluntary; he does not actually choose to take a substance that will in fact harm him. Feinberg maintains that Doe—who has expertise about whether the substance will cause physical harm—is entitled to withhold the drug. In the second scenario, Roe responds: 'That's just what I want. I want to harm myself.' In this case, Feinberg claims that Roe's decision *appears* to be non-voluntary. Roe's stated goal of harming himself is so odd that it gives rise to a presumption that he is deprived of the full use of his reflective faculties. Thus, Doe again is justified in withholding the drug, at least temporarily. In the third scenario, Roe responds: 'I don't care if [the drug] causes me physical harm. I'll get a lot of physical pleasure first, so much pleasure in fact, that it is well worth running the risk of physical harm.' Feinberg's appraisal of this final case is altogether different from that of the previous two. Since there is no basis on which to call Roe's decision non-voluntary, Feinberg is inclined to describe the case as 'easy'. No paternalistic interference in Roe's decision to take the pleasurable but dangerous drug is justified.

For present purposes, I am not concerned about whether one shares Feinberg's sympathies with soft paternalism, or is persuaded by his general objections to hard paternalism. Instead, my point is that any lesson to be learned from the foregoing three scenarios is of limited significance when we turn to questions of law. The distinction between hard and soft paternalism, although potentially helpful in identifying the conditions under which paternalism can be justified in personal relationships, is much less valuable in identifying the conditions under which legislators are justified in enacting laws for paternalistic reasons. This lack of relevance is a product of a phenomenon I have already noted: law is necessarily general and applicable to large numbers of persons whose circumstances vary in several crucial respects.

Perhaps the most obvious variable in the circumstances of the persons who are subject to law is their differing motivations for wanting to engage in the conduct the law would prohibit. Suppose that a legislator is weighing the arguments for and against proscribing the harmful but pleasurable drug described in the foregoing three scenarios. He scrutinizes Feinberg's reasoning and becomes persuaded of the evils of hard paternalism and the merits of soft paternalism. How does he apply what he has learned to the issue before him? Suppose that this legislator finds that a great many prospective users resemble Roe in the first of the three scenarios. Since such persons are misinformed about the health hazards of their decisions, the legislator will infer that their choices are not sufficiently voluntary. Thus, he will tend to favour proscription. But suppose that this legislator also finds that a small minority of prospective users resemble Roe in the second scenario. Such persons want to use the drug precisely because they desire to harm themselves. If the legislator is persuaded by Feinberg's analysis, he will conclude that the choices of these users are presumptively non-voluntary. Finally, suppose that this legislator also finds that the majority of prospective users conform to Roe in the third scenario. Such persons neither desire to harm themselves nor are misinformed of the health risks of their decisions. Like many persons who elect to take lifts rather than walk upstairs, or to eat fatty foods rather than salads, these prospective users have simply decided that the benefits of pleasure (or convenience or superior taste) outweigh the risks to their health. Since this legislator rejects hard paternalism, and finds that the preferences of these latter persons are sufficiently voluntary, he will tend to allow the drug to be used.

What conclusion, then, should this legislator reach about whether or not to enact the law? The proscription seems justified in its application to those persons whose choices are non-voluntary, but unjustified in its application to those persons whose choices are voluntary. Ideally, the legislator will search for a solution that manages to treat each person individually, so that the drug is permitted for those persons whose decisions are voluntary, but is banned otherwise. The drug might be distributed under a system of licensure, so that it would be available only to those adults who demonstrate their knowledge of the relevant risks. But this ideal solution encounters both pragmatic and principled difficulties. Consider the practical difficulties. Would a person be required to obtain a licence to use each drug—alcohol, tobacco, marijuana, and the like—that is potentially harmful? And why license only drugs? Would a person need a licence to ski, ride a bicycle, or play football? In short, licensing would be extraordinarily cumbersome, inefficient, and subject to error and abuse. Since the state cannot be expected to adjust its approach to the distinct circumstances of each person, it needs a default position. Prohibiting the drug unless the prospective user demonstrates the voluntariness of his decision has a paternalistic flavour. Perhaps, then, the default position should be to permit the drug unless the state has reason to believe that the decision of the prospective user is *not* voluntary.

The crux of the problem is as follows. In Feinberg's example of a personal relationship, the doctor is able to engage in a dialogue with each patient to ascertain the extent to which his choice is voluntary. If Roe proposes to undertake some activity but is unaware of its risks, Doe can provide him with information, and quiz him until he is confident that Roe understands the relevant facts. Virtually all deficiencies of knowledge can be rectified in the personal arena. But no such rectification is possible in law (Kennedy 1982). Certainly, cigarettes and dangerous products can contain warnings. Empirical research, however, provides ample indication that consumers seldom process such warnings. Doe can quiz Roe; the law cannot ensure that consumers pay attention to warnings. Since the state can hardly afford to initiate an extended conversation with individual citizens about each potentially harmful decision, it must adopt some policy in the absence of these dialogues.

What, then, should this legislator do? No answer can be derived directly from a theory of the conditions under which paternalism is justifiable in personal relationships. If this legislator decides to vote in favour of the law, he must engage in a *trade-off*—that is, he must balance his judgement about the merits of soft paternalism against the demerits of hard paternalism. The principles that govern these trade-offs—that govern the application of a theory of justified paternalism to legal contexts—might be described as *mediating maxims*. I will return to a discussion of these mediating maxims in Section IV; at this point, I simply point out the necessity of employing such principles if insights about the conditions under which paternalism is justified in personal relationships are to be applied to the domain of law.

This legislator will find additional important differences in the circumstances of persons. Some prospective users of the drug are adolescents, while others are adults. Every philosopher concedes that paternalistic intervention in the preferences of adolescents is justified more easily than in the preferences of competent adults. How should this legislator take account of this concession in his deliberations about whether to proscribe the drug? The most obvious solution is to adopt the kinds of regulations that govern the availability of alcohol and tobacco. The harmful but pleasurable drug would be permitted only for persons over a given age, typically 18 or 21. This solution is problematic. Whenever a substance is made available to adults, 'leakage' to adolescents is bound to occur. In other words, greater numbers of adolescents will succeed in using the drug illegally if it is permitted for adults than would manage to do so if it were prohibited for persons of all ages. Thus, this legislator will be tempted to proscribe the drug altogether if he is greatly concerned about its deleterious effects on adolescents. Again, such a legislator must engage in a trade-off—on this occasion, he must balance the freedom of adults against the welfare of adolescents. Some heretofore unidentified mediating maxim is required to govern the justifiability of whatever trade-off he decides to make.

To this point, I have described various kinds of differences in the circumstances of the persons whose preferences are disregarded by a given law, and how these differences create complications in attempts to apply to the domain of law a theory of justified paternalism derived from personal relationships. The differences I have mentioned thus far are all (roughly) psychological—law applies to persons of different degrees of sanity and maturity, with disparate motivations, and distinct levels of knowledge about the consequences of engaging in the activity to be proscribed. But purely physical differences between persons may be important as well. Because of physical dissimilarities between individuals, a given law may protect the welfare of some while jeopardizing that of others. Air bags in cars provide an excellent illustration of this phenomenon. The deployment of an air bag reduces the severity of injuries for the vast majority of persons involved in automobile accidents. In some kinds of collisions, however, persons who are very short are more likely to be injured by the deployment of the air bag than by the crash itself. Ideally, of course, air bags should be designed to benefit *all* occupants of cars. But engineers may be unable to design an air bag to realize this ideal. If a legislator decides to require air bags to protect the safety of persons involved in car accidents, he necessarily trades a reduction in some injuries for an increase in others. Alternatively, engineers may be able to design an air bag to benefit all occupants, but only at an exorbitant cost. If a legislator declines to require this expensive but optimal air bag, he necessarily balances the value of money against the desirability of reducing injuries.

The foregoing phenomenon provides an occasion to return to some of the difficulties in defining paternalism with which I began. Suppose that a legislator must vote for or against a regulation mandating that cars contain air bags. He is inclined to support the regulation because he believes that occupants of cars should be protected from injuries. But he is aware that this regulation will actually decrease the safety of a minority of persons. If he ultimately supports the law, should we categorize his motivation as paternalistic? That is, should we describe his reason *as paternalistic* when he knows he will jeopardize the welfare of some persons, because he knows he will promote the welfare of most of the persons in the group of those whose liberty is restricted? This question has no straightforward answer.

Consider additional difficulties in applying to law some of the familiar efforts to justify paternalism in personal relations. Gerald Dworkin proposes that what he calls 'future-oriented consent' is crucial in deciding when a parent is justified in treating his child paternalistically. According to this proposal, 'paternalism may be thought of as a wager by the parent on the child's subsequent recognition of the wisdom of the restrictions. There is an emphasis on what could be called future-oriented consent—on what the child will come to welcome rather than on what he does welcome' (Dworkin 1972: 76–7). This endeavour to justify paternalism in the context of the parent–child relationship is not without difficulties; I will mention only two. First, if the principle of 'future-oriented consent' is acceptable at all, why confine its application to the parent–child relationship? Suppose that an adult eventually comes to appreciate the paternalistic intervention of his friend. Why is such an interference not justified here as well? Moreover, the principle entails that the parent cannot know whether his paternalistic restriction is justified until long after he imposes it, when the child (hopefully) is sufficiently mature to make a judgement about its wisdom. Clearly, the parent would like some guidance about whether his restriction is justified at the moment he imposes it. Again, however, I am less interested in assessing this proposed justification in the context in which it was developed (namely, the parent–child relation) than to assess its potential application to law. The obvious difficulty in implementing a principle of future-oriented consent in the legal domain is the overwhelming likelihood that some but not all the persons whose liberty is restricted will eventually come to appreciate the wisdom of any given restriction. Apparently, such a law would then be justified with respect to those who subsequently welcome it, but not with respect to those who do not. This conclusion, however, does not take us very far. We still need to know: is the law justified or not?

In this section, I have argued that many of the distinctions that philosophers have believed to play a central role in attempts to justify paternalism in the context of personal relationships are less valuable when applied to matters of law. My point should not be overstated. A few such distinctions, if relevant to the justifiability of paternalism in personal relations, are relevant to legal paternalism as well. Consider, for example, the familiar distinction between action and omission. Philosophers have long debated whether this distinction has or lacks moral relevance. A parallel debate surrounds the justifiability of legislation—paternalistic legislation in particular. Some laws (presumably) enacted largely for the good of the persons whose liberty is restricted require them to perform a given action—to wear a helmet while riding a motorcycle, for example. Other laws with a similar rationale forbid persons to perform a given action—to borrow money at too high a rate of interest, for example. If the distinction between action and omission is (or is not) morally relevant in personal contexts, it probably has (or lacks) the same relevance when applied to matters of paternalistic legislation.

For the most part, however, we should not anticipate that the distinctions that have proved so helpful in attempts to identify the conditions under which paternalism is justified in personal contexts can be readily applied to assess the justifiability of paternalism in law.

4. PRINCIPLES TO JUSTIFY
LEGAL PATERNALISM

I have spoken frequently of the need to make trade-offs in adapting to law a theory about when paternalism is justified in personal relations. Difficulties arise in the legal realm that seldom if ever are replicated in paradigm cases in which one person treats another person paternalistically. I have suggested, for example, that a given law that disregards the preferences of some may simultaneously enable others to gain an objective that they want but know themselves to be unable to obtain. Moreover, a single law that constitutes hard paternalism in its application to *A*, and soft paternalism in its application to *B*, may not be paternalism of any kind in its application to *C*. In addition, one and the same law will restrict the liberty of both adolescents and adults. And a single law might increase the welfare of some of the persons whose liberty is restricted, but decrease that of others. Finally, some but not all the persons whose preferences are disregarded may eventually come to appreciate the wisdom of a given paternalistic statute. What verdict should be pronounced about such laws? Are they justified or unjustified *simpliciter*? In order to answer these questions, we must supplement a theory about the conditions under which paternalism is justified in personal relationships. Mediating maxims are needed to supplement the theory.

I will describe, and quickly dismiss, two very simple mediating maxims. The first is *absolutist*. According to the absolutist maxim, no paternalistic law should be enacted unless it is justified in its application to each and every person. Almost certainly, this maxim would preclude the state from enacting *any* instance of legal paternalism. Suppose that a few persons would choose to save a tiny amount of money by buying spectacles that would shatter on impact, thus creating serious risks to vision. The great majority of such persons, let us imagine, are simply misinformed of the relevant facts. But suppose that at least one person—call him Dan—fully understands the risks, but foolishly opts to buy the cheaper lens. The state regulation that bans these lenses represents hard paternalism to Dan. Can a philosopher who rejects hard paternalism in personal relations seriously conclude that this regulation must be unjustified, in so far as its rationale is paternalistic? I think not. Absolutism has little appeal in most normative enquiries; it fares no better in its application to paternalistic legislation (Goldman and Goldman 1990).

The second simple mediating maxim I will describe—and also dismiss—is *majoritarian*. Unlike absolutism, the majoritarian maxim does not give single individuals (like Dan) a trump over majorities, but, more sensibly, gives majorities a trump over minorities. Two examples should suffice to illustrate how this maxim might be applied. If more persons than not would eventually come to appreciate the wisdom of a given paternalistic restriction, the majoritarian maxim could readily adapt Dworkin's theory of future-oriented consent to the domain of law. The distinction between hard and soft paternalism could be salvaged by enacting only those laws that represent soft paternalism to the majority of persons whose preferences they disregard. And so on.

The application of the majoritarian maxim gives rise to some results that might or might not be acceptable. The number of adults whose liberty is restricted by a given law will nearly always be greater than the number of adolescents. Is the fact that an activity is deleterious to minors *never* a good reason to bar that activity altogether? Must the law tolerate the leakage to which I have referred, regardless of the extent to which the conduct is harmful to adolescents? Perhaps. Adults are treated like minors when they are prohibited from engaging in an activity on the ground that it is bad for minors. However this issue is ultimately resolved, the application of the majoritarian maxim seems clearly counter-intuitive in other kinds of cases. Return to my example of a law requiring persons to contribute a given percentage of their income to a state retirement plan. Recall that this statute represents hard paternalism to Jones, while enabling Smith to achieve a desired outcome. Suppose that the Joneses of the world outnumber the Smiths by a 3 to 2 ratio. Presumably, then, the majoritarian principle would condemn the state plan. The failure to implement this plan, however, would greatly increase the numbers of elderly persons who are impoverished. The spectre of a society with a large population of poor senior citizens may be unacceptable. To prevent this consequence, a legislator might well decide to endorse the state plan, notwithstanding its incompatibility with the majoritarian maxim.

Theorists who continue to embrace the majoritarian maxim might reply that, over time, persons would learn to save effectively for their own retirement, so that the numbers of impoverished senior citizens would eventually decline. I see no evidence for this optimistic prediction about the triumph of rationality when persons are left to their own devices. Instances in which adults tend to take inadequate care of themselves—by unhealthy diets, for example—are too numerous to discount. In any event, the transition costs in conducting this experiment are far too high. The plausibility of the majoritarian maxim is not sufficiently great to warrant the immediate (and perhaps permanent) increase in poverty among the elderly. Therefore, I conclude that the majoritarian maxim should be rejected. We still lack a principle to adapt into law a theory about the conditions under which paternalism is justified in personal relations.

One might hope that philosophers who have thought primarily about the justification of paternalism in personal contexts would have provided some guidance about the mediating maxims needed to translate their theories into the legal domain. Most moral philosophers, however, have tended to employ a deonotological framework to approach the issue of whether and under what circumstances paternalism can be justified in personal relationships. That is, they have rejected the supposition that paternalism is justified whenever it produces optimal results. Nonetheless, I believe that consequentialist reasoning is essential to develop the mediating maxims needed to justify paternalism in law. Consequentialism best allows us to recognize—and thereby to resist—the horrors of a world with large

numbers of impoverished senior citizens—even if that world contains less paternalism and more freedom.

It is worthwhile commenting on the general kinds of deontological objections
philosophers have tended to raise against the justifiability of paternalism in
personal relations. The most plausible objections invoke a conception of *personal
autonomy* with which paternalistic interferences are said to be incompatible.
Three difficulties surround these efforts. One must (a) identify what autonomy is,
(b) show why it is valuable, and (c) argue that its value is always greater than the
value of reducing whatever harm is prevented by the paternalistic restriction. Each
of these three difficulties is formidable.

Any philosopher who objects to some (or all) paternalistic interferences because
they infringe personal autonomy should be pressed to formulate the conception of
autonomy on which he relies. The supposed incompatibility between paternalism
and autonomy must be defended rather than presupposed. Of course, autonomy
might be *defined* so that its incompatibility with paternalism is guaranteed; one
might characterize autonomy as the freedom to do what one wants. According to
this conception, respect for autonomy requires complete deference to personal preferences (Husak 1980). I think that this conception of autonomy is implausible. Any
alternative conception, however, is likely to be compatible with some instances of
paternalism. I will not endeavour to support this claim in any detail; too many different versions of the principle of personal autonomy have been proposed (May
1994). But, even if we conclude that paternalism is incompatible with autonomy, we
should not condemn all instances of paternalism unless we are persuaded that
autonomy, as so construed, has value; indeed, it must have enough value to outweigh whatever good the instance of paternalism promotes. It seems unlikely that
the value of personal autonomy could be sufficiently great to outweigh *all* competing considerations that might lead a state to favour paternalistic legislation.

Suppose, however, that we conclude that the value of protecting autonomy is
greater than the disvalue of the harm to be prevented by each instance of paternalism. The next difficult issue is to ask how this conclusion can be translated into legal
policy. The difficulties here should be familiar. A general law restricts the liberty of
persons in very different circumstances. As I have indicated, a single law may violate the autonomy of some persons, while enabling others to attain a good they
want. If our primary objective is to protect autonomy, what should we conclude
about such a law? This kind of question points to the need for (yet unidentified)
mediating maxims.

I now want to propose that the concept of personal autonomy, which has figured
so prominently in philosophical endeavours to object to paternalism in personal
relations (Feinberg 1986), might actually provide the key to justifying some
instances of paternalism in law. Suppose we construe persons to be autonomous
when they make their own lives (Raz 1986). Philosophers have offered very different kinds of accounts of what it means for someone to 'make his own life', and how

anyone might succeed in this endeavour. On any explication, however, this conception of autonomy provides *a* reason to oppose instances of legal paternalism. The
ability of persons to make their own lives is decreased whenever they are subjected
to a legal interference for any reason—paternalistic or otherwise. At the same time,
however, this conception of autonomy provides a reason to *favour* some instances
of legal paternalism. Many restrictions on liberty will improve the opportunities of
persons to make their own lives by promoting what might be called the *conditions*
of autonomy—the conditions under which persons are likely to develop into
autonomous agents. Laws that limit the number and severity of physical injuries
help to preserve opportunities for persons to lead the lives they choose. For example, an athlete whose toes are cut off by a lawn mower without a safety guard has
lost a significant part of his ability to make his own life. Since the value of autonomy gives us a reason to create the conditions in which this sort of accident is less
likely to occur, we have a reason to enact a law that requires that lawn mowers
include safety guards. Thus, we have a reason to oppose this law, and a countervailing reason to support it—both of which are derived from the value of personal
autonomy. Whether one ultimately accepts or rejects this example (as well as other
examples) of legal paternalism depends largely on how one balances these conflicting reasons. Many factors enter into this difficult balancing. Of special significance,
however, is the means by which the paternalistic law is enforced—an issue to which
I will return in Section 5.

I propose, then, that the key to developing a theory of justified paternalism in
legal contexts is to understand how various paternalistic laws affect the conditions
of autonomy—that is, how they enhance or undermine the ability of persons to
make their own lives. This determination does not simply involve the counting of
heads—an alternative I dismissed when discussing the majoritarian maxim.
Instead, a paternalistic law may be justifiable because its contributions to the conditions of autonomy for the minority are more important than its detriments for
the majority. No precise formula for balancing these variables exists. I can only
identify some of the factors that are relevant to this determination, and illustrate
their application in one or two examples.

Consider the example of mandatory seat belts. Suppose that the majority of
occupants of cars will never be involved in an accident in which the use of a seat
belt would prove beneficial. If so, a law requiring that belts be worn can promote
the conditions of autonomy for only a minority. Still, I contend that the gains to the
minority are likely to outweigh the losses to the majority. Consider the trivial losses
to the majority who are made to fasten their seat belts, but will never benefit
thereby. They may dislike the feeling of restraint, resent the wrinkling of their
clothes, disapprove of the waste of a second or so of their time, and so on. But no
theory of liberty should deem these sacrifices to be especially serious; nothing of
great value has been lost. Now consider the enormous gains to the minority who
will benefit from the regulation. The injuries they will avoid will greatly enhance

their ability to make their own lives. If we really hope to create the conditions under which persons are likely to be able to lead lives of their own choosing, it is hard to see why we would condemn this example of paternalistic legislation.

Philosophers who agree so far will reach different judgements as other real (or hypothetical) examples of legal paternalism are evaluated. Consider a proposal to make occupants of cars wear the kinds of helmets that some states require of motorcyclists. Again, suppose that the majority of occupants will never be involved in an accident in which the use of a helmet would prove beneficial. When compared to seat belts, this law would impose greater losses for the majority in each of the three respects I have mentioned. Helmets give rise to greater feelings of restraint than belts, distort personal appearance more substantially, and take more time to install. Thus, the value of the liberties that are lost is somewhat greater. Is this imaginary statute therefore unjustifiable? I think so. But exactly where is the line to be drawn? Again, no precise answer to this question is possible, as reasonable minds will draw lines in very different places.

For example, reasonable minds have differed about whether paternalistic reasons ever suffice to prohibit adults from using drugs for recreational purposes (Husak 1989). This issue is noteworthy because of the sheer numbers of persons who are severely punished simply for using (or possessing) illicit substances. Some prohibitionists have advanced paternalistic reasons for waging an ongoing 'war on drugs'. The justifiability of drug proscriptions cannot be assessed without empirical data about the extent to which given substances create risks of physical and psychological harm. Moreover, the fact that some illicit drugs are addictive raises concerns about voluntariness, thereby bringing proscriptive laws under a rationale of soft paternalism.

I can only sketch the general line of enquiry I believe to be relevant if such issues are to be resolved. On my view, one must balance the significance of the various losses of freedom the law will impose against the resultant gains in the ability of persons to lead lives of their own creation. More specifically, attempts to evaluate instances of legal paternalism require, first, a set of principles about the value of different liberties; secondly, a theory about how given interferences affect the conditions under which persons are able to make their own lives; and, thirdly, some means to balance these (hopefully commensurable) values against one another. Small wonder that judgements about legal paternalism are so controversial!

5. PATERNALISM IN VARIOUS AREAS OF LAW

To this point, I have talked indiscriminately about paternalistic laws, with no indication of what *kind* of law is involved. But distinctions between kinds of law are tremendously important in endeavours to justify legal paternalism by applying the mediating maxims I have sketched above. In particular, paternalistic laws enforced by the **criminal** sanction are unlike those not backed by punishment.

A simple reason shows why paternalistic rationales seldom justify the enactment of a criminal law. One side of the balance in endeavours to justify legal paternalism involves a judgement about how the law in question affects the conditions of autonomy. Punishment—at least when it is severe—always undermines these conditions to an extraordinary degree. Persons are far less able to make their own lives when a criminal sanction is inflicted upon them. The punishment for violating a criminal law is almost always more detrimental to an offender's ability to make his own life than is the harm that he risks to himself by engaging in the proscribed conduct (Bayles 1974).

The following example will help to explain my reservations about paternalism as a rationale for criminal legislation. Suppose that some activity—boxing, for example—risks substantial injuries to persons who engage in it. Suppose also that some persons are foolishly inclined to perform this activity, perhaps because it is exciting, euphoric, or profitable. Why not protect these persons from their own foolishness by enacting a criminal statute to punish boxers (Dixon 2001)? My answer is simple. A criminal law merely proscribes behaviour, but cannot always prevent it. In a world of perfect deterrence, no instances of the proscribed activity would occur. Perfect deterrence, of course, is unattainable. The threat of criminal punishment may succeed in reducing the incidence of the activity, but some persons will persist in boxing, whatever the law may say. Suppose that Bill is one such person. What should be done to him if he is detected? Presumably, Bill must be punished, unless the state does not mean what it says in classifying the statute as criminal.

What might be the justification for punishing Bill? Two answers might be given. First, Bill's punishment might be justified in order to preserve whatever efficacy the criminal law has as a deterrent. But punishing Bill in order to deter others from following his foolish example can hardly be thought to promote the interests of Bill himself. That is, the state does not treat Bill paternalistically when he is punished to deter others. If the law purports to treat Bill paternalistically, punishment must be thought to be in *his* interest—which is the second possible answer to the question of how his punishment might be justified. This second answer, however, seems implausible. How can punishment be in Bill's interest? Is Bill really better off if he were punished than if he were free to box? The answer probably depends on further details about *how* Bill is punished. A small monetary fine would not seriously undermine Bill's ability to make his own life. If the threat of further fines induces him to stop boxing, the law will have succeeded in protecting the conditions of his autonomy. The difficulty, of course, is that Bill may continue to box even though he pays the fine. Suppose, then, that Bill is imprisoned. This mode of punishment has (perhaps!) a greater probability of successfully preventing him from continuing to box. But it is hard to believe that imprisonment is really in Bill's interest. Can a legislator believe that Bill is actually better off not boxing in jail than boxing out of jail?

If the answer to this question is negative, Bill's punishment cannot be justified paternalistically.

Only rarely can an affirmative answer be given to the foregoing kind of question. Almost no conduct that sane adults are voluntarily inclined to perform is so destructive of their autonomy that they are better off in jail. Perhaps a few counterexamples to this generalization can be found. Consider a promoter who offers enormous sums of money to induce persons to engage in gladiatorial contests to the death. I concede that the welfare of combatants would probably be enhanced by their imprisonment. Few examples in the real world, however, are analogous. Since paternalists should be unwilling to impose a 'cure' that is worse than a 'disease', they should not back paternalistic laws with the criminal sanction.

Criminal paternalism may be easier to justify, however, when it is indirect, and imposed on a third party. In the gladiator example, the state may imprison promoters who profit by persuading others to fight. Clearly, punishment would be designed to benefit the combatants, not the promoters. Criminal legislation might be easier to justify in such cases, since the state succeeds in promoting the conditions of autonomy of numerous persons by punishing a single individual. When paternalism is direct, however, criminal law should almost never be used.

Here again, paternalism in personal relations is unlike paternalism in law. Return to the case of the father who attempts to induce his stubborn daughter to eat her vegetables. What strategies are available to him? Clearly, a severe beating or a lengthy term of incarceration in a cupboard would cause her greater harm than the lack of vegetables in her diet. Thus, the father should resort to less extreme measures: he might forbid her to eat dessert, prevent her from watching television, or confine her to her room for a short period of time. These mild sanctions are legitimate means to accomplish his paternalistic end. If the father were to invoke more draconian devices, we would have good reason to suspect that he did not really have his daughter's best interests at heart. The criminal law, by contrast, rarely has such trivial sanctions available to it. Severe measures, such as imprisonment, are almost certain to be more harmful than the conduct for which they are imposed.

Since direct criminal paternalism is rarely justified, many of the more interesting questions about legal paternalism are not questions about the criminal law. Instead, they are questions about other areas of law. Sometimes, paternalistic rationales for law give rise to little dispute, as when states create and support social institutions to encourage persons to take better care of themselves. Health and safety regulations may be enacted, such as requirements that water contain fluoride. States can sponsor advertisements to discourage unhealthy behaviours such as excessive alcohol use. These sorts of regulations are not enforced through criminal penalties, and only occasionally have given rise to objections from philosophers who purport to dislike legal paternalism. The reluctance of these philosophers to complain about such examples probably indicates that they do not oppose legal paternalism altogether, but only direct legal paternalism enforced by the criminal sanction. On my view, these non-criminal modes of law are more easily justified because they can be given force without seriously undermining the autonomy of the persons who are subject to them.

Unquestionably, the particular safety regulation most often attacked by opponents of paternalism is the law in many states requiring occupants of cars to wear seat belts. Why is this law singled out so frequently? Seat-belt requirements, after all, are only the tip of the paternalistic iceberg in car regulations. Cars are required to conform to over 1,000 rules that mostly serve to protect the safety of occupants. Consider, for example, rules that require manufacturers to install shatterproof windshields and pads on dashboards and steering wheels. Philosophers who reject legal paternalism are rarely (if ever) heard to demand that consumers should be allowed to endanger themselves by having the option to drive with harder dashboards. Why, then, do these philosophers tend to complain so vociferously about seat-belt laws? I suspect that these laws are perceived as problematic because they require occupants to *do* something for their own good. Drivers must buckle a belt; nothing is required of drivers to 'activate' the padding in their interior. If seat belts buckled automatically when a door was closed, no *action* on the part of the occupant would be required, and quasi-criminal fines imposed on drivers who failed to buckle their belts would no longer be needed. A driver who disassembled the automatic mechanism could be treated like a driver who ripped the padding from his steering wheel. He would not be punished, but his car might fail to pass the inspection that most states currently require, and thus would not be certified as safe to drive.

Paternalistic rationales are prominent in civil contexts. In contract law, such rationales are often invoked against the enforcement of given kinds of agreements. Of course, agreements are not enforced unless the parties are competent (Wikler 1978). Some agreements are unenforceable, however, even when made by parties whose competence is unquestioned. Agreements about given kinds of subject matters—involving the sale of bodily organs, for example—are unenforceable. Other agreements involve legitimate subject matters, but contain terms or conditions that are unenforceable according to the doctrine of unconscionability. This doctrine allows a court not to enforce agreements that are one-sided, overreaching, or exploitive. Some terms in agreements cannot be waived, and thus are imposed as a matter of law. For example, a consumer cannot voluntarily relinquish his statutory right to be paid a minimum wage, or to repay a loan at less than the rate of usury. Nor can a consumer waive his statutory right to a 'cooling-off period' in a door-to-door sale. Seemingly, each of these aspects of contract law is underlied by a paternalistic rationale.

The famous issue posed by Mill and discussed by a host of subsequent commentators (Hodson 1981)—whether persons should be free to abdicate their freedom by voluntarily becoming slaves—is a question about the scope and limits of freedom of contract. Suppose that Sue agrees to become Jane's permanent slave. Courts have no reason to become involved as long as Sue remains content to keep her agreement; no law prevents persons from entering into a *de facto* arrangement of slavery. But what should the law do if Sue changes her mind and Jane seeks to enforce this agreement? In such an event, courts would declare the agreement unconscionable and unenforceable on grounds of public policy—presumably for paternalistic reasons.

A few legal philosophers have contested, however, whether the doctrine of unconscionability is really based on a paternalistic rationale. If they are correct, contract law can retain this doctrine without admitting to paternalism. Some have proposed that this doctrine can be derived from a commitment to economic efficiency (Zamir 1998). More plausibly, a judge might refuse to enforce an unconscionable agreement because of his unwillingness to facilitate and become implicated in the unfair arrangements of others (Shiffrin 2000). Here again, we see the difficulty of identifying a law (or a legal doctrine) as paternalistic.

Paternalism also appears to play a role in tort law—and has contributed to a blurring of the line between contract and tort. The doctrine of assumption of risk, for example, is not invoked very often in contemporary tort law (Sugarman 1997). Consumers are frequently unable to trade decreases in safety for lower prices. Some courts, for example, have allowed drivers of a car to recover compensatory damages for injuries that would not have occurred had their car been equipped with an air bag—even though the drivers seemingly had assumed the risk of injury by electing not to buy a safer but more expensive car. The erosion of such defences as assumption of risk in tort law might be explained by a growing acceptance of paternalism among the judiciary.

Although I have claimed that a criminal statute is almost never justified as an instance of direct paternalism, perhaps *defences* from criminal liability may be disallowed on paternalistic grounds. Rules that withhold defences for paternalistic reasons may or may not have a different impact on autonomy than rules that create criminal offences. Consider, for example, the defence of consent, which typically functions as a justification for persons who infringe a criminal statute. Consent is not a defence, however, to a number of crimes—most notably, those that prohibit *serious* bodily harm. The most frequently cited rationale for disallowing consent as a defence for these offences is that persons who acquiesce in such behaviour are acting contrary to their own interest.

The unwillingness of the law to allow consent as a justification for what is otherwise criminal behaviour has proved especially controversial in the context of mercy killings. The fact that the patients (or victims) of Dr Kevorkian consented to die is legally immaterial to his liability. A reason commonly given against allowing consent as a defence is that some people will agree to have their lives terminated for the wrong reasons. Some patients may actually prefer to die sooner rather than later in order to reduce their medical bills, and thus to preserve a larger inheritance for their heirs. Certainly, a great many patients who wish to end their lives have motives that seem perfectly reasonable. But many legislators are prepared to disregard the reasonable preferences of some fatally ill patients. They fear that a general policy of honouring these preferences would allow other patients to die whose preferences seem far less reasonable. Here again, trade-offs are needed to justify a general policy about assisted suicide and voluntary euthanasia.

Even the most far-reaching proposals to allow assisted suicide tend to include a residue of paternalism. Many commentators are persuaded that persons should be permitted to enlist the assistance of physicians to terminate their lives, but only when they satisfy certain conditions—that they be incurable and suffering from severe pain, for example. But why should persons not be allowed to seek assistance in ending their lives when they choose to die for other reasons—that is, even when they are *not* incurable or suffering from extreme pain? As long as their decision is sufficiently voluntary, opponents of paternalism will be hard-pressed to justify *any* restrictions on the availability of assisted suicide and euthanasia.

6. Moral Paternalism

What *kinds* of harms may be prevented by paternalistic legislation? If the state has the authority to use law to prevent any kinds of self-inflicted harms, I assume that personal injury and economic loss are among the kinds of harms that may be prevented. Far more controversial, however, is state action designed to improve character, or to prevent persons from engaging in wrongful or immoral conduct. The principle of *moral legal paternalism* authorizes the state to strive to make persons better off morally. The issue of whether the state may enact law with the objective of improving the morality of its citizenry has proved enormously divisive among political philosophers. Many (but not all) liberals have argued that the state lacks such authority, while *perfectionists* believe that some instances of moral paternalism are justified.

Some of the debate has centred on empirical grounds for doubting that the state should be granted the authority to use legislation to improve morality. The state could be mistaken, of course, in its empirical determination that fluoride reduces the incidence of tooth decay. But mistakes about matters of morality are more probable than mistakes about matters of fact. Before the state is granted the authority to prevent moral harm, citizens must have confidence that the state is likely to be correct in its determinations that given instances of conduct are immoral. Citizens should have reservations about moral paternalism to the extent that they are deeply divided about matters of morality.

Equally unsettled is the conceptual question of whether the morality of citizens *can* be improved by legislation. Many philosophers believe that it is impossible to force persons to be better from a moral point of view. They contend, roughly, that persons deserve moral praise only when they perform the right action for the right reasons. Clearly, the law can provide carrots and sticks to increase the probability that persons will perform the right action. Laws can proscribe wrongful acts such as theft, and potential offenders can be deterred by the threat of punishment. What is far more dubious, however, is whether the law can do much to ensure that persons act for the right reasons. Arguably, an agent is not improved morally unless he personally *endorses* the goods he chooses. A person who abstains from wrongful conduct because of the fear of punishment fails the endorsement condition, and does not deserve moral praise.

Whether endorsement is a precondition for moral praise—and how the endorsement condition can be satisfied—are enormously controversial. In what follows, however, I will assume that some version of the endorsement condition is true in order to pursue a different line of enquiry. The endorsement condition is frequently taken to provide a reason to believe that law cannot succeed in improving persons morally, and thus to provide a decisive objection to moral paternalism. This conclusion, however, does not follow. In the long run, at least, I believe that law *can* improve persons morally, the endorsement condition notwithstanding. That is, law can provide the means by which persons come to endorse the goods they pursue. After all, we come to endorse whatever values we have because of the influences to which we are subjected. Law can be an especially powerful such influence. Even though a person who performs the right action because of fear of legal sanctions may not immediately deserve moral praise, law may provide the mechanism by which he eventually comes to endorse the values he is initially compelled to adopt (Sher 1997). This phenomenon should be familiar. We should all recall occasions in which we were made to engage in some activity against our immediate preferences—to take a required course in college, for example—but subsequently came to appreciate its value. The same phenomenon may occur when we are forced to be good.

Disagreement about whether the law should strive to improve persons morally has been prominent in recent attempts to justify the institution of criminal punishment. Despite my rejection of paternalism as a rationale for criminal legislation, paternalistic rationales are occasionally invoked as a justification for the 'hard treatment' of punishment. Some philosophers (Morris 1981) have argued, for example, that punishment is partially justified in promoting the offender's 'identity as a morally autonomous person attached to the good'. Others (Duff 1999) contend that punishment should aim at the 'self-correction and self-reform' of offenders. Such theories encounter many problems (Dolinko 1999)—not the least of which is their commitment to perfectionism.

My concession that the law *can* be used to improve the morality of persons does not show that moral paternalism is thereby justified. I contend that instances of moral paternalism must be defended by the same theory I have sketched above. I have suggested that the justifiability of instances of legal paternalism should be assessed by balancing the significance of the various losses of freedom the law will impose against the resultant gains in the ability of persons to lead autonomous lives. I suspect that applications of this general theory will sometimes allow particular cases of moral paternalism. Consider the weights to be placed on each side of the scale. The freedom that is lost by laws that discourage immoral behaviour hardly seems to be of great value. The freedom to act wrongfully cannot be as significant as the freedom to act permissibly. Next, consider the other side of the equation—how these laws affect the conditions of autonomy—that is, the conditions under which persons are able to make their own lives. Wrongful choices may seem to be just as much a matter of self-creation as those deserving of moral praise. Nonetheless, I have reservations about describing as autonomous a choice that merits moral condemnation. If I am mistaken, and a wrongful choice *can* be autonomous, the autonomy that such a choice exemplifies does not seem to be especially valuable. Thus, some (non-criminal) instances of moral paternalism might pass my justificatory test. They result in insignificant sacrifices of freedom, without losses in the ability of persons to lead autonomous lives of value. Because of empirical misgivings about whether states can correctly distinguish moral from immoral behaviour, support for perfectionism should remain cautious and tentative. In principle, however, I conclude that the state has as much authority to enact paternalistic legislation to prevent moral harm as to prevent personal injury or economic loss.

REFERENCES

Archer, David (1990). 'Paternalism Defined'. *Analysis*, 50: 36.

Bayles, Michael (1974). 'Criminal Paternalism', in J. Roland Pennock and John W. Chapman (eds.), *Nomos XV: The Limits of Law*. New York: Lieber-Atherton, 174.

Buchanan, Allen (1989). *Deciding for Others: The Ethics of Surrogate Decision Making*. New York: Cambridge University Press.

Dixon, Nicholas (2001). 'Boxing, Paternalism, and Legal Moralism'. *Social Theory and Practice*, 27: 323–44.

Dolinko, David (1999). 'Morris on Paternalism and Punishment'. *Law and Philosophy*, 18: 345.

Duff, R. A. (1999). 'Punishment, Communication, and Community', in Matt Matravers (ed.), *Punishment and Political Theory*. Oxford: Hart Publishing Company, 48.

Dworkin, Gerald (1972). 'Paternalism'. *Monist*, 56: 64.

Feinberg, Joel (1985). *Harm to Others*. New York: Oxford University Press.

—— (1986). *Harm to Self*. New York: Oxford University Press.

Gert, Bernard, and Culver, George (1976). 'Paternalistic Behaviors'. *Philosophy and Public Affairs*, 6: 46.

Goldman, Michael, and Goldman, Alan (1990). 'Paternalistic Laws'. *Philosophical Topics*, 18: 65–78.

Hodson, John (1981). 'Mill, Paternalism, and Slavery'. *Analysis*, 41: 61.

Husak, Douglas (1980). 'Paternalism and Autonomy'. *Philosophy and Public Affairs*, 10: 27.

—— (1989). 'Recreational Drugs and Paternalism'. *Law and Philosophy*, 8: 353.

Kennedy, Duncan (1982). 'Distributive and Paternalist Motives in Contract and Tort Law'. *Maryland Law Review*, 41: 563.

Kleinig, John (1984). *Paternalism*. Totowa, NJ: Rowman & Allanheld.

May, Thomas (1994). 'The Concept of Autonomy'. *American Philosophical Quarterly*, 31: 133.

Mill, John Stuart (1859/1951). *On Liberty*. New York: E. P. Dutton & Co.

Morris, Herbert (1981). 'A Paternalistic Theory of Punishment'. *American Philosophical Quarterly*, 18: 18.

Raz, Joseph (1986). *The Morality of Freedom*. Oxford: Oxford University Press.

Sartorious, Rolf (1983) (ed.), *Paternalism*. Minneapolis: University of Minnesota Press.

Sher, George (1997). *Beyond Neutrality*. Cambridge: Cambridge University Press.

Shiffrin, Seana (2000). 'Paternalism, Unconscionability Doctrine, and Accommodation'. *Philosophy and Public Affairs*, 29: 205–50.

Sugarman, Stephen (1997). 'Assumption of Risk'. *Valparaiso University Law Review*, 31: 833.

VanDeVeer, Donald (1986). *Paternalistic Intervention*. Princeton: Princeton University Press.

Waldron, Jeremy (1989). 'Legislation and Moral Neutrality', in R. Goodin and A. Reeve (eds.), *Liberal Neutrality*. London: Routledge, 61–83.

Wikler, Daniel (1978). 'Paternalism and the Mildly Retarded'. *Philosophy and Public Affairs*, 8: 377.

Zamir, Eyal (1998). 'The Efficiency of Paternalism'. *Virginia Law Review*, 84: 229.

Case Cited

Lochner v. *New York*, 198 US 45 (1905).

CHAPTER 16

MULTICULTURALISM

JOHN ARTHUR

1. SOME GENEALOGY

FEW ideas are as open to different interpretations these days, or as controversial, as multiculturalism. Like many other 'isms'—socialism, conservativism, fascism—multiculturalism is a political movement as well as a set of philosophical, social, and political ideas. Before looking at the range of positions associated with multiculturalism, I want first to describe its historical origins and the social forces that came together to create it.

'Multiculturalism' is a term that has, in Nathan Blum's phrase, both 'great currency' and 'imprecise usage' (1991: 129). It is also a relatively new word, making its first recorded appearances in Canada and Australia during the 1970s, at a time when both countries were struggling to deal with large influxes of non-European immigrants and with a new-found appreciation of the mistreatment of their own indigenous peoples. By now, the word has become commonplace in public media and especially in academia. A search of major US newspapers and periodicals uncovers only forty references to the term in 1981, and 2000 in 1992 (Bernstein 1994: 4). It has also expanded into government and other institutions. The government of Canada now has a 'Department of Multiculturalism and Citizenship' and many universities include courses that discuss multiculturalism in their curricula. Some even boast administrators and student government representatives such as my own institution's 'Vice-President for Multicultural Affairs'.

Despite this wide usage, the term's meaning is very much open to dispute, as are the political and other claims that are often made in its name. According to the editors of a recent book, multiculturalism refers to what must be thought a philo-sophical commonplace: the idea that 'people in other cultures, foreign and domes-tic, are human beings, too—moral equals, entitled to equal respect and concern, and not to be discounted or treated as a subordinate caste' (Okin 1999: 4). Nathan Glazer expresses a similar position, taking 'We Are All Multiculturalists Now' as the title of an article and later a book in which he declares that multiculturalism 'has, in a word, won'. What has won—what he understands multiculturalism to mean— is simply 'a greater attention to minorities and women and their role in American history and social studies and literature classes' (Glazer 1997: 14). In a similar vein, Amy Gutman defines multiculturalism as recognition of the 'identities of cul-tural and disadvantaged minorities which in the United States means primarily African-Americans, Asian-Americans, Native Americans and women' (1994: 3). Emphasizing that it is a political movement as well as an intellectual position, Marilyn Friedman says multiculturalism has two primary goals: to promote diver-sity in education and to challenge the system of oppression (1995: 61).

But multiculturalism has not won wide acceptance, as many have supposed; others take a different attitude. Political commentator and author Andrew Sullivan wrote recently that 'A couple of decades of multiculturalism and the results are in. It doesn't work. Nobody buys it any more. Its most avid supporters are licking their wounds and recanting their past absurdities' (2000: 9). And historian James Caeser (1998: 155), while unconvinced that Sullivan is correct in supposing it is in retreat, explains that

Multiculturalism perpetuates a perverse psychology. Proof of victimization, established generally today by possession of some biological characteristic, is the basis of any claim to honor or position. . . . Multiculturalism blinds us to the (or a) meaning of our own history. In multicultural history, the heart of the American experience has been one of racism and biologism.

Trying to take a more distanced view, intellectual historian James Davidson Hunter (1991) argues that debates about multiculturalism are part of a larger war being waged between groups he calls the 'orthodox' and the 'progressives' over the future of America. The fields of conflict are many, he suggests, including family, education, free speech and the arts, law (where issues range from judicial activism to economic policy), and democratic politics. Behind this, he claims, are competing 'moral visions' whose subscribers disagree over how to interpret history and over the sources of moral authority. Richard Rorty, on the other hand, sees another and for him more troubling culture war travelling under the banner of multiculturalism. He identifies it as a dispute between 'postmodernists' who understand modern American society to be irredeemably evil and dominated by a corrupt elite versus 'typical left-wing Democratic professors' like Rorty himself who understand America more charitably and optimistically, believing that reforms may bring equality and decrease suffering (Rorty 2000: 17).

Given all this, it seems pretty clear that, on almost any plausible understanding of the term multiculturalism, the literal reading—the reference to many cultures—is misleading. Multiculturalism includes a set of political ideas that extend beyond what is often thought of as culture. A recent dictionary of cultural theory defines culture as the 'capabilities and habits acquired by man as a member of society' (Payne 1996: 2). Ronald Dworkin offers a similar if somewhat more precise understanding of culture: members of a common culture share a 'vocabulary of tradition and convention' (1985: 231). If that is what cultures are, then many topics surrounding multiculturalism are not cultural issues: gay rights, economic justice, abortion, affirmative action, and racism, while undoubtedly important, are not disputes grounded in different vocabularies and traditions.

That said, there does remain a sense in which multicultural concerns *are* at least indirectly tied to culture and cultural change. The entry for 'Multiculturalism' in *A Dictionary of Cultural and Critical Theory* states: 'The word "multiculturalism" can be seen as having referentiality, however ambitious or ambiguous, to transnational associations between the cultures of two or more nations.' This has meant that, thanks to 'the evolution of world history as evidenced by intercontinental exploding populations and general public recognition of the increasing number of nation-states, the underlying assumption of the intrinsic superiority of "Western tradition" has been necessarily called into question and reevaluated' (Payne 1996: 353). Interpreting a bit, we might take this to suggest that the political liberation movements of minorities, women, gays/lesbians, and the poor have all grown out of, and are in some sense an extension of, the greater awareness (and respect) among Western nations of cultural and other differences. That much, perhaps, these movements have in common.

All of which raises but does not really answer the question of how we are to explain the emergence of multiculturalism, viewed as a political movement. It seems clear that, while globalization and the increased awareness of other cultures that comes in its wake are part of the story, three other factors have also contributed to multiculturalism's emergence as an important social and ideological stance. The first is the civil-rights and women's movements of the 1960s and 1970s. In many ways, multiculturalism would be unimaginable without these. Equality and equal consideration came to be seen—especially after the murderous genocide of the Second World War—as an insistent demand of modern societies. This applied especially to religious and racial groups, and to the indigenous peoples of the New World. But the last third of the twentieth century also saw significant economic and social changes. Capitalism emerged as the dominant economic system worldwide, while the civil-rights and women's movements expanded to global decolonization. Technology exploded, providing far easier communication and transportation while increasing exponentially the amount of information that is widely available. The century also brought with it the destruction or weakening of ties to land and to work, as the proportion of people tied to land, through agriculture, declined sharply. Still another important factor in the rise of multiculturalism is immigration and the easy movement of labour that have transformed many Western democracies into far more diverse societies.

Multiculturalism, in the broadest sense, resulted from the confluence of these many factors, ranging from ideological and social to economic and technological. As might be expected given that history, a wide range of issues travel under the banner of multiculturalism, some of which are discussed elsewhere in this book. These include affirmative action, racism, gay rights, and regulation of hate speech, among many others. In what follows, however, I focus on the areas that are most distinctive to multiculturalism—namely, the problems associated with finding social and political arrangements appropriate to a 'multicultural' society, understood as a society made of divergent cultural groups. This topic is itself many faceted, and its pursuit will take us far afield into discussions of group rights, social solidarity, and personal identity. Before turning to those topics, however, we will look at education. Some of the earliest disputes over multiculturalism originated in and around schools and universities. They involved the curriculum, though they also reached into more theoretical questions about the nature and purposes of the study of social sciences and humanities.

2. Multiculturalism and Education

Two debates over school curricula, one in California and the other in New York, brought multiculturalism to prominence. In the late 1980s a group of students at Stanford University demanded that the Western Culture programme be replaced with one that emphasized the contributions of cultures that had previously been ignored or distorted. A committee was formed and eventually proposed a new required course that emphasized 'diversity'. Heated disagreement followed, including student disruptions of faculty meetings and a sit-in at the President's office. The university eventually adopted the diversity course. This required course was followed soon thereafter by other required courses at Stanford emphasizing race, gender, ethnic, and other forms of 'diversity'. Similar programmes were proposed and adopted across the country. Following on from the recognition of the value of diversity courses, other universities looked to other policies that they believed have an impact on students' educational experiences. Some adopted speech codes designed to prevent words from creating a hostile environment for students (and faculty) members of these groups.

The reaction of the more conservative and traditionally minded was often quite hostile. Then Secretary of Education William J. Bennett joined a chorus of criticism when he said in a talk at Stanford that the university's decision 'was not a product of enlightened debate, but rather an unfortunate capitulation to the campaign of pressure politics and intimidation . . . we have seen in this instance the closing of the Stanford mind . . . through bullying, threatening and name calling' (Bennett 1998: 38). Speech codes fared no better, with many of them being rejected by US courts as violating the guarantee of free speech under the first amendment.

Despite these criticisms, however, the multicultural movement has flourished on campuses across the USA. New interdisciplinary programmes in women's studies, Afro-American studies, gay/lesbian studies, and Hispanic studies emerged throughout the 1980s and 1990s. Affirmative action programmes were instituted, giving preference to 'under-represented' groups in university and college hiring, promotion, and student admission, although they have also come under increasing legal and political pressure.

Along with changes in the college curriculum have come changes in various disciplines themselves. Scholars throughout the humanities and social sciences are studying new topics and sometimes proposing alternative methodologies. Traditional, grand-scale histories of nations and military/political conflict have been supplemented, if not supplanted, by social history emphasizing the experiences of ordinary people—including especially non-Europeans and women.

Multiculturalism in all its many forms has also had an impact at primary and secondary schools. Almost any library these days will have shelves of books discussing the concept of a multicultural curriculum and how to address greater ethnic, religious, and linguistic diversity in schools. This is unsurprising: often schools are the first and among the most divisive sites where social and cultural disputes are played out. One key battleground for schools, as Stanford was for universities, was the New York State's 1989 *Curriculum of Inclusion*. Under pressure from legislators, Commissioner of Education Thomas Sobol appointed a committee to look into curricular issues as they affect black and hispanic students. The committee chose as its consultant Leonard Jeffries of the City University of New York, who is among the most adamant of the 'Afrocentrist' scholars. Part of his fame arose when he referred to 'white' people as 'ice people'. The report attacked 'Eurocentric' education, beginning with the statement that 'African Americans, Asian Americans, Puerto Rican/Latinos, and Native Americans have all been the victims of an intellectual and educational oppression that has characterized the culture and institution of the United States and the European American world for centuries' (Commissioner's Task Force on Minorities 1989).

Like the Stanford reform, this met with considerable criticism. Its controversial claims about the African origins of major scientific and other achievements were attacked in both the academy and the popular press. A second committee was created, which included more non-minorities. Its report too was controversial, and was denounced by one of its own members, historian Arthur Schlessinger Jr., among others. The second report, *One Nation, Many Peoples: A Declaration of Cultural Interdependence*, exposed some of the fault lines and political difficulties posed by multiculturalism. This second report attempted both to acknowledge that the USA is a single nation and also to affirm that it includes many, independent cultures. In doing so, it affirmed the existence of 'multiple perspectives' in the teaching of history. But one problem, according to a member of the committee, is that the only perspectives it included were the traditional 'multicultural' groups: it ignored the perspectives of urban versus rural, north versus south, farmers versus industrialists. Its focus on the Bill of Rights emphasized almost exclusively the ongoing struggle of some, not the achievements made under the Constitution (Glazer 1997).

The events at Stanford and in New York illustrate nicely the key issues embedded in the debates over multiculturalism and education. One question that emerges throughout the literature is the goal of multicultural education. Some defenders of multiculturalism take a modest view that multicultural education means no longer excluding the accomplishments of non-European cultures. These cultures have made genuine contributions and have influenced the course of history, so that to ignore them is to fail as educators. This assumes, then, that there is some basis on which to assess the (relative) accomplishment of a culture—something not all multiculturalists share, as we will see. On the other hand are those who see multicultural education in more political terms. They emphasize that among the causes of poor academic achievement of especially African-Americans is a lack of self-esteem. Multicultural education is meant to remedy that by highlighting the accomplishments of Africa, so that, for example, Egypt's contributions to civilization are often emphasized in 'Afrocentric' curricula.

3. MULTICULTURALISM AND THE POLITICS OF DIFFERENCE

In addition to education, another issue central to multiculturalism is political: how should governments 'recognize languages, draw boundaries, and distribute powers' in a multicultural society, including whether or not governments should acknowledge 'group rights' (Kymlicka 1995: 113). Should law be used to ensure the continuation of cultures? And, if so, what does that requirement mean in practice? Among those most closely associated with these political issues are Iris Marion Young and Will Kymlicka.

Young (1990: 186) is concerned with injustices experienced by groups, where groups are understood as sharing cultural forms, practices, and ways of life that give a common sense of identity or affinity. Young's particular interest is in those groups that are victims of injustice, specifically 'oppression' and 'dominance'. The former is defined as 'constraints on self-development'—that is, institutional processes preventing people from exercising certain capacities and skills—while domination occurs when groups are prevented from participating in the processes that determine 'the conditions of their action' (Young 1990: 37–8). The five different forms of injustice she identifies are exploitation (transfer of results of labour), marginalization (for example, unemployment), powerlessness, cultural imperialism, and violence. She identifies the groups that are subject to these injustices in the USA as including 'among others women, Blacks, Chicanos, Puerto Ricans and other Spanish-speaking Americans, American Indians, Jews, Lesbians, gay men, Arabs, Asians, old people, working-class people and the physically and mentally disabled' (Young 1990: 40).

This 'difference' vision of multicultural politics, which emphasizes the oppression of groups and the importance of membership to personal identity, is explored in detail in later sections of this essay. But, with respect to the specifics of Young's claims, three questions arise. First, the list of groups suffering injustice is extremely broad—so broad that virtually everybody belongs to a victimized group according to Young. The only American group *not* victimized by dominance and oppression is relatively young, non-working class, white, heterosexual, straight, non-Spanish speaking, non-Jewish males of European descent. Brian Barry (2001: 367) has recently concluded that by Young's account nearly 90 per cent of all Americans would be victims of the oppressive American political system. Nor, secondly, is it clear that these groups should be thought of as cultural groups with a shared sense of identity. Some, like old people, do share certain political interests, of course; but then so do children. To suggest a common culture and shared identity for these widely disparate persons, merely based on group membership, risks extending notions of culture and identity so broadly that they lose meaning. Finally, it is far from obvious that it is *as members of those groups* these people suffer injustices, when they do. To take an obvious example, many (though by now means all) old people may be thought to suffer some form of injustice, but why not suppose the injustice is due to poverty, or lack of medical care, rather than membership in the group 'the elderly'? Much the same could be said for other groups. Many Asians, Hispanics, Jews, gays, women, blacks and workers are flourishing, while some suffer what could be thought to be injustices. But again it is not clear their group membership is the source of the problems, rather than poverty. So it seems that many important philosophical issues revolve around the claimed injustices themselves, largely economic in nature, and not group membership and cultural identity.

Agreeing that Young's conception of cultural group is too broad to be of much use, Will Kymlicka offers a narrower definition of culture that emphasizes a common history and language. In that sense, his notion of cultural group closely resembles what we think of as a people or nation, with the implication that the elderly, gays, women, and other groups discussed by Young are irrelevant to his project. Kymlicka then uses this narrower understanding of cultural groups to defend 'self-government rights' and provide a level of political autonomy for groups in the form of control over their territory within a larger multinational state (for example,

Native Americans or French speakers in Quebec), the opportunity to defend themselves through control of immigration into their territory, education, and protection of their native language. He also offers a sympathetic account of the case for 'ensuring a voice for minorities' through political mechanisms that would secure minimal representation in democratic institutions and practices, and defends finding ways to accommodate minority cultures—for example, by allowing Sikhs to wear turbans while serving on the police force and increasing the self-esteem of minority children by expanding the school curriculum. But at the same time Kymlicka is also sympathetic to those who worry about the political effects of such a move on the attitudes of members of the majority, or doubt the assumption that the only people who can represent a cultural group are members of the group.

In defending these proposals, Kymlicka distinguishes 'multinational' from 'polyethnic' states. Multinational states have different cultures that are tied to the land, such as the English and French in Canada. In polyethnic states, members of different cultures are dispersed throughout the country. Group rights may vary, he argues, depending on which type the state is. Kymlicka then distinguishes three types of 'group differentiated' rights. 'Self-government rights' provide a level of political autonomy in the form of control over the territory of groups within multinational states. 'Polyethnic rights' extend beyond the universal rights against discrimination afforded all citizens to rights designated to benefit specific groups. Examples in this category would include demands for public funding of cultural practices and exemptions from laws disadvantaging particular groups (for example, Sunday closing laws, laws forbidding animal sacrifice, dress codes). A third category is 'representation rights', in which a particular level of representation in a legislative body is reserved for each cultural group (see also Guinier 1994).

Perhaps the most oft-heard objection to multiculturalism's emphasis on group difference in education and in politics is that it undermines a sense of shared citizenship. In his concession speech after the 2000 election, Al Gore said that the closeness of the election 'can serve to remind us that we are one people with a shared history and a shared identity' (2000: 12). But others, some of whom may be friends of multiculturalism, question Gore's assumption and doubt whether such a shared sense of identity and social solidarity can be sustained among the citizens of modern, multicultural nations—especially one that emphasizes group and ethnic identity.

4. CITIZENSHIP, NATIONALISM, AND CULTURAL IDENTITY

European nations face similar questions about group rights, stability, and national identity. A furore erupted recently in Britain, for example, with publication of a report by the Runnymede Trust titled 'The Future of Multi-Ethnic Britain'. After pointing out the growing cultural, religious, and ethnic diversity of Britain and wondering whether 'Britishness has a future', the report went on to say that 'A genuinely multi-cultural Britain needs to re-imagine itself' because Britishness has 'systematic, largely unspoken, racial connotations' (Runnymede Trust 2000). The report met with a storm of criticism in the popular press. Similar events have been reported in Germany, Italy, and France.

Europeans are confronting issues of stability and national identity in other contexts as well. One is the European Union. If such a super-national political project is to succeed, some claim, it must be accompanied by an increased sense of patriotic solidarity and mutual identification among Europeans as a historically and culturally distinct people. Yet 'Europe today', wrote Vaclav Havel (1993: 3), 'lacks an ethos', so that there is a weak sense of identity and little popular support for political integration. Suggestions that a new European identity should be cultivated has provoked different responses. Some oppose increased integration in the name of national sovereignty and occasionally cultural or ethnic identity; others seek to cultivate a sense of shared identity among Europeans. In his best-selling *Europe: A History*, for instance, Norman Davies (1996) argues for just the identity that Havel thinks is lacking. A third political and constitutional issue running alongside debates about multiculturalism and European integration is the gradual 'devolution' of power downward. In Great Britain this has put more power into the parliament in Scotland and the new assembly in Wales. Similar devolution is being considered elsewhere in Europe.

Questions about stability and diversity are important in many other areas of the world that have yet to achieve constitutional government. In Africa, Latin America, and parts of Eastern Europe and Asia, nations struggle to achieve the rule of law and stable constitutional government in the face of poverty, internal conflicts, religious, ethnic, and cultural diversity, and often international economic and military pressure. For these nations the problems of stability and legitimacy are especially acute, often seeming to dwarf the concerns of multiculturalists about protecting cultural identity in relatively prosperous and stable Western democracies.

These political and cultural changes have provoked a range of responses. While the European Union is defended in many circles, it is also sometimes attacked as an infringement on national sovereignty and identity, or by other critics who take a much more cosmopolitan position and attack all forms of patriotism, whether national or regional, as mere prejudice. Martha Nussbaum, for example, describes citizenship in a nation as a 'morally irrelevant characteristic' that should be replaced not with another, super-national loyalty to Europe, for instance, but instead with a sense of solidarity among *all* 'human beings in the entire world' (1996: 3). Whether such universalism is workable or attractive is, of course, controversial. Michael Sandel (1996), for instance, argues it is neither. For him, the devolution of political and other forms of authority to local governmental and voluntary associations represents the best hope for democratic government. Still another response to this, found in John Rawls's recent work (1999) on law of peoples, is to assume that the relevant political unit will remain the nation state, populated by a single people whose sense of common identity and social solidarity remain strong.

Where these controversies over national identity and changes in political structures will lead is anybody's guess, of course. But there is no doubt that the pressure on national identity has generated controversy, as illustrated by those who claim multiculturalism's emphasis on racial and ethnic identity threatens the shared sense of solidarity that provides the basis of citizenship. Arthur Schlesinger (1992), for example, writes of the 'disuniting of America', while sociologist Todd Gitlin (1995: 236) worries about the impact on democratic institutions:

Democracy is more than a license to celebrate (and exaggerate) difference. . . . It is a political system of mutual reliance and common moral obligations. . . . If multiculturalism is not tempered by a stake in the commons, then centrifugal energy overwhelms any commitment to a larger good. This is where multiculturalism has proved a trap even—or especially—for people in the name of whom the partisans of identity politics purport to speak.

The question is difficult and complex. Given a diverse, democratic nation state, how is it possible to maintain the requisite sense of social solidarity in a context of growing polarization and group consciousness? Some propose lessening immigration and implementing restrictive language laws as a solution, but others doubt that is a workable solution even if it were right. Jeffrey Spinner-Havel seeks a different solution. He begins with a description of the problem similar to Gitlin:

A multiculturalism that tries to create a society with several distinct cultures deeply threatens citizenship. In this kind of multicultural society, people are not interested in citizenship; they are not interested in making the state a better place for all; they care little about how public policies affect most people or about their fellow citizen. . . . What they have are fellow Jews, or fellow blacks, or fellow Muslims, or fellow Sikhs.   (Spinner-Havel 1999: 65)

To understand the problem, he argues, we must first distinguish two types of groups making two different demands on their fellow citizens. On the one hand are those that hope to protect their cultural practices in ways that cannot be accomplished except by separating themselves from the rest of society. One thinks here of the Amish, and some sects of Orthodox Jews. Other groups, however, reject separation and instead hope instead that their cultural practices, and by implication themselves, will be respected by the larger society. Groups that argue for reform of educational curricula because it has ignored their contributions in history books therefore need not be seen as demanding the maintenance of a distinct identity apart from the larger nation in the separatist sense. Indeed the opposite is the case: members of these groups want to be *included* in that common history, and hope to change the larger group so as to make that compatible with membership in a subgroup with which they also identify. They seek accommodation of a dual identity. Thus, when Captain Goldman demanded that he be allowed to wear a yarmulke in violation of Air Force rules, he sought ways for society to allow both forms of membership so that he might ultimately participate in both.

So demands for *accommodation* should be distinguished, Spinner-Havel (1999: 71) argues, from those who seek 'partial citizenship'—that is, who wish to ignore and be ignored by the larger society in order to live among themselves. That leads in turn to a second distinction. On the one hand are groups that neither involve themselves in politics nor demand benefits from government. They seek a bargain in which they ask for little or nothing, and expect as much in return—except to be left to organize their own affairs as they see fit. As such, they pose no threat to the larger society and may even contribute to it through trade or cultural contacts. Others, however, hope for a different sort of bargain. They hope to receive various benefits from the state, economic or otherwise, though like the first they are not interested in political participation or further social integration. That means, however, that they are therefore uninterested in the virtues essential to democratic government: toleration, concern for the well-being of others, and respect for others' rights. The danger to citizenship is greatest from these partial citizenship groups, Spinner-Havel claims, because of the reaction to them by the rest of society: as such groups grow and press demands for benefits, non-separatists will tend to withdraw themselves from essential institutions like public education and social welfare programmes into their own gated, segregated, and economically isolated communities.

This situation is best avoided, Spinner-Havel argues, when the majority seeks to encourage citizenship by accommodating groups rather than driving them into a stage of partial citizenship that risks provoking further, counter-reaction from the majority. This accommodation is important. A multicultural society is committed not only to allowing partial citizens to live within its borders (if that is what a group wants) but also to encouraging groups to become active citizens while at the same time and in so far as is reasonable accommodating their cultural needs.

A second, related problem involving multiculturalism and citizenship is the conflict between the duties of group membership and the duties of citizenship. Will Kymlicka, for instance, is concerned to set respect for individual rights alongside the demand to protect cultures and promote diversity. But included among the individual rights Kymlicka wants to defend is the right of members to reject the group, its beliefs, and its practices. To resolve the potential conflict, he distinguishes *external* protections of groups against the dominant culture from *internal* restrictions that would prevent groups from violating rights of their own members. So, for example, while it might be legitimate for government to promote the language of native Scots or the French in Quebec, it would not be acceptable 'internally' to forbid people moving to another region or to insist they speak a particular language in their homes.

Many would surely agree that no group, even those that pursue merely partial citizenship, should be allowed to establish whatever rules they want in governing themselves internally. But there are many other issues about which reasonable people will differ. These cover a wide range—from mandatory public education of older children and teaching evolution in schools to allowing animal sacrifice or religious practices that treat women differently from men. The US Supreme Court famously addressed this dilemma in a case involving the cultural rights of a group of Amish who demanded that their children be exempted from mandatory school attendance laws. As the court noted, protecting the Amish as a cultural group by exempting their families from mandatory school attendance rules that could threaten the group's existence can also be seen as violating the rights of Amish children, who someday may want to leave their group to join the larger society and will therefore need an education (*Wisconsin* v. *Yoder*, 1972). Conversely, laws protecting the free speech right of individuals like Salman Rushdie to criticize or even mock their own group may be seen as threatening the culture from outside, just as giving women in a group the right to civil divorce and child custody may be seen as either an external threat to the group or an internal protection of its members.

5. The Importance of Cultural Membership: Freedom, Identity, and Recognition

I want now to turn to a set of issues the last sections have had in the background, and ask why it is important that cultural identities be maintained. As I have hinted, Kymlicka's defence of group rights is predicated on liberalism's fundamental commitment to freedom, and particularly 'freedom [of individuals] to choose their own life plans' (1995: 80). Expanding on Dworkin's definition of culture as a 'shared vocabulary of tradition and convention', Kymlicka argues that liberalism must respect cultures because of their connections with people's ability to make meaningful choices about their ways of life. To lose a culture to which one is connected is to lose the prerequisites of choosing and thus realizing the values inhering in that culture, he claims. Joseph Raz makes the point more explicitly by linking culture with choice and freedom: 'Only through being socialized in a culture', he writes, 'can one tap the options which give life a meaning. By and large one's cultural membership determines the horizon of one's opportunities, of what one may become or (if one is older) what one might have been' (Raz 1994: 177). People thus have a need for a societal culture to provide what Kymlicka terms a 'context of choice'. Freedom involves 'making choices amongst various options, and our societal culture not only provides these options, but also makes them meaningful to us' (Kymlicka 1995: 83).

Jeremy Waldron (1993) questions this argument that governments should protect particular cultures. While agreeing with Kymlicka's premiss that everybody needs a culture to provide a 'context of choice', it is not at all clear, says Waldron, that the choice must come from within any *particular* culture. Waldron thus charges Kymlicka and other multiculturalists in effect with reifying the idea of culture. Indeed, Kymlicka himself acknowledges that it is 'natural and desirable for cultures to change as a result of decisions made by their members' (1995: 103). Going further, it might be argued that multicultural societies present a diverse variety of cultural materials, drawn from all over the world, and then integrated and in the process transformed into part of a diverse cultural polyglot. So at the very least one might question whether any *particular* stable culture is essential for people to maximize options. Immigrants and their descendants will sometimes have *different* options from members of the majority culture, but to understand the point of maintaining the culture as providing more options seems mistaken. It might actually offer fewer, though they would be different ones. Policies that seek to protect a particular culture may therefore have the effect of eventually reducing the options available to both the members of that culture and to the society at large. That would be true if, for instance, rather than contributing to and being shaped by the other cultures in the society the protected ones become insular and the society balkanized.

What we also may notice, then, are often opposing interpretations of 'liberal' cultures. Many multiculturalists see American culture as homogeneous, homogenizing, and threatening to minority cultures living within its boundaries (as well as beyond). Given that, it is important for people who do not participate in the dominant culture to be protected against its onslaught, whether inside the borders of the USA or beyond. The alternative interpretation sees American and other liberal multicultural societies not as homogeneous but as diverse and constantly changing— regularly absorbing into themselves the ideas, customs, music, tastes, and even religious practices of their diverse citizens. Describing his book *Satanic Verses*, Salman Rushdie expresses this attitude: the book, he wrote, 'celebrates hybridity, impurity, intermingling, the transformation that comes from new and unexpected combinations of human beings, cultures, ideas, politics, movies, songs. It rejoices in Mongrelization . . . a bit of this and that is how newness enters the world' (Joppke and Lukes 1999: 20). Viewed in that light, whatever else can be said about the lives of persons in liberal, Western cultures, they are not without options and freedom. We are, each of us, free to construct our identities from a huge array of materials.

But not all those who accept this picture of multicultural society's diversity and freedom find it agreeable. Michael Sandel in particular has mounted a critique of the 'liberal' conception of freedom, identity, and the self. In place of the Kantian and Rawlsian 'unencumbered' self, which is abstracted from any particular identity and social role and able to choose its associations and ultimately its identity, Sandel defends a different picture. His key claim is that, far from choosing our identities, they are in large measure assigned to us by history. Identities are created by virtue of membership in groups, including most importantly families, religious traditions, nations, and even civic organizations. Ignoring the fact of the historically and bio-logically encumbered self has important political consequences, according to Sandel. When liberalism addresses freedom of religion, for example, its mistaken conception of the unencumbered self freely choosing its identity ignores the fact that a religious person may have a duty to attend services, for instance, or wear a yarmulke. Thus, liberal court decisions that treat religion as an optional 'lifestyle choice' denigrate the importance of religion (Sandel 1996: 55–71). Liberalism's conception of the self also leads it to fail to appreciate the harm caused by hate speech, he argues. Because the self is understood not as unencumbered, abstract, rational chooser, liberalism can-not appreciate the cost to victims of one-on-one ethnic, religious, and racial attacks, or of generalized attacks on a group with which one is identified (Sandel 1996: 80–6).

Liberalism's failure to take seriously the encumbered nature of our identities leads to another problem, as well: it produces an overly narrow conception of obligations. While unencumbered selves have duties to keep promises and other contracts, as well as universal duties owed to all persons, they have no room to appreciate the special communal obligations of family, religion, and nation. These are historically grounded, he claims, and so cannot be taken seriously by the a-historical, unencumbered self imagined by liberals.

In determining our obligations, Sandel concludes, we must ultimately decide 'which of one's identities is properly engaged—as a parent or professional, follower of a faith or partisan of a cause, citizen of one's country or citizen of the world' (1996: 343). Inherent in that deliberative process is the problem of identity: we must 'attend to the content of the claims, their relative moral weight, and their role in the narratives by which the participants make sense of their lives' (Sandel 1996: 343–4). Human beings, he adds, are 'storytelling beings' whose lives and identities can make sense only when placed in the context of history (Sandel 1996: 351). Sandel summa-rizes his position this way: 'Community describes not just what they *have* as fellow citizens but also what they *are*, not a relationship they choose (as in a voluntary association) but an attachment they discover, not merely an attribute but a con-stituent of their identity' (1998: 150).

Sandel's core claim is that identification with a cultural or other group is a (if not the) central, defining feature of a person. But *why* must it be the case that people's identity is tied, through history, to cultural groups? One answer is suggested by Margalit and Raz, who emphasize that identification with a cultural group is more 'stable' than other traits we may have: group membership 'does not depend on achievements, and is a secure, easy basis for belonging' (1990: 447).

Politics could then become relevant, in this view, because of the link between group membership, identity, and social recognition. In general terms, identity refers to how we, as individuals, conceive of ourselves and of our relationships with others in our group. This can involve racial, ethnic, or religious identities, but it may include other professional and personal relationships and roles as well. Recognition, on the other hand, is concerned with how *others in society identify us* and, crucially, how members of society then react to that identity. Do they take a respectful, approving attitude, or a negative one? Does the negative attitude reflect prejudice—for example, racism or ethnic hatred?

The political implications of personal identity are explored in Charles Taylor's 'The Politics of Recognition' (1994), as he discusses the connections between the self, identity, and the political demand for 'recognition' (see also Honneth 1995). That demand for recognition, Taylor points out, is a relatively new claim that people have come to press in the political realm, though it has intellectual roots in Rousseau and Hegel. He distinguishes between the 'politics of equal recognition', in which people insist on formal equality, and the 'politics of difference', in which people demand recognition of what it is that makes them different from others. The politics of difference is not about what makes one *individual* different from others, but rather about the ethnic or cultural identity that distinguishes people, *qua members of that group*, from members of other groups. Taylor suggests that both forms of recognition are important, and argues that they share a common root because the demand for recognition of one's difference is itself an expression of the demand for treatment as an equal. (Whether or not society should ultimately respect a particular cultural tradition is an open question, he claims, although, as I will discuss shortly, he does believe there is a presumption in favour of doing so.)

Taylor thus claims that culture and the formation of identity are linked in virtue of the nature of the process of identity formation. He writes:

This crucial feature of human life [identity formation] is its fundamentally dialogical character. We become full human agents, capable of understanding ourselves, and hence of defining our identity, through our acquisition of rich human languages of expression. . . . We define our identity always in dialogue with, sometime in struggle against, the things our significant others want to see in us . . . the conversation with them continues within us as long as we live.   (Taylor 1994: 32–3)

These various claims, about the encumbered self, identity, and recognition, have met with a variety of criticisms. Some have objected to the understanding of the conception of identity, others to the political implications multiculturalists draw from the conception. Amartya Sen (1998: 14, 16), for example, attacks the multiculturalist notion of identity directly.

To insist on a particular canonical group identity, without reasoned support, would beg the question: why focus on this group only rather than another, of which the person may also be a member? A person can simultaneously have the identity of an Italian, a woman, a feminist, a vegetarian, a novelist, a fiscal conservative, a jazz fan, and a Londoner. . . . Often such choices are quite explicit, like when Mohandas Gandhi deliberately decides to give priority to his identification with Indians seeking independence from British rule over his identity as a trained barrister pursuing English legal justice.'

So to suggest that one's identity is strongly tied to a particular group—let alone a racial or ethnic group—misses the important, complex fact that we get our sense of self from choices we make among a range of different options. Sen might have added that the importance of 'group' is not nearly as important as multiculturalists suppose. A person whose identity is tied to bird watching, music, or sports, for instance, may resist the thought that membership in a group of like-minded persons is central, insisting instead that it is the commitment to the activity itself that provides a sense of identity.

Sen also questions Sandel's rejection of the liberal, choosing self. He argues that Sandel's understanding of the self as something we 'detect' rather than 'determine' runs counter to the fact that 'we do have a choice about our beliefs, associations and attitudes, and we must take responsibility for what we actually choose (if only implicitly)' (Sen 2000: 37). Kymlicka makes a similar point, stating that we must give due regard for people's ability to revise their 'deepest ends' and that 'no end is immune from potential revision' (1995: 91).

A further concern raised about multiculturalism's embrace of the politics of difference is the long-term effects of these ideas on social solidarity. Sen worries that to claim we merely discover our choices could lead to 'unquestioning loyalty and belief in precipitating atrocities and horrors'. He points specifically to the carnage in India during the pre-partition riots, when previously tolerant people became ruthless Hindus and fierce Muslims as a result of having 'discovered' their true identity, 'unhampered by reasoned humanity' (Sen 2000: 37).

It sometimes seems, then, that there are just two extremes: on the one hand is the encumbered self, bound by historical narrative and the obligations it brings, while the other pictures identity as a choice that is within our control. The truth, however, would seem to lie somewhere between. Keeping in mind the original understanding of identity as how each person conceives of him or herself, there is a sense in which our identity is within our control: we can choose to marry, pursue a particular career, get deeply involved in a charitable or political cause, or work to develop musical, athletic, or other talents. All these choices shape our sense of our selves. But what then of other facts about us that we cannot control, such as race, gender, and ethnicity? Here it seems clear that, while, on one hand, it is not in our control whether others see and identify us as belonging to that group, it nonetheless remains in our control whether we want to emphasize that fact above others or, if we choose, deny group membership's importance to our identity. That said, however, there are also limits to that control. Suppose a person is a member of a group that is not thought suitable, by society at large, for a certain role or pursuit. To insist on that choice, in those circumstances, would be to struggle against a headwind not felt by members of other groups. In that sense, our identity, while not defined by outsiders against our will, is at least encouraged. Our own reason and doubt may also make our chosen identity difficult to sustain, as when a religious believer, consumed with doubt or critical of the Church, reports she cannot remain among the faithful. While there is no external impediment to continued participation in the group, there is another, important sense in which membership is no longer an option from the person's own, subjective standpoint. Thirdly, and finally, society also plays an important albeit again an indirect role in shaping the identities of its members as it makes some options easily available while either discouraging or foreclosing others. Societies that use law or popular opinion to discourage popular culture or forbid participation in religious institutions, for example, limit the identity-defining roles available to their members. Other roles may be unavailable for economic reasons. As Joseph Raz (1994: 118) points out in another context, the role of miner (and its association with fraternity, the labour movement, hard work, and courage) may simply not be an option in some societies. So, while Sen is right to reject the fully encumbered self and emphasize the ways that identities are within our control, there are at least three important respects in which our identities are shaped and sometimes restricted by forces outside ourselves.

In the case of recognition (that is, how *society* identifies a person and then assesses that identity as opposed to how we identify ourselves) there seems to be less room for individual control. When society regards an immutable trait as central to identity, or as irrelevant, there may be little that the individual can do to affect that perception. Nor is it possible to exercise much control over society's evaluation of our identity, whether it is associated with an immutable group characteristic or a chosen activity or role. Some may try to win acceptance for their group by showing the errors in society's stereotypes, though the effects of such a programme may be small. The fact that society is racist or anti-semitic and therefore either shows no respect or, worse, vilifies one's identity cannot be easily changed. Strategies are available to try to mitigate these influences by associating only with people who take a different attitude from society's, as a group of neo-Nazis may do, and thereby make it easier to sustain a socially stigmatized identity.

6. MULTICULTURALISM AND OBJECTIVITY

The last issue I want to mention is less political than the others, though how it is answered may shape decisions about many of the topics I have already identified, including citizenship's potential conflict with multiculturalism and the rights of members against their group. It involves the vexing epistemological questions associated with determining the relative merits of different cultures: whether or not it is possible to make such a judgement and, if it is, how it should be made. This issue emerges in various contexts, but most clearly with the demand that people and institutions not just tolerate but respect differences and acknowledge the equal dignity or worth of each culture. Charles Taylor terms this the 'premise that we owe equal respect to all cultures' and admits that such a presumption is 'by no means unproblematic' (1994: 66). The difficulty is nowhere better illustrated than by a remark often attributed to Saul Bellow: 'When the Zulus produce a Tolstoy we will read him', or in Allan Bloom's phrase 'The Closing of the American Mind' (1987), which he used to describe the decline of standards in American education as it turned to multiculturalism in the curriculum. One response offered by multiculturalists to those who doubt the value of a particular culture is relativism. Indeed, relativism has long been part of the debate over multiculturalism for at least three reasons. First, multiculturalism has roots in the reaction against cultural and other forms of imperialism, and imperial powers are widely thought to have justified their misdeeds on grounds of cultural superiority. A second reason is ethical relativism's close association with relativistic social sciences like anthropology. The third reason is linked with identity politics. Once identification with a culture takes centre stage, authenticity is valued (in the sense of respecting and reflecting the ideals of the group). Truth and objectivity are then pushed to the background as each group relies on its own members' scholarship to give 'voice' to its unique perspective and concerns. Following this line, Stanley Fish claims that all cultures are equally worthy of respect on the grounds that we cannot make 'objective' judgements about cultures, but rather only ones from our particular cultural vantage point. People are 'defined' by their positions in a community and so cannot achieve a perspective 'independent of institutional assumptions' (Fish 1980: 320). Speaking specifically of multiculturalism, Fish claims that people can talk to one another only if they 'share a set of basic assumptions', including perhaps the 'decorums of Enlightenment rationalism' (Fish 1998: 79). Reject those culturally based norms and assumptions, he claims, and reasoned argument becomes impossible.

In one sense, of course, this is trivially true: reject the norms of rational argument, and there will be no rational argument. But Amy Gutman and Thomas Nagel also respond that this is both an inaccurate description of cultural disagreement and self-defeating. Using polygamy as an example, Gutman (1993) points out that the practice was in fact the subject of serious discussion and debate within Mormon culture. She thus doubts the familiar picture of societies as homogenous systems whose practices are beyond criticism either from within or outside. In a similar vein, Nagel (1997) observes that, while it is 'old as the hills' to make the point, multicultural relativism is self-defeating when it makes universal truth claims itself, such as Fish's claim that truth and meaning are always and everywhere reducible to particular cultures.

Rejecting those who claim we should respect cultures on the basis of relativism, Charles Taylor offers a different approach. Every society and culture, he points out, can go through periods of decline and improvement. And certainly not all are equally good at producing art or science, for example, let alone at respecting human rights and securing fair equality of opportunity and economic prosperity. But, if we reject relativism in favour of an external, objective assessment of cultures, how can we also think all cultures deserve equal respect? Taylor's answer is that respect is merely a presumption or 'starting hypotheses'—one that can be rebutted and whose validity must be demonstrated by the careful study of a culture. In making such cross-cultural comparisons, he emphasizes, we must broaden our horizons and be aware that our own criteria for valuation may rest on nothing more than prejudice in favour of the familiar. Our judgements to respect another culture, if they are to be sound, may therefore require us to question and eventually transform our own standards of evaluation. As further support for this presumption, he points out that it would be reasonable always to begin by assuming that any culture that has supported and animated the lives of its members for a decent period of time offers something of value, even if we as outsiders cannot yet appreciate or even comprehend what that value is. None of that is to say, however, that a culture must necessarily be valuable and worthy of respect. That conclusion must be earned, and everything depends on the merits of the particular case.

REFERENCES

Barry, B. (2001). *Culture and Equality: An Egalitarian Critique of Multiculturalism*. Cambridge, MA: Harvard University Press.

Bennett, W. J. (1988). Speech delivered at Stanford University, repr. in *National Review*, 27 May, 37–9.

Bernstein, R. (1994). *The Dictatorship of Virtue: Multiculturalism and the Battle for America's Future*. New York: Knopf.

Bloom, A. (1987). *The Closing of the American Mind*. New York: Simon & Schuster.

Blum, L. (1991). 'Philosophy and the Values of a Multicultural Community'. *Teaching Philosophy*, 14: 127–34.

Caeser, J. (1998). 'Multiculturalism and American Liberal Democracy', in A. Melzer, J. Weinberger, and R. Zinman (eds.), *Multiculturalism and American Democracy*. Lawrence, KS: University Press of Kansas, 139–56.

Commissioner's Task Force on Minorities (1989). *A Curriculum of Inclusion: Report of the Commissioner's Task Force on Minorities: Equity and Excellence* (Albany, NY: State Education Department).

Davies, N. (1996). *Europe: A History*. Oxford: Oxford University Press.

Dworkin, R. (1985). *A Matter of Principle*. Cambridge, MA: Harvard University Press.

—— (1986). *Law's Empire*. Cambridge, MA: Harvard University Press.

Fish, S. (1980). *Is there a Text in this Class?* Cambridge, MA: Harvard University Press.

—— (1998). 'Botique Multiculturalism', in A. Melzer, J. Weinberger, and R. Zinman (eds.), *Multiculturalism and American Democracy*. Lawrence, KS: University Press of Kansas, 69–88.

Friedman, M. (1995). 'Multicultural Education and Feminist Ethics'. *Hypatia*, 10: 56–68.

Gitlin, T. (1995). *The Twilight of Common Dreams: Why America is Wracked by Culture Wars*. New York: Henry Holt.

Glazer, N. (1997). *We are all Multiculturalists Now*. Cambridge, MA: Harvard University Press.

Gore, A. (2000). 'Concession Speech'. *International Herald Tribune*, 15 Dec., 12.

Guinier, L. (1994). *The Tyranny of the Majority: Fundamental Fairness in Representative Democracy*. New York: Free Press.

Gutman, A. (1993). 'The Challenge of Multiculturalism to Political Ethics'. *Philosophy and Public Affairs*, 22: 172–80.

——(1994) (ed.). *Multiculturalism*. Princeton: Princeton University Press.

Havel, V. (1993). 'Address to the General Assembly of the Council on Europe', trans. P. Wilson. *New York Review of Books*, 18 Nov.

Honneth, A. (1995). *The Struggle for Recognition: The Moral Grammar of Social Conflicts*. Cambridge, MA: MIT Press.

Hunter, J. D. (1991). *Culture Wars: The Struggle to Define America*. New York: Basic Books.

Joppke, C., and Lukes, S. (1999) (eds.), *Multicultural Questions*. London: Oxford University Press.

Kymlicka, W. (1995). *Multicultural Citizenship*. Oxford: Oxford University Press.

Margalit, A., and Raz, J. (1990). 'National Self-Determination'. *Journal of Philosophy*, 87: 439–61.

Melzer, A., Weinberger, J., and Zinman, R. (1996) (eds.), *Multiculturalism and American Democracy*. Lawrence, KS: University Press of Kansas.

Nagel, T. (1997). *The Last Word*. Oxford: Oxford University Press.

Nussbaum, M. C. (1996). 'Patriotism and Cosmopolitanism', in M. C. Nussbaum et al. (eds.), *For Love of Country: Debating the Limits of Patriotism*. Boston: Boston Beacon Press, 3–17.

Okin, S. M. (1999). 'Is Multiculturalism Bad for Women?', in J. Cohen, M. Howard, and M. C. Nussbaum (eds.), *Is Multiculturalism Bad for Women?* Princeton: Princeton University Press, 9–24.

Payne, M. (1996) (ed.). *A Dictionary of Cultural and Critical Theory*. Oxford: Blackwell.

Rawls, J. (1971). *A Theory of Justice*. Cambridge, MA: Harvard University Press.

——(1999). *The Law of Peoples*. Cambridge, MA: Harvard University Press.

Raz, J. (1994). *Ethics in the Public Domain*. London: Oxford University Press.

Rorty, R. (2000). *Philosophy and Social Hope*. New York: Penguin.

Sandel, M. (1996). *Democracy's Discontents: America in Search of a Public Philosophy*. Cambridge, MA: Harvard University Press.

——(1998). *Liberalism and the Limits of Justice*. 2nd edn. Cambridge: Cambridge University Press.

Scanlon, T. M. (1998). *What we Owe Each Other*. Cambridge, MA: Harvard University Press.

Schlesinger, A. (1992). *The Disuniting of America: Reflections on a Multicultural Society*. New York: Norton.

Sen, A. (1998). *Reason before Identity*. Oxford: Oxford University Press.

——(2000). 'Reason in East and West'. *New York Review of Books*, 20 July, 33–8.

Spinner-Havel, J. (1999). 'Cultural Pluralism and Partial Citizenship', in C. Joppke and S. Lukes (eds.), *Multicultural Questions*. London: Oxford University Press, 65–86.

Sullivan, A. (2000). 'United Colors of America'. *Sunday Times* (London), 15 Oct., 9.

Taylor, C. (1994). 'The Politics of Recognition', in A. Gutman (ed.), *Multiculturalism*. Princeton: Princeton University Press, 25–73.

Waldron, J. (1993). 'Minority Cultures and the Cosmopolitan Alternative'. *University of Michigan Journal of Law Reform*, 25: 751–93.

Young, I. M. (1990). *Multiculturalism and the Politics of Difference*. Princeton: Princeton University Press.

Case Cited

Wisconsin v. *Yoder*, 406 US 205 (1972).

CHAPTER 17

ECONOMIC JUSTICE

JONATHAN WOLFF

1. INTRODUCTION

ONCE upon a time the question of economic justice would have been: capitalism or communism? But it is now generally thought that the efficiency advantages of the capitalist free market are so profound that they render the question of the justice of communist systems irrelevant to present-day concerns (cf. Nove 1983, 1991). Under conditions of imperfect knowledge a price system is essential for signalling information about surplus and shortage of particular goods, relative to demand. A profit system is essential to give individuals an incentive to respond to changing prices. Accordingly, any attempt to produce according to a central plan—however rational this may seem in theory—will destroy both information and incentives. Prosperity presupposes markets (Hayek 1944, 1960, 1982; Friedman 1962; Friedman and Friedman 1980).

Yet it would be wrong to identify the market with pure capitalism, in which the exercise of property rights may lead to deep inequality. If we are concerned with both efficiency and justice we must determine how far we can depart from capitalist forms of the free market, in the name of justice, without losing 'too much' of its efficiency advantages (Carens 1980). Or we must find an account of justice that coincides, as far as possible, with the capitalistic free market (Nozick 1974).

Our topic, we can already see, is complex. Justice must be balanced against efficiency and perhaps other values. How this is to be achieved will form an important part of our subsequent discussion.

I am enormously grateful to Hugh LaFollette for round after round of detailed and insightful comment on various drafts. Michael Otsuka and Veronique Munoz Dardé also provided much-appreciated comments at various stages.

2. THEORIES OF ECONOMIC JUSTICE

How might we classify theories of economic justice? Perhaps the most common method is in terms of the institutions the theory recommends. Although this may, philosophically, appear somewhat superficial, it is understandable for political purposes. For example, libertarian theories—whatever their foundational assumptions—tend to be grouped together because of their advocacy of the minimal state, and their opposition to coercive, state-enforced, redistribution. In the opposing camp are broadly egalitarian interventionists, who typically defend some form of welfare state, although they too may differ greatly in foundational assumptions. Most recent major theorists of economic justice can be differentiated by the degree of intervention they advocate. Our main question, then, could be put in terms of whether there is a proper role for state intervention in the economy, and, if so, to achieve what ends?

It seems most natural to start with the idea of minimal intervention: what, after all, is wrong with the idea that the economy should simply be left to look after itself? Some people, as will shall see, claim that this would lead to injustice. But another reply is that the idea is incoherent. Any distribution presupposes a set of rights to possess and dispose of property. Accordingly at the minimum it will be the task of the government to determine which of the many possible property regimes is legitimate. Consequently there is no such thing as how the economy would be without government action. Now this is, of course, arguable. Perhaps there are natural rights, or ways of settling on a particular conventional set by custom and tradition. However, whether or not 'minimal intervention' has a natural claim to priority, it is, for us, a convenient starting point.

First a note about the structure of what follows. I will lay out what I take to be the core of a number of theories, and will also set out certain difficulties for each. In doing so I do not intend to suggest that all such theories are false, but to make clear that this is a field in which nothing has been firmly established. Advocates of the theories will think that they have good answers to the questions, and perhaps they have. I do not pretend to offer any final words.

3. LIBERTARIANISM

Libertarian theories start from the thought that, as far as possible, we should keep government out of individual lives. It is not for governments to tell us what we can do, provided that we respect the rights of others. In its general form this is not an economic doctrine, although arguably it has economic implications. In particular, it opposes coercive forms of redistribution of wealth and income. If the rich wish to give money to widows and orphans, then that is their own business, and, perhaps, to be admired. But it is illegitimately coercive for the state to seize the money of some and present it to others (except to rectify previous illegality). I shall take such anti-redistribution to be the economic linchpin of libertarianism.

Why should anyone favour such a policy? Here we will look at three groups of theories, based, respectively, on rights; neutrality; and consequences. We shall start with the rights-based and anti-consequentialist approach best known through the work of Robert Nozick (1974). His foundational assumption is that each one of us has rights of self-ownership, and the correlate absolute duty to respect the self-ownership of each other. From this he derives principles of justice, which truncate the legitimate functions of the state by denying that the state may rightfully impose any 'pattern' of property holdings.

Nozick's 'Entitlement Theory of Justice' has three parts. The first is an account of justice in initial acquisition, which explains how anyone can be the first owner of property. He appears to advocate something like the right of the first claimant, subject only to the 'weak Lockean proviso' that no one should be rendered worse off by the existence of private property than they would have been without property ownership. (For discussion, see Wolff 1991; see also Cohen 1995: chs. 1–3; Kymlicka 1990: ch 4; 2002: ch. 4; and the essays in Paul 1982.)

The second element is a principle of justice in transfer, which explains how property may pass from one legitimate owner to another. Nozick adopts the principle that a transfer is just if and only if it is both voluntary and does not violate the Lockean proviso. Thirdly, Nozick advances a principle of justice in rectification to deal with cases where one or other of the first two principles has been violated.

Nozick contrasts this theory of procedural justice with 'patterned' theories, in which justice requires conformity to a pattern, such as equality, or 'each according to his or her need'. Nozick argues that any attempt to impose a pattern of holdings will violate individual liberty, which, given the assumption of self-ownership, is unacceptable. In order to preserve a pattern we must either prohibit people from making pattern-breaking transactions, or forcibly redistribute property on a regular basis. Note, though, that regular redistribution will act as a disincentive to any transactions, and so may function, *de facto*, as equivalent to a prohibition. But whether we choose prohibition or redistribution, individual liberty is involuntarily sacrificed, and any involuntary sacrifice is a violation. Redistributive taxation, argues Nozick, is 'on a par with' forced labour. To take the fruits of one person's labour for the benefit of another is effectively to make one person work for another, without giving him any choice in the matter. In other cases where this happens it is described as slavery.

Is Nozick correct? Does every attempt to enforce a pattern of any sort really undermine liberty, and, if so, is this a decisive objection to patterned distributions? This position rests on the claim that property rights are in some way absolute, and any interference with property constrains its owner's self-ownership. By contrast, some will claim that property rights over external objects are 'softer' than, say, the rights one has over one's own body. We might agree with Nozick that only I have the right to decide what should happen to my own kidneys or eyes, but refuse to extend this reasoning to my claims over external objects, and thus accept modest taxation for certain purposes. What can Nozick do to argue that those who hold the contrary view are mistaken? The foundations of his theory appear to be the unargued assumption that we have rights to self-ownership that also provide a model for the rights we have over external objects (cf. Nagel 1982). Of course, he may be correct, but he does little, if anything, to establish this.

Others, however, have attempted to provide foundations for something like a Nozickian account of rights. Here I shall briefly introduce two interesting attempts. Loren Lomasky, in *Persons, Rights and the Moral Community* (1987) takes as basic the idea that people are to be conceived of as 'project pursuers', committing themselves to long-term ends, which determine both what they have reason to pursue and what is to count as an item of value for that person. In order to pursue projects, people need rights of non-interference: a protected 'moral sphere' in which they can pursue their goals, free from the demands of others. This, then, provides a foundation for a libertarian theory of rights. Although Lomasky recognizes that people might also require at least minimal access to economic goods, this, he claims, is insufficient to ground positive rights to welfare assistance. One reason for this is that duties of supply are far more onerous than duties of non-interference. Thus, he claims, although it is good to help the needy, they have no right to aid. (However, he does accept that there could possibly be circumstances in which such rights are generated, although this he seems to treat as a far-off possibility.)

A distinct attempt to provide foundations for a broadly Nozickian account of libertarian rights can be found in Jan Narveson's *The Libertarian Idea* (1988). Narveson, largely following Gauthier (1986), attempts to provide contractarian foundations for morality, and in Narveson's hands this is a morality of distinctly libertarian stripe. Contractarian theory must specify, first, the 'break point', or non-contractual situation, often called 'the state of nature' or 'baseline', and, secondly, the motivation of the parties that leads them to seek and reach agreement. For Narveson the break point is mutual indifference; how our lives would go if we had no interaction with each other. The motivation impelling us towards agreement is self-interest. Narveson then argues that a certain set of libertarian rights of mutual non-interference would be chosen from this initial situation, for it represents a strong Pareto improvement over the baseline (it makes everyone better off than they otherwise would be). People would retain the protection from each other that they have, by definition, in the non-contract situation, but immensely benefit from the possibility of cooperation under secure conditions of peace. In itself this seems very plausible, but are libertarian rights the only route to a strong Pareto improvement over this rather meagre pre-contract situation? If not, it is unclear how we are to select between different possible regimes. Furthermore, we may ask whether Narveson's baseline is to be preferred to other possibilities, such as mutual joint ownership of the earth, which may give very different outcomes (Gibbard 1976; Wolff 1992).

An alternative foundation for libertarianism does not try to deepen the justification of individual rights, but looks towards the idea of neutrality as an alternative basis. It is a commonplace among liberals that the state has no right to impose one person's conception of the good upon others. So, even if every member of the government is convinced of the absolute truth of Christianity, the state has no right to impose, or even encourage, Christian belief. One form of libertarianism attempts to extend this reasoning to theories of justice as well as theories of the good life. The state has no right to impose a scheme of redistribution, for this would be a way of imposing one group's values on another group who do not share them. Accordingly, the state may not intervene to redistribute property, for this would render it non-neutral and, hence, illiberal (Barry 1986).

This may look convincing if the state has a duty of neutrality. However, as remarked earlier, any set of property rights embodies a set of rules permitting and prohibiting certain actions. Hence libertarian schemes of property rights have an element of non-neutrality too, for they prevent some people from doing what they would otherwise wish to do. Arguably, then, it is not plausible to represent libertarianism as the perfect embodiment of neutrality.

Finally, many libertarians emphasize the beneficial consequences of a libertarian regime. One sees elements of this in the economic writings of von Hayek and Milton Friedman, which have much in common with more moderate forms of libertarianism (Hayek 1944, 1960, 1982; Friedman 1962; Friedman and Friedman 1980). It is also signalled in the title of Ayn Rand's *The Virtue of Selfishness* (1964), and the classical economic tradition of 'private vices, public virtues', where self-regard and non-intervention is said to benefit society as a whole. A recent version of this general approach has been developed by David Schmidtz (Schmidtz and Goodin 1998).

Schmidtz relies very heavily on the claimed benefits of a regime of individual responsibility. If people are required to take responsibility for their own lives, as they would be in libertarian society, then they will not develop an initiative-sapping dependency on the state, which is so wasteful of both resources and human potential. Thus we should look for institutions that, in Schmidtz's terminology, 'internalize' responsibility, making people responsible for their own fate. According to Schmidtz, a system of strong, individual, private property rights has exactly the right character. In more communal regimes, people have the incentive to reap benefits but avoid costs—that is, to consume as much as they can, while doing as little work as possible. Since they have no assurance that they will be in a position to benefit from their own efforts, why should they even try? In a properly regulated and enforced system of private property, one can benefit only from one's own efforts.

This interesting argument raises many questions. Does a system of internalizing responsibility contribute to general utility, or will everyone benefit, perhaps even to the point, in the long term, of making the worst off as well off as possible? If so, then we have an interesting convergence between libertarianism and the best-known representative of its philosophical opponent; Rawlsian liberal equality. We shall look at Rawls's theory in more detail shortly, but in the meantime we can note that Rawls's Difference Principle states that inequalities in income and wealth are permitted provided that they make the worst-off group as well off as possible (Rawls 1971, 1999). It is common to assume that the way to implement such a prin-ciple is through an extensive tax and welfare scheme. In effect, Schmidtz argues that this ignores the effects of such a scheme, and, in the medium to long term, the poor do best in a libertarian scheme in which all must take care of themselves. Thus the difference between Schmidtz and Rawls appears to come down to an empirical question about effective strategies.

4. NATURAL AND SOCIAL CONTINGENCY

Most critics of libertarianism claim that it leads to injustice. In discussing such a system (which he calls 'the system of natural liberty') John Rawls writes:

> The existing distribution of income and wealth, say, is the cumulative effect of prior distribu-tion of natural assets—that is, natural talents and abilities—as these have been developed or left unrealized, and their use favoured or disfavoured over time by social circumstances and such chance contingencies as accident and good fortune. Intuitively the most obvious injust-ice of the system of natural liberty is that it permits distributive shares to be improperly influ-enced by these factors so arbitrary from a moral point of view.   (Rawls 1971: 72; 1999: 62–3)

In this passage Rawls identifies two types of difficulty with the system of natural liberty. First, individual life prospects will be affected by 'social contingencies'—essentially the class, economic position, and character of one's parents. Secondly, such prospects are also affected by 'natural fortune': the talents and abilities with which one is born. Consider, on the one hand, someone born to a family of great wealth and culture, with high intelligence, drive, energy, and health, and, on the other, someone born into poverty, of low intelligence and poor health. We can reas-onably predict that the former will have a far greater chance of a successful life. But, according to Rawls, this is morally unjustified. Thus we should look for a distribu-tive scheme that does not generate such apparently unjust outcomes. (For discus-sion of Rawls, see especially the essays in Daniels 1975a.)

It would, I think, be a brave soul who would claim that such social and natural factors, such as parental support and native intelligence, have no effect at all on individual life prospects. To do so would, most likely, be based on the supposition that people make their own fates through their own sheer will. But, however sym-pathetic one might be to doctrines of personal freedom and responsibility, it is hard to believe that all differentials in life prospects can be explained this way.

The next step in Rawls's argument is to add a normative judgement to this factual claim: that differentials generated this way are unjust or unfair. Clearly this is a more controversial step, at least in the case of natural fortune. Some people genuinely believe that natural talent deserves financial reward. Rawls disagrees, and the final step in the argument is that it is one of the tasks of governments to remedy the unfairness of the natural and social lottery.

Now it is one thing to acknowledge that justice needs to mitigate the effects of social contingency and natural fortune. It is another thing to come up with a proposal that does this, especially when we remember that schemes need to be evaluated not only from the standpoint of how just they are but whether they promote efficiency. For example, we could respond to differential natural fortune by 'levelling down'—in this case, say, by medical intervention to destroy the advantages of the better off and ensure that no one has more ability or strength than those in the least fortunate group. Now this is not usually regarded as a serious possibility, although there is one sense in which it could be argued to create a more just world (cf. Temkin 1993). But, even if it is replied that such intervention violates rights, and so in that sense is unjust, there are other obvious objections, such as the resulting immense loss of talent and wealth within such a society. Rawls argues that, instead of eliminating individual advantages, we should find a way of turning them to everyone's advantage. But the main lesson is that the acceptance of the need to find a scheme to minimize the effect of social and natural contingencies on economic distribution does not yet tell us how this is to be done. Rawls's own theory is only one of a possible multitude.

5. Broad Egalitarianism

Theories that try to take up Rawls's challenge constitute what I shall call the 'broad-egalitarian' tradition. Any complete theory of this type needs to address at least five questions. The first is the question of the 'currency' of justice. Economic justice requires a just distribution of something. But of what? Of money? Of well-being? Of the satisfaction of needs? Perhaps giving people equal money will leave them unequal in well-being, for example (Dworkin 1981a). Which should we prefer?

The second is the question of 'pattern'. Do we think that justice requires an equal distribution of the currency? Or, as in Rawls's difference principle, do we think that we should aim to make the worst off as well off as possible, even if this leads to inequality? Or is there some other pattern for which we should strive?

The third question concerns responsibility. What role is there for individual responsibility in an account of justice? Suppose that, as a result of freely made choices, someone has less than others. Is this resulting distribution perfectly fair, or can there be a valid claim to have free choices subsidized? These are the three central issues that have concerned egalitarian theorists. However, a fourth issue and a fifth must also be addressed at some point. The fourth is: how should we remedy any injustice that has been identified? Many writers seem to assume that some form of compensation will be a universally appropriate remedy, but we will need to examine this in a little more detail. And, finally, how should the claims of justice be balanced against possibly conflicting values, such as efficiency?

6. The Question of Currency

The revitalization of egalitarianism began with detailed attention to a long-recognized problem: to make people equal in one respect is very likely to make them unequal in another respect. Yet the task of explicitly raising this issue, cataloguing possible, precisely formulated alternatives, and giving reasons against and in favour of them, was largely ignored until the work of Sen and Dworkin in the early 1980s (Sen 1980; Dworkin 1981a,b. But see also Scanlon 1975, and in retrospect we can see Rawls as making a highly sophisticated contribution to the same debate in Rawls 1971.) Since then we have seen a literature of increasing detail and sophistication that shows little sign of ending in consensus. (For a recent collection of important papers, see Clayton and Williams 2000.) As we shall see, there are four principal proposals, centring on: needs, preferences, resources, and basic capabilities, although there is no reason to think that these should exhaust the range of possibilities.

6.1 Need

Arguably the most intuitive understanding of the currency of justice is captured by Marx's phrase 'to each according to their need' (Marx 1875/1974; Williams 1979). On this view economic justice requires that everyone should have at least their essential needs satisfied, provided that this is possible. Now there are a number of objections that could be raised: perhaps there are some people who do not deserve to have their needs satisfied. Such people might include those who have been given what they need, but have wasted it in some way. However, let us put this thought to one side for the purposes of this section; it will reoccur under the heading of responsibility.

How good a theory of distributive justice is 'each according to his or her need'? It has to be admitted that it is rather vague. It is clear that people need food. But do they need a varied diet? We need shelter. But does a bare earth floor and no internal sanitation count? Or does it count in some places but not others? According to a recent survey in the UK, 85 per cent of people surveyed thought that a warm, water-proof coat was essential. But this means that 15 per cent of people didn't (Gordon et al. 2000). This shows how hard it is to achieve complete agreement even on the most basic needs.

But, even with complete agreement, the goal of satisfying basic needs hardly looks like a complete theory of economic justice, for this is a very minimal stand-ard. Perhaps the better theory is that everyone's needs should be satisfied to the same degree. But then we have a new difficulty: how do we devise an index that enables us to compare the 'need satisfaction' of everyone? If you have excellent food but mediocre housing, and I have boring food but luxurious accommodation, which one of us is better off in terms of need satisfaction?

Note that this difficulty affects not only the proposal that we should equalize need satisfaction, but also any proposal that requires us to identify differential levels of need satisfaction. A 'difference principle of need' that tells us to make the most needy person as less needy as possible, for example, clearly requires a 'need index'.

It may be that such indexing difficulties with the idea of need have led to its relat-ive neglect in recent writing (although I will argue later that it is becoming domi-nant again under different terminology). There are few theorists who advocate a need-based approach to justice (but see Doyal and Gough 1991). In order to find an index, theorists appear to have moved either to more objective, and thus measura-ble currencies, such as resources that can be measured in terms of economic value, or, conversely, to more subjective notions, such as preference satisfaction, which we shall consider now.

6.2 Preferences

Preference satisfaction theory is one branch of 'welfare' theories of which the other main branch is hedonism. Hedonism supposes that the currency of justice is hap-piness or pleasure. Although hedonism may seem appealing, it is generally rejected, like need theory, as being too vague for theoretical purpose. However, even if it may be very hard to say whether package *A* satisfies more of my needs, or makes me hap-pier, than package *B*, it should not be difficult to say which one, if either, I prefer. For a given individual, it is relatively unproblematic to derive a consistent prefer-ence ordering (here I ignore difficulties revealed by Kahneman and Twersky 1979, for example). Turning this into an interval scale—that is, a cardinal ordering—is more problematic, but it seems reasonably widely accepted that this can be done by considering the combinations of gambles that an individual is prepared to take. Suppose I have an apple. You then offer to exchange that apple for a 50 per cent chance of an orange (to be decided on a fair coin toss). Assuming that I have no particular taste for, or aversion to, gambling, and that I decide to accept the exchange, it would be reasonable to say that this means I rate the orange as at least twice as valuable, in terms of preference satisfaction or utility, as I do the apple. Extending this general approach, it is claimed to be possible to create a complete 'utility function', at least in principle, for each individual, over the whole range of goods and options that they may face. (The classic presentation is Von Neumann and Morgenstern 1944.)

Now, although this is, in one respect, an improvement over the idea of need satisfaction, it lacks its intuitive plausibility as a currency of justice. A problem is that justice will be held hostage to each individual's preferences, which can lead to counter-intuitive results. Consider Scanlon's example of a man who is starving to death, but his preference is not for food but to build a monument to his god. If we give him money, this is how he will spend it. But we are likely to say that, if he has a claim on society at all, it is for food and not for the means to build a monument. Scanlon's conclusion is that we operate with an 'objective' conception of well-being, as well as a subjective one, based on preferences, and in questions of distribution we rightly use the objective one (Scanlon 1975). Despite this some liberals may insist upon a subjective measure of preference satisfaction as the only properly neutral approach. (For an interesting attempt to develop an objective theory, see Hurka 1993.)

Yet the difficulty can be pressed when we consider Dworkin's examples of preferences that are very expensive to satisfy, and thus, if people are to achieve equal preference satisfaction (however it is measured), then there will have to be transfers of resources from those with cheap tastes to those with expensive tastes. The problem, then, is that preference-based theories must respond to how important goals are to the individuals who have them, however eccentric these individuals are, rather than any social or objective standard. So someone who thinks her life will go badly unless she undertakes space travel, or someone who can achieve satisfaction only by drinking vintage claret, will, it appears, be entitled to a greater share of society's resources than those with ordinary tastes. Now I should make clear that Dworkin uses these examples to help motivate the idea of equality of resources, rather than equality of need satisfaction, but they bring out what many claim to be the central difficulty with preference theory. It may be that preference theories can solve the indexing problem that plagues need theories, but in doing so they lead to apparent injustice.

It may even be an illusion to think that preference theories do solve the index problem, for, even if they allow us to say what would make a given individual better or worse off, justice needs interpersonal comparisons of utility. There is certainly no consensus on how this might be done, even in principle. And we would be utterly at a loss to see how governments could make such judgements except in the most crude and approximate terms. Indeed, governments no doubt find it easier by far to make rough judgements of need satisfaction. Thus, although preference theory may be more promising as a solution to the theoretical indexing problem, need theory does much better in practice.

6.3 Resources

Rawls and Primary Goods

Resource-based theories provide a much easier solution to the indexing problem, and one of the most prominent examples is John Rawls's use of the idea of 'primary goods'. Rawls defines primary goods as 'things that every rational man is presumed to want' (1971: 62; 1999: 54).[1] The idea is that, whatever else you want from life, the social primary goods—liberty, opportunity, the powers and prerogatives of office, the social basis of self-respect, income, and wealth—are 'all-purpose means' that will help you achieve your goals. This could be, and has been, contested (Nagel 1973; Schwartz 1973), but initially at least the key question is, even if this is so, why not use a metric of preference satisfaction, which is more directly addressed to what people want?

One problem is that, if we are to take people's preferences as the basic currency, we face the problem that some people have preferences of an extremely unpleasant nature; for example, racist or sexist preferences, or preferences for harm to particular other people. Yet, Rawls argues, surely people do not have the right that the state treats these preferences as having any positive weight at all.

A second argument is that his theory 'does not look behind the use which persons make of the rights and opportunities available to them…[for] it is assumed that members of society are rational persons able to adjust their conceptions of the good to their situation' (Rawls 1971: 94; 1999: 81). I understand this as the thought that, while society is responsible for ensuring that each individual has the means to a fulfilling life, whether, and how, an individual chooses to employ those means is a matter for that individual, rather than for society.

Thirdly, we need an uncontroversial way of deciding which group is worst off. Even if we accept there is no problem, in principle, of determining which group has the lowest level of preference satisfaction, there may, nevertheless, be disagreements about this at the public level. That is, preference satisfaction levels are not publicly accountable (Rawls 1971: 95; 1999: 81). This could lead to unwelcome and divisive public debate. Relying on wealth measures may overcome this problem.

A further reason appears in the final pages of *A Theory of Justice*: using a measure of happiness may leave people in a 'fool's paradise'—that is, an individual may be happy partly as a consequence of false beliefs (Rawls 1971: 549; 1999: 481). One may have one's preferences satisfied to a high degree, but only because those preferences are in some way deformed. This is often known as the problem of the 'happy slave' or the 'tamed housewife'.

---

[1] This is one issue on which the first edition of *A Theory of Justice* (1971) differs considerably from the revised edition (1999). However, although Rawls's now emphasises that the primary goods are what people need as citizens, rather than merely as rational agents, the changes do not affect the following. The most detailed account of Rawls's preferred understanding is given in Rawls (1982).

There seems no doubt that a primary goods metric has both technical (indexing) and philosophical advantages over at least some preference metrics. But is it good enough? We should ask two questions, in the context of the difference principle: first, does it identify a determinate worst-off group, and, secondly, does it identify the right group? As we will see, there are problems on both counts.

The difference principle distributes income and wealth. Now we might be able to identify the lowest income group, and we might be able to identify the lowest wealth group (in terms of accumulated assets), but we have no guarantee that they will be the same group. This creates a problem. Rawls largely circumvents this by ignoring issues of wealth, concentrating on income. Whether this is an acceptable strategy I cannot address here.

The other problem is more serious. Some people face uncertain or diminished life prospects, not through any shortage of social primary goods, but because they lack the natural talents and skills others take for granted. In particular, those who have physical disabilities may find they need expensive equipment that will use up even an average income, leaving nothing to spare for other needs. Indeed, the situation could be much worse; they could be well off in terms of primary goods, but still not even have enough to survive. Now Rawls is aware of this problem, and deliberately sets the parameters of his discussion under the simplifying assumption that no one is disabled. Unfortunately, he tells us nothing about how to develop the theory for the real world when that assumption is dropped. (For an attempt to take the discussion further, see Daniels 1985.)

Dworkin and Internal and External Resources

Partly in order to bring the disabled into the scope of the discussion, Ronald Dworkin introduces his theory of equality of resources. Taking the simple case first, where resources are identified with the external material resources of the world, how can we tell that resources are equally shared? It is no good trying to parcel goods out in equal bundles, because they are not all indefinitely divisible. So we need a way of setting things into diverse bundles that will, nevertheless, be regarded as equal. Dworkin's solution relies on the so-called envy test: if bundles of goods are parcelled up in such a way that no one prefers another's bundle, then we can say that the division of resources is equal. Now Dworkin recognizes that this is not perfect. If the available resources are much more suited to one person's lifestyle than another's, then one person might feel a legitimate grievance even if she does not prefer anyone else's bundle. However, at least in his initial presentation of this position Dworkin appears to set the envy test as a necessary condition of equality of resources.

So far, despite the introduction of a technical innovation, we do not have much progress over a primary goods metric. After all, one way of meeting the envy test is simply to give everyone equal income and wealth, and send them off to market. Progress comes at the next stage, when Dworkin takes up the question that Rawls sidelines: how do we bring people with disabilities into the picture? The conceptual move to handle this question is to treat each person's strengths and abilities as part of his resources. Someone who suffers from some sort of disability is, therefore, conceptualized as holding an inferior bundle of resources to others.

To address this, Dworkin adopts a version of Rawls's idea of the veil of ignorance, asking: what level of insurance would one take out against disability if one knew the prevalence, disadvantage, and cost of various forms of disability, but was unaware of whether one had, or would develop, any disability oneself? Clearly it would be rational to take out a certain level of insurance, but, Dworkin claims, not so much that the premium would hinder one's ability to lead a worthwhile life should one be, by good luck, able-bodied. Tax and welfare levels are set to mimic premium levels and payouts of the hypothetical insurance scheme.

This scheme has been much discussed and criticized (Tremain 1996; McLeod 1998). One concern is that the resulting distributions are unlikely to satisfy the envy test; compensation for disability is likely to be set at a level where people's lives do not go disastrously badly, rather than to provide the high level of compensation necessary to meet the test. This is generally how people insure in real life. But it is hard to see how this can be represented as a position of equality of resources. One may also question whether providing individuals with cash compensation is the most appropriate form of disability policy; many would argue that it does nothing to address exclusion, which is often thought to be the main problem for those with disabilities. Yet Dworkin should be applauded for taking the discussion on to this most difficult terrain, even if his own solution may not satisfy everyone.

In a different criticism of resource-based theory Cohen points out that in some cases welfare deficiency would seem to give rise to a valid claim for assistance, even when it cannot plausibly be theorized as a lack of a resource. But rather than return to preference theory Cohen coins the term 'advantage', which encompasses both resources and welfare, and people should be compensated for lack of advantage. While there is clear good sense in this proposal, it does little to help us over the difficulties we have found so far, in that it appears to compound the problems of index we need to overcome. In fairness to Cohen, however, his proposal is designed to respond to common intuitions about egalitarian justice, rather than to solve the index problem.

6.4 Basic Capabilities

Cohen, like many others in the debate, is highly sympathetic to Sen's account of 'basic capabilities'. Sen points out the obvious weakness in the primary goods metric: it ignores the fact that some people can make better use of the primary goods. In Sen's own terminology, Rawls's theory does not respond to different individuals' capabilities to function. Sen sets out a rather open-ended list of functionings;

as he puts it, a list of 'beings and doings'. 'The relevant functionings can vary from such elementary things as being adequately nourished, being in good health, avoiding escapable morbidity and premature mortality, etc., to more complex achievements such as being happy, having self-respect, taking part in the life of the community, and so on' (Sen 1992: 39). Those who need more resources to achieve an adequate level of functioning have a greater claim than those who can make do with lesser resources. The government's responsibility is not to ensure that everyone is, for example, well nourished, but to ensure that everyone has the capability to be well nourished. If people neglect to use their capabilities, that is their own affair. (On this point he is in agreement with Rawls and Dworkin.) One's capability to achieve a level of functioning is called one's capability set, and, in this view, the currency of justice is 'capability set'. Those who follow Sen and, for example, argue in favour of strict equality would argue that equality requires the equalization not of preference satisfaction, nor of resources, but of capability sets. (Sen's approach has been developed in more detail by Nussbaum: see, in particular, Nussbaum 2000.)

Now there seems something absolutely right about this. Yet there seems also something of a feeling that we have come full circle. How different is this to the idea that people should have their needs satisfied, or, rather, have the means to have their needs satisfied? And so it is no surprise to see that this proposal runs into the problems of the need approach. Despite the fact that Sen has possibly done more than anyone else to raise the questions of how to measure inequality (Sen 1973, 1982, 1992, 1997), we lack a convincing account of what it is to equalize capability sets. So, if strict equality of capability sets is the goal (and it is unclear in Sen whether this really is the case), then this approach fails to give us the precision we needed. And recall that this is a problem not only for those who favour equality, but for anyone who needs to make comparisons between different levels.

7. THE PATTERN

7.1 Equality

We have mentioned Rawls's difference principle several times: the idea that the worst off are to be made as well off as possible. While for Rawls the index for the worst off is stated in terms of primary goods, one could provide a difference principle of welfare, and so on.

Although Rawls's theory is often regarded as a theory of equality, it is also often regarded with suspicion by those who favour more radical equality, since it is clear that it does allow inequalities (see Daniels 1975b). How, then, should we classify his position? More recent work by Frankfurt (1987) and Parfit (1998) will help.

Although one may adopt a strict theory of equality Rawls does not adopt this because, he says, it may be possible to make everyone better off by departing from equality. If there is a general incentive that will allow people to become richer by working harder and this can be made to work for the benefit of everyone, through the right tax and redistribution scheme, for example, then we should allow the resulting inequality. This incentive argument is the converse of the 'levelling-down' argument that points out that, if our goal is to reach equality, then the most effective way of achieving this may be to destroy those things that make us unequal. The incentive argument, then, can be seen as a way of avoiding levelling down, which is often presented as a devastating objection to equality. (For further discussion, see Wolff 2001.)

7.2 Priority: Absolute and Qualified

Bearing in mind that Rawls's theory does allow inequalities, it clearly contrasts with one that prohibits them. Parfit has helpfully labelled Rawls's theory one of priority rather than equality: it gives priority to the worst off, rather than insisting on equality. Temkin (1993) had earlier used the term 'humanitarianism' to register the same point: a humanitarian theory, in this sense, is one that gives priority to the worst off. Indeed we can distinguish two forms of priority theory: absolute priority and qualified priority. Absolute priority states that we must always raise the position of the worst-off group if we can (although, as the composition of the worst-off group may change, it may be that some particular individuals will become worse off). However, there is another possibility, which we may call qualified priority. Suppose that in a given case it is possible to improve the lot of the great majority, but only at some very small, yet uncompensatable, cost to some who are worse off. Now it may be very hard to imagine such cases, but let us leave that to one side. The question is, should we allow a change that makes the worst-off group a little worse off, even though let us say everyone else is made much better off? An absolute prioritarian will have to say that we may not, but a qualified prioritarian can allow this. The worst off are given priority in decision making, but not so much that it swamps everything else. Parfit sees relative prioritarianism as a type of weighted utilitarianism. And the priority to the worse off becomes less urgent as they become, in absolute terms, better off.

7.3 Sufficiency

Thus we have, so far, three positions in play: equality, absolute priority, and qualified priority. Frankfurt introduces a fourth: that of sufficiency. Frankfurt objects to theories of equality on a number of grounds, including the idea that most people who claim to advocate equality are rather confused. The laudable aim of such people, he thinks, is not so much to eliminate inequality, as to eliminate poverty. What matters is not that people should have the same, but that they should have enough. Once everyone has enough, it does not much matter whether some people have more—even a lot more—than others. Furthermore, a concern for equality is, he says, 'alienating', requiring us to make comparisons with other people, rather than concentrate on how our own lives are going.

Sufficiency, then, seems an importantly distinct position. Yet it does raise questions. What is meant by 'sufficiency'? And can we define a level of sufficiency without reference to the holdings of another?

7.4 Unconditional Basic Income

An important variant of the sufficiency approach is that of 'unconditional basic income' favoured by Steiner (1994) and van Parijs (1995). The idea is that each citizen should receive a certain income from the state regardless of that citizen's other sources of income. Thus the unemployed and the well paid will both receive the same grant, which, ideally, should be set at a high enough level so as to replace as many other benefits as possible. So, unlike other benefits we have known it is unconditional on need, past work, present willingness to work, or ability to work. We will, in a common example, pay fit and healthy people to surf all day off Malibu.

Many people's initial response to this is to throw their arms up in horror at the apparent injustice of such income transfers from the hard-working to the idle, especially as the level of taxation needed to sustain basic income will be very high. However, the arguments are not all one way. One family of arguments for providing a guaranteed income claims that everyone should have the right to use the world's material resources; and, in particular, land and raw materials. To translate this into practice we imagine a global company, which owns the world, and in which each individual is a shareholder. Anyone who wishes to use part of the world's resources must pay rent into the global fund, and each individual should receive a shareholder's dividend financed by those payments. If we call this dividend 'unconditional basic income', we have an appealing rationale, in justice, for the scheme, despite its apparent injustice. This is not to say that the case for the justice of basic income has been made, but to point out that arguments are available on both sides.

A second family of arguments appeals to the possible beneficial effects of guaranteed income on the economy as a whole. One of the great apparent paradoxes of capitalism is that much of the most unappealing work is also the lowest paid. Intuitively we might think that poor conditions of work should be compensated by high pay. But in fact the same factors that keep conditions poor keep wages low: simply that there is a surplus of supply of labour over demand for it in the unskilled sectors. Employers have no incentives to improve conditions or raise pay if there is a ready stock of work-ers prepared to accept given pay and conditions. However, if everyone already had a decent income, and tax rates are high, no one will do unpleasant jobs unless wage rates for those jobs are very high. So it might be that unrewarding jobs become the highest paid on the economy (van der Veen and van Parijs 1986). Following out the consequences of this will take us beyond the scope of the present chapter, but they provide a second type of justification for basic income, even if the connection with justice is mediated through issues about just pay. But to recall, I introduced basic income as one important variety of a sufficiency pattern. It would not, I think, be endorsed by Frankfurt, although much is consistent with what he says.

7.5 Patterns of Justice, and Efficiency

Questions of justice and questions of efficiency are often intertwined, and it is not always easy to unravel what exactly is doing the work in any argument. To achieve a better understanding of the positions laid out so far it will be helpful to try to sep-arate elements of justice and elements of efficiency.

But, first, what exactly do we mean by efficiency? In common use efficiency sim-ply means non-wastage: getting the most output from the least input. However, two other thicker notions are often used in economic contexts: utility maximization and Pareto efficiency. The former holds that the most efficient system is the one that produces the highest sum of utility, while the latter claims that a situation is Pareto efficient if and only if no one can be made better off without making someone else worse off. A strong Pareto improvement makes everyone better off. How do these forms of efficiency help us to understand the patterns discussed so far?

There seems little question that the pattern of equality is defended as a pure the-ory of justice. The most common objection to it, of course, is that it is in some way inefficient. This, then, is a common argument for absolute priority, such as Rawls's difference principle. Perhaps our first objective is to achieve justice, but once we have done that we should make whatever Pareto improvements are possible. Rawls himself contends that the difference principle is compatible with Pareto efficiency, although he admits that this result requires some special assumptions, for, as a gen-eral claim, this is false in that some changes sanctioned by the difference principle will not be Pareto improvements. (Once we realize that a given individual may be in the worst-off group under one distribution, but not under another, we see that one individual may suffer a fall at the same time as the position of the worst-off group rises.) However, if we start with Rawls's argument that we should eliminate the contingencies of natural and social fortune, it may seem hard to represent the difference principle in itself as fair, strictly speaking, rather than as a reasonable way of turning unfairness to general advantage—for it remains true that, in a Rawlsian society, the naturally talented will generally have a better life.

On the other hand, if we think that a situation is just only if it is approved of by the person who fares worst within it, then the absolute priority afforded by the difference principle will in many cases, if not all, be the natural consequence. The difference principle aims to make the worst-off group as well off as possible. How could the worst off fail to approve of that? (This is to leave aside the annoying complication that the person worst off in one distribution may not have been worst off in another.)

Qualified priority reflects the thought that, even from the standpoint of the worst off, some complaints appear clearly unreasonable. It would be wrong, in this view, to protest against a trivial loss when the result would be that those better off than you would gain greatly by whatever it is that causes your loss. However, this looks less like a justice-based concern than one based on efficiency; this time in the utilitarian sense, rather than Pareto efficiency. Nevertheless, some claim that utilitarianism is itself a theory of justice.

Finally, it is also possible to represent sufficiency theory as a pure theory of justice too. Here, though, one must reject Rawls's argument that justice requires the elimination of natural and social fortune, for by this standard sufficiency allows unjust inequalities. Rather, one must say something like that the point of a system of justice is to give everyone a fair chance to lead a self-determining life. By this standard there could come a point where everyone does have enough, and justice is done, residual inequalities notwithstanding.

In somewhat surprising conclusion, if one adopts the appropriate deeper understanding of justice, each of equality, absolute priority, and even qualified priority, and sufficiency can be made at least to appear theories of justice unmixed with considerations of efficiency. However, a more natural understanding of each except equality is that they offer differing balances between justice and efficiency (either Pareto or utilitarian).

8. Responsibility

I mentioned Dworkin's objection that Rawls does not provide a way of addressing the needs of those who are disabled. A second important objection is that it provides benefits for the worst off irrespective of their responsibility for creating their own plight. It is true, as we have noted, that the primary goods metric makes individuals responsible for converting the means they are given into valuable ends. However, Dworkin argues that there is nevertheless a failure of responsibility too. The difference principle does not ask why someone is badly off. Perhaps it is his own fault: he decided to surf rather than take a job. If so, how can it be a requirement of justice to tax others to help him? So understood, the difference principle goes against the folk wisdom of the little red hen, and the ant and the grasshopper

(Rosen and Wolff 1999: 224), as does any theory that apparently divorces issues of distribution from issues of responsibility. It is this that fuels the libertarian critique of equality, as we have seen above.

Rawls (1993: 181–2 n.) is clearly concerned about this, and flirts with the idea of including leisure as a primary good. Those with a great deal of (voluntary) leisure could be stipulated as enjoying a good package of primary goods, irrespective of their possession of wealth and income. However, Rawls does not integrate this into his system as a whole and thus it has more of a status as a possibility than a proposal.

Dworkin's own solution is quite different. He argues that individuals must be held responsible for the 'true social costs' of their choices, and so, he says, distributions should be 'ambition sensitive' but 'endowment insensitive'. What this means is that one's possessions should not be affected by the level of natural abilities, strengths, or talents one has, but ought to be affected by the consequences of carrying out freely made choices. In particular, if one embarks on a risky course of action that is open to others, then one ought to be allowed to enjoy the benefits if it works, but suffer the costs if it fails. This diversion from equality is, in another respect, a way of understanding equality in a more dynamic way: over a life rather than at a particular time. If others have the opportunities I do, they cannot complain that they have been treated unequally if they fail to make use of them but I do. Cohen admires the way in which Dworkin has been able to find a place for issues of responsibility within an egalitarian position, suggesting: 'Dworkin has performed for egalitarianism the considerable service of incorporating within it the most powerful idea in the arsenal of the anti-egalitarian right: the ideas of choice and responsibility' (Cohen 1989: 933).

The distinction between option luck and brute luck is at the centre of Dworkin's scheme. Brute luck is how matters of natural chance fall out; option luck concerns matters of deliberately accepted risk. Dworkin's basic idea is that one should be insulated from the effects of good and bad brute luck, but should be able to gain and lose the effects of good and bad option luck. The next step is to point out that an insurance market is a way of converting brute luck into option luck. Thus, if an insurance market exists in which you can take out insurance against bad brute luck, but fail to do so, then you have converted the brute risk into option luck; you have decided to take on the risk yourself, in order to save money. Accordingly you have no claim for compensation if things turn sour.

We can see why the hypothetical insurance market is such an appealing way for Dworkin to handle the issue of disability. Indeed, he uses a different hypothetical insurance market to handle the case of low talent. Just as real insurance turns brute luck into option luck, hypothetical insurance is the closest way he can find of turning all brute luck into simulated option luck and thus to bring it under the same conceptual framework as the rest of his discussion.

In conclusion, then, on Dworkin's scheme equality requires that surfers should not be fed, on the assumption that these are freely made life choices, for which each individual should pay the true social costs. Dworkin uses these considerations both to argue for the place of responsibility within equality, and as an argument against equality of welfare (the problem of expensive tastes).

8.1 Currency Revisited

Although Richard Arneson accepts that responsibility must be incorporated within equality, he argues that it does not follow that the currency of egalitarian justice must be resources. He argues that Dworkin's argument in favour of equality of resources confuses two contrasts. Dworkin, as we have seen, contrasts equality of resources and equality of welfare, and his expensive tastes objection is taken as an argument in favour of equality of resources. Arneson correctly points out, however, that another distinction is also at work here: that between equality of outcome and equality of opportunity. Consider again the individual who deliberately develops an expensive taste, and, as a result, is worse off in terms of well-being. If we accept equality of welfare outcomes, there is now, implausibly, a reason to redistribute resources to the person with expensive tastes. But suppose our view is that everyone should have equal opportunity for well-being. In this case someone who deliberately cultivates expensive tastes has squandered the opportunity for well-being he once had. So, despite the fact that his welfare is lower than that of others, there is no case for redistribution as he has had equal opportunities with others. Thus the expensive-tastes objection, if it is taken as refuting equality of welfare, does not necessarily point us towards equality of resources. In Arneson's view, it is more naturally to be taken as an argument for *equality of opportunity for welfare*. In his view the distinction between luck and responsibility reveals a reason for favouring some sort of opportunity conception of equality. For Dworkin this is equality of opportunity for resources; for Arneson equality of opportunity for welfare. In Arneson's view (1989), if someone is born with expensive tastes, there is reason for subsidy, for he lacks the opportunities for welfare that others have.

Dworkin does not accept this criticism. He claims that we have a reason not to subsidize expensive tastes even if they are not deliberately cultivated (Dworkin 2000: 285–303). Although some expensive tastes become cravings so strong that they may be sufficient to count as disabilities, normal expensive tastes, he claims, are not candidates for compensation whatever their causal history. This remains an open area of disagreement.

8.2 Criticism of 'Luck Egalitarianism'

Dworkin, Arneson, and Cohen all agree, however, that issues of responsibility are vital to issues of justice (see also Rakowski 1991). This reflects their shared underlying belief that the point of justice is to eliminate the results of luck, and John

Roemer (1998) has probably gone the furthest in trying to work out how to make a scheme responsive to issues of responsibility. However, Elizabeth Anderson (1999) points out some strange consequences. People who have injured themselves as a result of their own choices have no claim in justice for assistance. Imagine someone who plays Sunday league football, and breaks his leg, which is a reasonably foreseeable risk. However, he failed to take out widely available insurance, and is unable to pay for medical bills; and unable to support himself as he cannot work. Does justice really judge that he should receive no support from the state? Consider another person who is blinded as a result of an accident that was her own fault. Does justice require us to withhold any benefits or privileges we extend to those who are blinded in accidents for which they are not to blame? This 'discrimination among the disabled' seems to follow from the extreme responsibility that is a consequence of following the luck perspective on justice, but is extremely unnerving.

Anderson's own solution is to say that each person is entitled to a level of basic support independent of issues of responsibility, whether or not they are responsible for their situation. But in a further twist she does not extend this generosity to those who refuse to work. So surfers will not be fed. For reasons we shall see, it is not clear that this is satisfactory.

Perhaps the most principled way of trying to reduce the strains of responsibility, while remaining within the justice perspective, comes from the basic income approach, based on joint world ownership. In this view, we have seen, we really are entitled to something for nothing, as a matter of justice. So at a certain low level responsibility is irrelevant. It kicks in only once everyone already has what they should have as a matter of basic income.

Even if justice requires responsibility, other values, such as respect for individuals, may require us not to enquire too readily into issues of responsibility (Wolff 1998). While justice needs to take responsibility into account, and this, in turn, requires a system of conditional benefits, the cost of implementing such a scheme may be too high in terms of their effects on other values. In particular, conditional unemployment benefit, which attempts to discriminate between those who deserve help and those who do not, may require humiliating enquiries into individual lives. Under conditions of low unemployment the only valid reason for claiming benefit would be unemployability, which presumably would have to be the consequence of low talent, or possibly an unfortunate personality. Thus those claiming state benefit would have to make 'shameful revelations' about themselves in order to qualify. (This difficulty, if it is one, also affects Anderson's proposal.) Therefore there may be reason to refrain from making the sort of enquiries that would be needed to implement a system of justice that caters to responsibility. Now it is possible to reply that, rather than conflicting with the requirements of justice, such considerations can be subsumed within a theory of justice (Arneson 2000). But the main point is that a scheme of economic distribution may need to be sensitive to a number of considerations beside justice, at least narrowly conceived.

However, to sum up the discussion so far, a theorist who identifies with the broad egalitarian tradition now has a variety of fairly precisely defined theories to choose from. We now have three dimensions along which one may vary one's theory: the currency, the pattern, and the attitude towards responsibility. So, for example, Richard Arneson once argued for equality of opportunity for welfare, but now argues for what he calls 'responsibility-catering prioritarianism' (Arneson 2000), which is a form of qualified priority, giving priority to the worst off unless they are responsible for their own plight. And the currency in this view is a form of welfare. Another possible view is sufficiency of basic capabilities, at a high level of sufficiency, which favours not taking responsibility into account unless it can be shown empirically that it would have unacceptable costs not to do so. These possibilities show the range of theories that can now be offered.

9. REMEDY

The question of remedy is rarely discussed, although there are important works that bear on it (Anderson 1993; Radin 1996; Frey 1997; Phillips 1999). The basic question is this: suppose that, by whatever theory we fasten on, a distribution can be shown to be unjust to an individual. Perhaps he has too little welfare, or a diminished stock of resources. What should we do? The general answer in the literature is that we should compensate; this, after all, is the remedy offered by the courts for injustice.

Yet what do we mean by 'compensate'? On a broad understanding this might merely mean 'repair by whatever means are available'. More strictly it means something like: provide the victim with money or some other goods that 'makes up for' the loss. It can make up for the loss by making the victim no worse off then they would have been without the harm. In Nozick's words (1974), full compensation makes the victim neither pleased nor sorry that the harm and following compensation have happened.

However, compensation in this sense is only one possible strategy for remedy. Consider someone whose poor level of access to education has qualified him to undertake only low-paid, and low-status, work. How do we remedy this injustice? Now we could give compensation, which would be, perhaps, enough money so that he does not mind being unqualified. Or we could offer something akin to restitution: that is a free, intensive course of education that would bring him up to the level of qualification sufficient to do more rewarding work. This seems distinct from compensation—it is closer to repair. A third alternative is also conceptually possible; to break the link between qualification and high pay and status. This, of course, requires concerted social action over a long period, and so would be part of a resolve to root out a type of injustice, rather than to remedy a particular instance.

It asks us to reorganize the world so that no differential rewards are the consequence of different levels of education or qualification. This, I say, would be to nullify the injustice. It is not to deny that there are remaining issues of justice in the distribution of education, but that we might be able to find ways of stopping injustice in that 'sphere' influencing distributions in another (cf. Walzer 1983; Miller and Walzer 1995; Miller 1999). Thus we see issues of social structure and culture 'intruding' into issues of economic justice. In sum, then, we should not assume that compensation is the only form of remedy for injustice. Repair (cure) and nullification are also in principle available. This is especially so in the case of disability. Those who are disabled might be offered medical remedy (cure) or financial compensation (in Nozick's sense) or we may take social action to try to ensure that those possessing certain physical or mental features do not suffer disadvantage.

10. The Natural and the Social

This discussion introduces a question that, in some sense, should have been the starting point, but is hard to bring to life without first having seen a range of theories. The question is: what does a theory of justice set out to achieve? We have largely concentrated on one answer, broadly derived from Rawls: the point of a theory of justice is to achieve a certain conception of fairness. In particular we should not allow distributions to be affected by matters that are arbitrary from a moral point of view. Developed by Dworkin, Cohen, and others, this becomes the demand to equalize luck.

Compare this, though, with the view of Iris Marion Young: '(in many political contexts) I suggest that social justice means the elimination of institutionalised domination and oppression' (1990: 15). Here, then, the focus is much less on whether or not fortune has smiled on a given individual but rather, what people do to each other through social and political structures (see also Nagel 1997; Anderson 1999).

So, on the one hand, we have the view that justice requires the elimination of undeserved difference in advantage. Many of these advantages will be the result of natural fortune. On the other hand, we have the view that justice requires the elimination of oppression. Oppression, of course, is a social matter. So, is justice about 'the natural' or 'the social'? The answer, surely, must be both.

It seems to me that we can understand this issue best in the following way. One's prospects in life are determined, we might say, both by the pieces one has to play with, and by the rules of the game. That is, one has certain resources, and holding those resources one finds oneself within certain social structures. Those structures create possible paths, contingent on holding the 'right' resources. The resources can be, following Dworkin, divided into two types: internal (talents and skills) and external (income and wealth). To illustrate, consider a nineteenth-century woman in London who had the intelligence and ambition to be a lawyer. Unfortunately the interaction of her internal resources (the fact that she was female) and the social structures within which she found herself, ruled out this goal for her, and the prospects of her leading a fulfilling life were diminished accordingly.

If we want, or feel we have a duty, to improve her fortunes, what can we do? Assuming we cannot change her sex (and would not wish to, even if we could), we seem to have two possibilities. One, obviously, is to change the rules about who can be a lawyer. The other is to offer some other compensation for this social barrier, perhaps to provide other goods, such as more money, to compensate her for her frustrated ambition. Even given other alternatives, changing the rules must seem the most satisfactory: social change to end oppression. This must have something to do with the idea we have of what it is to treat people properly; increased preference satisfaction is not always enough. Here, then, is a case where the problem is that social structures prevent people from flourishing, given their resource holding, and the remedy is to change that structure.

This provides a little more background to the distinctions made in the previous section, between compensation, cure, and nullification. Broadly, those who focus on the social aspects of injustice will look towards nullification as a form of remedy, in so far as it is ever possible. Those who see injustice in terms of natural fortune will tend to offer remedy at the level of resources—that is, in terms of cure (internal resources) or compensation (external resources). Although here I have only scratched the surface of this issue, which requires much more detailed treatment, there are clearly advantages in refusing to say that injustice is either exclusively a matter of natural ill-fortune, or exclusively a matter of socially constituted disadvantage. For why should there not be both types of cases, requiring different types of remedy?

REFERENCES

Anderson, Elizabeth (1993). *Value in Ethics and Economics*. Cambridge, MA: Harvard University Press.

——(1999). 'What is the Point of Equality?' *Ethics*, 109: 287–337.

Arneson, Richard (1989). 'Equality and Equality of Opportunity for Welfare'. *Philosophical Studies*, 56: 77–93.

——(2000). 'Egalitarian Justice versus the Right to Privacy'. *Social Philosophy and Policy*, 17/2: 91–119.

Barry, Norman (1986). *Classical Liberalism and Libertarianism*. London: Macmillan.

Carens, Joseph H. (1980). *Equality Moral Incentives and the Market*. Chicago: Chicago University Press.

Clayton, Matthew, and Williams, Andrew (2000) (eds.), *The Ideal of Equality*. London: Palgrave.

Cohen, G. A. (1989). 'On the Currency of Egalitarian Justice'. *Ethics*, 99: 906–44.

——(1995). *Self-Ownership, Freedom and Equality*. Cambridge: Cambridge University Press.

Daniels, Norman (1975a). *Reading Rawls*. Oxford: Blackwell.

—— (1975b). 'Equal Liberty and Unequal Worth of Liberty', in Daniels (1975a), 258–81.

—— (1985). *Just Health Care*. Cambridge: Cambridge University Press.

Doyal, Len, and Gough, Ian (1991). *A Theory of Human Need*. London: Macmillan.

Dworkin, Ronald (1981a). 'What is Equality? Part I: Equality of Welfare'. *Philosophy and Public Affairs*, 10: 185–246. Reprinted in Dworkin (2000).

—— (1981b). 'What is Equality? Part II: Equality of Resources'. *Philosophy and Public Affairs*, 10: 283–345. Reprinted in Dworkin (2000).

—— (2000). *Sovereign Virtue*. Cambridge, MA: Harvard University Press.

Frankfurt, Harry (1987). 'Equality as a Moral Idea'. *Ethics*, 98: 21–43.

Frey, Bruno (1997). *Not Just for the Money*. Northampton, MA: Edward Elgar.

Friedman, Milton (1962). *Capitalism and Freedom*. Chicago: Chicago University Press.

—— and Friedman, Rose (1980). *Free to Choose*. Harmondsworth: Penguin.

Gauthier, David (1986). *Morals by Agreement*. Oxford: Oxford University Press.

Gibbard, Alan (1976). 'Natural Property Rights'. *Nous*, 10: 77–86.

Gordon, David et al. (2000). *Poverty and Social Exclusion in Britain*. York: Joseph Rowntree Foundation.

Hayek, F. A. von (1944). *The Road to Serfdom*. London: Routledge & Kegan Paul.

—— (1960). *The Constitution of Liberty*. London: Routledge & Kegan Paul.

—— (1982). *Law Legislation and Liberty*. London: Routledge.

Hurka, Tom (1993). *Perfectionism*. Oxford: Oxford University Press.

Kahneman, D., and Tversky, A. (1979). 'Prospect Theory: An Analysis of Decision under Risk'. *Econometrica*, 45: 1623–30.

Kymlicka, Will (1990). *Contemporary Political Philosophy: An Introduction*. Oxford: Oxford University Press.

—— (2002). *Contemporary Political Philosophy: An Introduction*. 2nd edn. Oxford: Oxford University Press.

Lomasky, Loren (1987). *Persons, Rights and the Moral Community*. New York: Oxford University Press.

McLeod, Colin (1998). *Liberalism, Justice, and Markets*. Oxford: Oxford University Press.

Marx, Karl (1875/1974). *Critique of the Gotha Programme*, in *The First International and After*. Harmondsworth: Penguin.

Miller, David (1999). *Principles of Social Justice*. Cambridge, MA: Harvard University Press.

—— and Walzer, Michael (1995) (eds.). *Pluralism, Justice, and Equality*. Oxford: Oxford University Press.

Nagel, Thomas (1973). 'Rawls on Justice'. *Philosophical Review*, 82: 220–34.

—— (1982). 'Libertarianism without Foundations', in Paul (1982), 191–205.

—— (1997). 'Justice and Nature'. *Oxford Journal of Legal Studies*, 17: 303–21.

Narveson, Jan (1988). *The Libertarian Idea*. Philadelphia: Temple University Press.

Nove, Alec (1983). *The Economics of Feasible Socialism*. London: George Allen & Unwin.

—— (1991). *The Economics of Feasible Socialism Revisited*. London: Harper Collins.

Nozick, Robert (1974). *Anarchy, State, and Utopia*. Oxford: Blackwell.

Nussbaum, Martha (2000). *Women and Human Development*. Cambridge: Cambridge University Press.

Parfit, Derek (1998). 'Equality and Priority', in Andrew Mason (ed.), *Ideals of Equality*. Oxford: Blackwell, 1–20.

Paul, J. (1982) (ed.), *Reading Nozick*. Oxford: Blackwell.

Phillips, Anne (1999). *Which Equalities Matter?* Cambridge: Polity.

Radin, Margaret Jane (1996). *Contested Commodities*. Cambridge, MA: Harvard University Press.

Rakowski, Eric (1991). *Equal Justice*. Oxford: Oxford University Press.

Rand, Ayn (1964). *The Virtue of Selfishness*. New York: New American Library.

Rawls, John (1971). *A Theory of Justice*. Oxford: Oxford University Press.

——(1982). 'Social Unity and Primary Goods', in Sen and Williams (1982), 159–85.

——(1993). *Political Liberalism*. New York: Columbia University Press.

——(1999). *A Theory of Justice*. Rev. edn. Oxford: Oxford University Press.

Roemer, John (1998). *Equality of Opportunity*. Cambridge, MA: Harvard University Press.

Rosen, Michael, and Wolff, Jonathan (1999) (eds.), *Political Thought*. Oxford: Oxford University Press.

Scanlon, T. M. (1975). 'Preference and Urgency'. *Journal of Philosophy*, 72: 655–69.

Schmidtz, David, and Goodin, Robert (1998). *Social Welfare and Individual Responsibility*. Cambridge: Cambridge University Press.

Schwartz, Adina (1973). 'Moral Neutrality and Primary Goods'. *Ethics*, 83: 294–307.

Sen, Amartya (1973). *On Economic Equality*. Oxford: Oxford University Press.

——(1980). 'Equality of What?' in S. M. McMurrin (ed.), *The Tanner Lectures on Human Values*. Salt Lake City, UT: University of Utah Press. Reprinted in Sen (1982).

——(1982). *Choice, Welfare and Measurement*. Oxford: Blackwell.

——(1992). *Inequality Re-examined*. Cambridge, MA: Harvard University Press.

—— (1997). *On Economic Equality*. Expanded edn. Oxford: Oxford University Press.

——and Williams, Bernard (1982). *Utilitarianism and Beyond*. Cambridge: Cambridge University Press.

Steiner, Hillel (1994). *An Essay on Rights*. Oxford: Blackwell.

Temkin, Larry (1993). *Inequality*. New York: Oxford University Press.

Tremain, Shelley (1996). 'Dworkin on Disablement and Resources'. *Canadian Journal of Law and Jurisprudence*, 9: 343–59.

van der Veen, Robert, and van Parijs, Philippe (1986). 'A Capitalist Road to Communism'. *Theory and Society*, 15: 635–55.

van Parijs, Philippe (1995). *Real Freedom for All*. Oxford: Oxford University Press.

Von Neumann, J., and Morgenstern, O. (1944). *The Theory of Games and Economic Behavior*. Princeton: Princeton University Press.

Walzer, Michael (1983). *Spheres of Justice*. Oxford: Blackwell.

Williams, Bernard (1979). 'The Idea of Equality', in P. Laslett and W. G. Runciman (eds.), *Philosophy, Politics and Society*. 2nd ser. Oxford: Blackwell.

Wolff, Jonathan (1991). *Robert Nozick: Property, Justice and the Minimal State*. Cambridge: Polity.

——(1992). 'Not Bargaining for the Welfare State'. *Analysis*, 52: 118–25.

——(1998). 'Fairness, Respect and the Egalitarian Ethos'. *Philosophy and Public Affairs*, 27: 97–122.

——(2001). 'Levelling Down', in K. Dowding, J. Hughes, and H. Margetts (eds.), *Challenges to Democracy*. Basingstoke: Palgrave, 18–32.

Young, Iris Marion (1990). *Justice and the Politics of Difference*. Princeton: Princeton University Press.

CHAPTER 18

INTERGENERATIONAL JUSTICE

AXEL GOSSERIES

1. INTRODUCTION

WHAT is so special about the field of intergenerational justice for Rawls to claim that 'it submits any ethical theory to severe if not impossible tests' (1971: 284)? Justice between generations focuses on the moral rights and obligations of people who are born at different times, as, for example, international justice does with respect to those with different citizenships, and, more generally, those born in different places. What then are these difficult questions raised by our differences in 'temporal location'? Broadly, we can distinguish three subsets of issues.

The first debate (discussed in Section 2) has to do with the very *possibility* of intergenerational justice beyond our obligations towards members of other generations while they coexist with us. Here, we ask ourselves whether we owe anything to people who either have died already, or are not yet born. This problem does not only affect the relations between *distant* generations: as soon as my own parents have died and as long as my children are not yet born, I can ask myself 'why would I owe them anything?' Differences in temporal location mean that people may not exist at the same time—be it only during part of their life—which raises special ethical challenges.

I wish to thank especially Gustaf Arrhenius, Hugh LaFollette, Peter Momtchiloff, as well as an anonymous referee. I remain, of course, fully responsible for any remaining mistakes or inconsistencies.

The next two issues consist in attempts at answering a single question: what (if anything) do members of a generation owe members of another one? As the word 'generation' can be understood either as 'birth cohort'—that is, a set of people born within the same lapse of historical time—or as 'age group'—that is, a set of people being at the same stage of their biographical time—this question can indeed be answered from two angles (for example, Daniels 1988: 12–13; van Parijs 1996: 67–9). Sharing non-renewable resources such as oil between generations clearly belongs to the realm of justice between birth cohorts. In contrast, age discrimination on the job market will appear to most of us to belong mainly to the sphere of justice between age groups. These two spheres of intergenerational justice will be dealt with respectively in Sections 3 and 4.

2. Harm and Existence: The Possibility of Justice between Non-Contemporaries

2.1 Should We Care about the Past?

Let us thus address the first set of questions. There are essentially two difficulties related to our non-contemporaneity with *past* generations. We may have several reasons for looking at the past in the context of a theory of intergenerational justice. Suppose first that one community (for example, Afro-Americans or Australian aboriginals) has an average wealth level lower than that of another community (for example, Euro-Americans or Euro-Australians). And let us assume that this difference in wealth can be traced back to injustices done in the past by the ancestors of the wealthier community. Are not the current members of such a community morally bound to some reparation? Part of the answer rests upon whether people today can be held responsible for unjust actions from which they have benefited, but against which they were unable to do anything, since they did not exist at that time (see Bedau 1972; Waldron 1992; Thompson 2000). Suppose we provide a negative answer. It means that we may look for alternative approaches (for example, 'unjust enrichment' or more simply intra-generational distributive justice) to account for our obligations to improve the condition of the worst-off communities in society. But it may also have implications in deciding, for example, whether the citizens of a country should be bound to pay back an external public debt contracted by earlier governments that they never had a chance to elect.

This first issue is, however, not so much one of justice between generations (for example, between possibly careless Euro-Americans of today and their descendants who will have to pay the costs of such carelessness) as one of rectification between two groups *across* generations (for example, the alleged obligations of contemporary Euro-Americans towards today's Afro-Americans, because of what the ancestors of the former inflicted upon the ancestors of the latter). The other question, more genuinely *inter*generational, is whether our—now dead—ancestors can be *harmed* by some of our current actions (for example, destroying what they regarded as an architectural masterpiece for the sake of building a motorway). One might claim that if, whatever our actions, dead people can *never* be harmed, then no moral constraints on our actions could be derived from their past wishes or achievements. In other words, the question here is not whether we can *inherit* an obligation that a dead (group of) people had *towards some other (group of) people*. Instead, it is whether we can meaningfully *have* an obligation *towards our ancestors themselves*.

We can start from two assumptions: either dead people 'exist' (immortalism) or they do not (mortalism) (Mulgan 1999). As to the latter, there have been attempts by mortalists at defending the possibility of using a concept of (pre)posthumous harm (see Feinberg 1984; Waluchow 1986; Lamont 1998). Posthumous harms are possible only if there are posthumous properties (for example, interests). But, in order for the latter not to be free-floating properties, they need to be ascribed to *ante-mortem* persons. Now, it makes perfect sense to ascribe properties to people after their death. Saying that Ronald Reagan *is* one of the five last US presidents illustrates the fact that the way we *describe* persons may depend on subsequent events, including *posthumous* ones. However, once we ask *when* an *ante-mortem* person was *harmed* by a post-mortem action, we need to argue that the post-mortem harm took place *before* the person's death—that is, while she was alive. This requires a deterministic view ('it has been true since the beginning…'), which is hard to swallow. Admittedly, there are alternative ways of defending the idea of obligations towards dead people. Either we abandon the idea of 'posthumous harm' and argue for the possibility of posthumous duties in the absence of correlative harms. Or we adopt an immortalist view, which is probably what underlies the view of many of those who believe that dead people can be harmed.

What are the consequences of such views for a theory of intergenerational justice? For those—be they immortalists or not—who hold the view that dead people can be harmed, the question of our duties towards dead people should be regarded as an essential component in the definition of our intergenerational obligations. Not only would we *have* obligations towards the past. But the *content* of these obligations would affect the content of what we owe to the coming generations, both because resources devoted to caring for the dead (for example, managing cemeteries) will not be used for current and future people, and because of the consideration given to the dead's desires as to what should be transferred to our descendants (see Thompson 1999). The workers who died while building the pyramids or the soldiers who were killed on the battlefields for their country may understandably have wished that what they were working or fighting for be passed to future generations. While such wishes are certainly not *irrational*, does this entail that it would be *immoral* not to try to fulfil them (for example, Thompson 1999)? Moreover, it would require at least that we work out a plausible theory to address conflicts, for example, between the desires of remote and less remote past generations or between the ideas of the 'few' current human beings and those of the huge crowd of people who are now dead (for example, Bykvist 1998: 67–8). For those holding the contrary view that dead people *cannot* be harmed, intergenerational justice can be described as a story involving current and future generations only. This does not entail, however, that it would be a 'one-way story', for the existence of generational *overlap* is such that caring about the previous generation will not necessarily amount to caring for a non-contemporary generation. To conclude on this point, either one argues that we do not have obligations towards dead people, which shapes the scope of questions that a theory of intergenerational justice has to address. Or we consider that we do have obligations towards dead people, in which case we should explain *why* as well as *how* the wishes of all these dead people can be articulated between themselves as well as with those of people alive today. In addition, liberals may have to address the following challenge: how to design procedures (including voting procedures) that are such that the views of both 'mortalists' and 'immortalists' can be accommodated in society (see Mulgan 1999)?

2.2 Should We Care about the Future? The Non-Identity Challenge

There is a more serious difficulty, however. At first sight, one might expect that, given the temporal direction of causation (if any), acting now in a certain way (for example, burying radioactive waste unsafely) might clearly *harm* future people, even though they do not exist yet. There is, however, one *fact* that entails a challenge to the possibility of using a concept of harm with regard to future people. It is often overlooked that most of our actions not only affect *what* will end up being transferred to future people. They also affect the *identity* of these very people—that is, whether it is *this* or *that* person who will be conceived and born. Let us consider the following case. Two parents learn from their medical doctor that, if they were to conceive a child now, he would certainly be born blind. They can, however, follow a very cheap and painless treatment for two months, in which case they would be able to conceive a child who will certainly not be blind. The crucial fact is that, since it is another egg and another spermatozoa that would meet, this would be *another* child. The problem that the parents then face is the following. They are wondering why it would be *wrong* to conceive the (blind) child now. His life would certainly be worth living. And there would be no way to prevent him from being blind, other than not conceiving him. Conceiving another child with perfect vision could thus hardly be said to *improve* the situation of *this* child. How could the blind child then ever be said to have been harmed by his parents' decision to conceive him, if being born blind is the *best possible* genetic condition for *this* child?

This is the *non-identity challenge* (see for example, Parfit 1984: ch. 16). We find ourselves in *non-identity* cases whenever the absence of an allegedly harmful action would also have meant the non-existence of the allegedly harmed person. The key question is whether a moral/legal concept of harm can still be used in such circumstances (see for example, Woodward 1986; Shiffrin 1999). This does not only affect the assessment of 'procreative' actions. In fact, most of our actions, to the extent that they have an impact on the moment of our sexual intercourse, hence on which spermatozoa and which egg will meet, are also subject to this challenge. This is the case, for example, with transportation or energy policies. Thus, a car-addicted father could tell his daughter: 'well, I might have taken the bicycle and left you a cleaner environment; it is, however, unlikely that it would have been *you* whom I would be speaking to now; are you not then better off alive in a polluted environment than non-existent?' Does it not follow from the non-identity challenge that, whatever we do, we will not do anything wrong towards future people? If we want to avoid such a conclusion, we have at least two sets of strategies at our disposal. One consists in questioning the practical significance of the non-identity problem. Another consists in arguing that we can come up with meaningful accounts of *wrongful* actions that would not be *harmful* ones at the same time. We shall focus here on the first set of strategies, of which we shall mention three avenues.

One avenue consists in arguing that, in a wide amount of cases, *more than one action* could lead or have led to the conception of a given person. Even though it was *very unlikely* that this person would have been born had I acted otherwise (for example, given the huge number of competing spermatozoa), it was still *possible*. According, for example, to Roberts (1998: 26–7), we should restrict the scope of the non-identity challenge to cases where it would have been *impossible* for another person to have been conceived, had we acted otherwise. If this strategy appears to be too restrictive, introducing probabilities in the definition of the problem's scope may well be meaningful (see for example, Vallentyne 1987). A related way of restricting the scope of the non-identity problem consists in defending a distinction between *necessary* and *potential* people (for example, Arrhenius 2000: 141–5). Here, instead of arguing that the problem arises only with respect to an action that was *necessary* for the allegedly harmed person's existence, it is being argued that people who would necessarily have been born, whatever our actions had been, fall outside the scope of the non-identity argument. However, one may wonder whether anybody can ever be 'necessary' in this sense.

A second—more significant—avenue consists in focusing on cases where the future person's life can be expected *not to be worth living*. In this case, the use of a concept of harm is not being blocked by the non-identity circumstances. We do not need to show that, once born, this person could have had a *better* life. Showing that she has an irreversibly *bad* life will do. In such a case, there is no need for a comparison with an alternative state of the *same* person. It is enough to compare the person's current or expected condition with an absolute threshold. Whenever the child to be born can be expected to have a life irreversibly below such a threshold, the fact that the only way to prevent this is for this child not to exist does not entail that a concept of harm cannot be used.

This still leaves us with cases, like the 'blind-child' or the 'car-addicted-father' ones, where the expected life of the child *is* worth living. Let us mention in this respect a third avenue, which rests on two assumptions. The factual assumption is that there is generational *overlap*. This means that the car-addicted father, once his daughter has been conceived (and born), will still spend a significant amount of years with her. The normative assumption is that the fulfilment of some obligations should be assessed as soon as the child has been conceived, whereas, for other obligations, this may be done after conception. An example of the former is the possible obligation not knowingly to conceive a child with a given set of physical characteristics. As an illustration of the latter, let us mention our obligations towards the *next* generation. We may claim that, if our generation has the obligation to transfer to the next one a given basket of 'goods', it is only at the end of this generation's life that its fulfilment should be assessed. At least some flexibility should be left to each generation as to *when* (during its life) it should operate such transfers. We should make sure, however, that, on the day of our death, our obligations to the next birth cohort will have been fulfilled. Let us thus refer to these as *complete-life obligations*—that is, obligations the fulfilment of which should be assessed only at the end of our lives. Now, once we bring together the idea of generational overlap and the notion of complete-life obligations, the car-addicted-father case (and more generally energy-policy, transportation-policy, and so on cases) can be addressed as follows. We may consider that his 'pre-conception' pollution did not harm his daughter, given the non-identity circumstances. *However*, the father should not use this non-identity argument as an excuse for not taking action *after* conception took place in order to make sure that his complete-life obligations will turn out to have been fulfilled. Whatever he did before his daughter was conceived, if he turns out at the end of his life not to have fulfilled his intergenerational obligations as they apply to environmental matters, he will certainly have *harmed* his daughter. Given that he is able *to catch up* on the accumulated pre-conception pollution by taking post-conception measures, he should not be entitled to claim that the pollution eventually transferred to his daughter in violation of his intergenerational obligations was *necessary* for this daughter to have existed. This is how complete-life obligations towards the *next* generation can escape the non-identity challenge. And, if we are able to ground our obligations towards more remote generations on those we have towards the next generation (for example, based on the view that we should not act so as to prevent the next generation from being able to fulfil its own obligations), our obligations towards these more remote generations may also escape the non-identity challenge. Our theory of justice towards future people would thus have to rest entirely on our obligations towards members of the next generation, obligations towards subsequent generations being derived by transitivity.

One may, however, remain unconvinced by such a view, for at least two reasons. *First*, those who believe that the parents should have waited two months in the blind-child case are still left with no plausible account of the possible wrongness of the parents' impatience. *Secondly*, the solution proposed to deal with the 'car-addicted father' does not allow us to account for obligations towards remote people in a *direct* way, unless we adopt Roberts's approach mentioned above. We would have no direct obligations towards remote future generations, except the minimalist one of not acting in a way that would make their life *not worth living*. Thus, those who want to address these two worries may then have to develop a second strategy consisting either in proposing alternative concepts of harm or in arguing for the possibility of harmless wrongs. In the latter case, they need to explain how a given action can be wrong despite, in a sense, being bad for no one (Parfit 1984; Arrhenius 2000: ch. 8).

3. Theories of Justice between Birth Cohorts

It is one thing to decide *whether* we owe anything to the next generation(s). It is another to define *what* we owe them. Most standard theories of justice have tried to answer this difficult question. It will not be possible to provide an analysis of the variety of proposals. We shall focus on a comparison between a reciprocity-based and an egalitarian account of justice between generations. We shall then turn, on the one hand, to a brief discussion of alternative theories and, on the other hand, to implementation issues.

3.1 Indirect Reciprocity. On Borrowing the Earth from our Children . . .

To account for our obligations towards the next generations, one popular formula is: 'we borrow the earth from our children' (stewardship). This phrase formulates in an ambiguous and compressed form the idea that we owe *back* to our *children* something that they never gave us in the first place, since it is from our *parents* that we received it. The idea of *indirect* reciprocity accounts properly for this. It points at the fact that the generation that made us a debtor is not itself the final creditor generation. Contrary to what happens in a *direct* reciprocity context, it is not the same person (or set of persons) who benefited us in the first place and to whom we owe something back. This has an additional consequence: the indirect reciprocity 'open loops' can be put together into an intergenerational chain.

It is worth distinguishing two different uses of the notion in the intergenerational justice debate. At times, it is supposed to *justify the existence* of obligations towards future people. There is, indeed, nothing obvious in owing something to a (coming) generation that has not benefited us (yet) in any way. The maxim we can use in such a case is then: we owe something to the next generation *because* we received something from the previous generation (hereinafter the 'justificatory maxim'). At other times, the idea of indirect reciprocity is used to *define the content* of our obligations towards future generations: *what* we owe to future people is (at least) as much as what we have received from previous generations (hereinafter the 'substantive maxim').

This may seem a plausible way of accounting for our intergenerational obligations. However, we shall see, in line with Barry (1989), that it faces very serious challenges. *First*, the 'gift-obligation' objection asks whether *any* gift should give rise to corresponding obligations. Either it is a gift for which nothing is expected in return, in which case we would not be bound to anything. Or, if something is expected in return, the person who accepts the gift should be able at least to understand what it entails as well as to refuse such a gift. Can you expect a newborn to refuse 'gifts' for which she will be bound over for the rest of her life? Similarly, should we feel obliged to give life in turn because we benefited ourselves from such a gift?

The 'gift–obligation' objection is a strong objection. Is it the only one, however? The 'past–future' objection raises a second problem: even if we were to consider that gifts may justify obligations in return, why would it follow from the fact that it is from the *previous* generation that I received something that I should give it back to the *next* generation? At first sight, there is nothing in the definition of indirect reciprocity that requires such a temporal orientation. For example, given the fact of generation overlap, part or the whole of our obligations could be fulfilled on a *direct* reciprocity basis, to the benefit of the *previous* generation who benefited us in the first place (for example, through expensive elderly health care). In such a case, would it still be the case that we would owe the *next* generation *at least as much* as what we received from the previous generation? Perhaps not, since, under a reciprocity logic, we cannot owe more than what we initially received.

However, there is a 'zipper' counter-objection. If we start to reciprocate to members of the previous generations, they in turn will have to reciprocate to someone else if they are willing to comply as well with the reciprocity principle. They would otherwise have received at the end of their life more than they would have given (net intergenerational transfers). The problem is that the previous generation might not itself have any older (and still alive) generation beyond it. Hence, reciprocating might force *it* to violate the principle of reciprocity, because it would find no one further back in time to reciprocate to. This is unacceptable. The 'past–future' objection is thus not as robust as it may have seemed (for a fuller assessment, see Gosseries 2001). Still, the 'gift–obligation' one remains a very serious challenge. And a further difficulty is that reciprocity reduces justice to an equivalence in contributions, which is a core idea underlying, for example, contract law regimes. The logic of such a commutative view of justice is, however, far apart from a *distributive* one that typically underlies, for example, egalitarian theories. This has practical consequences, as we shall now see.

3.2 Rawls's Two-Stages Approach

Is there any plausible *distributive* theory of intergenerational justice? Let us look at Rawls's work, which is a cornerstone for the current debate. The author of *A Theory of Justice* (1971) devotes one section (sect. 44) to our topic and deals with both procedural and substantive issues. Although it is probably not the most interesting part, the *procedural* dimension of Rawls's intergenerational proposal gave rise to extensive discussion (English 1977; Routley and Routley 1977: 166–173; Paden 1977; Wissenburg 1999). The reader will remember that Rawls's idea of an 'original position under a veil of ignorance' provides a justificatory hypothetical device relying on a notion of counterfactual insurance (1971: sect. 24). To decide upon the principles of justice to be adopted, we have to imagine ourselves as if we did not know our gender, our social status, our talents, and so on. In the case of intergenerational justice, people in the original position are being asked to define 'how much they would be willing to save at each stage of advance on the assumption that all other generations are to save at the same rates' (Rawls 1971: 287). Rawls adds, however, two specifications, departing from the standard veil of ignorance. *First*, while ignoring *which* generation we are members of, we should assume that we are all members of the *same* generation. Why would this matter, since we do not know *which* generation we are in anyway? The reason invoked by Rawls—that it would otherwise 'stretch fantasy too far' (1971: 139)—is not very convincing and we should therefore not give too much importance to this 'present time of entry' assumption. What about the second specification? Rawls sidesteps the key assumption according to which the actors in the original position are to be regarded as 'mutually disinterested'. Instead, in the intergenerational context, we should regard ourselves as 'heads of families' having a 'desire to further the welfare of their nearest descendants' (1971: 128). This aims at solving the problem that *previous* generations may not have saved at the appropriate rate, that there is no way we could now force them to do so, and that—as a result—current generations, were they mutually disinterested, would not be willing to save at the appropriate rate either. It may also be hard to account for the obligations of the first generation on a mutual disinterest basis. Rawls subsequently abandoned this specification, however, assuming that, in an *ideal* world, previous generations are supposed to have saved at the appropriate rate (1993: 274). This, of course, does not solve the problem of how to account for the obligations of a mutually disinterested *first* generation, even in such an ideal world. It is significant, however, of the difficulties involved in justifying our intergenerational obligations from a 'mutual disinterest' perspective.

It is now time to turn to Rawls's *substantive* proposal, the *just savings principle*. Let us briefly look at how utilitarians would deal with the issue of just savings (see Ramsey 1928/1978; Fleurbaey and Michel 1999). Utilitarianism is concerned with maximizing the aggregate intergenerational utility, whatever the possible intergenerational inequalities that may follow. In an intertemporal context, there is a key fact: capital is productive, at least once you invest it properly. If you defer to next year (or century) the consumption of part of your capital, and if you invest it, you may well turn out being able to consume much more then. To put things simply, utilitarians tend systematically to defer consumption and invest in the future with the aim of increasing the intergenerational utility pie. This results—even in finite-number-of-generations models—in a sacrifice of early generations to the benefit of later ones—or to no one's benefit if the horizon is indefinite and if there is no satiety level (never-ending sacrifice). Utilitarians will thus call for the adoption of *positive* intergenerational savings rates, at least for the first generations, to the benefit of later generations, which either will never come (infinite horizon with no satiety level), or will be much better off as a result of this early saving. Is this not shockingly incompatible with (maximin) egalitarianism—that is, the idea that we should care in priority for the worst off and that inequalities are acceptable only when they are necessary to improve the situation of the worst off?

Rawls himself proposes a two-stages model. On the one hand, there is an accumulation phase where generations are required to adopt a *positive* savings rate—that is, to leave more than they received. Referring ambiguously to reciprocity language, he writes:

the process of *accumulation*, once it is begun and carried through, is to the good of all *subsequent* generations. Each passes on to the next a fair equivalent in real capital as defined by a just savings principle.... This equivalent is in return for what is received from previous generations that enables the later ones to enjoy a *better* life in a more just society.   (Rawls 1971: 288; emphasis added)

Then comes a steady-state stage where each generation is required only to leave at least as much as it received from its predecessors: 'once just institutions are firmly established, the net accumulation required falls to zero. At this point a society meets its duty of justice by maintaining just institutions and preserving their material base' (Rawls 1971: 287–8). Rawls adds: 'all generations are to do their part in reaching the just state of things beyond which no further net saving is required' (1971: 289). We thus have a clear two-stage model with an accumulation phase where net savings are required, followed by a steady-state stage where no net savings are expected.

A comparison with Ramsey's utilitarian model reveals that such a two-steps approach may be reached on strictly aggregative grounds, at least under the assumption of the existence of a satiety level or 'bliss point' beyond which further consumption does not bring more utility. And one key difficulty with Rawls's model is clearly the existence of such an accumulation phase. Why does Rawls resist from adopting a one-stage (maximin) egalitarian position on the issue? The idea of an accumulation phase seems in clear violation of maximin: not only would the earlier (poorer) generations be bound to larger efforts than later (richer) generations, but the worst-off people in a model without accumulation would certainly be better off than the generations finding themselves in such an accumulation phase, at least for the first of these generations. The superficial reason why Rawls abandons maximin is that, as he puts it, 'there is no way for the latter generation to improve the situation of the least fortunate first generation. The principle is inapplicable and it would seem to imply, if anything, that there be no saving at all' (1971: 291). The idea is thus that, since the worst-off generation is now dead and therefore out of reach, there is no way we will ever be able to satisfy the requirements of maximin. There is, however, a simple answer to this worry. We should simply shift to a less strict version of maximin called *leximin* (Sen 1970: 138). It says that, if the situation of the very worst off cannot be improved, we should then care about the next worst off, and so on. This in fact amounts to saying that the realm of intergenerational justice is between *accessible* generations—that is, cohorts whose situation can still be changed.

There is a more serious reason why Rawls abandons *a single-phase* theory. Without an accumulation phase, we would remain stuck at the level of wealth of prehistoric generations. The reason why Rawls advocates an accumulation phase is, however, not due to strictly aggregative motives. Instead, positive savings should stop as soon as we are in a situation capable of 'bringing about the full realization of just institutions and the fair value of liberty' (1971: 290). This rests, however, on the twofold *empirical* claim that, in the absence of such accumulation, the level of wealth of successive generations would be unacceptably poor *and* that such a level of wealth would be incompatible with the existence of just institutions and a just distribution. It is beyond the scope of the current chapter to provide a detailed examination of the validity of these two claims. However, it is far from excluded that Rawlsians be able to justify the need for an accumulation phase. (For further developments, see Gosseries 2001.)

3.3 Requiring a Zero Rate of Savings, in any Circumstances?

There is a second difficulty, however, with Rawls's substantive proposal. Even if we were able to justify on non-aggregative grounds the need for an accumulation phase, we would still need to know whether humanity is still in a state that requires accumulation. And we would also have to examine whether the prohibition of non-dis-savings proposed by Rawls as a principle to rule the steady-state phase is the one that maximin egalitarians should defend. This is the question we shall be briefly focusing on now.

Egalitarianism, be it of the 'strict' or the 'maximin' form, does not only prohibit dis-savings at steady-state stage. It should also *prohibit net positive savings*. As long as we remain within the ambit of a reciprocity-based approach, there is in principle nothing wrong with leaving to the next generation *more* than what was left to us by the previous generation. But as soon as we adopt a properly distributive theory, we should prohibit not only dis-savings, but also *savings* ('zero-rate' rule). Is there anything wrong, however, with freely sacrificing ourselves for our children? Were a generation *unanimously* deciding to do so, the egalitarian answer would certainly be 'no'. However, in the absence of such unanimity (which is likely), the surpluses transferred to the next generation could instead be transferred to the worst-off people of *our own* generation. And this is the key move. In other words, were maximin egalitarian redistribution effectively to take place within each generation (*intra*-generationally), the 'zero-rate' rule would be such that the worst off under it (whatever generation they are members of) would be better off than under any alternative rule. The next generation, inheriting just as much as we initially received ourselves, will be able in turn to apply maximin egalitarianism intra-generationally, so that the worst off in the next generation will not be worse off than the worst off in the current generation. Thus, in contrast with Rawls, being concerned for the worst off trans-generationally, hence for those of our own generation as well, leads us to prohibit both dis-savings *and savings* in steady-state stage.

As for any principle, the prohibition of both dis-savings and savings ('zero-rate' rule) suffers exceptions. We have already mentioned that, if a generation unanimously decided to adopt a positive savings rate or if maximin egalitarianism were not being applied *intra*-generationally, the principle should not necessarily be followed. There is, moreover, the striking fact that the amount of uncertainties as to what we in fact do transfer to future generations may call for a rate of positive savings, for the sake of prudence (on uncertainty issues, see Birnbacher 1988). Still, prudence should not be excessive, for it may well take place to the detriment of the currently worst off. Moreover, intergenerational maximin egalitarianism may require a departure in some cases from our 'zero-rate' rule, as long as an increase in intergenerational inequalities may be required for the sake of improving the condition of the worst-off people trans-generationally. Let us focus, however, on two further exceptions that are of special interest in so far as they illustrate differences between an egalitarian and a reciprocity-based rule.

First, there is the 'exogenous-disadvantage' exception. It refers to a hypothesis where—as a result of extremely reliable predictive models—the current generation can expect the next one to undergo a major climatic disaster (due, for example, to the fall of a meteorite) that will greatly reduce opportunities available to the next generation. *Ex hypothesi*, this impact is in no sense due to human activities (exogeneity). Under a reciprocity-based model, this should not change anything to our intergenerational obligations, for, as soon as we have given back as much as we received, that is it! The egalitarian view is different. If two countries exhibit great differences in natural resources, egalitarianism requires international redistribution. If two generations are likely to come across radically different environmental circumstances, it will similarly require intergenerational redistribution. Thus in our hypothesis of a 'predictable exogenous disadvantage' affecting the next generation, a *positive* rate of savings will be expected from the current generation, so that the worst-off generation of these two be better off than under an alternative distributive scheme. Of course, in the reverse situation—a temporary and non-repeatable exogenous disadvantage affecting the *current* generation—a *negative* rate of savings will be allowed and even required from the present generation.

The other interesting exception results from the fact that egalitarians should adopt a 'per capita' proviso. As soon as we have a growing population, transferring to the members of the next generation as much as we received ourselves will require the adoption of a *positive* savings rate. Conversely, when population declines, we should adopt a *negative* savings rate such that the worst off under this scheme would be better off than under any alternative scheme. Again, this contrasts with a reciprocity-based perspective: as long as we gave back as much as we received, it does not matter how many people will benefit from it. But the requirement of a positive savings rate in case of a growing population also raises the question as to the extent to which egalitarians should allow a population to grow, for a positive savings is necessarily adopted at the cost of the worst off in our generation. To what extent do we not have the obligation to deal with the existing worst off first before we procreate? Intergenerational ethics is therefore inevitably connected with population and procreation ethics, at least once we reject a reciprocity-based account of intergenerational justice.

3.4 From Theories...

So far, we have explored and discussed only the 'folk' reciprocity-based and the (maximin) egalitarian accounts as well as—to a lesser extent—the utilitarian account of our intergenerational obligations. There have been developments in the literature as well about how 'mutual advantage' (Gauthier 1986: 298–9; Sauvé 1995; Heath 1997; Arrhenius 1999) or 'communitarian' (de-Shalit 1995: 13–65) theories would deal with the matter. But it is probably on Lockean theories of legitimate appropriation that a few additional words are needed (see Elliott 1986; Wolf 1995). It is misleading to regard them as mere 'first-come, first-serve' theories. One of the so-called 'Lockean provisos' states that, for an original appropriation to be legitimate, 'at least as much and as good' should be left for others (Locke 1690/1980). How should this be interpreted in the intergenerational context? Does it mean that we should leave to the following generation at least as much as the *first* generation on earth appropriated per head? Or does it mean instead that we should leave our followers at least as much as *they* would have had in the absence of *any* earlier generation? The environment may well have changed quite a lot since prehistoric times, for reasons that partly have nothing to do with the activities of preceding generations. Still, there is another possible baseline. There is no reason—for a Lockean—why the current generation should make up for early degradations for which it would not be responsible, nor why it should be allowed simply to spoil for its own pleasure the whole product of historical accumulation. Should not Lockeans then simply advocate the rule according to which the current generation has to leave to the next generation at least as much as it received from the previous generation? More precisely, it should then transfer to its followers at least as much as they would have had had the current generation (as opposed to all the generations so far) neither degraded, nor improved, what it inherited. (For further developments, see Gosseries 2001). Interestingly enough, such a Lockean principle exhibits a surprising convergence with the reciprocity-based maxim.

This provides only an overview of a few competing theories on the matter. Further exploration is needed on a series of (practically relevant) theoretical issues. *First*, to what extent does the fact of intergenerational *overlap* affect the possibility and/or content of different theories? For example, it is essential in allowing for some forms of intergenerational contractarianism. *Secondly*, the *exogenous disadvantage* hypothesis provides a good example against which to test the behaviour of these various theories. The reciprocity-based and the Lockean theories of intergenerational justice are on the same side in this respect. And it helps to understand the idea that what the next generation ends up with is not strictly the result of what was transferred to it by the current one. *Thirdly*, the *population* dimension is a key element for any comprehensive intergenerational theory (see Narveson 1967; Parfit 1984: ch. 17; Wolf 1997; Fehige and Wessels 1998; Arrhenius 2000). While the indifference of reciprocity-based theories to the matter is patent, it is less clear how Lockeans should look at it (Vallentyne 2000: 13). And, as we have seen, once we realize that a growing population requires an egalitarian to adopt a positive savings rate, the morality of such a demographic growth is being brought under question. *Fourthly*, how can an egalitarian accept the possibility of *development* and growth, if she is not ready to endorse a 'two-stage' approach to intergenerational justice or if she adopts a 'zero-rate' rule at steady state? This is where intergenerational and international justice meet each other.

3.5 …to Practice

So far, we have discussed only the general 'shape' that intergenerational transfers should take, based on the idea of savings rate, defining when a generation should transfer more or less than it received. It is, of course, important to define a *metric* allowing us to compare what is left by a generation with what it initially inherited. It is clearly beyond the scope of this contribution to provide a detailed analysis of the possible metrics. Roughly, there are welfarist and resourcist metrics. The problem—for example, for an egalitarian—is that, as soon as we have to compare resources of a very different nature, we need some account of the respective value of these resources. One avenue consists in relying on hypothetical auctions with non-envy tests or notions such as undominated diversity (for example, van Parijs 1995: ch. 3). The issue is always to assess the extent to which two baskets of heterogeneous (internal and external) resources can be regarded as *equivalent*.

Heterogeneity is thus not a problem that occurs only in the intergenerational context. Is there, however, anything special about that context? We can mention three types of issues. First, it is clear that the heterogeneity of goods available for distribution is increased by a specific *cause* in the intergenerational context. Some resources are indeed *exhaustible*. And, unless we consider that they should, therefore, never be exploited, it is clear that at some point we have to substitute, for example, oil resources with *equivalent* technologies. This brings us to our second problem. To assess whether these substitution resources or technologies are equivalent, we need the possibility of an auction, be it a hypothetical one. Once we introduce the idea of non-contemporaneity, the intergenerational overlap opens the possibility of a (hypothetical) auction involving both the current and the next generation. Of course, there is an additional peculiarity: the preferences of the next generation's members are heavily influenced by the current generation, both through the education provided and through the fact that what is left and not left by the current generation will also influence the formation of the future generation's preferences. The third point is about the whole debate in environmental economics on 'strong' and 'weak' sustainability (for example, Norton 1999). Roughly, the question is whether there should be limits to substitutability, and whether we should apply our criterion of intergenerational justice (whichever it is) separately to natural and human-made capital, requiring that it be satisfied in each of these spheres. In fact, there are two angles from which to approach this difficult issue. On the one hand, we can try to develop some moral argument according to which *specific objects* should be preserved for future generations, and therefore treated separately in the 'equivalence' accountancy. It could be a chunk of virgin forest, a given species, or some remarkable cultural productions such as Brussels' Grand Place or the Tage bridge in Lisbon. The dividing line does not, therefore, have necessarily to do with a natural–cultural one. On the other hand, what one can value is the *diversity* of (types of) objects as such, whatever they are. Whether we let this or that species or monument disappear would not matter at all as long as a certain diversity of goods and options remains. This can in turn be justified on various grounds—for example, because the existence of a diverse world is essential for future generations to be free to form their preferences. Both strategies—the 'irreplaceable-object' and the 'diverse-world' ones—are extremely difficult ones.

But, unless at least one of them can be successfully brought to fruition, it does not seem that any limits to substitutability could meaningfully be defended.

Another important question is how we connect our theories of justice with practices such as 'generational accounting' (for example, Kotlikoff 1993) or the adoption of a 'positive social discount rate' in cost–benefit analysis. As to the former, the key point is whether we can use it without necessarily implementing a reciprocity-based strategy. As the 'exogenous-disadvantage' example illustrates, justice does not always require a benefit ratio from each generation that would be equal to zero (implying the absence of net transfers between the generations at stake). And it is even less acceptable to phrase things in terms of *equivalent* benefit ratios from one generation to the next, as the example of generations who would have the same but *higher than one* benefit ratio suggests. This could be the case of a succession of cohorts depleting resources to the same extent and without compensation. As to the adoption of a positive social discount rate, the key question is: to what extent does adopting such a positive discount rate entail giving less moral importance to future people than to present ones (for example, Cowen and Parfit 1992)?

4. Age, Justice, and the Complete-Life View

Oil-resources depletion and age discrimination in employment both raise inter-generational issues. Is it enough, however, to claim that the former has to do with justice between birth cohorts and the latter with justice between age groups? Age-based reforms (as any reforms) always have a cohortal impact. Raising the age for pension eligibility or cancelling age-based mandatory retirement, like cancelling compulsory military service, will advantage some birth cohorts over others. Similarly, *ageing* societies raise problems both of justice between cohorts (for example, what would be a fair evolution of the active population's contribution rate across different cohorts?) and of what can be called justice between age groups (for example, is there something like a fair contribution rate, assuming that each cohort would have the same active/inactive ratio?) (see Scharlach and Kaye 1997).

This just shows that the mere invocation of age does not help us define the specific field of justice between age groups, as opposed to justice between birth cohorts. Given the continuous correlation between age and date of birth, it is not obvious that such a task can ever be brought to fruition. One meaningful task to be assigned to 'justice between age groups' can, however, consist in a critical investigation on the *complete-life view*—that is, the (egalitarian) view, according to which, as long as people receive the same amount of a good over their whole life, justice will be met (for example, McKerlie 1993). To grasp the underlying intuition, let us compare age-based discrimination with, for example, racial discrimination. Both age and 'skin colour' are clearly *unchosen* features. However, under certain conditions (including the constancy of the discriminatory practice through time), the age-based discrimination may turn out *not* to be discriminatory *over complete lives*, because of the simple fact that we all age—while we generally do not change the colour of our skin during our life. Imagine two job applicants, Eileen and June, the latter being much younger. At first sight, one may be shocked by an employer who would prefer June for the mere reason that she is younger. However, it may well be that Eileen herself benefited from such a discriminatory practice ten years earlier, when she was then younger than the other applicants for another job. Transporting ourselves to the end of both Eileen's and June's lives, it may well turn out that they will have had equal access to employment over their life. Age discrimination is thus very different from other types of discriminations, as the former may turn out not to discriminate at all between people once we adopt a longitudinal, complete-life approach.

A full theory of justice between age groups needs to address two broad types of issue. First, we have to assess the extent to which age-based and seniority-based practices are in line with the complete-life view. And in doing so, we may well have to take into account the cohortal impacts of such practices (see Section 4.1). Secondly, can the complete-life view fully account for our intuitions as to how goods should be allocated between people of different age and therefore as well along people's lives? There are several reasons why it may not. Either we may adopt the radical view that the basic units of ethical concern are not whole lives but segments of people's lives (see Section 4.2). Or, assuming that complete-life egalitarianism is being complied with, the way some goods are allocated *along* people's lives may still raise extra problems of *justice*. In other words, equality over complete lives may be a necessary but not sufficient condition for a just allocation between age groups (see Section 4.3). We may also consider that, while some types of goods (for example, jobs) should be allocated on a complete-life egalitarian basis, others should not (for example, basic political rights) (see Section 4.4). Let us consider each of these issues in turn.

4.1 Life Profile and Lifespan

Even for those adopting the plainest complete-life (egalitarian) view, age-based practices will still constitute a whole field of investigation. It may well be that such practices would entail direct or indirect violations of complete-life egalitarianism. Let us begin with a distinction between *lifespan* and *life-profile* issues. Suppose that there is a policy of age rationing applied to a life-extending type of health care (for example, heart surgery). People who suffer from a given deadly disease will not be provided with access to surgery if they are above a certain age, say 65. This age-rationing practice does not allocate goods in a certain way *along* people's lives. What it does instead is to allocate directly *lengths* of life. It may be justified on at least two very different grounds. For utilitarians, this age-rationing policy will be the right one *if and only if* we can show that age is a good proxy for additional life expectancy and if this is likely to increase the aggregate utility in a given society. For egalitarians, based on the amount of resources that it is fair to allocate to life-extending intervention, we should try to equalize people's life expectancies, *ceteris paribus* and as long as those who have a poorer life expectancy cannot be held responsible for it. Age rationing in health care *might* be one way of equalizing lifespans, but not necessarily the best one. What matters is *not* the age of the respective candidates at the moment of the medical intervention. What matters, *ceteris paribus*, is how many years each of them will eventually turn out to have lived. To get a proper prognosis, other proxies might be better than age. Moreover, the complete-life account cannot simply aim at equalizing people's length of life regardless of huge differences in the quality of these lives. Age rationing would be acceptable only to the extent that it would serve complete-life maximin egalitarianism. This contrasts with, for example, Callahan's support (1987) to age rationing that relies, not on a reference to scarcity, but on the intuition that, for the elderly to have a meaningful life, they should serve the young, which implies also the sacrifice of their lives (for a critique, see Daniels 1996: 277). As to Daniels, he is reluctant to justify age rationing on egalitarian grounds. His reluctance rests with the example of two competing candidates for the same life-extending intervention (1996: 276). Suppose that none of them is more responsible than the other for her now fragile physical condition. The old person has never relied so far on medical services for which she has been paying her whole life, while the younger candidate has already benefited from several earlier interventions. To a 'desert-based' view claiming that the old should be chosen, egalitarians should respond that the old person was simply lucky enough never to have needed health care so far and that the younger candidate, if he had reached such an advanced age, may also have contributed in the same way to the financing of the health-care system. Daniels's reluctance may therefore not be justified.

In contrast to life-extending health-care rationing, when *employment benefits* are being allocated on the basis of age or seniority (that is, in-company age), it *does not* directly affect the (professional) lifespan of the people at stake. It primarily allocates access to employment benefits in a certain way *along* people's life. This is why age rationing of life-extending health care and age-based or seniority-based discrimination in employment raise different types of issues. Whereas the former 'merely' raises an issue of allocation *of lifespans*, only the latter raises a problem of allocation *across the lifespan* (what I call a 'life-profile' issue). With this distinction in mind, we can understand at least two things. Since age-based rationing of life-extending health care and age-based discrimination in access to employment benefits raise different issues, judgements on the former should not automatically be transposed to the latter (and conversely). Moreover, we are now able to perceive how egalitarians can assess age-based practices on a complete-life basis. Taking the

case of employment benefits, they will want to assess when discriminatory allocations *across* the (chronological) lifespans result in an unequal allocation of (professional) lifespans—that is, of the amount of years of access to employment benefits.
One will then typically try to debusk the various ways through which age-based or
seniority-based allocation of employment benefits can entail in certain circumstances inequalities over complete lives between workers. Take, for example, age-
based *mandatory retirement*. It is clear that, from the point of view of access to
employment benefits, it disadvantages those who either had to start working later
than others, or who had to interrupt their career for longer periods than others (for
example, because of repeated diseases). Take as well the 'last-in, first-out' seniority-
based layoff rule. It clearly disadvantages those who underwent external mobility
more frequently than others for reasons that they cannot be held responsible for.
We can thus identify categories of workers who are more affected than others by a
given age-based or seniority-based rule, through no fault of their own. From an
egalitarian point of view, such 'involuntary victims' constitute a prima facie case
against these practices.

Egalitarians should not stop here, however, for they are only halfway. Whatever
the metrics they choose (for example, resources), complete-life equality of access to
employment benefits is not the only thing that matters. Maximin egalitarians could
support such age-based or seniority-based practices if the latter are capable of—
and necessary for—improving the situation of the worst-off people in society (be
they workers or not) from the point of view of equality of resources *in general*, even
if this means that some workers will have a lesser access *to employment* than others,
for reasons beyond their control. For such a maximin argument to be successful,
several conditions are to be fulfilled. One of them is that there should be an efficiency case for such discriminatory practices. However, if we take, for example, the
age–productivity relationship, the empirical evidence is mixed (Levine 1989:
108–17). Moreover, these efficiency gains (if any) should be effectively redistributed
in line with maximin egalitarianism. Suppose that age-based discrimination effectively increases the productivity of companies, but that states are incapable of taxing these gains to redistribute them to society at large. In this case, egalitarians may
well be forced to advocate second-best policies aiming at prohibiting such age-
based or seniority-based discriminatory practices.

4.2 What Are the Fundamental Units of Ethical Concern?

So far, we have remained within the ambit of the complete-life paradigm. Let us now
turn to one radical way of questioning such a paradigm. It requires a fundamental
anthropological shift towards considering that we are in fact not necessarily the same
person during our whole life, that our physical continuity is not all that matters in
that respect (Parfit 1984: chs. 10–12). We can thus contrast the 'complete-life' view

with an 'inter-segment' one, according to which the real units of ethical concern should not be persons as we generally see them, but smaller units that can be called 'segments'. Thus, the reason why we should regard intra-life allocation as a genuine problem of *justice* is simply because it is about allocating resources, welfare, and so on between different segments that are the true units of ethical concern.

Several egalitarian 'segment-based' views have been proposed (McKerlie 1989, 1993; Daniels 1996: 264–9), the most consistent among them being the 'total-segments' one. It values equality between all segments of all lives. This means that equality should reign between the segments both from one period to the next one of the same person *and* between the different people at each period (for example, McKerlie 1989, 1993). This could require, for example, a flat income profile across people's lives, no age limits for access to education or employment, and so on. However, as Cupit puts it, 'it is hard to see that there is any inherent injustice in a system where people take their leave at different times, or receive presents celebrating their births on different days' (1998: 714). As such this is an objection more against an *egalitarian* 'inter-segment' view than against the view that segments should be regarded as the core units of ethical concern. Parfit has rightly noted that, for a *utilitarian*, the plausibility of inter-segmental sacrifice in common-sense ethical views would then logically entail the plausibility of interpersonal sacrifices for the sake of utility maximization (Parfit 1984: 340). In other words, the acceptability of sacrificing the life of an innocent to increase the well-being of twenty other people would get further credibility from considering that there is nothing wrong with working like mad at one moment of one's life for the sake of enjoying relaxed holidays later in one's life. Still, the idea that the fundamental units are 'segments' as opposed to 'full persons' is hard to swallow. Its defenders try to give it plausibility by providing examples such as the following one: suppose that a couple decides that each of them will take turns in having a dominant position, in a manner compatible with complete-life equality of powers (McKerlie 1993: 222). Does it mean that complete-life egalitarians could have nothing to object to such a 'switching-places' case? On egalitarian grounds perhaps not. But there may be something else going wrong with this domination relationship, notwithstanding the fact that it is equally shared. Hence, Daniels (1996: 269) is right when he says that such an example does not necessarily force us to shift to an inter-segment view. Do we not then dispose of any alternative to a fundamental anthropological shift to account for our moral intuitions for which the complete-life view cannot account?

4.3 Daniels's Prudential Lifespan Account

If we reject the reductionist strategy, do we fall back on a plain complete-life view? Two people may well have received the same amount of resources at the end of their lives. Still is it not the case that the fact that they would have received them differently across time might raise an additional problem of *justice*? This seems to be Daniels's view (1988, 1996: ch. 12). Equalization over complete lives certainly makes sense and it may entail that we be treated differently at different ages. Still, the way we may treat each age group differently should itself be subject to some additional constraints that cannot be derived directly from the complete-life view itself. How could we define and justify such constraints? For Daniels, justice between age groups should be dealt with not directly as an *interpersonal* issue. Instead, it should be looked at as a problem of *intra*-life allocation between *age stages*. What is just between the young and the old can then be defined by exploring what a prudent *intra*-life allocation would consist in. He specifies procedural constraints that should lead us to adopting a given substantive theory. The procedural approach consists in a 'veil-of-ignorance' strategy, including three specific informational restrictions. First, we should assume that we do not know *our age*. Secondly, we should act as if we ignored our current *conception of the good life* and of the good life plan. Thirdly, we should ignore our actual life expectancy and assume that we shall have a *normal lifespan*—that is, that we will go through each of the age stages (for example, Daniels 1988: 67). With these three informational constraints in mind, people in a hypothetical original position, knowing what their lifetime fair share of resources would be, are being asked to define what a prudential intra-life allocation would consist in.

The key outcome that is supposed to follow from such a procedure is the 'keeping-options-open' principle. As Daniels (1988: 58) puts it,

I want to assure myself at each stage of life of having an adequate chance to pursue whatever my plan of life is then. I must assure myself that at each stage of life I shall have a reasonable share of basic social goods which serve as the all purpose means of pursuing what I think is good. Keeping options open implies that I must be neutral or unbiased toward the different stages of life that I shall go through.

This principle of neutrality allows for some *revisability* of conceptions between the different age stages, hence for *differences* in conceptions between different age groups. As Daniels recognizes, this principle is not without its difficulties. Being committed to a single conception of the good life (1988: 58–9) or to a given insurance plan (1988: 55) may be required across different age stages, which is to a large extent incompatible with strong revisability. Otherwise, we would respectively have painstakingly invested in future realizations that would never take place, or have enjoyed life carelessly with the idea that we could always contract an insurance when the time of great risks would come. Daniels in fact restricts his 'keeping-options-open' view to requiring that, at each age stage, a *normal opportunity range* be guaranteed—that is, the array of life plans reasonable persons...are likely to construct for themselves' in a given society (1988: 69). Unexpectedly, it also implies an 'income preservation principle' requiring that 'post-retirement income levels (or standard of living) should approximate pre-retirement income levels (or standard of living), across the board for all levels of fair income shares' (1988: 122–3).

No doubt, the shift to an intra-life approach to justice between age groups has its merits. There are, however, at least two types of difficulties involved in Daniels's prudential lifespan account. *First*, why would a *prudent* intra-life allocation be a proper guide to a *just* inter-personal allocation (for example, Daniels 1996: 267)? It is clear that the shift to an intra-life approach helps us *see* the problem 'from the inside'. And envisaging the tragic choices that society has to make as if they were our own (painful) choices for our own life may render them more acceptable to us. What is less clear, however, is the extent to which, for example, the requirement of intra-life revisability underlying the 'keeping-options-open' principle *adds any independent support* to the liberal idea of neutrality towards the various conceptions of the good life plan. Is not the need for such neutrality already present at the outset behind the second informational restriction that will in turn lead to the 'keeping-options-open' principle? *Secondly*, on the substance of Daniels's account, to what extent is the 'keeping-options-open' principle acceptable and why would it require an *equality* between pre-retirement and post-retirement income levels? As we have said, some conceptions of a good life (plan) may not be compatible with this in so far as they require sacrificing an earlier or later part of one's life to the benefit of a given lifelong project. Egalitarians—contrary to utilitarians—are in principle not ready to sacrifice one person to the benefit of others. At the same time, why would they see anything wrong in a person sacrificing a part of her life to the benefit of achieving something greater over her life as a whole?

4.4 Articulating Three Intuitions

There is probably still a long way before a full theory of justice between age groups can be proposed. For such a theory to be plausible—and assuming that we leave the inter-segment view aside—at least three basic intuitions should be articulated: the 'complete life', the 'just profile', and the 'continuist' one. We have already been focusing explicitly on the (egalitarian) *complete-life* view—that is, on the intuition according to which for certain goods (for example, jobs) egalitarians should primarily focus on equalizing the access to such goods over people's complete lives. The *just-profile* intuition entails that this is not enough, for there can be good reasons for promoting a given type of allocation of certain goods along people's lives. Daniel's prudential lifespan view is one example: to each age, a certain option set should be attached. Child labour might provide another illustration, for, beyond concerns as to working conditions, there is a certain view that childhood should be preserved for playing and learning. A variety of considerations may lead us to promote a certain type of income or education profile over another. Some might be efficiency based (for example, for investing early in life in education) or paternalistic (favouring regular instalments over lump-sum allocation). There might also be a perfectionist view according to which there is a prime of life that corresponds with adulthood and that successes during the prime of life will determine the general success of one's whole life (Wilkinson 1994). Finally, there is the *continuist* view, according to which some rights and/or goods should be guaranteed to people *at any moment* in their life. Sufficientarians—that is, those concerned with the coverage of basic needs—will in principle adopt such a view. People should be guaranteed food and shelter whatever the reasons why they are unable to pay for themselves (for example, because they have consciously lost everything at the lottery). If this relies on a certain understanding of what respect for basic human dignity entails, it should be the case *all along* the person's life, even if shelter, for example, is not required for the person's physical survival. Similarly, voting rights may be considered so fundamental (and non-scarce) that—contrary to jobs—there is no valid reason (except competency-based ones) why voting rights should be restricted on an age basis (for example, Daniels 1996: 268; cf. van Parijs 1999). In the same line, what should we then think of the allocation of political power on a seniority basis? Not only do we need to clarify the connections and articulations between these three intuitions. We should also try to find out what non-egalitarian theorists (for example, utilitarians, libertarians) think about age-based practices.

5. CONCLUSION

Theories of intergenerational justice are clearly still at an early stage. A lot of focus has been devoted to issues such as the non-identity problem, which clearly raises fascinating puzzles that touch upon moral concepts as fundamental as the one of 'harm'. Justice between birth cohorts is a complex field where a great deal of research is still needed on issues such as the justification of an accumulation phase, the articulation with population ethics, the critical assessment of various notions of environmental sustainability, or the ethically aware use of tools such as generational accounting. But it is probably the domain of justice between age groups that is in need of the strongest research effort. We are still far from working out clearly why some goods should be allocated all along our lives while others need to be equalized only over complete lives. Whether connections between prudence and justice can be meaningfully drawn is still to be found out. And difficult problems such as care of the elderly and children's rights need to be precisely defined before being integrated in a full theory of justice between age groups. What is at stake is the variety of reasons why differential treatment may be attached to different ages. For each of them, we need to put into operation the tools of ethical assessment. Finally, while the theoretical challenges are numerous and fascinating, the practical relevance of such a theoretical debate is equally so. A whole set of policies, ranging from population to employment, health care, resource management, and environmental issues, are potentially affected by theoretical discoveries in this relatively new field of ethical research.

REFERENCES

Arrhenius, G. (1999). 'Mutual Advantage Contractarianism and Future Generations'. *Theoria*, 65: 25–35.

——(2000). 'Future Generations: A Challenge for Moral Theory'. PhD thesis, Uppsala: University Printers.

Barry, B. (1978). 'Circumstances of Justice and Future Generations', in R. Sikora and B. Barry (eds.), *Obligations to Future Generations*. Philadelphia: Temple University Press, 204–48.

——(1989). 'Justice as Reciprocity' in Barry, *Liberty and Justice*. Oxford: Oxford University Press, 211–41.

Bedau, H. (1972). 'Compensatory Justice and the Black Manifesto'. *Monist*, 56: 20–42.

Birnbacher, D. (1988). *Verantwortung für zukünftige Generationen*. Stuttgart: Reclam.

Bykvist, K. (1998). 'Changing Preferences: A Study in Preferentialism'. PhD thesis, Uppsala: University Printers.

Callahan, D. (1987). *Setting Limits: Medical Goals in an Aging Society*. New York: Simon & Schuster.

Cowen, T., and Parfit, D. (1992). 'Against the Social Discount Rate' in P. Laslett and J. Hishkin (eds.), *Justice between Age Groups and Generations*. New Haven: Yale University Press, 144–61.

Cupit, G. (1998). 'Justice, Age and Veneration'. *Ethics*, 108: 702–18.

Daniels, N. (1988). *Am I My Parents' Keeper? An Essay on Justice between the Old and the Young*. New York: Oxford University Press.

——(1996). *Justice and Justification: Reflective Equilibrium in Theory and Practice*. Cambridge: Cambridge University Press.

de-Shalit, A. (1995). *Why Posterity Matters: Environmental Policies and Future Generations*. London: Routledge.

Elliot, R. (1986). 'Future Generations, Locke's Proviso and Libertarian Justice'. *Journal of Applied Philosophy*, 3: 217–27.

English, J. (1977). 'Justice between Generations'. *Philosophical Studies*, 31: 91–104.

——(1991). 'What do Grown Children Owe their Parents?', in N. Jecker (ed.), *Aging and Ethics: Philosophical Problems in Gerontology*. Totowa, NJ: Humana Press, 147–70.

Fehige, C., and Wessels, U. (1998). 'Introduction to Possible Preferences', in C. Fehige and U. Wessels (eds.), *Preferences*. Berlin: De Gruyter, 367–82.

Feinberg, J. (1984). *The Moral Limits of the Criminal Law, i. Harm to Others*. Oxford: Oxford University Press.

Fleurbaey, M., and Michel, L. (1999). 'Quelques réflexions sur la croissance optimale'. *Revue économique*, 50: 715–32.

Gauthier, D. (1986). *Morals by Agreement*. Oxford: Oxford University Press.

Gosseries, A. (2001). 'What do We Owe the Next Generation(s)?' *Loyola of Los Angeles Law Review*, 35: 101–158.

Heath, J. (1997). 'Intergenerational Cooperation and Distributive Justice'. *Canadian Journal of Philosophy*, 27: 361–76.

Kotlikoff, L. (1993). 'Justice and Generational Accounting', in L. Cohen (ed.), *Justice across Generations: What Does it Mean?* Washington: American Association of Retired Persons, 77–93.

Lamont, J. (1998). 'A Solution to the Puzzle of When Death Harms its Victims'. *Australasian Journal of Philosophy*, 76: 198–212.

Levine, M. (1989). *Age Discrimination and the Mandatory Retirement Controversy*. Baltimore: Johns Hopkins University Press.

Locke, J. (1690/1980). *Second Treatise of Government*, ed. C. B. MacPherson. Indianapolis: Hackett Publishing Company.

McKerlie, D. (1989). 'Equality and Time'. *Ethics*, 99: 475–91.

——(1993). 'Justice between Neighboring Generations', in L. Cohen (ed.), *Justice across Generations: What Does it Mean?* Washington: American Association of Retired Persons, 215–25.

Mulgan, T. (1999). 'The Place of the Dead in Liberal Political Philosophy'. *Journal of Political Philosophy*, 7: 52–70.

Narveson, J. (1967). 'Utilitarianism and New Generations'. *Mind*, 76: 62–72.

Norton, B. (1999). 'Ecology and Opportunity: Intergenerational Equity and Sustainable Options', in A. Dobson (ed.), *Fairness and Futurity*. Oxford: Oxford University Press, 118–50.

Paden, R. (1997). 'Rawls's Just Savings Principle and the Sense of Justice'. *Social Theory and Practice*, 23: 27–51.

Parfit, D. (1984). *Reasons and Persons*. Oxford: Oxford University Press.

Ramsey, F. (1928/1978). 'A Mathematical Theory of Savings', in Ramsey, *Foundations: Essays in Philosophy, Logic, Mathematics and Economics*, ed. D. H. Mellor. London: Routledge & Kegan Paul, 261–81.

Rawls, J. (1971). *A Theory of Justice*. Oxford: Oxford University Press.

——(1993). *Political Liberalism*. New York: Columbia University Press.

Roberts, M. (1998). *Child versus Childmaker: Future Persons and Present Duties in Ethics and the Law*. Lanham, MD: Rowman & Littlefield.

Routley, R., and Routley, V. (1977). 'Nuclear Energy and Obligations to the Future'. *Inquiry*, 21: 133–79.

Sauvé, K. (1995). 'Gauthier, Property Rights, and Future Generations'. *Canadian Journal of Philosophy*, 25: 163–76.

Scharlach, A., and Kaye, L. (1997). (eds.) *Controversial Issues in Aging*. Boston: Allyn & Bacon.

Sen, A. (1970), *Collective Choice and Social Welfare*. Amsterdam: North-Holland Publishing Co.

Shiffrin, S. (1999). 'Wrongful Life, Procreative Responsibility, and the Significance of Harm'. *Legal Theory*, 5: 117–48.

Thompson, J. (1999). 'Inherited Obligations and Generational Continuity'. *Canadian Journal of Philosophy*, 29: 493–516.

——(2000). 'Historical Obligations'. *Australasian Journal of Philosophy*, 78: 334–45.

Vallentyne, P. (1987). 'Utilitarianism and the Outcomes of Actions'. *Pacific Philosophical Quarterly*, 68: 57–70.

——(2000). 'Introduction: Left-Libertarianism—a Primer', in P. Vallentyne and H. Steiner, *Left-Libertarianism and its Critics: The Contemporary Debate*. New York: Palgrave.

van Parijs, P. (1995). *Real Freedom for All: What (if Anything) can Justify Capitalism?* Oxford: Oxford University Press.

van Parijs, P. (1996). 'Du patrimoine naturel aux régimes de retraite. Quelle solidarité entre les générations?' in van Parijs, *Refonder la solidarité*. Paris: Le Cerf, 67–95.

——(1999). 'The Disfranchisement of the Elderly, and Other Attempts to Secure Intergenerational Justice'. *Philosophy and Public Affairs*, 27: 290–333.

Waldron, J. (1992). 'Superseding Historic Injustice'. *Ethics*, 103: 4–28.

Waluchow, W. J. (1986). 'Feinberg's Theory of "Preposthumous" Harm'. *Dialogue*, 25: 727–34.

Wilkinson, T. (1994). 'Age, Equality and the Prime of Life'. *Political Science*, 46: 91–104.

Wissenburg, M. (1999). 'An Extension of the Rawlsian Savings Principle to Liberal Theories of Justice in General', in A. Dobson (ed.), *Fairness and Futurity*. Oxford: Oxford University Press, 173–98.

Wolf, C. (1995). 'Contemporary Property Rights, Lockean Provisos and the Interests of Future Generations'. *Ethics*, 105: 791–818.

——(1997). 'Person-Affecting Utilitarianism and Population Policy; or, Sissy Jupe's Theory of Social Choice', in N. Fotion and J. C. Heller, *Contingent Future People: On the Ethics of Deciding Who Will Live, or Not, in the Future*. Dordrecht: Kluwer, 99–122.

Woodward, J. (1986). 'The Non-Identity Problem'. *Ethics*, 96: 804–31.

CHAPTER 19

....

PRIVACY

....

ANITA L. ALLEN

1. INTRODUCTION

....

PHILOSOPHERS of privacy have engaged in three interrelated, but distinguishable enterprises: (1) conceptual analysis, both descriptive and normative; (2) policy analysis, including analysis of issues raised by bioethics and new technologies; and (3) feminist analysis. Although all three have enjoyed periods of special prominence, even the earliest—conceptual analysis—has continued beyond its time of origin and prominence into the present day. A separate discussion of each enterprise follows this introduction.

Recognizing that strict definitions of 'privacy' are diverse and contested, I will use 'privacy' broadly to encompass the concepts, values, and phenomena most commonly discussed under its rubric, specifically: (1) freedom from government or other outside interference with personal life—decisional privacy; (2) seclusion, solitude, and bodily integrity—physical privacy; (3) confidentiality, anonymity, data protection, and secrecy of facts about persons—informational privacy; and (4) limits on the use of a person's name, likeness, identity, or other attributes of identity and exclusive possession—proprietary privacy (A. L. Allen 1997: 33). In its decisional, physical, informational, and proprietary senses, privacy is protected by law, but also by cultural norms, professional ethics, and business practices.

Ideas and ideals of privacy have played a role in religious, political, and legal thought for centuries. It has been portrayed variously as an ideal of solitary, reclusive, secret, or modest spiritual devotion and also as an ideal of right conduct (Konvitz 1966). James Fitzjames Stephen (1873) quipped that anything 'indecent' is an invasion of privacy. Privacy has also played a significant role in political thought as an ideal of limited government called for by moral autonomy, civil liberty, and civility (Feinberg 1983; G. Dworkin 1988). Today, civil libertarians cite John Stuart Mill's classic defence in *On Liberty* (1859) of decisional privacy rights for individuals acting in the domain of self-regarding conduct; and moral philosophers cite Immanuel Kant's familiar deontological theory of moral autonomy (G. Dworkin 1978, 1988).

The idea of privacy has played a role in constitutional thought, formulations of human rights, and both common and civil law. The US Supreme Court has recognized that five of the original Bill of Rights and the Fourteenth Amendment protect privacy interests. In US tort law, interests against intrusion upon seclusion, public disclosure of private fact, publications placing one in a false light, and misappropriation of a person's name, likeness, or identity are potentially protected through civil actions styled 'invasions of privacy'. Federal and state statutes protect interests in the privacy of records relating to, *inter alia*, health, finances, consumer transactions, Internet use, and taxes.

Scholarly interest in privacy was minimal prior to the 1960s. This was true throughout the English-speaking world. In the USA, the most cited scholarly article on the subject of the right to privacy was (and is) one Samuel Warren and Louis Brandeis (1890) published in the *Harvard Law Review*, calling for recognition of a right of privacy in tort law. However, in the 1960s, legal scholars began writing about privacy in significant numbers (Davis 1959; Beany 1962, 1966; Ernst and Schwartz 1962; Note 1963; Bates 1964; Hofstadter and Horowitz 1964; Dixon 1965; Kalven 1966; Negley 1966; Shils 1966; Long 1967; Nimmer 1968). William Prosser (1960) published a key article announcing the full flowering of four invasion-of-privacy torts. Early articles by Edward Bloustein (1964, 1978) and Charles Fried (1968) sought to identify the moral foundations of privacy in neo-Kantian principles of dignity and respect. Two of the few books on the subject of privacy from the period were sociologist Alan Westin's highly influential *Privacy and Freedom* (1967) and law professor Arthur Miller's *The Assault on Privacy* (1964).

Scholarly interest in organized conceptual understandings of privacy increased after 1970 (Bostwick 1976). Academic philosophers in the USA, UK and Australia began systematic study of privacy in the 1970s (Van den Haag 1971; Thomson 1975; Wasserstrom 1978; Berns 1979; Benn 1980, 1988; F. A. Allen 1984). Several anthologies devoted to privacy topics, including some substantially devoted to philosophical perspectives, were published in the 1970s, including issues of *Nomos* and *Philosophy and Public Affairs (PAPA)* (Ernst and Schwartz 1962; Pennock and Chapman 1971; McClellan 1976; Young 1978). Indeed, volume 6 of *PAPA* (1976) signalled the definitive arrival of privacy as a concept commanding serious, sustained philosophical dialogue. Some of the volume's seminal articles were later included in a useful anthology of legal and philosophical privacy perspectives assembled by Ferdinand Schoeman (1984a).

A number of books about privacy by interdisciplinary philosophers interested in public policy were published in the 1980s. Informational privacy was the subject of Sissela Bok's *Secrecy* (1983), although Bok contends that privacy and secrecy are distinct concepts. Bok's analysis of secrecy as intentional concealment closely examines the ethical value of non-disclosure in personal relationships, medicine, science, government, the military, journalism, and corporate life. Published in 1986, *Toleration and the Constitution* was David A. J. Richards's social contractarian analysis of constitutional freedoms and privacy. Rejecting 'original-intent' and 'plain-meaning' theories of constitutional interpretation, Richards argued that the eighteenth-century intellectual heritage of the US Constitution warrants contractarian jurisprudence. State action ought to be limited by a standard of rational agreement by autonomous moral agents. Properly interpreted, the Constitution requires wide tolerance of religion, free expression, and autonomous choices respecting consensual adult sex and reproduction. *Uneasy Access: Privacy for Women in a Free Society* (A. L. Allen 1988b), one of the first books about privacy to focus exclusively on gender issues, included a comprehensive survey of the philosophic literature. The book began with chapters surveying definitional accounts of the meaning and value of privacy and offering a perspective influenced by the work of Charlotte Perkins Gilman (1898/1986), Hannah Arendt (1958), Ruth Gavison (1980), and Jean Bethke Elshstain (1981). *Uneasy Access* argued that women have varied privacy interests and confront special obstacles to privacy at home, at school, on the streets, at work, in the media, in the courts, and while in the hands of police and prison officials. Important books by philosophers Julie Inness (1992), Ferdinand Schoeman (1992), Patricia Boling (1996), and Judith Wagner DeCew (1997) followed.

The paucity and then sudden bounty of privacy scholarship in the final few decades of the twentieth century require explanation. Developments in law, medicine, civil rights, and technology help to explain why scholars in law and philosophy turned to privacy studies. This is painstakingly true of scholars in the USA. However, US developments also had an impact on scholars from Canada (Flaherty 1972), Israel (Gavison 1980), Great Britain (Wacks 1980), and Australia (Benn 1971).

First, in the 1960s and 1970s the US Supreme Court popularized the idea of legal rights of privacy by relying upon the idea of constitutional rights of privacy to set the standards for lawful search and seizure (*Katz* v. *United States*, 1967), and to overturn laws criminalizing birth control (*Griswold* v. *Connecticut*, 1965), interracial marriage (*Loving* v. *Virginia*, 1967), the use of pornography in the home (*Stanley* v. *Georgia*, 1969), and abortion (*Roe* v. *Wade*, 1973). These precedents inspired later efforts to establish sexual privacy rights for gays and lesbians, including *Bowers* v. *Hardwick* (1986).

Secondly, the escalation of the cold war, the Vietnam conflict, and racial turmoil heightened concern about the government's techniques of espionage, surveillance, and social control. The surveillance technologies used for spying could also be used to monitor ordinary citizens and suspected criminals. The government's ability to discern the details of private lives through covert wiretapping, and powerful lenses, microphones, and cameras made citizens concerned about the fate of freedom and democracy. US Congress enacted the Omnibus Crime Control and Safe Street Act in 1967, permitting, but setting limits on, wiretapping and certain other forms of surveillance. (The Electronic Communication Privacy Act of 1986 and subsequent statutes have updated this major legislation.)

Thirdly, by 1970 some Americans had come to see computers as threats to informational privacy. Concerns over the 'databank' containing personal profiles emerged. The potential for unfair use of personal information and misinformation stored in commercial and government databanks led to federal laws including the Privacy Act of 1974, the Family Education and Right to Privacy Act of 1974, and the Right to Financial Privacy Act 1978. A national commission formed by federal lawmakers, the US Privacy Protection Study Commission, published its two-volume report, *Personal Privacy in an Information Society* in 1977. The report recommended that a list of 'fair information practices' govern the collection, storage, and use of personal information about individuals.

A fourth development increased scholars' interest in privacy: advances in medicine and health care. One category of advances enabled physicians to prolong the lives of terminally ill patients, critically injured patients, and fragile newborns. The ability to extend life created difficult bioethical questions about the allocation of decision-making authority about matters of life and death among patients, health-care providers, family members, and insurers. Conceptions of privacy and autonomy were adduced by some ethicists as relevant to the assignment of authority and responsibility. Medical advances of the 1960s and 1970s also enabled women and their physicians to prevent and safely to terminate pregnancy. Access to birth control and abortions was defended in the courts, in legislatures, on college campuses, and as a matter of women's privacy rights. The global AIDS epidemic and the International Human Genome Project increased interest in the use and abuse of medical information.

The World Wide Web as a popular social and commercial setting has made 'privacy policy' a household word (Berners-Lee 1999), as did aggressive, sensational, and confessional television journalism, which gained special popularity after 1990. The Watergate scandal had established investigative journalism as a major political force within American life. After Watergate, however, the scope of investigative journalism broadened and took on a more commercial slant. Journalists engaged in made-for-prime-time undercover efforts to reveal corporate and professional wrongdoing. Camera-toting journalists rode along with law enforcers and medical rescue missions. In addition, programmes in which guests reveal family problems, medical concerns, and personal relationships took over the airways. Other popular television programmes featured the interpersonal conflicts of children or adults, whether in competition or while living together communally. Programmes based on European models appeared in 2000, in which people lived in isolated settings with cameras trained on them twenty-four hours a day for extended periods. Because of television, events including the Clarence Thomas hearings, the O. J. Simpson murder trial, the impeachment trial of President William J. Clinton, and the deaths of Princess Diana and John F. Kennedy Jr., made the intimate lives of public figures and public officials everyone's business. Important ethical issues about the value of privacy and celebrity were raised by these developments. (A. L. Allen 1999*a,b,c,d*; Rosen 2000).

2. THE CONCEPTUAL ENTERPRISE

The enterprise of sustained conceptual analysis of privacy originated in the late 1960s and early 1970s in response to the societal developments just identified. The ethicists who undertook conceptual analysis sought to describe and define the meaning of the expression 'privacy', distinguishing it from other concepts, such as property, liberty, and secrecy. They also sought to define the value of privacy. Philosophers of the period often used the tools of ordinary language analysis associated with analytic philosophy's normative branches. Judith Thomson's article 'The Right to Privacy' (1975) is an apt example. In addition to normative concerns, philosophers explored Wittgensteinian, epistemic, and ontological privacy concerns, such as whether and how language or thought can be private (J. W. Cook 1965; A. Kenny 1966; Temkin 1981; Castiligione 1984; Fiser 1986).

2.1 Definitional Analysis: What 'Privacy' Means

In the 1970s and 1980s, philosophical writings about privacy issuing from the academy were often definitional. Philosophers maintained that making the ordinary language or ideal definitions of privacy clear and explicit was a useful first step to addressing vexing questions of law, policy, and ethics.

The definitional literature is illuminating, although no one definition of 'privacy' gained universal acceptance. Nor was there consensus about what would constitute an adequate definition. A number of critical surveys assessed attempts to define 'privacy' (McCloskey 1971; O'Brien 1979; Gavison 1980; Parent 1983*a*; Schoeman 1984*a*; A. L. Allen 1988*b*). Some philosophers thought that to define 'privacy' they must isolate necessary and sufficient conditions of correct usage or of the truth of propositions predicating privacy (Gerety 1977; Velecky 1978). Others sought informal or stipulative definitions. They claimed that formal definition need not precede practical legal or ethical analysis (Schoeman 1984*b*; Tomkovicz 1985). Wacks (1980) argued that the persistent search for definition is sterile.

'Privacy' has been broadly and inadequately defined as 'being let alone'—after the fashion of Warren and Brandeis's popularization (1890) of a definition they attributed to Judge Thomas Cooley. Following Alan F. Westin (1967: 7), scholars and policy analysts frequently defined privacy as 'control over or exclusive possession of information'.

'Privacy' can denote much more than information management. Yet information (that is, data) control is a leading conception of privacy in the age of the Internet and World Wide Web. Control-based definitions of privacy preceded the Internet. On Paul Siegel's model (1984), 'privacy' refers to control over self-regarding conduct: control over 'stimulus input' and control over 'stimulus output'. Stimulus input is what persons receive through their five senses; stimulus output is what persons do or say. He went on to argue that the normative key to privacy's value is not human dignity, as many have claimed, but human control.

Richard Parker argued that privacy deals essentially with not being sensed by others. Richard Hallborg (1986) defined privacy as the condition of being unobserved when one is 'in private', and the right to privacy as the right not to be observed when one is in private. Hallborg's definition problematically precludes attaching 'privacy' to interests in solitude, seclusion, anonymity, and confidentiality, and persons arguably possess these even while strolling public streets and utilizing recreational and commercial facilities. Concerns about privacy in public places have mushroomed in recent years and have led to laws aimed at the paparazzi photographers who trail public figures.

In law, philosophy, and the social sciences, definitions of 'privacy' in which the concept of restricted access plays a central role became commonplace in the 1980s. According to Ruth Gavison (1980: 428), 'in perfect privacy no one has any information about X, no one pays any attention to X, and no one has physical access to X'. Indeed, it does appear that we can characterize what is meant by physical and informational privacy in terms of the inaccessibility of persons, their mental states, or information about them to the senses or surveillance devices of others. So conceived, privacy can function as an 'umbrella' concept, encompassing subordinate concepts, each of which denotes a particular form of limited accessibility to others. Such subordinate concepts plausibly include seclusion, solitude, anonymity, confidentiality, modesty, intimacy, reserve, and secrecy. However, it has been argued that some or all of these concepts are not reducible to forms of privacy. Friedrich (1971) maintained that privacy is a form of secrecy, rather than the other way around. Bok (1983) has argued that secrecy is the wholly distinct concept of intentional concealment; and Bellman (1981) that secrecy is a metaphor and refers to a different way of treating knowledge rather than a different concept of privacy. The proponent of a narrow definition of legal privacy as 'not having undocumented personal knowledge about oneself possessed by others', William Parent (1983a,c) was a critic of 'restricted-access' definitions. Parent's alternative conception of privacy has been rejected as arbitrarily narrow (DeCew 1986; A. L. Allen 1988b). A common concern raised by restricted access and control-based definitions is that they typically do not invoke the idea of intimacy that is presuppposed by much of what we say and think about privacy (Inness 1992; Boling 1996).

The philosophers who undertook conceptual analysis were persuaded that they had something to contribute to urgent practical endeavours, such as the adjudication of constitutional cases. Seeking to expose the implicit moral and political theories of a judiciary espousing fundamental privacy rights and reasonable expectations of privacy, philosophers sometimes argued that the courts perpetuate confused and mistaken definitions of privacy. Indeed, the philosophy literature of the 1970s, 1980s, and 1990s includes lively debates among philosophers about whether the courts ought to continue decisional and proprietary uses of privacy, alongside the paradigmatic informational and physical uses. Physical and informational privacy are at issue in discussions of, for example, intrusion into the home, employer access to e-mail, unwanted surveillance or publicity, and employer use of drug or polygraph testing. Proprietary privacy is at issue in discussions of publicity rights and control over human tissues and DNA. Decisional privacy is at issue in discussions of the right to die, abortion, and sodomy statutes. The decisional use of 'privacy' has been particularly controversial. Here 'privacy' refers chiefly, not to restricted access to the five senses or surveillance devices of others, but to an aspect of liberty or autonomy—freedom from governmental or other outside interference with decision making and conduct regarding 'private' affairs.

What counts in a society as 'private' has obvious cultural dimensions (Westin 1967; Moore 1984; Johnson and Crowley 1986). In the West, philosophers in the liberal tradition, including John Stuart Mill (1859) and Ronald Dworkin (1985), have defended interests in a domain of unrestrained self-regarding conduct. Joel Feinberg (1983), who wrote extensively about the nature of moral harm, defended privacy as an aspect of liberty meriting constitutional protection. A number of theorists maintain that the decisional usage of 'privacy' mistakenly conflates privacy with liberty (Ely 1974; Parent 1983a,b,c). McCloskey (1971) argued that privacy cannot be adequately characterized as a species of liberty, particularly since protecting privacy requires constraints on liberty. Some efforts to restrict the kinds of interests that are called privacy interests have been political efforts aimed at keeping controversial practices such as abortion and homosexuality within the purview of restrictive public regulation (DeCew 1986; A. L. Allen 1992).

2.2 Normative Analysis: Why 'Privacy' is Important

Definitions of privacy are often offered as a prelude to accounts of why privacy is important. Moral philosophers maintain that respecting the many forms of privacy is paramount for respect for human dignity and personhood, moral autonomy, and a workable community life. Commentators often say that the high moral value of privacy is the justification for legal rights of privacy.

Social science suggests that virtually every human culture protects privacy (Westin 1967; Altman 1977; Moore 1984). The importance of privacy is partly a matter of psychological health and comfort. Physical and informational privacy practices serve to limit observation and disclosure deemed inimical to well-being (Altman 1976). Psychologists have long emphasized the unhealthful effects of depriving individuals of opportunities for socially defined modes of privacy (C. Schneider 1977). The value of privacy in relation to religion and theology was considered in the 1980s (Johnstone 1984; Sutherland 1984). At least one philosopher explored questions about the normative meaning of human privacy in the face of an omniscient God (Lackey 1984).

The many accounts of privacy's positive, affirmative value found in the literature can be grouped into several broad categories, as follows: (1) intrinsic value accounts; (2) reductionist accounts; (3) personhood creation and enhancement accounts; (4) relationship creation and enhancement accounts; (5) functionalist accounts. Accounts of types (3), (4), and (5) are by far the most common.

First, seemingly implausible intrinsic value accounts maintain that privacy has inherent or unanalysable value. These have been more often criticized (McCloskey 1971; Gavison 1980; Allen 1988*b*) than defended. Secondly, reductionist accounts, such as Judith Thomson's (1975), hold that the value of privacy can be understood by reference to other familiar values.

Thirdly, personhood-creation and personhood-enhancement accounts are especially popular with moral philosophers. These emphasize the value of privacy in relation to deontological norms of personhood and moral agency. Privacy is sometimes said to promote individuality, independent moral judgement, and the formation of self-concept (Kupfer 1987). For instance, Jeffrey Reiman defined 'privacy' as 'a social ritual by means of which an individual's moral title to his own existence is conferred' (1976: 39), while Benn (1971) claimed that privacy promotes respect for persons. Most commentators applaud Benn's account, but it has had noteworthy critics (McCloskey 1971; Hudson and Husak 1979). McCloskey doubted that there are sufficient empirical grounds for maintaining that privacy promotes personhood. Hudson and Husak denied that the principle of respect for persons could itself require privacy protection or give rise to particular privacy rights. However, Benn did not argue, as the criticism implies, that a general principle of respect grounds *indefeasible* moral or legal privacy rights.

Fourthly, relationship-creation (Fried 1968, 1970; Gernstein 1970, 1978) and relationship-enhancement (Rachels 1975) accounts stress the respects in which privacy promotes desirable social relations. Relationship creation/enhancement theories are sometimes ancillaries rather than alternatives to personhood creation/enhancement theories. Opportunities for privacy enables us to keep some persons at a distance so that we can enjoy intense intimacy with others, including friends, families, and spouses.

Fifthly, liberal functionalist accounts, exemplified by Westin (1967) and Gavison (1980), ascribe instrumental value to privacy corresponding to its many functions promoting the diverse interests of individuals, groups, and the state. Many philosophers point to the political morality of a limited, tolerant government as the moral basis of privacy rights against government control of sexuality, reproduction, and health care (Richards 1986). They say that a function of privacy is to make a certain kind of political community—a liberal, tolerant, non-discriminatory one—possible. Non-liberal functionalists reject pervasive liberal conceptions of privacy, but emphasize the significance of privacy otherwise understood for promoting norms of civility, democratic citizenship, and the common good (Sandel 1996; Etzioni 1999). Another functional value of privacy, this one stressed by economic theorists, is promoting efficiency through exclusive access to information needed to reward and further commercial enterprises.

Most defenders of privacy recognize that privacy is not an unqualified good and that privacy values may conflict with other important values. Several authors have attempted to defend privacy against claims that it is immoral or inconsistent with egalitarian modes of intimacy, family, or community (Weinstein 1971; Louch 1982; Boone 1983). A common theme in the defence of privacy is that privacy is a social as well as an individual good, and that privacy can be made consistent with regard for aggregate life and social responsibility. To take one example, philosophers have examined the consequences of the 'private' status of the family for moral education and equal opportunity (H. Cohen 1978; Fishkin 1983; Blits 1985; Montague 1988). Schoeman (1987) argued that children have individual moral privacy rights whose legal enforcement is not fundamentally at odds with desirable forms of family privacy and parental control. The truth of this is suggested by the US Children's Online Privacy Protection Act (2000), which requires parents to give consent before commercial web-site operators can collect personal data from children under 13. Parents function as guardians of young children's informational privacy. Teen privacy rights are more of a problem, where the law allows them full independent exercise. Many have argued otherwise in the context of teen abortion, but Schoeman concluded that the recognition of confidentiality rights for adolescents seeking professional medical or educational services does not undermine the intimacy of the parent–child relationship, but rather supports ideals of respect and love. One way to express love is by allowing and supporting independence.

2.3 Negative Critiques

Section 2.2 emphasized the analytic-style normative philosophical literature of the 1970s and early 1980s, which offered subtle accounts of the *positive* aspects of privacy from liberal points of view emphasizing personal autonomy, choice and individual rights. In the 1980s and 1990s, accounts of *negative* aspects of privacy accompanied both challenges to analytic methods of philosophy and critiques of liberalism from feminists, left-progressives, communitarians, and civic republicans.

Critics of liberalism say that the theory rests on an incorrigibly problematic distinction between public and private. Indeed, the public/private distinction is something of a myth (Radest 1979). The concept of privacy is sometimes depicted, however, as much more than a benign myth. Feminists charge that privacy rights are most often understood in the liberal tradition as strong, individual rights to freedom from government and community interference. Such rights would appear to obligate authorities and neighbours to turn a blind eye to the victimization—such as domestic violence—that takes place behind closed doors (Elshtain 1981; Okin 1982; MacKinnon 1984).

Sociologist Amitai Etzioni (1999: 7) offers a communitarian critique of US law: that 'immoderate champions of privacy have . . . engaged in rhetorical excesses [with] . . . significant and detrimental effects'. Those effects including 'delaying for years needed public actions by bottling them up in the courts'; blocking 'the introduction of other needed public policies', and having 'a chilling effect on the consideration of other public policies that would advance the public good'. To illustrate his points he argues that privacy advocates blocked HIV testing of newborns, opposed laws to alert communities when convicted child molesters move into the neighbourhood, blocked efforts to institute national ID cards or other identifiers, and opposed mandatory government access to encryption keys.

The rhetoric of 'fundamental rights' and 'sacred' rights of privacy found in US law invites communitarian criticism. But the appearance of such rhetoric in several landmark cases belies the courts' typical insistence upon balancing privacy interests in the name of national security, crime control, business needs, public health, the news, free speech, and administrative convenience. Moreover, the protection of some forms of privacy surely promote the common interest. Etzioni implicitly concedes this when he argues that medical records deserve more privacy than they get under current policy and practice.

From a civic republican perspective, Michael Sandel (1996) condemned the liberal reasoning found in privacy law. The liberal strain in constitutional decisions treats privacy rights as autonomy rights to individual self-determination. An older and more 'republican' vision of privacy, Sandel argued, sees privacy rights as rights that allow persons to flourish in families, intimate relationships, and communities that are constitutive of their identities. Sandel's critics worry that his attempt to revive the older, more republican understanding of privacy leaves us without a vocabulary for transforming oppressive and subordinating modes of traditional family and community life (Rosenblum 1998).

The left progressive critique, commonly forged by the critical legal studies movement, critical race theory, and feminist legal theory in the USA in the 1970s, 1980s, and 1990s, is founded on the general critique of the public/private distinction within liberal jurisprudence. First, it is unclear what ought to be classified as 'public' and what as 'private'. Privacy is incoherent, or at least indeterminate (Kennedy 1982; Peller 1985; Mensch and Freeman 1987). Family life is highly regulated by public law.

Marriage laws, divorce laws, child abuse and neglect laws, education requirements, adoption strictures—all these make the so-called private sphere a matter of public scrutiny and control. Left progressives warn that legal privacy rights cannot function as secure protections against intrusion in personal affairs. Secondly, government and other powerful elements within society interpret privacy as a negative liberty and use 'privacy' as an excuse for neglect of the interests of victims of those affairs. *DeShaney* v. *Winnebago Department of Social Services* (1989) exemplifies the liberal abrogation of collective responsibility for what are constructed as individual choices. A majority on the Supreme Court in the *DeShaney* case agreed that state government is not responsible for the consequences of its negligent failure to remove a child from the custody of his physically abusive father whose beatings led to irreversible brain damage. Thirdly, the quest for privacy is a quest for isolation and unaccountability that contradicts the inescapable social and spiritual nature of the self, and that is inimical to community flourishing (A. Cook 1990).

3. THE FEMINIST ENTERPRISE

The second enterprise, rooted in the politics of the 1960s, but flourishing in the academy in the 1980s and 1990s, is feminism. Feminist philosophers have focused on the relevance of privacy to egalitarian justice, explored the public/private distinction, advocated legal privacy rights to reproductive services, and often engaged in conceptual analysis and policy analysis. Anita Allen (1988b), for example, combined conceptual analysis, policy analysis and feminist analysis.

Theories of privacy and the private sphere have been one of the central contributions of feminist philosophy. In feminist theory, 'privacy' typically connotes the female predicament of domesticity—a set of social expectations for a life centred on home and family suggested but not strictly required by reproductive capacities. Some feminists view the concept of privacy as having an inherently conservative valence in the Western liberal societies, where it has had the greatest currency (Allen and Mack 1991). Feminists commonly argue that ideologies of 'privacy' have slowed the growth of the laws beneficial to vulnerable classes of women (Olsen 1989). The banner of privacy is said to wave away public intervention needed to address customary standards of behaviour that led to female under-participation in society outside the home and to male domination and violence behind closed doors. Feminist activists promulgated the slogan that 'the personal is political', to make the point that wrongs formerly shielded inside the male-dominated private sphere should be brought to light to collective redress.

While many women in the USA enjoy independent and egalitarian lifestyles, this was not always the case. Some women still lack basic equalities. Viewed historically, homes and families have been domains of power and privilege for men, particularly for men of economic means or social standing. Until the late twentieth century, Western law and custom allowed men to govern their household with a degree of freedom from outside interference rarely shared by women. For dependent children, servants, and slaves, the control exercised by male heads of household was nearly complete, in practice, if not in law.

Feminist philosophy has emphasized the inequality, subordination, and oppression that can exist in homes and families. Subject to the sovereignty of public political authority but themselves sovereigns over wives and children and other dependents, men easily subordinate others. The resultant 'patriarchy' is an oppressive society, in which many lead unfulfilled lives, vulnerable to unchecked abuse and domestic violence. Legal feminism has shared the concerns of philosophical feminism. Leading feminist legal theorists equate traditional ideas of privacy with barriers to escaping domestic confinement, traditional roles, and violence. Some legal feminists have argued that ideals of isolation, independence, autonomy, or individualism conflict with the reality women experience and obstruct egalitarian social justice (MacKinnon 1984). Women are not autonomous in the way men are. Child bearing, breast feeding, and heterosexual sex connect women physically and psychologically to others (West 1988). Other feminists claim that ideals of ethical care, compassion, and community responsibility—not privacy—dominate women's lives.

Many legal feminists blame the emphasis on privacy in abortion law for the failure of legal efforts to secure government funding for poor women's abortions (Olsen 1989; Colker 1992). Even pro-choice liberals sometimes oppose government funding for poor women's 'elective' abortions. For some, it is self-evident that a privacy right is not something the public should have to pay for. Philosophers have argued that the right to privacy, recognized by US courts, is a negative right *against* government decision making respecting procreation, not as a positive right *to* governmental programmes designed to make contraception and abortion services available (Sher 1982).

Though essentially sound, the feminist condemnation of privacy has been too categorical. The longing for personal, quiet time and personal decision making can linger long after the grip of patriarchy over women is loosened. While the quest for privacy can be isolating, it can also be rejuvenating in ways that make people more fit and ready for their roles in the family and community (Boone 1983). Feminists do not need to reject the language of public and private or the broad principles of inaccessibility, control and decisional autonomy that undergird privacy rights (McClain 1998). The lines between public and private are 'socially constructed', and as such they must be redrawn as necessary to further dignity, safety, and equality. Feminism rightly calls for a vigilant, critical stance towards whatever wears the privacy label. Feminists have good reason to be critical of what privacy has meant for women in the past, and what the rhetoric and jurisprudence of privacy rights can signal for the future. At the same time, one can see that women seeking greater control over their lives have already begun to benefit from heightened social respect for many forms of decisional privacy.

4. THE POLICY ANALYSIS ENTERPRISE

Privacy-related policy analysis commenced in the 1970s, alongside and in combination with the afore-discussed conceptual enterprise. The 'applied' philosophers who engaged in policy analysis were concerned about the precise roles accorded respect for privacy in law, government, medicine, and journalism. Applied philosophers sometimes combined conceptual analysis with policy analysis, by first clarifying the idea and value of privacy, and then making specific proposals for, for example, constitutional adjudication or medical ethics. The discussion of privacy in Bok's book *Secrecy* (1983) is a good example of policy analysis complemented by conceptual analysis.

4.1 Diverse Policy Domains

Concerns about privacy are pervasive in many policy contexts other than the one I will highlight—new technologies. Other key contexts include criminal justice and law enforcement, employment, business practices, journalism, and bioethics. In criminal justice and law enforcement, the justice of mandatory DNA testing and the use of thermal imaging technologies are but two of the recent policy questions that have found their way into American courts. A few philosophers have focused on privacy concerns raised by employment policies and practices. It has been argued that routine use of polygraphing violates the privacy rights of job applicants and employees. It has been argued that some uses of routine drug and alcohol testing unreasonably invade privacy. Smoking bans and dating restrictions also raise privacy concerns. Psychological testing raises privacy concerns, as do the increasing common practices of video surveillance and e-mail monitoring of employees. The ubiquity of computer use in the workplace has been of major concern to privacy watchdogs. Employers have access to the content of employee e-mail generated on network computers. Employers also have the capacity to store e-mail messages indefinitely and to track employee's Internet use generally, including all of the web sites they have visited. To complicate matters, employers have a legal right and responsibility to engage in some degree of e-mail monitoring to detect employee wrongdoing and productivity.

Privacy concerns are raised by the practice of retailers of using cameras, sometimes hidden cameras, to deter and detect shoplifting in fitting rooms and sexual encounters in bathrooms. Businesses also engage in credit checking and reporting practices that have implications for personal privacy. The US Fair Credit Reporting Act beneficially regulates such practices. A recent US statute, Title V of the Financial Services Modernization Act ('Gramm-Leach-Bliley'), requires banks, insurance companies, and investment firms to adopt privacy policies and to notify customers about those policies in writing. Another recent statute, the Health Insurance Porta-bility and Accountability Act, led to detailed regulations for the health-care industry mandating the security and privacy of medical records.

The non-consensual disclosure of the video movie rentals of Judge Robert Bork led Congress to enact the Video Privacy Protection Act. World Wide Web-based businesses collect vast amounts of personal information from Internet users seek-ing to make purchases or engage in other transactions (Bennett and Grant 1996). Airline companies, for example, collect names, addresses, credit card information, and travel plans and preferences. Book sellers collect telling information of the sort just described and, in addition, information about reading tastes. These can reveal ideological allegiances and personal preferences deemed personal and private. The US Federal Trade Commission has urged Congress to adopt statutes regulating per-sonal information on the Internet. Thus far, Congress has responded only with legis-lation related to children's privacy on line.

Contemporary journalism has been under fire for what many believe are egre-gious invasions of privacy. Yet the Code of Ethics promulgated by the Society of Professional Journalists exhorts members to avoid 'intrusion into anyone's privacy'. Although the code asserts the vital importance of the public's right to know, it also demands the protection of privacy. The code requires journalists to 'Recognize that gathering and reporting information may cause harm or discomfort'. After an instruction that journalists 'Recognize that private people have a greater right to control information about themselves than do public officials and others who seek power, influence or attention', the code observes that 'Only an overriding public need can justify intrusion into anyone's privacy'. This statement could be read to say that journalists must give presumptive priority to protecting privacy.

Is respect for privacy an appropriate ethical imperative for journalists? While few philosophers have taken on the ethics of journalism, it is an area ripe for analysis and enquiry. One might argue that journalism should stand for openness, trans-parency, and accountability, and for the 'public's right to know' rather than for privacy. The public's rights to know arguably include: the right to monitor govern-ment, public officials, political candidates, public figures, and businesses receiving government aid or affecting the public welfare conduct.

It is now a common practice for policy-makers and policy analysts to consider the privacy implications of competing public policies. Ethicists and bioethicists, like other policy analysts, evaluate policies in part by reference to how well they respect personal privacy. For example, one of the major focuses of discussions of the ethi-cal, legal, and social implications of the human genome project has been the impli-cations of genetic research for personal privacy. Recent proposals to standardize and digitize medical records have raised concerns about medical informational privacy, as did the move to managed care.

Philosophers have actively participated in the policy debates about decisional privacy, for example, in the abortion debate. Some philosophers are persuaded that the humanity of the fetus made life, rather than the privacy of the mother, the overriding consideration for shaping legal policy. Others are persuaded that, because the unborn are contained in the body of women, privacy should control the direction of policy, vesting the right to decide the fate of the unborn in the hands of pregnant women, not the state. Philosophers have also embraced wildly different stances on assisted suicide and the right to die. Some philosophers have urged as a matter of individual or family privacy that decisions about sustaining the life of persons in hopeless comas or suffering from terminal illnesses be left to patients and their intimates rather than to physicians, hospital staff, or the state. Privacy has also been cited in debates over decision making about the care of newborns born with severe abnormalities, and in the debates over prenatal testing and surrogate mothers.

4.2 New Technology

Ongoing developments in surveillance, communications, and, especially, computer technologies are spawning discussions about the humanistic significance of privacy and just approaches to its regulation. The ethicists who are entering this arena of policy analysis are undertaking debates about the possibility and desirability of traditional notions of privacy in the age of the video camera, cell phone, and the Internet. Judith Wagner DeCew's book *In Pursuit of Privacy: Law, Ethics, and the Rise of Technology* (1997) addresses the privacy implications of some of the new technologies, and also contains conceptual, policy, and feminist analyses. The interdisciplinary essays in *Technology and Privacy: The New Landscape* (Agre and Rotenberg 1997) include conceptual and policy analysis.

We confront daily technology-aided assaults on individual informational privacy perpetrated by governments, corporations, and the media. The courts have held that many aggressive and invasive journalistic practices must be permitted in the name of First Amendment freedom of the press and the public's right to know. The growth of the Internet has brought about a range of concerns about the fate of personal privacy. One concern is that government records containing personal information will appear on line, facilitating stalking, unwanted commercial solicitation, and identity theft. E-commerce—business conducted through the World Wide Web—requires that consumers yield personal information. Personal information must be provided to merchants to ensure identity and financial responsibility. E-businesses request and use personal information to target advertising to customers based on established patterns of Internet use and stated preferences. Privacy concerns raised by e-commerce are about both overt information-gathering practices and the often covert data collection though 'cookies', serial number detection and government or employer monitoring of e-mail and web browsing. All of these practices raise ethical concerns for public and private policy-makers.

As a society, we also confront voluntary abrogation of traditions of domestic privacy and modesty. Exhibitionism and indifference to privacy are a fixture of popular culture. People stroll about public places engaged in cellular telephone calls about intimate details of their lives. Television, radio, and cyberspace are domains in which ordinary individuals, performers, and professionals voluntarily share vast amounts of personal information with viewing and listening audiences. Confessional programmes, documentary-style programmes, and new journalism project the intimate lives of willing (and unwilling) subjects into the public arena. Television programmes and web sites that allow audiences to follow closely the daily lives of previously anonymous men and women are popular in the USA and other countries. The ethics and the etiquette of privacy are raised by these developments.

Fair Information Practices

Privacy advocates have urged that those who must collect personal information should avoid collecting information that segments of the public are likely to deem especially personal, such as social security numbers, health and genetic information, family financial information, and information about sexual orientation, religion, and race. Privacy advocates also call for businesses and government to commit themselves to standards that have come to be known as 'fair information practices'. Under typical models of fair information practices, these standards should be met to the extent possible.

1. The existence of data systems containing personal information should not be a secret.
2. Personal information should be collected only for narrow, specific purposes.
3. Personal information should be used only in ways that are similar to and consistent with the primary purposes for its collection.
4. Personal information should be collected only with the informed consent of the persons about whom the information is collected or their legal representative.
5. Personal information should not be shared with third parties without notice or consent.
6. For the sake of accuracy and relevancy, the duration of storage of personal information should be limited.
7. Individuals should have access to personal information about themselves and should be permitted to correct errors.
8. Those who collect personal data should ensure the security and integrity of personal data and systems.

Little analysis has been undertaken of what makes fair information practices 'fair'. In any case, holding business and government to what are termed fair information practices, and holding journalists to consensual privacy protection standards, do not erase ethical concerns about privacy. The anonymous and libertarian realm of cyberspace is proving to be a domain in which women and minorities are vulnerable to actual and virtual privacy abuses perpetrated by fellow users, chatters, and game-players (Brin 1998; Dibbell 1998; Kang 1998; Wallace 1999; Wertheim 1999; A. L. Allen 2000). Civility norms mindful of the injurious nature of boundary crossing in cyberspace are needed.

Defining Privacy for Cyberspace

The conceptual questions philosophers asked about privacy in the 1970s are being asked again, this time in direct response to concerns about data protection in cyberspace. What is privacy, why is it important, and what does respect for privacy require of us? Yet even before the development of cyberspace, one of the most quoted definitions of privacy was Alan Westin's (1967), equating privacy with control over information. Westin wrote of the 'claim of individuals, groups or institutions to determine for themselves when, how, and to what extent information about them is communicated to others'. Since definitions of privacy vary with purposes for definition, theorists have defined privacy in terms of control to complement their generally liberal views that just government and ideal social practices should promote individual control over personal data. A communitarian critic of liberalism and liberal conceptions of privacy might also define privacy as individual control over personal information, for purposes of emphasizing the privacy sacrifices demanded of participation in responsible communities.

The conception that privacy is essentially about maintaining control over personal data seems tailor made for cyberspace (Cavoukian and Tapscott 1997: 9; Berman and Mulligan 1999). Three claims about control of personal information are pervasive in discussions of privacy in cyberspace: (1) that the term 'privacy' *means* control (or rights of control) over the use of personal data or information; (2) that the expression 'right to privacy' *means* the right or claim to control the use of personal data or information; and (3) that the central aim of privacy regulation should be promoting individuals' control (or rights of control) over personal data or information. The three claims about control of personal information form a kind of paradigm in the significant sense that, individually and as a group, they cohere with liberal moral, political, and legal perspectives that emphasize wide sway for individual autonomy (A. L. Allen 2000).

'Privacy' can mean informational privacy, but also physical, decisional, and proprietary privacy. As a stipulative definition or a description of what many people worry about in the context of online communications, however, 'data control' has appeal. However, even for purposes of discussing issues in cyberspace, there are good reasons for rejecting the privacy-as-data-control paradigm.

To begin with, control over personal data is neither necessary nor sufficient for states of privacy to obtain. The person in control of her data might elect to share personal information with others. In 1999 a nurse chose to broadcast her double mastectomy live over the Internet, to educate the public about breast cancer. In 1998 a married woman chose to share the delivery of her third child with other expectant parents by delivering her baby live over the Internet.

Men and women have chosen to train 'Web cams' on the interiors of their dwellings and then sell or give away real-time images of their daily lives. While their cameras and computers broadcast images of them to others, they have no physical privacy to speak of, and others possess otherwise private information about their home life. Control is not sufficient for privacy, nor is it necessary. For example, 'a prison inmate locked in solitary confinement has privacy in the sense that he or she is often unobserved. But he or she has no control over personal information, since prison officials can initiate surveillance at will' (Schoeman 1984a: 3).

The privacy-as-data-control paradigm has practical limits. Internet users disclose a great deal of information when they purchase goods and services or send e-mail. Internet users do not control personal data to the extent that they do not understand all the ways their data can be collected from them as they travel in cyberspace and remain powerless to demand meaningful limits on third-party disclosures. Because of the unreliable and adhesive nature of privacy agreements, even people using sites that offer opportunities to pre-authorize or refuse data collection and third-party disclosures, or that give notice of such practices, do not really control personal information.

The privacy-as-data-control paradigm obscures the need for concern that people will want too little privacy, and also the concern that people will want too much privacy. A sense of moral responsibility for one's conduct and a desire for morally responsive public policies might lead to abandonment of enhancing individual data control as the central objective of privacy policy. For example, the demands of responsible employment place a moral limit on policies that might purport to give workers greater control over personal financial and health information. Moreover, our political obligations to our country and fellow citizens make that impossible. As James Rule and Lawrence Hunter have observed, 'if governments are expected to tax income or commerce . . . citizens can hardly expect control over information about their personal finances' (1996: 169–70). It would seem unwise to prohibit the constitutionally mandated decennial census-takers from collecting personal information about household income, welfare, social security, disaster relief, student loans, and so on.

Ethical qualms about the 'privacy-control' paradigm seem unavoidable, upon reflection. However, we ought not to adopt policies that compel us uncritically to yield personal data to every public and private sector actor who requests it. However, because personal information cannot and should not be completely controlled by individuals, it is both misleading and wrong to hold up 'privacy control' as such as a policy aim. Something very different and more complex than data control is the realistic aim of e-commere and marketing privacy policies. Precisely defining this 'something very different' is one of the most challenging tasks on the table for privacy theorists. Professor Amitai Etzioni (1999) concluded that policy-makers need to balance individual and entity interests in light of the common good. Paul Schwartz (2000) tries to get at this alternative to data control when he points to the need to think of privacy constitutively and to understand that respect for privacy requires contextual line-drawing. Privacy should be available, but well-ordered societies must require moral accountability.

5. CONCLUSION

Where, then, do the three enterprises stand? The conceptual enterprise remains vital, at least in its normative dimension. There is little demand for highly technical definitions of 'privacy'; but the demand for clear, persuasive accounts of the value of privacy is great. The feminist enterprise remains vital, too. Feminist scholars continue to refine and build on their signature critiques of privacy and the public/private distinction. The policy analysis enterprise is in its heyday. Privacy is important, but so, too, are public health and safety, efficient, accountable government, the free press, and freedom from terrorism. Philosophers can make useful, important contributions to the task of articulating just and ethical ascriptions of privacy rights.

REFERENCES

Adler, Shelden (1978). 'Toward a Constitutional Theory of Individuality: The Privacy Opinions of Justice Douglas'. *Yale Law Journal*, 87: 1579–600.

Agre, Philip E., and Rotenberg, Marc (1997) (eds.), *Technology and Privacy: The New Landscape*. Cambridge, MA: MIT Press.

Alderman, Ellen, and Kennedy, Caroline (1995). *The Right to Privacy*. New York: Random House.

Allen, Anita L. (1983). 'Women and Privacy, What is at Stake?', in Carol Gould (ed.), *Beyond Domination*. Totowa, NJ: Rowman & Allanheld.

—— (1987a). 'Rethinking the Rule against Corporate Privacy Rights: Some Conceptual Quandries for the Common Law'. *John Marshall Law Review*, 20: 607–39.

—— (1987b). 'Taking Liberties: Privacy, Private Choice and Social Contract Theory'. *University of Cincinnati Law Review*, 56: 461–91.

—— (1988a). 'Privacy, Surrogacy and the *Baby M* Case'. *Georgetown Law Journal*, 76: 1759–92.

—— (1988b). *Uneasy Access: Privacy for Women in a Free Society*. Totowa, NJ: Rowman & Littlefield.

—— (1991). 'Tribe's Judicious Feminism'. *Stanford Law Review*, 44: 179–203.

Allen, Anita L. (1992). 'Autonomy's Magic Wand: Abortion Law and Constitutional Interpretation'. *Boston University Law Review*, 72: 693–8.

——(1995). 'The Proposed Equal Protection Fix for Abortion Law: Reflections on Citizenship, Gender and the Constitution'. *Harvard Journal of Law and Public Policy*, 18: 419–55.

——(1996). 'Constitutional Privacy', in Dennis Patterson (ed.), *A Companion to Philosophy of Law and Legal Theory*. Oxford: Blackwell, 139–55.

——(1996). 'The Jurispolitics of Privacy', in Uma Narayan and Molly Shanley (eds.), *Reconstructing Political Theory*. Cambridge: Polity, 68–83.

——(1997). 'Genetic Privacy: Emerging Concepts and Values', in Mark Rothstein (ed.), *Genetic Secrets*. New Haven: Yale University Press, 31–59.

——(1998). 'Privacy', in Iris Young and Alison Jaggar (eds.), *A Companion to Feminist Philosophy*. Oxford: Blackwell, 456–65.

——(1999*a*). 'Coercing Privacy'. *William and Mary Law Review*, 40: 723–57.

——(1999*b*). 'Lying to Protect Privacy'. *Villanova Law Review*, 44: 161–88.

——(1999*c*). 'Privacy and the Public Official: Talking about Sex as a Dilemma for Democracy'. *George Washington Law Review*, 67: 1165–82.

——(2000). 'Gender, Privacy and Cyberspace'. *Stanford Law Review*, 52: 11–57.

——and Mack, Erin (1991). 'How Privacy Got its Gender'. *Northern Illinois Law Review*, 10: 441–71.

Allen, Francis A. (1984) '1984: The End of Intimacy: How Private Values and Private Lives are Threatened by the New Technology'. *Human Rights*, 11: 22.

Alschuler, Albert (1971). 'A Different View of Privacy'. *Texas Law Review*, 49: 872–82.

Altman, Irwin (1976). 'Privacy: A Conceptual Analysis'. *Environment and Behavior*, 8: 7–30.

——(1977). 'Privacy Regulation: Culturally Universal or Culturally Specific?' *Journal of Social Issues*, 33/3: 66–84.

American Law Institute (1926), *Restatement (Second) Torts*. Sections 652B, C, D, E.

Anderson, David (1999). 'The Failure of American Privacy Law', in Basil S. Markesinis (ed.), *Protecting Privacy*. Oxford: Oxford University Press, 139–68.

Andre, Judith (1986). 'Privacy as a Value and as a Right'. *Journal of Value Inquiry*, 20: 309–17.

Arendt, Hannah (1958). *The Human Condition*. Chicago: University of Chicago Press.

Baer, Judith (1999). *Our Lives before the Law: Constructing a Feminist Jurisprudence*. Princeton: Princeton University Press.

Bates, Alan (1964). 'Privacy—a Useful Concept?' *Social Forces*, 42: 429–33.

Bazelon, David (1978). 'Probing Privacy'. *Georgia Law Review*, 12: 589.

Beany, William (1962). 'The Constitutional Right to Privacy in the Supreme Court'. *Supreme Court Review*, 1962: 216.

——(1966). 'The Right to Privacy and American Law'. *Law and Contemporary Problems*, 31: 253–71.

Beardsley, Elizabeth L. (1971). 'Privacy: Autonomy and Selective Disclosure', in J. Roland Pennock and John W. Chapman (eds.), *Privacy: Nomos XIII*. New York: Atherton Press, 56–70.

Bellman, Beryl (1981). 'The Paradox of Secrecy'. *Human Studies*, 4: 1–24.

Benn, Stanley I. (1971). 'Privacy, Freedom and Respect for Persons', in J. Roland Pennock and John W. Chapman (eds.), *Privacy: Nomos XIII*. New York: Atherton Press, 1–26.

——(1980). 'Privacy and Respect for Persons: A Reply'. *Australasian Journal of Philosophy*, 58: 54–61.

—— (1988). *A Theory of Freedom*. Cambridge: Cambridge University Press.

Bennett, Colin, and Grant, Rebecca (1996) (eds.), *Visions of Privacy: Policy Choices for the Digital Age*. Toronto: University of Toronto Press.

Berman, Jerry, and Mulligan, Dierdre (1999). 'Privacy in the Digital Age: Work in Progress'. *Nova Law Review*, 23: 551–82.

Berners-Lee, Tim (1999). *Weaving the Web*. San Francisco: Harper.

Berns, Walter (1979). 'Privacy, Liberalism and the Role of Government', in Robert C. Cunningham (ed.), *Liberty and the Rule of Law*. College Station, TX: A & M University Press, 182–223.

Bien, Joseph (1980). 'Dewey and Marx, Two Notions of Community'. *Philosophy Today*, 24: 318–24.

Blaustein, Albert P., and Flanz, Gisbert H. (1994). *Constitutions of the Countries of the World: A Series of Updated Texts, Constitutional Chronologies and Annotated Bibliographies*. Dobbs Ferry, NY: Oceana Publications, Inc.

Blits, Jan H. (1985). 'Privacy and Public Moral Education: Aristotle's Critique of the Family'. *Educational Theory*, 35: 225–38.

Bloustein, Edward J. (1964). 'Privacy as an Aspect of Human Dignity: An Answer to Dean Prosser'. *New York University Law Review*, 39: 962–1007.

—— (1978). *Individual and Group Privacy*. New Brunswick, NJ: Transaction Books.

Bohn, Robert J. (1984). 'Recommendations of the Task Force on Privacy Human Sexuality, and Sex Education for Developmentally Disabled Persons'. *Journal Medical Humanities and Bioethics*, 5: 6–26.

Bok, Sissela (1983). *Secrets: On the Ethics of Concealment and Revelation*. New York: Pantheon Books.

Boling, Patricia (1996). *Privacy and the Politics of Intimate Life*. Ithaca, NY: Cornell University Press.

Boone, C. Keith (1983). 'Privacy and Community'. *Social Theory and Practice*, 9: 1–30.

Bostwick, Gary L. (1976). 'A Taxonomy of Privacy: Repose, Sanctuary, and Intimate Decision'. *California Law Review*, 64: 1447–83.

Brenkert, George G. (1981). 'Privacy, Polygraphs and Work'. *Business and Professional Ethics Journal*, 1: 19–36.

Brin, David (1998). *The Transparent Society: Will Technology Force Us to Choose between Privacy and Freedom*. Reading, MA: Addison-Wesley.

Bryant, Christopher (1978). 'Privacy, Privatization, and Self-Determination', in John Young (ed.), *Privacy*. Chichester, NY: Wiley.

Buss, Arnold (1980). *Self-Consciousness and Social Anxiety*. San Francisco: W. H. Freeman.

Castiglione, Robert L. (1984). 'Paul Weiss' Privacy: The Rediscovery of Human Being'. *Philosophy Today*, 28: 20–35.

Cavoukian, Ann, and Tapscott, Don (1997). *Who Knows: Safeguarding your Privacy in a Networked World*. New York: McGraw Hill.

Clark, Lorenne M. G. (1978). 'Privacy, Property, Freedom and the Family', in Richard Bronaugh (ed.), *Philosophical Law*. Westport, CT: Greenwood Press.

Cohen, Howard (1978). 'Children and Privacy', in Richard Bronaugh (ed.), *Philosophical Law*. Westport, CT: Greenwood Press

Cohen, Julie E. (1996). 'A Right to Read Anonymously'. *Connecticut Law Review*, 28: 981–1040.

Colker, Ruth (1989). 'Feminism, Theology, and Abortion: Toward Love, Compassion, and Wisdom'. *California Law Review*, 77: 1011–75.

Colker, Ruth (1992). *Abortion and Dialogue: Pro-Choice, Pro-Life, and American Law*. Bloomington, IN: Indiana University Press.

Cook, Anthony (1990). 'Beyond Critical Legal Studies: The Reconstructive Theology of Dr Martin Luther King, Jr.', *Harvard Law Review*, 103: 985–1044.

Cook, John W. (1965). 'Wittgenstein on Privacy'. *Philosophical Review*, 74: 281–314.

Davidson, David M., and Kunkel, Jean A. (1983). 'The Developing Methodology for Analyzing Privacy Torts'. *Hastings Journal of Communications and Entertainment Law (Comm/Ent)*, 6: 43–90.

Davis, Frederick (1959). 'What do we mean by "Right to Privacy"?' *San Diego Law Review*, 4: 1.

DeCew, Judith Wagner (1986). 'The Scope of Privacy in Law and Ethics'. *Law and Philosophy*, 52: 145–73.

——(1987). 'Defending the "Private" in Constitutional Privacy'. *Journal of Value Inquiry*, 21: 171–84.

——(1997). *In Pursuit of Privacy: Law, Ethics, and the Rise of Technology*. Ithaca, NY: Cornell University Press.

Derlega, Valerian J., and Chaikin, Alan L. (1977). 'Privacy and Self-Disclosure in Social Relationships'. *Journal of Social Issues*, 33: 102–15.

Dibble, Julian (1998). *My Tiny Life: Crime and Passion in a Virtual World*. New York: Holt & Company.

Dionisopolous, P. A., and Ducat, C. (1976). *The Right to Privacy*. St Paul, MN: West Publishing Company.

Dixon, R. (1965). '*Griswold* Penumbra: Constitutional Charter for an Expanded Right of Privacy?' *Michigan Law Review*, 64: 197–218.

Dunlap, M. C. (1982). 'Toward Recognition of a "Right to be Sexual"'. *Harvard Women's Rights Law Reporter*, 7: 245.

Dworkin, Gerald (1978). 'Privacy and the Law', in John Young (ed.), *Privacy*. John Chichester, NY: Wiley.

——(1988). *The Theory and Practice of Autonomy*. Cambridge: Cambridge University Press.

Dworkin, Ronald (1985). *A Matter of Principle*. Cambridge, MA: Harvard University Press.

Eichbaum, June A. (1979). 'Towards an Autonomy-Based Theory of Constitutional Privacy: Beyond the Ideology of Familial Privacy'. *Harvard Civil Rights–Civil Liberties Law Review*, 14: 361–84.

Elshstain, Jean Bethke (1981). *Public Man, Private Woman*. Princeton: Princeton University Press.

Ely, John H. (1974). 'The Wages of Crying Wolf: A Comment on *Roe* v. *Wade*'. *Yale Law Journal*, 82: 920–49.

Emerson, Thomas (1979). 'The Right to Privacy and Freedom of the Press'. *Harvard Civil Rights–Civil Liberties Law Review*, 14: 329–60.

Epstein, Richard (1978). 'Privacy, Property Rights, and Misrepresentations'. *Georgia Law Review*, 12: 455–74.

——(1980). 'Taste for Privacy: Evolution and the Emergence of a Naturalistic Ethic'. *Journal of Legal Studies*, 9: 665–81.

Ernst, Morris, and Schwartz, Alan (1962) (eds.), *Privacy—the Right to Be Let Alone*. New York: Macmillan.

Etzioni, Amitai (1999). *The Limits of Privacy*. New York: Basic Books.

Feinberg, Joel (1983). 'Autonomy, Sovereignty, and Privacy: Moral Ideals in the Constitution?' *Notre Dame Law Review*, 58: 445–92.

Felkenes, George (1987). 'Ethics in the Graduate Criminal Justice Curriculum'. *Teaching Philosophy*, 10: 23–36.

Fiser, Karen, B. (1986). 'Privacy and Pain'. *Philosophical Investigations*, 9: 1–17.

Fishkin, James S. (1983). *Justice, Equal Opportunity, and the Family*. New Haven: Yale University Press.

Flaherty, David H. (1972). *Privacy in Colonial New England*. Charlottesville, VA: University Press of Virginia.

Foddy, W. H. (1984). 'A Critical Evaluation of Altman's Definition of Privacy as a Dialectic Process'. *Journal for the Theory of Social Behavior*, 14: 297–308.

Francis, W. S. (1982). 'Of Gossips, Eavesdroppers, and Peeping Toms'. *Journal of Medical Ethics*, 8: 134–43.

Freund, Paul A. (1971). 'Privacy: One Concept or Many?' in J. Roland Pennock and John W. Chapman (eds.), *Privacy: Nomos XIII*. New York: Atherton Press, 182–98.

Fried, Charles (1968). 'Privacy'. *Yale Law Journal*, 77: 475–93.

——(1970). *An Anatomy of Values*. Cambridge, MA: Harvard University Press.

Friedrich, Carl (1971). 'Secrecy versus Privacy: The Democratic Dilemma', in J. Roland Pennock and John W. Chapman (ed.), *Privacy: Nomos XIII*. New York: Atherton Press, 105–20.

Garrett, Roland (1974). 'The Nature of Privacy'. *Philosophy Today*, 18: 263–84.

Gavison, Ruth (1980). 'Privacy and the Limits of Law'. *Yale Law Journal*, 89: 421–71.

Gerety, Thomas (1977). 'Redefining Privacy'. *Harvard Civil Rights–Civil Liberties Law Review*, 12: 233–96.

Gernstein, Robert (1970). 'Privacy and Self-Incrimination'. *Ethics*, 80: 87–101.

——(1978). 'Intimacy and Privacy'. *Ethics*, 89: 76–81.

Gilman, Charlotte Perkins (1898/1986). *Women and Economics*. New York: Harper & Row.

Goldstein, Leslie Friedman (1981). 'A Critique of the Abortion Funding Decision: On Private Rights in the Public Sector'. *Hastings Constitutional Law Quarterly*, 8: 313–42.

Grcic, Joseph M. (1986). 'The Right to Privacy: Behavior as Property'. *Journal of Value Inquiry*, 20: 137–144.

Greenawalt, Kent (1974). 'Privacy and its Legal Protection'. *Hastings Center Studies*, 2: 45–68.

Gross, Hyman (1971). 'Privacy and Autonomy', in J. Roland Pennock and John W. Chapman (eds.), *Privacy: Nomos XIII*. New York: Atherton Press, 169–82.

Gross, Robert A. (1991). 'Public and Private in the Third Amendment'. *Valparaiso University Law Review*, 26: 215–21.

Gurak, Laura (1997). *Persuasion and Privacy in Cyberspace, On-line Protests over Lotus Marketplace and the Clipper Chip*. New Haven: Yale University Press.

Habermas, Jurgen (1989). *The Structural Transformation of the Public Sphere: An Inquiry into a Category of Bourgeois Society*. Cambridge, MA: MIT Press.

Hague, Aminul (1986). 'The Concept of Epistemic Privacy'. *Journal of Indian Council of Philosophical Research*, 3: 160–5.

Hallborg, Robert B., Jr. (1986). 'Principles of Liberty and the Right to Privacy'. *Law and Philosophy*, 52: 175–218.

Henkin, Louis (1974). 'Privacy and Autonomy'. *Columbia Law Review*, 74: 1410–33.

Hill, Afred (1976). 'Defamation and Privacy under the First Amendment'. *Columbia Law Review*, 76: 1205–313.

Hirschleifer, Jack (1980). 'Privacy, its Origins, Function, and Future'. *Journal of Legal Studies*, 9: 649–64.

Hofstadter, Samuel, and Horowitz, George (1964). *The Right of Privacy*. New York: Central Books.

Houdek, F. G. (1985). 'The Right of Publicity: A Comprehensive Bibliography of Law-Related Materials'. *Hastings Journal of Communications and Entertainment Law (Comm/Ent)*, 7: 505–25.

Hudson, Stephen D., and Husak, Douglas N. (1979). 'Benn on Privacy and Respect for Persons'. *Australasian Journal of Philosophy*, 57: 324–9.

Huff, Thomas (1980). 'Thinking Clearly about Privacy'. *Washington Law Review*, 55: 777–94.

Ingham, Roger (1978). 'Privacy and Psychology', in J. Young (ed.), *Privacy*. Chichester, NY: Wiley.

Inness, Julie C. (1992). *Privacy, Intimacy, and Isolation*. New York: Oxford University Press.

Jensen, Ejner J. (1984). 'Privacy and the Power of Art'. *University of Toledo Law Review*, 15: 437–47.

Johnson, Jeffrey L., and Crowley, Donald W. (1986). '*TLO* and the Student's Right to Privacy'. *Educational Theory*, 36: 211–24.

Johnstone, Brian V. (1984). 'The Right to Privacy: The Ethical Perspective'. *American Journal of Jurisprudence*, 29: 73–94.

Kalven, Harry (1966). 'Privacy in Tort Law: Were Warren and Brandeis Wrong?' *Law and Contemporary Problems*, 31: 326–41.

Kang, Jerry (1998). 'Information Privacy in Cyberspace Transactions'. *Stanford Law Review*, 50: 1193–294.

Karafiel, Emile (1978). 'The Right to Privacy and the *Sidis* Case'. *Georgia Law Review*, 12: 513–34.

Kelman, Herbert (1977). 'Privacy and Research on Human Beings'. *Journal of Social Issues*, 33/3: 169–95.

Kennedy, Duncan (1982). 'The Stages of the Decline of the Public–Private Distinction'. *University of Pennsylvania Law Review*, 130: 1349–57.

Kenny, Anthony (1966). 'Cartesian Privacy', in George Pitcher (ed.), *Wittgenstein: Philosophical Investigations*. Notre Dame, IN: University of Notre Dame Press, 352–70.

Kenny, D. J. (1982). 'Confidentiality: The Confusion Continues'. *Journal of Medical Ethics*, 8: 9–11.

Konvitz, Milton R. (1966). 'Privacy and the Law: A Philosophical Prelude'. *Law and Contemporary Problems*, 31: 272–80.

Kupfer, Joseph (1987). 'Privacy, Autonomy, and Self-Concept'. *American Philosophical Quarterly*, 24: 81–9.

Lackey, Douglas (1984). 'Divine Omniscience and Human Privacy'. *Philosophy Research Archives*, 10: 383–92.

Laufer, Robert, and Wolfe, Maxine (1977). 'Privacy as a Concept and a Social Issue: A Multidimensional Developmental Theory'. *Journal of Social Issues*, 33/3: 22–42.

Latin, Howard (1976). *Privacy: A Selected Bibliography and Topical Index of Social Science Materials*. South Hackensack, NJ: F. B. Rothman.

Little, Rory K. (1981). 'Protecting Privacy under the Fourth Amendment'. *Yale Law Journal*, 91: 313–43.

Long, E. V. (1967). *The Intruders: The Invasion of Privacy by Government and Industry*. New York: Praeger.

Losito, William F. (1980). 'An Ethical Theory for Privacy in Educational Contexts'. *Philosophy of Education*, 36: 236–44.

Louch, A. R. (1982). 'Is Privacy Immoral?' *Human Rights*, 10: 17.

McClain, Linda (1998). 'Toleration, Autonomy, and Governmental Promotion of Good Lives: Beyond "Empty" Toleration to Toleration as Respect'. *Ohio State Law Journal*, 59: 19–132.

—— (1992). 'The Poverty of Privacy'. *Columbia Journal of Gender and Law*, 3: 119–74.

McClellan, Grant S. (1976) (ed.), *The Right to Privacy*. New York: H. W. Wilson Co.

McCloskey, H. J. (1971). 'The Political Ideal of Privacy'. *Philosophical Quarterly*, 21: 303–14.

—— (1980). 'Privacy and the Right to Privacy'. *Philosophy*, 55: 17–38.

MacKinnon, Catharine (1984). '*Roe* v. *Wade*: A Study in Male Ideology', in Jay Garfield and Patricia Hennessey (eds.), *Abortion: Moral and Legal Perspectives*. Amherst: University of Massachusetts Press, 45–54.

—— (1987). *Feminism Unmodified: Discourses on Life and Law*. Cambridge, MA: Harvard University Press.

Mann, Steve (1998). 'Reflectionism and Diffusionism: New Tactics for Deconstructing the Video Surveillance Superhighway'. *Leonardo*, 31/2: 93–102.

Margulis, Stephen (1977). 'Conceptions of Privacy: Current Status and Next Steps'. *Journal of Social Issues*, 33/3: 5–21.

Masud, M. Khan R. (1974). *The Privacy of the Self, Papers on Psychoanalytic Theory and Technique*. New York: International Universities Press.

May, Larry (1980). 'Privacy and Property'. *Philosophy in Context*, 10: 40–53.

Mayer, Michael F. (1972). *Rights of Privacy*. New York: Law-Arts Publishers.

Mensch, Elizabeth, and Freeman, Allen (1987). 'The Public–Private Distinction in American Law and Life'. *Buffalo Law Review*, 36: 237–57.

Mill, John Stuart (1859). *On Liberty*, ed. Elizabeth Rapaport. Indianapolis: Hackett Publishing, 1978.

Miller, Arthur (1971). *The Assault on Privacy*. Ann Arbor: University of Michigan Press.

Mohr, Richard D. (1987). 'Why Sex is Private: Gays and the Police'. *Public Affairs Quarterly*, 1: 57–81.

Montague, Phillip (1988). 'A Child's Right to Privacy'. *Public Affairs Quarterly*, 2: 17–32.

Moore, Barrington (1984). *Privacy: Studies in Social and Cultural History*. Armonk, NY: M. E. Sharpe.

Morton, Andrew (1999). 'Much Ado about Newsgathering: Personal Privacy, Law Enforcement, and the Law of Unintended Consequences for Anti-Paparazzi Legislation'. *University of Pennsylvania Law Review*, 147: 1435–72.

Mulligan, Edward Thomas (1984/5). '*Griswold* Revisited in the Light of *Uplinger*: An Historical and Philosophical Exposition of Implied Autonomy Rights in the Constitution'. *New York University Review of Law and Social Change*, 13: 51–82.

Negley, Glenn (1966). 'Philosophical Views on the Value of Privacy'. *Law and Contemporary Problems*, 31: 319–25.

Newman, M., and De Chabris, G. Marks (1987). 'Employment and Privacy: A Problem for our Time'. *Journal of Business Ethics*, 6: 153–63.

Nimmer, Melville (1968). 'The Right to Speak from Times to Time: First Amendment Theory Applied to Libel and Misapplied to Privacy'. *California Law Review*, 56: 935–67.

Note (1963). 'The Right of Privacy: Normative and Descriptive Confusion in the Defense of Newsworthiness'. *University of Chicago Law Review*, 30: 722–34.

O'Brien, David (1979). *Privacy, Law and Public Policy*. New York: Praeger Special Studies.

—— (1980). *The Right of Privacy: Its Constitutional and Social Dimensions*. Austin, TX: Tarleton Law Library, School of Law, University of Texas, Austin.

Okin, Susan Moller (1982). 'Women and the Making of the Sentimental Family'. *Philosophy and Public Affairs*, 11: 65–88.

Olsen, Frances (1989). 'Unraveling Compromise'. *Harvard Law Review*, 103: 105–35.

Parent, W. A. (1983*a*). 'A New Definition of Privacy for the Law'. *Law and Philosophy*, 2: 305–38.

——(1983*b*). 'Privacy, Morality and the Law'. *Philosophy and Public Affairs*, 12: 269–88.

——(1983*c*). 'Recent Work on the Concept of Privacy'. *American Philosophical Quarterly*, 20: 341–56.

Parker, Richard B. (1974). 'A Definition of Privacy'. *Rutgers Law Review*, 27: 275–96.

Peck, Robert S. (1984). 'Extending the Constitutional Right to Privacy in the New Technological Age'. *Hofstra Law Review*, 12: 893–912.

Peller, Gary (1985). 'The Metaphysics of American Law'. *California Law Review*, 73: 1152–290.

Pember, Don (1970). *Privacy and the Press*. Seattle: University of Washington Press.

Pennock, J. Roland, and Chapman, John W. (1971) (eds.), *Privacy: Nomos XIII*. New York: Atherton Press.

Peters, Thomas, A. (1999). *Computerized Monitoring and Online Privacy*. Jefferson, NC: McFarland & Co.

Pine, Rachael C., and Law, Sylvia A. (1992). 'Envisioning a Future for Reproductive Liberty: Strategies for Making the Rights Real'. *Harvard Civil Rights–Civil Liberties Law Review*, 27: 407–63.

Posner, Richard (1978). 'The Right to Privacy'. *Georgia Law Review*, 12: 393–422.

——(1979). 'Privacy, Secrecy and Reputation'. *Buffalo Law Review*, 28: 1–56.

——(1981). *The Economics of Justice*. Cambridge, MA: Harvard University Press.

Post, Robert (1989). 'The Social Foundations of Privacy: Community and Self in the Common Law Tort'. *California Law Review*, 77: 957–1010.

Prosser, William (1960). 'Privacy'. *California Law Review*, 48: 383–423.

Rachels, James (1975). 'Why Privacy is Important'. *Philosophy and Public Affairs*, 4: 323–33.

Radest, Howard B. (1979). 'The Public and the Private: An American Fairy Tale'. *Ethics*, 89: 280–91.

Rehnquist, William (1974). 'Is an Expanded Right to Privacy Consistent with Fair and Effective Law Enforcement?' *Kansas Law Review*, 23: 1–22.

Reiman, Jeffrey H. (1976). 'Privacy, Intimacy, and Personhood'. *Philosophy and Public Affairs*, 6: 26–44.

Richards, David A. J. (1979*a*). 'Sexual Autonomy and the Constitutional Right to Privacy: A Case Study in Human Rights and the Unwritten Constitution'. *Hastings Law Journal*, 30: 957–1018.

——(1979*b*). 'Unnatural Acts and the Constitutional Right to Privacy: A Moral Theory'. *Fordham Law Review*, 45: 1281–348.

——(1986). *Toleration and the Constitution*. New York: Oxford University Press.

Roberts, Dorothy E. (1991). 'Punishing Drug Addicts Who Have Babies: Women of Color, Equality, and the Right of Privacy'. *Harvard Law Review*, 104: 1419–82.

Roberts, John M., and Gregor, Thomas (1971). 'Privacy: A Cultural View', in J. Roland Pennock and John W. Chapman (eds.), *Privacy: Nomos XIII*. New York: Atherton Press, 199–225.

Rohr, John A. (1974). 'Privacy, Law and Values'. *Thought*, 49: 353–73.

Rosen, J. (2000). *The Unwanted Gaze: The Destruction of Privacy in America*. New York: Random House.

Rosenblum, Nancy (1998). 'Fusion Republicanism', in Anita L. Allen and Milton Regan (eds.), *Debating Democracy's Discontent*. Oxford: Oxford University Press, 273–88.

Rotenberg, Marc (1999). *The Privacy Law Sourcebook: Unites States, International Law, and Recent Developments*. Washington: Electronic Privacy Information Center.

Rubenfeld, Jed (1989). 'The Right of Privacy'. *Harvard Law Review*, 102: 737–807.

Rule, James, and Hunter, Lawrence (1996). 'Towards Property Rights in Personal Data', in Colin J. Bennett and Rebecca Grant (eds.), *Visions of Privacy: Policy Choices for the Digital Age*. Toronto: University of Toronto Press, 169–70.

Sandel, Michael (1996). *Democracy's Discontent*. Cambridge, MA: Harvard University Press.

Scanlon, T. (1975). 'Thomson on Privacy'. *Philosophy and Public Affairs*, 4: 315–22.

Schneider, Carl D. (1977). *Shame, Exposure, and Privacy*. Boston: Beacon Press.

Schneider, Elizabeth M. (1991). 'The Violence of Privacy'. *Connecticut Law Review*, 23: 973–99.

Schoeman, Ferdinand (1983). 'Privacy and Criminal Justice Policies'. *Criminal Justice Ethics*, 2: 71–84.

——(1984a). *Philosophical Dimensions of Privacy: An Anthology*. Cambridge: Cambridge University Press.

——(1984b). 'Privacy: Philosophical Dimensions'. *American Philosophical Quarterly*, 21: 199–214.

——(1987). 'Adolescent Confidentiality and Family Privacy'. *John Marshall Law Review*, 20: 641–60.

——(1992). *Privacy and Social Freedom*. Cambridge: Cambridge University Press.

Schwartz, Paul M. (2000). 'International Privacy and the State'. *Connecticut Law Review*, 32: 815.

——and Reidenberg, Joel R. (1996). *Data Privacy Law*. Charlottesville, VA: Michie.

Senchuk, Dennis M. (1986). 'Privacy Regained'. *Philosophical Investigations*, 9: 18–35.

Shattuck, John (1977). *Rights of Privacy*. Skokie, IL: National Textbook Co.

Sher, George (1981). 'Subsidized Abortions: Moral Rights and Moral Compromise'. *Philosophy and Public Affairs*, 10: 361–72.

——(1982). 'Our Preferences, Ourselves'. *Philosophy and Public Affairs*, 12: 34–50.

Shils, Edward (1966). 'Privacy: Its Constitutional Vicissitudes'. *Law and Contemporary Problem*, 31: 281–307.

Siegel, Paul (1984). 'Privacy: Control over Stimulus Input, Stimulus Output, and Self-Regarding Conduct'. *Buffalo Law Review*, 33: 35–84.

Simmel, Arnold (1971). 'Privacy is not an Isolated Freedom', in J. Roland Pennock and John W. Chapman (eds.), *Privacy: Nomos XIII*. New York: Atherton Press, 71–87.

Smith, Robert Ellis (1997). *Compilation of State and Federal Privacy Laws*. Providence, RI: Privacy Journal.

Solomon, Toby (1985). 'Personal Privacy and the 1984 Syndrome'. *Western New England Law Review*, 7: 753–90.

Spiro, Herbert J. (1971). 'Privacy in Comparative Perspective', in J. Roland Pennock and John W. Chapman (eds.), *Privacy: Nomos XIII*. New York: Atherton Press, 121–48.

Stephen, James Fitzjames (1873). *Liberty, Equality and Fraternity*. London: Smith, Edler, & Co.

Stigler, George (1980). 'An Introduction to Privacy in Economics and Politics'. *Journal of Legal Studies*, 9: 623–44.

Stone, Geoffrey (1976). 'The Scope of the Fourth Amendment: Privacy and the Police Case of Spies, Secret Agents, and Informants'. *American Bar Foundation Research Journal*, 1193–271.

Sunstein, Cass R. (1992). 'Neutrality in Constitutional Law (with Special Reference to Pornography, Abortion, and Surrogacy)'. *Columbia Law Review*, 92: 1–52.

Sutherland, Stewart R. (1984). 'Religion, Experience and Privacy'. *Religious Studies*, 20: 121–32.

Swire, Peter, and Litan, Robert E. (1998). *None of your Business: World Data Flows, Electronic Commerce, and the European Privacy Directive*. Washington: Brookings Institution Press.

Sykes, Charles, J. (1999). *The End of Privacy*. New York: St Martin's Press.

Tefft, S. (1980) (ed.). *Secrecy, a Cross Cultural Perspective*. New York: Human Sciences Press.

Temkin, Jack (1981). 'Wittgenstein on Epistemic Privacy'. *Philosophical Quarterly*, 31: 97–109.

Thom, James A., and Thorne, Peter G. (1986). 'Privacy Principles: Tacit Assumptions under Threat'. *Journal of Law and Information Science*, 2: 68–82.

Thomson, Judith Jarvis (1975). 'The Right to Privacy'. *Philosophy and Public Affairs*, 4: 295–314.

Tomkovicz, James J. (1985). 'Beyond Secrecy for Secrecy's Sake: Toward an Expanded Vision of the Fourth Amendment Privacy Province'. *Hastings Law Journal*, 36: 645–737.

Tribe, Laurence (1973). 'Forward: Toward a Model of Roles in the Due Process of Life and Law'. *Harvard Law Review*, 87: 1–53.

Turkington, Richard, and Allen, Anita L. (1999). *Privacy Law*. Minneapolis: West Publishing Co.

US Private Protection Study Commission (1977). *Personal Privacy in an Information Society*. Washington: US Printing Office.

Van den Haag, Ernest (1971). 'On Privacy', in J. Roland Pennock and John W. Chapman (eds.), *Privacy: Nomos XIII*. New York: Atherton Press, 149–68.

Velecky, Lubor (1978). 'The Concept of Privacy', in John Young (ed.), *Privacy*. Chichester, NY: Wiley.

Vickery, Alan B. (1982). 'Breach of Confidence: An Emerging Tort'. *Columbia Law Review*, 82: 1426–86.

Wacks, Raymond (1980). 'Poverty of "Privacy" '. *Law Quarterly Review*, 96: 73–89.

——(1989). *Personal Information: Privacy and the Law*. Oxford: Oxford University Press.

Wallace, Patricia (1999). *The Psychology of the Internet*. Cambridge: Cambridge University Press.

Warren, Samuel, and Brandeis, Louis D (1890). 'The Right to Privacy'. *Harvard Law Review*, 4: 193–220.

Wasserstrom, R. A. (1978). 'Privacy: Some Arguments and Assumptions', in Richard Bronaugh (ed.), *Philosophical Law: Authority, Equality, Adjudication, Privacy*. Westport, CT: Greenwood Press.

Watson, Gerald G. (1986). 'The Ninth Amendment: Source of a Substantive Right to Privacy'. *John Marshall Law Review*, 19: 959–81.

Weinstein, Michael (1971). 'The Use of Privacy in the Good Life', in J. Roland Pennock and John W. Chapman (eds.), *Privacy: Nomos XIII*. New York: Atherton Press, 88–104.

Weisman, Alisa M. (1982). 'Publicity as an Aspect of Privacy and Personal Autonomy'. *Southern California Law Review*, 55: 727–68.

Wellington, Harry (1973). 'Common Law Rules and Constitutional Double Standards: Some Notes on Adjudication'. *Yale Law Journal*, 83: 221–311.

Wells, K., and Merritt, F. S. (1980–1). 'Individual Rights'. *Urban Lawyer*, 13: 713–21.

Wertheim, Margaret (1999). *The Pearly Gates of Cyberspace: A History of Space from Dante to the Internet*. New York: W. W. Norton.

West, Robin (1988). 'Jurisprudence and Gender'. *University of Chicago Law Review*, 55: 1–72.

——(1990). 'Forward: Taking Freedom Seriously'. *Harvard Law Review*, 104: 43–106.

Westin, Alan (1967). *Privacy and Freedom*. New York: Atheneum Press.

Williams, Joan (1991). 'Gender Wars: Selfless Women in the Republic of Choice'. *New York University Law Review*, 66: 1559–634.

Young, John Baldwin (1978) (ed.). *Privacy*. Chichester, NY: Wiley.

Zebrowski, Martha K. (1978). 'Commentary on Rosen's "The Complaint Client"'. *Values Ethics Health Care*, 3: 8–16.

Zimmerman, Diane (1983). 'Requiem for a Heavyweight: A Farewell to Warren and Brandeis's Privacy Tort'. *Cornell Law Review*, 68: 291–367.

Cases Cited

Bowers v. Hardwick, 478 US 186 (1986).

DeMay v. Roberts, 46 Mich. 160, 9 NW 146 (1881).

DeShaney v. Winnebago Department of Social Services, 489 US 189 (1989).

Eisenstadt v. Baird, 405 US 438 (1972).

Griswold v. Connecticut, 381 US 479 (1965).

In Re Baby M, 109 NJ 396, 537 A.2d 1227 (1988).

Katz v. United States, 386 US 954 (1967).

Loving v. Virginia, 388 US 1 (1967).

Planned Parenthood v. Casey, 112 Sup. Ct. 2791 (1992).

Roe v. Wade, 410 US 113 (1973).

Stanley v. Georgia, 394 US 557 (1969).

CHAPTER 20

CORPORATE
RESPONSIBILITY

PATRICIA H. WERHANE
R. EDWARD FREEMAN

1. INTRODUCTION

FOUNDED in 1906, the family-owned company Malden Mills is one of the last textile mills located in Lawrence, Massachusetts. Most of the US textile industry, formerly located in the north-east of the country, has moved to the South or to Asia, where non-unionized workers and cheaper wages keep these mills competitive. However, Malden Mills, under the direction of Aaron Feuerstein, chose to stay in Lawrence where his family had always operated this business, and the mill continued to be a unionized workplace.

During the early 1980s, because of fierce competition in the traditional fabric business, Malden Mills had to lay off workers and was almost bankrupt. Still, Feuerstein did not close the plant. Instead, he turned to the union, his engineers, and his managers and asked them for ways to help the company become more efficient. Given that challenge, Malden Mills' engineers created a new fabric, Polartec©, a patented thermal polyester fleece fabric. This fabric became an almost instant success in the winter clothing market. In the meantime, with the cooperation of the union, Malden Mills' employees were able to reduce the labour component of all fabric production to under 10 per cent of costs. As a result, by 1995, with reduced labour costs and the expanding demand for Polartec©, Malden Mills had increased its labour force to 2,900 people in Lawrence and 3,200 people worldwide. Its sales rose to $400 million a year and it became highly profitable (Narva 1996).

Then, on 11 December 1995, during the celebration of Feuerstein's seventieth birthday, the ageing Lawrence factory partially burned, putting most of its workers out of jobs. Feuerstein faced a new dilemma. The insurance company would pay only about half of the $300 million needed for rebuilding the factory. Feuerstein had to decide whether to go into debt to rebuild the factory.

The day after the fire, Feuerstein announced that he would rebuild the factory as quickly as possible. In the meantime he continued to pay the wages and benefits of his out-of-work employees. Within three months of the fire, the company was again producing Polartec©, and most of the workers had jobs at the new plant (Goozner 1996: 27).

In the late 1970s the pharmaceutical company Merck developed a highly success-ful anti-parasitic drug, ivermectin, used for attacking worms and other parasites in animals. After testing this drug extensively on a number of animal parasites, the leading researcher on ivermectin, Dr William Campbell, concluded that a version of ivermectin might be successful in combating onchocerciasis or 'river blindness'. River blindness is a disease transmitted by the bite of black flies that breed near rivers. When the flies bite humans, they leave the larvae of a parasitic worm, which then burrows into the skin. The worms multiply under the skin, causing terrible itching and eventually blinding its human victims. Between eighteen million and twenty-five million people have river blindness, and almost 100 million are in dan-ger of becoming infected. Unfortunately, almost all of these people live in very poor countries in remote areas of the world.

The director of research at Merck, Roy Vagelos, quickly realized that if this drug was developed the customer base would be almost exclusively people in developing countries where river blindness was prevalent. These customers had no income, and the countries in which they lived were among the poorest in the world. On a nor-mal schedule it takes about ten years and up to $350 million to develop and perfect a drug for humans. Ordinarily Merck did not proceed with a drug that did not have a promised customer base returning at least $20 million in profit per year to the company.

However, the edict of George Merck, which had become the *de facto* corporate mission at Merck, stated, 'We try never to forget that medicine is for the people. It is not for the profits. The profits follow, and if we have remembered that, they have never failed to appear. The better we have remembered it, the larger they have been' (Bollier et al. 1991: 3).

After almost ten years, a successful version of ivermectin for humans, called Mectizan, was developed. All along, Merck had thought that, if it developed a suc-cessful product, the World Health Organization (WHO) or some other international or US organization would help fund the development, testing, manufacturing, and/or distribution of the drug. However, the WHO had just invested several million dollars in fly eradication in countries with large river blindness infections without success, and it was unwilling to invest further money even to test the drug. No other agency came forward, so Merck initiated and funded drug testing in human subjects.

Much to Campbell's delight, Mectizan proved to be highly successful. It arrested the growth of river blindness in victims infected with the parasite, and prevented it from occurring altogether when given to children. Producing the drug was relatively inexpensive, and taking one pill a year was all that was needed for the drug to be effective.

Still, even at $1 a dosage, no organization was willing to help Merck in funding the drug, so Merck decided to give the drug away. Its next problem was distribution, since neither those infected with river blindness nor their governments were capable of administering Mectizan. Setting up distribution channels in remote areas was a complex task. Finally, helped by international organizations, Merck instigated a multi-year programme to distribute the drug (Bollier et al. 1991; Bollier 1996: 280–94). By the end of 1999 Merck had succeeded in giving away over 400 million doses of Mectizan. According to the WHO, river blindness, like smallpox, is becoming 'extinct' (Merck Annual Report 1999: 30).

We begin with these two cases because each illustrates a situation where a company or its CEO was faced with ethical challenges, but the circumstances surrounding each challenge were out of the ordinary. Feuerstein neither caused nor was responsible for the factory fire. Merck knew little about river blindness, and the disease struck populations far removed from communities to whom Merck was ordinarily connected or responsible. Still, each made what we would consider audacious decisions. In each case what was done was beyond what is ordinarily morally expected of businesses and business people. Traditionally, companies have not been obligated to pay workers' wages when a factory is destroyed. Pharmaceutical companies are not ordinarily expected to investigate and produce drugs for diseases that have no expected pay-offs to the companies.

Given these examples of what appear to be responsible behaviour, we shall explore the dimensions of corporate responsibility. We will begin by studying the nature of organizations, such as corporations, to determine whether, or in what ways, corporations, like individuals, are morally responsible. We will explore the scope of corporate responsibility—to think about what responsibilities corporations have or should have, and whether one can understand those responsibilities as residing in the corporation or in individuals acting on behalf of the corporation. We shall investigate what factors contribute to corporate moral decision making and how these play a role in corporate responsibility.

2. CORPORATE RESPONSIBILITY AND BUSINESS ETHICS

The study of corporate responsibility has its roots in business ethics, in business law, and in more social-science-oriented approaches to corporate social responsibility: business and society (Goodpaster 1997; T. McMahon 1997). Technically defined, business ethics is the study of the relationship between ethics and economics and the analysis of the role of ethical decision making in commerce. The subjects of business ethics include individuals, professionals, managerial decision makers, corporations, governments, public policy, and the natural environment. Business ethics is normative and descriptive. It evaluates individual and corporate behaviour, and practices in which managers and corporations ought or ought not to engage, and it engages in behavioural and sociological studies of what, in fact, managers and companies do. It also describes and evaluates corporate-government, corporate-community and corporate-natural environment interactions (Goodpaster 1984; Werhane 1996).

The study of corporations and corporate responsibility focuses on the middle range of business ethics and contains three overlapping approaches. The first is a meta-analysis of the nature of a corporation in order to answer the question of whether one can hold a corporation, like an individual person, morally responsible. The second is a study of positive and negative corporate obligations and the resulting scope of corporate responsibility. The third is a more descriptive analysis of corporate mission, culture, climate, and roles, and an exploration of how these factors contribute to corporate moral accountability. It is not always useful clearly to separate these dimensions as some would have. The way that corporations work, and the nature of corporations, are surely relevant to how they could work. Fact and value, theory and practice, are inevitably intertwined in applied ethics.

2.1 What is a Corporation?

In the USA, the modern publicly owned corporation is an association given legal status by a state charter to operate as a single unit with limited liability over an indefinite period of time. Corporations have unique property arrangements because they are owned by shareholders whose interests are represented by the oversight of a board of directors. Corporations, on the other hand, are usually managed by other persons hired specifically for that task. Shareholders or their representatives on boards of directors usually do not participate in the day-to-day operations of the firm. (We will use the terms 'firm' and 'corporation' interchangeably in this chapter.)

The unlimited life and shareholder limited liability, all granted by laws in the USA, raise some interesting ethical issues on the macro-level (Sollars, forthcoming). However, our main purpose is not to engage in a macro-analysis of corporations but to focus on organizational responsibility.

2.2 Corporate Moral Agency

In the law, at least in the USA, corporations are by and large treated as fictional persons, although they are granted unlimited 'life' by their state charters. This means that, for purposes of legislation and litigation, corporations are treated as single units, not as aggregates or conglomerates. Corporations have also been granted some constitutional rights guaranteed to individual persons, including equal protection, due process, freedom of speech, and freedom from self-incrimination and unreasonable search (O'Kelley 1979; M. Phillips 1992). This theory, called the 'concession theory', grants artificial personhood but not necessarily moral personhood to corporations. The legal analogy between corporations and persons raises the question whether corporations are sufficiently like individual persons to be considered moral as well as legal agents.

2.3 Are Corporations Merely Aggregates?

It is sometimes argued that, unlike legal personhood, artificial personhood does not imply moral agency, since a corporation is not a distinct entity having its own personality, intentions, rights, and liabilities. Rather, a corporation is merely a collection or an aggregate of individuals who voluntarily get together for the purposes of convenience, efficiency, and limited liability to conduct business. The term 'corporation' is merely a convention used to describe the particular legal contractual relationship represented by the voluntary association (Hessen 1979; Velasquez 1983; Keeley 1988). According to this theory, the decisions and actions of individuals within a corporation and through its board of directors cause corporate 'action'. A board of directors represents shareholder interests. It can change the direction, scope, or size of an organization, or even shut it down. But a corporation itself does not act independently of its members. Everything that occurs in and through the corporation is a result of individual decision making, individual action, or individual omission. Therefore, according to this analysis, all so-called corporate 'actions' can in principle be traced ultimately to individuals, each of whom plays a different role in shaping the direction of the association or aggregate. The corporation is merely the sum of these individual actions and of the complex interactions between them. Of course, these may be very complex transactions to trace. And, since there are uncertainty and bounded rationality among the actors, in fact we may not be able to trace these causal chains.

A second formulation of the aggregate view of the corporation is implied from the thesis that a corporation is a 'nexus of contracts' (Coase 1937). According to this view, corporations are formed in order effectively to coordinate market exchanges and to reduce and make more efficient transaction costs of those exchanges through team production and organization. The corporation is best conceptualized as a nexus of implied and explicit contracts between employees, investors, suppliers, and other stakeholders and the firm (Boatright 1999a,b). According to some theorists, these contracts can be analysed into contracts that are between individual actors and agents. The 'corporation' is just a shorthand way of referring to where these individual contracts and relationships may intersect (Bratton 1989; Millon 1990; see also M. Phillips 1992: 438–9; C. McMahon 1995: 541–54).

The implication of the aggregate theory in both formulations for an evaluation of corporate moral agency is the following: if a corporation is an association of individuals or a nexus of contracts between individuals, then, when the association 'acts', moral responsibility could in principle be traced back to the individual or individuals making the decision. Questions about corporate moral agency could in principle be questions about the moral agency of persons who own, manage, work for, contract with, or have other agency or contractual relationships with a corporation. Therefore, any description of corporate moral agency, moral responsibility, or institutional rights simply restates the individual responsibilities and rights of corporate constituents.

It has been argued by some that the problem with the aggregate theory is that it is an incomplete account of corporate action. It erroneously identifies the causal roles of individuals in corporate contract arrangements and decision making with outcomes of that process: corporate action. Yet this is too narrow an interpretation of the aggregate theory. Even if there are no 'real entities' (whatever this may mean) around called 'corporations', this does not imply that one cannot make sense out of describing the corporation as some sort of unit or collective. For instance, the clever aggregate theorist such as Sollars (forthcoming) may well respond that individuals in the corporate context may act under conditions of uncertainty, and that they do not always know all the alternatives, options, and causal chains that are open to them. Individual actors are boundedly rational. Thus, 'the corporation' serves as an important shorthand, an important vocabulary in which to conduct certain kinds of activity such as praising and blaming when it is virtually impossible to trace outcomes of actions to particular individuals. There is no reason to believe that we could do away with 'corporation-talk' and replace it with 'individual-talk' in the same way that we cannot reduce 'mind-talk' to 'body-talk', yet we believe that 'brains' or 'bodies' are the underlying entity (see Coleman 1990; Dennett 1995: 82).

2.4 Corporations as Moral Agents

There are a number of senses in which we ordinarily think of firms as moral agents. Like individuals, corporations set goals. These goals are often defined in a mission statement, delineated in policies, or operationalized in the corporate culture and activities in which the corporation is engaged. In ordinary language we refer to corporations as actors, and we hold them, like individuals, responsible. For example, we say that Ford failed to act when it did not initially change the design of the Pinto despite its knowledge about the unfortunate placement of its gas tank. We praise 3M for its environmental programmes or DuPont for initiating an alliance of chemical companies to improve environmental and social performance.

We hold companies, like individuals, accountable for their actions. Dow Corning, not simply its executives, was held morally as well as legally liable for an allegedly harmful silicone breast implant it manufactured and sold (Stocker et al. 2000); as it turned out, a number of scientific studies have shown that implants cause no known dread disease (Angell 1996). Given that, we now exempt Dow Corning from these liabilities—that is, we 'forgive' the company (Spencer et al. 1999: 26).

2.5 Are Corporations Moral Persons?

Because we treat firms as moral agents, it is tempting to conclude that, like their biological counterparts, they are moral *persons*. In his well-cited article 'The Corporation as a Moral Person' and in later work (French 1979, 1984), Peter French makes such an argument. According to French, a legal person is defined as an eliminable 'subject of a right' (French 1979: 210). Eliminable subjects 'cannot dispose of their rights, cannot administer them…' (French 1979: 210). From this definition French suggests that a moral person might be defined as a non-eliminable subject of a right, an agent capable of alienating or disposing of her rights and administering them—that is, a subject to whom one ascribes moral responsibility. By moral responsibility French has in mind accountability 'relationships [that] hold reciprocally and without prior agreements among moral persons' (French 1979: 211). In order to be a moral person—that is, an agent who participates in morally accountable relationships for which one is responsible—one must, according to French, be an intentional agent. Thus, French argues, intentionality is a necessary condition for moral agency. When we apply this analysis to corporations, we see that a corporation is a moral person if it is an intentional agent, if it engages in reciprocal responsibility relationships, and if it is a non-eliminable subject of a right (French 1984).

The contention that corporations are moral persons raises serious difficulties. If a corporation is a moral *person*, what is the status of employee persons? Are they lesser moral persons? An employee, by this reasoning, could be a moral person of grade one, MP_1, a corporate committee making decisions an MP_2, and so on, so that a corporation would be an MP_n. A corporation would be allowed to do as it pleased so long as it did not interfere with the freedoms of other corporations (other MP_ns). But, by this reasoning, a corporation could interfere with the freedoms of individual moral persons without moral violation, because, being MP_ns, corporations would have *more* in the way of moral personhood and thus freedom than persons or MP_1s (Werhane 1985). French's analysis appears to give too much to corporations in the way of moral personhood, so that individuals end up having less moral status than corporations. The consequences of such reasoning are that corporate power is legitimated just because of its lofty ontological status (C. McMahon 1995). This is not to imply that most firms would exercise this power wrongly, but that possibility is one that individual persons might not relish.

It turns out that, by appealing to the notion of intentionality as French uses it, corporate moral personhood makes little sense. Because of the various applications of intentional language, it is useful to call those phenomena that exhibit intentional behaviour, 'intentional systems'. The contemporary philosopher Daniel C. Dennett defines an intentional system as 'a system whose behaviour can be—at least some-times—explained and predicted by relying on ascriptions to the system of beliefs and desires (and hopes, fears, intentions, hunches...)' (Dennett 1978: 3). Dennett says further that this definition of an intentional system does not imply that all so-called intentional systems really have beliefs and desires. Rather, his point is that one can best explain and predict the behaviour of a variety of phenomena by describing this behaviour in terms of intentional beliefs and desires. Dennett's description of intentional systems is helpful because it shows how taking what he calls an 'intentional stance' can accurately describe and predict certain kinds of activities such as the actions of organizations such as corporations. This is similar to the sophisticated defence of the aggregation view of the corporation.

According to this reasoning, one could call a corporation an intentional system because one can predict corporate behaviour through intentional descriptions. For example, one can use intentional language to describe actions that have allegedly been ascribed to corporate activities. For example, the social and environmental havoc in Nigerian oil fields has sometimes been ascribed to Shell, although there are many fac-tors that created this situation. Focusing on Shell's involvement, one could employ expressions such as: did Shell intend to contribute to social and environmental havoc in its Nigerian oilfields? Although one could also describe the same corporate behavi-our using other modes of description, there are nevertheless good reasons to describe corporate actions and omissions through the language of intentionality. The good reasons, however, are not because a corporation is a moral person, but rather because corporations act as single units and exhibit intentional behaviour (Werhane 1985).

Many corporations appear to 'think about' their desires, beliefs, and goals, and some corporations or persons acting on behalf of corporations seem to engage in moral deliberation and self-analysis as well. For example, during the silicone breast implant controversy, Dow Corning, the leading manufacturer of silicone breast implants, debated about the morality and feasibility of manufacturing implants. Of course, Dow Corning the firm did not literally engage in self-reflection and moral self-analysis about breast-implant manufacture; rather its constituents (the board, managers, employees, and legal agents) did so on behalf of the corporation. Dow Corning's so-called 'corporate actions' were a result of these deliberations, which subsequently directed actions of persons who functioned as agents for the corpor-ation. To continue the example, Dow Corning was responsible for the manufacture of silicone breast implants. But the corporation, in fact, did not design, manufac-ture, or market implants; engineers and other employees working at Dow Corning did so. Still, we hold Dow Corning responsible, because the persons who made implants were acting as agents on behalf of the corporation. We then say that the corporation performed intentional actions. But literally the actions were a result of the activities of a collection of persons or groups operating on behalf of Dow Corning. Thus the intricate web of intentional behaviour exhibited in corporate decision-making procedures coupled with resulting actions by agents on behalf of the corporation produce corporate 'actions'.

Firms also engage in reciprocal accountability relationships with their various stakeholders. For example, firms engage in relationships with their managers and employees, contracting or trading working conditions, wages, and benefits for productivity and managerial judgement, where each party is accountable to the other for these expectations. Firms engage in similar relationships with clients or customers, trading goods or services for remuneration, and with shareholders, trading growth and profitability for capital. But, like all corporate intentional behaviour, these relationships are between collections of individuals acting on behalf of the corporate entity and the respective stakeholders.

Corporations also enjoy legal rights such as the right freely to exist, own property, engage in commerce, and even go out of business. The result is that corporations exhibit intentional behaviour, engage in reciprocal accountability relationships, are subjects of rights, and are said to act. But their so-called intentions, their accountability relationships, and their 'actions' are the collective result of decisions made by individual persons. Their rights are assigned to an artificial entity, not to any individual person. The corporation is an *eliminable* subject, because, without persons, corporate 'actions' literally could not occur. Thus, corporations are moral agents, but not moral persons.

2.6 Collective Moral Agency

The charter and the founders of a corporation set the initial corporate goals and initiate the business of the organization as a corporation. Often firms, like Merck, will develop mission statements or an ideology will develop from statements or actions of some of the company founders. Hewlett Packard's founders' edict that they manage by 'walking around' has become the management philosophy at Hewlett Packard. In the complex decision-making processes that occur within a corporation, corporate goals change, mission statements become depersonalized corporate philosophy, and a corporate 'character' develops. Together these activities and phenomena create an organizational culture defined as 'the customary or traditional ways of thinking and doing things, which are *shared* to a greater or lesser extent by all members of the organization and which new members of the organization must *learn* and at least partially accept in order to be accepted into the service of the firm' (Jacques 1951: 166).

One component of an organizational culture is what some organizational theorists call the 'ethical climate' of an organization, the functional analogue of the

character of an individual. A person's character is exhibited in a group of traits connected with practical choice and action. Similarly, an organization's ethical climate
is defined by the shared perceptions of how ethical issues should be addressed and
what is ethically correct behaviour for the organization (Victor and Cullen 1988).
Just as personal ethics may guide what an individual will do when faced with moral
dilemmas, corporate ethical climate guides or can influence what an organization
and its constituents will do when faced with issues of conflicting values. Ethical climate includes both content—the shared perceptions of what constitutes ethical
behaviour—and process: how ethical issues will be dealt with (Spencer et al. 1999).

Except for very small corporations, managerial actions are often role related—
that is, they are actions performed 'for the corporation' or with some corporate mission or goals in mind rather than for personal satisfaction. Corporate decision
making and action are often a result of the functions of disparate groups within a
corporation, so that an action of one part of a corporation is a function, in part, of
actions of another group within an organization. Thus, again the sophisticated
aggregate theorist can claim that 'roles' mediate the uncertainty and bounded
rationality of corporate actors. One is uncertain of outcomes, or one is uncertain
of the particular causal chain one is setting in motion, so one 'acts for the corporation' in conjunction with many others acting for the same set of reasons. Often the
final set of action plans or policies, evolving from combinations and permutations
of individual primary actions done on behalf of impersonal aims, cannot be identified merely with the sum of the original individual tasks. This is because of the
role-related anonymity, uncertainty, and bounded rationality of the individual
actions. In addition, these individual actions can be changed through the corporate
culture, climate, and actions of other individuals and groups in other divisions of
the corporation, and the ways in which goals are interpreted at each stage of activity. Thus the *reasons* for the corporate 'action' often cannot be explained merely by
itemizing individual constituent actions. The result is corporate 'activity' or policy
that is a secondary action, an action ascribed to the collective, the firm, even though
the collective itself did not literally authorize the action. Thus collective action may
not be identical to individual action because of the role-related nature of managerial decision making and the impersonal character of the authorization process.

The notion of collective action is helpful in understanding why one often holds
a corporation and not merely its managers and agents primarily responsible for its
'actions', even though these actions are secondary actions that a corporation is
unable to perform 'by itself'. While individual action is necessary for collective or
corporate action, and while the totality of individual actions on behalf of a corporation is sufficient for such action, except in the smallest corporations no one individual action is sufficient for a secondary action, and each individual input becomes
transformed as it mixes with other constituent and agent input and as corporate
'directives' are interpreted. The result is often (but not always) collective action different from the actions of its constituents. Thus, at least in principle, it is possible

that there could be questionable outcome of corporate decision making that is the result of a series of blameless individual actions. For all these reasons, then, corporate action is sometimes usefully described as 'collective action', the rationale for which cannot be redescribed in terms of the actions of individual managers and agents, even though these are nevertheless necessary and sufficient for a corporation to function.

Because corporations 'act', because corporations are intentional systems engaged in reciprocal relationships with their stakeholders, and because firms have some rights analogous to individual rights, the fact that, under law, corporations are treated as quasi-persons is not surprising. However, although corporations indeed have some of the characteristics of persons, they lack the autonomy necessary to perform primary actions, and they are eliminable subjects, both conditions necessary to be ascribed full moral personhood.[1]

2.7 Collective Moral Responsibility

Because corporate 'actions' are collective actions, a corporation is not an independent moral agent. Unlike individual actions, which are presumed to be free choices of autonomous agents, corporate 'action' is an outcome of groups of choices of constituents and agents acting on behalf of the corporation—that is, it is sometimes 'collective action'. Because collective actions are, in a derivative way, actions of persons, they can be moral or immoral actions, and one may evaluate them accordingly. Corporate actions that are collective actions can be praiseworthy or blameworthy even though it is not useful to ascribe moral personhood to the corporation.

Corporations, like individuals, do not always 'respond' positively or negatively to moral pressures, because corporate moral agency is not independent of the moral input of corporate culture, and its managers and agents. Moral reactions of persons are necessary (but not sufficient) for collective moral reaction. The kind and degree of corporate moral 'action' and moral 'response' depend on the kinds and degrees of primary constituent moral actions and reactions. For example, many employees at Shell did not feel responsible in any way for Shell's alleged questionable activities in Nigeria the firm was supposed to have abetted. Some did not even recognize that there is a moral issue in this case. Therefore, Shell as a collective did not initially 'respond' morally to allegations about its Nigerian policies, because at Shell there was no amalgamation of individual moral indignation at the time that initiated a corporate moral 'reaction' to these accusations (Moldoveanu and Paine 2000). This explanation would not excuse Shell or its managers from any alleged moral culpability, but this pathology helps to explain how a corporate culture and role

---

[1] Much of this section on 'corporate moral agency' was derived from Werhane (1985). It has been revised extensively, but parts are reprinted by permission of the author.

assignments can create moral blindness. Still, although they sometimes appear to take morally neutral stances, and do not always 'recognize' moral demands, corporations as collectives are made up of persons who can 'act' as moral agents, and therefore are morally responsible. Moral blindness does not excuse a corporation from moral responsibility, just as it does not excuse rational free individual moral agents.

3. Corporate Responsibility

3.1 The Shareholder Thesis and Moral Minimalism

If corporations are collective moral agents and if the CEO or top management of a corporation can act as a 'stand-in' for corporate actions, it is tempting to ascribe to the corporation responsibilities paralleling those we ascribe to individuals. However, there are some qualifications to be considered before jumping to that conclusion. First, corporations are *merely* collective moral agents; they cannot act autonomously without individual or collective action. Secondly, corporations are created for a certain set of purposes; their goals are not as malleable as ordinary human intentions and goals. Thirdly, the property relationships of corporations— that is, the fact that they, unlike human moral agents, are owned by shareholders— means that corporations have reciprocal obligations to their shareholders to create value. Thus the very nature of the firm may bring with it specific moral obligations, making additional obligations problematic. It is tempting to conclude, then, that the primary obligations of corporations are to their shareholders. Indeed, the economist Milton Friedman is famous for his edict that the *only* responsibility of managers is to maximize value, usually economic value or profits, for shareholders, although even Friedman argues that managers' and thus corporate fiduciary duties to shareholders should be constrained by law, ethical custom, and social mores (Friedman 1970). We shall call this view a minimalist conception of corporate responsibility.

What is the extent of such minimalism? The grandfather of free enterprise and business ethics, Adam Smith, argued that markets, commerce, and commercial enterprises will succeed under conditions of 'natural liberty...[in which] all systems... of restraint...[are] completely taken away' (Smith 1776/1791/1976: 687, IV.ix.51). However, Smith goes on in the same passage to qualify that statement, arguing that, in commerce, 'every man, *so long as he does not violate the laws of justice*, is left perfectly free to pursue his own interest...' (emphasis added). Further, according to Smith, market exchanges are justified only under the rule of law, and only if individual managers, owners, and others engaged in commerce act with prudence and a respect for basic rights, honour contracts, avoid causing net harms, and conduct business fairly (Werhane 1991). These provisos appear to be fairly minimalist, but, if one thinks, practically, of conducting enterprise with a healthy respect for rights, which would mean considering the negative rights of employees, customers, and shareholders equally, with a consequentialist respect for the negative harm principle, which, today, would involve respect for the natural environment as well as worker and consumer safety, and with the operationalized ideal of fair play, one may be quite far from the minimalist conception of corporate responsibility that is often ascribed to Friedman (Smith 1776/1791/1976; Werhane 1991).

3.2 Corporate Responsibility as Role Responsibilities

While a minimalist interpretation of corporate responsibility is still popular, the business ethics and the management literature have by and large gone beyond this perspective. It would appear that the responsibility of a corporation, as a collective moral agent with at least a vaguely defined set of purposes and fiduciary responsibilities to shareholders, can be analysed and limited to roles and role responsibilities. 'Role' refers 'to constellations of institutionally specified rights and duties organized around an institutionally specified social function... [where] an institution [is any public system or social arrangement that] includes rules that define offices and positions which can be occupied by different individuals at different times' (Hardimon 1994: 334–5).

Families (however defined), professions, trades and trade unions, corporations, churches, and states are all institutions. Each has socially defined role obligations. Additionally corporations, like most other institutions, have role obligations specified by their mission, policies, and procedures. These help to clarify, rank, and specify obligations to various stakeholders, including obligations to communities in which they operate. The roles of corporations are related to their function, their mission, and their goals. As with individuals, we hold corporations morally responsible for carrying out their role responsibilities. When the baby food manufacturer Beech-Nut some years ago was found to make apple juice that contained almost no *apple* juice, it was held liable for that oversight (Halliday and Paine 1992). Similarly, Union Carbide has been held responsible for the Bhopal disaster because, it is argued, it was within the confines of the company's role responsibilities as a manufacturer of dangerous chemicals to have instituted safety measures that would have prevented this accident from occurring.

Role obligations, while important, are not enough, by themselves, to explain corporate responsibility. There are two reasons for this. First and most obviously, one could create a corporation whose mission and/or role obligations were abhorrent. There are obvious examples: Krupp Steel, which used slave labour during the Second World War. The Beech-Nut case is a more benign but equally egregious example where managers confused corporate role obligations to maximize shareholder returns with standards of common-sense morality.

There is a second reason why role obligations are insufficient to explain corporate responsibility. We sometimes hold companies responsible for untoward consequences of their actions, even when at first sight it appears not to be within their role responsibilities. For example, H. B. Fuller manufactured a glue in Honduras called Resistol. The product was abused by Honduran street children and sniffed as a drug. The resulting glue-sniffing street children were called 'Resistoleros'. Fuller argued that they were making glue, not drugs, and that they sold glue only in large containers to legitimate wholesalers. In addition, the street children sniffed many kinds of glue, not just Resistol. While it was true that Fuller's glue was repackaged and sold to children, it was not because of any intentional action Fuller had taken (Bowie and Lenway 1999). Still, even with well-defined role responsibilities, we raise ethical questions about Fuller's responsibility not to create further harms to Honduran street children. That is, we judge Fuller not merely on its role responsibilities, but on the responsibilities that result from its role-defined operations. We raise evaluative questions about firms even when they are performing their roles in a seemingly exemplary manner. That is, we judge firms from the point of view of common-sense morality, not merely on the basis of their roles and role responsibilities.

As David Luban carefully argues, we can and should use those same tools of common morality for judging organizations as we use for evaluating individuals. Paralleling individual moral evaluation, we can assess organizations such as corporations, their roles, and their mission or the ends they allegedly serve (Luban 1988: chs. 6, 7). This sort of assessment relies on appeals to those rules or precepts that most of us, stepping out of our roles and judging others, would regard as rules for how we and others ought to behave, such as equal respect for persons, avoidance of harm, respect for rights and fairness, honouring contracts, and respect for property, however particularly defined (Walzer 1994). According to Luban, we can evaluate any corporate role, its role-defined obligations, and its mission, as well as whatever acts the corporate role, the role duties it requires of its managers, and/or its mission seem to demand. At each step we evaluate the corporate role, individual corporate-defined role obligations, and the organization mission or ends in terms of both what justifies the mission, corporation, role, obligation, or act, and, secondly, what the mission, corporation, role, obligation, or act justifies. For example, while Beech-Nut's corporate mission seems to be sound, we evaluate the misinterpretation of role obligations at Beech-Nut. In the H. B. Fuller case we evaluate the consequences of its execution of its role responsibilities.

3.3 Corporate Responsibility and Integrative Social Contracts Theory

One promising approach to corporate responsibility is called Integrative Social Contracts Theory. First proposed in the seventeenth century by Thomas Hobbes, social contract theory rests on the idea that, in theory at least, human beings consent to join together in societies and at least tacitly to agree to laws and regulations so that they can live in harmony and achieve their own ends in relation to others. As it relates to corporate responsibility, social contract theory focuses primarily not on how corporations are constituted, but instead on their status in society. According to this position as initially proposed by Thomas Donaldson, in brief, because a corporation is sanctioned by society to operate in a given community, the corporation makes some implicit commitments to that community. These commitments form the basis for a social contract between corporations and society. A corporation is allowed to exist because it is thought that 'the benefits from authorizing the existence of productive organizations outweigh the detriments of doing so. ... From the standpoint of society, the goal of a productive organization may be said to be *to enhance the welfare* of *society through a satisfaction* of *consumer and worker interests*' (Donaldson 1982: 49).

Society has high expectations for corporations, and, because they are allowed to exist and operate freely, corporations have obligations to achieve these expectations. A corporation that does not live up to its side of the bargain is not performing its obligations within the community, and thus is not upholding its contract.

The social contract theory's emphasis on the obligations of corporations provides an important insight into the scope of corporate moral responsibility, but the theory assumes that corporations are moral agents, while being less clear as to what this agency entails. Moreover, while the theory focuses on external corporate–societal relationships, one has to account for corporate responsibility to its employees, shareholders, and customers as well. Such work has recently been developed by Thomas Donaldson and Thomas Dunfee through what they call Integrative Social Contracts Theory (ISCT). Summarized, ISCT is based on the following assumption:

All rational humans aware of the bounded nature of their own rationality would consent to a hypothetical social contract, encompassing a 'macrosocial contract', that would preserve for individual economic communities significant moral free space in which to generate their own norms of economic conduct, through actual 'microsocial contracts'.   (Donaldson and Dunfee 1995: 89)

Donaldson and Dunfee argue that there are basic moral minimums or hypernorms that govern all social relationships on the macro-level. What those are is subject to debate, but moral minimums such as not causing gratuitous harm, honouring contracts, respecting or at least not denigrating basic rights, and treating people and organizations fairly are candidates for hypernorms (Donaldson and Dunfee 1995: 95–6). Such hypernorms provide the moral baseline for organizational action and also govern organizational interrelationships. On a micro-level, within particular societies, and, by analogy, within particular organizations, there is what Donaldson and Dunfee call 'moral free space' dictated by the community or organization in question. Although subject to compatibility with moral minimums or hypernorms, communities and firms can spell out specific norms, acceptable customs, and agreements among themselves. Again, on the micro-level these are tacit agreements, since one seldom sits down, in a community or in an organization, to spell out or vote on these arrangements.

There are a number of useful concepts from ISCT that are worth emphasizing: the idea of a hypothetical social contract (or the expectations that follow from that idea), the notion of tacit consent, and the notion of moral minimums, an idea developed by Michael Walzer (1994). In most societies, corporations have been allowed to come into being and operate because we believe in expanding and improving our well-being. Therefore, one could conclude that there is a tacit social contract between companies and the societies in which they operate to carry out that mission. For instance, we find ourselves angry when a firm fails in its mission or becomes distracted with concerns for expansion or profitability that seemingly cause harms. ISCT explains the source of our anger and concerns, and helps to justify those conclusions. While the notion of a hypernorm is somewhat unclear, following Walzer and others, the idea of a moral minimum is an appealing one. Moral minimums are invaluable as justifications for making and evaluating moral judgements that cross organizational, cultural, or ethnic boundaries, and they make possible corporate role evaluation.

What is less helpful is ISCT's idea of a moral free space on the micro-level, a space that could allow the production of untoward actions by less than perfect firms. Moral free space, for example, allows for the domination of role morality in the organizational and cultural domains. While role morality has an important function in organizations, one must be able to evaluate roles and role obligations by more general moral principles than those merely generated by role norms in an allegedly moral free space. The connection between role morality and more general moral evaluations of those domains remains indeterminate, and ISCT does not thoroughly work out that link. In discussing corporate responsibility, we need to be much more explicit than ISCT about what is acceptable on the micro-level in the allegedly moral free space.

3.4 Corporate Responsibility and Employee Rights

Because corporate action is derived from collections of individual actions, it is tempting to argue that the *primary* responsibilities of firms are, or should be, to their employees and managers, those who initiate corporate action. These responsibilities are often formulated as reciprocal obligations between firms and their employees. Employees and managers have certain role responsibilities, job specifications defining their responsibilities at work. These include role responsibilities to perform efficiently and productively in the workplace, not to cause unwarranted or slanderous disturbances, and not to engage in activities that would put the corporation out of business.

Accompanying employee and managerial role responsibilities are correlative reciprocal responsibilities of an employer—that is, a corporation—to its employees and managers. These include, of course, the obligation to pay employees fairly for their work. In addition, corporations have role responsibilities to recognize employee moral rights claims to entry and exit, voice, safety, information, and due process, and, some argue, participation in corporate decision making (Werhane 1985; C. McMahon 1994; Radin and Werhane 1997). What is interesting is that these are moral role responsibilities arising not merely from an employer's legal obligations to its employees but from the fact that employees and managers, like firms, are moral agents; indeed they are moral *persons* (Werhane 1985).

It is difficult not to exaggerate corporate responsibilities to employees and managers, since corporate agency and action are derived from employee and manager moral agency and action. However, the shortcoming with this approach is that it prioritizes corporate responsibility in ways that tend to neglect other corporate responsibilities, in this case, responsibilities to shareholders, to customers, to suppliers, and to communities. A stakeholder view, on the contrary, tries to balance corporate responsibilities, rather than to focus on one area of obligation.

3.5 Corporate Responsibility and Stakeholder Theory

Stakeholder language, originating in the business strategy literature and summarized in a book on strategy (Freeman 1984), has become standard management language, even in corporate annual reports. Challenging the position that a manager's primary responsibility is to maximize profits, or that the primary purpose of a firm is to maximize the welfare of its shareholders, stakeholder theory argues that the *goal* of any firm and its management is, *or should be*, the flourishing of the firm and *all* its primary stakeholders.

> The very purpose of a firm [and thus its managers] is to serve as a vehicle for coordinating stakeholder interests. It is through the firm [and its managers] that each stakeholder group makes itself better off through voluntary exchange. The corporation serves at the pleasure of its stakeholders, and none may be used as a means to the ends of another without full rights of participation of that decision . . .   (Evan and Freeman 1988: 104)

Widely defined, stakeholders are 'Groups or individuals who benefit from or are harmed by, and whose rights are violated or respected by, corporate actions' (Freeman 1999: 250). The core thesis of stakeholder theory is the normative claim that the interests of all the parties involved in any transaction ought to be considered in determining corporate responsibility. In order to determine how an individual or a firm ought to act or react in a particular situation, it is necessary first to identify each of the parties (individual and collective) with whom the organization interacts and what each party has at stake. In a modern business corporation the primary or most important stakeholders commonly include employees, management, owners/shareholders, customers, and, usually, suppliers and the community.

Mitchell, Agle, and Wood (1997) have argued that prioritizing stakeholders further helps to sort out and clarify a firm's priorities so that not every person, group, or other organization affecting or affected by the company in question is equally important as a stakeholder. One way to prioritize stakeholder claims is to examine an organization's purpose and mission, ranking stakeholders in terms of who has legitimate or appropriate claims, who is essential to that mission and to the survival and flourishing of the organization, and who is most affected by corporate decision making. The apparent instrumentality of the prioritization deals only with part of what is important in stakeholder relationships. In fact, the intent of stakeholder theory is largely normative.

The descriptive accuracy of the theory presumes the truth of the core normative conception, in so far as it presumes that managers and others act (*or should act*) as if all stakeholders' interests have intrinsic value. In turn, recognition of these ultimate moral values and obligations gives stakeholder management its fundamental normative base (Donaldson and Preston 1995: 74). Let us assume for our purposes that all stakeholders in question are individuals or groups (including institutions) made up of individuals. If stakeholder interests have intrinsic value, then, in every stakeholder relationship, the 'stakes [that is, what is expected and due to each party] of each are reciprocal [although not identical], since each can affect the other in terms of harms and benefits as well as rights and duties' (Freeman 1999: 250).

Obligations between stakeholders and stakeholder accountability notions are derived on two grounds. First and obviously, stakeholder relationships are relationships between persons or groups of persons. So the firm and each of its stakeholders are reciprocally morally accountable to each other just because they are people. What is distinctive about stakeholder relationships, however, is that these relationships entail additional obligations because of the unique and specific organizationally defined and role-defined relationships between the firm and its stakeholders. For example, an organization has obligations to its employees because they are human beings *and* because they are employees of the organization (R. Phillips 1997). Conversely, because of their organizationally defined roles, employees and managers have role obligations to the organization that employs them and its other stakeholders *as well as* ordinary moral obligations to that organization and its other stakeholders.

Stakeholder theory raises a thorny issue. Is a stakeholder analysis, even an instrumental analysis, merely self-referential? That is, could one make a case for an organization that prioritized its stakeholders in terms of its mission and recognized reciprocal accountability relationships between the organization and its primary stakeholders, but engaged in untoward or even evil activities? In evaluating stakeholder claims, Evan and Freeman, two of the initiators of stakeholder theory, initially took a Kantian approach, arguing that, because stakeholder relationships are relationships between individuals or groups of individuals, any decision must be one that affords equal respect to persons and their rights, valued for their own sake. In addition, autonomy, respect for individuals, procedural fairness, informed consent, and respect for contractual agreements are means tests for stakeholder relationships. Additionally, in a properly constructed stakeholder arrangement, stakeholders should have viable avenues for self-governance and recourse.

Robert Phillips has developed a standard of fairness as the normative basis for stakeholder relationships. This principle, derived from Rawls's theory of justice, argues that

Whenever persons or groups of persons voluntarily accept the benefits of a mutually beneficial scheme of co-operation requiring sacrifice or contribution on the parts of the participants and there exists the possibility of free-riding, obligations of fairness are created among the participants in the co-operative scheme in proportion to the benefits accepted. (R. Phillips 1997: 57; emphasis deleted)

Decisions that affect various stakeholders must meet these minimum standards of respect for individuals, fairness of procedures and outcomes, informed consent, and availability of recourse. These formal considerations of a fairness standard provide a set of externally derived minimum guidelines or moral minimums for evaluating organizations and stakeholder decisions: for judging some of them morally acceptable or morally problematic.

Stakeholder theory contributes to our thinking about corporate responsibility in the following ways. First, it challenges the minimalist model of corporate responsibility from a normative and a descriptive point of view. It claims that corporations actually do create value for stakeholders (not merely shareholders) and that there are good reasons for their doing so. Secondly, it helps to prioritize those affecting and affected by the organization, in particular, usually employees, managers, customers, and shareholders, without being preoccupied with one set of stakeholders. Stakeholder theory spells out reciprocal accountability relationships connected to organizational accountability that takes into account that firms' stakeholders are individuals as well as organizations. Finally, stakeholder theory eliminates the micro/macro distinction and the idea of a moral free space introduced by ISCT by developing evaluation tools within the organization based on its mission and externally as well.

3.6 Corporate Responsibility as Social Responsibility

If firms, like ordinary individuals, are subject to moral evaluation that goes beyond role responsibilities, it is tempting to identify corporate responsibility as social responsibility or to analogize the corporate responsibility in terms of corporate citizenship parallel to individual citizenship. Because they have the privilege of incorporation and rights to engage in commerce within a social context, it is often argued that firms have social responsibilities as well as role, fiduciary, and legal obligations (e.g. Eells and Walton 1961; Carroll 1979).

The difficulty is in defining the range of those responsibilities. Are these merely negative obligations not to cause harm, be unfair, and so on, or are there positive corporate obligations to communities in which they operate? If so, what is the extent of these obligations? Adam Smith suggested that corporate responsibility consists primarily of negative responsibilities not to create a net set of harms or violations of rights. Other more contemporary thinkers contend that the corporate social responsibility is limited to 'bringing corporate behaviour up to a level where it is congruent with prevailing social norms, values, and expectations of performance' (Sethi 1975: 62). At the other end of the spectrum, some argue that corporations have responsibilities beyond what is minimally required: responsibilities to address social problems and actively improve the social and natural environment (Tichy et al. 1997).

The latest emphasis in that literature is to try to define corporate social responsibility through a notion of corporate citizenship. Corporate citizenship can be defined as 'limited rights, privileges, duties, and obligations consistent with these [business] organizations' primary mission of supporting individual autonomy and goal attainment, and institutional viability, especially by "defense against common enemies" such as social injustice' (Wood and Logsdon 2002).

Corporate citizenship has even been defined as aiming 'to enhance the quality of community life through active, participate organized involvement' (Tichy et al. 1997: 3). The notion of corporate citizenship, at least as exemplified in these two definitions, is that it is not yet well developed. While these appear to be fairly benign definitions, they raise the question of the extent to which firms have obligations to address social injustices. We have argued that corporations have responsibilities to their primary stakeholders as defined by their mission and activities, and as restrained by precepts of common morality. Fuller has responsibilities to make a good glue, just as Beech-Nut has responsibilities to put apple juice in a product so named. Each has responsibilities not to create or abet human-rights violations or cause egregious harms. These are also the responsibilities of ordinary citizens. We often require or expect more of ordinary citizens—that they participate in community and political activities and engage in practices that encourage social justice. But are these also requirements of corporate citizens? Moreover, while as citizens, ordinarily we have a set of community and political responsibilities, internationally these responsibilities are circumscribed by the sovereignty of other nations. We are critical of individuals as well as countries that interfere with other nations, and similarly we are critical of firms that expand their sovereignty internationally. So even if we limit corporate citizenship to citizenship in the country from which a company operates (its 'home' country), one must take care before overascribing positive corporate responsibilities. Corporate responsibility that overextends itself into paternalism can be liberty-limiting, as examples of 'company towns' in the late nineteenth and early twentieth centuries should remind us. On an international level, multinational firms that exert economic power in small countries can also find themselves engaged in political interference as well. This does not mean that any company should encourage, abet, or contribute to harmful practices, but corporations are ordinarily not experts in politics or macroeconomics, and the question of national sovereignty cannot be ignored. There is a thin line between corporate responsibility and imperialism.

There are difficulties, then, in thinking about firms as citizens, since, as we have argued at length, corporations are different from individuals. There are particular dangers when one tries to use the notion of corporate citizenship for multinational or global companies that operate in many countries. A more fruitful approach is to evaluate whether a particular set of activities is expected, desirable, or questionable as part of corporate social responsibility. One can ask questions such as the following:

• Is this activity necessary in order to conduct business?
• Is it necessary to redress harms caused by the company?
• Are the activities (or activity) within the scope of the firm's expertise and knowledge?
• Can they be carried out without harming the firm's basic enterprises?
• Can such activities be carried out without interfering with social fabric, or community, or national autonomy?
• Does this set of activities pass a stakeholder and community 'publicity test'? That is, can we make these activities public? Will the firm's stakeholders including its shareholders applaud or disapprove? (see Werhane 1994: 141)

Corporate social responsibility is not unimportant. But, like any corporate activity, any so-called socially responsible activity should be evaluated, and not every allegedly good work is within the preview of every firm; indeed some should be avoided.

3.7 Corporate Responsibility and the Limits of Minimalism

Given the foregoing discussion, we can conclude that corporations, like persons, have obligations to persons and institutions other than their shareholders; if we accept stakeholder theory, these obligations are defined by corporate mission and role obligations, and precepts of common-sense morality. But why should any corporation interested in efficiency, productivity, survival, growth, and profitability take seriously its moral obligations to stakeholders other than shareholders beyond minimal requirements? And why should its shareholders allow such moral 'indulgences'?

In their 1994 book, *Built to Last: Successful Habits of Visionary Companies*, James C. Collins and Jerry I. Porras studied the characteristics of the 'visionary companies' (as identified by polling CEOs of 700 major corporations), and examined how these companies differed from other 'comparison companies'. Collins and Porras define a visionary company as the premier organization in its respective industry, as being widely admired by its peers, and as having a long track record of making a significant impact on the world around it. Each of the visionary companies chosen by the CEO poll has faced setbacks, and each has made mistakes. Still, the long-term financial performance of each has been remarkable. A dollar invested in a visionary company stock fund on 1 January 1926, with dividends reinvested, and making appropriate adjustments for when the companies became available on the stock market, would have grown by 31 December 1990 to $6,356. That dollar invested in a general market fund would have grown to $415.

What was different about visionary companies as compared to the comparison companies? Each operates in the same market and each has relatively the same opportunities. What is critical for the visionary or successful companies, according to Collins and Porras's findings, is that a visionary company is driven by an ideology that 'it lives, breathes, and expresses in all it does. ... A visionary company almost religiously preserves its core ideology—changing it seldom, if ever' (Collins and Porras 1994: 8). Moreover,

contrary to business school doctrine, 'maximizing shareholder wealth' or 'profit maximization' has not been the dominant driving force or primary objective through the history of the visionary companies. Visionary companies pursue a cluster of objectives, of which making money is only one—and not necessarily the primary one. Yes, they seek profits, but they are equally guided by a core ideology—core values and a sense of purpose beyond just making money. Yet, paradoxically, the visionary companies make more money than the more purely profit-driven comparison companies.   (Collins and Porras 1994: 8)

4. CONCLUSION

The notion of corporate responsibility is essential so that we can account for our ordinary language that holds companies as well as individuals morally responsible. We not only want to praise or blame individual managers, but we also want a philosophical mechanism to explain collective responsibility as well. The notion of collective moral agency does that work. At the same time, there are limits to what we can expect from corporations, just as there are limits to individual moral responsibilities. However, it may be the case that a minimalist attitude is not conducive to best practices, and indeed it appears that in visionary companies the attitude towards certain kinds of values is far from minimalist. These companies are more imaginative, more creative, and, for the most part, more responsible as well.

However, one question remains concerning corporate responsibility: can business do 'good works?' It is easy to wonder whether it is asking too much of companies to engage in good works beyond engaging in corporate best practices. However, we do find examples of supererogatory behaviour in business; for example, 3M with a twenty-five-year record of positive environmental initiatives; Steelcase, the largest manufacturer of office furniture in the world, which now makes environmentally compostable materials; Unilever, which has developed a Triple Bottom Line accounting mechanism that measures equally economic, social, and environmental outcomes; and Merck, whose 'gift' of over 400 million doses of Mectizan, a cure for river blindness, to people in remote developing countries has virtually stamped out that disease. These good works, and the many others that we have not mentioned, are a real threat to corporate moral minimalism. Each is part of that company's best practices; each has to do with the expertise of the firm in question, and, indeed, in many cases the 'good works' enhance the competitive advantage of that firm by enhancing or broadening that expertise. Each presents a model for corporate responsibility that goes beyond what is ordinarily expected while staying within the boundaries and scope of company capabilities.

References

Angell, Marcia (1996). *Science on Trial*. New York: W. W. Norton & Co.

Boatright, John (1999a). *Ethics in Finance*. Malden, MA: Blackwell.

—— (1999b). 'Does Business Ethics Rest on a Mistake?' *Business Ethics Quarterly*, 9: 583–92.

Bollier, David (1996). *Aiming Higher*. New York: American Management Association.

—— Weiss, Stephanie, and Hanson, Kirk O. (1991). 'Merck and Co'. Harvard University Graduate School of Business Administration Case No. 9-991-021. Boston: Harvard Business School Press.

Bowie, Norman, and Lenway, Stephanie (1999). 'H. B. Fuller in Honduras: Street Children and Substance Abuse', in Thomas Donaldson and Patricia H. Werhane (eds.), *Ethical Issues in Business*. 6th edn. Englewood Cliffs, NJ: Prentice Hall.

Bratton, William (1989). 'The "Nexus of Contracts" Corporation: A Critical Appraisal'. *Cornell Law Review*. 74: 407–65.

Carroll, Archie (1979). 'A Three-Dimensional Model of Corporate Performance'. *Academy of Management Review*. 4: 497–505.

Coase, Ronald (1937). 'The Nature of the Firm'. *Economica*, NS 4: 386–405.

Coleman, James (1990). *Foundations of Social Theory*. Cambridge, MA: Harvard University Press.

Collins, James C., and Porras, Jerry I. (1994). *Built to Last: Successful Habits of Visionary Companies*. New York: Harper Business.

Dennett, Daniel C. (1978). *Brainstorms: Philosophical Essays on Mind and Psychology*. Cambridge, MA: MIT Press.

—— (1995). *Darwin's Dangerous Idea*. New York: Simon & Schuster.

Donaldson, Thomas (1982). *Corporations and Morality*. Englewood Cliffs, NJ: Prentice Hall.

—— and Dunfee, Thomas (1995). 'Integrative Social Contracts Theory: A Communitarian Conception of Economic Ethics'. *Economics and Philosophy*, 11/1: 85–112.

—— and Preston, Lee (1995). 'The Stakeholder Theory of the Corporation: Concepts, Evidence, and Implications'. *Academy of Management Review*, 20: 65–91.

Eells, Richard, and Walton, Clarence (1961). *Conceptual Foundations of Business*. Homewood, IL: Richard D. Irwin.

Evan, William, and Freeman, R. Edward (1988). 'A Stakeholder Theory of the Modern Corporation: Kantian Capitalism', in Tom Beauchamp and Norman Bowie, *Ethical Theory and Business*. 3rd edn. Englewood Cliffs, NJ: Prentice Hall.

Freeman, R. Edward (1984). *Strategic Management: A Stakeholder Approach*. Boston: Pitman Publishing.

—— (1994). 'The Politics of Stakeholder Theory: Some Future Directions'. *Business Ethics Quarterly*, 4: 409–22.

—— (1999). 'Stakeholder Theory and the Modern Corporation', in Thomas Donaldson and Patricia H. Werhane (eds.), *Ethical Issues in Business*. 6th edn. Upper Saddle River, NJ: Prentice Hall, 247–57.

French, Peter A. (1979). 'The Corporation as a Moral Person'. *American Philosophical Quarterly*, 16/3: 207–15.

—— (1984). *Collective and Corporate Responsibility*. New York: Columbia University Press.

Friedman, Milton (1970). 'The Social Responsibility of Business is to Increase its Profits'. *New York Times Magazine*, 13 Sept.

Goodpaster, Kenneth (1984). 'The Concept of Corporate Responsibility', in T. Regan (ed.), *Just Business*. New York: Random House, 292–323.

—— (1997). 'Business Ethics', in P. Werhane and E. Freeman (eds.), *Encyclopedic Dictionary of Business Ethics*. Oxford: Blackwell, 51–7.

Goozner, Merrill (1996). 'The *mensch* of Malden Mills Inspires'. *Chicago Tribune*, 26 Dec. 1, 27.

Halliday, Bronwyn, and Paine, Lynn Sharp (1992). 'Beech-Nut Nutrition Corporation'. Harvard Graduate School of Business Administration Case No. 9-392-084. Boston: Harvard Business School Press.

Hardimon, Michael (1994). 'Role Obligations'. *Journal of Philosophy*, 91/7: 333–63.

Hessen, Robert (1979). *In Defense of the Corporation*. Stanford, CA: Hoover Institution Press.

Jacques, E. (1951). *The Changing Culture of a Factory*. New York: Dryden Press.

Keeley, Michael (1988). *A Social-Contract Theory of Organizations*. Notre Dame, IN: Notre Dame University Press.

Luban, David (1988). *Lawyers and Justice*. Princeton: Princeton University Press.

McMahon, Christopher (1994). *Authority and Democracy*. Princeton: Princeton University Press.

—— (1995). 'The Moral Status of Organizations'. *Business Ethics Quarterly*, 5: 541–54.

McMahon, Thomas (1997). 'History of Business Ethics', in P. Werhane and E. Freeman (eds.), *Encyclopedic Dictionary of Business Ethics*. Oxford: Blackwell, 317–20.

Millon, David (1990). 'Theories of the Corporation'. *Duke Law Journal*, 2: 201–62.

Mitchell, R. K., Agle, Bradley, and Wood, Donna (1997). 'Toward a Theory of Stakeholder Identification and Salience: Defining the Principle of Who and What Really Counts'. *Academy of Management Review*, 22: 853–86.

Moldoveanu, Mihnea, and Paine, Lynn Sharp (2000). 'Royal Dutch/Shell in Nigeria'. Harvard Graduate School of Business Administration Case No. 9-399-126. Boston: Harvard Business School Press.

Narva, Richard (1996). 'The Real Story on Malden Mills'. *Genus Resources, Inc.*, www.genusresources.com/msepcv_7.html.

O'Kelley, Charles R., Jr. (1979). 'The Constitutional Rights of Corporations Revisited: Social and Political Expression and the Corporation after *First National Bank* v. *Bellotti*'. *Georgetown Law Review*, 67/5: 1347–84.

Phillips, Michael (1992). 'Corporate Moral Personhood and Three Conceptions of the Corporation'. *Business Ethics Quarterly*, 2: 435–59.

—— (1995). 'Corporate Moral Responsibility'. *Business Ethics Quarterly*, 5: 555–76.

Phillips, Robert (1997). 'Stakeholder Theory and a Principle of Fairness'. *Business Ethics Quarterly*, 7: 51–66.

—— (Forthcoming). 'Normative Stakeholder Theory: Toward a Conception of Stakeholder Legitimacy'. *Business Ethics Quarterly*, 12.

Radin, Tara, and Werhane, Patricia (1997). 'Employment at Will and Due Process', in Tom Beauchamp and Norman Bowie (eds.), *Ethical Theory and Business*. 5th edn. Englewood Cliffs, NJ: Prentice Hall, 275–83.

Sethi, S. Prakash (1975). 'Dimensions of Corporate Social Performance: An Analytical Framework'. *California Management Review*, 17/3: 58–64.

Smith, Adam (1776/1791/1976). *The Wealth of Nations*, ed. R. H. Campbell and A. S. Skinner. Oxford: Oxford University Press.

Sollars, Gordon (forthcoming). 'Proportional Liability'. *Journal of Business Ethics*.

Spencer, Edward, Mills, Ann, Rorty, Mary, and Werhane, Patricia (1999). *Organization Ethics for Health Care*. New York: Oxford University Press.

Stocker, Julie, Gorman, Michael, and Werhane Patricia H. (2000). 'Dow Corning Corporation Breast Implant Design' in Michael Gorman, Matthew Mehalik, and Patricia H. Werhane (eds.), *Ethical and Environmental Challenges to Engineering*. Englewood Cliffs, NJ: Prentice Hall.

Tichy, Noel M., McGill, Andrew R., and St Clair, Lynda (1997) (eds.), *Corporate Global Citizenship: Doing Business in the Public Eye*. San Francisco: New Lexington Press.

Velasquez, Manuel G. (1983). 'Why Corporations Are Not Morally Responsible for Anything They Do'. *Business and Professional Ethics Journal*, 2/3: 1–18.

Victor, Bart, and Cullen, J. (1988). 'The Organizational Bases of Ethical Work Climates'. *Administrative Science Quarterly*, 33: 101–25.

Walzer, Michael (1994). *Thick and Thin*. Notre Dame, IN: Notre Dame University Press.

Werhane, Patricia H. (1985). *Persons, Rights, and Corporations*. Englewood Cliffs, NJ: Prentice Hall.

—— (1991). *Adam Smith and his Legacy for Modern Capitalism*. New York: Oxford University Press.

—— (1994). 'The Moral Responsibility of Multinational Corporations to be Socially Responsible', in W. Michael Hoffman, Judith Kamm, Robert Frederick, and Edward Petry (eds.), *Emerging Global Business Ethics*. Westport, CT: Quorum Books.

—— (1996). 'Business Ethics', in *Encyclopedia of Philosophy*. New York: Macmillan Publishing.

Wood, D., and Logsdon, J. (2002). 'Business Citizenship: From Individuals to Organizations'. *Ethics and Entrepreneurship*, Ruffin Series 3. Charlottesville, VA: Philosophy Documentation Center, 59–94.

CHAPTER 21

WHISTLEBLOWING

MICHAEL DAVIS

1. INTRODUCTION

WHISTLEBLOWING is not so much a settled practice as a growing collection of acts in search of a unifying analysis. Indeed, there is even disagreement concerning which acts belong to the collection. So, for example, a recent text in business ethics, in the course of distinguishing between 'internal' and 'external' whistleblowing, gives as an example of internal whistleblowing '[the] engineers for Morton Thiokol [stressing] to their superiors, prior to the launch, the seriousness of their concerns about launching the shuttle in low temperatures' (Adams and Maine 1998: 175–6) One of these engineers, Roger Boisjoly, has become a sort of paradigm of whistleblowing, but the act that won him that status was not objecting to the launch of the *Challenger* the night before it exploded, but testimony about that night given to the Rogers Commission several months later.

Since texts generally try to avoid controversial examples, this example is informative. The text has treated responding honestly but negatively to a superior's question as whistleblowing (rather than as simply part of an engineer's job). This mistake—if that is what it is—is evidence that 'whistleblowing' (in the sense relevant here) is, like many other relatively new terms, far from having a settled definition (Elliston et al. 1985). Any attempt to make sense of the concept of whistleblowing must in part be an attempt to shape the concept, to legislate usage. In so far as legislating usage involves balancing a number of considerations, it is no less likely to create controversy than other forms of legislating are. Rational people can disagree about how much weight to give this or that consideration.

This state of things seems to disallow any hope of an analysis of whistleblowing that is both interesting and uncontroversial. What I can do, what I shall try to do, is give one informed observer's sense of how whistleblowing should be understood, what moral and practical problems whistleblowing (so understood) raises, and how those problems might be resolved. The chief test of my recommendations is whether they help us understand whistleblowing better, not whether they fit usage. Usage is nonetheless relevant: if my recommendations stray too far from usage, I will be talking about something other than whistleblowing.

2. THE METAPHOR OF 'WHISTLEBLOWING'

The term 'whistleblowing' (in the sense that interests us) is plainly metaphorical. What is the metaphor? There are at least three candidates. One is a train sounding its whistle to warn those on the track to get off. This whistleblowing is a morally unambiguous warning (such as the engineers at Thiokol gave their superiors on the night before the *Challenger* exploded). Its emphasis is on sounding an alarm. Another candidate metaphor emphasizes wrongdoing. In many sports, referees blow a whistle to signal a foul, stopping play. The whistle does not sound an alarm but merely starts the process of penalizing the foul. A third candidate for the whistleblowing metaphor combines elements of the first two. The police officer blows his whistle to stop wrongdoing but—unlike the referee—he also sounds an alarm. The sound of his whistle should bring help, both ordinary citizens and other police, so that the officer can, for example, catch a purse snatcher.

What is striking about this list of candidates for the metaphor underlying the term 'whistleblowing' is that none seems appropriate. The first reduces whistle-blowers to mere alarmists. The second treats whistleblowers as 'referees'—that is, as neutrals charged with enforcing the 'rules of the game'. Whistleblowers are never that. Well, almost never. A few whistleblowers—for example, internal auditors—do have jobs rather like referees. Such exceptions need not concern us. Like other whistleblowers, they become whistleblowers not when they sound an alarm but when they sound it out of approved channels. A whistleblower is, then, more like a 'member of the team' who calls a foul on his own teammates, usurping the role of referee (Bok 1980: 2–7). The police officer, like the referee, is not a 'member of the [wrongdoer's] team'. 'Whistleblowing' seems to have slipped its etymological mooring.

3. JUSTIFICATION IN GENERAL

Given that neither usage nor etymology is much help in understanding whistle-blowing, how are we to construct the unifying analysis we desire? Whistleblowing is a practical concept. It seems to identify a kind of conduct, one in need of justification. So, I think the best way to understand whistleblowing is to begin with the problem of justification. What we must look for is a conception in which whistleblowing is always in need of justification and at least sometimes capable of it. We should, if possible, try to construct that conception so that one form of justification is good for all examples of justified whistleblowing (and only for those). That justification will, in effect, define what we mean by 'whistleblowing' strictly so called.

We may distinguish three (related) senses in which an act may be 'justified'. First, an act may be something morality permits. Many acts—for example, writing a letter to a friend—are morally justified in this weak sense. They are (all things considered) morally all right, though some of the alternatives are morally all right too (writing to a parent or eating lunch). Second, acts may be morally justified in a stronger sense. Not only is doing them morally all right, but doing anything else instead is morally wrong. These acts are *morally required*. Third, some acts, though only morally justified in the weaker sense, are still required, all things considered. They are mandatory because of some non-moral consideration. They are rationally (but not morally) required.

Generally, we do not *need* to justify an act unless we have reason to think it wrong (whether morally wrong or wrong in some other way). So, for example, I do not ordinarily need to justify writing a letter to a friend, though I would if I intend to include comments likely to offend him. We also do not need a justification if we believe the act in question wrong. We do not need a justification because, in so far as an act is wrong, justification is impossible. The point of justification is to show an act to be right when its rightness has been put in (reasonable) doubt. In so far as we believe the act wrong, we can only condemn or excuse it. To condemn it is simply to declare it wrong. To excuse it is to show that, while the act was wrong, the doer had good reason to do it, could not help doing it, or for some other reason should not suffer the response otherwise reserved for such a wrongdoer.

To say that an act needs justification is not to say that the alternatives do not require justification too. Occasionally, we must choose in circumstances where all the alternatives, even doing nothing, are objectionable (each in its own way). In such circumstances, several of the alternatives may be justifiable, though each for somewhat different reasons. We choose with difficulty, perhaps risking much we value, but we do not risk choosing unjustifiably (or, at least, do not risk that any more than we normally do).

4. Why a Justification of Whistleblowing?

Most acts, though what morality permits or requires, need no justification. There is no reason to think them wrong. Their justification is too plain for words. How then are we to understand whistleblowing so that it becomes clear why we have *theories* of its justification? What general reasons do we have to think whistleblowing morally problematic?

4.1 Revealing

Whistleblowing always involves revealing information that would not ordinarily be revealed. But there is nothing morally problematic about that: after all, revealing information not ordinarily revealed is one function of science. Whistleblowing always involves, in addition, an actual (or at least declared) intention to prevent something bad. There is nothing morally problematic in that either. That may well be the chief way we use information.

4.2 Honest Organization

What seems to make whistleblowing morally problematic is its organizational context. A mere individual cannot blow the whistle (in any interesting sense); only a member of an organization, whether a current or a former member, can. Indeed, she can blow the whistle only on her own organization (or some part of it). So, for example, a police officer who makes public information about a burglary ring, though a member of an organization, does not blow the whistle on the burglary ring (in any interesting sense). She simply alerts the public. Even if she came by the information working undercover in the ring, her revelation would not be whistleblowing. While secret agents, spies, and other infiltrators need a moral justification for what they do, the justification they need differs from that whistleblowers need. Infiltrators gain their information under false pretences. They need a justification for that deception. Whistleblowers generally do not gain their information under false pretences.

What if, instead of being a police officer, the revealer of information about the burglary ring were an ordinary member of the ring? Should we count such an informer as a whistleblower? I think not. Even a burglar who, having a change of heart, volunteers information about his ring to the police or the newspaper, does not need to justify his act in the way the whistleblower does. The burglary ring is a criminal organization. The whistleblower's organization never is, though it may occasionally engage in crime (knowingly or by inadvertence). Helping to destroy a criminal organization by revealing its secrets is morally less problematic than whistleblowing.

4.3 Trust

What then is morally problematic about the whistleblower's organizational context? The whistleblower cannot blow the whistle using just any information obtained in virtue of membership in the organization. A clerk in Accounts who, happening upon evidence of serious wrongdoing while visiting a friend in Quality Control, is not a whistleblower just because she passes the information to a friend at the *Tribune*. She is (without something more) more like a self-appointed spy. She seems to differ from the whistleblower, or at least from clear cases of the whistleblower, precisely in her relation to the information in question.

To be a whistleblower is, I think, to reveal information with which one is *entrusted*. This is not to say that there are no arguments for counting the friend from Accounting as a whistleblower, only that those arguments will have to convert her into someone trusted with the information. Perhaps, for example, the departments are so small that people in Accounts frequently pass through Quality Control and therefore have almost as much access to Quality Control documents as people in Quality Control do. That the organization trusted the person from Accounts with information from Quality Control seems relevant to deciding whether her revelation of that information would be whistleblowing (Koehn 1998: 210–14).

4.4 Not Self-Interested

Whistleblowing needs justification because it involves a breach of trust. But there is more to its need for justification than that. The whistleblower does not breach that trust to save his own skin (for example, to avoid perjury under oath); that is what a 'stool pigeon' does. Of course, for some purpose, for example, a whistleblower protection act, it may be convenient to include among whistleblowers those who reveal information to save their own skin (Burke 1997). But, for developing a general theory of justified whistleblowing, such cases are uninteresting. Avoiding contempt of court or Congress generally provides sufficient justification for testifying about serious wrongdoing; avoiding perjury provides sufficient justification for testifying truthfully. Indeed, avoiding contempt and avoiding perjury together seem to provide a stronger justification for revealing information with which one has been trusted than (as we shall see) the standard theory of whistleblowing (or my alternative) does. If we keep to our strategy of looking for a definition of whistleblowing that includes only those acts that share a common justification, we must exclude from whistleblowing (strictly so-called) all revealing of organizational information done to protect the revealer from harm. Those who reveal to protect themselves have a special excuse (or justification) for what they do, self-interest.

The (ordinary) whistleblower has no such *excuse*. She claims to be *justified* in revealing what she reveals. If she cannot honestly make that claim, her revelation is not (or, rather, should not be counted as) whistleblowing (and so, not justified as whistleblowing), but something analogous, much as pulling a child from the water is not a rescue, even if it saves the child's life, when the 'rescuer' merely believes himself to be salvaging old clothes.

4.5 Summary of Characteristics

What makes whistleblowing morally problematic, if anything does, is this high-minded but unexcused misuse of the whistleblower's position in a generally law-abiding, morally decent organization, an organization that prima facie deserves the whistleblower's faithful service, as a burglary ring does not. The whistleblower takes his concern out of channels that he has a prima facie moral obligation to remain within. At least part of what makes whistleblowing morally interesting is this conflict between faithful service and other prima facie moral claims.

4.6 Disloyalty

This faithful service to the organization is commonly referred to as 'loyalty' (or 'organizational loyalty'). There is now a small literature on loyalty generally (see e.g. Fletcher 1993). The literature on loyalty to organization is much smaller. For our purpose, we may define (organizational) loyalty as (in part at least) a willingness to act for the organization as one would be justified in acting if all reasonable doubts were resolved in the organization's favour. The 'warm feeling' we associate with loyalty arises from thinking of the object of loyalty in this favourable way. An organization that does not seem to deserve our faithful service even when thought of in this favourable way (probably) does not deserve it at all.

Loyalty so defined is a kind of bias (a radical discounting of evidence)—and so, always in need of justification. The justification of organizational loyalty has its own problems. Most organizations understand their employees as instruments rather than members, raising deep questions about the point of organizational loyalty. Why should I have warm feelings for an organization that regards me as a mere instrument? How can I reasonably trust such an organization (Baron 1984)? While justifying whistleblowing is easier the less loyalty one owes the organization in question, we will learn more about whistleblowing if we focus on the harder cases, those where we admit significant obligations of loyalty. So, that is what I do here.

4.7 Contested Disloyalty

The whistleblower must reveal information the organization does not want revealed. But, in any actual organization, 'what the organization wants' will be contested, with various individuals or groups asking to be taken as speaking for the organization. To be a whistleblower, one must at least temporarily lose an argument about what the organization wants. The whistleblower is often at once loyal to the organization (from his own perspective) and disloyal to it (from its official perspective).

The whistleblower must also go out of approved channels—but which channels are approved may itself be controversial. Indeed, the very notion of 'internal whistleblowing' depends on a distinction within the organization between approved channels and others somehow available. So, for example, in one organization, an employee may be able to appeal from his boss's decision directly to one of the vice-presidents without anyone labelling him a whistleblower. In another organization, or even in the same organization on another day or for another issue, a similar employee may have his appeal to a similar vice-president labelled as whistleblowing. Internal whistleblowers often become whistleblowers only after losing an argument about whether a certain internal channel is all right, an argument they might have won in an organization better designed to use the information the employee has.

So, the whistleblower, whether external or internal, is disloyal only in a sense—the sense the winners of the internal argument get to dictate. What can justify such disloyalty? That, apparently, is the question upon which we must focus to understand whistleblowing.

5. THE STANDARD THEORY

Credit for the theory of whistleblowing now standard generally goes to Richard De George, though Norman Bowie (1982: 143) seems to have published it about the same time. According De George (1990: 200–14), whistleblowing (as we have defined it) is morally permissible when:

(S1) The organization to which the would-be whistleblower belongs will, through its product or policy, do serious and considerable harm to the public (whether to users of its product, to innocent bystanders, or to the public at large);

(S2) The would-be whistleblower has identified that threat of harm, reported it to her immediate superior, making clear both the threat itself and the objection to it, and concluded that the superior will do nothing effective; and

(S3) The would-be whistleblower has exhausted other internal procedures within the organization (for example, by going up the organizational ladder as far as allowed)—or at least made use of as many internal procedures as the danger to others and her own safety make reasonable.

Whistleblowing is morally required (according to the standard theory) when, in addition:

(S4) The would-be whistleblower has (or has accessible) evidence that would convince a reasonable, impartial observer that her view of the threat is correct; and

(S5) The would-be whistleblower has good reason to believe that revealing the threat will (probably) prevent the harm at reasonable cost (all things considered).

Why is whistleblowing morally required when these five conditions are met? According to the standard theory, whistleblowing is morally required, when it is, because 'people have a moral obligation to prevent serious harm to others if they can do so with little cost to themselves' (De George 1990: 200). In other words, whistleblowing meeting all five conditions is a form of 'minimally decent samaritanism' (a doing of what morality requires) rather than 'good samaritanism' (going well beyond the moral minimum) (Singer 1972; Gewirth 1978: 217–30; Smith 1990).

A few writers have pointed out that the relation between the first three conditions and the full five does not seem to be that between the morally permissible and the morally required (Goldberg 1988). If, for example, the whistleblower lacks evidence that would convince a reasonable, impartial observer of the threat in question (S4), her whistleblowing could not prevent harm. Since it could not prevent harm, her whistleblowing would not be even morally permissible: what could make morally permissible an attempt to help a stranger when the attempt will probably fail and the cost be high both to the would-be samaritan and to those to whom she owes a competing obligation? The most that can be said for blowing the whistle where only conditions S1–S3 are met seems to be that the whistleblower has an excuse when (without negligence) she acts on inadequate evidence. So, the better view seems to be that S1–S5 state sufficient conditions for morally required whistleblowing even though S1–S3 do not state sufficient conditions for morally permissible whistleblowing but (at best) for morally excusable whistleblowing.

The standard theory is not a *definition* of whistleblowing or even of justified whistleblowing. The theory purports to state sufficient conditions, but not necessary conditions (a 'when' but *not* an 'only when'). These conditions are supposed to identify only the central cases of morally justified whistleblowing. Other cases will have to be identified another way, presumably by arguments from analogy; the weaker the analogy, the less central the case. Since a theory that identified only most cases of whistleblowing in some such way would be quite useful, we cannot object to the theory merely because it is incomplete or messy in this way. Incomplete and messy only in this way, it would be about as useful as theories of practical ethics ever are.

6. SOME PROBLEMS WITH THE STANDARD THEORY

I shall now identify three paradoxical consequences of the standard theory. These paradoxes are, I believe, together enough to make appealing the alternative I will then offer.

6.1 Burden

The first paradox concerns a commonplace of the whistleblowing literature. Whistleblowers are not minimally decent samaritans. If they are samaritans at all, they are good samaritans. They always act at considerable risk to career and generally at considerable risk to their financial security and personal relations.

In this respect, as in many others, Roger Boisjoly is typical. Boisjoly blew the whistle on his employer, Morton Thiokol, when he volunteered information, in public testimony before the Rogers Commission, that Morton Thiokol did not want him to volunteer. As often happens, both his employer and many who relied on it for employment reacted hostilely. Boisjoly had to say goodbye to the company town, to old friends and neighbours, and to building rockets; he had to start a new career at an age when most people are preparing for retirement.

Since whistleblowing is generally costly to the whistleblower in some such large way as this, the standard theory's minimally decent samaritanism provides *no* justification for the central cases of whistleblowing. That is the first paradox, what we might call 'the paradox of burden'.

6.2 Harm

The second paradox concerns the prevention of 'harm'. According to the standard theory, the would-be whistleblower must seek to prevent 'serious and considerable harm' in order for the whistleblowing to be even morally permissible. There seems to be a good deal of play on the term 'harm'. The harm in question can be physical (such as death or disease), financial (such as loss of or damage to property), and perhaps even psychological (such as fear or mental illness). But there is a limit to how much the standard theory can stretch 'harm'. Beyond that limit are 'harms' like injustice, deception, and waste. As morally important as injustice, deception, and waste can be, they do not seem to constitute the 'serious and considerable harm' that requires someone to become even a minimally decent samaritan.

Yet, many cases of whistleblowing, perhaps most, are not about preventing serious and considerable physical, financial, or psychological harm. For example, by the time Boisjoly testified before the Rogers Commission, the seven astronauts were beyond help, the shuttle programme was suspended, and any further threat of physical, financial, or psychological harm to the 'public' was—after discounting for time—negligible. Boisjoly had little reason to believe his testimony would make a significant difference in the booster's redesign, in safety procedures in the shuttle programme, or even in reawakening concern for safety among NASA employees and contractors. The *Challenger*'s explosion was much more likely to do that than anything Boisjoly could do. What Boisjoly could do in his testimony, what I think he tried to do, was prevent falsification of the record.

Falsification of the record is harm in a sense (a setback to an interest), especially in a record as historically important as that the Rogers Commission was to produce. But falsification is harm only in a sense that almost empties 'harm' of its distinctive meaning, leaving it more or less equivalent to 'moral wrong'. (We all have an interest in others acting morally.) Of course, falsification has a connection with other interests as well. Falsification increases the likelihood that (ordinary) harm will occur. All else being equal, we are safer acting on the truth than against it. But the question now is not whether falsity in Rogers Commission's record would increase the likelihood of harm, but whether that remote and uncertain harm is consistent with the standard theory's approach to justifying whistleblowing.

The proponents of the standard theory must mean more by 'harm' than any possible harm, however remote and uncertain. They must because protecting from such harm is more than the minimally decent samaritan does; indeed, more than even the good samaritan did. So, we should not be surprised that De George explicitly restricts himself 'to products and practices that produce or threaten serious harm or danger to life and health' (1990: 210). The standard theory is strikingly narrower in its grounds of justification than many (relatively) uncontroversial examples of justified whistleblowing suggest it should be. That is the second paradox, the 'paradox of missing harm'.

6.3 Failure

The third paradox is related to the second. In so far as whistleblowers are understood as people out to prevent harm, not just to prevent moral wrong, their chances of success are poor. Whistleblowers generally do not prevent much harm (or at least the harm they seek to prevent). In this too, Boisjoly has become a paradigm of whistleblowers. In so far as we can identify cause and effect, even now we have little reason to believe that—whatever his intention—his testimony actually prevented any harm. So, if whistleblowers must have, as the standard theory says (S5), 'good reason to believe that revealing the threat will (probably) prevent the harm', then the history of whistleblowing virtually rules out the moral justification of whistleblowing. That is certainly paradoxical in a theory purporting to state sufficient conditions for the central cases of justified whistleblowing. Let us call this 'the paradox of failure'.

7. AN ALTERNATIVE: COMPLICITY

Collect all the relatively uncontroversial cases of whistleblowing: is there anyone in these cases who, like the clerk from Accounts, just happened upon key documents in a cover-up? The answer is few, if any: whistleblowers (generally) are not mere third parties like the good samaritan. They are generally deeply involved in the activity they reveal. (See, for example, the collections of whistleblowing cases: Westin 1981; Glazer and Glazer 1989.) This involvement suggests that we might understand whistleblowing better if we understand the whistleblower's obligation to derive from *complicity* in wrongdoing rather than from the ability to prevent harm.

Any complicity theory of justified whistleblowing has two obvious advantages over the standard theory. One is that (moral) complicity itself presupposes (moral) wrongdoing, not harm. So, a complicity justification automatically avoids the paradox of missing harm, fitting the facts of whistleblowing better than a theory that, like the standard one, emphasizes prevention of harm.

Second, complicity invokes a more demanding obligation than the ability to prevent harm does. We are morally obliged to avoid doing moral wrongs. When, despite our best efforts, we nonetheless find ourselves engaged in some wrong, we have an obligation to do what we reasonably can to set things right. If, for example, I cause a traffic accident, I have a moral (and legal) obligation to call for help, stay at the scene till help arrives, and render first aid (if I know how), even at substantial cost to myself and those to whom I owe my time, and even with little likelihood that anything I do will help much. Just as a complicity theory automatically avoids the paradox of missing harm, it also automatically avoids the paradox of burden.

What about the third paradox, the paradox of failure? That depends on the details of the theory. I must therefore offer a formulation before I can show that, unlike the standard theory, the complicity theory can avoid the paradox of burden. Here is my formulation of the *complicity theory*:

You are morally required to reveal what you know to the public (or to a suitable agent or representative of it) when:

  (C1) what you will reveal derives from your work for an organization;
  (C2) you are a voluntary member of that organization;

(C3) you believe that the organization, though legitimate, is engaged in a serious moral wrong;

(C4) you believe that your work for that organization will contribute (more or
less directly) to the wrong if (but *not* only if) you do not publicly reveal
what you know;

(C5) you are justified in beliefs C3 and C4; and

(C6) beliefs C3 and C4 are true.

8. Major Differences between the Two Theories

The complicity theory so formulated differs from the standard theory in several
ways worth pointing out here.

8.1 Source of Information

The first is that, according to C1, what the whistleblower reveals must derive from
his work for the organization. This condition distinguishes the whistleblower from
the spy (and the clerk from Accounts). The spy seeks out information in order to
reveal it; the whistleblower learns it as a proper part of doing the job the organization has assigned him. The standard theory, in contrast, has nothing to say about
how the whistleblower comes to know of the threat she reveals (S2). For the standard theory, spies are just a kind of whistleblower. The standard theory can, of
course, be amended to exclude spies, but the reason for the amendment will be
usage, not (as with complicity theory) a consideration internal to the theory itself.

8.2 Employee

A second way in which the complicity theory differs from the standard theory is
that the complicity theory (C2) explicitly requires the whistleblower to be a *voluntary* participant in the organization in question. Whistleblowing is not—according
to the complicity theory—an activity in which slaves, prisoners, or other involuntary participants in an organization engage. In this way, the complicity theory
makes explicit something implicit in the standard theory. The whistleblowers of the
standard theory are generally 'employees'; employees are voluntary participants in
the organization employing them.

What explains this difference in explicitness? For the samaritanism of the standard theory, the voluntariness of employment is extrinsic. What is crucial is the ability to prevent harm. Whistleblowers must be employees only to satisfy usage. For the complicity theory, however, the voluntariness is intrinsic. The obligations deriving from complicity varies with the voluntariness of the participation in wrongdoing. Consider, for example, a teller who helps a gang rob her bank because they have threatened to kill her if she does not: she does not have the same obligation to break off her association with the gang as someone who has freely joined it. The voluntariness of ordinary employment means that the would-be whistleblower's complicity is more like that of one of the gang than like that of the conscripted teller.

There are, of course, degrees of voluntariness. Even a loaded gun pointed at one's head leaves one free to choose (in some sense). But that is much less voluntariness than typical of the employment relation. The complicity theory does not require us to choose one sense of voluntariness within this range. It merely requires us to adjust the strength of obligation arising from complicity to the degree of voluntariness—and, I think, to recognize (as common sense does) that some people—slaves, prisoners, inmates in mental hospital, students in a school, and the like—are simply not voluntarily involved in the organization that holds them.

Do I claim that slaves, prisoners, inmates in a mental hospital, or students in a school cannot blow the whistle—or, at least, cannot do so justifiably? Well, not exactly. That the usual lists of whistleblowers include no involuntary participants in wrongdoing is, I think, important evidence for the claim that involuntary participants cannot blow the whistle. But, since how we have used a term does not determine how we can use it (especially a term like 'whistleblowing' where usage is still evolving), that evidence is hardly decisive. What I think is clear is that involuntary participants will not have the same obligation of loyalty as the typical whistleblower; hence, any theory justifying their 'going public' will have a somewhat different structure from the theory developed here.

What about *voluntary* participants who are not employees, such as unpaid volunteers in a political campaign? While the complicity theory clearly counts them as capable of justified whistleblowing, the standard theory must make some ad hoc provision. This is another weakness of the standard theory.

8.3 Wrong, not Harm

A third way in which the complicity theory differs from the standard theory is that the complicity theory (C3) requires moral wrong, not harm, for justification. The wrong need not be a new event (as a harm must be if it is to be *prevented*). The wrong might, for example, consist in no more than silence about facts necessary to correct a continuing injustice. If the revelation seems likely to prevent harm as well, or to help undo the effect of some injustice as well, that will, of course, strengthen the justification, making better a justification already good enough. But, according to complicity theory, such good consequences are not necessary for justification.

The complicity theory (C3) does, however, follow the standard theory in requiring that the predicate of whistleblowing be 'serious'. Under the complicity theory, minor wrongdoing can no more justify whistleblowing than can minor harm under the standard theory. While organizational loyalty cannot forbid whistleblowing, it does forbid 'tattling'—that is, revealing minor wrongdoing.

8.4 Success

A fourth way in which the complicity theory differs from the standard theory, the most important, is that the complicity theory (C4) requires that the whistleblower believe her work will have contributed to the wrong in question if she does nothing but does *not* require that she believe that her revelation will prevent (or undo) the wrong. The complicity theory does not require any belief about what the whistleblowing can accomplish (beyond ending complicity in the wrong in question). The whistleblower reveals what she knows to end complicity in the wrong, not to prevent the wrong as such (whether to end complicity in past wrong or to prevent complicity in some ongoing or future wrong). She can prevent complicity (if there is any to prevent) simply by 'publicly' revealing what she knows. The revelation itself breaks the bond of complicity, the secret partnership in wrongdoing, that makes her an accomplice in her organization's wrongdoing (something her mere departure from the organization cannot do).

We are, of course, assuming the standard case of whistleblowing where complicity involves only information. We can imagine more complicated cases where, in addition to information, there are benefits from the wrongdoing (say, a bonus derived from past wrongdoing). In such complex cases, revealing information (including the bonus) may not be all that is morally required to end complicity. Even so, it will, I think, end the complicity relevant to whistleblowing. The complicity theory thus avoids the third paradox, the paradox of failure, just as it avoided the other two.

8.5 Public

A fifth difference between the two theories is in the interpretation of the term 'public'. While neither theory includes an analysis of 'public', the standard theory explicitly follows usage in understanding the public as existing *outside* the organization. Whistleblowing is not necessarily 'going public', but it is always revealing information to someone who is both able and willing to do something to end the danger to some outsiders ('users of [the organization's] product...innocent bystanders, or...the public at large' (S1)). For the standard theory, the only difference between internal and external whistleblowing is that, in internal whistleblowing, the receiver of information is, though out of channels, still within the organization, while in external whistleblowing she is not. For the standard theory, whistleblowing cannot be justified as a way to protect the organization. Whistleblowing is necessarily 'public spirited'.

For complicity theory, in contrast, whistleblowing is not necessarily 'public spirited'. For complicity theory, 'public' means only 'persons whose knowledge of the wrongdoing will end the whistleblower's complicity' in it. The organization itself can be the public in this sense if, for example, a department has radically inflated the sale figures it sends to the board of directors. While internal whistleblowing may concern a public wrong (in the ordinary sense of 'public'), it may as easily concern a wrong to the organization. When it does, the whistleblower will be disloyal not to the organization as a whole but only to the part he is in.

I find this difference between the two theories puzzling. The samaritanism that, according to the standard theory, underwrites the moral obligation to blow the whistle seems to allow coming to the rescue of one's own organization as well as to the rescue of complete strangers. The only explanation I can see for the standard theory's excluding such 'internal whistleblowing' from the category of whistleblowing strictly so-called is that such a 'whistleblower' has a stronger obligation to sound an alarm than the standard theory provides: loyalty to the organization as a whole. If this is the reason for the standard theory's exclusion of 'private-spirited whistleblowing', we have a good explanation of why complicity theory should include such whistleblowing. Because the obligation to end complicity in wrongdoing is much stronger than the obligation to rescue, the complicity theory offers a justification of 'private-spirited' whistleblowing at least rivalling in strength one relying on loyalty.

8.6 Evidence

The sixth difference between the complicity theory and the standard theory is closely related to the fourth. Because publicly revealing what one knows breaks the bond of complicity, the complicity theory does not require the whistleblower to have enough evidence to convince others of the wrong in question. Convincing others, or just being able to convince them, is not, as such, an element in the justification of whistleblowing.

The complicity theory does, however, require (C5) that the whistleblower be (epistemically) justified in believing both that his organization is engaged in wrongdoing and that he will contribute to that wrong unless he blows the whistle. Such (epistemic) justification may require substantial physical evidence (as the standard theory says) or just a good sense of how things work. The complicity theory does not share the standard theory's substantial evidential requirement (S4).

8.7 Accuracy

In one respect, however, the complicity theory clearly requires more of the whistle-blower than the standard theory does. The complicity theory's C6—combined with C5—requires not only that the whistleblower be *justified* in her beliefs about the organization's wrongdoing and her part in it, but also that she be *right* about them. If she is mistaken about either the wrongdoing or her complicity, her revelation will not be justified whistleblowing. This consequence of C6 is, I think, not as surpris-ing as it may seem. If the would-be whistleblower is mistaken only about her own complicity, her revelation of actual wrongdoing, being otherwise justified, merely fails to be justified *as whistleblowing* (much as a failed rescue, though justified as an attempt, cannot be justified as a rescue). If, however, she is mistaken about the wrongdoing itself, her situation is more serious. Her belief that wrong is being done, though fully justified on the evidence available to her, cannot justify her dis-loyalty. All her justified belief can do is *excuse* her disloyalty. In so far as she acted with good intentions and while exercising reasonable care, she is a victim of bad luck. Such bad luck will leave her with an obligation to apologize, to correct the record (for example, by publicly recanting the charges she publicly made), and other-wise to set things right.

8.8 Channels

The complicity theory says nothing on at least one subject about which the standard theory says much: going through channels before publicly revealing what one knows. But the two theories differ less than this difference in emphasis suggests. If going through channels would suffice to prevent (or undo) the wrong, then it cannot be true (as C4 and C6 together require) that the would-be whistleblower's work will contribute to the wrong if she does not publicly reveal what she knows. Where, how-ever, going through channels would *not* prevent (or undo) the wrong, there is no need to go through channels. Condition C4's if-clause will be satisfied. For the com-plicity theory, going through channels is a way of finding out what the organization will do, not an independent requirement of justification. That, I think, is also how the standard theory in fact understands it. So, for example, De George says: 'By reporting one's concern to one's immediate superior or other appropriate person, one preserves and observes the regular practices of firms, which on the whole pro-mote their order and efficiency; this fulfills one's obligation of minimizing harm, and *it precludes precipitous whistleblowing*' (De George 1990: 211; emphasis added).

8.9 Morally Required

Another difference between the two theories worth mentioning here is that the complicity theory is only a theory of morally required whistleblowing, while the standard theory claims as well to define circumstances when whistleblowing is morally permissible but not morally required. This difference is another advantage that the complicity theory has over the standard theory. The standard theory, as we saw, has trouble making good on its claim to explain how whistleblowing can be morally permissible without being morally required.

8.10 Non-Consequentialism?

A last difference between the two theories worth mentioning here is that the standard theory is 'consequentialist' (concerned with reducing harm) while the complicity theory is not. This does not mean that which theory of whistleblowing one favours must be determined by the general moral theory one already accepts. There may be good consequentialist reasons for adopting the complicity theory, just as there may be good consequentialist reasons for obeying the law. Perhaps organizations that seek to do what is right (according to non-consequentialist standards) are much more likely to maximize overall well-being than organizations that try to maximize overall well-being directly. There may also be good non-consequentialist reasons for adopting the standard theory, just as there are good non-consequentialist reasons for paying attention to the harm you cause however unintentionally.

9. KINDS OF WHISTLEBLOWING

In ordinary usage, 'whistleblower' is a term capacious enough to allow for the following distinctions: internal or external; justified or unjustified; accurate or inaccurate; anonymous or open; well intentioned or not well intentioned. What happens to these distinctions once we adopt the complicity theory, treating as the central (or clear) cases of whistleblowing those the theory identifies as justified whistleblowing? For some of these distinctions, the answer is plain.

9.1 Internal, External

The distinction between internal and external whistleblowing, though somewhat different under complicity theory than under the standard theory, remains (as already explained).

9.2 Justified, Unjustified

The distinction between justified and unjustified whistleblowing also remains. But the complicity theory will assign some cases (for example, Boisjoly's testimony before the Rogers Commission) to the justified category that the standard theory assigns to the unjustified (given certain plausible assumptions about testimony, knowledge, and complicity). The complicity theory may also assign some cases of whistleblowing to the unjustified category that the standard theory assigns to the justified—in particular those cases in which the whistleblower was (epistemically) justified in her belief but in fact wrong about the existence of wrongdoing. In so far as whistleblowing is inaccurate on any essential matter, it is, according to the complicity theory (but not the standard theory) unjustified (though it may still be excused).

9.3 Anonymity

What about anonymous whistleblowing? For the standard theory, revealing what one knows about danger does not require revealing one's identity. The famous anonymous informant of the Watergate scandal, 'Deep Throat', was, according to the standard theory, a whistleblower (or, at least, would have been if the scandal involved a threat of harm of the sort the standard theory requires). For complicity theory, however, Deep Throat's status is more equivocal. His anonymity means we do not know whether he was revealing what he learned in the course of his work or what he learned by going out of his way. Even if we knew that he was not a free-lance spy, his status would still be equivocal. In so far as he betrayed a trust the organization put in him, he would—objectively—have ended his complicity. He would, in that respect, resemble a whistleblower. But, in so far as neither the organization nor anyone else knows of that betrayal (because his anonymity prevents their knowing), he remains complicit in everyone's eyes but his own. His 'whistle-blowing', even if justified, cannot be justified in the straightforward way ordinary whistleblowing is. His conduct requires a justification of the deception anonymity generally brings with it. That, perhaps, is reason enough to declare 'anonymous whistleblowing' only an analogue of whistleblowing strictly so-called.

9.4 Motive

What about the last of our distinctions, that between well-intentioned and ill-intentioned whistleblowing? Interest in this distinction depends, I think, on the standard theory's distinction between permissible and required whistleblowing. Because, under the standard theory, an agent is sometimes morally free to engage or not engage in whistleblowing, the question naturally arises why the whistle-blower did not keep quiet when keeping quiet was morally permissible. One obvious answer is, 'She was disgruntled.' For the complicity theory, however, the justified whistleblower has a complete explanation of her conduct as soon as she has shown that it is morally justified: she is simply doing what she should. Enquiry into what other reasons she might have is, even if historically interesting, beside the point morally. We cannot, for example, complain of Roger Boisjoly's honesty even if he gave honest testimony in part to make his enemies squirm. Doing what honesty requires, once recognized as such, needs no justification.

But (it may be objected), whistleblowing is never as morally simple as honesty. Whistleblowing always involves disloyalty or betrayal of trust. Part of recognizing an act as whistleblowing is recognizing moral claims inconsistent with it. It is these other claims that make us want to know more about the motivation of the whistle-blower, to be sure she really means well.

I agree with this explanation of why we want to be sure the whistleblower means well. What I deny is that, assuming her justification is satisfactory, we need enquire further. Under the complicity theory (and, indeed, under S1–S5 of the standard theory), the whistleblower has already given loyalty its due when she has shown her whistleblowing to be morally required.

There may, of course, be special reasons for not blowing the whistle beyond those the theory of whistleblowing is concerned with—for example, the harm whistle-blowing may do to innocent parties. In such cases, the whistleblower may face a dilemma (in the strict sense): two (apparently) inconsistent moral requirements. But, even in such a case, the moral requirement to blow the whistle would not differ from honesty (understood as the requirement not to lie, cheat, or steal). Sometimes we cannot both be honest and protect innocent parties from harm. When we cannot, we are not therefore free to choose either of the dilemma's horns. We are instead under an obligation to choose the lesser evil or invent a better option (one that takes us 'between the horns of the dilemma'). We should enquire into an agent's motive only if we think he made the wrong choice. That he 'meant well' will mitigate the blame. That he had a bad motive confirms us in our initial judgement that he deserves blame for doing what he should not have done.

10. WHISTLEBLOWER AS BAD NEWS

Given this analysis, how are we to explain why so many organizations are so hard on whistleblowers? After all, on this analysis, whistleblowers are simply doing what morality requires. Most organizations do not react with the same hostility to other manifestations of good character such as fairness or temperance.

10.1 Self-Interest

The most common answer is that those who mistreat whistleblowers do so because they expect to benefit from having fewer whistleblowers. The self-interest of individuals or their organization explains the mistreatment.

Though no doubt part of the truth, this explanation is, I think, only a small part. We are in general far from perfect judges of self-interest. Our judgement does not improve simply because we assume an organizational role. We can still be quite irrational. So, for example, in *Moral Mazes*, Robert Jackall (1988) grimly recounts what happened to several executives with bad news to tell their respective organizations. Though each discovered wrongdoing it was his duty to discover, reported it through channels, and saw the wrongdoer punished, though none of them was responsible for the wrong reported, and though the organization was better for the report, the lucky among Jackall's executives had their part in the affair forgotten. Some paid with their careers (Jackall 1988: 105–33).

10.2 Irrationality

We generally think of information as power—and it is. But thinking of information that way is no small achievement when the information wrecks our plans. Even experienced managers can find themselves telling subordinates, 'I don't want to hear any more bad news.'

The rationality of organizations is an ideal never more than partially achieved. We must keep that in mind if we are to understand what happens to so many whistleblowers. An organization that would ruin Jackall's simple bringers of bad news is not likely to respond well to the whistleblower—even if, as often happens, the whistleblower serves the organization's long-term interests. The whistleblower is, after all, not only a bearer of bad news; he *is* bad news.

10.3 Harm Whistleblowing Does

Discussions of whistleblowing tend to emphasize the undeniable good the accurate whistleblower does (both directly, by revealing wrongdoing, and indirectly, by deterring further wrongdoing). The incidental harm tends to be overshadowed, perhaps because so much of it seems deserved. The harm done by inaccurate whistleblowing has received much less attention, perhaps because organizations do not like to admit publicly that they have suffered.

Whatever the reasons for ignoring the bad news about whistleblowing, the fact remains that much of it is ignored and, for our purposes, the bad news is crucial. So, let us recall how much bad news there is: whistleblowing is always proof of organizational trouble. Employees do not go out of channels unless the channels at least *seem* inadequate. Whistleblowing is also proof of management failure. Usually several managers directly above the whistleblower will have heard his complaint, tried to deal with it in some way, and failed to satisfy him. However managers view the whistleblower's complaint, they are bound to view their own failure to 'keep control' as a blot on their record. Whistleblowing is also bad news for those on whom the whistle is blown. What they were peacefully doing in obscurity is suddenly in the spotlight. They will have to participate in investigations and 'damage control' that would not otherwise demand their scarce time. They will have to write unusual reports, attend special meetings, worry about the effect of publicity on their own career, and face the pointed questions of spouse, children, and friends. And they may have to go on doing such things for months—or even years.

10.4 Bias

In so far as whistleblowing has such effects, no one within the organization will be able to hear the whistleblower's name without thinking unpleasant thoughts. No manager will be able to make a decision about the whistleblower without having bad associations colour her judgement. The whistleblower not only makes conscious enemies within his organization; he can also create enormous biases against himself, biases very hard to cancel by any formal procedure.

10.5 Distrust

What must the whistleblower have become to blow the whistle? At the very least, he must have lost faith in the organization. If he had kept faith, he would have accepted whatever decision came through channels—at least once he had exhausted all means of appeal.

For anyone who has been a loyal employee for many years, losing faith in the organization is likely to be quite painful—rather like the disintegration of a marriage. My impression is that few whistleblowers take their job thinking that they might some day have to blow the whistle. They seem to start out as loyal employees—perhaps more loyal than most. One day something happens to shake their loyalty. Further shocks follow until loyalty collapses, leaving behind a great emptiness. While managers tend to think of whistleblowers as traitors to the organization, most whistleblowers seem to feel that, on the contrary, it is the organization that has betrayed them (Near and Miceli 1996).

This bad news implies more. Before the whistleblower was forced to blow the whistle, she trusted the organization. She took its good sense for granted. That is no longer possible. Faith has become suspicion. Since what we call 'organizational authority' is precisely the ability of the organization to have its commands taken more or less on faith, the 'powers that be' now have as much reason to distrust the whistleblower as she has to distrust them. She no longer recognizes their authority. She is much more likely to blow the whistle than before. She is now an alien presence within the corporate body.

Something equally bad may happen to relations between the whistleblower and her fellow workers. Whistleblowing tends to bring out the worst in people. Some friends become implacable enemies. Others hide, fearing 'guilt by association'. Most, perhaps, simply lose interest, looking on the whistleblower as they would on someone dying of cancer. These desertions can leave deep scars. And, even when they do not, they leave the whistleblower an outsider, a loner in an organization in which isolation for any reason makes one vulnerable.

11. Helping the Whistleblower and the Organization

All this bad news suggests some hard questions. How can a whistleblower work as before with people whose loyalty he no longer shares? How can fellow workers treat him as they did before when he is no longer quite one of them? How can he hope for promotion, or even retention, in an organization in which he can put no trust, in which he has no friends, and for which he is likely to make further trouble? There are at least three responses to the problem these questions point to: legal protection, a different employer, and rehabilitation. Let us consider these in order.

11.1 Laws

Some governments have adopted laws or regulations to protect whistleblowers. Generally, these prohibit 'reprisals'. The penalty for reprisal, though generally not high, may make organizations more careful how they treat whistleblowers. But, like most legal measures, these are much more effective against overt acts than against general ill-will (Mallin 1983; Devine and Aplin 1988; Near and Miceli 1995).

11.2 New Job

The second response to the whistleblower's unhappy position within an organization is to find the whistleblower another job. That is seldom easy. Potential employers shun known whistleblowers. That alone makes finding a new job hard. Then, too, the whistleblower may not be as good an interviewee as before. Many whistleblowers seem to signal the bad news even when they do their best to conceal it. They may, for example, sound emotionally exhausted, ask questions that suggest distrust, or just seem prickly. They are like people going through a bad divorce.

11.3 Rehabilitation

Since few potential employers want someone else's troubles, we must draw the paradoxical conclusion that the whistleblower's best hope for continuing her career may be her old employer. That the old employer may be her best hope is the chief reason to support laws protecting whistleblowers. Though a law can offer the whistleblower little direct protection, it can prod the organization to think about rehabilitating the whistleblower. This, however, is still a small hope. The organization can rehabilitate the whistleblower *only if* it can re-establish her loyalty to the organization and her trust in those with whom she must work. That is not easy.

Clearly, the organization itself must change enough for the whistleblower to have good reason to believe that she will not have to go out of channels again. The changes will probably have to be substantial, including such formal arrangements as a 'hot line' or 'open-door policy'. Most organizations automatically resist such changes. But, even if they did not, such formal changes are not likely to be enough to re-establish the whistleblower's personal relations with superiors, subordinates, and fellow workers. What is needed in addition is something like marriage counselling: group therapy to expose and resolve all the feelings of betrayal, distrust, and rejection whistleblowing inevitably generates.

Some government agencies have required employees involved in a whistleblowing case to participate in such group therapy. The results so far have not been good. Managers, especially, seem to view such therapy as just one more hoop to jump through on the way to the inevitable. To work, the therapy probably needs to be voluntarily undertaken by all participants, something not easily legislated. That is why even this best hope for the whistleblower, rehabilitation, is still a faint hope.

11.4 Alternatives?

We need to find better ways to protect whistleblowers. In the long run at least, peace between the whistleblower and the organization is as good for the organization as for the whistleblower. The whistleblower is not really an enemy. An organization that has whistleblowers needs them. The whistleblower is like the knock at the door that wakes one in a house on fire—unwelcome, but better than sleeping till the fire reaches the bed. An organization that punishes its whistleblowers blinds itself to troubles better faced. So, for example, when the Bay Area Transit Authority (BART) fired three electrical engineers for going out of channels to inform BART's own governing board of trouble with the software that was to run its new operatorless trains, it merely turned a technical problem into a scandal waiting to happen. When a train jumped the tracks after rushing through a station at which it was supposed to stop, BART had to face the technical problem the engineers had identified, to deal with public concern over the operatorless trains, and to explain why it had ignored the problem until then. Had BART promptly heeded the whistleblowers before they blew the whistle, it would only have had the technical problem to deal with.

To say that whistleblowers generally tell an organization what it needs to know is not to deny the disadvantages of whistleblowing described earlier but to explain why we should try to make whistleblowing unnecessary rather than try to prevent whistleblowing in other ways. Among the ways to make whistleblowing less necessary are, first, organizational arrangements that increase the number of channels open for resolving disputes that might grow into whistleblowing, and, secondly, ethics programmes (and other educational strategies) that help prevent organizational practices from having even the appearance of wrongdoing.

12. History

Even though the newspapers seem to be reporting cases of whistleblowing about as often as in the preceding decades, scholarly interest in whistleblowing seems to have been in decline since the early 1990s. (So, for example, Amazon.com lists no book about whistleblowing published after 1989.) I am not sure why that should be. Doubtless, one reason I am not sure is that I do not understand why whistleblowing became a hot topic only in the 1960s or why we chose that odd term for the phenomenon it names.

One common explanation for the term's recent appearance is that it names a new response to a new phenomenon, the large organization. That explanation seems to me clearly wrong. Large organizations—church, army, government—have existed continuously in the West since the Middle Ages. We can even identify historical personages who are at least arguably whistleblowers. Consider, for example, Martin Luther. While still a Catholic monk, he publicly sounded an alarm about corruption in the Catholic Church by (as the legend goes) nailing his ninety-five theses to the door of the court church at Wittenberg in 1517. Why do I not feel inclined to call him a whistleblower?

We will probably understand whistleblowing better once we have a good history of it. But how that history turns out will depend in part on the theory of whistleblowing historians bring to it. I have, I hope, added to their options—as well as to the options of others interested in whistleblowing.

REFERENCES

Adams, David M., and Maine, Edward W. (1998) (eds.), *Business Ethics for the 21st Century*. Mountain View, CA: Mayfield Publishing Company.

Baron, Marcia (1984). *The Moral Status of Loyalty*. Debuque, IO: Kendall/Hunt.

Bok, Sisela (1980). 'Whistleblowing and Professional Responsibilities'. *New York University Education Quarterly*, 11 (Summer), 2–7.

Bowie, Norman (1982). *Business Ethics*. Englewood Cliffs, NJ: Prentice Hall.

Burke, Anna Mae Walsh (1997). '*Qui Tam*: Blowing the Whistle for Uncle Sam'. *Nova Law Review*, 21: 869–913.

De George, Richard T. (1990). *Business Ethics, 3rd edn*. New York: Macmillan.

Devine, Thomas M., and Aplin, Donald G. (1988). 'Whistleblower Protection—the Gap between the Law and Reality'. *Harvard Law Journal*, 31: 223–39.

Elliston, Frederick, et al. (1985). *Whistleblowing Research: Methodological and Moral Issues*. New York: Praeger.

Fletcher, G. P. (1993). *Loyalty: An Essay on the Morality of Relationships*. London: Oxford University Press.

Gewirth, Alan (1978). *Reason and Morality*. Chicago: University of Chicago Press.

Glazer, Myron Peretz, and Glazer, Penina Migdal (1989). *The Whistleblowers: Exposing Corruption in Government and Industry*. New York: Basic Books.

Goldberg, David Theo. (1988). 'Tuning in to Whistle Blowing'. *Business and Professional Ethics Journal*, 7 (Summer), 85–94.

Jackall, Robert (1988). *Moral Mazes*. New York: Oxford University Press.

Koehn, Daryl (1998). 'Whistleblowing and Trust: Some Lessons from the ADM Scandal', in Adams and Maine (1998), 210–14.

Mallin, Martin H. (1983). 'Protecting the Whistleblower from Retaliatory Discharge'. *Journal of Law Reform*, 16 (Winter), 277–318.

Near, Janet P., and Miceli, Marcia P. (1995). 'Effective Whistle-Blowing'. *Academy of Management Review*, 20: 679–708.

——(1996). 'Whistle-Blowing: Myth and Reality'. *Journal of Management*, 22: 507–26.

Singer, Peter (1972). 'Famine, Affluence, and Morality'. *Philosophy and Public Affairs*, 7 (Spring), 229–43.

Smith, Patricia (1990). 'The Duty to Rescue and the Slippery Slope'. *Social Theory and Practice*, 16 (Fall), 19–41.

Westin, Alan F. (1981). *Whistle-Blowing! Loyalty and Dissent in the Corporation*. New York: McGraw-Hill.

PART V

JUSTICE AND INTERNATIONAL RELATIONS

CHAPTER 22

IMMIGRATION

CHANDRAN KUKATHAS

1. INTRODUCTION

ON 2 April 2001, 48-year-old Mr Shahraz Kayani doused his body with petrol and set himself alight at the entrance to Parliament House in Canberra. Mr Khayani was a recent migrant, who had arrived in Australia on a visitor's visa from Pakistan in 1995 and soon after applied for refugee status—having alleged harassment by the police in his native country for having friendly relations with members of the banned Ahmedi religious sect. Soon after winning the right to remain in Australia, Mr Kayani tried to secure permission to have his wife and young children immigrate, but his case was not regarded favourably (the Department of Immigration and Multicultural Affairs twice refusing his applications for his family to join him, in 1997 and 1999); and the bureaucracy's processes were slow. A Commonwealth Ombudsman's report in August 2000 was favourable to his case, and Mr Kayani lodged another application, but the whole process then had to start again from scratch. Driven to the point of madness (a letter from a Canberra health service had contacted the office of the Minister for Immigration and Multicultural Affairs the week before, concerned that Mr Kayani was suicidal), he tried to protest at the delay, and to draw attention to his despair by self-immolation. He succeeded, at the cost of horrific injury, in making headline news, and in having his family brought to Australia to be by his hospital bed. Shortly afterwards he died of the massive infections his body suffered as a result of burns. He did not, however, succeed in changing the attitude of the Australian government to his case; and for his family the attraction of coming to Australia died with him.

The Kayani case is a noteworthy one not only because it is a particularly tragic story in the larger saga of global population movements in the twentieth and twenty-first centuries—though tragic it undoubtedly is—but also because it brings into sharp relief the great range of questions, and ethical and political dilemmas, that make up the immigration issue. Immigration cases are rarely handled expeditiously, but what had complicated Mr Kayani's application to have his family come to Australia was that his middle daughter, Annum, 10, had cerebral palsy and failed to meet the health standards for entry into the country. Moreover, the Immigration Department had estimated that the cost of lifelong care for the disabled charge would come to A$750,000 (US$400,000). Immigration officials are able to waive health objections, but when lifetime health costs exceed A$250,000 (US$120,000) a ministerial waiver is required. (Although Mr Kayani had said that the family would look after the child at its own expense, his initial application for entry had been lodged under the Humanitarian Scheme, which meant that treatment for the 10 year old would be the government's responsibility once she arrived in Australia.) Mr Kayani had been told on 6 March 2001 that his case had been passed to the minister's office for a final decision, but on checking with the office on 29 March he was informed that the file had not yet arrived, leading him to suspect that he was being given the runaround by the bureaucracy.

The day after Mr Kayani's dramatic suicide attempt in front of Parliament, the Minister for Immigration stated that he had no intention of deciding the third application for Annum under pressure from the hospitalized man's family or from human-rights groups. Subsequently, the family was granted a three-month visa so that Mr Kayani's wife and three daughters could visit him and, as it turned out, attend his funeral.

The Kayani case is not unusual. Half of all immigration worldwide is made up of the movement of refugees (Zolberg 2001: 407) and a good deal more is made up of people fleeing war, famine, natural disasters, economic development projects, human-rights violations, or simply poverty. Immigration involves not simply moving across borders from one country to another but asserting a claim to be allowed to settle, temporarily or permanently, within the boundaries of another state. Such claims cannot be made without engaging the governments, bureaucracies, and laws of those states. Often, many of these claims force governments to subject themselves to international law, and challenge their domestic policies. If they are welfare states, immigrants can pose an important challenge to their budgetary concerns; if they are culturally homogeneous, immigrants may come to be seen as threats to cultural integrity and the sense of national identity; and, whether they are wealthy states or poor ones, immigrants provoke the question: do we have more to gain by excluding outsiders than by admitting them?

It is in political circumstances such as these that the ethical issue of immigration arises. How one responds to it, and answers the most important questions it throws forward, will depend significantly on how one views the state, and its place in the international order (Norman, this volume). The ethical issue in immigration is thus not simply a matter of one's stance as an individual but a question of what political institutions and international laws should be promoted or upheld.

2. WHAT IS IMMIGRATION?

The movement of people is a fact of history as old as humanity, but immigration as we know it now is a more recent phenomenon. International migration is not merely a matter of physical relocation but a change of jurisdiction from one state to another (Zolberg 2001: 407). To migrate is to cross a border, or borders, demarcating the bounds of national political authority. For this to be possible, or even imaginable, it is necessary for those boundaries to exist; and, in that respect, immigration is no older than the modern nation state. This is not to suggest, let it be emphasized, that the movement of people—as groups and as individuals—has not always been a part of the human story in all parts of the world. It has (Sassen 1999). But a world of clearly defined states, with sharply (even if not always uncontroversially) demarcated boundaries, is a recent development. While some scholars do trace the origin of the nation as far back as medieval times in Europe (Schulze 1994; Hastings 1997), few would deny that it did not emerge as a dominant form of political organization at least until the Peace of Westphalia in 1648 (Krasner 1995). And, even then, it was some time before Europe itself was dominated by states rather than a mixture of empires, kingdoms, city states, and leagues (Spruyt 1998). The Italian and German states were creations of the nineteenth century, Austria and Hungary of the twentieth, and the majority of the countries that hold seats in the General Assembly of the United Nations are products of the postcolonial era that began in 1945.

Yet even so it would be misleading to think of modern immigration as beginning with the modern state, for, while the Peace of Westphalia may have established the principle of sovereign authority within geographically defined territories, it was some time before states became fully capable of knowing precisely where their borders were and controlling movements across them (Morris 1998: 31). The Napoleonic Inquiry of 1808–13, which attempted to establish France's manpower resources, reveals the extent of the migrations of labour (both seasonal and permanent) across Europe at the time, but also shows us how little the state knew of its own geography, and how little control it exercised over that movement (Sassen 1999: 7–32). Passports did not appear until the great states of Europe were locked in war in 1914 (Torpey 2000). It was only with the emerging flood of refugees in the inter-war period that serious thought was given to the security problems posed by the large-scale movement of peoples. It was world war and its aftermath that shaped immigration, international immigration law, and immigration policy in the twentieth century.

In considering immigration as an ethical issue at the beginning of the twenty-first century, however, we should think of it as something distinctively modern, for it is the question of state control of the movement of people that dominates public policy. Certainly, in earlier times movement was not entirely at the discretion of individuals. Slaves and vassals were assigned to their lords and their lands in ancient and medieval times. And even more recently the English Poor Law (1601) provided for 'settlement' of beggars in a parish, whose duty it was to care for them. But immigration controls as we know them now were not known. Immigration is best defined, then, as the movement of a person or persons from one state into another for the purpose of temporary or permanent settlement. More than 100 million people currently live outside the states of which they are citizens (Trebilcock 1995: 219). But many others also move between countries as visitors, businessmen, tourists, actors, sportswomen, or artists—without any intention of settling even briefly in a new country. Immigrants are people whose aim is to stop rather than simply to pass through. This distinction itself reveals the difficulty of identifying immigrants and separating them from other people on the move. Some immigrants may return home after only a few weeks, having decided that their new surroundings were not for them, or because circumstances (a broken marriage, a death in the family) forced them to leave. On the other hand, tourists, foreign students, and itinerant workers may find themselves staying for years and settling permanently. Many Chinese and Indians in Malaya regarded themselves (and were regarded) as sojourners, who would eventually return to their native lands—though most never would. The definition of immigrant is not one that admits of further precision.

Furthermore, not all immigrants are the same or seek the same thing, and they can fall into many different categories. First, as noted earlier, not all migration is voluntary. We might divide migrants into three categories: those who are *forced* to leave their countries (for example, evacuees from war zones, or slaves), those who are *impelled* to leave (for example, refugees or indentured labourers), and those who leave freely (for example, people moving in search of better opportunities or enticed by offers to resettle elsewhere) (Peterson 1958; Parnwell 1993: 25). Of course, people do not always fall neatly into these categories, and the categories themselves depend on judgements on matters of degree. How desperate do things have to become before someone can be regarded as impelled to move rather than moving freely? The Irish who moved to the USA during the potato famine moved for good reason, even if they moved freely; and they might not have moved at all had circumstances been different.

Secondly, not all migrants seek the same legal status in the states to which they move. Some seek full citizenship of their newly adopted countries. Others seek full citizenship, but without any intention of relinquishing their original citizenship and propose to maintain a dual or multiple nationality (Hammar 1985). Asylum-seekers may want only temporary refuge and the right to work until they are able to return (though many may also see no prospect of going back) to their homes. But many want simply the right to travel and work in a foreign country, whether as guest workers (perhaps to remit money to relatives at home) or as more or less temporary resident aliens.

Thirdly, not all immigration is legal. Significant numbers of people reside in countries other than their own after they have entered them without authorization, or simply in view of the fact that they have not returned home after their visas or entry permits have expired. However, it would be a mistake to assume that persons turning up at the border without visas are 'illegal immigrants', since it is not illegal to travel to the borders of any state or to seek asylum as a refugee. Mexican workers without authorization crossing the border in search of work in the USA are illegal immigrants; but asylum-seekers landing on the shores of Florida or Western Australia are not.

In addressing the ethical issue of immigration, then, we are asking about the morality of admitting persons into (and out of) the state, for any of these reasons and under any of these conditions. Therefore, there may be no single answer about the morality of immigration—it will require taking positions on a number of different matters. What stance one takes will often depend upon—or shape—one's general views about the nature of the state.

3. The Argument for Open Borders

On the question of who should be admitted into the state, the most straightforward answer is simply: anyone who wishes to enter (Dowty 1987). Political borders should not exclude persons from entering (or leaving) a given territory or restrict the movement of persons or populations. There are at least two perspectives from which open borders have been defended: liberal egalitarianism and libertarianism. Both of these are universalist standpoints, holding that such rights and duties as we possess apply globally rather than within a more restricted domain (Goodin and Pettit 1986; Goodin 1988; 1992: 7–9).

From a liberal egalitarian perspective, there are several reasons to favour open borders (Carens 1987). First, egalitarianism demands that the earth's resources be distributed as equally as possible, and one particularly effective mechanism for facilitating this is freedom of movement. It is unlikely that such a distribution could be adequately effected merely by foreign aid from rich nations to poor, even if governments were to become committed to such programmes. But freedom of movement would enable the poor to go where resources and opportunities are more plentiful. 'If we cannot move enough money to where the needy people are, then we will have to count on moving as many of the needy people as possible to where the money is' (Goodin 1992: 8).

Secondly, liberal egalitarians see freedom to move as an important freedom in itself. In a liberal society, individual freedom to pursue one's own projects and shape one's own life, as long as one does not interfere with the freedom of others to do the same, is particularly valued. To deny someone freedom of movement is to deny him or her that opportunity (Carens 1992: 26).

Thirdly, egalitarianism mandates not only a world of reduced economic, political, and social inequalities but also a world in which opportunity is equal. Free movement gives everyone an entitlement to pursue opportunities wherever they may be found. It is a matter of good fortune that one happens to be a member of a state in which opportunities are plentiful, and one is not only able but has a right not available to outsiders to take advantage of such opportunities. Economists might say that members of states capture the rents that come with membership, since they can keep out those who might compete with them for those opportunities. Rents are the gains one makes by exercising one's exclusive access to a resource—gains that would typically be higher than those made in competition in an open market. (Technically, rents are gains above opportunity cost. From a universalist egalitarian point of view, members of states have no special claims upon those rents.)

Libertarians reach very similar conclusions from a very different starting point. The central principles of libertarianism are the principle of freedom of contract, and the principle of the right to hold (justly acquired) private property (Nozick 1974; Steiner 1994). For libertarians like Hillel Steiner, national boundaries have no less—and no more—significance than the boundaries distinguishing private property. In the case of private property, holding just title entitles a person to admit or refuse admission to any others who wish to set foot on his property. Thus the state is not entitled to deny me the right to admit anyone, including 'foreigners', onto my property—just as it is not entitled to force me to accept people I do not want on my property. In such a world, immigration has to be free to the extent that states cannot rightly deny people the right to contract with others to use (or enter) their property. If there is a role for the state, it is in the enforcement of property rights rather than in restricting them (Steiner 1992).

Both these general approaches recognize, of course, that in the world as it is open borders may not be feasible. Political realities may not permit it, since the general public of the wealthy nations are unlikely to accept unrestricted immigration. Nor, for that matter, do open borders serve the security concerns and the economic interests of states. So theory must consider some second-best option—guided, however, by the principle of open borders.

Despite this similarity, there are important differences between the libertarian and the liberal egalitarian perspectives on open borders. The libertarian view assumes a very small role for the state, which is charged essentially with the task of protecting rights of property and enforcing contracts, and so does not have to concern itself with the problem of immigrant claims on the resources of the public. When there is no extensive public property, and no welfare state, persons entering the state can do so only because they have contracted with members of the state and are able to support themselves, or because they are the beneficiaries of private charity.

In contrast the liberal egalitarian, envisaging a more extensive state (concerned, among other things, with promoting equality within the state), must consider how far the resources of the public are to be made available to immigrants. Thus liberal egalitarians must consider very carefully the claims of migrants not only to enter the state but also to join the state. Joining a libertarian state might be likened to joining a football or bowling league: one gains little more than the right to play or compete. Joining a liberal egalitarian state might be likened to joining a club or a guild, which provides one with access to benefits financed in part by the accumulated wealth of the association.

Because of this difference, liberal egalitarians are more likely to accept that there is reason to restrict entry, for they see a more positive role for the state in addressing the claims of particular interests in society. Thus they might reason, as does Goodin (a defender of open borders and a strong proponent of the welfare state): every state ought, perhaps, to have a welfare state, but a generous welfare state always runs the risk of being swamped by immigrants if people can enter the country freely from abroad. Closed borders may, therefore, be justified in order that the country be able to pursue 'ideals for which other nations of the world are not yet ready' (Goodin 1992: 11). For writers like Goodin, this second-best option is justifiable as a matter not of principle but of pragmatism (Goodin 1992: 11). The reason why liberal egalitarians would generally accept immigration restrictions is not that they attach special value to the state but because no other policy is feasible (Goodin 1988).

4. THE CASE FOR RESTRICTIONS ON POPULATION MOVEMENT

Nonetheless, many have argued that there is a stronger case for restricting population movement. There are many kinds of reasons why immigration restrictions might generally be defended—economic, political, cultural. All of these reasons terminate in an assertion of the importance of preserving the integrity of the state.

One common reason why immigrants are viewed with suspicion by the general population of any country is that migrants are seen as an economic threat: taking scarce jobs, absorbing welfare resources, and driving up prices. Countries with substantial migrant inflows thus often see the emergence of anti-immigrant parties (such as Pauline Hanson's One Nation Party in Australia) or exclusionist immigration and settlement policies (Castles 1995). Three questions are salient here. First, are the economic consequences of immigration positive or negative—for the receiving country, and also globally? Secondly, how is the economic effect of immigration to be measured? And, thirdly, how are the distributional consequences to be considered.

There is a wide consensus among economists that the global consequences of free movement are positive, since, on standard models of international trade, competitive labour markets encourage a more efficient use of resources (Galbraith 1985; Simon 1990). What is more contentious, however, is whether all nations benefit from immigration. The economic advantages of migrant inflows include an increase in the size of the pool of labour—particularly if it is skilled—and an expansion in the size of the domestic market. The disadvantages may include the cost of supporting aged or infirm immigrants (or those who will not continue working for long before starting to consume more welfare benefits in retirement than they will contribute in lifetime taxes), the cost of educating them (particularly if language training is necessary), and the costs in health-care services (particularly for refugees or migrants fleeing war zones). Such costs may increase as immigrants acquire the right to petition the state to have their relatives reunited with them in their new country. These disadvantages obtain particularly in states with extensive public health, welfare, and education services.

But, even if one disregarded the costs of welfare provision, the economic impact of immigration may be negative for other reasons. The consequences for the working of the labour market may not always be advantageous. Obviously immigration will not be beneficial if there is little demand for labour, whether in general or within particular labour markets. It may also work to the disadvantage of workers in those markets into which immigrants are likely to move, driving down wages. It would also increase the bargaining power of employers vis-à-vis native workers (Vroman 1995: 213–15). Labour has generally been hostile to immigration while business has usually regarded it more favourably. In countries like Australia and the USA business has often been prepared to turn a blind eye to illegal immigration, while labour unions have seen it as a threat that needs to be addressed.

Immigration may also be costly because of the strain greater numbers place on public facilities, from beaches, parks, and public highways, to sewerage services and pollution controls. (In Australia, for example, immigration is viewed by many environmentalists as a threat to Australia's delicate ecology.) These effects may be exacerbated when such goods are publicly controlled and underpriced. This, however, brings us to the problem of how the costs are to be measured. When publicly owned facilities are underpriced (or not priced at all) it is very difficult to establish the value of the goods and services consumed by immigrants. But is also difficult to work out the cost of immigration without determining how to calculate the value of returns to public assets. Should one consider the returns on the investments made by earlier generations (which exist in the form of roads, public buildings, police and fire stations, for example)? If such facilities were financed by earlier generations and the returns are now passed on to current taxpayers in the form of lower tax rates, all members of the present generation benefit. Immigrants coming into such an arrangement are then sharing in a boon that would otherwise have been available only to natives. On the other hand, one might regard these facilities as if they were financed by a bond issue repaid over the life of the building out of current tax revenue, which means that there is no intergenerational transfer resulting from taxation. If so, immigrants paying tax would have to be regarded as contributors to the cost of construction. Which conceptual understanding should we adopt in trying to determine the costs and benefits of immigration? Indeed, what view should we take on the question of who receives the returns on earlier public investment: government employees, or politicians, or all current taxpayers, or some current taxpayers, or beneficiaries of the programmes? How these (possibly unanswerable) questions are answered will make an important difference to whether migrants are viewed as having a favourable or unfavourable effect on the rest of the populace with regard to any given facility. Equally, of course, one would have to consider the extent to which migrants incur liabilities—say, by acquiring an obligation to pay taxes needed to repay public debt.

The difficulty of making calculations of economic cost makes debate about the economic consequences problematic at best, and at worst inconclusive. But other arguments against open immigration do not turn on questions of measurement. For some environmentalists, for example, the protection of nature is something that ought not to figure in economic calculations but should be regarded as a fundamental value. One particularly important argument, however, is the cultural argument for restricting immigration. More open borders and the free movement of peoples threaten to undermine the cultural distinctiveness of nations. Countries that are particularly favoured as migrant destinations are thus especially vulnerable to cultural transformation by the arrival of large numbers of people with foreign customs, languages, and religious traditions. Indeed, immigration may be a threat to national identity (Brimelow 1995: 202–33).

As Brian Barry points out, mass migration at the very least 'has the effect of changing the recipient area' (1992: 281). Immigrants from similar backgrounds often cluster together, forming enclaves or significant minorities in major cities. Immigration turned Melbourne into the second largest Greek city in the world (after Athens); and many major Western metropolises, such as Vancouver, San Francisco, Sydney, and New York, have 'chinatowns'. As immigrants swell in numbers, the ethnic, religious, ethical, and political character of the country's population also changes—particularly if immigrants do not assimilate but seek to maintain their own cultural traditions.

There are several reasons why this might be a serious concern. One important reason is that a certain level of social solidarity is necessary if the state is to work well. A particularly robust argument putting this point is developed by David Miller. According to Miller, states are needed to pursue social justice. Nation states have a special standing, he argues, 'because where a state is constituted in such a way that its citizens share a common national identity, the resulting political community has three features that make the application of principles of social justice feasible and fruitful' (Miller 1999: 18). First, because national identities tend to create strong bonds of solidarity, the community thus formed 'becomes a natural reference group when people ask themselves whether the share of resources they are getting is fair or not' (Miller 1999: 18). Secondly, national political cultures include a range of shared understandings that are essential for principles of social justice. And, thirdly, nation states can help provide an assurance to each that others will show a similar restraint in following fair principles and procedures of social justice. For Miller, the conclusion to be drawn here is not that immigration must be stopped but that it ought to be limited 'according to the absorptive capacities of the society in question' (Miller 1995: 129). But some conservative critics go further to claim that only an end to immigration can prevent the influx of different peoples from destabilizing a society's practices and institutions (Casey 1982).

A different kind of reason for concern about the influx of culturally different immigrants is not so much that cultural diversity will be socially destabilizing but that it will be politically and economically deleterious. When the host nation is a wealthy and politically stable country to which migrants are naturally attracted, it may be that the host's wealth is no accident but the product of economic and political institutions that are conducive to stability and wealth creation. Immigration from countries whose people do not share the values that are needed to underpin such institutions may well create a society in which those institutions can no longer be sustained. In this regard, immigration may have the effect of killing the goose that lays the golden egg. Thus, James Buchanan points out (without himself arguing for or against immigration barriers), 'the effects of adding new members extend well beyond those that might be measured in economic terms and . . . they become especially important in modern democratic states' (1995: 65). In order to evaluate any immigration policy, one must consider the consequences of the impact of new arrivals on political culture.

Finally, any immigration policy, it is argued, must consider the possibility that a large influx of culturally different people will simply cause unrest and ethnic or religious conflict, since unassimilated people with alien customs will often be regarded as threats or treated with suspicion if they appear in large numbers (Blainey 1984). A reasonable regard for peace suggests that large-scale migration of culturally different people may have to be managed with great care—and this may require careful attention to the numbers allowed into a society in an age of cheap mass transport. A number of options seem open to societies attracting immigrants in significant numbers: to control and reduce the intake but leave immigrants to be selected at random and to enjoy the freedom to live as they please; to admit considerable numbers, but require immigrants to assimilate; or to adopt some variation that involves controlling numbers to some degree and managing the process of acculturation of immigrants to the host society, and the transformation of the society as it is in turn changed by the diversity of newcomers. Which of these strategies should be adopted is the subject of considerable debate in Western societies today, and is central to the question of multiculturalism, which dominates much contemporary discussion both in academic philosophy and in public policy.

5. Immigration and Multiculturalism: Citizenship and Social Cohesion

This brings us immediately to the issue of how immigrants should be treated in the countries in which they settle—and what obligations they incur as members of their new society. This is a complex issue, which becomes even more complex and controversial when immigrants are culturally different from the majority of people in the society. Countries around the world differ very substantially in their attitudes to aliens in their midst. Some, like the USA, Canada, and Australia, generally allow immigrants to become citizens within a short space of time, and indeed encourage them to do so. Others, like Japan, are loath to grant citizenship rights to people not of indigenous (in this case, Japanese) descent. (People of Korean origin born to ancestors who have lived in Japan for several generations are still generally unable to gain Japanese citizenship.) Germany has welcomed people of German ancestry, but has been reluctant to grant citizenship rights to Turks born and raised in Germany (usually as the children of 'guest workers'). Israel sees as fundamental to its national being the 'law of return', according to which people of Jewish descent have an unconditional right to citizenship of the Israeli State, but does not recognize any similar right of citizenship for Arab members of the society.

Countries also differ not only in their attitudes to immigrant claims to citizenship but also in their attitudes to the question of how, and how far, immigrants ought to be assimilated into the society they have entered. France, for example, maintains strongly assimilationist policies, requiring immigrants of all cultural stripes to conform to French social and political practice. The USA, less overtly, accepted until recently a similar public philosophy according to which all immigrants would eventually become American citizens, who would not so much cleave to their own ethnic or cultural traditions as blend into the 'melting pot' that was the American pluralist tradition. Canada and Australia, however, explicitly rejected assimilation as a defensible social policy in favour of multiculturalism. By the 1990s, the USA had done much the same (Glazer 1997).

In one way or another, then, contemporary debates about the place of immigrants in modern society are dominated by the question of multiculturalism. The important questions here are as follows. Under what terms and conditions should migrants be allowed to enter a society? What cultural claims can they properly make? And under what circumstances should they be granted citizenship? Since it is immigration to wealthy, Western, democratic societies that has dominated the issue of movement of peoples (for few people willingly move to poor or politically unstable countries), these questions are often raised as challenges for liberal democratic theory as much as for Western societies themselves.

The most important theoretical effort to address the question of multiculturalism over the 1990s was that of Will Kymlicka (1995, 1998). One of the most significant problems confronting liberal democracies is how to address the desire for immigrants to retain their own cultural traditions in the society of which they have become members. Particularly when such immigrants have deep religious commitments, there may even arise conflicts between the demands of their religion and the requirements of the law. Sikhs, for example, may wish to continue to wear turbans and so be unable to comply with laws mandating helmets for motorcyclists. Or Muslims may wish to have the slaughtering of (some) animals conform not so much to Western standards of humane treatment as to their own religious requirements. On what basis should laws determine the different rights and duties of a culturally diverse populace? The problem is made more complicated by the fact that many societies also contain cultural groups—indeed, minorities—who are not immigrants: indigenous peoples, such as Aborigines, or cultural minorities, such as the Quebecois in Canada.

Kymlicka's theory (1995) holds that a distinction needs to be drawn between ethnic minorities and national minorities. Immigrants who form minority cultures in their new societies are ethnic minorities, while people like the Quebecois and the Inuit in Canada are national minorities. National minorities may have their concerns (grievances) addressed by being given a measure of self-government within the polity, and perhaps also by special representation in the political system. But ethnic minorities may claim mainly 'polyethnic rights', which do not include rights of self-government but do encompass exemptions from some legal requirements in recognition of their cultural or religious interests, and special entitlements to enable them to uphold their cultural distinctiveness, or their religious or linguistic traditions.

According to Kymlicka's theory, immigrants ought to be welcomed as citizens. But citizenship itself needs to be differentiated so that the rights of citizens can be specified with greater precision and cultural sensitivity. One of the reasons for this, Kymlicka argues, is that a failure to distinguish different kinds of citizen rights may make it difficult to treat immigrants fairly without incurring the suspicions of native citizens who fear the erosion of their own rights by the granting of privileges to outsiders. In Canada, for example, the failure to recognize the distinction between national and ethnic minorities meant that French Canadians feared that multiculturalism would reduce their claims of nationhood to the level of immigrant ethnicity, while other Canadians feared that it would mean treating immigrant groups as nations (Kymlicka 1995: 17).

What, however, is the basis for distinguishing the claims of immigrant cultural minorities from those of non-immigrant minorities in a culturally diverse society? In Kymlicka's theory, immigrants should be regarded as essentially voluntary entrants into the society, who are, thus, obliged to conform to the political arrangements that exist. Society's political institutions should accommodate them, and as far as possible help them adjust by subsidizing their efforts to hold on to their languages and to their cultural heritage. But immigrants cannot claim any right to govern themselves in the way that indigenous peoples or nations like the Quebecois can.

One important difficulty with Kymlicka's theory stems from the problem of distinguishing clearly between immigrants and non-immigrants (Kukathas 1997). To put it at its simplest, the question is: who is an immigrant? An obvious answer might be: someone who was born abroad. But this clearly will not do, since it does not take into account the fact that many children are born abroad to parents temporarily resident outside their country of citizenship, yet cannot be regarded as immigrants when they accompany their parents on their return. And what of people who were born abroad but entered the country as children and grew up as citizens? (I was born in Malaysia but have lived in Australia all my adult life and for half my childhood, and find it difficult to think of myself as an immigrant.) Indeed, how long does one retain one's status as an immigrant? Furthermore, how should we regard the children of immigrants born in the country in which their parents have resettled? Are they also immigrants, and so entitled to the rights immigrants have? Or do we only recognize such entitlements for some—perhaps the children of recently arrived immigrants?

Now Kymlicka can reasonably note that the point of his theory is to identify differential rights not for immigrants as such but rather for cultural minorities. The point of distinguishing immigrants from natives is to make clear that immigrant *cultures* may not claim the same rights (of self-government) as national minorities. Yet, at the same time, the recognition of special or differential rights for some cultural minorities also means drawing distinctions between citizens who hail from different ethnic immigrant backgrounds. If ethnic minorities are to be given special rights, why only certain ethnic minorities? If Vietnamese immigrants in Australia are to be given resources to assimilate (say, through subsidized English-language classes), and also resources to maintain their cultural heritage (say, through community grants for cultural festivals), why should similar opportunities not be made to people of English, or Scottish, or Irish descent? Indeed, why should there not be as much recognition granted to those who simply regard themselves as Australian? On what basis are some groups favoured, if all are members of groups whose forebears were immigrants? Concerns of this sort led to the National Multicultural Advisory Council of Australia recommending that, if multiculturalism was to be a politically successful public policy, it would have to persuade all citizens that it was not a policy that favoured recent immigrants but held advantages for all Australians (National Multicultural Advisory Council 1999).

The problem is more complex still in other countries that contain minorities who do not easily fall into either of Kymlicka's categories. African-Americans came to the USA as slaves and their descendants are neither immigrants nor the children of immigrants nor indigenous national minorities. In Fiji, ethnic Indians make up 45 per cent of the population and have been a presence on the islands for more than a century, yet cannot readily be described as immigrants, having few ties to India, and having long been an important political and cultural force in the country. In South Africa, both minority white and majority black peoples are descended from immigrants to the region.

The issue, however, is not only one of the distribution of resources or the subsidizing by one culture of another. It is also a matter of whose language, traditions, symbols, and beliefs should take prominence in the public image of the state. It is in this regard that the point of Kymlicka's theory becomes most clearly apparent. It seems only natural that those who have been members of a state since its earliest inception should be able to set the terms of its political organization, while those who have come more recently should be treated well but not allowed to become self-governing communities. Some theory is needed to describe the different kinds of claim immigrants, natives, and indigenous peoples can rightly make, so that the state can be rightly ordered.

Kymlicka's suggestion is that immigrants are essentially *voluntary* members of the society of which they are a part, while indigenous peoples or national minorities are involuntarily incorporated members. On the face of it, this is a helpful and plausible distinction. Clearly, Aborigines in Australia were involuntarily incorporated into the new-found colonies and then the Federation, while the Greeks and Italians came voluntarily, seeking opportunities for a better life. But even this distinction is tested when one considers that many immigrants do not come voluntarily: children, refugees, displaced persons fleeing war or famine, all move less because they want to than because they are forced to by others or by circumstances. Equally, some national minorities have every opportunity to choose voluntarily between living as adherents of a minority culture or as cosmopolitans. Middle-class Aboriginals, who are highly educated professionals, for example, can often choose to live not as Aborigines but as cosmopolitan urban-dwellers; and many Quebeckers have a choice between living as French-speakers in their own province and living as cosmpolitans abroad. If this is so, it is not the voluntariness of their choices that sets immigrants apart and provides the basis for their differential treatment in a multicultural society.

The difficulty, in the end, is working out how immigrants fit into a culturally diverse society. If they are expected simply to enter and assimilate into the mainstream of society, this makes demands to which many immigrants are unwilling to agree. (Australia's own assimilationist policies were abandoned in the 1970s partly because many immigrants began to return home to Europe, feeling that they had been unable to hold on to their cultural heritage after a working life spent away from their country of origin.) Yet, if immigrants are given the right to uphold their own customs and traditions, this might threaten social cohesion or, at the very least, hasten a cultural transformation of the host society that natives find unwelcome.

The complexity of the matter is perhaps well illustrated by Canadian practice. Canada welcomes a great diversity of immigrants, and has a policy of multiculturalism that accommodates the cultural concerns of many different peoples. At the same time, however, Quebec requires its immigrants to assimilate much more thoroughly if they wish to become members of Quebec society (Carens 2000: 107–39). Multiculturalism may require that immigrants be allowed to retain their cultural and linguistic traditions under a regime of differentiated citizenship. Yet a regime of differentiated citizenship that allows autonomy to national minorities like Quebec may also require that some immigrants not be entitled to that same opportunity. In the end, no more consistent system may be possible, since the claims of migrants have to be considered not only against the interests and demands of natives, but also against the structure of political authority within a society.

6. Refugees and Humanitarian Aid

In no area of immigration policy is political authority more seriously tested, however, than in the area of refugee policy. According to various United Nations organizations and international human-rights groups, more than forty million people in the world today are displaced persons. Janie Hampton estimates there were 20–22 million internally displaced people in the world in 1998, while the United Nations Commissioner for Refugees estimates twenty-one million displaced people living outside their countries of origin at that time (Hampton 1998). Living in terrible conditions, having been forced to leave their homes because of civil or international war, political conflict, 'ethnic cleansing', human-rights violations, natural disasters, or economic development projects, these people have little security and few prospects (Skran 1995: 70). The problem for many of these people is that, as refugees fleeing war or persecution, they are unable to have their 'basic rights' addressed by their own political communities, either because those communities are in turmoil, or because they are themselves victims of regimes from which they are now trying to escape.

Ethical discussion of the refugee issue might usefully begin with the 1951 UN Convention relating to the Status of Refugees, to which some 140 countries are now signatories. Three elements of the convention need special mention. First, the convention defines a refugee as any person who

owing to a well-founded fear of being persecuted for reasons of race, religion, nationality, membership of a particular social group or political opinion, is outside the country of his nationality and is unable, or owing to such fear, is unwilling to avail himself of the protection of that country; or who, not having a nationality and being outside the country of his former habitual residence as a result of such events, is unable or, owing to such fear, is unwilling to return to it.   (Article 1A2)

Secondly, the convention requires (Article 31) that signatory nations not impose any penalties on refugees who, coming directly from a territory where their life or freedom was threatened, have entered the state's territory without authorization, provided that they present themselves to the authorities and show cause for their illegal entry or presence. Thirdly, the convention expressly prohibits (Article 33) the expulsion or return (*refoulement*) of a refugee to frontiers or territories 'where his life or freedom would be threatened on account of his race, religion, nationality, membership of a particular social group or political opinion'. In sum, the convention requires its signatory members to admit and care for, within carefully defined limits, anyone who appears at their doors who is genuinely a refugee. This means granting such persons rights of various kinds, from rights to welfare no worse than those enjoyed by other aliens in the country, to rights of access to courts of law, to rights to own property and to practise their own religion.

A number of important issues arise out of this convention, but it is worth noting at the outset that the consequence of states becoming signatory to it is that they thereby relinquish (in principle) a significant measure of control over their own borders. No asylum-seeker may be turned away, and any such person with a well-founded fear of persecution (and who is not a criminal who poses a threat to society) is someone signatory states are obliged to accept. It is this particular consequence that has made the provisions of the convention not only controversial but also, all too often, imperfectly honoured.

The very definition of a refugee has been a matter of controversy from the outset. The convention definition reflects the concerns of Europeans dealing with people caught in the circumstances of the two world wars, when refugees were, by and large, 'the persecuted victims of highly organized predatory states' (Shacknove 1985: 276). Yet refugees might also, in reality, include many who are not the victims of persecution but simply people fleeing war, famine, or environmental catastrophe. For this reason, the Organization of African Unity adopted a very different definition, according to which a refugee was a person who 'owing to external aggression, occupation, foreign domination or events seriously disturbing public order in either part or the whole of his country of origin or nationality, is compelled to leave his place of habitual residence in order to seek refuge in another place outside his country of nationality' (OAU Convention Governing the Specific Aspects of Refugee Problems in Africa, adopted 10 September 1969 (UNTS no. 14691), Article 1(2); quoted in Shacknove 1985: 275–6). Bosnians fleeing civil war are thus captured by this definition in a way that they are not by the 1951 UN Convention.

Yet even this definition is flawed in so far as it does not include as refugees those who are not yet outside their countries of habitual residence: internally displaced people (Kurdish victims of the Iraqi regime of Saddam Hussein, for example) who have not had the chance to flee across borders or seek international assistance. A better definition might be the one offered by Matthew Gibney, for whom the term denotes 'those people who require a new state of residence, either temporarily or permanently, because if forced to return or stay at home they would, as a result of either the inadequacy or brutality of their state, be persecuted or seriously jeopardize their physical security or vital subsistence needs' (1999: 170–1). One particular merit of this definition is that it also includes as refugees those forced to flee in anticipation of a repression they rightly foresee. (It would also encompass those persons recognized in international law as refugees *sur place*: those persons who are unable to go back home because events in their country since their original temporary departure have left them with a well-founded fear of persecution should they return.)

The problem with expanding the definition of refugee, however, is that its most obvious consequence will be to increase the number of people who will be able to claim refugee status. Already many nations are unwilling to regard those fleeing generalized violence or famine as 'genuine' refugees deserving of protection. In recent years, Guatemalans, Salvadoreans, and Haitians have all been detained and sent home because they were not held to be victims of persecution (although the USA is not a signatory to the 1951 Convention). And German courts have ruled that 'fear of torture is not sufficient grounds for claiming fear of persecution with respect to Turkish asylum applicants, since torture is commonly inflicted on all prisoners in Turkey and not just on political prisoners' (Chalk 1998: 155). States in general are looking to narrow rather than widen the definition of refugee to enable them more easily to discriminate among those clamouring for aid. When the number of claimants is overwhelming, and some basis for discrimination has to be found, a narrow definition of the legitimate claimants looks like a reasonable solution.

Ethically, however, this approach to the question of definition must be regarded as dubious, for it misses the point of seeking a definition in the first place. The purpose of a definition in this case is not to facilitate policy or resolve or alleviate resource problems. The purpose of seeking a proper definition is to ensure that justice is done by correctly identifying who is deserving of our concern. Even if triage is going to be necessary, we do not begin by deeming those we cannot save to be healthy. This is not to say that utilitarian considerations have no place in morality; but to the extent that they do it is important that they not intrude in ways that compromise morality altogether. In questions of punishment, for example, it may be quite appropriate to determine the character and level of punitive measures by taking careful note of the likely consequence of any penalty inflicted. The justification for the practice of punishment may itself rest on utilitarian considerations. But the question of *who* is to be punished cannot rest on such considerations: only the guilty may rightly be punished. The purpose of any investigation into such matters must be, first, to identify correctly who is guilty. Only then can justice be done. And so it is with the question of the definition of 'refugee'. We evince a concern about refugees because we recognize that there are categories of people who are in need of special assistance. In this case it is because they can no longer avail themselves of resources to which they might ordinarily be expected to have access. The aim of definition should be to capture the spirit of this concern. Only then should we turn to the question of how, with our limited resources (if they are, indeed, so limited), best to serve the interests of those the legitimacy of whose claims we have already established.

Whatever the merits of this view, however, most states have not shown themselves interested in expanding the definition of refugee, and many have been unwilling even to abide by the terms of the convention to which they are signatory. In August 2001 the Australian government turned away a boatload of asylum-seekers rescued by the Norwegian vessel, the *Tampa*, which had sailed with its human cargo into Australian territorial waters. Had the asylum-seekers set foot on Australian territory, they would have been in a position to appeal for recognition as refugees, so the vessel carrying them was diverted to Nauru. Australia would prefer to select its quota of refugees not from the ranks of boat people landing unauthorized on its shores, but from the ranks of official applicants to its offshore refugee admission programme. And, like many European governments, it is looking for measures to discourage people from seeking asylum—particularly when they do so with the help of 'people-smugglers'.

The dilemma here, in the first instance, is that, if one is party to the 1951 Convention, one is obliged to take in anyone who is a genuine refugee, regardless of how many are found to have valid claims. Yet, with the numbers of people fleeing persecution numbering in the millions, the potential number of applicants may be overwhelming. Even for rich nations, the political problem posed by the prospect of hundreds of thousands of refugees landing on shore is significant—particularly when such persons will then have entitlements to welfare services, and rights to bring in members of their family.

After the *Tampa* had been turned away, a majority of the Australian population indicated, in a series of opinion polls and in the November 2001 general election dominated by the refugee issue, its support of the government's policy of refusing to allow boats containing asylum-seekers to land on Australian territory. Australians did so even though this policy ran against the spirit, if not the letter, of the 1951 convention to which Australia is signatory. At the same time, European governments have been looking to find ways to discourage refugees from entering the European Union. Some of these governments have also been discussing whether or not they should follow Australia's lead and establish detention centres into which asylum-seekers would be placed until their refugee status is determined, despite the many criticisms that have been raised against detention both as policy and in practice (Mares 2001).

On the face of it, the ethical question of how to deal with refugees is one that ought to admit of an easy answer—particularly for the wealthy and stable nations of the world. People who are fleeing for their lives, or seeking relief from war or natural disaster, should surely be helped. It is a principle that is enshrined in numerous international declarations, some of which have legally binding force. At the very least, it would seem, those who are themselves unwilling or unable to help the desperate or the destitute should not stand in the way of others who are willing and able. It is at this point, however, that ethical principle comes up against political reality. And, while philosophers who have maintained the importance of the nation and its integrity have nonetheless distinguished refugees from migrants, as special cases deserving of particular humanitarian concern, this argument has not made enough of a difference to alter national policies. Though philosophers like Michael Walzer have suggested that 'toward some refugees, we may well have obligations of the same sort that we have toward fellow nationals' (1983: 49), governments and citizens have generally not been persuaded. Refugees may be immigrants of a more desperate kind; but they are immigrants all the same.

It is at this point that the example of people like Mr Kayani becomes salient. In one sense, it would appear a straightforward matter of giving a greater preference to the resettlement claims of asylum-seekers like Mr Kayani for the sorts of reasons Michael Walzer would invoke. Those who fear persecution and are fearful for their own safety need to be helped immediately. But, once they are granted the right to stay, they pose many of the same sorts of challenges other migrants do—along with some others of their own. Refugees typically want to be reunited with their families, as do many other immigrants who seek to bring relatives to join them in their adopted country. In many cases they can impose substantial burdens on sections of the community either by their entry into some labour markets; or by their impact on housing markets; or by the pressure they might exert on existing publicly provided services, from parks to sewerage. Though such effects may matter only in the short term, and be amply compensated by the positive economic effects of immigration, the short-term effects may be significant politically. And morally. The people whose welfare is most affected adversely by some refugee immigrants may be the least well-off members of society rather than the well to do. A further complication is added when one considers that many refugees are people who are severely injured or traumatized and likely to add signficantly to the state's welfare burden.

In one respect, it is easy to say that wealthy countries ought to be ready to shoulder the burden of caring for those people described so graphically by Hannah Arendt. Referring to the European refugees created by the outbreak of the First World War, those groups who, 'unlike their predecessors in the religious wars, were welcomed nowhere and could be assimilated nowhere', she observed: 'once they had left their homeland they remained homeless; once they had left their state they became stateless; once they had been deprived of their human rights they were rightless, the scum of the earth' (Arendt 1960: 267). Surely the rich countries of the world should be able to shoulder such a burden—in a world in which the GDPs in 2000 of Australia ($410 billion with its eighteen million people) or Norway ($163 billion with its four million people) simply dwarf those of Rwanda ($1.8 billion for eight million people) or Tajikistan ($2.1 billion for six million people)—when their average members are wealthy beyond most people's dreams (all statistics from O'Driscoll et al. 2001). But the problem is that burdens taken on by states do not naturally fall upon those who can most readily—or willingly—carry them.

7. Answering the Immigration Question

It should be clear by now that immigration is an issue that is fraught with ethical difficulties, in part because the questions it raises are numerous and complex, but also because the stakes are high. Political stability, economic progress, human freedom, and individual survival all hang in the balance. But ethical questions may not be evaded just because they are difficult. So something ought to be said about how we might begin to address this one in particular.

Our starting point, I suggest, should be a recognition of our common humanity, and the idea that both the resources of the earth and the cooperation of our fellows are things to which no one has any privileged entitlement. Some are born better able to secure these blessings, but this is an accident of history. And, while history cannot be ignored, nor ought its accidents to be entrenched. Among the accidents that ought not to be entrenched are those that set boundaries dividing and confining populations, for these imaginary lines have never proven particularly enduring, and their ethical significance ought to be viewed with some scepticism. We should start, then, by assuming that the movement of peoples should be free.

There are three reasons why we should accept this starting point—though each is unquestionably controversial. First, from a utilitarian point of view, this is most conducive to human welfare in the long term. It would be a better world if people could go where there are opportunities to improve their welfare, and if the poorest were the last ones to be denied the freedom to pursue them. It would be a better world if the persecuted could flee their persecutors, who could not confine them within their borders simply by reminding them they are not welcome elsewhere. It would be a better world if those who wish to be with others for whom they care are not denied that opportunity by barriers forbidding the spontaneous reshaping of communities.

Secondly, if there is nonetheless a justification for political organizations such as the state, we should recognize that its point is to bring moral order into the world. Immanuel Kant (1797/1978) held that every person was under an obligation to enter a moral order or what he called a juridical condition, for it is only in a condition in which human beings relate to one another through law that moral life is possible. In this regard, we should recognize the admission into a juridical order of peoples fleeing conditions of lawlessness as an important obligation if we are to have a world in which the principle of living under law is honoured.

Thirdly, we should recognize that, while we may disagree about the nature and extent of our duties to aid or cooperate with our fellows, such duties exist nonetheless. And, while we cannot always be required to shoulder duties others may wish to impose upon us, we should not stand in the way of those who wish themselves to fulfil their duties to others as they conceive them. There might be important limits to the extent to which states may require us to contribute to the welfare of others; but there can be little justification in principle for the state denying us the opportunity to help others ourselves. To the extent that barriers to immigration—to the free movement of people—do precisely this, they are unjustified.

In this regard, it is worth remembering that, in the end, although ethical *discussion* must, from a practical point of view, begin with a recognition of national and international law, ethical *reflection* begins before this. Mere treaties, like the 1951 Convention, are pretty weak arguments, morally. The are just contracts: once one has signed them, one is bound by them (until one has complied with the 'notice' requirements and formally withdrawn from the treaty regime); but there is no particular reason, morally, to have to sign them, necessarily. Here it is worth noting that the USA has admitted significant numbers of refugees since the end of the Second World War without ever having signed the 1951 Refugee Convention. In the end, borders should be more open than they are not because national or international law demands it but because other, more substantial, ethical considerations obtain.

These are the basic reasons for taking a starting point that favours open immigration. But starting points are not finishing points. We do not live in a world in which all ethical options are open, for it is a world in which people have made their lives not on the basis of philosophical first principles, but on the assumption that existing laws and the expectations they have generated are more or less reliable. Yet the starting point advocated here suggests not that existing expectations be overthrown in the name of open borders, but that we approach immigration issues with a view to answering the question: how can the barriers be lowered? It also suggests that claims about the special signficance—let alone the sanctity—of borders do not provide a compelling justification for denying people the right to enter a society. They provide no justification at all.

8. Immigration as a Dilemma in Political Ethics

People have always been suspicious of strangers, and the arrival or presence of outsiders has typically provoked a hostile response from at least some members of the host community. The American 'know-nothings' of the nineteenth century were no less wary of foreigners than were the citizens of European countries or of Japan of the twentieth. Yet it is equally true that human history is the story of the intermingling of peoples. But what has made the movement of foreigners the ethical issue that it is today is the emergence of the modern, sovereign, nation state. Immigration poses a dilemma for such states because the demands *of* membership do not sit well with demands *for* membership (Kraut 2001).

There is, however, a further twist to this tale. The past three centuries have seen the rise of the sovereign state, as the seventeenth-century European model of international political society has found itself replicated across the planet. Yet, as the world has become a world of states, that world has increasingly become one regulated by law. Most states are not only members of the United Nations and related international organizations, but also signatories to international treaties or members of international regimes (such as that founded by the 1951 Convention concerning the treatment of refugees). In many ways, states have relinquished elements of their sovereignty by exercising their sovereign right to do so. They have signed agreements governing the ways in which they may wage war, what restrictions they may impose on the import and export of goods, what pollutants they may discharge into the oceans and the atmosphere, and what resources they may take from the sea. In this era of increasingly compromised national sovereignty (Krasner 1995), national membership—membership of the sovereign state itself—may be the one aspect of sovereignty to which states will cling most tenaciously. For as long as membership has value—and clearly it is of greater value in some states than it is in others—immigration will pose a dilemma. Paradoxically, it may be the nations whose ethical principles are most open to the free movement of peoples who will find that dilemma the most troubling.

References

Arendt, Hannah (1960). *The Origins of Totalitarianism*. New York: Meridian.

Barry, Brian (1992). 'The Quest for Consistency: A Sceptical View', in Brian Barry and Robert E.Goodin (eds.), *Free Movement: Ethical Issues in the Transnational Migration of People and Money*. University Park, PA: Pennsylvania State University Press, 279–87.

Blainey, Geoffrey (1984). *All for Australia*. Sydney: Methuen.

Brimelow, Peter (1995). *Alien Nation: Common Sense about America's Immigration Disaster*. New York: Random House.

Buchanan, James (1995). 'A Two-Country Parable', in Warren F. Schwartz (ed.), *Justice in Immigration*. Cambridge: Cambridge University Press, 63–6.

Carens, Joseph H. (1987). 'Aliens and Citizens: The Case for Open Borders'. *Review of Politics*, 49/2: 251–73.

——(1992). 'Migration and Morality: A Liberal Egalitarian Perspective', in Brian Barry and Robert E. Goodin (eds.), *Free Movement: Ethical Issues in the Transnational Migration of People and Money*. University Park, PA: Pennsylvania State University Press, 25–47.

——(2000). *Culture, Citizenship and Community: A Contextual Exploration of Justice and Evenhandedness*. Oxford: Oxford University Press.

Casey, J. (1982). 'One Nation: The Politics of Race'. *Salisbury Review*, 1: 23–8.

Castles, Stephen (1995). 'How Nation-States Respond to Immigration and Ethnic Diversity'. *New Community*, 21/3: 293–308.

Chalk, Peter (1998). 'The International Ethics of Refugees: The Case of Internal or External Political Obligation'. *Australian Journal of International Affairs*, 52/2: 149–63.

Dowty, Alan (1987). *Closed Borders: The Contemporary Assault on Freedom of Movement*. New Haven: Yale University Press.

Galbraith, Kenneth (1985). *Immigration*. Harmondsworth: Penguin.

Gibney, Matthew J. (1999). 'Liberal Democratic States and Responsibilities for Refugees'. *American Political Science Review*, 93/1: 169–81.

Glazer, Nathan (1997). *We are All Multiculturalists Now*. Cambridge, MA: Harvard University Press.

Goodin, Robert E. (1988). 'What's so Special about our Fellow Countrymen?' *Ethics*, 98: 663–86.

—— (1992). 'If People were Money? . . .', in Brian Barry and Robert E. Goodin (eds.), *Free Movement: Ethical Issues in the Transnational Migration of People and Money*. University Park, PA: Pennsylvania State University Press, 6–22.

—— and Pettit, P. (1986). 'The Possibility of Special Duties'. *Canadian Journal of Philosophy*, 16: 651–76.

Hammar, Tomas (1985). 'Dual Citizenship and Political Integration'. *International Migration Review*, 19/13: 358–50.

Hampton, Janie (1998) (ed.), *Internally Displaced People: A Global Survey*. London: Earthscan.

Hastings, Adrian (1997). *The Construction of Nationhood: Ethnicity, Religion and Nationalism*. Cambridge: Cambridge University Press.

Kant, Immanuel (1797/1978). *The Metaphysical Elements of Justice*, trans. John Ladd. Indianapolis: Bobbs-Merrill.

Krasner, Stephen (1995). 'Compromising Westphalia'. *International Security*, 20/3: 115–51.

Kraut, Alan M. (2001). *The Huddled Mases: The Immigrant in American Society, 1880–1921*. 2nd edn. Arlington Heights, IL: Harlan Davidson.

Kukathas, Chandran. (1997). 'Multiculturalism as Fairness: Will Kymlicka's *Multicultural Citizenship*'. *Journal of Political Philosophy*, 5/4: 406–27.

Kymlicka, Will (1995). *Multicultural Citizenship: A Liberal Theory of Minority Rights*. Oxford: Oxford University Press.

—— (1998). *Finding our Way: Rethinking Ethnocultural Relations in Canada*. Don Mills, Ontario: Oxford University Press.

Mares, Peter (2001). *Borderline: Australia's Treatment of Refugees and Asylum Seekers*. Sydney: University of New South Wales Press.

Miller, David (1995). *On Nationality*. Oxford: Oxford University Press.

—— (1999). *Principles of Social Justice*. Cambridge, MA: Harvard University Press.

Morris, Christopher W. (1998). *An Essay on the Modern State*. Cambridge: Cambridge University Press.

National Multicultural Advisory Council (1999). *Australian Multiculturalism for a New Century: Towards Inclusiveness*. Canberra: Australian Government Printing Service.

Nozick, Robert (1974). *Anarchy, State and Utopia*. Oxford: Blackwell.

O'Driscoll, Gerald P., Holmes, Kim R., and Kirkpatrick, Melanie (2001). *2001 Index of Economic Freedom*. Washington and New York: Heritage Foundation and *Wall Street Journal*.

Parnwell, Mike (1993). *Population Movements in the Third World*. London: Routledge.

Petersen, W. (1958). 'A General Typology of Migration'. *American Sociological Review*, 23/3: 266.

Sassen, Saskia (1999). *Guests and Aliens*. New York: New Press.

Schulze, Hagen (1994). *States, Nations and Nationalism from the Middle Ages to the Present*. Oxford: Blackwell.

Shacknove, Andrew (1985). 'Who is a Refugee?', *Ethics*, 95/2: 274–84.

Simon, Julian (1990). *The Economic Consequences of Immigration*. Oxford, Blackwell.

Skran, Claudena M. (1995). *Refugees in Inter-War Europe: The Emergence of a Regime*. Oxford: Oxford University Press.

Spruyt, Hendrik (1998). *The Sovereign State and its Competitors*. Princeton: Princeton University Press.

Steiner, Hillel (1992). 'Libertarianism and the Transnational Migration of People', in Brian Barry and Robert E. Goodin (eds.), *Free Movement: Ethical Issues in the Transnational Migration of People and Money*. University Park, PA: Pennsylvania State University Press, 87–94.

——(1994). *An Essay on Rights*. Oxford: Blackwell.

Trebilcock, Michael J. (1995). 'The Case for a Liberal Immigration Policy', in Warren F. Schwartz (ed.), *Justice in Immigration*. Cambridge: Cambridge University Press, 219–46.

Torpey, John (2000). *The Invention of the Passport: Surveillance, Citizenship and the State*. Cambridge: Cambridge University Press.

Vroman, Susan (1995). 'Some Caveats on the Welfare Economics of Immigration Law', in Warren F. Schwartz (ed.), *Justice in Immigration*. Cambridge: Cambridge University Press, 212–18.

Walzer, Michael (1983). *Spheres of Justice: A Defence of Pluralism and Equality*. Oxford: Blackwell.

Zolberg, Aristide (2001). 'International Migration', in Joel Krieger (ed.), *The Oxford Companion to Politics of the World*. 2nd edn. Oxford: Oxford University Press, 407–12.

CHAPTER 23

NATIONAL
AUTONOMY

WAYNE NORMAN

1. INTRODUCTION

WHAT rights do nations have to govern themselves and to control specific territories and the people living on these territories? What limits are there on these rights and on the activities of national communities and their political leaders? What projects can be justified primarily by appeals to the interests and identities of nations? We could call a well-reasoned answer to these questions a normative theory of national autonomy or national self-determination, which in turn is a central part of a normative theory of nationalism.

It would be an understatement to note that political philosophers are far from any consensus about the broad content of a theory of national autonomy. Almost every central concept in, and assumption underlying, the above questions is contested. There are disputes about what nations are, or even if there are such things as nations (Brubaker 1996: 13–22). And where there is agreement about that, there are still disputes on the ground about, for example: which particular minority and majority communities within the state qualify as nations; which nation or nations various groups of individuals belong to; and which particular chunks of territory

I am grateful for the financial support of the Social Sciences and Humanities Research Council of Canada; and for the institutional support of the Center for Social Innovation, Stanford University, where I wrote this chapter as a Visiting Scholar.

'belong' to different national communities. Then there are questions about the relevance of nationhood or nationality when assigning rights and duties to groups, and also about the relation between group rights and individual rights within a democratic system (Baker 1994; Barry 2001). In short, when it comes to national autonomy, there is still as much disagreement about what the proper questions are as there is about the best answers.

A large part of the explanation for this normative and conceptual free-for-all lies in the fact that this subject matter in contemporary political philosophy is barely a decade old. The first book ever published by an English-speaking philosopher on the ethics of secession (a central issue of national autonomy) appeared in 1991 (Buchanan 1991), and the first major philosophical book in the post-war era on the morality of nationalism was published in 1993 (Tamir 1993). That said, there has been a veritable explosion of intellectual activity on these issues since the early 1990s. (The bibliographies of five recent books—Couture et al. 1998; Kymlicka and Norman 2000; Levy 2000; Kymlicka 2001; Moore 2001—average about eighteen pages in length, and consist mainly of references from the 1990s.) This explosion has obliterated most of the walls between traditional disciplines like philosophy, political science, sociology, law, and history. It has become such a commonplace for scholars of nationalism from these different fields to interact with one another in the same conferences, journals, and collected volumes that they no longer think of themselves as exemplifying 'interdisciplinarity'.

All of this has led to a certain amount of intellectual anarchy in normative nationalist studies. As Hilliard Aronovitch observes, 'The flow of work on nationalism threatens now to inundate even the avid reader of it and forces one to ask whether in its wake we have gained a beachhead or lost all ground on which to stand' (2000a: 457). I think that there is now a solid beachhead. There has been a tremendous amount of progress since the early 1990s in refining both the agenda of issues for a normative evaluation of nationalism and the most plausible theories of the rights and limitations of national autonomy. Before we turn to these practical and institutional issues, though, it is worth examining briefly the larger question of the nature of nationalism and the challenges it poses for the modern liberal-democratic state and for normative theories appropriate for such states.

2. NATIONALISM: A BRIEF HISTORY IN POLITICAL THOUGHT

It has been said that in the nineteenth century everybody could agree on what democracy was and everybody was against it (even J. S. Mill), whereas, in the mid-twentieth century, nobody could agree on what democracy was but everybody was for it (even the leaders of the People's Democratic Republic of (North) Korea) (Graham 1986). This was partly the result of shifting values, no doubt; but also of shifting—and shifty—meanings. Similar generalizations are approximately true for nationalism. Roughly speaking, nationalism had a very good press from its earliest mentions by political philosophers in the eighteenth century until its fascist perversion in the middle part of the twentieth century. Although not all nationalists were liberals during this period (for example, Rousseau and Fichte were not), almost all liberal theorists were nationalists (from the authors of the *Federalist Papers* to J. S. Mill, Giuseppe Mazzini, and Ernest Barker) and nationalism was associated with progress, enlightenment, and the unity of great nation states. But all of this changed when fascists and Nazis ensured that nationalism would be, for most political thinkers for more than four decades, synonymous with authoritarianism and racism. The only progressives willing to use the language of nationalism in the post-war decades were those sympathetic with movements of 'national liberation' and decolonization. As late as 1993, the editors of the *Blackwell Companion to Contemporary Political Philosophy* could declare that 'nationalism—still less racism, sexism or ageism—does not figure [in the *Companion*], on the grounds that it hardly counts as a principled way of thinking about things' (Goodin and Pettit 1993: 7).

But by 1993 this blanket dismissal of nationalism was already being rethought all over the academic world. For many, perhaps the majority, of theorists publishing on the topic, 'liberal nationalism' went from oxymoron to pleonasm almost overnight. In retrospect this is quite surprising. Most philosophers evaluating nationalism in the 1990s had little or no academic training in the history or sociology of nationalism, and were no doubt drawn to the subject in part by the urgency of the violent images of ethnic nationalism on their TV screens every night. Philosophers, who had not taken nationalism seriously as a progressive ideology because of Hitler, were now taking an interest, in a way, because of Milosovic and Zhirinovski. (It should be noted that in the decade or so preceding the fall of the Berlin Wall there was something of a renaissance of nationalist studies among a small but extraordinary group of social scientists, including Nairn 1977; Breuilly 1982; Anderson 1983/1991; Gellner 1983; Horowitz 1985; Hobsbawm 1990; A. Smith 1991; and the essays republished in Connor 1994. These books served as 'Nationalism 101' for most philosophers entering the field.)

What then explains the relative sympathy for nationalism in so many of the 'first wave' of philosophical evaluations of the idea in the early 1990s? (This first wave included Kymlicka 1989, 1995a; Margalit and Raz 1990; Miller 1993, 1995; Tamir 1993; Taylor 1993; Canovan 1996; also many of the authors in influential collections edited by McKim and McMahan 1997; Couture et al. 1998; Moore 1998; Beiner 1999.) The core of the explanation is that these theorists distinguished between, if you will, 'good' and 'bad' forms of nationalism. What they tried to show, in general, was that the 'good' forms, often called 'civic nationalism', had a long and venerable history in the liberal tradition and in liberal-democratic societies. Like the fish that fails to see the water it swims in, liberal theorists in the post-war era had taken the bonds of national identity for granted. They simply assumed that society is a 'cooperative scheme in perpetuity', in which 'membership is a given' and 'fixed', and in which the

citizens 'will [all] lead their [entire] lives' (Rawls 1971). That is, they assumed the existence of social cohesion without giving much thought to how such 'social cement' was
generally created in modern states (that is, through decades or centuries of nation
building), or of how to deal with the challenges to political unity posed by ethnocultural groups that do not accept that their membership in the state should be taken
'as a given, in perpetuity'. In short, both nation-state nationalism (the kind that tries
to build political and cultural ties of identity in an otherwise heterogeneous society)
and minority-group nationalism (the kind that tries to build a national consciousness within a minority 'stateless nation', and leads to demands for autonomy) seemed
worth a fresh look: the former, because it appeared to be a hidden presupposition
for the stable liberal state; and the latter, because it threatened that state, though perhaps in ways that good democrats would have to respect.

Other trends in political philosophy and political events in Western democracies
fuelled the interest in the evaluation of both nation-state and stateless-nation varieties of nationalism. The debates between liberals and communitarians, which were
a main attraction in political philosophy throughout the 1980s, had become increasingly stale and abstracted from actual political life by the end of that decade. Many
of the participants in these debates reconvened in the 1990s under the rubrics of citizenship and diversity. (For surveys of these debates, see Kymlicka and Norman
1994, 2000.) In both cases, the nature of political and cultural *identity* became a central issue, probably for the first time in mainstream Anglo-American political philosophy. (In earlier eras it was more common to talk about national *character* than
identity; see Hume, J. S. Mill, Renan, and Barker.) Those discussing the nature and
demands of citizenship began to focus on the bonds of solidarity and identity in
pluralistic modern states, and on a politics of citizenship that looked much like civic
nationalism. Meanwhile, for the first time since the Second World War, philosophers had begun to devote serious attention to minority rights (see e.g. Kymlicka
1989, 1995*b*; Baker 1994; Spinner 1994; Phillips 1995; Bennett 1998; Williams 1998);
with the ultimate minority rights being those demanded by minority nationalists—
namely, self-government within the larger state, or secession from it.

These academic concerns about citizenship, diversity, and nationalism were also
in many ways responding to, and drawing case studies from, the changing political
landscape in most Western democracies at the end of the twentieth century
(Aronovitch 2000*a*: 460). Multiculturalism, feminism, and debates about 'political
correctness' in the USA were challenging the nature of, and need for, a common
melting-pot approach to American identity. And many multinational democracies,
including Canada, the UK, Belgium, Spain, and Switzerland, were attempting (not
always successfully) major constitutional revisions, usually in response to demands
from national minorities for increased autonomy. At the same time the traditional
nation states of Western Europe were in the process of voluntarily delegating real
sovereignty and national autonomy to the European Union (as it would come to be
called), not always with the blessings of nationalists among their own citizens.
Finally, to these events we can add the need for Western states to develop policies for

when to recognize the new states emerging from the first wave of secessions—in the former Soviet Union, Czechoslovakia, Yugoslavia, and Ethiopia—since President Wilson's support for 'national self-determination' following the First World War. All in all, the 1990s was a busy decade for the theory and practice of citizenship, national identity, secession, and federation in multinational states. And almost all of these challenges look likely to continue well into the twenty-first century: all of the minority-nationalist and secessionist movements in the West remain as strong and active now as they were in the 1990s; the European Union faces the dual task of consolidating its role in Western Europe while expanding to the east; and immigration continues to make all Western societies more diverse while challenging their traditional national identities.

3. NATIONS AND NATIONALISM

It is natural for philosophers to want to define nationalism as a *normative principle* (to wit, one that asserts that nations have a right to autonomy or self-determination). This, after all, is how we have traditionally defined other 'isms', like liberalism and socialism. Indeed, this intuition would be confirmed if one read no further than the first line of Ernest Gellner's influential book where he asserts that 'Nationalism is primarily a political principle, which holds that the political and national unit should be congruent' (1983: 1; see also Hechter 2000: 7). From here, presumably, one would attempt to nail down the definition of 'nation' or 'national unit', and then start to enquire about what rights and duties this kind of group should have. Unfortunately, matters never get to be that straightforward with this most peculiar of 'isms'. If we read on a little further in Gellner's book, we learn something with which most historians and sociologists now agree: that 'it is nationalism which engenders nations, and not the other way round' (1983: 55; see also Brubaker 1996: 17). As Gellner continues over the page: 'Nationalism is not what it seems, and above all it is not what it seems to itself. The cultures it claims to defend and revive are often its own inventions, or are modified out of all recognition' (1983: 56). How can nationalism be defined in terms of the rights (or rightful aspirations) of nations, but also be the 'thing' that creates and shapes nations and their aspirations?

Part of the apparent confusion in Gellner's various claims about nationalism here (and we could pluck similar passages out of most sociological studies of nationalism) is that he is using the term 'nationalism' to pick out three different kinds of things: a principle, a full-blown ideology, and a political movement. This shifting sense of nationalism is not uncommon in nationalist studies. The historical sociologist Anthony Smith has noticed the term being used to refer to a *process*, a kind of *sentiment* or *identity*, a *form of political rhetoric*, an *ideology*, a *principle* or set of principles, and a kind of *social-political movement* (A. Smith 1991: 72). Obviously these sorts of things are related, and we can see why we would want to use the adjective 'nationalist' to describe phenomena of all these kinds, even if we decide to reserve the noun 'nationalism' for only one of them. So, in addition to evaluating a principle of national self-determination, a normative theory of nationalism will be concerned with the nature and value of national identities, political attempts to forge them, and the rhetoric and ideologies that are used in such attempts.

Now this chapter is primarily concerned with the issue of national autonomy, and for this reason we shall leave to the side important issues for a normative theory of nationalism that concern the ethics of nation building (what Smith called the 'whole process of forming and maintaining nations'). (For pioneering explorations of some of the issues in the ethics of nation building, see Kymlicka 1995a: ch. 9; Miller 1995: ch. 3; Callan 1997: ch. 5; Norman 1999, forthcoming; Moore 2001: ch. 5; Weinstock 1999.) But the lingering question posed earlier remains. How are we to approach this principle about the rights of nations when the very idea of 'nation'—and the existence and character of any particular nation—seems to be the product of nationalist ideology and politics? To approach this question, some analysis of the concept of nation is in order.

Nations are a subset of human communities. In general, theorists try to distinguish nations from mere ethnic and racial groups, on the one hand, and communities defined entirely by political and territorial boundaries, on the other. (It should be clear by now that I am not using the term 'nation' to be synonymous with 'state', although the word is often used this way; for example, in the name 'United Nations'. Of course, in a few cases the membership of a given nation and a given state—say, Iceland—may be nearly co-extensive.) Most theorists are inclined to accept that national communities tend to have a number of special traits, such as those enumerated in a definition by Anthony Smith, where a nation is a 'named population sharing an historic territory, common myths and historical memories, a mass, public culture, a common economy and common legal rights and duties for all members' (A. Smith 1991: 14). Other traits often shared by members of a national community can include language, religion, and ethnicity.

But at least since J. S. Mill's discussion 'Of Nationality' (1862/1972) and Ernest Renan's *Qu'est-ce qu'une nation?* (1882/1939), most theorists, including Smith, have acknowledged that any such list of characteristics is open to exceptions: there will always be, among other things, some obvious nations that lack at least one of the characteristics. It is now common to think that all these 'objective' markers of nationhood are merely conditions that tend to foster the real necessary, and perhaps even sufficient, condition for being a nation—namely, the existence of what Max Weber (1948) called a 'community of sentiment'. Certain communities qualify as nations because of the way the members think about their fellow members and about the group itself: 'nations are the artefacts of men's convictions and loyalties and solidarities' (Gellner 1983: 7). Ultimately, communities are nations when a significant percentage of their members think they are nations. And virtually all theorists agree that part of what it is to think about your community as a nation is to assume that it requires the political means to exercise control over its destiny.

Most sociologists and philosophers now follow Benedict Anderson's evocative (though frequently misunderstood) idea of the nation as a kind of 'imagined community'. Nations are *imagined* in the sense that 'the members of even the smallest nation will never know most of their fellow-members, meet them, or even hear of them, yet *in the minds of each lives the image of their communion*' (Anderson 1991: 6; emphasis added). But 'imagined' certainly does not mean 'imaginary'. Following Anderson (1983/1991) and Tamir (1995: 421), Margaret Moore notes that 'many, if not most, communities, except the very smallest, are imagined. . . . Religious communities are imagined; my university is imagined; even my extended family is imagined. But they may all be important, and legitimate, bases of identification' (2001: 13).

One of the challenges for sociologists and social psychologists is to explain the obvious emotional receptivity of people to these 'invented' myths and 'fabricated antiquities' (Anderson 1993: 615). 'Why were so many very ordinary people willing to lay down their lives for nations of whom [*sic*] their grandparents had never heard?' (Anderson 1993: 615). And why is it that some attempts to make people identify with a given nation take hold, while others do not? Why, for example, should the majority of Croatian Yugoslavs at some point come to identify more with Croatia than Yugoslavia; why should northern Italians continue to identify more with Italy than with Lombardia or 'Padania', despite the persistent efforts of the Northern League? Why do most Catalans identify strongly with both Catalonia and Spain? Given the myriad forms that national identities and nationalist cultures can take, it is difficult even to conceive of social scientists providing the kind of robust, general answers to these questions that could provide meaningful explanations in particular cases. (See Hardin 1995 for a brave and interesting game-theoretic account.) *Why* any particular national identity can become so natural and so compelling for ordinary citizens is difficult to explain; but the fact that national identities *are* often so compelling is beyond dispute, even if it has been consistently under-appreciated by 'progressive' intellectuals over the past century. Marxists were dismayed to see the working classes fight against each other under their respective national flags in the First World War (rather than joining hands across borders to fight the 'common enemy'—the capitalists). And liberals, like Michael Ignatieff (1993: 5), were crestfallen when the collapse of Communism seemed at first to bring not the promise of democracy but only ethnonationalist violence.

At least part of what troubles philosophers about considering special rights for national groups is the generally accepted fact that these 'imaginary communities' called nations are the products of more or less deliberate projects of identity shaping by political elites. As Arthur Ripstein puts it, 'nations are imagined by the few for the many. In doing this, national[ist] leaders come close to the task that Rousseau assigns to the legislator: that of coming up with traditions through which people can recognise each other as fellow citizens' (1997: 210). Andrew Levine (overstating the case, no doubt, and with a deliberate nod to Freud) argues that 'typically, nationalisms are deliberately contrived and promoted. They are the work of political entrepreneurs who mould populist longings for communal forms appropriate to modern life in nationalist directions. In short, it is real-world politics, not psychological necessity, that explains this distinctively modern way of "valorizing an illusion" ' (Levine 1998: 361). Now a full evaluation of the implications of this claim would require a foray into the ethics of nation building—about the permissible means of identity shaping—which lies beyond the scope of this chapter. It is, however, appropriate to consider the relevance of taking seriously the existence of an identity that is a social construction (for example, by granting rights to groups that identify themselves as nations).

The standard response to this issue, which has been explored at length by Miller (1995) and Moore (2001: 42–6), is that there is nothing unusual in normative theory about working with socially constructed phenomena. Virtually all (if not, by definition, all) of our identities are social constructions, including our identities as citizens, elected officials, officers of the court, criminals, and what have you. This does not make these things less real or something that ethical theories should not deal with. The fact that the cash in my wallet is a social construction—something the existence and value of which is dependent on the beliefs of individual humans—does not mean that I have no more right to it than you have. Moore rightly questions both the truth of the strong elite-manipulation view of national identities, and the utility of this hypothesis for people with a liberal world view. For one thing, she argues, this view 'fails to come to grips with the reasons for its success—rather than that of other forms of identity, which presumably can also be manipulated'. More seriously, she argues:

this line of criticism [the elite-manipulation view] fails to treat people with respect, as agents capable of making decisions over their own destiny. Perhaps in a society in which all sources of information are controlled by the state, the elite-manipulation argument makes sense, but in a society with relatively open avenues of communication, and open political debates—that is, liberal-democratic societies—it is hard to describe nationalism in this way and maintain the basic assumptions about autonomy and rationality and reasonableness of all agents, which is central to both liberalism and democratic theory. (Moore 2001: 44)

Of course, the hypothesis in question does not literally fail to treat people with respect, the way, say, a police officer or a piece of legislation might. And there is nothing in principle contradictory for a liberal in believing that actual people are less than fully rational and can be duped by the ideologies of political opponents. But Moore seems to be onto something here. Most citizens of advanced Western democracies embrace a national identity—whether of the majority nation (for example, Britain), or the minority (for example, Scotland), or both—including most relatively clear-thinking liberal democrats. The way that people think about their nation and their identification with it is a matter of continual public debate and is therefore constantly evolving. There may be something non-rational about identifying with a community of mostly strangers, but it does not seem necessarily irrational. After all, what is the liberal alternative: identifying with a community of citizens within one's state in a way that does not shade into a national identity, or with humankind? Is one to imagine that these identities could become widely embraced without elite manipulation?

Given the existence of multiple, and sometimes overlapping, communities with strong national bonds within the same state, what special status or rights are such communities entitled to? For the remainder of this chapter we will focus for the most part on whether *minority* national communities have special rights to autonomy or self-determination. This focus is based largely on the fact that majority communities, in most democracies, already control the reins of sovereign state power—although it must be said that the question of the rights of majority communities within multinational states has received less than its fair share of attention in the recent literature (see Resnick 1998, 2000).

4. WHAT (IF ANYTHING) IS SPECIAL ABOUT NATIONS?

If we are to accept any principles of national autonomy that give national communities the right to maintain or promote their cultures through self-government, then it would seem that there must be something 'special' about *national* communities. That is, something that gives nations important political rights not granted to other kinds of groups and communities defined solely by, for example, ethnicity, religion, mother tongue, sexual preference, or political ideology. In the liberal-democratic tradition, for nations to be special in the relevant way, they must ultimately make a difference for individual members of the nation. (History provides numerous examples of non-liberal-democratic nationalist movements that felt *their particular* nation or race was 'special' and deserving of rights to dominate other nations; but it goes without saying that no such views find favour with philosophical defenders of nationalism today.) When political philosophers refocused their attention on nationalism around the time of the fall of the Berlin Wall, they quickly came up with three possible links between core liberal values and the special characteristics of national cultures.

First, there is the link between a healthy cultural context and liberal commitments to freedom, autonomy, and well-being. As Kymlicka (1989: 165) argued in his paradigm-shifting book, *Liberalism, Community, and Culture*:

Our language and history are the media through which we come to an awareness of the options available to us, and their significance; and this is a precondition of making intelligent judgements about how to lead our lives. In order to make such judgements, we do not explore a number of different patterns of physical movement, which might in principle be judged in abstraction from any cultural structure. Rather we make these judgements precisely by examining the cultural structure, by coming to an awareness of the possibilities it has, the different activities it identifies as significant.   (see also Margalit and Raz 1990: 449; Tamir 1993: 73–4; Kymlicka 1995a: 85–93)

The philosophers sympathetic to the demands for national autonomy think of nations as the most robust manifestations of these 'cultural structures'—sometimes called 'encompassing groups' (Margalit and Raz 1990) or 'societal cultures' (Kymlicka 1995a). Their basic argument for some form of liberal nationalism is quite simple: if liberals care about individual autonomy and well-being, then they must be concerned about a healthy cultural context required for meaningful options, and therefore about the health of the national cultures that provide this context of choice.

The second way some liberal political philosophers have tried to answer the question 'what's so special about nations?' extends the argument just sketched. It emphasizes the way that individuals *identify* with their national culture, and how their sense of self-respect (a Rawlsian primary good) is tied up with the respect shown to their nation. Tamir (1993: 73) sketches the argument quite bluntly:

Membership in a nation is a constitutive factor of personal identity. The self-image of individuals is highly affected by the status of their national community. The ability of individuals to lead a satisfying life and to attain the respect of others is contingent on . . . their ability to view themselves as active members of a worthy community. A safe, dignified, and flourishing national existence thus significantly contributes to their well-being.

Charles Taylor (1993: 49) makes a similar case on behalf of linguistic national minorities:

The language/culture that defines our identity must be one that can command our allegiance. We have to see it as valuable. If it comes to be depreciated in our eyes and if it remains the indispensable pole of our identity, we are in a catastrophic position, one in which we cannot avoid depreciating ourselves, tied as we are to an impoverished culture.

Both Tamir and Taylor see these claims about this link between the state of a national culture, on the one hand, and individual members' self-respect and well-being, on the other, as a premise in arguments for national self-determination. They continue their arguments on behalf of nationalists from the passages just quoted thusly:

The right of national self-determination can be fully realised only if the national group is recognised by both members and non-members as an autonomous source of human action and creativity, and if this recognition is followed by political arrangements enabling members of the nation to develop their national life with as little external interference as possible.   (Tamir 1993: 74)

For nationalists, this [self-identification via the nation] is necessary and indispensable, and the remedy can therefore only be the promotion of the national culture.   (Taylor 1993: 50)

We will discuss concrete rights to self-determination in the next two sections. I note these arguments primarily to show just how 'special' nations are taken to be here: their role in a healthy sense of identity and self-respect is thought to be so crucial it underwrites extensive political rights for minority national communities.

The third reason nations are treated as special by some liberal theorists concerns a point mentioned early on in this chapter: national identities can provide the kind of social cement presupposed by well-functioning liberal-democratic institutions. This argument has its roots in J. S. Mill's chapter 'Of Nationality, as connected with Representative Government' (1862/1972). Its most important recent exponent is David Miller (1995: 70):

the ethical implications of nationality differ from those of *lesser* [i.e. non-national] communities ... The potency of nationality as a source of personal identity means that its obligations are strongly felt and may extend very far—people are willing to sacrifice for their country in a way that they are not for other groups and associations.   (emphasis added)

For Miller, this special feature of national identity also leads almost directly to a central argument 'favouring national self-determination,' one that is particularly appealing for liberal-democrats (see also Barry 1983; Canovan 1996):

Where a nation is politically autonomous, it is able to implement a scheme of social justice; it can protect and foster its common culture; and its members are to a greater or lesser extent able collectively to determine its common destiny. Where the citizens of a state are also compatriots [share the same sense of nationality], the mutual trust that this engenders makes it more likely that they will be able to solve collective action problems, to support redistributive principles of justice, and to practise deliberative forms of democracy. Together these make a powerful case for holding that the boundaries of nations and states should as far as possible coincide.   (Miller 1995: 98)

As we see, all three of these arguments for the 'specialness' of nations are meant to appeal to liberal-democrats. Not surprisingly, not all liberal political philosophers find them convincing. It is worth distinguishing two related objections, one of which suggests that other liberal values are betrayed by these arguments, and another that believes these arguments are undermined when we focus on some of the basic features of the concept of nation.

Allen Buchanan takes up the former objection in an article that provides a sceptical answer to the question of its title, 'What's So Special About Nations?'(1998a). He argues that liberal nationalists may have shown that national communities can provide important conditions for the autonomy, well-being, self-respect, and solidarity of their members; but they have not shown that this makes them *special*—because membership in other kinds of identity groups can provide similar benefits. Indeed, many members of a given nation may place much more stock in other aspects of their identity (based on, say, their religion, sexual preference, occupation, or what have you), and may derive all the benefits (or costs) of membership in these other identity groups that Kymlicka, Tamir, Taylor, and Miller associate with nations. Given this 'dynamic pluralism' of identities, Buchanan (1998a: 294) argues:

Singling out nations as such as being entitled to self-government is nothing less than a public expression of the conviction that allegiances and identities have a single, true rank order of value, with nationality reposing at the summit. So to confer a special right of self-government on those groups that happen to be nations is to devalue all other allegiances and identifications. And to devalue these . . . is to show less than equal respect to the persons whose allegiances and identifications they are.   (see also Brighouse 1998: 374–80)

(Recall Miller's comparison between nations and '*lesser* communities', in a quote earlier.) Buchanan believes that this argument holds true even if nations are 'encompassing groups' that 'provide unity and integration for, rather than compete with, the other identities that individuals may have' (Buchanan 1998a: 297). As Jacob Levy puts it, the difficulty with the arguments of liberal nationalists like those we have explored is that they 'do not uniquely pick out the nation as the sole or primary object of that partiality and loyalty. . . . Instead they justify . . . loyalty to and partiality to all those groups to which one belongs that cooperatively produce valuable goods, that warrant gratitude, or that have a shared sense of history and shared attachment to a piece of land' (Levy 2000: 76).

Liberal-nationalist arguments look most convincing, Levy points out, when the alternative to strengthening the national identity or self-government for a given group is 'imagined to be either undifferentiated humanity or alienated individualism' (Levy 2000: 71). Consider, for example, how the first and third arguments for the 'specialness' of national membership invite us to imagine how difficult it would be: (in the first) for a person to have to make autonomous choices in the absence of *any* cultural context that teaches her to value certain ways of life, or (in the third) for a society to support just redistributive schemes if there were *no* bonds of solidarity among the individuals making up the society. But, in fact, it is rarely the case, at least in the developed democracies of the West, that groups or societies face the choice between having a particular identity reinforced, on the one hand, and having no identity or community structure, on the other. As a political movement, nationalism rarely comes into play unless there are rival claims on some individuals' or groups' national identity and loyalty. In other words, nationalisms usually come in pairs: with minority nationalists trying to convince individuals that, say, Quebec, Scotland, Catalonia, Flanders, Brittany, Kurdistan, or Nagaland is the nation they truly belong to; and 'nation-state' nationalists trying to stoke these same individuals' pride in their membership in the Canadian, British, Spanish, Belgian, French, Turkish, or Indian state and nation. In most democratic states where minority nationalism is alive and well, members of the minority communities have genuinely divided loyalties; they feel Québécois *and* Canadian, Catalan *and* Spanish, and so on. So the alternative to 'minority cultural preservation' (or, alternatively, to nation-state building) is not undifferentiated humanity or alienated individualism, but rather membership in 'some other community to which [they] also have some attachment' (Levy 2000: 71). Or, more to the point, the alternative to the nationalist's dream that individuals cherish only one 'true' national identity is that they continue (perhaps happily) to juggle more than one national identity, along with their many other important identities.

We would not want to push this argument too far. Though members of most national minorities in the West have overlapping national identities, they are rarely indifferent about relative importance of these identities. It is no critique of nationalism to imagine that there would be no loss if minorities just 'quietly' assimilated into the larger nation-state identity, the way, say, the Cornish became English. For one thing, this would amount to a particularly unsympathetic apology for *majority* nationalism. Furthermore, it is unrealistic in our world to expect such assimilations to happen voluntarily. According to the sociologist of nationalism Walker Connor, there is not a single example of a group relinquishing its minority national consciousness since the early twentieth century; and this despite some of the most horrific forms of oppression against minorities who refuse to relinquish their identity (Connor 1994: 53–4). But not only is it a kind of brute fact that minorities with a national self-conception do not assimilate *en masse*; to do so, even for an individual, is very often quite difficult and costly, especially when this requires mastering a second language and overcoming the stigma and discrimination that often greet minority nationals trying to make it in the larger society. This kind of obstacle to equal opportunities raises obvious issues of justice for liberals (see Taylor 1993: 50; Kymlicka 1995a: 82–93).

These arguments against the 'specialness' of national identity and nations do not point directly to any particular political conclusion concerning (*a*) how minority or majority nations should be treated, (*b*) what kind of nation building is appropriate within such communities, or (*c*) what sorts of political structures (if any) they should have to permit self-government. What they are meant to undermine is the validity of certain overly simple patterns of argument in favour of the self-determination of nations (especially minority nations): namely, the idea that national communities deserve special rights because of their special ability to provide a cultural context of choice, a social basis of self-respect, and/or a particularly sticky form of social cement. Again, such arguments for national autonomy seem quite unconvincing, especially when it comes to 'adjudicating between claims— usually over territory—by rival national communities' (Moore 2001: 47). Other arguments for justifying self-government for particular national communities may fare better. Over the next two sections we will consider when groups, national or otherwise, might qualify for the most concrete rights to self-determination— namely, the right to secede or the right to substantial degree of political autonomy within a multinational state.

In the end, we probably should not be surprised at the difficulty in coming up with a convincing, abstract, general answer to the question of what is special about nations. The very peculiar definition of nation accepted by most contemporary scholars should be the first clue. These various imagined communities—around the world and back in time for the last two or three centuries—have very little empirical content in common, apart from the fact that their members have come to think of their groups as nations. Nationalists in one will point to shared language as the basis of their sense of nationhood; in another to shared religion or ethnicity or to a common history living under certain institutions, and so on. (And, as Levy (2000: 79) has noted, it is because each national movement attaches identity significance to different empirical features that two or more national groups or nationalist movements can 'lay claim' on some of the same individuals; each denying the others' claims.) The only generally accepted necessary conditions for nations are that (most of their) members (*a*) think they are a nation, and (*b*) think they ought to be allowed to govern themselves. But it is normally a rather dubious moral argument to claim that you have a right to something merely because, in effect, you *think* you ought to have it.

On the other hand, that is at least partly what democracy is about. And as long as national (or other) identities influence citizens' political choices, there is a prima facie reason to take them seriously. In short, whether nations in general are all 'special' in the same way and in a way that distinguishes them from other kinds of groups and communities is beside the point. There may nevertheless be good grounds for permitting particular national communities (be they majorities or minorities within their states) rights to control their destinies.

5. SECESSION

Secession is the withdrawal of a population *and its territory* from the domestic constitutional law of one state, and its accession to the full status as a new state under international law. (In the case of an irredentist secession, the seceding territory and its people join up with a neighbouring 'kin' state.) All theorists sympathetic to the demands of national minorities for autonomy or self-determination, including those who were arguing that nations were 'special' in the preceding section, are quick to point out that national self-determination does not always, or even usually, require secession. Without doubt, though, secession is the most full-blooded form of autonomy for national minorities; and the ultimate, if usually unrealistic, dream of minority nationalists everywhere.

Almost totally ignored in the history of political philosophy until the 1990s, these issues have inspired a small boom of research and publishing since Allen Buchanan sparked the debates with his book *Secession: The Morality of Political Divorce from Fort Sumter to Lithuania and Quebec*, in 1991. I think it is safe to say that we have largely made up for lost time now. There is no more consensus about the morality of secession than there is about any other issue in political philosophy, but the main rival theories and critiques have now been developed in sophisticated form, and the agenda of issues looks to be pretty well filled out.

When philosophers first turned to this issue, it is likely that most were expecting to find a relatively small, discrete, neglected problem in applied political theory—like a thread protruding from a nearly completed garment needing to be tied and snipped. Instead, they found a loose thread so integral to the whole that pulling it in the wrong direction might just unravel everything. Rawls once made explicit what most political philosophers since Hobbes have merely presupposed: that the frontiers of their discipline coincide, more or less, with the unchanging frontiers of the nation state. 'I assume that the boundaries of these schemes [of justice] are given by the notion of a self-contained national community', he wrote (Rawls 1971: 457), where 'national community', in typical American parlance, means the state. As I noted at the outset, like most philosophers, he developed his theory for a society that is a 'cooperative scheme in perpetuity', in which 'membership is a given' and 'fixed', and in which the citizens 'will [all] lead their [entire] lives'. But what happens to liberal theory and the theory of justice when not all groups within the national (that is, state) community want to be contained by it, or to have their membership assumed as a given? Or, perhaps more to the point, what does it take to try to *make* the overwhelming majority of citizens in a culturally pluralistic state think of their state (or nation) as a cooperative scheme in perpetuity? And what can be done by the state to discourage, dissuade, or even disarm those who might actively try to break the state up? None of these questions evokes obvious or simple answers, and yet they go to the heart of liberal-democratic statecraft. This is presumably what Brian Barry had in mind when he recommended a recent collection of new essays on secession (Lehning 1998) for the 'special significance' of its using the issue of secession 'as a way of exploring deep questions about the nature and value of political community' (Lehning 1998: p. xii).

Yet even more recently Barry (2001: 137) himself has opined that there is:

no distinctive liberal theory of political boundaries at the level of principle.... What liberalism is about is how polities, however constituted, should be run.... All it has to say about boundaries is that they are better the more conducive they are to the creation and maintenance of a liberal political order within them. Whether that requires units that are large or small, heterogeneous or homogeneous, is a pragmatic question. There is not going to be any generally applicable answer.

This view suggests that philosophers will not have much to contribute to normative questions about secession (even if thinking about secession may sharpen their theories about the importance of community). Buchanan would surely disagree, citing a number of fundamental liberal principles that would seem, prima facie, to have a bearing on the rights of people to alter international borders through secession. 'A political philosophy [such as liberalism] that places a pre-eminent value on liberty and autonomy, that highly values diversity, or that holds that legitimate political authority in some sense rests on consent must either acknowledge a right to secede or supply weighty arguments to show why a presumption in favour of such a right is rebutted' (Buchanan 1991: 4).

Many leading social scientists involved in ethnic-conflict studies side with Barry, who himself quotes Brubaker warning that 'Good institutional design is more likely to be subverted than informed by grand architectural principles like the principle of national self-determination or the principle of nationality' (Brubaker 1998, quoted in Barry 2001: 137). Donald Horowitz is subtler in his disdain for some of the early writings by philosophers on secession. He does not wish 'to exhibit hostility to the efforts of philosophers on such issues in general—for moral reasoning is needed'; but his years of studying the dynamics of actual conflicts between ethnic groups leave him with no patience for 'a priori methods that seem appropriate for other problems [of political philosophy but are] utterly unsuitable to this problem' (Horowitz 1997/1998: 199).

Horowitz is being a little grumpier than he needs to be here. Many philosophers have also joined in criticisms of normative theories of secession that seem to tumble too innocently from abstract principles and 'a priori methods' (see e.g. Buchanan 1991, 1997, 1998a,b; Beiner 1998; Freeman 1998; Norman 1998a, 2001a; Weinstock 2001). Horowitz is probably correct, though, in framing the issue as one hinging on moral methodology. The content of a theory of secession seems to be very closely linked to the choice of some basic assumptions about moral methodology, and, in particular, about whether it is best to engage in so-called institutional or non-institutional' moral argument (see Philpott 1995, 1998; Buchanan 1997; Copp 1998; Moore 1998, 2001: 203–6; Norman 1998a). I will say more about this distinction and its relevance below. Suffice it to say here that the very idea of *institutional* moral reasoning challenges the stark dichotomy between a principled and a pragmatic approach—it is meant to be principled *and* pragmatic.

Most normative theories of secession now fit into three basic categories (there are also a few hybrid theories mixing elements of these three theories):

- *Nationalist theories of secession*, which hold that a territorially concentrated group may secede if and only if it is a nation, and the majority of members of the nation (or inhabitants on the territory it proposes to take with it) want to secede.
- *Choice theories of secession*, which hold that (with certain caveats) any geographically defined group may secede if and only if the majority of its members choose to.
- *Just-cause theories of secession*, which hold that a group has a right to secede only if it has 'just cause'; for example, if it has been the victim of systematic and continuing discrimination or exploitation, or if its territory had been illegally incorporated into the larger state against its will (subject to a kind of 'statute of limitations' clause of 'within recent memory').

Of course, actual theories of these three types are loaded with details, including caveats and compromises that try to meet some of the challenges of institutionalizing the theory in the real world. Nevertheless, these three categories capture some essential features of the spirit behind different normative approaches to secession. In particular, as Buchanan (1997) has emphasized, there is a big difference between thinking of secession as a *primary* right, in the first two, and a *remedial* right, in the third. Groups (and a majority of their members) need only want a state of their own in order to gain the right to secede, according to nationalist and choice theorists; but for just-cause theorists the group must have suffered an injustice for which secession is the only reasonable remedy. (Daniel Weinstock has called this a distinction between 'just 'cos' and 'just-cause' theories!)

Since 1991 there have now been two or three go-rounds of criticisms and replies between partisans of these three types of theories, and there is not space to summarize all the most sophisticated moments of these debates here. It is worth noting that there are very few philosophical defenders of nationalist theories of secession (see Nielsen 1993; Gilbert 1998)—even amongst those who were willing to argue that nations are 'special' and deserving of some vaguely defined realm of self-determination (e.g. Kymlicka, Tamir, Miller, Taylor). Of course, this is still the basic self-justification for most actual secessionist movements, almost all of which are rooted in ethno-cultural communities. Arguments of the sort marshalled against the 'specialness' of nations are telling against nationalist theories of secession—particularly those pointing out (*a*) the violations of equality that come from privileging one type of identity group over others, as well as (*b*) those that worry about the extent to which the existence of a nation is the product of deliberate political projects to forge a national consciousness. After all, if being a nation gives you special rights, and being a nation is a function of people thinking they are a nation, then nationalist entrepreneurs will be given enormous incentives to try to construct a national consciousness even where one does not really exist (as, say, in Corsica, Wales, or Northern Italy). Another frightening implication of the nationalist theory is that literally thousands of ethnolinguistic and ethnoreligious groups in the world would gain access to a right to secede if this theory were sound. A typical state in the developing world contains upwards of twenty-five ethnic groups with at least the potential to develop a national self-awareness, and most are intermixed in the way the ethnic populations of Bosnia and Rwanda were. Can anyone really believe that the world would be a better place (with democracy flourishing where it now struggles to find minimal nourishment) if this principle were enforced in international law?

Similarly, perhaps the most intuitively telling criticism of choice theories is that they would grant rights of secession to even more groups than the 5,000 or so that might accede to this status under the nationalist theory. And in so doing they would be encouraging secessionist politics (including disingenuous secessionist blackmail) from all sorts of groups that would not even dream of seceding in the absence of the currency of the choice theory itself.

Now to argue in this way against choice and nationalist theories is to engage in so-called institutional moral reasoning: evaluating political principles in large part by evaluating the institutions they would justify, taking into consideration the dynamic effects of these institutions in society (including perverse incentives they might encourage). Half of the institutional moral argument against nationalist and choice theories is that it is almost beyond conceivability that anything like them could be embodied in a desirable, practicable, form of international law and practice; and that is not just because existing states prefer the status quo. The other half of the argument is that, if these theories *were* instantiated in practice, the world would be much worse off than it is currently. Nationalist and choice theorists do sometimes try to deny that the currency of their theories would have horrendous consequences, but almost without exception they begin by justifying their theories not for their good consequences in the world, but rather on the basis of 'non-institutional' moral reasoning from more basic abstract liberal principles: for example, from arguments about the 'specialness' of nations in the case of nationalist theories, and from principles of democracy (Copp 1997), individual autonomy (Philpott 1995), and freedom of association (Beran 1984; Gauthier 1994; Wellman 1995), in the case of choice theorists.

One way to sum up the above case for a just-cause theory of secession over the nationalist and choice rivals is to say that only the just-cause theory comes close to justifying a reasonable institutional response to secessionist politics. If constitutional and international law allowed only groups with just cause to secede and enforced their right to do so, then the world would be improved in a number of significant respects: many oppressed groups would find their oppressors easing off (since central authorities would not want to be providing these groups with just cause), and those that continued to be oppressed would be given a safe state of their own; states would lose their current incentives to deny their minorities basic rights and political autonomy, since these groups would not be able to use this autonomy to launch successful secessionist movements; similarly, states would lose much of their incentive to try (usually without much success) coercively to assimilate ethnocultural minorities; and states would not have to worry about restricting the free circulation of minorities within the state in order to prevent them forming territorially concentrated majorities. All of this seems for the good. By contrast, the only benefit of codifying and enforcing nationalist and choice theories would be that they too would allow oppressed groups to seek a safe haven in a new state of their own. But all the other positive effects and incentives of institutionalizing just-cause theories would be reversed if choice or nationalist theories were institutionalized: oppression would be encouraged in cases where it could intimidate minorities from mounting a secessionist or nationalist movement; and assimilationist policies would still look attractive to states, as would restrictions on mobility (or encouraging members of the majority group to flood into the traditional homeland of the minority, as happened in Croatia and Serbia in the early 1990s) and the refusal to grant minority rights. (For a fuller version of arguments like these, see Buchanan 1997: 52–5; Norman 1998a: sect. 5). Of course, in the background of all real-world concerns about secession is the fear of Yugoslav-like levels of interethnic violence.

It should be noted, however, that, for all the attention to realism and pragmatism by just-cause theorists, these theories still leave us some distance from the actual institutions for secession that should be instituted in constitutional or international law. The main reason for this is that the theory ties the right to secession to the existence of a just cause; but who in the real world is qualified—and accepted by all parties in a given dispute—to determine when a group has suffered sufficient injustice that only secession can provide the appropriate remedy (Buchanan 1991; Norman 1998a; Moore 2001: 147–8)? Determinations of justice and injustice in the historical relations between groups are, of course, deeply contested. When designing actual institutions (say, for the constitution of a multinational democratic state) just-cause theorists are likely to rely on popular support for secession as a proxy, albeit a fallible one, for the movement's having just cause. They may, for example, specify that for a province to secede from a federation there must be a referendum with two-thirds of the voters in the province choosing to secede. Interestingly (and ironically) enough, such an approach to institutional design is sometimes favoured by choice theorists, who are at pains to show how their theories would not unduly encourage a wave of secessions.

For an indication of the complex practical and normative challenges facing those who would reform international law to deal in a fairer way with secessionist demands (and the demands of states to have their sovereignty and borders preserved), readers can turn to Buchanan (1997, 1998b), Musgrave (1997), or Copp (1998), among others. For an interesting elaboration of how the basic constitutional principles of a liberal-democratic, federal state can be extended to deal with secessionist politics in domestic law, one can hardly do better than the monograph-length Opinion of the Supreme Court of Canada from 1998. This opinion followed a federal government 'Reference' on the legality of secession in a country whose constitution is silent on the issue. (Very few constitutions deal explicitly with secession. Many rule out the very possibility by declaring the country to be 'Indivisible'. For good international surveys of this aspect of constitutional law, see Suksi 1993; Monahan and Bryant 1996.) In its carefully reasoned Opinion—which surprisingly found favour with both federalists and separatists—the court argued that the federal government of Canada would have a constitutional obligation to negotiate the secession of a province if a referendum in the province produce a 'clear majority' voting 'Yes' on a 'clear question'. More interesting, from a political philosopher's point of view, is the moral and legal reasoning leading to this conclusion. The court believed that this conclusion followed from an understanding of each of the four basic principles of Canadian constitutional law: federalism; democracy; constitutionalism and the rule of law; and respect for minorities (para. 32; for more analysis of this document, see Brown-John 1999; Walters 1999; Moore 2001; Norman 2001a).

Of course, it goes without saying that the constitutional traditions of other demo-cratic states would not permit such a generous interpretation of the democratic right of secession. The judges' arguments in the Opinion do suggest, nevertheless, that the stark alternative (suggested by Brubaker and Barry) for normative theoriz-ing about secession between 'grand architectural principles', on the one hand, and mere 'pragmatic' argument, on the other, is overdrawn. There is much for political philosophers and legal theorists to contribute to debates about secession, including the debate about whether it is appropriate or even desirable for the constitution of a democratic multinational state to include some sort of clause to regulate seces-sionist contests (see Buchanan 1991: ch. 4; Sunstein 1991, 2001; Bauböck 1999; Aronovitch 2000b; Norman 2001a, in press; Weinstock 2001).

6. Self-Determination without Secession

As we have seen, there are differences of opinion among political philosophers about when groups have a right to secede. But virtually all theorists of secession express the hope that even groups with a right of secession will typically choose not to (or not to be forced to choose to) exercise the right. It is a commonplace to think of minority national communities as having a general right to self-determination, but it is also assumed that there are many ways that such a right can be fully exer-cised within a multinational state. In fact, those most 'conservative' (if you will) about the right of secession—including most just-cause theorists, as well as ethnic-conflict analysts like Horowitz—also tend to be most 'liberal' about rights to concrete forms of self-determination and autonomy for minorities within the state. In this final section we will survey very quickly some of these forms of internal autonomy as well as some of the issues for thinking about their justification and legitimacy.

For national minorities that are territorially concentrated, the desired form of autonomy is usually conceived of in terms of some kind of federal arrangement. In history, federalism has taken dozens of forms (see Watts 1998), but we will focus here on federal systems that: (a) allow one or more minority groups to form the majority in a federal subunit (call this a province; although they are also called states, cantons, autonomous regions, and so on); and (b) divide legislative and/or administrative jurisdictions between central and provincial governments, with some powers shared between both levels of government. By allowing national minorities to have exclusive or shared responsibility for important powers (such as education, health and welfare, or language policy), such federal systems can be said to divide sovereignty. Of course, the devil is in the details: to decide whether a given federal arrangement provides an appropriate degree of autonomy for a national minority, we have to consider how it handles the following concrete issues.

- How are the borders of the subunits determined? Do they correspond to 'traditional homelands' for national minorities, or are they culturally arbitrary or intended to dilute or diffuse the autonomy of minorities? Are there democratic provisions for changing provincial boundaries?
- What specific powers are given to the central and to the provincial governments, and how are the two orders of governments to coordinate their activities? Does the minority have sufficient control over jurisdictions with cultural and linguistic significance? Does the federal government retain powers sufficient to make the political and economic union work, and to promote some form of pan-state identity and solidarity? Do provinces controlled by national minorities have powers not shared by other provinces?
- What representation do the provinces, the citizens of the provinces and members of national minority groups have within central federal institutions like the parliament, the supreme court, the civil service, and the military? Are minorities guaranteed certain levels of representation (e.g. a certain percentage of seats in parliament or judges on the supreme court)? Are they over-represented in terms of population?
- What role do the provinces (or specifically the minorities' provinces) have in the amending formula for the constitution? Can they veto changes that would affect, e.g. the division of powers or other provincial rights?
- Is there a constitutional provision permitting the secession of a province under democratic conditions?
- How are national minorities and majorities reflected in and recognized by the major symbols of the state, such as its name, its flag, its constitutional preamble, and its official languages and/or religions?
- What minority rights and citizenship rights are available to those who are minorities within the political jurisdiction of either the majority or minority (e.g. for Serbs in Kosovo, or for Kosovars in Serbia)?

It goes without saying that these are hugely complicated normative and political questions. It is often not even clear what kind of normative theory should be appealed to when we search for institutional answers. If very general or abstract normative considerations are useful here, they must surely be applied in ways that permit very different answers for different cultural, political, and historical cases. One good explanation for puzzlement in the face of these issues is that they are among the most neglected in all political philosophy. There has never been a book published by a major academic press by a philosopher in the English-speaking tradition on federalism (although normative issues have received airing in works by political scientists like Wheare 1963; Riker 1964; Friedrich 1968; Forsythe 1981). The fact that citizens in federal or federalizing states discuss these institutional issues in a rich normative language has sparked the interest of a number of political philosophers in the last decade (see e.g. Taylor 1991/1993, 1992; Norman 1994, 1995*a,b*, 1998*b*, 2001*b*; G. Smith 1995, 2000; Kymlicka 1998*a,b*, 2000*b*; Fosses and Requejo 1999; Requejo 1999; Weinstock 1999, 2001; Bauböck 2000; and the essays in Gibbins and Laforest 1998 and Gagnon and Tully 2001). The quasi-federalization of the European Union has also spawned a sizeable recent literature on issues that are equally relevant for many federal states (see e.g. A. Smith 1993; Hesse and Wright 1996; MacCormick 1999; Eriksen and Fossum 2000; van Parijs 2000). Another body of recent normative explorations of federalism comes from the political-theory communities within a number of federal or quasi-federal states that have undergone attempts at major reforms in recent years—most notably in Canada, Switzerland, Belgium, Spain, the UK, and Australia. Despite this flurry of recent activity towards a normative theory of federalism, however, it is fair to say that few authors claim to have done much beyond either, on the one hand, the cataloguing of relevant issues for future enquiry, or, on the other, addressing very specific issues within specific federal contexts. Of course, in the space that remains I can scarcely do even that here.

Interestingly enough, there is a rather grand tradition of federalist theory beginning in the Renaissance, which includes important works by thinkers like Althusius (1603/1995), Pufendorf (1679/1934), Montesquieu (1748/1989), Rousseau (1782/1917), Kant (1795/1996), the authors of the *Federalist Papers* (Publius 1787–88/1961), Tocqueville (1835/1990), Acton (1859/1922), and J. S. Mill (1862/1972), as well as a number of middle-ranking political thinkers in the twentieth century. (For surveys of this intellectual tradition, see Forsythe 1981; Elazar 1987; Karmis and Norman, forthcoming.) That these running debates are largely unknown to students in the history of political thought—even as other works by these authors sit proudly in the canon—says much about the centralized, nation-state bias that has dominated the agenda of political philosophy over the last century or two. It must also be said that one would have a difficult time extracting directly from these classic works the kind of normative theorizing that would help one ground a solution for the basic institutional issues (outlined above) facing the multinational democratic federation in today's world. These works were written for different contexts, and in many ways for a different world. At best, we get a passionate defence of federalism as a kind of ingenious compromise that allows us to combine the advantages of large states (especially military and economic security) with the advantages of small republics (more democratic deliberation and virtuous citizenship activity, a richer sense of community), while avoiding the pitfalls of both. But until recently there was relatively little written about the challenges of constructing a federation that could cope with the often contradictory demands of minority and majority identities and nation-building projects.

If we think of multinational democratic federations as the best alternative to secession, then they must allow national minorities a significant degree of autonomy to manage their societies and their identity. This implies, for example, the ability to control language and cultural policy within their jurisdiction, as well as to have a significant, if not deciding, say over all levels of education. But federalism will not turn out to be a good alternative to secession if federal arrangements are inherently unstable—and, in particular, if they give leaders of minorities opportunities for nation building that naturally lead to demands for secession (Kymlicka 1998b; 2001: ch. 5); or if they give the central government the means to frustrate most minority identity-strengthening projects. What we see in most democratic states with traditions of autonomy for national minorities is that individual members of these minorities tend to have significant identities and loyalties to both overlapping communities. The ultimate challenge is to find constitutional mechanisms and a political culture that will nurture both attachments in a way that is stable over the long run. This raises a number of conceptual and philosophical issues concerning, for example, the role of group rights in a theory of justice, and the place of considerations of stability in such a theory (see Arel 2001; Karmis and Gagnon 2001; Norman 2001b; Patten 2001). Philosophers should also be called upon to clarify clashing arguments from equality that are pervasive in constitutional debates in federal states. It is often not possible, for example, to satisfy demands that individual citizens, provinces, and ethnocultural communities all be treated equally by constitutional arrangements and policies. And yet it is far from clear how equality and inequality can be traded off in a principled way between these levels. Surely, for example, it cannot be the case that the equality of individual citizens always trumps other considerations since, by its very nature, federalism creates subunits with powers and rights of their own. (To take a simple example: the equal status of states in the USA expresses itself in the right of each state to two federal Senators; but this means that a citizen of a very small state has more 'voting weight' in the federal Congress than does a citizen in a large state. In this case, the equality of states trumps the equality of citizenship. In theory, equality of citizenship is represented in the other chamber of the US Congress, the House of Representatives, where electoral districts have roughly the same population wherever they are in the country.)

In most parts of the world—where minorities have been historically abused under undemocratic regimes—the idea of national autonomy through federalism looks to even sympathetic observers like an impossible dream. Federalism is, for example, an 'F'-word throughout the multiethnic states of Eastern and Central Europe (see Kymlicka 2000a,b; Kymlicka and Opalski 2001). Even looking at the long-standing democratic societies in the West, it is not clear whether we should be pessimistic or optimistic about the possibility of federations that are both generous in the autonomy they grant to national minorities and stable. On the one hand, there is still no clear-cut case of a long-standing democratic federation breaking up. But, on the other hand, some of these states (e.g. Canada, Belgium, Spain) have seen a steady historical rise in secessionist sentiments among national minorities taking full advantage of their constitutionally protected autonomy.

7. Conclusion

After barely a decade of serious attention in most of the English-speaking philosophical world to issues of national autonomy, there are still more questions than answers. But it must be considered progress that there is a growing consensus on what the agenda of major questions and issues should look like. The basic conceptual debates about the nature of nations, nationalism, and group rights are now winding down, as are debates about whether nations are 'special' and whether this issue matters. Debates about secession have evolved significantly and produced at least three identifiable 'schools' of thought. In all likelihood, most future discussions of secession will deal more specifically with justifying institutional recommendations in constitutional and international law.

The least developed of all issues of national autonomy concern the appropriate forms of self-determination within a federal or quasi-federal multinational state—and these issues also seem destined to treatment primarily within the context of domestic and international institutions. With some 5,000 ethnocultural groups in the world, and a limited capacity and willingness in the international community to sanction the emergence of new states, creative forms of internal autonomy provide the most realistic alternative to the systematic injustice that most of these minority groups have experienced throughout the history of the modern state. That said, philosophers are still a long way from articulating robust theories of 'federal justice' that can guide deliberations on the basic design issues for the stable multinational federal state. We have not focused in this chapter on the context of globalization. The integration of global and continental economies leads to somewhat contradictory prospects for federalism and federal theory. On the one hand, it challenges the need for small cultural communities to remain within larger states in order to secure economic prosperity. But, on the other, international *economic* integration leads to calls for a certain amount of *political* integration that can amount to quasi-federal arrangements between previously sovereign states (such as in the European Union and even in the North American Free Trade zone). These sorts of arrangements give national *majority* groups (such as the English in the UK, or English-speaking Canadians) a sense of their own cultural vulnerability, and this could lead to hitherto rare reflections on the kind of autonomy they need within the state and its superstate organizations.

References

Acton, Lord (1859/1922). 'Nationality', in J. Figgis and R. Laurence (eds.), *The History of Freedom and Other Essays*. London: Macmillan, 270–300.

Althusius, J. (1603/1995). *Politica*, ed. and trans. Frederick S. Carney. Indianapolis: Liberty Fund. Relevant extracts reprinted in Karmis and Norman (forthcoming).

Anderson, B. (1983/1991). *Imagined Communities: Reflections on the Origins and Spread of Nationalism*. Rev. edn. London: Verso.

—— (1993). 'Nationalism', in J. Krieger (ed.), *Oxford Companion to Politics of the World*. Oxford: Oxford University Press, 614–19.

Arel, D. (2001). 'Political Stability in Multinational Democracies: Comparing Language Dynamics in Brussels, Montreal and Barcelona', in Gagnon and Tully (2001), 614–19.

Aronovitch, H. (2000*a*). 'Nationalism in Theory and Reality'. *Philosophy of the Social Sciences*, 30/3: 457–79.

—— (2000*b*). 'Why Secession is Unlike Divorce'. *Public Affairs Quarterly*, 14/1: 27–37.

Baker, J. (1994) (ed.), *Group Rights*. Toronto: University of Toronto Press.

Barker, E. (1922). *National Character and the Factors in its Formation*. London: Methuen & Co.

Barry, B. (1983). 'Self-Government Revisited', in D. Miller and L. Siedentop (eds.), *The Nature of Political Theory*. Oxford: Oxford University Press, 121–54.

—— (2001). *Culture and Equality*. Cambridge, MA: Harvard University Press.

Bartkus, V. O. (1999). *The Dynamic of Secession*. Cambridge: Cambridge University Press.

Bauböck, R. (1999). 'Self-Determination and Self-Government'. Unpublished TS.

—— (2000). 'Why Stay Together? A Pluralist Approach to Secession and Federation', in Kymlicka and Norman (2000), 366–99.

Beiner, R. (1998). 'National Self-Determination: Some Cautionary Remarks Concerning the Rhetoric of Rights', in Moore (1998), 158–80.

—— (1999) (ed.), *Theorizing Nationalism*. Albany, NY: SUNY Press.

Bennett, D. (1998) (ed.), *Multicultural States: Rethinking Difference and Identity*. London: Routledge.

Beran, H. (1984). 'A Liberal Theory of Secession'. *Political Studies*, 32: 21–31.

—— (1998). 'A Democratic Theory of Political Self-Determination for a New World Order', in Lehning (1998), 32–59.

Breuilly, J. (1982). *Nationalism and the State*. Manchester: Manchester University Press.

Brighouse, H. (1998). 'Against Nationalism', in Couture et al. (1998), 365–405.

Brown-John, C. (1999). 'Self-Determination, Autonomy and State Secession in Federal Constitutional and International Law'. *South Texas Law Review*, 40: 567–601.

Brubaker, R. (1996). *Nationalism Reframed: Nationhood and the National Question in the New Europe*. Cambridge: Cambridge University Press.

—— (1998). 'Myths and Misconceptions in the Study of Nationalism'. In Moore (1998), 233–65.

Buchanan, A. (1991). *Secession: The Morality of Political Divorce from Fort Sumter to Lithuania and Quebec*. Boulder, CO: Westview Press.

Buchanan, A. (1997). 'Theories of Secession'. *Philosophy and Public Affairs*, 26/1: 30–61.

—— (1998*a*). 'What's so Special about Nations?', in Couture et al. (1998), 283–310.

—— (1998*b*). 'Democracy and Secession', in Moore (1998), 14–33.

Callan, E. (1997). *Educating Citizens: Political Education and Liberal Democracy*. Oxford: Oxford University Press.

Canovan, M. (1996). *Nationhood and Political Theory*. Cheltenham: Edward Elgar.

Carens, J. H. (2000). *Culture, Citizenship, and Community: A Contextual Exploration of Justice as Evenhandedness*. Oxford: Oxford University Press.

Connor, W. (1994). *Ethnonationalism*. Princeton: Princeton University Press.

Copp, D. (1997). 'Democracy and Communal Self-Determination', in McKim and McMahan (1997), 277–300.

Copp, D. (1998). 'International Law and Morality in the Theory of Secession'. *Journal of Ethics*, 2: 219–45.

Costa, J. (2001). 'On Theories of Secession: Minorities, Majorities, and the Multinational State'. Paper presented to the 97th Annual Meeting of the American Political Science Association, San Francisco.

Couture, J., Nielsen, K., and Seymour, M. (1998) (eds.), *Rethinking Nationalism* (*Canadian Journal of Philosophy*, supp. vol. 22). Calgary: University of Calgary Press.

Elazar, D. (1987). *Exploring Federalism*. Tuscaloosa, AL: University of Alabama Press.

Eriksen, E., and Fossum, J. (2000) (eds.), *Democracy in the European Union: Integration through Deliberation?* London: Routledge.

Fichte, J. (1807–8/1922). *Addresses to the German Nation*, trans. R. Jones and G. Turnbull. La Salle, IL: Open Court Publishing.

Forsythe, M. (1981). *Union of States: The Theory and Practice of Confederation*. London: Leicester University Press.

Fosses, E., and Requejo, F. (1999) (eds.), *Asimetría federal y estado plurinacional*. Madrid: Editorial Trotta.

Freeman, M. (1998). 'The Priority of Function over Structure: A New Approach to Secession', in Lehning (1998), 12–31.

Friedrich, C. (1968). *Trends of Federalism in Theory and Practice*. New York: Praeger.

Gagnon, A., and Tully, J. (2001) (eds.), *Multinational Democracies*. Cambridge: Cambridge University Press.

Gauthier, D. (1994). 'Breaking Up: An Essay on Secession'. *Canadian Journal of Philosophy*, 24: 357–72.

Gellner, E. (1983). *Nations and Nationalism*. Ithaca, NY: Cornell University Press.

Gibbins, R., and Laforest, G. (1998) (eds.), *Beyond the Impasse: Toward Reconciliation*. Ottawa: Institute for Research in Public Policy.

Gilbert, P. (1998), *The Philosophy of Nationalism*. Boulder, CO: Westview.

Goodin, R., and Pettit, P. (1993) (eds.), *Blackwell Companion to Contemporary Political Philosophy*. Oxford: Blackwell.

Graham, K. (1986). *The Battle of Democracy*. Brighton: Wheatsheaf.

Hardin, R. (1995). *One for All: The Logic of Group Conflict*. Princeton: Princeton University Press.

Hechter, M. (2000). *Containing Nationalism*. Oxford: Oxford University Press.

Hesse, J., and Wright, V. (1996) (eds.), *Federalizing Europe? The Costs, Benefits, and Preconditions of Federal Political Systems*. Oxford: Oxford University Press.

Hobsbawm, E. (1990). *Nations and Nationalism since 1780*. Cambridge: Cambridge University Press.

Horowitz, D. (1985). *Ethnic Groups in Conflict*. Berkeley and Los Angeles: University of California Press.

——(1997/1998). 'Self-Determination: Politics, Philosophy, and Law'. Repr. in Moore (1998), 181–214.

Hume, D. (1777/1987). 'Of National Characters', in David Hume, *Essays, Moral, Political and Literary*, ed. Eugene F. Miller, Indianapolis'. Liberty Fund, 197–215.

Ignatieff, M. (1993). *Blood and Belonging: Journeys into the New Nationalism*. London: Penguin.

Kant, Immanuel (1795/1996). 'Toward Perpetual Peace', in *Practical Philosophy*, trans. and ed. Mary J. Gregor. Cambridge: Cambridge University Press, 311–52.

Karmis, D., and Gagnon, A. (2001). 'Federalism, Federation and Collective Identities in Canada and Belgium: Different Routes, Similar Fragmentation', in Gagnon and Tully (2001), 137–75.

—— and W. Norman (forthcoming) (eds.), *Theories of Federalism*. New York: Palgrave.

Kymlicka, W. (1989). *Liberalism, Community, and Culture*. Oxford: Oxford University Press.

—— (1995*a*). *Multicultural Citizenship*. Oxford: Oxford University Press.

—— (1995*b*) (ed.), *The Rights of Minority Cultures*. Oxford: Oxford University Press.

—— (1998*a*). 'Western Political Theory and Ethnic Relations in Eastern Europe', in M. Opalski (ed.), *Managing Diversity in Plural Societies: Minorities, Migration and Nation-Building in Post-Communist Europe*. Ottawa: Forum Eastern Europe, 275–322.

—— (1998*b*). 'Is Federalism a Viable Alternative to Secession?', in Lehning (1998), 111–50.

—— (1998*c*). *Finding our Way: Rethinking Ethnocultural Relations in Canada*. Toronto: Oxford University Press.

—— (2000*a*). 'Nation-Building and Minority Rights: Comparing East and West'. *Journal of Ethnic and Migration Studies*, 26/2: 183–212.

—— (2000*b*). 'Federalism and Secession At Home and Abroad'. *Canadian Journal of Law and Jurisprudence*, 13/2: 207–24.

—— (2001). *Politics in the Vernacular: Nationalism, Multiculturalism and Citizenship*. Oxford: Oxford University Press.

—— and Norman, W. (1994). 'Return of the Citizen: Recent Work in Citizenship Theory'. *Ethics*, 104/2: 352–81.

—— (2000) (eds.), *Citizenship in Diverse Societies*. Oxford: Oxford University Press.

—— and Opalski, M. (2001) (eds.), *Can Liberal Pluralism be Exported? Western Political Theory and Ethnic Relations in Eastern Europe*. Oxford: Oxford University Press.

Lehning, P. (1998) (ed.), *Theories of Secession*. London: Routledge.

Levine, A. (1998). 'Just Nationalism: The Future of an Illusion', in Couture et al. (1998), 345–64.

Levy, J. (2000). *The Multiculturalism of Fear*. Oxford: Oxford University Press.

MacCormick, N. (1999). *Questioning Sovereignty: Law, State and Nation in the European Commonwealth*. Oxford: Oxford University Press.

McKim, R., and McMahan, J. (1997) (eds.), *The Morality of Nationalism*. New York: Oxford University Press.

Margalit, A., and Raz, J. (1990). 'National Self-determination'. *Journal of Philosophy*, 87/9: 439–46.

Mazzini, G. (1995). 'The Duties of Man', in O. Dahbour and M. Ishay (eds.), *The Nationalism Reader*. Atlantic Highlands, NJ: Humanities Press, 87–97.

Mill, J. S. (1862/1972). 'Considerations of Representative Government', in H. B. Acton (ed.), *Utilitarianism, Liberty, Representative Government*. London: Dent, 188–428.

Miller, D. (1993). 'In Defence of Nationality', *Journal of Applied Philosophy*, 10/1: 3–16.

—— (1995). *On Nationality*. Oxford: Oxford University Press.

—— (1998). 'Secession and the Principle of Nationality', in Couture et al. (1998), 261–82.

Monahan, P., and Bryant, M. (1996). *Coming to Terms with Plan B: Ten Principles Governing Secession*. Toronto: C. D. Howe Institute.

Montesquieu, Baron de (1748/1989). *The Spirit of the Laws*, trans. and ed. Anne M. Cohler, Basia Carolyn Miller, and Harold Samuel Stone. Cambridge: Cambridge University Press.

Moore, M. (1998) (ed.), *National Self-Determination and Secession*. Oxford: Oxford University Press.

—— (2001). *The Ethics of Nationalism*. Oxford: Oxford University Press.

Musgrave, T. (1997). *Self-Determination and National Minorities*. Oxford: Oxford University Press.

Nairn, T. (1977). *The Break-up of Britain*. London: New Left Books.

Nielsen, K. (1993). 'Secession: The Case of Quebec'. *Journal of Applied Philosophy*, 10: 29–43.

Norman, W. (1994). 'Toward a Philosophy of Federalism', in Baker (1994), 79–100.

——(1995a). 'The Morality of Federalism and the European Union'. *Archiv für Rechts- und Sozialphilosophie*, 59: 202–11.

——(1995b). 'The Ideology of Shared Values', in J. Carens (ed.), *Is Quebec Nationalism Just?* Montreal and Kingston: McGill-Queen's University Press, 137–59.

——(1998a). 'The Ethics of Secession as the Regulation of Secessionist Politics', in Moore (1998), 34–61.

——(1998b). 'Federalism and Confederalism', in Edward Craig (ed.), *Routledge Encyclopedia of Philosophy*. London: Routledge, iii. 572–4.

——(1999). 'Theorizing Nationalism (Normatively)', in Beiner (1999), 51–66.

——(2001a). 'Secession and (Constitutional) Democracy', in F. Requejo (ed.), *Democracy and National Pluralism*. London: Routledge, 84–102.

——(2001b). 'Justice and Stability in Multination States', in Gagnon and Tully (2001), 90–109.

——(forthcoming). 'From Nation-Building to National Engineering: The Ethics of Shaping Identities', in A. Dieckhoff (ed.), *Nationalism, Liberalism and Pluralism*. Lanham, MD: Lexington Books.

——(in press). 'Domesticating Secession', in S. Macedo (ed.), *Secession and Self-Determination, Nomos XLV*. New York: NYU Press.

Patten, A. (2001). 'Liberal Citizenship in Multinational Societies', in Gagnon and Tully (2001), 279–98.

Phillips, A. (1995). *The Politics of Presence: Issues in Democracy and Group Representation*. Oxford: Oxford University Press.

Philpott, D. (1995). 'In Defense of Self-Determination'. *Ethics*, 105: 352–85.

——(1998). 'Self-Determination in Practice', in Moore (1998), 79–102.

Pufendorf, S. (1679/1934). *De jure naturae et gentium libri octo*, ed. James Brown Scott, trans. C. H. and W. A. Oldfather. Oxford: Oxford University Press.

Publius [J. Madison, A. Hamilton, J. Jay] (1787–8/1961). *Federalist Papers*. New York: Mentor, 1961.

Rawls, J. (1971). *A Theory of Justice*. Cambridge, MA: Harvard University Press.

Renan, E. (1882/1939). 'What is a Nation?', in A. Zimmern (ed.), *Modern Political Doctrines*. Oxford: Oxford University Press, 187–205.

Requejo, F. (1999). 'Cultural Pluralism, Nationalism and Federalism: A Revision of Democratic Citizenship in Plurinational States'. *European Journal of Political Research*, 39/2: 255–86.

Resnick, P. (1998). 'Majority Nationalities within Multinational States: The Challenge of Identity'. Paper presented at the conference on *Mythologies of Identity and Contexts of Power*, organized by the CSIC, Madrid, Oct.

Resnick, P. (2000). 'Recognition & Ressentiment: On Accommodating National Differences within Multinational States'. Paper presented at Europa Mundi conference on 'Democracy, Nationalism and Europeanism', Santiago de Compostela, 21–23 June.

Riker, W. (1964). *Federalism: Origins, Operation, Significance*. Boston: Little, Brown & Co.

Ripstein, A. (1997). 'Context, Continuity, and Fairness', in McKim and McMahon (1997), 209–26.

Rousseau, J.-J. (1782/1917). 'Judgement on Saint-Pierre's Project for Perpetual Peace', in *A Lasting Peace through the Federation of Europe*, trans. and ed. C. E. Vaughan. London: Constable, 36–112.

—— (1772/1985). *The Government of Poland*, trans. Willmoore Kendall. Indianapolis: Hacket Publishing Co.

Smith, A. (1991). *National Identity*. Harmondsworth: Penguin.

—— (1993). 'A Europe of Nations—or the Nation of Europe'. *Journal of Peace Research*, 30/2: 129–35.

Smith, G. (1995) (ed.), *Federalism: The Multiethnic Challenge*. London: Longman.

—— (2000). 'Sustainable Federalism, Democratization, and Distributive Justice', in Kymlicka and Norman (2000), 345–65.

Spinner, J. (1994). *The Boundaries of Citizenship: Race, Ethnicity and Nationality in the Liberal State*. Baltimore: Johns Hopkins University Press.

Suksi, M. (1993). *Bringing in the People: A Comparison of Constitutional Forms and Practices of the Referendum*. London: Martinus Nijhoff.

Sunstein, C. (1991). 'Constitutionalism and Secession'. *University of Chicago Law Review*, 58: 633–70.

—— (2001). 'Should Constitutions Protect the Right to Secede?'. *Journal of Political Philosophy*, 9/3: 350–5.

Supreme Court of Canada (1998). *Reference re Secession of Quebec*, SCC no. 25506, 20 Aug. [Opinion].

Tamir, Y. (1993). *Liberal Nationalism*. Princeton: Princeton University Press.

—— (1995). 'The Enigma of Nationalism'. *World Politics*, 47: 418–40.

Taylor, C. (1991/1993). 'Shared and Divergent Values'. Repr. in Taylor (1993), 155–86.

—— (1992). 'The Politics of Recognition', in A. Gutmann (ed.), *Multiculturalism and the 'Politics of Recognition'*. Princeton: Princeton University Press, 25–74.

—— (1993), *Reconciling the Solitudes: Essays on Canadian Federalism and Nationalism*, ed. G. Laforest. Kingston and Montreal: McGill-Queen's University Press.

Toqueville, A. de (1835/1990). *Democracy in America*, i. ed. Phillips Bradley and Daniel Boorstin. New York: Vintage.

van Parijs, P. (2000). 'Must Europe be Belgian? On Democratic Citizenship in Multilingual Polities', in C. McKinnon and Iain Hampsher-Monk (eds.), *The Demands of Citizenship*. London: Continuum, 235–53.

Walters, M. (1999). 'Nationalism and the Pathology of Legal Systems: Considering the *Quebec Secession Reference* and its Lessons for the United Kingdom'. *Modern Law Review*, 62/3: 371–96.

Watts, R. (1998). 'Examples of Partnership', in Gibbins and Laforest (1998), 359–93.

Weber, M. (1948). 'The Nation', in H. Gerth and C. Wright-Mills (eds. and trans.), *From Max Weber: Essays in Sociology*. London: Routledge & Kegan Paul, 171–9.

Weinstock, D. (1999). 'Building Trust in Divided Societies'. *Journal of Political Philosophy*, 7/3: 287–307.

—— (2001), 'Constitutionalizing the Right to Secede'. *Journal of Political Philosophy*, 9/2: 182–203.

Wellman, C. (1995). 'A Defense of Secession and Political Self-Determination'. *Philosophy and Public Affairs*, 24/2: 142–71.

Wheare, K. (1963). *Federal Government*. 4th edn. Oxford: Oxford University Press.

Williams, M. (1998). *Voice, Trust and Memory: Marginalized Groups and the Failings of Liberal Representation*. Princeton: Princeton University Press.

CHAPTER 24

INTERNATIONAL ECONOMIC JUSTICE

DEBRA SATZ

1. INTRODUCTION

THERE are pervasive and increasing inequalities between countries. Of a total world GNP in 1989 of some $18 trillion, the two richest countries—the USA and Japan—accounted for $8.2 trillion, or 45 per cent, while the forty-four least developed countries had a share of world income of less than 0.6 per cent. The combined GDP of the poorest 180 countries was less than the GDP of one country—the USA—in 1996. If we were to contrast the degree of global and domestic income inequality, two observations would stand out. First, the absolute level of world income inequality is extremely high and considerably higher than the inequalities observed within most nations. Secondly, intra-national income differences are a relatively minor source of world income inequality. If all intra-nation income inequality were abolished, roughly 70 per cent of global income inequality would remain. Most income inequality in the world, then, is accounted for by the differences between nations and not by differences within them (Anand 1993).

Why are these facts important? Economic inequalities in dimensions such as income and wealth matter only in so far as they reflect differences in people's real standard of living. Consider the living standard differences for the average person born into different countries in terms of mortality and morbidity, literacy, access to adequate nutrition, and the extent of political and civil freedoms. Life expectancy in rich countries averages 77 years, while in sub-Saharan Africa it is 48. (In 1990, the country with the lowest life expectancy in the world was Guinea-Bissau: 39 years.) Although income is an imperfect proxy for some of the important dimensions of a person's standard of living (for example, health, disability, and public goods), it is a rough indicator for many others (for example, access to nutrition). Moreover, although many poor countries could conceivably provide for the basic needs of their citizens, it remains true that most of the world's people (who live on less than $2 per day) lack access to the minimum goods needed to feed, clothe, and shelter themselves. Robert McNamara, writing in the 1978 *World Bank Development Report*, described the condition of the world's poorest as 'a condition of life so characterized by malnutrition, illiteracy, disease, squalid surroundings, high infant mortality and low life expectancy as to be beneath any reasonable definition of human decency' (McNamara 1978: p. iii). In contrast, in the USA alone there are over 350,000 households with a net worth of $10 million or more (and many have correspondingly high incomes) and in most of the advanced countries no one lives on $2 per day.

The magnitude of economic inequalities between nations raises a number of crucial questions. Some of these questions are empirical. What best explains the origins and persistence of such enormous disparities between countries? What measures, if any, are available to alleviate the material inequalities between nations? To what extent are the sources of these inequalities rooted in conditions beyond any single nation's control?

Other questions are philosophical. Are any of the economic inequalities between nations unjust? If so, why? Why should we care about economic inequalities between strangers—people with whom we will never interact—and ourselves? What role should states and nations play in our thinking about justice? Should we take their existence into account or focus our concern only on the well-being of individuals?

These theoretical questions arise with special urgency when we reflect on the everyday practices of most countries and their citizens. Consider the fact that the wealthy countries give extremely little development aid and that the majority of movements for greater distributive equality have tended to focus almost exclusively on inequalities within national borders. While this focus would pose no special moral problem if it were simply motivated by self-interest or expediency, it is frequently justified in moral terms. It is often argued, for example, that we have special obligations to our own families, communities, and societies and that these obligations are weightier and more extensive than our obligations to other people (Scheffler 1997). To those who take the idea of global justice seriously, these claims of special responsibility can seem like merely self-serving rationalizations. Can the claim that shared citizenship gives rise to special obligations be justified? And, even if so, how do we balance these obligations against the needs, sometimes more urgent, of strangers?

While many would criticize the current global distribution of income and wealth in which over a billion people live in conditions of desperate and degrading poverty, there is disagreement as to whether the central problem with it is extreme poverty or inequality. On one view, we have the same reasons to press against global inequality as we do to protest economic inequalities between our own citizens: each violates the moral equality of persons (Beitz 1979; Pogge 1989). Other theorists draw a distinction between what we owe to our own citizens and what we owe to strangers. Strangers are owed some absolute threshold of material resources, but the global gap between rich and poor is not itself a source for concern (Miller 1995). Perhaps attending to this disagreement is not an immediately urgent problem, since almost no country gives close to the amount of international aid required if the globe's poorest are to achieve even bare subsistence. (Many years ago the United Nations set a target for the developed nations of 0.7 per cent of GDP to be given for development aid. Only a handful of nations—for example, Denmark and the Netherlands—meet or surpass this target. Most countries fail even to get near it. The USA gave 0.1 per cent of GDP for aid in 1999.) Yet, whether we think the problem with international inequality is inequality or poverty does ultimately have implications for the international policies and institutions we should advocate.

Deciding what we mean by international economic justice, then, requires an analysis of the moral relevance of the fact that some inequalities exist between fellow citizens who share a state and some are between strangers from different states with whom we may have no reciprocal relations of any kind. We also need to consider how a theory of international distributive justice is related to our theories of domestic economic justice. More generally, in what contexts do we think that economic inequality (as opposed to poverty) is unjust and for what reasons?

Complicating things further, how we answer at least some of the philosophical questions will depend upon our answers to the empirical questions. For example, if the deprivations and disparities in the world were inevitable products of natural scarcity and not due to human institutions, then some would hold that they are not unjust, but only tragic. Alternatively, if—as seems to be the case—the current global distribution is not inevitable, then it seems that we can and should hold it up to moral scrutiny and criticism. This chapter will explore the philosophical issues posed by international economic inequalities, but I will begin by sketching out some of the empirical controversies that bear on these issues.

2. Why Is there so much Economic Inequality among Nations?

There is no consensus as to what explains the huge differences in average incomes and life prospects around the globe. The relative importance of various factors—natural resource endowments, technology, human capital, political and economic culture, and position in the international economy—is itself the subject of dispute. Settling the dispute is complicated by the fact that domestic economies are embedded in a global division of labour and thus subjected to trade relations, international financial institutions, and foreign capital markets. It is thus difficult to disentangle the domestic from the international influences of a society's economic condition. Furthermore, we do not even fully understand how and why such huge differences in income and wealth once created can continue to persist, especially given that information and technologies can, at least theoretically, move rapidly across state borders.

Most social scientists would agree that a key factor in explaining the disparity is the rise of Europe several centuries ago. But there continues to be significant disagreement as to what itself explains that rise. Adam Smith and Henri Pirenne stressed the role of trade in the development of the West, while others such as Max Weber emphasized the importance of a distinct culture with a rational, individualistic world view. For those inspired by Weber, such as David Landes (1998), the most important determinants of a society's economic condition lie in its political culture, religious and moral traditions, and the character of its people. For still others, such as Karl Marx, it was the fact that only the social relations and institutions of Europe were transformed into capitalism that explains the rise of the West.

In his magisterial book *Guns, Germs and Steel*, Jared Diamond (1997) attempts to give a new answer to this question, as posed to him by his New Guinean friend Yali. Yali asks, 'Why is it that you white people developed so much cargo (i.e., material goods) but we black people had little cargo of our own?' Diamond argues that we cannot put the answer down to the inherent superiority of white people (as nineteenth-century racists assumed), to culture, to trade, to modern institutions, or even to a few lucky decisions. Rather, he suggests that we must look to geography, demography, and epidemiology for an answer. In the aftermath of the ice age, people in a small area of what is now northern Iraq and eastern Turkey had access to a unique combination of plants and large animals. As human population grew, they also domesticated themselves to the animals' germ cultures. Over the next few millennia, the entire package of people, crops, animals, germs, and weapons spread across Eurasia's east–west access. People in other parts of the world never had the opportunity to develop the same package; as Eurasians spread into the Pacific, the Americas, and Africa, their lethal germs and weapons meant that the people they encountered never stood a chance. The course of human history was basically set by 10,000 BC; this early history made it inevitable that by 1972 the Eurasians would have all the cargo.

This is an intriguing thesis, but Diamond never explains why it was only the western end of the Eurasian land mass that took off. Nor is it obvious that, without capitalism and the Industrial Revolution, the West would look as different from parts of the rest of the world (for example, Central Africa) as it does.

Whatever theory of the origins of international inequality one has, it is important to acknowledge that theft, conquest, and exploitation have also contributed to its extent. As examples, consider the history of colonialism and the fact that trade relations between countries have rarely been free and competitive. I will discuss the bearing of historical factors such as theft and fraud on international economic justice below. As we will see, some philosophers (and ordinary people) believe that international inequality and/or poverty is only an injustice if someone acted unjustly in bringing it about.

In addition to controversies about the ultimate causes of international inequality, there are debates as to how best to understand what maintains it. These debates are significant because they steer us towards different remedies for eradicating the inequality. For example, if current inequality were due to differences in traditional resources like commodities and energy, then perhaps we should advocate for the more equitable redistribution of these resources. But it is most likely that the primary explanation for the low rate of wages in poor countries is the low productivity of human labour there. If that is indeed the case, then many resource transfer programmes may have little direct effect. Instead, we should be supporting the development of human capital, through investment and the establishment of institutions (that is, a democratic political state, markets, a free press, and a public education system) that will improve the prospects for internal economic production.

It is unfortunate that most philosophical theorizing about international inequality takes place without consideration of the causal factors underwriting that inequality. For example, Peter Singer, whose work, more than any other philosopher's, has consistently called attention to the importance of international economic justice, advocates resource transfers by rich individuals to poor countries. But, short of coping with emergency situations brought on by famine and flood, it is questionable whether such transfers would do much long-term good in the absence of new institutions and additional labour-market opportunities in the poor countries.

In considering the proximate causes of international inequality, and in advocating solutions, it is especially important that we keep in mind the dynamic effects of any remedies we choose. What may look reasonable when viewed as a short-term measure of relief may have long-term dynamic negative effects. For example, pressures exerted on transnational companies to pay their foreign workers higher wages may drive these companies to go to countries without wage restrictions, setting one poor country against another and fuelling what, in other contexts, has been called a 'race to the bottom'.

3. Against International Economic Justice

3.1 Statism and Nationalism

There has been surprisingly little written by political philosophers and social scientists on the subject of international economic justice; indeed, there has been little written on international justice as a whole. One reason for this omission is that the dominant paradigms in political philosophy and social policy have been either statist or nationalist. Statists argue that states should be conceived as sovereign entities, exercising absolute jurisdiction with respect to the populations and resources that fall within their borders. Nationalists argue that the nation is an ethical community for its members and that accordingly our obligations lie with members of our own nation. Both nationalists and statists tend to be hostile towards international economic redistribution, believing either that the very idea of international justice does not make any sense or that our primary loyalties are to those at home.

The statist conception of our obligations of justice can be found in the writings of theorists of international relations such as Hans Morgenthau (1952) and Kenneth Waltz (1959). The central justification for this position, however, goes back to Thomas Hobbes. Hobbes famously argued that, in the absence of a sovereign power with the authority to enforce its laws, each individual has a right to do whatever is necessary for her own self-preservation. Statists draw an analogy between the individual and the state and argue that, in the international realm, in the absence of a world state to enforce norms, each and every state may do whatever it deems necessary for its own survival. Furthermore, in the absence of shared institutions, states have no obligations to help each other at all.

As Brian Barry (1999) has observed, the morality of states is analogous to universal egoism for individuals. Just as the latter doctrine directs all individuals to pursue their interests, statists argue that every state has a right to arrange its own affairs as it wishes, to pursue its own interests, and to hold absolute sovereignty over its own territory. This principle of 'state autonomy' yields strong barriers to international economic redistribution. In particular, it leaves natural resources in the hands of whoever controls the territory on which they are found and has no place for a principle of economic distribution between states. Surprisingly, statism has no theory about how even the boundaries of states should be drawn: it simply takes them as given.

A quite different argument for a state-centred approach to distributive justice takes off not from facts about the external international environment, but from two internal features of states: that they are coercive institutions and that they claim to speak for the entire political community. In order to legitimate its coercive power, Ronald Dworkin (1986) argues that states must treat their citizens with equal regard and must act only according to principles that all citizens can accept. The distributive egalitarian obligations of individuals to each other, on Dworkin's view, stems only from their participation in a common state. It is only as fellow citizens—seeking to justify the uses of coercive power to each other—that they must be committed to sharing equally their benefits and burdens. In the absence of shared membership in a state, Dworkin holds that a person has no duties with respect to justice at all. While Dworkin does not deny that individuals in different countries and national institutions have duties of charity towards each other—to alleviate famines or human-rights disasters—he does not believe that they have duties of justice. This is not a merely terminological distinction, since it means that economic equality is not an appropriate goal of international redistribution; rather, redistribution aims to achieve only a threshold level of sufficiency.

Nationalists are also opposed to international redistribution, asserting absolute collective ownership rights over their national territories. Nationalists believe that, on the basis of some kind of shared identity—whether based on 'blood' or 'belonging'—individuals have special obligations to each other that they do not have to others. These obligations may or may not track actually existing states—in practice, many nationalist movements have been hostile to existing state boundaries, arguing that those boundaries are most often illegitimate and do not reflect genuine communities. The value of a nation is precisely that it constitutes a community, a language, and a culture—contexts that are indispensable for individual human flourishing. Academic defenders of this view include Michael Walzer (1983), Charles Taylor (1992), and David Miller (1995), although the roots of the ideas are found in the German romantic nationalists of the nineteenth century.

3.2 Objections

Although statism and nationalism are very influential in international relations theory and practice, they each rest on controversial factual and moral premises. In fact, the international realm is not a Hobbesian state of war of all against all and there is a surprising amount of international cooperation. States ratify treaties, negotiate trade agreements, and engage in joint peacekeeping enterprises. There are thus shared norms that appear to be self-reinforcing, and do not require a single common authority. There is also substantial interdependence between states. The internal affairs of many countries are influenced by the policies of other nations, especially by their trade policies. Thus, contrary to statist assumptions, very few states are self-sufficient: most states engage in cooperative relationships with others, relationships that give rise to at least some moral obligations, such as the obligation not to engage in cheating and theft. These empirical facts undermine not only the more Hobbesian-derived arguments for statism, but those statist arguments emphasizing the link between domestic justice and state legitimacy. Views such as Dworkin's are plausible only to the extent that states coerce their own and only their own members and hence need to be legitimated only to those members. In the modern world, however, very few states, if any, exercise complete sovereignty with respect to their populations. Most of the world's states are highly dependent on economic and political interaction with other states, and are permeable to quasi-political institutions such as the World Bank, the International Monetary Fund, the World Trade Organization, and GATT among others (Murphy 1998). Some states also directly support corrupt regimes elsewhere. If Dworkin's distributive equality is motivated by a concern for preventing illegitimate coercion, then it is hard to see why this concern should necessarily run out at state borders. Whether it does run out will depend on the nature of the relationships that exist between trans-state institutions and states and between states and each other. This cannot be decided in abstraction from facts, by philosophical argument alone. Later in this chapter I will consider theories that allow for states to matter intrinsically in the ways that Dworkin captures, but that do not deny a role for international economic justice.

Nationalism also runs into problems, given the factual situation of mankind. Nationalities are everywhere 'mottled'—dispersed, in flux, and overlapping—and it is difficult if not impossible to map nations into states. In practice, any territory that includes one national group will almost invariably include members of at least one other. At the very least, giving every nation its own state will either lead to some people being only second-class citizens or will require massive immigration and relocation programmes, perhaps on a scale of 'ethnic cleansing'. More deeply, nationalism is itself not a pre-political given, but depends on human action and intervention (Kiss 1996).

Inefficiencies, as well as other problems arising from sheer scale, render a world government undesirable. The natural conditions of humanity—its diversity of values and conceptions of the social good—also render world sovereignty unlikely. But, even in the absence of shared government, it does not seem true that there are no hard international norms capable of motivating states and others to act. There is a strong consensus among the member states of the United Nations that the sovereignty of states is not absolute: for example, states that engage in genocide against members are liable to sanction and intervention. In practice, the debate is not over whether there are any international norms, but which ones there are. We can view different human-rights norms as articulating different conceptions of humanity's aspirations. These norms also provide goals that can orient our behaviour even when we know that the globe's ability to stand by and enforce such norms is weak in the absence of stronger international institutions.

3.3 Entitlement and Charity

Some philosophers hold a historical entitlement theory of distribution in which, if goods were justly acquired (that is, without force or fraud), then their present distribution is just, no matter how unequal it is (Nozick 1971). The rich countries, if they acquired their wealth justly, have a right to that wealth and it would be wrong to force them to redistribute it without their consent. In the absence of any past theft or fraud, the current distribution of world income may be unfortunate, but it is not unjust. According to such theories, what we (in the rich countries) owe to others (in the poor countries) depends on whether the economic inequalities between nations are the result of robbery and plunder or arise from differences that are freely pursued. Entitlement theories stress what people and states do to one another, rather than any particular outcomes.

Certainly, colonialism, slavery, and unfair trade policies have contributed to global economic inequality. Many nationalist movements have called for 'reparations', on the ground that territory and resources that were properly theirs (according to some entitlement theory) were stolen. But a large percentage of the disparities between nations are probably best explained by differences in labour productivity, technology, political institutions, and capital accumulation—differences that might have existed even in the absence of the alleged theft. So, an entitlement theory might well be hostile to international economic justice, depending on the facts. However, entitlement views hold that we are free to help the poor, so long as we do so voluntarily, and such charity is often held to be commendable. In fact, some entitlement proponents go further and argue that, although the current distribution of world income is not unjust, individuals have moral duties of charity to aid those who are in need. (As noted above, statists and nationalists can also embrace duties of charity.)

3.4 Objections

There are some powerful reasons to reject voluntary charity as a satisfactory solution to the problems of world destitution and massive inequality. Many of these reasons stem from problems with the entitlement theory itself.

In the first place, the theory does not question the basic entitlements of the rich to what they are asked to donate. But why should we accept these? Property rights are not facts of nature, but human institutions designed to serve human purposes. So, as with all institutions with profound and inescapable effects on the lives of human beings, they stand in need of justification. Why should we accept property rights that leave a majority of the world's population on the brink of starvation?

Secondly, it seems implausible to rest all the moral force behind a property claim on the historical chain of events that led to it. Does it undermine a person's claim to a good if fifty generations back in the causal chain someone cheated? Moreover, taking the historical criterion seriously (that is, no past force or fraud), it is unlikely that the claim of any state to its territory is legitimate. Such a criterion would wreak havoc on all existing political entities.

Thirdly, most entitlement theories are silent on the question of how much charity an individual should give. They leave it up to each person to decide not only how much to give, but also to whom to give. This is not only problematic since there is no assurance that the giving will be adequate to the need, but it also fails to recognize that for much of the world's poverty the solution is not simple income transfer but the development of human capabilities in the poor nations.

One objection that has been made to charitable (and other) resource transfers to the poor nations—whether these are voluntary or conceived of as morally required—is that these are likely to be worse than ineffective, prompting a spiralling population of people and exhausting the supply of food and other natural resources for everyone (Hardin 1974). This argument turns on a number of assumptions— including assumptions about the mechanisms that produce rising population and assumptions about the rate of technological change. It also appears to assume that there is an inevitable link between more aid to the poor and rising population. However, research shows that one of the most effective ways to decrease population growth is to educate women in the poor countries, a measure that often requires the transfer of resources. Nonetheless, there are important questions concerning how to balance our obligations to those now living with what we owe to future generations. These questions are especially important in the context of the dilemmas faced by many developing societies where there can be trade-offs between present and future GDP. Is there a minimum level of welfare that the government of these societies should assure all its citizens, regardless of the opportunity cost in future growth output? Interestingly, the question of what we owe to future generations has some clear parallels to that of what we owe to the strangers we do not know and will never meet. I do not discuss these parallels in this chapter, but see the essays in Sikora and Barry (1978) for elaboration.

4. Extending Economic Justice across Borders

Some theorists reject the extreme discontinuity that statists and nationalists posit between domestic and global justice. These theorists hold that we do have some obligations of justice in the international domain, including obligations to the world's poorest. But they differ as to the nature and scope of these obligations.

4.1 Cosmopolitan Theorists

At one end lies a view I will call cosmopolitanism. Cosmopolitans hold that our fundamental concern is for individuals and their well-being, and that it is irrelevant what part of the world these individuals happen to be in. Just as race/ethnicity, gender, and social class are irrelevant from the point of view of what a person deserves, so too is her country of origin. Moreover, cosmopolitans accord no moral privilege to domestic societies. There is no bright line separating theories of domestic and international economic justice. Instead, any differences between local and global obligations will be derived from pragmatic considerations about what works in different contexts. Robert Goodin (1988), for example, defends special obligations to compatriots, but sees this 'merely as an administrative device for discharging our general duties more efficiently'.

Cosmopolitans differ among themselves as to what moral theory best takes everyone's interests equally into account as well as to the institutions that would be best suited to bringing about a just international distribution. Peter Singer, perhaps the best-known cosmopolitan, draws on utilitarianism, while others such as Charles Beitz and Thomas Pogge take John Rawls's social contractarian theory of justice as their starting point. But each of these theorists agrees that existing political and economic structures have no intrinsic value apart from what they do for the lives of individuals.

Singer focuses on the role of individual action, rather than institutions, in redressing international inequality. In his seminal paper, 'Famine, Affluence and Morality' (1972), he establishes an individual obligation to provide aid to the world's poor from two premisses: (1) suffering and death from lack of food and medical care are bad; and (2) if we can prevent something bad from happening without sacrificing something 'morally significant', then we ought, morally, to do it. He gives the following example as an application of this principle: if I see a child drowning in a shallow pond and I can wade in and save her, but my shoes will get dirty, then I ought to save her. It would be unconscionable to allow minor considerations like dirty shoes to outweigh the good of saving a child's life. Singer then draws an analogy between the person who refuses to save a drowning child for fear of getting her shoes dirty and those of us who live in the advanced countries and contribute nothing to the plight of starving Bengali refugees. The vast majority of the people in developed countries spend money on frivolous goods—the equivalent of clean shoes—in lieu of life-saving food and basic medicines for the Bengalis. By living as we do, we in effect allow the Bengalis to drown for the sake of our new shoes.

This is a powerful argument in the area of international economic justice for radical redistribution from the rich to the poor. Moreover, the case for this redistribution is independent of issues of responsibility (it does not matter how the Bengali ended up poor), distance (it does not matter whether the Bengali is in front of you or 10,000 miles away, as long as you can save him), and reciprocity (it does not matter whether you and the Bengali are involved in any cooperative relations at all). Indeed, there is a stronger interpretation of Singer's principle (that he himself favours) whereby you should help the Bengali refugee up to the point where you sacrifice something of 'comparable moral importance'. On that interpretation, the distributive implication is that we should more or less equalize economic resources on a global scale. It is not merely our clean shoes we should give up, but our standard of living more generally.

Some philosophers have found this argument implausible. Some question whether my lack of causal responsibility for the Bengali's plight makes no difference and others point out that Singer's principle may be excessively demanding, especially in a world where others do not do their part. For example, if I stand by the ocean day and night, I can save more children from drowning than if I teach my philosophy classes. But must I so devote myself to saving drowning children? How much aid is reasonable?

The strongest philosophical arguments against Singer's view question the obligation to equalize distribution (the strong version of his principle) in the absence of any engagement between the parties in a cooperative practice. Consider the following example. Two islands, A and B, with similar initial wealth and population size, give rise to different rates of growth because of their respective inhabitants' preferences for work and leisure. Island A prospers and generates a large surplus while on island B people produce only enough to meet their basic needs. Why should people on island A now be obligated to transfer resources to island B? While it seems reasonable to ensure that the basic needs of island B are met, perhaps because the satisfaction of such needs is a basic right (Shue 1996), it seems unfair to ask island A to give over more (Rawls 1999).

While Singer's account generates our obligations of distributive justice from the greater needs of others whoever they are, Beitz (1979) and Pogge (1989) believe that our obligations are greatest to those with whom we cooperate or otherwise interact. They emphasize the fact that we all live in nations that regularly stand in economic relationships with other nations. In their view, it is the fact that we engage in ongoing cooperative ventures that span nations that gives rise to significant global obligations. Without interaction, the obligations we would have to strangers, while non-trivial, would be markedly less than those we have to our compatriots.

In addition to stressing the importance of interdependence and interaction in generating the demand for global justice, both Beitz and Pogge place their emphasis, not on the actions of individuals, but on institutions. Rather than encouraging individuals to engage in acts of individual transfer, they focus on criticizing the institutional arrangements that support the unjust distribution of global benefits and burdens. My primary obligation is not to give more money to Oxfam, or to stand at the beach saving children, but to work to support the creation of just institutions, both at home and abroad. This emphasis has the merit of connecting with what are arguably the main empirical deterrents to growth in the poor countries: the lack of institutions to facilitate human capital formation. Institutional mechanisms of tax and transfer can also be designed to specify each individual's fair share, thus addressing the worry of Singer's critics that his view provides no clear guidance to exactly how much we owe each other.

On the basis of their assumption that global interaction parallels domestic interaction, Beitz and Pogge support the application of John Rawls's difference principle to the international realm. According to this principle, inequalities in certain resources (including income and wealth) are justified only to the extent that they are compatible with equal basic liberties and fair equality of opportunity and they maximize the position of the least well-off individual (Rawls 1971).

The conclusion that we ought to advocate a global difference principle depends on a close parallel between the basic domestic institutions and arrangements of a society and those in the international realm. Critics might plausibly argue that, while both domestic society and international society are marked by interaction, they nonetheless differ in significant ways that make the simple extension of domestic justice to international justice implausible. Thus, whereas what Rawls calls a society's 'basic structure' has an important role in shaping human identity and aspirations, most economic interactions between countries do not have the effect of educating children, communicating respect, and preparing individuals to take on the responsibilities of citizens. The extent and nature of the interactions between persons matter, not simply the fact of their existence.

Furthermore, it seems likely that international societies are marked by far less convergence on fundamental values than is found in a single society. Much of that divergence finds expression in differing conceptions of legitimate social order. For example, many societies are marked by a conception of the social good in which not all members are given equal status. So critics might also challenge such cosmopolitan theories to find a way of balancing their commitment to univocal principles of distributive justice with a principle of toleration for divergent conceptions of the social good that help legitimate a country's government. How cosmopolitans strike that balance will have consequences for the attractiveness of their theory, its usefulness to us now, and its moral force.

One final version of cosmopolitanism comes from the perspective of human rights. Theorists of human rights begin from the idea that we are a common humanity, sharing aspirations, vulnerabilities, and essential capacities. On the basis of that ideal, they believe that we can articulate the basic claims of human beings— the rights and powers that human beings need in order to preserve their status as members of this human community.

The content of these claims has been interpreted both minimally and maximally. Minimally, these claims can consist in immunities from torture, arbitrary arrest, imprisonment, and killing. More robustly, some have argued that these claims include entitlements to the material resources and freedoms needed to live and develop their capacities. So understood, human rights would have a powerful global redistributive dimension, obligating the wealthy nations to ensure the basic subsistence of the world's poorest (Shue 1996). The major instruments for the international protection of human rights are the Universal Declaration of Human Rights (1948), the International Covenant on Civil and Political Rights (1966), and the International Covenant on Economic, Social, and Cultural Rights (1966).

Cosmopolitan theorists have tended to strike a somewhat abstract stance, setting out a moral orientation, but not detailing much in the way of concrete policy proposals or new institutional designs. Thus, they have had little to say about vexing problems of immigration policy (for example, what distinctions can the USA reasonably draw between its own citizens, permanent residents, legal and illegal immigrants and refugees from persecution?), trade policy, and any costs of 'globalization' for US workers. (I consider the latter below.)

One intriguing exception to this tendency to abstraction is Thomas Pogge's recent proposal for 'A Global Resources Dividend' (1994). The basic idea of such a dividend is that, 'while each people owns and fully controls all resources within its national territory, it must pay a tax on any resources it seeks to extract'. States would thus be asked to pay taxes on natural resources in proportion to 'how much value they take from the planet'. The proceeds from this tax would then be targeted to aid the global poor. Interestingly, this tax can be supported on forward-looking con-sequentialist grounds, on grounds of basic human rights, and on historical backward-looking grounds: as recognition of the arbitrariness of current ownership of natural resources.

4.2 Rawls's *Law of Peoples*

John Rawls sets out a different position from both the cosmopolitans and the stat-ists in his recent book *The Law of Peoples* (1999). Unlike the statists, he rejects the idea of traditional sovereign states, with their rights to complete internal autonomy as well as their right to go to war to pursue their own interests. Instead, he sees states as subordinate to a reasonable law of 'peoples'—that is, a form of international law, which allows them to go to war only in self-defence and which places limits, derived from human rights, on their internal sovereignty. Unlike the cosmopolitan theorists who build their case for international economic justice out of a concern with indi-viduals, Rawls's focus is on peoples. 'Peoples' are not states; they do not have absolute sovereignty, and they have an inherent 'moral nature', by which Rawls means that they affirm a conception of the social good and constrain their actions by considerations of reasonableness embedded in their public cultures. For most purposes, however, the concept can be interpreted as referring to a society with a common political culture organized as a state.

Rawlsian international theory is based on the idea of a division of labour between international and domestic society. Principles of international justice must show equal respect and concern for all peoples, but states have primary responsibility for caring for individuals. Thus, the principles of international justice are to be justi-fied by considering the fundamental interests of those societies to whom they apply, and not directly to the individuals who live in those societies.

While peoples must be reasonable—they must respect the inevitable plurality of cultural values as well as the human rights of individuals—Rawls believes that international justice does not require that they all be liberal. Rather, principles of reciprocity require that we not impose conditions on others that they could reas-onably reject. This means that we must tolerate decent but non-liberal societies with fundamentally different conceptions of the social good than our own. Rawls refers to these societies as 'decent hierarchical peoples'. Such societies respect basic human rights, but do not regard their members as free and equal citizens. They include societies that privilege an established religion, give unequal citizenship to women and members of ethnic minorities, and whose governmental authority is not subject to the criteria of democratic legitimacy.

What principles of global justice would reasonable and decent peoples agree to regulate their relationships by? Rawls imagines an international 'original position' in which all reasonable peoples are represented. *The Law of Peoples* outlines eight principles that they would choose, including principles governing the morality of war, the ethics of statesmanship, and the international distribution of resources. For the purposes of the topic of this chapter, international economic justice, two principles are crucially important:

1. 'Peoples are to honor human rights' (including 'the means of subsistence', personal liberty, including liberty of conscience, and equal treatment under law); and
2. 'Peoples have a duty to assist other peoples living under unfavorable conditions that prevent their having a just or decent political and social regime'.

In practice, these two principles probably imply a system of international development assistance, financed by transfers from the rich countries.

While Rawls's requirements are demanding, it is important to note his theory's differences with cosmopolitanism. As I noted above, cosmopolitans see the fundamental unit of concern as the individual and insist that our moral obligations directly consider the interests of individuals. They, therefore, see no reason why the distributive requirements of international justice should be any less stringent than those that domestic justice imposes. Yet, Rawls draws a sharp line between the economic distributive principles he sees as applying in a domestic context and those that he believes should govern the relations between peoples. In particular, his international principles contain neither an egalitarian distributional element, nor the familiar Rawlsian liberal principles of justice—that is, the fair value of political liberty, an adequate scheme of basic liberties for equal citizens, and fair equality of opportunity. While our domestic theory of justice requires that institutions constrain inequalities, international justice requires only that a minimum threshold be reached by the poor nations. Moreover, international justice is 'agnostic' as to the extent of allowable inequality within other societies: it simply sets a minimal baseline given by the need for all to respect human rights (Beitz 2000).

How does Rawls's theory fare when compared with cosmopolitan views of international distributive justice? His theory is vulnerable to several objections.

First, it can be argued that Rawls's theory fails to recognize that the advanced countries are causally implicated in at least some part of the plight of the world's poor. Although, as I mentioned at the outset of this chapter, there is substantial disagreement as to the sources of economic backwardness, it is clear that developing societies are enmeshed in the global division of labour. Foreign capital markets, international financial institutions like the World Bank and the International

Monetary Fund, as well as its trade relations, influence a society's economic condition. These transnational institutions are not facts of nature, but human institutions in need of justification. Why should the world's poor accept status quo arrangements as opposed to some alternative under which they would fare better?

Secondly, some of this global interaction occurs even at the level of individual behaviour. People do not simply participate in domestic political institutions. Some of our shared cooperative activities with others involve transnational institutions such as the international labour market and multinational corporations. For example, as workers, many of us collaborate in an international division of labour jointly contributing to the manufacture of certain goods. In cases of joint production and collaboration, it is arguable that merely respecting human rights of foreign workers is not enough: we have duties of fair play to reciprocate in contexts in which we work together with others and benefit from their cooperation.

Not only are individuals and nations intermeshed around the globe, but also some goods are, by their nature, 'international public goods'. Consider the good of a sustainable environment or that of scientific research on deadly contagious diseases. These goods cannot be easily partitioned between the various countries, and often give rise to positive or negative externalities. Moreover, such goods are now generally recognized as playing a crucial role in determining and/or influencing the well-being of the world's poor. But some principle of justice will be needed to regulate and distribute the benefits and burdens created by such goods. (It is estimated, for example, that changing precipitation patterns and a hotter climate will disrupt crop harvests, trigger an increase in heat waves, floods, droughts, fires, and pest outbreaks, and cause sea levels to rise anywhere from 15 to 94 centimetres, placing island nations and Bangladesh at considerable risk.) But Rawls's theory says nothing about such cases, save that the parties to all treaties be viewed as 'equals'. This is a serious, and in my view highly damaging, omission for Rawlsian international theory.

A third objection criticizes the theory's focus on peoples as opposed to individuals. In rejecting the global application of his difference principle, Rawls appeals to the unfairness of asking one society to transfer resources to another society. Thus he invites us to consider two countries at the same level of wealth that have the same population size. The first decides to industrialize while the latter does not. Assuming that both societies made their decisions freely, Rawls asks whether the industrializing society should be taxed to give funds to the pastoral one. That, he says, 'seems unacceptable'. By contrast, he does find such transfers acceptable—even required by justice—in domestic society. (Against libertarian critics of A Theory of Justice (1971), Rawls argued that it is perfectly acceptable for a person who has worked hard to achieve her wealth to be taxed in order to support someone who has led a more leisurely life among the worst-off members of society.)

Of course, this example of the citizens of two poor countries freely choosing different development strategies is empirically dubious: the world's poorest countries are often ruled by despots who are corrupt to their core. Further, the example also abstracts away from any international influences on the two countries' decisions. But, even granting the example's empirical premisses, it seems objectionable to hold individuals responsible for choices they themselves did not make or did not make alone. For example, my country's development policy might be a path-dependent result of past choices by earlier generations: why should I now pay the cost (Beitz 2000)?

Relatedly, to address the needs of individual persons, it is insufficient to transfer assets to poor countries when one knows that the governments of those countries will appropriate them or otherwise prevent them from going to the poor people within their borders. Even if the problem is hunger and destitution and not equality, we must care about the distributions within countries and not simply between them. Indeed, some recent work in economics suggests that inequality may be bad for economic growth (Birdsall et al. 1995).

Nonetheless, Rawls seems right to stress that economic equality, as opposed to economic sufficiency, is important only in certain contexts. For example, in the domestic context, economic equality is important to secure because it underwrites the fair conditions for democratic politics. In that context, economic equality plays a role in ensuring that each citizen has equal opportunity to influence an election. (In countries such as the USA, where the costs of elections are not publicly subsidized, unequal income allows the wealthy to wield disproportionate power over the electorate.) But this equal ability is relevant only between those who are directly subject to the coercive policies imposed by that election, and usually, but not necessarily, these are the citizens of a particular state. It is of no intrinsic importance to me to be able to exercise the equal opportunity for political influence with a French citizen in the French elections and thus economic inequalities between the French and the Americans seem less pertinent.

Against this point, it can be objected that a world with large inequalities of wealth (and perhaps related inequalities of military power) renders the domestic institutions of the poorer nations vulnerable to corruption from abroad. Perhaps large global inequalities allow the wealthy nations to interfere with the domestic political institutions of poorer nations in order to influence and control them. Thus, the importance domestic democratic legitimacy may have consequences for international distribution.

This objection might lead to a revised principle, which considered the different contexts in which inequality (and not merely deprivation) undermined the basic freedoms of individuals. Differences in the obligations we have to our co-nationals and strangers would not be absolute, but a matter of degree. Notice that this revised principle is not identical to the Rawlsian difference principle—it does not require that all inequalities in primary goods between the two countries be justified in terms of their effects on the least well-off person regardless of the country he is in. In particular, it does not require that citizens in the poorer country have the resources necessary to influence the elections in the richer country, nor even that they have the resources necessary to have a fair go at occupying social and economic positions in the richer country. Rawlsian international justice thus amended regis-ters the moral importance of states as a context for equality, but need not accept an absolute restriction on equality in the international sphere.

Finally, Rawlsian theory might fare better than cosmopolitan theory in being more 'realistic'—that is, in having a greater chance of gaining international adher-ents. It requires no new international institutions, and leaves a wide berth for non-democratic forms of society. The challenge for Rawls's theory is to show that this realism does not come at the price of principle: that it does not represent an accom-modation to injustice and cultural relativism. Some believe that it cannot meet this challenge (Barry 2001).

5. AGENT-CENTRED INTERNATIONAL JUSTICE

Some of the theories I discussed (such as that of Peter Singer) abstract away from questions of the causes of harms and disadvantages. By contrast, according to some views of distributive justice, burdens that are quite indistinguishable for their recipi-ents can nonetheless differ greatly in their moral significance. In such views, their significance will depend on whether they are imposed through (our) social and political institutions or whether they arise in some other way.

Entitlement theories stress our causal connections to harms, but they are not the only such theories that can incorporate an agent-relative point of view. Kantian the-ories can do this (as do Beitz and Pogge to a degree), as well as backwards-looking theories that stress reparative justice and compensation. On such theories, it is an agent's relationship to others' burdens that matter. We are most implicated in the social injustice that we directly participate in. What we are required to do to stop distant suffering is therefore greater and our obligation stronger when social institu-tions avoidably contribute to this suffering and also when we cooperate in upholding these institutions.

Is this kind of agent relativity plausible? To get a sense of what it entails, let us return to the Rawlsian thought experiment where there are self-contained countries with minimal interactions. Assume that all countries provide for their citizens above a satisfactory minimum, but nevertheless in each of them there remains some injustice. An agent-relative approach would argue that you have a stronger reason to uphold the just institutions of your own society rather than those of other soci-eties, and a stronger reason to fight for the erasure of institutional injustice at home, which your taxes helped impose, rather than injustices abroad. Many twentieth-century social movements have drawn on the idea that causal responsibility effects moral responsibility in especially targeting injustices at home.

While countries' causal histories and the obligations that they engender are not the whole story of international justice (for some of the reasons rehearsed above), they do represent relevant considerations. Consider that many people find it plausible that the German government bears special responsibility for what has happened to its former Jewish citizens and that it pays reparations to survivors. Likewise, we generally hold people more responsible (*ceteris paribus*) when they violate a promise than when they simply fail to perform an action.

6. GLOBALIZATION DEBATES

Questions of international economic justice become especially pressing in the context of the phenomena popularly called 'globalization'. Globalization is essentially a set of developments that have as their common element the international integration of markets for goods, services, and capital. Many economists have heralded globalization as a mechanism for development and poverty reduction, particularly for the world's poorest nations. At the same time, broad segments of many societies, especially but not exclusively in the more developed countries, have been putting up a fight to the internationalization of their local economies.

Each of the perspectives outlined above has at least some implications for the question of what our attitude towards globalization should be. Yet, there has thus far been little fleshing out of these perspectives in the context of the complex economic and social factors that bear on internationalization of markets. The issues are complicated, as in the case of economic development generally, because many of the debates around globalization centre on empirical disagreements—disagreements that persist even among those who share the common goal of reducing global poverty.

Many parties to the debate start with different assumptions. Because mainstream economists see the liberalization of capital flows in terms of the principles of competitive markets, they thus see gains from lifting restrictions on capital mobility. Even if workers in the country sending capital abroad lose, workers in the recipient country will gain. Moreover, since with mobility capital will move to the highest return, theoretically the efficiency created will allow the gainer to compensate the loser. By contrast, critics see globalization in terms of the principles of monopoly and asymmetric bargaining power, where capital is mobile and labour immobile: they thus see no contradiction in workers everywhere being made worse off as a result, despite the gains from efficiency.

Let us suppose, for the sake of argument, that globalization poses no issue of monopoly power in the classical sense. What ethical issues does globalization raise from the different perspectives that we have considered on international economic justice? How should we respond to an international economic process in the context of the existence of separate nations with their own norms, governments, and citizens?

Nationalists and statists would probably support import restrictions if it could be shown that free trade has some costs to domestic jobs and wages. For example, American autoworkers in the 1980s asked car-buyers to 'Buy American—The Job You Save May Be Your Own', while other Buy American campaigns sprang up around the USA. Campaigns such as these focus on protecting national jobs and ignore the costs of such protectionist strategies to foreign workers (and other domestic workers who now pay higher prices for goods). Indeed, such campaigns often aim to restrict not only the entry of foreign goods into the national economy, but also foreign workers themselves. Protectionism, thus understood, can look like a self-serving strategy by American workers to hold on to their privileged position in the global economy, especially if we accept the (disputed) premiss that there are no issues of monopoly power.

But even under the assumption of classical markets with a large number of small agents, not all statist concerns with internationalization should be viewed as crass protectionism. A concern with trade relations might also be motivated by democratic aspirations—that is, by a desire by a population to exercise democratic control over their nation and their economic lives. Consider that countries have different norms governing and constraining their domestic economies—as reflected in workplace practices, legal rules, and social safety nets. What should we do when international trade undermines the norms implicit in domestic practices? One way of viewing the current opposition to globalization in the name of 'fair trade' is as an assertion of a domestic procedural norm. For example, one objection (among many) to child or sweatshop labour abroad is that it is an unfair way of imposing a burden on others—namely, the adult workers such labour replaces. Likewise, poor countries faced with unilateral global rules on development might prefer to put more of their loans into education or a minimum safety net than international lenders accept. They might want to use selective protectionist strategies to protect fledgling industries, as the USA did in the first half of the twentieth century. Not all 'statist' arguments must amount to protectionist strategies designed to hold on to material privilege; they can be motivated by independent values.

In *Has Globalization Gone Too Far?*, Dani Rodrik (1997) asks us to consider two cases. In the first case, a US company outsources much of its operation to Honduras, laying off its American workers who find other jobs, and employing 12-year-old children at the very low prevailing wages in its new location. In the second case, the company moves its plant just north of the Mexican border and brings in 12-year-old children from Honduras as temporary migrants. Other than that the second case involves breaking US law, Rodrik asks us to consider whether there is any significant differences between the two cases. While most economists would accept the legitimacy of such outsourcing but have trouble with allowing migration under the terms of the second example, Rodrik argues that this position is inconsistent. In both cases, the 'comparative advantage' of the Honduran workers is created by institutional choices that conflict with some norms in the importing country. As a prevailing norm, Americans do not believe that it is acceptable to reduce the living standards of American workers by taking advantage of labour standards that are far below those standards we have adopted for ourselves (Rodrik 1997: 34). What makes the geographical location of the violation of this procedural norm relevant?

Cosmopolitans and statists may differ precisely as to how we should respond to these varying procedural norms. They may therefore differ as to whether or not it is morally permissible for local norms about legitimate procedures to block income transfers that might benefit those who are the most disadvantaged. Is it legitimate to refuse to engage in trade relations with countries whose labour standards are inconsistent with those of the host country? This can be an especially pressing question where the norms of the recipient country (that is, child labour) impose costs on citizens (that is, adult workers) in the exporting country.

Even if it is conceded that statists have a point in emphasizing the legitimacy of local procedural norms, cosmopolitans are correct to alert us to the importance of considering the effects of our actions on the world's least disadvantaged. For example, if our objection to child labour is motivated out of sympathy for the children involved (and not only concern for our own workers), then we must be sensitive to the likely effects on a ban on child labour. Will it drive children into far worse situations like child prostitution? Is there some way of raising standards and conditions in the poor countries without penalizing those who are most vulnerable?

Debates over globalization also raise questions of how to aggregate benefits and burdens. Is it enough that a poor country's overall GDP is rising, or must we pay special attention to how that GDP is distributed among individuals? Cosmopolitans tend to focus on the effects of policies on individuals, not states, and thus to emphasize intra-country distribution as key. It is not enough for the GDP of Ghana to rise, if the lives of many Ghanaians become worse through social dislocation and the collapse of basic services.

Thus far, I have provisionally granted the assumption that there is little or no market power in the international realm. But those who see pockets of monopoly power throughout the economy have powerfully criticized this assumption. Examples of asymmetric market power include the bargaining advantages that mobile capital has over less mobile labour, the power of local moneylenders, and the power wielded by the wealthy with their governments. Such market power can also arise from the fact that some people are more dependent (and desperate) on a transaction occurring than others and thus more likely to accept terms that are unfair.

Additionally, international trade and labour practices are rife with examples of forced agreements, coercion, exploitation, and simply taking advantage of the least fortunate. It is unclear to what extent some of the poorest nations have benefited from the pilfering/trading of the scarce commodities that are found within their borders. Consider the squalid encounter between the global high-tech economy and the Congo over coltan, a heavy mud that is a superb conductor of electricity. A recent report to the United Nations Security Council, reported in the *New York Times*, claimed that coltan perpetuates the Congo's civil war. The report said the war 'has become mostly about access, control and trade' of minerals, especially coltan. The incentive to grab coltan and get rich has overwhelmed security concerns, and money from coltan funds fuels and augments the war efforts that wreak havoc on most of the population (*New York Times Magazine*, 12 Aug. 2001). Coltan is simply the latest booty in a history in which the Congo has been plundered for ivory, rubber, diamonds, and gold. In the 1960s, to secure access to cobalt and copper, the CIA helped assassinate the Congo's first democratically elected president, Patrice Lumumba. While coltan does bring some money into the Congo's impoverished economy, most of the money has gone to warlords and profiteers.

Of course, trade can help the Congo, and alleviate poverty. But the crucial question is under what conditions? What trade and aid policies best foster economic growth and empower the poor in countries like the Congo? Within international institutions—such as the World Bank, the World Trade Organization, and the International Monetary Fund—there has been insufficient attention to including the voices of the poor.

7. CONCLUSION

Considering the legitimacy of the world's economic distribution from the perspective of its destitute millions places pressure on what has been called 'everyone's favorite moral conviction'—that is, the view that there is nothing wrong with the lives we lead (Pogge 1989). Moreover, the unequal situation between the poorest people and ourselves is not simply a general problem about distribution and justice: it is an extreme case, involving extreme and urgent needs. I have argued that the condition of the world's poorest is morally wrong, even if no one did anything wrong (like theft) to bring it about. I have also argued that in some contexts it is reasonable to think that the inequality between the wealthy nations and the poor nations is unjust. But, whether one accepts that argument, it is clear that, even on the other grounds of reparative justice, charity, or human rights, we are not doing enough for the world's poor.

REFERENCES

Anand, Sudhir (1993). 'Inequality between and among Nations'. Paper prepared for Workshop on 'Economic Theories of Inequality'. Stanford University.

Barry, Brian (1999). 'Statism and Nationalism: A Cosmopolitan Critique', in I. Shapiro and L Brilmayer (eds.), *Global Justice*. New York: New York University Press, 12–66.

——(2001). *Culture and Equality*. Cambridge, MA: Harvard University Press.

Beitz, Charles (1979). *Political Theory and International Relations*. Princeton: Princeton University Press.

——(2000). 'Rawls' Law of Peoples', *Ethics*, 110: 669–96.

——Cohen, Marshall, Scanlon, Thomas, and Simmons, John (1985) (eds.), *International Ethics*. Princeton: Princeton University Press.

Birdsall, Nancy, Ross, David, and Sabot, Richard (1995). 'Inequality and Growth Reconsidered: Lessons from East Asia'. *World Bank Economic Review*, 9/3: 477–508.

Diamond, Jared (1997). *Guns, Germs and Steel*. New York: W. W. Norton.

Dworkin, Ronald (1986). *Law's Empire*. Cambridge, MA: Harvard University Press.

Goodin, Robert (1988). 'What is so Special about our Fellow Countrymen?' *Ethics*, 98: 663–867.

Kiss, Elizabeth (1996). 'Five Theses on Nationalism', in Ian Shapiro and Russell Hardin (eds.), *Political Order*. New York: New York University Press, 288–332.

Landes, David (1998). *The Wealth and Poverty of Nations*. New York: W. W. Norton.

McNamara, Robert (1978) (ed.), *World Bank Development Report*. New York: World Bank.

Miller, David (1995). *On Nationality*. Oxford: Oxford University Press.

Morgenthau, Hans (1952). *In Defense of the National Interest*. New York: Knopf.

Murphy, Liam (1998). 'Institutions and the Demands of Justice'. *Philosophy and Public Affairs*, 27: 251–91.

Nozick, Robert (1971). *Anarchy State and Utopia*. New York: Basic Books.

Pogge, Thomas (1989). *Realizing Rawls*. Ithaca, NY: Cornell University Press.

——(1994). 'A Global Resources Dividend', in D. Crocker and T. Linden (eds.), *The Ethics of Consumption*. Totowa, NJ: Rowman & Littlefield, 501–36.

Rawls, John (1971). *A Theory of Justice*. Cambridge, MA: Harvard University Press.

——(1999). *The Law of Peoples*. Cambridge, MA: Harvard University Press.

Rodrik, Dani (1997). *Has Globalization Gone Too Far?* Washington: Institute for International Economics.

Sen, Amartya (1999). *Development as Freedom*. Cambridge, MA: Harvard University Press.

Scheffler, Samuel (1997). 'Relationships and Responsibilities'. *Philosophy and Public Affairs*, 26: 189–209.

Shue, Henry (1996). *Basic Rights*. 2nd edn. Princeton: Princeton University Press.

Sikora, R., and Barry, B. (1978) (eds.), *Obligations to Future Generations*. Philadelphia: Temple University Press.

Singer, Peter (1972). 'Famine, Affluence and Morality'. *Philosophy and Public Affairs*, 1: 229–43.

Taylor, Charles (1992). 'The Politics of Recognition', in Amy Gutmann (ed.), *Multiculturalism and the Politics of Recognition*. Princeton: Princeton University Press, 25–73.

Unger, Peter (1996). *Living High and Letting Die: Our Illusion of Innocence*. New York: Oxford University Press.

United Nations Development Programme (1997, 1998, 1999, 2000). *Human Development Report*.

Waltz, Kenneth (1959). *Man, State and War*. New York: Columbia University Press.

Walzer, Michael (1977). *Just and Unjust Wars*. New York: Basic Books.

——(1983). *Spheres of Justice*. New York: Basic Books.

CHAPTER 25

....

WORLD HUNGER

....

NIGEL DOWER

1. SCENE SETTING

....

IT might be thought that the central question for applied ethics raised by world hunger should be: do the affluent in rich countries have obligations to alleviate hunger in poor countries, and if so, to what extent? This was indeed the central question in the 1970s when philosophers became engaged with the issue. It was for instance the main theme of the influential collection *World Hunger and Moral Obligation* (Aiken and LaFollette 1977). Since then the debate has broadened and other issues have come to be seen as important. This is illustrated by the second edition of the above work entitled *World Hunger and Morality* (Aiken and LaFollette 1996) (though 'second edition' is a little misleading as most of the essays are new ones reflecting this change of emphasis). This broadening of the debate, partly associated with the work of Amartya Sen (e.g. Sen 1981, 1990), came with the recognition that the causes of hunger and poverty are complex, that the conditions of successful aid are not easy to achieve especially when it becomes politicized in situations of conflict, that institutional and political changes are necessary at both national and international levels, and that development is itself a highly contested concept, not at all to be identified simply with economic growth. Since all these factors raise normative questions about who ought to do what, the original question 'Ought the affluent to help the poor in another country?' may be seen as too narrow and rather misleading for a number of reasons.

First, the question itself is in danger of polarizing the world too much—that is, of suggesting that the affluent live in rich countries and the poor live in poor countries, whereas the truth is that there are very poor people in rich countries and very affluent people in poor countries. The way we conceptualize the world is itself an ethical issue.

Secondly, if the question is seen as *the* ethical question in this area, it commits the fallacy of 'misplaced concreteness' (Crocker 1996) in excluding other key issues. The real issues are not about hunger as such, certainly not about rushing food aid in when there are famines and emergencies. Hunger, though a great evil in itself, is indicative of extreme poverty, which is evil in many other respects: the nature of poverty, the respects in which it is bad, and the factors that cause it are all immensely complex. This complexity shows that the appropriate responses are not necessarily the provision of food (except in emergencies), or even the increase in food production for an area (which agencies like Oxfam may promote). Many value issues are raised by these matters (see e.g. Mephan 1996; Toyne and O'Neill 1998). If aid or government programmes have an emphasis on long-term development, part of the rationale for this may be the *prevention* of future problems of hunger, malnutrition, or more generally poverty, rather than solving pre-existing problems, temporary or chronic. The nature of development is in part an ethical issue, and in fact some issues raised by hunger are now discussed within the framework of an emerging area of enquiry called 'development ethics' (Aman 1991; Goulet 1995).

Thirdly, even if we focus on hunger, the same complex picture emerges. Much of Sen's work had been on famines, in which he developed the leading idea of entitlements as the bundle of commodities that an individual commands (e.g. Sen 1996). His work brought attention to the fact that hunger and starvation generally occurred in situations in which there was enough food; the poor simply did not have access to it. The 'political economy of hunger' (the title of a three-volume book co-edited by Sen and Drèze, recently republished in an abbreviated form in one volume (Drèze and Sen 1990–1; Drèze et al. 1995), is concerned with the human role in most problems to do with poverty—whether it is the state's unwillingness to intervene in appropriate ways (an unwillingness generally checked in countries where a free press is able to monitor what is happening), or the unequal distribution of food within a family where the males command greater access to available food.

Hunger then usually occurs in situations in which food is available. However, the very poor have neither the food themselves nor the resources to purchase it. Nor do they exist in a social environment in which the community or the government provides food. But the food may exist all around them. Of course, in rare situations individuals or groups may be without food, and either others do not know this or cannot get food to them. That is, others lack either knowledge or capacity. Examples might be a real lifeboat situation or a community cut off by severe flooding. However, in normal circumstances this is not the case. Most hunger occurs where there is in fact food in the area.

What practical conclusions should we draw from this? At one level the issue has to do with *making food available to the hungry*. In the short term this may be a matter of political and community will and organization, supplemented, in emergencies, by the transfer of food from elsewhere (in the country or the world) by government or aid agencies. In the longer term it is a matter of enabling the hungry to have better access to food on a regular basis, which may involve a wide range of measures to do with education, transfers of technologies, new agricultural methods, new seeds, and so on, or land reform, government work schemes, and so on. That is, the poor are enabled to grow more food themselves or have better resources for acquiring food. A large measure of responsibility for creating these better conditions of course lies with governments in poor countries and with local organizations as well. But clearly there are at least three broadly different ways in which inputs for those outside the country have an important role. First, official aid programmes (if appropriate) will provide the resources and expertise for these things to happen. Secondly, non-governmental organizations (NGOs) also do the same thing, though generally through smaller-scale projects. Thirdly, the policies pursued by other countries (and by transnational companies) have a major impact, for good or ill, on the economic conditions within a poor country, and thus on the extent to which governments, organizations, and individuals within poor countries can pursue such policies. For many thinkers, then, the changes that are needed are essentially political or more generally institutional, both at national and international levels (see e.g. Attfield and Wilkins 1992).

Do these complexities that raise a range of ethical issues in 'development ethics' then displace the question about the responsibilities of the individual? My own conclusion is that they do not. She has an important role, which might be summarized as her being citizen, consumer, and humanitarian—citizen in respect of her role in influencing political decisions, consumer in respect of her role in influencing the kinds of economic relations that people have in one county vis-à-vis those in another, and humanitarian in respect of her wish, through solidarity with the rest of humanity, to make direct contributions to alleviate distant problems, typically through voluntary agencies.

The question is still central largely because the extent to which NGOs and governments pursue such aid programmes, and the extent to which the policies of government and financial institutions pursue benign economic policies in the global economy, are an important function of what individuals in rich countries regard as ethically important. Let us suppose at this point—as I shall later defend—that individuals in rich countries have significant obligations to help alleviate world hunger. (We need not go as far as Peter Singer, who, in his seminal paper 'Famine, Affluence and Morality', in 1972, discussed more fully below, essentially argues that we should do 'as much as we can'.)

Does the fact that in large measure addressing problems of hunger involves complex development processes, political changes, and so on, in any way reduce the importance of what individuals are prepared to do in rich countries? Not at all. If one holds the view that one has significant obligations, then one's obligations are not less. Rather they are channelled into different kinds of activity. Let us grant that political change—national and international—is what is needed. What this means is that I should as an active citizen take part in politics in my own country in order to further appropriate changes internationally or join an NGO working on the issue. But note two things about this. First, nothing follows from this about not contributing one's time and resources to help alleviate hunger and poverty more directly—for example, by contributing to voluntary organizations. Secondly, suppose one held that contributing to charity actually did no good at all, nothing follows about not doing as much as one would have done through such charities in the sphere of effective action—namely, political or institutional action; the amount of time, energy, and resources one puts into political activity (or into an NGO) could be as extensive as you like. The fact that what is appropriate is far more complex than the 'traditional financial contribution to charity' model suggests does not get rid of the thorny problems concerning the extent of obligation at all—it merely makes one's responsibilities more complicated.

2. SINGER'S ARGUMENT

In 1971 Singer argued in the article referred to above that the affluent should use their resources to help save the lives of those dying from starvation, up to the point of marginal utility. He used the illustration of a lecturer passing a pond in which a child is drowning and argues that, for anyone who accepts the ethical intuition that the lecturer ought to save the drowning child, the following principle should be accepted: 'if it is our power to prevent something bad from happening, without sacrificing anything of comparable moral importance, we ought, morally, to do it.' But, if we accept this principle, we must in consistency accept that we should save the lives of starving people in other countries and go on doing so until we are sacrificing something of equal moral importance. The fact that the hungry elsewhere in the world are distant or unknown makes no difference.

Although there can be much dispute as to what equal moral importance is and whether 'significance' would make the principle more acceptable, the acceptance of the principle would revolutionize one's life. Thus, even if one saw duties of truthtelling or respect for property as having greater moral importance, or even if one gave *some* priority to special relations with family, one would still have obligations to use one's resources far in excess of what even normally generous people do. The principle was so formulated to appeal to non-consequentialists as well as consequentialists, but, for reasons to be explained later on, it is essentially consequentialist. In a later expanded version of the argument in his book *Practical Ethics* (1979), Singer considers, but does not fully endorse, a rather different style of argument, which comes to much the same conclusion—namely, what is called the 'negative actions' thesis. That is, there is no intrinsic difference between causing someone to die and letting someone die when one could intervene to prevent her from dying, so failing to save a life is 'morally equivalent to murder'. Ted Honderich (1976) and John Harris (1980) advanced similar arguments at much the same time to the effect that we need to accept a conception of negative violence as well as positive violence. Whether or not it is acceptable to one's intuition to see letting someone die as a form of *violence*, the more fundamental point remains. If one accepts as many consequentialists do that one is responsible for what one knows (or ought reasonably to know) will happen as a result of what one does or refrains from doing, then there is not going to be much ethical difference between what one does knowingly in an active way and what one lets happen where one is aware of this (or ought reasonably to be aware of it) and one could act to prevent that happening.

3. Objections to Singer's Argument

Singer's position can be criticized for a number of reasons. First, it seems to have the difficulty (which it shares with Utilitarianism) of providing the wrong kind of reason for caring for the hungry, by making this care impersonal because it is simply a contingent means towards maximizing the good, or, in Singer's case, of preventing evils as long as one does not sacrifice something of an equivalent value. Secondly, given Singer's wider account of good and evil in terms of preference utilitarianism, it presupposes an unduly restrictive account of what is bad about poverty and hunger. Thirdly, it involves a principle that is too 'demanding' and conflicts with what is generally taken to be the place of morality within a human life. Of these three objections, the third is the most serious.

Perhaps the first difficulty is one that is merely apparent. There is an 'impersonalness' about the account of why one should help that seems to overlook that the reason for helping the poor—a reason acceptable to the poor themselves—is because it is something owed to them or because they are a direct object of altruistic concern. If, however, a 'maximizing' consequentialism can recognize that a person's actual motives in morally correct action are richer than that of 'maximizing' and that the fundamental principle endorses acting on other motives such as personal altruistic motives, the 'impersonalness' can be removed. Certainly Singer's own principle is so formulated as to make the prevention of evil a direct object of concern, and the other considerations can be seen as preconditions or side constraints. On the contingency issue, it needs to be recognized that this is actually a feature of any ethical theory that acknowledges that one's duty might sometimes be not to act on a personal altruistic motive because of other overriding considerations.

With regard to the second criticism, it may or may not be a criticism of Singer's approach that the criteria for good and evil are understood in terms of preference satisfaction/frustration (or pleasure/pain and suffering in older versions of utilitarianism). Certainly, death is bad because it curtails a life that could have contained the continuation of worthwhile experiences, and hunger and disease, apart from being the causes of death, are bad because they cause the experiences of pain and suffering and the frustration of preferences. However, as we note later on, much of development ethics focuses on the question of whether this kind of characterization of human well-being is adequate as a criterion of good development, or as an explanation of the evil of poverty. For instance, various forms of bodily malfunction, such as disease, illness, or physical incapacities, may be evils *in themselves* quite apart from their effects—suffering and failure to satisfy desires. The limitation to or undermining of the exercise of rational autonomy may also constitute a serious evil in its own right. However, even if it is accepted that Singer's account of the good is limited, the central thrust of Singer's argument remains: however 'good' and 'evil' are understood, the prevention of untimely death and the prevention of continued suffering in other parties is in most circumstances a lesser evil to that of allowing them to continue, and therefore we ought to prevent them.

The main difficulty with this aspect of Singer's argument—one that is also shared by act utilitarianism—is that it requires agents to act again and again to the point where more harm would be done by so acting. The 'iterative' nature of the argument can be questioned, as it is by Cullity, since, whatever persuasive power the analogy has, it derives from the fact that there is one child not countless children (Cullity 1996). However, he thinks that an alternative 'aggregative' interpretation concerning the overall impact of a course of action would still leave one with extensive obligations. Two types of argument are often stressed against either version of the claim that we have such relentless obligations: first, one has rights (or even duties) to oneself to continuing to pursue one's own life or to pursue one's own projects (Arthur 1996) in what Fishkin called a 'robust zone of moral indifference' (1986). To put it another way, the difficulty with this kind of consequentialist reasoning is that it leaves little or no moral 'space' in which what one does is neither morally required nor morally forbidden (Dower 1983). Secondly, special relations to family and friends or indeed members of immediate communities are an important part of the ethical life, and, in fulfilling obligations in relation to these, one may sometimes be justifiably giving priority to the lesser good of these than the greater good of those not so related.

This raises one of the most general issues in moral philosophy, which concerns the interpretation of what is generally (though not universally) accepted as a basic starting point to moral thought—namely, the equal moral status of all human beings. Singer's underlying position, which he applies to all areas of applied ethics, is 'equal consideration of interests', which suggests that, even when for practical reasons one does give priority to one's self or to some particular others, this always has to be justified as consistent with the principle of equal consideration. For instance, parental caring for children may be seen as an effective means towards creating an overall outcome in which everyone's interests are given equal weight. On the other hand, it is not self-evident that the equal moral status of all humans entails this way of looking at things. Others may hold that, so long as a certain status of all human beings is respected in one's actions, then, consistent with this, one is free to give special priority to self and some others; a corollary of this is that part of the equal status that all humans have is the equal right to pursue a life in which priority is given to self and some others.

Of course, in most ethical systems, *some* duties of benevolence to strangers and those who are distant and unknown are recognized, but generally to anyone who is not a robust consequentialist (as Singer is) the idea of benevolence as being relentless and demanding 'as much as you can' is simply not accepted. Singer's principle does not, as he intended it, generally attract those whose ethical systems are more complex than straightforwardly consequentialist, though there are some who so argue (Kagan 1991). It is certainly worth noting that, as a point of moral logic, accepting a plurality of duties allows for the possibility of accepting a duty of benevolence that is as extensive as possible consistent with those other duties. It does not, of course, require one to accept such an 'extensive' interpretation of benevolence, and generally those who accept a plurality of duties do not accept this. (What would have to be missing from any such non-consequentialist ethic would be any significant right to pursue one's own projects or give one's own interests any special priority.) The general merit of Singer's argument, which makes his original article a *locus classicus* (frequently reprinted), is that it presses on us the need to take seriously the category of *negative responsibility*. If we are not, as few are, persuaded that we ought to intervene *as much as we can*, we need to accept that some such intervention is a dimension to the moral life; then the challenge is: how much and in what ways?

4. ARGUMENTS AGAINST AID

Before turning to an examination of other positive accounts of the nature of our obligations to alleviate hunger and poverty more generally, it is worth pausing to consider the kinds of arguments supporting the claim that the affluent in a rich country do not have obligations to alleviate hunger and poverty in another poor country, nor correspondingly that rich countries have a duty to give aid to poor countries for the same reason.

In respect to individuals, the arguments fall into three distinct categories which for moral analysis it is important to distinguish. The conclusion that the rich should help the poor in another country may be resisted on three grounds: (1) aid does not work: aid is ineffective and does no good; (2) libertarianism: we should not accept a moral theory that postulates a duty of *general* benevolence towards other people, whether they live in one's own country or not; and (3) obligations are not global in scope: whatever one's obligations within one's own society or country, these obligations are either non-existent or much weaker in respect of people living outside one's own country. It will be noted that the first argument is not as such a moral argument but a *factual* claim, and a controversial one at that; the second is a normative claim about the *content* of one's ethical norms; and the third is a claim about the *scope* of moral obligations and in effect about how moral obligations arise in respect to other people.

4.1 Aid does not Work

Garrett Hardin's argument in essays like 'Lifeboat Ethics: The Case against Helping the Poor' (1977) exemplifies the first type of argument, though in fact his arguments are a blend of empirical claims and normative claims. The first empirical claim is that rich countries are like lifeboats in being able to maintain their carrying capacity in terms of food supplies only if they refuse to share what they have with the poor of the third world, who are drowning in the sea around them (where sharing might be done either by passing food out as aid or by allowing open access immigration). The normative claim involved in Hardin's analysis here relies on the lifeboat analogy to justify the supposed right of affluent nations to take the line of refusing to help those outside their borders. The second empirical claim is that providing food aid to the hungry does no good for the hungry; indeed, it makes things worse, because by helping to keep them alive one is merely contributing to greater problems in the future because populations will expand even more rapidly, thus creating the conditions for even greater famines and suffering in the future.

Amongst the various objections that can be raised to this line of argument, I will mention two. The first argument, which combines the *empirical* claim with the *moral* claim associated with lifeboats, gets much of its force from the simplicity of the metaphor, which is wholly inadequate to the complexities of the world situation. Poor people are not in any case in the sea but in other lifeboats—that is, countries. As Aiken (1996) has argued, the wealth of rich countries is intimately connected with complex patterns of trade and exchange between all countries, and the implied ethic of self-sufficient countries is simply inapplicable. Our extensive involvement with other countries simply prevents us from seeing ourselves as not belonging to the same ethical domain as other countries. This renders us ethically responsible (in part) for what happens in other countries, if we both accept a duty to alleviate suffering where it is possible to do so, and also accept that this is possible vis-à-vis the distant poor. The latter claim is what is disputed in Hardin's second argument.

In response to the second argument, two things are worth noting; first, as O'Neill observes, this is a consequentialist argument claiming that non-intervention is optimific in the long run. Now, whether this is right or wrong, the basis of the argument here is not that different from that of Singer, which is also consequentialist; the only difference is that they each have radically different readings of the empirical facts (O'Neill 1989). Secondly, Hardin's reading of the facts seems to be implausible, at least if we see famine relief in the wider context in which it needs to be seen. To be sure, if food aid were something conducted in total isolation from any other policies, such aid might in many cases have the consequences Hardin predicts. But food aid does not happen in isolation. Hardin himself is well aware that there are good arguments for development assistance (he quotes 'give a man a fish you feed him for a day; teach him to fish and he feeds himself for a lifetime'), but does not seem to see the corollary of this: food aid *coupled with* development aid does not have the negative consequences that he associates with food aid on its own.

The argument against aid that it does not work is, of course, more elaborate than I have made out. It does not merely depend on claims that it compounds problems in the long run; it also depends on claims that it leads to wider environmental problems (and there is another very big set of issues here concerning the links between poverty and environmental degradation). The argument is also based on a certain reading of the aid record as being a chapter of disasters, and is backed by a certain kind of conceptual claim made by Peter Bauer and others that aid by its very nature undermines genuine development, for the simple reason that aid creates dependency whereas proper development for the poor involves empowerment and autonomy (e.g. Bauer 1984).

The reply to this kind of reasoning needs to be of the following form: we need to distinguish between the claim that aid cannot work and the claim that it generally does not work. Since it would be extraordinary to claim that no forms of 'assistance' actually assisted those they were trying to assist, we cannot conclude that overseas aid is necessarily bad for those who are aided. We therefore need to distinguish between good and bad forms of aid. And, so long as this is recognized, anyone who accepts a general duty of benevolence and wants to help a certain target group of people suffering from extreme hunger should simply recognize a derivative duty to become informed about which forms of aid are successful and which not. The duty to give aid contains within it the duty to be informed. (An uninformed or ill-informed good will, *pace* Kant, may not be as good as a well-informed good will.) It is not enough to say this and nothing more. After all, if relatively few forms of aid did actually work and it was hard work finding out what these were, a moral agent might well not support aid programmes to help alleviate distant poverty as much as she might, were there plenty of effective programmes around and properly known about. Whilst I hold that the record of donor programmes is on balance reasonably positive and so I am inclined to think that this kind of objection from 'difficulty' can be answered, it is clear that one's position on this depends more upon factual information than on what ethical theorizing can establish (Riddell 1987).

4.2 Libertarianism

The second kind of objection to the idea of a duty to help the distant poor depends on a rejection of the idea of general benevolence as part of one's ethical code. In recent years this kind of position has come to be associated with the label 'libertarianism'. However, libertarianism has at least two forms to it, one a political interpretation, the other an ethical interpretation (though in another sense they are both ethical in the sense of being normative). The political interpretation has to do with what the state may legitimately do; on this view, associated, for example, with Nozick, the state cannot legitimately take more than minimum amount of freedom from its subjects, since subjects will consent only to what is necessary to protect their rights to liberty (Nozick 1974). This entails that any action dependent on progressive taxation aimed at redistributing wealth from the better off to the worse off is unjust, and so a fortiori any attempt by the state to transfer wealth raised by taxation to benefit poor people in other countries is ruled out as unacceptable. Such a doctrine about the limits on legitimate state power leaves open of course the possibility that individuals might, on the same overall ethical theory, have duties of benevolence towards others, whether in their own society or in others. But here the obligations would be seen as obligations voluntarily assumed by the individual not coerced by state taxation.

Whilst political libertarianism then is consistent with a more robust account of benevolent duties in individuals, it often goes hand in hand with a more basic libertarian position at the level of individual morality (Narveson 2000). That is, the individual is seen as having nothing or little in the way of general obligation to help others when they need help. Here we need to distinguish carefully general obligations of benevolence from specific obligations to particular others. The latter may exist in virtue of such facts as the natural ties of family obligation, obligations assumed between friends, and duties of service entered into by formal agreement. This philosophy that might be summed up as 'the duty not to cause harm but no duty to come to the aid of those harmed' can be seen as a minimalist moral theory, and to be motivated by a certain kind of conventionalist or contractual conception of how morality arises (Harman 1977). If each person is seen as entering into a contract to cooperate for mutual advantage, the duty to come to the aid of others is not seen as vital as the duty not to harm others (in their person, reputation, or property) clearly is. If such an ethic is accepted, there are two alternative consequences so far as one's attitude towards others in need is concerned; one might indeed sometimes be motivated by compassion or concern to help them, but this would be beyond any call of duty and depend on one's altruistic impulses; or one might simply remain indifferent to the plight of others.

What should one make of such responses to human suffering, whether on one's doorstep or in distant lands? Two arguments out of many may be mentioned here.

Starting with the political argument, a general strategy is to try and show that implicit in the values accepted by the libertarian is in fact a commitment to give aid to those whose life and liberty are undermined. Sterba, for instance, who generally pursues a 'reconciliationist' path, has argued that, if we recognize that, whilst the rich may wish to exercise their liberty to keep their wealth, the poor may also wish to exercise their liberty to take wealth from the rich in order to feed themselves and escape extreme poverty, so some kind of compromise needs to be struck in which some wealth is redistributed and everyone's liberty is given a value (Sterba 1996; see also Shue 1996b).

There are similar arguments against the moral claim that we have no moral duty to help others. Either the libertarian is driven into acknowledging her position as essentially egoistic because the lives and liberties of others are in fact of no value to her. Or she must acknowledge that the lives and liberties of other humans—indeed any other humans anywhere—have a value and that morality has something to do with promoting and protecting these values. Since the latter involves maintaining or creating the conditions necessary for these values to be realized, and these conditions include both stable social structures and material conditions, such as access to resources including especially food, one at least should have some obligation to promote these conditions. Of course the libertarian can still interpret the right to life and liberty as something to which we are ethically committed, but claim that all that we are ethically committed to is a duty of non-interference. That is, these rights are merely negative rights; we must not deprive people of their liberty or their lives. But such a move, though possible, then leaves one with having to accept that the value of life and liberty does not have much normative force, since it does not include the value of the effective exercise of liberty or the effective enjoyment of a life.

4.3 Obligations Are not Global in Scope

The third kind of resistance to the claim that the rich in the north have an obligation to alleviate hunger and poverty in the south rests on a variety of considerations intended to show that we do not really belong to a global moral community, or at least to one that is as robust and as meaningful as the particular moral and political communities in which we all live and from which we derive our primary moral obligations and allegiances. Thus obligation towards those in other countries is either denied or regarded as marginal. Some of the arguments relate to what states should do, some to what individuals should do (though the arguments are connected).

International Scepticism and Internationalism

So far as states are concerned, out-and-out realists will deny that states have any obligations to other states: in the absence of a world 'common power' (in Hobbes's sense), there is either no morality (because morality requires the enforceability of common rules) or, if there is, the norms of morality are generally overridden by the right to maintain national interests because we live in an insecure world. If aid is given, it is either because of strategic interests that are gained or because governments need to be sensitive to the sentiments of their electorate when these require responses to disaster and some development assistance. However, in reply, we should note that, apart from the fact that enforceability is not a prerequisite of obligation, the image of a radically insecure world assumed here does not fit the facts of globalization in the beginning of the twenty-first century—300 years on from the kind of world conceptualized by Hobbes and other architects of realism (see Dower 1998).

More plausible and more prevalent is what is known as the 'internationalist' paradigm, which asserts that there is a morality of states that has evolved in the last few hundred years, but it is a limited morality based largely on the agreements of states themselves, stressing sovereignty and non-intervention. Part of its orientation comes from the recognition of political pluralism and more generally cultural relativism: since visions of the good and of social order vary significantly throughout the world, the function of the international community is to maintain peace and international order and not to promote more specific agendas. In so far as a duty to aid other countries is concerned, this may be acknowledged, but it is, at least as things stand now, a limited one, since it is based on two factors. First, it is based on the development of international humanitarian and human right law and on specific international agreements (like rich countries giving 0.7 per cent of GNP in official aid, agreed in the 1970s but never fully lived up to anyway), and, secondly, it is based on what a country's electorate may indicate should be done. Of course, citizens may have a variety of reasons for wanting aid, but the chances are that it is because a significant number accept a thesis that wealthy countries and wealthy individuals in them should give some support to alleviate hunger and poverty.

Cosmopolitan Replies

From the point of view of the cosmopolitan, these developments are to be welcomed but do not go far enough. The cosmopolitan is someone who sees the whole world as one moral community in which individuals have (even though many do not recognize this) obligations towards fellow human beings anywhere, and that governments of rich countries, for instance, have obligations to give aid that are a function of the basic moral vision of a world community rather than a function of what their electorates happen to be thinking. Cosmopolitanism is in part a moral doctrine with implications for political theory and how international relations are justified. This is striking, for instance, in attempts to apply Rawls's theory to international relations by Beitz (1979) and Pogge (1989). These theories develop a conception of global justice that requires significant redistribution of the world's resources in favour of poor countries, as do other theories such as that of Brian Barry (1989, 1995), who founds his global theory on the principle of impartiality.

The cosmopolitan approach is also a political or institutional conception in its own right; if we are members or citizens (*polites*) of a world community, we need to develop appropriate institutions through which to express our commitments. Apart from developing stronger inter'national' institutions, the increasing role of international NGOs and of networks of concerned individuals (using the Internet, for instance) is seen both as morally important and as something that is developing anyway (Held and McGrew 2000).

Much of the recent literature that has a bearing on the international commitment to tackle the problems of hunger and poverty actually focuses on the issues of institutional globalization. There are various discourses around—like that of global civil society (Linklater 1998), cosmopolitan democracy (Held 1995), global governance (Commission on Global Governance 1995), and global citizenship (Hutchings and Dannreuther 1998)—but they all have a bearing on the development in individuals of a cosmopolitan identity and set of loyalties. It should be noted that the development of these does not establish the relevant global ethic; rather, they presuppose it and give it embodiment and therefore more effective expression with more people coming to accept it. The ethic itself may well be one that has been around for a long time or one that is seen as in some sense timelessly valid (Nussbaum et al. 1996).

Many of the main ethical theories have been implicitly global or cosmopolitan in approach. This is true of utilitarianism (already discussed in connection with Singer), Kantianism, human-rights theories, the ethical systems of the major religions, and more recent approaches such as biocentrism. They may not always style themselves 'cosmopolitan', but they contain the two central features essential to a cosmopolitan or global ethic: first, some commitment to universal values (for example, a core conception of what human well-being consists in) and, secondly, some commitment to obligations that in principle are global in scope (Dower 1998). The position of virtue ethics in this regard is open, in that there is no reason why such an approach should not be global in approach, and is so, for instance, in the thinking of Martha Nussbaum and in much neo-Aristotelian thinking about development ethics. On the other hand, there is nothing in the general approach that entails that the virtues have to be understood as involving relationships of a global nature. Many of our familiar ethical systems are like this, but not all of them. Before attending to some of these as alternatives to utilitarianism, I need to round off the consideration of arguments against global obligation at the level of the individual.

Relativist and Communitarian Objections

There are broadly two sources of resistance: relativism (and lying behind this certain forms of postmodern thinking) and communitarianism. Relativism essentially disputes the first premise of a global ethic, by denying that there are universal values; and communitarianism disputes the second premise, by denying that we have significant obligations towards those outside our own community, since obligations arise from shared traditions.

Relativism no doubt has a point in stressing that conceptions of the good and of moral norms do vary somewhat and that there is no reason to suppose that all conceptions need to be the same. But this does not preclude recognition that there is a common core of elements of human well-being (such as freedom from hunger) that are universal, both in the sense of being accepted universally and in the sense of 'being universally the same about human beings'. Nor does it preclude the idea that there might be obligations across borders to attend to those common elements, such as the removal of hunger.

Communitarianism has been much in vogue of late, both as a response to liberalism (Sandel 1982) and as a response to cosmopolitanism (though that does not make cosmopolitanism necessarily liberal) (Brown 1992). There are two strategies for replying to it. The first is to turn it on its head by arguing that cultural globalization has already created the conditions of global community and, more generally, the existence of multiple communities to which individuals may belong. The second is to argue that, whatever shared traditions may do to give particular shape to obligations and to give motivation to agents, morality arises from facts that are universal as opposed to the facts based on the particularity of a shared culture. These universal facts include the fact that we have common vulnerabilities and the fact that we interact with one another as agents, recognizing one another as agents, irrespective of whether 'the other' belongs to one's own immediate community or not. The issues are complex and it is not possible to pursue them here (but see Dower 1998).

Let us now turn to some other positive approaches that avoid some of the difficulties with the kind of view presented by Singer but do not withdraw, for libertarian, relativist, or communitarian reasons, from accepting significant obligation.

5. KANTIANISM

Onora O'Neill has become one of the best-known modern exponents of a broadly Kantian approach to the problems of world hunger and poverty (e.g. O'Neill 1989). Several features of her account are worth highlighting. First, the condition of extreme poverty and neediness is one of disempowerment, an undermining of rational agency or autonomy. Secondly, one of the significant causes of this condition, apart from the contributions made by natural causes, are the actions of other agents, who often take advantage of the poor's weakness and ignorance, by deceiving them and coercing them. Thirdly, as moral agents we have duties ourselves not only not to coerce or deceive others but also to respect the rational agency of others like the poor by taking action to remove the conditions that undermine rational agency. This involves both supporting appropriate aid programmes, and opposing the actions of agencies such as transnational companies that themselves deceive and coerce the poor. Fourthly, as a theory of agency, it focuses on the perspective of the agent not that of the poor (as opposed to rights theories that focus on the poor) and, fifthly, it makes the point that agencies with moral responsibility are not merely individuals but also corporate agents such as governments and companies.

This strong account provides a useful corrective to the earlier account we considered. The emphasis on the point that the problem for the poor is disempowerment and lack of rational autonomy gives us a richer account of why poverty is an evil. It also gives us guidance about what sorts of aid programme are more likely to be successful—namely, those that treat the poor as agents contributing to the solution to their own problems rather than as merely passive recipients whose suffering is being relieved by the actions of others. On the other hand, precisely this emphasis gives rise to a problem that is opposite to that facing utilitarianism mentioned earlier, since the impression may be gained that the reason why extreme suffering (hunger, illness), disease, and frustration of preferences is bad is because they undermine rational agency; that is, they are causes of or indications of what is bad and it is this other 'bad' state that gives rise to the obligation to do something about it. Yet, suffering, disease, and failure in the satisfaction of preferences are all bad in and of themselves. Kant's own formulation of the categorical imperative in terms of treating people as ends not merely means invites this difficulty since it is as rational ends that we have the values to be respected. It may be that latter-day Kantians such as O'Neill and recently Korsgaard (1996) are right to feel this limitation can be circumvented within a Kantian framework (a similar issue arises vis-à-vis the status of animals), but the point remains that a rounded account is needed of why poverty is an evil to be addressed. The point at issue is whether from a Kantian framework one can treat the fact that human beings (like animals) are physically vulnerable, finite beings capable of suffering as providing the grounds for duty, independent of the fact that humans are rational agents.

The other point to be made, which turns out to be a problem for almost any theory in this area, is that of determining how much any individual is obligated to take action, beyond herself not coercing and not deceiving. Kant, of course, sees benevolence as helping those in need as something we are required as a matter of imperfect duty to engage in (on pain of rational inconsistency, since we will that, were we in need, we would be helped). He had in mind no doubt the situation of someone placed before one in need, rather like the drowning child in Singer's example; but, of course, if one included all those situations where one could help those in need indirectly (here's Oxfam's address; here's my cheque book . . .), the duty of benevolence would quickly become an iterative or maximizing duty in the manner of Singer, and, although the reasoning would be different, the general effect on affluent agents might be much the same. Since it is unlikely that either Kant or Kantians intend this interpretation, we are left with the question: how much should I take action to further the conditions of autonomy for the poor? Clearly O'Neill sees us being proactive about our obligations, so one is left with a rather open-ended invitation. This may be how things have to stand, though it is possible that other theories will fare better on this issue.

6. HUMAN RIGHTS

Let us now turn to human rights as another approach to the issue. A number of writers in recent years have found it appropriate to defend the case for aid on the basis of human rights (Nickel 1996; Shue 1996b; Li 1996). This is partly because human-rights discourse has become very well established in international arenas, and is reflected in much international law and many regional conventions. This does not, of course, show that as a moral theory human-rights theory is any better than rival theories, since the existence of human-rights law and indeed support for its development could come from many different theories.

Is there a right to food? It would seem that, if there are any rights at all that belong to all humans as such and are natural in the sense that they pertain to what is essential to a human leading a life as a human, then the right to food would be amongst them. Food, as Shue points out, is both a vital and a vulnerable good—and these are the goods we think of as constitutive of a person's basic rights (Shue 1996b). Such a right to food, like more generally a right to life, is not merely a negative right—a right not to have food taken from one—but a positive right to have food available to one. Such a general right, it is argued, correlates with a general duty on the part of others to bring it about that the right is realized. As Shue argued in another work (1996a), such socially basic rights are the minimum demand of all humanity on all humanity.

How much then should the individual do? As Shue notes, there are really two alternatives: limitless duties or limited duties. The problem with the former is that it would become totally exhausting with all the problems attendant on Singer's position of 'as much as you can'. On the other hand, if one has a duty only to do one's share of what would be necessary if everyone in a position to do so did their share, that hardly seems enough, particularly in a world where palpably most people are not doing their share. In any case, there are immense problems about working out what one's share would be—pro rata according to one's wealth, a fixed amount for people above a certain income level, or what?

These problems become compounded when we recognize that trying to work out how much money or wealth each individual should contribute is going about the problem in the wrong way: it assumes that cumulative impacts from individuals will solve the problems of hunger and poverty. This is unlikely, since it would not

alter the political and institutional structures within which poverty is often perpetuated. If the right to food is to be realized, many structural changes are needed. This
is linked to the point that, whereas all people have negative duties not to deprive
people of what they have a right to, it is not clear that the positive duty to protect
people from being deprived of rights rests primarily with ordinary people rather
than state agencies. This is particularly so with regard to standard threats that are
anticipatable by public measures. On the other hand, if we take to heart the spirit
of Shue's position mentioned earlier that basic rights are the minimum demand of
all on all, there is certainly much that individuals can do that is consistent with seeing the larger tasks belonging to various agencies. And, in so far as state agencies are
not doing, or cannot do, all that is necessary, the matter comes back to individuals:
how far does one act to change things? These complexities do not remove the pivotal role of the individual and hence the need to stress that the ethical basis is *cosmopolitan*, both in stressing obligations that are global in scope and in stressing the
importance of seeing oneself as a member or 'citizen' of the world community.

There does not appear to be any magic answer or formula here for determining
how much or what individuals should do—either in the case of rights or in other
theories. Since 'doing one's share' is almost meaningless and 'doing all one can'
unacceptable, the matter may have to be left to individual conscience—with circumstance, opportunity, solidarity with, and knowledge of one group rather than
another and so on making a difference. That is not to say that there are not other
ways of tackling the 'how-much?' question, but these are not pursued here. Leaving
it to individual conscience does not, however, make it simply a subjective matter, so
that someone could decide not to do anything at all. The broad parameters are
given—significant obligation, a global scope, and so on—and what is needed is
Aristotelian 'judgement' about time and place in regard to what have traditionally
been called imperfect or meritorious duties.

One of the factors that makes things open-ended is that, although almost anyone
who is willing to talk of basic moral rights or human rights will assert a right to
food as basic, it is rather less clear how many other rights are to be admitted as
basic—political liberty, religious freedom, having a family of whatever size one
wants, environmental security, work, education, health, rule of law and due process,
personal safety, culture. Although, to use UN jargon, all such rights are said to be
'indivisible' and such that each is mutually supportive of the others, in reality hard
choices have to be made as to which rights are given priority.

Although human-rights theories are important because they firmly locate the
focus of attention on individuals whose good is meant to be the point of other
agents having duties (Mackie 1984), there is a sense in which such theories are
incomplete in that they presuppose, but do not provide, an account of what human
good or well-being consists in. This is borne out by the fact that there can be serious disputes as to what are the basic rights to be recognized. Thus the richness or
adequacy of a theory of rights will in part be a function of the richness or adequacy

of the theorist's account of what human well-being consists of, which relies on a wider theory of value drawn from other theories (or elements in them) being considered here.

7. Neo-Aristotelianism

We noted earlier that in certain respects a utilitarian account of well-being in terms of pleasure/pain and/or preference satisfaction was one-sided, as was the Kantian account in terms of the exercise of rational autonomy, but that each picked out something important. We could simply combine the insights of the two. On the other hand we have a distinctive approach to thinking about human well-being in the context of development issues which attempts to provide a fully rounded account. This is the neo-Aristotelian approach developed *inter alia* by Amartya Sen (1993), Martha Nussbaum (1992) and David Crocker (for a survey of the approach of Sen and Nussbaum, see Crocker 1992), sometimes referred to as the 'capabilities' approach. It certainly addresses ethical issues raised by hunger and famine, but the set of issues here is a somewhat broader set of issues from those that are concerned with the duty of individuals, in that what is important is the identification of the appropriate kinds of development policies for tackling the problems (Crocker 1996). Such prescriptions have a direct relevance to the work of governments in poorer countries, to aid agencies, and to the international community in terms of bilateral and multilateral support.

The broader model of appropriate development (in which appropriate responses to famine feature as a part) focuses on the fact that human beings have a wide range of capabilities or capacities that need to be developed and exercised in what is called 'functionings', if human beings are to live well. These capabilities range over many dimensions of human flourishing, from proper bodily functioning, adequate nutrition, range of pleasures, exercise of rational powers in a variety of ways, creativity, friendship, participation in community, and so on.

The appeal of this approach is that it gets beyond the quantificational approach of much standard economic analysis and it gets beyond a rather too abstract characterization of human well-being in the other *ethical* critiques of standard economic analysis. Thus it stresses that you cannot measure development in terms of quantity of income or for that matter quantities of food. A given income may enable many functionings in one case but rather fewer in another. Different bodies require different levels of food intake for nutritional health. On the other hand, abstract accounts in terms of pleasure, utility, preference satisfaction, or exercise of choice do not get to the heart of the matter—precisely what it is that is needed for a person's capacities to be properly exercised.

8. DEVELOPMENT ETHICS

What this approach illustrates is a more general feature of much recent writing in the field of what is called 'development ethics'—namely, the assertion that development is essentially a normative concept, and that the account of well-being needed by which to measure whether 'progress' is made is significantly more complex than the standard models of economic growth suppose. The capabilities approach also claims as one of its merits that its critique of standard economic growth models is more effective than the relatively formalistic accounts of well-being in terms of utility, pleasure, preference satisfaction (utilitarianism), or choice (liberalism). Within the emerging literature on development ethics, this claim is disputed.

What is generally agreed within development ethics as a self-conscious academic discourse is the claim that development as the process of socio-economic change that is pursued by governments (and other agencies) stands in need of critical assessment. Development cannot simply be seen as economic growth. Even those who defend that model are challenged to justify it in terms of the values it is meant to serve. The various analyses of 'good' development based on utilitarian thinking, human needs, Kantianism, basic rights, capabilities, and so on have a large amount in common in critically assessing economic growth models—in so far as simple growth may not map appropriately and therefore not bring about appropriately increases in human well-being (Aman 1991). This is either because it lacks a proper principle of just distribution, or, even if it did have that (as 'growth-with-equity' models claimed to do), it may, for instance, involve increases of income but, because of social dislocation, fail to bring increases in well-being. Each ethical model will claim it properly identifies the criteria for assessing 'progress'. To what extent any one of them would, if generally adopted, lead to development that was more of an improvement on standard economic models than those based on other ethical models is difficult to determine. At any rate, the general import of 'development ethics' is to be seen as salutary in that it effectively puts the mainstream economic approach in the ethical spotlight, enabling or challenging the latter to recognize the value assumptions implicit in its own approach.

Whilst the capabilities approach presents what may be seen as the most complex model of human well-being by which to measure and define development, it is not clear that it provides the full ethical picture unless it is supplemented with other ethical insights. Although its strong point is the account of the assumptions about 'well-being' implicit in development, it leaves two key issues relatively unattended—first, the nature, extent, and justification of the duty of others to facilitate this development (already noted), and, secondly, the issue of 'just distribution'. Granted that we have an adequate account of human well-being, there still remains the question of how the conditions of well-being are to be distributed. This leads to the familiar controversies between welfarists and libertarians. I would note only that the issue is an important one both at national and at international levels.

Whilst the presuppositions about the 'good' in an account like Rawls's may be criticized by the capabilities approach, the key question in Rawls—what is a just distribution of whatever well-being constitutes?—remains. It does not go away because the capabilities approach focuses on another issue. At an international level the issues are also rather important, since the ethical character of foreign policy is at stake. Foreign policy affects the conditions for development in other countries profoundly, so that the extent to which countries are willing to accept some ethical principle requiring the sharing of wealth between rich and poor countries will make a profound difference. Charles Beitz (1979) and Thomas Pogge (1989) amongst others have attempted to develop an account of global distributive justice, extending Rawls's own model to the global level. Now, whether one accepts this kind of approach to global justice or develops another one, the point remains that this issue reflects a very wide interpretation of the 'normative' aspects of development—certainly development discourse is not merely about 'the good', it is about 'the right' as well.

9. Further Issues

The main focus has been on the ethical basis for concern for world hunger. But, if we accept that rich individuals and rich governments have significant obligations, there remain a number of further ethical issues that arise from this and that are worthy of mention in rounding off the discussion. These issues can be seen as arising from different dimensions. First, there is the issue: who is to be helped? Secondly, there is the issue relating to the question: what is the relationship between the goal of alleviating hunger/poverty and other morally defensible goals in public policy and/or private pursuit? There are several possibilities here: in some cases, other goals may be seen as complementary to, if not providing a wider context for, this goal, such as general policies of global trade. In some cases, there may be competition for resources between these goals and other goals, such as the pursuit of peace. In other cases, there may be direct conflict between these goals and other goals such as the preservation of a natural habitat.

9.1 Who Is to be Helped?

Whether we accept a very extensive obligation to help alleviate world hunger/poverty or a more limited but significant obligation, the issue arises: since we cannot help more than a small percentage of people, who should be helped? The same issue will arise for any government trying to determine where to send its aid. It may be thought that this is not really an ethical issue but a pragmatic issue. Granted that there is some arbitrariness about which group gets chosen to be given help, what will determine the choice will be factors like opportunity and effectiveness. An individual may choose an aid agency to support because its record is good or because there is an active branch in her locality. The agency or a government department might choose a development project because of historical relations or because it has access to a given area and believes the target group has the right motivation to benefit, and so on. Such selection is consistent with the principle that *all* the poor are equally deserving of our attention or have the same basic rights to assistance.

On the other hand, the poor might not be seen as all equally 'deserving', in the sense that there may be certain features of the poor or their situation that reduce their claim on us—for example, they do not make any efforts themselves, or are involved in a civil war or other dangerous pursuits, or have a different religious or political affiliation.

In practice this distinction may not be very clear. One complex example is the UK Government's policy on foreign aid as revealed in its 1997 White Paper entitled *Eliminating World Poverty* (DFID 1997). Entry into partnership agreements with third-world countries is made dependent upon their governments adopting 'good governance'—human-rights protection, transparency, and some form of democratic process and accountability. Although this is very different from older and more common forms of conditionality of aid (for example, aid linked to donor goods and services), it is nevertheless, whether justified or not, a form of conditionality. Although this may look like a *pragmatic* selection of some countries and not others—that is, because countries adopting these values are more likely to tackle extreme poverty effectively—it can also be seen as an ideological preference for those countries that already share or are willing to adopt the donor's values. More generally, any attempt by countries, agencies, and individuals to select groups to help on the basis of a shared value system—similar religion, church, or political ideology—is selecting a target group for reasons *over and above* the duty to reduce the evil of hunger and poverty, since that duty alone would not suffice to differentiate it from other needy groups.

9.2 The Wider Context

We have already noted that discussions of hunger and poverty need to be situated in wider discussions of the nature and dynamics of development itself. But they also need to be situated in wider discussions of the whole range of interactions between rich countries and poor countries, particularly in the economic sphere. The trade relations between countries impact powerfully on the economic prospects of poor countries and poor people within them; given the imbalance of power, the terms of trade often favour richer countries. More particularly, the control of biotechnology by large transnationals raises ethical issues about the effects of such control, especially through the use of patents. Transnational companies operate extensively in poorer countries and this raises a cluster of ethical issues to do with such things as workers' conditions and environmental protection (as witnessed by recent controversies surrounding meetings of the World Trade Organization). Last but not least, third-world-debt servicing is one of the major modern contributory factors towards endemic poverty. Apart from any other ethical arguments for cancelling such debt (as the movement Jubilee 2000 argued), there is a marked paradox in a situation in which governments and international lending institutions expect payment back at far higher levels than the levels of official aid given in return. There is a strong argument for making this dimension of foreign policy—aid, debt relief, and trade generally—consistent with itself. Otherwise the rationale for aid is undermined.

9.3 Other Objectives

Policies aimed at reducing hunger and poverty are not, of course, the only policies that governments or individuals may feel a moral obligation to pursue vis-à-vis the well-being of those outside their country. Policies aimed at combating human-rights violations, or at curbing environmental degradation (whether for anthropocentric or biocentric reasons), or at building peace may be seen as equally important. Although these goals may be seen to complement each other—at least most of the time—it needs to be recognized that, given a limited amount of resources, they do compete for priority as objects of direct attention.

9.4 Conflict

There may be times, however, in which there is a direct conflict between the goal of hunger or poverty alleviation and other goals that are seen as ethically important. Perhaps the most obvious area for this is environmental concerns of certain kinds. Holmes Rolston (1996), for instance, raised the prospect of conflict between the preservation of species and habitats and letting poor people destroy these to preserve their livelihoods, and he argued that sometimes the preservation of species took precedence. This is a more serious ethical issue than one of mere competition for limited resources (though often 'development-versus-environment' dilemmas are of the latter nature), since the condition for the fulfilment of one goal may be precisely the denial of the condition for the fulfilment of another goal. (Conflicts over issues to do with 'place' are often like this—for example, over rival claims to religious sites and conflicts over traditional cultural sites wanted for commercial exploitation.) Not all conflicts can be resolved in a 'win–win' way.

On the other hand, the general message to be gained from considering both competition for resources and deeper conflicts is the need to find ways of reducing the number of such dilemmas that have to be resolved in 'win–lose' outcomes. Thus there is a need to develop structures locally, nationally, and internationally, in which such dilemmas are less likely to emerge—for example, by trying to promote policies that genuinely pursue 'sustainable development' (see e.g. Dobson 1998, 1999; Holland et al. 2000). This requires at the very least an integrated ethical approach.

If the arguments outlined in this chapter are right, the need ethically to address hunger and extreme poverty will feature centrally in such an integrated approach.

10. Conclusion

The conclusion falls into two parts. I first indicate where I think the overall argument has led. Secondly, I comment on how the discussion illustrates certain features of applied ethics itself.

10.1 The Overall Argument

In this chapter I have attempted primarily to survey the main issues and the main positions taken on these, at least in recent discussions in Western academic communities, and to indicate the strengths and weaknesses in the various positions taken. In the course of this a general position has emerged that I regard as defensible, though I am aware that it needs a fuller defence than is given here.

Whilst modern analyses of aid and development show that the response to hunger cannot be simply that of the affluent using their resources to enable the hungry to get food, the ethical challenge to affluent individuals still remains. This is both because they are able to influence the political and institutional processes that are needed to tackle the conditions of hunger and extreme poverty, and because there is still ample room for appropriate humanitarian responses of a personal kind. What then are the nature and extent of this obligation or responsibility? Although the various accounts such as utilitarianism, Kantianism, and neo-Aristotelianism each provide insights into the complex nature of well-being and thus into what makes hunger and extreme poverty evils, a human-rights framework provides us with an account of why we should care about the evils that befall others. Since there seems good reason neither to adopt a maximizing principle that we should do all we can nor to adopt a minimalist 'do only that which is needed were everyone to do their share' (let alone to adopt a libertarian view that denies general benevolence altogether), we are left with the claim that we have a significant though indeterminate obligation to help alleviate hunger and extreme poverty. An important part of the account needs to be the recognition that, since relativism and international realism need to be rejected, we belong to one global ethical domain or 'global community', so that the obligations of general caring that are part of what it is to belong to a moral community extend to the global level.

10.2 Applied Ethics

Discussion of the ethical issues surrounding world hunger have amply illustrated the kinds of issues that are central to applied ethics.

First, differences in what individuals ought to do or what governments ought to do may be partly a matter of empirical disagreement (for example, two utilitarians might disagree about what the long-term effects of giving food aid will be) and partly a matter of disagreement about ethical principles (for example, a libertarian may reject the idea that we have extensive duties to give aid to strangers, although a utilitarian might assert this).

Secondly, thinkers might agree that hunger ought to be alleviated by contributions from the affluent, but disagree on their reasons for this: thus a utilitarian might see addressing hunger as the most effective way to promote the greatest balance of good over evil in the world, whereas a human-rights theorist or a Kantian may argue that what we do vis-à-vis the hungry is something owed to them specifically.

Thirdly, it illustrates well the powerful attractions of as well as problems with examples based on vivid metaphors and with arguments based on intuitions one is supposed to have in connection with these examples—two examples being the obligation to save a child drowning in a pond and the rights of individuals on a lifeboat with limited supplies.

Fourthly, discussion of world hunger quickly shows that applied ethics is in some respects misdescribed, since it is not the application of pre-set values or principles to some set of problems. The exercise may well engage one's thinking about ethics generally. Taking a careful look at an issue and checking what one might initially think about the issue against wider considerations may well lead to a deepening or modification of what one says about the basic norms of morality as well as about the nature of morality, or lead to a modification of what one thinks about the issue. For instance, one's conception of moral community may well be modified, given conceptions of community often assumed in recent communitarian debates with liberals and/or cosmopolitans. Thus one's conception of morality has to be such as to make sense of the considered judgements in a given area.

Fifthly, as we saw in Section 10.4, ethical discussions cannot be isolated. There we were concerned with the need to integrate discussions about what ought to be done about world hunger with those about other global issues to do, for instance, with the environment, peace, or human rights. Thus, although applied ethics is by its nature specialized in focus—hence this chapter amongst many others in this book—it is clear that its inner drive is nevertheless towards an ethical synthesis in the final analysis.

References

Aiken, W. (1996). 'The "Carrying Capacity" Equivocation', in Aiken and LaFollette (1996), 16–25.

—— and LaFollette, H. (1977) (eds.), *World Hunger and Moral Obligation*. Englewood Cliffs, NJ: Prentice Hall.

—— —— (1996) (eds.), *World Hunger and Morality*. Englewood Cliffs, NJ: Prentice Hall.

Aman, K. (1991) (ed.), *Ethical Principles for Development: Needs, Capacities and Rights*. Upper Montclair, NJ: Institute for Critical Thinking, Montclair State University.

Arthur, J. (1996). 'Rights and the Duty to Bring Aid', in Aiken and LaFollette (1996), 39–50.

Attfield, R., and Wilkins, B. (1992) (eds.), *International Justice and the Third World*. London: Routledge.

Barry, B. (1989). *Theories of Justice: A Treatise on Social Justice,* i. Hemel Hempstead: Harvester Wheatsheaf.

—— (1995). *Justice as Impartiality: A Treatise on Social Justice*, ii. Oxford: Oxford University Press.

Bauer, P. (1984). *Rhetoric and Reality*. London: Weidenfeld & Nicolson.

Beitz, C. R. (1979). *Political Theory and International Relations*. Princeton: Princeton University Press.

Brown, C. (1992). *International Relations Theory: New Normative Approaches*. New York: Harvester Wheatsheaf.

Commission on Global Governance (1995). *Our Global Neighbourhood*. Oxford: Oxford University Press.

Crocker, D. (1992). 'Functioning and Capability—the Foundation of Sen's and Nussbaum's Development Ethic'. *Political Theory*, 20/4: 584–612.

—— (1996). 'Hunger, Capability and Development', in Aiken and LaFollette (1996), 211–30.

Cullity, G. (1996). 'The Life-Saving Analogy', in Aiken and LaFollette (1996), 51–69.

DFID (1997). Department for International Development, *Eliminating World Poverty*. London: HMSO.

Dobson, A. (1998). *Justice and the Environment*. Oxford: Oxford University Press.

—— (1999) (ed.). *Fairness and Futurity*. Oxford: Oxford University Press.

Dower, N. (1983). *World Poverty Challenge and Response*. York: Ebor Press.

—— (1998). *World Ethics—the New Agenda*. Edinburgh: Edinburgh University Press.

Drèze, J., and Sen, A. (1990–1) (eds.), *The Politics of Hunger*. 3 vols. Oxford: Oxford University Press.

—— —— and Hussain, A. (1995) (eds.), *The Politics of Hunger—Selected Essays*. Oxford: Oxford University Press.

Engel, J. R., and Engel, J. B. (1990) (eds.), *Ethics of Environment and Development: Global Challenges and International Responsibilities*. London: Belhaven Press.

Fishkin, J. (1986). 'Theories of Justice and International Relations: The Limits of Liberal Theory', in A. Ellis (ed.), *Ethics and International Relations*. Manchester: Manchester University Press, 1–12.

Goulet, D. (1995). *Development Ethics—Theory and Practice*. London: Zed Books.

Hardin, G. (1977). 'Lifeboat Ethics: The Case against helping the poor', in Aiken and LaFollette (1977), 5–15.

Harman, G. (1977). *The Nature of Morality*. New York: Oxford University Press.

Harris, J. (1980). *Violence and Responsibility*. London: Routledge & Kegan Paul.

Held, D. (1995). *Democracy and Global Order*. Cambridge: Polity.

—— and McGrew, D. (2000) (eds.), *The Global Transformations Reader*. Cambridge: Polity.

Holland, A., Lee, K. and McNeill, D. (2000). *Global Sustainable Development in the Twenty-first Century*. Edinburgh: Edinburgh University Press.

Honderich, T. (1976). *Violence for Equality*. Harmondsworth: Penguin.

Hutchings, K., and Dannreuther, R. (1998) (eds.), *Cosmopolitan Citizenship*. London: Macmillan.

Kagan, K. (1991). *The Limits of Morality*. Oxford: Oxford University Press.

Korsgaard, C. (1996). *The Sources of Normativity*. Cambridge: Cambridge University Press.

Li Xiaorong (1996). 'Making Sense of the Right to Food', in Aiken and Lafollette (1996), 153–70.

Linklater, A. (1998). 'Cosmopolitan Citizenship', in Hutchings and Dannreuther (1998), 35–59.

Mackie, J. L. (1984). 'Can there be a Right-Based Moral Theory?', in J. Waldron (ed.), *Theories of Rights*. Oxford: Oxford University Press, 168–81.

Mephan, B. (1996) (ed.), *Food Ethics*. London: Routledge.

Narveson, J. (2000). 'Libertarianism', in H. LaFollette (ed.), *The Blackwell Guide to Ethical Theory*. Oxford: Blackwell 306–24.

Nickel, J. (1996). 'A Human Rights Approach to World Hunger', in Aiken and LaFollette (1996), 171–85.

Nozick, R. (1974). *Anarchy, State and Utopia*. Oxford: Blackwell.

Nussbaum, M. (1992). 'Human Functioning and Social Justice: in defense of Aristotelian Essentialism'. *Political Theory*, 20/2: 202–46.

—— et al. (1996). *For Love of Country*. Boston: Beacon Press.

O'Neill, O. (1989). *Faces of Hunger*. London: Allen & Unwin.

Pogge, T. (1989). *Realizing Rawls*. New York: Cornell University Press.

Rawls, J. (1971). *A Theory Justice*. Oxford: Oxford University Press.

Riddell, R. (1987). *Foreign Aid Reconsidered*. London: James Currey.

Rolston, H. (1996). 'Feeding People versus Saving Nature?', in Aiken and LaFollette (1996), 248–67.

Sandel, M. J. (1982). *Liberalism and the Limits to Justice*. Cambridge: Cambridge University Press.

Sen, A. (1981). *Poverty and Famines*. Oxford: Oxford University Press.

—— (1993). 'Capability and Wellbeing', in A. Sen and M. Nussbaum (eds.), *Quality of Life*. Oxford: Oxford University Press, 30–53.

—— (1995). 'Food, Economics & Entitlements', in Drèze et al. (1995), 56–68.

—— (1996). 'Goods and People', in Aiken and LaFollette (1996), 186–210.

Shue, H. (1996a). *Basic Rights: Subsistence, Affluence and US Foreign Policy*. 2nd edn. Princeton: Princeton University Press.

—— (1996*b*). 'Solidarity among Strangers and the Right to Food', in Aiken and LaFollette (1996), 113–32.

Singer, P. (1972). 'Famine, Affluence and Morality'. *Philosophy and Public Affairs*, 1/3: 229–43; repr. in Aiken and Lafollette (1996), 26–38.

—— (1979). *Practical Ethics*. Cambridge: Cambridge University Press.

Sterba, J. (1996). 'Global Justice', in Aiken and LaFollette (1996), 133–52.

Toyne, J., and O'Neill, H. (1998) (eds.), *A World without Famine?* London: Macmillan.

PART VI

LIFE AND DEATH

CHAPTER 26

EUTHANASIA AND PHYSICIAN-ASSISTED SUICIDE

MARGARET P. BATTIN

1. INTRODUCTION

SOMETHING is amiss with the debate over euthanasia and physician-assisted suicide. When it emerged into public consciousness in the mid-1970s, the debate got off to a rousing start, as philosophers, doctors, theologians, public-policy theorists, journalists, social advocates, and private citizens became embroiled in the debate. On the one side were liberals, who thought physician-assisted suicide and perhaps voluntary active euthanasia were ethically acceptable and should be legal; on the other side were conservatives, who believed assisted dying was immoral and/or dangerous to legalize as a matter of public policy. Over the several decades in which this debate has been accelerating it has achieved a lively, florid richness, both as a philosophical dispute and as a broad, international public issue.

That is the good part. In this chapter I want to explore the richness of this debate by showing something of the terrain of the debate and the figures who have inhabited it, both the public figures and the academic ones partly behind the scenes. But I also want to explore the not-so-good part. I am particularly concerned with what has gone wrong in this debate—or, more precisely, what has not gone quite right just yet.

2. THE DEVELOPMENT OF THE ARGUMENT IN THE ASSISTED-DYING DEBATE

Although disputes over the moral status of suicide are found as far back as the First Intermediate Period of ancient Egypt, some two millennia BC, the debate about *physician-assisted* euthanasia and *physician-performed* suicide is new, occupying academic and public attention primarily in the late twentieth century and the early twenty-first. The emergence of this issue reflects a basic shift in the epidemiology of human mortality, a shift away from death due to parasitic and infectious disease (ubiquitous among humans in all parts of the globe prior to about 1850) to death in later life of degenerative disease (Olshansky and Ault 1987)—especially heart disease and cancer, which now together account for almost two-thirds of deaths in the developed countries. In earlier periods of human history, physicians could do little to stave off death; now, improvements in public sanitation, the development of immunization, the development of antibiotics, and the many technologies of modern medicine have combined to lengthen the human lifespan, particularly in the developed world. For much of human history, life expectancy hovered between 20 and 40; in the developed countries, at the beginning of the twenty-first century, it is nearing 80 and, unless infectious disease becomes more prevalent again, is expected to increase. The result is that, in the developed world, with its sophisticated health-care systems, the majority of the population in these countries dies at comparatively advanced ages of degenerative diseases with characteristically long downhill courses, marked by a terminal phase of dying. On average, people die at older ages and in slower, far more predictable ways, and it is this new situation in the history of the world that gives rise to the assisted-dying issues to be explored here.

The debate over euthanasia and physician-assisted suicide pits arguments about autonomy and about relief of pain and suffering on the 'for' side, versus arguments about the intrinsic wrongness of killing, threats to the integrity of the medical profession, and potentially damaging social effects on the 'against' side.

Principal arguments *for* are:

- the argument from autonomy (Section 3.1);
- the argument from relief of the pain and suffering (Section 3.5).

Principal arguments *against* are:

- the argument from the intrinsic wrongness of killing (Section 3.2);
- the argument from the integrity of the profession (Section 3.3);
- the argument from potential abuse: the slippery-slope argument (Section 3.4).

It is to this overall schema that I will be referring in exploring the five component arguments to be examined below, which I will treat in the order indicated above, for reasons that will become evident later on. It is this overall schema that I will also have in mind in suggesting what seems to have gone wrong with the assisted-dying debate—or, rather, has not gone quite right just yet.

The focused debate over physician-assisted dying began in the wake of the civil-rights movements of the late 1960s and early 1970s, as many formerly disenfranchised or disregarded groups sought recognition of rights or a greater range of rights than had previously been accorded them: blacks, women, people from religious minorities, people with disabilities, and—gradually—medical patients, including patients with terminal illnesses. As in all these groups, the quest for greater respect and a greater range of rights developed with increasing force. With the new availability of antibiotics and technologies like intravenous lines, respirators, and dialysis machines, medicine's capacity to extend the lives of dying patients had begun to increase, but patients themselves were still regarded as 'patients'—comparatively passive subjects of medicine's ministrations. They were rarely understood as agents of autonomous control, but rather as naive and frightened parties appropriately treated in paternalistic ways. In the 1960s, patients with fatal illnesses were rarely (only about 10 per cent of the time) told the truth about fatal prognoses. Consent for experimentation was often ignored (as in the infamous Tuskegee syphillis study), and consent for therapeutic treatment—fully informed and fully voluntary consent—comparatively rarely sought. Truth telling and autonomy were hardly central values of medicine; doctors were expected to do what they thought was best for patients, and—believing patients would be harmed if told they were dying—routinely hid fatal diagnoses and urged patients to go on fighting as long as they could.

Gradually, however, it came to be recognized that continuing all-out treatment could be painful, dehumanizing, and pointless. Thanks in large part to Elizabeth Kübler-Ross's influential book *On Death and Dying* (1969), by the mid-1970s it was becoming socially possible to talk openly about death. Kübler-Ross had described a series of five stages through which the person who learns he or she is terminally ill will pass in facing death (denial; anger; bargaining; depression; and a final stage she called detachment but that became popularly known as acceptance); Kübler-Ross held that it was better for patients if the fact that they were dying was openly acknowledged. The California Natural Death Act of 1976 marks one of the earliest legal recognitions of this changing social perception, since it enabled the patient who knew the truth to decline or discontinue treatment that might otherwise prolong the process of dying; the law served to protect their physicians from prosecution for failure to treat. State by state, similar 'living-will' legislation began to permit terminally ill patients to make advance choices about withholding and withdrawing treatment, now that, with increasing frequency, they were being told the truth that they were dying.

During this long process of transformation, several central figures emerged to argue in favour of physician-assisted suicide. British journalist Derek Humphry, widely recognized as the founder of the right-to-die movement, published *Jean's Way* (1978), describing in heart-rending detail his assistance in the suicide of his first wife, dying of cancer. By 1980, then in Los Angeles, Humphry founded the Hemlock Society, a grassroots organization committed to the legalization of physician-assisted suicide. The first philosophical voices in the new debate began to be heard as well: philosophers like Tom Beauchamp, Ray Frey, Dan Brock, David Mayo, and myself, in the USA, and those like John Harris and Jonathan Glover in the UK, Carlos Prado in Canada, and Helga Kuhse and Peter Singer in Australia, all began to weigh in, largely supporting an autonomy-based view. Although they developed their views in somewhat different ways and responded quite differently to the various objections raised, they all subscribed to what might be called the argument from self-determination or autonomy. And, of course, they all faced the same objections from opponents.

The argument from autonomy is the first of the five components of the overall debate outlined above, one of the two principal arguments on the 'for' side. Because even this one component is too complex to examine fully here, I present it just as a schematic outline and will discuss only the more significant parts; it should be evident that its sequences of argument/objection/counter-objection could be extended in great detail through many more sub-arguments and counter-counter-objections.

3. COMPONENTS OF THE ASSISTED-DYING ARGUMENT

3.1 The Argument from Autonomy (For)

Just as a person has the right to determine as much as possible the course of his or her own life, a person also has the right to determine as much as possible the course of his or her own dying. If a terminally ill person seeks assistance in suicide from a physician freely and rationally, the physician ought to be permitted to provide it.

- *Objection.* True autonomy is rarely possible, especially for someone who is dying. Not only are most choices socially formed, but in terminal illness depression and other psychiatric disturbances are likely to be a factor.
  - *Counter-objection.* Even if many choices are socially shaped, they must be respected as real choices.
  - *Counter-objection.* Rational suicide is possible, and it is possible for patients to make choices about dying without distortion by depresssion.

- *Objection.* One cannot impose on another an obligation to do what is morally wrong, even if one's own choice is made freely and rationally. Since suicide is wrong, the physician can have no obligation to assist in it.
  - *Counter-objection.* This merely assumes, but does not prove, that suicide in circumstances of terminal illness is morally wrong.
  - *Counter-objection.* The physician is not obligated to provide assistance in dying, but should be free to do so if he or she wishes.

Autonomy, involving both freedom from restriction (liberty) and the capacity to act intentionally (agency), is the central value to which this argument appeals, and respect for a person's autonomous choice the social principle it entails. In the context of end-of-life medical care, respecting autonomy for the dying patient not only means honouring as far as possible that person's choices concerning therapeutic and palliative care, including life-prolonging care if it is desired, but could also mean refraining from intervening to prevent that person's informed, voluntary, self-willed choice of suicide in preference to a slow, painful death, or even providing assistance in realizing that choice. Certainly, respect for autonomous choice had been understood (most fully by Kant) to involve respect for rational self-governance, and to be limited (as Mill had pointed out) by the harm principle: respect for a person's autonomous choice does not license just any old act—not crazed acts and not acts that harm others. But the principle does insist that free, considered, individual choice, where one is the architect of one's own life and the chooser of one's own deepest values, must be respected—including, at least as proponents interpret the principle, choices of physician-assisted suicide.

The early theorists were particularly concerned with what was called the issue of 'rational suicide'. The question was whether a person could rationally choose to die or whether such a choice was always a product of depression, a frequent concomitant of terminal illness that narrows one's view of the range of alternative futures, when the irrationality of the choice is compounded by the fact that the person making this choice can have no objectively confirmable belief about what might happen to him after suicide, at least assuming an agnostic view about whether there is or is not an afterlife. Certainly, such issues had been discussed as early as the time of Lucretius, but they took a new, more psychiatrically informed focus in the light of twentieth-century clinical theories of depression and other mental illness, as well as postmodernist claims that seemingly autonomous choices are actually socially formed. Could suicide be rational and rationally chosen? Could it be the product of a fully autonomous choice? Advocates of physician-assisted suicide said yes, taking this as a mainstay of their position.

The most direct, immediate response to the concept of 'rational suicide' was an objection to suicide itself on religious and ethical grounds, an objection most forcefully pursued by Catholic thinkers. This is the opening argument of the 'against' side in the schema above.

3.2 The Argument from the Intrinsic Wrongness of Killing (Against)

> The taking of a human life is simply wrong (witness the commandment 'Thou shalt not kill'); since suicide is killing, suicide is also wrong.
>
> - *Objection.* But killing is socially and legally accepted in self-defence, war, capital punishment, and other situations; if it can be accepted there it could be accepted where it is the voluntary, informed choice of the person who would be killed.
>   - *Counter-objection.* In self-defence, war, and capital punishment, the person killed is guilty; in assisted suicide, the person killed is innocent.

Killing is understood as morally wrong in virtually all cultures and religious systems. Judaism, Christianity, Islam, Hinduism, Buddhism, Confucianism, and many other religious traditions prohibit killing; so do the moral and legal codes of virtually all social systems. Since suicide is a form of killing, this argument observes, suicide—and with it assisted suicide—is wrong ('sinful', 'taboo', 'reviled by God', and so on) as well. However, although this view is shared by all the major world traditions, it has been Roman Catholicism that has been most active in the political debate over physician-assisted suicide in Europe and the USA.

According to the teachings of Catholicism, suicide violates the biblical commandment 'Thou shalt not kill'. Self-killing can never be permitted, even in painful terminal illness, although if it is caused by depression or other psychopathology it may be excused from ecclesiastical penalties like denial of funeral rites. It was Augustine in the early fifth century who first interpreted the commandment as a prohibition of suicide. Aquinas, in the thirteenth century, developed an extensive argument against suicide, arguing that, because 'everything loves itself' and seeks to remain in being, suicide is unnatural, that suicide injures the community, and that suicide rejects God's gift of life. From Aquinas on, the position of the Catholic Church has been quite uniform: unless someone is driven by insanity and hence excused from blame, suicide is always wrong. (In practice, the Catholic Church has often assumed that suicide victims were emotionally disturbed or mentally ill, and on that ground has withheld blame and permitted church rites to be performed.) Catholic contributors to the contemporary debate over physician-assisted suicide in terminal illness, like Kevin Wildes (1993), John Finnis (1995), and John Noonan (1998), held this view; physician-assisted suicide, even if it could be 'rational', would still, in this view, be gravely wrong.

Proponents of physician-assisted suicide pointed out that, while killing is morally and legally regarded as wrong in general, in some exceptional circumstances— for instance, in war, self-defence, and (though now more controversially) capital punishment—it is accepted as morally permissible. Other religious traditions have different ranges of exceptions, though most accept killing in (legitimate) war and in self-defence. But, the objection goes, if killing could be morally acceptable in some or all of these circumstances like war, self-defence, and capital punishment, why not self-killing or self-directed killing in painful terminal illness, when the killing would be for good reason and any assistance offered in performing it occurs at the express request of the 'victim'?

A Catholic response, employed by a number of writers, seeks to distinguish between killing of the 'innocent' and killing of those who, guilty of aggressive or immoral actions, are not. Proponents of physician-assisted suicide point out that this gives a curious result: on this reasoning, 'innocent' patients who are terminally ill could not have physician-assisted suicide no matter how fervently they wanted it, but 'guilty' ones presumably could. Catholic thinkers appear to have found this response trivializing of the religious concept of innocence, and have made little response.

While the Catholic Church opposed directly caused dying even in painful terminal illness and had always held that suffering can be of redemptive value, the Church did not ignore the issue about pain. In 1958, Pope Pius XII issued his famous statement to anaesthesiologists 'The Prolongation of Life', in which he employed the traditional Principle of Double Effect to argue that, while death must never be intentionally caused, the physician may licitly use drugs for the control of pain even though foreseeing—though not intending—that this will cause an earlier death. The Pope was referring in particular to the use of opiates, especially morphine, which, it was widely understood, could depress respiration and so cause death. The principle of double effect rests on the observation that an act may have two ('double') or more effects, both an intended effect and a foreseen but unintended effect (as when a child is given castor oil: the intended effect is preservation of health; the foreseen but unintended effect is the bad taste of the medicine). Rigorously stated, the principle of double effect requires that four conditions be met: (1) the action must not be intrinsically wrong; (2) the agent must intend only the good effect, not the bad one; (3) the bad effect must not be the means of achieving the good effect; and (4) the good effect must be 'proportional' to the bad one—that is, outweigh it. The principle was used to argue that a dying patient could always be assured of an easy death, if given morphine with the intent to relieve his or her suffering, even if that were to mean that the death might occur earlier; this would still be to intend the good effect only—relieving the suffering—while the bad effect, death, was merely foreseen, not intended. Whether this was a tenable distinction was a subject of considerable dispute, but its role in the argument was clear: to deflect claims that death hastened with pain-killing drugs involved killing a human being.

Meanwhile, during the period in which this stage of the argument over assisted dying was being most forcefully argued, social expectations regarding terminal illness shifted from the earlier view that the dying patient ought to fight on as long as possible to the new view that forgoing treatment and discontinuing treatment were permissible, indeed acceptable and even normal. The 1976 case of Karen Ann Quinlan raised the issue of discontinuing the respirator for a permanently coma-tose patient; within a decade or so, discontinuation of respiratory support was to become routine. Over the years, not starting treatment, or, having once started, stopping treatment of all sorts became more common. While the earliest technolo-gies to be regarded in this way were the conspicuous, highly invasive ones like dia-lyzers and respirators ('tubes and machines'), the practice gradually came to include withholding and withdrawing of all forms of life-sustaining treatment. Once it had become possible to recognize terminal illness as terminal, to discuss the approach of death with the patient, and to recognize that continuing treatment might pro-long the process of dying but not stave off death altogether, it became increasingly possible to plan to 'negotiate' death. Respirators could be unplugged, dialysis dis-continued, chemotherapy avoided, antibiotics and pressors simply not used. Most controversially, artificial nutrition and hydration could fail to be started, or discon-tinued once it was already in use.

Such practices were often referred to as 'letting die', not 'killing'. Though the prin-ciple of double effect that was held to draw an adequately bright line between them was inherited from Catholic thought, it was widely embraced in secular bioethics. Letting die seemed sharply distinguished from killing: to turn off the respirator was not to kill the patient, but simply to let the patient die of the underlying disease. The killing/letting-die distinction was supposed to draw an important line, to which virtually all conservatives in the debate subscribed; patients must never be deliberately, intentionally killed, but, if treatment were withheld or withdrawn, they could be allowed to die of natural causes—namely, the underlying disease.

However, early on in the debate, James Rachels had attacked this view in a short but highly influential paper that appeared in the *New England Journal of Medicine* (1975). Imagine, he wrote in this now-famous paper, Smith and Jones, both of whom stand to inherit a sizeable fortune from their respective 6-year-old cousins, should the cousins die. One evening, while his cousin is taking his bath, Smith sneaks into the bathroom and drowns him. Meanwhile, Jones is also plan-ning to drown his own cousin, who is also taking a bath, but, as Jones sneaks into the bathroom, the child hits his head and slips under the water. Jones does nothing to save him. Now both children are dead. Smith has killed his cousin; Jones has merely allowed his cousin to die. But both are seriously, equally wrong. Hence it cannot be, Rachels argued, that the distinction between killing and letting die is adequate to discriminate between ethically unacceptable and ethically acceptable cases, and indeed in some cases killing may be ethically more defensible than letting die.

Among such cases, proponents of legalization chorused, could be cases of painful terminal illness. In some such cases, they argued, the voluntary, deliberate termina-tion of life involved in physician-assisted suicide or active voluntary euthanasia—even though they involve killing—could be ethically better than simply withdrawing treatment and thus consigning a pain-racked patient to a miserable end by letting the underlying disease cause death.

Opponents of assisted dying, religious and secular, have had little success in answering Rachels's point, especially as it has been developed more fully by later proponents, except to reaffirm the killing/letting-die distinction and to insist that pain can always be controlled (for a number of analyses, see Steinbock and Norcross 1994). They have turned instead to other points of opposition, particularly two closely related concerns about the consequences of legalization. The first of these, the argument concerning the integrity of the medical profession, is the second of the principal arguments against physician-assisted suicide; it has played a major role in the public opposition of physicians' groups like the AMA in opposing legalization.

3.3 The Argument from the Integrity of the Profession (Against)

Doctors should not kill; this is prohibited by the Hippocratic Oath. The physician is bound to save life, not take it.

- *Objection.* In its original version the Hippocratic Oath also prohibits doctors from performing surgery, providing abortifacients, and taking fees for teaching medicine. If the Oath can be modified to permit these practices, why not assistance in suicide, where the patient is dying anyway and seeks the physician's help?
  - *Counter-objection.* To permit physicians to kill patients would undermine the patient's trust in the physician.
    - *Counter-counter-objection.* Patients trust their physicians more when they know that their physicians will help them, not desert them as they die.

'Doctors should not kill!' thundered physicians like Willard Gaylin, Leon Kass, Edmund Pellegrino, and Mark Siegler (1988). For some opponents of assisted dying, this reflects a religiously based moral judgement about the intrinsic wrongness of killing; for others, it is the underlying axiom of medical practice to which the Hippocratic Oath alludes in stipulating that the physician 'shall give no deadly drug, not even when asked for it'. For still others, it reflects concerns about the pressures under which physicians operate and the kinds of incentives to which they are subject. For example, Diane Meier, MD, a former proponent, changed her position to oppose legalization on the grounds that the conditions of medical practice in modern urban hospitals—immense time pressures, financial incentives against expensive treatment, little ongoing relationship with patients, and so on—could so severely compromise physician judgement in the matter of assisting a patient in dying that medical integrity would be sacrified. For example, she noted, some 25 per cent of people in New York City have no health insurance. Many other physicians have made similar points, aware as they are of the circumstances in which they now practise. Although the argument concerning the integrity of the medical profession is closely related to the slippery-slope argument about the potential for abuse, since it intimates that doctors will become more callous in their treatment of patients, it is also an argument focused on the nature of trust. Patients will be unable to trust their physicians, the argument about integrity claims, since the nature of the physician's role will have changed to permit killing; this is to disrupt something essential to the bond that is established in the physician–patient relationship. Not only will it undermine trust, but it will change the physician as well, from healer to killer, from trusted helper to untrustworthy threat. On this argument, assisting in suicide or performing euthanasia will not only cause physicians personal anguish, as is sometimes observed in the Netherlands, but it will also lead to the corruption of their very nature as physicians.

Opponents, still stung by Rachels's dismantling of the theoretical distinction between killing and letting die, also began to emphasize more fully the second element of this counter argument, an issue present in the debate from the start. This was the 'slippery-slope' claim that to allow even the few sympathetic cases of physician-assisted suicide or euthanasia where the patient fully autonomously chose it and would be spared great pain—these are the most compelling cases—would lead by gradual degrees down a slippery slope towards widespread abuse. Patients would be pressured by overwrought family members, callous physicians, or cost-conscious insurers into choosing an assisted death when they did not really want to die at all. They would be made to feel superfluous, burdensome, as if they *ought* to make such a request, or they might be forced into it by greedy heirs or circumstances deliberately made intolerable. This component of the overall argument, the third of the principal arguments against physician-assisted suicide, is a complex argument containing a variety of sub-arguments. It is the weightiest in the opposition's case—and, I believe, the one to be taken with greatest earnestness by all.

3.4 The Argument from Potential Abuse: The Slippery-Slope Argument (Against)

Permitting physicians to assist in suicide, even in sympathetic cases, may lead to situations in which patients are killed against their will.

- *Objection.* A basis for these predictions must be demonstrated before they can be used to suppress personal choices and individual rights.
  - *Counter-objection.* The bases for these predictions are increasing cost pressures, as well as greed, laziness, insensivity, prejudice, and other factors affecting physicians, family members, health-care institutions, and society.

- *Counter-counter-objection.* It is possible, with careful design, to erect effective protections against abuse by doctors, families, institutions, or society.
- *Counter-objection.* Vulnerable patients will be socially programmed to think of themselves as unworthy to remain alive, and the elderly, the chronically ill, the disabled, and others will be manœuvred into choosing to end their lives.
  - *Counter-counter-objection.* Only patients with documented terminal illnesses would be allowed this option.
    - *Counter-counter-counter-objection.* Restrictions of this sort cannot be enforced; pressures to die would spread beyond the terminally ill.

Slippery-slope arguments involve predictive empirical issues about possible future abuse. *If you let practice A happen now,* these arguments hold, *consequences B will occur, and they will be very, very bad.* To carry weight, there must be evidence to support such an argument; slope arguments take both causal and precedential forms in their efforts to provide such evidence, insisting either that practice *A* will cause consequence *B*, or that permitting practice *A* will set a precedent in the presence of which other causal forces will produce consequence *B*. Many versions of slope arguments in the end-of-life context point either to the suggestive character that some acts of assisted dying would have, thus causing more killing to occur, or to the way in which permitting some acts of assisted dying would loosen the barriers against killing and thus permit such forces as greed, impatience, prejudice, and so on to operate to produce killing on a wider scale.

The risks would be particularly great, many have argued, for those in vulnerable groups. For instance, Susan Wolf has sought to show that the impact of legalization would fall particularly heavily on women; Adrienne Asch has worried about the impact on people with disabilities; Leslie Francis has been concerned about the elderly. Still others have pointed to the likely impact of legalization on blacks and other racial minorities, on people with chronic illnesses, on people with mental illnesses, on people with developmental delays, and so on. To legalize assisted-dying practices at all would start the slide down this very treacherous slope, they have argued, particularly affecting vulnerable groups.

Patients need not even be members of vulnerable categories to be at risk of pressures from family, physicians, institutions, or social expectations in general. John Hardwig's well-known piece 'Is There a Duty to Die?' (1997) explored the way in which a person might come to think it appropriate to choose to end his life rather than constitute a 'burden' to his family. Were physician-assisted suicide a legal possibility, opponents argued, the pattern of reasoning Hardwig explores in his own case would also become expected of others in general. One would come to believe one had a 'duty to die'.

Virtually all opponents of assisted dying have employed some form of slippery-slope argument. For some, like Dan Callahan, Sissela Bok, and Yale Kamisar, the slippery-slope argument is a supplement to the view that intentionally causing death is morally wrong. For others, like Art Caplan, it is the central one: Caplan says that he would not object to physician aid-in-dying were it not for the risks of abuse. Much the same view characterized *When Death is Sought*, the report of the New York State Task Force on Life and the Law (1994), which took the risk of abuse as its primary reason for recommending against legalization of physician-assisted suicide. Similarly, the Canadian Supreme Court held in the 1993 case *Rodriguez* v. *British Columbia* that, although ALS patient Sue Rodriguez had good reason to want to end her life, the court could not permit her to do so because of the risks for others this would entail.

Even some proponents of physician-assisted suicide have been alert to the risks of the slippery slope. For instance, in an early paper titled 'Manipulated Suicide', I outlined the various mechanisms of potential abuse, including domestic abuse by families, professional abuse by physicians, and institutional abuse by health-care institutions, insurers, and government agencies, though I did not draw the conclusion that assisted dying ought therefore to be prohibited (Battin 1994: 195–204). Indeed, like many other proponents, I believe legalization and the openness it brings are the best protection against such abuse.

In the early days of the physician-assisted suicide debate, fuel was fed to the fire by data emerging from abroad: the Netherlands was beginning to recognize the legitimacy of voluntary active euthanasia and physician-assisted suicide. In a series of cases, euthanasia was increasingly legally tolerated, even though technically illegal, provided it met the guidelines for 'due care' established by the courts and the Royal Dutch Medical Association. The guidelines required that the patient's choice be voluntary and enduring; that the patient be undergoing or about to undergo intolerable suffering; that the patient have full information about his or her condition and prognosis; that all alternatives for relieving the suffering that are acceptable to the patient have been tried; that a second, independent physician be consulted; and that the physician report the action to the appropriate authorities. The physician who was faced with a conflict of duties between the obligation to prolong life and the obligation to relieve suffering would not be prosecuted for ending or helping end the patient's life under these guidelines, provided he or she acted with due care.

As news from the Netherlands began to reach the rest of the world, so did rumour. Opponents reacted to the developments in Holland with horror and also with distortion. Some, like Richard Fenigsen, a Dutch cardiologist, intimated that 20,000 people a year were being killed against their will; such grossly distorted claims were entertained or repeated by detractors around the world—for example, John Keown in England and a wide network of right-to-life writers in the USA.

The Dutch Government issued a broad, systematic empirical study of end-of-life decisions known as the Remmelink Report in 1990 and again in 1995 (published in Dutch in 1991 and 1996, in English in 1992 and 1996: see van der Maas et al.); these studies found that, in the decade studied, somewhat over 3 per cent of deaths were due to deliberately hastened death: voluntary active euthanasia, about 2,300 cases, 2.4 per cent of the total annual mortality of 135,000; physician-assisted suicide, about 400 cases, or 0.3 per cent; and 'life-terminating treatment', where there was no current explicit request, about 950 cases, about 0.7 per cent (data from the 1995 study). In the 1990 study, there had been about 1,000 cases of euthanasia without current explicit consent; these notorious 'thousand cases' came to occupy a central role in the opponents' case against legalization in the USA and elsewhere, despite the fact that these cases nearly all involved people who had made antecedent enquiries or who were no longer competent and could no longer make requests (Pijnenborg et al. 1993). Proponents' pleas to look at the actual data emanating from the Netherlands, which does not exhibit a pattern of abuse and shows no victimization of vulnerable groups, have largely fallen on deaf ears.

Slippery-slope arguments are often extremely effective in swaying public opinion, and have been central to the opposition's case. Proponents, however, have argued that there is no adequate evidence to support the case against legalization of physician-assisted suicide and euthanasia, and what little evidence there is— especially that from the Netherlands—seems to cut the other way. The second report of the Remmelink Commission, covering all forms of assisted death in the Netherlands between 1990 and 1995, found that the rates of euthanasia and assisted suicide had not changed substantially since the first report five years earlier, and concluded that, 'in our view, these data do not support the idea that physicians in the Netherlands are moving down a slippery slope' (van der Maas et al. 1996: 1705). To the opposition's rebuttal that these studies covered only a decade and that the real danger lay in the future, proponents replied that the conclusions of slippery-slope arguments about social change can never be confirmed in advance of the future they predict. But neither can they be disconfirmed, at least in the broad social contexts in which they are usually used, and they have tremendous—though often unwarranted—persuasive power. Furthermore, slippery-slope arguments tend to be one-sided: used in the contexts of social debate, such arguments are almost always employed to present evidence favouring one side of a picture but not evidence favouring the other, and hence do not invite comparisons of value or probability assessment among various predicted outcomes. By their very nature, slippery-slope arguments tend to be unreliable—though, of course, this does not entail that the bad consequences predicted could not materialize.

The difficulties of slippery-slope arguments are well known to social commentators. Particularly troubling is the issue of the appropriate weight to be given to slope arguments versus other considerations. Suppose slippery-slope evidence did suggest that some patients would be abused—how should this weigh against the freedoms of other patients to make specific end-of-life choices? Slippery-slope arguments hold that practice A should be prevented in order to prevent undesirable outcome B, but in their usual forms do not assess arguments about the moral consequences of suppressing A, nor the relative likelihood that B and A will occur.

Meanwhile, heightened awareness of the conditions of dying invited renewed focus on the second central argument made by proponents for the ethical accept-ability and legalization of assisted dying, which for some time had formed the core of its intuitive appeal. No patient should have to endure pointless terminal suffer-ing, proponents of assisted dying argued, and, if pain cannot be controlled, then the patient should be able to avoid such suffering by means of an earlier, easier death. With this we return to the second principal component of the argument in favour of physician-assisted suicide, the argument that pain and suffering ought to be relieved where possible, sometimes also called the argument from mercy.

3.5 The Argument from Relief of Pain and Suffering (For)

No person should have to endure pointless terminal suffering. If the physician is unable to relieve the patient's suffering in other ways acceptable to the patient and the only way to avoid such suffering is by death, then as a matter of mercy death may be brought about.

- *Objection.* Thanks to techniques of pain management developed by Hospice and others, it is possible to treat virtually all pain and to relieve virtually all suffering.
  - *Counter-objection.* 'Virtually all' is not 'all'; if some pain or suffering cannot be treated, there will still sometimes be a need to avoid them by directly caused death.
    - *Counter-counter-objection.* Complete sedation can be used where pain cannot be controlled.
      - *Counter-counter-counter-objection.* Complete sedation means complete obtundation, and, because the patient can no longer communicate or perceive, is equivalent to causing death. If these are permitted, why not more direct methods of bringing about death?

- *Objection.* Even if it involves pain and suffering, the dying process can be valuable as a positive, transformative experience of new intimacy and spiritual growth.
  - *Counter-objection.* There can be no guarantee of a positive, transformative experience.

Allowing patients to try to avoid pain and suffering, proponents argued, would in some cases mean allowing physician-assisted suicide and, a few also argued, allow-ing euthanasia as well, at least euthanasia in its root sense, *eu-thanatos*, Greek for 'good death'. (Although in the USA and other countries the term 'euthanasia' was often understood in its post-Nazi sense as referring to politically motivated geno-cidal killing, in contrast, 'euthanasia' has been understood in the Netherlands in the Greek sense of 'good death.') The Netherlands provided a relevant example: In the Netherlands, euthanasia and physician-assisted suicide were coming to be legally tolerated for a person facing intolerable suffering (though not necessarily termi-nally ill), where that suffering could not be relieved by any methods acceptable to the patient (a patient with amyotrophic lateral sclerosis (ALS), or Lou Gherig's dis-ease, could not be forced onto a respirator, for example): the avoidance of suffering was what was central. What counted as intolerable suffering was to be defined by the patient; there were no objective criteria for this.

As the increasing acceptance of assisted dying in the Netherlands was coming to light, so also was a greater range of empirical data in the USA and elsewhere about what actually was happening to dying patients. The conditions of dying in America were bad: inadequately treated pain was rampant, choices were ignored, patients were consigned to 'living deaths' hooked to tubes and machines, and medical sci-ence in its relentless drive for progress ignored the human well-being of dying patients in favour of prolonging merely biological life. As the SUPPORT study of 1995 found, half of conscious patients in a sample of tertiary-care hospitals were reported by family members to have suffered moderate to severe pain (though this may have involved other symptoms as well) at least 50 per cent of the time during their last three days of life (SUPPORT Principal Investigators 1995). The conditions of dying in America, as in many countries with advanced, highly technologically developed health-care systems, were often inhumane. Small wonder that some patients might want to avoid them by an earlier, easier death.

In the public mind, however, the issue of physician-assisted suicide had come to be associated with the name of Jack Kevorkian, MD, a retired anesthesiologist who, more perhaps than any other person, kept the issue before the press. Kevorkian was a crusader for legalization of physician-assisted suicide: again and again, he assisted the suicides of people suffering from conditions ranging from Alzheimer disease to ALS. He responded to patients' claims of untreatable, intolerable suffering; like the Dutch, he did not require that the patient be terminally ill. Over a period of years, Kevorkian provided assistance in the suicides of well over 100 people; he was tried repeatedly, but it was not until he performed euthanasia by injecting a lethal drug (rather than assisted in suicide by providing means of death that the patient could operate him or herself) on nationwide television in 1998 that he was convicted of second-degree murder and imprisoned. Kevorkian served in the minds of many as the spectre of what could go wrong with physician-assisted suicide, though he was a hero to others.

If Kevorkian was seen by some as the bad doctor, there was a good doctor on the scene too, Timothy Quill, MD. Quill provided his leukaemia patient Diane with a prescription for a lethal drug, which she took some months later, and he then described his role in her death in the *New England Journal of Medicine* (Quill 1991).

The ensuing legal events became one of the central episodes in the history of the development of the assisted-dying argument: a New York State grand jury simply refused to indict him. Articulate in expressing his conviction that a bad death should be treated as a 'medical' emergency—that is, that it is urgent that the physician act to help the patient avoid terminal suffering and pain—Quill also holds the view that a physician's assistance in suicide should be a 'last resort', that final measure to turn to when all other ways of avoiding suffering have failed. Quill has become one of the central, though more moderate, figures among proponents.

The argument from mercy, that pain and suffering are to be relieved, is understood to support the claim that good medicine involves helping a patient avoid pain and suffering in dying, and that it is within the physician's role as reliever of suffering to help a patient achieve an easier death. This concern is also central in the view of a number of other physicians. Marcia Angell, MD, associate editor and then acting editor of the *New England Journal of Medicine*, Christine Cassel, MD, and Howard Brody, MD, are among the more moderate voices on the scene, subscribing to Quill's view that physician-assisted suicide should be viewed as a 'last resort', something to turn to only in the most difficult cases. Even if rare, such proponents argue, physician-assisted dying nevertheless needs legal protection. Still others believe it may be a reasonable, normal way of bringing life to an end.

But pain can be controlled, objects a chorus of physicians on the other side, opposing any form of assisted dying. Cicely Saunders, MD, one of the earliest and most revered figures in the controversy, has not merely claimed that pain can be controlled but has pioneered effective ways of doing so: she developed the Hospice technique, especially effective with cancer pain, of administering pain medication before the onset of pain symptoms, making it possible to break the cycle of recurrent breakthrough pain. Saunders is a true pioneer, having done perhaps more than any other to change the actual circumstances of dying in modern, highly technologically developed societies—the grim circumstances that provoked the original movement concerning voluntary euthanasia and assisted suicide. Palliative care, now a recognized medical speciality, focuses first on the recognition, treatment, and prevention of pain: its practitioners advocate better attention to pain management in terminally ill patients, more reliable assessment of pain, the use of escalating, ladder-type schedules of pain management, antecedent interception of pain before it begins (the technique pioneered by Hospice), and more thorough training of physicians and restructuring of provider incentives to provide better pain management. Palliative care also involves attention to the question of what to do in those cases in which pain cannot be adequately managed: here, it advocates the use of pain control even in contexts in which it is foreseen, though not intended, that a shorter life may result; and, in very extreme cases, it accepts the use of terminal sedation: sedating the terminally ill patient into unconsciousness, and then withholding or withdrawing artificial nutrition and hydration that would be required to keep an unconscious patient alive.

The first Hospice in the USA was opened in 1974, and since that time work in palliative care has been carried on by a wide range of pain specialists, including palliative-care and Hospice physicians like Kathleen Foley, MD, and Joanne Lynn, MD, both known for their work on pain, pain assessment, and social issues related to pain. Like many others who are opposed to the legalization of physician-assisted suicide and any form of euthanasia, these pain-specialist physicians see the solution to the public debate in improved methods of pain control, symptom control, and increased resources for pain research, as well as more thorough instruction for medical students and physicians in pain-control techniques, destruction of myths about addiction, and other forms of progress in palliative care. Better pain control means less call for assisted suicide, they say.

Pain control techniques do not always work, retort proponents of aid-in-dying. There are still some situations in which perfect pain control is not possible, and in any case there is an immense gap between theoretical capacities for pain control and the actual situations of dying. Not all patients receive the kind of expert palliative care that is theoretically possible, and in some cases even the theory is inadequate. Timothy Quill's urging that a bad death be regarded as a medical emergency is not an idle abstraction: there really are cases in which pain and suffering are intolerable.

To this charge, opponents of physician-assisted suicide—for example, philosopher Bernard Gert and physician Ira Byock—recommend the practice known as terminal sedation. Terminal sedation, they insist, allows the patient whose pain is intolerable to find relief, but still preserves the delicate line between killing and letting die. Terminal sedation has been the last-resort darling of many opponents in the debate.

Proponents of physician-assisted suicide—philosophers Gerald Dworkin and R. G. Frey come to mind—issue a double rejoinder. First, terminal sedation hardly preserves the line between killing and letting die: by sedating a patient and then failing to provide nutrition or hydration, the physician is foreseeably and deliberately ending his life; there is no safe line here. They claim that 'those who oppose medically assisted dying themselves favor policies that cannot be morally distinguished from the policies we favour and they oppose' (Dworkin et al. 1998: 3). Dworkin and Frey's move here exposes the confusion of the opposition in trying to draw a line between allowing to die (which the opposition accepts) and causing to die (which it says it rejects); terminal sedation is functionally equivalent to killing the patient— that is, causing the end of his life. David Orentlicher puts the point more boldly: to accept terminal sedation, as the US Supreme Court did in its joint decision (1997) in *Washington* v. *Glucksberg* and *Vacco* v. *Quill*, is to 'embrace euthanasia'.

Secondly, perhaps more importantly, the unsatisfactoriness of recourse to terminal sedation shows that the avoidance of pain is not all there is to the debate. For some, maybe most, patients who seek assistance in dying, pain is not the issue as much as its control. This view—in many ways, a return to the autonomist view with which the debate started—is to some degree borne out by the data from the

Netherlands covering the period 1985–95 and from Oregon, where physician-assisted suicide has been legal since 1997. In the Netherlands, according to the Remmelink studies, pain is a factor in the choices of patients who receive euthanasia or assisted suicide in less than half the cases; it is the sole factor in just a tiny fraction. In the period during which assisted suicide has been legal in Oregon—from 1997 through 2001 there were ninety-one cases (Hedberg et al. 2002)—there is no evidence that there were any cases for pain alone. Patients fear future pain and want to avoid future hard deaths; but for most of them, it is retaining control, remaining capable of being the architects of their own lives, that is central. Even if all pain could be controlled—as terminal sedation will do, though in a way that proponents find unacceptable—this would not resolve the issue. Rather, the issue has to do with respecting terminally ill patients' own choices about how they want to die, rather than—as proponents would put it—forcing them to accept their physicians' or health-care institutions' models of appropriate terminal care.

In a sense, the debate at the moment stands right here. It is a stand-off between, on the one side, opponents who rely on the claim that pain can be controlled and that improvements in pain-control capacities are what is needed, and, on the other side, proponents who insist that the real issue is not only pain but autonomy, self-determination, and personal control.

4. THE SKEWED NATURE OF THE DEBATE

Most of these arguments on both sides of the debate, including the five principal arguments sketched so far, merit exploration in much greater detail. This has been a schematic review, intended to provide a road map for fuller exploration. But the components of the argument examined so far must also all be seen as part of a larger, overall argument, a larger argument whose structure has itself become problematic. This is an issue about how the debates are conducted and what turf, so to speak, they occupy.

Take, as a specimen of the difficulty, the book *Euthanasia and Physician-Assisted Suicide: For and Against* (Dworkin et al. 1998), which, while admirable in many respects, illustrates the central problem at the core of the assisted dying debate. The authors of this short volume are three well-known philosophers mentioned earlier, Gerald Dworkin, R. G. Frey, and Sissela Bok. It is an excellent book, and its distinguished authors argue with considerable clarity, rigour, and sensitivity about many of the deepest issues in the euthanasia debates. This book has everything central to the debate: discussions of the difference between killing and letting die, the distinction between foreseeing and intending, the tenuous relationship between allowing and causing. It discusses the principle of double effect, the risks of the slippery slope, the delicate matter of the integrity of the medical profession. Indeed, this small book is an excellent model of the entire debate.

But its structure tells us much about the debate as a whole. On the first page of the first chapter of this little book, Dworkin—arguing on the 'for' side of the issue, attacks the opposition, represented in this case by Kass, Siegler, and the view of other opponent physicians that 'doctors should not kill'. Only a few pages later, at the beginning of the second short chapter, Frey, likewise arguing the 'for' side of the debate, also begins by attacking the opposition: he shows how the opposition's position concerning pain control and terminal sedation fails to be coherent, and why, as we have seen earlier, the normative asymmetry often alleged between them does not hold. However, Sissela Bok, defending the 'against' view in the second part of the book, does something different: while she reviews some of the sorts of arguments Dworkin and Frey make, she largely addresses concerns about the social effects of acceptance or legalization of physician-aided dying.

All three authors are making moves entirely characteristic of the current debate, including all the moves we have already discussed here. What both Dworkin and Frey do, on the 'for' side, is to move straight to the attack against their opponents. Their argument is an adroit *reductio* in which contradictions in the opponents' position are exposed, pointing out that, although opponents of physician-assisted suicide say they do not accept physician-assisted suicide or euthanasia, they in fact accept practices like terminal sedation that are functionally equivalent to these. But, in running this clever, sophisticated argument, Dworkin and Frey, on the 'for' side, make a problematic move of their own. What they do is *assume* the principles on which their side of the argument is based, principles of autonomy and freedom from suffering, without explicitly or directly defending these principles.

We might assume that this defence would be easy to mount. The principle of autonomy, or self-determination, or liberty, is a familiar, fundamental principle in ethical theory, and might seem to need little direct defence. So too, it might be argued, is the principle that pain and suffering ought to be relieved where possible, perhaps a straightforward utilitarian claim. But neither Dworkin nor Frey, both philosophers of considerable distinction and skill, defends these issues directly, though here is where the really interesting philosophical work might occur.

Meanwhile, Bok, defending the 'against' position, exploits its strongest point: the slippery-slope argument sketched above that the legalization or acceptance of euthanasia or physician-assisted suicide would lead to pressures on vulnerable patients, that people would be edged or forced into dying when that was not their choice. While Bok considers other arguments, this is her central claim. Bok's concerns are important, crucial ones. But they are the only ones she considers decisive: thus one cannot join the discussion with her about anything else except this issue. Thus, both in their 'attack' against the opposition's position and in their direct discussion of the points Bok will raise, Dworkin and Frey are as it were lured into fighting the rest of the battle on what is essentially Bok's turf, the slippery-slope set of concerns about social effects. They score points against elements of her position; but she gains the home-court advantage. Consequently, although defeated in the initial manœuvre and outclassed in the technical argumentation over the issues of causation and intention, Bok in a sense wins the day, even though the arguments she uses about the slippery slope are not fully persuasive. Her achievement lies in the fact that she is able to cast the slippery-slope issue as the *central* one, the one on which, it is assumed, views about legalization will stand or fall. Both sides end up allowing the slippery-slope issues of abuse to take the main court, and, implicitly, to be the issue on which practical policy measures like legalization turn. Dworkin and Frey argue that the slippery-slope argument does not succeed; Bok argues that it does; but all seem to agree that, if it did succeed, it would prove decisive in issues of policy. While this one small book—and it is a text intended for classroom use at that, in a series designed as 'For and Against'—is only a small part of the immense literature on euthanasia and physician-assisted suicide, it is uncannily representative of the skewed nature of the debate. This skewed argument is the not-so-good part of the debate I have wanted to explore.

There are two distinct problems with this relocation of the debate over euthanasia and physician-assisted suicide on slippery-slope turf. For one thing, as we have seen, slippery-slope arguments involve predictive empirical issues about possible future abuse, and the evidence for such claims cannot be firm; however, slippery-slope arguments cannot be disconfirmed either, at least not in the weak sense that undesirable consequences B could always follow A, whether or not they were actually caused by A or caused by some other force in the presence of A as a precedent. Slippery-slope arguments are always around; they rarely dissipate until long after the social change in question has already taken place. However, because of their power to persuade, especially in a broad, public context, slippery-slope arguments tend to block out other major concerns that should be regarded as central too, or perhaps as still more central. Thus, on both counts, the structure and location of the debate skew the answer.

There is an additional problem with the for-and-against structure of the euthanasia debate, also mirrored in the Dworkin, Frey, and Bok book. This structure of adversarial debate is used effectively in many areas of human discourse, including philosophy and in particular bioethics. A *for-and-against* argumentative format is not just a universally good idea; rather, a *for-and-against* format may or may not be appropriate to a particular topic, depending on, among other things, the degree of infancy or maturity of the debate. A new social and ethical issue, just breaking open into explicit debate when it may have been festering unrecognized beneath the surface of public consciousness for years, needs the kind of philosophical exploration that *for-and-against* analysis yields: the elements of the debate need to be isolated, identified, catalogued, and critiqued. But after a debate begins to mature, it becomes time to pursue attempts at resolution: here, the search should be for common elements, points of agreement, ways of reaching both practical and theoretical consensus about the issue at hand. There have been many, many *for-and-against* works on the issue of physician-aided dying, including treatises, popular articles, edited collections, and assemblages of amicus briefs to the US Supreme Court. The Dworkin, Frey, and Bok volume, like much of my own work, properly counts among these. Certainly, the debate has evolved considerably over time, so that proponents are less likely to argue for absolute-autonomy views that patients should be free to do whatever they want and are more likely to support guidelines and safeguards for the practice of physician-assisted suicide, while opponents are less likely to argue that patients have an obligation to try to continue to live at whatever cost and more likely to accept death-hastening strategies like disconnecting ventilators or undergoing terminal sedation. But there are comparatively few works that attempt to seek genuine consensus, though I believe the debate has now matured enough to demand them. New, evolved structures of reflective consideration, not just debate, will suit the issue better; it is time for all of us to move on.

5. THE POSSIBILITY OF CONCESSION AND COMPROMISE

Two things must happen in the debate over physician-aided dying if it is to avoid calcification and extended political friction, as has been the case, for example, with the abortion debate. It has one advantage over the abortion debate that makes resolution seem more plausible; in the assisted-dying debate, unlike the abortion debate, there is no third party analogous to the fetus whose ontological status and vulnerability to harms are under dispute. However, in many other ways the assisted-dying debate has many of the trappings of the abortion debate: noisy rhetoric, hostile sides entrenched over an issue constructed as 'choice' versus 'killing', and (though this remains more pronounced for the abortion debate) the development of a political 'litmus test' over the issue.

Nevertheless, there are some things that would make the assisted-dying debate far more open to resolution. First, the debate needs to enlarge the range within which it is conducted. This involves expanding the scope of the issue or issues that are seen as central beyond slippery-slope concerns to the positive case that is offered for accepting and legalizing euthanasia and/or physician-assisted suicide. There are basic philosophical issues here about autonomy and self-determination, freedom and control, about the moral issues in suicide: these need direct scrutiny.

As I have said, one might think these would be easy to defend. After all, the central notions of liberty—of self-determination and autonomy, about freedom to choose how to live one's life—are said to be central to the liberal traditions of

Western culture. Here, popular discussion in the physician-assisted suicide debate may have an edge over academic dispute: chatlines, letters to the editor, popular books, and other vehicles of public discussion are full of ringing appeals to freedom, self-determination, and 'get-government-off-my-back' conceptions of individual liberty in matters of dying. But the philosophers are strangely reluctant to take these issues on, knowing, of course, how complex they can be. What is the appropriate scope of individual autonomy, anyway? This is an issue under debate throughout the entire history of philosophy, but still ready for fresh re-examination in the light of the new circumstances of dying.

Indeed, the discussion of autonomy in the context of death and dying might even help illuminate the issue of autonomy in general. If there are certain kinds of actions, like enslavement or murder, that one ought not to undertake, is bringing about one's own death one of them? How is such action to be described, in any case: as 'suicide', or 'self-deliverance', or 'aid-in-dying', or 'hastened death', or in any of the various euphemisms and derogatory labels employed in the public debates? Does an individual have a basic right to (try to) avoid pain and suffering, and, if so, is this perhaps the obverse of the right to pursue happiness, or is it rooted in some deeper, more basic interest? If, as Buchanan and Brock (1989) have argued, competence in decision making is task specific (one may be competent to decide whom to have watch the delivery of one's baby but not competent to decide what anaesthetic to use, or competent to refuse treatment but not competent to balance one's cheque book), the question remains whether competence to decide on a course of medical action that will result in one's death (like physician-assisted suicide while in severe, terminal pain) requires a high standard of competence (as is often assumed), or a low one, so that a terminally ill patient who is suffering severely and wants to die need not meet demanding standards of competence. It is not that these issues are unknown in the academic debates over physician-aided dying, but that they have not been cast as *central*; it is the slippery-slope argument that has been largely cast as central, when it may well be secondary to these more fundamental conceptual issues. This is not to say that the slippery-slope argument is not important; it is, enormously so. But it is not the only important thing about this issue. Of course, to restructure the debate so that these more fundamental issues become central does not entail that the debate will be resolved in favour of the 'pro' side, but means only that the debate must focus more directly on the deeper issues at hand.

A centrist, consensus position beyond this for-and-against polarization may already seem to be emerging, particularly in practical medical contexts. The palliative-care movement in particular, as we have already seen, claims to offer a solution to the end-of-life dilemmas over pain and suffering that seem to have given rise to the issues of euthanasia and physician-assisted suicide in the first place: better pain control will mean less call for physician-assisted suicide, and, until such time as the science of pain control has been perfected, measures like terminal sedation can always be employed in cases of intractable terminal pain.

But while there is some progress here—indeed real growth—towards a more mature phase of the debate, I do not think its direction will be straight ahead. In almost every way the new attention being given to palliative care is an excellent development. But the construction of the position dedicated to palliative care as a *centrist* position is not, I think, fully warranted. It may seem to be so, since it elides the distinction between killing and letting die and thus may appear to dissolve it. But palliative care does not provide a compromise between the 'pro' and 'con' positions, at least not an adequate compromise, and it is not really centrist. While it permits more extensive pain control, and while it permits actions that are functionally equivalent to euthanasia and physician-assisted suicide, it still does not permit active euthanasia or physician-assisted suicide in the senses that many advocates have in mind. Palliative care answers just one of the underlying concerns of the 'pro' side, relief from pain and suffering; it does not address the other basic principle, autonomy, very well at all, particularly since such ostensible compromises as terminal sedation have the effect of placing the patient in a position of absolute loss of control while undergoing the sedation process. After all, many thinkers support the legalization of physician-assisted suicide and/or voluntary active euthanasia because they support the desire that some terminally ill patients express for control over the timing, character, and circumstances of their deaths—not so much because they fear pain, but because they want to be the architects of the ends of their lives. The palliative-care movement certainly represents progress towards a partial consensus, but it does not yet represent full resolution of the issues between the 'for' and 'against' sides of the debate.

A more mature phase of the intellectual discussion may also seem to be beginning. Some works advance the discussion towards resolution by reserving judgement on the theoretical and policy issues while exploring the realities of concrete application, whether the practices in question are legalized or remain underground. For example, the report of the American Psychological Association's task force on physician-assisted suicide includes an extended discussion of the multiple roles psychologists can play in end-of-life decisions as well as the practical considerations and challenges they face in becoming more active in the end-of-life arena. (American Psychological Association Working Group on Assisted Suicide 2000). The US Supreme Court's 1997 joint decision in *Washington* v. *Glucksberg* and *Vacco* v. *Quill* may also seem to be a comparatively mature, consensus-seeking decision, since it did not actually side with either the 'pro' or the 'con' factions in the debate (although, because the decision held that there is no constitutional right to physician-assisted suicide, it is sometimes seen as defeat for the 'pro' side); rather, it sidestepped the moral issue by turning the matter over to the individual states.

However, many discussions that claim to or are perceived to seek consensus are not fully successful: they still want resolution on one side or the other of the same continuing battle. For example, Linda Emanuel's 'Facing Requests for Physician-Assisted Suicide' (1998*a*) advises physicians how to deal with patients who seek assistance in suicide, and thus to some extent allows recognition of the issue, but, after a lengthy series of steps designed to deflect the patient into other forms of care, tells physicians to reject the request if it persists at the end: this is not compromise or resolution; this is to side with the 'against' faction, even after a seemingly sensitive discussion. More negatively, the Supreme Court's decision can be read not as paving the way for resolution, but as evasion of the issue. Meanwhile, also apparently unwilling to cooperate in the search for resolution, some writers on the 'pro' side continue to call for legalization without much attention to slippery-slope issues at all. It is difficult to find a writer with a foot firmly planted on each side of the fence, or, better still, for whom there is no longer any fence at all. I do not yet see the kind of genial, comprehensive summation of the issue that is sensitive to the concerns of both sides, one that manages synthesis without ignoring or trivializing the principal concerns on both sides, one that could be called a real resolution of the issues, one that could elicit consensus and agreement at both policy and practical levels.

On the contrary, many authors seem to assume the problem will just go away, if pain control can be suffficiently improved and medicine's enthusiasm for prolonging life beyond a reasonable point can be restrained. Others see a political pattern of worsening escalation as conservative politicians consider federal measures that would preclude the use of scheduled drugs for the purpose of ending life, leading Hemlock, Ergo!, Last Rights Publications, the Voluntary Euthanasia Research Foundation, and other right-to-die groups in the USA and abroad to develop new technologies for bringing about death that do not rely on prescription drugs at all. (I have discussed both these points at greater length elsewhere; for the first, see Battin 1998; for the second, see Battin 2001.) These 'NuTech' methods under development by the more resolute proponents include devices like hypoxic masks and tents, plastic bags (the 'Exit Bag'), helium inhalation devices, scuba-based 'Debreathers', and other technologies for producing an easy death; they can be operated by family members or friends or by the patient him or herself. These NuTech measures have the effect of taking the matter of assisted suicide out of the hands of physicians altogether: the deed can be done within the intimate circle of patient, family, or friends, and the medical establishment is no longer involved. Like the Pain Relief Promotion Act and its successors developed by opponents of physician-assisted suicide, NuTech ups the stakes on the proponent side as well: the matter is now beyond medicine's control.

Perhaps real resolution is not possible and consensus a silly dream. But perhaps resolution and consensus are possible; it is the moment at which the current discussion ought to begin in earnest to try to seek them, and in the final section I want to sketch how I think this resolution might proceed. After all, these are not trivial social issues, and the circumstances in which these dilemmas arise—where, as a result of the epidemiological transition in the causes of mortality, death at the conclusion of long, terminal illness awaits an ever-increasing proportion of the population in the developed world—are what the future increasingly brings.

6. Can the Dispute over Physician-Assisted Suicide be Resolved?

In my optimistic moments, I do think it is possible to reach resolution in this debate in a way that will satisfy most of the concerns of most parties to the debate. Consider the principal tension: autonomy, on the one hand, versus the risks of the slippery slope, on the other. Relief of pain, I think, along with concerns about the integrity of the medical profession and the moral status of killing, are comparatively secondary, since pain control is not really an *issue*, but a matter of practical inadequacy (virtually all parties agree that pain control and access to it ought to be improved), since the intrinsic-wrongness-of-killing argument falls to its counterexamples of war and self-defence without adequate rebuttal, and since concerns about the integrity of the medical profession are so closely related to slippery-slope concerns. At root, what remains is a tension between what the patient really wants, at the deepest, most reflective level, and what limitations may be placed on his or her choices to protect the interests of other parties or society as a whole.

These are real tensions, not to be minimized; they explain why the slippery-slope issues have such prominence. But the tension can be reduced by reinspecting the temporal location of decision making about dying. Typically, medicine has been structured so that decisions about aspects of terminal care are delayed as long as possible, often until a crisis occurs and a decision must be made immediately. By this time, the patient is in distress, the family is in distress, and many peripheral aspects of the decision are swept aside. Advance directives play some role, but they have many deficiencies: they may have been executed in casual, inadequately informed circumstances, they may be too specific, too general, or not fully clear; and in any case they are often ignored. But, in typical decision-making situations, things need to be done right away: doctors are busy; schedules are tight; the readings on the monitors are already slipping. Decision making in crisis is different in character from reflective decision making well in advance, and part of what gives rise to the current tension over end-of-life decision making is the fact that institutional structures and conventional medical practice favour urgent, last-minute decision making rather than reflective anticipation. It is an institutional pattern, not necessarily a human one.

But the decisions at hand are decisions about issues basic to end-of-life care—about whether it may be acceptable to forgo or discontinue treatment in order to let death occur; about whether one should always try to obliterate pain completely, even at the cost of obliterating consciousness, or regard some pain as acceptable; about whether forgoing nutrition and hydration is a welcome strategy or a repugnant charade; and about whether active aid-in-dying is morally permissible or morally wrong. Patients—that is, people—often form their ideas about these things long in advance, indeed long before the start of an illness that might lead to practical questions about dying, and what they develop is a kind of personal philosophy about these issues—a more general, reflective view, often idiosyncratically their own, a view broad and deep enough to govern specific practical questions.

If decision making takes place earlier, in the more leisured space of life when real reflection is possible, it is far less likely to be decision making that is warped by intense institutional or familial pressures. Of course, patients cannot decide the precise details of their care far in advance, since it is not clear what illnesses and what circumstances will arise. And, of course, some patients change their minds over time, sometimes in response to specific life experiences. Just the same, patients can certainly indicate the kinds of things they would seek and they would avoid—their personal view, a view they develop and refine over time. To convey this personal philosophy is, we might say, to articulate a 'personal end-of-life policy'—it is to express what sorts of things one would favour and what one would not. This is not quite the same thing as executing an advance directive—that is, executing a restrictive, stipulative document with legal force and thus incurring many of the difficulties of combining formal advance directives with physician aid-in-dying (Francis 1993); it is rather a matter of making one's basic values and preferences a matter of record in one's medical history and in one's family's or friends' ongoing lore, revising it if it evolves, as the basis for all further discussion. Factors that contribute to one's 'personal policy' may include one's religious convictions or the absence of them, one's sense of the meaning of life, one's personal style as a risk-taker or risk-minimizer, and so on, but are hardly reducible to these. Advance reflective decision making—or, better, *advance personal policy making*, as it might be called, both satisfies the principle of autonomy but protects against the slippery slope, the two deepest core concerns in the debate. Some people will want the kind of terminal care that emphasizes palliation and uses only a limited range of means; others will want direct, open assistance in the self-termination of their own lives; still others will want many options in between. Advance directives in the conventional sense capture only a part of this, and they are characteristically executed much further along in a terminal process; they govern specific medical procedures once a terminal course has begun. *Advance personal policy making* is grander, if you will; it involves the antecedent, lifelong, philosophically reflective exploration and articulation of one's deeper commitments about living and dying, alert to shifts it may undergo but sensitive to the most basic elements of one's convictions. Advance directives, limited and specific as they characteristically are, might be seen as the tip of the personal-choice iceberg, so to speak—the telltale symptom of an underlying personal philosophy that could be expressed as a personal policy, but hardly the whole thing.

A second component is also necessary for full resolution. Briefly sketched, it involves the notion of a social 'default' disposition for troubling cases concerning death and dying. A default specifies what happens if no contrary instructions are specified instead: it is what you get if you do not choose something else. As I plan to argue in fuller detail later, a consensus might articulate a default policy about treatment of the dying, and this would be the standard, 'normal' way to resolve dilemmas about the prolongation of life, the control of pain, and so on, in the modern, industrialized world, where life characteristically ends after a prolonged period of deterioration or terminal illness. But the very notion of 'default' presupposes that there are other options as well, and a default arrangement is morally tolerable *only* provided it offers a fuller range of choice. (If there are no other options, it can hardly be said to be a 'default'.) Thus I can imagine an approach that concedes to conservatives some unease about the slippery slope and allows the establishment of a default (such a default might, for example, permit withholding and withdrawing treatment as well as the use of 'double-effect' opiates in controlling pain), but that does not establish terminal sedation or physician-aided dying as a norm; it would have to ensure that options remain open for alternative ways of approaching death. These alternatives would have to include both more conservative and more liberal options: seeking more extensive treatment even where it is viewed as futile, seeking terminal sedation, seeking physician-assisted suicide, and (perhaps) seeking voluntary active euthanasia. That there be other options besides the default, both more conservative and more liberal, is a non-negotiable demand.

I hardly have space here to explore this conjecture in full detail, but it is the kind of direction in which I think the discussion of euthanasia and physician-assisted suicide should now go, in both the public and the academic areas. The benefits of polarized, *for-and-against* discussion have now been largely gained in ongoing argument about assisted dying; it is time to turn to exploring the possibilities for resolution. *Advance personal policy making* together with public policy that recognizes a *default-with-other-options* may be only one of these, though I think it is a promising combination for both theory and practice. Certainly, there may be other fruitful avenues for exploration, but it is high time to turn to the consideration of such possibilities. After all, the majority of people in developed countries will die the kinds of deaths from diseases with long terminal courses in which these issues arise, and it is crucial to find ways of resolving the debates. If these debates continue to fuel public polarization and political controversy, it could make all our deaths worse; if resolution can be found, that would be a gain for us all.

References

American Psychological Association Working Group on Assisted Suicide and End of Life Decisions (2000). *Report to the Board of Directors*. Washington: American Psychological Association; http://www.apa.org/pi/aseolf.html.

Angell, Marcia (1997). Editorial: 'The Supreme Court and Physician-Assisted Suicide—the Ultimate Right'. *New England Journal of Medicine*, 336: 50–3.

Arras, John D. (1997). 'Physician-Assisted Suicide: A Tragic View'. *Journal of Contemporary Health Law and Policy*, 13: 361–89.

Asch, Adrienne (1998). 'Distracted by Disability'. *Cambridge Quarterly of Health Care Ethics*, 7/1: 77–87.

Baron, C. H., Bergstresser, C., Brock, D. W., Cole, G. F., Dorfman, N. S., Johnson, J. A. et al. (1996). 'A Model State Act to Authorize and Regulate Physician-Assisted Suicide'. *Harvard Journal of Legislation*, 33: 1–34.

Battin, Margaret P. (1982). *Ethical Issues in Suicide*, Englewood Cliffs, NJ: Prentice Hall; rev. edn. 1985; trade-titled *The Death Debate* (1996).

—— (1994). *Least Worst Death: Essays in Bioethics on the End of Life*. Oxford: Oxford University Press.

—— (1998). 'Physician-Assisted Suicide: Safe, Legal, Rare?', in Battin et al. (1998), 63–72.

—— (2000). 'On the Structure of the Euthanasia Debate: A Review of Dworkin, Frey, and Bok: *Euthanasia and Physician-Assisted Suicide. For and Against*', in Review Symposium on Euthanasia and Physician-Assisted Suicide. *Journal of Health Politics, Policy, and Law*, 25/2: 415–30.

—— (2001). 'New Life in the Assisted-Death Debate in the US: Scheduled Drugs vs. NuTech', in A. Klijn, F. Mortier, M. Trappenburg, and M. Otlowski (eds.), *Regulating Physician-Negotiated Death* (special issue of *Recht der Werkelijkheid, Dutch/FlemishJournal of Law & Society*). s-Gravenhage: Elsevier, 49–63.

—— Rhodes, Rosamond and Silvers, Anita (1998). *Physician-Assisted Suicide: Expanding the Debate*. New York: Routledge.

Beauchamp, Tom L. (1996) (ed.), *Intending Death: The Ethics of Assisted Suicide and Euthanasia*. Upper Saddle River, NJ: Prentice Hall.

—— and Perlin, Seymour (1978) (eds.), *Ethical Issues in Death and Dying*. Englewood Cliffs, NJ: Prentice Hall.

Brock, Dan W. (1993). *Life and Death: Philosophical Essays in Biomedical Ethics*. Cambridge: Cambridge University Press.

Brody, Howard (1992). 'Assisted Death—a Compassionate Response to a Medical Failure'. *New England Journal of Medicine*, 327: 1384–8.

Buchanan, Allen E., and Brock, Dan W. (1989). *Deciding for Others: The Ethics of Surrogate Decision Making*. Cambridge: Cambridge University Press.

Byock, Ira (1997a). 'Physician-Assisted Suicide is not an Acceptable Practice', in R.F. Weir (ed.), *Physician-Assisted Suicide*. Bloomington, IN: University of Indiana Press, 107–35.

—— (1997b). *Dying Well: The Prospect for Growth at the End of Life*. New York: Riverhead Books.

Callahan, Daniel (1992). 'When Self-Determination Runs Amok'. *Hastings Center Report*, 22: 52–5.

—— (1993). *The Troubled Dream of Life: Living with Mortality*. New York: Simon & Schuster.

—— (1997). 'Self-Extinction: The Morality of the Helping Hand', in Robert F. Weir (ed.), *Physician-Assisted Suicide*. Bloomington, IN: University of Indiana Press, 69–85.

Campbell, Courtney S. (1992). 'Sovereignty, Stewardship, and the Self: Religious Perspectives on Euthanasia', in R.I. Misbin (ed.), *Euthanasia: The Good of the Patient, the Good of Society*. Frederick, MD: University Publishing Group, 165–82.

Caplan, Arthur L., Snyder, Lois and Faber-Langedoen, K. (2000). 'The Role of Guidelines in the Practice of Physician-Assisted Suicide'. University of Pennsylvania Center for Bioethics Assisted Suicide Consensus Panel. *Annals of Internal Medicine*, 132: 476–81.

Cassel, Christine K., and Meier, Diane E. (1990). 'Morals and Moralism in the Debate over Euthanasia and Assisted Suicide'. *New England Journal of Medicine*, 323: 750–2.

Cassell, Eric J. (1991). *The Nature of Suffering and the Goals of Medicine*. New York: Oxford University Press.

Conwell, Yates, and Caine, Eric (1991). 'Rational Suicide and the Right to Die—Reality and Myth'. *New England Journal of Medicine*, 325/15: 1100–3.

Dresser, Rebecca, and Whitehouse, Peter J. (1994). 'The Incompetent Patient on the Slippery Slope'. *Hastings Center Report*, 24/4: 6–12.

Dworkin, Gerald, Frey, R. G., and Bok, Sissela (1998). *Euthanasia and Physician-Assisted Suicide: For and Against*. Cambridge: Cambridge University Press.

Dworkin, Ronald (1993). *Life's Dominion—an Argument about Abortion and Euthanasia*. London: HarperCollins.

——Nagel, Thomas, Nozick, Robert, Rawls, John, Scanlon, Thomas, and Thomson, Judith Jarvis (1997). 'Assisted Suicide: The Philosophers' Brief'. *New York Review of Books* (27 Mar.), 41–7; also in Battin et al. (1998), app. C.

Emanuel, Ezekiel J., and Battin, Margaret P. (1998). 'What are the Potential Cost Savings from Legalizing Physician-Assisted Suicide?' *New England Journal of Medicine*, 339/3: 167–72.

——Fairclough, D. L., Daniels, E. R., and Clarridge, B. R. (1996). 'Euthanasia and Physician-Assisted Suicide: Attitudes and Experiences of Oncology Patients, Oncologists, and the Public'. *Lancet*, 347: 1805–10.

Emanuel, Linda L. (1998a). 'Facing Requests for Physician-Assisted Suicide: Toward a Practical and Principled Clinical Skill Set'. *Journal of the American Medical Association*, 280/7: 643–47.

——(1998b) (ed.), *Regulating How We Die: The Ethical, Medical, and Legal Issues Surrounding Physician-Assisted Suicide*. Cambridge, MA: Harvard University Press.

Feldman, Fred (1992). *Confrontations with the Reaper: A Philosophical Study of the Nature and Value of Death*. New York: Oxford University Press.

Fenigsen, Richard (1989). 'The Case against Dutch Euthanasia'. *Hastings Center Report*, 19: suppl. 22–30.

Field, M. J., and Cassel, Christine (1997) (eds.), *Approaching Death: Improving Care at the End of Life*. Washington: National Academy of Science Press.

Finnis, John (1995). 'A Philosophical Case against Euthanasia' and other essays in Keown (1995b), 23–36, 46–56, 62–72.

Foley, Kathleen M. (1991). 'The Relationship of Pain and Symptom Management to Patient Requests for Physician-Assisted Suicide'. *Journal of Pain and Symptom Management*, 6: 289–97.

——(1997). 'Competent Care for the Dying Instead of Physician-Assisted Suicide'. *New England Journal of Medicine*, 336/1: 54–8.

——and Hendin, Herbert (1999). 'The Oregon Report. Don't Ask Don't Tell'. *Hastings Center Report*, 29: 37–42.

Foot, Philippa (1984). 'Killing and Letting Die', in Jay L. Garfield and Patricia Hennessey (eds.). *Abortion and Legal Perspectives*. Amherst, MA: University of Massachusetts Press, 177–85.

Francis, Leslie Pickering (1993). 'Advance Directives for Voluntary Euthanasia: A Volatile Combination?' *Journal of Medicine and Philosophy*, 18/3: 297–322.

Gaylin, Willard, Kass, Leon R., Pellegrino, Edmund D., and Siegler, Mark M. (1988). 'Doctors Must Not Kill'. *Journal of the American Medical Association*, 259: 2139–40.

Gert, Bernard, Bernat, James L., and Mogielnicki, R. Peter (1994). 'Distinguishing between Patients' Refusals and Requests'. *Hastings Center Report*, 24/4: 13–15.

Glover, Jonathan (1977). *Causing Death and Saving Lives*. Harmondsworth: Penguin.

Gomez, Carlos F. (1991). *Regulating Death: Euthanasia and the Case of the Netherlands*. New York: Free Press.

Gorovitz, Samuel (1992). *Drawing the Line: Life, Death, and Ethical Choices in an American Hospital*. New York: Oxford University Press.

Hardwig, John (1997). 'Is There a Duty to Die?' *Hastings Center Report*, 27/2: 34–42.

Harris, John (1975). 'The Survival Lottery'. *Philosophy*, 50/191: 81–7.

——(1985). *The Value of Life*. London: Routledge & Kegan Paul.

Hedberg, Katrina, Hopkins, David and Southwick, Karen (2002). 'Legalized Physician-Assisted Suicide in Oregon, 2001'. *New England Journal of Medicine*, 346/6: 450–2, also citing data and references for previous years.

Hendin, Herbert (1996). *Seduced by Death: Doctors, Patients, and the Dutch Cure*. New York: W. W. Norton.

Humphry, Derek (1984–6). *Let Me Die Before I Wake*. Eugene, OR: Hemlock Society.

——(1992). *Final Exit: The Practicalities of Self-Deliverance and Assisted Suicide for the Dying*. New York: Dell.

——and Clement, Mary (1998). *Freedom to Die: People, Politics, and the Right-to-Die Movement*. New York: St Martin's Press.

——with Wickett, Ann (1978). *Jean's Way*. London and New York: Quartet Books.

Kamisar, Yale (1958). 'Some Non-Religious Views Against Proposed "Mercy Killing" Legislation'. *Minnesota Law Review*, 42: 966–1004.

Kamm, Frances M. (1993). *Morality, Mortality*. New York: Oxford University Press.

Kass, Leon (1993). 'Is There a Right to Die?' *Hastings Center Report* (Jan.–Feb.), 34–43.

Keown, John (1995a). 'Euthanasia in the Netherlands: Sliding Down the Slippery Slope?' *Notre Dame Journal of Law, Ethics, and Public Policy*, 9/2: 407–48.

——(1995b). *Euthanasia Examined: Ethical, Clinical, and Legal Perspectives*. Cambridge: Cambridge University Press.

Kluge, Eike-Henner (1975). *The Practice of Death*. New Haven: Yale University Press.

Kübler-Ross, Elizabeth (1969). *On Death and Dying*. New York: Macmillan.

Kuhse, Helga (1987). *The Sanctity-of-Life Doctrine in Medicine: A Critique*. New York: Oxford University Press.

——and Singer, Peter (1994). *Individuals, Humans, Persons: Questions of Life and Death*. Sankt Augustin: Academia Verlag.

Lynn, Joanne (1986) (ed.), *By No Extraordinary Means: The Choice to Forgo Life-Sustaining Food and Water*. Bloomington, IN: Indiana University Press.

——(1992). 'Should Doctors Hasten Death?' *Dartmouth Medicine*, 17/2: 34–41.

Mayo, David J. (1983). 'Contemporary Philosophical Literature on Suicide: A Review'. *Suicide and Life-Threatening Behavior*, 13/4: 313–45.

——and Wikler, Daniel (1979). 'Euthanasia and the Transition from Life to Death', in M. Robinson and J. Pritchard (eds.), *Medical Responsibility: Paternalism, Informed Consent, and Euthanasia*. Clinton, NJ: Humana Press, 720–35.

Meier, Diane E. (1992). 'Physician-Assisted Dying: Theory and Reality'. *Journal of Clinical Ethics*, 3/1: 35–7.

Miller F. G., Quill, T. E., Brody, H., Fletcher, J. C., Gostin, L. O., Meier, D. E. (1994). 'Regulating Physician-Assisted Death'. *New England Journal of Medicine*, 331: 119–23.

Misbin, Robert I. (1992). *Euthanasia: The Good of the Patient, The Good of Society.* Frederick, MD: University Publishing Group.

Momeyer, Richard W. (1988). *Confronting Death.* Bloomington, IN: Indiana University Press.

New York State Task Force on Life and the Law (1994). *When Death is Sought: Assisted Suicide and Euthanasia in the Medial Context.* Albany, NY: New York State Task Force on Life and the Law.

Noonan, John T. (1998). 'Dealing with Death'. *Notre Dame Journal of Law, Ethics, and Public Policy,* 112/2: 387–400.

Nuland, Sherwin B. (1994). *How We Die: Reflections on Life's Final Chapter.* New York: Knopf.

Olshansky, S. Jay, and Ault, A. Brian (1987). 'The Fourth Stage of the Epidemiologic Transition: The Age of Delayed Degenerative Disease', in Timothy M. Smeeding et al. (eds.), *Should Medical Care Be Rationed By Age?* Totowa, NJ: Rowman & Littlefield, 11–43.

——Rogers, R. G., Carnes, B. A., and Smith, L. (2000). 'Emerging Infectious Diseases: The Fifth Stage of the Epidemiologic Transition?' *World Health Statistics Quarterly,* 51/2–4: 207–17.

Orentlicher, David (1997). 'The Supreme Court and Physician-Assisted Suicide: Rejecting Assisted Suicide but Embracing Euthanasia'. *New England Journal of Medicine,* 337: 1236–9.

Pijnenborg, Loes, van der Maas, Paul J., van Delden, Johannes J. M., and Looman, Caspar W. N. (1993). 'Life Terminating Acts without Explicit Request of Patient'. *Lancet,* 341: 1196–9.

Pius XII (1958). 'The Prolongation of Life' (address to a congress of anaesthesiologists), in *The Pope Speaks,* 4/4: 393–8.

Prado, C. G. (1998). *The Last Choice: Preemptive Suicide in Advanced Age.* 2nd edn. Westport, CT: Praeger.

Quill, Timothy E. (1991). 'Death and Dignity—a Case of Individualized Decision Making'. *New England Journal of Medicine,* 324/10: 691–4.

——(1996). *A Midwife through the Dying Process: Stories of Healing and Hard Choices at the End of Life.* Baltimore: Johns Hopkins University Press.

——Cassel, Christine, and Meier, Diane E. (1992). 'Care of the Hopelessly Ill—Proposed Clinical Criteria for Physician Assisted Suicide'. *New England Journal of Medicine,* 327/19: 1380–4.

——Dresser, Rebecca, and Brock, Dan W. (1997). 'The Rule of Double Effect—a Critique of its Role in End-of-Life Decision Making'. *New England Journal of Medicine,* 337: 1768–71.

Rachels, James (1975). 'Active and Passive Euthanasia'. *New England Journal of Medicine,* 292: 78–80. (Follow-up articles in Steinbock and Norcross 1994.)

——(1986). *The End of Life: Euthanasia and Morality.* New York: Oxford University Press.

Rosenberg, Jay F. (1982). *Thinking Clearly About Death.* Englewood Cliffs, NJ: Prentice Hall.

Saunders, Cicely (1976). 'Living with Dying'. *Values and Ethics in Health Care,* 1: 227–42.

Singer, Peter (1987). 'Uncertain Voyage', in Philip Pettit (ed.), *Metaphysics and Morality.* New York: Blackwell, 154–72.

Society for Health and Human Values (1995). *Physician-Assisted Suicide: Toward a Comprehensive Understanding.* Report of the Task Force on Physician-Assisted Suicide of the Society for Health and Human Values. *Academic Medicine,* 70: 583–90.

Steinbock, Bonnie, and Norcross, Alastair (1994) (eds.), *Killing and Letting Die.* 2nd edn. New York: Fordham University Press.

SUPPORT Principal Investigators (1995). 'A Controlled Trial to Improve Care for Seriously Ill Hospitalized Patients: The Study to Understand Prognoses and Preferences for Outcomes and Risks of Treatments (SUPPORT)'. *Journal of the American Medical Association,* 274/20: 1951–98.

Tolle, Susan W., and Snyder, Lois (1996). 'Physician-Assisted Suicide Revisited: Comfort and Care at the End of Life', in Lois Snyder (ed.), *Ethical Choices: Case Studies for Medical Practice*. Philadelphia: American College of Physicians, 17–23.

van der Maas, Paul J., van Delden, Johannes J. M., and Pijnenborg, Loes (1992). *Euthanasia and other Medical Decisions Concerning the End of Life: An Investigation Performed upon Request of the Commission of Inquiry into the Medical Practice Concerning Euthanasia* [known as the Remmelink Report], published in full in English as a special issue of *Health Policy*, 22/1–2.

van der Maas, Paul J. et al. (1996). 'Euthanasia, Physician-Assisted Suicide and Other Medical Practices Involving the End of Life in the Netherlands, 1990–1995' [known as the second Remmelink Report]. *New England Journal of Medicine*, 335/22: 1699–705.

van der Wal, Gerrit et al. (1996). 'Evaluation of the Notification Procedure for Physician-Assisted Death in the Netherlands'. *New England Journal of Medicine*, 335/22: 1706–11.

Wanzer, Sidney H., Federman, D. D., Adelstein, S. J., Cassel, C. K., Cassem, E. H., Cranford, R. D. et al. (1989). 'The Physician's Responsibility toward Hopelessly Ill Patients: A Second Look'. *New England Journal of Medicine*, 320: 844–8.

Weir, Robert F. (1997) (ed.), *Physician-Assisted Suicide*. Bloomington, IN: Indiana University Press.

Wildes, Kevin W. (1993). 'Conscience, Referral, and Physician-Assisted Suicide'. *Journal of Medicine and Philosophy*, 18/3: 323–8.

Wolf, Susan (1996). 'Physician-Assisted Suicide in the Context of Managed Care'. *Duquesne Law Review*, 34: 455–79.

Cases Cited

Rodriguez v. British Columbia 519, 3 SCR (1993).

Vacco v. Quill, 521 US 793, 117 S. Ct. 2293 (1997).

Washington v. Glucksberg, 521 US 702, 117 S.Ct. 2258 (1997).

CHAPTER 27

CAPITAL PUNISHMENT

HUGO ADAM BEDAU

1. INTRODUCTION

UNDERSTANDING and justifying capital punishment need to proceed from within a larger framework that can be and often is left implicit. That framework consists of one's views about punishment generally; only within that context can one adequately face the narrower issues peculiar to understanding and justifying the death penalty. If punishment as such could not be justified, then a fortiori neither could the death penalty. If punishment generally serves certain purposes or functions, then presumably so does the death penalty. Not so conversely, however. The death penalty might not be justified, but that need not put in doubt the justification of punishment in general (Bedau 1991). In the remarks below, the discussion will proceed on two assumptions. First, the general features defining punishment within a legal system will be taken for granted (Hart 1968; Feinberg 1970). Secondly, the function and purposes of the death penalty will be assumed to be those shared by punishments generally.

2. PUNISHMENT AS THE PREVENTION OF CRIME

A system of punishment is often thought to be justified on the ground that it provides protection for law-abiding persons by helping to prevent crime, and that it does this either by incapacitation or by deterrence (or both). So, too, with the death penalty. Utilitarians and other consequentialists generally support the practice of punishment on one or both of these preventive grounds (Bentham 1830/1838), and the debate over the death penalty has often been focused on whether this form of punishment is especially effective in either of these two ways.

The issue, of course, is an empirical one. Few students of the actual practice of punishment would dispute the claim that some punishments sometimes prevent some persons from committing some crimes (Gibbs 1975). But that generalization is so vague that it sheds no light whatever on the interesting question: is the death penalty a more effective preventive than alternative punishments (typically consisting of what are believed to be less severe punishments, such as long-term imprisonment, and especially life imprisonment without the possibility of parole (LWOP))? What is disputed, in other words, are issues of *marginal prevention*, and especially whether the evidence offered by sociologists, psychologists, criminologists, and other social scientists settles the dispute one way or the other.

3. Deterrence

Most modern research on the marginal deterrent effect of the death penalty has been conducted in the USA and falls into two distinct periods. The earlier research (from 1919 to the early 1970s) compared homicide rates in abolition versus death-penalty jurisdictions, in a given jurisdiction before and after an execution, and in a given jurisdiction before and after abolition or re-enactment of the death penalty. No change in homicide rates owing to the death penalty was detected in any of this research. The more recent period (1973–97) was inaugurated by investigations purporting to show that each execution during the middle decades of this century 'resulted, on average, in 7 or 8 fewer murders' (Ehrlich 1975: 414). Subsequent reinvestigation and further study, however, have more than cast doubt on the adequacy of those findings (Bailey and Peterson 1997). Various special features of the methodology (multiple regression analysis) employed were widely criticized, as were the adequacy of the aggregate national data on which the methodology relied. The most recent attempt to establish that lawful executions result in a reduction in murder (Layson 1985) has been shown to suffer from much the same defects as the earlier research in this vein (Fox and Radelet 1989). The ideal research project to settle the question whether executions cause a decline in criminal homicides (and a greater decline than with LWOP) has yet to be defined and in any case probably would be impossible to carry out. Meanwhile, professional criminologists are in virtually complete agreement that there is no convincing empirical evidence that the death penalty is a deterrent marginally superior to long-term imprisonment (Radelet and Akers 1996).

Running head-on into collision with research purporting to show a deterrent effect is other research purporting to show that executions have a 'brutalization' effect. This provocative claim (perhaps first proposed in a newspaper article by Karl Marx in 1853 (see Marx 1853/1959)) has been supported both by statistical evidence (Bowers 1988; Bowers and Pierce 1980) and by clinical interviews with persons who committed murder because, they said, they were afraid to commit suicide and wanted the state to execute them (Diamond 1975; Solomon 1975; West 1975).

The moral question raised by considerations of deterrence (marginal or otherwise) is whether the threat of punishment and carrying out that threat (provided certain specified conditions are satisfied) are justified. (This is not a problem unique to the death penalty.) From a Kantian point of view, the objection is obvious: attempting to lower the crime rate by deterrence or incapacitation flagrantly violates the categorical imperative, because it uses a person (in this case, the convicted murderer) solely as a means to the ends of others (greater public safety through incapacitation or deterrence). The Kantian defender of the death penalty can reply that, although only retributive considerations justify any punishment, if there are also superior crime reduction effects thanks to the death penalty, those effects are a legitimate bonus and are not part of the intention in choosing to punish murder with death rather than with some lesser penalty.

4. INCAPACITATION AND RECIDIVISM

So far as the issue of incapacitation is concerned, the death penalty obviously has no rival. Not only do dead men tell no tales; dead men commit no crimes. Punishment of any other sort still permits the offender to cause harm, even if such harm is only slight, remote, and infrequent. There are, however, both empirical and moral questions raised by the practice of incapacitative punishments. First, there is no guarantee that using incapacitation as a punishment prevents any crime(s). To close the gap between incapacitation and prevention, we need to know what crimes would have been committed by the offender had he or she not been incapacitated. Little research on this counterfactual condition relevant to the death-penalty controversy has been carried out. The best such research (Marquart and Sorenson 1989) was carried out in the USA. It shows that, as of 1987, out of some 453 murderers on death row in 1972 but not executed because of constitutional infirmities in their sentences, 209 had committed 'aggravated assaults' either in the general prison population or while on parole. In addition to these felonies, the former death-row prisoners also committed half a dozen criminal homicides. The remaining ex-death-row murderers (244) either committed no crimes, or their recidivism went undetected, or their crimes were 'against institutional order' (escape, riot, strike).

A somewhat different picture emerges from US government statistics, which report that roughly one in eleven of those currently under sentence of death for murder had a prior conviction of criminal homicide (US Bureau of Justice Statistics 2001). Given such data, it is reasonable to conclude that had that tenth (roughly 370) of the current death-row prisoners (3,700 in 2000) been executed after their first conviction of criminal homicide, several hundred innocents would never have been killed (at least, not by those recidivists). But there is no way to identify in advance which convicted killers will recidivate; predictions of future violence are plagued with false positives (Monahan 1978). Whether any of these recidivist killers had been sentenced to LWOP is not reported (if they had been, their victims must have been other inmates or prison staff or visitors). So long as LWOP is an available sentence for first-degree murder, incapacitation by the death penalty is not necessary to prevent recidivist murder by the vast majority of these offenders. As for the policy options, they reduce to three: (1) return to a mandatory death penalty, in order to execute all convicted murderers (and other capital felons, if any), or (2) execute none and try to improve methods of predicting future violence among incarcerated offenders in order to reduce recidivism in prison and after release (if any), or (3) continue (or, as the case may be, resume) sentencing convicted murderers to death and execute some of them, with little or no rational connection between the likelihood a given offender will become a recidivist murderer and the decision of whether to sentence him to death.

The first alternative, like any attempt to effect greater safety for the general public by incapacitating a select few, clearly violates the categorical imperative because it uses these prisoners purely as a means to the ends of others. Non-Kantians might at this point raise a different objection: is such a strategy to achieve perfect incapacitation worth the cost? If such a policy were adopted not on retributive grounds (that is, on the ground that a murderer deserves to die) but on consequentialist grounds (that is, that society is better off running zero risk from murder by recidivist murderers), other questions must be asked. Is society really ready for such a draconian penal policy? Do the crimes prevented constitute enough harm avoided to be worth the price of executing an entire class of offenders (especially when it is reasonable to believe that only a small fraction of the class would otherwise have killed again)?

A perfect criminal justice system—a system that was not arbitrary or discriminatory or given to punishing the innocent, and thus unlike our actual system (Bedau and Radelet 1987; Radelet et al. 1992/1994; Radelet and Bedau 1998)—might arguably claim the right to enforce a mandatory death penalty for convicted murderers. But would it be justified to exercise that right when the evidence shows that homicidal recidivism among convicted murderers is infrequent? Undeniably, there is recidivism among convicted murderers—in death-penalty jurisdictions as well as in abolition jurisdictions. Yet the same evidence shows that recidivism among convicted murderers is infrequent. As a result, a mandatory death penalty for anyone convicted of criminal homicide would result in the execution of thousands of convicted murderers, but without any very large reduction in the number of criminal homicides (or other felonies). Since we have no way of knowing who among the convicted murderers will murder again if not executed, a policy of mandatory execution for murder would involve executing thousands without much evident benefit (apart from deterrence and other considerations, of course). The sober truth is that perfect incapacitation of convicted murderers (via the death penalty) does not guarantee *any* reduction in criminal homicide (by avoidance of recidivist murder).

5. DESERT

Intuitively, making the punishment *fit* the crime seems a fundamental requirement of justice, and seemingly the surest way to do this is to make the punishment *like* the crime—like it in the kind and quality of deprivation it imposes on the guilty offender. This is the strategy of the classic idea of *lex talionis*: justified punishments are like the crimes for which they are inflicted. Where murder is concerned, such punishments as whipping, maiming, solitary confinement, and other severe deprivations fail this test; intuitively, none of them 'fits' murder at all or as well as death does. So, where the crime is murder, we can make the punishment fit the crime most closely by using the penalty of death. On this basis, it is argued, murderers deserve to die—that is, the punishment they deserve is death (Davis 1996; Pojman 1998; Reiman 1998).

This reasoning is open to various objections, epistemological and otherwise.

5.1 The argument is really a form of special pleading. In general, society places little or no weight on making the punishment like the crime in order to make it fit the crime, and for good reasons. Arson, burglary, embezzlement, child abuse, serial or multiple murder, treason, espionage, and tax evasion are among the scores of crimes deserving severe punishment. But it is impossible to make any of them punishable by a punishment that 'fits', a punishment like the crime. So on what ground, in the face of such difficulties, can one defend the proposition that nevertheless the murderer must be punished with death, because only that punishment is sufficiently like the crime? Why this exception?

5.2 The argument relies on an unproved premiss. How do we know what punishment the murderer deserves, or indeed whether he deserves any punishment at all? One way to answer this question is to turn to whatever punishment is specified by law for the crime(s) of which the offender has been convicted. We might call this *legal desert* and argue that an offender deserves whatever punishment the law provides. But this notion of desert, while fully intelligible and readily applied, is entirely unsatisfactory from the moral point of view. It has the obvious objection that the deserved punishment for murder in Michigan (no death penalty) is not the punishment deserved next door in Illinois and Indiana (both death-penalty jurisdictions).

What we need is a concept of *moral desert*, a concept with general application and sufficient to enable us to answer (at least in theory) two questions: who deserves to be punished, and what punishment does he or she deserve? Abstractly considered, we can answer the first question this way: whoever is guilty of a crime and has no excuse or justification deserves to be punished. But the second question is not so easily answered. No doubt those guilty of the graver crimes deserve the severer punishments; this principle of proportionality has widespread appeal. However, there is no unique way in which to interpret this principle; 'the worse the crime, the more severe the deserved punishment' is a principle consistent with an infinite number of alternative punishment schemes (Pincoffs 1977; Bedau 1978), some of which do not involve the death penalty (von Hirsch 1976) even if others do (Davis 1996). As things stand, we are not agreed as to what punishment a given offender—a given murderer, say—morally deserves. The factors that must be taken into account in order to specify what a given murderer morally deserves are unsettled territory; the role of an abused childhood, for example, in mitigating an otherwise 'deserved' punishment is highly controversial. Desert sceptics understandably deny there is any rational or unique answer to these questions and for that reason reject desert as a normative principle on which to construct the penalty schedule.

5.3 The argument verges on circularity. Some who assert that murderers *deserve* death do so as their way of declaring that society *ought* to punish murderers with death, or that it is *right* to do so. If that is what their claim about desert really means, then appealing to the offender's desert ceases to be a reason for the death penalty. 'Murderers ought to be punished with death because they deserve to die' makes sense whether or not it is true; 'murderers ought to be punished with death because they ought to' is too obviously circular to make any sense.

5.4 The argument is inconclusive. Even if it were true that a murderer could be said morally to deserve to be put to death, how is it argued that we (always?) *ought* to give him what he deserves? Does this not dismiss out of hand any consideration of forgiveness, not to mention other and lesser considerations? It seems to follow from this retributivist position that it is *wrong* (because *unjust*) for victims to forgive their victimizers. Of course, where murder is the crime, the victim cannot forgive the murderer (unless, which is highly unlikely, it were done in advance of the crime). By means of what argument do we show that 'justice' always necessarily trumps mercy and precludes forgiveness? Or suppose that it were enormously expensive to give an offender the punishment he deserves; ought we, must we, pay that price anyway?

Suppose it were enormously expensive even to find out what a given murderer deserves; ought we, must we, pay that price? Public resources are a scarce commodity; on what ground do we argue that giving offenders the punishment they deserve takes high (the highest?) priority in the allocation of public expenditures? 'Everyone always ought to get the punishment he or she deserves' does not, on reflection, have the finality to it that retributivists would have us believe.

With this general discussion of crime prevention and desert behind us, we are in a position to give a closer look at the arguments for and against capital punishment. Debate over the death penalty is usually constructed out of a complex mixture of factual generalizations, common-sense conjectures, and hypotheses, in conjunction with various normative principles and social goals. Leaving entirely to one side religious and sectarian arguments for and against the death penalty (except for the discussion below in Section 6.4), let us consider first some of the typical claims made by those who support the death penalty, in contrast to the claims made by those who oppose it, assuming for the sake of the argument that the death penalty is confined to the punishment of murder (even though historically it has been used to punish an immense variety of crimes) and that any considerations arising from the different methods of inflicting the death penalty can be ignored.

6. ARGUMENTS FOR THE DEATH PENALTY

Since the mid-eighteenth century in Europe, the initiative in arguing over the death penalty has been taken by those who are opposed to it; complacent acceptance of whatever is the current use of the death penalty has put its defenders in an essentially reactive posture. Let us reverse that procedure here and look first at the arguments favouring the death penalty. (Not all the authors cited for the arguments below are to be credited with originating the argument in question.)

6.1 The death penalty because of its severity and finality is more feared than imprisonment and deters some prospective murderers not deterred by the threat of imprisonment (van den Haag 1986). To put this another way, common sense tells us that, since people fear the death penalty more than they fear a punishment of imprisonment, they will be deterred more by the risk of incurring the death penalty than by the risk of imprisonment (Davis 1996; Pojman 1998).

Comment. This is an empirical proposition, and it immediately raises the question of what evidence there is to support it. (*a*) There is some anecdotal evidence given by arrested felons in police custody, for example, that they used toy guns, or no guns, rather than real guns, because using the latter might result in a felony murder and thus the risk of the death penalty. Whether such testimony is self-serving (telling the police what the arrestee believed they wanted to hear) or otherwise unreliable is uncertain. (*b*) Even if the death penalty is more feared than any less severe, humane punishment, it is obvious that thousands do not fear it enough to deter them. Criminal homicide statistics in the USA for the 1990s show that roughly 15,000 killers per year (that is, all those who commit criminal homicide in death-penalty jurisdictions) are not deterred by the threat of the death penalty. (*c*) It is possible that the death penalty is feared more than long-term imprisonment; even so, it may be that the punishment of life imprisonment is still severe enough to deter all those who can be deterred by any punishment (Conway 1974). (*d*) The deterrent effect of a punishment is not determined solely by its *severity* (or its severity relative to an alternative punishment), but also by the *certainty* and *celerity* of its imposition. The delays and uncertainty that surround infliction of the death penalty are a direct result of inescapable worries arising from its irrevocable character; these obstacles to maximum deterrence are not shared to the same extent by a punishment of imprisonment. As for improving the deterrent efficacy of the death penalty, that is impossible without 'hurry-up' procedures that will sacrifice the often-frail defences available to the accused that due process of law is intended to provide (Amsterdam 1999).

However, let us grant the original claim for the sake of the argument. Two fundamental problems remain. First, is it not plausible to assume that what this heightened fear of death provides to the would-be killer is, first and foremost, an incentive not to get caught? Only if it is also believed there is a high degree of certainty of arrest and conviction will this fear create a greater degree of deterrence. As things actually stand in American society today, a would-be murderer has one chance in three of not being arrested, and if arrested one chance in three of not being convicted of capital murder (US Federal Bureau of Investigation 1998).

Secondly, if fear of the death penalty is such a powerful deterrent and if deterrence is the primary consideration in our choice of punishments, why not threaten murderers with a still more frightening punishment, such as death preceded by torture, or death by means of a thousand cuts, or by burning at the stake? After all, if death is feared more than imprisonment because it is more painful (or a greater deprivation) than prison, then death by torture ought to be feared even more than death by lethal injection. If the only or the dominant consideration is instilling fear in would-be offenders, on what ground do we reject a system of really terrifying punishments? (Surely, not merely on the ground that the US Constitution forbids 'cruel and unusual punishments'; see the discussion in Section 7.8 below.)

If the reply is that death preceded by torture is not a 'humane' punishment, then that invites this rejoinder: to rule out torture on the ground of its inhumanity is to accept tacitly some principle or criterion of humanely tolerable punishments. To do that is to open the possibility that the upper bound to morally permissible punishments might rule out the death penalty as well.

6.2 Let us agree that we do not have convincing evidence to show that the death penalty is a better deterrent than imprisonment. Even so, we ought to choose the death penalty—it is our 'best bet' (van den Haag and Conrad 1983; van den Haag 1986; Pojman 1998). Our situation is as follows. Either the death penalty is a better deterrent or it is not (we don't know which). And either we choose to adopt the death penalty or we do not. This yields four possibilities: (1) death is the better deterrent, and we choose death as the punishment for murder; (2) death is the better deterrent, but we reject the death penalty; (3) death is not the better deterrent, but we choose it anyway, and (4) death is not the better deterrent and we choose a lesser punishment. Our task is to choose between the pair of outcomes (1) and (3), or the pair of outcomes (2) and (4). Assume that each outcome has the same a priori probability as the other three. Defenders of the death penalty claim that the rational choice is the pair (1) and (3)—that is, we ought to choose the death penalty because the outcomes are better whether or not the death penalty is a better deterrent.

Why? Because the value to society of the outcomes in the pair (1) and (3) is greater than for the outcomes (2) and (4). After all, innocent lives are worth more than guilty murderers' lives, and so the losses in outcome (2) are considerably greater than the gains; we must avoid outcome (2) at all costs. (The only possible gain in outcome (2) is that we run no risk of executing a few who are innocent.) The only way to avoid outcome (2) is to choose the pair (1) and (3). In outcome (1), the gains are much greater than the losses (which consist only in the deaths of murderers who deserve death anyway, plus the deaths of any who were wrongly convicted and executed). As for outcome (3), the loss is relatively slight; a few convicted murderers (guilty or innocent) are executed despite the fact that the general public gains no greater protection thanks to these executions. As for outcome (4), the gain is slight—no innocent murder convicts are executed—and the loss is zero. If we combine the gains and losses in the pair of outcomes (2) and (4), the losses clearly exceed the gains. We maximize the prospect of greatest gains and least losses if we choose to bet that the death penalty is a better deterrent, and that means choosing in favour of outcomes (1) and (3).

Comment. This argument, popularized (and perhaps invented) by Ernest van den Haag, has attracted more than its share of attention among philosophers, probably because it is so neat and abstract, appears to acknowledge our ignorance about deterrence, and caters to a common-sense belief that murderers are 'worth less' than their victims (Conway 1974; Bayles 1991; Pojman 1998). In several respects it is reminiscent of Pascal's Wager, a philosophical stalking horse for more than three centuries. Nevertheless, the argument has its weaknesses. (*a*) It is not clear that the argument applies to the real world of discretionary death indictments, plea bargains, trials, convictions, sentences, appeals, and executions—including execution of the innocent. And, if the argument does not apply to a world with these features, then it must be discarded as irrelevant. (*b*) Even if all four possible outcomes have equal a priori probability, the extensive search by social scientists for evidence of a special deterrent effect in the death penalty and their failure to date to discover any such evidence (recall Section 3) suggests that these four possible outcomes do not have the equal empirical probability. Awarding equal probability to the death penalty as a specially effective deterrent really just sidesteps the available empirical evidence. If we grant that the empirical probability favours outcomes (3) and (4), then it is not so clear that rationality requires us to prefer the pair of outcomes (1) and (2). (*c*) What the death penalty does is to risk the lives of innocent defendants wrongly convicted, without any scientific basis for believing that there is a commensurate gain in extra protection through deterrence. For all we know, everyone who is deterrable (and thousands evidently are not) is deterrable by a long prison sentence, in which case executing any prisoners produces no extra social protection (leaving aside any role for incapacitation to avoid recidivism). (*d*) If the death penalty brutalizes society, as some would have us believe, then the extent to which that result occurs has to be weighed against the conclusion of the Best Bet argument and the benefits it points to in extra deterrence. (*e*) Finally, if the death penalty as used in the USA should turn out to be a better marginal deterrent than long-term imprisonment, how can society be entitled to get the benefit of that extra deterrence when it is the product of a system riddled with injustice, maladministration, and error (see Section 7.6)?

6.3 It would be quite reasonable to support the death penalty if an execution of the guilty convict brought the victim back to life. If so, it seems unreasonable not to support it if an execution prevented, say, a hundred innocent persons from being murder victims (Pojman 1998).

Comment. Yes, it would be rational to support the death penalty if executing the murderer brought back to life the murder victim. But, since the death penalty has no such benefits and since there is no convincing evidence that the death penalty is a marginally superior deterrent, the alleged inconsistency can be ignored. What remains, however, just under the surface is the tacit accusation that opponents of the death penalty really do not care about the safety of the general public, much less the plight of the victims and their surviving loved ones. If they did (so the objection goes), they would be willing to embrace executions were it shown with reasonable assurance that executions actually did deter criminals undeterred by any less severe punishment. But embracing the death penalty on grounds of deterrent effectiveness ignores the risk of executing the innocent. (After all, the deterrent effect of a penalty is achieved by punishing the innocent as well as by punishing only the guilty, provided it is generally believed that the convicted defendants really are guilty.) And this leads to the following *tu quoque*: it is irrational to support the death penalty as a superior deterrent in the absence of convincing evidence to that effect and in the face of documented cases where innocent persons have been arrested, tried, convicted, sentenced to death, and executed.

6.4 Hundreds of thousands abstain from murder because they regard it with horror. One great reason why they regard it with horror is that murderers are hanged (J. F. Stephens, quoted favourably by van den Haag 1986).

Comment. If the idea of regarding murder with 'horror' means being horrified at the gross immorality of murder, disgusted and appalled at the thought of being a murderer (with the deserved opprobrium that implies), it is difficult to believe such a reaction is explained by a general awareness that convicted murderers are executed. Being aware that one is liable to punishment if one commits a criminal act does not teach that the act is *wrong*; what it teaches is that the act is *risky*. Awareness of the immorality of murder is best explained by awareness of the facts that murder is the killing of another human being without consent of the victim and that it causes the victim the gravest irremediable harm. Anyone can immediately see that murder violates familiar and common-sense moral principles, such as the Golden Rule. Awareness of that violation, not the punishment threatened for it, is what arouses moral 'horror' at murder.

6.5 Murderers have forfeited their right not to be killed (Pojman 1998).

Comment. The claim is familiar and looks plausible. No doubt we want a doctrine of forfeiture of rights in order to make punishment a legitimate possibility (lest the deprivations imposed in the name of punishment be themselves violations of the offender's rights). But there are at least two problems. (*a*) The claim invites us to say as well: rapists forfeit their right not to be raped, muggers forfeit their right not to be mugged, torturers forfeit their right not to be tortured, and so on. Surely, this is a *reductio ad absurdum* of the original claim, as there is no way with consistency to assert the claim in isolation in order to avoid embracing these ugly parallels. Tacit reliance on *lex talionis* can be discerned in the background. (*b*) We have to ask: if the murderer forfeits his right not to be killed, does he not also forfeit a right not to be killed in a long, drawn-out manner, say by crucifixion, particularly if he killed his victim in some such savage and cruel manner? Why are we not entitled to inflict death on the murderer in whatever horrible fashion he chose to inflict on his victim? Why does he not forfeit a right to be put to death promptly, painlessly, and with such dignity as circumstances permit? The very questions only need to be asked in order to see that there are upper bounds to permissible punishments that we ignore or flout at our peril. Why do those bounds not rule out modern, sanitized modes of inflicting the death penalty as well as cruel methods of carrying it out?

6.6 If I violate the rights of others, I therefore lose the same rights. Thus, if I am a murderer, I have no right to live (Primoratz 1989*a*).

Comment. This remark expresses the idea (without using the word) of forfeiture of rights, by far one of the most influential weapons in the armoury of those who support capital punishment. Undeniably, the general idea of the forfeiture of rights is a feature of any theory of rights worth taking seriously. More controversial, however, is whether any or all rights one possesses *can* be forfeited. Philosophers at least since John Locke (1632–1704) have insisted that we have certain inalienable natural or human rights; our right to life is usually said to be such a right. A few philosophers have gone further and insisted that we also have certain unforfeitable rights; the best candidate for such a right is whatever right is taken to be constitutive of our status as moral agents (Vlastos 1962; Morris 1981). Do we or do we not, then, forfeit our very status as moral agents by virtue of committing a terrible crime, such as murder? (Remember, only moral agents are capable of immoral conduct. Or are we to believe that, by behaving immorally, one can cease to be a moral agent?) Is it possible to retain our status as a moral agent, despite being a murderer, and yet forfeit our right to life? These questions have no standard answer.

6.7 If the murderer forfeits his right to life by violating the right of another to life, then society is justified in imposing the worst type of punishments on the murderer (Pojman 1998).

Comment. The issue here is not what the *murderer deserves*; it is rather what *we are free* to do to him given his forfeiture of rights. Notice that this argument treats forfeiture of the right to life as a sufficient condition of justifiably executing the murderer. To do so is to treat the murderer's forfeiture of his right as the only relevant (or the dominant) moral consideration in deciding what we ought to do to him. Furthermore, according to this argument, we are permitted to inflict cruel ('the worst type of') punishments. No doubt a more charitable interpretation of this argument would have it that, thanks to forfeiture of rights by the murderer, society is justified in inflicting 'the worst type' of morally permissible punishments. But on what basis are we to draw the line between morally permissible and morally impermissible punishments? Indeed, on what ground are we to conclude that the death penalty is among the permissible rather than the impermissible punishments? Either way, with or without the more charitable interpretation proposed above, the argument falls short.

6.8 Since the value of human life is not commensurable with other values, there is only one truly equivalent punishment for murder, namely death (Primoratz 1989a).

Comment. Although actuaries employed by insurance companies routinely put a dollar amount on the value of a human life (or limb), the rest of us are unlikely to share their confidence. Doubts on that score to the side, the incommensurabilty of values is not confined to the value of human life. Surely, being unraped, unassaulted, unkidnapped are also 'not commensurable with other values'. So the incommensurability of the value of human life is not unique. No doubt we can say that the value of not being murdered is *greater* than the value of not being raped, and greater than the value of not being kidnapped, and so on. But, whatever reason there is to believe that 'the only truly equivalent punishment for murder' is death, is equally a reason for believing that the only truly equivalent punishment for rape is—being raped, and so on. Thus we encounter, once again, only a slightly disguised form of the old doctrine of *lex talionis*.

6.9 Since the murderer cannot plausibly claim a right to life for himself, neither can anyone else do that on his behalf (Primoratz 1989*b*).

Comment. Let us grant that it is unfair to claim a right for oneself that one is unwilling to grant to others similarly situated. Let us further grant that it is unreasonable to expect someone whose right has been violated to respect the comparable right of the violator. But these concessions about rights do not suffice to tell us what the victim or society ought to do about the violation of the victim's rights. We can reach a decision on this crucial point only by means of some further normative premiss, such as this: morality poses no objection to punishing a murderer with death. That proposition, however, is not obviously true, because our rights do not exhaust the relevant moral considerations concerning what we ought to do (Thomson 1990); those other moral considerations remain to be examined.

6.10 Since it is morally right to be angry with criminals and to express that anger publicly, officially, and in an appropriate manner, this may require the worst of them to be executed (Berns 1979).

Comment. Is the world really a better, healthier place, thanks to the expression of anger at violent criminals by their victims or by third parties on behalf of the victims? Ought we to teach our children to cultivate the emotion of anger at wrongdoers and encourage and help them to find ways to express that anger 'in an appropriate manner'? What *is* an 'appropriate' expression of anger? And what is its proper target? (Think of the old saw, 'Hate the sin, love the sinner'.) The feeling and expression of resentment—seeing oneself as an undeserving victim of another's immoral conduct and objecting to it—is understandable. So is moral indignation— seeing another as an undeserving victim of someone's immoral conduct and objecting to it. But both resentment and indignation are moral emotions—that is, they are regulated by moral considerations, in contrast to anger and revenge. These latter know no bounds; thus it might be said that they are *always* inappropriate, even if they are often excusable. After the anger, then what? (Consider the admonition, 'Anger in haste, repent at leisure'.) Or is one supposed to cultivate and sustain anger, relishing the feeling, savouring the excitement, and then act accordingly? Surely, this is a recipe for disaster in both moral and political relations.

6.11 If humans do not possess some kind of intrinsic value—say the image of God—then we have the right to rid ourselves of those who egregiously violate the necessary conditions for civilized living (Pojman 1998).

Comment. No doubt murderers, rapists, kidnappers, muggers, and other persons guilty of crimes against the person 'egregiously violate the necessary conditions for civilized living'. But—as the story of Cain's punishment for the murder of his brother Abel teaches (Gen. 4: 8–16)—there is more than one way to 'rid' ourselves of their presence among us. In most capital punishment jurisdictions (China is a conspicuous exception), convicted murderers are routinely sentenced to prison. Only a small fraction is sentenced to death. Are they the worst among the bad, the most dangerous, the least likely to be incapacitated by prison, the least likely to be deterred by the threat of any punishment less severe than death? The empirical evidence suggests otherwise; at most, some among those sentenced and executed are 'the worst among the bad', but many of the others clearly are not. (The criteria for their selection as death-row convicts had little or nothing to do with the above considerations.) Basing penal policies on purely secular considerations (as the argument assumes) does not free us from the constraints of reflective morality. Dostoevsky's Ivan Karamazov was wrong in thinking that, if God is dead, everything is permitted.

6.12 Persons in the Rawlsian Original Position behind a Veil of Ignorance would choose to live in a society with the death penalty for murder (Cooper and King-Farlow 1989).

Comment. If this reasoning were correct, it would tend to show that the death penalty is a fair or just punishment. But is it correct? Consider the following general facts about contemporary USA (such information must be available if one is to decide on any social policies behind the Veil): at the end of the twentieth century, there were annually (*a*) about 18,000 victims of criminal homicide, (*b*) 200–300 convicted murderers sentenced to death, and (*c*) 100 or so executed. Furthermore, (*d*) an uncertain percentage of all persons arrested, tried, convicted, sentenced to death, and executed are innocent, (*e*) there is no empirical evidence that the death penalty is a better deterrent than long-term imprisonment, (*f*) there is no empirical evidence that prisoners, guards, visitors are more at risk in the prisons of non-death-penalty jurisdictions than in the prisons of death-penalty jurisdictions, and (*g*) there is no empirical evidence that the police are less at risk in death-penalty jurisdictions than in jurisdictions without the death penalty. There is empirical evidence that (*h*), if one is non-white or poor, one has a greater likelihood of being arrested, indicted, tried, convicted, and sentenced to death than if one is white and rich, and that (*i*) capital trial juries tend to make up their minds about the punishment the accused deserves even before the defendant is convicted; they do not understand the judge's instructions on how to decide between a life and a death sentence for the defendant they have just convicted; and even when they do understand those instructions they do not always follow them (Bowers 1995; Bowers et al. 1998). Furthermore, there is (*j*) a slightly greater likelihood of being a murder victim or a member of a victim's family than being a murderer or a member of a murderer's family, (k) a greater likelihood of being found guilty, sentenced to death, and executed than being innocent but found guilty, sentenced to death, and executed, (l) a greater likelihood of being poor rather than rich and thus at greater risk of being a murder victim and of being a murderer, and (m) a greater likelihood of being white rather than non-white, and to that extent at less risk of being a murder victim or a murderer sentenced to death.

Would a rational, self-interested person averse to running great risks conclude that he or she would be better off in a society with the death penalty for murder (in a discretionary, not mandatory, form) than in a society with no punishment for murder more severe than LWOP? Were one to turn out to be a murderer, it is reasonable to assume that self-interest would dictate that one would prefer prison to death. Were one to turn out to be a murder victim, one might wish the murderer to be punished equivalently, thus favouring the death penalty. ('Might' because, improbable as it may seem, many survivors of murder victims are on record avowing that they do not want the murderer of their loved one to be put to death.) But, given the nearly equal likelihood of these two possibilities (and the small likelihood of being either a murderer or a murder victim), there is not much to tip the scale for or against the death penalty. These considerations suggest that there is no clear and convincing reason for wanting to live in a society that has the (discretionary) death penalty for murder, because there is no evidence of gain in security from the greater severity of the punishment over LWOP, and because there is evidence that the system is not fail-safe. Therefore, if Rawlsian contractarianism is the correct way to determine whether a social policy is fair, then it is unclear whether the death penalty in contemporary USA passes this test. To the extent similar considerations apply to other Western societies, the same verdict follows.

A somewhat more definite result emerges if we view the task of thinking behind a Veil of Ignorance (as Rawls does) as designed to help us make a choice among *principles* and only indirectly a choice for or against the death penalty as a *policy*. In this context, the issue concerns the choice of principles governing state interference with individual liberty, privacy, and autonomy. It seems reasonable to suppose that behind the Veil it would be in the rational self-interest of everyone to choose a principle empowering the state to make minimal coercive interferences and then only in pursuit of paramount social goals. As will be argued below (see Section 8), adoption of such a principle given the relevant facts yields a strong—indeed, the best— argument against the death penalty.

6.13 The death penalty is a symbolic affirmation of the humanity of both victim and murderer (van den Haag 1985b).

Comment. The death penalty does nothing for the murder victim, and it has very diverse effects on the victim's surviving friends and family. So how execution of the murderer 'symbolically affirms' the humanity of the victim (something that life in prison presumably fails to do) is unclear. As for the 'humanity of the murderer' and its symbolic affirmation in his execution, that seems to be manifest in two ways. First, executing him shows him that he is not superhuman and hence not invulnerable to the kind of harm he inflicted on the victim. But, as that harm was a wrongful harm, it is not immediately clear why inflicting similar harm is not also a wrongful harm even when it is done through the criminal justice system. Secondly, finding the defendant guilty and sentencing him or her to death treats the defendant as a fully responsible moral agent at the time of the crime and at the time of execution. It would presumably be inhumane to execute an insane or otherwise non-responsible offender. However, not all those actually executed qualify as fully responsible moral agents even if they do not qualify as legally insane (consider the cases of Alvin Ford in Florida in 1991 (Miller and Radelet 1993)) and Ricky Ray Rector in Arkansas in 1992 (Frady 1993). The claim in (13) is true, if at all, only in an ideal system of capital punishment; it is quite false as a description of every known actual system.

In any case, this consideration does not exhaust the symbolic significance of the death penalty. For its opponents the death penalty symbolizes ultimate and unlimited power over the individual by an impersonal government that operates 'the machinery of death' (Justice Blackmun, dissenting in *Callins* v. *Collins*, 1994). Execution is not the only way 'symbolically to affirm the humanity of victim and murderer'. Why should we believe it is the best way?

7. ARGUMENTS AGAINST THE DEATH PENALTY

As the discussion in Section 6 shows, rebuttals to arguments for the death penalty amount to arguments against it. But not all the reasons for opposing the death penalty emerge in the clearest light if they are limited to the role of rebuttal argumentation. If the abolitionist seizes the initiative, the kinds of reasons that typically emerge include the following, each of which warrants a closer look. (Most of the arguments cited below, being part of the popular discourse on the subject, are not supported by a citation to any source.)

7.1 Governments have no right to use the death penalty.

Comment. This is perhaps the oldest argument against the death penalty, having been used by Cesare Beccaria (1738–94) in his path-breaking monograph, *On Crimes and Punishments* (1764/1995), the first notable attack on the death penalty. Beccaria argued that no rationally self-interested person would choose to live in a society that uses the death penalty (he might be its victim), and, since society has no right to do anything other than what its members would permit, therefore society (and its agent, government) has no right to adopt the death penalty. This conclusion may indeed be true, but the argument for it is inconclusive because it relies on a highly contested principle of legitimate government—namely, that a government has the right to threaten and inflict harm in punishment only to the extent that a rationally self-interested person would permit it to do so.

There are other problems with this claim. (*a*) It can be viewed as a theorem from a generally pacifist axiom forbidding all forms of punishment; if it is so viewed, it is unlikely to attract many supporters. (*b*) Few would deny that one's liberty and property are valuable to the owner, and yet the state has the right to take one's liberty and property as punishment. If so, then why not life as well? Either claim (1) is false, or the state has no right to punish at all, or there is something peculiar—indeed, unique—about taking life as punishment that is absent where taking liberty or property as punishment is concerned. (*c*) There is some danger of hidden circularity here. If one argues 'The death penalty is wrong because no one has the right to use it', that is coherent and possibly true. But if one tries to explain why the government has no right to use this punishment by claiming that it is morally wrong, then one is arguing in a circle, presupposing the very thing to be proved. (*d*) If the death penalty were a better preventive of crime than any alternative punishment less severe, some would argue that *salus populi suprema rex* and so government does have the right to use the threat of death as a deterrent.

7.2 The death penalty ought to be abolished because it violates the offender's right to life.

Comment. There are two major objections to this claim. (*a*) It would be a plausible argument if (but only if) one could defend the proposition that the right to life is *absolute*—that is, there are no moral considerations that could ever outweigh this right. But this seems unlikely. Consider self-defence or intervention as a third party on behalf of someone at risk of death by the lethal aggression of another. Are we to believe that it is always wrong—and, in particular, that no one ever has the right—to avoid being a victim of unjust life-threatening aggression by acting so as to disable the aggressor by taking his life? No one but an absolute pacifist believes this; and it seems highly irrational in any case. (*b*) Defenders of the death penalty will argue (see above, Sections 6. 5–7) that, since murderers forfeit their right to life, only the innocent can find protection of their interests through their right to life. Precisely how the critic of the death penalty is to respond to this objection is unclear.

Nevertheless, the idea of a universal human right to life is of use to the opponent of the death penalty in the following way. It does seem reasonable to argue that in a very general way the burden of proof always falls on those who would take human life under whatever conditions. (To suppose that neither side of the argument has any burden of proof, or that the burden falls on those who would not kill other human beings, is too implausible to be worth discussing.) If so, then it is morally necessary for the advocates of the death penalty to explain why certain human lives ought to be taken as punishment.

7.3 The death penalty ought to be abolished because it ignores the value of human life.

Comment. This claim invites the challenge: what value is there in the life of a convicted murderer? As an empirical fact, given the great variety of persons convicted of murder, and the variations in their education, intelligence, dangerousness, talent, character, abilities, self-control, socialization, and so on, there is no plausible generalization to cover all cases and thus answer the question unequivocally. Empirical evidence amply sustains only this vague generalization: some convicted murderers can live a life of considerable value, to themselves and to others (the famous case in the 1920s of Nathan Leopold (1958) is a stellar and by no means unique example). But there are others, many others, whose lives are of little if any value to society, and of dubious value to themselves—as their suicidal despondency or their maladjustment to prison life indicates. The variable and often indeterminable value in the life of a convicted murderer makes it impossible to use this consideration across the board as a basis for rejecting the death penalty in all cases.

Again, however, opponents of the death penalty can rescue something of use to their argument. It is plausible to take as a baseline that each human life is (or could be) of value both to the person whose life it is and to others in the social environment. This puts the burden of argument on those who would endorse killing some persons on the ground that the disvalue of their lives manifestly outweighs whatever value their lives have. To be sure, judging the value versus the disvalue of a given human life is neither simple nor uncontroversial. Still, we have to countenance the possibility that, as a matter of empirical fact, we cannot reasonably believe the value of the life of *every* convicted murderer outweighs whatever is of disvalue in that life.

7.4 The death penalty is wrong because it flouts the sanctity of human life.

Comment. Unlike the other claims and arguments discussed in this section, this one is not secular. The sanctity of human life is a religious concept, especially familiar to Jews, Christians, and Muslims because of the biblical doctrine that man is made in the 'image of God' (Gen. 9: 6). Secular moral theory cannot use this concept, any more than it can pass judgement on the legitimacy of this religious norm. What can be said, however, is that the logic of the doctrine of the sanctity of human life puts the burden of argument on those biblical monotheists who believe in the death penalty, not on their co-religionists who would invoke this idea to protest the death penalty. In this connection, it is especially interesting to consider the argument of the recent papal encyclical, *Evangelium vitae, The Gospel of Life* (1995). In this treatise, Pope John Paul II argued that, in the absence of 'necessity' to protect human life, there is no justification for a penalty that takes lives, even the lives of murderers. The Pope reminds us of the story of Cain and Abel (Gen. 4: 8–16); God punishes the murderer Cain with a curse, a stigma, and exile—but not death. No other biblical passage relevant to the death penalty involves a decree by God on the punishment of a guilty murderer in the way this passage does.

7.5 The death penalty is an affront to human dignity.

Comment. The concept of human dignity has played a surprisingly neglected role in modern moral philosophy; partly for this reason an appeal to human dignity in public discussion and debate often runs the risk of being merely a rhetorical flourish. What counts as respect for, in contrast to violations of, human dignity is far from clear. In sharp contrast to the role of rights, values, justice, virtues, and their several overlapping and interwoven norms, the concept of dignity is underdeveloped and inadequately integrated into the rest of normative moral theory.

Elsewhere (Bedau 1992), it has been suggested that the claim (7.5) above might be fleshed out as follows. First, it is an affront to the dignity of a person to be forced to undergo catastrophic harm at the hands of another when, before the harm is imposed, the former is entirely at the mercy of the latter, as is always the case with legal punishment. Secondly, it offends the dignity of a person to be punished according to the will of a punisher free to pick and choose arbitrarily among offenders, so that only a few are punished very severely when all deserve the same severe punishment if any do. Thirdly, it offends the dignity of a person to be subjected to a severe punishment when society shows by its actual conduct in sentencing that it no longer regards this punishment as the best or the only legitimate punishment for that crime. Finally, it is an affront to human dignity to impose very severe punishment on an offender when it is known that a less severe punishment will achieve all the purposes it is appropriate to try to achieve by punishing anyone in any manner whatsoever.

If there is an argument (such as the one above) against the death penalty on the ground of its affront to human dignity, it remains to be seen whether such an argument by itself would be sufficient to outweigh, say, an argument for the death penalty based on considerations of deterrence and incapacitation, or on desert.

7.6 The death penalty is wrong because its history shows that it cannot be administered fairly.

Comment. The available evidence strongly confirms the claim, and it is this claim that is probably the most influential of all the arguments against the death penalty for those who oppose it at present. From the decision of the prosecution on whether to seek the death penalty to the decision of the executive on whether to extend clemency, the administration of the death penalty—at least in the USA—has been and remains significantly 'deregulated'. A wide variety of independent observers has reached this conclusion (Weisberg 1984; White 1991; Paternoster 1991; Bright 1994, 1995; International Commission of Jurists 1996; American Bar Association 1997; Acker et al. 1998). Few who have studied the matter carefully believe that this complex problem can be remedied by procedural reforms.

However, the implicit claim is that the deregulation characteristic of the death penalty is more pronounced or in some other way worse than the (de)regulation of long-term prison sentences. If there is evidence to support this claim, it is obscure and underdeveloped. Nevertheless, it seems reasonable to grant that, if the death penalty is a more severe sanction than LWOP, then *ceteris paribus* its mismanagement is worse than whatever mismanagement characterizes administration of the alternative punishment.

But is this deficiency, even if true, a sound basis on which to abolish the death penalty? Critics of the objection in claim (7.6) above are quick to point out that it is addressed entirely to the administration of this form of punishment, and not to the death penalty itself. They will add that every form of punishment meted out by the criminal justice system involves errors and mistakes in its administration; the death penalty is hardly unique in suffering from such shortcomings. They will argue further that the maladministration of the death penalty is not an argument for its abolition. Opponents of the death penalty will reply that it is artificial to distinguish between a flawless death-penalty system (possible only in an ideal world utterly remote from ours) and the actual flawed systems under which we live and have always lived, and in which real persons are put to death by a system that seems to resist significant reforms and improvements. There is no such thing as 'the death penalty itself'; there are only the actual systems under law, warts and all. Any attempt to distinguish the death penalty as such from the death penalty as actually administered under law in a given jurisdiction distracts us from the evaluation of the death penalty in the only forms we actually have it (Black 1981). Friends of the death penalty divide over whether this problem (especially as it involves seemingly irreducible racism) is so grave as to undermine whatever merit there is in the death penalty taken abstractly as a just punishment (Berns 1979; van den Haag 1986).

7.7 Even though murderers do deserve the death penalty, it is desirable for a modern state to refuse to impose such punishments, because such punishments are inconsistent with the civilizing process characteristic of modern states (Reiman 1998).

Comment. This argument, which might be called the Advancement of Civilization Argument, owes its inspiration to the French sociologist Émile Durkheim (1858–1917). His so-called 'laws of penal evolution' claim in part that, the more advanced a civilization becomes, the less it practises brutal corporal punishments. Cruel punishments, like torture, cause great pain and require the utter subordination of the punished to the punisher. From this point of view, the death penalty is like torture, a retrograde and counter-civilizing practice. 'Torture is to be avoided not only because of what it says about what we are willing to do to our fellows, but also because of what it says about us who are willing to do it' (Reiman 1998: 115). Thus the refusal to carry out lethal punishments even on those who arguably deserve them contributes significantly to this civilizing process.

One advantage of this argument is that it can concede the chief demand of the retributivist—we know what punishment murderers deserve; it is the punishment most like their crime—while arguing that other considerations have a predominant role in determining whether society ought to use this mode of punishment. The result is this: although murderers *deserve* to die, and thus society has a *right* to sentence them to death and execute them, society *ought not* to do so (and certainly has no duty to do so), because the system we use to determine who ought to be executed is itself fundamentally unjust. The death-penalty system in the USA is fundamentally flawed, so that the justice of the death penalty taken in the abstract is undermined by the injustice of its actual administration. (This final step in the Advancement of Civilization Argument amounts to recycling the empirical considerations central to the argument in Section 7.6.)

Abolitionists who are also desert sceptics need not reject this argument, because its main features remain intact whether or not one endorses the retributivist features it embraces. They are independent of any advancement of civilization effects that forswearing the death penalty allegedly produces. On the other hand, there is some danger of circularity in this argument. Using abandonment of cruel practices like torture as a criterion of a civilized society guarantees that the death penalty cannot survive in a civilized society, provided that the analogy to torture is accepted. But some will surely reject the analogy, just as others will grant that civility is incompatible with barbaric punitive practices but will deny that the death penalty is necessarily barbaric: what is so barbaric (they will reply) about a substantially painless execution by lethal injection?

7.8 The death penalty in the USA is wrong because it violates constitutional protections.

Comment. If this claim is meant to be an accurate statement of the status of the death penalty at the beginning of the twenty-first century, as seen by the Supreme Court in its role as the ultimate legal interpreter of the Constitution and the Bill of Rights, then it is false. Beginning with its decision in *Furman* v. *Georgia* (1972), the court has whittled away at the permissible scope of death penalties. But the court also ruled by a majority of 7 to 2 in *Gregg.* v. *Georgia* (1976) that the death penalty *per se* is not in violation of the eighth amendment prohibition of 'cruel and unusual punishments'. The court has also implicitly rejected any suggestion that the death penalty inherently violates some other constitutional provision, such as 'due process of law' (fifth amendment), 'equal protection of the laws' (fourteenth amendment), or unenumerated rights of the person (ninth amendment). It is, of course, possible to argue (as some have) that the court is wrong, and that it has misinterpreted these provisions of the Constitution (Black 1981; Bedau 1985, 1992, 1996).

From the moral point of view, however, these constitutional considerations really are beside the point. Even if the US Constitution were interpreted by some future Supreme Court to rule out the death penalty, one would still have to face the question whether such interpretations were based on sound moral theory. 'Ought we to abolish the death penalty?' cannot be answered with any finality merely by a decision of the Supreme Court to the effect that, contrary to *Gregg* and related cases, the death penalty really is inherently inconsistent with the Constitution and the Bill of Rights.

7.9 The death penalty is wrong because it violates international standards of permissible and humane punishment.

Comment. The death penalty in the USA and in several foreign countries, as administered, is clearly in violation of international human-rights standards. Those standards prohibit execution of anyone under 18, whereas several US jurisdictions permit juveniles under 18 but over 16 to be executed (National Coalition to Abolish the Death Penalty 1997). They also prohibit execution of the mentally disabled. US law makes no exception for women, whereas international human-rights law forbids their execution. The US Government has ratified the International Covenant on Civil and Political Rights with explicit reservations on these two issues, reservations that have been challenged by other signatory nations (Schabas 1997). In 1999, the UN Human Rights Commission voted for a worldwide moratorium on executions; the USA was one of eleven nations voting against this resolution.

However, as with the constitutional objections to the death penalty discussed above, objections based on international human-rights law are of interest from the moral point of view only to the extent that the human-rights laws in question are persuasive and can be incorporated into a sound normative moral theory (Nickel 1987). As with legal norms generally, international human-rights norms are not ultimate but are at best only penultimate considerations.

7.10 The death penalty ought to be abolished because conditions on death row are morally intolerable.

Comment. There are two versions of this argument. One stresses the fact that conditions on the death rows of death-penalty prisons in many nations leave much to be desired. These conditions have a harmful and enduring effect on most of those who have to undergo them, especially when death-row prisoners in the USA may spend a decade or more before their cases are finally resolved. The other argument simply points to the long duration of life under a death sentence for many prisoners, and claims that, no matter how decent death-row conditions are, the long delay in reaching a final disposition (execution or some form of relief) is itself a cruel and inhumane treatment. Friends of the death penalty will deny that these conditions are beyond remedy, and will insist that the remedy need not lie in abolition of the death penalty. Is it not more plausible to argue, they will say, that, if the conditions on death row are truly inhumane and intolerable, then they ought to be remedied as swiftly and completely as possible—and that their remedy is entirely a separate issue from abolishing the death penalty? Abolitionists using this argument must defend the proposition that these conditions by the very nature of the case cannot be adequately remedied, and that the only remedy is not only to dismantle death row but to abolish the death penalty itself. But is that true? Surely, it is not unreasonable to reply that, quite apart from abolishing the death penalty, prisons ought to abolish wretched and indecent conditions of incarceration, period.

7.11 The death penalty is too expensive to support.

Comment. Executions are indeed much cheaper than long-term imprisonment, if all one counts in the cost is the pro-rated salary of the prison personnel as they monitor each death-row prisoner and prepare for and carry out a death sentence, plus whatever material costs are involved (food and security while on death row, a dose of lethal gas, lethal injection, a dozen rifle bullets, electricity, or the hangman's rope) and other pro-rated costs. A much better way to think about the cost of the death penalty is to calculate the costs of a criminal justice *system* in which *every* murder indictment raises the question of whether the accused is to be tried as a first-degree murderer and thus be made vulnerable to a death sentence. This requires tracking the typical costs of murder trials and subsequent appeals in which the death penalty is sought versus the comparable costs incurred in murder trials and appeals in jurisdictions without the death penalty. Research by several different investigators that takes these considerations into account reveals that a typical modern death penalty system in the USA is far more expensive than an alternative system of LWOP (Dieter 1994). Thus the claim advanced in (11) is true, so far as current calculations permit.

   If, however, justice or other moral considerations showed that a death penalty system really is required, then deciding between its abolition and retention in favour of the less expensive system would represent a refusal to finance a requirement of justice. The only way in which the greater costs of a death-penalty system constitute a relevant criticism of that system is if the death penalty can also be criticized on moral grounds.

7.12 The risk of executing the innocent, however small, is too large a risk to run.

Comment. Calculating the risk of wrongful execution is very difficult. During the twentieth century in the USA, that risk may have been quite small: out of over 7,000 executions, only a few hundred have been carefully examined, and of these 0.3 per cent ($=$ 24 cases) seem highly probable to have involved an execution of the innocent (Bedau and Radelet 1987). How should we tell whether this risk is too large to accept? Are abolitionists in danger of exaggerating the risk of erroneous executions? Perhaps. Imperfect though the system is, for every person believed to be innocent but executed in recent years, seven or eight innocent prisoners under sentence of death were vindicated in time to be released; some of these defendants narrowly escaped wrongful execution (Radelet et al. 1992). Were the death penalty known to be a superior deterrent to imprisonment, one might argue that risking the lawful deaths of a few innocent prisoners (but of course not *known* to be innocent) is worth the added protection for hundreds of innocent citizens (recall the argument in Section 6). But the evidence on deterrence prevents that argument (see above, Section 3).

Some defenders of the death penalty (van den Haag 1986) concede that the death penalty may occasionally fall upon the innocent, but they argue that this is not a reason to abolish the death penalty, any more than it is a reason to prohibit automobiles and trucks from the highways when we know that statistical lives will be lost in traffic accidents. This objection, however, overlooks two important points. (*a*) Highway traffic provides many incontrovertible social benefits, whereas it is arguable whether the death penalty provides any (or any that outweigh its costs, economic and otherwise). (*b*) The death penalty is an intentionally lethal system, whereas the use of high-speed vehicles, highway design, and traffic regulations involves no such intention at all. Since highway deaths are accidental, not intentional, the provocative comparison is irrelevant.

8. The Best Argument for Abolition

Whatever argument one regards as the best argument for or against the death penalty is bound to reflect one's beliefs about the best argument for a system of punishment generally. Accordingly, it may be most useful to end this discussion with an examination of what may be the best argument currently available in favour of abolition, an argument that best merges empirical generalizations and norms, practical as well as abstract considerations.

1. Governments ought to use the least restrictive means—that is, the least severe, intrusive, violent methods of interference with personal liberty, privacy, and autonomy—sufficient to achieve compelling state interests.
2. Reducing the volume and rate of criminal violence—especially murder—is a compelling state interest.
3. The threat of severe punishment is a necessary means to that end.
4. Long-term imprisonment is less severe and restrictive than the death penalty.
5. Long-term imprisonment is sufficient to accomplish (2).
6. Therefore, the death penalty—more restrictive, invasive, and severe than imprisonment—is unnecessary; it violates premiss (1).
7. Therefore, the death penalty ought to be abolished.

The seven steps of this argument have been elaborated elsewhere (Bedau 1999) and are of rather different character. Premiss (1) states a fundamental liberal principle of state intervention at least as old as John Stuart Mill's essay *On Liberty* (1859/1975).

Premiss (2) states a goal any society must pursue if it hopes to endure. Premiss (3) is an empirical proposition generally accepted and warranted not only by common sense but by reflection on the conditions of social order. Premiss (4) is an empirical proposition supported by evidence from the behaviour of death-row prisoners (who rarely attempt suicide and rarely dismiss their lawyers in order to 'volunteer' for execution). Premiss (5), also an empirical generalization, is based on experience with abolition of the death penalty in many societies, including several states in the USA. Conclusions (6) and (7) follow accordingly. The argument overall is entirely forward looking and allots no role to retribution or desert in the general justification of punishment (and a fortiori none in justifying the death penalty), although the argument can accommodate these ideas in deciding who ought to be punished (namely, all and only the guilty who lack a credible excuse or justification).

This argument is not invulnerable to criticism. Premiss (5) and thus the conclusion in step (6) will of course be rejected by those who believe in the deterrent superiority of the death penalty when compared with LWOP or other forms of long-term imprisonment. But, this criticism aside, the basic objection to this argument by defenders of the death penalty will not focus on contesting any of the other steps in the argument; they have no reason to quarrel with premisses (1), (2), or (3). Nor do they have reason to quarrel with step (4); defenders of the death penalty must believe this empirical claim, or else their support of the death penalty involves preferring what they believe to be the less severe punishment. As for step (5), some will accept and others will contest this premiss. Conclusions (6) and (7) are unavoidable given the prior steps. Where does this leave the defenders of the death penalty?

The focus of their objections will be on what this argument entirely omits—namely, any reference to the unique (or, less extravagantly, the relatively superior) fit between the penalty of death and the crime of murder, and the feelings of outrage and indignation provoked by crimes against the person, especially by murder. Thus, the inference to the conclusion in (6) can be blunted by asserting and defending further premisses (FP) such as these:

(FP1) to the greatest degree possible, a punishment ought to reflect the gravity of the crime,

(FP2) a punishment reflects the gravity of the crime to the extent that the loss or deprivation it imposes on the offender is equivalent to the loss or deprivation the crime imposed on the victim, and

(FP3) the death penalty expresses public outrage and indignation at murder as well as what the murderer deserves better than any (tolerably humane) form of imprisonment, such as LWOP.

Opponents of the death penalty probably cannot accept (FP1); and, if they reject this premiss, it does not matter whether they accept or reject (FP2). What they cannot do is accept both these premisses and still oppose the death penalty (unless they were to defend some such implausible view as that murder does not impose on the victim as great a loss or deprivation as the death penalty imposes on the offender). They must then either reject (FP3) or come up with a reason why this true premiss is nonetheless not dispositive, because countervailing considerations prevail. They might reach that conclusion if the following were also true:

(FP4) The death penalty brutalizes society and provokes disrespect for human life within prisons and among the general public.

Were some such empirical generalization true, one might plausibly argue that it cancels (or at least puts into doubt) the importance of (FP3).

If the discussion of this section is correct, then even the best argument against the death penalty is not beyond challenge. Deciding which side of the dispute has the better of the argument will require further reflection on the moral and political norms and empirical generalizations employed in the various arguments for and against abolition, restoration, retention, or revision of the death penalty.

REFERENCES

Acker, James R., Bohm, Robert M., and Lanier, Charles S. (1998) (eds.), *America's Experiment with Capital Punishment: Reflections on the Past, Present, and Future of the Ultimate Penal Sanction*. Durham, NC: Carolina Academic Press.

American Bar Association (1997). 'Recommendation and Report'. *Law and Contemporary Problems*, 61: 219–31.

Amsterdam, Anthony G. (1999). 'Selling a Quick Fix for Boot Hill: The Myth of Justice Delayed in Death Cases', in Austin Sarat (ed.), *The Killing State: Capital Punishment in Law, Politics, and Culture*. New York: Oxford University Press, 148–83.

Bailey, William C., and Peterson, Ruth D. (1997). 'Murder, Capital Punishment, and Deterrence: A Review of the Literature', in Hugo Adam Bedau (ed.), *The Death Penalty in America: Current Controversies*. New York: Oxford University Press, 135–61.

Bayles, Michael D. (1991). 'A Note on the Death Penalty as the Best Bet'. *Criminal Justice Ethics*, 10: 7–10.

Beccaria, Cesare (1764/1995). *On Crimes and Punishments, in Beccaria On Crimes and Punishments and Other Writings*, ed. R. Davies. Cambridge: Cambridge University Press, 1–113.

Bedau, Hugo Adam (1978). 'Retribution and the Theory of Punishment'. *Journal of Philosophy*, 75: 601–20.

——(1985). 'Thinking of the Death Penalty as a Cruel and Unusual Punishment'. *University of California Davis Law Review*, 18: 873–925.

——(1991). 'Punitive Violence and its Alternatives', in James B. Brady and Newton Garver (eds.), *Justice, Law, and Violence*. Philadelphia: Temple University Press, 193–209.

——(1992). 'The Eighth Amendment, Human Dignity, and the Death Penalty', in Michael J. Meyer and William A. Parent (eds.), *The Constitution of Rights: Human Dignity and American Values*. Ithaca, NY: Cornell University Press, 145–77.

——(1996). 'Interpreting the Eighth Amendment: Principled vs. Populist Strategies'. *Thomas M. Cooley Law Review*, 13: 780–813.

—— (1997) (ed.), *The Death Penalty in America: Current Controversies*. New York: Oxford University Press.

—— (1999). 'Abolishing the Death Penalty Even for the Worst Murderers', in Austin Sarat (ed.), *The Killing State: Capital Punishment in Law, Politics, and Culture*. New York: Oxford University Press, 40–59.

—— and Radelet, Michael L. (1987). 'Miscarriages of Justice in Potentially Capital Cases'. *Stanford Law Review*, 40: 21–179.

Bentham, Jeremy (1830/1838). 'Rationale of Punishment', in *The Works of Jeremy Bentham*, ed. John Bowring. London: Simpkin, Marshall, & Co., i. 388–525.

Berns, Walter (1979). *For Capital Punishment: Crime and the Morality of the Death Penalty*. New York: Basic Books.

Black, Charles L., Jr. (1981). *Capital Punishment: The Inevitability of Caprice and Mistake*. 2nd edn. New York: W. W. Norton.

Bowers, William J. (1988). 'The Effect of Executions is Brutalization, Not Deterrence', in Kenneth C. Haas and James A. Inciardi (eds.), *Challenging Capital Punishment: Legal and Social Science Approaches*. Newbury Park, CA: Sage, 49–89.

—— (1995). 'The Capital Jury Project: Rationale, Design, and Preview of Early Findings'. *Indiana Law Journal*, 70: 1043–103.

—— and Pierce, Glenn L. (1980). 'Deterrence or Brutalization: What is the Effect of Executions?' *Crime and Delinquency*, 26: 453–84.

—— Sandys, Marla, and Steiner, Benjamin D. (1998). 'Foreclosed Impartiality in Capital Sentencing: Juror's Predispositions, Guilt-Trial Experience, and Premature Decision Making'. *Cornell Law Review*, 83: 1476–556.

Bright, Stephen B. (1994). 'Counsel for the Poor: The Death Sentence Not for the Worst Crime but for the Worst Lawyer'. *Yale Law Journal*, 103: 1835–83.

—— (1995). 'Discrimination, Death and Denial: The Tolerance of Racial Discrimination in Infliction of the Death Penalty'. *Santa Clara Law Review*, 35: 433–83.

Conway, David A. (1974). 'Capital Punishment and Deterrence: Some Considerations in Dialogue Form'. *Philosophy and Public Affairs*, 3: 431–3.

Cooper, W. E., and King-Farlow, John (1989). 'A Case for Capital Punishment'. *Journal of Social Philosophy*, 20: 64–76.

Davis, Michael (1996). *Justice in the Shadow of Death: Rethinking Capital and Lesser Punishments*. Lanham, MD: Rowman & Littlefield.

Diamond, Bernard L. (1975). 'Murder and the Death Penalty'. *American Journal of Orthopsychiatry*, 45: 712–22.

Dieter, Richard C. (1994). *Millions Misspent: What Politicians Don't Say About the High Cost of the Death Penalty*. Rev. edn. Washington: Death Penalty Information Center.

Ehrlich, Isaac (1975). 'The Deterrent Effect of Capital Punishment: A Question of Life or Death'. *American Economic Review*, 85: 397–417.

Feinberg, Joel (1970). 'The Expressive Function of Punishment', in Feinberg, *Doing and Deserving: Essays in the Theory of Responsibility*. Princeton: Princeton University Press, 95–118.

Fox, James Alan, and Radelet, Michael L. (1989). 'Persistent Flaws in Econometric Studies of the Deterrent Effect of the Death Penalty'. *Loyola of Los Angeles Law Review*, 23: 29–44.

Frady, Marshall (1993). 'Death in Arkansas'. *New Yorker*, 22, Feb. 105–18, 119–26, 128–33.

Gibbs, Jack P. (1975). *Crime, Punishment, and Deterrence*. New York: Elsevier.

Hart, H. L. A. (1968). 'Prolegomena to the Principles of Punishment', in Hart, *Punishment and Responsibility: Essays in the Philosophy of Law*. New York: Oxford University Press, 1–27.

International Commission of Jurists (1996). *Administration of the Death Penalty in the United States*. Geneva: International Commission of Jurists.

John Paul II (1995). *The Gospel of Life (Evangelium vitae)*. New York: Random House.

Layson, Stephen K. (1985). 'Homicide and Deterrence: An Examination of the United States Time-Series Evidence'. *Southern Economic Journal*, 52: 68–9.

Leopold, Nathan F., Jr. (1958). *Life Plus 99 Years*. New York: Doubleday.

Marquart, James W., and Sorensen, Jonathan R. (1989). 'A National Study of the *Furman*-Commuted Inmates: Assessing the Threat to Society from Capital Offenders'. *Loyola of Los Angeles Law Review*, 23: 5–28.

Marx, Karl (1853/1959). 'Capital Punishment', in Lewis S. Feuer ed. *Marx and Engels: Basic Writings on Politics and Philosophy*, New York: Anchor Books, 485–9.

Mill, John Stuart (1859/1975). 'On Liberty', in David Spitz (ed.), *John Stuart Mill On Liberty: Annotated Text Sources and Background Criticism*. New York; W. W. Norton, 1–106.

Miller, Kent S., and Radelet, Michael L. (1993). *Executing the Mentally Ill: The Criminal Justice System and the Case of Alvin Ford*. Newbury Park, CA: Sage.

Monahan, John (1978). 'The Prediction of Violent Criminal Behavior: A Methodological Critique and Prospectus', in Alfred Blumstein, Jacqueline Cohen, and Daniel Nagin (eds.), *Deterrence and Incapacitation: Estimating the Effects of Criminal Sanctions on Crime Rates*. Washington: National Academy of Sciences, 244–69.

Montague, Phillip (1995). *Punishment as Societal-Defense*. Lanham, MD: Rowman & Littlefield.

Morris, Herbert (1981). 'A Paternalistic Theory of Punishment'. *American Philosophical Quarterly*, 18: 263–72.

Nathanson, Stephen (1987). *An Eye for An Eye? The Morality of Punishing by Death*. Totowa, NJ: Rowman & Littlefield.

National Coalition to Abolish the Death Penalty (1997). *Human Rights and Human Wrongs: The Sentencing of Children to Death in the US: A Report*. Washington: National Coalition to Abolish to Death Penalty.

Nickel, James W. (1987). *Making Sense of Human Rights: Philosophical Reflections on the Universal Declaration of Human Rights*. Berkeley and Los Angeles: University of California Press.

Paternoster, Raymond (1991). *Capital Punishment in America*. New York: Lexington Books.

Perlmutter, Martin (1996). 'Desert and Capital Punishment', in John Arthur (ed.), *Morality and Moral Controversies*. 4th edn. Upper Saddle River, NJ: Prentice Hall, 390–7.

Pincoffs, Edmund L. (1977). 'Are Questions of Desert Decidable?', in J. B. Cederblom and William L. Blizek (eds.), *Justice and Punishment*. Cambridge, MA: Ballinger, 75–88.

Pojman, Louis P. (1998). 'For the Death Penalty' and 'Reply to Jeffrey Reiman', in L. P. Pojman and J. Reiman, *The Death Penalty: For and Against*. Lanham, MD: Rowman & Littlefield, 1–66, 133–49.

Primoratz, Igor (1989a). *Justifying Legal Punishment*. Atlantic Highlands, NJ: Humanities Press.

——(1989b). 'Murder is Different'. *Criminal Justice Ethics*, 8: 48–63.

Radelet, Michael L., and Akers, Ronald L. (1996). 'Deterrence and the Death Penalty: The Views of the Experts'. *Journal of Criminal Law and Criminology*, 87: 1–16.

——and Bedau, Hugo Adam (1998). 'The Execution of the Innocent'. *Law and Contemporary Problems*, 61: 105–24.

————and Putnam, Constance E. (1992/1994). *In Spite of Innocence: Erroneous Convictions in Capital Cases*. Boston, MA: Northeastern University Press.

—— Lofquist, William S. and Bedau, Hugo Adam (1996). 'Prisoners Released from Death Rows since 1970 Because of Doubts about their Guilt'. *Thomas M. Cooley Law Review*, 13: 907–66.

Reiman, Jeffrey (1998). 'Why the Death Penalty Should Be Abolished in America' and 'Reply to Louis J. Pojman', in L. P. Pojman and J. Reiman, *The Death Penalty: For and Against*. Lanham, MD: Rowman & Littlefield, 67–132, 151–63.

Schabas, William A. (1997). *The Abolition of the Death Penalty in International Law*. 2nd edn. Cambridge: Cambridge University Press.

Solomon, George F. (1975). 'Capital Punishment as Suicide and as Murder'. *American Journal of Orthopsychiatry*, 45: 701–11.

Sorrell, Tom (1987). *Moral Theory and Capital Punishment*. Oxford: Blackwell.

Thomson, Judith Jarvis (1990). *The Realm of Rights*. Cambridge, MA: Harvard University Press.

US Bureau of Justice Statistics (2001). *Capital Punishment 2000*. Washington: Department of Justice.

US Federal Bureau of Investigation (1998). *Crime in United States—1997*. Washington: US Government Printing Office.

van den Haag, Ernest (1985a). 'Refuting Reiman and Natanson'. *Philosophy and Public Affairs*, 14: 165–76.

—— (1985b). 'The Death Penalty Once More'. *University of California Davis Law Review*, 18: 957–72.

—— (1986). 'The Ultimate Punishment: A Defense'. *Harvard Law Review*, 99: 1662–9.

—— (1990). 'Why Capital Punishment?' *Albany Law Review*, 54: 501–14.

—— and Conrad, John P. (1983). *The Death Penalty: A Debate*. New York: Plenum Press.

Vlastos, Gregory (1962). 'Justice and Equality', in Richard Brandt (ed.), *Social Justice*. Englewood Cliffs, NJ: Prentice Hall, 31–72.

von Hirsch, Andrew (1976). *Doing Justice: The Choice of Punishments*. New York: Hill & Wang.

Weisberg, Robert (1984). 'Deregulating Death'. *Supreme Court Review 1983*, 305–95.

West, Louis Jolyon (1975). 'Psychiatric Reflections on the Death Penalty'. *American Journal of Orthopsychiatry*, 45: 689–700.

White, Welsh S. (1991). *The Death Penalty in the Nineties: An Examination of the Modern System of Capital Punishment*. Ann Arbor: University of Michigan Press.

Cases Cited

Callins v. *Collins*, 510 US 1141 (1994).

Furman v. *Georgia*, 408 US 238 (1972).

Gregg v. *Georgia*, 428 US 153 (1976).

CHAPTER 28

WAR

HENRY SHUE

1. INTRODUCTION

THE three fundamental ethical questions about war concern the justification of the resort to war, the justification of the conduct of war, and the relation between the resort to a war and the limits on its conduct. These three questions are as follows. When, if ever, is one either permitted or obligated to resort to war? If the resort to war is ever justified, what are the limits on how a war may be fought? Are these limits on its conduct a necessary condition of a just war, or might extreme situations arise in which some of these limits may justifiably be ignored?

Some of the arguments for the conclusion that war is never permissible, much less obligatory, rest on features of war that are not unique to it. Wars kill and maim human beings, destroy human artefacts, and degrade and distort the natural environment. If it is always wrong to kill another human being intentionally or carelessly, or always wrong to degrade the environment unnecessarily or carelessly, then obviously war, which inflicts both these harms in great magnitude, is always wrong. Such arguments are among the several plausible grounds of pacifism, the view that war is never justified. Obviously, precise accounts of the wrongness of killing vary in their ultimate grounds, and pacifism admits of significantly different varieties (Holmes 1990). Equally obviously, questions of when, if ever, any killing of other persons is justified are supremely important. If somehow an abstract analysis of those questions at a perfectly general level could lead to the conclusion that no, or almost no, killing of human beings can ever be justified, then we would need pursue no further the distinctive features of war. Here, nevertheless, we will focus on the issues raised by what is distinctive about war, for the following reason.

While it may initially appear obvious that one ought to discuss 'killing as such' (or 'environmental destruction as such') before discussing the usually large-scale killing and destruction in war, it is evident upon reflection that there is no such thing as 'killing as such'. Stabbings in drunken brawls, assassinations of murderous dictators, executions by hired hit men, neonaticides by mothers with post-partum depression, military occupations of lands that are the homes of other people, and military defences against attempted military occupations are all cases of killing other human beings. Yet these concrete cases are so different from each other that it is at least conceivable that some are justified and some are not, because some of the differences among them may be more significant than their similarities. The suggestion that one should somehow begin with 'killing as such' is, in my view, just bad philosophy and is in any case not practical ethics, which attempts to arrive at concrete conclusions about what kind of person to be and how to act in the here and now.

Clearly, we have persuasive ways of explaining why the avoidable death of a human being is normally sad and often tragic. In this sense, there is a presumption against killing. Yet we have no way to conclude, in advance of the consideration of possible exceptions, that killing is always wrong. Whether it is always wrong depends on whether there are any justified exceptions to the general presumption against it, and one can determine that only by examining the respective cases for the various proposed exceptions. Certain types of wars are among the most import-ant of those proposed exceptions. While a few romantic defenders of war have tried to argue that something like the alleged glory of war or of victory in war, or some individual heroism and selfless sacrifice evoked only by war, can make war, all things considered, a good thing, such romantics are now mostly appropriately neglected. It is essential never to forget the eerie magnetism that often accompanies, and seems even to be parasitic upon, the fear and horror of participation in risking and inflict-ing death in combat, an experience that often strikes those who have it as far and away the most significant of their lives, the one time that what they did mattered the most (Gray 1959/1998).

Nevertheless, apart from sheer romantic foolishness, serious justifications for the resort to war are all, in effect, excuses for doing what, without the excuse, would be unforgivable and even with the excuse is at least deeply regrettable, usually tragic, possibly a necessary evil. In other words, justifications for the resort to war begin from the acknowledgement that the infliction of death and destruction is normally wrong and can, at best, be justified only as an exception to the general rules against the infliction of such harms. The question whether the resort to war is ever justi-fied takes the form of an enquiry into whether actions that in ordinary circum-stances would be wrong are, in the special context of some kinds of war, either not the kind of action they appear to be and therefore not strictly speaking wrong (not the intentional or careless killing of innocent persons and therefore not evil) or are indeed wrong but nevertheless justifiable here, all things considered (necessary evil). In order to reach practical conclusions we will explore these special contexts, the varieties of war.

2. JUSTIFIED RESORT AND JUSTIFIED CONDUCT

Western writers on war tend mechanically to point out that doctrines about justified resort, or recourse, to war were categorized by medieval Christian thinkers as *jus ad bellum*—and doctrines about the proper limits on the conduct of war, as *jus in bello*. This ritual use of Latin terminology tends not only sometimes to make urgent matters seem archaic and academic but usually to be positively misleading in so far as it strongly suggests that the medieval Christian views are for some reason especially authoritative, at least as starting points, when many were by any reasonable standard outrageous or are irrelevant to contemporary war. While, for example, the historically influential lectures in 1539—never published in his own lifetime—of Francisco de Vitoria were in their temporal context progressive both in their condemnation of the genocidal slaughters of indigenous Americans by Vitoria's compatriot conquistadors and their condemnation of attacks based simply upon religious difference, they nevertheless defend the proposition that 'a Christian may lawfully fight and wage war' (Vitoria 1539/1991: 297) with such contentions as the following: 'The same proof holds true also for offensive war; that is to say, not only war in which property is defended or reclaimed, but also war in which vengeance for an injury is sought' (Vitoria 1539/1991: 297–8). In other words, the reclamation of lost property and the infliction of vengeance are adequate reasons for starting wars; the indigenous Americans, on the other hand, had done Spain no harm and did not deserve their murderous fate at the hands of the Spanish explorers. On *jus in bello* Vitoria is similarly torn between two worlds, the world of universal humanity and the world of struggle between the civilized and the uncivilized. Vitoria reaches the progressive conclusion 'that even in wars against Turks we may not kill children, who are obviously innocent, nor women, who are to be presumed innocent . . .' (1539/1991: 315), but only after struggling in deadly seriousness with the proposition, rejected in the end, that 'it is lawful to kill people who are innocent, but may yet pose a threat in the future. For example, the sons of Saracens are harmless, but it is reasonable to fear that when they reach manhood they will fight against Christendom' (1539/1991: 316).

Of course, the stratagem of preventive slaughter of 'enemy children' goes deep in the Western tradition. Noting the uncanny similarity with the rationale given by extremist Hutu for the murder of even the Tutsi children during the Rwandan genocide of 1994, Mahmood Mamdani recalls *Numbers* 31: 7–18 (Jewish *Torah*; Christian *Old Testament*) for us:

They warred against Median, as the Lord commanded Moses, and they slew every male. . . . And [they] took captive the women . . . and their little ones. . . . And Moses said unto them, Have you saved all the women alive? Behold, these caused the children of Israel . . . to commit trespass against the Lord . . . Now therefore kill every male among the little ones, and kill every woman that hath known man . . . But all the women children that have not . . . keep alive for yourselves.   (Mamdani 2001: 9)

The 'stark savagery' (McCoubrey 1998: 9) of Moses' reprimands of the military commanders of the ancient Hebrews for not having executed all the children who were males and all the women who were not virgins, among this enemy group, is a chilling reminder of why one ought not to be simply reverential of the Western tradition. Western religion contains its fair share of barbarity, like this twisted notion that massacres of helpless prisoners could be divine commands, a notion that unfortunately was still powerfully alive in the overwhelmingly Christian nation of Rwanda in the last decade of the twentieth century and evidently helped to fuel the final genocide in that century of awful state-sponsored exterminations.

Moses' orders for his military to go back and slaughter more women and children is also a stunning paradigm of the horrors that result when a decision to resort to war is unconstrained by limits on the conduct of war. A sense that one's war is holy because God is on one's side easily slides into a sense that this end justifies absolutely any means and thus no holds are barred, not even the annihilation of whole groups of 'enemies' through systematic slaughter. Modern discussions of war, by contrast, have often insisted that, however fully justified the resort to war, it is morally permissible to fight a war only if it can be, and is, conducted within firm limits. Justified conduct—that is, compliance with the limits on the conduct of war—is a strictly necessary condition of justified war. Both sets of moral tests, the tests for resort and the tests for conduct, must separately be met (cf. Johnson 1999).

The main alternative is the position that the resort to war can be so fully, and so urgently, justified that one or more of the limits on the conduct of war may be violated and yet the war as a whole still be justified. This alternative has been popularized by Michael Walzer for situations he has influentially labelled 'supreme emergencies' (1977/2000: 228–68); and John Rawls, for example, has now unquestioningly adopted Walzer's category (Rawls 1999: 98–9). To his great credit, Michael Walzer made the deep tension between 'the two kinds of justice' (1977/2000: 232) the organizing principle of his now-classic *Just and Unjust Wars*. His assertion that 'the dualism of *jus ad bellum* and *jus in bello* is at the heart of all that is most problematic in the moral reality of war' (Walzer 1977/2000: 21) seems, however, to concede more theoretical disunity than needs to exist and to miss potential unifying connections that I hope to bring out below. Thus I will argue in the end that Walzer's resolution of the tension is dangerously wrong, and that his formulation of the issue as 'dualism' rather than tension is unfortunate. Walzer has nevertheless made it far more difficult simply to settle into the unresolved dichotomy and taken us a significant distance down the road to a unified resolution. Because I want to continue his struggle towards a unified theory, I will not follow the usual pattern, available in a number of fine books, of discussing resort and conduct separately and then trying somehow to put together in the end what have long been held apart. I will instead attempt to integrate issues about acceptable conduct and acceptable resort whenever possible, from the beginning.

3. DISCRIMINATION

Perhaps the single most widely acknowledged specific constraint on war today is non-combatant immunity, or discrimination, which is normally taken to be a part of—indeed, the heart of—the justified conduct of war. Under international law as it is now in force, the fighting of a war is justifiable only if attacks are made only upon legitimate targets. To attack only legitimate targets is to fight with discrimination: one must discriminate between legitimate and illegitimate and attack only the legitimate. The only legitimate targets are military objectives, and among human beings the only military objectives are combatants, not non-combatants. Non-combatants have legal, and moral, immunity from attack—hence, 'non-combatant immunity'.

Now the preceding paragraph simply indicates the interconnections of a number of the terms of art used in discussing war. The philosophical issues still remain untouched. The 'principle of non-combatant immunity' and 'the principle of discrimination', or 'distinction', are often used interchangeably, although strictly speaking the principle of discrimination is broader, covering discrimination among property and objects, as well as persons, that may and may not be the object of attack. However, those who speak of 'discrimination' usually have people, not property, in mind, unless they explicitly mention property. The most recent revision of the international law governing the conduct of war, now legally in force, was the addition in 1977 after long negotiations of two protocols to the four 1949 Geneva Conventions, yielding the formal designation: the 1977 Geneva Protocols I and II Additional to the Geneva Conventions of 1949. Protocol I, Article 51, 2, says: 'The civilian population as such, as well as individual civilians, shall not be the object of attack. Acts or threats of violence the primary purpose of which is to spread terror among the civilian population are prohibited' (Roberts and Guelff 2000: 448). This is one central, current, legally binding expression of what a philosopher would normally describe as non-combatant immunity. Non-combatants are legally protected by being excluded from the class of legitimate targets.

Naturally, Article 51 is only one strand in a complex web of legal protections. Article 52 goes on to property in general: 'Civilian objects shall not be the object of attack or of reprisals.' Article 53 concerns 'protection of cultural objects and of places of worship'; and Article 54 covers 'protection of objects indispensable to the survival of the civilian population', including the following:

It is prohibited to attack, destroy, remove or render useless objects indispensable to the survival of the civilian population, such as foodstuffs, agricultural areas for the production of foodstuffs, crops, livestock, drinking water installations and supplies and irrigation works, for the specific purpose of denying them for their sustenance value to the civilian population or to the adverse Party, whatever the motive, whether in order to starve out civilians, to cause them to move away, or for any other motive.   (Roberts and Guelff 2000: 450)

And in a two-article chapter (Articles 57 and 58) devoted to 'Precautionary Measures', Protocol I significantly requires: 'In the conduct of military operations, *constant care* shall be taken to spare the civilian population, civilians and civilian objects' (emphasis added). This eloquent legal requirement of 'constant care' places a heavy burden of what Walzer has similarly called 'due care' (Walzer 1977/2000: 156) on the military, as Article 50 had already done in saying: 'In case of doubt whether a person is a civilian, that person shall be considered to be a civilian.' The requirement of constant care echoes a central theme in writing about the morality of war going back, in Western thinking, at least to Hugo Grotius in 1625: 'One must take care, so far as is possible, to prevent the death of innocent persons, even by accident' (Grotius 1625/1972: 87 (bk. III, ch. XI, art. VIII)). In Ancient Hindu civilization essentially the same point was conveyed movingly two millennia earlier in the *The Laws of Manu* by a graphically specific list of excluded targets; warriors may not strike, among many others, 'anyone asleep, without armour, naked, without a weapon, not fighting, looking on, or engaged with someone else' (*The Laws of Manu* 1991: 137–8 (ch. 7, verse 92)).

This introductory discussion of non-combatant immunity raises many broader issues, some of which we need to take up. First, a relatively superficial observation reveals one of the deep concerns about provisions regarding the legality and morality of war. Lists tend, by implication, to include as well as to exclude. When the Hindu *The Laws of Manu* says that one is not to strike one 'not fighting, looking on', the implication would be, even if there were no explicit discussion of the question, that one may strike one who is not just looking on but is taking part in the fight. The lists of persons and objects that are not legitimate targets in the 1977 Protocol I Additional would strongly suggest that there are legitimate targets, even if there were not in fact a crucial explicit definition in Article 52, 2:

Attacks shall be limited strictly to military objectives. In so far as objects are concerned, military objectives are limited to those objects which by their nature, location, purpose, or use make an effective contribution to military action and whose total or partial destruction, capture, or neutralization, in the circumstances ruling at the time, offers a definite military advantage.   (Roberts and Guelff 2000: 450)

Objects that make an effective contribution to military action for the adversary and whose destruction offers a concrete and immediate military advantage to one's own side may be destroyed. This includes some so-called 'dual-purpose' objects that make a contribution to civilian life as well as to military action; in spite of their undoubted civilian function, such dual-purpose objects may be treated as military objectives because of their military function, if thwarting that function at that time 'offers a concrete and immediate military advantage'.

This is an instance of a far broader tendency that provides one of the most important grounds for doubt about the ethics of discussing the ethics of war: accounts of justifiable war rule wars in just as definitely as they rule wars out. Ian Clark has perceptively noted 'the dual function of just war theory both as a form of permission and as a form of restraint' (1988: 35). A line is being drawn; and, while the wars on one side of the line are declared to be unacceptable, the wars on the other side are declared acceptable. The purpose of discussing the ethics of war may often be to attempt to define acceptable wars very narrowly, as the 1977 Protocol I Additional generally does, even though Article 52, 2, has been argued to be insufficiently (Dunlap 2000b), and excessively (Shue, forthcoming a), permissive. Evidently, in the abstract, far more kinds of possible warfare are ruled out than are ruled in. And the list of 'civilian objects' is longer than the list of 'military objectives'. But these abstract points are of little or no consequence. One question that a morally serious person wants answered is: do the uses to which the laws and the books distinguishing acceptable from unacceptable wars are put do more to encourage wars that might otherwise not be fought or more to discourage wars that might otherwise be fought? Or, rather, are the horrors wreaked in the permitted wars so intolerably great—and so pointless or self-defeating, producing new injustices to fuel new wars (Welch 1993)—that the hypothetically avoided wars count in reality for little?

This is a difficult issue about, among other things, the relation between philosophical and legal ideas, their likely uses, and historical reality. I raise the question, not in order to answer it, but because those concerned with practical ethics must consider such questions. Just as there is no guarantee that, because professors lecture about ethical theories, students become better persons rather than merely becoming more glib defenders of superficial relativism, there is no guarantee that, because philosophers write defences of more humane warfare, and lawyers formulate protocols to conventions legally limiting warfare to certain forms but not others, war will in fact become either less frequent or less cruel. Pacifists rightly worry, I believe, that even 'narrow' permissions may still in practice permit much too much. The issue is complicated by the obvious fact that much actual warfare clearly violates even the most widely accepted moral and legal principles. War crimes are crimes only because there is in fact extensive international law governing the conduct of and resort to war. Many of the bloodiest actions—for instance, the land battles of Loos and the Somme (Coates 1997: 214–21) in the First World War, 'that savage war of attrition' (Coates 1997: 253), and the air attacks on Dresden, Hiroshima, and Nagasaki in the

Second World War (Walzer 1997/2000: 251–68)—were clear violations of fundamental principles of acceptable warfare. Why, then, blame the philosophers and lawyers who formulated the principles that were violated?—blame the violators!

But this is far too simplistic. The pacifist's worry here is this: while it is true that the philosophers and the lawyers did not, of course, authorize the violation of their own principles, they authorized the attempt—often, in reality, the failed attempt—to conduct a war in accord with those principles. The theorists counselled the dogs of war to behave, but what counts is that they unleashed them. The pacifist's argument here is that, when one unleashes the dogs of war, telling them to have a clean fight, what one actually gets almost always, for whatever reasons, is a dirty fight. And, knowing this, one ought simply not to unleash them.

Now this is a dialectic that has more stages than space here allows us to enter. Of course, war is never fought entirely—often, not even largely—in accord with the laws, much less the moral principles, that reasonably seem to apply. But it is still far from clear whether matters would improve if everyone counselling moderation advocated abolition instead. Does anyone need to unleash the dogs of war or will they in any case find their own ways to get loose? If so, might they heed at least some of the counsels of moderation while ignoring the defence of pacifism? And so on. I raise the issue because I believe that, as we examine what amounts to the question 'what would be the most tolerable form war could take?', we would do well to keep in mind the underlying question 'and is that form tolerable enough?' While I would not suggest in the least that moral and legal positions should always and only be judged by the likely effects of their advocacy on the behaviour of others, the ethics of war is a case in which those effects are especially great. Every nation's armies, marines, navies, and air forces have manuals on the laws of war, and many professional militaries study them with great seriousness. The causal connections here, as elsewhere, between beliefs and behaviour are complex and difficult to understand. But it is abundantly clear both that, while many do not, many of those who fight wars do in fact attempt to fight them as they believe they ought to be fought; and that understanding of how they ought to be fought is often at least partly shaped by the reflections embodied in ethical and legal writings about war. In the less than confident hope that such reflection may do more good than harm, let us turn now to other issues raised by the introductory discussion of non-combatant immunity.

Secondly, who exactly—or as exactly as the nature of the case admits—are the 'civilians' that the 1977 Protocol I Additional excludes from among legitimate targets of attack and the 'non-combatants' that the principle of non-combatant immunity declares morally immune from intentional harm (leaving until the later discussion of 'double effect' the other important and difficult element: 'intentional')? In medieval Western discussion, those who are not to be targeted or intentionally harmed were given a label in Latin that has been translated as the 'innocent', a translation that, while not incorrect, has inordinately bedevilled philosophical discussion, although international law has fortunately ignored it, in favour of 'civilians'. We should first try to put aside the confusions sown by 'innocent'. 'Innocent' is the negation of 'nocent', and the 'nocent' (nocere) are those harming (Coates 1997: 235). So the innocent are those who are doing no harm. The principle of non-combatant immunity is a reaffirmation of the morally foundational 'no-harm' principle. One ought generally not to harm other persons. Non-combatant immunity says one ought, most emphatically, not to harm others who are themselves not harming anyone. This is as fundamental, and as straightforward, and as nearly non-controversial, as moral principles can get. Thus, to employ the preferable legal term, since civilians are not part of the military threat, civilians may not be attacked, as elements of the military may be attacked. Those who are harming may themselves be harmed, as necessary, in order to put a stop to the initial harm.

Discussion goes off the track if the term 'innocent' is taken to be the opposite of 'guilty', rather than the opposite of engaged in harming, and especially if it is taken to refer to some subjective guiltiness. People then wonder whether, for example, a citizen who voted for a regime that has tried to attack and hold some other group's land is guilty in a relevant sense. But, while a citizen is indeed responsible for the people and measures for which she votes, and so might be guilty of supporting a regime that initiated an unjust war, she is not for that reason subject to military attack. Execution-by-B52 is not the appropriate penalty for bad politics. More fundamentally, the issue is not punishment. Perhaps the supporters of governments that launch unjust wars do deserve some kind of punishment; it has often been thought that some of the tax revenues they pay ought to be taken, after the war is over, as reparations for their victims and perhaps also as punishment for them (although the long-term wisdom of such punitive policies is highly debatable). Perhaps the leaders of the government ought to be tried for war crimes, if indeed they launched a blatant aggression, but before they are punished—certainly, before they are killed—they should receive a fair trial. One of many reasons military action ought no longer to be viewed as a form of punishment—as, for example, Vitoria and many earlier Western thinkers did view it—is that it is unavoidably punishment without a trial, and capital punishment, in many cases, at that. The medieval Western view of war as a form of punishment is a large part of the problem; for centuries the 'nocent', as distinguished from the 'innocent', were indeed those engaged in harming and therefore deserving of punishment in the form of military assault.

The question to which the principle of non-combatant immunity is the answer is no longer 'who deserves to suffer or possibly to be killed through military action, because of the degree of their guilt?' The question is 'who needs to be harmed now in order to stop the harm that was already under way?' Possibly no one—if a stop can be put to the harm under way without further harm, this is very much to the good. But, at most, harm may be inflicted on those who are themselves inflicting harm. What happens to others, some of whom may be far more guilty for the occurrence of the harms than those actually carrying out the harms, is another, non-military matter. Military people often describe their job as placing themselves 'in harm's way'. This is intended to be quite literally true. Justified military action consists in confronting those engaged in doing harm and stopping them, if necessary by harming them instead. The soldier places herself between the perpetrator and the intended victim and stands in the way of the harm. To protect the originally threatened victim, and herself, she may harm the threatening perpetrator as much as necessary (but no more—hence, the complementary principle of proportionality, to which we will come later).

As Walzer makes admirably clear (1977/2000: 135–7, 144–7), the mystery is not: how could anyone be immune from attack in the midst of a war? Or, how do we explain non-combatant immunity? What needs to be explained is combatant non-immunity. What needs to be justified is the killing, not the 'constant care' to avoid more killing. 'The theoretical problem is not to describe how immunity is gained, but how it is lost. We are all immune to start with; our right not to be attacked is a feature of normal human relationships. That right is lost by those who bear arms "effectively" because they pose a danger to other people. It is retained by those who don't bear arms at all' (Walzer 1977/2000: 145 n.). All human beings are morally immune from physical assaults designed to injure or kill them. What needs to be explained is why there should be any exception to this general rule and, if so, what exactly the terms of the exception are. The explanation provided by contemporary theories of justified war is that those, and only those, engaged in efforts to harm others without justification may themselves justifiably be harmed to the extent necessary to prevent further unjustified harm. Justified military action stands in harm's way, shielding intended victims from the harm. It is justified harm protecting against unjustified harm, justified by the protection it provides. Theologian Paul Ramsey (1968/1983: 143–4) put it beautifully:

The justification of participation in conflict at the same time severely limited war's conduct. What justified also limited! Since it was for the sake of the innocent and helpless of the earth that the Christian first thought himself obliged to make war against an enemy whose objective deeds had to be stopped, since only for their sakes does a Christian justify himself in resisting by any means even an enemy-neighbor, he could never proceed to kill equally innocent people as a means of getting at the enemy's forces. Thus was twin-born the justification of war and the limitation which surrounded non-combatants with moral immunity from direct attack. Thus was twin-born the distinction between combatant and non-combatant in all Christian reflection about the morality of warfare. This is the distinction between legitimate and illegitimate military objectives. The same considerations which justify killing the bearer of hostile force by the same stroke prohibit non-combatants from ever being directly attacked with deliberate intent.

I believe that Ramsey's conception of 'twin-born' justification and limitation is a brilliant insight into the underlying unity of justified resort to war and justified conduct of war, the unity that is broken by the doctrine of 'supreme emergency' proposed by Walzer and accepted by Rawls, to which I return later. For now we need to continue to look specifically at the prohibition of attacks upon civilians, or non-combatant immunity. Obviously non-Christians cannot ground their solidarity with the rest of humanity in exactly the same conception that 'everyone is my neighbour'—so that even my enemy is my 'enemy-neighbour'—that theologian Ramsey believed in, but I have already offered above a non-Christian version of the same fundamental logic—namely, that the purpose of justified military action is the interposition of force between those on the way to inflicting harm and their intended victims, Ramsey's 'innocent and helpless of earth'. As already indicated, Walzer, like me in not relying on specifically Christian grounding, explains and justifies non-combatant immunity by appeal to fundamentally the same logic of protecting potential victims by harming those, and only those, who are on the way to inflicting harm—those who 'pose a danger to other people'.

It will be noted that this account of the matter works only from the point of view of combatants fighting on the right side of a war, an instance of the inseparability of justified conduct and justified resort. Only they are in fact placing themselves in harm's way—those on the other side are on the way to do harm and need to be prevented. But, since the rules for the conduct of war apply to both sides, do we not need some account of the matter that makes sense from the other side? No, we do not. If one believes that one is fighting on the wrong side of a war—the side whose resort to war is not justified—then one ought to desist. One does not need a special set of rules about how to conduct oneself while doing something one knows one ought not to be doing. If one believes one ought not to be fighting, because the side for which one is fighting has no adequate justification for fighting, one ought to stop. Clearly, 'to stop' may be extremely difficult and highly dangerous, but unfortunately there is no cure for that.

Unfortunately, too, many people have mistakenly believed that they were on a right side when they were on a wrong side. In quite a few wars, surely, both sides are wrong—neither has any business killing people and destroying things, given what is actually at stake between them; and the combatants on both sides are misguided or have been misled. But there is no general cure for false belief, either, and sadly this includes false beliefs about war. If one believes that one is fighting where the resort to war is justified, then one ought to fight within the limits governing war. If one believes that one is fighting where the resort to war is not justified, then one needs, not a special set of rules for people who are wrong, but a way to escape. One can ask both sides to abide by the same rules because one can ask that no one engage in war unless they believe they must. One of the most tragic aspects of war is that many individually decent people—usually, young people—have killed others, believing in good faith that they had to do it, and then been killed themselves in wars that should never have been fought and would never have been fought if everyone involved had known the truth. One might well think this is another reason for pacifism. It is surely, at the very minimum, another powerful reason for abiding by the principle of proportionality, to which we will come later, even in the case of 'enemy' combatants (Ramsey's 'enemy-neighbours'), many of whom act in total good faith.

4. DOUBLE EFFECT

The two principles at the core of the morality of the conduct of war are discrim-ination, at which we have looked in the previous section, and proportionality, at which we will look in the succeeding section. The most influential manner in which to arrange the intersection of discrimination with proportionality is provided by the doctrine, or principle, of double effect (Coates 1997: 239–64). Since propor-tionality is the final of the four elements in double effect, and discrimination is central to the second and third of the four, the analytic framework of double effect provides us with a natural bridge between the two fundamental substantive con-siderations, discrimination and proportionality.

The analytic framework of double effect is the site of profound and passionate disagreement; and judgements about the morality of war as a whole often pivot upon judgements about double effect, which is sometimes dismissed as the prover-bial loophole through which one can (literally) drive a tank (Lackey 1989: 66–8; Norman 1995: 91, 107, 204) and sometimes embraced as a complex synthesis of two ineliminable kinds of moral concern onesidedly oversimplified in opposite direc-tions by, respectively, so-called deontological ethics and so-called consequentialist ethics (Coates 1997: 239–64; Walzer 1977/2000: 151–6). Double effect mandates the consideration of four factors (Coates 1997: 241–2; Walzer 1977/2000: 153).

The first factor is the nature of the act performed itself, which must be morally good or at least morally indifferent—in traditional terms, not intrinsically evil. Since many people today would be mystified by the notion that an action has any essential nature, much less an essential moral character, this factor tends to be ridiculed or ignored. However, Coates persuasively argues that read simply as the injunction to be quite clear about exactly what is being done under the usual gov-ernmental euphemisms and public-relations obfuscations—like 'collateral dam-age'—the first analytic move required by double effect is highly salutary in two respects. It raises the threshold that any moral justification must cross, and it tests the plausibility of the assertions about intentions that constitute the second and third factors in double-effect analysis. First, 'an accurate, complete and impartial account of the physical or pre-moral structure of the act, eschewing euphemistic and tendentious description and focusing clearly and exactly on its total human costs', sets an appropriately high threshold for any justifications of the act that are to follow (Coates 1997: 243). Secondly, this clear-eyed physical accuracy, specificity, and completeness of description may also serve to disconfirm, or 'give the lie to', claims about intention at the next two stages of analysis. On this demystified inter-pretation of the first factor, the injunction to begin by looking very hard at exactly what is being done, however these deeds are being categorized, is invaluable, espe-cially as an antidote to over-reliance upon assertions about intentions that lie at the core of the second and third factors, which I will now discuss together.

The second and third factors to be examined, according to double effect, are complementary and not fully separable. Both concern right intention: the second, the end intended; the third, the means intended. Together the second and third factors require that the actual morally unacceptable effects of a military action, specifically described as the first element of the analysis, should not have been intended either for their own sake—as an end—or as a means to an intended end. Only the morally acceptable effects of the action may have been intended as either end or means. This can be made somewhat less obscure through the examination of three issues: the criterion of morally acceptable effects, the meaning of intention, and the significance of intention. Most of what is done during war—the killing and injuring of human beings, the destruction of buildings and equipment—would be utterly unacceptable in any other context. Morally acceptable effects of military action are best understood by means of the principle of discrimination already discussed: persons and property may be attacked only if they are legitimate targets, and they are legitimate targets only if they are at least partly military, not entirely civilian; 'dual-purpose' facilities—like bridges, oil refineries, and electricity-generating plants—with both a civilian and a military function, may often be treated in accord with their military function. Right intention, within the double-effect analysis, is specified as intention to attack only legitimate targets—intention to abide by the principle of discrimination. All harm to civilians and all damage to purely civilian objects must have been unintended.

'Unintended' means not any part of one's plan or design. 'The relevant conception of intent is this: an action or aspect of an action is intentional if it is a part of the plan on which one freely acts. That is to say, what one tries to bring about in acting, whether it be the goal one seeks to realize or the means one chooses to realize that goal, is intended' (Finnis et al. 1987: 79). The 'acid test', as Coates (1997: 244) puts it, 'is whether or not the agent has anything to gain from the evil effect itself. . . . There can be no doubt that, if it were possible to achieve the good consequences without the evil effects, that would be the course of action which he or she would prefer.'

Why does the double-effect analysis attach so much significance to this distinction between the intended effect and the unintended effect? Why is the analysis structured into double effects, intended ones, and unintended ones? Both philosophical and political justifications are available. The more philosophical answer would appeal to the kinds of grounds offered for the more deontological elements of morality—that we value not only consequences but also certain kinds of agents and their respectful ways of treating other persons, so that, when consequences that are clearly bad result from an action, we are interested not only in the consequences themselves but also in whether the agent of those consequences was disrespectful or otherwise evil, having intended them, or was good or respectful and caused them only unintentionally.

The more political answer is that, if the principle of discrimination were interpreted exclusively in terms of consequences, with no distinction between intended and unintended consequences, and simply forbade damage to at least partly civilian objects and the death or injury of civilians, it would be such a stringent requirement that it would make the fighting of wars impossible. 'Cause no harm to civilians' would be, not a constraint upon war, but a prohibition of war. And, rightly or wrongly, the social role of the principles of war is to limit, not to eliminate, war. In order to play this role, they cannot make demands that are incompatible with fighting wars—indeed, with fighting them successfully. The principle of discrimination in war, as ordinarily understood, prohibits all harm to civilians that is intentionally caused but permits harm to civilians that is both unintentional and proportional. And thus we come to the fourth factor in the double-effect analysis: the unintentional damage, even when it is indeed unintentional, must also be proportional to the good achieved.

The fourth factor, proportionality, at least partially deflects one common criticism of double effect misunderstood as allowing virtually any consequences as long as they were not intended. The second and third factors, not intending the bad consequences as end or means, are sometimes misinterpreted as if they meant merely something like crossing one's fingers behind one's back while bringing the consequences about; it might then be thought that, as long as one keeps, in effect, crossing one's fingers, one can wreak any havoc one likes. This would indeed be an irresponsible denial of one's own agency in bringing about the bad consequences, but this is not the meaning or role of intention in any defensible version of double effect. Proportionality comes into the double-effect analysis precisely in order to hold the agent responsible, to some degree, for the unintended effects as well as the intended effects (Coates 1997: 244, 246). Unintended morally unacceptable effects are limited, while intended morally unacceptable effects are forbidden. Agents are responsible for all the effects of their choices, but the responsibility is more stringent with regard to what one intends. It is not even entirely clear what it could mean to try entirely to prohibit all unintended bad consequences, since one simply does not control all the consequences of much of what one does. Walzer's proposal, mentioned earlier, that one should take 'due care', even to the point of running additional risks to oneself, in order to avoid unintended bad consequences is already a quite stringent standard (Walzer 1997/2000: 156).

5. PROPORTIONALITY

Principles of proportionality lie, along with the principle of non-combatant immunity (and of discrimination more generally), at the heart of the morality of war. 'Principles of proportionality' is plural because a macro-level test concerning the resort to war, as well as the micro-level test concerning the conduct of war, which constitutes the fourth factor—just discussed—within the double-effect analysis, are thought each to apply independently (Coates 1997: 167–88, 208–33). One must both ask prior to going to war, would the evil to be prevented by military action in this case be worth engaging in a war overall, and ask throughout any war engaged in, would this particular military engagement make a sufficiently great contribution to potential victory to be worth the death and destruction likely to result? Several questions immediately arise.

First, one might suspect that, if each of the parts is proportional, the whole will be proportional, and that there is, consequently, no need for separate tests for resort and conduct. If each battle conducted is proportional, it might be thought, then the war as a whole will be proportional. It seems to me, however, that the respective criteria of 'proportional' are not identical across the two tests, even though the same term is used, and that consequently the proportionality of the parts, judged separately and then aggregated, is not the same as the proportionality of the whole.

In judging proportional conduct of war (*jus in bello*, if Latin is preferred), on the one hand, the standard by which the death and destruction from a specific operation are assessed is a standard that already grants considerable weight to a kind of military rationality—which means are rational in the light of the military end sought—and that is therefore relatively permissive. The general idea is: given that forces are engaged in a certain area, it is very important that the adversary not be able, for example, to attack them on the flank, and therefore it is very important that, say, the bridge providing access to that flank be destroyed. Consequently, while this bridge is also important to the civilians who need it perhaps to bring their products to market, its importance as a military transport link may readily outweigh its importance as a commercial link. The micro-level test, while not unimportant, as we will see below, is tipped in favour of the military action on the general presumption that, since the fighting has by then been initiated, forces cannot justifiably be denied permission to do so very much of what they would now need to do in order to succeed. There is a strong flavour of the notion that, since the end has at this stage already been willed, one must now will most reasonable means, where 'reasonable means' is interpreted largely in terms of military rationality. It is generally assumed that, once people have been placed in a dangerous situation by having been sent into battle, one cannot then deny them considerable discretion to do what at the time they consider reasonable in order to accomplish their assigned task without undue danger to themselves. In addition, this is a judgement of proportionality that cannot but be left in the first instance to military commanders.

On the other hand, the consideration of proportionality at the macro-level, recourse to war (*jus ad bellum*), does not yet have built in the element of military rationality, because this prior decision to proceed militarily has not yet been made and is indeed precisely the decision still to be made. As the ratio of good likely to be achieved—or, more likely, harm to be prevented—to harm likely to be done in the process is weighed, the macro-level assessment of overall damage can, and should, count the potential aggregate damage, bearing clearly in mind the relative permissiveness of the micro-level proportionality standard for conduct of war. Accordingly, one might judge that the likely total death and destruction from recourse to a war, each individual battle of which would satisfy proportionality by the relatively permissive standard of 'proportional' applicable to the conduct of individual engagements, would be disproportional by the tougher standard of 'proportional' applicable to the whole war. In this way, the whole can be disproportional in spite of each part's being proportional.

At the level of the conduct of a war, a military leader must give considerable weight to genuine military requirements, but, in deciding initially whether to resort to war, a political leader must bear in mind only that, if warfare is indeed launched, such militarily oriented weight will indeed virtually have to be given in individual engagements. That it will be given is one reason not to unleash the dogs of war. The micro-level judgements of proportionality must be made by military people already engaged in a military mission and will understandably be somewhat narrow. The macro-level judgement about whether to employ military force at all ought to be made by political leaders engaged in a fully comprehensive moral assessment: is what is at stake worth a war, given everything we know about how war tends to go, even at best?

The second question about proportionality is 'who, and what, counts?' Here too, I believe, the answer varies between proportional recourse and proportional conduct (further confirming that 'proportional' is non-univocal in its two applications). The answer to the question 'who counts?' at the level of recourse to war is remarkable and is a powerful expression of the substantive moral universality underlying the principle of proportionality (as well as the principle of discrimination). Everyone counts: combatants and non-combatants, one's own, the adversary's, and those of neutrals—indeed, the entire international community (O'Brien 1981: 27–8; Coates 1997: 168). Consideration should even include, I believe, future generations who will be affected by precedents set. The decision to go to war may entail—this is a difficult issue I can pursue only a little in the next paragraph—thenceforward discounting to some degree the value of the lives of at least the combatants for the adversary. The principle of discrimination, of course, prohibits discounting the lives of any non-combatants, adversarial, friendly, or neutral. Be the future discounting, if war is initiated, as it may, no discounting ought to enter into the decision to go to war. All the death, injury, and destruction that the war under consideration is likely to bring—'theirs' and 'ours'—go into the balance against any harm the war can reasonably be expected to prevent. It is specifically wrong to consider only one's own national interest. The simplistic modern moral position sometimes referred to as 'prescriptive realism'—namely, that each nation always ought to consider only its own national interest—is in direct conflict with the far older morality of war—specifically with proportionality in the recourse to war, when literally everyone affected counts equally.

The answer to the question 'who counts?' at the level of proportional conduct of war must be different, because the fighting of a war must aim to a considerable degree at 'the destruction of the forces'—in plain language, the killing and wounding of the combatants and the destruction and immobilization of the equipment—of the adversary. A military force attempts to avoid casualties to its own side and to inflict casualties on the other side. Proportionality in the conduct of a war cannot conceivably mean the equal counting of friend and foe alike. If this is unacceptable, war is unacceptable. Proportionality can, then, here mean only: no more casualties than necessary inflicted on the other side. Even enemy casualties ought not to be excessive, but the standard of 'excessive' is heavily influenced by what it is expected to take to attain military objectives vital to victory for one's own side.

Once again, I am not suggesting that the standard of proportional conduct can or does have no bite at all as a limit: it clearly prohibits, for example, the pointless slaughter of defeated fighters, and of course the execution of prisoners of war. And it prohibits wars of attrition in which what passes for military strategy is merely an attempt to kill as many opposing troops as possible. Coates puts this eloquently: 'The moral permissibility of the war of attrition (not merely a war with an attritional element, but a war in which attrition defines the entire strategy) must be in grave doubt. . . . The policy of attrition serves as a blank cheque . . . the policy is profligate and disproportionate by design' (1997: 220). And later: 'what lies behind this criterion of proportionality—as it lies behind just war thinking as a whole—is a basic respect for life urged on all those who engage in war. It demands economy in the use of force . . .' (Coates 1997: 227). Such restrictions are far from totally insignificant. Because of them, wars aimed at maximum 'body counts', like the US war in Vietnam, are utterly unacceptable. One may discount the value of the lives of the combatants on the opposing side to some degree—certainly commanders ought strongly to favour their own combatants—but the life of no human being is discounted entirely. No person is simply to be 'wasted'.

The third, and primary, doubt about the principles of proportionality, both proportional recourse and proportional conduct, is, however, whether they are too vague to be as significantly limiting as they should be. At both levels a quite unspecific balancing of expected good—or, bad expected to be prevented—and bad expected to be done in the process must be conducted. In general, any injunction simply 'to balance the good against the bad and to decide which is greater' leaves much to discretion. Of course, algorithms cannot be provided for fundamental decisions, and at some point it is indeed necessary to rely upon some kind of practical judgement. Two specific worries suggest, unfortunately, that the making of proportionality judgements concerning war may be somewhat less disciplined than would be desirable. First, the standard(s) for what is proportional are unspecified, which primarily affects the proportionality of the conduct of a war. Secondly, what must be balanced is incommensurable, which mainly concerns the proportionality of the recourse to war.

Proportionality is, first, never provided with any determinate standard. Most worrying, it is fairly clear that avoiding excessive harm, which is the negative way in which proportionality is ordinarily understood, does not even entail doing more good than harm. It allows accomplishing some important good while causing greater harm, provided only that the harm caused was no greater than necessary to accomplish the good in question. Suppose that ten of our troops are trapped by thirty of their troops and that the only means of rescuing all ten of ours is to kill all thirty of theirs. Very few military commanders would, I believe, hesitate to kill thirty of the adversary to save ten of their own. Obviously, however, there is one respect in which three times as much harm as good is being done: thirty human lives are being taken in order to save ten human lives. As excessive loss of life is normally judged in the context of the conduct of war, however, I think that this would not be considered in the least excessive if, *ex hypothesi*, no less harmful means to the same end were available. This is an example of my earlier comment that the understanding of proportional conduct is heavily weighted towards a kind of military rationality. I am neither challenging the particular judgement that in the midst of deadly combat it is reasonable to inflict thirty deaths upon the adversary's troops in order to avoid suffering ten deaths among one's own nor denying that the requirement of inflicting no more losses than necessary imposes some not-very-stringent limit that is better than no limit at all. I am simply underlining the fact that what are generally accepted as non-excessive losses to impose upon an adversary in the midst of war are still great human losses.

Indeed, it is precisely because I grant that one cannot reasonably send young people into deadly conflict under orders to be extremely careful not to inflict the slightest unnecessary losses upon the adversary—certainly they must err on the sides of both self-preservation and military victory, if they are to fight at all—that I suggest that the standard of proportionality for recourse to war (*jus ad bellum*) is so different from the standard for the conduct of war (*jus in bello*). That is, it is precisely because 'not excessive' at the level of specific operations definitely does not mean 'more good than harm' that it is absolutely essential that the judgement about proportional recourse be understood as answering the question whether whatever is at stake is worth the fighting of a war, with all expectable losses on all sides counted. It must be the case that fighting the war is, all things considered, better than not fighting the war. Even here, however, the standard tends to be unspecified and is, in fact, very difficult to specify, in part because of the incommensurability of the various matters at stake.

Secondly, quite often, obviously, less destruction of artefacts, less damage to the environment, and many fewer human deaths and injuries would result if no war were fought. Yet a refusal to resist the depredations of a ruthless aggressor might lead to many—even if fewer—deaths and injuries, plus the loss of political independence for one's state and the loss of liberty for many individual persons. How much independence and liberty is worth how many additional deaths and injuries? Judging

from actual human decisions through history, many persons have in fact been willing to risk their own lives and to take the lives of those threatening them in order to
preserve the autonomy of their group and their own individual liberty. This is not
the place to try to determine definitively whether the customary balancing of incom-
mensurables like, to put it most grandly, liberty and life is or is not reasonable. Yet
that is part of what would be involved in settling upon a more determinate standard
of proportionality in recourse to war. At the same time, it is extremely important not
to assume that the stakes in most wars are in fact nearly so glorious; often the conflict is merely over something like the price of oil, but many are misled by groundless rhetoric about freedom into fighting and dying nevertheless (Klare 2001).

6. Justified Resort and 'Supreme Emergency'

Three considerations are central in contemporary discussion of whether a resort to
war can be justified. First, as we have just seen, the resort to military action must be
judged to be proportional overall: more likely than not to prevent more harm than it
causes, counting all the death and destruction, intentional and unintentional, on all
sides without nationalistic discounting. Secondly, and now virtually taken for
granted, the resort to war must be a defence against an aggression directed at oneself
or others. Thirdly, and currently highly controversial, it must be possible to conduct
this defence discriminately: the *jus ad bellum* is conditional upon compliance with *jus
in bello*. The first consideration, proportional resort, was discussed above in contrast
with proportional conduct; the most controversial third element will be discussed
below. We begin with the least controversial requirement: defence against aggression.

The firm contemporary requirement that warfare is permissible only in response
to aggressive attack represents a significant historical change. Until relatively recently
in human history, a variety of 'just causes' for resort to war were each widely thought
acceptable. These included the punishment of previous wrongdoing, the spread of
true religion, the maintenance of a balance of power, and the recovery of unjustly
taken assets, especially territory. Although the full explanation for the relatively
abrupt and sharp narrowing of acceptable grounds for going to war to the single
ground of defence against aggression would range far beyond the scope of this analysis, the date of the narrowing is quite clear: the widespread acceptance upon the conclusion of the Second World War in 1945 of the Charter of the United Nations, which
explicitly and firmly restricts justifiable resort to war to national defence. Partly in
shock and revulsion that the attrition strategy imposed upon combatants in the
trenches of the First World War had been succeeded in only a few decades by the terror bombing, nuclear and non-nuclear, visited upon civilians in Asia and Europe in
the Second World War, in both cases by the self-proclaimed defenders of civilization,

many concluded at the time that, with the conduct of war appearing to be out of control, the better hope was to control the resort to war. If no nation committed aggression, no nation would be forced to defend itself. Subsequently, of course, the principles for the conduct of war were also powerfully and widely reaffirmed in the Geneva Conventions (1949) and the Geneva Protocols Additional to the Geneva Conventions (1977), condemning in retrospect much of the conduct of both world wars and recognizing that, one way or another, wars will continue to start.

Perhaps the most serious conceptual difficulty about the prohibition of aggressive war concerns timescale: what can be construed by one side as aggression can be presented by the other as a delayed defence against an alleged earlier aggression. This is particularly tempting in the case of 'lost' territory to which some 'historic' right can be claimed by a party that was earlier unable to defend itself successfully. The intent of the UN Charter is, nevertheless, quite clear: whatever the rights and wrongs of the status quo, the status quo is not to be changed by military force. Many national borders are admittedly the outcomes of previous wars, many of them blatantly aggressive, but the fighting of additional wars is the one solution that can no longer be allowed. Any changes will have to be made peacefully.

The third issue about the resort to war returns us again to the third of the most fundamental ethical questions about war mentioned at the beginning of this chapter: the relation between the resort to war in a particular case and the limits on its conduct. Is the limited conduct of the war always a necessary condition of a justified resort to war, or do certain extreme situations excuse the violation of one or more of the limits on the conduct of war that otherwise apply? In what is probably the single most influential discussion of the morality of war in the last half century, Michael Walzer's *Just and Unjust Wars* has suggested, as indicated earlier, that, in the extreme circumstances of what he calls 'supreme emergencies', a defensive war may be fought indiscriminately—that is, one may violate the principle of discrimination by intentionally attacking the innocent, if—and, of course, only if—a victorious defence seems otherwise unlikely and one can nevertheless abide by the (vague) principle of proportionality.

The type of indiscriminate attack ordinarily in question is air attack with missiles and bombs, although the tactics adopted by the USA in Afghanistan in 2001–2 made the choice of locations assaulted by special operations forces very important as well. In the wealthiest militaries, increasing percentages of missiles and bombs operate with some form of precision guidance. Precision guidance, however, means only that munitions are more likely to strike the target at which they are aimed; it is, therefore, increasingly important whether the target at which they are aimed is a military objective. It is useful to distinguish three general kinds of attacks, according to whether their intended targets are military, civilian, or both ('dual purpose'). First, missiles and bombs used directly against opposing military forces are intended to produce either defeat or what is called 'denial'; denial is coerced surrender brought about through a more partial destruction of military forces, prior to a literal defeat through the still more complete physical destruction of military forces. Secondly, missiles and bombs used against civilians and purely civilian objects are said to be used for 'punishment'; this is usually called 'strategic bombing'. The hypothesis is that at some level of civilian death and destruction 'will' may break, or morale may collapse, and somehow lead to a surrender even prior to sufficient destruction of military forces to produce denial or defeat. Thirdly, missiles and bombs may be used against so-called dual-purpose objects—that is, infrastructure like electricity-generating plants and oil refineries that serve both military and civilian purposes; as we have noted above, dual-purpose infrastructure may, according to the 1977 Geneva Protocol I, Article 52, 2, legally be a military objective in spite of the fact that it serves civilian functions as well as military ones (Roberts and Guelph 2000: 450).

On the one hand, it is essential that, while considering hypothetical cases, one not inadvertently convey a false impression about the facts (Donagan 1994). Very few of the claims made for the effectiveness of strategic, or 'punishment', bombing— bombing intended to destroy the morale or to break the will to resist of societies— turn out to have any empirical grounding (Pape 1996; Mueller 1998). Strategic bombing usually fails at one of two points. First, often morale is raised, not lowered, just as the attacks on the World Trade Center on 11 September 2001 stiffened, rather than weakened, the resolve of the US population. Secondly, even if the will of the general population were broken by attacks on civilian targets, the general population often has no political mechanism by which to force their own government to end a war it is still capable of fighting. This is especially true if the government is authoritarian— the German and Japanese citizens subjected to British and US terror bombing dur- ing the Second World War could not have influenced their governments even if their resolve had been weakened (Pape 1996; Carr 2002). NATO's bombing of Serbia in 1999 may be one case in which attacks upon dual-purpose targets contributed to one type of military success primarily because of the civilian damage done, although it is far from clear that the same success could not have been attained by other means (Hosmer 2001; Shue, forthcoming a). On the other hand, it may be of at least theor- etical interest to consider the hypothetical instance in which limited bombing for 'punishment'—that is, indiscriminate but still proportionate attacks upon civilians—was indispensable to victory against an aggressor.

Here I believe we must distinguish more sharply than Walzer (or Rawls, who merely follows him) does between two different cases on the basis of what is at stake in the war (Orend 2000b: 128–9; Shue, forthcoming b). Ex hypothesi, one is fighting defens- ively against an aggression and is accordingly the just side, by the criteria for resort to war, in a conflict in which the other side is clearly unjust. Two kinds of cases may still be distinguished on the basis of the price of defeat, the first type in which defeat means only the loss of the control of a sovereign state of one's own and the second type in which defeat leads to enslavement, massacre, or even genocide. Naturally the loss of one's own sovereign state may in some instances be only the prelude to enslavement or massacre; these are then cases of the second, not the first, type. However, without minimizing the severity of the loss of control of one's own state, foreign conquest by even a highly repressive foreign power that does not lead on to massacre or genocide—that is, a case of the first type—is often endurable and seems clearly preferable to the slaughter of innocents that would be constituted by attacks upon civilians, even in the highly unlikely situation in which such indiscriminate attacks were the most effective form of resistance to aggression. This is for two reasons.

First, while an individual might freely choose to sacrifice his own life for the sake of protecting the communal autonomy of his own (or some other) group, to inflict death upon any significant number of innocent third parties who were not part of any threat to anyone's community's autonomy, for the sake of communal autonomy would be justifiable only if communal autonomy were a more ultimate value than many lives of individual (innocent) persons. I see no reason to believe that communal autonomy matters more than large numbers of individual human lives.

Secondly, and crucial in this context, to permit the violation of the principle of discrimination in cases of what we might think of as ordinary defeats—defeats of the first type—as distinguished from the extraordinary, second kind of defeat that would be followed by massacre or enslavement, runs a serious risk of giving away entirely the game of trying to limit war. Walzer himself has put the fundamental point with eloquent clarity: 'It is not always possible to do whatever is required to win.... The rules of war may at some point become a hindrance to the victory of one side or another. If they could then be set aside, however, they would have no value at all. It is precisely then that the restraints they impose are most important' (1997/2000: 195).

The pivotal issue is the severity of the defeat one can reasonably be expected to suffer without resorting to the killing of other innocent people in an effort to save oneself. Walzer, I believe, conflates defeats of the crucially different two types. If ever it were clear, as it never yet in history has in fact been, that attacking the innocent could be the only effective way to save one's group from genocide, one might be forgiven for carrying out the attacks. But, unlike that purely hypothetical, ahistorical conceivability, a defence of political independence could never excuse such a slaughter of the innocent, even if the slaughter were in some unimaginable way an effective defence. In conflating the two types of defeat, Walzer, and Rawls in following him, risk undermining the fundamental limit on the conduct of war.

7. 'Humanitarian' Military Intervention

Most recent conflicts have been domestic, not international (Wheeler 2000), and have consisted either of civil war or of assaults by a government on a portion of its own citizenry, as in the ethnic cleansing in the Balkans in the 1990s (Silber and Little 1996; Independent International Commission on Kosovo 2000; Booth 2001) and the catastrophic genocide in Rwanda in 1994 (African Rights 1995; Des Forges 1999; Melvern 2000). The modern international system has been dominated by the Eurocentric notion of the sovereign state to such an extent that sovereign states appear to be a natural arrangement even though they are only one of several possible arrangements (Reus-Smit 1999). Within the system oriented around state sovereignty a fundamental principle is non-intervention by one state into the affairs that properly fall within the sovereignty of another state. What was described in the preceding section on justified resort to war as now 'the least controversial requirement: defence against aggression' reflects the centrality of sovereignty and non-intervention. Aggression is the violation of the principle of non-intervention, which is the guard for sovereignty. Under the Charter of the United Nations only the Security Council may authorize military action across state borders that is not clearly a defence against aggression. The Security Council may, under chapter VII of the Charter, authorize military action in the face of a threat to international peace, prior to the occurrence of aggression. But strictly speaking only a threat to international peace—and no amount of domestic conflict—may ground an authorization of force under chapter VII, although some tendency is developing for the Security Council to treat desperate domestic conditions, such as the Somalian famine in 1992, as if they were threats to international peace irrespective of whether they are in fact.

Even so, these aspects of the 1945 Charter are coming under increasing pressure. On the one hand, the UN Security Council is a blatantly undemocratic institution totally dominated by the five states with permanent vetoes over anything proposed, which happen to be the first five states acquiring nuclear weapons (the USA, Russia, the UK, France, and China) and which constitute an odd assortment of past, present, and possibly future major military powers containing only a minority of the world's population and no representatives at all from two continents and at least two major religions. The lack of democracy, and the allocation of the veto purely on the basis of national military power, within the Security Council make any moral authority behind its legal authority exceedingly thin, especially in so far as the permanent veto appears to rest on the proposition that might makes right.

On the other hand, during the second half of the twentieth century the conviction grew that not only should the external sovereignty of the state be limited by the principle of non-intervention—and the prohibition against aggression—but that the internal sovereignty of the state ought to be conditional on some minimal level of respect for the human rights of the persons living under its power and conditional, at the very least, on the state's not in effect committing aggression against its own people through genocide, enslavement, massacre, ethnic cleansing, or intentional famine. The growing conviction that 'internal aggression' as well as external aggression ought somehow to be countered has led to important debates over the justification of 'humanitarian' military intervention. Where a predatory state not only fails to protect the basic rights of the people under its power but is itself attacking them, what protection can there be other than the interposition of power from outside the state? Then this would have to be a form of military action that is justified, which means that it is not aggression, but that is also not an instance of self-defence against aggression (Luban 1980/1985). As Luban suggested, it is not clear that the authors of the UN Charter foresaw the contemporary need for a category of justified resort to military force that is neither aggressive nor self-defensive, but is instead an attempted rescue of persons victimized by their own state.

The solution in the abstract is quite straightforward: the privileges of sovereignty can be understood to be conditional not only upon non-predatory external behaviour—non-aggression—but also upon non-predatory internal behaviour, like refraining from genocide and ethnic cleansing within national borders. Paul Ramsey's logic of twin-born justification and limitation, as I characterized it above, seems applicable in principle: 'justified military action stands in harm's way, shielding intended victims from the harm. It is justified harm protecting against unjustified harm, justified by the protection it provides.' In the instance of 'humanitarian' military intervention, the intervenors, acting upon a default duty, protect people against the very state that failed in its own primary duty to protect them and even in the universal duty not to attack them. The difficulties concern the practical ethics: the specific modalities of any military interventions against states that have forfeited aspects of their internal sovereignty by predatory domestic policies, especially the fundamental political question 'who decides?' Is Security Council authorization necessary for a form of military action the Charter does not seem to have foreseen?

The most important instance in the final decade of the twentieth century was the intervention that never happened or, more accurately, the abandonment of genocide victims by the Security Council decision, under heavy pressure from the USA and the UK, to withdraw, rather than to reinforce, a UN peacekeeping force that was already in place when the genocide began: Rwanda, in 1994 (Power 2002). That existing force was inadequate for its mission because the USA had insisted, when the force was authorized in October 1993, that it be kept small and cheap and be given a much weaker mandate than the Arusha Agreement, which it was supposed to implement, depended on (Adelman and Suhrke 1996: 89 n. 65; United Nations 1996: 169–201; Melvern 2000: 85; Barnett 2002: 71; Power 2002: 341–3).

Shame at the betrayal of nearly a million Rwandans to their deaths, and at this failure in 1994 to keep the oft-repeated promise of 'never again', was one explicit motivation for the intervention into Serbia in 1999 by NATO, led by the USA and the UK, the two permanent members of the Security Council that had most vigorously advocated the pull-out of UN peacekeepers from Rwanda as the genocide began. While the NATO intervention was grounded in the ethnic cleansing conducted against the Kosovar Albanians by the Serbian state—their own sovereign government—it had two troubling features, one procedural and one substantive. First, NATO acted without clear, explicit authorization by the Security Council in the knowledge that a request for authorization would in fact have been vetoed. Secondly, in the first such extended military action in history, NATO intervened only with airpower: bombers and missiles. No ground troops were sent in to protect the Kosovars, several hundred thousand of whom were driven from the country after the intervention began but then mostly returned shortly after the intervention ended (Roberts 1999; Daalder and O'Hanlon 2000; Ignatieff 2000; W. K. Clark 2001). The central substantive controversy had two empirical elements. Did NATO's unwillingness to risk ground troops in combat produce a failure to provide protection against expulsion for the Kosovar Albanians that ground troops could have provided? And did the use exclusively of airpower, especially plane flights at relatively high altitudes designed to keep the planes and pilots safe from attack, produce greater civilian casualties among Kosovars or Serbians than 1977 Geneva Protocol I's requirement of 'constant care' permits (Amnesty International 2000; Ronzitti 2000; International Criminal Tribunal for Yugoslavia 2001)? Those for whom the answers to the two empirical questions are troubling find themselves returned to the question that has been the theme of this chapter: to what extent can the resort to military force be justified in cases in which the conduct of the force cannot be fully justified? But in this case the end of the resort to force is, not self-defence, but rescue.

References

1977 Geneva Protocol I Additional to the Geneva Conventions of 12 August 1949 (1977). In Roberts and Guelff (2000); at http: icrc.org/ihl.nsf/WebCONVFULL?OpenView.

Adelman, Howard, and Suhrke, Astri (1996). *The International Response to Conflict and Genocide: Lessons from the Rwanda Experience, Study 2: Early Warning and Conflict Management.* Copenhagen: Joint Evaluation of Emergency Assistance to Rwanda, DANIDA; http:\\www.um.dk\danida\evalueringsrapporter\1997_rwanda.

African Rights (1995). *Rwanda: Death, Despair and Defiance.* Rev. edn. London: African Rights.

Amnesty International (2000). *'Collateral Damage' or Unlawful Killings? Violations of the Laws of War by NATO during Operation Allied Force* [NATO/Federal Republic of Yugoslavia], EUR 70/18/00. London: Amnesty International.

Barnes, Jonathan (1982). 'The Just War' in Norman Kretzmann, Anthony Kenny, and Jan Pinborg (eds.), *Cambridge History of Later Medieval Philosophy.* Cambridge: Cambridge University Press, 771–84.

Barnett, Michael (2002). *Eyewitness to a Genocide: The United Nations and Rwanda.* Ithaca, NY: Cornell University Press.

Baylis, John, and O'Neill, Robert (2000) (eds.), *Alternative Nuclear Futures: The Role of Nuclear Weapons in the Post-Cold War World.* Oxford: Oxford University Press.

Booth, Ken (2001a). 'Ten Flaws of Just Wars', in Ken Booth (ed.), *The Kosovo Tragedy: The Human Rights Dimensions.* London: Frank Cass, 314–24.

—— (2001b) (ed.), *The Kosovo Tragedy: The Human Rights Dimensions.* London: Frank Cass.

Carr, Caleb (2002). *The Lessons of Terror: A History of Warfare against Civilians: Why It Has Always Failed and Why It Will Fail Again*. New York: Random House.

Center for Defense Information (2000). *National Missile Defense: What Does It All Mean?* Washington: Center for Defense Information.

Clark, Ian (1988). *Waging War: A Philosophical Introduction*. Oxford: Oxford University Press.

Clark, Gen. Wesley K. (2001). *Waging Modern War: Bosnia, Kosovo, and the Future of Combat*. New York: Public Affairs.

Coates, A. J. (1997). *The Ethics of War*. Manchester: Manchester University Press.

Daalder, Ivo H., and O'Hanlon, Michael E. (2000). *Winning Ugly: NATO'S War to Save Kosovo*. Washington: Brookings Institution Press.

Des Forges, Alison (1999). *'Leave None to Tell the Story': Genocide in Rwanda*. London: Human Rights Watch.

Donagan, Alan (1991). 'Moral Absolutism and the Double-Effect Exception'. *Journal of Medicine and Philosophy*, 16, 495–509.

——(1994). 'The Relation of Moral Theory to Moral Judgments: A Kantian Review', in *The Philosophical Papers of Alan Donagan, ii. Action, Reason, and Value*, ed. J. E. Malpas. Chicago: University of Chicago Press, 194–216.

Dunlap, Charles J., Jr. (2000a). 'Kosovo, Casualty Aversion, and the American Military Ethos: A Perspective'. *Journal of Legal Studies*, 95–107.

——(2000b). 'The End of Innocence: Rethinking Noncombatancy in the Post-Kosovo Era'. *Strategic Review*, 9–17.

Finnis, John, Boyle, Joseph, and Grisez, Germain (1987). *Nuclear Deterrence, Morality and Realism*. Oxford: Oxford University Press.

Friedman, Leon (1972) (ed.), *The Laws of War: A Documentary History*. 2 vols. New York: Random House.

Gray, J. Glenn (1959/1998). *The Warriors: Reflections on Men in Battle*. Lincoln, NE: University of Nebraska Press.

Grotius, Hugo (1625/1972). *The Law of War and Peace, Bk. III*, in Leon Friedman (ed.), *The Law of War: A Documentary History*, i. New York: Random House, 16–146.

Hartigan, Richard Shelly (1983). *Lieber's Code and the Law of War*. Chicago: Precedent Publishing.

Holmes, Robert L. (1989). *On War and Morality*. Princeton: Princeton University Press.

——(1990). *Nonviolence in Theory and Practice*. Prospect Heights, IL: Waveland Press.

Hosmer, Stephen T (2001). *The Conflict over Kosovo: Why Milosevic Decided to Settle When He Did*. Project Air Force Series on Operation Allied Force, MR-1351. Santa Monica: RAND.

Howard, Michael, Andreopoulos, George J., and Shulman, Mark R. (1994) (eds.), *The Laws of War: Constraints on Warfare in the Western World*. New Haven: Yale University Press.

Ignatieff, Michael (2000). *Virtual War: Kosovo and Beyond*. New York: Henry Holt.

Independent International Commission on Kosovo (2000). *Kosovo Report: Conflict, International Response, Lessons Learned*. Oxford: Oxford University Press.

International Criminal Tribunal for Yugoslavia (2001). *Final Report to the Prosecutor by the Committee Established to Review the NATO Bombing Campaign against the Federal Republic of Yugoslavia*. The Hague: International Criminal Tribunal for Yugoslavia; http://www.un.org/icty/pressreal/nato061300.htm.

Johnson, James Turner (1999). *Morality and Contemporary Warfare*. New Haven: Yale University Press.

Jokic, Aleksandar (2001) (ed.), *War Crimes and Collective Wrongdoing*. Malden, MA: Blackwell.

Kenny, Anthony (1985). *The Logic of Deterrence*. Chicago: University of Chicago Press.

Klare, Michael T. (2001). *Resource Wars: The New Landscape of Global Conflict*. New York: Henry Holt.

Lackey, Douglas P. (1989). *The Ethics of War and Peace*. Englewood Cliffs, NJ: Prentice Hall.

The Laws of Manu (1991). Trans. Wendy Doniger. London: Penguin.

Lee, Steven P. (1993). *Morality, Prudence, and Nuclear Weapons*. Cambridge: Cambridge University Press.

Lichtenberg, Judith (1994). 'War, Innocence, and the Doctrine of Double Effect'. *Philosophical Studies*, 74: 347–68.

Luban, David (1980/1985). 'Just War and Human Rights', in Charles R. Beitz, Marshall Cohen, et al. (eds.), *International Ethics: A Philosophy and Public Affairs Reader*, 195–216.

——— (2002). 'Intervention and Civilization: Some Unhappy Lessons of the Kosovo War', in Ciaran Cronin and Pable de Greiff (eds.), *Deliberative Democracy and Transitional Politics: Beyond the Nation-State Paradigm*. Cambridge, MA: MIT Press.

McCoubrey, Hilaire (1998). *International Humanitarian Law: Modern Developments in the Limitation of Warfare*. 2nd edn. Aldershot: Ashgate.

McNamara, Robert S. (2000). 'Reflecting on War in the Twenty-first Century: The Context for Nuclear Abolition', in John Baylis and Robert O'Neill (eds.), *Alternative Nuclear Futures: The Role of Nuclear Weapons in the Post-Cold War World*. Oxford: Oxford University Press, 167–82.

Mamdani, Mahmood (2001). *When Victims Become Killers: Colonialism, Nativism, and the Genocide in Rwanda*. Princeton: Princeton University Press.

Melvern, Linda (2000). *A People Betrayed: The Role of the West in Rwanda's Genocide*. London: Zed Books.

Miller, Richard B. (1992) (ed.), *War in the Twentieth Century: Sources in Theological Ethics*. Louisville, KY: Westminster/John Knox Press.

Moxley, Charles J., Jr. (2000). *Nuclear Weapons and International Law in the Post Cold War World*. Lanham, MD: Austin & Winfield.

Mueller, Karl (1998). 'Denial, Punishment, and the Future of Air Power'. *Security Studies*, 7: 182–228.

National Conference of Catholic Bishops (1983). *The Challenge of Peace: God's Promise and our Response, A Pastoral Letter*. Washington: US Catholic Conference.

Norman, Richard (1995). *Ethics, Killing and War*. Cambridge: Cambridge University Press.

O'Brien, William V. (1981). *The Conduct of Just and Limited War*. New York: Praeger Publishers.

Orend, Brian (2000a). *War and International Justice: A Kantian Perspective*. Waterloo, Ont.: Wilfrid Laurier University Press.

——— (2000b). *Michael Walzer on War and Justice*. Montreal: McGill-Queen's University Press.

Pape, Robert A. (1996). *Bombing to Win: Air Power and Coercion in War*. Ithaca, NY: Cornell University Press.

Politi, Mauro, and Nesi, Giuseppe (2001) (eds.), *The Rome Statute of the International Criminal Court: A Challenge to Impunity*. Brookfield, VT: Ashgate.

Power, Samantha (2001). 'Bystanders to Genocide: Why the United States Let the Rwandan Tragedy Happen'. *Atlantic Monthly* (Sept.), 84–108; http:\\www.theatlantic.com\issues\ 2001\09\power.htm.

—— (2002). 'A Problem from Hell': America and the Age of Genocide: New York: Basic Books.

Quinn, Warren S. (1989). 'Actions, Intentions, and Consequences: The Doctrine of Double Effect'. *Philosophy and Public Affairs*, 18: 334–51.

Ramsey, Paul (1968/1983). *The Just War: Force and Political Responsibility*. Savage, MD: Rowman & Littlefield.

Rawls, John (1999). *The Law of Peoples with 'The Idea of Public Reason Revisited'*. Cambridge, MA: Harvard University Press.

Reus-Smit, Christian (1999). *The Moral Purpose of the State: Culture, Social Identity, and Institutional Rationality in International Relations*. Princeton: Princeton University Press.

Roberts, Adam (1999). 'NATO's "Humanitarian War" over Kosovo'. *Survival*, 41: 102–23.

—— and Guelff, Richard (2000) (eds.), *Documents on the Laws of War*. 3rd edn. Oxford: Oxford University Press.

Ronzitti, Natalino (2000). 'Is the Non Liquet of the Final Report to the Prosecutor by the Committee Established to Review the NATO Bombing Campaign against the Federal Republic of Yugoslavia Acceptable?' *International Review of the Red Cross*, 82: 840.

Russell, Frederick H. (1975). *The Just War in the Middle Ages*. Cambridge: Cambridge University Press.

Scarry, Elaine (1985). *The Body in Pain: The Making and Unmaking of the World*. New York: Oxford University Press.

Schaffer, Ronald (1985). *Wings of Judgment: American Bombing in World War II*. New York: Oxford University Press.

Schell, Jonathan (1998). *The Gift of Time: The Case for Abolishing Nuclear Weapons*. New York: Henry Holt.

Shue, Henry (forthcoming *a*). 'Bombing to Rescue? NATO's 1999 Bombing of Serbia', in Deen Chatterjee and Don Scheid (eds.), *Ethics and Foreign Intervention*. Cambridge: Cambridge University Press.

—— (forthcoming *b*). 'Liberalism: The Impossibility of Justifying Weapons of Mass Destruction', in Sohail Hoshemi and Steven Lee (eds.), *Ethics and Weapons of Mass Destruction*. Princeton: Princeton University Press.

Silber, Laura, and Little, Allan (1996). *Yugoslavia: Death of a Nation*. New York: Penguin.

Thomas, Ward (2001). *The Ethics of Destruction: Norms and Force in International Relations*. Ithaca, NY: Cornell University Press.

United Nations (1996). *The United Nations and Rwanda 1993–1996*. New York: United Nations.

Vitoria, Francisco de (1539/1991). 'On the Law of War', in Francisco de Vitoria, *Political Writings*, ed. Anthony Pagden and Jeremy Lawrance. Cambridge: Cambridge University Press, 293–327.

Walzer, Michael (1977/2000). *Just and Unjust Wars: A Moral Argument with Historical Illustrations*. 3rd edn. New York: Basic Books.

Welch, David A. (1993). *Justice and the Genesis of War*. Cambridge: Cambridge University Press.

Wells, Donald A. (1992). *The Laws of Land Warfare: A Guide to the US Army Manuals*. Westport, CT: Greenwood Press.

Wheeler, Nicholas J. (2000). *Saving Strangers: Humanitarian Intervention in International Society*. Oxford: Oxford University Press.

INDEX

....

abortion vii, xv, 2, 6, 10, 18, 38, 41, 74, 76, 112–17, 120–2, 124–9, 131–5, 137, 138, 153, 156, 157, 173, 237, 238, 243, 268, 415, 487, 491, 493, 496, 499, 504–7, 509, 512, 693, 701

adoption 36, 81, 117, 137, 151, 154, 468, 471, 474, 495, 719

adultery xv, 17, 19, 20, 41, 70, 241

affirmative action viii, xiii, 6, 7, 9, 226, 230, 231, 253, 264, 272–83, 285, 287–99, 415–17

    gender-based 229, 273, 288–92, 367

    race-based 248–50, 262

    rationale for 37, 100, 104, 109, 119, 124, 131, 133, 213, 374, 392–4, 405, 408, 410, 444, 449, 462, 463, 469, 473, 488, 506, 511, 516, 517, 524, 528, 534, 536, 598, 629, 644, 650, 664, 693, 694, 725, 752

    stigma 289, 290, 292, 297, 357, 370, 371, 603, 723

agape 43, 44, 49, 50, 52–4, 56, 58, 59, 62, 68, 69

aggression 28, 231, 236, 366, 367, 582, 721, 742, 752–7

AIDS 37, 130, 183, 184, 488

Allen, Anita L. viii, xi, 159, 268, 269, 355, 411, 457, 485–7, 489–92, 495, 501, 503, 504, 509, 511, 512, 601, 604, 668, 700

Almond, Brenda vii, xi, 70, 77, 82, 85

Altman, Andrew viii, xi, 358, 492, 504

Alzheimer's disease 174

Americans with Disabilities Act (ADA) 303, 320

Anderson, Elizabeth S. xv, 32, 33, 39, 311, 312, 316–18, 324, 341, 353, 453–6, 504, 593, 597, 615

animal experimentation 163, 166, 168–71, 176, 179, 184–6

animals vii, 21, 43, 48, 117, 161–80, 182–7, 189, 191, 195–7, 213, 256, 323, 326, 515, 578, 623, 657

anthropology 70, 87, 430

Anti-Semite and Jew 270

Appiah, Anthony 254, 258, 259, 269

Aquinas, St Thomas 16, 39, 78, 85, 114, 678

Archard, David vii, xi, 36, 37, 39, 91, 102, 110

Arendt, Hannah 487, 504, 585, 588

Aristotle 43, 46, 50, 53, 57, 67, 68, 204, 256, 257, 269

friendship xii, 8, 28, 43, 46, 50–3, 56–63, 65, 67–9, 105, 180, 660

generosity 67, 453

pleasure 16, 19, 20, 23, 26, 30, 31, 37, 40, 43–6, 48–50, 52, 59, 82, 366, 395, 396, 441, 472, 530, 648, 660, 661

virtues xii, 3, 44, 45, 50, 60, 67, 68, 110, 174, 223, 252, 323, 324, 326, 376, 423, 437, 655, 723

Arneson, Richard 315–18, 324, 452–4, 456

Arthur, John viii, xi, 413, 417, 422, 486, 509, 597, 648, 667, 700, 732

artificial insemination 159, 243

Audi, Robert 378–80, 383

Augustine, St 16, 43, 78, 85, 678

autonomy ix, 7, 32, 37, 45, 68, 82, 86, 100, 102, 105–8, 110, 112, 125, 131, 137, 152, 153, 160, 199, 322, 334, 337, 364, 365, 376, 377, 402, 403, 405–8, 411, 412, 419, 420, 486, 488, 491, 493, 494, 496, 501, 504, 506–10, 524, 532–4, 581, 591, 592, 594–6, 598–601, 603, 604, 606, 608, 610–15, 625, 633, 648, 651, 656–8, 660, 674–7, 690, 691, 693–5, 697, 698, 719, 752, 755

    drugs xiv, 28, 239, 397, 404, 411, 516, 527, 679, 696, 700

    euthanasia ix, xii, 10, 114, 134, 153, 167, 409, 673, 674, 680, 682, 684–96, 699–704

    moral rights 126, 173, 174, 195, 197, 198, 459, 511, 530, 659

    utilitarianism 170, 357, 447, 450, 458, 468, 483, 617, 630, 647, 648, 655, 657, 661, 665

Badhwar, Neera K. vii, xii, 42, 52, 67, 68

Barry, Brian 214, 419, 431, 437, 456, 466, 482, 575, 588–90, 592, 601, 605, 606, 610, 615, 625, 629, 637, 642, 654

basic rights xv, 125, 257, 525, 529, 608, 642, 658, 659, 661, 663, 668, 756

Battin, Margaret P. ix, xii, xv, 326, 673, 684, 696, 700, 701

Beauchamp, Tom L. 172, 185, 186, 537, 538, 676, 700

Beauvoir, Simone de 75, 76, 79, 85, 227, 242

Bedau, Hugo Adam ix, xii, 267, 270, 460, 482, 705, 708, 710, 723, 725, 727, 728, 730–3
Beitz, Charles 622, 630, 631, 634, 636, 637, 642, 654, 662, 667, 760
Bell Curve, The 262, 269, 270, 283, 284, 286, 298
benevolence 46, 67, 649–52, 657, 666
Benn, S. I. 486, 492, 504
Bentham, Jeremy 8, 84, 173, 196, 326, 654, 667, 706, 731
Berkeley, George 68, 69, 85, 159, 187, 297, 298, 301, 317, 326, 355, 616, 732
biocentrism 191, 215, 655
birth cohort 143, 460, 464
Blum, Lawrence A. 67, 68, 413, 431
Bok, Sissela 276, 297, 299, 487, 490, 505, 540, 563, 683, 689–93, 700, 701
Bosnia 607, 759
Brandt, Richard B. 733
Brown v. *Board of Education* 299
Buchanan, Allen 149, 159, 315, 325, 395, 411, 576, 588, 592, 601, 602, 604–7, 609, 610, 615, 694, 700
Buckley, William F. 371, 383

Callahan, Daniel 114, 134, 137, 159, 482, 683, 700
Callan, Eamon 106, 108, 110, 596, 615
Canada 321, 370, 382, 413, 420, 577, 578, 581, 589, 594, 609, 612–14, 616, 617, 619, 676
capital punishment ix, 6, 9, 10, 351, 678, 679, 705, 711, 715, 720, 730–3, 742
capitalism xvi, 192, 250, 362, 415, 433, 448, 457, 483, 537, 538, 623
Carens, Joseph 433, 456, 571, 572, 581, 588, 615, 618
Carter, Alan 378, 380, 383
censorship 39, 233, 243, 256, 364, 382, 588, 646, 715
Challenger 539, 540
character 15, 21, 45, 46, 50, 53, 56–9, 62–4, 69, 74, 91, 92, 97, 98, 105, 123, 190, 253, 255, 256, 276, 340, 341, 376, 409, 427, 437, 438, 522, 523, 557, 575, 583, 594, 596, 615, 616, 623, 662, 683, 695, 697, 712, 722, 728, 745
    differences in 74, 140, 250, 283, 316, 359, 397, 398, 459, 471, 476, 479, 620, 622–4, 628, 636, 666
    social basis of 443, 603
charity 573, 625, 627, 628, 641, 646
childhood xi, 24, 26, 36, 66, 91–5, 98, 100, 109–11, 156, 195, 255, 256, 480, 579, 710
children vii, xi, xiii, 16–18, 26, 27, 33, 36, 37, 48, 51, 56, 58, 59, 71–3, 76–83, 85–7, 91, 92, 94–111, 125, 130, 135, 137–9, 142–4, 146–52,
155–8, 160, 170, 173, 182, 183, 196, 197, 227, 229, 231, 233, 240–2, 244, 256, 259, 263, 265, 268, 270, 277, 280, 281, 283, 291, 296, 302, 304, 308, 309, 320, 360, 377, 391, 419, 420, 424, 459, 465, 470, 482, 488, 493, 496, 505, 516, 527, 536, 559, 567, 577, 579, 580, 630–2, 639, 640, 648, 649, 680, 717, 736, 737
China 84, 756
Chomsky, Noam 362, 383
Christianity 158, 186, 189, 437, 678
citizenship xiv, 40, 87, 108, 109, 298, 339, 369, 370, 373, 378–85, 413, 420–3, 432, 493, 504, 532–4, 538, 570, 577–9, 581, 588–90, 594, 595, 611–13, 615, 617–19, 621, 634, 655, 668
Clinton, William Jefferson 16, 489
cloning 118–20, 123, 141–8, 150, 151, 154–60, 162
closed borders 573, 589
coercion 16, 27, 40, 106, 153, 234, 312, 347, 627, 640, 760
Cohen v. *California* 360, 383
colonialism 623, 628, 760
communitarianism xii, 334, 655, 656
compassion 67, 221, 267, 496, 505, 652
compensation 126, 202, 246, 264, 296, 317, 346, 348, 379, 440, 445, 451, 452, 454–6, 474, 637
    affirmative action viii, xiii, 6, 7, 9, 226, 230, 231, 253, 264, 272–83, 285, 287–99, 415–17
    property rights 198–200, 433, 435–7, 457, 483, 484, 506, 511, 572, 628
compensatory rights 311, 314, 315, 318
competition 124, 231, 255, 275, 276, 278, 281, 285, 289, 488, 514, 572, 662, 664, 665
complicity 549–57
considered judgements 5, 666
consistency:
    abortion vii, xv, 2, 6, 10, 18, 38, 41, 74, 76, 112–17, 120–2, 124–9, 131–5, 137, 138, 153, 156, 157, 173, 237, 238, 243, 268, 415, 487, 491, 493, 496, 499, 504–7, 509, 512, 693, 701
    euthanasia ix, xii, 10, 114, 134, 153, 167, 409, 673, 674, 680, 682, 684–96, 699–704
    free movement 572, 574, 575, 587–90
contraception 18, 38, 75, 76, 129, 133, 237, 496
contractarianism 472, 482, 719
Copp, David 39, 606, 608, 609, 615, 616
corporate responsibility viii, 8, 514, 516, 517, 525–30, 532–7
corporations xvi, 8, 197, 249, 250, 254, 363, 499, 516–30, 532–6, 538, 635
cosmopolitanism 629, 632, 634, 654, 656
Cottingham, John 340, 354

counterfactual 467, 707
crime 27, 72, 82, 95, 235, 244, 331–3, 335, 337–45,
    347–51, 354–7, 366, 370, 488, 494, 506, 543,
    705, 707, 709–11, 716, 720, 721, 723, 729, 731–3
    causes of 36, 189, 366, 418, 624, 637, 643, 648,
        656, 657, 696
    and drugs xiv
Cruzan, Nancy 369, 494
Cullity, Garrett 648, 667
cultural identity 419–21, 427, 594
currency of justice 440–2, 446

Daniels, Norman 159, 309, 310, 325, 438, 444,
    446, 457, 460, 476, 478–82, 701
date rape 27, 28, 41
Davis, Michael ix, xii, 147, 151, 159, 340, 342, 354,
    385, 486, 506, 539, 709–11, 730, 731, 733
death ix, xii, 10, 35, 46, 71, 100–2, 117, 123, 127,
    134, 142, 175, 185, 191, 203, 349, 406, 442, 461,
    464, 483, 488, 547, 570, 630, 648, 671, 674,
    675, 677, 679–82, 684–9, 693, 694, 696–8,
    700–33, 735, 739, 747–9, 752, 754, 755, 758, 761
DeCew, Judith Wagner 11, 487, 490, 491, 506
Deigh, John 346, 354
Dennett, Daniel 6, 11, 336, 354, 519, 521, 536
dependency approach to equality 241–2
desert 340, 343, 344, 354, 357, 476, 681, 709–11,
    723, 725, 729, 732
    and punishment 334, 340–3, 348, 355, 357,
        411, 732
development assistance 634, 651, 654
Dewey, John 284, 286, 297
Diamond, Jared 623, 642, 707, 731
difference feminists 226, 232, 233, 236, 240
difference principle 105, 438, 439, 441, 444, 446,
    449, 450, 631, 635, 636
discrimination viii, xv, xvi, 2, 7, 8, 34, 74, 78, 129,
    130, 144, 153, 155, 176, 199, 202, 219, 220,
    227–30, 233–5, 241–3, 245, 247, 248, 250, 253,
    264, 270, 272–5, 277, 279–83, 288–90, 292–7,
    301, 303, 310, 314, 319–21, 325, 326, 359, 367,
    420, 453, 460, 474–7, 483, 583, 603, 606, 731,
    738, 745–7, 749, 753, 755
diversity feminists 226, 227, 230, 232, 233, 235,
    238, 239, 241
divorce 17, 27, 72, 73, 76, 82, 85–7, 102, 239–41,
    244, 424, 495, 561, 604, 615
dominance feminism 220, 226–7
Donagan, Alan 189, 754, 759
Donaldson, Thomas xvi, 527–9, 531, 536, 537
double effect 9, 114, 679, 680, 690, 699, 741, 745,
    747, 760, 761
Dower, Nigel ix, xii, 643, 648, 654–6, 667

drugs xiv, 28, 239, 397, 404, 411, 516, 527, 679,
    696, 700
    and addiction 69
    and crime 333
    legalization of 676, 684–7, 689, 691, 695
    right to use 57, 171, 448, 720, 721
dualism 18, 737, 738
Duff, R. A. viii, xiii, 331–9, 341, 342, 345–7,
    349–54, 356, 357, 410, 411
Dworkin, Gerald 398, 411, 506, 512, 589, 689,
    690, 701
Dworkin, Ronald xiv, xiv, 68, 159, 315, 319, 325,
    383, 415, 444, 457, 461, 491, 506, 536, 625, 642,
    701, 732, 761

ecology 191, 192, 194, 195, 203–5, 208, 209, 214,
    215, 483, 574
economic justice viii, ix, 415, 430, 433, 434,
    439–41, 455, 620, 622, 624, 627–30, 633,
    634, 638
    and equality 84, 297, 367, 381–3, 431, 452, 456,
        457, 496, 590, 615, 642
    and international relations ix, xv, 10, 565, 642,
        667, 668
    property rights 198–200, 433, 435–7, 457, 483,
        484, 506, 511, 572, 628
    veil of ignorance 319, 445, 467, 479, 718
egalitarianism 264, 439, 440, 451, 452, 468, 470,
    471, 475–7, 571, 572
email 491, 497, 500, 502
empirical data 3, 6, 7, 10, 31, 404, 687
entitlement theory 435, 627, 628
environmental ethics xiv, 3, 188–95, 201, 203–15
    and justice 105, 299, 354, 355, 357, 433, 450, 481,
        482, 537, 641, 760
equality viii, xv, 10, 30, 73, 74, 78, 80, 84, 106, 192,
    194–6, 215, 216, 220–2, 224, 241–3, 247, 258,
    265, 272, 275, 276, 280, 282, 288–90, 292, 297,
    309, 312, 322, 324–6, 366, 367, 370–2, 374, 378,
    380–3, 385, 414, 415, 427, 430, 431, 435, 438,
    442, 444–52, 454, 456–8, 475, 477, 478, 480,
    483, 484, 496, 510–12, 573, 590, 607, 613, 615,
    621, 622, 626, 631, 634, 636, 637, 642, 668
    of all human beings 43, 648, 649
    of animals 21, 161–7, 171–9, 182–7, 196, 197,
        213, 657
    of opportunity 97, 275, 276, 282, 288–92, 310,
        312, 430, 452, 454, 456, 458, 631, 634
    of resources 315, 318, 437, 442, 444–6, 452, 454,
        456, 457, 476–9, 574, 576, 580, 583, 629, 634
    utilitarianism 170, 357, 447, 450, 458, 468, 483,
        484, 617, 630, 647, 648, 655, 657, 661, 665
eros 50, 61, 62, 65, 66, 68, 69

ethical theory 8, 9, 11, 191, 193, 355, 459, 508, 537, 538, 647, 652, 668, 691
eugenics 152, 153, 159, 326
euthanasia ix, xii, 10, 114, 134, 153, 167, 409, 673, 674, 680, 682, 684–96, 699–704
    active 10, 25, 26, 98, 114, 141, 246, 249, 273, 274, 277, 423, 474, 533, 595, 600, 646, 647, 663, 673, 678, 680, 684, 685, 695, 697, 699
    duty to die 683, 702
    involuntary 125, 295, 298, 435, 477, 550, 551
    passive 25, 26, 195, 223, 657, 675, 703
    and religion viii, 224, 358, 359, 381, 382
    slippery slope arguments 685, 692
    voluntary 45, 78, 99, 102, 173, 199, 237, 278, 295, 347, 395–7, 409, 421, 426, 435, 451, 500, 518, 530, 549–51, 570, 578, 580, 628, 645, 646, 673, 675, 677, 678, 680, 684, 685, 688, 695, 696, 699, 701
Eze, Emmanuel 254, 269

fairness 84, 96, 105, 211, 257, 278, 280–3, 287, 289, 290, 295, 297, 431, 445, 455, 483, 484, 527, 532, 538, 557, 589, 618, 667
families vii, 8, 72, 75–7, 81, 83, 85, 91, 103–7, 109, 111, 227, 228, 239, 260, 290, 296, 302, 322, 424, 425, 467, 492, 494, 496, 526, 585, 621, 683, 684
    economic justice viii, ix, 415, 430, 433, 434, 439–41, 455, 620, 622, 624, 627–30, 633, 634, 638
    feminism xv, xvi, 29, 34, 39–41, 73, 75, 80, 86, 87, 222, 225, 243, 495, 496, 509, 594
favouritism 275, 277
Feinberg, Joel 213, 383, 411, 506, 731
Feinberg, Walter 272–99
feminism xv, xvi, 29, 34, 39–41, 73, 75, 80, 86, 87, 222, 225, 243, 495, 496, 509, 594
    families vii, 8, 72, 75–7, 81, 83, 85, 91, 103–7, 109, 111, 227, 228, 239, 260, 290, 296, 302, 322, 424, 425, 467, 492, 494, 496, 526, 585, 621, 683, 684
    pornography 16, 24, 29–31, 34, 37, 39, 41, 232–4, 237, 243, 360, 363, 365–9, 371, 385, 487, 512
    rape 16, 27–31, 34, 35, 39–41, 125, 235, 236, 238, 243, 244, 351, 368, 717
    sexual harassment xi, 24, 234, 235, 243, 274
    speech codes 369, 416, 417
fetus xiv, 112–15, 117, 120–2, 124–8, 131, 137, 139, 141, 142, 145, 146, 153, 157, 173, 224, 238, 239, 499, 693
    moral status of xiv, 8, 53, 91, 94, 109, 112, 113, 121, 124, 128, 131, 134, 137, 138, 144, 157, 163, 196, 344, 537, 563, 648, 649, 674, 697
    potential of 119, 222, 239, 286, 303

right to life 10, 237, 257, 325, 653, 658, 716, 717, 721
Finnis, John 78, 86, 120, 134, 366, 383, 746, 759
Fish, Stanley 122, 209, 361, 362, 383, 430, 431, 593, 651
Fiss, Owen 365, 372, 383
food aid 644, 650, 651, 666
food chain 163
forgiveness 356, 710
Foucault, Michael 24–6, 35, 39, 40, 73, 351, 355
Frankfurt, Harry 45, 53, 56, 68, 446, 447, 449, 457
free market 433
free movement 572, 574, 575, 587–90
free speech 358–65, 367–9, 371, 372, 376, 378, 381, 383–5, 414, 417, 424, 494
    consistency 256, 364, 382, 588, 646, 715
free will 11
freedom viii, 27, 30, 35, 64, 74, 75, 81, 82, 94, 96, 98, 100, 106, 107, 152, 233, 238, 242, 267, 296, 299, 336, 338, 339, 341, 347, 358–61, 363, 364, 370, 372, 375–7, 379, 381–5, 388, 389, 392–4, 398, 402, 404, 407, 410–12, 424–6, 438, 456–8, 483, 485, 486, 488, 491, 494, 496, 499, 503–6, 511–13, 518, 520, 571, 572, 576, 582, 586, 589, 599, 608, 614, 642, 652, 656, 659, 677, 691, 693, 694, 702, 752
Freeman, Edward, R. viii, xiii, 514, 530, 531, 537
Freud, Sigmund 39, 102, 110, 598
Frey, R. G. vii, xiii, 161–3, 165, 175, 186, 196, 197, 213, 454, 457, 676, 689–93, 700, 701
Fried, Charles 101, 110, 486, 492, 507
friendship xii, 8, 28, 43, 46, 50–3, 56–63, 65, 67–9, 105, 180, 660
    duties of 151, 423, 436, 578, 617, 625, 626, 628, 635, 646, 649, 652

Gauthier, David 436, 457, 471, 482, 483, 608, 616
Gellner, Ernest 593, 595, 596, 616
genetic engineering 139, 141–5, 151, 152, 156, 157, 162–5
gender inequality/sexual discrimination and:
    education 220–7
    family 239–41
    reproduction 226
    sexuality 231–6
    work 227–31
Gert, Bernard 388, 411, 689, 701
Glazer, Nathan 414, 418, 431, 549, 563, 577, 589
Glover, Jonathan 6, 11, 115, 134, 676
Goldman, Alan 23, 339, 355, 400, 411, 422
good life 100, 180, 181, 294, 437, 479, 480, 512
Good Samaritan 548, 549
Goodin, Robert E. 213, 437, 458, 571, 573, 588–90, 593, 616, 629, 642

Goodpaster, Kenneth 190, 213, 516, 517, 537
Gosseries, Axel viii, xiii, 459, 467, 469, 472, 482
Gould, Stephen J. 41, 255, 262, 263, 269, 284,
    298, 503
Goulet, Dennis 644, 668
Gutman, Amy 102, 107, 108, 110, 269, 414, 430, 432

Habermas, Jügen 507
habit 255, 305
Hampton, Jean 341, 342, 346, 350, 355, 356,
    581, 589
harassment xi, 16, 24, 234, 235, 243, 274, 280, 567
Hardin, Garrett 650, 651, 668
Hargrove, Eugene 189, 190, 198–200, 213
Harris, John vii, xiii, 112, 113, 115, 116, 129, 131, 134,
    137, 159, 173, 186, 257, 269, 647, 668, 676, 702
Harsanyi, John 210–12, 214
Hart, H. L. A. 332, 333, 336, 337, 342, 355, 357, 383,
    411, 705, 731
hate speech xi, 360, 363, 369–71, 385, 416, 426
Hayek, Friedrich xiv, 433, 437, 457
Hegel, Georg Wilhelm Friedrich 78, 86, 104, 254,
    339, 355, 427
historical injustice 294
Hobbes,Thomas 100, 101, 110, 527, 605, 625, 654
holism 207, 208
Holm, Søren vii, xiv, 112, 113, 134, 137, 159
holocaust 295
homosexuality 21, 24, 25, 36, 491
Honderich, Ted 340, 353, 355, 647, 668
honesty 15, 60, 67, 349, 557
human capital 228, 622, 624, 631
human dignity 481, 490, 491, 505, 723, 730
human life 18, 70, 118, 135, 164, 167, 172, 176–85,
    202, 242, 374, 377, 427, 647, 678, 716, 721, 722
  quality of 164, 165, 167, 170, 172, 174–80, 182–5,
    230, 285, 304, 306–8, 325, 326, 476, 533,
    668, 709
  sanctity of 278, 722
  value of 20, 22, 23, 44, 48, 49, 56, 62, 110, 117,
    134, 135, 148, 162–4, 167, 173, 175, 177, 178,
    180–6, 194, 231, 264, 304, 318, 322, 363, 373,
    374, 380, 398, 402–4, 416, 430, 473, 487,
    489, 491–3, 497, 503, 509, 574, 596, 598,
    605, 626, 634, 653, 701, 716, 722, 749, 750
human rights 41, 191, 193, 196, 385, 430, 486, 504,
    505, 508–10, 533, 568, 581, 585, 626, 627,
    632–5, 641, 655, 658, 659, 664–8, 716, 726, 732,
    756, 758–60
Hume, David 40, 104, 254, 594, 616
humility 221, 223, 231
hunger ix, 8, 636, 643–9, 651, 653–8, 660, 662–8
Hurka, Thomas 442, 457
Hursthouse, Rosalind 174, 186

Husak, Douglas viii, xiv, 340, 355, 387, 402, 404,
    411, 492, 508

immigration ix, 416, 420, 422, 567–78, 581,
    585–90, 595, 627, 632, 650
impartiality 8, 84, 326, 654, 667, 731
  family and friends 164, 181, 648
  racism xvii, 34, 176, 196, 199, 245–57, 263–70,
    283, 293, 370, 382, 414–16, 427, 593, 724
in vitro fertilization 136–8
incapacitation 335, 338, 706–9, 714, 723, 732
individual liberty 79, 435, 694, 719, 752
individual responsibility 437, 439, 458
individualism 288, 496, 603
inequality 29, 30, 59, 148, 225, 227, 249, 265, 283,
    291, 297, 310, 316, 326, 367, 374, 381, 382, 433,
    439, 446–8, 458, 496, 613, 620–4, 628, 630,
    634, 636, 641, 642
infanticide 113, 117, 131, 135
infants 43, 45, 97, 165, 171, 172, 182, 183, 261
inherent value 47–9, 56, 194, 196, 197
insanity 678
integrity 15, 22, 24, 33, 51, 62, 125, 138, 150, 160,
    205, 208, 215, 500, 568, 573, 585, 674, 681, 682,
    691, 697
intentions 114, 251, 252, 293, 347, 518, 521, 522,
    525, 554, 745, 761
intergenerational justice xiii, 459–62, 466, 467,
    469, 471–3, 481, 484
international borders 605
International Covenant on Civil and Political
    Rights 632, 642, 726
International Covenant on Economic, Social,
    and Cultural Rights 632, 642
international trade 574, 639, 640
intimates 499, 682
intuitionism 4, 5, 11
invasion of privacy 486, 508

journalism 487, 488, 497, 498, 500
just war 734, 740, 750, 758, 760, 761
justice viii, ix, xii–xvi, 10, 11, 28, 38, 40, 41, 59, 67,
    74, 85, 86, 91, 103–5, 109–11, 113, 124, 155, 159,
    161, 193, 198, 199, 201–3, 212, 213, 215, 231, 241,
    242, 246, 257, 263, 264, 270, 277, 293, 295,
    298, 299, 303, 308, 310–12, 315–17, 321–7, 331,
    336–8, 341, 348–50, 352–7, 364, 369, 377, 379,
    394, 415, 427, 430, 432–5, 437, 439–43, 445,
    446, 448–50, 452, 453, 455–62, 464–9, 471–5,
    478–84, 495–7, 503, 507, 510, 511, 525, 532, 533,
    537, 565, 575, 576, 583, 588–90, 601, 603, 605,
    609, 613, 615, 618–22, 624–35, 637–9, 641,
    642, 654, 662, 667, 668, 708–10, 720, 732–5,
    727, 730–3, 737, 760, 761

Kamm, Frances Myrna 5, 11, 538, 702
Kant, Immanuel 16, 17, 19, 21, 22, 30, 32, 40, 45,
    47, 62, 78, 86, 168, 254, 586, 589, 612, 616, 651,
    657, 677
  equality of persons 272, 622
  personal relations 84, 398–402, 406, 547, 561
Kass, Leon 149, 159, 307, 325, 681, 691, 701, 702
Kevorkian, Jack 408, 687
Keynes, Alfred 281, 298
killing 114–17, 120–2, 124, 127, 134, 182, 186, 209,
    213, 576, 632, 674, 678–83, 687, 689, 690, 693,
    695, 697, 702, 703, 715, 722, 730, 731, 734–6,
    743, 744, 746, 750, 755, 760
  infanticide 113, 117, 131, 135
  wrongness of 27, 121, 122, 131, 132, 465, 674,
    678, 681, 734
kindness 58, 67, 221
King, Martin Luther, Jr. 110, 199, 374, 384, 506,
    718, 731
Kittay, Eva Feder 241–3, 322, 326
Kleinig, John 395, 412
Kukathas, Chandran ix, xiv, 567, 579, 589
Kymlicka, Will xiv, 295, 298, 418–20, 423–5, 428,
    435, 457, 578, 579, 589, 592–4, 596, 599, 600,
    602, 603, 607, 612, 613, 615, 617, 619

labour 33, 34, 199, 200, 227, 236, 237, 243, 250,
    275, 279, 296, 302, 310, 326, 391, 416, 419, 429,
    514, 526, 623, 624, 628, 633–5, 638–40
  forced 26, 29, 57, 134, 183, 184, 201, 237, 239,
    295, 296, 302, 308, 352, 373, 391, 394, 410,
    435, 477, 559, 570, 580, 581, 583, 610, 640,
    682, 687, 691, 723, 753
labour market 310, 624, 635
LaFollette, Hugh i, v, 11, 57, 60, 67, 68, 83, 84, 86,
    110, 164, 186, 411, 456, 482, 589, 643, 667–9
land ethic 213
law xi–xv, 8, 11, 16, 18, 37, 40, 41, 70, 71, 75, 76, 78,
    81, 82, 86, 99, 100, 107, 110, 111, 125, 129, 133,
    134, 137, 153, 159, 160, 185, 206, 211, 226,
    233–6, 238, 241, 243, 244, 250, 260, 264, 271,
    301, 303, 306, 307, 314, 320, 324–7, 333–6, 338,
    339, 341, 343–5, 348, 353–8, 365, 366, 369–71,
    373, 375, 378–85, 387, 390–4, 396–412, 414,
    418, 421, 422, 429, 432, 457, 458, 467, 482, 483,
    485–90, 493, 494, 496, 497, 499, 503–13, 516,
    517, 524, 525, 536–8, 544, 555, 561, 563, 568,
    570, 578, 582, 583, 586–8, 592, 604, 607–9,
    614–17, 619, 633, 634, 639, 642, 654, 658, 659,
    675, 684, 700, 702–5, 709, 710, 712, 724–6,
    730–3, 738, 740, 741, 759–61
  concept of 49, 57, 70, 74, 75, 77, 78, 83, 92,
    193, 197, 206, 223, 242, 245–8, 250, 253, 257,
    333, 355, 402, 412, 417, 461–4, 490, 494,

    495, 507, 510, 512, 539, 596, 601, 677, 679,
    710, 723
  and euthanasia xii, 409, 674, 685, 692, 695,
    699–702
Lawrence, Charles 324, 369, 383–5, 431, 432
laziness 683
legal rights 165, 187, 197, 240, 241, 487, 491,
    522, 596
Leopold, Aldo 191, 198, 214, 722, 732
Levy, Jacob 42, 592, 602–4, 617
Lewis, C. S. 43, 45, 59, 60, 65, 68, 256, 338,
    355, 732
libel 509
liberal feminism 222
liberalism xii, xiv, 40, 81, 103, 110, 111, 384–6, 424,
    426, 432, 456–8, 483, 493, 494, 501, 505, 595,
    598, 599, 605, 617, 656, 661, 686, 761
libertarianism 434, 435, 437, 438, 456, 457, 483,
    571, 572, 652, 668
Locke, John 78, 86, 98, 101, 102, 110, 115–17, 199,
    200, 376, 384, 471, 716
Lockean proviso 435
love vii, 8, 17–19, 23, 33, 39–69, 82, 85–7, 103, 105,
    148, 149, 156, 157, 180, 232, 233, 493, 505,
    668, 717
  and morality 68, 86, 134, 355 536, 563, 588, 616,
    630, 642, 643, 667, 703, 739, 759
  and sex 39, 41, 82, 86, 281, 282, 505
loyalty 64, 268, 421, 428, 544, 545, 551–3, 557,
    559–61, 563, 602
luck 289, 316, 317, 445, 451–3, 455, 554
lying 19, 142, 198, 655

MacIntyre, Alasdair 203, 214, 322, 323, 326
MacKinnon, Catherine 29–31, 40, 143, 159, 231,
    233–5, 238, 243, 367, 368, 494, 496, 509
McMahan, Jeff 134, 146, 159, 210, 516, 593, 615, 617
McNaughton, David 4, 11
Malcolm X 267, 270
managed care 499, 704
Marcuse, Herbert 362, 384
marginal cases 163, 164, 172, 182–4, 186
Marquis, Don 116, 122, 135
marriage 16–20, 27, 32, 39–41, 70, 72, 73, 75–9, 81,
    82, 85–7, 102, 105, 111, 225, 233, 239–41, 244,
    268, 269, 286, 366, 383, 487, 495, 559, 561, 570
Marx, Karl xvi, 104, 281, 298, 373, 374, 384, 440,
    457, 505, 623, 707, 732
masturbation 21, 22
Matsuda, Mari 364, 384
meaning of life 698
medical care 308, 419, 630, 677, 703
medicine xii, xv, xvi, 4, 70, 73, 76, 149, 160,
    163, 165, 185, 186, 226, 294, 297, 309, 487,

488, 497, 515, 674, 675, 679–81, 687, 688, 697,
    699–704, 759
  and abortion xv, 18, 41, 112, 237, 487, 496, 505
  wrongness of killing 121, 122, 674, 678, 681, 734
merit 105, 230, 275, 276, 280, 288, 290–2, 316, 343,
    377, 583, 631, 649, 690, 724
metaphors 666
meta-ethics 2, 9
Mill, John Stuart 79, 84, 86, 103, 107, 111, 221, 243,
    363, 384, 394, 407, 411, 412, 491, 509, 514,
    592–4, 601, 612, 617, 677, 732
Miller, David 455, 457, 509, 575, 576, 589, 593,
    596, 598, 601, 602, 607, 615, 617, 622, 626,
    642, 702, 732, 760
minimalism 525, 534, 536
monogamy 19, 20, 40
Moore, G. E. 298, 341, 342, 356, 491, 492, 509,
    592, 593, 596–8, 603, 606, 609, 615–18
moral agency 116, 492, 517–20, 522, 524, 530,
    535, 536
moral community 168–70, 173, 174, 176–8, 180,
    183, 191, 196, 436, 457, 653, 654, 666
  animals vii, 21, 43, 48, 117, 161–80, 182–7, 189,
    191, 195–7, 213, 256, 323, 326, 515, 578,
    623, 657
moral deliberation 5, 521
moral education 103, 104, 346, 355, 356, 493, 505
moral imagination xvi, 9
moral status vii, xiv, 7, 8, 10, 53, 89, 91, 93–5, 98,
    109, 112, 113, 115, 120, 121, 124, 127, 128, 131,
    134, 135, 137–9, 144, 157, 163, 185, 187, 196, 344,
    520, 537, 563, 648, 649, 674, 697
  of animals 21, 161–7, 171–9, 182–7, 196,
    197, 213, 657
  of the fetus xiv, 112, 113, 115, 121, 122, 124,
    126–8, 137, 145, 157, 238, 499
  of groups 8, 247, 248, 261, 265, 301, 419, 420,
    422, 423, 524, 579, 599, 604, 607
Morris, Herbert 338–41, 346, 349, 350, 356,
    410–12
motherhood 159, 237, 240
multiculturalism xiv, 110, 265, 384, 413–18, 420–3,
    429–32, 577–9, 581, 589, 594, 617, 619, 642
Murphy, Jeffrey G. 332, 333, 338, 340–2, 350–2,
    356, 626, 642

Naess, Arne 191, 194, 195, 214
Nagel, Thomas 21, 22, 40, 333, 356, 359, 384, 430,
    432, 436, 443, 455, 457, 701
Narveson, Jan 436, 457, 472, 483, 652, 668
nationalism xiv, 420, 589–96, 598–600, 602, 603,
    614–19, 624, 626, 627, 642
nationalist movements 599, 604, 626, 628
Native Americans 256, 260, 268, 295, 414, 417, 420

natural law 16, 18, 37, 78, 86, 365, 366, 383
negative rights 313–15, 526, 653
Nicholson, Linda 74, 86, 87, 219, 244
Nielsen, Kai 592, 607, 616, 618
Norman, Wayne ix, xiv, 159, 309, 325, 421, 456,
    457, 536, 537, 545, 563, 569, 589, 591, 592,
    594, 596, 606, 609, 610, 612–15, 617–19, 745,
    758, 760
Nozick, Robert xvi, 64, 65, 69, 101, 105, 111, 198,
    199, 296, 298, 433, 435, 436, 454, 457, 458, 572,
    589, 627, 642, 652, 668, 701
nuclear power 188, 189, 193
Nussbaum, Martha 7, 11, 31, 32, 40, 59, 68, 69, 326,
    378, 379, 384, 421, 432, 446, 457, 655, 660, 668

obedience 255, 256, 339
objectivity 40, 429, 430
obscenity 30, 31
Okin, Susan Moller 74, 86, 109, 111, 384, 414, 432,
    494, 510
open borders 571–3, 575, 587
oppression 24, 26, 27, 80, 98, 191, 224, 240, 257,
    312, 363, 364, 367, 369, 381, 414, 417–19, 455,
    456, 496, 603, 608
OXFAM 631, 644

pacifism 734, 741, 744
parents 5, 48, 51, 56, 71, 72, 75, 77, 82–7, 91,
    98–110, 130, 142, 146–51, 155–8, 171, 172, 238,
    249, 256, 260, 268, 304, 305, 377, 438, 459,
    462, 465, 482, 493, 502, 579
Parfit, Derek 446, 447, 457, 463, 465, 472, 474,
    477, 478, 482, 483
passive euthanasia 703
Passmore, John 189–91, 215
paternalism viii, 95, 97, 110, 152, 387–412, 533
patriarchy 496
paedophilia 22, 39
people with disabilities viii, 300–5, 307, 310, 313,
    315, 316, 320, 326, 445, 675, 683
personhood 27, 62, 63, 75, 115–20, 122, 123, 127,
    128, 133, 135, 165, 377, 379, 491, 492, 518, 520,
    521, 524, 538
Pettit, Philip xiv, 331, 336, 337, 342, 354, 356, 571,
    589, 593, 616, 703
physicians 189, 228, 285, 294, 302, 409, 488, 499,
    674, 675, 681–5, 688, 689, 695, 696, 703
Pineau, Lois 27, 28, 41
Plato 65, 69, 78, 102, 113, 134, 225, 226, 257, 355
pleasure 16, 19, 20, 23, 26, 30, 31, 37, 40, 43–6,
    48–50, 52, 59, 82, 366, 395, 396, 441, 472, 530,
    648, 660, 661
Pogge, Thomas W. 622, 630, 631, 637, 641, 642,
    654, 662, 668

Pojman, Louis 213, 215, 709, 711, 713–17, 732, 733
political authority 101, 496, 569, 581, 606
politics of difference 87, 327, 418, 427, 428, 432, 458
population growth 629
pornography 16, 24, 29–31, 34, 37, 39, 41, 232–4, 237, 243, 360, 363, 365–9, 371, 385, 487, 512
postmodern feminism 224–5
positive rights 314, 436
potentiality argument 119, 120, 123, 183
poverty 76, 84, 148, 202, 229, 250, 265, 277, 287, 296, 308, 401, 419, 421, 438, 448, 457, 509, 568, 621, 622, 624, 628, 641–4, 646–9, 651, 653–9, 662–8
primary goods 443–6, 450, 451, 456, 458, 636
Primoratz, Igor 23, 41, 82, 86, 336, 337, 344, 353, 356, 715–17, 732
privacy viii, xi, 20, 38, 84, 102, 103, 456, 485–513, 719, 728
property rights 198–200, 433, 435–7, 457, 483, 484, 506, 511, 572, 628
proportionality 124, 273, 349–51, 353, 710, 743–5, 747–53
prostitution xv, 17, 18, 23, 29, 32–4, 41, 72, 233, 234, 243, 640
prudence 470, 481, 525, 760
punishment vii, ix, xiii, xiv, 6, 8–10, 27, 91, 255, 266, 267, 331–57, 405, 406, 410–12, 583, 678, 679, 705–7, 709–26, 728–33, 742, 752, 754, 760
    abolition 78, 168, 351, 352, 354, 706, 708, 724, 726–30, 733, 741, 760
    and desert 711
    deterrence theory 345, 730–2
    equal treatment 104, 202, 232, 258, 383, 634
    excuses 38, 252, 256, 356, 735
    proportionality principle 124, 273, 349–51, 353, 710, 743–5, 747–53
    retribution theory 357
    utilitarianism 170, 357, 447, 450, 458, 468, 483, 484, 617, 630, 647, 648, 655, 657, 661, 665
Purdy, Laura 40, 86, 97, 98, 111, 137, 159, 326

quality of life 164, 165, 167, 170, 172, 174–80, 182–5, 304, 307, 308, 325, 326, 668
Quill, Timothy 687–9, 695, 702, 703
Quine, W. V. 11

race:
    and DNA 491
    and IQ 262
    mixed xvii, 270
Rachels, James 115, 119, 172, 187, 232, 362, 363, 367, 369, 381, 382, 416, 492, 494, 500, 510, 680, 703

racial discrimination viii, 245, 253, 264, 277, 475, 731
    affirmative action viii, xiii, 6, 7, 9, 226, 230, 231, 253, 264, 272–83, 285, 287–99, 415–17
    civil-rights movement 248
    criminal punishment 331, 348, 405, 410
racial stereotypes 266
racism xvii, 34, 176, 196, 199, 245–57, 263–70, 283, 293, 370, 382, 414–16, 427, 593, 724
    classic 32, 79, 84, 112, 186, 189, 195, 248, 301, 442, 486, 612, 709, 737
    concept of 49, 57, 70, 74, 75, 77, 78, 83, 92, 193, 197, 206, 223, 242, 245–8, 250, 253, 257, 333, 355, 402, 412, 417, 461–4, 490, 494, 495, 507, 510, 512, 539, 596, 601, 677, 679, 710, 723
    construction of 29, 224, 589, 695
    definitions of 207, 208, 248, 250, 252, 253, 374, 485, 489–91, 501, 503
    environmental xii–xvi, 3, 140, 141, 148, 149, 155, 188–99, 201–15, 253, 254, 263, 270, 284, 372, 464, 471, 473, 481, 482, 519, 521, 536, 538, 582, 651, 659, 664, 735
    forms of 4, 21, 24–6, 29, 42, 46, 50, 56, 59, 62, 66, 94, 105, 113, 223, 232, 247, 252, 265, 283, 303, 334, 336, 359, 360, 362–5, 368, 369, 375, 379, 382, 416, 419, 421, 423, 427, 430, 433, 434, 437, 445, 447, 449, 472, 488, 490, 491, 493, 494, 497, 540, 593, 598, 601, 603, 610, 614, 637, 648, 651, 655, 663, 680, 689, 696, 721, 729
    institutional 6, 153, 167, 202, 249–55, 257, 267, 291, 293, 294, 303, 310, 358, 363, 373, 418, 430, 519, 533, 592, 606, 608, 609, 611, 612, 614, 631, 632, 637, 640, 643, 645, 646, 655, 659, 665, 684, 697, 698, 707, 761
    and justice 105, 299, 354, 355, 357, 433, 450, 481, 482, 537, 641, 760
    mens rea 248–55, 257, 264
    unacknowledged 255, 256
radical feminism 222–4
rape 16, 27–31, 34, 35, 39–41, 125, 235, 236, 238, 243, 244, 351, 368, 717
    date rape 27, 28, 41
    feminism xv, xvi, 29, 34, 39–41, 73, 75, 80, 86, 87, 222, 225, 243, 495, 496, 509, 594
    and pornography 31, 371
Rawls, John 103, 104, 111, 210, 212, 215, 257, 270, 296, 298, 336, 356, 364, 374, 379, 380, 385, 422, 432, 438–40, 443, 444, 446, 447, 449–51, 455–9, 467–70, 483, 594, 605, 618, 631–6, 642, 662, 668, 701, 719, 737, 743, 754, 755, 761
Raz, Joseph 364, 378, 385, 402, 412, 424, 426, 429, 432, 593, 600, 617

recidivism 707, 708, 714

reciprocity 32, 47, 173, 180, 196, 242, 327, 354, 465–8, 470–2, 474, 482, 630, 633

reflective equilibrium 5, 482

refugee 568–70, 574, 580–5, 587–90, 630, 632

Regan, Tom 166, 170, 173, 184, 187, 190, 192, 196, 197, 213, 215, 325, 511, 537

Reliman, Jeffrey 492, 510, 709, 724, 732, 733

religious beliefs:
   euthanasia ix, xii, 10, 114, 134, 153, 167, 409, 673, 674, 680, 682, 684–96, 699–704
   homosexuality 21, 24, 25, 36, 491
   value of lives 177, 182, 186

reparations 296, 298, 628, 638, 742

repentance 347, 348

reproduction xvi, 21, 22, 27, 76, 80, 85, 86, 102, 124, 133, 134, 137, 139, 142, 149, 150, 152, 158–60, 222, 223, 225, 236, 238, 487, 493

right to life 10, 237, 257, 325, 653, 658, 716, 717, 721

Roe v. *Wade* 238, 243, 487, 509, 513

Rolston, Holmes 190, 193, 202, 203, 208, 215, 664, 668

Rorty, Richard 68, 69, 74, 414, 432, 520, 538

Ross, W. D. 4, 11, 642, 675, 702

Rousseau 41, 92, 94, 111, 225, 226, 427, 593, 597, 612, 618

Russell, Bertrand 18, 19, 41, 167, 187, 642, 761

sameness feminists 226, 230, 232, 233, 235, 236, 238, 240

Sandel, Michael 111, 377, 385, 421, 422, 425, 426, 432, 493, 494, 511, 656, 668

Sartre, Jean Paul 79, 255, 256, 267, 270

Satz, Debra ix, xiv, 620

Savage Inequalities 263, 270

Scanlon, T. M. 359, 432, 440, 442, 458, 511, 642, 701

scepticism 97, 653

Schauer, Frederick 360, 363, 385

Scheffler, Samuel 621, 642

Schmidtz, David 437, 438, 458

Schoeman, Ferdinand 84, 87, 486, 487, 489, 493, 502, 511

secession xiv, 592, 594, 595, 604–19

self-awareness 57, 58, 607

self-defence 257, 721, 757, 758

self-development 221, 418

self-esteem 29, 48, 224, 267, 418, 420

self-interest 68, 436, 544, 558, 719

Sellars, Wilfred 6, 11, 355

Sen, Amartya 138, 315, 326, 427–9, 432, 440, 445, 446, 458, 469, 483, 642–4, 660, 667, 668

sentience 126, 127, 190, 191

sexuality vii, 15, 17, 18, 21, 23–30, 32–6, 38–40, 67, 70, 82, 225, 231, 232, 234, 236, 244, 269–71, 366, 493, 505
   conceptual analysis of 489
   marital commitment 22
   morality of xv, 25, 38, 159, 170, 269, 275, 325, 409, 410, 412, 436, 472, 493, 563, 571, 592, 604, 605, 615, 617, 618, 625, 634, 654, 700, 731, 732, 739, 743, 745, 747, 749, 753
   value of 20, 22, 23, 44, 48, 49, 56, 62, 110, 117, 134, 135, 148, 162–4, 167, 173, 175, 177, 178, 180–6, 194, 231, 264, 304, 318, 322, 363, 373, 374, 380, 398, 402–4, 416, 430, 473, 487, 489, 491–3, 497, 503, 509, 574, 596, 598, 605, 626, 634, 653, 701, 716, 722, 749, 750

shareholders 517, 522, 525, 526, 528, 530–2, 534

Sher, George 341, 357, 410, 412, 496, 511

Shrader-Frechette, Kristin vii, 188, 189, 191, 198, 200, 202–5, 207, 208, 215

Shrage, Laurie vii, 15, 34, 41

Shue, Henry ix, xv, 631, 632, 642, 653, 658, 668, 734, 740, 754, 761

Silvers, Anita 300, 305, 307, 311–15, 317, 321, 324–7, 696, 700, 701

Singer, Peter 38, 42, 43, 45, 53, 55, 69, 115, 135, 161, 165, 173, 186–7, 190, 196, 203, 213, 215, 546, 563, 624, 630, 637, 642, 645–7, 649, 651, 655–7, 669, 676, 702, 703

slavery 7, 24, 35, 247, 250, 255, 260, 269, 294–6, 408, 411, 435, 628

slippery slope arguments 685, 692
   abortion vii, xv, 2, 6, 10, 18, 38, 41, 74, 76, 112–17, 120–2, 124–9, 131–5, 137, 138, 153, 156, 157, 173, 237, 238, 243, 268, 415, 487, 491, 493, 496, 499, 504–7, 509, 512, 693, 701
   euthanasia ix, xii, 10, 114, 134, 153, 167, 409, 673, 674, 680, 682, 684–96, 699–704
   free speech 358–65, 367–9, 371, 372, 376, 378, 381, 383–5, 414, 417, 424, 494

Smith, Adam ix, xii, xvi, 199, 326, 525, 533, 538, 623, 730–3, 761

smoking 153, 378, 497

Soble, Alan 23, 41, 65–9

social contract 78, 503, 528, 529

social roles 78

social solidarity 416, 420, 422, 428, 575

socialism 364, 374, 413, 457, 595

speciesism 118, 176

speech codes 369, 416, 417

Spinner-Havel, Jeffrey 422, 423, 432

stakeholder theory 530–2, 534, 535–8

Steele, Shelby 275, 299

Stocker, Michael 69, 520, 538

suicide ix, xii, 4, 6, 7, 167, 183, 409, 499, 568,
    673–97, 699–704, 707, 729, 733
Sunstein, Cass 360, 365, 367, 369, 372, 385, 512,
    610, 619
Supreme Court 17, 108, 115, 233, 238, 267, 268,
    295, 301, 303, 307, 320, 321, 360, 369–71, 377,
    378, 381, 394, 424, 486, 487, 495, 504, 609,
    611, 619, 684, 689, 693, 699, 703, 725, 726, 733

Tamir, Yael 382, 385, 592, 593, 597, 600, 602,
    607, 619
taxation 76, 435, 436, 448, 575, 652
tenBroek, Jacobus 300–4, 306, 312, 320, 323, 326
Thomson, Judith Jarvis 124, 135, 486, 512, 701,
    717, 733
Tong, Rosemarie viii, xv, 219, 236, 243, 244
Tonry, Michael 349, 350, 356, 357
Tuana, Nancy vii, xvi, 15, 39

Unger, Peter 203, 215, 642
United Nations 98, 569, 581, 588, 622, 627, 641,
    642, 752, 756, 757, 759, 761
utilitarianism 170, 357, 447, 450, 458, 468, 483,
    484, 617, 630, 647, 648, 655, 657, 661, 665

Vallentyne, Peter 463, 472, 483
van Parijs, Philippe 448, 449, 458, 460, 473, 481,
    483, 612, 619
vegetarianism 162
Velleman, David J. 47, 48, 62, 69
violence xv, 24, 26, 27, 34, 35, 40, 134, 160, 232, 235,
    248, 255, 360, 367, 369, 381, 382, 419, 494–6,
    511, 583, 597, 609, 647, 668, 708, 730, 738
virtue ethics 212, 655
virtues xii, 3, 44, 45, 50, 60, 67, 68, 110, 174, 223,
    252, 323, 324, 326, 376, 423, 437, 656, 723
Vlastos, Gregory 43, 50, 51, 69, 716, 733
von Hirsch, Andrew 335, 336, 338–41, 343–5,
    347–51, 353, 357, 710, 733

Wachbroit, Robert vii, xvi, 136, 137, 140, 151,
    153, 160
Waldron, Jeremy 351, 357, 392, 412, 424, 425, 432,
    460, 484, 668
Walzer, Michael 455, 457, 458, 527, 529, 538, 585,
    590, 626, 642, 737–9, 741, 743–5, 747, 754, 755,
    760, 761
war ix, 2, 10, 102, 153, 189, 302, 307, 359, 379, 404,
    414, 415, 487, 526, 568–70, 574, 580–2, 584,
    585, 588, 590, 592–5, 597, 626, 633, 634, 641,
    642, 663, 678, 679, 697, 734–45, 747–56,
    758–61
Warren, Mary Anne 115, 173, 196, 197, 215
Wasserman, David vii, xv, xvi, 136, 137, 146, 151,
    153, 160, 315, 316, 326
Wasserstrom, Richard 19, 41, 486, 512
Wenz, Peter 193, 201, 202, 215, 254, 270
Werhane, Patricia viii, xvi, 514, 517, 520, 521,
    525–7, 530, 534, 536–8
whistleblowing ix, 8, 539–63
Williams, Bernard 264, 411, 458, 689, 701, 731
Williams, Patricia 68, 86, 250, 325, 487, 505,
    509, 512
wishful thinking 55, 184
Wolff, Jonathan viii, xvi, 319, 327, 384, 433,
    435, 437, 447, 451, 453, 458
Wollstonecraft, Mary 79, 87, 221, 225, 226, 244
Wolterstorff, Nicholas 380, 386
working class 290, 419
World Bank 201, 626, 634, 641, 642
World Health Organization (WHO) 188, 515, 516
World Wide Web 488, 490, 498
World Trade Organization (WTO) 212

Young, Iris Marion 70–2, 74, 81, 87, 239, 244, 294,
    302, 311, 312, 315, 327, 418, 419, 432, 455, 458

Zack, Naomi viii, xvii, 245, 247, 256, 258–62,
    268–71

Lightning Source UK Ltd.
Milton Keynes UK
UKHW03f0811190818
327271UK00011B/342/P